Ellicott's
COMMENTARY
ON THE
WHOLE BIBLE

A VERSE BY VERSE
EXPLANATION

EDITED BY
CHARLES JOHN ELLICOTT

Introduction by
DR. HERBERT LOCKYER

VOLUME I

Genesis — Numbers

WIPF & STOCK · Eugene, Oregon

Wipf and Stock Publishers
199 W 8th Ave, Suite 3
Eugene, OR 97401

Ellicott's Commentary on the Whole Bible Volume I
Genesis - Numbers
By Ellicott, Charles J.
ISBN 13: 978-1-4982-0136-0
Publication date 3/18/2015
Previously published by Cassell, 1897

This is a reprint of the 1959 Zondervan edition. Originally
published in 1897 by Cassell as A Bible Commentary for
English Readers.

INTRODUCTION

As I journey back through almost half a century of Christian witness, of the many books that helped to shape my ministry, none has been so eagerly consulted as the volumes comprising Ellicott's *Bible Commentary for English Readers,* now known as "Ellicott's Commentary on the Whole Bible." This valuable eight-volume set is conspicuous among Commentaries for its adherence to the divine inspiration of Holy Scripture; its conservative approach to foundational truths; its comprehensive treatment of books, chapters and verses.

Charles John Ellicott, compiler of and contributor to this renowned Bible Commentary, was one of the most outstanding conservative scholars of the 18th century. He was born at Whitwell near Stamford, England, on April 25, 1819. He graduated from St. John's College, Cambridge, where other famous expositors like Charles Simeon and Handley Moule studied. As a Fellow of St. John's, he constantly lectured there. In 1847, Charles Ellicott was ordained a Priest in the Church of England. From 1841 to 1848, he served as Rector of Pilton, Rutlandshire. He became Hulsean Professor of Divinity, Cambridge, in 1860. The next three years, 1861 to 1863, he ministered as Dean of Exeter, and later in 1863 became the Lord Bishop of Gloucester and Bristol.

Conspicuous as a Bible Expositor, he is still well known for his Critical and Grammatical Commentaries on Galatians, Ephesians, Philippians, Colossians, Thessalonians and Philemon. Other printed works include *Modern Unbelief, The Being of God, The History and Obligation of the Sabbath.*

This unique Bible Commentary is to be highly recommended for its worth to Pastors and Students. Its expositions are simple and satisfying, as well as scholarly. Among its most commendable features, mention should be made of the following:

It contains profitable suggestions concerning *the significance of names* used in Scripture. Take, for example, this dissertation on the divine name in Exodus 3:13-14:

"What is His name? — In Egypt, and wherever polytheism prevailed, every god had, as a matter of course, a name. Among the Israelites hitherto God had been known by titles, as *El* or *Elohim,* "the holy One." *Shaddai,* "the Powerful"; *Jahveh* or *Jehovah,* "the Existent." These titles were used with some perception of their meaning; no one of them had as yet passed into a proper name . . . *I Am That I am* — It is generally assumed that this was given to Moses as the full name of God. But perhaps it is rather a deep and mysterious statement of His nature . . . *I Am,* assumed as a name implies —

1. An existence different from all other existence. "I am, and there is none beside Me" (Isa. 45:6).
2. An existence out of time, with which time has nothing to do (John 8:58).
3. An existence that is real, all other being shadowy.
4. An independent and unconditional existence, from which all other is derived, and on which it is dependent.

Symbolism is another phase of Bible Study we need to handle sanely. Seeing the Scriptures abound in Symbolism, we need a safe guide in all interpretation of same. Chosen at random is this illustration from Ellicott's commentary on God bearing His children as on eagle's wings (Exod. 19:4; Deut. 32:11).

"When its young are first fledged, the eagle is said to assist them in the flight by flying beneath them, so that they may settle upon its wings or back, if necessary. God means that He has bestowed upon His people the same tender and powerful care, has borne them up mightily when they might have fallen, supported them in their first flight as fledgings, and so saved them from disaster."

Much could be said regarding the expositional advantages of the Commentary before us. All who preach the Word should strive after correct interpretation and practical application. Turning to Ellicott's comment on Numbers 31:6, here is what we gather about "the holy instruments"—

"The reference may be only to the silver trumpets, or it may include other sacred instruments. This was emphatically a holy war; and we may learn, from the command given to the Israelites to take with them 'the holy instruments,' that they who would engage in the war against sin and Satan must 'take to them the whole armour of God' (Eph. 6:13)."

It would take more space than allowed here to extol the homiletical worth of this Commentary. Divisions of themes and verses are notable in this eight-volume set. Israel, we are told, sinned ten times (Numbers 14:21-23). Here is Ellicott's division of this portion:

> "Some have explained the words these ten times by adding to the eight murmurings which are recorded:
>
> 1. At the Red Sea (Exod. 14:11, 12).
> 2. At Marah (Exod. 15:23).
> 3. In the wilderness of Sin (Exod. 16:1).
> 4. At Rephidum (Exod. 27:1).
> 5. At Horeb (Exod. 32).
> 6. At Taberah (Num. 11:1).
> 7. At the graves of lust (Num. 11:4).
> 8. At Kadesh (Num. 14) — the transgressions of certain individuals.
>
> It is more probable, however, that the number *ten* is used here as elsewhere (Gen. 31:7) as denoting a full measure."

No pastor's study should be without this set of beneficial expositions. We have no hesitation in affirming that Seminaries, Bible Institutes and Christian Colleges adding Ellicott's Commentary on the Whole Bible to their library will prove it to be the most sought after work of its kind. Students for the ministry will not be long in discovering the rich mine of truth its pages contain.

HERBERT LOCKYER

Genesis

BY

VERY REV. R. PAYNE SMITH, D.D.

Exodus

BY

REV. GEORGE RAWLINSON, M.A.

Leviticus

BY

THE REV. C. D. GINSBURG, LL.D.

Numbers

BY

REV. C. J. ELLIOTT, M.A.

CONTENTS

	PAGE
Preface	vii
General Introduction	xiii
Introduction to the Pentateuch	xxv
Introduction to Genesis	3
Genesis	11
Excursus on Notes to Genesis	176
Introduction to Exodus	187
Exodus	192
Additional Notes to Exodus	334
Introduction to Leviticus	341
Leviticus	343
Introduction to Numbers	475
Numbers	485

PREFACE

THE present Commentary on the Old Testament, of which this is the First Volume, is based on the same principles, and designed for the same class of readers, as the companion Commentary on the New Testament.

In the Preface to that Work, the general aims and objects of the Commentary were set forth with some fulness. It was stated that the Commentary was designed for that large and increasing class of cultivated English readers who, believing the Holy Scriptures not only to contain God's Word, but to be God's Word, do earnestly desire to realise that Word, and to be assisted in applying it to their own spiritual needs, and to the general circumstances and context of daily life around them.

It was further stated that its object was also to meet some of the deep needs of the present time, especially of that large, and—as we fear it must again be said—increasing class of readers, who are conscious that chilling doubts have crept into the soul, and that modern criticism has seemed to them to make it doubtful whether Scripture is what it claims to be; not merely a truthful record of God's dealings with man, but a power to make man wise unto salvation through faith which is in Christ Jesus. For these, and for such as these, it was stated that much that would be put forward in the Notes, and especially the manner in which it would be put forward, would be found especially helpful. Difficulties would be fairly met; removed where they could be removed; left, simply and frankly, where it did not appear that God had yet vouchsafed to us the means of doing more than modifying them, or reducing their gravity and magnitude.

These were the two great objects of the Commentary on the New Testament—to bring home to the believing the life and power of God's Word, and to set forth the truth of that Word to those whose belief had become shaken or impaired. And these are the two great objects of the present Commentary; but, as the very nature of the subject-matter will necessitate, in somewhat altered aspects and proportions. First, for this obvious reason, that while we unhesitatingly maintain with Origen * that the whole of the Sacred Scriptures make up one perfectly adjusted "instrument of God," we nevertheless recognise with that great teacher that the perfect harmony of the blessed instrument is due to the accordant diversity of the sounds. Though the Old Testament and the New Testament are the Word of the same Spirit, though their general end and object are one, yet, as Hooker † clearly points out, there is this momentous difference, that the Old Testament did make wise by teaching salvation through Christ that should come, the New Testament by teaching that Christ the Saviour is come. Secondly, because the difficulties connected with the Old Testament are much more serious than those connected with the New Testament, and must, by the nature of the case, occupy more of the special attention of the interpreter.

The main difficulties connected with the Old Testament may briefly be summed up as scientific,

* Origen, *Comment. in Matt.* v. 9 (Fragm.), Vol. III., p. 241 (ed. Delarue).
† Hooker, *Laws of Ecclesiastical Polity*, Book I., chap. xiv. 4.

historical, and moral—all of which, in their turn, are constantly presenting themselves to the interpreter, and, at the very least, demand of him something more than mere passing notice and recognition.

The scientific difficulties mostly connect themselves with the narrative of the emergence of the world and of the totality of things around us, and with the place which man holds in the order and system of nature of which we have more immediate cognisance. The origination of the human race, its antiquity, its dispersions, and its developments, are all subjects which are forced upon the attention of the candid interpreter, and which must be dealt with, even in the necessarily circumscribed limits of a commentary, with distinctness and candour. The day for the so-called reconciliations of Scripture and Science, or, in other words, for wide assumptions as to the statements of Scripture, and shallow and superficial answers to inferences drawn from real or supposed discoveries, has now passed away. The interpreter is now remanded to the simple and holy words into which tradition, or imperfect knowledge, may have imported a meaning which they never were intended to bear. He is reminded, ere he attempts either defence or reconciliation, that his duty is to set forth in clearness and truth that and that only which, by the ordinary principles of human thought and of human language, the words on which he is meditating really express; and when he has done this, he is bidden to remember that it is also his duty not to recognise as truths of science what as yet are no more than working hypotheses, nor to invest with the high character of established theories, brilliant generalisations which are still regarded by eminent men of science as, at best, only partially verified. The duty of the faithful interpreter is to set forth the apparent meaning of that which lies before him with all candour, breadth, and simplicity; to be severely truthful, and to wait. The disclosures of science are as yet only partial and fragmentary. Their drift and tendency, however, indisputably lead us to this conviction, that, with fuller knowledge, much that at present prevents our fully realising the harmony between the revelation of God in the book of Nature, and the revelation of God in His own inspired Word, will entirely pass away. We must, then, often be content to wait. He that has sent the dream will, in His own good time, send the interpretation thereof.

We do not disguise that there are difficulties; we do not deny that there are subjects, such, for instance, as the antiquity of the human race, in regard of which our first impressions derived from Scripture do not *appear* to be coincident with some of the results of modern discovery. These things we deny not. But this, on the other hand, we assert with unchanging confidence, that by very far the greater portion of the so-called opposition between Religion and Science is due to bias, preconception, and literalism, on one side, and, on the other side, to an elevation, often studiously antagonistic, of plausible hypothesis into the higher domain of universally received and established theory.

Scarcely less in magnitude and importance are the numerous historical difficulties which present themselves in the inspired narrative, whether as connected with supposed discrepancies with generally accepted secular history, or as presented by what are claimed to be ascertained facts as to the early origination of the human race, or as *ipso facto* forced upon the modern reader by the inherent improbabilities of the story. This last-mentioned class of difficulties is, it need hardly be said, always connected with the miraculous portions of the narrative, and more especially with the presence of miracles when appearing in what would seem to be ordinary human history. In the earlier books of Scripture, this form of difficulty is not felt to be so trying to the faith. In the youth of the world many things seem admissible, which at a later period seem startling and incongruous. The presence of the supernatural may be felt to be partially explicable in the case of the one portion of the narrative, but inexplicable in the case of the other. The age of the miraculous is assumed to have passed away, and its startling recurrence in the ordinary stream of human history, in the narratives of wars, or the annals of established kingdoms, often raises uneasy feelings in the minds of really earnest and religious readers—feelings which, at a time such as the present, may be entertained far more widely than we may, at first sight, be disposed to admit.

Difficulties such as these must, it is plain, often traverse the path of an interpreter; and it will be found by the readers of this Commentary that they have been neither evaded nor ignored. In regard of the first two forms of historical difficulty, it may be observed that the remarkable additions to the records of ancient history that have been disclosed within the present generation, and the still more remarkable documents that relate to what may not improperly be called a pre-historic period, will be found to have been used soberly and critically, wheresoever their testimony might be judged to be available. It will be found also that they are of the highest evidential importance. Not only do they supply the interpreter with hitherto undiscovered demonstrations of the faithfulness and truth of the inspired record, where it might otherwise have seemed most open to criticism, but even suggest inferences as to the early migrations and settlements of the great human family, which are shadowed forth in the brief and mainly genealogical notices of the opening chapters of Holy Scripture. Just as true science, apart from mere speculative inferences or unverified hypotheses, has of late been permitted, in many striking discoveries, to bear its testimony to the Divine truth of the earliest pages of the world's history, so has recent archæology been enabled to throw a light upon the pages that follow it. Nay, even in regard to the grave difficulty connected with the presence of the supernatural and miraculous in the current of what might be deemed ordinary national history, even in this respect recent historical research has indirectly ministered light and reassurance. It has shown that in numerous details the holy narrative is now proved to be in strict accordance with independent secular history; and in showing this, it suggests the important consideration that if Scriptural statements are thus to be relied on in one portion of the narrative, there is at least a presumption of a very high order that they deserve to be believed and relied upon in the other. And the more so, when it is borne in mind that the narrative of Holy Scripture is the record of the providential government of the world rather than of the events and issues of merely human history. These combined considerations will go far, in any candid mind, to alleviate the doubts that may have arisen from the presence of the miraculous, where experience might have seemed to suggest that it was due only to the misconceptions or credulity of the writer.

The moral difficulties connected with the details of many events that come before us in the Old Testament are not lightly to be passed over. They can, however, only properly be dealt with in connection with the whole narrative of which they form a part. Still, this may be said generally, that while, on the one hand, each portion of the Holy Scriptures of the Old Testament presents to us, faithfully and truthfully, the morality and civilisation of the age to which that portion refers, there is, on the other hand, plainly to be traced a Divine working by which the standard is persistently raised both in the individual and in the nation. The *præparatio evangelica* was continuous and progressive; the passage from the days of comparative ignorance to those in which the blessed teaching of the Sermon on the Mount was proclaimed in the ears of men, was by steady gradation and providential advance. There was no period in which, whether in regard of spoken word or entailed consequence, God left Himself without a witness: but the testimony of each witness became fuller and clearer as the centuries rolled onward; and as the time drew nigh when the mystery of salvation was to be fully disclosed to the children of men, the light shone forth clearer and clearer even unto the perfect day.

This broad consideration, which will be illustrated in numerous instances in the Notes of the present volume, and of those that will follow it, will be found to go far to remove the greater part of the moral difficulties of the Old Testament. Individual cases, in which there may seem to have been a positive Divine command to do that which, on the principles of the New Testament, must be condemned and forbidden, will still remain, and must be dealt with in their proper places, and with all the circumstances of their true historical connection. Even, however, in regard of these, this general remark may rightly be made, that the command and the contemporary moral estimate of the act commanded can never be dissociated by any equitable thinker, and that the recognition of this simple fact will certainly modify, if it does not completely remove, some of the greater difficulties connected with the subject.*

Such are the three main classes of difficulties which from time to time present themselves to the earnest student of the Old Testament. They differ in many important particulars from the difficulties connected with the New Testament, and are, we fear, seriously felt by many who accept without any conscious hesitation the broader outlines of Christianity. Thus felt, and thus admitted into the general current of thought, they contribute to that silent and often unconscious depreciation of the Divine authority of the Old Testament, which is certainly disclosing itself in our own times, even among those who might claim to be considered religiously-minded readers and thinkers. To such as these—and their number, it is to be feared, is yearly increasing—this Commentary will be found to supply a help that is sorely needed, and that is likely, by the very manner in which that help is offered, to exercise a permanently good effect on those who may seek for it. As in the Commentary on the New Testament, difficulties are fairly met. Where a full answer to the questions that may arise can distinctly be given, it is given; where only such reasonable considerations can be urged as qualify the force of objections, and suggest, though they may not as yet completely supply, the true explanation, there the limited state of our present knowledge, and so of our power of wholly removing the difficulty, is placed clearly before the reader; where, as in the case of numerical statements and other and similar details, startling objections at once present themselves, there the possibility, and even likelihood, of transcriptional errors is pointed out, and the statement left as it has come down to us—still needing elucidation, but, as the whole aspect of recent discovery warrants us in believing, in due time fully to receive it.

But here, as was done in the case of the Commentary on the New Testament, it is proper to state with all distinctness, that though the truth is so dear to the writers of this Commentary that they have never allowed themselves to set forth explanations in which they themselves have not the fullest confidence, no one is, for one moment, to expect to find any traces of unfixed or vacillating opinions as to the true nature and authority of this portion of God's Holy Word. As was said in the Preface to the Commentary on the New Testament, so may it be said with equal force here, that each member of our present company knows on Whom and in What he has trusted, and is persuaded, with all that deep conviction which the study of this blessed Book ever bears to the humble and reverent, that heavenly truth is present in every part and portion, even though he himself may not be able to set it forth in all its brightness. This, it is plainly avowed, is the presumption and *præjudicium* under which the work of the interpreter has been done throughout this Commentary. That presumption, however, has never interfered with the most exact discharge of the duty of the faithful interpreter; nay—for truth will bear any investigation—it has even encouraged and enhanced it.

But it is far indeed from the sole aim of this Commentary to remove or attenuate the difficulties that are to be found in the Old Testament. No; as in the Notes on the New Testament, so here, it has been the main object of the writers to bring the blessed teaching of the Sacred Volume home to the heart and soul of the reader; to show how He that was to come

* See Mozley, *Lectures on the Old Testament*, Lect. X., p. 236 *seq.*

is the guiding light, the quickening principle, the mystic secret of the long ages of preparation; how history typified, and rite foreshadowed, and prophesy foretold; how, in a word, salvation is the orient light under which all the mysteries of the Old Dispensation become clear and intelligible.

Especially is it our hope that some momentous truths in relation to the Old Testament will be found to have been brought out with fresh force and perspicuity, and that not so much by isolated notes or special disquisitions, as by the whole tone and tenour of the Commentary. There was never a time when this was more needed. It is not now merely by outward foes that the Divine authority of the Old Testament is impugned and its teaching invalidated: Christians are now being taught by Christians to regard the history of the Old Testament as no more than the strange annals of an ancient people, that have no more instruction for us than the histories of the nations among whom they dwelt. Nay, more, the very moral scope and bearing of that Law, from which it has been said that "one jot or tittle shall in no wise pass away till all things be accomplished," is boldly called in question in the very precincts of Christian controversy. It is well, then, that the simple and earnest reader should have within reach a Commentary professedly plain, popular, and uncontroversial, which by the very tenour of its interpretation, and the reverent candour of its discussion, should assist in maintaining in the foreground those broad truths relative to the Old Dispensation which it is the especial care of modern criticism to keep out of sight and to ignore. We allude more particularly to these three great truths: First, that the history of the Old Testament is not merely the history of an ancient nation, but the history of a nation that was, as it were, the church of humanity, and in which and through which dawned the true future and true hope of mankind; secondly, that the Divine government of that nation, and the law to which it was to be subordinated, are to be estimated, not by the isolated consideration of individual facts or commands, but by the scope, purpose, and final issues of that law and that government which history incontrovertibly discloses; and lastly, and almost inferentially, that the revelation which God vouchsafed to His chosen people, and partially, through them, to the widespread nations of the earth, was progressive and gradual, and that the Old Testament is the record of the long preparation of mankind for that for which every true heart in every age had dimly longed for—redemption and salvation through Jesus Christ.

These three great truths, the first of which was felt, especially in the later days, by the very Jews themselves,* will be presented to the reader in constantly recurring aspects and with every variety of illustration. Though but seldom definitely formulated, though felt rather than enunciated, they will, nevertheless, be found to form the sort of spiritual warp and woof of the Commentary, and to give life and continuity to the interpretation. They will be seen to be what they are—not principles previously agreed upon, not personal preconceptions persistently maintained, but great and fundamental truths, which the inspired Word itself discloses, and which become patent through the medium of faithful and appreciative interpretation.

Such is our Commentary. It now only remains necessary to make a very few comments on those details of the responsible work which may seem to require it.

In regard of the learned and able body of men who have, to the great advantage of the student, consented to take part in this Commentary, the same general remark may be made that was made in the Preface to the Commentary on the New Testament, viz., that each writer is responsible for his own notes and his own interpretation. It has been the care of the Editor to help each writer, so far as he had power to do so, to set forth his interpretation with clearness and precision. No attempt has been made, where similar ground has been passed

* See Note on Leviticus, chap. xx. 26.

over by two independent writers, to bring about any conventional uniformity of comment or interpretation. The tenour and context of each passage—and it is rare indeed that the tenour and context of two passages are exactly alike—have been regarded as those elements which each writer must be considered utterly free to use as conditioning the details of interpretation. The result may be, here and there, some trivial differences in the subordinate features of the interpretation, yet only such differences as help to bring out what may ultimately be regarded as the closest approximation to the true facts of the case. In many passages it is from this sort of *concordia discors* that the real meaning is most clearly ascertained. In these and all similar details it has been the especial care of the Editor so to place himself in the same point of view with each writer, as to supply most effectively assistance where it might seem to be needed, and, in offering suggestions or proposing alterations, to do so with a due regard to the position deliberately taken up by the writer. Reconsideration has, from time to time, been suggested; but where such reconsideration has seemed to the writer to confirm him in his original view, there that view has never been interfered with.

As in the case of the New Testament, an Introduction has been prefixed to each portion, in which the general tenour of the inspired writing, and those details which might help to set it forth most clearly to the reader, are specified with as much fulness as the nature of this Commentary will permit. Where, also, the subject-matter has seemed to require it, an Excursus has been appended to the Notes for the purpose of helping the more critical reader, and supplying a detail that could not be given elsewhere consistently with the general character of the Work. It has never been forgotten that this Commentary is popular in its general aspect, and designed for the English reader rather than for the professed scholar. Modern controversies, therefore, and the subtler criticisms to which portions of Holy Scripture, especially the prophetical portions, have recently been subjected, are treated broadly and generally, and more with reference to the results arrived at than to the procedure by which those results were obtained. Detailed investigations of hyper-critical objections, or elaborate confutations of theories which common sense or common honesty seems to predispose us at once to repudiate, would obviously be out of place in this Commentary. Nothing, however, has been kept back from the reader. All opposing statements that seem to be of any weight whatever are candidly set forth, and plainly answered whensoever and wheresoever the material for a conclusive answer has been found to exist. That difficulties will in part still remain may be frankly conceded; but even in regard of them this remark may certainly be made—that it is the *plain tendency* of modern historical discovery to attenuate or remove them.

The broad purpose and the structure of the Notes remain the same as in the Commentary on the New Testament. Exegetical details, linguistic discussions, and the refutations of competing interpretations, are, for the most part, if not entirely, avoided; while, on the other hand, all those more general considerations which seem likely to bring home the sacred words more closely to the heart of the reader, are set forth with as much fulness as our limits will allow. Scripture faithfully interpreted is the best evidence for the truth of Scripture, and on that defence no anxious soul has ever rested in vain.

We now (for I well know that my dear brethren and associates would desire to be joined with me in this closing paragraph) humbly commit this work to Almighty God, praying earnestly and devoutly that it may be permitted to set forth the truth of the living Oracles of God, and may minister to the deeper adoration of Him who spake through patriarchs and prophets, the Holy and Eternal Spirit, to whom, with the Father and the Son, be all glory for evermore.

C. J. ELLICOTT
(GLOUCESTER AND BRISTOL).

GENERAL INTRODUCTION

I. The Problem to be Solved.—It is not altogether an easy task to write an Introduction to the Old Testament as a whole which shall not trench on the province of those who have to deal with the several books of which it is composed. Questions as to the date and authorship of those books must obviously be reserved for a later and fuller discussion, or be answered only provisionally. What is now proposed accordingly is to deal with the volume which we know by that name, as containing all that has come down to us from the time of Moses to that of Malachi (or, perhaps, later), of the literature of the Israelites: to trace the growth of that literature in the several stages of its expansion: to note the process by which, after the return of the Jews from Babylon, the work of gathering up the fragments that remained ended, to use a suggestive phrase, in the "survival of the fittest;" and to point out the gradual growth and crystallisation of the idea that the books so collected, the library thus formed, had an authoritative completeness, which was not to be impaired either by addition or diminution, and formed, in the language of a later time, the *Canon** of the Holy Scriptures. That inquiry being completed, with the subsidiary points which present themselves for discussion as to the order, titles, and classification of the books, there will remain the further question how it came to pass that other books, known as those of the Apocrypha, or as deutero-canonical, came to be added to the list, and to meet with a wide, though not an universal, acceptance. Lastly, there will come the inquiry as to the influence of the new revelation which we connect with the name of Christ upon the thoughts and language of mankind in relation to the books that were the authoritative documents of the old revelation. A short notice of the versions in which for long centuries they were chiefly studied, and of the materials which were at hand when the desire to go back to the original sources of knowledge prompted scholars and theologians to study the sacred books of Israel in the Hebrew which was the speech of Israel's noblest days, and lastly of the several attempts which have been made to reproduce them in our English speech, will complete our survey of the subject.

II. The Literature of the Patriarchal Age.—Whether there were any written records in the earliest age of that people, in the period commonly known as the patriarchal, is a question on which we cannot speak with certainty. We have no Hebrew inscriptions of that period, and the Moabite Stone, with its records of the reign of Mesha, a contemporary of Ahab, is, perhaps, the earliest record in any cognate alphabet. Egypt, however, had, at that time, its hieroglyphics, and Assyria its cuneiform characters. Coming as Abraham did from Ur of the Chaldees, and sojourning in Egypt, as the honoured chieftain of a tribe, he may well have appropriated some elements of the culture with which he came in contact. The purchase of the cave of Machpelah (Gen. xxiii. 17—20) implies a documentary-contract, and the record of the conveyance bears a strong resemblance to the agreements of like nature which we find in the old inscriptions of Nineveh, and the Hittite capital, Carchemish (*Records of the Past*, i. 137; ix. 91; xi. 91). The commerce of the Midianites (Gen. xxxvii. 28) would scarcely have been carried on without written accounts. If the name of Kirjath Sepher (City of Scribes, or Book-city—Josh. xv. 15, 16; Judges i. 11, 12) could be traced so far back it would prove that there was a class of scribes, or a city already famous for its library. The episode of the invasion of the cities of the plain by the four kings of the East (Gen. xiv.) has the character of an extract from some older chronicle. The "book of the generations of Adam" (Gen. v.) and other like genealogical documents, tribal, national, or ethnological (Gen. x., xi. 10—32; xxii. 20—24; xxv. 1—4; xxxvi.), indicate a like origin. The Book of Job is, perhaps, too doubtful in its date to furnish conclusive evidence, but if not pre-Mosaic it, at least, represents fairly the culture and the thought of a patriarchal age, outside the direct influences of Mosaic institutions, and there the wish of the sufferer that his words might be "printed in a book" (Job xix. 23); that his adversary had "written a book," *i.e.*, that his accuser had formulated an indictment (Job xxxi. 35), shows the use of writing in judicial proceedings. On the whole, then, it seems probable that when Jacob and his descendants settled in the land of Goshen they had with them at least the elements of a literature, including annals, genealogies, and traditions of tribal history, together with fragments of ancient poems, like the song of Lamech (Gen. iv. 23, 24) and the blessing of Jacob (Gen. xlix.). The Book of Genesis was probably composed largely out of the documents that were thus preserved.

III. Literature of Israel at the Time of the Exodus.—At the time of the exodus from Egypt there can be little doubt that Israel had its historiographers and its poets, as well as its framers and transcribers of laws. Without entering into disputed questions as to the authorship or editorship of books, it can scarcely admit of doubt that the song of Moses, in Exod. xv., has the ring of a hymn of victory written at the time; that at least the first section of the Law (Exod. xx.—xxiii.) dates from the earliest dawn of Israel's history; that the genealogies and marching orders of Num. i., ii., x., and xxvi., and the record of the offerings of the several tribes in Num. vii and viii., and of the encampments of the wandering in Num. xxxiii., are contemporary records. Incidental notices indicate the process by which these records were made, and there is no reason to suppose that they are the out-growth of a later age. After the defeat of the

* The word means primarily, it may be noted, a reed or measuring rod, and thus passes into the figurative sense of a standard or rule. So we have the canons of art, of ethics, and of grammar. The canons passed by Councils were rules for worship or action. The canons (*canonici*) of cathedral or collegiate churches were men bound by a fixed rule of life. This word is first applied to Scripture by Amphilochius (A.D. 330) and Jerome. Canonical books are those admitted into the Canon, as the rule or standard of Truth.

Amalekites, Moses is commanded to "write it for a memorial in *the* book" (Heb.), which was to contain the mighty acts of the Lord (Exod. xvii. 14). After the first instalment of legislation, he "wrote all the words of the Law," presumably in the same book, which is now designated as "the Book of the Covenant" (Exod. xxiv. 3—5). Passing over the more explicit statements of Deuteronomy (xvii. 18, 19; xxviii. 58—61; xxix. 19, 20, 27; xxx. 10), as not wishing to discuss here the questions which have been raised as to the authorship and date of that book, we have incidentally in Josh. xxiv. 26 a notice of a "Book of the Law of God," which was kept in the sanctuary, and had a blank space in which additions might be made from time to time as occasion might require. In addition to these traces of records, partly historical and partly legislative, we have extracts from other books now lost, which indicate the existence of a wider literature, the well-digging song of Num. xxi. 17, 18, the hymn of victory over the Amorites, commemorating their early victories over Moab (Num. xxi. 27, 28), both probably taken from the "Book of the Wars of the Lord" (Num. xxi. 14), which seems to have been the lyric record of the achievements which the historians narrated in prose. On the whole, then, there would seem to be ample grounds for believing that on their entry into the land of Canaan the Israelites brought with them, not indeed the whole Pentateuch in its present form, but many documents that are now incorporated with it, and which served as a nucleus for the work of future compilers.

IV. Hebrew Literature under the Judges.—The period that followed the settlement of the Israelites in Canaan was not favourable to the growth of what we call literature. A population half-pastoral and half-agricultural, with few cities of any size, and struggling for existence under repeated invasions, had not the leisure out of which literary culture grows. In the list of conquered kings, however (Josh. xii.), and in the record of the division of the lands, which forms, as it were, the Doomsday Book of Israel (Josh. xiii.—xxi.), we have documents that bear every trace of contemporary origin, and show that the work of the annalist had not ceased. The Book of the Wars of the Lord apparently found a successor in a collection of heroic *sagas* known as the Book of Jasher (the just or upright), from which extracts are given in Josh. x. 13 and 2 Sam. i. 18, and may have been the unrecognised source of many of the more poetical elements of history that now appear in the Pentateuch. The mention of those who "handle the pen of the writer" in the song of Deborah (Judges v. 14) might suggest at first, like the name of Kirjath-Sepher, the thought of a recognised class of scribes, but scholars are agreed that the words should be translated as "those that wield the rod of the ruler;" and it is obvious that, except as registering the muster-rolls or chronicling achievements, such a class could have found no place in Deborah's song of triumph. That song itself, with the stamp of originality and contemporaneousness impressed on every line, shows that among the women of Israel the genius that had shown itself in Miriam, the part taken by female singers in triumphal processions (Judges xi. 34; 1 Sam. xviii. 7) and in funeral lamentations (2 Sam. i. 24; Jer. xxii. 18), each of which called for words appropriate to the occasion, naturally tended to the development of this form of culture, and in the song of Hannah (1 Sam. ii. 1—10) we may probably trace its influence, intermingled with that of the higher inspiration of the moment.

V. The Schools of the Prophets.—With the institution of the schools of the prophets traditionally ascribed to Samuel, the culture of Israel advanced as by leaps and strides. They were to its civilisation, besides all that was peculiar to their vocation, what the Orphic brotherhoods and the Homeridæ were to that of Greece—what universities and cathedrals and monasteries were to that of mediæval Europe. Their work of worship, uniting as it did both song and music, developed into the Book of Psalms which we retain, and into the lost art of Hebrew music of which the titles to the Psalms (*e.g.*, Neginoth, Nehiloth, Sheminith, Gittith, Muthlabben, &c.) present so many traces. The language of unpremeditated praise in which their work apparently began, though even then not without a certain order (1 Sam. x. 5; xix. 20), passed before long first into the more deliberate work of the reporter, and afterwards into that of a man who sits down to compose a hymn. A like process, we cannot doubt, went on with the preaching which formed another part of the prophet's work. In the earlier days the prophet comes and goes and speaks his message, and leaves but the scantiest records, as probably in the record of the work of the "angel" (better "messenger") of the Lord in Judges ii. 1; v. 23; and in the words of Jehovah, which must have come from some human lips, in x. 11. In the second stage in that of the schools of the prophets, he utters, as throughout the history of Samuel, Elijah, and Elisha, what he has to say in the presence of his disciples, and they take down his words, but the prophet himself is a preacher rather than a writer. In the third the prophet is himself the author, either writing with his own hand (Isa. viii. 1), or employing still the help of an amanuensis (Jer. xxxvi. 1—4). In this way we may trace to the schools of the prophets, as to a fountain-head, a large portion of the Psalms and of the prophetic books of the Old Testament. It was natural under the conditions in which they lived that their influence should spread to the hereditary caste of the tribe of Levi, who had been set apart for the ministries of worship. The founder of the prophetic schools, himself a Levite, formed a link between the two, and from the days of Heman, Asaph, and Jeduthun (1 Chron. vi. 33; xv. 16—22, 41; xxv. 1—3) under David, to those of the sons of Korah under Jehosaphat and Hezekiah (2 Chron. xx. 19), the Levites appear to have furnished their full quota to the minstrelsy of Israel, that minstrelsy being described in one memorable passage as belonging to the functions of a prophet (1 Chron. xxv. 3). The fact that David himself had been trained in those schools—that from earliest youth (1 Sam. xvi. 17—23) to extreme old age (2 Sam. xxiii. 1—7) his life was illumined with the stars at once of prophecy and of verse, made his advent to the throne the golden time of Hebrew literature. The king was known not only as the conqueror and the ruler, but as the "sweet psalmist of Israel," and every form of composition found in him at once a master and a patron. The consciousness of national life which was thus developed, found expression, as it has always done in the analogous stages of the growth of other nations, in the form of history. Men felt that they had at once a future and a past. One man felt drawn to search out the *origines* of his people, and another to record the events in which he and his fathers had actually been sharers. There were the formal official annals, the Books of the "Chronicles," the work, probably, for the most part of the priests, and therefore dwelling largely on the organisation of the Temple, and the changes made during periods of religious reformation under the kings of Judah and Israel. And besides these we have traces of a copious literature, chiefly the work of prophets, and therefore viewing the history of the people from the prophet's standpoint of faith in a righteous order working through the history of the nation, such as has been described above, in the books of Nathan the prophet and Gad the seer (1 Chron. xxix. 29); the book of the Acts of Solomon (1 Kings xi. 41); the prophecy of Ahijah the Shilonite (2 Chron. ix. 29); the visions of Iddo the seer (*ibid.*); the prophecy of Jonah, not found in the book that bears his name (2 Kings xiv. 25); the book of Shemaiah the prophet (2 Chron. xii. 15); of Iddo the seer, concerning genealogies (*ibid.*), and a third book by the same writer (2 Chron. xiii. 22); the book of Jehu the son of Hanani (2 Chron. xx. 34); the acts of Uzziah and Hezekiah, by Isaiah, the son of Amoz (2 Chron. xxvi. 22; xxxii. 32); and the lamentations of Jeremiah for Josiah (2 Chron. xxxv. 28).

Working side by side with each other, and taking each a wider range than the mere register of events which was the work of the "recorder" of the king's court (2 Sam. viii. 16; Isaiah xxxvi. 22), the priests and the prophets, the same man often uniting both characters, laid the foundations of the historical literature of Israel, as the monks did of the history of mediæval Europe. In addition to their work as preaching the word of Jehovah they left their impress on the music and psalmody of the people, on its battle-songs and lamentations, and delighted to trace out the sequence of events in the history of the people as indicating the conditions of true greatness and the fulfilment, more or less complete, of the laws of a righteous government.

VI. The Wisdom-literature of Israel.—The accession of Solomon opened yet another region of culture. The world of nature—from the cedar of Lebanon to the hyssop on the wall (1 Kings iv. 33), the apes and peacocks from the far East, the gold and precious stones from Ophir, the tin that came from Tarshish (Spain)—presented objects for a natural, almost for a scientific, curiosity, which led to registering phenomena, and inquiring into their causes. Contact with nations of other races and creeds, a wider experience of the chances and changes of human life, led to the growth of an ethical wisdom which, after the manner of the East, embodied itself in the form of proverbial maxims. Here also we have traces of a far wider literature than that which now remains with us. But a comparatively small portion of the "three thousand" proverbs of Solomon survives in the book which bears that title (1 Kings iv. 33), that book including also (1) a collection of maxims that was made in the reign of Hezekiah (Prov. xxv.—xxix.), and proverbs, apparently from the wisdom of other countries, that bear the names of Agur and of Lemuel (Prov. xxx. 1; xxxi. 1). To this period and these influences we may probably assign also, if not the authorship, yet the appearance in the literature of Israel of the grand drama which we know as the Book of Job,* dealing with the problem of man's life and the moral government of God from another standpoint than that of the Mosaic Law, and the poem, also dramatic in form, and portraying, at least in its outer framework, the working of human love and its triumph over many obstacles, which we know as the Song of Solomon.†

VII. The Law Forgotten.—So far the literature that thus grew up was in harmony with the faith in Israel, but its wider and more cosmopolitan character tended to a greater laxity; and it would seem that in course of time there came to be a natural conflict between the new literature and the old, as there was between the worship of Jehovah, as the God of Abraham, of Isaac, and of Jacob, and that of Moloch and Chemosh, of Baal and Ashtaroth, which formed one of the perils of this wider culture, and to which kings like Solomon, Ahaz, and Manasseh gave a wrongful preference. The Book of the Law of the Lord, in whatever form it then existed, fell into comparative oblivion. The reformation under Jehoshaphat brought it again into a temporary prominence (2 Chron. xvii. 9), and it is natural to assume that a devout king like Hezekiah cultivating as he did both the psalmody and the sapiential literature which were identified with the faith of Israel (Prov. xxv. 1), and guided by a teacher like Isaiah, would not be neglectful of the older book (or books) which was the groundwork of both. The long reign of Manasseh, however, did its work alike of destruction and suppression, and when the Book of the Law of the Lord was discovered in some secret recess in the Temple during the progress of Josiah's reformation (2 Kings xxii. 8; 2 Chron. xxxiv. 14), it burst upon the people, with its warnings and its woes, with the startling terrors of an unknown portent. What that book was, is one of the problems which must be reserved for discussion in its proper place in the course of this Commentary. It may have been the whole Pentateuch as we now have it, or, as the prominence given to its prophecies of evil might indicate, the Book of Deuteronomy, as the work of Moses, or, as the bolder criticism of our time has suggested, the work of a contemporary who, confident that he was reproducing the mind of Moses, that the spirit of the lawgiver was speaking through him, did not hesitate to assume his character and speak as in his name, as at a later date, certainly in the Book of Wisdom, and possibly also in Ecclesiastes, the teachers of wisdom spoke with no fraudulent *animus* in the name of Solomon.

VIII. The Literature of the Northern Kingdom.—It lies in the nature of the case that we have fuller materials for tracing the history of Hebrew literature in the kingdom of Judah than in that of Israel. The culture of the northern kingdom was of a lower type. The apostasy of Jeroboam alienated from the outset the priests and Levites, who supplied the chief materials of a learned class, and the "lowest of the people" (1 Kings xii. 31), who were made priests of the high places, and of the calves of Bethel and of Dan, were not likely to supply its place. But here also, it must be remembered, there were official historiographers attached to the royal court, schools of the prophets which, under the guidance of Elijah and Elisha, maintained the worship of Jehovah as hymn-writers and as preachers, writers of songs for the feasts of princes and of nobles of a far other character than that of the songs of Zion (Amos vi. 5; viii. 10), probably even a literature as profligate and as sceptical as that of the European Renaissance (Hosea viii. 12; ix. 9, 10). The conquest of the kingdom of Israel by the Assyrians, the events which we sum up as the captivity of the Ten Tribes, swept off alike the good and the evil elements of that literature. If, as in the case of some of the Psalms (probably, *e.g.*, Ps. lxxx.) and the writings of prophets like Hosea and Amos, whose lives and work were cast in the northern kingdom, some of it has survived, it was probably because the remnant of Ephraim that was left took refuge in

* See essay on "The Authorship of the Book of Job," in *Biblical Studies*, by the present writer.

† Ecclesiastes, though purporting to be the work of Solomon, belongs, in the judgment of most recent critics, to a later date, and is therefore not mentioned in the text as belonging to the Salmonic literature.

Judah (2 Chron. xxx. 18) at a time when Hezekiah was carefully gathering up (as we have seen in the case of the Book of Proverbs) all fragments that remained of the older and nobler literature of the people, that nothing might be lost.

IX. The Babylonian Exile.—The capture of Jerusalem by the Chaldæans under Nebuchadnezzar must have wrought a like destruction in Judah or Jerusalem. The royal library of Jerusalem, of which we possibly find a trace as suggesting the symbolism of the house of wisdom with its "seven pillars" (comp. Prov. ix. 1), must have perished in the flames, as that of Alexandria, at a later period, did under Omar, and with it much that would have thrown light on the history and religion of Israel has passed away, never to be recovered. All, however, was not lost. The most precious books were, as in all ages, not those that were only on the shelves of a public library, but those that were treasured up by individual men as the guides and counsellors of their life. The priests, Levites, prophets, and psalmists of Israel, carried with them into Babylon the books which they held most sacred. They were known to have with them the "songs of Zion" (Ps. cxxxvii. 3), and were expected to sing them at the bidding of their conquerors. A priest-prophet, like Ezekiel, may well have had with him the Book of the Law to which he appeals (Ezek. v. 6; xx. 11), the documents which served as the basis of his ideal realisation of the Holy Land, of Jerusalem, and of the Temple (Ezek. xl.—xlviii.). A scribe like Baruch, over and above his work as committing to writing the prophecies of his master Jeremiah (Jer. xxxvi. 4, 32), was not likely to be unmindful of the books which, like Deuteronomy and some of the earlier prophets, formed the basis of that master's teaching. A prince like Daniel, "skilful in all wisdom, and cunning in knowledge, and understanding science" (Dan. i. 4), must, in the nature of the case, have been trained in the books in which the wisdom of his people was enshrined (Dan. vi. 5; ix. 13). To the influence of these three men at the beginning of the captivity it was, we may believe, due that the Jewish exiles did not shrink into a degraded and unlettered caste, that they preserved what they could of the sacred books of their fathers, now more precious to them than ever. Under their training or, at least, with the memory of their work ever before his eyes, grew up the man whose relation to those books is absolutely unique.

X. The Work of Ezra.—Round the name of Ezra there has gathered much that is obviously legendary and fantastic; but the traditions, wild as they are, are such as cluster round the memory of a great man, and indicate the character of his work. To him, according to those legends, it was given to dictate, as by a special inspiration, all the sacred books that had been destroyed by fire and perished from the memories of men (2 Esdr. xiv. 21, 44; Iren. *adv. Hær.* iii. 21, 2; Tertull. *de Cult. Fœmin.* 1, 3.) He had, besides this, dictated to an esoteric circle of disciples seventy other books of a mystic and apocalyptic character (2 Esdr. xiv. 46). He was the president of the Great Synagogue, which included every notable name of the period, and to which the traditions of later rabbis assigned the whole work of the restoration of religion at Jerusalem, the institution of synagogues, the settlement by authority of something like a canon of books that were to be accounted sacred (art. *Synagogue, Great,* in Smith's *Dict. of Bible*). In the more authentic records his work is naturally confined within narrower limits, but it lies in the same direction. He brings the people together on his return to Jerusalem, and has the Book of the Law read to them publicly (Neh. viii. 1—5), and appoints interpreters to expound its meaning (Neh. viii. 8) and cause the hearers "to understand the reading." It is an open question whether their work was confined to translating from the older Hebrew into the later Aramaic, which became from this time the spoken language of the Jews, or extended to a paraphrase of the text, such as afterwards took shape in the books known as Targums (interpretations or paraphrases). In any case the work of Ezra, as the restorer of the religion of Israel, must have been one of immense importance. To him, with scarcely a shadow of a doubt, we owe the preservation of the books which we now have as the anthology of a wide literature, the *Reliquiæ Sacræ* of the older days of Israel, probably the completion out of many documents of the Books of Kings and Chronicles, one from the prophetic, the other from the priestly standpoint; one dealing generally with the history of both Israel and Judah, as the record of the Divine government of the people, the other more fully with that of Judah only.

XI. Completion of the Old Testament Canon.—As yet, however, we do not find, except in relation to the Book of the Law, the idea of a closed Canon, to which no addition could rightfully be made. Not to speak of the writings which belong to Ezra's own period, and in some of which he probably took part as compiler, editor, or writer, the Books of Ezra and Nehemiah, the prophecies of Haggai and Zechariah, the psalm of the Babylonian exiles (Ps. cxxxvii.), the Books of Kings and Chronicles), we have, of later date, the history of Esther and the prophecy of Malachi. In the judgment of many scholars, the Book of Daniel belongs wholly or in part to the time of the Maccabees, and some of the Psalms are ascribed by not a few critics to the same period. The authorship of Ecclesiastes has been brought by some critics as low as the reign of Ptolemy Philopator, by others even to that of Herod the Great. In regard to the last-named book there are traces of a dispute among the rabbis whether it was or was not to be admitted among the sacred books (see *Ecclesiastes* in the *Cambridge School Bible,* p. 27), and the same holds good (the difficulty in each case arising out of the contents of the book) of the Song of Solomon. The discussion ended, however, in the recognition of their claims, and at the time when the history of the New Testament opens it may fairly be assumed that, for the Jews of Palestine at least, the books of the Old Testament were as we now have them,* and were known as being emphatically the Scriptures (Matt. xxi. 42; xxii. 29; Luke xxiv. 27, 32), the holy writings (2 Tim. iii. 15). They were divided popularly into the Law and the Prophets (Matt. xi. 13; xxii. 40; Acts xiii. 15), or more fully into the Law, the Prophets, and the Psalms (Luke xxiv. 44). Traces of a like classification are found in the preface to the apocryphal Book of Ecclesiasticus, where we read more vaguely of the "law, the prophets and the other books." Upon these the rabbis, first of Jerusalem and afterwards of Tiberias and Babylon, concentrated their labours, which bore fruit in the *Targumim* and *Midrashim;*

* So Josephus (*c. Apion.* 1, 8) enumerates (1) the five books of Moses, (2) the thirteen Prophets, in which the Minor Prophets are reckoned as a single book, and the historical books treated as prophetic, and (3) four which contain hymns and directions of life. The last group would seem to imply the non-recognition of some one of the Hagiographa, probably Ecclesiastes or the Song of Solomon. A list framed according to our present Canon would give *five* such books.

the first being of the nature of simple paraphrases, intermingled, as regards those of the later books of the Old Testament, with much legendary matter; and the *Midrashim*, or commentaries, which collect the often discordant expositions that had been given orally by the rabbis. The writings thus reverenced served as the basis of Jewish education, and were read in the synagogues of Palestine (Acts xv. 21). Under these the Christ, as man, increased in wisdom and knowledge. These were the ultimate standard of appeal for Apostles and evangelists. The argument of St. Paul in 2 Cor. iii. 14, and of the writer of the Epistle to the Hebrews (chap. viii. 13; ix. 15), fixed, for Christians at least, on the books thus collected the title of the Old Covenant, the Old Testament, as distinguished from the New.

XII. Jewish Classification of the Old Testament Books.—At a later date, probably in the ninth century after Christ, from the scribes of the *Masora* (= Tradition—*i.e.*, the text as it had been handed down) or revised text of the sacred books, the sacred books received a new and more complete classification, which is retained in all existing copies, written or printed, of the Hebrew text, as follows:—

(1) The *Torah*, or Law, including the books of the Pentateuch, the title of each being taken from its opening words:—

(*a*) *B'reshith* ("In the beginning")=Genesis.
(*b*) *Velle Sh'moth* ("Now these are the names") =Exodus.
(*c*) *Vayikra* ("And he called") =Leviticus.
(*d*) *B'Midbar* ("In the wilderness")=Numbers.
(*e*) *D'bharim* ("The words") =Deuteronomy.

(2) The Prophets, subdivided thus:—

(*a*) Elder { Joshua. Judges. 1 and 2 Samuel. 1 and 2 Kings.
(*b*) Later.
(*a*) Greater { Isaiah. Jeremiah. Ezekiel.
(*β*) Lesser. The twelve Minor Prophets.

(3) The *K'thubim* (= Writings), subdivided as follows:—

(*a*) Psalms.* Proverbs. Job.
(*β*) The five *Megilloth*,† or Rolls { Ruth. Lamentations. Ecclesiastes. Esther. Song of Songs.
(*γ*) Daniel. Ezra. Nehemiah. 1 and 2 Chronicles.

In part the principle of this classification is natural enough, but it presents some peculiarities. (1) The fact that five books so dissimilar in character were grouped together under the title of *Megilloth* finds a possible explanation in the survival of some doubts, such as we have seen in the case of Ecclesiastes and the Song of Songs, as to their full Canonical authority; perhaps also in the reverence for the mystical meaning of the number five, shown also in the arrangement of the Pentateuch and the Psalms.* (2) The position of Daniel, as separated from the other prophets, may possibly have had a like origin, the doubt in this case being strengthened for the later rabbis by the use made by Christians of its Messianic predictions.

XIII. The Work of the Masoretic Scribes.—In addition to this work of classification, the Masoretic scribes (1) carefully revised the text, copying what they found in MSS. of authority, even where they judged it faulty, under the title of the *K'thib*, or text *to be written*, while they wrote in the margin what seemed to them a preferable reading as the *K'ri*, or text *to be uttered*, when the passage was read aloud. (2) They introduced an elaborate system of subdivisions: (*a*) the Pentateuch was divided into 54 *Parashioth*, or sections, the number being chosen so as to give a lesson for synagogue use on each Sabbath of the Jewish intercalary year; this division had probably been in use from the time when the *Torah* was first publicly read in the synagogues (Acts xv. 21); (*b*) the prophets in like manner were divided into the same number of sections, known in this case as *Haphtaroth*; (*c*) throughout the whole of the Hebrew Canons there ran a more minute division into *Pesukim*, or verses, for convenience of reference in writing or preaching. These were reproduced in the edition of the Latin Vulgate, printed by Stephens in 1555, were adopted by the translators of the Geneva Bible in 1560, and afterwards appeared in the Bishops' Bible of 1563, and the Authorised version of 1611, the earlier English printed versions having had only on each page the letters A, B, C, D at equal intervals, as we see in the early editions of Plato and other books. The division into *Parashioth* and *Haphtaroth*, being adapted entirely for synagogue uses (Acts xiii. 15). has naturally never gained acceptance in the Christian Church, and for many centuries the Law and the Prophets were written without any subdivision, till circ. A.D. 1240, when Cardinal Hugh de St. Cher divided each book into sections of convenient length which, combined, as above stated, with the Hebrew *Pesukim*, give us our familiar chapter and verse arrangement. It may be added that the first Hebrew Bible was printed at Soncino in A.D. 1477, just in time to serve as the basis first of Luther's translation, and afterwards, in varying degrees, of the successive English versions. It is true of the Church and people of England that they have received the books of the Old Testament from the fountain-head of what became known in the Reformation controversies by the almost technical term of the "Hebrew verity." The careful revision of the text between the sixth and the ninth centuries after Christ by the Masoretic scribes, and the scrupulous exactness of most Jewish copyists, have minimised the chances of variation in the text, and the result of the collation of MSS. of the Old Testament presents in this respect a marked contrast to that of a like process in dealing with the MSS. of the New.

XIV. The LXX. Version of the Old Testament.—We must not forget, however, that for many

---

* Divided, after the manner of the Pentateuch, into five distinct sections, indicated by the word Amen in Psalms xli., lxxii., lxxxix., and the doxology of Psalm cv.

† So called because each book was written on a parchment roll for synagogue or private use.

* The liturgical use of the *Megilloth* as read, each book being read as a whole, on appointed days, may have helped to determine the arrangement. The order was as follows:—(1) The Song of Solomon on the eighth day of the Feast of the Passover, (2) Ruth on the second day of Pentecost, (3) Lamentations on the ninth day of the month Ab, (4) Ecclesiastes on the third day of the Feast of Tabernacles, (5) Esther on the Feast of Purim. (Delitzsch on *Isaiah*, p. 3. Eng. translation.)

centuries the influence of the Old Testament in the Christian Church was chiefly exercised through the medium of two versions, each of which calls for a brief notice. And (1) there is the Greek version, commonly known as the Septuagint, and referred to more briefly as the LXX. The name has its origin in a narrative more or less legendary which has come down to us bearing the name of Aristeas, who writes as an Alexandrian Jew.* Ptolemy Philadelphus, King of Egypt (B.C. 277), it was said, wished to enrich his library with a translation of the religious books of the Jews, who formed an important section of the population of his kingdom. With this view he wrote to the high priest of the Temple at Jerusalem requesting him to send competent translators. Seventy-two scribes of repute, six from each of the twelve tribes, were accordingly despatched. They were received by the king on their arrival at Alexandria with every mark of honour, and separate chambers were assigned to them, in which each, apart from the others and with no communication with them, was to execute his task. They worked for seventy-two days, and when they met to compare the results of their labours it was found, according to a later form of the legend preserved by Irenæus (iii. 24), but not in the narrative of Aristeas, that they had all agreed *verbatim et literatim* in the same version. The result was ascribed to the guidance of an immediate inspiration, and the book was accordingly received as having a Divine authority equal to that of the original. Over and above the introduction into this story of a supernatural element working contrary to the analogy of God's general method in revealing His will and wisdom to mankind, there are obviously many elements of improbability. It is not certain that the Hebrew Canon of Scripture was at this time definitely settled. The narrative has a suspicious likeness to the legend already referred to, that Ezra had, from memory, or by inspiration, reproduced the whole of that Canon in its completeness. The volume now known includes many writings which are not in that Canon, and some of which are confessedly of later date. The authority of the version was never acknowledged by the Jews of Palestine. To them this translation of the sacred books into the language of the heathen seemed an act of sacrilege, a sin as great as the worship of the golden calf. They appointed a day of fasting and humiliation to be held annually for this profanation, as they did for the destruction and desecration of the Temple. (Walton's *Prolegomena*, ix.) Passing from legendary history to the safer region of reasonable conjecture, what probably occurred was this. The Jews, who had settled in Alexandria in great numbers, and who occupied, as they did afterwards at Rome, a distinct quarter of the city, learnt to speak and think in Greek. They lost their familiarity with the ancient Hebrew, and with the Aramaic of the Targums. They wanted to read their sacred books both privately and in their synagogues in what was now their own language. The action of Ezra and his successors in paraphrasing or translating those books seemed to give a sanction to the principle of translation. The five books of the Law, soon coming to be regarded as a single yet five-fold volume, and therefore known as the Pentateuch, were, as being read in the synagogues every Sabbath, the first to be translated, and were followed in due course by the Prophets, in the wider sense in which that name was employed in the Hebrew classification. The *K'thubim*, now known to the Alexandrian Jews by the Greek equivalent of *Hagiographa*, or Holy Writings, were, as far as we can judge, the last to come under the translator's hands. It is probable enough that copies of the translation were placed in the royal library at Alexandria, and this served as a starting-point for the legend of Aristeas. The want which was thus met at Alexandria was felt wherever the Jews, known as Hellenistæ or Greek-speaking Jews, were settled in the cities of Asia, Greece, or Italy. Even in Palestine itself Greek was freely spoken, and there were many synagogues at Jerusalem, as we see in Acts vi. 9, consisting entirely of these Hellenistæ. The natural result was that there also the LXX. version found acceptance with all but the more bigoted and prejudiced rabbis, who, as we have seen, anathematised it. Its texts were freely quoted, we cannot doubt, in the disputes between St. Stephen and his opponents in those Hellenistic synagogues (Acts vi. 9). Even St. Paul, though a Hebrew of the Hebrews, habitually used and quoted it. It served as the groundwork of religious education of Jewish children like Timotheus (2 Tim. iii. 15), who were growing up in heathen cities. It may have been familiar even to our Lord and to His Galilean disciples.

It would be out of place to enter here into any detailed discussion of the merits of the LXX. version as a translation. It is not without the defects which attach in greater or less measure to all human workmanship. Sometimes, after the manner of the Targum, it gives a paraphrase instead of a translation, toning down strong expressions, and removing difficulties. Sometimes it mistakes the meaning of the Hebrew, or appears to have been based upon a different text from that which the Masoretic scribes have handed down to us. Sometimes, notably in the history of Jeroboam, and in some chapters of Daniel, as in Bel and the Dragon, and the History of Susannah and the Elders, and in some of the headings of the Psalms, it inserts what is not now found in the Hebrew text. In the case of Jeremiah the whole arrangement of chapters differs from that of the Hebrew. What is yet more noteworthy, it treats the Hebrew Canon as one which was not yet closed, and includes in the same volume, and with no note of inferiority, books which are not found in it, and which are represented by what we now know as the Apocrypha;* and, these books being intermingled with the others, the order of the books is different from that of the Hebrews.

XV. The Apocrypha.—The Alexandrian Jews, it is clear, looked on the Hebrew books as a *Bibliotheca Sacra*, a library of the sacred literature of their nation, and did not hesitate, as occasion offered, to place, as it were, on the shelves of that library what seemed to them precious, either as recording the dealings of God for and with His people, as in 1 Esdras, Tobit, Judith, 1 and 2 Maccabees, or the utterances of the wise of heart, whether pseudonymous, like the Wisdom of Solomon, or compilations with the name of the editor, like the Wisdom of the Son of Sirach (Ecclesiasticus), or devotional fragments like the Prayer of Manasseh, which is found in some, though not in all, MSS. of the LXX. It is, of course, open to question how far they were right in exercising this freedom at

* The narrative of Aristeas has been printed by Havercamp in his edition of Josephus, by Hody (*De Bibliorum Textibus Originalibus*), and elsewhere.

* The word, which primarily means "hidden" or "secret," was probably applied in the first instance to books that claimed, like those alluded to in 2 Esdr. xiv. 44, a mysterious and esoteric character. When these came to be looked on as of questionable authority, the word was used, with a touch of sarcasm, as equivalent to "spurious." Another but less natural explanation is that the name indicated the fact that the books to which it was applied were not, like the Canonical books, read publicly in the church, but privately and in secret.

all; how far they were wise in the use they made of it. The fact that they inserted all the books of the Hebrew Canon is, at all events, valuable as a testimony to the authority of the older Scriptures, and they can claim, as those of the Apocryphal books cannot, the *consensus* alike of the Hebrew and Hellenistic Jews. It might have been well, indeed, to have acknowledged their higher prerogative by placing them, as Protestant churches have done, in a separate group, as standing in this respect on a lower level. On the other hand, we owe to this action of the LXX. translators the preservation of whatever was most valuable in the literature of Judaism between the close of the Old Testament and the beginning of the New, and are thus able to trace the continuous education that was preparing the way for the higher revelation which was made known to men in Christ.

XVI. The Apocrypha in the Eastern Church.—The absence of any earlier MSS. of the LXX. than those of the fourth or fifth century makes it difficult to say when the complete collection thus formed appeared as a single volume. The fact that Josephus (though, as a Greek writer, he must have been familiar with the Greek version of the sacred books, and largely uses some of the additions, as in the history of the Maccabean period) adheres, as stated above, to the Hebrew Canon when he gives a list of them, shows that he, of Palestinian birth, at once a priest and a Pharisee, did not admit the claims of the later books to stand on the same level as the earlier. The writers of the New Testament, as was also natural from their education and training, write in much the same way, never quoting the books that we know as the Apocrypha, as authoritative, or honouring them with the title of Scripture; while yet, as is shown by a comparison of the Epistle to the Hebrews with the Wisdom of Solomon, they borrow largely from their phraseology, or allude, as the writer of that epistle does, to facts recorded in their history (Heb. xi. 35), or cite, as St. James seems to do, some of their utterances of wisdom. (See *St. James* in the *Cambridge School Bible*, pp. 32, 33.) If, as many critics, from Luther onwards, have thought, Apollos was the writer of the Epistle to the Hebrews, it was perhaps natural that he should use the books of the Alexandrian Canon more freely than the other writings of the New Testament. It lies on the surface, however, that the New Testament writers, while recognising the supreme authority of the books of the Hebrew Canon, do not shrink from using freely books that were neither in that Canon nor the Alexandrian, and refer, *e.g.*, to some lost version of the history of the Exodus, which contained the names of Jannes and Jambres (2 Tim. iii. 8), to some legendary record of the dispute between Michael the archangel and Satan after the death of Moses (Jude, verse 9), and to a prophecy ascribed to Enoch (Jude, verse 14) found in the book that bears his name, and which, after having been hidden and forgotten for centuries, was found by the traveller Bruce in an Ethiopian version, and has since been translated by Archbishop Laurence in 1838, and edited by various hands.

The history of the Christian Church follows mainly on the same lines. Its writers used freely all the books that belonged to the sacred literature of the Jews, whether Hebrew or Hellenistic. As the earliest MSS. of the LXX. version, such as the Sinaitic, the Vatican, and the Alexandrian, show, they recognised, as adapted for the worship of the Church, for its lessons and its sermons, the Alexandrian Canon with all its numerous additions. The Greek Church, as was natural, has continued to use it, as its only text of the Scriptures of the Old Testament. On the other hand, the more critical writers who studied Scripture in the light of history, recognised, tacitly or expressly, the difference between the Hebrew Canon and the additions. Justin Martyr (in this instance we trace the influence of his birth and training in Palestine) never quotes the latter. Melito of Sardis (circ. A.D. 160) omits them altogether, with the exception of the Wisdom of Solomon, in his catalogue of the Old Testament writings. It may be noted also that he omits the names of Nehemiah and Esther. Probably they were included under the general name of Esdras. Origen in like manner confines his list to the twenty-two books of the Hebrew Canon. The Council of Laodicea (A.D. 363), possibly under the influence of the tradition which originated with Melito, excluded all the Apocryphal books except the Epistle to Baruch, which seems to have been regarded as an integral part of the Book of Jeremiah.

XVII. The Apocrypha in the Western Church.—The history of the Latin Church runs, to a great extent, parallel with that of the Greek, in its relation to the Old Testament Canon. The earliest converts in Rome and its Latin-speaking provinces, northern Africa being the most prominent of these, were either Hellenistic Jews, or proselytes who had passed through Hellenistic Judaism on their way to the faith of Christ, and they therefore naturally adopted the Alexandrian rather than the Hebrew Canon. The early Latin Fathers, Tertullian and Cyprian, quote the Apocryphal books freely as Scripture. Augustine follows them in his general use of the books, gives a list which includes the additions, but, possibly under the influence of his great contemporary Jerome, draws a line of distinction between them and those of the Hebrew Canon, confining the adjective "Canonical" to the latter, and speaking of the others as "received by the Church, though not by the Jews," as on a lower level than "the Law, and Psalms, and the Prophets, to which the Lord bore His witness" (*De Doct. Christ.* ii. 8, 13). The Old Latin version, however, as made, not from the Hebrew, but from the Greek, reproduced the same books, and in the same order as we find them in the LXX.

XVIII. The Vulgate Version of the Old Testament.—With the appearance of Jerome on the scene, we find a marked difference of thought and language, though not of action. With the natural instincts of a scholar he determined to translate from the original, and not from a Greek version of it. He settled in Palestine for the completion of his great work, and learnt Hebrew from Jewish teachers. He found that their Canon was not the same as that with which he was familiar, that the books which it contained were characterised by a higher and more venerable antiquity, and had been cited, as the others had not been cited, by the writers of the New Testament, and by Christ Himself. He had the courage, accordingly, to run counter to the prevailing traditions of the Western Church, and drew a hard and fast line between the two groups of books, as standing on a different footing, and applicable to different uses. The Hebrew books alone were Canonical, the others were only "ecclesiastical." The one might be used to establish a doctrine, the others (in language with which the sixth Article of the Church of England has made us familiar) were to be read only "for example of life and instruction of manners." (*Prolog. Galeat. Dialog. in Libros*

Salomonis.) In practice, however, Jerome was content to follow on the old lines, and the Vulgate included the same books as the older version had done, and in the same order. One book, indeed, now known as the Second Book of Esdras, was thrown into a position of marked inferiority. Jerome speaks of it with undisguised contempt. It is rarely found in MSS. of the Latin Vulgate. It, with the 1 Esdras of our Apocrypha, and the Prayer of Manasses, of all the Apocryphal books, was excluded by the Council of Trent from the list of Canonical books, and these have consequently disappeared from most editions of the Latin version of the Old Testament printed for the use and under the sanction of the Roman Church.*

In regard to the other books of the Alexandrian Canon, however, the Council of Trent (*Sess.* iv.), in its antagonism to the rising criticism of the period, accepted the action rather than the teaching of Jerome, and, in stronger language than had ever been used before, declared that they were to be received with the same reverence and honour as the other Canonical books, and pronounced its anathema on all who should teach otherwise. The Reformed Churches, as might be expected, took the other line. Luther placed them in a group by themselves, and for the first time affixed to them the title of Apocrypha. The English version followed in the line of Luther, and adopted his nomenclature. In one remarkable instance, indeed, we trace a feeling of hesitation showing itself in a somewhat curious blunder. In the preface to Cranmer's Bible the books had been described as Apocrypha, and the usual explanation of that term had followed. In correcting the proofs, apparently, the thought had occurred to the editor that it would be better to use a more respectful title, and the word was altered, and so, when the volume was published, the reader was informed that the books "were called *Hagiographa*" (= Holy Writings, the title commonly given to the *K'thubim* of the Hebrew Canon), "because they were read not publicly, but, as it were, in secret." That blunder, however, was not repeated, and the word Apocrypha retained its place in the printed versions of the Old Testament. In 1542, the sixth of what were then the forty-two Articles of the Church of England, deliberately adopted, in the words that have been already quoted, the distinction which Jerome had been the first to draw; and without using the term Apocrypha (its reticence in this respect is noteworthy), spoke of them as "the other books," which were not Canonical, and therefore were not to be used "to establish any doctrine." Practically, however, the Church of England, by appointing lessons to be read from some of the books, both in the older and, in a more limited measure, in the more recent lectionary, has treated the books in question with more honour than any other Reformed Church; and with some of her leading divines—*e.g.*, Cosin—the term "deutero-canonical" has commended itself as more accurately describing their character than the more familiar Apocrypha.

XIX. English Versions of the Old Testament.—The history of the English translations of the Old Testament may, for our present purpose, be very briefly told. In Wycliffe's version the Old Testament was assigned to his friend and disciple Nicholas de Hereford, but the work was apparently interrupted, probably by a citation to appear before Archbishop Arundel, in A.D. 1382, and ends abruptly in the middle of the Epistle of Baruch. It was completed and revised by Richard Purvey in A.D. 1388, and took its place in what was commonly known as Wycliffe's Bible. It was based entirely on the Vulgate, neither Hebrew nor Greek being at that time accessible to English students; and a crucial instance of this appears in its rendering of Gen. iii. 15, as "*she* shall trede thy head." The statement in the preface, "that, by witnesse of Jerom, of Lire" (Nicholas de Lyra, the great mediæval commentator), "and other expositoures, the texte of our boke discordeth much from the Ebrew," shows, however, a consciousness that something more was wanted, and that the true idea of a translation implied that it should be made from the original. The work of Tyndale was naturally concentrated chiefly on the New Testament, but there is abundant evidence throughout his writings that he had studied Hebrew with a view to the translation of the Old. As a first experiment he published a translation of Jonah, and (circ. 1530–1) this was followed by the Pentateuch. He did not proceed further. Traces of his labours as a student are found, however, in many casual notes throughout his later works; in a table of Hebrew words, with their meanings, prefixed to his translation of the Pentateuch; notably in a remark (preface to *Obedience of a Christian Man*) which shows how fully he had entered into the genius of the language: "The properties of the Hebrew tongue agreeth a thousand time more with the English than with the Latin. The manner of speaking is in both one, so that in a thousand places thou needest not but to translate the Hebrew word for word."

The work which was thus begun by Tyndale was taken up by Coverdale. His aim, however, was a less lofty one. His translation did not profess to be made from the original text either of the Old or the New Testament, but "from the Douche and the Latine," *i.e.*, from Luther and the Vulgate. It would seem, however, that he attained in the course of his labours a wider knowledge than that with which he started, and in a letter to Cromwell (*Remains*, p. 492. Parker Soc.) he speaks of himself as acquainted "not only with the standing text of the Hebrew, but with the interpretation of the Chaldee and the Greek" (*i.e.*, with the Targums and the LXX.), "and with the diversity of reading of all texts." Luther's version was, however, dominant in its influence. Thus, to give a few examples of special interest:—"Cush," which in Wycliffe, Tyndale, and the Authorised version, is uniformly rendered "Ethiopia," is in Coverdale "the Morians' land," after Luther's "Mohrenland" (= land of the Moors) (Ps. lxviii. 31; Acts viii. 27, &c.), and appears in this form accordingly in the Prayer Book version of the Psalms. The proper name Rab-shakeh passes, as in Luther, into "the chief butler" (2 Kings xviii. 17; Isa. xxxvi. 11). In making the sons of David "priests" (2 Sam. viii. 18) he followed both his authorities. "Shiloh," in the prophecy of Gen. xlix. 10, becomes "the worthy," after Luther's "der Held." "They houghed oxen" takes the place of "they digged down a wall," in Gen. xlix. 6. The singular word "lamia" (=a vampire sorceress that sucked the blood of children) is taken from the Vulgate as the rendering of the Hebrew *ziim* ("wild beasts" in Authorised version) in Isa. xxxiv. 14. The "tabernacle of witness," where the Authorised version has "congregation," shows the same influence. It was perhaps under the same guidance that his language as to the Apocrypha lacks the sharpness of that of the more zealous Reformers.

* In the classification of the Tridentine list of books, 1 Esdras =Ezra of the Authorised version, 2 Esdras=Nehemiah, while 3 and 4 Esdras answer to the 1 and 2 Esdras of the English Apocrypha.

Baruch is placed with the Canonical books after Lamentations. Of the rest, he says that "they are placed apart," as "not held in the same repute" as the other Scriptures; but this is only because there are "dark sayings" in them, which seem to differ from the "open Scripture." He has no wish that they "should be despised or little set by." "Patience and study would show that the two were agreed."

Coverdale's version was first printed, probably at Zurich, in 1535; other editions appeared in 1537, 1539, 1550, 1553. The plural form "Biblia" appears in the title-page—possibly, however, in its later use as a singular feminine. There are no notes, no chapter-headings, no division into verses. The letters A, B, C, D, in the margin, as in the early editions of the Greek and Latin authors, are the only helps for finding places. Marginal references point to parallel passages. The Old Testament, especially in Genesis, has the attraction of wood-cuts. Each book has a table of contents prefixed to it.

In the year 1537 a large folio Bible appeared, as edited and dedicated to the king by Thomas Matthew. No one of that name appears at all prominently in the religious history of the period, and this suggests the inference that the name was pseudonymous, adopted as a veil to conceal the real translator. There is abundant evidence, external and internal, identifying this translator with John Rogers, the proto-martyr of the Marian persecution, and a friend and disciple of Tyndale. As far as the Old Testament is concerned, it seems to have been based, but with an independent study of the Hebrew, upon the previous versions of Tyndale (so far as that extended) and Coverdale. Signs of a more advanced knowledge are found in the explanations given of technical words connected with the Psalms, Neginoth, Shiggaion, Sheminith, &c. Ps. ii. is printed as a dialogue. The names of the Hebrew letters are prefixed to the verses in the acrostic chapters of Lamentations. Reference is made to the Chaldee paraphrase (Job vi.), to Rabbi Abraham (Job xix.), to Kimchi (Ps. iii.). After being printed abroad as far as the end of Isaiah it was taken up as a business speculation by Grafton and Whitchurch, the king's printers, and patronised by Cranmer and Cromwell. Through their influence, and probably through the fact that Rogers' name was kept in the background, it obtained, in spite of notes which were as strongly Protestant as any of Tyndale's, the king's sanction, and a copy of it was ordered to be placed in every church at the cost of the incumbent and the parishioners. It was accordingly the first Authorised version.

Taverner's version (1539), based upon "the labours of others," whom, however, he does not name, was probably undertaken in deference to the wishes of the more moderate Reformers, who were alarmed at the vehemence of some of Rogers' notes, and yet wished for a more accurate version, and one more definitely based upon the original, than Coverdale's. It left no marked impress on the theology or literature of the time, and its chief interest lies perhaps in the fact that, alone of all the English versions of the Bible, it was the work of a layman.

In the same year as Taverner's, and coming from the same press, appeared an English version of the Bible, in a more stately folio, printed after a more costly fashion, bearing a higher name than any previous edition. The title-page is an elaborate engraving, the spirit and power of which indicate the hand of Holbein. The king, seated on his throne, is giving the *Verbum Dei* to the bishops and doctors, and they distribute it to the people, while bishops, doctors, and people are all joining in cries of *Vivat Rex*. It declares the book to be "truly translated after the verity of the Hebrew and Greek texts," by "divers learned men, expert in the foresaid tongues." A preface, in an edition of 1540, with the initials T. C., implies the archbishop's sanction. In a later edition (Nov., 1540) his name appears on the title-page, and the names of his coadjutors are given, Cuthbert (Tonstal), Bishop of Durham, and Nicholas (Heath), Bishop of Rochester. In the translation of the Old Testament there is, as the title-page might lead us to expect, a greater display of Hebrew than in any previous version. The books of the Pentateuch have their Hebrew names given, *B'reshith* ("In the beginning") for Genesis, *Velle Sh'moth* ("And the names") for Exodus, and so on. 1 and 2 Chronicles, in like manner, appear as *Dibre Haiamim* ("Words of days"). The strange mistake caused by the substitution of *Hagiographa* for *Apocrypha*, for which this version is memorable, has been already noticed. The sanction given to the book, and the absence of any notes (though a marginal hand [☞] indicated an intention to supply them some day), naturally gave it a greater popularity than had been acquired by any previous version. In 1541 it appears as "authorised," to be "used and frequented" in every church in the kingdom. It was the Authorised version of the English Church till 1568, the interval of Mary's reign excepted. From it were taken most, if not all, the portions of Scripture in the Prayer Books of 1549 and 1552. The Psalms as a whole, the quotations from Scripture in the Homilies, the sentences in the Communion Service, and some phrases elsewhere, still preserve the remembrance of it.

Cranmer's version, however, did not satisfy the more zealous Reformers. Its size made it too costly. There were no explanatory or dogmatic notes. It followed Coverdale too closely, and failed, therefore, in spite of the profession of the title-page, to represent the Hebrew of the Old Testament, or the Greek of the New. The English refugees at Geneva accordingly—among them Whittingham, Goodman, Pullain, Sampson, and Coverdale himself—undertook the task of making a new translation of the whole Bible. They entered on what they call their "great and wonderful work" with much "fear and trembling." It occupied them for more than two years. The New Testament was printed at Geneva in 1557; the whole Bible in 1560. Of all the versions prior to that of 1611 the Geneva gained the most general acceptance. Not less than eighty editions were printed between 1558 and 1611, and it kept its ground for some time even against the Authorised version. The causes of this popularity are not far to seek. The volume was, in all its editions, cheaper and more portable—a small quarto, or octavo, instead of the large folio of Cranmer's "Great Bible." It was the first version that laid aside the obsolescent black-letter, and appeared, though not in all the editions, in Roman type. It was the first which, following the Hebrew example, recognised the division into verses, so dear to preachers and to students. It was accompanied, in most of the editions after 1578, by a Bible Dictionary of considerable merit. The notes were often really helpful in dealing with the difficulties of Scripture, and were looked upon as spiritual and evangelical. It was, accordingly, the version specially adopted by the great Puritan party through the whole reign of Elizabeth and far into that of James. In regard to the Old Testament it may be noted that it attempted to reproduce the exact form of Hebrew names, such as Izhak (Isaac), Jaacob, and the like. The English edition, published by Barker, became popularly known as the

"Breeches" Bible, from its use of that word instead of "aprons" in Gen. iii. 7.

Archbishop Parker, though he had supported an application from the publisher of the Geneva Bible for a licence to reprint in 12mo, was not satisfied, and contemplated, as he stated at the time, "one other special Bible for the churches, to be set forth as convenient time and leisure should permit." In the meantime, he said, "it would nothing hinder, but rather do good, to have diversity of translations and readings" (Strype's *Life of Parker*, iii. 6). With the help, accordingly, of eight bishops, with some deans and professors, Cranmer's Bible, which was avowedly taken as the basis, was carefully revised, and the book appeared in a magnificent folio in 1568. It was adorned by portraits of Elizabeth and the Earl of Leicester, with a map of Palestine, with not a few wood engravings, with an elaborate set of genealogical tables, prepared by Speed the antiquary, under the direction of Hugh Broughton, the greatest Hebrew scholar of the century. It adopted the verse division of the Geneva Bible. Alone of all the versions it classified the books, both of the Old and New Testaments, under the headings of legal, historical, sapiential, and prophetical. Like the Geneva, it aimed at a more accurate representation of the Hebrew of Old Testament names, as, *e.g.*, in Heva (Eve), Isahac, Urijahu. The bulk and cost of the Bishops' Bible tended to confine its use to the churches, in all of which it was ordered to be used. It never entered into anything like a practical competition with the Geneva version.

Of the Douay version of the Old Testament, published in 1609, by Roman Catholic scholars, as the complement of the Rhemish New Testament of 1582, there is not need to say much. It was based on the Vulgate, not on the Hebrew. The style was disfigured by pedantic Latinisms, and strange "ink-horn" phrases. It left no mark on the thought and language of the English people.

The history of the Authorised version of 1611 presents, in one respect, a striking contrast to the history of those which had preceded it. They had an average duration of about ten years each, and each then gave way to its successor. It has commanded the reverence and admiration of all English-speaking nations for more than two centuries and a half. Till within the last ten years no attempt even has been made at a revision. It must be admitted that it had just claims to this reverence. If it did not bear the impress of the genius of a single mind, as Tyndale's did, it was, to balance that defect, the outcome of the labours of scholars far more numerous and better qualified than had ever been joined together before for a like purpose. The list of the forty-seven members of the revising company included well-nigh every man of scholarly mark in England. Andrews, Saravia, Overal, Montague, and Barlow represented the "higher" party in the Church; Reinolds, Chaderton, and Lively that of the Puritans. Culture and scholarship unconnected with party were represented by Sir Henry Savile and John Boys. It was, perhaps, wise on the part of the revisers, with a view to the general acceptance of their work, that they confined themselves to the task of translating, and avoided the risk and responsibility of interpreting. Had they given notes after the manner of the Geneva Bible, they would certainly have offended one school of thought in their own generation, and might have laid a stumbling-block in the way of those that were to come. In that case we might have had the tremendous evil of a whole body of exegesis reflecting the Calvinism of the Synod of Dort, the absolutism of James I., the high-flying prelacy of Bancroft. As it was, they left the work of the interpreter free and unfettered for all time to come.*

In that part of their work with which we are now more immediately concerned, the version of the Old Testament, the translators of 1611 were relatively more successful than in dealing with the New. The Hebrew scholarship of the time stood on a higher level than the Greek, and the reverence which men felt for what was known in their controversies with Rome as the "Hebrew verity" made them look to the original text as the basis of their work, caring little for the LXX. or the Vulgate. Making allowance for the inherent difficulties of their work, they succeeded in a marvellous degree in reproducing the loftiness and grandeur of the prophets and psalmists of Israel, and through that success have enriched the thoughts and language of the theological, and even of the non-theological, literature of England. They did not, however, claim finality for their work, and those who would urge that claim now on their behalf, as a bar to further revision, are unfaithful at once to their teaching and their example. It cannot be questioned that their work, excellent as it was, is yet capable of improvement. The labours of Gesenius, and Furst, and Ewald have given us better lexicons and grammars than those of the seventeenth century. The literature of England, and yet more of Germany, presents a vast mine of exegetical apparatus, which cannot be without an influence for good upon the work of revision. The company of revisers to whom the Old Testament was committed represented a higher average of Semitic scholarship than that of 1611. The comparative scantiness of variations in the Hebrew text, the comparative simplicity of Hebrew grammar, free their work from occasions of controversy and offence which, rightly or wrongly, made more difficult the revision of the New Testament as issued in 1881. The Old Testament revision, which was issued four years later, from the causes mentioned, was far less complex. The work of revision began in 1870, and an edition of the Bible published in 1876 by Messrs. Eyre and Spottiswoode, "with various readings and renderings from the best authorities," under the editorship of Messrs. Cheyne, Clarke, Driver, and Goodwin, gave evidence of the added help and inspirational enlightenment to be derived from an earnest and scholarly revision, of the light thrown upon obscurities, and the loyalty with which the past was respected.

XX. The Authority and Inspiration of the Old Testament.—Such, briefly, is the history of the volume which we have come to know throughout Christendom as the Old Testament. It remains, in conclusion, to say a few words as to the nature of its claims on the attention of the thoughtful reader, and the temper in which it should be studied. It need hardly be said that if it came before us only as embodying all that remains of the literature of Israel in its brightest and palmiest days, it would have for us an interest beyond that which attaches (with the one exception of the New Testament) to any other of what are known as the sacred books of the history of mankind. It is something more than a collection of liturgical hymns like the Vedas of India, or the Zend-Avesta of the Parsees; something more than the

* I am bound to acknowledge my obligations for much of the information as to the English versions of the Bible, to the article *Version, Authorised*, in Smith's *Dictionary of the Bible*, and to the works on the same subject by Dr. Westcott and Dr. Moulton.

utterances of a single mind, reflecting its various moods and phases, like the Koran, or than the proverbial maxims which represent the teaching of Confucius, or the mystic legends which make up the sacred books of Buddhism. It represents, to say the least, the whole life—political, religious, and literary—of a people of singular gifts, and it has sustained the life of that people through the long succession of centuries. It embodies their strivings after wisdom, their aspirations after the Eternal, their belief in a Divine order asserting itself among the disorders of mankind. It has formed the basis of a religion wider than its own, and through Christendom has permeated the thoughts and feelings of the most civilised portion of mankind. It has left its impress upon their laws, their polity, their creeds. Were it nothing more than this, it would deserve and would repay the study of any thoughtful student of the religious history of mankind. But for us it is something more, much more, than this. It has its highest outcome in the life, the teaching, the character of Christ, and of those whom He sent to be His apostles and evangelists. That life and character were, humanly speaking, fashioned under its influence; they fulfilled all its dim foreshadowings and inextinguishable hopes, stamped it with the supreme sanction of His authority as a Divine revelation of the will and mind of God. It was not, indeed, a full revelation, for God "had provided some better thing for us" (Heb. xi. 40), and He who had "in sundry times and divers manners" spoken in times past to the fathers (Heb. i. 1), spake in the last days to us through the Son; but it was taken by that Son Himself as the norm and standard of His teaching (Matt. v. 17), as prophetic of His work. He testified that Law and Prophets and Psalms spake of Him (Luke xxiv. 27; John v. 39, 46), that they bore their witness to His Divine Sonship, that they prophesied, sometimes distinctly, sometimes in parables and dark sayings, of His sufferings and death and resurrection. Its sayings sustained Him in His conflict with evil (Matt. iv. 1—10; Luke iv. 1—12), in His endurance of shame and obloquy and pain (Matt. xxvi. 54; Luke xxiii. 37). Its brightest visions of a Divine kingdom of peace and purity and blessedness were, He taught men, (Luke iv. 21), realised in the kingdom which He founded, in the company of believers in Him, which, as the Church of the living God, was founded upon the Eternal Rock. And the witness which He thus bore was carried on by His Apostles. They taught men to find new and deeper meanings in the types of Jewish ritual, in the aspirations of psalmists, in the visions of prophets (Epistle to the Hebrews, *passim*). For them the Holy Scriptures of the Old Testament were "able to make men wise unto salvation through faith which is in Christ Jesus, and, being inspired of God," were "profitable for doctrine, for reproof, for correction, for instruction in righteousness" (2 Tim. iii. 16, 17). They taught that prophecy "came not of old time" (or indeed at any time) "by the will of man, but that holy men of God spake as they were borne on by the Holy Spirit" (2 Pet. i. 21).

"Inspired of God." That thought has, we know, been fruitful in many controversies. On the one hand, there have been theories of inspiration which have minimised or excluded the human element; which have made prophets, lawgivers, apostles, evangelists, only the machines through which the Divine Spirit uttered His own words; and have seen, accordingly, in every statement of fact as regards history or nature, an oracle of God not to be questioned or debated; in the title even of every book, that which was a bar to any inquiry into its authorship or date. On *à priori* grounds it has been argued that a revelation from God must, in the nature of the case, include all the subordinate accessories that cluster round it, that it was not worth giving at all unless it were infallible in everything. That mechanical theory of inspiration has, it is believed, but little to recommend it, except that it meets the craving of men for an infallible authority; and that craving, as we know, goes farther, and leads to a demand for an infallible interpreter of the infallible book. The *à priori* assumption goes beyond the limits of what is in itself reasonable and right. We are in no sort judges, as Bishop Butler has taught us (assuming that God willed to impart to mankind a knowledge of Himself), of the methods and the forms, the measures and degrees in which that knowledge would be imparted (*Analogy*, ii. 6). And the theory is, to say the least, at variance with the impression made on us by the books themselves. They bear, as strongly as the books of any other literature, the stamp of individual character. They indicate, in not a few cases, the labours of compilation and editing which brought them into their present form. They reflect the thoughts and feelings of the times in which they were severally written. They are from first to last intensely national in their character.

What has been called, in contrast with this hypothesis, the theory of a dynamic inspiration,* presents, it is believed, a more satisfactory solution of the problem, one more in harmony with reason, with analogy, with the facts of the case, with the teaching of the Bible itself. The term requires, it may be, a few words of explanation. What is meant is this, that the writers of the Old and New Testaments were not mere machines, but men of like passions with ourselves; each with his own thoughts, temperament, character; each under a training that developed the gifts which he thus possessed by nature, or acquired by education and experience; but that there was, mingling with and permeating all that was essentially his own, a Power above himself, quickening all that was true and good in him to a higher life, so guiding him that he did the work to which he was called faithfully and well, making known to men what he was commissioned to declare as to the mind of God and His dealings with mankind, in such form and in such measure as men were able to receive it. On this view of the case, criticism may enter on its work free and unfettered; may rightly study the "manifold," the "very varied" wisdom of God (Eph. iii. 10) working through all diversities of human gifts and character; may learn, in the temper of a reverential courage, to distinguish between the accidental and the essential, the letter and the spirit, the temporal and the eternal. As the teaching of the New Testament corrects and completes what was partial and imperfect in the Old, even in relation to what was its highest subject-matter, so the student of science and history may enter on his work without fear, not surprised or startled if he finds in the records of the Old Testament not a scientific account of the origin of the universe and the history of mankind, but broad and general statements, to be recognised hereafter in their right relation to the perfect Truth, which is mighty and will prevail.

E. H. PLUMPTRE.

---

* See especially Westcott's *Introduction to the Study of the Gospels:* Introduction.

INTRODUCTION

TO

THE PENTATEUCH

The Pentateuch derives its name from a word in the Greek language as spoken at Alexandria, signifying "the five-fold book," and with this agrees the fact that the breaking of it up into five parts was apparently the work of the Alexandrian translators. The titles of these parts at the present day are all taken from their version, the LXX., while in the Hebrew itself there is no trace of any such arrangement, and though the division has been accepted for the sake of convenience, the names of the several books are simply the opening words. Thus Genesis is called *Berêshith*, that is, In the beginning; Exodus, *Eleh Sh'moth*, These are the names; Leviticus, *Wayikra*, And he called; Numbers, *Bemidbar*, In the wilderness; and Deuteronomy, *Eleh Haddebarim*, These are the words. Everywhere in the Bible it is spoken of as a whole, of which the name occurs once only before the Captivity, in 2 Kings xxii. 8, where it is called "the book of the Torah," or Law. Naturally, after the return from Babylon, when the state had to be reconstituted, and the kingly office was virtually abolished to make way for a more exact observance of the Mosaic institutions, a more frequent reference is made to it, and we find it fully described as "the book of the Torah of Moses, which Jehovah had commanded to Israel" (Neh. viii. 1), and as "the book of the Torah of Jehovah" in 2 Chron. xvii. 9.

At that period we have full evidence that the Pentateuch was accepted by Ezra and the Jews returning from Babylon as the fundamental law of the children of Israel, and that its influence was so paramount that the members of the royal family laid no claim to the throne of David. Jewish tradition also asserts that Ezra and the men of the Great Synagogue settled the texts both of it and of their other Scriptures, and, to use a modern phrase, re-edited them, adding many remarks to elucidate the meaning, which in our days would be placed as foot-notes at the bottom, but which were incorporated into the body of the work. Were such a thing possible, nothing could be more interesting than for us to possess the original text of the Pentateuch. Even as it is, the vocabulary is to some extent different from that of later books, and there still remain numerous traces of archaic grammatical forms and inflexions different from those of later times, even though the Masorites have done much to obliterate them. But when we find that the autograph copies of the Apostolic Epistles, which existed in Tertullian's days (*Tert. de Praescrip.* xxxvi.), have long passed away, we must be content with the Old Testament as we find it, though the hope is held out to us of the discovery of copies anterior to the Masoretic Recension. And even as it is, we have no reason to suppose that it has ever been falsified, or that it was treated by Ezra with anything but the most reverent respect; and the Samaritan Pentateuch and the LXX. version prove to demonstration that we at this day have the Pentateuch just as it was several centuries before the advent of Christ.

Confessedly, then, in the days of Ezra, the Pentateuch was regarded as the work of Moses, and as given by the command of Jehovah. (See Neh. viii. 1—8.) We find, also, that the reading of it, with the interpretation into the Aramaic tongue, occupied a whole week (*ibid.* 18). But the assertion that it was "the Torah of Moses" may be interpreted in two ways. It may mean that Moses was the virtual author, the various laws having been enacted or even written by him, though the collection and arrangement of the book was left to others; or it may mean that he was also the actual composer of the work, and that at his death he left the Pentateuch, not in a loose and scattered condition, but such, in the main, as we now have it.

It is incumbent upon us, therefore, first of all to examine the evidence of the book itself, and we find towards the end of it a most important passage. In Deut. xxxi. 24—26 we read that "when Moses had made an end of writing the words of this Torah in a book until they were finished," he commanded the Levites to "take this book of the Torah and put it by the side of the Ark of the Covenant." Now these words show that Moses did not leave his laws unarranged, but himself collected them. There is previously allusion made to the practice of Moses to keep written accounts of memorable events, as in Exod. xvii. 14, where in the Hebrew we are told not of "a book," but of "the book," the official record of Israel's doings. In a similar manner, in Exod. xxxiv. 27, Num. xxxiii. 2, we find the assertion that the more important events which took place in the wilderness were recorded in writing by the commandment of Jehovah. But the evidence of the present passage is much more express, for it speaks of Moses completing the writing of the Torah. It no longer, however, speaks of *the book*, but of *a book*, as if from the official narratives and other sources Moses had compiled and digested into one volume both the history of Israel's selection to be God's people, and also the laws by which they were to be governed. This book is also referred to in Deut. xvii. 18. The autograph copy of Moses was to be laid up "by the side of the Ark" (Deut. xxxi. 26); but "the priests, the Levites" were also to have a copy for their use, and of this again a copy was to be made for the king's guidance.

The meaning of the words in Deut. xxxi. seems plainly to be that the actual writing by the hand of Moses ceased at the end of chap. xxx. Following it, we have in the other four chapters a history of his last days, and especially of the appointment of Joshua to be his successor. There are also preserved in them "the song of Moses," and "the blessing wherewith he blessed the children of Israel" before his death. These two compositions would probably be on separate rolls, and may have been for many years the companions and occupation from time to time of Moses in the wilderness. It would only be after their solemn delivery at the close of his life that they would be reverently added to the Torah, together with the account of the prophet's last actions, and of his death. The person who was charged to do this was, according to the tradition of the Syriac Church, Moses' successor, Joshua, for to their copies of the Pentateuch this Note is always attached, that it was "written by Moses, but arranged and completed by Joshua bar Nun his minister." Moses may even have often employed him as his scribe, just as Jeremiah employed Baruch, and as St. Paul constantly used the hands of others. But the testimony of the book itself is full and complete as to the authorship of Moses, and we may add in passing that we know of no one except Moses who could have written a psalm so sublime as that in chap. xxxii. The author of it stands on a level as high as that of David and Isaiah, and such writers are not produced every day, and are each too strong and masterly for any one but themselves to have written their compositions.

It does not, of course, follow that we have the Pentateuch just in every minute particular as it left the hands of Moses and Joshua, and we must therefore examine the limitations of such changes. It seems, then, to have been the case that additions were made to certain documents to complete them. Thus, for instance, I have shown the probability of the two genealogies contained in Gen. xxxvi. 31—43 having been added in later times. And nothing was more natural; for the Pentateuch was a great document, and the title-deed of the nation's possession of Palestine; and the records contained in it would from time to time be completed and brought down to later times by proper authority. With regard to the work of Ezra, we can well understand that after so great a calamity as the destruction of Jerusalem and the burning of the Temple, one of the most pressing needs of the nation would be a correct copy of their Law. Fortunately there had been an interval of eleven years between the carrying away of Jewish captives by Nebuchadnezzar and the fall of Zedekiah, and during this period there had been a thriving community of exiles growing up at Babylon, to whose piety the prophet Jeremiah makes frequent reference. One of their first cares would be to supply themselves with copies of their Law, but many of these would be made hurriedly, and Ezra, in his anxiety to make the people understand their Torah (Neh. viii. 1—8), would also certainly endeavour to give them a text as correct as possible. In this work he was assisted, according to Jewish tradition, by three prophets, Haggai, Zechariah, and Malachi, by the prince Zerubbabel, the high priest Jeshua, the son of Jozedek, and others, to the number in all of twelve. A full account of this tradition is given by Buxtorf, in his *Tiberias*, chap. x., with the authorities in proof of it. It was accepted by St. Jerome, and is too reasonable in itself, and too directly confirmed by the passages in Nehemiah referred to above, to be lightly disregarded. Excepting, however, the addition of notes by Ezra and the men of the Great Synagogue, and the completion of documents, we can find no trace of change or alteration in the text as written by Moses.

It has been thought, however, that the book referred to in Deut. xvii. 18, xxxi. 24, 26, was the book of Deuteronomy only. In the LXX. version the words in chap. xvii. 18 rendered "a copy of this law" are translated by "this Deuteronomy." Jerome also, no mean authority, in the Vulgate renders them "a Deuteronomy of this law." We may, however, dismiss this passage, because it is quite possible that the priests may have had an abstract of the law for their guidance, which contained only the ritual and legal portions of the Pentateuch; and that the king was to make a copy of this for his instruction and direction in giving judgment in cases brought before his tribunal. But neither here, nor still less in the thirty-first chapter, can I see any probability of "this book" being that of Deuteronomy. For Deuteronomy consists of three addresses delivered by Moses to the people at the very end of their forty years' wanderings in the wilderness. There had probably been a sojourn of many years in Kadesh (Numb. xx. 1), during which, while the headquarters of each tribe were with Moses, the mass of the people was wandering in search of pasture for their flocks in the wildernesses of Paran and Zin. At the end of this sojourn Moses made preparations for the conquest of Palestine; but it was probably during this lengthened period of repose that he digested into one book the patriarchal documents which he had brought with him from Egypt (for the exodus was made in so orderly a manner, and with such careful preparation, though hurried at last, that even Joseph's bones were not forgotten), and also the written records that he had himself made of the events of which he had been the centre. Probably there, too, he wrote these addresses, or at least arranged the subjects of them; but when he "made an end of writing the words of this law in a book until they were finished," the reference would naturally be, not to the three addresses, which, after they had been delivered, would, of course, be added to the words of the law, but to the whole history. And this is confirmed by the fact, already referred to, that there are no traces in the Bible itself of the division into five parts made by the translators of the LXX. And granting, as we do, that in Deuteronomy the popular side of the Mosaic ordinances is exhibited, and their more kindly and social aspect made prominent, as was natural when, in his last addresses, the prophet was commending them to the hearty acceptance of a stiff-necked and wilful people, yet there is no proof that Deuteronomy ever was regarded as the Torah itself; and the supposition that it is meant by "the Book of the Torah" in 2 Kings xxii. 8, and not the whole Pentateuch, is based upon no other foundation than the fact that Jeremiah does especially refer to Deuteronomy; and it is a convenient matter for the critics to find some one to whom they may assign a deliberate forgery.

We find, then, the assertion in the Pentateuch of the Mosaic authorship, and upon this point we must remember that the forgery of writings did not begin until books were marketable commodities, and men made money by their sale. Literary forgeries are comparatively modern things, and the art was first practised on a large scale by the Jews in Egypt. In the Bible it is most rare to find any account given either of the writer of a book, or of the circumstances under which it was composed. Nor is it easy to find a time when the forgery could have been made; for after the settlement of the nation in Palestine its civilisation declined. When it left Egypt its chiefs were men who had profited necessarily by the flourishing state of literature there. Not a year passes without fresh proofs being brought to light of the greatness of that "wisdom of the Egyptians," in which Stephen tells us that Moses was learned (Acts vii. 22). But there is no reason for supposing that the Israelite chiefs were dependent upon the Egyptians for a knowledge of the art of writing. Not only had Abraham been brought up at a place where writing was in daily use, but it was no unknown matter in Palestine. The Phœnicians not only introduced their alphabet into Greece, but were the inventors of parchment prepared from the skins both of sheep and goats (*Herod.* v. 58). The introduction of writing materials—so portable compared with the old tablets of clay—must have done much to popularise literary arts, and even more so must the use of papyrus in Egypt. It was not so much the discovery of printing, as of paper, which brought the darkness of mediæval times to a close. As long as the material was so expensive as parchment, copying by hand was not more costly than printing would have been; for it is the multiplication of copies, by reason of our possession of an inexpensive material, that makes the printing of books so cheap. But parchment was a great improvement upon the materials previously in use, and the method of preparing it would not have been invented unless there had been a demand for a convenient writing material. Accordingly, in the Egyptian monuments, the Hittites, who were the leading people of Palestine, are repeatedly mentioned both as scribes and as authors; and it is interesting to find that the document referred to in Gen. xxiii. 17, and which has all the exactness of a written contract, was a covenant between Abraham and the chiefs of this very nation.

We suppose, however, that no one now, after the flood of light thrown upon ancient Chaldea and Egypt, and still more recently upon the nation of the Hittites, doubts the fact that Moses and all high-born Israelites were well acquainted with the art of writing; or even that the Semitic race was in advance of most other nations in this respect. As the words for *ink* and *book* (*sepher*, comp. the name of the Hittite town, Kirjath-Sepher, Introd. to Genesis, p. 9) are common to almost all the Semitic dialects, we need feel no difficulty in accepting the statement of Herodotus, that it was a Semitic people who invented a writing material capable of being made into books, and also the simple contrivances for inscribing characters upon it. But their verb "to write," like those in Greek and Latin, means to *cut in*, or *dig*, and belongs to the older age, when the materials for writing were either of clay or plaster (still used in Deut. xxvii. 2), or tablets of wood or metal (Is. viii. 1, where the word rendered *roll* is a metal plate), or the smoothed surface of rocks (Job xix. 24). But after the conquest of Palestine the Israelites seem to have gradually declined in all the arts of civilisation. Deborah, indeed, appears as an educated woman; and we find that the priests had preserved at Shiloh writing and other remains of more polished days. But when we read, in the song of Deborah, of Zebulon producing men who "handle the pen of the writer" (Judges v. 14), most persons are aware that the words really mean "the sceptre or baton of the musterers" of the army. Generally the book of Judges describes the Israelites as hardly bestead, and constantly fighting for their very existence; and it was not till the days of Samuel, the great restorer of Israel, that we find the civilisation of the nation reviving, and Samuel himself writing "the manner of the kingdom in a book, and laying it up before Jehovah" (1 Sam. x. 25).

Samuel, a man of extraordinary ability, and trained from his early infancy in the tabernacle of Shiloh, undoubtedly could have written the Pentateuch as far as acquaintance with the arts of writing and literary composition go. We will suppose even that the documents brought by Moses out of Egypt, and the memorials written by his hand in the wilderness, were all stored up at Shiloh, and, therefore, that he possessed that knowledge of Egypt which is so marked an element of the Pentateuch; but if so, what object could Samuel have had in falsifying those documents, and in asserting that Moses himself had made them into a book? The knowledge of Egypt and of the Sinaitic wilderness manifested in the Pentateuch is abundant and precise. If, for instance, we take the plagues of Egypt, we find that almost every one of them is founded upon natural occurrences there, utterly unknown in Palestine; and that the Divine intervention consisted in the intensifying of their force, and in their rapid sequence. But Samuel could have had no personal knowledge of these Egyptian phenomena, nor of the many Egyptian customs referred to in the Pentateuch, exact parallels to which are to be found in books like Brugsch's *History of Egypt* and Wilkinson's *Manners and Customs of the Ancient Egyptians*. Even in the hands of practised forgers there are sure to be numerous unintentional proofs of the want of personal knowledge, of the misuse of knowledge obtained second-hand, and of the obtrusion of ideas taken from the state of things among which the forger was living. The more the Pentateuch is searched by hostile critics, and supposed examples of this ignorance brought forth and examined, the more clear becomes the proof that the writer had a thorough acquaintance both with Egypt and with the wilderness of Sinai. And so exact and intimate is this knowledge, that we look in vain elsewhere for a person or an age when it would have been possible, without records written in Egypt, to have composed this book.

If, however, Samuel found Mosaic documents in the tabernacle at Shiloh, and rescued them, and subsequently compiled them into a volume, then we have in the Pentateuch substantially the work of Moses; but we fail altogether in finding a reason why this great and good man should deliberately represent his own work as that of another. For though the restorer of Israel, he nowhere appears as the restorer of the Mosaic institutions. On the contrary, there are occasions in which, as in the offering of sacrifices, he does not conform to the Mosaic Law. On no occasion do we find him endeavouring to restore a central place of worship, such as was contemplated by Moses, and had existed at Shiloh. On the contrary, the ark was left by him at Kirjath-jearim for twenty years; and it was first Saul, and then David, who restored to it something of its Mosaic importance. There are proofs of the existence of the Mosaic Law and institutions in the time of Samuel, but they are never obtruded upon our notice, and must be searched for. The great work of Samuel was the foundation of the schools of the prophets. The need of them was forced upon his attention by the decay of the nation in all literary arts, but even here he did not build upon the old lines. It was not men of the tribe of Levi whom he chose for his purposes; on the contrary, the doors of entry to his schools stood open to all. Nor was it at a central sanctuary that he gathered the flower of the nation round him to instruct them in the learning which he had been taught at Shiloh. Nor do we find in the Pentateuch any preparations for Samuel's work, or allusion to it. It was distinctly an addition to the Mosaic institutions, and was forced upon Samuel by the lapse of the nation into barbarism.

At the return from Babylon there was an attempt made to keep exactly to the Mosaic lines, but never before. For what we have said of Samuel holds good of the times of the kings. There never was, until the return from exile, any age in which the Law of Moses commanded the universal assent of the people. In the times of the judges the anarchy and distress of the nation were too great; and subsequently the kings may have regarded the Mosaic Law as a matter to be left to the priests. They certainly do not seem, as a rule, to have observed the precept in Deut. xvii. 18, which required each one of them to write out for himself a copy of the Levitical Law. Written copies were probably rare, and the knowledge of it was preserved by its being learnt by heart in the prophetic schools. Many critics have, in fact, made this their main ground of objection to the authenticity of the Pentateuch. They have said, that had it existed in the times of the kings, there must have been a more complete observance of it. But the attempt thus made to assign a later date to its fabrication is itself met in the most complete way. For we have clear proof that it existed under the kings, not only in Judah but also in Israel.

This proof consists partly in the manner in which the Levitical Law is referred to by the prophets Hosea and Amos. The former was a contemporary of Isaiah, but was an Israelite, and addressed his words entirely to the kingdom of the ten tribes. Amos was himself a member of the tribe of Judah, but his mission was to Israel, and he too prophesied in the days of Jeroboam II., whose victories extended the empire of Samaria to the widest limits to which it ever attained. Now these two prophets, in the narrow compass of a few chapters refer to a large number of the most distinctive points in the books of Leviticus and Deuteronomy. I shall not enter minutely into this argument, because it has been demonstrated in so satisfactory a manner by Bishop Brown in the Introduction to the Pentateuch in the Speaker's Commentary. He has shown there that throughout the Old Testament Scriptures, and especially in these prophetical books, there is a perpetual reference to the Mosaic Law. Beginning with the book of Joshua, he carefully examines each subsequent scripture, and shows that the Pentateuch underlies the whole of them, and that its very words were constantly in the minds of the writers. Probably only a few picked men could read and write. We know how in mediæval Europe these arts became rare; and the result necessarily was that the influence of the Christian Scriptures diminished, but it never entirely ceased. In Judah and Israel probably the want of education was far greater; still, even there, copies, we may be sure, of their sacred books existed, if not generally, yet at the chief prophetic schools, and neither the knowledge of them nor their influence ever entirely died out.

But there is a second clear proof that the Pentateuch was known and received in the kingdom of the ten tribes, namely, that of this book alone there exist, first, copies written in the Samaritan characters; and secondly, a translation into the Samaritan dialect. It is, unfortunately, here very difficult to arrive at certain conclusions, because there exists no critical edition of the Samaritan Pentateuch, but, like the LXX., the Peshito-Syriac, and the Vulgate, scholars are content to leave the text in uncertainty, though materials have in some cases been collected for future use; nearly twenty manuscript copies are known to exist in Europe of the Samaritan Pentateuch, but the only text available f r use is that in Walton's Polyglot;* while even greater obscurity rests upon many questions connected with the Samaritan Targum. While no book is read and studied as the Bible, yet not one tithe of the care and labour devoted to the text of the New Testament has been expended upon these versions, which, from the absence of ancient Hebrew manuscripts, are our most important means for verifying the text of the Old Testament Scriptures.

Still, some things are certain. For, first, these Samaritan manuscripts are written in the same characters as those used by the Jews before the Babylonian exile. Even in Jerusalem the use of their old alphabet did not immediately die out; for the inscriptions upon the Maccabean coins are still in the Samaritan characters, though the Babylonian square writing may have superseded it for ordinary purposes. In the Talmud (Tract. Sanhedrin xxi. b) it is said, that "whereas the Torah was originally given to Israel in the Hebrew writing, and the holy language, in the days of Ezra the Israelites changed it into the Assyrian writing and the Aramaic language." As the words *Hebrew writing* might be equivocal, the Rabbi goes on to explain it by a term which signifies that found in these Samaritan copies of the Law. But, besides this change of the characters, we notice that the authorship also of the Chaldee Targum is referred to Ezra. But both assertions must be taken in a very limited sense. The Chaldee paraphrase undoubtedly grew out of the custom begun by Ezra, of translating the Torah, that is, the Pentateuch, into the Aramaic language, that the people might understand the sense (Neh. viii. 8). But centuries passed away before it was committed to writing under the name of "the Targum of Onkelos." All, nevertheless, that Onkelos did was to give in written form that which had long been handed down by tradition; and one reason which probably moved him to it was, that, though in the great schools, like that of Tiberias, there was an exact knowledge of the text, yet that elsewhere variations were growing up. Just, then, as the Aramaic paraphrase was the work of centuries, though it began in the customs of Ezra, so it was but slowly that the new writing took the place of the old, and the use of the sacred characters was probably long retained in the copying of the Scriptures, even though the more easy method of writing was growing into common use. So, in the Syriac Church, the Estrangelo character was still employed, both for the Scriptures and ritual books, long after simpler alphabets were in other matters universally prevalent.

The fact, therefore, that the Samaritan Pentateuch is written in the old characters† does not settle its date. The Samaritans may have obtained it from Ezra, or even at some later period; but nothing is more probable than that copies of the Pentateuch remained in Israel after the deportation by Shalmanezer of the ten tribes. The schools of the prophets had been, from the days of Elijah, particularly strong there, and we have seen that Hosea knew the Pentateuch well, and that most of the Levitical institutions were observed by the kings of the house of Jehu, as was to be expected, considering that they had been placed upon the throne by Elijah's influence. When transcripts of these manuscripts were subsequently made, the scribes would be sure to regard Ezra's text as the most correct and authoritative, and its readings would prevail wherever Samaritan prejudices were not interfered with.‡ But, passing these probabilities by, we have also to take into consideration the fact that the Samaritans could no more understand the book to which they gave complete

* Mr. Petermann published, at Berlin, an edition of the Samaritan Pentateuch; and the Rev. J. W. Nutt has edited, from a Bodleian MS., some fragments of a Samaritan Targum, with an interesting introduction treating upon Samaritan history and literature.

† Ancient examples of these may be seen in the Moabite stone, the Siloam inscription (B.C. 700), and other facsimiles, in the Oriental Series of the Palæographical Society.

‡ The Samaritan Pentateuch, nevertheless, has a text so much more like that of the LXX. than the Hebrew, that many scholars have concluded that the LXX. version was made from a Samaritan manuscript.

allegiance, than could the Jews, and that they too had their paraphrase. There is much obscurity as to the history of this version, because copies—of even fragments of it—though multiplying, are still extremely rare; but Gesenius places its date about the middle of the first century of our era. The Targum of Onkelos was probably not committed to writing until a century later; for up to that time there are numerous variations in the citations made from it in the Talmud. Such was sure to be the case as long as the preservation of it was entrusted to the memory, and there existed opposing schools of interpretation; but all such diversities would die out as soon as the Targum was committed to writing, according to the tradition of the leading school. But what we are anxious to point out is, that in both cases the things themselves are far older than the date when they took written form.

It is exceedingly probable that the Samaritan paraphrase, as long as it was a matter of tradition, would be more or less influenced by the Chaldee Targum, as being the translation of the greater authority. Such, in fact, we find to have been the case. But granting this, there still remain facts of which there can be no reasonable doubt. We cannot doubt but that "the book of the Torah of Moses" (Neh. viii. 1), was the authoritative rule of faith and practice, both in Samaria and Jerusalem, on the return from Babylon, nor that its language, nevertheless, was unintelligible to the mass of the people, and that the custom grew up in Judea of translating it to them, and that this translation gradually became fixed and settled, and finally was committed to writing as the Targum of Onkelos. As this Targum includes the whole Pentateuch, and nothing besides, it also seems plain that the Torah of Moses was the whole Pentateuch, and not some portion of it. Equally, too, the Samaritans acknowledged the Pentateuch as their one sacred book, rejecting the other scriptures; and, moreover, they adhered to the use of the old characters common to all the Jews before the exile. As they too could not understand the old language, they likewise had an Aramaic version for common use, agreeing to a considerable extent with that of Onkelos. But, surely, neither Jew nor Samaritan would have accepted a book as their rule of faith, and as the national law in civil matters also, unless it had held that same position in previous time. It was the strictness of the Mosaic Law in the matter of mixed marriages which made Nehemiah drive away from Jerusalem men of high rank, including a grandson of the high priest Eliashib (Neh. xiii. 28). Some have even supposed that it was this person, called by Josephus (*Antiq.* xi. 7, 8), "Manasseh, the brother of the high priest," who carried the Pentateuch to Samaria, and that his father-in-law, Sanballat, made him there high priest of the temple on Mount Gerizim. But no attempt was made to excise from the Pentateuch, or even to soften down, its severe enactments; nor neither would he have carried it with him into banishment, nor would the Samaritans have accepted from men who treated them as an inferior and mongrel race, a book which, while attaching to them this disgrace, yet claimed their obedience, unless the claims of that book to be Israel's law were indefeasible. But if so, we really carry the Pentateuch back at once to the date of the divided kingdom. Jeroboam, as was but natural, did his best to weaken the hold of the Mosaic Law upon his subjects; but his method was not the abrogation of it, but the substitution at Bethel and Dan of centres corresponding to Jerusalem, and his calves were imitations of the cherubim in the tabernacle. The placing of the ark at Jerusalem had been the work of David, and probably was regarded with hostility by the powerful tribe of Ephraim, as being an act injurious to that supremacy which they had ever claimed, and of which the placing of the ark at Shiloh had been a symbol. Politically, therefore, they would approve of having national centres of worship, and Bethel, a holy place, consecrated by Jacob's dream there, and admirably situated on the mountains of Ephraim upon the high road to Jerusalem, and distant only twelve miles from it, was chosen with consummate statesmanship as the site for the rival sanctuary. But so strong was the hold of the Mosaic Law in its exactness upon the people, that not only the Levites, who were displaced by the throwing open of the priesthood to all alike, but all the best of the people, withdrew gradually from the northern kingdom and settled in Judah. These facts are indeed given in the Chronicles (2 Chron. xi. 13—17), which were compiled from old documents after the return from exile, but they account for the subsequent strength of Judah; nor is there any doubt but that the numerous authorities there referred to were records kept by the old prophets, and that the history in the books of Chronicles was copied from them. And thus we find no period between the return from exile and the division of the kingdom, when such an act as the supposed forgery of the Pentateuch could have been committed. For at the one period we find Jew and Samaritan agreeing in receiving it as the book of Divine Law, to which their obedience was due; and at the other we find Jeroboam constrained to set up an imitation of its central worship, but the people divided in their views, some accepting his institutions, but the more religious portion even abandoning their property that they might go where the Law of Moses was more faithfully kept. Even those who kept the annals of the kings, and who were far less influenced by respect for the Levitical law than the writer of the Books of Chronicles, branded Jeroboam as the man who made Israel to sin, because for worldly policy he violated the religious ordinances of the nation. Though willing to break away from their allegiance to David and his house, large numbers were unwilling to break away from what was far older than David, namely, the Mosaic Law. Between the days of Jeroboam and those of Ezra there never was a time when the rival kingdoms would have agreed to accept as their national law anything that had not been handed down to them as such by their fathers from immemorial times; and there was just as little possibility of this agreement after a rival temple had been set up on Mount Gerizim.

If, nevertheless, the Pentateuch be a forgery, the earlier chapters in Genesis could have been forged only after or during the exile at Babylon. It is true, indeed, that the Chaldee legends of Creation, of the Flood, of the Tower of Babel, &c., have come to us from Assyria, but they were current certainly in Babylonia as well. The whole imagery, the tree of life, the cherubim, the sword of flame which turned every way, the site of Paradise, the fashion of the ark, all this and much beside is Chaldaic to the uttermost; but who could believe that out of legends so grossly polytheistic as those lately brought to light any one could frame a history so elevated in its pure monotheism, so grand in its conception of the manner of the working of the Most High, as these first chapters of the Pentateuch? But supposing that this stupendous act of authorship had been performed, we come in the course of a few chapters to an equally exact knowledge of ancient Egypt. Scene after scene is presented to us of which we find the exact representations existing to this day on ancient monuments. How could a forger at Babylon have known of them? So precise is this knowledge that we find horses mentioned in the history of Joseph, and in Jacob's blessing, but not enumerated among the gifts bestowed by Pharaoh on Abraham. This is just one of the points in which a forger would fail; he would certainly have enumerated horses among the presents made to Abraham, whereas really they were introduced into Egypt in the interval between Abraham's visit and Joseph's betrayal by his brethren. We find, too, the author of Genesis equally accurate in his description of the life of an Arab sheik; and, finally, he takes the chosen race down to Egypt, and is just as exact in his knowledge of daily life there. We have referred before to the plagues of Egypt, and to the natural phenomena which underlie them; and with each advance in our knowledge of Egyptian manners and literature the more complete is the confirmation given to the exactness of the picture of Egyptian life. But soon the scene is changed. The exodus takes place, and again there is the same accuracy as regards the desert. Professor Palmer, with exceptional advantages for the examination of the question, comes to the conclusion that "whether we look at the results obtained in physical geography alone, or take into consideration the mass of facts which the traditions and nomenclature disclose, we are bound to admit that the investigations of the Sinai expedition do materially confirm and elucidate the history of the exodus" (Palmer, *The Desert of the Exodus*, i. p. 279). And again, "In the case of Sinai, physical facts accord with the inspired account" (*ibid.*). He concludes also his second volume by saying that he has "purposely abstained from discussing any of the objections brought against the truth of the narrative of the exodus, because he believes that geographical facts form the best answer to them all"* (p. 530).

Falsehood is sure to be detected by the growth of knowledge, and a forged document will sooner or later have the veil stripped away from it, and stand forth in its hideous baseness. No cleverness can prevent this. It may impose upon people for a time, but when a critical examination is made, a hundred proofs are brought to light, showing the date, the country, and the purpose of the forger. Nor would the detection be less certain if the Pentateuch was, as others suggest, a curious medley of many different ages, and of works by many hands. As it is, the Bible stands ever upon surer ground as knowledge grows. Thus, the survey of the desert of the exodus, undertaken by the Ordnance Survey Department, and the scientific examination of Palestine so thoroughly carried out under the auspices of the committee of the Palestine Exploration Fund, have proved that the geography of these two regions not only agrees with the Biblical account, but enables us clearly to understand narratives which before were full of difficulty. When the minute criticism of Scripture began, the critics heaped together so large a number of specious objections, and had so many plausible reasons for putting everything where they did not find it, and for breaking up and distributing among a host of people† who had never been heard of, what had come down to us as one work, that believers were alarmed, and began to fear that the Bible would be torn from them, and that faith would come to be a belief in that which their reason told them was untrue. Undoubtedly we have had to part with some popular interpretations of the Scripture, but these were no more part of Scripture than the popular theology of Rome which rests the papal claims upon an interpretation of Matt. xvi. 18, or purgatory upon 1 Cor. iii. 13—15. But the examination of this mass of objections, and the large and rapid growth of knowledge, have both tended to place the Bible upon a more sure foundation. As we know more of the history and geography, and also of the literature, of the countries in which the scenes of the Bible are laid, we are ever receiving fresh confirmation of its truth; and as the outward and material form of the Book in which God has enshrined His truth daily receives fresh confirmation, we can with more undoubting faith rest our hearts upon those spiritual verities which are revealed therein for the salvation of our souls.

In conclusion, the Pentateuch covers so vast a space of ground, takes us to so many dissimilar countries, and sets before us the habits and manners of so many different races of men, that we know of no man who could have written it except Moses, and of no period in Jewish history when it could have been penned except when Egypt and the wilderness were fresh in the writer's mind. It is not worth arguing whether Joshua might not have compiled it from records left by Moses, because not only is this contradicted by the testimony of all future times, but it makes Joshua deliberately tell a falsehood in saying that Moses was the author (Deut. xxxi. 24), without the slightest purpose or object to be gained by it. The book would stand on equally sure footing if, as some think, these words refer only to Deuteronomy, and the rest was arranged and completed by Joshua and Eleazar. But I can see little proof of this, though probably these two men would cause transcripts to be made. And as for Genesis, it seems to be entirely the work of Moses; for we have there knowledge indeed beyond the range of his natural faculties, and which tradition would not have handed down correctly, but for the possession of which he satisfactorily accounts; for, excepting the first narrative of creation, he describes all the rest as *tôldôth*, genealogical documents, which he did not compose, but from which, using mainly, as seems certain, their very words, he compiled the history so necessary for his purpose, of the choice of the family of Abraham to be God's peculiar people: and necessary also for the integrity of Holy Scripture; because without the Book of Genesis we should know neither what was the end and object for which the Israelites were made into a nation, nor what was the blessing which God through them was preparing to bestow upon mankind.

Now these documents, Moses, as the ruler of the nation, would of course have had in his charge. He had, too, at Kadesh abundant leisure for the work. No man besides was so thoroughly permeated with the sense of Israel's high and unique calling. He had the literary ability and skill. The revelation to him of the name I AM as that of Israel's covenant God accounts for the importance attached to the name in Genesis, and the discrimination in its use. And, finally, his position as the leader of a discontented people, whom he had brought out of Egypt to brave hardships in the wilderness, required of him the proof that he was accomplishing the original purpose for which Abraham had been called away from Ur, and his race made into a great nation. And if Moses wrote Genesis he would not stop there, but would naturally proceed to digest into a connected narrative the other records of the great events of which he had been the eye-witness, in order that the nation which he had formed might be impressed with

* This eminent scholar was assassinated in Upper Egypt in the year 1882; his travels in the desert of the exodus have confirmed in a remarkable manner the truth and fidelity of the history of Israel's wanderings there as given in the Pentateuch.

† Thus Ewald distributes the Pentateuch and Joshua among seven different authors, and tells you when and where they lived.

the sense of its nearness to Jehovah, and of the work it had to do for him.

These are broad and solid considerations, which far outweigh all the difficulties which critics have brought forward upon the other side. In a book so old there must be difficulties, and we cannot tell what have been its fortunes during the vast period of its existence. We know that God's providence has not miraculously interfered to preserve for us an absolutely certain text of the New Testament. At this very time a warm controversy is raging as to whether that text is to be settled by the authority of two or three of the great uncial manuscripts, or whether we are to abide substantially by that of Erasmus, founded upon what was the received text of subsequent times. So, too, may scribes have made errors and mistakes in copying a book so vastly more ancient, but none of material importance.

For, as regards the Old Testament, we may claim, on the authority of the LXX., combined with the Targum of Onkelos and the Samaritan Pentateuch and Targum, that we have the Pentateuch such as it was in Ezra's days. But before this time we have probabilities only, and such slight proof as arises from the collation of the passages in which the Law is referred to with the words of the Pentateuch itself. There is no reason for supposing that there was ever any wilful falsification of the national law; but it has passed through many a trying time, and we do not know how manuscripts were treated in those old days, nor how many of the illustrative notes which we ascribe to Ezra may really have been added long before.

But thus the discovery of the "book of the law" in the Temple acquires fresh interest. We read that the effect upon the mind of king Josiah of the reading of the denunciations contained therein was so great that he rent his clothes, and sent a solemn embassy to inquire of Jehovah. Now it has been well pointed out * that this is an argument against there existing a very considerable knowledge of the Pentateuch in those days. Manasseh, in his violent and persecuting reign, had probably destroyed as many copies of it as he could find, and had suppressed the schools of the prophets. Still, even so, many would survive who knew the Pentateuch by heart. Probably one important part of the instruction given in these schools was the committal to the memory, if not of the whole, yet of large parts of the Pentateuch; and the teachers would learn it in its entirety. The priests would similarly be, to a considerable extent, acquainted with it, though their methods of sacrifice may have been mainly learnt by practice. Now Josiah was but eight years old when he restored the worship of Jehovah, and as his father, Amon, had "served idols" like Manasseh (2 Kings xxi. 21), but was so unpopular that his own servants slew him, the king's acts at first must have been chiefly the result of the counsels of the pious men who had gathered round him, and who were now the dominant party because of the re-action against Amon. It is probable, therefore, that not very much was done until the king was older, and in his eighteenth year threw the whole energy of his noble character into the work of reformation. It was about this time that the copy of the Torah was found in the Temple, and though Josiah had doubtless heard portions of it recited before, yet now for the first time the whole was before him, and he listened with awe to the threatenings against the nation in case it lapsed into idolatry, which were actually so soon to be fulfilled. These threatenings are indeed contained in Deuteronomy, but we have no authority for dividing this portion from the rest. It was probably the whole Torah that was found, and we cannot wonder at the excitement caused by the discovery when we remember that the reign of Manasseh lasted fifty-five years, and that he was a bitter enemy of the religion of Jehovah. Under such a monarch, at a time when books were very rare, it must have been only very old people, who belonged to Hezekiah's days, and a few secretly trained by them, that would still have the Pentateuch written in their memories.

Now if, as there is reason for supposing, this was the autograph copy of Moses that had been laid up beside the ark, we have every probability for the conclusion that the copies of the Law possessed by the exiles at Babylon had a text founded on the original manuscript. Most other copies had perished, and though this was doubtless reverently stored up again in the Temple near the ark, we can see by the writings of Jeremiah that he had diligently studied it, and he would take care that those in captivity, over whose welfare he watched so carefully, would also have transcripts of this great treasure. And thus this narrative gives us the assurance that the Pentateuch has come down to us in an authentic form. No doubt this particular copy perished when the Temple was burnt by Nebuchadnezzar, but not until it had done its work. Nor would other manuscripts be wanting; for as the schools of the prophets arose again from their ruins, many an old copy of the Pentateuch would be brought forth from its hiding-place. There may have been insertions here and there which Ezra regarded as authorised additions, because placed there by prophetical hands. But we have no reason to suppose that these were of any great extent or importance; and certainly this copy found by Josiah is our security that we have the work of Israel's lawgiver much as it left his hands. The idea broached by some that Jeremiah forged the book, and that it was therefore Deuteronomy only, is disproved by the character of the man, and by the local knowledge which is as remarkable in Deuteronomy as in the rest of the Pentateuch.

There are numerous other considerations which all confirm the foregoing conclusions, but to which we can only briefly refer. Such points are the numerous divergences between the blessing of Jacob and that of Moses. The one belongs exactly to the age of the Patriarch, gives vent to his feelings at the misconduct of his sons, magnifies Judah as the future head of the nation, and yet shows no knowledge of the time when, under David, this prediction was fulfilled. In the blessing of Moses, Levi stands well nigh foremost in the abundance of his happiness, while Simeon, who had been classed with him by Jacob, absolutely disappears. Moreover, Ephraim holds the place which was actually his until the days of David; and the relative importance of the tribes is different from that of the sons of Jacob in their father's eyes. Authentic documents are sure to have these divergences, and if these two are genuine, they were separated by many centuries. If fabricated, such divergences would be avoided.

We find also that the family of the lawgiver ends in obscurity, while that of the brother holds an office of great and lasting power. The headship of the tribe of Levi is bestowed by Moses upon Aaron and his sons, and not upon his own children. His own tribe, too, is represented as lying under Jacob's curse. This is changed into a blessing but the Levites remain destitute of all political importance; they have no tribal government, and are even left dependent upon the

* See article *Pentateuch* in *Smith's Dictionary of the Bible.*

goodwill and religious feeling of their countrymen. As the result, Jeroboam's change of policy drives them away from ten of the tribes in poverty and humiliation. Now this dispersion of the Levites throughout the tribes, and the refusal to them of a share of the conquered territory in Palestine, is absolutely unintelligible upon any other supposition than that they had more than an equivalent in their religious privileges. But these privileges pre-suppose the Levitical law, and represent it as firmly established in the hearts of the people at the time of the conquest of Canaan. Levi would not have abandoned his tribal independence and his share of the conquered lands unless the Israelites had looked upon the Mosaic institutions as the law that was to be permanently in force throughout their territory.

Arguments such as this might be greatly multiplied; but I will only add that the silence of the Pentateuch is as remarkable as its knowledge of the manners and peculiarities, and the physical geography of the many regions it describes to us. There is, indeed, here said to be an exception. For in the book of Deuteronomy the probability is clearly set forth that the Israelites would not be content with that somewhat loose organisation of independent tribes which Moses arranged for them, but would demand a king. But they had seen Egypt governed by a king; there were kings in all the countries round. Moses himself had been king virtually (Deut. xxxiii. 5), and Balaam had described Israel's greatness by representing his king as greater than the monarch of what was then the mighty race of the Amalekites (Numb. xxiv. 7). Moses, surrounded by nations ruled by kings, must have often reflected upon the problem of the national government. He deliberately preferred a more free form, but it was impossible for him to put from him the thought of the likelihood that the nation would wish for and demand a form of government which, while it gave up some domestic advantages, was all important in war. The miserable state of things under the Judges actually arose from the want of a strong central rule (Judges xxi. 25), and would have been avoided if Joshua had been made king, or probably if Gideon had not, out of regard to the Mosaic principles, declined the offered crown (Judges viii. 23). But, excepting this foreboding of the longing for a king, the Pentateuch has no allusion to subsequent events or institutions. Even prophecy, which in time became, with the priesthood and the king, the third power in the state, has no allusions made to it. It existed. Moses was himself a prophet; the seventy elders received the gift (Numb. xi. 16, 25), but only on one special occasion* as the proof of their appointment. Of it, such as it became after the time of Samuel, there is no single word; and generally the Pentateuch is true to its own time, and contains no indications, casual or otherwise, of any later age.

Granting, then, that there are difficulties in the text, as was to be expected in a work written more than three thousand years ago, and difficulties in criticism and interpretation, yet the conclusion seems sure, that we have in the Pentateuch the work of Moses, and that we have it substantially as it left his hands.

* The words rendered, "they did not cease," really mean that they did not continue to prophesy.

THE FIRST BOOK OF MOSES, CALLED

GENESIS

INTRODUCTION

TO

THE FIRST BOOK OF MOSES, CALLED

GENESIS

THE Book of Genesis is a record of the highest interest, not only as being probably the oldest writing in the world, but also because it is the foundation upon which the whole Bible is built. As well the Jewish as the Christian religions have their roots in this book, and there is even no doctrine of Christianity, however advanced, which is not to be found, at least in outline, therein. Written in the very infancy of the human race, made subject, as are all the Scriptures, to the external conditions of their times, bearing upon its very surface proofs that the art of writing was in its infancy, and the science of arithmetic scarcely advanced beyond its first principles, it nevertheless contains the germ of every future truth of revelation, while, in accordance with the law which regulates the growth and development of the written Word, it never goes beyond the limits which were afterwards to be reached. No portion of Genesis has to be omitted as inconsistent with the truth which was subsequently to be revealed. Necessarily, the truths it teaches are imperfect and incomplete, for this is the rule of all the Old Testament Scriptures (Heb. i. 1); but they are the proper preparation for the brightening light that was to illuminate the world.

This consistency of Holy Scripture with itself is made the more remarkable by the fact that in Genesis we have records of an age far anterior to the exodus from Egypt. Though the hand be the hand of Moses, the documents upon which the narrative is founded, and which are incorporated in it, date from primæval times. Upon them Moses based the Law, and subsequently the prophets built upon the Pentateuch the marvellous preparation for Christ. But though given thus "by diverse portions and in diverse manners," through a vast period of time, and under every possible variety of culture and outward circumstance, the Bible is a book which from first to last is at unison with itself. It grows, proceeds onward, develops, but always in the same plane. It is no national anthology, full of abrupt transitions and violent contrasts, with the writings of one age at variance with those of another, and with subsequent generations ashamed of and destroying what went before. Rather like some mighty oak it has grown slowly through long centuries, but with no decaying limbs, no branches which have had to be lopped away. Christianity has developed, also. Starting from a far higher level, and amid a riper culture, it too has expanded its creed; but all those developments which are more than the arrangement and consistent expression of its first teaching are rejected by the most enlightened portions of Christendom as corruptions at variance with the truth.

Judaism also has had its development in the Talmud, but the development is inferior to the starting-point, and is marred by a curious admixture of puerility. From Genesis to Malachi there is in Holy Scripture a steady and homogeneous growth, advancing upwards to a stage so high as to be a fit preparation for the full sunshine of the Gospel; and in the Book of Genesis we find the earliest stages of this work founded upon pre-Mosaic documents. We read there of the forming of a being in the image of God, of the fall of that being, of the promise given of restoration, and of the first steps taken towards the fulfilment of that promise; and not only is the foundation thus laid for future revelation, but many a pregnant hint is given of the course which that revelation would follow. But though thus preserving for us records of vast antiquity, the Book of Genesis is arranged upon a definite plan. Having set man before us as the goal of creation, but nevertheless as incapable of serving God aright and of saving himself by his natural powers, and thereby attaining to the end and purpose for which he was made, it next lays the foundation for the plan of supernatural religion by the promise made to Eve in the very hour of her punishment, of a Deliverer who should arise from her seed. Thenceforward the fulfilment of this promise is steadily kept in view; and while much valuable subsidiary knowledge is bestowed upon us, yet so directly does Moses advance onward to his purpose, that by the end of Genesis we have the family chosen to be the depositaries of revelation located in an extensive and fertile region, wherein they were to multiply into a nation. So essential is the Book of Genesis to the Bible, that without it Holy Scripture would be scarcely intelligible: with this introduction all is orderly and follows in due course.

As regards its contents, it consists of an account of creation given in chaps. i.—ii. 3, and, as we have shown in *Excursus D*, of ten histories, called in the Hebrew *Tôldôth*, or genealogies, written each in its own style, and with a distinct local colouring, but with evident marks of arrangement for a settled purpose. To account for these differences of style numerous theories have been devised, one of which especially has exercised the ingenuity of a large number of writers, among whom the best known in this country is Bishop Colenso. Discarding, or not observing, that the book itself asserts that it consists of eleven parts, the beginning of each of which is carefully noted, these commentators have attempted to divide Genesis into portions according to the prevalence in them severally of the names of Elohim and Jehovah. With this theory they also combined attempts to settle the dates of the Elohist and the Jehovist, generally bringing them down to a late period, and endeavouring to find in Holy Scripture some person or persons who might be credited with what was virtually a forgery.

This theory has been often met and refuted on its own ground; but this is an age of a most rapid increase of knowledge, and the exhumed libraries of ancient Chaldea and Egypt have at last exhibited to our wondeing eyes records parallel to those which we find in the opening book of Holy Scripture. Orthodox commentators, like Vitringa, had indeed long regarded it as probable that "Moses had certain records or traditions referring to the patriarchal ages which he incorporated into his history" (Bishop Browne, *Speaker's Commentary*, p. 2); but there were so many difficulties in the way of believing that even the art of writing was known in those ancient days, that thoughtful men spoke diffidently on a subject so obscure. Often was the lament uttered that we had no contemporaneous literature that would remove some of the darkness which enwrapped man's early history. But the light has now come. Written on tablets and cylinders of clay, and therefore virtually indestructible, there lay beneath the mounds that mark where populous cities once occupied the Assyrian plains, the libraries of famous kings, in which are found not only translations of ancient Accadian * works, but written records of a king of Ur, which are said by Mr. Sayce to be about three thousand years anterior to the Christian era (*Chaldean Account of Genesis*, ed. Sayce, p. 24). We now know that writing was in such common use at Ur when Abraham dwelt there, that all the common transactions of business were inscribed on tablets, and numerous specimens of written contracts, contemporaneous with or anterior to the days of Abraham, may now be found among the Assyrian curiosities in our libraries. It has thus become highly probable that Abraham, when leaving that great and cultured mart of commerce, Ur of the Chaldees, would carry his library with him. He left Ur for religious reasons. Its religion had degenerated into idolatry, and we find in the Chaldean accounts of creation and of the flood a polytheism utterly abominable. Now, whence did Terah and Abraham obtain the better knowledge which made them hate idolatry, and abandon their homes at Ur because of its growing prevalence there? What answer more probable than that it was in these records, which teach so nobly and impressively the unity and omnipotence of the Creator? At what date the Semitic family of Eber crossed the Tigris and migrated to Ur we do not know, but they found there in the Accadians not a Semitic but an Elamite race. Probably they tried to teach them the great truth that God is one; but in proportion as the people there wandered farther into idolatry, so would they hate and persecute an alien family who rejected their many gods; and as the result Terah and his sons and clan withdrew. But their departure was voluntary (chap. xi. 31), and they took with them their wealth, and doubtless also the tablets on which was inscribed the knowledge which had made them stand firm amidst the corruption which encompassed them around, and which was the real cause of their emigration.

The Chaldaic records extend to the end of chap. xi. 26, though much light is also thrown by our enlarged knowledge of Chaldean history upon the invasion of Palestine by Chedorlaomer (chap. xiv.). From chap. xi. 27 to chap. xxxvii. 1, the surroundings of Abraham, Isaac, and Jacob are those of Arabian sheiks. From chap. xxxvii. 2 to the end the colouring is in the main Egyptian, and in all three sections it is not only the general aspect that is thus Chaldaic, Arabian, or Egyptian; but even the minuter points are true to the time and place. And the result of our increased knowledge is that numerous difficulties are now cleared away. They used to be difficulties only because of our ignorance, but it seemed to give a triumph to the sceptic if the believer could only answer,—We have no sufficient knowledge, and must be content to wait, resting our faith meanwhile upon those parts of revelation where contemporaneous knowledge has been vouchsafed. Nay, even the believer has often been restless and discontented because questions have been asked which were not easy to answer; or, what is worse, because well-meaning defenders of the faith have given answers evidently insufficient, and savouring more of the controversialist than of the seeker after truth. Even now our increased knowledge has not removed all difficulties, nor is it to be expected that there ever will be a time when our faith will have no trial to undergo. But in this trial it is an aid to our faith if we find that increased knowledge lessens our difficulties; and, as a matter of fact, nothing so profits by each fresh discovery as the Bible. If Galileo cleared away many a mistaken gloss put upon Scripture to make it accord with the Ptolemean solar system, so have the astronomers and geologists of the present day enabled us at last to see something of the grandeur and majesty of the Biblical account of creation. And our increased knowledge of the country where Abraham and his clan so long sojourned, and of the land where his descendants grew into a nation, is like sunshine illuminating a region where before we had only twilight and shadow.

We shall gain a better idea of the nature of the book, as well of the difficulties with which it abounds as also of the light cast upon them by our increased knowledge, if we pass, at least, the two first portions of which it consists somewhat fully in review before our eyes, concluding with some general remarks.

The first narrative is the history of creation, as told in chaps. i.—ii. 3. It consists of eight parts, of which the first, after affirming that God is the Creator of all things, and consequently that matter is not eternal, describes the first stage of creation as a void and formless waste. Chaos is a Greek notion, arising out of their theory that matter was uncreated and eternal. Now no language can convey a notion of a state of existence destitute of all shape, order, and arrangement; but it is sketched with marvellous beauty as an abyss, a depth without bounds, veiled in darkness, but in which the Spirit of God is hovering over the waters to quicken them with life. Without moisture life on our planet cannot exist; but we must not put any commonplace interpretation upon these abysmal waters. They were still void, empty, formless; but the words show that God had called into being in this dark abyss the matter out of which the universe was to be shaped, and that His power was present there to mould and quicken it. Upon this noble preface, which annihilates most of the dogmas of heathenism, of Greek philosophy, and of pseudo-Christian heresy, follow the six creative days, and the day of holy rest.

In the division of our Bible into chapters, with a carelessness only equalled by that perversity which has formed the ninth chapter of Isaiah out of the end and the beginning of two incongruous prophecies, the seventh day's rest is separated from the account of the six working days, and thus the very purpose of the narrative is concealed. Slowly and gradually we see in it the earth passing through successive stages, until it becomes the abode of a being made in the image of God. Mechanical laws are first of all imposed upon

* The Accadians were the primitive inhabitants of Chaldea, and were descendants of Japheth. Ur was one of their chief cities. It is uncertain at what date the Chaldeans, who were a Semitic race, gained the ascendency there.

created matter, and as gravitation draws the particles together, the friction produces electricity, and with it light and heat. In union next with chemical laws, they sort and arrange the materials of this our earth, and break it up into land and sea. On the third day, the creative energy for the second time manifests itself, and vegetable life is called into being; and on the fourth day there was apparently a long pause, during which the atmosphere was purified by means of vegetation, till the sun and moon shone upon the hardening surface, and made it capable of bearing more advanced types of plants, quickly followed on the fifth day by the lower forms of animal life. Finally, when the work of the sixth day was far advanced, and the mammalia had been called into existence, the Creator takes solemn counsel, and by special intervention man is created to be the ruler and governor of all that had been made. From the first he is set forth as a religious being, made in God's likeness; and on the seventh day God rests, to hallow for man his weekly rest. We are now living in this seventh day of God, and it will go on until the advent of the day of the Lord. During this day of rest the creative energy pauses, and no being higher than man is called into existence. We know not how long it may continue, nor what may follow it; but we know that God's days are not as our days. The record is not a geological treatise, but a hymn of praise to God, magnifying His mighty works, indicating man's high relation to Him, and hallowing the weekly Sabbath, which is man's day of rest, just as the whole period of time which has followed upon the creation of man unto the present time is God's day of rest. In it He creates no new being, fashions nothing higher than man, but He still protects and maintains all created things: for in the work of providence and grace God resteth not. (See John v. 17.)

Other minor purposes are, indeed, kept in view. The teaching that God made the sun and moon, and that they are placed under servitude for man's use, coupled with the scarcely grammatical insertion of the words "the stars also," in verse 16, reading like a marginal note thrust into the text, all this had plainly for its object the prevention of the idolatrous veneration of the heavenly luminaries. And it succeeded. Everywhere else the sun and moon and planets were worshipped with Divine honours. Even we Christians call the names of the days of the week after them. The Jew, better taught by this first chapter of Genesis, never fell into this error. To him the heavens declared God's glory, and the firmament displayed His handywork (Ps. xix. 1).

So in verse 21 there is a protest against the worship of the crocodile, the animal especially meant by the word translated *whales*. Now here we have one of the many indications of the hand of Moses. If it was this record which kept Eber and his race free from the debasing superstition of star-worship, and which made Terah and his family quit their home at Ur of the Chaldees, so by the insertion of these words Moses protected the Israelites from the animal worship so prevalent in Egypt. Equally they needed protection from the attractions of star-worship (Amos v. 25, 26), and found it where the patriarchs had found it of old.

The history of creation is, however, never expressly called a document, as are the other ten portions of the book, and it may have been entirely revealed to Moses. Such was long my own opinion, but there are two considerations which seem to tend in a contrary direction.

For, first, this narrative seems essential as the groundwork for the faith of the patriarchs. Not necessarily in the form in which we now have it, and which was given it by the hand of Moses, but in some form. And as it must have been inspired, if it was to be the foundation for man's faith, we may well believe that Moses, being guided by the same Divine inspiration, would not make any other changes in it than such as would render it more fit to do God's work in all succeeding times. If, then, the patriarchs possessed this narrative mainly such as it now is, they had a document of so great weight and authority as would account for their rejection of idolatry and their persistence in the belief of one sole Deity. For it is not, like the Oriental cosmogonies, a speculative attempt to solve the great difficulty of creation, namely, how a Being perfect and infinite, "with whom can be no variation" (James i. 17), changed from the passive state of not willing the existence of the universe, to the active state of willing it; and how, with almighty power and boundless goodness, He called into being a world imperfect, and marred by sorrow and sin. It is no subtile device of thinking that we find, but absolute knowledge given with authority, and of which the one purpose is to show that man from the first stood in a near relation to God, was made for converse with Him, and must set apart a portion of his time for his Creator's service. Such a narrative stands outside the physical sciences, in which man is to attain to knowledge by his own exertions. But whenever truth is reached, either in physics or in metaphysics, we could not believe a book to be inspired which was incapable of being shown to be in accordance with truth. In every age the Bible speaks to men according to their knowledge, and our increased knowledge of astronomy and geology has shown that there are profound verities in the Biblical account of Creation, concerning which even the ablest commentators without this knowledge spake with stammering lips and unintelligent tongue.

As then such absolute knowledge could have been given only by inspiration (see Job xxxviii. 4), it would be a document, whenever bestowed, that must from the first have been highly prized and religiously preserved. And if it was essential to the faith of the patriarchs it would be bestowed upon them, and probably, from early times, was a treasure in the family of Shem. Even long before the Flood, Enoch was a prophet who attained to a remarkable nearness to God, and foretold a day of judgment (Jude 14, 15). There were also other inspired men through whom God spake, and whose words would probably be recorded; and their teaching, carefully preserved, would account for the purity of the religious belief of the Semitic family as a whole, and especially for that of the race of Eber. God has made it the law of His working that He ever employs secondary causes, and the chastened monotheism of Abraham's faith must have had something to produce it. Subsequently he was himself the recipient of revelations, but these were vouchsafed to him because he was fit for them. If he possessed this narrative of creation, his pure creed, his noble character, his trustful abandonment of his home, all become intelligible. And living in a highly-civilised, though heathen, community, and in an age when the commonest transactions of life were inscribed on tablets and cylinders of clay, there is no difficulty in believing that Abraham had the record in writing, and that it was preserved until the days of Moses. And Moses, instinct with prophetic power, has placed it upon the forefront of revelation, and being himself a prophet, would record it in such a form as would make it fit for the permanent use, first, of the Jewish, and then of the Christian Church.

But had we only these considerations they would not

go beyond the bound of a moderate probability. We have, in the second place, to examine the bearing upon revelation of the Babylonian Legend of the Creation. Now the actual tablets deciphered by Mr. George Smith are of a comparatively late date, being of the time of Assurbanipal, a contemporary of Manasseh, the son of Hezekiah, in the seventh century before Christ; but the narrative is the Assyrian form of a far older legend.* It is grossly and even childishly polytheistic, describes the creation of the gods, and gives divine honours to the heaven, the earth, and the sea, as the three supreme deities; but in other parts there is so close a resemblance to much in the record in Genesis, that we cannot doubt that they stand in some relation to one another. The library of Assurbanipal consisted either of tablets robbed from other libraries, or of translations made from older and mainly from Accadian works: and as our acquaintance becomes greater with the vast materials brought from Assyria, but unfortunately existing in a very fragmentary state, other Creation-tablets will probably be found, giving us the legend in many forms. What we already possess makes us aware that an account of Creation in remarkable agreement with that in Genesis existed in Assyria,† but with all its sobriety and its pure monotheism gone. The legend is as corrupt as it could well be. But whence came it? We can hardly doubt that the land whence the Assyrians obtained it was Ur of the Chaldees, Abraham's erewhile home. He had probably inherited the document, and with loving zeal tried to teach it to the Elamites in Ur, that they might know that their star-worship was the worship of the creature instead of the Creator: and it was this probably which exposed him to persecution, and so God called him away, to preserve the pure faith for future times. But if the revelation be no older than the time of Moses, and was given to him in the wilderness of Sinai when writing the Pentateuch, it would be difficult to account for the possession by the Chaldees of so much of the inspired narrative. And the same holds good of the Chaldean Legends of the Flood, of the Tower of Babel, and of other narratives in Genesis.

To one of these we must next briefly call attention. The narrative of the invasion of Palestine by Chedorlaomer has called forth much satirical comment on the part of critics. What could be said in defence of a story which described a king of Elam, a sort of Switzerland lying south and east of Assyria and Persia, as carrying his arms through a region so difficult as that which lay to the north of Babylonia, and onward to the shores of the Mediterranean Sea? Moreover, this mountaineer is represented as having among his vassals a king of Shinar, so that Babylon must have been subject to him. But we have now ancient documents deciphered for us which show that about the time of Abraham the kings of Elam were the paramount power in Asia, and that the plain of Babylonia was parcelled out among numerous towns, whose petty kings were subject to them. According to the Assyrian records the Elamite supremacy lasted for several centuries, and was not finally overthrown until B.C. 1270; and about Abraham's time one of their kings named Kudur-Mabuk actually claimed the title of "Lord of Phœnicia," or Palestine (see *Excursus E*), so that we have the most complete corroboration of the Biblical narrative. The names also which occur in the history are all explained by what we now know of the language of this ancient people; and we probably have in Gen. xiv. a contemporary record, carefully preserved from Abraham's times. As the title "Lord of Phœnicia" attests the victories of Kudur-Mabuk, we conclude that he it was who imposed upon the cities of the plain the tribute which Kudur-Lagomar endeavoured to enforce.

But leaving these Assyrian legends, let us revert to the contents of the Biblical narratives of Creation. And here it would altogether exceed our limits if we attempted to show the agreement of the record in Genesis with the proved facts of science.* It must suffice to state briefly a few salient points.

First, then, the creative words in the opening record of Genesis are laws. God speaks, and not only is it done, but the law is immutably settled for all future time. The law given on the first day apparently was that grand universal law of gravitation, giving rise, as the result of the closer cohesion of matter, to electrical and chemical forces, whence spring most of the phenomena of existence. The law given on the second day was not a new departure of creative energy, but simply marks a point reached by the law given on the first. Accepting the nebular hypothesis as the only theory which satisfactorily accounts for the phenomena of Creation, there was a vast period of time during which the condensation of matter produced mainly heat and light, and only at last would our planet be so far advanced as for there to be an open "expanse" around it, and solids and fluids beginning to cohere within this ring. On the third day a further stage is reached. The strata formed by gravitation are broken up, partly by chemical and partly by mechanical forces, and dry land appears. This is followed by a new creative act, calling vegetable life into existence, and giving it its laws. For the higher forms of vegetation were not reached until man appeared on the earth, when "God planted a garden," and made not only fruit trees, but also all the nobler vegetation, described as "every tree that is pleasant to the sight," to grow out of the ground (chap. ii. 8, 9). After the pause of the fourth day animal life is created, extending through two Divine days, until man finally appears. As on the fourth day so on the seventh, there is no new creative energy displayed, but the laws previously given move on in their mighty power. And they are immutable, because they are the ever-present will of the immutable God.

There are then but three acts of creative power, of which the first is the calling of matter into existence, as recorded in verse 1. Matter is next made subject to laws by which it is so arranged and combined as to form an orderly world, in opposition to the waste and empty abyss through which it was at first dispersed. The next creative act is the bestowal of vegetable life, narrated in verse 11. The third and final act is the bestowal of animal life, recorded in verse 20. To this I would venture to add the creation of the human reason, and of the spiritual nature of man.

* "Every copy of what we will term the Genesis Legends yet found was inscribed, with one exception, during the reign of Assurbanipal, from B.C. 670: but it is stated and acknowledged on all hands that most of these tablets are not the originals, but only copies from earlier texts" (Sayce, *Chald. Gen.*, p. 16). This king's library consisted of not less than 10,000 inscribed tablets (*ibid.* 15).

† Mr. Sayce, *Chald. Gen.*, p. 312, considers that Chaldea was the original home of the narratives concerning Creation, the Flood, the Tower of Babel, &c.

* Dr. Kinns, in his interesting work, *Moses and Geology*, shows that the fifteen creative events recorded by Moses correspond in order with their place in science. He also shows that the chances against their being so arranged almost defy the power of numbers to express.

All the rest is but arrangement; but in these four acts we attain to results which no force of mechanical or chemical laws could produce. When some time ago it was argued that life might have come to our earth from an aërolite, scientific men thereby confessed that there was nothing upon this our globe to account for it. But as the materials of aërolites are much the same as those of the earth, and as they are in fact parts of our solar system, we must go outside them: and ever onwards until we find it where alone it is to be found, and where Moses placed it, in God.

But if thus the cosmogony in the Book of Genesis sets before us a gradual advance in creation, giving us its successive stages, and its immutable laws, and marking the introduction from time to time into the abyss of new forces, and especially of life, are we to accept evolution as the best exposition of the manner in which God wrought? I answer that the theologian has nothing to do with such questions. The unwise disputes between science and theology almost always arise from scientific men crying aloud that some new theory just hatched is a disproof of the supernatural, and from theologians debating each new theory on the ground of scriptural exposition. It is but just to the author of the theory of evolution to say that he never made this mistake. Really, every scientific hypothesis must be proved or disproved on the ground of science alone; but when the few survivors of the very many theories which scientific men suggest have attained to the rank of scientific verities, then at last the necessity arises of comparing them with Holy Scripture: for we could not believe it to be the Word of God if it contradicted the book of nature, which also comes from Him. God is truth, and His revealed Word must be true.

Now evolution is very far from having attained to the rank of a scientific verity; it is at most an interesting and ingenious theory. But should it ever win higher rank, the second account of creation is in its favour. While in the first Elohim appears in all the grandeur of the Divine majesty, creating, first, matter by a word, and then life, and finally the rational soul; in the second He appears as the Divine artificer. All is slow and gradual. He forms man, builds up the woman, plants a garden, makes trees to grow. The two accounts undoubtedly are meant to supplement one another, and it is remarkable that while the second compresses the whole of creation into one day, it nevertheless represents it as a patient and lengthy process; and when Adam was placed in the terrestrial paradise vegetable life had reached the fruit tree, and animal life had advanced to cattle—animals, that is, fit for domestication. And we have another mark of duration of time in the fact that the waters had not only formed channels for themselves, but that these had become so fixed and settled that two of the rivers of Eden exist and bear the same names at the present day.

Unfortunately for its temperate discussion, evolution is now enwrapped by many of its partisans in the ugly pellicle of materialism, and for this there is in the Bible no place. While, therefore, I am content to leave all the processes of creation to those who make the material universe the object of their intelligent study, I object to their crossing beyond their proper limits, which they do in arguing that our enlarged knowledge of matter and its laws militates with a belief in a governing and law-giving mind: for material science can penetrate no farther than to the phenomena of nature. It is the noble teaching of the Book of Genesis that creation was the work of an All-wise and Almighty intelligence, and that the Infinite Mind, which we reverently call God, even called matter into being, and gave it those laws which scientific men study so wisely. I am content to believe everything which they prove in their own domain; but when they make assumptions in regions where they are but trespassers, it is mere waste of time to dispute with them. But I cannot say this without at the same time acknowledging the immense obligation under which theologians lie to the masters of the sciences of astronomy and geology; for they have enlarged our ideas, brushed away many a crude popular fallacy, and enabled us to understand more and more of the perfect ways of God.

Leaving, therefore, the theory of evolution to be proved or disproved on scientific grounds, we must next observe that much light is thrown upon the Biblical account of creation by our increased knowledge of the literature of Babylonia. We have seen that the form of the narrative and the arrangement of the work of creation into six days had for one main object the hallowing of the seventh day's rest. We are now aware that the division of time into weeks of seven days, and the weekly day of rest, is of extreme antiquity. Accadian tablets of very early date show that the Sabbath was strictly observed in times anterior to those of Abraham. The Babylonian story of the flood gives to the number *seven* as marked an importance as is assigned to it in the narrative in Genesis. There is, however, this striking difference. In the Accadian tablets the seven days of the week are connected with the sun, the moon, and the five planets which were all then known. Our own days of the week, as mentioned before, bear testimony to the general prevalence of this idolatry of the heavenly bodies. So, also, the Babylonian narrative of the flood is intensely polytheistic. In the Book of Genesis we have the purest monotheism, without a trace of even the most ancient and most seductive forms of heathenism.

In the second narrative, chaps. ii. 4—iv. 26, creation appears only as a subsidiary part of the history. For following the rule usual in the *tôldôth*, it is the description of that which follows upon the name given in the title. The *tôldôth* of Adam is the history of his descendants up to the flood; that of Terah is the history of Abraham; that of Jacob is the story of Joseph. So the *tôldôth* of creation is the narrative of the lives of Adam and Eve until their posterity was divided into the two lines of Seth and Cain. Naturally, therefore, creation appears as the work of a single day, though the stages recorded are all slowly reached, and have reference to the care taken by God of our first parents. If the mist period is referred to, when the ball of the earth was so hot as to drive off from it the water in the form of vapour to the far side of the expanse, this is in contrast with the cool garden, shaded by forest trees, planted with choice kinds of fruit, and watered by rivers running in settled channels. Precious products of the earth are also mentioned, gold and pearls, and precious stones, because such things adorn civilised life. Beasts and birds, too, are there, because upon them Adam exercised his budding intelligence. But even in Paradise Adam is not represented as being possessed of high metaphysical powers; on the contrary, he is described as in a very rudimentary state, and with his intellect undeveloped. He does not even know the difference between right and wrong, one of the very first things a child learns, though a child generally learns it in much the same way as Adam did, by doing something wrong and incurring punishment. But neither is he without use of reason, for he studies the animals, and names them after their peculiar gifts or ways. He holds, too, a simple communion with God, who walks with him in the garden; and thus, again, man appears from the very first as a religious being, capable of and actually having intercourse with the Deity.

But amongst numerous points of surpassing interest in this second narrative, one of the most remarkable is the name given to the Deity. In the first narrative God is Elohim, a term expressive of universal might. Elohim is God in His omnipotence. In the second narrative it is Jehovah-Elohim. Now the name Jehovah holds a mysterious place in Revelation. It is, if we may reverently so speak, the personal name of God. It is no general title drawn from His attributes, but something individual, representing God, first as a person, and secondly as holding personal relations to man. The Israelites correctly expressed this when they said to Joshua, "Jehovah is our God" (Josh. xxiv. 18). It was no abstraction which they worshipped, but a definite being, who stood to them in a fixed and definite relation.

But though the meaning is clear, the history of the name is full of difficulties.* For in Exod. vi. 2, 3, while revealing Himself to Moses as Jehovah, God says that He manifested Himself to the patriarchs as *El-Shaddai*, "but by my name Jehovah was I not known to them." Now this is startling when we find in Genesis, not only the origin of the name carefully recorded, and a note given of the time when it first was ascribed to Deity (chap. iv. 26), but even its general occurrence joined, nevertheless, with the utmost discrimination in its use. Even if the names El-Shaddai, El-'Olam, El-'Elyon, are those most prominent in the history of Abraham, yet it was Jehovah who first called him from Ur (chap. xii. 1); and when after the Elamite invasion a covenant was made between God and Abraham, not only did God say, "I am Jehovah," but Abraham also addressed Him as Adonai - Jehovah (chap. xv. 7, 8), wrongly rendered in our version "Lord God."

Strangely enough, the only name compounded with Jehovah, which occurs before the time of Moses, is that of Jochebed ("Jehovah is glory"), his own mother (Exod. vi. 20). There may, of course, have been others, for the names of very few persons have been preserved. But the existence of even this one name shows that the title Jehovah was in use, and was highly honoured, and perhaps even that it was becoming more common. But the difficulty is apparent rather than real, and disappears upon an examination of the right meaning of the words in Exod. vi. 3. For if we turn to our Bibles, and examine the manner in which the word "name" is employed there, we shall find, as has been pointed out in innumerable places by commentators, that in Hebrew the name stands for the thing. What is really intended by the passage in Exodus is that the peculiar use of the name Jehovah, which had long been in process of formation, was now fully established; and whereas the Deity had hitherto been El-Shaddai, the Mighty One, henceforth, as their covenant-God, He was to be addressed as Jehovah. It had always been a title round which loving memories clustered, and which had been used with a deep sense of its importance. God had now brought out the meaning of the name in a way in which it had never been interpreted before. Eve had used it of her child, calling him "He shall be" (Gen. iv. 1); but she had been bitterly disappointed. God now applies it to Himself; for when asked by Moses what was the special epithet by which he was to proclaim Him to the Israelites in Egypt, He answered, "I shall be that I shall be" (Exod. iii. 14). It was a name pointing onward to a future manifestation of Himself, and mysteriously indicating that the fulfilment of the promise in chap. iii. 15 would be by an incarnation of Deity. Jehovah is the third person of that which God spake in the first person, and henceforward it was to be the peculiar title of the Deity in His covenant relation with Israel, because in it were mysteriously summed up all those Messianic hopes which the prophets were to unfold. Israel's covenant-God was one "who would become" the Immanuel, God manifest in the flesh.

The words, then, in Exod. vi. 2, 3, indicate that a great culmination had been reached. The Elohim of their fathers (Exod. iii. 13), who had been worshipped under various titles, but who had chiefly been known as the Omnipotent, is henceforward to have a special title, indicative of a close relation between Him and His people. They were at length a nation, and were to have, in a few years, a country of their own; and instead of the general monotheism of the patriarchs, they were to worship still one God, but under a title that set forth, not some special attribute, but that He would manifest Himself more clearly and fully to them in time to come. It is the theocratic name, and could reasonably be given only when the theocracy was about to be constituted. And thus the care and discrimination so clearly shown in Genesis in the use of the names Jehovah and Elohim is explained, and is a strong argument for the Mosaic authorship. Had we a mere jumble of extracts from a Jehovist and an Elohist, no such exactness would have been possible; for it would have been a mere matter of chance which name was employed. As it is they often appear in close juxtaposition, but each correctly used. And in this second narrative of creation, the reason for the unusual title Jehovah-Elohim is plain. God is no longer the Omnipotent, calling matter and life into existence, and giving them laws which cannot be broken; He is a loving being, arranging and providing for man's good and happiness, taking care of the most perfect of His creatures, and revealing Himself to him as his Friend. Even more important is it to notice that in this narrative the foundation is laid for the Gospel, and that the special office of Jehovah, and the reason of the name, are indicated in chap. iii. 15. And they are given in relation to all mankind; for this is a distinguishing point of the Book of Genesis, and one that indicates most plainly that its origin was prior to the giving of the Law, that while it prepares for the theocracy, it ever represents God as the God of all the world. There is none of that exclusiveness of view which grew up subsequently in the Jewish Church: the very noblest form which is presented to us is that of Melchizedek, the king-priest of a Gentile town, and who on that account is the fit type of Christ, in whom once again the bonds of union with God's Church became as wide as the world.

The remaining *tôldôth* have been, I trust, sufficiently considered in the notes. I would only, in conclusion, warn the reader against expecting that all difficulties can be cleared away. If our view be true, that Moses had before him ancient written documents, some of which had even been carried by the family of Eber to the rich and civilised city of Ur, while others, like the *tôldôth* of the patriarchs, were recorded in their tents, then we possess in Genesis the oldest and most venerable literature in the world. There is no reason for supposing that the patriarchs could not write. Abraham

* Upon its origin see *Excursus B.*

came from a place where writing flourished; nor were the Canaanites an uneducated people. It was they who carried letters to Greece, and we still use in the main their alphabet. Nor are there wanting indications of this in their history; for the town Debir, to the west of Hebron, was called Kirjath-Sepher—*i.e.*, Book-town—by the Canaanites (Josh. xv. 15); and Kirjath-Sannah (*ibid.* 49), a word hard to interpret, but which many explain as meaning that some material for writing was prepared there. But independently of this, Abraham would not readily lose an art well known to him; his son and grandson were both men of domestic habits; and before Jacob's death the Israelites were settled in learned Egypt.

Many of the difficulties that have been felt in the narrative refer to numbers and matters of chronology. Now God did not bestow upon men a perfect system of numeration, but left it to them to discover it for themselves. And neither Hebrews, Greeks, nor Romans did discover it; but the Arabs, comparatively a few centuries ago, invented for us that simple but accurate method which we now employ. The Hebrews at the present day express numbers by letters. Thus Aleph is put for one, Beth for two, Yod for ten, Koph for one hundred, and the highest number they can thus indicate is four hundred by Tau. Above four hundred they can only add letters together, or try to make them express higher numerals by dots. But we do not know when this system began, nor even when their alphabet attained to its full complement of twenty-two letters. In what way numbers were previously indicated is an entire mystery, and probably the earlier genealogies of mankind were of the nature of a *memoria technica*, and had to be explained by oral teaching. Moreover, the great object of these lists of names was not chronology but genealogy. To this the patriarchs attached the highest value, and their justification lies in the genealogy of our Lord. From the call of Abraham it is possible to construct a chronology that cannot be far wrong, difficult as it may be to make 1 Kings vi. 1 accord with Acts xiii. 20. Previously to that date all is uncertain, and while in a religious point of view we have everything that we want, it is as impossible to construct a scientific chronology of the world from the records in Genesis, as it is to construct from those same records a scientific geology or astronomy. The Bible refuses to be put to purposes for which it was never intended.

Of numerous interesting points which remain, I will notice but one, namely, the morality of the book of Genesis. And here we must start with the acknowledged principle that there is progress throughout the Bible, and that as the light of revelation was gradually given, so with it was there a growth in morality. The least in the kingdom of heaven is in this respect greater than John the Baptist, just as he in his moral level was higher than all who had gone before (Matt. xi. 11). If then we look for a morality in the Book of Genesis as pure as that of the Gospel, we shall look in vain; and in doing so must reject our Lord's contrast in the Sermon on the Mount between His teaching and that of the great and good of old times. Yet the morality of the Book of Genesis is absolutely high, and is also such as would lead on to higher stages. Note how from the first the idea of the family, which many regard as quite modern, is the root and centre of the patriarchal life. Polygamy, that great curse of the Oriental home, is from the first discountenanced. In the earthly paradise we have but one loving pair, and the woman is described as the man's counterpart (chap. ii. 18), and so as his equal. The law of marriage is given in terms so stringent and binding (chap. ii. 24) that our Lord could add nothing to them, though He draws out their force (Matt. xix. 5, 6). When polygamy appears it is in a Cainite family, marked by arrogance and cruelty. If Abraham takes to him a concubine, it is at his wife's suggestion, and for the purpose of having offspring, and not for lust. Isaac, though long without offspring, remains faithful to his barren wife. And, subsequently, when Jacob marries two sisters, though his conduct falls far below the level of Christian morality, yet he regarded Rachel as his lawful wife unjustly withheld from him; and while he had little love for Leah, and took greatly to heart the fraud practised upon him, and to which she had lent herself, yet he did not cast her away, but took care of her, treated her with honour, and finally, it would seem, reciprocated her affection. And so as regards the handmaids, while the picture is even offensive to Christian feeling, we again notice that the dominant idea was that of offspring, and that it was the act of the wives at a time when each considered herself barren, and had for its purpose the increase of their family. There is nothing in it of a low and sensual character, and it seems even then to have been regarded as abnormal; for Jacob's sons return again to the practice of monogamy. In all the pride and power of viceroyalty, Joseph is content with one wife.

As regards slavery, Abraham receives gifts of slaves from Pharaoh (chap. xii. 16), in addition to those which he had brought with him from Haran, and has so large a household as to be able to take with him for the battle with Chedorlaomer three hundred and eighteen trained servants born in his own house (chap. xiv. 14). Apparently, too, there was even a trade in slaves (chap. xvii. 27). Such was also the case when the New Testament was written, and the apostles were content to provide for the kind treatment of the slave, while enunciating principles which naturally led to the stern disapproval of it in course of time, though its suppression was long delayed by human greed. Now in the Book of Genesis we find nothing like the predial slavery which has disgraced modern times. The slave, whether "born in the house or bought with money," was to share in all the religious privileges of his master. The express command was given that he should be circumcised, and admitted into covenant with his master's God (chap. xvii. 13). Undoubtedly a large mass of the Israelite nation was sprung from those who had thus formed the families of the patriarchs; and we can imagine nothing that would more alleviate the lot of the "servant," would increase his own self-respect, and insure his kindly treatment, than the feeling that he thus worshipped the same God as his master, and was bound up with him in the same religious brotherhood. We do not wonder after this at finding that not his nephew Lot, but a home-born slave was next in authority to Abraham over his tribe, and his prospective heir if he had no son (chap. xv. 2, 3). Nor does it surprise us that Sheshan, a highborn descendant of Hezron, should give his daughter in marriage to a slave (1 Chron. ii. 35); nor that his slave, Ziba, should have been the representative of the house of Saul until David called Mephi-bosheth, the son of Jonathan, out of obscurity, and restored him to his rank (2 Sam. ix. 2, &c.).

In the denial of their wives both Abraham and Isaac fail as regards truthfulness. It is undoubtedly the case that wherever men occupy a position of danger, they are too apt to have recourse habitually to artifice to insure their safety. In the East to this day it is well-nigh the universal rule to give false answers, not merely to escape from peril, but even simply to conform to the supposed wishes of the questioner. We may well suppose that the few men of the Semitic race, surrounded by an overwhelming number of Elamites and aliens at Ur, and in the plains of Babylonia, were exposed to this temptation; and probably truthfulness in the face of danger and death is a heroic virtue which we have learned from Christian martyrs. But while we thus find the patriarchs deficient in this high quality, the two narratives condemn their want of faith. In both cases their ruse involves them in danger and difficulty. They are reproved by heathen mouths, and learn that truthfulness would have been their wisest policy.

Finally, the sacrifice of Isaac by his father has often been condemned in unmeasured terms. We have here, they say, the father of the faithful tempted to commit a crime, which every dictate of a pure conscience would have condemned. Human sacrifice is the blackest outcome of fanaticism and morbid superstition, and no supposed revelation would justify a deed opposed to the laws of natural religion, and absolutely wrong in itself. A command requiring the commission of a crime ought in all cases, without exception, to be disobeyed. But, first of all, the supposed effect of a justification of human sacrifice never has resulted from the patriarch's example. No Jew ever derived from it the conclusion that there might be circumstances under which a father might offer his child to God. The conclusion which they deduced from the occurrence was "that God would provide" the great sacrifice (chap. xxii. 14, see Notes). How can an act be immoral from which no immoral consequences have resulted, and which has ever been so interpreted as to condemn the very practice which these critics supposed that it favoured? But in sober truth, there are far higher considerations involved in this history. The Bible must and always will be the object of constant attack from those who stand outside it, but what, may we ask, has been the view of Abraham's conduct inside the Church? We may safely say that there, by Jew of old, and Christian now, it has ever been regarded as the crowning act of Abraham's life. To it we believe that our Lord referred when He said, "Your father Abraham rejoiced to see my day: and he saw it, and was glad" (John viii. 56). For there the whole mystery of God's redeeming love was set forth, and while only the great facts were recorded as a parable, for men to muse over until the interpretation came, we may conclude from our Lord's words that to Abraham was revealed the interpretation of the solemn mystery in which he had taken part. We have repeatedly pointed out that in the Book of Genesis we have the germ of every future doctrine of revelation. This would not be true if we had not in this narrative the anticipation of the teaching that "God so loved the world that He gave His only begotten Son, that whosoever believeth in Him should not perish, but have everlasting life.' (John iii. 16).

THE FIRST BOOK OF MOSES, CALLED

GENESIS

CHAPTER I.—(1) In the [a] beginning
God created the heaven and the earth.
(2) And the earth was without form, and
void; and darkness *was* upon the face
of the deep. And the Spirit of God
moved upon the face of the waters.

[a] Ps. 33. 6; & 136. 5; Acts 14. 15; & 17. 24; Heb. 11. 3.

THE CREATIVE WEEK (chaps. i. 1—ii. 3).

(1) **In the beginning.**—Not, as in John i. 1, "from eternity," but in the beginning of this sidereal system, of which our sun, with its attendant planets, forms a part. As there never was a time when God did not exist, and as activity is an essential part of His being (John v. 17), so, probably, there was never a time when worlds did not exist; and in the process of calling them into existence when and how He willed, we may well believe that God acted in accordance with the working of some universal law, of which He is Himself the author. It was natural with St. John, when placing the same words at the commencement of his Gospel, to carry back our minds to a more absolute conceivable "beginning," when the work of creation had not commenced, and when in the whole universe there was only God.

God.—Heb., *Elohim.* A word plural in form, but joined with a verb singular, except when it refers to the false gods of the heathen, in which case it takes a verb plural. Its root-meaning is *strength, power;* and the form *Elohim* is not to be regarded as a *pluralis majestatis,* but as embodying the effort of early human thought in feeling after the Deity, and in arriving at the conclusion that the Deity was One. Thus, in the name *Elohim* it included in one Person all the powers, mights, and influences by which the world was first created and is now governed and maintained. In the Vedas, in the hymns recovered for us by the decipherment of the cuneiform inscriptions, whether Accadian or Semitic, and in all other ancient religious poetry, we find these powers ascribed to different beings; in the Bible alone Elohim is one. Christians may also well see in this a foreshadowing of the plurality of persons in the Divine Trinity; but its primary lesson is that, however diverse may seem the working of the powers of nature, the Worker is one and His work one.

Created.—Creation, in its strict sense of producing something out of nothing, contains an idea so noble and elevated that naturally human language could only gradually rise up to it. It is quite possible, therefore, that the word *bârâ,* "he created," may originally have signified to *hew* stone or *fell* timber; but as a matter of fact it is a rare word, and employed chiefly or entirely in connection with the activity of God. As, moreover, "the heaven and the earth" can only mean the totality of all existent things, the idea of creating them out of nothing is contained in the very form of the sentence. Even in verses 21, 27, where the word may signify something less than creation *ex nihilo,* there is nevertheless a passage from inert matter to animate life, for which science knows no force, or process, or energy capable of its accomplishment.

The heaven and the earth.—The normal phrase in the Bible for the universe (Deut. xxxii. 1; Ps. cxlviii. 13; Isa. i. 2). To the Hebrew this consisted of our one planet and the atmosphere surrounding it, in which he beheld the sun, moon, and stars. But it is one of the more than human qualities of the language of the Holy Scriptures that, while written by men whose knowledge was in accordance with their times, it does not contradict the increased knowledge of later times. Contemporaneous with the creation of the earth was the calling into existence, not merely perhaps of our solar system, but of that sidereal universe of which we form so small a part; but naturally in the Bible our attention is confined to that which chiefly concerns ourselves.

(2) **And the earth.**—The conjunction "and" negatives the well-meant attempt to harmonise geology and Scripture by taking verse 1 as a mere heading; the two verses go together, and form a general summary of creation, which is afterwards divided into its several stages.

Was is not the copula, but the substantive verb *existed,* and expresses duration of time. After creation, the earth existed as a shapeless and empty waste.

Without form, and void.—Literally, *tohu* and *bohu,* which words are both substantives, and signify *wasteness* and *emptiness.* The similarity of their forms, joined with the harshness of their sound, made them pass almost into a proverb for everything that was dreary and desolate (Isa. xxxiv. 11; Jer. iv. 23). It expresses here the state of primæval matter immediately after creation, when as yet there was no cohesion between the separate particles.

Darkness.—As light is the result either of the condensation of matter or of vibrations caused by chemical action, this exactly agrees with the previous representation of the chaos out of which the earth was to be shaped. It existed at present only as an incoherent waste of emptiness.

The deep.—*Tĕhôm.* This word, from a root signifying confusion or disturbance, is poetically applied to the ocean, as in Ps. xlii. 7, from the restless motion of its waves, but is used here to describe the chaos as a surging mass of shapeless matter. In the Babylonian legend, Tiâmat, the Hebrew *tĕhôm,* is represented as overcome by Merodach, who out of the primæval anarchy brings order and beauty (Sayce, *Chaldean Genesis,* pp. 59, 109, 113).

The Spirit of God.—Heb., *a wind of God, i.e.,* a mighty wind, as rendered by the Targum and most Jewish interpreters. (See Note on chap. xxiii. 6.) So the *wind of Jehovah* makes the grass wither (Isa. xl. 7); and so God makes the winds His messengers (Ps. civ. 4). The argument that no wind at present existed because the atmo-

(3) And God said, [a]Let there be light: and there was light. (4) And God saw the light, that *it was* good: and God divided [1]the light from the darkness. (5) And God called the light Day, and the darkness he called Night. [2]And the evening and the morning were the first day.

a 2 Cor. 4. 6
1 Heb., *between the light and between the darkness.*
2 Heb., *And the evening was, and the morning was,* &c.

sphere had not been created is baseless, for if water existed, so did air. But this unseen material force, wind (John iii. 8), has ever suggested to the human mind the thought of the Divine agency, which, equally unseen, is even mightier in its working. When, then, creation is ascribed to the wind (Job xxvi. 13; Ps. civ. 30), we justly see, not the mere instrumental force employed, but rather that Divine operative energy which resides especially in the Third Person of the Holy Trinity. But we must be upon our guard against the common error of commentators, who read into the text of these most ancient documents perfect doctrines which were not revealed in their fulness until the Gospel was given. It is a marvellous fact that Genesis does contain the germ of well-nigh every evangelical truth, but it contains it in a suggestive and not a completed form. So here this mighty energising wind suggests to us the thought of the Holy Ghost, and is far more eloquent in its original simplicity than when we read into it a doctrine not made known until revelation was perfected in Christ (John vii. 39).

Moved.—Heb., *fluttered lovingly.* (See Deut. xxxii. 11.) This word also would lead the mind up to the thought of the agency of a Person. In Syriac the verb is a very common one for the incubation of birds; and, in allusion to this place, it is metaphorically employed, both of the waving of the hand of the priest over the cup in consecrating the wine for the Eucharist, and of that of the patriarch over the head of a bishop at his consecration. Two points must here be noticed: the first, that the motion was not self-originated, but was external to the chaos; the second, that it was a gentle and loving energy, which tenderly and gradually, with fostering care, called forth the latent possibilities of a nascent world.

The Creative Days.

(3) **And God said.**—Voice and sound there could be none, nor was there any person to whom God addressed this word of power. The phrase, then, is metaphorical, and means that God enacted for the universe a law; and ten times we find the command similarly given. The beauty and sublimity of the language here used has often been noticed: God makes no preparation, He employs no means, needs no secondary agency. He speaks, and it is done. His word alone contains all things necessary for the fulfilment of His will. So in the cognate languages the word *Emir*, ruler, is literally, *speaker*. The Supreme One speaks: with the rest, of hear is to obey. God, then, by speaking, gives to nature a universal and enduring law. His commands are not temporary, but eternal; and whatever secondary causes were called into existence when the Elohim, by a word, created light, those same causes produce it now, and will produce it until God recalls His word. We have, then, here nature's first universal law. What is it?

Let there be light: and there was light.—The sublimity of the original is lost in our language by the cumbrous multiplication of particles. The Hebrew is *Yhi ôr wayhi ôr.* Light is not itself a substance, but is a condition or state of matter; and this primæval light was probably electric, arising from the condensation and friction of the elements as they began to arrange themselves in order. And this, again, was due to what is commonly called the law of gravitation, or of the attraction of matter. If on the first day electricity and magnetism were generated, and the laws given which create and control them, we have in them the two most powerful and active energies of the present and of all time—or possibly two forms of one and the same busy and restless force. And the law thus given was that of gravitation, of which light was the immediate result.

(4) **And God saw.**—This contemplation indicates, first, lapse of time; and next, that the judgment pronounced was the verdict of the Divine reason.

That it was good.—As light was a necessary result of motion in the world-mass, so was it indispensable for all that was to follow, inasmuch as neither vegetable nor animal life can exist without it. But the repeated approval by the Deity of each part and portion of this material universe (comp. Ps. civ. 31) also condemns all Manichæan theories, and asserts that this world is a noble home for man, and life a blessing, in spite of its solemn responsibilities.

And God divided . . .—The first three creative days are all days of order and distribution, and have been called "the three separations." But while on the first two days no new thing was created, but only the chaotic matter (described in verse 2) arranged, on day three there was the introduction of vegetable life. The division on the first day does not imply that darkness has a separate and independent existence, but that there were now periods of light and darkness; and thus by the end of the first day our earth must have advanced far on its way towards its present state. (See Note, verse 5.) It is, however, even more probable that the ultimate results of each creative word are summed up in the account given of it. No sooner did motion begin, than the separation of the air and water from the denser particles must have begun too. The immediate result was light; removed by a greater interval was the formation of an open space round the contracting earth-ball; still more remote was the formation of continents and oceans; but the separations must have commenced immediately that the "wind of Elohim" began to brood upon and move the chaotic mass. How far these separations had advanced before there were recurrent periods of light and darkness is outside the scope of the Divine narrative, which is not geological, but religious.

(5) **God called the light Day . . . Night.**—Before this distinction of night and day was possible there must have been outside the earth, not as yet the sun, but a bright phosphorescent mass, such as now enwraps that luminary; and, secondly, the earth must have begun to revolve upon its axis. Consequent upon this would be, not merely alternate periods of light and darkness, but also of heat and cold, from which would result important effects upon the formation of the earth's crust. Moreover, in thus giving "day" and "night" names, God ordained language, and that vocal sounds should be the symbols of things. This law already looks forward to the existence of man, the one being on earth who calls things by their names.

(6) And God said, [a]Let there be a [1]fir-
mament in the midst of the waters, and
let it divide the waters from the waters.
(7) And God made the firmament, and
divided the waters which *were* under
the firmament from the waters which
were above the firmament: and it was
so. (8) And God called the [b]firmament
Heaven. And the evening and the
morning were the second day.

a Ps. 136. 5; Jer. 10. 12; & 51. 15.

1 Heb., *expansion.*

b Jer. 51. 15.

And the evening and the morning.—Literally, *And was an evening and was a morning day one*, the definite article not being used till verse 31, when we have "day the sixth," which was also the last of the creative days.

The word "evening" means a *mixture.* It is no longer the opaque darkness of a world without light, but the intermingling of light and darkness (comp. Zech. xiv. 6, 7). This is followed by a "morning," that is, a *breaking forth* of light. Evening is placed first because there was a progress from a less to a greater brightness and order and beauty. The Jewish method of calculating the day from sunset to sunset was not the cause, but the result of this arrangement.

The first day.—A creative day is not a period of twenty-four hours, but an *æon*, or period of indefinite duration, as the Bible itself teaches us. For in chap. ii. 4 the six days of this narrative are described as and summed up in one day, creation being there regarded, not in its successive stages, but as a whole. So by the common consent of commentators, the seventh day, or day of God's rest, is that age in which we are now living, and which will continue until the consummation of all things. So in Zech. xiv. 7 the whole Gospel dispensation is called "one day;" and constantly in Hebrew, as probably in all languages, *day* is used in a very indefinite manner, as, for instance, in Deut. ix. 1. Those, however, who adopt the very probable suggestion of Kurtz, that the revelation of the manner of creation was made in a succession of representations or pictures displayed before the mental vision of the tranced seer, have no difficulties. He saw the dark gloom of evening pierced by the bright morning light: that was day one. Again, an evening cleft by the light, and he saw an opening space expanding itself around the world: that was day two. Again darkness and light, and on the surface of the earth he saw the waters rushing down into the seas: that was day three. And so on. What else could he call these periods but days? But as St. Augustine pointed out, there was no sun then, and "it is very difficult for us to imagine what sort of days these could be" (*De Civ. Dei*, xi. 6, 7). It must further be observed that this knowledge of the stages of creation could only have been given by revelation, and that the agreement of the Mosaic record with geology is so striking that there is no real difficulty in believing it to be inspired. The difficulties arise almost entirely from popular fallacies or the mistaken views of commentators. Geology has done noble service for religion in sweeping away the mean views of God's method of working which used formerly to prevail. We may add that among the Chaldeans a cosmic day was a period of 43,200 years, being the equivalent of the cycle of the procession of the equinoxes (Lenormant, *Les Origines de l'Histoire*, p. 233).

(6) **A firmament.**—This is the Latin translation of the Greek word used by the translators of the Septuagint Version. Undoubtedly it means something solid; and such was the idea of the Greeks, and probably also of the Hebrews. As such it appears in the poetry of the Bible, where it is described as a mighty vault of molten glass (Job xxxvii. 18), upheld by the mountains as pillars (*ibid.* xxvi. 11; 2 Sam. xxii. 8), and having doors and lattices through which the Deity pours forth abundance (chap. vii. 11; Ps. lxxviii. 23). Even in this "Hymn of Creation" we have poetry, but not expressed in vivid metaphors, but in sober and thoughtful language. Here, therefore, the word rendered "firmament" means an *expanse.* If, as geologists tell us, the earth at this stage was an incandescent mass, this expanse would be the ring of equilibrium, where the heat supplied from below was exactly equal to that given off by radiation into the cold ether above. And gradually this would sink lower and lower, until finally it reached the surface of the earth; and at this point the work of the second day would be complete.

(7) **God made the firmament.**—This wide open expanse upon earth's surface, supplied by the chemistry of nature—that is, of God—with that marvellous mixture of gases which form atmospheric air, was a primary necessity for man's existence and activity. In each step of the narrative it is ever man that is in view; and even the weight of the superincumbent atmosphere is indispensable for the health and comfort of the human body, and for the keeping of all things in their place on earth. (See Note, verse 8.) And in this secondary sense it may still rightly be called the firmament.

The waters which were under the firmament . . . the waters which were above the firmament.—While this is a popular description of what we daily see—namely, masses of running water congregated upon earth's surface, and above a cloudland, into which the waters rise and float—it is not contrary to, but in accordance with, science. The atmosphere is the receptacle of the waters evaporated from the earth and ocean, and by means of electrical action it keeps these aqueous particles in a state of repulsion, and forms clouds, which the winds carry in their bosom. So full of thoughtful contrivance and arrangement are the laws by which rain is formed and the earth watered, that they are constantly referred to in the Bible as the chief natural proof of God's wisdom and goodness. (See Acts xiv. 17.) Moreover, were there not an open expanse next the earth, it would be wrapped in a perpetual mist, unvisited by sunshine, and the result would be such as is described in chap. ii. 5, that man could not exist on earth to till the ground. The use, however, of popular language and ideas is confessedly the method of Holy Scripture, and we must not force upon the writer knowledge which man was to gain for himself. Even if the writer supposed that the rains were poured down from an upper reservoir, it would be no more an argument against his being inspired than St. Mark's expression, "The sun did set" (Mark i. 32), disproves the inspiration of the Gospels. For the attainment of all such knowledge God has provided another way.

(8) **God called the firmament** (the expanse) **Heaven.**—This is a Saxon word, and means *something heaved up.* The Hebrew probably means the *heights*, or upper regions, into which the walls of cities nevertheless ascend (Deut. i. 28). In verse 1, "the heaven" may include the abysmal regions of space; here it means the atmosphere round our earth, which, at a distance of about forty-five miles from the surface, melts away into the

(9) And God said, [a]Let the waters
under the heaven be gathered together
unto one place, and let the dry *land*
appear: and it was so. (10) And God
called the dry *land* Earth; and the
gathering together of the waters called
he Seas: and God saw that *it was* good.
(11) And God said, Let the earth bring
forth [1]grass, the herb yielding seed,
and the fruit tree yielding fruit after his
kind, whose seed *is* in itself, upon the
earth: and it was so. (12) And the earth
brought forth grass, *and* herb yielding
seed after his kind, and the tree yielding
fruit, whose seed *was* in itself, after his
kind: and God saw that *it was* good.
(13) And the evening and the morning
were the third day.

a Ps. 33. 7; & 136. 6; Job 38. 8.

1 Heb., *tender grass.*

imponderable ether. The work of the second day is not described as being good, though the LXX. add this usual formula. Probably, however, the work of the second and third days is regarded as one. In both there was a separation of waters; but it was only when the open expanse reached the earth's surface, and reduced its temperature, that water could exist in any other form than that of vapour. But no sooner did it exist in a fluid form than the pressure of the atmosphere would make it seek the lowest level. The cooling, moreover, of the earth's surface would produce cracks and fissures, into which the waters would descend, and when these processes were well advanced, then at the end of the third day "God saw that it was good."

(9) **Let the waters . . . be gathered together.**—The verb, as Gesenius shows, refers rather to the condensation of water, which, as we have seen, was impossible till the surface of the earth was made cool by the radiation of heat into the open expanse around it.

Unto one place.—The ocean bed. We must add the vast depth of the ocean to the height of the mountains before we can rightly estimate the intensity of the forces at work on the third day. Vast, too, as the surface of the ocean may appear compared with the dry land, it is evidently only just sufficient to supply the rain necessary for vegetation. Were it less, either the laws of evaporation must be altered, with painful and injurious effects, or much of the earth's surface would be barren.

Let the dry land appear.—Simple as this might appear, it yet required special provision on the part of the Creator; for otherwise the various materials of the earth would have arranged themselves in concentric strata, according to their density, and upon them the water would have reposed evenly, and above it the air. But geologists tell us that these strata have been broken up and distorted from below by volcanic agencies, while the surface has been furrowed and worn by the denuding power of water. This was the third day's work. By the cooling of the crust of the earth the vast mass of waters, which now covers two-thirds of its surface, and which hitherto had existed only as vapour, began to condense, and pour down upon the earth as rain. Meanwhile the earth parted with its internal heat but slowly, and thus, while its crust grew stiff, there was within a mass of molten fluid. As this would be acted upon by the gravity of the sun and moon, in just the same way as the ocean is now, this inner tidal wave would rupture the thin crust above, generally in lines trending from north-east to south-west. Hence mountain ranges and deep sea beds, modified by many changes since, but all having the same final object of providing dry land for man's abode.

(11) **Let the earth bring forth grass.**—This is the second creative act. The first was the calling of matter into existence, which, by the operation of mechanical and chemical laws, imposed upon it by the Creator, was arranged and digested into a cosmos, that is, an orderly and harmonious whole. These laws are now and ever in perpetual activity, but no secondary or derived agency can either add one atom to the world-mass or diminish aught from it. The second creative act was the introduction of life, first vegetable, and then animal; and for this nothing less than an Almighty power would suffice. Three stages of it are enumerated. The first is *deshe*, not "grass," but a mere greenness, without visible seed or stalk, such as to this day may be seen upon the surface of rocks, and which, when examined by the microscope, is found to consist of a growth of plants of a minute and mean type. But all endogenous plants belong to this class, and are but the development of this primary greenness. Far higher in the scale are the seed-bearing plants which follow, among which the most important are the cerealia; while in the third class, vegetation reaches its highest development in the tree with woody stem, and the seed enclosed in an edible covering. Geologists inform us that cryptogamous plants, which were the higher forms of the first class, prevailed almost exclusively till the end of the carbonaceous period; but even independently of this evidence we could scarcely suppose that fruit-trees came into existence before the sun shone upon the earth; while the cerealia are found only in surface deposits in connection with vestiges of man. Vegetation, therefore, did not reach its perfection until the sixth day, when animals were created which needed these seeds and fruits for their food. But so far from there being anything in the creative record to require us to believe that the development of vegetation was not gradual, it is absolutely described as being so; and with that first streak of green God gave also the law of vegetation, and under His fostering hand all in due time came to pass which that first bestowal of vegetable life contained. It is the constant rule of Holy Scripture to include in a narrative the ultimate as well as the immediate results of an act; and moreover, in the record of these creative days we are told what on each day was new, while the continuance of all that preceded is understood. The dry land called into existence on the third day was not dry enough to be the abode of terrestrial animals till the sixth day, and not till then would it bear such vegetation as requires a dry soil; and the evidence of geology shows that the atmosphere, created on the second day, was not sufficiently free from carbonic acid and other vapours to be fit for animals to breathe, until long ages of rank vegetation had changed these gases into coal. When, then, on the third day, "God said, Let the earth bring forth grass . . . herb yielding seed . . . tree." He gave the perfect command, but the complete fulfilment of that command would be gradual, as the state of the earth and the necessities of the living creatures brought forth upon it required. For in God's work

(14) And God said, Let there be lights
in the firmament of the heaven to divide
[1] the day from the night; and let them
be for signs, and for seasons, and for
days, and years: (15) and let them be
for lights in the firmament of the hea-
ven to give light upon the earth: and
it was so. (16) And God made two great
lights; the greater light [2] to rule the
day, and the lesser light to rule the
night: *he made* the stars also. (17) And
God set them in the firmament of the
heaven to give light upon the earth,
(18) and to [b] rule over the day and over
the night, and to divide the light from
the darkness: and God saw that *it was*
good. (19) And the evening and the
morning were the fourth day.

(20) And God said, [c] Let the waters
bring forth abundantly the [3] moving
creature that hath [4] life, and fowl *that*
may fly above the earth in the [5] open

a Deut. 4. 19; Ps. 136. 7.

1 Heb., *between the day and between the night.*

2 Heb., *for the rule of the day, &c.*

b Jer. 31. 35.

c 2 Esd. 6. 47.

3 Or, *creeping.*

4 Heb., *soul.*

5 Heb., *face of the firmament of heaven.*

---

there is always a fitness, and nothing with Him is hurried or premature.

(14) **Let there be lights** (luminaries) **in the firmament** (or expanse) **of the heaven.**—In Hebrew the word for light is *ôr*, and for luminary, *ma-ôr*, a light-bearer. The light was created on the first day, and its concentration into great centres must at once have commenced; but the great luminaries did not appear in the open sky until the fourth day. With this begins the second triad of the creative days. Up to this time there had been arrangement chiefly; heat and water had had their periods of excessive activity, but with the introduction of vegetation there came also the promise of things higher and nobler than mechanical laws. Now, this fourth day seems to mark two things: first, the surface of the earth has become so cool as to need heat given it from without; and secondly, there was now a long pause in creation. No new law in it is promulgated, no new factor introduced; only the atmosphere grows clearer, the earth more dry; vegetation does its part in absorbing gases; and day by day the sun shines with more unclouded brilliancy, followed by the mild radiance of the moon, and finally, by the faint gleamings of the stars. But besides this, as the condensation of luminous matter into the sun was the last act in the shaping of our solar system, it is quite possible that during this long fourth day the sun finally assumed as nearly as possible its present dimensions and form. No doubt it is still changing and slowly drawing nearer to that period when, God's seventh day of rest being over, the knell of this our creation will sound, and the sun, with its attendant planets, and among them our earth, become what God shall then will. But during this seventh day, in which we are now living, God works only in maintaining laws already given, and no outburst either of creative or of destructive energy can take place.

Let them be for signs—*i.e.*, marks, means of knowing. This may be taken as qualifying what follows, and would then mean, Let them be means for distinguishing seasons, days, and years; but more probably it refers to the signs of the zodiac, which anciently played so important a part, not merely in astronomy, but in matters of daily life.

Seasons.—Not spring, summer, and the like, but regularly recurring periods, like the three great festivals of the Jews. In old time men depended, both in agriculture, navigation, and daily life, upon their own observation of the setting and rising of the constellations. This work is now done for us by others, and put into a convenient form in almanacks; but equally now as of old, days, years, and seasons depend upon the motion of the heavenly orbs.

(15) **To give light.**—This was to be henceforward the permanent arrangement for the bestowal of that which is an essential condition for all life, vegetable and animal. As day and night began on the first day, it is evident that very soon there was a concentrating mass of light and heat outside the earth, and as the expanse grew clear its effects must have become more powerful. There was daylight, then, long before the fourth day; but it was only then that the sun and moon became fully formed and constituted as they are at present, and shone regularly and clearly in the bright sky.

(16) **He made the stars also.**—The Hebrew is, *God made two great lights . . . to rule the night; and also the stars.* Though the word "also" carries back "the stars" to the verb "made," yet its repetition in our version makes it seem as if the meaning was that God now created the stars; whereas the real sense is that the stars were to rule the night equally with the moon. But besides this, there was no place where the stars—by which the planets are chiefly meant—could be so well mentioned as here. Two of them, Venus and Mercury, were formed somewhere between the first and the fourth day; and absolutely it was not till this day that our solar system, consisting of a central sun and the planets, with their attendant satellites, was complete. To introduce the idea of the fixed stars is unreasonable, for it is the planets which, by becoming in their turns morning and evening stars, rule the night; though the fixed stars indicate the seasons of the year. The true meaning, then, is that at the end of the fourth day the distribution of land and water, the state of the atmosphere, the alternation of day and night, of seasons and years, and the astronomical relations of the sun, moon, and planets (with the stars) to the earth were all settled and fixed, much as they are at present. And to this geology bears witness. Existing causes amply suffice to account for all changes that have taken place on our globe since the day when animal life first appeared upon the earth.

(20) **Let the waters . . . in the open firmament.**—The days of the second creative triad correspond to those of the first. Light was created on the first day, and on the fourth it was gathered into light-bearers; on the second day air and water were called into being, and on the fifth day they were peopled with life; lastly, on the third day the dry land appeared, and on the sixth day it became the home of animals and man.

Bring forth abundantly the moving creature that hath life.—Literally, *let the waters swarm a swarm of living soul.* But the word *soul* properly signifies "breath," and thus, after the long pause of the fourth day, during which vegetation was advancing under the ripening effects of solar heat, we now hasten onward to another creative act, by which God called into being creatures which live by breathing. And as vegetation began with a green tinge upon the rocks, so doubtless animal life began in the most

firmament of heaven. (21) And God
created great whales, and every living
creature that moveth, which the waters
brought forth abundantly, after their
kind, and every winged fowl after his
kind: and God saw that *it was* good.
(22) And God blessed them, saying, [a] Be
fruitful, and multiply, and fill the
waters in the seas, and let fowl multiply
in the earth. (23) And the evening and
the morning were the fifth day.
(24) And God said, Let the earth bring
forth the living creature after his kind,
cattle, and creeping thing, and beast of
the earth after his kind: and it was so.
(25) And God made the beast of the earth
after his kind, and cattle after their
kind, and every thing that creepeth upon

a ch. 8. 17; & 9. 1.

---

rudimentary manner, and advanced through animalcules and insects up to fish and reptiles. The main point noticed in the text as to the living things produced on this day is their fecundity. They are all those creatures which multiply in masses. It does not, however, follow that the highest forms of fish and reptiles were reached before the lowest form of land animal was created. All that we are taught is that the Infusoria and Ovipara preceded the Mammalia. As the most perfect trees may not have been produced till the Garden of Eden was planted, so the peacock may not have spread his gaudy plumes till the time was approaching when there would be human eyes capable of admiring his beauty.

And fowl that may fly.—Heb., *and let fowl*, or winged creatures, *fly above the earth*. It does not say that they were formed out of the water (comp. chap. ii. 19). Nor is it confined to birds, but includes all creatures that can wing their way in the air.

In the open firmament.—Literally, *upon the face of the expanse of heaven*—that is, in front of it, upon the lower surface of the atmosphere near to the earth.

(21) **God created great whales.**—Whales, strictly speaking, are mammals, and belong to the creation of the sixth day. But *tannin*, the word used here, means any *long* creature, and is used of serpents in Exod. vii. 9, 10 (where, however, it may mean a crocodile), and in Deut. xxxii. 33; of the crocodile in Ps. lxxiv. 13, Isa. li. 9, Ezek. xxix. 3; and of sea monsters generally in Job vii. 12. It thus appropriately marks the great Saurian age. The use, too, of the verb *bârâ*, "he created," is no argument against its meaning *to produce out of nothing*, because it belongs not to these monsters, which may have been "evolved," but to the whole verse, which describes the introduction of animal life; and this is one of the special creative acts which physical science acknowledges to be outside its domain.

After their kind.—This suggests the belief that the various genera and species of birds, fishes, and insects were from the beginning distinct, and will continue so, even if there be some amount of free play in the improvement and development of existing species.

(22) **Be fruitful, and multiply.**—This blessing shows that the earth was replenished with animal life from a limited number of progenitors, and probably from a small number of centres, both for the flora and for the fauna.

(23) **The fifth day.**—Upon the work of the first four days geology is virtually silent, and the theories respecting the physical formation of the world belong to other sciences. But as regards the fifth day, its testimony is ample. In the lowest strata of rocks, such as the Cambrian and Silurian, we find marine animals, mollusca, and trilobites; higher up in the Devonian rocks we find fish; in the Carbonaceous period we find reptiles; and above these, in the Permian, those mighty saurians, described in our version as *great whales*. Traces of birds, even in these higher strata, if existent at all, are rare, but indubitably occur in the Triassic series. We thus learn that this fifth day covers a vast space of time, and, in accordance with what has been urged before as regards vegetation, it is probable that the introduction of the various genera and species was gradual. God does nothing in haste, and our conceptions of His marvellous working are made more clear and worthy of His greatness by the evidence which geology affords.

(24) **Let the earth bring forth.**—Neither this, nor the corresponding phrase in verse 20, necessarily imply spontaneous generation, though such is its literal meaning. It need mean no more than that land animals, produced on the dry ground, were now to follow upon those produced in the waters. However produced, we believe that the sole active power was the creative will of God, but of His *modus operandi* we know nothing.

On this sixth creative day there are four words of power. By the first, the higher animals are summoned into being; by the second, man; the third provides for the continuance and increase of the beings which God had created; the fourth assigns the vegetable world both to man and animals as food.

The creation of man is thus made a distinct act; for though created on the sixth day, because he is a land animal, yet it is in the latter part of the day, and after a pause of contemplation and counsel. The reason for this, we venture to affirm, is that in man's creation we have a far greater advance in the work of the Almighty than at any previous stage. For up to this time all has been *law*, and the highest point reached was *instinct;* we have now freedom, reason, intellect, speech. The evolutionist may give us many an interesting theory about the upgrowth of man's physical nature, but the introduction of this moral and mental freedom places as wide a chasm in his way as the first introduction of vegetable, and then of animal life.

The living creature, or rather, *the creature that lives by breathing*, is divided into three classes. The first is "behêmâh," *cattle:* literally, the *dumb* brute, but especially used of the larger ruminants, which were soon domesticated, and became man's speechless servants. Next comes the "creeping thing," or rather, *moving thing*, from a verb translated *moveth* in verse 21. It probably signifies the whole multitude of small animals, and not reptiles particularly. For strictly the word refers rather to their number than to their means of locomotion, and means a *swarm*. The third class is the "beast of the earth," the wild animals that roam over a large extent of country, including the carnivora. But as a vegetable diet is expressly assigned in verse 30

the earth after his kind: and God saw
that *it was* good.
(26) And God said, [a]Let us make man
in our image, after our likeness: and
let them have dominion over the fish of
the sea, and over the fowl of the air,
and over the cattle, and over all the
earth, and over every creeping thing
that creepeth upon the earth. (27) So God
created man in his *own* image, in the
image of God created he him; [b]male
and female created he them. (28) And
God blessed them, and God said unto
them, [c]Be fruitful, and multiply, and re-
plenish the earth, and subdue it: and
have dominion over the fish of the sea,
and over the fowl of the air, and over
every living thing that [1]moveth upon
the earth. (29) And God said, Behold, I
have given you every herb [2]bearing seed,
which *is* upon the face of all the earth,
and every tree, in the which *is* the fruit

[a] ch. 5. 1; & 9. 6; 1 Cor. 11. 7; Eph. 4. 24; Col. 3. 10.

[b] Matt. 19. 4; Wisd. 2. 23.

[c] ch. 9. 1.

[1] Heb., *creepeth.*

[2] Heb., *seeding seed.*

---

to the "beast of the earth," while the evidence of the rocks proves that even on the fifth day the saurians fed upon fish and upon one another, the record seems to point out a closer relation between man and the graminivora than with these fierce denizens of the forest. The narrative of the flood proves conclusively that there were no carnivora in the ark; and immediately afterwards beasts that kill men were ordered to be destroyed (chap. ix. 5, 6). It is plain that from the first these beasts lay outside the covenant. But as early as the fourth century, Titus, Bishop of Bostra, in his treatise against the *Manichees*, showed, on other than geological grounds, that the carnivora existed before the fall, and that there was nothing inconsistent with God's wisdom or love in their feeding upon other animals. In spite of their presence, all was good. The evidence of geology proves that in the age when the carnivora were most abundant, the graminivora were represented by species of enormous size, and that they flourished in multitudes far surpassing anything that exists in the present day.

(26) **Let us make man.**—Comp. chap. xi. 7. The making of man is so ushered in as to show that at length the work of creation had reached its perfection and ultimate goal. As regards the use of the plural here, Maimonides thinks that God took counsel with the earth, the latter supplying the body and Elohim the soul. But it is denied in Isa. xl. 13 that God ever took counsel with any one but Himself. The Jewish interpreters generally think that the angels are meant. More truly and more reverently we may say that this first chapter of Genesis is the chapter of mysteries, and just as "the wind of God" in verse 2 was the pregnant germ which grew into the revelation of the Holy Ghost, so in Elohim, the many powers concentrated in one being, lies the germ of the doctrine of a plurality of persons in the Divine Unity. It is not a formal proof of the Trinity, nor do believers in the inspiration of Holy Scripture so use it. What they affirm is, that from the very beginning the Bible is full of such germs, and that no one of them remains barren, but all develop, and become Christian truths. There is in this first book a vast array of figures, types, indications, yearnings, hopes, fears, promises, and express predictions, which advance onwards like an ever-deepening river, and when they all find a logical fulfilment in one way, the conclusion is that that fulfilment is not only true, but was intended.

Man.—Hebrew, *Adam.* In Assyrian the name for man is also *adamu*, or *admu*. In that literature, so marvellously preserved to our days, Sir H. Rawlinson thinks that he has traced the first man up to the black or Accadian race. It is hopeless to attempt any derivation of the name, as it must have existed before any of the verbs and nouns from which commentators attempt to give it a meaning; and the *adâmâh*, or "tilled ground," of which we shall soon hear so much, evidently had its name from Adam.

In our image, after our likeness.—The human body is after God's image only as being the means whereby man attains to dominion: for dominion is God's attribute, inasmuch as He is sole Lord. Man's body, therefore, as that of one who rules, is erect, and endowed with speech, that he may give the word of command. The soul is first, in God's *image.* This, as suggesting an external likeness, may refer to man's reason, free-will, self-consciousness, and so on. But it is, secondly, in God's *likeness*, which implies something closer and more inward. It refers to man's moral powers, and especially to his capacity of attaining unto holiness. Now man has lost neither of these two. (Comp. chap. ix. 6; 1 Cor. xi. 7; James iii. 9.) Both were weakened and defiled by the fall, but were still retained in a greater or less degree. In the man Christ Jesus both were perfect; and fallen man, when new-created in Christ, attains actually to that perfection which was his only potentially at his first creation, and to which Adam never did attain.

Let them have dominion.—The plural here shows that we have to do not with Adam and Eve, but with the human race generally. This, too, agrees with the whole bearing of the first chapter, which deals in a large general way with genera and species, and not with individuals. This is important as an additional proof that God's likeness and image belong to the whole species man, and could not therefore have been lost by the fall, as St. Augustine supposed.

(27) **Created.**—This significant verb is thrice repeated with reference to man. It indicates, first, that man has that in him which was not a development or evolution, but something new. He is, in fact, the most perfect work of the creative energy, and differs from the animals not only in degree, but in kind, though possessing, in common with them, an organised body. And next, it indicates the rejoicing of the Deity at the completion of His purpose.

(29) **Every herb bearing seed . . . every tree.**—Of the three classes of plants enumerated in verse 11, the two most perfect kinds are given to man for his food; while in verse 30 the birds and animals have not merely the cryptogamous plants of the first class, but every *green herb* granted to them for their sustenance. We are not to suppose that they did not eat seeds and fruits, but that the fundamental supply for the maintenance of animal life was the blade and leaf, and that of human life the perfected seed and ripe fruit. Man is thus from the first pointed out as of a higher organisation than the animal; and the fact that his food is such as requires preparation and cooking has been the basis, not merely of most of the refinements of life, but

of a tree yielding seed; [a]to you it shall
be for meat. (30) And to every beast of
the earth, and to every fowl of the air,
and to every thing that creepeth upon
the earth, wherein *there is* [1]life, *I have
given* every green herb for meat: and it
was so.

(31) And [b]God saw every thing that he
had made, and, behold, *it was* very good.
And the evening and the morning were
the sixth day.

CHAPTER II.—(1) Thus the heavens
and the earth were finished, and all the
host of them. (2) [c]And on the seventh
day God ended his work which he had
made; and he rested on the seventh
day from all his work which he had
made. (3) And God blessed the seventh
day, and sanctified it: because that in
it he had rested from all his work which
God [2]created and made.

(4) These *are* the generations of the

a ch. 9. 3.

1 Heb., *a living soul.*

b Ecclus. 39. 16.

c Ex. 20. 11; & 31. 17; Deut. 5. 14; Heb. 4. 4.

2 Heb., *created to make.*

---

even of the close union of the family. For what would become of it without the common meal?

But undoubtedly the food originally assigned to man was vegetable; nor was express leave given to eat flesh until after the flood. Nevertheless the dominion given to man, in verse 28, over fish, bird, and animal, made it lawful for him to use them for his food; and the skins with which Adam and Eve were clothed on their expulsion from Paradise prove that animals had been already killed. After the fall, Abel's sacrifice of the firstlings of his flock, and *of the fat thereof,* leads irresistibly to the conclusion that the flesh was eaten by the offerer and his family. In ancient times this was the rule. Flesh was not the staple of man's diet, but the eating of it was a religious ceremony, at which certain portions were offered to God and burnt on His altar, and the rest consumed by man as the Deity's guests. So we may well believe that until the flood the descendants of Seth partook of flesh rarely, and only at a sacrifice, but that after the flood a more free use of it was permitted.

(31) **Behold, it was very good.**—This final blessing of God's completed work on the Friday must be compared with the final words of Christ spoken of the second creation, upon the same day of the week, when He said "It is finished." Next we must notice that this world was only *good* until man was placed upon it, but then became *very good.* This verdict, too, had respect to man as a species, and is not therefore annulled by the fall. In spite, therefore, of the serious responsibilities attendant upon the bestowal of freewill on man, we believe that the world is still for purposes of mercy, and that God not only rejoiced at first, but "shall rejoice in His works" (Ps. civ. 31). (Comp. Ps. lxxxv. 10; Rom. v. 15, &c.)

II.

The Sabbath.

(1) **Were finished.**—The first three verses of this chapter form part of the previous narrative, and contain its Divine purpose. For the great object of this hymn of creation is to give the sanction of the Creator to the Sabbath. Hence the ascribing of rest to Him who wearies not, and hence also the description of the several stages of creation as days. Labour is, no doubt, ennobled by creation being described as work done by God; but the higher purpose of this Scripture was that for which appeal is made to it in the Fourth Commandment, namely, to ennoble man's weekly rest. Among the Accadians, Mr. Sayce says (*Chald. Genesis,* p. 89), the Sabbath was observed—so ancient is its institution—but it was connected with the sun, moon, and five planets, whence even now the days of the week take their titles, though the names of Scandinavian deities have been substituted in this country for some of their old Latin appellations. Here every idolatrous tendency is guarded against, and the Sabbath is the institution of the One Almighty God.

The host of them.—The word translated *host* does not refer to military arrangement, but to numbers gathered in crowds. This crowded throng of heaven sometimes means the angels, as in 1 Kings xxii. 19; oftener the stars. Here it is the host both of heaven and earth, and signifies the multitudes of living creatures which people the land, and seas, and air.

(2) **God ended his work.**—Not all work (see John v. 17, and Note *in loc.*), but the special work of creation. The laws given in these six days still continue their activity; they are still maintained, and there may even be with them progress and development. There is also something special on this seventh day; for in it the work of redemption was willed by the Father, wrought by the Son, and applied by the Holy Ghost. But there is no creative activity, as when vegetable or animal life began, or when a free agent first walked erect upon a world given him to subdue.

The substitution, in the LXX. and Syriac, of the *sixth* for the seventh day, as that on which God ended His work, was probably made in order to avoid even the appearance of Elohim having put the finishing touches to creation on the Sabbath.

(3) **Sanctified it.**—That is, separated it from ordinary uses, and hallowed it. Legal observance of the Sabbath did not begin till the days of Moses (Exod. xxxi. 13, xxxv. 2); but this blessing and sanctification were given prior to any covenant with man, and by Elohim, the God of nature, and not Jehovah, the God of grace. The weekly rest, therefore, is universal, permanent, and independent of the Mosaic law.

Which God created and made.—Literally, *created to make.* God created the world in order to make and form and fashion it. There is a work of completion which follows upon creation, and this may still be going on, and be perfected only when there is a new heaven and a new earth.

The Generations of the Heavens and of the Earth (chaps. ii. 4—iv. 26).

After the hymn of creation the rest of the Book of Genesis is divided into ten sections of very unequal length, called *tôldôth,* translated by the LXX. *the Book of Genesis,* or generation, whence the title given by St. Matthew to his Gospel. (See note on chap. v. 1.) This title, however, does not mean a genealogical list of a person's ancestors, but the register of his posterity. As applied to the *heavens and the earth,* it signifies the history of what followed upon their creation.

(4) **When they were created.**—Heb., *in,* or upon, *their creation.*

heavens and of the earth when they were
created, in the day that the LORD God
made the earth and the heavens, (5) and
every plant of the field before it was in
the earth, and every herb of the field
before it grew: for the LORD God had
not caused it to rain upon the earth,
and *there was* not a man to till the
ground. (6) But [1]there went up a mist
from the earth, and watered the whole
face of the ground.
(7) And the LORD God formed man [2]*of*
the [a]dust of the ground, and breathed
into his nostrils the breath of life; and
[b]man became a living soul.
(8) And the LORD God planted a garden

[1] Or, *a mist which went up from*, &c.

[2] Heb., *dust of the ground.*

[a] 1 Cor. 15. 47.

[b] 1 Cor. 15. 45.

In the day.—Viewed in its several stages, and with reference to the weekly rest, there were six days of creation, which are here described as one day, because they were but divisions in one continuous act.

The Lord God.—Jehovah-Elohim. (See *Excursus* at the end of this book.)

(5) **And every plant . . .**—The Authorised Version follows the LXX. in so translating this as to make it simply mean that God created vegetation. The more correct rendering is, "There was no shrub of the field (no wild shrub) as yet on the earth, and no herb of the field had as yet sprung up." The purpose of the writer is to prepare for the planting of the paradise, though geology teaches us the literal truth of his words. When the earth was so hot that water existed only in the form of vapour, there could be no vegetation. Rain began on the second day; on the third the vapours were so largely condensed as for the waters to form seas; and on the same day vegetation began to clothe the cool, dry surface of the ground. To understand these opening words, we must bear in mind that the object of the narrative is not now the formation of the world, but man's relation to Jehovah, and thus the long stages of creation appear but as one day's work.

(6) **A mist.**—This mist, as we learn from Job xxxvi. 27, where the same word is translated *vapour*, is the measure and material of the rain, and thus there was already preparation for the Divine method of watering the earth, and making it capable of producing food for man. But, as we gather from chap. i., vast periods of indefinite length intervened between the first rain and the creation of man; and in each of them numerous series of animals were introduced, adapted each to the geologic condition of its time. All this now is rapidly passed over, and three points only lightly touched: namely, first, the earth saturated with vapour, and unfit for man; secondly, the vapour condensing into rain, and the earth growing fit for man; thirdly, man.

(7) **And the Lord God formed man of the dust of the ground.**—Literally, *formed the man* (adam) *dust from the ground.* In this section the prominent idea is not that of producing out of nothing, but of *forming,* that is, shaping and moulding. So in verse 19 Jehovah forms the animals, and in verse 8 He plants a garden. As Elohim is almighty power, so Jehovah is wisdom and skill, and His works are full of contrivance and design. As regards man's body, Jehovah forms it *dust from the ground:* the *adâmâh,* or fruitful arable soil, so called from Adam, for whose use it was specially fitted, and by whom it was first tilled. But the main intention of the words is to point out man's feebleness. He is made not from the rocks, nor from ores of metal, but from the light, shifting particles of the surface, blown about by every wind. Yet, frail as is man's body, God—

. . breathed into his nostrils the breath of life.—The life came not as the result of man's bodily organisation, nor as derived by evolution from any other animal, but as a gift direct from God.

And man became a living soul.—The word translated "soul" contains no idea of a spiritual existence. For in chap. i. 20, "creature that hath life," and in verse 24, "the living creature," are literally, *living soul.* Really the word refers to the natural life of animals and men, maintained by breathing, or in some way extracting oxygen from the atmospheric air. And whatever superiority over other animals may be possessed by man comes from the manner in which this living breath was bestowed upon him, and not from his being "a living soul;" for that is common to all alike.

The whole of this second narrative is pre-eminently anthropomorphic. In the previous history Elohim commands, and it is done. Here He forms, and builds, and plants, and breathes into His work, and is the companion and friend of the creature He has made. It thus sets before us the love and tenderness of Jehovah, who provides for man a home, fashions for him a wife to be his partner and helpmate, rejoices in his intellect, and brings the lower world to him to see what he will call them, and even after the fall provides the poor outcasts with clothing. It is a picture fitted for the infancy of mankind, and speaking the language of primæval simplicity. But its lesson is for all times. For it proclaims the love of God to man, his special pre-eminence in the scale of being, and that Elohim, the Almighty Creator, is Jehovah-Elohim, the friend and counsellor of the creature whom He has endowed with reason and free-will.

(8) **The Lord God planted a garden.**—The order followed in the text, namely, man first and the garden afterwards, is not that of chronology, but of precedence. In verse 15 we find that the garden was ready as soon as man needed a home. It was a separate plot of ground, fenced off from the rest of Eden, and planted with trees and herbs that were of choicer kinds, more fit for food, and more beautiful in foliage and blossom, than elsewhere. The word Paradise, usually applied to it, is a Persian name for an enclosed park, such as the kings of Persia used for hunting.

Eastward in Eden.—This does not mean in the eastern portion of Eden, but that Eden itself was to the east of the regions known to the Israelites. The name "Eden," that is, pleasure-ground, occurs elsewhere, but for regions not identical with that in which the paradise was situated (2 Kings xix. 12; Isa. xxxvii. 12, li. 3; Ezek. xxvii. 23; Amos i. 5). Of its site no certain conclusions have been established, and probably the flood so altered the conformation of the ground as to make the identification of the four rivers impossible. But there can be no doubt that an eastern district of Asia is meant, and that the details at the time the narrative was written were sufficient to indicate with sufficient clearness where and what the region was. The rendering of several

eastward in Eden; and there he put
the man whom he had formed. (9) And
out of the ground made the LORD God
to grow every tree that is pleasant to
the sight, and good for food; the tree
of life also in the midst of the garden,
and the tree of knowledge of good and
evil. (10) And a river went out of Eden
to water the garden; and from thence
it was parted, and became into four
heads. (11) The name of the first *is*
[a]Pison: that *is* it which compasseth the
whole land of Havilah, where *there is*
gold; (12) and the gold of that land *is*
good: there *is* bdellium and the onyx
stone. (13) And the name of the second
river *is* Gihon: the same *is* it that com-
passeth the whole land of [1]Ethiopia.

a Ecclus. 24. 25.

1 Heb., *Cush.*

---

versions *in the beginning* instead of *eastward* is untenable.

(9) **Every tree that is pleasant to the sight, and good for food.**—It has often been noticed that while the ancients do not seem to have had much taste for the beauty of the landscape, they greatly admired large and umbrageous trees. This feeling seems like a reminiscence of the joy of our first parents when they found themselves in a happy garden, surrounded by trees, the beauty of which is even more commended than the fact placed second, that they supplied wholesome and nutritious food. Two trees in the centre of the garden had marvellous qualities; for "the tree of life" had the power of so renewing man's physical energies that his body, though formed of the dust of the ground, and therefore naturally mortal, would, by its continual use, live on for ever. The other, "the tree of knowledge of good and evil," must have acquired this name after the fall. As long as Adam and Eve were in their original innocence they had no knowledge of evil, nor could any mere mental development bestow it upon them. They must either feel it in themselves, or see it in others, before they could know it. We conclude, then, that this was the tree to which God's command, that they should not eat of it (comp. chap. iii. 3), was attached; and only by the breach of that command would man attain to this higher knowledge, with all the solemn responsibilities attached to it. Besides this, each tree had a symbolic meaning, and especially the tree of life (Rev. ii. 7, xxii. 2). The Chaldean legends have preserved the memory of this latter tree, and depict it as the *Asclepias acida*, whence the *soma* juice is prepared.

(10) **A river went out of Eden.**—Out of the large region of which the garden formed a part. The tenses, too, are present, as if the main features of the country remained unchanged: "a river goeth forth from Eden, and thence outside of it is parted, and becometh four main streams." The idea is that of a stream rising in Eden, and flowing through the Paradise, and at some distance outside of it divided into four great rivers. This has made many suppose that the site of Paradise was in the Persian Gulf, in a region now submerged; and the Babylonian legends actually place it there, at Eridu, at the junction of the Tigris and Euphrates. The two other rivers they suppose to have been the Indus and the Nile, represented by the two coasts of the Persian Gulf. Sir H. Rawlinson suggests the Babylonian province of Gan-duniyas, where four rivers may be found; but in neither case could the ark have floated against the current of the flood up to the highlands of Armenia. We must add that many authors of note have regarded the whole as symbolical, among whom is the famous Syriac writer, Bar-Hebraeus, who regards it as a description of the human body.

(11, 12) **The name of the first is Pison.**—"The full-flowing" (Gesenius), or "free-streaming" (Fürst). Neither derivation has much authority for it in the Hebrew language, and we must wait for the true explanation till the cuneiform inscriptions have been more thoroughly examined. As two of the four rivers of Paradise rise in Armenia, so we must probably seek the other two there; but the conjectures of commentators have thus far suggested no probable identification of this stream.

Compasseth.—This word, without strictly meaning *to go round*, gives the idea of a devious course (comp. 1 Sam. vii. 16; Cant. iii. 3), as if the river had now reached a level plain.

Havilah may mean *sandy land* (Delitsch), or *circuit region.* There seems to have been more than one country of this name; but the most probable is that in South-Western Arabia, afterwards colonised by the Joktanites (chap. x. 29), which this river skirted rather than traversed. But we know of no such river, rising in Armenia or elsewhere, which answers to this description now. Besides gold of great purity, pronounced emphatically "good," this land produced "bdellium," a scented gum, to which manna is compared (Num xi. 7), though the meaning even there is uncertain.

Instead of *bedolach*, bdellium, the Syriac reads *berulchê*, that is, the same word in the plural, but with *d* instead of *r*. These two letters being very similar, not merely in the square Hebrew alphabet now in use, but in the original Samaritan characters, are constantly interchanged in manuscripts; and as *berulchê* means *pearls*, the sense agrees better with the other productions of Havilah, gold and onyx stones. As *bedolach* is a quadriliteral, while Hebrew words have only three root letters, we must look to the Accadian language for its true signification, if this be really the right reading.

The onyx stone.—Though there is considerable authority for this translation, yet probably the LXX., supported by most ancient authorities, are right in regarding this gem as the beryl of a light green colour (leek-stone, LXX.). The root signifies something *pale*, while the onyx has its name from its markings resembling those of the human nail.

(13) **Gihon,** "the river that bursts forth," has been supposed to be the Nile, because it is said to wind about Ethiopia (Cush). According to this view, there was originally no break between Asia and Africa, and the Nile, entering Abyssinia from Arabia, took thence a northerly course, and traversed Egypt. But Cush is now known to have signified at this period the southern half of Arabia, and it was not until later times that the name was carried by colonists to Abyssinia. Moreover Gihon, in Arabic Jaihan, is a common name among the Arabs for a river, and perhaps the Oxus is here meant, which flowed northward from Armenia into the Caspian. Mr. Sayce, however, thinks it is the Araxes, "the river of Babylon," which flowed westward into the desert of Cush, in Arabia (*Chald. Gen.*, p. 84).

(14) And the name of the third river *is*
Hiddekel: that *is* it which goeth [1]to-
ward the east of Assyria. And the
fourth river *is* Euphrates.
(15) And the LORD God took [2]the
man, and put him into the garden of
Eden to dress it and to keep it.
(16) And the LORD God commanded the
man, saying, Of every tree of the garden
[3]thou mayest freely eat: (17) but of the
tree of the knowledge of good and evil,
thou shalt not eat of it: for in the day
that thou eatest thereof [4]thou shalt
surely die.

1 Or, *eastward to Assyria.*
2 Or, *Adam.*
3 Heb., *eating thou shalt eat.*
4 Heb., *dying thou shalt die.*
a Ecclus. 36. 24.
5 Heb., *as before him.*
6 Or, *the man.*
7 Heb., *called.*

(18) And the LORD God said, *It is* not
good that the man should be alone; I
will make [a]him an help [5]meet for him.
(19) And out of the ground the LORD God
formed every beast of the field, and
every fowl of the air; and brought
them unto [6]Adam to see what he would
call them: and whatsoever Adam called
every living creature, that *was* the name
thereof. (20) And Adam [7]gave names to
all cattle, and to the fowl of the air,
and to every beast of the field; but for
Adam there was not found an help
meet for him.

---

(14) Of the "Hiddekel" and "Euphrates" there is no doubt: the former is the Tigris, or Tigres, which is a mere Graecising of its Oriental name, Daglath in Arabic, and Deklath in Syriac, and in the Targum of Onkelos. The word Hiddekel is startling as being a quadriliteral, but the Samaritan Codex reads *the Dekel,* that is, it has the article instead of the Hebrew Kheth. Mr. Sayce accepts the uncertain reading Hiddekel, and says (*Chald. Gen.*, p. 84) that *Hid* is the Accadian name for river. *Dekel,* Tigris, is said to mean an arrow. The Samaritan reading is probably right.

Euphrates.—No description is given of this as being the largest and best known of Asiatic rivers. Hence, probably, the Pison and Gihon were but small streams. *Euphrates* is the Greek manner of pronouncing the Hebrew *Phrath,* the first syllable being simply a help in sounding the double consonant. In Accadian it is called *Purrat,* and means "the curving water," being so named from its shape.

(15) **And the Lord God took the man** (the adam), **and put him into the garden of Eden.**—The narrative now reverts to verse 8, but the word translated *put* is not the same in both places. Here it literally means *He made him rest,* that is, He gave it to him as his permanent and settled dwelling.

To dress it and to keep it.—The first word literally means *to work it;* for though a paradise, yet the garden had to be tilled and planted. Seeds must be sown and the cultivated plots kept in order; but all this really added to Adam's happiness, because the adâmâh, as yet uncursed, responded willingly to the husbandman's care. The other word, "to keep it," implies, however, some difficulty and danger. Though no unpropitious weather, nor blight nor mildew, spoiled the crop, yet apparently it had to be guarded against the incursion of wild animals and birds, and protected even against the violence of winds and the burning heat of the sun.

(16, 17) **The Lord God commanded.**—Probation is the law of man's moral condition now, and it began in Paradise, only the conditions there were different. (See *Excursus* at end of this book.)

In the day. . .—Used, as in verse 4, for an indefinitely long period. But just as on the third day God gave the whole law of vegetation, though trees as the highest development of that law may not have been reached until after the appearance of animal life on the earth, so the law of man's mortal life came into existence with the eating of the forbidden fruit. Contemporaneously with that act, man passed from the paradisiacal state, with the possibility of living for ever, into the mortal state, with the certainty sooner or later of dying. It was a new condition and constitution of things which then commenced, and to which not Adam only, but also his posterity was subject. And thus this command resembles the words of Elohim in the first chapter. By them the fundamental laws of the material universe were given and established for all time; and the word of Jehovah-Elohim equally here was a law, not for the day only on which Adam broke the command, but for all men everywhere as long as the world shall last.

(18) **It is not good . . .**—In these words we have the Divine appointment of marriage, and also the declaration that the female is subsequent in order of production to the male, and formed from him. In chaps. i. 27, v. 2, the creation of male and female is represented as having been simultaneous. She is described as "a help meet for him:" Heb., *a help as his front,* his reflected image, or, as the Syriac translates it, *a helper similar to him.* The happiness of marriage is based, not upon the woman being just the same thing as the man, but upon her being one in whom he sees his image and counterpart.

(19) **Out of the ground.**—The adâmâh; thus the physical constituents of the animals are the same as those of the body of man. Much curious speculation has arisen from the mistaken idea that the order here is chronological, and that the animals were created subsequently to man, and that it was only upon their failing one and all to supply Adam's need of a companion that woman was called into being. The real point of the narrative is the insight it gives us into Adam's intellectual condition, his study of the animal creation, and the nature of the employment in which he spent his time. Then finally, at the end of verse 20, after numerous animals had passed before him, comes the assertion, with cumulative force, that woman alone is a meet companion for man.

(20) **And Adam gave names.**—Throughout this chapter Adam is but once mentioned as a proper name; and the regular phrase in the Hebrew is *the adam,* that is, the man, except in the last clause of this verse. In verse 23 there is a different word for man, namely, *ish.* We must not confine this giving of names to the domestic animals, nor are we to suppose a long procession of beasts and birds passing before the man, and receiving each its title. Rather, it sets him before us as a keen observer of nature; and as he pursues his occupations in the garden, new animals and birds from time to time come under his notice, and these he studies, and observes their ways and habits, and so at length gives them appellations. Most of these titles

(21) And the LORD God caused a deep
sleep to fall upon Adam, and he slept:
and he took one of his ribs, and closed
up the flesh instead thereof; (22) and the
rib, which the LORD God had taken
from man, [1]made he a woman, and
brought her unto the man. (23) And
Adam said, This *is* now bone of my
bones, and flesh of my flesh: she shall
be called Woman, because she was
[a]taken out of Man. (24) [b]Therefore shall
a man leave his father and his mother,

[1] Heb., *builded.*

[a] 1 Cor. 11. 8.

[b] Matt. 19. 5; Mark 10. 7; 1 Cor. 6. 16; Eph. 5. 31.

---

would be imitations of their cries, or would be taken from some marked feature in their form or plumage, or mode of locomotion. Adam is thus found possessed of powers of observation and reflection upon the natural objects round him; though we may justly doubt his being capable of the metaphysical discourses put into his mouth by Milton in the *Paradise Lost.*

But for Adam.—In this one place there is no article, and our version may be right in regarding it as a proper name. Among the animals Adam found many ready to be his friends and domestic servants; and his habits of observation had probably this practical end, of taming such as might be useful. Hence the omission of all notice of reptiles and fish. But while thus he could tame many, and make them share his dwelling, he found among them no *counterpart of himself,* capable of answering his thoughts and of holding with him rational discourse.

(21) **And the Lord God caused a deep sleep** (comp. Job iv. 13, where it is the same word) **to fall upon Adam.**—Heb., the man.

One of his ribs.—The word is never translated *rib* except in this place, but always *side, flank.* This is the true meaning also of the Latin word by which it is rendered in the Vulgate, *costa,* as shown in the French *côte,* and our *coast.* Both the Greek and Syriac also translate by words which primarily signify the *side,* but derivatively the *rib.* Woman was not formed out of one of man's many ribs, of which he would not feel the loss. She is one side of man; and though he may have several sides to his nature and character, yet without woman one integral portion of him is wanting.

Closed up the flesh instead thereof.—Literally, *closed up flesh under it,* that is, in its place. This does not mean that man now has flesh where before he had this *side,* but that a cavity was prevented by drawing the flesh on the two edges close together. Metaphysically it means that man has no compensation for what was abstracted from him, except in the woman, who is the one side of his nature which he has lost.

(22) **Made he a woman.**—Heb., *he built up into a woman.* Her formation is described as requiring both time and care on the heavenly artificer's part. Thus woman is no casual or hasty production of nature, but is the finished result of labour and skill. Finally, she is brought with special honour to the man as the Creator's last and most perfect work. Every step and stage in this description is intended for the ennoblement of marriage. Woman is not made from the adâmâh, but from the adam. She is something that he once had, but has lost; and while for Adam there is simply the closing of the cavity caused by her withdrawal, she is moulded and re-fashioned, and built up into man's counterpart. She brings back more than the man parted with, and the Creator Himself leads her by the hand to her husband. The anthropomorphic language of these early chapters is part of that condescension to human weakness which makes it the rule everywhere for inspiration to use popular language. He who made heaven and earth by the fiat of His will must not be understood as having literally moulded the side taken from Adam as a sculptor would the plastic clay; nor did He assume human form that He might place her at man's side. Much of this may indeed have been represented to Adam's mind in the trance into which he had fallen; but the whole narrative has a nobler meaning, and the practical result of its teaching was that neither woman nor marriage ever sank into that utter degradation among the Jews which elsewhere aided so greatly in corrupting morals and men.

(23) **This is now.**—Literally, *this stroke,* or *beat of the foot* in keeping time. It means, therefore, *this time,* or colloquially, *at last.* Adam had long studied the natural world, and while, with their confidence as yet unmarred by human cruelty, they came to his call, grew tame, and joined his company, he found none that answered to his wants, and replied to him with articulate speech. At last, on waking from his trance, he found one standing by him in whom he recognised a second self, and he welcomed her joyfully, and exclaimed, "This *at last* is bone of my bones, and flesh of my flesh:" that is, she is man's counterpart, not merely in feeling and sense—his flesh—but in his solid qualities. In several of the Semitic dialects *bone* is used for *self.* Thus, in the *Jerusalem Lectionary* (ed. Miniscalchi, Verona, 1861) we read: "I will manifest my bone unto him" (John xiv. 21), that is, myself; and again, "I have power to lay it down of my bone" (John x. 18), that is, of myself. So, too, in Hebrew, "In the selfsame day" is "in the bone of this day" (chap. vii. 13). Thus *bone of my bones* means "my very own self," while *flesh of my flesh* adds the more tender and gentle qualities.

She shall be called Woman (Ishah), **because she was taken out of Man** (Ish).—Adam, who knew that he was an Ish (see *Excursus* at end of this book), called the woman a "female Ish." The words of our Version, *man* and *woman* (perhaps womb-man), represent with sufficient accuracy the relation of the words in the original.

(24) **Therefore shall a man leave . . .**—These are evidently the words of the narrator. Adam names this new product of creative power, as he had named others, but he knew nothing about young men leaving their father's house for the wife's sake. Moreover, in Matt. xix. 5, our Lord quotes these words as spoken by God, and the simplest interpretation of this declaration is that the inspired narrator was moved by the Spirit of God to give this solemn sanction to marriage, founded upon Adam's words. The great and primary object of this part of the narrative is to set forth marriage as a Divine ordinance. The narrator describes Adam's want, pictures him as examining all animal life, and studying the habits of all creatures so carefully as to be able to give them names, but as returning from his search unsatisfied. At last one is solemnly brought to him who is his counterpart, and he calls her *Ishah,* his feminine self, and pronounces her to be his very bone and flesh. Upon this, "He who at the beginning made

and shall cleave unto his wife: and they shall be one flesh. (25) And they were both naked, the man and his wife, and were not ashamed.

CHAPTER III.—(1) Now the serpent was more subtil than any beast of the field which the LORD God had made. and he said unto the woman, [1]Yea, hath God said, Ye shall not eat of every tree of the garden? (2) And the woman said unto the serpent, We may eat of the fruit of the trees of the garden: (3) but of the fruit of the tree which *is* in the midst of the garden, God hath said, Ye shall not eat of it, neither shall ye touch it, lest ye die. (4) [a]And the serpent said unto the woman, Ye shall not surely die: (5) for God doth know that in the day ye eat thereof, then your eyes shall be opened, and ye shall be as gods, knowing good and evil. (6) And when the woman saw that the tree *was* good for food, and that it *was* [2]pleasant to the eyes, and a tree to be desired to make *one* wise, she took of the fruit thereof, [b]and did eat, and gave also unto her husband with her; and he

1 Heb., *Yea, because,* &c.

a 2 Cor. 11. 3; 1 Tim. 2. 14.

2 Heb., *a desire.*

b Ecclus. 25. 24; 1 Tim. 2. 14.

---

them male and female" pronounced the Divine marriage law that man and wife are *one flesh.*

THE TEMPTATION AND FALL.

(25) **They were both naked.**—This is the description of perfect childlike innocence, and belongs naturally to beings who as yet knew neither good nor evil. It is not, however, the conclusion of the marriage section, where it would be indelicate, but the introduction to the account of the temptation, where it prepares the way for man's easy fall. Moreover, there is a play upon words in the two verses. Man is *arom* = naked; the serpent is *arum* = crafty. Thus in guileless simplicity our first parents fell in with the tempting serpent, who, in obvious contrast with their untried innocence, is described as a being of especial subtilty.

III.

(1) **Now the serpent.**—Literally, *And.* The Hebrew language, however, is very poor in particles, and the intended contrast would be made plainer by rendering "Now they were both naked (*arumim*) . . . but the serpent was subtil (*arum*), more than every beast of the field." This quality of the serpent was in itself innocent, and even admirable, and accordingly the LXX. translate *prudent;* but it was made use of by the tempter to deceive Eve; for, it has been remarked, she would not be surprised on finding herself spoken to by so sagacious a creature. If this be so, it follows that Eve must have dwelt in Paradise long enough to have learnt something of the habits of the animals around her, though she had never studied them so earnestly as Adam, not having felt that want of a companion which had made even his state of happiness so dull.

And he said unto the woman.—The leading point of the narrative is that the temptation came upon man from without, and through the woman. Such questions, therefore, as whether it were a real serpent or Satan under a serpent-like form, whether it spake with a real voice, and whether the narrative describes a literal occurrence or is allegorical, are better left unanswered. God has given us the account of man's temptation and fall, and the entry of sin into the world, in this actual form; and the more reverent course is to draw from the narrative the lessons it was evidently intended to teach us, and not enter upon too curious speculations. We are dealing with records of a vast and hoar antiquity, given to man when he was in a state of great simplicity, and with his intellect only partly developed, and we cannot expect to find them as easy to understand as the pages of modern history.

Yea, hath God said . . .?—There is a tone of surprise in these words, as if the tempter could not bring himself to believe that such a command had been given. Can it really be true, he asks, that Elohim has subjected you to such a prohibition? How unworthy and wrong of Him! Neither the serpent nor the woman use the title —common throughout this section—of Jehovah-Elohim, a sure sign that there was a thoughtful purpose in giving this appellation to the Deity. It is the impersonal God of creation to whom the tempter refers, and the woman follows his guidance, forgetting that it was Jehovah, the loving personal Being in covenant with them, who had really given them the command.

(5) **Ye shall be as gods.**—Rather, *as God,* as Elohim himself, in the particular quality of knowing good and evil. It was a high bait which the tempter offered; and Eve, who at first had answered rightly, and who as yet knew nothing of falsehood, dallied with the temptation, and was lost. But we must not comment too severely upon her conduct. It was no mean desire which led her astray: she longed for more knowledge and greater perfection; she wished even to rise above the level of her nature; but the means she used were in violation of God's command, and so she fell. And, as usual, the tempter kept the promise to the ear. Eve knew good and evil, but only by feeling evil within herself. It was by moral degradation, and not by intellectual insight, that her ambitious wish was fulfilled.

(6) **And when the woman saw . . . she took.**—Heb., *And the woman saw . . . and she took,* &c. In this, the original form of the narrative, we see the progress of the temptation detailed in a far more lively manner than in our version. With awakened desire the woman gazes upon the tree. The fruit appears inviting to the eye, and possibly was really good for food. The whole aspect of the tree was beautiful; and, besides, there was the promise held out to her that it possessed the mysterious faculty of developing her intellectual powers. To this combined influence of her senses without and her ambition within she was unable to offer that resistance which would have been possible only by a living faith in the spoken word of God. She eats, therefore, and gives to her husband—so called here for the first time—and he eats with her. The demeanour of Adam throughout is extraordinary. It is the woman who is tempted—not as though Adam was not present, as Milton supposes, for she has not to seek him—but he shares with her at once the gathered fruit. Rather, she is pictured to us as more quick and observant, more open to impressions, more curious and full of longings than the

did eat. (7) And the eyes of them both
were opened, and they knew that they
were naked; and they sewed fig leaves
together, and made themselves [1]aprons.
(8) And they heard the voice of the
LORD God walking in the garden in the
[2]cool of the day: and Adam and his
wife hid themselves from the presence of
the LORD God amongst the trees of the
garden. (9) And the LORD God called
unto Adam, and said unto him, Where
art thou? (10) And he said, I heard thy
voice in the garden, and I was afraid,
because I *was* naked; and I hid myself.
(11) And he said, Who told thee that thou
wast naked? Hast thou eaten of the
tree, whereof I commanded thee that
thou shouldest not eat? (12) And the man
said, The woman whom thou gavest *to be*
with me, she gave me of the tree, and
I did eat. (13) And the LORD God said
unto the woman, What *is* this *that* thou
hast done? And the woman said, The
serpent beguiled me, and I did eat.
(14) And the LORD God said unto the
serpent, Because thou hast done this,
thou *art* cursed above all cattle, and
above every beast of the field; upon thy
belly shalt thou go, and dust shalt thou
eat all the days of thy life: (15) and I
will put enmity between thee and the
woman, and between thy seed and her

1 Or, *things to gird about.*

2 Heb., *wind.*

man, whose passive behaviour is as striking as the woman's eagerness and excitability.

(7) **The eyes of them both were opened.**—This consciousness of guilt came upon them as soon as they had broken God's commandment by eating of the forbidden fruit; and it is evident from the narrative that they ate together; for otherwise Eve would have been guilty of leading Adam into sin after her understanding had been enlightened to perceive the consequences of her act. But manifestly her deed was not without his cognisance and approval, and he had shared, in his own way, her ambition of attaining to the God-like. But how miserably was this proud desire disappointed! Their increased knowledge brought only shame. Their minds were awakened and enlarged, but the price they paid for it was their innocence and peace.

They sewed fig leaves together.—There is no reason for supposing that the leaves were those of the pisang (*Musa paradisiaca*), which grow ten feet long. Everywhere else the word signifies the common fig-tree (*Ficus carica*), one of the earliest plants subjected to man's use. More remarkable is the word *sewed.* The Syriac translator felt the difficulty of supposing Eve acquainted with the art of needlework, and renders it, "they stuck leaves together." But the word certainly implies something more elaborate than this. Probably some time elapsed between their sin and its punishment; and thus there was not merely that first hasty covering of themselves which has made commentators look about for a leaf large enough to encircle their bodies, but respite sufficient to allow of something more careful and ingenious; and Eve may have used her first advance in intellect for the adornment of her person. During this delay they would have time for reflection, and begin to understand the nature of the change that had taken place in their condition.

Aprons.—More correctly, *girdles.*

(8) **And they heard the voice of the Lord God walking in the garden.**—The matter-of-fact school of commentators understand by this that there was a thunderstorm, and the guilty pair hearing for the first time the uproar of nature, hid themselves in terror, and interpreted the mighty peals as meaning their condemnation. Really it is in admirable keeping with the whole narrative; and Jehovah appears here as the owner of the Paradise, and as taking in it His daily exercise; for the verb is in the reflexive conjugation, and means "walking for pleasure." The time is "the cool (literally, *the wind*) of the day," the hour in a hot climate when the evening breeze sets in, and men, rising from their noontide slumber, go forth for labour or recreation. In this description the primary lesson is that hitherto man had lived in close communion with God. His intellect was undeveloped; his mental powers still slumbered; but nevertheless there was a deep spiritual sympathy between him and his Maker. It is the nobler side of Adam's relationship to God before the fall.

Hid themselves from the presence of the Lord God.—This does not imply a visible appearance, for the whole narrative is anthropomorphic. The Fathers, however, saw in these descriptions the proof of a previous incarnation of the Divine Son (see Note on chap. xii. 7). Next, we find in their conduct an attempt to escape from the further result of sin. The first result was shame, from which man endeavoured to free himself by covering his person; the second was fear, and this man would cure by departing still farther from God. But the voice of Jehovah reaches him, and with rebuke and punishment gives also healing and hope.

(11) **Who told thee that thou wast naked?**—Adam had given as his excuse that which was really the consequence of his sin; but by this question God awakens his conscience, and makes him feel that what he had described as a want or imperfection was really the result of his own act. And as long as a man feels sorrow only for the results of his actions there is no repentance, and no wish to return to the Divine presence. God, therefore, in order to win Adam back to better thoughts, carries his mind from the effect to the sin that had caused it.

(12, 13) **She gave me . . .**—There is again in Adam the same passiveness which we noticed on verse 6. He has little sense of responsibility, and no feeling that he had a duty towards Eve, and ought to have watched over her, and helped her when tempted. It is a mistake to suppose that he wished to shift the blame, first upon Eve, and then upon God, who had given her to him; rather, he recapitulates the history, as if, in his view, it was a matter of course that he should act as he had done (see on verse 20), and as if he had no sense that there was any blame whatever attaching to any one. His conscience still seems utterly unmoved. Far nobler is the woman's answer. She acknowledges that she had been led astray, and, under the influence of the serpent's deceit, had broken God's commandment.

(14, 15) **Unto the serpent.**—As the serpent had tempted our first parents purposely and consciously in

seed; it shall bruise thy head, and thou
shalt bruise his heel.
(16) Unto the woman he said, I will
greatly multiply thy sorrow and thy conception; in sorrow thou shalt bring forth
children; and thy desire *shall be* [1] to thy
husband, and he shall [a] rule over thee.
(17) And unto Adam he said, Because

[1] Or, *subject to thy husband.*

[a] 1 Cor. 14. 34.

order to lead them into sin, he stood there without excuse, and received a threefold penalty. The outward form of the condemnation is made suitable to the shape which the tempter had assumed; but the true force and meaning, especially in the last and most intense portion of the sentence, belong, not to the animal, but to Satan himself. The serpent is but the type: diabolic agency the reality. First, therefore, the serpent is condemned to crawl. As he is pronounced to be "cursed above (or rather, *among*) all cattle"—that is, the tame animals subjected to man's service—and also "among all beasts of the field"—that is, the wild animals, but a term not applicable to reptiles—it has been supposed that the serpent was originally erect and beautiful, and that Adam had even tamed serpents, and had them in his household. But such a transformation belongs to the region of fable, and the meaning is that henceforward the serpent's crawling motion is to be to it a mark of disgrace, and to Satan a sign of meanness and contempt. He won the victory over our guileless first parents, and still he winds in and out among men, ever bringing degradation with him, and ever sinking with his victims into deeper abysses of shame and infamy. Yet, even so, perpetually he suffers defeat, and has, secondly, to "lick the dust," because his mean devices lead, as in this place, only to the manifestation of God's glory. In the *Paradise Lost* Milton has made Satan a hero, though fallen; really he is a despicable and mean-spirited foe, whose strength lies in man's moral feebleness. Finally, there is perpetual enmity between the serpent and man. The adder in the path bites man's heel, and is crushed beneath his tramp. It has been noticed that in spite of the beauty and gracefulness of many of the species, man's loathing of them is innate; while in hot countries they are his great enemy, the deaths in India, for instance, from snake-bites being many times more than those caused by the carnivora.

Her seed . . . shall bruise thy head.—We have here the sum of the whole matter, and the rest of the Bible does but explain the nature of this struggle, the persons who wage it, and the manner and consequences of the victory. Here, too, we learn the end and purpose for which the narrative is cast in its present form. It pictures to us man in a close and loving relation, not to an abstract deity, but to a personal and covenant Jehovah. This Being with tender care plants for him a garden, gathers into it whatever is most rare and beautiful in vegetation, and, having given it to him for his home, even deigns at eventide to walk with him there. In the care of this garden He provides for Adam pleasant employment, and watches the development of his intellect with such interest as a father feels in the mental growth of his child. Day by day He brings new animals within his view; and when, after studying their habits, he gives them names, the Deity shares man's tranquil enjoyment. And when he still feels a void, and needs a companion who can hold with him rational discourse, Jehovah elaborately fashions for him, out of his own self, a second being, whose presence satisfies all his longings. Meanwhile, in accordance with the universal law that hand in hand with free-will goes responsibility, an easy and simple trial is provided for man's obedience. He fails, and henceforward he must wage a sterner conflict, and attain to victory only by effort and suffering. In this struggle man is finally to prevail, but not unscathed. And his triumph is to be gained not by mere human strength, but by the coming of One who is "the Woman's Seed;" and round this promised Deliverer the rest of Scripture groups itself. Leave out these words, and all the inspired teaching which follows would be an ever-widening river without a fountain-head. But necessarily with the fall came the promise of restoration. Grace is no after-thought, but enters the world side by side with sin. Upon this foundation the rest of Holy Scripture is built, till revelation at last reaches its corner-stone in Christ. The outward form of the narrative affords endless subjects for curious discussion; its inner meaning and true object being to lay the broad basis of all future revealed truth.

As regards the reading of the Vulgate and some of the Fathers, *ipsa conteret*, "she shall bruise," not only is the pronoun masculine in the Hebrew, but also the verb. This too is the case in the Syriac, in which language also verbs have genders. Most probably a critical edition of the Vulgate would restore even there *ipse conteret*, "he shall bruise."

Like a large proportion of the words used in Genesis, the verb is rare, being found only twice elsewhere in Scripture. In Job ix. 17 the meaning seems plainly to be *to break*, but in Ps. cxxxix. 11, where, however, the reading is uncertain, the sense required is *to cover* or *veil*, though Dr. Kay translates *overwhelm*. Some versions in this place translate it *observe;* and the Vulgate gives two renderings, namely, "She shall *bruise* thy head, and thou shalt *lie in ambush* for (his or her) heel" (gender not marked—*calcaneo ejus*). The translation of the Authorised Version may be depended upon as correct, in spite of its not being altogether applicable to the attack of a natural serpent upon a wayfarer's heel.

(16) **Unto the woman he said.**—The woman is not cursed as the serpent was, but punished as next in guilt; and the retribution is twofold. First, God greatly multiplies "her sorrow and her conception," that is, her sorrow generally, but especially in connection with pregnancy, when with anguish and peril of life she wins the joy of bringing a man into the world. But also "thy desire shall be to thy husband." In the sin she had been the prime actor, and the man had yielded her too ready an obedience. Henceforward she was to live in subjection to him; yet not unhappily, because her inferiority was to be tempered by a natural longing for the married state and by love towards her master. Among the heathen the punishment was made very bitter by the degradation to which woman was reduced; among the Jews the wife, though she never sank so low, was nevertheless purchased of her father, was liable to divorce at the husband's will, and was treated as in all respects his inferior. In Christ the whole penalty, as St. Paul teaches, has been abrogated (Gal. iii. 28), and the Christian woman is no more inferior to the man than is the Gentile to the Jew, or the bondman to the free.

(17, 18) **Unto Adam** (without the article, and therefore a proper name) **he said.**—Lange thoughtfully

thou hast hearkened unto the voice of
thy wife, and hast eaten of the tree, of
which I commanded thee, saying, Thou
shalt not eat of it: cursed *is* the ground
for thy sake; in sorrow shalt thou eat
of it all the days of thy life; (18) thorns
also and thistles shall it [1]bring forth to
thee; and thou shalt eat the herb of the
field; (19) in the sweat of thy face shalt
thou eat bread, till thou return unto the
ground; for out of it wast thou taken:
for dust thou *art*, and unto dust shalt
thou return.
(20) And Adam called his wife's name
[2]Eve; because she was the mother of all
living. (21) Unto Adam also and to his
wife did the LORD God make coats of
skins, and clothed them.
(22) And the LORD God said, Behold,
the man is become as one of us, to know
good and evil: and now, lest he put
forth his hand, and take also of the

1 Heb., *cause to bud.*

2 Heb., *Chavah.*

remarks that while the woman was punished by the entrance of sorrow into the small subjective world of her womanly calling, man is punished by the derangement of the great objective world over which he was to have dominion. Instead of protecting his wife and shielding her from evil, he had passively followed her lead in disobeying God's command; and therefore "the ground," the *adâmâh* out of which Adam had been formed, instead of being as heretofore his friend and willing subject, becomes unfruitful, and must be forced by toil and labour to yield its produce. Left to itself, it will no longer bring forth choice trees laden with generous fruit, such as Adam found in the garden, but the natural tendency will be to degenerate, till "thorns" only "and thistles" usurp the ground. Even after his struggle with untoward nature man wins for himself no paradisiacal banquet, but must "eat the herb of the field" (Job xxx. 4); and the end of this weary struggle is decay and death. In the renewed earth the golden age of paradise will return, and the tendency of nature will no longer be to decay and degeneration, but to the substitution unceasingly of the nobler and the more beautiful in the place of that which was worthless and mean (Isa. lv. 13).

(19) **Dust thou art . . .**—It appears from this that death was man's normal condition. A spiritual being is eternal by its own constitution, but the argument by which Bishop Butler proves the soul to be immortal equally proves the mortality of the body. Death, he says, is the division of a compound substance into its component parts; but as the soul is a simple substance, and incapable of division, it is *per se* incapable of death (*Analogy*, Part I., chap. i.). The body of Adam, composed of particles of earth, was capable of division, and our first parents in Paradise were assured of an unending existence by a special gift, typified by the tree of life. But now this gift was withdrawn, and henceforward the sweat of man's brow was in itself proof that he was returning to his earth: for it told of exhaustion and waste. Even now labour is a blessing only when it is moderate, as when Adam kept a garden that spontaneously brought forth flowers and fruit. In excess it wears out the body and benumbs the soul, and by the pressure of earthly cares leaves neither time nor the wish for any such pursuits as are worthy of a being endowed with thought and reason and a soul.

(20) **Adam called his wife's name Eve.**—Heb., *Chavvah;* in Greek, *Zoë.* It has been debated whether this name is a substantive, *Life* (LXX.), or a participle, *Life-producer* (Symm). Adam's condition was now one of death, but his wife thereby attained a higher value in his sight. Through her alone could human life be continued, and the "woman's seed" be obtained who was to raise up man from his fall. While, then, woman's punishment consists in the multiplication of her "sorrow and conception," she becomes thereby only more precious to man; and while "her desire is to her husband," Adam turns from his own punishment to look upon her with more tender love. He has no word for her of reproach, and we thus see that the common interpretation of verse 12 is more than doubtful. Adam throws no blame either on Eve or on his Maker, because he does not feel himself to blame. He rather means, "How could I err in following one so noble, and in whom I recognise Thy best and choicest gift?" And with this agrees verse 6, where Adam partakes of the fruit without hesitation or thought of resistance. And so here he turns to her and calls her *Chavvah,* his life, his compensation for his loss, and the antidote for the sentence of death.

(21) **Coats of skins.**—Animals, therefore, were killed even in Paradise; nor is it certain that man's diet was until the flood entirely vegetarian (see Note on chap. i. 29). Until sin entered the world no sacrifices could have been offered; and if, therefore, these were the skins of animals offered in sacrifice, as many suppose, Adam must in some way, immediately after the fall, have been taught that without shedding of blood is no remission of sin, but that God will accept a vicarious sacrifice. This is perhaps the most tenable view; and if, with Knobel, we see in this arrival at the idea of sacrifice a rapid development in Adam of thought and intellect, yet it may not have been entirely spontaneous, but the effect of divinely-inspired convictions rising up within his soul. It shows also that the innocence of our first parents was gone. In his happy state Adam had studied the animals, and tamed them and made them his friends; now a sense of guilt urges him to inflict upon them pain and suffering and death. But in the first sacrifice was laid the foundation of the whole Mosaical dispensation, as in verse 15 that of the Gospel. Moreover, from sacrificial worship there was alleviation for man's bodily wants, and he went forth equipped with raiment suited for the harder lot that awaited him outside the garden; and, better far, there was peace for his soul, and the thought—even if still but faint and dim—of the possibility for him of an atonement.

(22) **As one of us.**—See Note on chap. i. 26. By the fall man had sunk morally, but grown mentally. He had asserted his independence, had exercised the right of choosing for himself, and had attained to a knowledge without which his endowment of free-will would have remained in abeyance. There is something painful and humiliating in the idea of Chrysostom and other Fathers that the Deity was speaking ironically, or even with insult (Augustine). All those qualities which constitute man's likeness to God—free-will, self-dependence, the exercise of reason and of choice—had

tree of life, and eat, and live for ever:
(23) therefore the Lord God sent him forth
from the garden of Eden, to till the ground
from whence he was taken. (24) So he drove
out the man; and he placed at the east
of the garden of Eden Cherubims, and
a flaming sword which turned every way,
to keep the way of the tree of life.

CHAPTER IV.—(1) And Adam knew
Eve his wife; and she conceived, and
bare Cain, and said, I have gotten a man

been developed by the fall, and Adam was now a very different being from what he had been in the days of his simple innocency.

Lest he put forth his hand.—Adam had exercised the power of marring God's work, and if an unending physical life were added to the gift of free-will now in revolt against God, his condition and that of mankind would become most miserable. Man is still to attain to immortality, but it must now be through struggle, sorrow, penitence, faith, and death. Hence a paradise is no fit home for him. The Divine mercy, therefore, commands Adam to quit it, in order that he may live under conditions better suited for his moral and spiritual good.

(23) **To till the ground.**—This is the same word as that rendered "dress" in chap. ii. 15. Adam's task is the same, but the conditions are altered.

(24) **So he drove out the man.**—This implies displeasure and compulsion. Adam departed unwillingly from his happy home, and with the consciousness that he had incurred the Divine anger. It was the consequence of his sin, and was a punishment, even if necessary for his good under the changed circumstances produced by his disobedience. On the duration of Adam's stay in Paradise, see *Excursus* at end of this book.

He placed.—Literally, *caused to dwell.* The return to Paradise was closed for ever.

At the east of the garden of Eden.—Adam still had his habitation in the land of Eden, and probably in the immediate neighbourhood of Paradise. (Comp. chap. iv. 16.)

Cherubims.—The cherub was a symbolical figure, representing strength and majesty. The ordinary derivation, from a root signifying to *carve, grave,* and especially to *plough,* compared with Exod. xxv. 20, suggests that the cherubim were winged bulls, probably with human heads, like those brought from Nineveh. We must not confound them with the four living creatures of Ezekiel's vision (Ezek. i. 5), which are the "beasts" of the Revelation of St. John. The office of the cherub here is to guard the Paradise, lest man should try to force an entrance back; and so too the office of the cherubs upon the mercy-seat was to protect it, lest any one should impiously approach it, except the high-priest on the Day of Atonement. The four living creatures of the Apocalypse have a far different office and signification.

IV.

The Founding of the Family, and Commencement of the Non-Paradisiacal Life.

(1) **She . . . bare Cain, and said. . .**—In this chapter we have the history of the founding of the family of Cain, a race godless and wanton, but who, nevertheless, far outstripped the descendants of Seth in the arts of civilisation. To tillage and a pastoral life they added metallurgy and music; and the knowledge not only of copper and its uses, but even of iron (verse 22), must have given them a command over the resources of nature so great as to have vastly diminished the curse of labour, and made their lives easy and luxurious.

I have gotten a man from the Lord.—Rather, *who is Jehovah.* It is inconceivable that *eth* should have here a different meaning from that which it has in chap. i. 1. It there gives emphasis to the object of the verb: "God created *eth* the heaven and *eth* the earth," that is, *even the heaven and even the earth.* So also here, "I have gotten a man *eth* Jehovah," *even Jehovah.* The objection that this implies too advanced a knowledge of Messianic ideas is unfounded. It is we who read backward, and put our ideas into the words of the narrative. These words were intended to lead on to those ideas, but they were at present only as the germ, or as the filament in the acorn which contains the oak-tree. If there is one thing certain, it is that religious knowledge was given gradually, and that the significance of the name Jehovah was revealed by slow degrees. (See on verse 26.) Eve attached no notion of divinity to the name; still less did she foresee that by the superstition of the Jews the title Lord would be substituted for it. We distinctly know that Jehovah was not even the patriarchal name of the Deity (Exod. vi. 3), and still less could it have been God's title in Paradise. But Eve had received the promise that her seed should crush the head of her enemy, and to this promise her words referred, and the title in her mouth meant probably no more than "the coming One." Apparently, too, it was out of Eve's words that this most significant title of the covenant God arose. (See *Excursus* on names *Elohim* and *Jehovah-Elohim,* at end of this book.)

Further, Eve calls Cain "a man," Heb., *ish,* a being. (See on chap. ii. 23.) As Cain was the first infant, no word as yet existed for child. But in calling him "a being, even the future one," a lower sense, often attached to these words, is not to be altogether excluded. It has been said that Eve, in the birth of this child, saw the remedy for death. Death might slay the individual, but the existence of the race was secured. Her words therefore might be paraphrased: "I have gained a man, who is the pledge of future existence." Mankind is thus that which shall exist. Now, it is one of the properties of Holy Scripture that words spoken in a lower and ordinary sense are often prophetic: so that even supposing that Eve meant no more than this, it would not exclude the higher interpretation. It is evident, however, from the fact of these words having been so treasured up, that they were regarded by Adam and his posterity as having no commonplace meaning; and this interpretation has a suspiciously modern look about it. Finally, in Christ alone man does exist and endure. He is the perfect man,—man's highest level; so that even thus there would be a presage of immortality for man in the saying, "I have gained a man, even he that shall become." Grant that it was then but an indefinite yearning: it was one, nevertheless, which all future inspiration was to make distinct and clear; and now, under the guidance of the Spirit, it has become the especial title of the Second Person in the Holy Trinity.

from the LORD. (2) And she again bare
his brother [1]Abel. And Abel was [2]a
keeper of sheep, but Cain was a tiller
of the ground.
(3) And [3]in process of time it came to
pass, that Cain brought of the fruit of
the ground an offering unto the LORD.
(4) And Abel, he also brought of the
firstlings of his [4]flock and of the fat
thereof. And the LORD had [a]respect
unto Abel and to his offering: (5) but
unto Cain and to his offering he had
not respect. And Cain was very wroth,
and his countenance fell. (6) And the
LORD said unto Cain, Why art thou
wroth? and why is thy countenance
fallen? (7) If thou doest well, shalt thou
not [5]be accepted? and if thou doest not

1 Heb., *Hebel.*
2 Heb., *a feeder.*
3 Heb., *at the end of days.*
4 Heb., *sheep or goats.*
a Heb. 11. 4.
5 Or, *have the excellency?*

---

(2) **Abel.**—Of this name Dr. Oppert imagined that it was the Assyrian *Abil,* a son. Really it is *Hebel;* and there is no reason why we should prefer an Assyrian to a Hebrew etymology. An Accadian derivation would have been important, but Assyrian is only a Semitic dialect, and *Abil* is the Hebrew *ben. Hebel* means a thing *unstable, not abiding,* like a breath or vapour. Now, we can scarcely suppose that Eve so called her child from a presentiment of evil or a mere passing depression of spirits; more probably it was a title given to him after his untimely death. Giving names to children would become usual only when population increased; and it was not till a religious rite was instituted for their dedication to God that they had names given to them in their infancy. Even then Esau was changed to Edom, and Jacob to Israel, while previously such names as Eber and Peleg, and earlier still Jabal and Jubal, must have been given to those who bore them from what they became. Such names too as Esau, Jacob, and most of those borne by Jacob's children, seem to have been playful titles, given them in the women's tents by quick-witted nurses, who caught up any chance words of the mother, until at length it became the Jewish rule for women to name their children. Probably, therefore, it was only after Abel's death that his sorrowing relatives called him the *Breath* that had passed away.

Abel was a keeper of sheep, but Cain was a tiller of the ground.—As Adam was 130 years old when Seth was born (chap. v. 3), there was a long period for the increase of Adam's family (comp. verses 14—17), and also for the development of the characters of these his two eldest sons. In the one we seem to see a rough, strong nature, who took the hard work as he found it, and subdued the ground with muscular energy; in the other a nature more refined and thoughtful, and making progress upwards. Adam had already tamed animals in Paradise: to these Abel devotes himself, tends them carefully, and gains from them ample and easy means of sustenance, higher in kind even than the fruits of Paradise. Round these two the other sons and daughters of Adam group themselves, and Cain seems already to have had a wife when he murdered his brother (verse 17).

(3, 4) **In process of time.**—Heb., *at the end of days*: not at the end of a week, or a year, or of harvest-time, but of a long indefinite period, shown by the age of Adam at the birth of Seth to have been something less than 130 years.

An offering.—Heb., *a thank-offering, a present.* We must be careful not to introduce here any of the later Levitical ideas about sacrifice. All that we know about this offering is that it was an act of worship, and apparently something usual. Now, each brought of his own produce, and one was accepted and one rejected. Why? Much ingenuity has been wasted on this question, as though Cain erred on technical grounds; whereas we are expressly told in Heb. xi. 4 that Abel's was the more excellent sacrifice, because offered "in faith." It was the state of their hearts that made the difference; though, as the result of unbelief, Cain's may have been a scanty present of common produce, and not of first-fruits, while Abel brought "firstlings, and of the fat thereof," the choicest portion. Abel may also have shown a deeper faith in the promised Deliverer by offering an animal sacrifice: and certainly the acceptance of his sacrifice quickened among men the belief that the proper way of approaching God was by the death of a victim. But Cain's unbloody sacrifice had also a great future before it. It became the *minchah* of the Levitical law, and under the Christian dispensation is the offering of prayer and praise, and especially the Eucharistic thanksgiving. We have already noticed that Abel's sacrifice shows that flesh was probably eaten on solemn occasions. Had animals been killed only for their skins for clothing, repulsive ideas would have been connected with the carcases cast aside to decay; nor would Abel have attached any value to firstlings. But as soon as the rich abundance of Paradise was over, man would quickly learn to eke out the scanty produce of the soil by killing wild animals and the young of his own flocks.

The Lord had respect.—Heb., *looked upon,* showed that He had seen it. It has been supposed that some visible sign of God's favour was given, and the current idea among the fathers was that fire fell from heaven, and consumed the sacrifice. (Comp. Lev. ix. 24.) But there is real irreverence in thus filling up the narrative; and it is enough to know that the brothers were aware that God was pleased with the one and displeased with the other. More important is it to notice, first, that God's familiar presence was not withdrawn from man after the fall. He talked with Cain as kindly as with Adam of old. And secondly, in these, the earliest, records of mankind religion is built upon love, and the Deity appears as man's personal friend. This negatives the scientific theory that religion grew out of dim fears and terror at natural phenomena, ending gradually in the evolution of the idea of a destructive and dangerous power outside of man, which man must propitiate as best he could.

(5) **Cain was very wroth.**—Heb., *it burned to Cain exceedingly*: that is, his heart was full of hot indignant feelings, because of the preference shown to his younger brother.

(7) **If thou doest well.**—This most difficult verse is capable of a satisfactory interpretation, provided that we refuse to admit into this ancient narrative the ideas of a subsequent age. Literally, the words mean, *If thou doest well, is there not lifting up?* It had just been said that his countenance fell; and this *lifting up* is often elsewhere applied to the countenance. (Comp. Job x. 15, xi. 15.) "Instead, then, of thy present gloomy

well, sin lieth at the door. And [1] unto
thee *shall be* his desire, and thou shalt
rule over him.
(8) And Cain talked with Abel his
brother: and it came to pass, when
they were in the field, that Cain
rose up against Abel his brother,
and [a]slew him. (9) And the LORD said
unto Cain, Where *is* Abel thy brother?
And he said, I know not: *Am* I my
brother's keeper? (10) And he said, What
hast thou done? the voice of thy bro-
ther's [2]blood crieth unto me from the
ground. (11) And now *art* thou cursed

1 Or, *subject unto thee.*

a Wisd. 10. 3; Matt. 23. 35; 1 John 3. 12; Jude 11.

2 Heb., *bloods.*

---

despondent mood, in which thou goest about with downcast look, thou shalt lift up thy head, and have peace and good temper beaming in thine eyes as the result of a quiet conscience." The second half of the verse is capable of two meanings. First: "if thou doest not well, sin lieth (croucheth as a beast of prey) at the door, and its desire is to thee, to make thee its victim; but thou shalt rule over it, and overcome the temptation." The objection to this is: that while sin is feminine, the verb and pronouns are masculine. There are, indeed, numerous instances of a verb masculine with a noun feminine, but the pronouns are fatal, though most Jewish interpreters adopt this feeble explanation. The other interpretation is: "If thou doest not well, sin croucheth at the door, that is, lies dangerously near thee, and puts thee in peril. Beware, therefore, and stand on thy guard; and then *his* desire shall be unto thee, and thou shalt rule over *him.* At present thou art vexed and envious because thy younger brother is rich and prosperous, while thy tillage yields thee but scanty returns. Do well, and the Divine blessing will rest on thee, and thou wilt recover thy rights of primogeniture, and thy brother will look up to thee in loving obedience." (Comp. the loving subjection of the wife in chap. iii. 16.)

We have in this verse proof of a struggle in Cain's conscience. Abel was evidently outstripping him in wealth; his flocks were multiplying, and possibly his younger brothers were attaching themselves to him in greater numbers than to Cain. Moreover, there was a more marked moral growth in him, and his virtue and piety were more attractive than Cain's harsher disposition. This had led to envy and malice on the part of Cain, increased, doubtless, by the favour of God shown to Abel's sacrifice; but he seems to have resisted these evil feelings. Jehovah would not have remonstrated thus kindly with him had he been altogether reprobate. Possibly, too, for a time he prevailed over his evil tempers. It is a gratuitous assumption that the murder followed immediately upon the sacrifice. The words of the Almighty rather show that repentance was still possible, and that Cain might still recover the Divine favour, and thereby regain that pre-eminence which was his by right of primogeniture, but which he felt that he was rapidly losing by Abel's prosperity and more loving ways.

(8) **And Cain talked with Abel his brother.**—Heb., *And Cain said unto Abel his brother.* To this the Samaritan Pentateuch, the LXX., the Syriac, and the Vulg. add, "Let us go out into the field;" but neither the Targum of Onkelos nor any Hebrew MS. or authority, except the Jerusalem Targum, give this addition any support. The authority of the versions is, however, very great: first, because Hebrew MSS. are all comparatively modern; and secondly, because all at present known represent only the Recension of the Masorites. Sooner or later some manuscript may be found which will enable scholars to form a critical judgment upon those places where the versions represent a different text. If we could, with the Authorised Version, translate "Cain talked with Abel," this would imply that Cain triumphed for a time over his angry feelings, and resumed friendly intercourse with his brother. But such a rendering is impossible, as also is one that has been suggested, "Cain told it unto Abel his brother": that is, told all that had passed between him and Jehovah. Either, therefore, we must accept the addition of the versions, or regard the passage as at present beyond our powers.

It came to pass, when they were in the field.—The open, uncultivated land, where Abel's flocks would find pasture. We cannot suppose that this murder was premeditated. Cain did not even know what a human death was. But, as Philippson remarks, there was a perpetual struggle between the husbandmen who cultivated fixed plots of ground and the wandering shepherds whose flocks were too prone to stray upon the tilled fields. Possibly Abel's flocks had trespassed on Cain's land, and when he went to remonstrate, his envy was stirred at the sight of his brother's affluence. A quarrel ensued, and Cain, in that fierce anger, to fits of which he was liable (verse 5), tried to enforce his mastery by blows, and before he well knew what he was doing, he had shed his brother's blood, and stood in terror before the first human corpse.

(9) **And the Lord said unto Cain, Where is Abel thy brother?**—It is the beauty of these early narratives that the dealings of the Deity with mankind are all clothed in an anthropomorphic form, for the reasons of which see Note on chap. ii. 7. It seems, then, that Cain at first went away, scarcely conscious of the greatness of his crime. He had asserted his rights, had suppressed the usurpation of his privileges by the younger son, and if he had used force it was his brother's fault for resisting him. So Jacob afterwards won the birthright by subtilty, and would have paid the same fearful penalty but for timely flight, and rich presents afterwards. But Cain could not quiet his conscience; remorse tracked his footsteps; and when in the household Abel came not, and the question was asked, Where is Abel? the voice of God repeated it in his own heart, Where is Abel, *thy brother?*—brother still, and offspring of the same womb, even if too prosperous. But the strong-willed man resists. What has he to do with Abel? Is he "his brother's keeper?"

(10) **Thy brother's blood crieth unto me.**—The sight he has seen of death cleaves to him, and grows into a terror; and from above the voice of Jehovah tells him that the blood he has shed calls aloud for vengeance. Thus with the first shedding of human blood that ominous thought sprang up, divinely bestowed, that the earth will grant no peace to the wretch who has stained her fair face with the life stream of man. But "the blood of Jesus speaketh better things than that of Abel" (Heb. xii. 24). The voice of one cried for justice and retribution: the other for reconciliation and peace.

(11, 12) **And now** (because of thy crime) **art thou cursed from the earth.**—Heb., *from the adâmâh,* or

from the earth, which hath opened her
mouth to receive thy brother's blood
from thy hand; (12) when thou tillest
the ground, it shall not henceforth yield
unto thee her strength; a fugitive and
a vagabond shalt thou be in the earth.
(13) And Cain said unto the LORD, [1]My
punishment *is* greater than I can bear.
(14) Behold, thou hast driven me out this
day from the face of the earth; and
from thy face shall I be hid; and I shall
be a fugitive and a vagabond in the
earth; and it shall come to pass, *that*
every one that findeth me shall slay me.
(15) And the LORD said unto him, There-
fore whosoever slayeth Cain, vengeance
shall be taken on him sevenfold. And
the LORD set a mark upon Cain, lest any
finding him should kill him.

(16) And Cain went out from the pre-
sence of the LORD, and dwelt in the land
of Nod, on the east of Eden. (17) And
Cain knew his wife; and she conceived,
and bare [2] Enoch: and he builded a city,

1 Or, *My iniquity is greater than that it may be forgiven.*

2 Heb., *Chanoch.*

---

cultivated ground. Cain was the first human being on whom a curse was inflicted, and it was to rise up from the ground, the portion of the earth won and subdued by man, to punish him. He had polluted man's habitation, and now, when he tilled the soil, it would resist him as an enemy, by refusing "to yield unto him her strength." He had been an unsuccessful man before, and outstripped in the race of life by the younger son; for the future his struggle with the conditions of life will be still harder. The reason for this follows: "a fugitive and a vagabond shalt thou be in the earth." Restless and uneasy, and haunted by the remembrance of his crime, he shall become a wanderer, not merely in the *adâmâh*, his native soil, but in the earth. Poverty must necessarily be the lot of one thus roaming, not in search of a better lot, but under the compulsion of an evil conscience. Finally, however, we find that Cain's feelings grew more calm, and being comforted by the presence of a wife and children, "he builded a city," and had at last a home.

(13, 14) **My punishment** (or *my iniquity*) **is greater than I can bear.**—Literally, *than can be borne*, or "forgiven." It is in accordance with the manner of the Hebrew language to have only one word for an act and its result. Thus *work* and *wages* are expressed by the same word in Isa. lxii. 11. The full meaning, therefore, is, "My sin is past forgiveness, and its result is an intolerable punishment." This latter idea seems foremost in Cain's mind, and is dwelt upon in verse 14. He there complains that he is driven, not "from the face of the earth," which was impossible, but from the *adâmâh*, his dear native soil, banished from which, he must go into the silence and solitude of an earth unknown and untracked. And next, "from thy face shall I be hid." Naturally, Cain had no idea of an omnipresent God, and away from the *adâmâh* he supposed that it would be impossible to enjoy the Divine favour and protection. Without this there would be no safety for him anywhere, so that he must rove about perpetually, and "every one that findeth me shall slay me." In the *adâmâh* Jehovah would protect him; away from it, men, unseen by Jehovah, might do as they liked. But who were these men? Some commentators answer, Adam's other sons, especially those who had attached themselves to Abel. Others say that Adam's creation was not identical with that of chap. i. 27, but was that of the highest type of the human race, and had been preceded by the production of inferior races, of whose existence there are widespread proofs. But others, with more probability, think that Cain's was a vain apprehension. How could he know that Adam and his family were the sole inhabitants of the earth? Naturally he expected to find farther on what he had left behind; a man and woman with stalwart sons: and that these, regarding him as an interloper come to rob them, and seeing in his ways proof of guilt, would at once attack and slay him.

(15) **The Lord said unto him, Therefore.**—Most of the versions have *Not so*, which requires only a slight and probable change of the Hebrew text.

Sevenfold.—Cain's punishment was severe, because his crime was the result of bad and violent passions, but his life was not taken because the act was not premeditated. Murder was more than he had meant. But as any one killing him would mean murder, therefore the vengeance would be *sevenfold*: that is, *complete*, seven being the number of perfection. Others, however, consider that Cain's life was under a religious safeguard, seven being the sacred number of creation. In this we have the germ of the merciful law which set cities of refuge apart for the involuntary manslayer.

The Lord set a mark upon Cain.—This rendering suggests an utterly false idea. Cain was not branded nor marked in any way. What the Hebrew says is, "And Jehovah set," that is, appointed, "unto Cain a sign, that no one finding him should slay him." In a similar manner God appointed the rainbow as a sign unto Noah that mankind should never again be destroyed by a flood. Probably the sign here was also some natural phenomenon, the regular recurrence of which would assure Cain of his security, and so pacify his excited feelings.

(16) **Cain went out from the presence of the Lord.**—See Note on chap. iii. 8. Adam and his family probably worshipped with their faces towards the Paradise, and Cain, on migrating from the whole land of Eden, regarded himself as beyond the range of the vision of God. (See Note on verse 14.)

The land of Nod.—*i.e.*, of wandering. Knobel supposes it was China, but this is too remote. Read without vowels, the word becomes India. All that is certain is that Cain emigrated into Eastern Asia, and as none of Noah's descendants, in the table of nations in chap. x., are described as having travelled eastward, many with Philippson and Knobel regard the Mongol race as the offspring of Cain.

CAIN AND HIS DESCENDANTS.

(17) **Cain knew his wife.**—As Jehovah had told Eve that He would "greatly multiply her conception" (chap. iii. 16), we cannot doubt but that a numerous offspring had grown up in the 130 years that intervened between the birth of Cain and that of Seth, the *substitute* for Abel. As a rule, only the eldest son is mentioned in the genealogies, and Abel's birth is chronicled chiefly because of his tragical end, leading to the enactment of the merciful law which followed and to the sundering of the human race. One of Adam's daughters

and called the name of the city, after
the name of his son, Enoch. (18) And
unto Enoch was born Irad: and Irad
begat Mehujael: and Mehujael begat
Methusael: and Methusael begat [1]La-
mech.

(19) And Lamech took unto him two
wives: the name of the one *was* Adah,
and the name of the other Zillah.
(20) And Adah bare Jabal: he was the
father of such as dwell in tents, and *of
such as have* cattle. (21) And his brother's
name *was* Jubal: he was the father of
all such as handle the harp and organ.
(22) And Zillah, she also bare Tubal-cain,
an [2]instructer of every artificer in

1 Heb., *Lemech.*

2 Heb., *whetter.*

---

apparently clave unto her brother, in spite of the solemn decree of banishment passed upon him, probably, by his father, and followed him in his wanderings as his wife, and bare him a son, whom they called "Enoch." Now this name, in Hebrew *Chanoch*, is of the utmost importance in estimating Cain's character. It means *train* in Prov. xxii. 6 ("Train up a child"), but is used in Deut. xx. 5 of the *dedication* of a house; and thus Cain also calls his city "Enoch," *dedicated.* But in old times the ideas of training and dedication were closely allied, because teaching generally took the form of initiation into sacred rites, and one so initiated was regarded as a consecrated person. Though, then, the wife may have had most to do with giving the name, yet we see in it a purpose that the child should be a trained and consecrated man; and Cain must have now put off those fierce and violent habits which had led him into so terrible a crime. We may add that this prepares our minds for the rapid advance of the Cainites in the arts of civilisation, and for the very remarkable step next taken by Cain.

He builded a city.—Heb., *was building*, that is, *began to build a city.* There was not as yet population enough for a city, but Cain, as his offspring increased, determined that they should dwell together, under *training*, in some *dedicated* common abode. He probably selected some fit spot for the acropolis, or citadel, to be the centre of his village; and as *training* is probably the earlier, and *dedication* the later meaning, Cain appears as a wise ruler, like Nimrod subsequently, rather than as a religious man. His purpose was much the same as that of the builders of the Tower of Babel, who wanted to keep mankind together that they might form a powerful community. It is worth notice that in the line of Seth, the name of the seventh and noblest of that race, is also Enoch, whose training was a close walk with God.

(18) **Unto Enoch was born Irad.**—Cain was building a city, *'Ir*, and it was this probably which suggested the name *'Irad.* It has little in common with Jared, as it begins with a harsh guttural, usually omitted in English because unpronounceable, but which appears as *g* in Gomorrah. Possibly 'Irad means *citizen;* but these names have been so corrupted by transcribers that we cannot feel sure of them. Thus, here the LXX. calls 'Irad Gaïdad, and the Syriac 'Idor. In the list that follows, the names Mehujael (Samaritan *Michel*, Syriac *Mahvoyel*), Methusael, Enoch, and Lamech (Heb., *Lemech*), have a certain degree of similitude with those in the line of the Sethites, whence many commentators have assumed that the two lists are variations of the same original record. But it is usually a similarity of sound only with a diversity of meaning. Thus Mehujael, *smitten of God*, answers to Mahalaleel, *glory to God;* Methusael, *God's hero*, to Methuselah, *the armed warrior.* Even when the names are the same, their history is often most diverse. Thus in the Cainite line Enoch is *initiation* into city life, in the Sethite into a life of holiness; and the Cainite polygamist Lemech, rejoicing in the weapons invented by his son, is the very opposite of the Sethite Lemech, who calls his son Noah, *quiet, rest.*

(19—22) **Lamech took unto him two wives.**—Whether polygamy began with Lamech is uncertain, but it is in keeping with the insolent character of the man. The names of his wives bear testimony to the existence, even at this early date, of considerable refinement; for I can scarcely believe that we need go to the Assyrian dialect for the meaning of two words for which Hebrew suffices. They are explained in Assyrian as being *edhatu*, "darkness," and *tzillatu*, "the shades of night." In Hebrew Adah means *ornament*, especially that which is for the decoration of the person; while Zillah means *shadow*, which agrees very closely with the Assyrian explanation. Both have distinguished children. Jabal, Adah's eldest son, took to a nomadic life, whence his name, which means *wanderer*, and was looked up to by the nomad tribes as their founder. The difference between their mode of life and that of Abel was that they perpetually changed their habitation, while he remained in the neighbourhood of Adam's dwelling. The younger, "Jubal," that is, the *music-player*, "was the father of all such as handle the harp and organ." Of these instruments, the *kinnôr*, always translated "harp" in our version, was certainly a stringed instrument, a guitar or lyre. The other, in Hebrew *'ugab*, is mentioned only in Job. xxi. 12, xxx. 31; Ps. cl. 4. It was a small wind instrument, a reed or pipe.

The son of Zillah attained to higher distinction. He is the first "sharpener (or hammerer) of every instrument of copper and iron." Copper is constantly found cropping up in a comparatively pure state upon the surface of the ground, and was the first metal made use of by man. It is comparatively soft, and is easily beaten to an edge; but it was long before men learned the art of mixing with it an alloy of tin, and so producing the far harder substance, bronze. The alloy to which we give the name of brass was absolutely unknown to the ancients. The discovery of iron marks a far greater advance in metallurgy, as the ore has to be smelted, and the implement produced is more precious. The Greeks in the time of Homer seem to have known it only as a rarity imported from the north; and Rawlinson (Anc. Monarchies, i. 167) mentions that in Mesopotamia, while silver was the metal current in traffic, iron was so rare as to be regarded as something very precious. The name of this hero is "Tubal-cain." In Ezek. xxvii. 13, Tubal brings copper to the mart of Tyre, and in Persian the word means copper. Cain is a distinct name from that of Adam's firstborn, and means, in most Semitic languages, *smith;* thus Tubal-cain probably signifies *copper-smith.*

The sister of Tubal-cain was Naamah.—The same as Naomi (Ruth i. 2), and meaning *beauty, loveliness.* As women are not mentioned in the genealogies, and as no history follows of this personage, her name must be given as an indication that a great advance had been made, not only in the arts, but also

brass and iron: and the sister of Tubal-
cain *was* Naamah. (23) And Lamech said
unto his wives,
Adah and Zillah, Hear my voice; ye
wives of Lamech, hearken unto my
speech:
For [1]I have slain a man to my wound-
ing, and a young man [2]to my hurt.
(24) If Cain shall be avenged sevenfold,
truly Lamech seventy and sevenfold.
(25) And Adam knew his wife again;
and she bare a son, and called his name
[3]Seth: For God, *said she*, hath ap-
pointed me another seed instead of Abel,
whom Cain slew. (26) And to Seth, to
him also there was born a son; and he
called his name [4]Enos: then began men
[5]to call upon the name of the LORD.

CHAPTER V.—(1) This *is* the [a]book
of the generations of Adam.
In the day that God created man, in
the likeness of God made he him;
(2) [b]male and female created he them;

1 Or, *I would slay a man in my wound, &c.*

2 Or, *in my hurt.*

3 Heb., *Sheth.*

4 Heb., *Enosh.*

5 Or, *to call themselves by the name of the LORD.*

a 1 Chron. i. 1.

b Wisd. 2. 23.

in the elegancies of life. Women could not have been mere drudges and household slaves, nor men coarse and boorish, when Naamah's beauty was so highly appreciated. The Rabbins have turned her into a demon, and given free play to their imagination in the stories they have invented concerning her.

(23, 24) **Lamech said . . .**—Following quickly upon music, we have poetry, but it is in praise of ferocity, and gives utterance to the pride of one who, by means of the weapons forged by his son, had taken violent revenge for an attack made upon him. Many commentators, however, regard the poem as hypothetical. "Were any one to wound me, I would with these weapons slay him." It would thus be a song of exultation over the armour which Tubal-cain had invented. It more probably records a fact, and is intended to show that, side by side with progress in the material arts, moral degradation was going on. Cain's own act is spoken of, not as a sin to be ashamed of, but as a deed of ancient heroism: not comparable, however, with the glory of Lamech, whose wrath shall be ten-fold. The poetry is vigorous, and marked by that parallelism which subsequently became the distinguishing quality of Hebrew verse. It should be translated:—

> "Adah and Zillah, hear my voice,
> Ye wives of Lemech, give ear unto my rede.
> For I have slain a man for wounding me:
> Even a young man for bruising me.
> Truly Cain shall be avenged sevenfold,
> And Lemech seventy and sevenfold."

It is remarkable that both of the words used for the attack upon Lamech refer to such wounds as might be given by a blow with the fist, while his word means to pierce, or run through with a sharp weapon. "Young man" is literally *child*, but see on chap. xxi. 14.

With this boastful poem in praise of armed violence and bloodshed, joined with indications of luxury and a life of pleasure, the narrator closes the history of the race of Cain.

SUBSTITUTION OF SETH FOR ABEL.

(25) **Another seed instead of Abel, whom Cain slew.**—Cain, the firstborn, and Abel, who had outstripped him in prosperity, were both lost to Adam. But instead of the third son succeeding to the place of the firstborn, it is given to one specially marked out, probably by prophecy, just as Solomon took the rights of primogeniture over the head of Adonijah.

Seth.—Heb., *Sheth*, that is, *appointed, substituted*: he was thus specially designated as the son who was to be the chief over Adam's family.

(26) **He called his name Enos.**—Heb., *Enosh*, that is, *man*. We thus find language growing. Up to this time there had been two names for *man:* Adam, which also in Assyrian—another Semitic dialect—has the same meaning, as Sir H. Rawlinson has shown: and Ish, a *being*. (See on chap. ii. 23.) We have now Enosh, which, according to Fürst and others, signifies *mortal;* but of this there is no proof. Most probably it is the generic word for man, and is used as such in the Aramaic dialects. Thus in Syriac and Chaldee our Lord is styled *bar-enosh*, the son of man: not the son of a mortal, but the son of man absolutely.

Then began men (Heb., *then it was begun*) **to call upon the name of the Lord** (Jehovah).—That is, the notion of Divinity began now to be attached to this name, and even in their worship men called upon God as Jehovah. Eve, as we have seen, attached no such idea to it; and when, in chap. iv. 3, we read that Cain and Abel brought an offering to Jehovah, these are the words of the narrator, who in the story of the fall had expressly styled the Deity Jehovah-Elohim, that is, Jehovah-God, or more exactly, "the coming God," in order to show that Elohim and Jehovah are one. Two hundred and thirty-five years had elapsed between the birth of Cain and that of Enos, and men had learned a truer appreciation of the promise given to their primal mother, in chap. iii. 15, than she herself had when she supposed that her first child was to win back for her the Paradise. Probably they had no exact doctrinal views about His person and nature; it was the office of prophecy "by divers portions" to give these (Heb. i. 1). But they had been taught that "He who should be" was Divine, and to be worshipped. It is the hopeless error of commentators to suppose that Eve, and Enos, and others, knew all that is now known, and all that the inspired narrator knew. They thus do violence to the plainest language of Holy Scripture, and involve its interpretation in utter confusion. Read without these preconceived notions, the sense is plain: that the name Jehovah had now become a title of the Deity, whereas previously no such sacredness had been attached to it. It was long afterwards, in the days of Moses, that it became the personal name of the covenant God of the Jews.

V.

PATRIARCHAL GENEALOGY FROM ADAM TO NOAH.

(1) **This is the book of the generations of Adam.**—See on chap. ii. 4, and *Excursus* on the Books of Generations.

In the likeness of God.—Man is now a fallen being, but these words are repeated to show that the

and blessed them, and called their name
Adam, in the day when they were
created.
(3) And Adam lived an hundred and
thirty years, and begat *a son* in his own
likeness, after his image; and called his
name Seth: (4) [a]and the days of Adam
after he had begotten Seth were eight
hundred years: and he begat sons and
daughters: (5) and all the days that
Adam lived were nine hundred and
thirty years: and he died.
(6) And Seth lived an hundred and
five years, and begat [1]Enos: (7) and
Seth lived after he begat Enos eight
hundred and seven years, and begat
sons and daughters: (8) and all the
days of Seth were nine hundred and
twelve years: and he died.

a 1 Chron. i. 1, &c.

1 Heb., *Enosh.*

2 Heb., *Kenan.*

3 Gr., *Maleleel.*

4 Heb., *Jered.*

(9) And Enos lived ninety years, and
begat [2]Cainan: (10) and Enos lived after
he begat Cainan eight hundred and fif-
teen years, and begat sons and daugh-
ters: (11) and all the days of Enos were
nine hundred and five years: and he
died.
(12) And Cainan lived seventy years,
and begat [3]Mahalaleel: (13) and Cainan
lived after he begat Mahalaleel eight
hundred and forty years, and begat sons
and daughters: (14) and all the days of
Cainan were nine hundred and ten
years: and he died.
(15) And Mahalaleel lived sixty and
five years, and begat [4]Jared: (16) and
Mahalaleel lived after he begat Jared
eight hundred and thirty years, and
begat sons and daughters: (17) and

Divine likeness was not therefore lost, nor the primæval blessing bestowed at his creation revoked. As man's likeness to God does not mainly consist in moral innocence (see on chap. i. 26), it was not affected by the entrance into the world of sin, except so far as sin corrupted the vessel in which this great gift was deposited. (Comp. 2 Cor. iv. 7.)

(3) **In his own likeness, after his image.**—That is, Adam handed down to his posterity that Divine likeness which he had himself received.

Seth.—See on chap. iv. 25.

(5) **The days that Adam lived were nine hundred and thirty years.**—The numbers in the Bible are involved in great difficulty, owing to the Hebrew method of numeration being to attach numerical values to letters, and add them together; and as the words thus formed are unmeaning, they easily become corrupted. Hence there is a great discrepancy in the numbers as specified by the three main authorities, the Hebrew text making the length of time from the expulsion from Paradise to the flood 1656 years, the Samaritan text only 1307, and the LXX. 2262, while in almost all cases they agree in the duration of the lives of the several patriarchs. There is, however, an appearance of untrustworthiness about the calculations in the LXX., while the Samaritan transcript must rank as of almost equal authority with the Hebrew text itself. St. Jerome, however, says that the best Samaritan MSS. in his days agreed with the Hebrew, but none such have come down to us.

Not only is there no doubt that the Bible represents human life as vastly prolonged before the flood, while afterwards it grew rapidly briefer, but it teaches us that in the Messianic age life is to be prolonged again, so that a century shall be the duration of childhood, and a grown man's ordinary age shall be as the age of a tree (Isa. lxv. 20, 22). On the other hand, we may accept the assertion of physiologists that such as man is now, a period of from 120 to 150 years is the utmost possible duration of human life, and that no strength of constitution, nor temperance, nor vegetable diet could add many years to this limit. Hence many have supposed that in the early Biblical genealogies races or dynasties were meant, or that at a time when there were only engraved cylinders or marks scratched on stones or impressed on bricks as modes of writing, a few names only were selected, each one of whom, by the length of years assigned to him, represented an indefinitely protracted period. In proof that there was something artificial in these genealogies, they point to the fact that the *tôldôth* of Adam are arranged in ten generations, and that the same number of generations composes the *tôldôth* of Shem (chap. xi. 10—26); while in our Lord's genealogy names are confessedly omitted in order to produce three series, each of fourteen names. It is also undeniable that in Hebrew genealogies it was the rule to omit names. Thus the genealogy of Moses contains only four individuals: Levi, Kohath, Amram, Moses (1 Chron. vi. 1—3); while for the same period there are eleven descents given in the genealogy of Jehoshuah (*Ibid*, vii. 23—27). All this is sufficient to convince every thoughtful person that we must not use these genealogies for chronological purposes. They were not drawn up with any such intention, but to trace the line of primogeniture, and show whose was the birthright. But the longevity of the antediluvian race does not depend upon these genealogies alone, but is part of the very substance of the narrative. It has too the evidence in its favour of all ancient tradition; but it is one of the mysteries of the Bible. We learn, however, from chap. vi. 3 that it did not prove a blessing, and we possibly are to understand that a change took place at the time of the flood in man's physical constitution, by which the duration of his life was gradually limited to 120 years.

We ought to add that modern scholarship has proved the identity of the names of the numbers up to ten in the three great families of human speech. Above ten they have nothing in common. It seems, therefore, to follow that primæval man before the confusion of tongues had no power of expressing large numbers. Hence in these lists the generations are limited to ten, and hence too the need of caution in dealing with the mystery which underlies the protracted duration of the lives of the patriarchs.

(9) **Enos lived ninety years.**—This proves that the years could not have been mere revolutions of the moon, as some have supposed. So Cainan was only

all the days of Mahalaleel were eight
hundred ninety and five years: and he
died.
(18) And Jared lived an hundred sixty
and two years, and he begat Enoch:
(19) and Jared lived after he begat Enoch
eight hundred years, and begat sons
and daughters: (20) and all the days of
Jared were nine hundred sixty and two
years: and he died.
(21) And Enoch lived sixty and five
years, and begat [1] Methuselah: (22) and
Enoch walked with God after he begat
Methuselah three hundred years, and
begat sons and daughters: (23) and all
the days of Enoch were three hundred
sixty and five years: (24) and [a] Enoch
walked with God: and he *was* not; for
God took him.
(25) And Methuselah lived an hundred
eighty and seven years, and begat
[2] Lamech: (26) and Methuselah lived
after he begat Lamech seven hundred
eighty and two years, and begat sons
and daughters: (27) and all the days of
Methuselah were nine hundred sixty
and nine years: and he died.
(28) And Lamech lived an hundred
eighty and two years, and begat a son:
(29) and he called his name [3] Noah, saying,
This *same* shall comfort us concerning
our work and toil of our hands, because
of the ground which the LORD hath
cursed. (30) And Lamech lived after he
begat Noah five hundred ninety and five
years, and begat sons and daughters:
(31) and all the days of Lamech were
seven hundred seventy and seven years:
and he died.
(32) And Noah was five hundred years
old: and Noah begat Shem, Ham, and
Japheth.

1 Gr., *Mathusala.*

a Ecclus. 44. 16; Heb. 11. 5.

2 Heb., *Lemech.*

3 Gr., *Noe.*

---

seventy years of age at the birth of his son, and Mahalaleel sixty-five. In the LXX. no patriarch has a son until he is at least 162 years of age, so that the supposition there would be more tenable.

(18) **Jared.**—Heb., *Yered.* This name is supposed to mean the *descent,* especially of water. Hence many have endeavoured to show that he is the Indian water-god *Varuna;* but competent modern commentators regard all such Aryan expositions as exploded. Mr. Sayce tells us that the word in Assyrian means *servant* (*Chald. Gen.* 311), but this is not quite satisfactory. Until, however, this very ancient Semitic dialect is thoroughly explored, we are scarcely in a position to speak with certainty as to these old names.

Further, he was 162 years of age when he begat Enoch. It is probable from this that Enoch was not the eldest son, but that the birthright became his because of his special excellencies. It is also to be observed that Enoch holds the seventh place from Adam, seven being the number of perfection; that he attains to the highest rank among the patriarchs; and that he passes over into immortality without death.

(24) **Enoch walked with God.**—This is translated in the LXX., "Enoch pleased God," whence comes the "testimony" quoted in Heb. xi. 5. Really it gives the cause of which the Greek phrase is the effect; for it denotes a steady continuance in well-doing, and a life spent in the immediate presence of and in constant communion with God. (See Note on chap. iv. 18.)

God took him.—Instead of the mournful refrain *and he died,* coming like a surprise at the end of each of these protracted lives, we have here an early removal into another world, suggesting already that long life was not the highest form of blessing; and this removal is without pain, decay, or death into the immediate presence of God. Thus one of Adam's posterity after the fall succeeded in doing, though, doubtless, not without special help and blessing from the Almighty, that wherein Adam in Paradise had failed. We learn, too, from Jude 14, 15, that Enoch's was a removal from prevailing evil to happiness secured. Already, probably, the intermarriages between the Cainites and Sethites had begun, and with it the corruption of mankind. Philippson, while regarding the phrase "God took him" as a euphemism for an early death, yet finds in it an indication of there being another life besides this upon earth. We may further add that Enoch's translation took place about the middle of the antediluvian period, and that his age was 365, the number of the days of the year. As, however, the Hebrew year consisted of only 354 days, and the Chaldean of 360, the conclusion that Enoch was a solar deity has no solid foundation to rest upon. But see Note on chap. viii. 14.

(29) **He called his name Noah.**—This is the first recorded instance, since the days of Eve, of a child being named at his birth, and in both cases the name ended in disappointment. Noah brought no rest, but in his days came the flood to punish human sin. We have already noticed that this longing of Lamech for comfort is in strong contrast with the arrogance of his namesake of the race of Cain. (Comp. chap. iv. 18.)

This same shall comfort us . . . of our hands.—These words form a couplet in the Hebrew, and rhyme like the Arabic couplets in the Koran.

The ground (adâmâh) **which the Lord hath cursed.**—It is usual to style this section Elohistic, because it so evidently takes up the narrative at chap. ii. 3. Yet, first, the writer distinctly refers to chap. iii. 17, where it is Jehovah-Elohim who curses the ground; and next he uses the name Jehovah as equivalent to God, according to what we are told in chap. iv. 26. Here, then, as in several other places, the idea that Genesis can be arranged in two portions, distinguished as Elohistic or Jehovistic, according to the name of God employed in them, entirely breaks down. It is remarkable, also, that the word for "toil" in Lamech's distich is the same as that rendered *sorrow* in chap. iii. 16, 17, and that it occurs only in these three places.

(32) **Noah was five hundred years old.**—No reason is given why Noah had no son until he had attained to so ripe an age, nor, in fact, does it follow that he might not have had other sons, though unworthy of sharing his deliverance. It is remarkable also that neither of the three sons who were with him in the ark had offspring until after the flood. (See chap. xi. 10.)

CHAPTER VI.—(1) And it came to
pass, when men began to multiply on
the face of the earth, and daughters
were born unto them, (2) that the sons
of God saw the daughters of men that
they *were* fair; and they took them
wives of all which they chose. (3) And
the LORD said, My spirit shall not

From them have sprung the three great lines into which the human family is divided. Shem means *name*: that is, fame, glory; and he, as the owner of the birthright, was the progenitor of our Lord. Ham, the *dark-coloured*, was the ancestor of the Egyptians, Cushites, and other black races of Arabia and Africa. Japheth, the *widener*, but according to others the *fair*, though the youngest son, was the ancestor of most of the races of Europe, as well as of some of the chief nations of Asia.

VI.

(1) **When men** (the adam) **began to multiply.**—The multiplication of the race of Adam was probably comparatively slow, because of the great age to which each patriarch attained before his first-born was brought into the world: though, as the name given is not necessarily that of the eldest, but of the son who enjoyed the birthright, it does not follow that in every case the one named was absolutely the eldest son. There may have been other substitutions besides that of Seth for Cain; and Noah, born when his father was 182 years of age, seems a case in point. He was selected to be the restorer of mankind because of his piety, and may have had many brothers and sisters older than himself. Each patriarch, however, begat "sons and daughters," and as we find Cain building a city, he must have seen, at all events, the possibility of a considerable population settling round him. It was probably, as we saw above, about the time of Enoch that the corruption of the family of Adam began to become general.

(2) **The sons of God . . . .**—The literal translation of this verse is, *And the sons of the Elohim saw the daughters of the adam that they were good* (beautiful); *and they took to them wives whomsoever they chose.* Of the sons of the Elohim there are three principal interpretations: the first, that of the Targums and the chief Jewish expositors, that they were the nobles, and men of high rank; the second, that they were angels. St. Jude, verse 6, and St. Peter, 2 Ep., ii. 4, seem to favour this interpretation, possibly as being the translation of the LXX. according to several MSS. But even if this be their meaning, which is very uncertain, they use it only as an illustration; and a higher authority says that the angels neither marry nor are given in marriage. The third, and most generally accepted interpretation in modern times, is that the sons of the Elohim were the Sethites, and that when they married for mere lust of beauty, universal corruption soon ensued. But no modern commentator has shown how such marriages could produce "mighty men . . . men of renown;" or how strong warriors could be the result of the intermarriage of pious men with women of an inferior race, such as the Cainites are assumed to have been.

The Jewish interpreters, who well understood the uses of their own language, are right in the main point that the phrase "sons of the Elohim" conveys no idea of moral goodness or piety. Elohim constantly means *mighty ones* (Exod. xv. 11, marg.). (Comp. *ib.* xii. 12, marg., xxi. 6, xxii. 8, 9, where it is translated *judges*; *ib.* 28, 1 Sam. ii. 25, where also it is translated *judge.*) In Job i. 6 the "sons of Elohim" are the nobles, the idea being that of a king who at his durbar gathers his princes round him; and, not unnecessarily to multiply examples, the "sons of the Elim," the other form of the plural, is rightly translated *mighty ones* in Ps. xxix. 1.

Who, then, are these "mighty ones?" Before answering this question, let me call attention to the plain teaching of the narrative as to what is meant by the "daughters of men." It says: "When the adam began to multiply, and daughters were born unto them, the sons of the Elohim saw the daughters of the adam . . . . and took them wives," &c. But according to every right rule of interpretation, the "daughters of the adam" in verse 1 must be the same as the "daughters of the adam" in verse 2, whom the sons of the Elohim married. Now, it seems undeniable that the adam here spoken of were the Sethites. The phrase occurs in the history of Noah, just after giving his descent from Adam; Cain is absolutely passed over, even in the account of the birth of Seth, who is described as Adam's firstborn, such as legally he was. The corruption described is that of the Sethites; for the Cainites have already been depicted as violent and lustful, and their history has been brought to an end. Moreover, in verse 3, "the adam with whom God will not always strive" is certainly the family of Seth, who, though the chosen people and possessors of the birthright, are nevertheless described as falling into evil ways; and their utter corruption finally is the result of the depravation of their women by a race superior to themselves in muscular vigour and warlike prowess.

Where, then, shall we find these men? Certainly among the descendants of Cain. In chap. iv. 17—24, we find Cain described as the founder of civil institutions and social life: the name he gives to his son testifies to his determination that his race shall be trained men. They advance rapidly in the arts, become rich, refined, luxurious, but also martial and arrogant. The picture terminates in a boastful hero parading himself before his admiring wives, displaying to them his weapons, and vaunting himself in a poem of no mean merit as ten times superior to their forefather Cain. His namesake in the race of Seth also indites a poem; but it is a groan over their hard toil, and the difficulty with which, by incessant labour, they earned their daily bread. To the simple "daughters of the adam," these men, enriched by the possession of implements of metal, playing sweet music on harp and pipe, and rendered invincible by the deadly weapons they had forged, must have seemed indeed as very "sons of the Elohim." The Sethites could not have taken the Cainite women according to their fancy in the way described, protected as they were by armed men; but the whole phrase, "whomsoever they would," reeks of that arrogancy and wantonness of which the polygamist Lamech had set so notable an example. And so, not by the women corrupting nobler natures, but by these strong men acting according to their lust, the race with the birthright sank to the Cainite level, and God had no longer a people on earth worthy of His choice.

(3) **And the Lord said.**—As the Sethites are now

always strive with man, for that he also
is flesh: yet his days shall be an hun-
dred and twenty years. (4) There were
giants in the earth in those days; and
also after that, when the sons of God
came in unto the daughters of men, and
they bare *children* to them, the same
became mighty men which *were* of old,
men of renown.

(5) And GOD saw that the wickedness
of man *was* great in the earth, and *that*
[1] every imagination of the thoughts of
his [a] heart *was* only evil [2] continually.
(6) And it repented the LORD that he had
made man on the earth, and it grieved
him at his heart. (7) And the LORD
said, I will destroy man whom I have
created from the face of the earth; [3] both
man, and beast, and the creeping thing,
and the fowls of the air; for it repenteth
me that I have made them. (8) But Noah
found grace in the eyes of the LORD.

1 Or, *the whole imagination.* The Hebrew word signifieth not only *the imagination,* but also *the purposes and desires.*

a ch. 8. 21; Matt. 15. 19.

2 Heb., *every day.*

3 Heb., *from man unto beast.*

---

the fallen race, it is their covenant Jehovah who determines to reduce the extreme duration of human life to that which, under the most favourable sanitary influences, might still be its normal length.

My spirit shall not always strive with man.—The meaning of this much-contested clause is really settled by the main purpose and context of the verse, which is the Divine determination to shorten human life. Whether, then, God's spirit be the animating breath spoken of in chaps. ii. 7, vii. 22, whereby human life is sustained, or the spiritual part of man, his conscience and moral sense—God's best gift to him—in opposition to his flesh, the struggle henceforward is not to be indefinitely prolonged. In the first case, the struggle spoken of is that between the elements of life and death in the body; in the second, it refers to the moral probation to which man is subject. The versions generally take the former meaning, and translate "shall not dwell," or "abide"; but there is much in favour of the rendering "shall strive," though the verb more exactly means *to rule, preside over, sit as judge.* Literally, then, it signifies that the Divine gift of life shall not rule in man "for ever;" that is, for a period so protracted as was antediluvian life. (Comp. Deut. xv. 17, &c.)

With man.—Heb., *with the adam:* spoken with especial reference to the Sethites.

For that he also is flesh.—So all the versions; but many commentators, to avoid an Aramaism which does not occur again till the later Psalms, translate, "in their erring he is (= they are) flesh." But no reason for shortening human life can be found in this commonplace assertion; and if Abraham brought these records with him from Ur, we have an explanation of the acknowledged fact that Aramaisms do occur in the earlier portions of the Bible. Man, then, is "also" flesh, that is, his body is of the same nature as those of the animals, and in spite of his noble gifts and precedence, he must submit to a life of the same moderate duration as that allotted them.

(4) **Giants.**—Heb., *Nephilim,* mentioned again in Num. xiii. 33, and apparently a race of great physical strength and stature. Nothing is more probable than that, at a time when men lived for centuries, human vigour should also show itself in producing not merely individuals, but a race of more than ordinary height. They were apparently of the Cainite stock, and the text carefully distinguishes them from the offspring of the mixed marriages. The usual derivation of the name is from a root signifying *to fall;* but Lenormant (*Origines de l'Histoire,* p. 344) prefers *pâlâ,* which means "to be wonderful," and compares the Assyrian *naptû,* "unique in size," often found in the cuneiform inscriptions as the denomination of an ogre.

The same became mighty men.—Heb., *They were the mighty men that were of old, men of name.* "Gibborim," *mighty men* (see chap. x. 8), has nothing to do with stature, but means heroes, warriors. It is also generally used in a good sense. The children of these mixed marriages were a race of brave fighting men, who by their martial deeds won for themselves reputation.

(5) **And God saw.**—Really, *And Jehovah saw.*

Imagination.—More exactly, *form, shape.* Thus every idea or embodied thought, which presented itself to the mind through the working of the heart—that is, the whole inner nature of man—"was only evil continually"—Heb., *all the day,* from morning to night, without reproof of conscience or fear of the Divine justice. A more forcible picture of complete depravity could scarcely be drawn; and this corruption of man's inner nature is ascribed to the overthrow of moral and social restraints.

(6) **And it repented the Lord.**—If we begin with the omniscience and omnipotence of God as our postulates, everything upon earth must be predestined and immutably fore-ordained. If we start with man's free will, everything will depend upon human choice and action. Both these sides must be true, though our mental powers are too limited to combine them. In Holy Scripture the latter view is kept more prominently in the foreground, because upon it depends human responsibility. Thus here, the overwhelming of mankind by a flood, and the subsequent abbreviation of life, is set before our eyes as painful to the Deity, and contrary to His goodwill towards men, but as necessitated by the extreme depravity of even the chosen Sethite race.

(7) **I will destroy.**—Heb., *delete, rub out.*

From the face of the earth.—Heb., *the adâmâh,* the tilled ground which man had subdued and cultivated.

Both man, and beast.—Heb., *from man unto cattle, unto creeping thing, and unto fowl of the air.* The animal world was to share in this destruction, because its fate is bound up with that of man (Rom. viii. 19—22); but the idea of the *total* destruction of all animals by the flood, so far from being contained in the text, is contradicted by it, as it only says that it is to reach to them. Wild beasts are not mentioned in this enumeration, probably because the domestic cattle would be the chief sufferers.

Creeping thing.—Not necessarily reptiles. (See Note on chap. i. 24.)

(8) **But Noah found grace.**—This is the first place where grace is mentioned in the Bible, and with these words ends the *Tôldôth Adam.* It has traced man from his creation until his wickedness was so great that the Divine justice demanded his punishment. But it concludes with words of hope. Jehovah's purpose was not extermination, but regeneration; and with Noah a higher and better order of things was to begin.

(9) These *are* the generations of Noah:
[a] Noah was a just man *and* [1] perfect
in his generations, *and* Noah walked
with God. (10) And Noah begat three
sons, Shem, Ham, and Japheth.
(11) The earth also was corrupt before
God, and the earth was filled with
violence. (12) And God looked upon the
earth, and, behold, it was corrupt; for
all flesh had corrupted his way upon the
earth.
(13) And God said unto Noah, The end
of all flesh is come before me; for the
earth is filled with violence through
them; and, behold, I will destroy them
[2] with the earth. (14) Make thee an ark
of gopher wood; [3] rooms shalt thou
make in the ark, and shalt pitch it
within and without with pitch. (15) And
this *is the fashion* which thou shalt
make it *of*: The length of the ark *shall
be* three hundred cubits, the breadth of
it fifty cubits, and the height of it thirty
cubits. (16) A window shalt thou make
to the ark, and in a cubit shalt thou
finish it above; and the door of the ark
shalt thou set in the side thereof; *with*
lower, second, and third *stories* shalt

a Ecclus. 44. 17; 2 Pet. 2. 5.

1 Or, *upright.*

2 Or, *from the earth.*

3 Heb., *nests.*

THE GENERATIONS OF NOAH (chaps. vi. 9, ix. 28).

(9) **Noah was a just man and perfect in his generations.**—"Just" is, literally, *righteous*, one whose actions were sufficiently upright to exempt him from the punishment inflicted upon the rest of mankind. "Perfect" means *sound, healthy*, and conveys no idea of sinlessness. It answers to the Latin *integer*, whence our word integrity, and not to *perfectus*.

Generations (*dôrôth*) is not the same word as at the beginning of the verse (*tôldôth*), but simply means *his contemporaries*. And this he was because—

Noah walked with God.—See Note on chap. v. 22.

(11) **The earth.**—This is the larger word, and it occurs no less than six times in these three verses, thus indicating a more widespread calamity than if adâmâh only had been used, as in verse 7. But the earth that "was corrupt before God" was not the whole material globe, but that part which man, notably the *gibborim* of verse 4, had "filled with violence." Whithersoever man's violence had spread, there his home and all his works, his builded cities, his tilled land, his cattle and stores, must be entirely swept away. An absolutely new beginning was to be made by Noah, such as Adam had to undertake when he was expelled from Paradise. The reason of this necessity is next given.

(12) **All flesh had corrupted his way upon the earth.**—These material things were incapable alike of moral good or evil, but man had made them the instruments of working his carnal will, and because of the associations connected with them they must be effaced, or *rubbed out*. (See Note on verse 7.)

(13) **The end of all flesh is come before me.**—A metaphor taken from the customs of earthly kings. Before an order is executed the decree is presented to the sovereign, that it may finally be examined, and if approved, receive the sign manual, upon which it becomes law.

I will destroy them.—Not the verb used in verse 7, but that translated *had corrupted* in verse 12. It means "to bring to ruin, devastate."

With the earth.—Rather, *even the earth*: *eth*, as in chap. iv. 1. The meaning is, "I will bring them to nought, even the whole present constitution of earthly things."

(14) **Make thee an ark.**—*Têbâh*, a word so archaic that scholars neither know its derivation, nor even to what language it belongs. It is certain, however, that it was an oblong box, not capable of sailing, but intended merely to float. In the Chaldean account of the deluge, the language everywhere is that of a maritime people: the history in Genesis is as plainly the work of a people living inland.

Of gopher wood.—Heb., *trees* (or beams) *of gopher*. This is also a word which occurs nowhere else, but means the cypress (*Cupressus sempervirens*), a tall, upright evergreen tree, of great durability, and anciently much valued for shipbuilding.

Rooms.—Literally, *nests*, small cells or cabins, arranged in three tiers, so that the interlacing of the timbers might aid in holding the whole structure together.

Pitch.—That is, *natural bitumen*. The ark therefore must have been built in some country where this natural product is easily obtainable, as in Assyria.

(15) **Cubits.**—The cubit is the length of the arm from the elbow to the tip of the middle finger. As, further, it was regarded as one-fourth of a man's height, we may safely compute it at eighteen inches, except where the sacred or longer cubit is expressly mentioned. Thus the ark was 450 feet long, 75 broad, and 45 in depth. The *Great Eastern* is much larger, being 680 feet in length. However simple her construction, there would be great difficulty in building so large a vessel, from the danger of her breaking her back, especially in the tempestuous weather which followed.

(16) **A window.**—Not the word so rendered in chaps. vii. 11, viii. 2, which means a *lattice*; nor that in chap. viii. 6, which means an *aperture*; but "zohar," *light, brightness*. In the dual, *double-light*, it is the usual word for "midday," but it does not occur elsewhere in the singular. It was evidently a means, not merely of lighting the ark, but also of ventilating it; for as it was thickly covered within and without with bitumen—a point strongly insisted upon in the *Chaldean Genesis*—the two lower storeys would be so ill supplied with air as to be fit only for stores and ballast, and the upper storey alone capable of being inhabited. If this *zohar* was an open space one cubit in height, running all round the ark, and formed by not boarding over the upright beams, it would have given a sufficient supply of air, and being protected by the overhanging eaves of the roof—for the ark had no deck—would not have admitted any serious amount of rain. So in the *Chaldean Genesis* the ark has no deck, but a roof (p. 281).

Above.—Or, *upward*. The word is one of those reduplicated forms by means of which the Hebrew language expresses so much within a little compass. Consisting of only six letters, it is nevertheless a compound of five particles, and signifies *from to upward*: that is, thou shalt finish it (the ark, as is shown by

thou make it. (17) And, behold, I, even
I, do bring a flood of waters upon the
earth, to destroy all flesh, wherein *is* the
breath of life, from under heaven; *and*
every thing that *is* in the earth shall
die. (18) But with thee will I establish
my covenant; and thou shalt come into
the ark, thou, and thy sons, and thy
wife, and thy sons' wives with thee.
(19) And of every living thing of all
flesh, two of every *sort* shalt thou
bring into the ark, to keep *them* alive
with thee; they shall be male and
female. (20) Of fowls after their kind,
and of cattle after their kind, of every
creeping thing of the earth after his
kind, two of every *sort* shall come unto
thee, to keep *them* alive. (21) And take
thou unto thee of all food that is
eaten, and thou shalt gather *it* to
thee; and it shall be for food for thee,
and for them.
(22) [a] Thus did Noah; according to all
that God commanded him, so did he.

a Heb. 11. 7.

---

the gender) from beneath, working upwards till the last cubit, which is not to be finished, but left open for ventilation and light.

The door, on which also much stress is laid in the Chaldean account as being essential for the protection of the inmates (p. 281), was to be at the side, and probably extended throughout the three storeys, two-thirds of which, however, might be closed as soon as the lower storeys had received their freightage of provisions. Besides this door, there must also have been apertures to admit of cleaning the cells in which the animals were confined and removing their litter, but of such lower arrangements no mention is made.

It is not necessary to suppose that Noah and his three sons built this vast vessel with their own hands. He was probably a powerful chieftain, and many of the Sethites may have given him aid. Implements of iron had been invented by the Cainites, and on the intermarriage of the two lines would be brought into general use. It is difficult, however, to understand how four men could feed, clean, and give water to a very large collection of animals for so many months. Without scrupulous attention to such matters, a murrain would have broken out, and as only two of many species were taken into the ark, the loss of any one of these animals would have been equivalent to the destruction of the race. The narrative, however, implies that the health of man and beast throughout the twelve months was perfect; and probably the number of the animals received into the ark was less than is commonly supposed.

(17) **A flood.**—*Mabbul,* another archaic word. It is used only of the deluge, except in Ps. xxix. 10, where, however, there is an evident allusion to the flood of Noah.

Every thing that is in the earth shall die.—That this by no means involves the theory of a universal deluge has been shown with admirable cogency by Professor Tayler Lewis in "Lange's Commentary." His view is that the writer described with perfect truthfulness that of which he was either an eye-witness, or of which he had received the knowledge by tradition; or lastly, that he recorded in his own language the impressions divinely inspired in his mind by God. "We have no right," he adds, "to force upon him, and upon the scene so vividly described, our modern notions or our modern knowledge of the earth, with its Alps and Himalayas, its round figure, its extent and diversities, so much beyond any knowledge he could have possessed or any conception he could have formed." The excursus is too long even for condensation, but we may add, first, that the idea of unnecessary miracle is contrary both to the wisdom of the Almighty, and to what we actually find in the Bible with respect to the exercise of supernatural power; and, secondly, that the narrative itself repeatedly negatives the theory that the flood extended to any great distance beyond the regions then occupied by man. Moreover, it is in exact accordance with the use of words in Holy Scripture that the large term, *the earth,* is limited to the earth as known to Noah and his contemporaries. We shall also discover in what follows reason for believing that the account originally came from one who was an eye-witness; and the extreme antiquity of the language is a proof that it was committed to writing at a time long anterior to the age of Moses.

(18) **My covenant.**—There had been no covenant with Adam or with the Sethites, but in the higher state of things which began with Noah, man was to hold a more exactly defined relation to God; and though they had begun to attach the notion of Deity to the name Jehovah in the days of Enos (chap. iv. 26), yet it was not till the time of Moses that it became the distinct title of God in covenant with man. Of this relation a necessary result was revelation, as in no other way could there be a communication between the two contracting parties. Hence the Bible is called "The Old and New Covenant," or "The Old and New Testament," the Greek term being of wider meaning than either word with us, and signifying either an agreement between the living or the document by which a testator disposes of his property after his death (Heb. ix. 16, 17). The title of covenant is more applicable to the Scriptures of the prior dispensation, which contain a series of such relations, all preparing for the last and best and most perfect, which was a Testament ratified in the blood of Christ.

(19–22) **Of every living thing of all flesh, two . . .**—The vast size of the ark and the wide terms used of the animals to be collected into it, make it evident that Noah was to save not merely his domestic cattle, but many wild species of beasts, birds, and creeping things. But the terms are conditioned by the usual rules for the interpretation of the language of Holy Scripture, and by the internal necessities of the event itself. Thus the animals in the ark could not have been more in number than four men and four women could attend to. Next, the terms exclude the carnivora (see also Note on chap. ix. 5). Not only was there no supply of animals taken on board to feed them, but half-tamed as they would have been by a year's sojourn in the ark, they would have remained in Noah's neighbourhood, and very soon have destroyed all the cattle which had been saved, especially as far and wide no other living creatures would have existed for their food. But if miracles are to be invoked to obviate these and similar difficulties, not only would it have been easier to save Noah and the denizens of the ark by one display of supernatural

CHAPTER VII.—(1) And the [a]LORD said unto Noah, Come thou and all thy house into the ark; for thee have I seen righteous before me in this generation. (2) Of every clean beast thou shalt take to thee by [1]sevens, the male and his female: and of beasts that *are* not clean by two, the male and his female. (3) Of fowls also of the air by sevens, the male and the female; to keep seed alive upon the face of all the earth. (4) For yet seven days, and I will cause it to rain upon the earth forty days and forty nights; and every living substance that I have made will I [2]destroy from off the face of the earth.

(5) And Noah did according unto all that the LORD commanded him. (6) And Noah *was* six hundred years old when the flood of waters was upon the earth. (7) And Noah went in, and his sons, and his wife, and his sons' wives with him, into the ark, because of the waters of the flood. (8) Of clean beasts, and of beasts that *are* not clean, and of fowls, and of every thing that creepeth upon the earth, (9) there went in two and two unto Noah into the ark, the male and the female, as God had commanded Noah. (10) And it came to pass [3]after seven days, that the waters of the flood were upon the earth.

(11) In the six hundredth year of Noah's

a 2 Pet. 2. 5.

1 Heb., *seven seven.*

2 Heb., *blot out.*

3 Or, *on the seventh day.*

---

power, but the ark was the means provided by God for this purpose; and if He wrought thus far by human instrumentality, in accordance with the usual law of the Divine working on earth, to help out the human means employed by repeated acts of omnipotence would have been to proclaim it as insufficient. It does not follow from this that no special providence watched over and guided the ark; such providence is often exercised now, but it works through and in accordance with the ordinary laws by which God governs the world.

VII.

(1) **Come thou.**—The task of building the ark is over, and after a week, to be spent in collecting animals and birds, Noah is to take up his abode in it. Many commentators suppose that 120 years were spent in the work; but this view arises from an untenable interpretation of chap. vi. 3, which really fixes the future duration of human life.

(2) **Of every clean beast**—Heb., *of all clean cattle*—**thou shalt take to thee by sevens**—Heb., *seven seven.*—This probably does not mean *seven pairs* of each, though many commentators so interpret it, but seven of each kind. If, however, *seven pairs* be the right interpretation, but few species could have been included, as to attend properly to so large a number of animals would have been beyond the power of Noah and his sons. But which were the clean beasts? There can be no reference here to the Levitical law, which had respect to human food; nor to animals tamed and untamed, as all alike are called cattle; but probably the clean cattle were such as from the days of Adam and Abel had been offered in sacrifice. Thus provision was made for Noah's sacrifice on his egress from the ark, and also for his possession of a small herd of such animals as would be most useful to him amid the desolation which must have existed for a long time after the flood. The clean beasts would therefore be oxen, sheep, goats; the unclean, camels, horses, asses, and such other animals as stood in some relation to man. Of birds, the dove would especially be clean.

It has been pointed out that these more full and specific orders are given in the name of Jehovah, whereas most of the narrative of the flood is Elohistic, and hence it has been assumed that some Jehovist narrator added to and completed the earlier narrative. These additions would be chap. vii. 1—6, the last clause of verse 16, Noah's sacrifice in chap. viii. 20—22, and the cursing of Canaan in chap. ix. 18—27. Now, it is remarkable that the sacrifice is as integral a portion of the *Chaldean Genesis* as the sending forth of the birds (*Chaldean Genesis*, p. 286), and is thus indubitably older than the time of Moses. Still, there is nothing improbable in Moses having two records of the flood before him, and while the division of Genesis into Elohistic and Jehovistic portions usually breaks down, there is a *primâ facie* appearance of the combination of two narratives in the present history, or, at least, in this one section (chap. vii. 1—6).

(4) **Forty days.**—Henceforward forty became the sacred number of trial and patience, and, besides the obvious places in the Old Testament, it was the duration both of our Lord's fast in the wilderness and of His sojourn on earth after the Resurrection.

Every living substance.—The word "living" is found neither in the Hebrew nor in the ancient versions, and limits the sense unnecessarily. The word is rare, being found only thrice, namely, here, in verse 23, and in Deut. xi. 6. It means *whatever stands erect.* Thus God "destroys"—Heb., *blots out* (see on chap. vi. 7)—not man and beast only, but the whole existent state of things—"from the face of the earth"—Heb., *the adâmâh*, the cultivated and inhabited ground. This section is much more limited in the extent which it gives to the flood, not including reptiles, or rather, small animals, among those saved in the ark, and confining the overflow of the waters to the inhabited region.

(6) **Noah was six hundred years old.**—It follows that Shem was about one hundred years of age (comp. chap. v. 32), and his two brothers younger; but all were married, though apparently without children. (Comp. chap. xi. 10.)

(8) **Beasts.**—Heb., *of the clean cattle and of the cattle that was not clean.* In the *Chaldean Genesis*, Xisuthrus takes also wild animals, seeds of all kinds of plants, gold and silver, male and female slaves, the "sons of the best," and the "sons of the people" (pp. 280—283). There it is a whole tribe, with their chief, who are saved—here one family only.

(10) **After seven days.**—Said, in Jewish tradition, to have been the seven days of mourning for Methuselah, who died in the year of the flood.

(11) **In the second month.**—That is, of the civil year, which commenced in Tisri, at the autumnal

life, in the second month, the seventeenth
day of the month, the same day were all
the fountains of the great deep broken
up, and the [1]windows of heaven were
opened. (12) And the rain was upon the
earth forty days and forty nights. (13) In
the selfsame day entered Noah, and
Shem, and Ham, and Japheth, the sons
of Noah, and Noah's wife, and the three
wives of his sons with them, into the
ark; (14) they, and every beast after his
kind, and all the cattle after their kind,
and every creeping thing that creepeth
upon the earth after his kind, and every
fowl after his kind, every bird of every
[2]sort. (15) And they went in unto Noah
into the ark, two and two of all flesh,
wherein *is* the breath of life. (16) And
they that went in, went in male and
female of all flesh, as God had com-
manded him: and the LORD shut him
in.

(17) And the flood was forty days upon
the earth; and the waters increased,
and bare up the ark, and it was lift up
above the earth. (18) And the waters
prevailed, and were increased greatly
upon the earth; and the ark went upon
the face of the waters. (19) And the
waters prevailed exceedingly upon the
earth; and all the high hills, that *were*
under the whole heaven, were covered.
(20) Fifteen cubits upward did the waters
prevail; and the mountains were covered.

1 Or, *flood-gates.*

2 Heb., *wing.*

---

equinox. The flood thus began towards the end of October, and lasted till the spring. The ecclesiastical year began in Abib, or April; but it was instituted in remembrance of the deliverance from Egypt (Exod. xii. 2, xxiii. 15), and can have no place here. The year was evidently the lunar year of 360 days, for the waters prevail for 150 days (chap. vii. 24), and then abate for 150 days (chap. viii. 3). Now, as the end of the first period of 150 days is described in chap. viii. 4 as the seventeenth day of the seventh month, whereas the flood began on the seventeenth of the second month, it is plain that the 150 days form five months of thirty days each. But see farther proof on chap. viii. 14.

The fountains of the great deep broken up (Heb., *cloven*), **and the windows** (*lattices*) **of heaven were opened.**—This is usually taken by commentators as a description of extraordinary torrents of rain, related in language in accordance with the popular ideas of the time and of the narrator himself. The rains poured down as though the flood-gates which usually shut in the upper waters were thrown open, while from the abysses of the earth the subterranean ocean burst its way upwards. But the words at least suggest the idea of a great cosmic catastrophe, by which some vast body of water was set loose. Without some such natural convulsion it is very difficult to understand how the ark, a vessel incapable of sailing, could have gone against the current up to the water-shed of Ararat. As the annual evaporation of the earth is also a comparatively fixed quantity, the concentrated downpour of it for forty days and nights would scarcely have produced a flood so vast as the deluge of Noah evidently was. It is thus probable that there was, besides the rains, some vast displacement of water which helped in producing these terrific effects.

We shall have occasion subsequently to notice the exactness of the dates (chap. viii. 14). Tradition might for a short time hand them down correctly, but they must soon have been committed to writing, or confusion would inevitably have crept in.

(13) **In the selfsame day.**—Heb., *in the bone of this day.* (See Note on chap. ii. 23.)

(14) **Every beast.**—Heb., *every living thing* (as in chap. viii. 1), but probably we are to supply "of the field," and thus it would mean the wild animals.

The cattle.—*Behêmâh.* (See Note on chap. i. 24.)

Creeping thing.—Not specially reptiles, but all small animals (see *ibid.*). The last clause literally is, *every fowl after its kind, every bird, every wing;* whence some understand it as meaning three kinds of winged beings: birds generally, next singing-birds, and lastly, bats, insects, and other such creatures. It more probably means "birds of all sorts."

(16) **The Lord** (*Jehovah*) **shut him in.**—The assigning to Jehovah of this act of personal care for Noah is very remarkable. In the *Chaldean Genesis* (p. 283), the Deity commands Xisuthrus to shut himself in.

(17–19) **The waters increased . . .**—The swelling of the flood is told with great power in these verses, but every stage and detail has reference to the ark, as if the author of the narrative was one of those on board. First, the "waters increased," and raised up the ark till it floated. Next, "they became strong and increased exceedingly"—the word rendered "prevailed" really signifying the setting in of mighty currents (see on chap. viii. 1), as the waters sought the lower ground—and at this stage the ark began to move. Finally, they "became strong exceedingly, exceedingly," rushing along with ever-increasing force, and carrying the ark high above every hill in its course. Of these it is said—

All the high hills, that were under the whole heaven, were covered.—Interpreting this by the English Version, many regard it as a proof of the deluge having been universal. But omitting the well-known fact that in the Bible the word "all" means much less than with us, we must also remember that the Hebrew language has a very small vocabulary, and "the whole heaven" means simply *the whole sky.* We with our composite language borrow a word for it from the Greek, and say "the whole horizon," that is, the whole heaven, bounded by the line of the spectator's vision. So then here. Far and wide, in every direction, to the utmost reach of the beholder's gaze, no mountain was in sight. All was a surging waste of flood. But there is no idea here of the mountains of Auvergne, with the ashes of old-world volcanoes still reposing upon their craters, extinct from a time probably long anterior to the creation even of man. The mountains were those of the Noachian world, as limited as the Roman world of Luke ii. 1, or even more so.

(20) **Fifteen cubits upward.**—This apparently was the draught of the ark, computed after it had settled

(21) [a] And all flesh died that moved upon
the earth, both of fowl, and of cattle,
and of beast, and of every creeping
thing that creepeth upon the earth,
and every man: (22) all in whose nos-
trils *was* [1] the breath of life, of all
that *was* in the dry *land*, died.
(23) And every living substance was
destroyed which was upon the face of
the ground, both man, and cattle, and
the creeping things, and the fowl of
the heaven; and they were destroyed
from the earth: and [b] Noah only re-
mained *alive*, and they that *were* with
him in the ark. (24) And the waters pre-
vailed upon the earth an hundred and
fifty days.

CHAPTER VIII.—(1) And God re-
membered Noah, and every living thing,
and all the cattle that *was* with him in
the ark: and God made a wind to pass
over the earth, and the waters asswaged;
(2) the fountains also of the deep and the
windows of heaven were stopped, and
the rain from heaven was restrained;
(3) and the waters returned from off the
earth [2] continually: and after the end of
the hundred and fifty days the waters
were abated. (4) And the ark rested in

a Wisd. 10. 4.

1 Heb., *the breath of the spirit of life.*

b Wisd. 10. 4; 2 Pet. 2. 5.

2 Heb., *in going and returning.*

---

in the region of Ararat. Fifteen cubits would be about twenty-two feet, and as the ark floated onward without interruption until it finally grounded, there must have been this depth of water even on the highest summit in its course. Continuous rains for forty days and nights would scarcely produce so vast a mass of water, unless we suppose that the *adâmâh* was some low-lying spot of ground whither the waters from many regions flowed together; but this is negatived by the ark having travelled into Armenia. In England the whole average mean rainfall in a year is not more than twenty-eight or thirty inches in depth. If we suppose this amount to have fallen in every twenty-four hours, the total quantity would be about 100 feet. Such a rain would denude the mountains of all soil, uproot all trees, sweep away all buildings, dig out new courses for the rivers, completely alter the whole surface of the ground, and cover the lower lands with débris. Wherever there was any obstacle in their way, the waters would deepen in volume, and quickly burst a passage through it. But as they would be seeking the lower grounds during the whole forty days, it is difficult to understand how they could cover any of the heights to the depth of twenty-two feet, unless there were some cosmic convulsion (see Note on verse 11), by which the waters from the equator were carried towards the poles, and in this way there would be no difficulty in the ark being carried against the current of the Tigris and Euphrates up to the high lands of Armenia.

(23) **Every living substance.**—*Every thing that stood erect.* (See Note on verse 4.)

Upon the face of the ground.—The *adâmâh*, the portion subdued to his use by the *adam*, man.

(24) **Prevailed.**—Heb., *were strong*, as in verse 18. The rains lasted forty days; for one hundred and ten more days they still bore up the ark, and then it grounded. But though still mighty, they had by this time "abated" (see chap. viii. 3), inasmuch as, instead of covering the hills to the depth of nearly four fathoms, the ark now had touched dry land. Again, then, the narrative seems to give the personal experiences of some one in the ark.

VIII.

(1) **God.**—*Elohim.* On the Jehovistic theory, one would have expected Jehovah here. (See *Excursus.*)

Every living thing.—See Note on chap. vii. 14.

The waters asswaged.—Heb., *became still.* It is plain from this that the "strength" of the waters, described in chap. vii. 24, has reference to the violent currents, which still existed up to the end of the one hundred and fiftieth day, after which they ceased.

A wind (comp. the creative wind in chap. i. 2) began to blow as soon as the rains ceased, or even before, as must necessarily have been the case with so vast a disturbance of the atmosphere; but its special purpose of assuaging the waters only began when the downpour was over. This wind would affect the course of the ark, but scarcely so strongly as the currents of the water.

(3) **The waters returned from off the earth.**—This backward motion of the waters also seems to indicate that a vast wave from the sea had swept over the land, in addition to the forty days of rain.

Were abated.—Heb., *decreased.* Those in the ark would notice the changing current, and would know, by their being aground, that the flood was diminishing. But it was not till the first day of the tenth month that the tops of the mountains were seen. This slow abatement of the waters and their stillness, described in verse 1, makes it probable that the ark had grounded on some land-locked spot.

(4) **The seventh month, on the seventeenth day of the month.**—As the months had each thirty days (see Note on verse 14), this makes exactly 150 days (see chap. vii. 11). The seventh civil month would be Abib; and the *Speaker's Commentary* notices the following remarkable coincidences:—"On the 17th day of Abib the ark rested on Mount Ararat; on the 17th day of Abib the Israelites passed over the Red Sea; on the 17th day of Abib, Christ, our Lord, rose again from the dead."

Ararat.—If in chap. xi. 2 the Authorised Version is right in saying that the descendants of Noah travelled "from the east" to Shinar, this could not be the Ararat of Armenia. Moreover, we are told that the word in Assyrian means "highland," and thus may signify any hilly country. In the *Chaldean Genesis* the ark rests upon Nizir, a region to the east of Assyria, the highest peak of which, now named Elwend, is called in the cuneiform texts "the mountain of the world" (*Chaldean Genesis*, p. 307). The rendering, however, "from the east," is by no means certain, and many translate "eastward," and even the Authorised Version renders the word *east*, that is, eastward, in chap. xiii. 11. In 2 Kings xix. 37 "Ararat" is translated Armenia; but it is more correctly described in Jer. li. 27 as a country near Minni, that is, near Armenia. There are in this region two mountains of great altitude, the Aghri-Dagh and the Kara-Dagh, the highest of which is

the seventh month, on the seventeenth
day of the month, upon the mountains
of Ararat. (5) And the waters [1]decreased
continually until the tenth month: in
the tenth *month*, on the first *day* of the
month, were the tops of the mountains
seen.

(6) And it came to pass at the end of
forty days, that Noah opened the window
of the ark which he had made: (7) and
he sent forth a raven, which went forth
[2]to and fro, until the waters were dried
up from off the earth. (8) Also he sent
forth a dove from him, to see if the
waters were abated from off the face of
the ground; (9) but the dove found no
rest for the sole of her foot, and she re-
turned unto him into the ark, for the
waters *were* on the face of the whole
earth: then he put forth his hand, and
took her, and [3]pulled her in unto him
into the ark. (10) And he stayed yet
other seven days; and again he sent
forth the dove out of the ark; (11) and
the dove came in to him in the evening;
and, lo, in her mouth *was* an olive leaf
pluckt off: so Noah knew that the
waters were abated from off the earth.
(12) And he stayed yet other seven days;
and sent forth the dove; which returned
not again unto him any more.

(13) And it came to pass in the six hun-
dredth and first year, in the first *month*,
the first *day* of the month, the waters
were dried up from off the earth: and
Noah removed the covering of the ark,

1 Heb., *were in going and decreasing.*

2 Heb., *in going forth and returning.*

3 Heb., *caused her to come.*

17,260 feet above the sea-level; and naturally legend chooses this as the place where the ark settled. But the inspired narrative says that it rested "upon the mountains of Ararat," upon some chain of hills there, and seventy-three days afterwards Noah found himself surrounded by an amphitheatre of mountains, the word used in verse 5 being emphatic, and signifying "the tops of the mountains became distinctly visible," and not that they had just begun to emerge. For, doubtless, after so vast a flood, mists and vapours would for a long time prevail, and shut out the surrounding world from Noah's view.

The Targum of Onkelos and the Syriac translate "on the mountains of Carduchia." This range, which separates Armenia from Kurdistan, is regarded by many authorities as the hills really meant, because, as they are nearer the place whence the ark started, the difficulty regarding the course taken by it is not so insuperable.

(5) **Seen.**—See Note on verse 4.

(6) **Noah opened the window.**—Not the *zohar* of chap. vi. 16, but an aperture. He had waited forty days after seeing the heights around him rising clearly into the air, and then, impatient of the slow subsidence of the waters, Noah at last sent forth a raven to bring him some news of the state of the earth. This bird was chosen as one strong of flight, and also, perhaps, because anciently regarded as prophetic of the weather; besides this, it is easily tamed, and as Noah retained its mate he had security for its return. And so it seems to have done, for it is described as going "forth to and fro." Each night it returned to the ark, and probably to its old perch near the female. The *Chaldean Genesis* agrees with many commentators and the ancient versions in supposing that the raven did not return, finding abundant food in the floating dead bodies (*Chaldean Genesis*, p. 286); but this is contrary to the Hebrew. The versions must have had a negative in their copies, and have read, "which went forth, going, and not returning." The present Hebrew text is, however, consistent with itself; for it adds, "until the waters," &c. This must mean that as soon as the earth was dry this going to and fro ceased.

(8, 9) **He sent forth a dove . . .**—From the nature of its food, the raven had not brought back to Noah any special information; but as the dove feeds on vegetable products, he hopes that he shall learn by her means what is the state of "the ground," the low-lying *adâmâh.* But as this species of bird does not fly far from its home, except when assembled in vast numbers, it quickly returned, finding water all around. This proves that the ark had not settled upon a lofty eminence; for as it had been already aground 120 days, and as within another fortnight the waters had "abated from off the earth," it could only have been in some valley or plain among the mountains of Ararat that the waters were thus "on the face of the whole earth," the larger word, yet which certainly does not mean here the whole world, but only a very small region in the immediate neighbourhood of the ark. For, supposing that the raven was sent out one week before the dove, forty-seven days (see verse 6) would have elapsed since Noah beheld the glorious panorama of mountain heights all around, and seven days afterwards the dove brought him a fresh-plucked olive-leaf. Yet, literally, the words are, *for waters were upon the face of the whole earth.* Plainly these large terms in the language of the Bible are to be limited in their interpretation by the general tenor of its narratives. For a similar conclusive instance, comp. Exod. ix. 6 with *ibid.* 19, 20.

(10—12) **Again he sent forth the dove . . .**—When, after another week's delay, Noah again sent forth the dove, it remained away until "the time of evening," finding both food and ground on which it could alight near the ark. It was not till nightfall that it came home, bringing to him "an olive leaf pluckt off," or, possibly, *a fresh olive-leaf.* The olive-tree, which grows abundantly in Armenia, is said to vegetate under water; but what Noah wanted to learn was, not whether the topmost boughs were emerging from the flood, but whether the soil beneath was becoming free from water. Now, after a seven days' interval, when Noah again sent forth the dove, she did not return, "because the ground was dry." It is thus plain that the olive-tree had had plenty of time on some of the higher lands, while the flood was subsiding, to put forth new leaves. From this event the olive-leaf, thus sent by the regenerated earth to Noah in proof that she was ready to yield herself to him, has been ever since, among all mankind, the symbol of peace.

(13) **The first day of the month.**—It will be plain to any one studying the following table that this

and looked, and behold, the face of the
ground was dry. (14) And in the second
month, on the seven and twentieth day
of the month, was the earth dried.
(15) And God spake unto Noah, saying,
(16) Go forth of the ark, thou and thy
wife, and thy sons, and thy sons' wives
with thee. (17) Bring forth with thee
every living thing that *is* with thee,
of all flesh, *both* of fowl, and of cattle,
and of every creeping thing that creepeth
upon the earth; that they may breed
abundantly in the earth, and be fruitful
and multiply upon the earth. (18) And
Noah went forth, and his sons, and his
wife, and his sons' wives with him:
(19) every beast, every creeping thing,
and every fowl, *and* whatsoever creepeth
upon the earth, after their [1] kinds, went
forth out of the ark.

(20) And Noah builded an altar unto
the LORD; and took of every clean
beast, and of every clean fowl, and
offered burnt offerings on the altar.

1 Heb., *families.*

---

was exactly one month after the day on which Noah, for the third time, sent out the dove (verse 12):—

The flood commenced in the second month, called Marchesvan, on day 17.		
The waters prevail during 150 days = 5 months, unto month 7, day 17.		
Mountain-tops seen on month 10, day 1, *i.e.*, after	73	days.
Noah sends out raven at end of . .	40	„
Dove thrice sent out, at intervals of 7 days . . . . . . =	21	„
	134	„

But from the seventeenth day of the seventh month to the first day of the first month of the following year, there are:—

Of the seventh month	13	days.
Five months of 30 days each . . =	150	„
First day of new year	1	„
	164	„

It was thus very slowly that the earth returned to its normal state. The intervals of seven days between the sending forth of the birds prove that the division of time into weeks was fully established, and also suggests that religious observances were connected with it.

The covering of the ark.—The word is elsewhere used of the covering of skins for the Tabernacle (Exod. xxvi. 14; Num. iv. 25), and it has probably a similar meaning here. To have removed the solid framework of the roof would have been a very laborious task, and still more so to have broken up the roof itself. But as the asphalte employed for filling up the interstices between the beams in the hulk of the ark would have been difficult to manage for the roof, it was apparently protected from the rain by a covering, probably of skins sewn together.

No one can read the narrative without noticing that Noah is not only described as shut up within the ark, but as having very slight means of observing what was going on around. Had there been a deck, Noah would have known exactly the state of the flood, whereas, peeping only through the *zohar*, he seems to have been able to see but little, possibly because his sight was obstructed by the overhanging eaves of the roof. Thus the freshly-plucked olive-leaf was like a revelation to him. But when these skins were taken off, there were numerous apertures through which he could obtain an uninterrupted view, and he "looked, and, behold, the face of the *adâmâh* was dry."

(14) **In the second month, on the seven and twentieth day of the month.**—That is, fifty-seven days after Noah removed the covering, and a year and eleven days after the flood began. The word rendered "dried" at the end of this verse is different from that translated "dried up" and "dry" in verse 13, and marks a further stage in the process. It should be translated, *was thoroughly dry.*

There is in this year and eleven days a curious fact. It is reasonably certain that thirty days were reckoned to a month. But as a matter of fact, twelve lunar months do not make 360 days, but only about 354. Probably, therefore, the day of the new moon was often twice counted, as the last of the old month and the first of the new. But if to these 354 days we add 11, that is, from the 17th to the 27th of the second month. the result is exactly a full solar year of 365 days.

(15—19) **Go forth . . .**—At the end of exactly a solar year, thus curiously rectified, Noah, his family, and all the animals belonging to the Noachian world-circle are to leave the ark. The vast extent of the flood, and the total destruction of all that had existed before, is indicated by the repetition of the primæval command, in chap. i. 22, "to be fruitful and multiply upon the earth." Whatever the flood may have been with respect to the whole globe, it was to Noah and his race absolutely a new beginning of things.

(20) **Noah builded an altar unto the Lord** (*Jehovah*).—The account of this sacrificial act is said to have been an interpolation of the Jehovist. Really it forms an integral portion of the numerous traditions of the flood. Thus in the *Chaldean Genesis*, after the sending forth of a dove, a swallow, and a raven, we read (p. 280):—

> "I sent them forth to the four winds; I sacrificed a sacrifice; I built an altar on the peak of the mountain."

This extreme antiquity of sections ascribed to the Jehovist, and supposed to be an after-thought, is seriously detrimental to the whole theory.

One result of the flood was to sweep away all traces of the earthly paradise and of the subsequent abode of Adam; and it is probable also that Noah was removed far away from his previous home by the floating of the ark. Thus to him and his family it was a new earth, with no holy places, no spots hallowed by the past history of man. He therefore determines to consecrate the earth to Jehovah, who had been the object of the worship of his family since the days of Enos, and therefore builds an altar, the first mentioned in the Bible. By so doing he provided for future generations a central spot and sanctuary, round which their religious ideas would group themselves. The animals offered were probably the seventh of all clean kinds (see Note on

(21) And the LORD smelled [1]a sweet savour;
and the LORD said in his heart, I will
not again curse the ground any more for
man's sake; for the [a]imagination of
man's heart *is* evil from his youth;
neither will I again smite any more every
thing living, as I have done. (22) [2] While
the earth remaineth, seedtime and har-
vest, and cold and heat, and summer and
winter, and day and night shall not
cease.

CHAPTER IX.—(1) And God blessed
Noah and his sons, and said unto
them, [b] Be fruitful, and multiply, and
replenish the earth. (2) And the fear of
you and the dread of you shall be upon
every beast of the earth, and upon every
fowl of the air, upon all that moveth
upon the earth, and upon all the
fishes of the sea; into your hand
are they delivered. (3) Every moving
thing that liveth shall be meat for you;
even as the [c] green herb have I given
you all things. (4) [d] But flesh with the
life thereof, *which is* the blood thereof,

1 Heb., *a savour of rest.*

a ch. 6. 5. Matt. 15. 19.

2 Heb., *As yet all the days of the earth.*

b ch. 1. 28; & 8. 17.

c ch. 1. 29.

d Lev. 17. 14.

---

chap. vii. 2). With Noah's burnt offerings we must not connect any of the later Levitical ideas. Apparently it was a simple thank-offering, the dominant thought of which was the hallowing man's future life by commencing it with worship. It thus contained within it the presage that a better state of things had now begun. Subsequently the thank-offering became a feast, at which the offerer and his family partook of the victim as Jehovah's guests; and as God during this sacrifice gave Noah permission to eat flesh (chap. ix. 3), it is probable that such was the case now, and that the eating of flesh was inaugurated in this solemn way. We have, however, previously seen reason to believe that the flesh of animals had occasionally been eaten before, though not as an ordinary article of diet.

(21) **A sweet savour.**—Heb., *a smell of satisfaction.* The idea is not so much that the sacrifice gave God pleasure as that it caused Him to regard man with complacency. The anger at sin which had caused the flood was now over, and there was peace between heaven and earth.

Said in his heart.—Heb., *to his heart:* that is, *Jehovah determined with himself, came to the settled purpose.* (Comp. chap. xvii. 17.)

For the imagination of man's heart is evil from his youth.—See chap. vi. 5. There seems at first sight to be an inconsistency between the two passages, and the Jehovist is accused of here contradicting the Elohist. For in the former place man's inborn sinfulness is described as an aggravation of his offence, while here it is used as a reason for mercy. But it is a characteristic of the Bible that it states the two sides of every principle with abrupt simplicity, and most heresies have arisen from seizing upon one side only, and omitting the other from view. Man is one whose every imagination of the heart is only evil continually. (Comp. Matt. xv. 19.) In the antediluvian world, with death indefinitely postponed, these imaginations had been unrestrained, and had therefore led to habitual and inveterate sin; and so justice at last had smitten it. But when man strives against them, and sin is the result of infirmity, then mercy heals and grace strengthens the penitent. When man, therefore, began his renewed life by hallowing it with religion, God saw therein the pledge of a struggle on his part after holiness, and the proof that the world would never again become totally corrupt. In this changed state of things human weakness was a reason only for mercy, and God gave the promise that so long as the world shall last, so total a destruction of man and his works upon it shall never again take place by the same agency.

(22) **While the earth remaineth . . .**—The traditional interpretation of this verse among the Jews represents the year as divided into six seasons. But this is untenable; for in Palestine itself there are two seed times, the winter crops being put into the ground in October and November, and the summer crops in January and February. Really the verse describes those great alternations upon which the well-being of the earth depends, whether considered absolutely, as of light and darkness, cold and heat, or with reference to man's labours, as of sowing and harvesting; or relatively with respect to vegetation, winter being earth's time of rest, and summer that of its activity.

As regards these promises, Delitsch considers that they probably came to Noah as strong inward convictions in answer to his prayers during the sacrifice.

IX.

(1) **God blessed Noah.**—The blessing bestowed upon Noah, the second father of mankind, is exactly parallel to that given to our first father in Gen. i. 28, 29, ii. 16, 17, with a significant addition growing out of the history of the past. There is the same command to fill the world with human life, and the same promise that the fear of man shall rest upon the whole animated creation; but this grant of dominion is so extended that the animals are now given to man for his food. But just as there was a restriction as regards Adam's food, the fruit of the tree of knowledge being refused him, so now there is a prohibition against the eating of blood. The addition is the sanctity given to human life, with the evident object of guarding against such a disruption of the human race as was the result of Cain's murder of Abel. Thus, then, man starts afresh upon his task of subjugating the earth, with increased empire over the animal world, and with his own life more solemnly guarded and made secure.

(4) **But flesh. . . .**—The words are remarkable. "Only flesh in its soul, its blood, ye shall not eat." The Authorised Version is probably right in taking *blood* as in apposition to *soul,* which word means here the principle of animation, or that which causes an animal to live. This is God's especial gift; for He alone can bestow upon that aggregation of solids and fluids which we call a body the secret principle of life. Of this hidden life the blood is the representative, and while man is permitted to have the body for his food, as being the mere vessel which contains this life, the gift itself must go back to God, and the blood as its symbol be treated with reverence.

shall ye not eat. (5) And surely your
blood of your lives will I require; at the
hand of every beast will I require it,
and at the hand of man; at the hand
of every man's brother will I require the
life of man. (6) [a] Whoso sheddeth man's
blood, by man shall his blood be shed:
[b] for in the image of God made he man.
(7) And you, be ye fruitful, and multiply;
bring forth abundantly in the earth,
and multiply therein.

(8) And God spake unto Noah, and to
his sons with him, saying, (9) And I,
behold, I establish my covenant with
you, and with your seed after you;
(10) and with every living creature that
is with you, of the fowl, of the cattle,
and of every beast of the earth with
you; from all that go out of the ark, to
every beast of the earth. (11) And [c] I
will establish my covenant with you;
neither shall all flesh be cut off any
more by the waters of a flood; neither
shall there any more be a flood to
destroy the earth. (12) And God said,
This *is* the token of the covenant which
I make between me and you and every
living creature that *is* with you, for
perpetual generations: (13) I do set my
bow in the cloud, and it shall be for a
token of a covenant between me and the
earth. (14) [d] And it shall come to pass,
when I bring a cloud over the earth,
that the bow shall be seen in the cloud:
(15) and I will remember my covenant,
which *is* between me and you and every
living creature of all flesh; and the
waters shall no more become a flood to
destroy all flesh. (16) And the bow shall
be in the cloud; and I will look upon it,
that I may remember the everlasting
covenant between God and every living
creature of all flesh that *is* upon the
earth. (17) And God said unto Noah,

a Matt. 26. 52; Rev. 13. 10.

b ch. 1. 27.

c Isa. 54. 9.

B.C. 2348.

d Ecclus. 43. 11, 12.

---

(5) **Your blood of your lives. . .**—This verse should be translated: "And surely your blood, *which is* for your souls, will I require (*i.e.*, avenge); from every beast will I require it, and from man: even from a man's brother will I require the soul of man," as from Cain. "Your blood, which is for your souls," means that it is the means for the maintenance of the animal life within them. As it is, then, the support of man's life, an animal which sheds it becomes guilty, and must be slain; and still more must those animals be destroyed which prey upon man. Thus there is a command given for the extirpation of the carnivora at the time when the more peaceful animals had just been saved. The last clause literally is . . . *at the hand of man, at the hand of one that is his brother, will I require the soul of man.* This has nothing to do with the avenger of blood. The near kinsman is here the murderer, and the commandment requires that even such an one should not be spared.

(6) **By man . . .**—This penalty of life for life is not to be left to natural law, but man himself, in such a manner and under such safeguards as the civil law in each country shall order, is to execute the Divine command. And thus protected from violence, both of man and beast, and with all such terrible crimes forbidden as had polluted Adam's beginning, Noah in peace and security is to commence afresh man's great work upon earth.

(9) **I, behold, I establish my covenant . . .** The covenant between God and man is thus solemnly introduced as Elohim's personal act. No covenant is mentioned as existing between Elohim and the antediluvian world; but distinctly now there is a step onward in all respects, and man, in the renovated earth after the flood, is brought nearer to God by being admitted into covenant with Him. And not only is man included in the covenant, but, first, those animals which had been with Noah in the ark; and, secondly, those which had not been admitted there. For the words of verse 10 are: "From all that go out of the ark unto every beast of the earth" (the larger world). To such straits are those reduced who hold to the theory of a universal deluge, that Kalisch argues that it means the fish, as if fishes would be destroyed by a second flood any more than they were by the first. Plainly, the words imply the existence of a larger world-sphere than that in connection with Noah, and give the assurance that not only those now providentially preserved, but the animals everywhere, shall never again be in danger of a similar extinction.

(12) **This is the token of the covenant.**—The word rendered "token" really means *sign,* and is a term that has met with very unfortunate treatment in our Version, especially in the New Testament, where—as, for instance, in St. John's Gospel—it is too frequently translated *miracle.* Its meaning will be best seen by examining some of the places where it occurs: *e.g.,* Gen. xvii. 11; Exod. iii. 12, xii. 13, xiii. 16; Num. xvii. 10; Josh. ii. 12; Job xxi. 29; Pss. lxv. 8, lxxxvi. 17, cxxxv. 9; Isa. xliv. 25. In the majority of these places the sign, or token, is some natural occurrence, but in its higher meaning it is a proof or indication of God's immediate working. On proper occasions, therefore, it will be supernatural, because the proof of God's direct agency will most fitly be some act such as God alone can accomplish. More frequently it is something natural. Thus the sign to the shepherds of the birth of a Saviour, who was "the anointed Jehovah" (Luke ii. 11), was their finding in a manger a babe wrapped in swaddling clothes, a thing of the most simple and ordinary kind. We may dismiss, then, all such curious speculations as that no rain fell before the flood, or that some condition was wanting necessary for producing this glorious symbol. What Noah needed was a guarantee and a memorial which, as often as rain occurred, would bring back to his thoughts the Divine promise; and such a memorial was best taken from the natural accompaniments of rain. We may further notice with Maimonides that the words are not, as in our version, "I do set," but *my bow I have set in the cloud:* that is, the bow which God set in the cloud on that day of creation in which He

This *is* the token of the covenant, which
I have established between me and all
flesh that *is* upon the earth.
(18) And the sons of Noah, that went
forth of the ark, were Shem, and Ham,
and Japheth: and Ham *is* the father of
[1] Canaan. (19) These *are* the three sons
of Noah: and of them was the whole
earth overspread.
(20) And Noah began *to be* an husband-
man, and he planted a vineyard: (21) and
he drank of the wine, and was drunken;
and he was uncovered within his tent.
(22) And Ham, the father of Canaan, saw
the nakedness of his father, and told his
two brethren without. (23) And Shem
and Japheth took a garment, and laid
it upon both their shoulders, and went
backward, and covered the nakedness of
their father; and their faces *were* back-
ward, and they saw not their father's
nakedness. (24) And Noah awoke from
his wine, and knew what his younger
son had done unto him. (25) And he said,

Cursed *be* Canaan; a servant of ser-
vants shall he be unto his brethren.

1 Heb., *Chenaan.*

---

imposed upon air and water those laws which produce this phenomenon, is now to become the sign of a solemn compact made with man by God, whereby He gives man the assurance that neither himself nor his works shall ever again be swept away by a flood.

But a covenant is a contract between two parties; and what, we may ask, was the undertaking on man's part? The Talmud enumerates several of the chief moral laws, which it supposes that Noah was now bound to observe. More truly it was a covenant of grace, just as that in chap. vi. 18 was one simply of mercy. What then might have been granted simply as a promise on God's part is made into a covenant, not merely for man's greater assurance, but also to indicate that it was irrevocable. Promises are revocable, and their fulfilment may depend upon man's co-agency; a covenant is irrevocable, and under no circumstances will the earth again be destroyed by water.

The rainbow appears in the *Chaldean Genesis*, but in a heathenish manner:—

> "From afar the great goddess (Istar) at her approach
> Lifted up the mighty arches (*i.e.*, the rainbow) which Anu had created as his glory.
> The crystal of those gods before me (*i.e.*, the rainbow) never may I forget."—*Chald. Gen.*, p. 287.

(18) **Ham is the father of Canaan.**—Though human life had thus begun again upon a firmer footing, yet evil and discord were soon to reappear, though in a milder form. No brother sheds a brother's blood, but in the next generation sin breaks forth afresh, and the human family is disunited thereby, the descendants of Canaan taking the place of the Cainites—without, indeed, their striking gifts, but nevertheless as a race foremost in trade and commerce. After enumerating the three sons of Noah, we are told: "Of"—more correctly, *from*—"them was the whole earth overspread," that is, *peopled.*

(20, 21) **Noah began to be an husbandman.**—Rather, *Noah, being a husbandman* (Heb., *a man of the adâmâh*), *began to plant a vineyard.* Noah had always been a husbandman: it was the cultivation of the vine, still abundant in Armenia, that was new. Scarcely aware, perhaps, of the intoxicating qualities of the juice which he had allowed to ferment, he drank to excess, and became the first example of the shameful effects of intemperance.

(21) **He was uncovered** is, literally, *he uncovered himself.* It was no accident, but a wilful breach of modesty.

(22, 23) **Ham . . . saw . . . and told.**—The sin lay not in seeing, which might be unintentional, but in telling, especially if his purpose was to ridicule his father. His brothers, with filial piety, "take a garment," the loose outer robe or cloak enveloping the whole body, and with reverent delicacy walk backwards, and lay it upon their father's person.

(24) **Noah . . . knew what his younger son had done unto him.**—Heb., *his son, the little one.* This can only mean his youngest son. So it is applied to Benjamin in chaps. xlii. 34, xliii. 29, and to David in 1 Sam. xvi. 11, where the words literally are, *there remaineth yet the little one.* Now Ham was not the youngest son, but Japheth; and it is not Ham who is cursed, but Canaan. So far from Ham being accursed, his descendants were building mighty cities, such as Egyptian Thebes, Nineveh, and Babylon, were rearing palaces, digging canals, organising governments, and founding empires at a time when the descendants of Japheth were wandering over Europe with no better weapons than implements of flint and bone. The application of the curse to Ham seems to have been suggested to commentators by the degradation of the African race in modern times, and especially by the prevalence of negro slavery: but anciently the converse was the case, and for centuries the Egyptians, a Hamite race, made the Israelites serve them.

We must not extend, therefore, to Ham the curse pronounced upon Canaan. But what had Canaan done to deserve it? As *the son, the little one,* was not Ham, so certainly it was not Japheth, but probably it was Canaan. He was the youngest son of Ham, and in Hebrew "son" is occasionally used for grandson (Gen. xxix. 5, xxxi. 55), and so he might be described as Noah's youngest son, being the youngest member of his family. Origen quotes a tradition that Canaan was the first who saw Noah's exposure, and that he told it to his father. Aben Ezra says that Canaan had done worse than mock, though the Scripture does not in words reveal his crime. With some such surmise we must be content; and the meaning seems to be, "Noah awoke from his wine, and knew what (Canaan) his youngest son (or grandson) had done unto him; and it was a deed so shameless that he said, 'Cursed be Canaan.'"

(25) **Cursed be Canaan.**—The prophecy of Noah takes the form of a poem, like Lamech's boast in chap. iv. In it Ham is passed over in silence, as though his unfilial conduct, recorded in verse 22, made him unworthy of a blessing, while it was not so wicked as to bring on him a curse. The whole weight of Noah's displeasure falls on Canaan, whose degraded position among the nations is thrice insisted upon.

A servant of servants. That is, the most abject of slaves. This was fulfilled in the conquest of

(26) And he said,
Blessed *be* the LORD God of Shem;
and Canaan shall be [1] his servant.
(27) God shall [2] enlarge Japheth, and
he shall dwell in the tents of Shem;
and Canaan shall be his servant.
(28) And Noah lived after the flood
three hundred and fifty years. (29) And
all the days of Noah were nine hundred
and fifty years: and he died.

[1] Or, *servant to them.*

[2] Or, *persuade.*

CHAPTER X. — (1) Now these *are*
the generations of the sons of Noah,
Shem, Ham, and Japheth: and
unto them were sons born after the
flood.

Canaan by Joshua, but the race had nevertheless a great future before it. The Hittites were one of the foremost nations of antiquity, and the Sidonians, Tyrians, and Phœnicians were such famous traders, that Canaanite is in our version translated *merchant*, without even a note in the margin (*e.g.*, Prov. xxxi. 24). But the whole race was enslaved by one of the most terrible and degrading forms of idolatry, and as Shem's blessing is religious, so possibly is Canaan's curse. Lenormant (Manual of Ancient History of the East, ii. 219) says of their religion, "No other people ever rivalled them in the mixture of bloodshed and debauchery with which they thought to honour the Deity." He also quotes Creuzer, who says, "The Canaanite religion silenced all the best feelings of human nature, degraded men's minds by a superstition alternately cruel and profligate, and we may seek in vain for any influence for good it could have exercised on the nation."

(26) **Blessed be Jehovah.**—The greatness of Shem's blessing is shown by its taking the form of a hymn of praise to Jehovah, the personal God; and the patriarch's fervent outburst of thanksgiving was a presage of the hallelujahs that were to arise unto God from all mankind for the birth of that son of Shem in whom all nations were to be blessed. The following words should be translated, *And let Canaan be their servant*, the servant both of Shem and Japheth. (See margin.)

(27) **God shall enlarge Japheth.**—First, the Deity is here *Elohim*, following upon *Jehovah* in the preceding verse, and that with extraordinary exactness. Jehovah has never been the special name of the Deity worshipped by the race of Japheth, though doubtless it is the Greek *Zeus* and the Latin *Jove*. But it soon became the proper title of God in covenant with the race of Shem. It is plainly impossible to divide this most ancient poem into Elohistic and Jehovistic sections, and the theory, however plausible occasionally, fails in a crucial place like this. Next, there is a play upon the name of Japheth, or rather, *Yepheth*, our translators having made the same mistake as in changing Hebel into Abel. The Hebrew is *Yapheth Elohim l'Yepheth*, "God enlarge the enlarger" (not "God shall enlarge"). While, then, it is the special blessing of Shem that through him the voice of thanksgiving is to ascend to Jehovah, the God of grace; it is Elohim, the God of nature and of the universe, who gives to Japheth wide extension and the most numerous posterity. If the most ancient civilisation and the earliest empires in Egypt and on the Tigris were Hamite, the great world-powers of history, the Chaldean, the Medo-Persian, the Greek and Roman, the Hindoo, were all of Japhetic origin, as are also the modern rulers of mankind.

He shall dwell in the tents of Shem.—(Rather, *let him dwell*). In one sense Shem now dwells in the tents of Japheth: for the Jews, the noblest representatives of Shem, dwell dispersed in Aryan countries; and except in the Arabian peninsula, once Cushite, the Shemites have no home of their own. But the religious privileges of their race now belong to the family of Japheth. Carried by Jewish missionaries, like St. Paul, throughout the Roman world, they have become the property of the leading members of the Aryan race; and thus Japheth takes possession of the tents which by right of primogeniture belonged to Shem. For "to dwell in the tents of Shem" is not so much to share them as to own them; and if the Jews retain some degree of faith, it has lost with them all expansive power; while the right interpretation of their Scriptures, and as well the maintenance as the propagation of the religion of their Messiah, are now in the hands of the descendants of Japheth. Yet Shem does not lose all pre-eminence: for again we read—

Canaan shall be his servant (rather, *their*).—If Shem lose the foremost place of primogeniture, he is still a brother, and Canaan but a slave.

(29) **All the days of Noah.**—While Noah attained to the same age as the antediluvian patriarchs, 950 years, human life was fast diminishing. The whole life-time of Shem was 600 years; that of Peleg, a few generations afterwards, only 239. After him only one man, Terah, is described as living more than 200 years, and of his age there is great doubt. (See Note on chap. xi. 32.) Thus before Shem's death the age of man was rapidly shortening, and things were settling down to that condition in which they are set before us in profane literature.

X.

THE ETHNOLOGICAL TABLE (chaps. x. 1—xi. 9).

These are the generations (the *tôldôth*) **of the sons of Noah.**—The importance of this "table of the nations" can scarcely be over-estimated; and while numerous exceptions were taken only a few years ago to many of its details, the vast increase of human knowledge in recent times has proved not merely its general credibility, but the truth of such startling facts as the possession by the race of Ham not only of the Arabian peninsula, but of the country on the Tigris and Euphrates. Its position is very remarkable. It stands at the end of grand traditional records of the mighty past, but belongs to a period long subsequent, giving us a picture of the division of the world at a time when nations and kingdoms had become settled, and their boundaries fixed; and it couples this with the confusion of tongues, difference of language being the great factor in this breaking up of the human race. Now, it is important to remember that it is not a genealogical table. It concerns peoples, and not individuals, and no names are mentioned which were not represented by political organisations. Generally even the names are not those of men, but of tribes or nations. We must also bear in mind that it works *backwards*, and not forwards. Taking the nations at some particular time, it groups them together, and classifies them according to the line to which they belonged.

As regards the order, it begins with Japheth, the

(2) [a] The sons of Japheth; Gomer, and Magog, and Madai, and Javan, and Tubal, and Meshech, and Tiras. (3) And the sons of Gomer; Ashkenaz, and Riphath, and Togarmah. (4) And the sons of Javan; Elishah, and Tarshish, Kittim,

a 1 Chron. 1. 5.

youngest son—for never was there a translation more opposed to the undeviating rule of such sentences than that of our version in chap. x. 21. "Shem . . . the brother of Japheth the elder," instead of "Shem, the elder brother of Japheth." But Japheth is here placed first because so little was known of the nations sprung from him. It gives, moreover, the mere first division into main lines, and then, in spite of the grand future that awaited his descendants, it dismisses them in brief haste to their homes on the Black and Mediterranean seas. It next takes Ham. Now, Ham was to the family of Noah what Cain was to that of Adam: first in all worldly accomplishments, last in all the gifts of piety. Settling upon the Nile, the Tigris, and Euphrates, his progeny raised up mighty cities, while the Japhethites were wandering in barbarous hordes over Europe, and the Shemites were pasturing their cattle upon the chalk-downs of Syria; whence, nevertheless, they soon came to do battle with the Hamites for the possession of Mesopotamia. Of the Hamites, it brings the history down to the time of their settlement in Canaan, but as it mentions Sodom and Gomorrah as still standing, the document must be prior to the time of the destruction of those cities, eighteen centuries and more before Christ; while, as it describes the Canaanites as even then in possession of Palestine, and as formed into tribes in much the same way as just before the time of Moses, it is evident that a much longer period must have elapsed between the flood and the birth of Abraham than is supposed in the ordinary chronology put in the margin of our Bibles. As the line of Shem was to be traced in subsequent *tôldôth*, it is not carried down so far as that of Ham, but stops at a great dividing line, at which the family breaks up into the race of Joktan and that of Peleg. To the former it ascribes thirteen nations, while the race of Peleg is left for future histories. The names of the Joktanite tribes also indicate the lapse of a lengthened period of time, as they abound in Arabic peculiarities.

(1) **Shem, Ham, and Japheth.**—This is the undeviating arrangement of the three brothers. (See Note on chaps. ix. 24, x. 21.)

(2) **The sons of Japheth.**—Of these, seven main divisions are enumerated, some of which are subsequently sub-divided; they are—

1. **Gomer,** whose name reappears in the Cimmerians. Their original settlement was between Magog and Madai, that is, between the Scythians and the Medes. After remaining some time on the Caspian and Black Seas, on which latter they have left their name in the Crimea, a powerful branch of them struck across the centre of Russia, and, skirting the Baltic, became the Cimbri of Denmark (whence the name of the Chersonesus Cimbrica, given to Jutland), the Cymry of Wales, &c. Generally they are the race to which the name is given of Celts.

2. **Magog.** The Scythians, who once possessed the country north and south of the Caucasus. The Russians are their modern representatives, being descended from the Sarmatians, a Scythic race, with a small admixture of Median blood.

3. **Madai.** The Medes, who dwelt to the south and south-west of the Caspian. *Mada*, in the Accadian language, means *land*, and it was in the Median territory that Kharsak-Kurra, "the mountain of the East," was situated, on which the Accadians believed the ark to have rested, whence possibly Media took its name, being "the land" above all others (*Chald. Gen.*, p. 196).

4. **Javan,** that is, Ionia, the land of the Greeks.

5. **Tubal.** The Tibareni, on the south-east of the Black Sea.

6. **Meshech.** The Moschi, a people of Colchis and Armenia.

7. **Tiras.** According to Josephus and the Targum, the Thracians. Other races have been suggested, but this is probably right; and as the Getae, the ancestors of the Goths, were Thracians, this would make the Scandinavian race the modern representatives of Tiras.

In this enumeration the race of Japheth is described as occupying Asia Minor, Armenia, the countries to the west as far as the Caspian Sea, and thence northward to the shores of the Black Sea. Subsequently it spread along the northern shores of the Mediterranean and over all Europe. But though unnoticed by the writer, its extension was equally remarkable towards the east. Parthia, Bactria, the Punjab, India, are equally Japhethite with Germany, Greece, and Rome; and in Sanscrit literature the Aryan first showed that genius, which, omitting the greatest of all books, the Semitic Bible, has made this race the foremost writers in the world.

(3) **Gomer** has three main divisions:—

1. **Ashkenaz,** a region in the neighbourhood of Armenia (Jer. li. 27), whence, following the course of Japhethite migration, the race seems to have wandered into Germany. The derivations are all most uncertain; but the Jews call the Germans Ashkenazites, and are probably right.

2. **Riphath,** in 1 Chron. i. 6, is called Diphath (see Dodanim, below). Riphath is probably right, and the inhabitants of the Riphæan Mountains (the Carpathians?) are the people meant. They were Celts.

3. **Togarmah.** Certainly Armenia.

(4) **Javan** has four main divisions:—

1. **Elishah,** a maritime people of Greece. Traces of the name occur in Aeolis and in Elis, a district of the Peloponessus. Some boldly identify with Hellas. The isles of Elishah are mentioned in Ezek. xxvii. 7.

2. **Tarshish.** At so early a period this could scarcely be Tartessus, but is more probably the Tyrseni, or Tyrrheni, a race once powerful in Italy, Corsica, Sardinia, and finally in Spain. Probably Tartessus, at the mouth of the Guadalquiver, in Spain, was founded by them, and took from them its name. At this time they were apparently a small tribe of the Javanites; but while Elishah followed the sea-coast and colonised Greece, Tarshish took a course so far inland to the north of the Danube that it did not reach the sea until it had come to the northern districts of Italy.

3. **Kittim.** A plural, like Madai. The Kittim were a maritime race, who colonised Cyprus, the chief city of which was Kitium, and probably other islands and coast-districts of the Mediterranean. There was a Kitium also in Macedonia; and Alexander is called King of the Kittim in 1 Macc. i. 1.

4. **Dodanim.** Another plural. The right reading is probably Rodanim, as in many MSS. in 1 Chron. i. 7, and in the LXX., and the Samaritan here. R and D are so constantly interchanged in proper names, owing to the similarity of their shape, that no depen-

and Dodanim. (5) By these were the
isles of the Gentiles divided in their
lands; every one after his tongue, after
their families, in their nations.
(6) [a] And the sons of Ham; Cush, and
Mizraim, and Phut, and Canaan. (7) And
the sons of Cush; Seba, and Havilah,
and Sabtah, and Raamah, and Sab-
techah: and the sons of Raamah;
Sheba, and Dedan. (8) And Cush begat
Nimrod: he began to be a mighty one
in the earth. (9) He was a mighty
hunter before the LORD: wherefore it
is said, Even as Nimrod the mighty
hunter before the LORD. (10) And the
beginning of his kingdom was [1] Babel,

[a] 1 Chron. 1. 8.

[1] Gr., *Babylon.*

---

dence can be placed upon the reading. The Rodanim would be the Rhodians.

(5) **Isles of the Gentiles.**—The word rendered "isles" means *any maritime region.* As there were no Gentiles at this time, the phrase should be translated "the coast-lands of the nations."

(6) **Ham.**—Many derive this word from a Hebrew root, and explain it as signifying *hot, sunburnt,* and so swarthy. Japheth they connect with a word signifying *to be fair;* and so Ham is the progenitor of dark races, Japheth of those of a fair complexion, while the olive-coloured spring from Shem. More probably it is *Chemi,* the old name of Egypt, "the land of Ham" (Ps. lxxviii. 51), called by Plutarch Chemia, and was taken from the *black* colour of the soil.

The Hamites are grouped in four principal divisions:—

1. **Cush.** Aethiopia, but not that of Africa, but of Asia. The home of the Cushites was on the Tigris and Euphrates, where Nimrod raised them to great power. Thence they spread into the southern peninsula of Arabia, and crossing the Red Sea at a later date, colonised Nubia and Abyssinia. In the Bible Cush is watered by the Gihon (Gen. ii. 13); and Zipporah, the wife of Moses, and daughter of a priest of Midian, is in Num. xii. 1 called a Cushite. Their high rank in old time is marked by the place held by them in the *Iliad* of Homer.

2. **Mizraim.** Egypt. In form the word is a dual, and may point to the division of the country into Upper and Lower Egypt. If we choose to interpret a Hamite word by a Hebrew root, it may signify the *narrowed land,* but it is safer to leave these words till increased knowledge shall enable us to decide with some security upon their meaning. For the ancient name of Mizraim see verse 6, and for its extent see verse 14. From the study of the skulls and bodies of a large number of mummies Brugsch-Bey in his recent history has come to the conclusion that the ancient Egyptians did not belong to any African race, but to the great Caucasian family, "but not of the Pelasgic or Semitic branches, but of a third, Cushite." He adds that the cradle of the Egyptian nation must be sought in Central Asia.

3. **Phut.** The Lybians of North Africa.

4. **Canaan.** See Note on verses 15—19.

(7) **Sons of Cush.**—Of Cush there are five sub-divisions, of which one is again parted into two. These are—

1. **Seba.**—The name at this time of an Arabian tribe, which subsequently migrated into Africa, and settled in Meroë, which, according to Josephus, still bore in his days this appellation. They also left their name on the eastern side of the Red Sea, not far to the north of the Straits of Bab-el-Mandeb.

2. **Havilah,** upon the river Pison (chap. ii. 11), was undoubtedly a region of Arabia, situated probably upon the Persian Gulf. Havilah is again mentioned in verse 29.

3. **Sabtah.**—Probably Hadramaut, in Arabia Felix. (See Note on verse 26.)

4. **Raamah,** on the Persian Gulf, was divided into Dedan upon the south-west and Sheba in the centre, while Havilah lay upon the north-west side. Of these, Sheba subsequently rose to fame as the kingdom of the Himyarite Arabs.

5. **Sabtechah.**—Apparently still more to the south of Dedan, but placed by some on the eastern side of the gulf.

Thus, then, at the time when this table was written the southern half of Arabia was Cushite, and a swarthy race of men is still found there, especially in Yemen and Hadramaut, far darker than the light brown Arabians. Migrating from place to place along the sea-shore, the passage of the Cushites into Nubia and Abyssinia was easy. But their chief home was, at this period, in Mesopotamia, and the cuneiform inscriptions have now revealed their long struggle there with men of the race of Shem.

(8) **Cush begat Nimrod.**—This does not mean that Nimrod was the son of Cush, but only that Cush was his ancestor. In the days of Nimrod population had become numerous, and whereas each tribe and family had hitherto lived in independence, subject only to the authority of the natural head, he was able, by his personal vigour, to reduce several tribes to obedience, to prevail upon them to build and inhabit cities, and to consolidate them into one body politic.

He began to be a mighty one.—Heb., *gibbor*= warrior. (See Note on chap. vi. 4.) The LXX. translate *giant,* whence in fable Nimrod is identified with the Orion of the Greeks, in Hebrew Chesil, and in Arabic Jabbar; but this identification is entirely fanciful, as is probably the idea that he is the Izdubar of the Chaldean legends (*Chald. Genesis,* p. 321). Following the unscholarlike method of explaining Hamite names by Hebrew roots, commentators interpret Nimrod as meaning *rebel;* but the Biblical narrative speaks rather in his commendation, and the foolish traditions which blacken his reputation date only from the time of Josephus. Mr. Sayce connects his name with the Accadian town Amarda (*Chald. Gen.,* p. 191).

(9) **He was a mighty hunter.**—When men were still leading a pastoral life, and were but poorly armed, the war with wild beasts was a most important and dangerous occupation. Probably from single combats with fierce animals, Nimrod, now recognised as a public benefactor, was led to organise hunts upon a large scale, and so, like Romulus, became the chief of a band of the most spirited and vigorous shepherds. With their aid, he next undertook the more serious duty of introducing order and rule among men who had hitherto lived in scattered groups without control, and without the means of suppressing feuds and of punishing deeds of violence.

Before the Lord.—A strong superlative. (Comp. chap. xiii. 13.)

(10) **The beginning of his kingdom.**—Nimrod's empire began with the cities enumerated in this verse, and thence extended into Assyria, as is mentioned in

and Erech, and Accad, and Calneh, in
the land of Shinar. (11) Out of that land
[1] went forth Asshur, and builded Nine-
veh, and [2] the city Rehoboth, and Calah,
(12) and Resen between Nineveh and Ca-
lah: the same *is* a great city. (13) And
Mizraim begat Ludim, and Anamim,
and Lehabim, and Naphtuhim, (14) and

1 Or, *he went out into Assyria.*

2 Or, *the streets of the city.*

verse 11. First, then, he established his sovereignty "in the land of Shinar:" that is, in Babylonia, the lower portion of Mesopotamia, as distinguished from Assyria, the upper portion. It is called *Sumir* in the cuneiform inscriptions. In Micah v. 6 Babylonia is called "the land of Nimrod." His cities there were four.

Babel.—That is, *Bab-ili,* "the gate of God," the literal translation in Assyrian of its previous Accadian name, Ca-dimirra (*Chald. Gen.*, p. 168). In chap. xi. 9 the word is derisively derived from a Hebrew root meaning *confusion*, because of the confusion of tongues there.

Erech.—"At the time of the opening of the Izdubar legends, the great city of the south of Babylonia was Urak, called in Genesis Erech" (*Chald. Gen.*, p. 192). It was ravaged by Kudur-nankhunte, king of Elam, in the year B.C. 2280, according to an inscription of Assurbanipal (B.C. 670). It lies about thirty leagues to the south-east of Babylon, and is now called Warka. From the numerous mounds and remains of coffins discovered there, it is supposed to have been the early burial-place of the Assyrian kings. (See also Rawlinson's *Ancient Monarchies*, i., pp. 18, 156.)

Accad.—This name, which was meaningless fifty years ago, is now a household word in the mouth of Assyriologers; for in deciphering the cuneiform literature it was found that many of the works, especially in the library of Sargon, were translations from an extinct language; and as these were deciphered it gradually became evident that before any inhabitants of the Semitic stock had entered Chaldea it had been peopled by the Accadians, a black race, who had been "the builders of its cities, the inventors of the cuneiform system of writing, and the founders of the culture and civilisation afterwards borrowed by the Semites" (*Chald. Gen.*, p. 19). This Sargon, who was king of Agané, in Babylonia, about B.C. 1800, is of course a different person from the Ninevite Sargon mentioned in Isa. xx. 1, who also was the founder of a noble library about B.C. 721; and as the Accadian language was already in his days passing away, this earlier or Babylonian Sargon caused translations to be made, especially of those works in which the Accadians had recorded their astronomical and astrological observations, and placed them in his library at Agané. Previously also "Semitic translations of Accadian works had been made for the library of Erech, one of the earliest seats of Semitic power" (*Ibid*, p. 21). Mr. Sayce places the conquest of Shinar by the Semites at some period two or three thousand years before the Christian era, and thus the founding of these cities and the empire of the Accadians goes back to a still more remote date, especially as the struggle between them and their conquerors was a very prolonged one (*Ibid*, p. 20).

Calneh.—The Calno of Isa. x. 9, where the LXX. read, "Have I not taken the region above Babylon and Khalanné, where the tower was built?" It was thus opposite Babylon, and the site of the tower of Babel (see *Chald. Gen.*, p. 75, and Note on chap. xi. 9). The other place suggested, Ctesiphon, is not in Shinar, but in Assyria.

(11, 12) **Out of that land went forth Asshur.**—So the LXX., Syriac, and Vulg.; but the Targum and most modern authorities rightly translate, "Out of that land he went forth into Assyria." We have here nothing to do with Asshur the son of Shem (see verse 22), but are occupied with Nimrod and the Hamites, who, after firmly establishing themselves in Babylonia, subsequently extended their influence northward. This is confirmed by the cuneiform inscriptions, which prove that the southern portion of Mesopotamia was the chief seat of the Accadians, while in Assyria they came at an early date into collision with the Shemites, who drove them back, and ultimately subjugated them everywhere. It is not necessary to suppose that this spread of Hamite civilisation northward was the work of Nimrod personally; if done by his successors, it would, in Biblical language, be ascribed to its prime mover.

The Assyrian cities were:—

1. **Nineveh.**—So happily situated on the Tigris that it outstripped the more ancient Babylon, and for centuries even held it in subjection.

2. **The city Rehoboth.**—Translated by some *Rehoboth-Ir*, but with more probability by others, "the suburbs of the city:" that is, of Nineveh, thus denoting already the greatness of that town.

3. **Calah.**—A city rebuilt by Assur-natzir-pal, the father of Shalmaneser, and interesting as one of the places where the Assyrian kings established libraries (*Chald. Gen.*, p. 26). The ruins are still called Nimroud.

4. **Resen.**—The "spring-head." Of this town nothing certain is known. Canon Rawlinson places it at Selamiyah (*Anc. Mon.*, i. 204), a large village half-way between Nineveh and Calah. As the vast ruins scattered throughout Mesopotamia are those of Assyrian buildings, Resen, though "a great city" in Hamite times, might easily pass into oblivion, if never rebuilt by the conquerors.

(13, 14) With Mizraim are connected seven inferior African races, the names of which are given in the plural, namely:—

1. The **Ludim.**—There were two races of this name: one Semitic, descended from Lud, the son of Shem (verse 22), and mentioned in Isa. lxvi. 19; the other Hamite, and subject to the Pharaohs (Jer. xlvi. 9; Ezek. xxx. 5). They seem to have inhabited the Nile valley, but their exact position is unknown.

2. The **Anamim.**—Knobel gives some reasons for supposing this race to have inhabited the Delta.

3. The **Lehabim.**—Probably the same as the Lubim of 2 Chron. xii. 3, xvi. 8; Dan. xi. 43; Nahum iii. 9. Their home was on the western side of the Delta.

4. The **Naphtuhim.**—Knobel explains these as "the people of Phthah, the deity worshipped at Memphis." If so, they were the true Egyptians, as Egypt is Kah-Phthah, "the land of Phthah," or more correctly, according to Canon Cook, Ai-Capth. (See Note on Capthorim.)

5. The **Pathrusim.**—People of Pathros, or Upper Egypt. According to Canon Cook, Pa-t-res means "the land of the south."

6. The **Casluhim.**—Probably the people of Cassiotis, a mountainous district to the east of Pelusium.

7. The **Philistim.**—The word Philistine means *emigrant*, and is translated *alien, foreigner*, by the LXX.

Pathrusim, and Casluhim, (out of whom came Philistim,) and Caphtorim. (15) And Canaan begat [1] Sidon his firstborn, and Heth, (16) and the Jebusite, and the Amorite, and the Girgasite, (17) and the Hivite, and the Arkite, and the Sinite, (18) and the Arvadite, and the Zemarite, and the Hamathite: and afterward were the families of the Canaanites spread abroad. (19) And the border of

[1] Heb., *Tzidon.*

We are here told that they came into Palestine as colonists from the Casluhim; but in Jer. xlvii. 4, Amos ix. 7, they are described as a colony from Caphtor. Probably the first Philistine settlers in Gerar (Gen. xxvi. 1), and in the towns conquered by Judah (Judges i. 18), were Casluchians; but afterwards, at the time when they struggled with Israel for empire, in the days of Samson, Eli, and Saul, there had been a second and larger immigration from Crete. As they seem to have spoken a Semitic tongue, they had apparently adopted the language of the Canaanites among whom they had settled, and especially of the Avim (Deut. ii. 23). The objection to their being of Egyptian origin, brought from their neglect of the rite of circumcision, has but little weight. The Israelites all but discontinued it (Josh. v. 5), and colonists escaped from the dominion of the priests might gladly dispense with such a custom. There is also much reason for believing that the institution of circumcision in Egypt was of a date subsequent to this emigration.

8. The **Caphtorim** are generally connected with Crete, but Egyptologers derive the name from Kah-Phthah, "the land of Phthah." According to this, the Caphtorim, like the Naphtuhim, would have been true Egyptians, and the Delta, with Memphis, for their capital, would have been their original home. The need of expansion, joined to the seafaring habits learnt on the shores of the Delta, may easily have led them to colonise Crete, while others of the race were going as settlers into Palestine. It is worth notice that while Cyprus and Rhodes are given to the sons of Javan (verse 4), no mention is there made of Crete.

It is plain from this survey that Mizraim at this time was not of very great extent, these seven tribes being confined to the lands closely bordering on the Delta and the upper part of the Nile valley. There is nothing to indicate that the great city of Thebes had as yet come into existence.

(15—18) **Canaan.**—The meaning of this name is uncertain, as, most probably, it is a Hamitic word: if derived from a Semitic root, it may mean the *lowland.* Though the Canaanites spoke a Semitic tongue at the time when we find them in Palestine, yet the assertion of the Bible that they were Hamites is confirmed by the testimony of profane writers, who say that their original home was on the Indian Ocean. They had probably been driven thence by the pressure of Semitic races, with whose language they had thus already become familiar; and when, farther, they found a Semitic people thinly spread over Palestine, they may, while absorbing them, have been confirmed in the use of their tongue. So, subsequently, Abraham gave up Syriac for Hebrew; and though these are kindred dialects, yet they are often remote enough from one another (see Gen. xxxi. 47). On the other hand, the whole character of the Canaanite religion and thought was Hamitic, and while they were active in commercial pursuits, and in culture far in advance of the Greeks, to whom they gave their alphabet, they were intensely sensuous in their worship and voluptuous in their manners. They are divided into eleven tribes, namely:—

1. **Sidon.**—This is remarkable as being the only town mentioned in the account either of Mizraim or of Canaan. All the rest are apparently the names of tribes still wandering about; and thus we gain a clearer idea both of the antiquity of this early record, and also of the great advance made by Nimrod in founding so many cities. Sidon, situated on the sea-shore, about thirty miles north of Tyre, became thus early a settled community and the seat of social life, because of its advantages for fishing (whence its name is derived), and also for commerce.

2. **Heth.**—The Kheta, or Hittites, a powerful race, whose language and monuments have recently become the object of careful study. They seem subsequently to have possessed not only Syria, but a large portion of Asia Minor. (See Note on chap. xxiii. 3, 5.)

3. **The Jebusite.**—This race held the territory afterwards occupied by Benjamin, and retained Jerusalem until the time of David (2 Sam. v. 6—9. See Note on chap. xiv. 18.)

4. **The Amorite.**—Or rather, *Emorite*, that is, mountaineer. Next to the Kheta, or Hittites, they were the most powerful race in Palestine, holding the hill country of Judea, where they had five kings (Josh. x. 5), and a large district on the eastern side of the Jordan (2 Sam. ix. 10).

5. **The Girgasite.**—Mentioned in Josh. xxiv. 11, but otherwise unknown.

6. **The Hivite.**—At Sichem (chap. xxxiv. 2), at Gibeon (Josh. ix. 7), and near Hermon and Lebanon (Josh. xi. 3; Judges iii. 3).

7. **The Arkite.**—Also in Lebanon.

8. **The Sinite.**—A small tribe in the same neighbourhood.

9. **The Arvadite.**—A more important people, inhabiting the island Aradus.

10. **The Zemarite.**—An obscure people, inhabiting Samyra, in Phœnicia.

11. **The Hamathite** whose city, Hamath, was the capital of Northern Syria. It was situated on the river Orontes, and though called Epiphaneia by the Macedonians, still retains its ancient name. The Kheta subsequently gained the supremacy at Hamath, and had their capital in the immediate neighbourhood.

Afterward were the families of the Canaanites spread abroad.—This may mean either that they spread inwards, or may refer to the numerous colonies of the Tyrians on the Mediterranean. While in Babylonia the Hamites are described as black, this branch was called Phœnicians, from their ruddy colour, in contrast with the olive-coloured Semitic stock. As they came by sea from the Indian Ocean, their earliest settlement was on the coast, and thus Sidon is called "the first-born" of Ham. Thence they advanced into the interior, and though few in number, absorbed by their superior culture the inhabitants of Palestine. It is probably this expansion inwards which is here referred to.

(19, 20) **The border . . .**—The boundaries given are Sidon in the north, Gerar and Gaza in the south and south-west, and thence to the Dead Sea. The only Lasha known is a place famous for its hot springs on

the Canaanites was from Sidon, as thou
comest to Gerar, unto [1]Gaza; as thou
goest, unto Sodom, and Gomorrah, and
Admah, and Zeboim, even unto Lasha.
(20) These *are* the sons of Ham, after their
families, after their tongues, in their
countries, *and* in their nations.
(21) Unto Shem also, the father of all the
children of Eber, the brother of Japheth
the elder, even to him were *children* born.
(22) The [a]children of Shem; Elam, and
Asshur, and [2]Arphaxad, and Lud, and
Aram. (23) And the children of Aram;
Uz, and Hul, and Gether, and Mash.
(24) And Arphaxad begat [3]Salah; and
Salah begat Eber. (25) [b]And unto Eber
were born two sons: the name of one
was Peleg; for in his days was the earth
divided; and his brother's name *was*
Joktan. (26) And Joktan begat Almodad,
and Sheleph, and Hazarmaveth, and
Jerah, (27) and Hadoram, and Uzal, and
Diklah, (28) and Obal, and Abimael, and
Sheba, (29) and Ophir, and Havilah, and
Jobab: all these *were* the sons of Jok-
tan. (30) And their dwelling was from
Mesha, as thou goest unto Sephar a
mount of the east. (31) These *are* the

1 Heb., *Azah.*

a 1 Chron. i. 17.

2 Heb., *Arpachshad*

3 Heb. *Shelah.*

b 1 Chron. i. 19.

---

the east of the Red Sea. Though the Phœnicians may have occupied this town on their way to Palestine, it could not have been one of their boundaries, so that it is probably some place destroyed in the convulsion which overthrew the cities of the plain. We must notice also that while Sidon is given as the northern limit, both Aradus and Hamath were considerably above it. It is probable, therefore, that both the Arvadite and the Hamathite were still wandering tribes without settlements when this table was drawn up.

(21–23) **Shem . . . the brother of Japheth the elder.**—Really, *the elder brother of Japheth.* Though the rules of Hebrew grammar will admit of no other rendering, it is remarkable that both the Syriac and the Vulg. make the same mistake as our own version. In designating Shem as "the father of all the children of Eber," attention is called to the fact that the descendants of Peleg, his elder son, are omitted from this table, and reserved for the *Tôldôth Shem.* (See chap. xi. 10.)

The nations descended from Shem were:—

1. **Elam.**—According to Mr. Sayce (*Chald. Gen.*, p. 196), "the primitive inhabitants of Elam were a race closely allied to the Accadians, and spread over the whole range of country which stretched from the southern shores of the Caspian to the Persian Gulf." But just as the Semitic Asshur expelled a Hamite race from Assyria, so another branch of this conquering family occupied Elymais. It is now called Chuzistan, and was the most easternly of the countries occupied by the Semites. But see Excursus to chap. xiv. on the conquests of the Elamite Chedorlaomer.

2. **Asshur.**—This Semitic stock seems to have been the first to settle on the Tigris, as the Hamites were the first to settle on the Euphrates. Finally, as we have seen (verse 11), they conquered the whole country.

3. **Arphaxad.**—Heb., *Arpachshad.* We may dismiss the idea that he was connected with the region called Arrapachitis, for this correctly is Aryapakshata, "the land next the Aryans." Really he appears as the ancestor of Eber and the Joktanite Arabs.

4. **Lud.**—Probably the Lydians, who, after various wanderings, settled in Asia Minor.

5. **Aram.**—As Asshur means *plain*, so Aram means *highland.* It was originally the name of the Lebanon ranges, and thus Damascus is called Aram in 2 Sam. viii. 5. Subsequently the race so extended itself as to possess Mesopotamia, a lowland country, but called, as early as Gen. xxiv. 10, "Aram of the two rivers." The greatness of Aram will be best seen by examining those places in our version where *Syria* and *Syrian* are spoken of, and which, in the Hebrew, are really Aram.

To the Aramæan stock belonged also four outlying dependencies—(1) Uz, the land of Job, a district in the northern part of Arabia Deserta; (2) Hul and (3) Gether, regions of which nothing is known; and (4) Mash, a desert region on the western side of the Euphrates (*Chald. Gen.*, p. 276).

(24) **Arphaxad begat Salah.**—Heb., *Shelah.* The rest of the chapter is devoted to giving an account of the settlements of the Joktanite Arabs, who formed only one, apparently, of the races sprung from Arphaxad, as in this table even the Hebrews are omitted, although Eber's birth is given with the view of showing that the right of primogeniture belonged not to Joktan, but to Eber. The name Arphaxad, as we have seen (verse 22), at present defies all explanation. For the rest, see the *Tôldôth Shem*, chap. xi. 10—26.

(25) **Peleg; for in his days was the earth divided.**—This may refer to the breaking up of the race of Shem into separate nations, which severally occupied a distinct region; and so, while Joktan took Arabia, and in course of time expelled the Hamites from that country, Asshur, Aram, and Peleg occupied the regions on the north and north-west. But as Peleg, according to the *Tôldôth Shem*, was born only 101 years after the flood, Noah's family could scarcely have multiplied in so short a time to as many as 500 people; and Mr. Cyril Graham considers that the name refers to "the first cutting of some of those canals which are found in such numbers between the Tigris and the Euphrates." This is made more probable by the fact that Peleg in Hebrew means *water-course.*

(26–31) **Joktan.**—"The little one," as being a younger son. Of the thirteen divisions of his family, few are of any importance, though several of the names are curious from their connection with the Arabic language. The Joktanite country was Arabia Felix, or Yemen, and as the people led a pastoral life without founding cities, the traces of their tribal names are insignificant. Those worth noting are Almodad, because it has the full form of the article, retained as *Al* in Arabic, but shortened in Hebrew into *Ha.* Hazarmaveth, "the court of death," so called because of the unhealthiness of its climate, is now Hadramaut. Abimael means "the father of Mael." While in Hebrew and Syriac men took the name of their father, in Arabic they often take the name of a son, with *Abu* or *Abi* ("father of") prefixed. Sheba, the region afterwards famous for its commerce and its wealth of spices and precious stones. A Sheba also occurs among the

sons of Shem, after their families, after
their tongues, in their lands, after their
nations.
(32) These *are* the families of the sons
of Noah, after their generations, in their
nations: and by these were the nations
divided in the earth after the flood.

CHAPTER XI.—(1) And [a] the whole
earth was of one [1] language, and of one
[2] speech.
(2) And it came to pass, as they
journeyed from the east, that they
found a plain in the land of Shinar; and
they dwelt there. (3) And [3] they said one
to another, Go to, let us make brick,
and [4] burn them throughly. And they
had brick for stone, and slime had they
for morter. (4) And they said, Go to,
let us build us a city and a tower, whose
top *may reach* unto heaven; and let us
make us a name, lest we be scattered

[a] Wisd. 10. 5.

[1] Heb., *lip.*

[2] Heb., *words.*

[3] Heb., *a man said to his neighbour.*

[4] Heb., *burn them to a burning.*

---

race of Ham (see verse 7). Ophir: the name, probably, at first of a district of Oman in Arabia, but afterwards given to some port in India or Ceylon, from some fancied similarity. Havilah: some commentators consider that this is the same district as that previously occupied by the Cushites (verse 7); others argue that the two Havilahs are distinct, and that this is the region called *Chawlân*, in Northern Yemen. It is, however, certain that the Hamites possessed this country prior to its being occupied by the Joktanites.

(32) **After their generations.**—Heb., *according to their Tôldôth.* This makes it probable that each family preserved in some way an historical record of its descent; and as this table is called the *Tôldôth of the Sons of Noah,* it was probably formed by a comparison of numerous *Tôldôth,* each showing the descent of various members of the three great families into which the sons of Noah were divided.

XI.

(1) **The whole earth.**—That is, *all mankind.* After giving the connection of the various races of the then known world, consisting of Armenia, the regions watered by the Tigris and Euphrates, the Arabian peninsula, the Nile valley, with the districts closely bordering on the Delta, Palestine, the Levant, and the islands of Cyprus, Rhodes, and Crete; with Lud on his journey to Asia Minor, and the Japhethites breaking their way into Europe through the country between the Caspian and the Black Sea: after this, we go back to the reason of this dispersion, which is found in the confusion of tongues.

Of one language, and of one speech.—Literally, *of one lip, and of words one:* that is, both the pronunciation and the vocabulary were identical. As regards this primitive language, whereas but a few years ago the differences between the Sanscrit and the Semitic tongues were regarded as irreconcilable, recent inquiries tend to show that both have a common basis.

(2) **As they journeyed.**—The word literally refers to the pulling up of the tent-pegs, and sets the human family before us as a band of nomads, wandering from place to place, and shifting their tents as their cattle needed fresh pasture.

From the east.—So all the versions. Mount Ararat was to the north-west of Shinar, and while so lofty a mountain could not have been the spot where the ark rested, yet neither could any portion of Armenia or of the Carduchian mountains be described as to the east of Babylonia. The Chaldean legends make the ark rest on Mount Nizir, or Elwend, on the east of Assyria; and though Ararat may possibly signify *Aryaverta,* "Holy Land," yet the transference of the name from Elwend to Armenia is not easily explicable. Moreover, the Bible elsewhere seems to point to Armenia as the cradle of the human race. Most modern commentators, therefore, translate *eastward,* and such certainly is the meaning of the word in chap. xiii. 11, where also the versions, excepting our own, render *from the east.*

Land of Shinar.—See on chap. x. 10. The whole of Chaldea is a level plain, and the soil immensely rich, as it is an alluvial deposit, which still goes on forming at the head of the Persian Gulf, at the rate of a mile in a period estimated at from seventy to thirty years (Rawlinson, *Anc. Mon.,* i. 4). A strip of land 130 miles in breadth has been added to the country, by the deposit of the earth washed down by the Tigris and Euphrates, since the time when Ur of the Chaldees was a great port.

(3) **Let us make brick, and burn them throughly.**—Heb., *for a burning.* Bricks in the East usually are simply dried in the sun, and this produces a sufficiently durable building material. It marks a great progress in the arts of civilisation that these nomads had learned that clay when burnt becomes insoluble; and their buildings with "slime," or native pitch, for cement would be virtually indestructible. In fact, Mr. Layard says that at Birs-Nimroud it was scarcely possible to detach the bricks one from another, as the cement by which they were united was most tenacious (*Nineveh and Babylon,* p. 499).

(4) **A tower, whose top may reach unto heaven.**—The Hebrew is far less hyperbolical: namely, *whose head* (or top) *is in the heavens,* or skies, like the walls of the Canaanite cities (Deut. i. 28). The object of the builders was twofold: first, they wished to have some central beacon which might guide them in their return from their wanderings; and secondly, they had a distinctly ambitious object, for by remaining as one nation they would be able to reduce to obedience all the tribes now perpetually wandering away from them, and so would "make them a name." We may, indeed, dismiss the silly stories of Josephus about their defiance of God and Nimrod's impiety, and the purpose of escaping a second deluge, for all which there is not the least vestige of authority in the sacred record; but we undoubtedly find a political purpose of preventing that dispersion of mankind which God had commanded (chap. i. 28), and of using the consequent aggregation of population for the attaining to empire. There was probably some one able and ambitious mind at the bottom of this purpose, and doubtless it had very many advantages: for it is what is now called centralisation, by which the individual sacrifices his rights to the nation, the provinces to the capital, and small nations are bound together in one empire, that the force of the whole body may be brought to bear more rapidly and effectually in carrying out the will of the nation or of the ruler, as the case may be. Nimrod's efforts at a later

abroad upon the face of the whole earth.
(5) And the LORD came down to see the
city and the tower, which the children
of men builded. (6) And the LORD
said, Behold, the people *is* one, and they
have all one language; and this they
begin to do: and now nothing will be
restrained from them, which they have
imagined to do. (7) Go to, let us go
down, and there confound their lan-
guage, that they may not understand
one another's speech. (8) So the LORD
scattered them abroad from thence upon
the face of all the earth: and they left
off to build the city. (9) Therefore is
the name of it called [2]Babel; because
the LORD did there confound the lan-
guage of all the earth: and from thence
did the LORD scatter them abroad upon
the face of all the earth.

B.C. cir. 2247.

1 That is, *Confusion.*

---

date were successful (chap. x. 10—12); and when we remember the blood-stained course of some of his cities, we may well doubt whether, with all its present advantages, this centralisation really promotes human happiness.

(5–7) **The Lord came down.**—The narrative is given in that simple anthropological manner usual in the Book of Genesis, which so clearly sets before us God's loving care of man, and here and in chap. xviii. 21 the equity of Divine justice. For Jehovah is described as a mighty king, who, hearing in His upper and heavenly dwelling of man's ambitious purpose, determines to go and inspect the work in person, that having seen, he may deal with the offenders justly. He views, therefore, "the city and the tower;" for the city was as important a portion of their purpose as the tower, or even more so. The tower, which, no doubt, was to be the citadel and protection of the city, was for the latter's sake to give the people a sense of strength and security. Having, then, inspected the tower and the city nestling round it, the Deity affirms that this centralisation is injurious to man's best interests, and must be counteracted by an opposite principle, namely, the tendency of mankind to make constant changes in language, and thereby to break up into different communities, kept permanently apart by the use of different tongues. At present "it is one people, and there is one lip to all of them, and this is what they begin to do," &c. Already there are thoughts among them of universal empire, and if thus the spread of mankind be hindered, and its division into numerous nations, each contributing its share to the progress and welfare of the world, be stopped, man will remain a poor debased creature, and will fail utterly in accomplishing the purpose for which he was placed upon earth. "Go to," therefore, He says, in irony of their twice repeated phrase, "we will go down, and make their speech unintelligible to one another." Now, though there is no assertion of a miracle here, yet we may well believe that there was an extraordinary quickening of a natural law which existed from the first. This, however, is but a secondary question, and the main fact is the statement that the Divine means for counteracting man's ambitious and ever-recurring dream of universal sovereignty is the law of diversity of speech. In ancient times there was little to counteract this tendency, and each city and petty district had its own dialect, and looked with animosity upon its neighbours who differed from it in pronunciation, if not in vocabulary. In the present day there are counteracting influences; and great communities, by the use of the same Bible and the possession of the same classical literature, may long continue to speak the same language. In days also when communication is so easy, not only do men travel much, but newspapers and serials published at the centre are dispersed to the most distant portions of the world. In old time it was not so, and probably Isaiah would not have been easily understood thirty miles from Jerusalem, nor Demosthenes a few leagues from Athens. Without books or literature, a little band of families wandering about with their cattle, with no communication with other tribes, would quickly modify both the grammar and the pronunciation of their language; and when, after a year or two, they revisited the tower, they would feel like foreigners in the new city, and quickly depart with the determination never to return. And to this day diversity of language is a powerful factor in keeping nations apart, or in preventing portions of the same kingdom from agreeing heartily together. And thus at Babel the first attempt to bind the human family into one whole came to an ignominious end.

(8) **The Lord** (Jehovah) **scattered them abroad from thence upon the face of all the earth: and they left off to build the city.**—The tendency of men, as the result of a growing diversity of language, was to separate, each tribe holding intercourse only with those who spake their own dialect; and so the Divine purpose of occupying the world was carried into effect, while the project of this ambitious knot of men to hold mankind together was frustrated, and the building of their tower ceased.

(9) **Therefore is the name of it called Babel.**—Babel is, in Aramaic, Bab-el, *the gate of God,* and in Assyrian, Bab-ili (chap. x. 10). It is strange that any one should have derived the word from Bab-Bel, *the gate of Bel,* for there is no trace that the second *b* was ever doubled; moreover, Bel is for Baal; and though we Westerns omit the strong guttural, because we cannot pronounce it, the Orientals would preserve it. *El* is the regular Semitic word for God—in Assyrian, *Ili;* in Arabic, *Ilah;* in Syriac, *Aloho.* So far from diminishing, this increases the force of the Scriptural derivation. Man calls his projected city Bab-el, *the gate*—that is, the court—*of God;* God calls it Babble; for in all languages indistinct and confused speech is represented by the action of the lips in producing the sound of *b.* The exact Hebrew word for this was *balbal*—the Greek verb, *bambaino;* the Latin, *balbutio;* and a man who stammered was called *balbus.* The town, then, keeps its first name, but with a contemptuous meaning attached to it; just as Nabal (1 Sam. xxv. 25) may really have had his name from the *nabla,* or harp, but from the day that his wife gave it a contemptuous meaning Nabal has signified only folly.

The Babylonian legends are in remarkable agreement with the Hebrew narrative. They represent the building of the tower as impious, and as a sort of Titanic attempt to scale the heavens. This means that the work was one of vast purpose; for there is something in the human mind which attaches the idea of impiety to all stupendous undertakings, and the popular feeling is

(10) [a] These *are* the generations of
Shem: Shem *was* an hundred years old,
and begat Arphaxad two years after the
flood: (11) and Shem lived after he begat
Arphaxad five hundred years, and begat
sons and daughters. (12) And Arphaxad
lived five and thirty years, and be-
gat Salah: (13) and Arphaxad lived
after he begat Salah four hundred and
three years, and begat sons and daugh-
ters. (14) And Salah lived thirty years,
and begat Eber: (15) and Salah lived
after he begat Eber four hundred and
three years, and begat sons and daugh-
ters. (16) [b] And Eber lived four and
thirty years, and begat [c] Peleg: (17) and
Eber lived after he begat Peleg four
hundred and thirty years, and begat
sons and daughters. (18) And Peleg
lived thirty years, and begat Reu:
(19) and Peleg lived after he begat Reu
two hundred and nine years, and begat
sons and daughters. (20) And Reu
lived two and thirty years, and be-
gat [d] Serug: (21) and Reu lived after
he begat Serug two hundred and seven
years, and begat sons and daughters.
(22) And Serug lived thirty years, and
begat Nahor: (23) and Serug lived after
he begat Nahor two hundred years, and
begat sons and daughters. (24) And
Nahor lived nine and twenty years, and
begat [e] Terah: (25) and Nahor lived after
he begat Terah an hundred and nine-
teen years, and begat sons and daugh-
ters. (26) And Terah lived seventy
years, and [f] begat Abram, Nahor, and
Haran.

[a] 1 Chron. 1. 17.
[b] 1 Chron 1. 19.
[c] Called Luke 3. 35, *Phalec.*
[d] Luke 3. 35. *Saruch.*
[e] Luke 3. 34, *Thara.*
[f] Josh. 24. 2; 1 Chron. 1. 26.

always one of rejoicing at their failure. The gods therefore destroy at night what the builders had wrought by day; and finally, Bel, "the father of the gods," confounds their languages. It is remarkable that the very word used here is *bâlal* (or perhaps *bâlâh*), and thus the meaning of "confusion" would attach to the word equally in the Assyrian as in the Hebrew language (*Chald. Gen.*, p. 166).

One question remains: Was the tower of Babel the temple of Bel destroyed by Xerxes, and which was situated in the centre of Babylon? or was it the tower of Borsippa, the site of which was in one of the suburbs, about two miles to the south? This tower was the observatory of the Chaldean astronomers, and its name, according to Oppert, means "the tower of languages." We incline to the belief that this ruin, now called the Birs-Nimrud, was the original tower, and that the temple of Bel was a later construction, belonging to the palmy times of the Chaldean monarchy. An account of it will be found in Sayce, *Chald. Gen.*, pp. 169, 170, and in Rawlinson, *Anc. Mon.*, i. 12, 21, &c.

The Tôldôth Shem.

(10–26) **These are the generations of Shem.**—Here also, as in chap. v., there is a very considerable divergence between the statements of the Hebrew, the Samaritan, and the Septuagint texts. According to the Hebrew, the total number of years from Shem to the birth of Abram was 390, according to the Samaritan, 1,040, and according to the LXX., 1,270. These larger totals are obtained by adding, as a rule, one hundred years to the age of each patriarch before the birth of his eldest son, and the LXX. also insert Cainan between Arphaxad and Salah. The virtual agreement of two authorities, coming from such different quarters as the Samaritan transcript and the LXX. version is remarkable, but scholars have long acknowledged that these genealogies were never intended for chronological purposes, and that so to employ them leads only to error.

Like the genealogy of Seth, in chap. v., the *Tôldôth Shem* also consists of ten generations, and thus forms, according to Hebrew ideas respecting the number ten, a perfect representation of the race. With the exception of Arphaxad (for whom see chap. x. 22), the names in this genealogy are all Hebrew words, and are full of meaning. Thus—

Salah means *mission*, the sending out of men in colonies to occupy new lands.

Eber is the *passage*, marking the migration of the head-quarters of the race, and the crossing of some great obstacle in its way, most probably the river Tigris. With this would begin the long struggle between the Semitic and Hamitic races in Mesopotamia.

Peleg, *division*, may be a memorial of the separation of the Joktanite Arabs from the main stem, but see Note on Chap. x. 25. Through him the rights of primogeniture passed to the Hebrews.

Reu, *friendship*, seems to indicate a closer drawing together of the rest after the departure of Joktan and his clan, which probably had been preceded by dissensions.

Serug, *intertwining*, may denote that this friendship between the various races into which the family of Shem was by this time divided was cemented by intermarriage.

Nahor, *panting, earnest struggle*, indicates, most probably, the commencement of that seeking after a closer communion with God which made his descendants withdraw from contact with the rest and form a separate community, distinguished by its firm hold of the doctrine of the unity of the Godhead. From the words of Joshua (Josh. xxiv. 2) it is plain, not only that idolatry was generally practised among the descendants of Shem, but that even Nahor and Terah were not free from its influence. Yet, probably, the monotheism of Abraham was preceded by an effort to return to the purer doctrine of their ancestors in Nahor's time, and the gods which they still worshipped were the teraphim, regarded both by Laban and Rachel (chap. xxxi. 30, 34) as a kind of inferior household genius, which brought good luck to the family.

Terah, *wandering*, indicates the commencement of that separation from the rest caused by religious differences, which ended in the migration of Abram into Canaan.

In **Abram**, *high-father*, we have a prophetic name, indicative of the high purpose for which the father of the faithful was chosen. There is a difficulty about the date of his birth. We read that "Terah lived seventy

(27) Now these *are* the generations of Terah: Terah begat Abram, Nahor, and Haran; and Haran begat Lot. (28) And Haran died before his father Terah in the land of his nativity, in Ur of the Chaldees. (29) And Abram and Nahor took them wives: the name of Abram's wife *was* Sarai; and the name of Nahor's wife, Milcah, the daughter of Haran, the father of Milcah, and the father of

---

years, and begat Abram, Nahor, and Haran;" and in verse 32 that "the days of Terah were two hundred and five years." But St. Stephen says that Terah died in Haran before Abram's migration (Acts vii. 4), and in chap. xii. 4 we are told that Abram was seventy-five years of age when he departed from that country. Either, therefore, Terah was a hundred and thirty years old when Abram was born—and Abram was a younger, and not the older son—or the Samaritan text is right in making the total age of Terah a hundred and forty-five years. The latter is probably the true solution: first, because Nahor died at the age of a hundred and forty-eight, and it is not probable that Terah so long outlived him; for human life, as we have seen, was progressively shortening after the flood: and secondly, because Abram, in chap. xvii. 17, speaks of it as almost an impossibility for a man to have a son when he is a hundred years old. Had he been born when his father was a hundred and thirty, he could scarcely have spoken in this way.

THE TÔLDÔTH TERAH.

(27) **Now these are the generations.**—This *tôldôth*, which extends to chap. xxv. 11, is one of the most interesting in the Book of Genesis, as it gives us the history of the patriarch Abraham, in whom God was pleased to lay the foundation of the intermediate dispensation and of the Jewish Church, by whose institutions and psalmists and prophets the light of true religion was to be maintained, and the way prepared for the coming of Christ. But though Abraham is the central figure, yet the narrative is called the *Tôldôth Terah,* just as the history of Joseph is called the *Tôldôth Jacob* (chap. xxxvii. 2). The explanation of this is, not that we have in it the history of Lot, and of Moab and Ammon, which are mere subsidiary matters; but that it connects Abraham with the past, and shows that, through Terah and the *tôldôth* which ended in him, he was the representative of Shem.

Terah begat Abram.—Commentators, in their endeavour to make St. Stephen's assertion in Acts vii. 4 agree with the numbers of the Hebrew text, have supposed that Abram was not the eldest son, and that the first place was given him because of his spiritual preeminence. But this is contrary to the rules of the Hebrew language, and the failure of the attempt to deprive Shem of his birthright by a mistranslation of chap. x. 21 confirms Abram's claim to the same prerogative.

(28) **Haran died before his father.**—Heb., *in the presence of his father.* This is the first recorded instance of a premature death caused by natural decay.

In Ur of the Chaldees.—*Ur-Casdim.* A flood of light has been thrown upon this town by the translation of the cuneiform inscriptions, and we may regard it as certain that Ur is now represented by the mounds of the city of Mugheir. When first we read of this city, it was inhabited by a population of Accadians, a Turanian race, sprang probably from an early offshoot of the family of Japheth; but in course of time it was conquered by men of the Semitic family, who from thence overran the whole of Shinar, or Babylonia, and expelled from it the descendants of Cush. Mr. Sayce (*Chald. Gen.*, p. 20) puts this conquest at some very uncertain date, two or three thousand years before Christ; but the establishment of a powerful monarchy under a king named Lig-Bagas, and the consolidation under his sway of several petty kingdoms, into which Chaldea had been previously split up, he places with some confidence at 3,000 years before the Christian era (*ibid.*, p. 24). Now, there are in our museums inscribed bricks and engraved cylinders actually from the library of Lig-Bagas, and we learn that the Accadian literature was still older; for many of the works found at Agané are translations from it: and thus all those difficulties as to the antiquity of the art of syllabic writing which used to exist when men had nothing better to judge by than Egyptian picture-writing have passed away. Abraham migrated from a town which was then a famous seat of learning, and where even the ordinary transactions of life were recorded on tablets of terra-cotta. Very probably, therefore, he carried with him bricks and cylinders inscribed with these ancient records. We are no longer, therefore, surprised at the striking similarity between the narratives in the Book of Genesis prior to the migration of Abraham and those preserved in the cuneiform inscriptions. But the believer in inspiration cannot fail to be struck also at their dissimilarity. The cuneiform inscriptions are polytheistic, acknowledging twelve superior gods, and of gods inferior a countless multitude. The Semitic race is accused of adding to these a number of goddesses, chief among whom were Beltis, the wife of Bel, and Istar, the planet Venus. Of all this there is no trace in the Biblical records; nor is there in the whole Chaldean literature anything so grand and Divine as the thoughts expressed in the opening words of Genesis: "In the beginning God created the heaven and the earth."

As Ur is an Accadian word, we must reject all Semitic interpretations of its meaning; we must further add that Mr. Rawlinson gives reasons for believing that its early importance was due to its being a great maritime emporium (*Anc. Mon.*, i. 27). It was, we read, a walled town, and the great port for the commerce of the Persian Gulf, while round it lay a marvellously rich country, said to be the original home of the wheat-plant, and famous for its dates and other fruits. Its being called Ur-Casdim, "Ur of the Chaldees," shows that they had already won it from the Accadians when Terah dwelt there. Its subsequent name, Mugheir, probably means "mother of bitumen"—that is, producer of it.

(29) **Iscah.**—Not the same as Sarai, for we learn in chap. xx. 12 that she was Abraham's half-sister—that is, a daughter of Terah by another wife. Nor was she Lot's wife, as Ewald supposed, for she was his full sister. Marriages between near relatives seem to have been allowed at this time, and were perhaps even common for religious reasons (see chaps. xxiv. 3, 4, xxviii. 1, 2), but not marriages between those actually by the same mother. Thus Abraham takes his half-sister to wife, and Nahor his niece. Iscah, like Naamah (chap. iv. 22), was probably eminent in her time, but for reasons not recorded.

Iscah. (30) But Sarai was barren; she
had no child. (31) And Terah took
Abram his son, and Lot the son of
Haran his son's son, and Sarai his
daughter in law, his son Abram's wife;
and they went forth with them from
[a] Ur of the Chaldees, to go into the land
of Canaan; and they came unto Haran,
and dwelt there. (32) And the days of
Terah were two hundred and five years:
and Terah died in Haran.

B.C. cir. 1921.

a Neh. 9. 7; Judith 5. 7; Acts 7. 4.

b Acts 7. 3.

c ch. 18. 18. & 22. 18; Acts 3. 25; Gal. 3. 8.

CHAPTER XII.—(1) Now the [b] LORD
had said unto Abram, Get thee out of
thy country, and from thy kindred, and
from thy father's house, unto a land
that I will show thee: (2) and I will
make of thee a great nation, and I will
bless thee, and make thy name great;
and thou shalt be a blessing: (3) and I
will bless them that bless thee, and curse
him that curseth thee: [c] and in thee
shall all families of the earth be blessed.

---

(31) **They went forth with them.**—This may possibly mean that they went forth in one body; but the phrase is strange, and the Samaritan, followed by the LXX. and Vulg., by a slight transposition of the letters reads, "And he (Terah) brought them forth."

Haran.—The Charran of Acts vii. 4, that is, Carrhae in North-west Mesopotamia, about twenty geographical miles south-east of Edessa. The name must not be confounded with that of Haran, the father of Lot, as really it is in the Heb. *Kharan*, and was so called in Accadian times, in which language the word means "road," being, according to Mr. Sayce, the key of the highway from the east to the west. It was both a very early and a very late outpost of Chaldean power. (Tomkins' *Studies on Times of Abraham*, 55*ff.*)

Terah's migration was partly perhaps a movement of a tribe of the Semites northwards (see Note on verse 28), made restless by the Elamites, who about this time overran Western Asia; but chiefly it had a religious motive: for Ur was the especial seat of the worship of the moon-god, Sin; and though Terah had not attained to the purity of Abraham's faith, yet neither was he altogether an idolater. But why did they intend "to go into the land of Canaan?" As Abram subsequently continued this migration in simple dependance upon God's guidance (chap. xii. 1), it was probably the Divine rather than the human purpose that is here expressed. Still, there may have been some tradition in the family, or knowledge handed down from patriarchal times, which made them look upon Canaan as their land of hope; and the expedition of Amraphel, king of Shinar, and others against the south of Palestine, recorded in chap. xiv. 1—16, and confirmed by our large present knowledge of these popular movements, shows that we must not assume that, far removed from one another as were Babylonia and Canaan, therefore they were lands mutually unknown. We gather also that the Divine summons came to Abram in Ur (see chap. xv. 7; Neh. ix. 7; Acts vii. 2), but we learn in chap. xii. 1 that his final destination was not then definitely told him.

(32) **The days of Terah.**—See note on verse 26. According to the Samaritan text, Abram left Haran in the same year as that in which Terah died. Nahor had probably joined Terah about this time, as we find him subsequently settled in Haran (chap. xxiv. 10); and moreover, Abram is expressly commanded to leave "his kindred and his father's house," whereas all those who are mentioned by name as going with Terah shared in Abram's subsequent migration. (See verse 31.)

XII.

(1) **Now the Lord had said unto Abram.**—Heb., *And Jehovah said unto Abram.* There is no new beginning; but having briefly sketched the family from which Abram sprang, and indicated that he had inherited from them the right of primogeniture, the narrative next proceeds to the primary purpose of the Tôldôth Terah, which is to show how in Abram Jehovah prepared for the fulfilment, through Israel, of the protevangelium contained in the promise made to Eve at the fall (chap. iii. 15). The rendering "had said" was doubtless adopted because of St. Stephen's words (Acts vii. 2); but it is the manner of the Biblical narrative to revert to the original starting point.

Thy country.—A proof that Abram and his father were no new settlers at Ur, but that the race of Shem had at this time long held sway there, as is now known to have been the case.

Thy kindred.—This rendering is supported by chap. xliii. 7; but it more probably means *thy birthplace.* It is the word translated "nativity" in chap. xi. 28, where its meaning is settled by the prefixed "land;" and the sense is probably the same here. If so, the command certainly came to Abram at Ur, though most of the versions suppose that it happened at Haran.

A land that I will shew thee.—In chap. xi. 31 it is expressly said that the land was Canaan, but possibly this knowledge was concealed from the patriarch himself for a time, and neither he nor Terah knew on leaving Ur what their final destination would be.

(2, 3) **Thou shalt be a blessing.**—More correctly, *Be thou a blessing.* The promises made to Abram are partly personal and partly universal, embracing the whole world. In return for all that he abandons he is to become the founder of a powerful nation, who will honour his name, and teach the inheritors of their spiritual privileges to share in their veneration for him. But in the command to "be" or "become a blessing," we reach a higher level, and it is the glory of Abram's faith that it was not selfish, and in return for his consenting to lead the life of a stranger, he was to be the means of procuring religious privileges, not only for his own descendants, but also "for all families of the earth" (Heb., *of the ground—the adâmâh*). Not for the earth as the material universe, but solely in its connection with man. Wherever man makes his home upon it, there, through Abram, spiritual blessings will be offered him.

I will bless . . .—These words indicate relations mysteriously close between Jehovah and Abram, whereby the friends and enemies of the one become so equally to the other. But in the second clause our version has not noticed an essential difference between the verbs used. They occur together again in Exod. xxii. 28, and are there more correctly rendered by "revile" and "curse." The one word signifies to treat lightly and contemptuously, the other to pronounce a curse, usually in a judicial manner. We might, therefore, translate, "I will curse—pass a sentence of re-

(4) So Abram departed, as the LORD had
spoken unto him; and Lot went with
him: and Abram *was* seventy and five
years old when he departed out of
Haran. (5) And Abram took Sarai his
wife, and Lot his brother's son, and all
their substance that they had gathered,
and the souls that they had gotten in
Haran; and they went forth to go into
the land of Canaan; and into the land
of Canaan they came.
(6) And Abram passed through the land
unto the place of Sichem, unto the
plain of Moreh. And the Canaanite

---

jection upon—him that speaketh lightly of, or revileth thee."

In thee shall all families of the earth be blessed.—Some authorities translate, "shall bless themselves;" but there is a different conjugation to express this meaning, and no reason exists for forcing it upon the text. Henceforward Abram and the nation sprung from him were to be the intermediaries between God and mankind, and accordingly revelation was virtually confined to them. But though the knowledge of God's will was to be given through them, it was for the benefit of all the families of every race and kindred distributed throughout the habitable world, the *adâmâh* (Rom. iii. 29, x. 12, &c.).

(4) **Abram . . . departed out of Haran.**—The command given him in Ur may have been repeated in Haran; but more probably Abram had remained there only on account of Terah. At his death (see note on chap. xi. 26) he resumed his migration northward.

(5) **Their substance that they had gathered.**—Not cattle only, but wealth of every kind. As we have no data about the migration of Terah, except that it was after the death of Haran, and that Haran left children, we cannot tell how long the family rested at their first halting place, but it was probably a period of several years; and as Abram was "very rich in silver and in gold," he had apparently engaged there in trade, and thus possibly knew the course which the caravans took.

The souls that they had gotten.—Heb., *had made.* Onkelos and the Jewish interpreters explain this of proselytes, and persons whom they had converted to the faith in one God. Such might probably be in Abram's company; but the most part were his dependents and slaves (comp. chap. xiv. 14,), though the word "slave" suggests a very different relation to us than that which existed between Abram and his household. Their descendants were most certainly incorporated into the Israelitish nation, and we have direct testimony that Abram gave them careful religious training (chap. xviii. 19). Thus the Jewish traditions record a fact, and by acknowledging Abram's household as proselytes admit their claim to incorporation with the race.

Into the land of Canaan they came.—Slowly and leisurely as the cattle with their young and the women and children could travel, Abram would take his way along the 300 miles which separated him from Canaan. The ford by which he crossed the Euphrates was probably that at Jerabolus, the ancient Carchemish, as the route this way is both more direct and more fertile than either that which leads to the ferry of Bir or that by Thapsacus. The difficulty of passing so great a river with so much substance, and people, and cattle would give fresh importance to his title of "the Hebrew," *the passer over,* already his by right of descent from Eber, so named from the passage of the Tigris. More correctly, these names are 'Eber and 'Ebrew, and have nothing in common with "Heber the Kenite" (Judg. iv. 11). From Carchemish Abram's route would lie to the south-west, by Tadmor and Damascus; and Josephus (*Antiq.*, i. 7) has preserved the legend that "Abram came with an army from the country beyond Babylon, and conquered Damascus, and reigned there for a short time, after which he migrated into the land of Canaan." In Eliezer of Damascus we have a reminiscence of Abram's halt there (chap. xv. 2). But it could not have been long, for Mr. Malan (*Philosophy or Truth*, pp. 98—143) has conclusively shown by the dates in Holy Scripture that only about a year elapsed between Abram's departure from Kharan and his settlement in Canaan.

(6) **The place of Sichem.**—Heb., *Shechem.* This word signifies "shoulder," and was the name of the ridge uniting Mounts Ebal and Gerizim, the summits of which are about two miles apart. As the name is thus taken from the natural conformation of the ground, it may be very ancient. The modern name of the place is Nablous, a contraction of Flavia Neapolis, a title given it in honour of Vespasian. Mr. Conder (*Tent Work in Palestine*, i. 61) describes the valley as an oasis of remarkable beauty and luxuriance, but set, like Damascus, in a desert, and girt around by strong and barren mountains.

The plain of Moreh.—Heb., *the oak of Moreh.* It was here that Jacob buried the strange gods brought by his household from Haran (chap. xxxv. 4), and here, too, Joshua set up the stone of testimony (Josh xxiv. 26; Judges ix. 6); but as in Deut. xi. 30 the oaks (wrongly translated in most places in our version "plains") are described in the plural, it is probable that the word is to be taken as a collective for an oak grove. Such shady spots were favourite places for the tents of the wandering patriarchs. A famous terebinth, called after Abram's name, long existed at Mamre, and under it, in the time of Vespasian, the captive Jews were sold for slaves. It disappeared about A.D. 330, and no tree now marks the site of Abram's grove. The Hebrew word, however, for terebinth is *elâh,* while that used here is *êlôn.* It was probably the *quercus pseudococcifera* (see Tristram, *Nat. Hist. of Bible*, p. 369). This tree often grows to a vast size.

Moreh.—Literally, *teacher* (Isa. ix. 15). Probably in this cool grove some religious personage had given instruction to the people. In Judges vii. 1 we find a place called the "teacher's hill," and it is thus possible that among a people so religious as the race of Shem, men from time to time arose revered by the people as teachers of holiness. Such an one was Melchisedech.

The Canaanite was then in the land.—This is no sign of post-Mosaic authorship, nor a later interpolation, as if the meaning were that the Canaanite was there at that time, but is so no longer. What really is meant is that Abram on his arrival found the country no longer in the hands of the old Semitic stock, but occupied by the Canaanites, who seem to have gained the ascendancy, not so much by conquest as by gradual and peaceful means. We gather from the Egyptian records that this had taken place not very long before Abram's time. In the early inscriptions we read only of the Sati and Aamu, both apparently Semitic races, the latter name being derived from the Heb. *am,* "people." Sub-

was then in the land. (7) And the LORD appeared unto Abram, and said, [a]Unto thy seed will I give this land: and there builded he an [b]altar unto the LORD, who appeared unto him.

(8) And he removed from thence unto a mountain on the east of Beth-el, and pitched his tent, *having* Beth-el on the west, and Hai on the east: and there he builded an altar unto the LORD, and called upon the name of the LORD.

(9) And Abram journeyed, [1]going on still toward the south.

(10) And there was a famine in the land: and Abram went down into Egypt to sojourn there; for the famine *was* grievous in the land. (11) And it came to pass, when he was come near to enter into Egypt, that he said unto Sarai his wife, Behold now, I know that thou *art* a fair woman to look upon: (12) therefore it shall come to pass, when the Egyptians

a ch. 13. 15.

b ch. 13. 4.

1 Heb., *in going and journeying.*

sequently we find frequent mention of the Amaor and the Kheta—that is, the Amorites and Hittites, evidently in Abram's time the two most powerful races of Canaan. (See Tomkins' *Studies,* 82*ff.*) For their previous wanderings, see on chap. x. 15—19.

(7) **The Lord appeared unto Abram.**—This is the first time that any appearance of the Deity is mentioned. Always previously the communications between God and man had been direct, without the intervention of any visible medium. Thus, God *commanded* Adam (chap. ii. 16); Adam and Eve *heard* His voice (chap. iii. 8), and He *called* them (*ib.* 9); He *said* unto Cain (chap. iv. 6—9); unto Noah (chaps. vi. 13, vii. 1), and *spake* unto him (chaps. viii. 15, ix. 8): but henceforward we read repeatedly of a Divine appearance, and this visible manifestation is subsequently connected with the phrase "an angel of Jehovah" (see chaps. xvi. 7, xxii. 11, &c.), and less frequently "an angel of God" (chap. xxi. 17; Judges vi. 20, xiii. 9). Upon the question whether this was a created angel, or whether it was an anticipation of the incarnation of Christ, see Excursus on "Angel of Jehovah" at end of this book.

There builded he an altar unto the Lord.—By so doing he took possession of the land for Jehovah, and consecrated it to Him. The altar would, further, be a place of public worship and of sacrifice. In a similar spirit Noah had taken possession of the renovated earth (chap. viii. 20).

(8) **He removed.**—Broke up his encampment. No special reason for this need be sought; it was the usual condition of the nomad life, and Abram's wealth in cattle would make frequent changes necessary. His first long halt was in the hill country between Beth-el and Hai, or rather Ai, as in Josh. viii. 1—3. The numerous almond-trees, whence the former town took its early name of Luz, the remains of aqueducts and other works for irrigation, and the strength of the town of Ai in Joshua's days bear witness to the ancient fertility of the district, though said now to be uninviting. Here, too, Abram made open profession of his faith, and worshipped with his household at an altar dedicated to Jehovah.

(9) **Toward the south.**—The Negeb, or dry land, so called because the soil being a soft white chalk, the rains sink through it, and even in the valleys run below the surface of the ground. Though treeless, it is still rich in flocks and herds, but the water has to be collected in tanks and cisterns (Conder, *Tent Work,* ii. 87).

ABRAM'S VISIT TO EGYPT.

(10) **There was a famine in the land.**—This famine must have happened within a few years after Abram reached Canaan; for he was seventy-five years of age on leaving Haran, and as Ishmael, his son by an Egyptian slave-woman, was thirteen years old when Abram was ninety-nine, only about eight years are left for the events recorded in chaps. xii.—xvi. As rain falls in Palestine only at two periods of the year, the failure of either of these seasons would be immediately felt, especially in a dry region like the Negeb, and at a time when, with no means of bringing food from a distance, men had to depend upon the annual products of the land. As Egypt is watered by the flooding of the Nile, caused by the heavy rains which fall in Abyssinia, it probably had not suffered from what was a mere local failure in South Palestine; and Abram, already far on his way to Egypt, was forced by the necessity of providing fodder for his cattle to run the risk of proceeding thither. In Canaan he had found a thinly scattered Canaanite population, for whom probably he would have been a match in war; in Egypt he would find a powerful empire, and would be at the mercy of its rulers. It is a proof of Abram's faith that in this necessity he neither retraced his steps (Heb. xi. 15), nor sought a new home. For he went to Egypt with no intention of settling, but only "to sojourn there," to remain there for a brief period, after which with returning rains he would go back to Canaan.

(11—13) **Thou art a fair woman.**—For the word *yephath,* rendered "fair," see on chap. ix. 27. Though its general meaning is *beautiful,* yet there can be no doubt that the light colour of Sarai's complexion was that which would chiefly commend her to the Egyptians; for she was now past sixty, and though vigorous enough to bear a son at ninety, yet that was by the special favour of God. As she lived to the age of 127 (chap. xxiii. 1), she was now about middle age, and evidently had retained much of her early beauty; and this, added to the difference of tint, would make her still attractive to the swarthy descendants of Ham, especially as they were not a handsome race, but had flat foreheads, high cheek-bones, large mouths, and thick lips. Twenty years later we find Abram still haunted by fears of the effects of her personal appearance (chap. xx. 2), even when living among a better-featured race. From chap. xx. 13 it appears that on leaving Haran Abram and Sarai had agreed upon adopting this expedient, which seems to us so strangely contrary to the faith which the patriarch was at that very time displaying. He abandons his birthplace at the Divine command, and starts upon endless wanderings; and yet, to protect his own life, he makes an arrangement which involves the possible sacrifice of the chastity of his wife; and twice, but for God's interference, this painful result would actually have happened. Perhaps Abram may have depended upon Sarai's cleverness to help herself out of the difficulty; but such a mixture of faith and weakness, of trust in God in abandoning so much and trust in worldly policy for preservation in a foreseen

shall see thee, that they shall say, This
is his wife: and they will kill me, but
they will save thee alive. (13) Say, I
pray thee, thou *art* my sister: that it
may be well with me for thy sake; and
my soul shall live because of thee.
(14) And it came to pass, that, when
Abram was come into Egypt, the
Egyptians beheld the woman that she
was very fair. (15) The princes also of
Pharaoh saw her, and commended her
before Pharaoh: and the woman was
taken into Pharaoh's house. (16) And he
entreated Abram well for her sake: and
he had sheep, and oxen, and he asses, and
menservants, and maidservants, and she
asses, and camels. (17) And the LORD
plagued Pharaoh and his house with great
plagues because of Sarai Abram's wife.
(18) And Pharaoh called Abram, and said,
What *is* this *that* thou hast done unto
me? why didst thou not tell me that she
was thy wife? (19) Why saidst thou, She
is my sister? so I might have taken her
to me to wife: now therefore behold thy
wife, take *her*, and go thy way. (20) And

B.C. cir. 1920.

---

danger, cannot but make us feel how much of infirmity there was even in a character otherwise so noble.

(13) **My sister.**—True literally, as Sarai was Terah's daughter (chap. xx. 12), but absolutely false, as it implied that she was wholly his sister, and therefore not his wife.

(14, 15) **Pharaoh** is not the name of a person, but was the title borne by all the Egyptian monarchs.

(15) **The princes . . . commended her before Pharaoh.**—In the days of Abram Canaan was the highway to Egypt, and so large an immigration of men of the Semitic stock found their way thither that they overspread the whole Delta, and finally, under the name of the Hyksôs, made themselves masters of the throne of the Pharaohs, and retained their supremacy for several centuries. To keep out these hordes, Amenemhai had built a chain of fortresses, with a connecting wall; and though probably, as M. Chabas concludes (*Rev. Arch., XVᵉ Année*, Livr. i. 7), the Hyksôs had already in Abram's time attained to empire, nevertheless, on arriving at this wall, so powerful a sheik, with so large a following, would be interrogated by the Egyptian scribes, and a report sent to the Pharaoh. The word *sar*, translated here *prince*, is common to the Babylonian, Egyptian, and Hebrew languages; but while in Babylonia it was the title of the sovereign, in Egypt it was applied to subordinate officers, such as those in command at these fortresses. By one of these Abram would, no doubt, be conducted into Pharaoh's presence; and on one of the sepulchres at Benihassan we find an exactly parallel occurrence in the presentation of a nomad prince, evidently of Semitic origin, who, with his family and dependents, is seeking the Pharaoh's protection, and is received by him with honour. As women did not at that time go veiled in Egypt, this custom not having been introduced there till the Persian conquest, the officers at the frontier would have full opportunity of seeing Sarai, and would, no doubt, mention the extraordinary lightness of her complexion.

The most probable derivation of the word *Pharaoh* is that which identifies it with a symbol constantly used in inscriptions to indicate the king, and which may be read *per-ao* or *phar-ao*. It signifies, literally, the double house, or palace. This would be a title of respect, veiling the person of the monarch under the name of his dwelling, in much the same manner as we include the sovereign and his attendants under the name of the Court. For the arguments in favour of this derivation, see Canon Cook's Excursus on the Egyptian words in the Pentateuch, at the end of Vol. I. of the *Speaker's Commentary*. He also gives there the reasons for his opinion, in opposition to that of M. Chabas, that the Pharaoh in whose days Abram visited Egypt was an early king of the twelfth dynasty, some time anterior to the usurpation of the Hyksôs.

(16) **He entreated Abram well.**—Heb., *did good to Abram*. It was usual to give the relatives a sum of money when taking a daughter or sister to wife. The presents here show that Pharaoh fully believed that he was acting lawfully, while the largeness of them proves that Sarai, in spite of her years, was looked upon as a valuable acquisition. Among the presents are "asses." The charge on this account brought against the author of "inaccuracy," as if asses were not known at this time in Egypt, is disproved by the occurrence of representations of this animal on the tombs of Benihassan: we have proof even that they were numerous as far back as when the Pyramids of Gizeh were built. The horse is not mentioned, and the earliest representation of one is in the war-chariot of Ahmes, the first Pharaoh of the eighteenth dynasty, who expelled the Hyksôs. Male and female slaves are, curiously enough, introduced between "he-asses" and "she-asses." As she-asses were especially valuable, perhaps these and the camels were looked upon as the monarch's choicest gifts.

Camels are not represented on the monuments, and are said not to thrive well in Egypt; but the Semitic hordes who were peopling the Delta would certainly bring camels with them. Many, too, of the Egyptian monarchs—as, for instance, those of the twelfth dynasty—held rule over a great part of the Sinaitic peninsula, and must have known the value of the camel for transporting heavy burdens in the desert, and its usefulness to a nomad sheik like Abram. (See chap. xxiv. 10.)

(19) **So I might have taken her to me to wife.**—The Hebrew is, *and I took her to me to wife*: that is, I took her with the intention of making her my wife. During the interval before the marriage Pharaoh and his household were visited with such marked troubles that he became alarmed, and possibly Sarai then revealed to him her true relationship to Abram. We find in Esth. ii. 12 that in the case of maidens there was a probation of twelve months duration before the marriage took place, and Sarai was probably saved by some such formality. The conduct of Pharaoh is upright and dignified; nor ought we to disbelieve his assurance that he had acted upon the supposition that Sarai might lawfully be his. The silence of Abram seems to indicate his consciousness that Pharaoh had acted more righteously than himself, and yet his repetition of the offence (chap. xx.) shows that he did not feel much self-reproach at what he had done; nor, possibly, ought we to judge

Pharaoh commanded *his* men concerning
him: and they sent him away, and his
wife, and all that he had.

CHAPTER XIII. — (1) And Abram
went up out of Egypt, he, and his wife,
and all that he had, and Lot with him,
into the south. (2) And Abram *was* very
rich in cattle, in silver, and in gold.
(3) And he went on his journeys from the
south even to Beth-el, unto the place
where his tent had been at the beginning,
between Beth-el and Hai; (4) unto the
[a] place of the altar, which he had made
there at the first: and there Abram
called on the name of the LORD.
(5) And Lot also, which went with
Abram, had flocks, and herds, and tents.
(6) And the land was not able to bear
them, that they might dwell together:
for their substance was great, so that
they could not dwell together. (7) And
there was a strife between the herdmen
of Abram's cattle and the herdmen of
Lot's cattle: and the Canaanite and
the Perizzite dwelled then in the land.
(8) And Abram said unto Lot, Let there
be no strife, I pray thee, between me
and thee, and between my herdmen and
thy herdmen; for we *be* [1] brethren. (9) *Is*
not the whole land before thee? sepa-
rate thyself, I pray thee, from me: if
thou wilt take the left hand, then I will
go to the right; or if *thou depart* to the
right hand, then I will go to the left.
(10) And Lot lifted up his eyes, and be-
held all the plain of Jordan, that it *was*
well watered every where, before the
LORD destroyed Sodom and Gomorrah,
even as the garden of the LORD, like the

B.C. cir. 1918.

a ch. 12. 7.

1 Heb., *men brethren.*

---

his conduct from the high standpoint of Christian morality. When, however, commentators speak of it as Abram's fall, they forget that he arranged this matter with Sarai at the very time when he was quitting Haran (chap. xx. 13).

XIII.

ABRAM'S RETURN FROM EGYPT AND HIS SEPARATION FROM LOT.

(1–4) **He went on his journeys.**—Or, *according to his stations,* which the Vulgate very reasonably translates, "by the same route by which he had come." This route was first into the south, the Negeb, which is virtually a proper name, and thence to the spot between Beth-el and Ai mentioned in chap. xii. 8.

At the first does not mean that this was the first altar erected by Abram, but that he built it on his first arrival there. His first altar was at Shechem. As regards his wealth, while his cattle had been greatly increased in Egypt, he had probably brought the silver and gold with him from Mesopotamia. Gold, however, was plentiful at that time in Egypt, but silver rare.

(5, 6) **Lot.**—He, too, had possibly received presents in Egypt, for we find him rivalling his uncle in wealth; and the "tents" show that he had numerous followers, and, like Abram, was the chief of a powerful clan. The repetition that "the land was not able to bear them," and that "they could not dwell together," implies that the difficulty had long been felt before it led to an open rupture.

(7) **The Perizzite.**—We find mention in the Bible both of Perazites, translated *villages,* in 1 Sam. vi. 18, Esth. ix. 19; and of Perizzites, who are sometimes opposed to the Canaanites, as here and in chap. xxxiv. 30, and sometimes described as one of the tribes settled in Palestine (Exod. iii. 8, 17; Josh. xvii. 15; Judges iii. 5). They are not mentioned among the races descended from Canaan, and probably were the earlier inhabitants of the country, who, being a pastoral people, possessed of no towns, were not able to make head against the Hamite settlers, but maintained themselves in the open country. Perazite and Perizzite are probably the same word, and both signify *lowlander,* though finally they were driven to the mountains (Josh. xi. 3). As the Canaanites devoted their main strength to a maritime life and trade, they would not attempt to extirpate these natives, but would be content with driving them into the interior. As thus some districts would be occupied by the dominant Canaanites, and others by these aborigines, two such large clans as those of Abram and Lot would find it difficult to discover unoccupied land enough to provide pasture for their cattle. The land must have been very thinly peopled for it to have been possible for them to do this, even when they had arranged to dwell apart.

(8, 9) **Let there be no strife.**—It is evident that Lot was beginning to take part with his herdmen, and regard himself as an injured man. But Abram meets him with the utmost generosity, acknowledges that their growth in wealth rendered a separation necessary, and gives him his choice. And Lot accepts it. Instead of feeling that it was due to his uncle's age and rank to yield to him the preference, he greedily accepts the offer, selects the region that seemed to offer the greatest earthly advantages, but finds in the long run that it has perils which far outweigh its promises of wealth and pleasure.

(10) **The plain of Jordan.**—This word, *Ciccar,* literally means the *circuit,* or, as it is translated in St. Matt. iii. 5, "the region round about Jordan," and, according to Mr. Conder (*Tent Work,* ii., p. 14), is the proper name of the Jordan valley, and especially of the plain of Jericho. It is now called the Ghor, or *depression,* and is one of the most remarkable districts in the world, being a deep crack or fissure, with chalk rocks upon the western and sandstone on the eastern side, over which lies limestone, geologically of the age of our greensand formation. It is thus what is technically called by miners a fault, the formations on the two sides having been displaced by some tremendous convulsion of nature. Most of the valley lies below the level of the Mediterranean, the Sea of Galilee being, by Mr. Conder's observations, about 682 feet below it, and the Dead Sea no less than 1,292 feet. As the watershed to the south rises to a level of 200 feet above the Mediterranean, all egress for the waters is thereby cut off, and there are numerous proofs that at some distant period the whole

land of Egypt, as thou comest unto
Zoar. (11) Then Lot chose him all the
plain of Jordan; and Lot journeyed
east: and they separated themselves
the one from the other. (12) Abram
dwelled in the land of Canaan, and Lot
dwelled in the cities of the plain, and
pitched *his* tent toward Sodom. (13) But
the men of Sodom *were* wicked and
sinners before the LORD exceedingly.

(14) And the LORD said unto Abram,
after that Lot was separated from him,
Lift up now thine eyes, and look from
the place where thou art northward, and
southward, and eastward, and westward:
(15) For all the land which thou seest, [a] to
thee will I give it, and to thy seed for
ever. (16) And I will make thy seed
as the dust of the earth: so that if a
man can number the dust of the earth,
then shall thy seed also be numbered.
(17) Arise, walk through the land in the
length of it and in the breadth of it;
for I will give it unto thee.

(18) Then Abram removed *his* tent, and
came and dwelt in the [1] plain of Mamre,
which *is* in Hebron, and built there an
altar unto the LORD.

a ch. 12. 7 & 26. 4; Deut. 34. 4.

1 Heb., *plains*.

---

valley, about 150 miles in length, was a succession of large lakes. But even in Abram's days the Jordan poured down a far larger volume of water than at present; for by the loss of its forests the climate of Palestine has become much more dry than of old, and regions once fertile are now barren. And as the supply of water has become less than that lost by evaporation, the Dead Sea has gradually receded, and left around it arid wastes covered over with incrustations of salt.

As the garden of the Lord.—Mr. Palmer (*Desert of the Exodus*, p. 465) describes the fertility of the Jordan valley as follows:—"Although the immediate vicinity of the Dead Sea is barren enough, the Ghor, or deep depression at the northern and southern extremities, teems with life and vegetation; and even where the cliffs rise sheer up from the water's edge, streams of fresh water dash down the ravines, and bring the verdure with them almost to the Salt Sea's brink." The same writer (p. 480) has also shown conclusively, with Mr. Grove, Dr. Tristram, and others, that Sodom and Gomorrha were at the northern end of the lake, and not, as was previously supposed, at the southern. For the Ciccar is strictly the part of the Ghor near Jericho, and as the Dead Sea is forty-six miles in length, its southern extremity was far away out of sight. Moreover, Lot was standing some miles away to the north-west, on the high ground between Beth-el and Ai, whence "the northern end of the Dead Sea, and the barren tract which extends from the oasis of Jericho to it and the Jordan, are distinctly visible" (Dr. Tristram, *Sunday at Home*, 1872, p. 215). This "barren tract" was once the Ciccar, and the traces of ancient irrigation and aqueducts attest its former fertility. It was upon this district, "well watered everywhere," that Lot gazed so covetously, and its richness is indicated by a double comparison: for, first, it was like Jehovah's garden in Eden, watered by its four rivers; and next, it was like Egypt, rendered fertile by artificial means.

As thou comest unto Zoar.—This makes no sense whatsoever. No person on the route to Egypt could possibly take Zoar in his way; and of the five cities of the plain this was the least like Paradise. The Syriac has preserved the right reading, namely, Zoan. This city, however, was called Zor, or Zar, by the Egyptians (*Records of the Past*, viii. 147), and was situated on the eastern side of the Tanaitic branch of the Nile, at the head of a fertile plain, called "the field of Zoan" in Ps. lxxviii. 12. Through this rich and well-watered region Lot had lately travelled in Abram's company, and the luxuriant vegetation there made it not unworthy to be compared with Paradise.

(11) **Lot journeyed east.**—This is the word translated "eastward" in chap. ii. 8, and "from the east" in chap. xi. 2. Here it can only mean *towards the east*.

(12, 13) **Lot dwelled in the cities of the plain.**—Heb., *of the Ciccar*. Not as yet within their walls, but in their neighbourhood, and evidently with a longing "toward Sodom," where, in chap. xix., we find him sitting in the gate as a citizen, and with his tent changed to a house. While, then, Abram continued to lead a hardy life as a stranger upon the bracing hills, Lot sighed for the less self-denying habits of the city; and probably, when he had descended into the Ghor, the enervating climate, which so developed the sensual vices of the people as to make them "sinners before Jehovah" (see on chap. x. 9), disposed Lot also to quit his tent, and yield himself to a luxurious and easy manner of living.

(14) **The Lord said unto Abram.**—The departure of Lot was certainly a great grief to Abram; for he lost thereby the companionship of the relative who had shared his abandonment of his country, and whom, probably, in his childless state, he had regarded as his heir. Jehovah, therefore, consoles him by a more definite promise of the possession of the whole land of which he had so generously given Lot the choice, and by the assurance that his own seed should be numerous as the dust of the earth. We may also feel sure that as Lot was deteriorating, so Abram was drawing nearer to God, and walking more closely with Him; and hence the fuller assurance of the Divine blessing.

(17) **Walk through the land.**—Repeated change of scene is not merely one of the pleasures of the nomad life, but also a necessity; for the uplands, covered with rich herbage in the spring, are usually burnt up in summer, and in the winter are exposed to driving winds and rain-storms. In these journeyings Abram is now to have the tranquil pleasure of feeling that his seed will inherit each beautiful spot that he visits, and that he is taking possession of it, and hallowing it for them.

(18) **The plain of Mamre.**—(Heb., *oaks of Mamre*. See on chap. xii. 6). Mamre was an Amorite, then living, and as he was confederate with Abram, it was apparently with the consent of the Amorites, and by virtue of the treaty entered into with them, that Abram made this oak-grove one of his permanent stations.

Hebron.—That is, *alliance*. Hebron was perhaps so called from the confederacy formed between Abram and the Amorites, and was apparently the name not only of a city, but of a district, as the oaks of Mamre are described as being "in Hebron." For its other name, Kirjath-arba, see note on chap. xxiii. 2.

CHAPTER XIV.—(1) And it came
to pass in the days of Amraphel king of
Shinar, Arioch king of Ellasar, Chedor-
laomer king of Elam, and Tidal king of
nations; (2) *that these* made war with
Bera king of Sodom, and with Birsha
king of Gomorrah, Shinab king of Ad-
mah, and Shemeber king of Zeboiim, and
the king of Bela, which is Zoar. (3) All
these were joined together in the vale
of Siddim, which is the salt sea.
(4) Twelve years they served Chedor-
laomer, and in the thirteenth year they
rebelled. (5) And in the fourteenth year
came Chedorlaomer, and the kings that
were with him, and smote the Rephaims
in Ashteroth Karnaim, and the Zuzims
in Ham, and the Emims in [1] Shaveh

1 Or, *the plain of Kiriathaim.*

XIV.

Invasion of the Jordan Valley by Chedorlaomer, King of Elam.

(1) **It came to pass.**—Connected with the settlement of Lot in the Jordan valley is one of the most remarkable episodes in the whole of the Bible, derived either from Canaanite records, or, as Mr. Sayce thinks (*Chald. Genesis,* p. 72), from those of Babylon. The latter view is made the more probable by the fact that Amraphel, though but a subject king, is placed first; and the way in which the patriarch is described in it, as "Abram the Hebrew," seems certainly to suggest that we have to do here with a narrative of foreign origin.

Its incorporation with the history admirably sets forth the consequences of Lot's choice in the troubles, and even ruin, which overtook him, the bravery and power of Abram, and his generosity to the rescued kings. It is also most interesting, as showing Abram's relation to the Amorites, among whom he lived, and the existence in Palestine of a Semitic population, who still worshipped "the most high God," and over whom one of the noblest figures in the Old Testament was king. The narrative is Jehovistic, for Abram calls God *Jehovah El Elion,* but is, nevertheless, of such ancient date as to forbid the acceptance of the theory which regards the occurrence of the name Jehovah as a proof of later authorship. Upon Elam and the conquests and route of Chedorlaomer, see Excursus at end of this book.

Amraphel.—An Accadian name, which Lenormant has found on Babylonian cylinders, and which he explains as meaning "the circle of the year."

Shinar.—See on chap. x. 10.

Arioch.—*i.e., Eriaku,* which in Accadian means "servant of the moon-god." He was king of Ellasar, *i.e.,* Al-Larsa, *the city of Larsa,* now called Senkereh. It is situated on the left bank of the Euphrates, in Lower Babylonia, and has contributed some very ancient tablets to the collection in the British Museum. The name occurs again in Dan. ii. 14.

Tidal.—More correctly in the LXX., *Thargal,* that is, Tur-gal, *the great son* (Sayce). In the Syriac he is called "Thargil, king of the Gelae," the latter being a mistake, through reading Gelim for Goïm. This word does not mean "nations," but is a proper name, spelt *Gutium* in the inscriptions, "by which the Accadians designated the whole tract of country which extended from the Tigris to the eastern borders of Media, including the district afterwards known as Assyria" (*Chald. Gen.,* p. 197).

(2) **Bera king of Sodom.**—The failure of the attempt to explain the names of these five kings, and of the cities over which they ruled (with one or two exceptions), by the help of the Hebrew language makes it probable that the inhabitants of the Ciccar were either Canaanites who had come from the sea-coast, or men of some Hamite stock who had colonised this region from the east. The latter is the more probable view, as they do not seem to have had much affinity either with the Amorites or with the Jebusites, their neighbours.

(3) **All these were joined together.**—Were united in a confederacy, and so formed a pentapolis, or group of five allied towns, like the Philistine league with its five lords (1 Sam. vi. 16—18).

The vale of Siddim.—Mr. Conder (*Tent-work,* ii. 16) says that the name *Sidd* is still given by the Arabs to the cliffs or banks of marl which run along the southern edge of the plain of Jericho; and with this agrees Aben-Ezra's explanation, who derives the word from the Hebrew *sid,* chalk. Mr. Conder searched throughout the Ciccar for traces of the ruined cities, but in vain; and "the gradual rise of the level of the plain, caused by the constant washing down of the soft marl from the western hills, would effectually," he thinks, "cover over any such ruins." He found, however, copious springs of water upon the north-western side of the lake, and considers that the five cities were in their neighbourhood.

Which is the salt sea.—From these words commentators have rashly concluded that the vale of Sodom was swallowed up by the Dead Sea; but not only is no such convulsion of nature mentioned in chap. xix., but Abram is described as seeing the Ciccar-land not submerged, but smoking like a furnace (verse 28). Probably "the vale of Siddim" was the name of the whole district in which these sidds, or bluffs, are situated, and which extend round all the northern shores of the lake. Mr. Conder, after tracing the lines of former beaches, which show that the Dead Sea has long been shrinking in extent, tells us (*Tent-work,* ii. 43) that geologists hold that it had reached its present condition long before the days of Abram. It still, indeed, covered a much larger space, for the rains at that time were far more copious in Palestine than at present; but it no longer extended over the whole Arabah, as, by the evidence of these beaches, was once the case.

(4) **They served.**—That is, *paid a yearly tribute,* that they might be exempt from Chedorlaomer's marauding expeditions (see 2 Kings xviii. 7). There must, therefore, have been envoys going from time to time to and fro from the Jordan valley to Shinar.

(5) **The Rephaims.** — Described as an Amorite tribe (Amos ii. 9) of great stature, settled in Bashan, where Moses conquered them (Josh. xiii. 12). We find them also on the other side of Jordan, in Mount Ephraim (Josh. xvii. 15), on the western side of Jerusalem (Josh. xv. 8, xviii. 16; 2 Sam. v. 18, 22), and even among the Philistines (2 Sam. xxi. 16, 18). In many of these places the word is wrongly translated *giants.* From this wide dispersion of them we may safely conclude that they belonged to the earlier settlers in the land,

Kiriathaim, (6) and the Horites in their
mount Seir, unto [1] El-paran, which *is*
by the wilderness. (7) And they returned,
and came to Enmishpat, which *is*
Kadesh, and smote all the country of
the Amalekites, and also the Amorites,
that dwelt in Hazezon-tamar.

(8) And there went out the king of
Sodom, and the king of Gomorrah, and
the king of Admah, and the king of
Zeboiim, and the king of Bela (the same
is Zoar;) and they joined battle with
them in the vale of Siddim; (9) with
Chedorlaomer the king of Elam, and
with Tidal king of nations, and Am-
raphel king of Shinar, and Arioch king
of Ellasar; four kings with five. (10) And
the vale of Siddim *was full of* slimepits;
and the kings of Sodom and Gomorrah
fled, and fell there; and they that re-
mained fled to the mountain. (11) And
they took all the goods of Sodom and
Gomorrah, and all their victuals, and
went their way. (12) And they took Lot,
Abram's brother's son, who dwelt in
Sodom, and his goods, and departed.

(13) And there came one that had
escaped, and told Abram the Hebrew;
for he dwelt in the plain of Mamre the
Amorite, brother of Eshcol, and brother
of Aner: and these *were* confederate
with Abram. (14) And when Abram
heard that his brother was taken cap-
tive, he [2]armed his [3]trained *servants*,
born in his own house, three hundred
and eighteen, and pursued *them* unto

1 Or, *the plain of Paran.*

B.C. cir. 1913.

2 Or, *led forth.*

3 Or, *instructed.*

---

and that only their rulers, like Og (Josh. ix. 10), were Amorites.

Ashteroth Karnaim.—*The two-horned Astarte,* the Phœnician Venus, identified by the Rephaim with the moon. Her worship had, no doubt, been introduced by the Amorites. This city was the capital of Og (Deut. i. 4), and is called *Be-Eshtera,* "the house of Astarte," in Josh. xxi. 27. Its remains have been found at Tell-Ashtereh, in the Hauran, about two leagues from the ancient Edrei.

The Zuzims.—Called in Deut. ii. 20 Zamzummim, where they are identified with the Rephaim, of which stock they were an inferior branch. Their capital, *Ham,* has been identified with Hameitât, about six miles to the east of the lower part of the Dead Sea (Tristram, *Land of Moab,* p. 117).

The Emims.—Of these also we read in Deut. ii. 10, 11: "The Emim . . . also were accounted Rephaim, as the Anakim."

In Shaveh Kiriathaim.—More probably, *in the plain of Kiriathaim.* This city, given to the tribe of Reuben (Num. xxxii. 37), was, upon the decay of the Israelites upon the east of Jordan, re-occupied by the Moabites (Jer. xlviii. 1), who had taken it from the Emim.

(6) **The Horites.**—*Cave-men,* the aboriginal inhabitants of Mount Seir, subsequently conquered by the Edomites (Deut. ii. 12, 22). The miserable condition of these earth-men is described in Job. xxx. 3—8.

El-paran.—This forest of oaks (or terebinths) was on the edge of the great wilderness, and reached to within three days' journey of Sinai (Num. x. 12, 33).

(7) **They returned.**—More correctly, *they turned,* as they did not go back by the same route, but wheeled towards the north-west.

Enmishpat.—*The fountain of justice,* because at this spring the ancient inhabitants of the country used to meet to settle their disputes. It was also called Kadesh, probably the 'Ain Qadis described by Professor Palmer. It was a great stronghold, and both a sanctuary and a seat of government. It has been visited lately by Mr. Trumbull, for whose account see Palestine Exploration Fund, Quarterly Statement, July, 1881, pp. 208—212.

The Amalekites. — Saul had to pursue these wandering hordes into the recesses of Paran (1 Sam. xv. 7), but they were evidently now in possession of the Negeb of Judea.

Hazezon-tamar, *the felling of the palm,* is certainly the same as Engedi (2 Chron. xx. 2). For descriptions of this wonderful spot, so dear to Solomon (Cant. i. 14), see Conder, *Tent-work,* ii. 135; Tristram, *Land of Israel,* 281; and for its strategical importance, Tristram, *Land of Moab,* 25.

(8) **They joined battle with them.**—Heb., *they set themselves in array against them.* As the five kings left their cities to do battle with the invaders "in the vale of Siddim," it is plain, as was said in verse 3, that the vale embraces a far wider extent of country than merely the site of the five cities.

(10) **The vale of Siddim was full of slimepits.**—That is, of holes whence bitumen had been excavated. Layers of this natural asphalte, well known both to the Greeks and Romans as *pix Judaica,* Judean pitch, still exist on the western side of the Dead Sea; and the places whence it had been dug out, and which are often very deep, formed dangerous impediments in the way of the defeated side.

(13) **One that had escaped.**—Heb., *the escaped;* not any one in particular, but the fugitives generally. As Sodom lay at the north-western end of the Dead Sea, the region where Abram was dwelling would be their natural place of refuge.

Abram the Hebrew.—That is, *the immigrant* (from beyond the Euphrates), but also his patronymic from Eber, who in like manner had crossed the Tigris. It was, no doubt, the usual title of Abram among the Canaanites, and has been preserved from the original document, whence also probably was taken the exact description of Lot in verse 12.

The plain of Mamre . . . these were confederate with Abram.—Heb., *the oak of Mamre* (see chap. xiii. 18), and *lords,* or *owners of a covenant.* Abram had not occupied Mamre without the consent of the dominant Amorites, and probably there was also a league for mutual defence between him and them.

(14) **Abram . . . armed . . .**—Heb., *led forth,* or literally, *let them loose, let them pour forth,* the verb indicating both their number and also their haste. The word for *trained* comes from the same root as the name Enoch, for which see note on chap. iv. 17. As Abram's cattle would often be exposed to danger from

Dan. (15) And he divided himself against
them, he and his servants, by night, and
smote them, and pursued them unto
Hobah, which *is* on the left hand of
Damascus. (16) And he brought back
all the goods, and also brought again
his brother Lot, and his goods, and the
women also, and the people.

(17) And the king of Sodom went out
to meet him after his return from the
slaughter of Chedorlaomer, and of the
kings that *were* with him, at the valley
of Shaveh, which *is* the [a] king's dale.
(18) And [b] Melchizedek king of Salem
brought forth bread and wine: and he
was the priest of the most high God.
(19) And he blessed him, and said, Blessed
be Abram of the most high God, pos-
sessor of heaven and earth: (20) and
blessed be the most high God, which
hath delivered thine enemies into thy
hand. And he gave him [c] tithes of all.

a 2 Sam. 18. 18.

b Heb. 7. 1.

c Heb. 7. 4.

---

the Amalekites, who throughout the Biblical history appear as a race of inveterate plunderers, there is no reason to doubt that these men were trained and practised in the use of weapons. This large number of servants born in his house, and of an age capable of undergoing the fatigues of a rapid pursuit, added to the older men left to defend and take care of the cattle, proves that Abram was the chieftain of a powerful tribe.

Dan.—There is a city of this name in Gilead, mentioned in Deut. xxxiv. 1, but this is probably the better known town at the source of the Jordan, also called Laish (Judges xviii. 29). For having swept the hill country on his march southwards, Chedorlaomer would now plunder the rich vale of the Jordan as his final exploit. Dan is about 140 miles from Hebron, where Abram began his march.

(15) **Hobah . . . on the left hand of Damascus.**—That is, *to the north*, as the Hebrews looked eastward in defining the quarters of the heaven. The victory had thus been followed up with great energy, the pursuit having lasted, according to Josephus, the whole of the next day and night after that on which the attack was made. At Hobah the mountains cease, and the great plain of Damascus begins, and further pursuit was therefore useless.

(17) **The slaughter.**—Heb., *the smiting*, that is, the defeat of Chedorlaomer.

The valley of Shaveh.—That is, the valley of the plain (see on verse 5). It was the place where Absalom erected his pillar (2 Sam. xviii. 18), and lay on the northern side of Jerusalem, probably where the Kedron valley widens out. Its other name, "the king's dale," may have been given it from this meeting of the kings of Salem and Sodom with the victorious Abram; but Onkelos, with far greater probability, considers that it was so called because upon this level ground the kings of Judah in subsequent times assembled and exercised their forces.

(18) **Melchizedek king of Salem.**—There is a Salem near Scythopolis in the tribe of Ephraim, near to which John baptised (John iii. 23, where it is called *Salim*), and Jerome mentions that some local ruins there were said to be the remains of Melchizedek's palace. But such traditions are of little value, and we may feel certain that the place was really Jerusalem (Ps. lxxvi. 2); for it lay on Abram's route homeward, and was within a reasonable distance of Sodom, which, as we have seen, lay in the Ciccar of Jericho, at the northern end of the Dead Sea. Salem is a common name for towns in Palestine (Conder, *Tent-work*, i. 91), and the village in Ephraim is too remote to have been the place of meeting.

In Melchizedek we have a type of Christ (Ps. cx. 4; Heb. v. 6, 10, vii. 1—21), and so venerable is his character and aspect that Jewish tradition identified him with the patriarch Shem, thus reconciling also to themselves his superiority over their forefather Abraham. But this idea is contradicted by Heb. vii. 3. He was more probably the king of some Semitic race who still occupied Salem, but from whom it was at a subsequent period wrested by the Jebusites, who called it Jebus, after the name of their ancestor (Judges xix. 10, 11). Up to David's days it seems to have still had a titular king (2 Sam. xxiv. 23), and upon his conquest of it its old name reappears, but with a prefix, and henceforward it was known as Jeru-salem, that is (probably), *the possession of Salem.*

The typical value of Melchizedek's priesthood lies not merely in his being "king of righteousness and king of peace," but even more in his priesthood being universal, limited by no external ordinances, and attached to no particular race or people. Moreover, he is a king-priest (Ps. cx.), and by taking precedence of Abram. and blessing him, and receiving of him tithes, he became the representative of a higher priesthood than any that could spring from Abram's loins.

Bread and wine.—The representatives of food of all kinds, both liquid and solid. Though the primary object of this offering was the refreshing of the bodies of Abram's men, and of the prisoners wearied with their long march to and fro, yet we cannot but recognise in it a foreshowing of the bestowal by Christ, the antitype, upon His Church of the spiritual food of His most blessed Body and Blood.

Priest of the most high God.—Heb., *of El 'elyon.* The mention of the term *priest* (used here for the first time) shows that some sort of sacrificial worship existed at Salem. Sacrifice had, however, been practised before; for Abel had acted as a priest when offering his firstlings, and Abram at the various altars which he built. Apparently, however, Melchizedek had been set apart for the priesthood in some more definite way. *El 'elyon* means "the supreme God," and though the two words are so similar in English, they are altogether unlike in Hebrew. In Ps. vii. 17 the epithet *'elyon* is applied to Jehovah. With that precision in the use of the names of Deity which we have so often noticed before, Melchizedek is described as a priest of *El 'elyon*, the Supreme Ruler of the universe; but Abram swears by *Jehovah El 'elyon*, thus claiming that Jehovah was that Supreme Deity whom Melchizedek served, though without the special knowledge of Him which the patriarch possessed.

(19) **Possessor.**—Literally, *creator*, or *framer*. It is a poetical word, as are also those for "delivered" and "enemies." The form of the blessing, moreover, is poetical, as it is arranged in parallel clauses.

(20) **He gave him tithes.**—Abram thus consecrated the war by a thank-offering to God, Who had

(21) And the king of Sodom said unto
Abram, Give me the [1] persons, and take
the goods to thyself. (22) And Abram
said to the king of Sodom, I have lift up
mine hand unto the LORD, the most high
God, the possessor of heaven and earth,
(23) that I will not *take* from a thread
even to a shoelatchet, and that I will
not take any thing that *is* thine, lest
thou shouldest say, I have made Abram
rich: (24) save only that which the young
men have eaten, and the portion of the
men which went with me, Aner, Eshcol,
and Mamre; let them take their portion.

CHAPTER XV.—(1) After these
things the word of the LORD came unto
Abram in a vision, saying, Fear not,
Abram: I *am* thy shield, *and* thy exceeding
[a]great reward. (2) And Abram
said, Lord GOD, what wilt thou give me,
seeing I go childless, and the steward
of my house *is* this Eliezer of Damascus?
(3) And Abram said, Behold, to me thou
hast given no seed: and, lo, one born
in my house is mine heir. (4) And, behold,
the word of the LORD *came* unto
him, saying, This shall not be thine
heir; but he that shall come forth out
of thine own bowels shall be thine heir.
(5) And he brought him forth abroad,
and said, Look now toward heaven, and
tell the stars, if thou be able to number
them: and he said unto him, [b] So shall

1 Heb., *souls*

a Ps. 16. 5.

b Rom. 4. 18.

---

given him the victory. But he also, by paying tithes, acknowledged the priesthood of Melchizedek, and that the God Whom he served was the true God. See Heb. vii. 4—11.

(21) **Give me the persons.**—To this day it is the rule among the Arabs that, if a camp be plundered, any-one who recovers the booty gives up only the persons, and takes the rest for himself. But Abram, with noble generosity, will accept nothing. The "lifting up of the hand" to give solemnity to an oath is mentioned here for the first time.

(24) **The young men . . . the men which went with me.**—The former are Abram's 318 servants, and they are to take only their food. The latter are the Amorites, and they are to have their fair share of the spoil.

We must notice in Abram's policy that, while Lot had joined himself to the Canaanites, he stood aloof, ready to help on fit occasion, but even so maintaining his independence, and refusing to draw the bonds of friendship close together. Such, too, was the true policy of the people sprung from him. Standing apart from all nations, they were to trust in Jehovah alone for the maintenance of their liberty and rights; and so long as they did thus act they found in Him peace and security.

XV.

JEHOVAH'S COVENANT WITH ABRAM.

(1) **After these things.**—After the war with Chedorlaomer.

The word of the Lord came (Heb., *was*) **unto Abram.**—This phrase, used so constantly afterwards to signify revelation, occurs here for the first time. The revelation on this occasion is made by night (verse 5), not however in a dream, but in a trance, in which the senses of Abram were closed to all earthly impressions and he became passive in the hands of the Almighty. Up to this time Abram had received only general promises of offspring, and of the land being the possession of his seed; but years were passing by, and the fulfilment of his hopes remained distant as ever. By the war with the Elamite king he had also made for himself powerful enemies; and though the immediate result was fortunate, yet many Canaanite nations may have witnessed with displeasure so remarkable an exhibition of the power and energy of an "immigrant." And thus the time had come when the patriarch needed and obtained more formal assurances, first, of the bestowal upon him of offspring (verses 1—6), and, secondly, of the future possession of Palestine (verses 18—21).

(2) **Lord God.**—Not *Jehovah Elohim*, but *Lord Jehovah*, "Lord" being the ordinary title of respect. Usually Jehovah takes the vowels of *'donai*, "lord," but as the two words occur here together, it takes the vowels of *Elohim*, whence the translation in our version, in obedience to a superstition of the Jews (chap. iv. 1).

What wilt thou give me?—There is a slight tone of complaint in these words. Jehovah promised Abram a "reward great exceedingly." He answers that no reward can really be great so long as he has no heir.

I go childless.—Either, *I am going to my grave childless* (Ps. xxxix. 13), or better, *I continue to be, pass my days, in childlessness.*

The steward of my house.—Heb., *the ben-meshek of my house.* Ben-meshek is generally explained as meaning "the son of possession," that is, the possessor, owner of my house when I die. Other authorities derive *meshek* from a verb signifying "to run about," as if it was Eliezer's business to go to and fro in execution of Abram's orders. The term is rare, and has evidently been chosen for the play of words upon *Dammesek* = Damascus. Perhaps this may also explain the last words, which literally are, *he is Damascus Eliezer.* Grammatically it should have been, "he is the Damascene Eliezer," but this would have spoiled the assonance between *ben-meshek* (probably pronounced *bemmeshek*) and *Dammesek.*

(3) **One born in my house.**—This is a mistake. Those born in Abram's house were his servants (chap. xiv. 14). The Hebrew is, *the son of my house,* my house-son, not born of me, but the chief of the house next to myself, and its representative. Eliezer was probably born at Damascus.

(5) **He brought him forth.**—There is no reason for regarding this as a poetical description of a merely mental emotion. With his senses dormant, but alive to every spiritual impression, Abram feels himself led forth from the tent into the open space around, and is there commanded to count the stars. As a matter of fact, the stars visible to the naked eye are not very numerous, but they have ever been a received metaphor

thy seed be. (6) And he [a]believed in
the Lord; and he counted it to him for
righteousness.
(7) And he said unto him, I *am* the
Lord that brought thee out of Ur of the
Chaldees, to give thee this land to in-
herit it. (8) And he said, Lord God,
whereby shall I know that I shall in-
herit it? (9) And he said unto him,
Take me an heifer of three years old,
and a she goat of three years old, and
a ram of three years old, and a turtle-
dove, and a young pigeon. (10) And he
took unto him all these, and divided
them in the midst, and laid each piece
one against another: but the birds
divided he not. (11) And when the fowls
came down upon the carcases, Abram
drove them away.
(12) And when the sun was going down,
a deep sleep fell upon Abram; and, lo,
an horror of great darkness fell upon
him. (13) And he said unto Abram,
Know of a surety [b]that thy seed shall
be a stranger in a land *that is* not their's,
and shall serve them; and they shall
afflict them four hundred years; (14) and
also that nation, whom they shall serve,
will I judge: and afterward shall they
come out with great substance. (15) And

a Rom. 4. 3; Gal. 3. 6; James 2. 23.

b Acts 7. 6.

---

for an infinite multitude, probably because, as men gaze, they perpetually see the faint radiance of more and more distant constellations. Thus they cannot be counted, and Abram's seed was to be countless, because of the vastness of its number.

(6) **He believed in the Lord** (in Jehovah) . . . —We have here the germ of the doctrine of free justification. Abram was both a holy man and one who proved his faith by his works; but nevertheless the inspired narrator inserts this reflection, not after the history of the offering of Isaac, but in the account of this vision, where all that Abram did was to believe, and for that belief's sake was accounted righteous before God. For the definite conclusions deduced from this verse by St. Paul see Rom. iv. The quotation there is from the LXX., and gives the general sense, but the correct rendering of the Hebrew is that given in our version.

(8) **Lord God.**—Heb., *Lord Jehovah*, as in verse 2.

Whereby shall I know that I shall inherit it?—Jehovah had required Abram to leave his home in Ur of the Chaldees on a general promise of future endowment with the land of Canaan. Abram now asks this question, not from want of faith, but from a desire for a more direct confirmation of the promise and fuller knowledge of the details. What Abram, therefore, receives is an exact and circumstantial prophecy, made in the form of a solemn covenant.

(9, 10) **Take me an heifer** . . .—This form of making a covenant was probably that usual in Babylonia, and thus Abram received the assurance of his inheritance by means of a ceremonial with which he was familiar. But in most ancient languages men are said to *cut* or *strike* a covenant, because the most solemn formula involved either the cutting of victims in two, or striking them dead, as was the Roman manner. The severing of the bodies was not, as some suppose, to represent the two parties; but, as explained in Jer. xxxiv. 18—20, it set forth the penalty of perjury, and was usually accompanied by the imprecation upon the covenant-breaker of a destruction as complete, as that which had befallen the slaughtered animals. There is no mention in this place of a sacrifice, although the animals are those subsequently set apart for sacrifice by the Levitical law. The heifer, she-goat, and ram at three years old would each have attained its full maturity; but there may be a further symbolic meaning in there being three animals each three years old.

Laid each piece . . .—More exactly, *and laid each half over against the other.* The birds were not divided; but as there were two, Abram probably placed one on one side and one on the other.

(11) **And when the fowls** . . .—Heb., *And the birds of prey came down upon the carcases, and Abram scared them away.* Had there been a sacrifice the fire would have kept the vultures from approaching; but the bodies lay exposed, and Abram therefore kept guard over them, lest the purpose of the ceremonial should be frustrated by any want of respect shown to the outward symbols.

(12) **When the sun was going down.**—The time described was the evening following the night on which he had received the assurance that his seed should be countless as the stars. He had then, in his trance, also asked for some security that Canaan should be the heritage of his posterity, and in answer had received the command to arrange, upon a large scale, the ceremonial of a solemn treaty-making. The morning had been spent in the performance of the command, and afterwards he had watched, probably for several hours, by the side of the divided bodies, uncertain what would happen, but occupied in driving away the vultures, which gathered from all quarters round the abundant feast. At sunset the revelation came to him, not in a waking trance, as on the previous night, but in "a deep sleep," and with those accompaniments of terror so powerfully described in Job iv. 12—16, and which the creature cannot but feel when brought near to the manifest presence of the Creator (Dan. x. 8).

Lo, an horror of great darkness fell upon him.—Heb., *lo, a terror, even great darkness, falling upon him.* The terror was not mental so much as bodily, caused by a deep gloom settling round him, such as would be the effect of an eclipse of the setting sun, and shutting all mortal things away from his view.

(13) **Four hundred years.**—The exact duration of the sojourn in Egypt was 430 years (Exod. xii. 40, 41), and with this agrees the genealogy of Jehoshua (1 Chron. vii. 23—27).

(14) **That nation.**—Had it been expressly revealed that the country that would afflict them was Egypt, the patriarchs might have been unwilling to go thither; but the reference to the plagues in the denunciation of judgment, and to the spoiling of the Egyptians in the promise that they should "come out with great substance" (Exod. xii. 36), gave detail sufficient for future guidance, and for their assurance in time to come that the promise had been fulfilled.

(15) **Thou shalt go to thy fathers in peace.**—Abram's ancestors had died in Babylonia, but the

thou shalt go to thy fathers in peace;
thou shalt be buried in a good old age.
(16) But in the fourth generation they
shall come hither again: for the iniquity
of the Amorites *is* not yet full. (17) And
it came to pass, that, when the sun
went down, and it was dark, behold a
smoking furnace, and [1] a burning lamp
that passed between those pieces.
(18) In the same day the LORD made a
covenant with Abram, saying, [a] Unto
thy seed have I given this land, from
the river of Egypt unto the great river,
the river Euphrates: (19) the Kenites,
and the Kenizzites, and the Kadmonites,
(20) and the Hittites, and the Perizzites,
and the Rephaims, (21) and the Amorites,
and the Canaanites, and the Girgashites,
and the Jebusites.

1 Heb., *a lamp of fire.*

a ch. 12. 7, & 13. 15, & 26. 4; Deut. 34. 4.

CHAPTER XVI. — (1) Now Sarai
Abram's wife bare him no children: and

---

phrase, used here for the first time, evidently involves the thought of the immortality of the soul. The body may be buried far away, but the soul joins the company of its forefathers in some separate abode, not to be absorbed, but still to enjoy a personal existence. (Comp. chap. xxv. 8.) A similar, but more exact, distinction between the body and the spirit is drawn in Eccles. xii. 7.

(16) **The fourth generation.**—Heb., *dôr.* (See Note on chap. vi. 9.) As the four generations are identical with the four centuries of verse 13, we have here an undesigned testimony to the long duration of human life. So Abram was 100 years old when Isaac was born, and Isaac was 60 at the birth of his children, and Jacob 64 years of age at his marriage. But the word *dôr* had probably come down from a remote antiquity, and, like the Latin word *seculum*, signified a century.

The iniquity of the Amorites.—As the chief and leading tribe, they are used here for all the Canaanite nations. We learn from this declaration that the Canaanites were not extirpated by any wilful decree to make room for Israel, but as an act of justice, like that which, because of their moral depravity, overwhelmed the Sethites with a flood. So, subsequently, Israel and Judah had each to bear a punishment in accordance with their sinfulness; and so, throughout the history of the world, whenever nations settle down in vice and corruption, the decay of their institutions follows upon that of their morals, and they either waste away or give place to some more manly race of conquerors. The conquest of Canaan by Israel was parallel to that of the enervated Roman empire of the West by the Germans; only we see the preparation for it, and God's purpose explained; and we also see that if the Amorites had not made the scale of justice weigh down heavily, they would not have been deprived of their country.

(17) **A smoking furnace.**—The word really means the circular firepot which Orientals use in their houses to sit round for purposes of warmth. This one was wreathed in smoke, out of which shot "a burning lamp" (Heb., *a torch of flame*). For not two symbols, but only one, passed between the divided carcases. Abram had probably passed between them immediately after arranging them, and now Jehovah does the same. Fire is the recognised symbol of the Deity, as in the burning bush, the pillar of fire, the lightnings on Mount Sinai, &c.

(18) **The Lord made a covenant.**—Heb., *Jehovah cut a covenant.* Abram had divided the slaughtered animals, and Jehovah, by passing between them, made the whole act His own.

The river of Egypt.—That is, the Nile. In the Hebrew the Wady-el-Arish, on the southern border of Simeon, is always distinguished from the Nile, though the distinction is neglected in our version. Thus, in Num. xxxiv. 5; Josh. xv. 4; Isa. xxvii. 12 (where alone an attempt is made at accuracy by translating *stream*), the Hebrew has, *the torrent of Egypt*, that is, a stream full after the rains, but dry during the rest of the year. For a description of these torrent-beds see Isa. lvii. 5, 6, where in verse 5 the word is translated *valleys*, and in verse 6 *stream*. The word used here signifies a river that flows constantly; and Abram's posterity are to found a kingdom conterminous with the Nile and the Euphrates, that is, with Egypt and Babylonia. If these bounds are large and vague, we must also remember that they are limited by the names of the ten nations which follow. Between the Nile and the Euphrates, the territories of these ten tribes is alone definitely bestowed upon Abram.

(19) **The Kenites.**—An Arab race, found both among the Amalekites in the south (1 Sam. xv. 6) and among the tribes of Naphtali and Zebulon in the north (Judges iv. 11), and even in Midian, as Jethro, the father-in-law of Moses, is called a Kenite (Judges i. 16). Balaam speaks of them as being a powerful nation (Num. xxiv. 21), and this wide dispersion of them into feeble remnants seems to show that they were a race of early settlers in Canaan, who, like the Rephaim, had been overpowered and scattered by subsequent immigrants. They were uniformly friendly to Israel.

The Kenizzites.—The chief fact of importance connected with this race is that Caleb was a Kenezite (Num. xxxii. 12). Apparently with his clan he joined the Israelites at the Exodus, and was numbered with the tribe of Judah. *Kenizzite* and *Kenezite* are two ways of spelling the same Hebrew word, the former being right.

The Kadmonites.—This may mean either an *eastern* or an *ancient* people, of whom we know nothing.

For **the Perizzites** see chap. xiii. 7; for **the Rephaims,** chap. xiv. 5; and for the rest, chap. x. 15—18.

XVI.

THE SON OF THE BONDWOMAN.

(1) **Now Sarai.**—The history of Abram is given in a succession of brief narratives, written possibly by the patriarch himself; and though papyrus was known at Ur (*Trans. Soc. Bibl. Arch.*, i. 343, ii. 430), yet the absence of any convenient writing material for ordinary use would oblige men in those ancient days to content themselves with short inscriptions, like those tablets of clay brought from Ur, many of which now in the British Museum are said to be considerably older than the time of Abram. The narrator would naturally make but few alterations in such precious documents, and hence a certain amount of recapitulation, like that which we find in the Books of Samuel, where

she had an handmaid, an Egyptian,
whose name *was* Hagar. (2) And Sarai
said unto Abram, Behold now, the
LORD hath restrained me from bearing:
I pray thee, go in unto my maid; it may
be that I may [1] obtain children by her.
And Abram hearkened to the voice of
Sarai. (3) And Sarai Abram's wife took
Hagar her maid the Egyptian, after
Abram had dwelt ten years in the land
of Canaan, and gave her to her husband
Abram to be his wife. (4) And he went
in unto Hagar, and she conceived: and
when she saw that she had conceived,
her mistress was despised in her eyes.
(5) And Sarai said unto Abram, My
wrong *be* upon thee: I have given my
maid into thy bosom; and when she
saw that she had conceived, I was des-
pised in her eyes: the LORD judge
between me and thee. (6) But Abram
said unto Sarai, Behold, thy maid *is* in
thy hand; do to her [2] as it pleaseth
thee. And when Sarai [3] dealt hardly
with her, she fled from her face.
(7) And the angel of the LORD found
her by a fountain of water in the wilder-
ness, by the fountain in the way to

1 Heb., *be builded by her.*

2 Heb., that which *is good in thine eyes.*

B.C. cir. 1911.

3 Heb., *afflicted her.*

again we have not a narrative from one pen, but the arrangement of materials already ancient. As, however, the Divine object was the revealing to mankind of the way by which God would raise up man from the fall, the narrator would be guided by inspiration in his choice of materials, and in the omission of such things as did not fall in with this purpose; and the evident reverence with which he deals with these records is a warrant to us of their genuineness. Such additions as the remark that the "Valley of Shaveh" was many centuries later called "the King's Dale" (chap. xiv. 17; 2 Sam. xviii. 18) are generally acknowledged to have been the work of Ezra and the men of the Great Synagogue, after the return from the exile.

Hagar.—As this word apparently comes from the Arabic verb *to flee,* it cannot have been her original name, unless we suppose that she really was an Arab fugitive who had taken refuge in Egypt. More probably she was an Egyptian woman who had escaped to Abram when he was in the Negeb, and had then received this appellation, which virtually means *run-away.*

(2) **That I may obtain children by her.**—Heb., *that I may be builded by her.* The words, *ben*=a son, *bath* (originally *banth*)=a daughter, *baith* (*banith*) =a house, and *bânâh*=to build, all belong to the same root in Hebrew, the idea being that the children build the house, and give a man the pledge of continuance. Until late times the tent was the habitation, while the house was the family (chap. vii. 1). Thus the phrase "to build a man *a sure house*" meant, to give him lasting prosperity (1 Sam. ii. 35). Hence, too, the close connection between building and the bestowal of children in Ps. cxxvii. As then the children of a woman bestowed by her mistress upon the husband were regarded as belonging to the wife (chap. xxx. 3), Sarah, despairing of bearing a son herself, as she was now seventy-five, and had been ten years in Canaan, concluded that her heir was to be born of a substitute.

As regards the morality of the act, we find that marriage with one wife was the original law (chap. ii. 24), and that when polygamy was introduced it was coupled by the inspired narrator with violence and licence (chap. iv. 19). Monogamy was the rule, as we see in the households of Noah, Terah, Isaac, and others; but many, like Esau and Jacob, allowed themselves a greater latitude. In so doing, their conduct falls below the level of Christian morality, but every one's actions are strongly influenced by the general views of the people among whom he lives; and in Abram's case it must be said in his defence that, with so much depending on his having offspring, he took no steps to obtain another wife, but remained content with the barren Sarai. When he did take Hagar it was at his wife's request, and for a reason which seemed to them adequate, and even religious. Rachel subsequently did the same for a much lower motive. The consent of the wife was in such cases all-important; and so in India, in ancient times, it was necessary to make a second marriage valid (see Wilson's *Hindu Theatre,* i. 179).

(3) **Abram had dwelt ten years in the land of Canaan.**—He was now, therefore, eighty-five years of age (see verse 16 and chap. xii. 4), and this long delay had not only tried his faith, but brought him and Sarai to the conclusion that the promised seed was to be obtained by other means.

(4) **Her mistress was despised.**—Hagar, we are told in verse 3, was to be, not Abram's concubine, but his wife. She was to be Sarai's representative, and though now she would hold the highest place in the household next to Sarai, because of this relation to Abram, yet she would continue to be Sarai's maid. But no sooner had she conceived, than, proud of her superiority over her mistress, she wished to overthrow this arrangement, and, at all events, acted as if she was Abram's wife absolutely, and thrust Sarai aside.

(5) **My wrong be upon thee.**—That is, *May the wrong done to me be avenged upon thee.* Sarai's act had been one of self-denial for Abram's sake, and now that it has led to her being treated insolently she makes Abram answerable for it.

(6) **Sarai dealt hardly with her.**—The verb is translated *afflicted* in Exod. i. 11 and Isa. lx. 14; its more exact meaning is, *Sarai humbled her,* that is, reduced her to her original condition. It was quite right that as Hagar had abused her elevation, Abram should make her yield to Sarai all due respect and submission; but in making her resume her old position as a slave, Sarai was possibly dealing unkindly with her (but see on verse 9). In running away Hagar not only showed the untamable love of freedom which Ishmael inherited from her, but apparently was repeating the act from which she had her name.

(7) **The angel of the Lord.**—Heb., *of Jehovah.* (See Excursus at end of Book.)

In the way to Shur.—Hagar evidently fled by the usual route leading from Hebron past Beer-sheba to Egypt. The wilderness was that of Paran, in which Kadesh was situated. The fountain by which Hagar was sitting was on the road to Shur, which is a desert on the eastern side of Egypt, forming the boundary of the territory of the Ishmaelites (chap. xxv. 18) and of the Amalekites (1 Sam. xv. 7, xxvii. 8), and reached

Shur. (8) And he said, Hagar, Sarai's
maid, whence camest thou? and whither
wilt thou go? And she said, I flee from
the face of my mistress Sarai. (9) And
the angel of the LORD said unto her,
Return to thy mistress, and submit thy-
self under her hands. (10) And the angel
of the LORD said unto her, I will multi-
ply thy seed exceedingly, that it shall
not be numbered for multitude. (11) And
the angel of the LORD said unto her,
Behold, thou *art* with child, and shalt
bear a son, and shalt call his name [1]Ish-
mael; because the LORD hath heard thy
affliction. (12) And he will be a wild
man; his hand *will be* against every
man, and every man's hand against
him; [a] and he shall dwell in the presence
of all his brethren. (13) And she called
the name of the LORD that spake unto
her, Thou God seest me: for she said,
Have I also here looked after him that
seeth me? (14) Wherefore the well was
called [b][2] Beer-lahai-roi; behold, *it is*
between Kadesh and Bered.
(15) And Hagar bare Abram a son: and
Abram called his son's name, which
Hagar bare, Ishmael. (16) And Abram
was fourscore and six years old, when
Hagar bare Ishmael to Abram.

CHAPTER XVII. — (1) And when
Abram was ninety years old and nine,
the LORD appeared to Abram, and said
unto him, I *am* the Almighty God;
[c] walk before me, and be thou [3] perfect.

1 That is, *God shall hear.*

a ch. 25. 18.

b ch. 24. 62.

2 That is, *The well of him that liveth and seeth me.*

B.C. cir. 1910.

B.C. cir. 1898.

c ch. 5. 22.

3 Or, *upright,* or, *sincere.*

---

by the Israelites soon after crossing the Red Sea (Exod. xv. 22; Num. xxxiii. 8). It is now called *J'afar*.

(8) **Whence camest thou?**—It is noteworthy that in these Divine communications God's knowledge of all the circumstances is not presumed, but the person visited is led on to tell them. This adds very much to the freshness and poetry of the narrative. Here, however, in the address, *Hagar, Sarai's maid*, the angel, at least, shows that he is aware who she is, and also reminds her of what she had forgotten, that in bestowing her upon Abram Sarai did not cease to be her mistress.

(9) **Submit thyself.**—Heb., *humble thyself.* It is the verb translated *dealt hardly* in verse 6. The angel therefore commands her to take the position which Sarai was forcing upon her; and by so doing proves to us that there had been no personal maltreatment. Commentators have taken this notion, not from the Hebrew, but from the English Version.

(10) **I will multiply thy seed.**—We have here the purpose of the Divine manifestation. Abram's son must not be mixed up with and lost among the debased population of Egypt, but must be the father of a free people; and Hagar will now submit to her lot as a slave, that she may secure liberty for her offspring.

(11) **Ishmael.**—That is, *God heareth.* Like Samuel, Ishmael received his name from the events of his mother's life, and not from anything in his own. There was, however, no rule in this matter, and the naming of children in the Book of Genesis is very diversified.

(12) **He will be a wild man.**—Heb., *he will be a wild-ass man.* The wild ass of the Arabian deserts is a very noble creature, and is one of the animals selected in the Book of Job as especially exemplifying the greatness of God (Job xxxix. 5—8). Its characteristics are great speed, love of solitude, and an untamable fondness of liberty. It is thus the very type of the Bedaween Arabs, whose delight is to rove at will over the desert, and who despise the ease and luxury of a settled life.

His hand will be against every man . . .—The Bedaween can be bound by no treaties, submit to no law, and count plunder as legitimate gain. Nevertheless—

He shall dwell in the presence of all his brethren.—That is, he shall maintain his independence, and his descendants shall continue to exist as a free race in the presence of the other Abrahamic nations. Many commentators, however, consider that the more exact rendering is, *he shall dwell to the east of all his brethren.* This is certainly the meaning of the word in chap. xxv. 6, but does not suit equally well there in verse 18.

(13) **Thou God seest me.**—Heb., *Thou art El Roï,* that is, a God of seeing. Not as Onkelos paraphrases it, "Thou art a God that sees all things," but "Thou art a God that permits Himself to be seen." For so Hagar proceeds herself to explain the name, *Do not I still see after seeing?* With all the love of an Oriental for dark sayings, Hagar plays upon the word "*roï*," but her meaning is plain: "Do I not see, and therefore am alive, and not even blinded, nor bereft of sense and reason, though I have seen God."

(14) **Beer-lahai-roi.**—That is, *Well of the living-seeing* (of God), the well where God has been seen, and the beholder still lives. It became afterwards a favourite dwelling-place of Isaac (chap. xxv. 11), and was probably, therefore, surrounded by pastures, but its site has not been identified. For Kadesh see chap. xiv. 7. Bered is absolutely unknown.

XVII.

CONFIRMATION OF THE COVENANT BY THE SACRAMENT OF CIRCUMCISION.

(1) **Abram was ninety years old and nine.**—Thirteen years, therefore, had passed by since the birth of Ishmael, who doubtless during this time had grown very dear to the childless old man, as we gather from the wish expressed in verse 18.

I am the Almighty God.—Heb., *El shaddai.* The word is Archaic, but there is no doubt that it means *strong so as to overpower.* Besides its use in Genesis we find it employed as the name of Deity by Balaam (Num. xxiv. 4, 16); by Naomi (Ruth i. 20); and in the Book of Job, where it occurs thirty-one times. We may thus regard it as "one of the more general world-wide titles of the Most High" (Speaker's Commentary). In Exod. vi. 3 it is said, with evident reference to this place, that El shaddai was the name of God revealed

(2) And I will make my covenant between
me and thee, and will multiply thee ex-
ceedingly. (3) And Abram fell on his
face: and God talked with him, saying,
(4) As for me, behold, my covenant *is*
with thee, and thou shalt be a father of
[1] many nations. (5) Neither shall thy
name any more be called Abram, but
thy name shall be Abraham; [a] for a
father of many nations have I made
thee. (6) And I will make thee exceed-
ing fruitful, and I will make nations of
thee, and kings shall come out of thee.
(7) And I will establish my covenant be-
tween me and thee and thy seed after
thee in their generations for an ever-
lasting covenant, to be a God unto thee,
and to thy seed after thee. (8) And I
will give unto thee, and to thy seed
after thee, the land [2] wherein thou art a
stranger, all the land of Canaan, for an
everlasting possession; and I will be
their God.

(9) And God said unto Abraham, Thou
shalt keep my covenant therefore, thou,
and thy seed after thee in their genera-
tions. (10) This *is* my covenant, which
ye shall keep, between me and you and
thy seed after thee; [b] Every man child
among you shall be circumcised. (11) And
ye shall circumcise the flesh of your
foreskin; and it shall be [c] a token of the

1 Heb., *multitude of nations.*

a Rom. 4. 17.

2 Heb., *of thy sojournings.*

b Acts 7. 8.

c Acts 7. 8; Rom. 4. 11.

to the patriarchs, but that He was not known to them by His name Jehovah. Here, nevertheless, in a passage said by commentators to be Elohistic, we read that "Jehovah appeared to Abram, and said to him I am El shaddai." But the very gist of the passage is the identification of Jehovah and El shaddai, and the great object of the manifest care with which Moses distinguishes the Divine names seems to be to show, that though Jehovah became the special name of Elohim in His covenant relation to Israel after the Exodus, yet that the name was one old and primeval (chap. iv. 26), and that the God of revelation, under various titles, was ever one and the same. And so is it now, though we, by following a Jewish superstition, have well-nigh forfeited the use of the name Jehovah, so greatly prized of old (chap. iv. 1).

Walk before me.—The same verb as that used of Enoch (chap. v. 22), and of Noah (chap. vi. 9), but the preposition *before* implies less closeness than *with*. On the other hand, Noah was described as "perfect among his contemporaries" (*ibid.*), while Abram is required still to strive after this integrity (see Note on chap. vi. 9).

(2) **I will make my covenant.**—In chap. xv. 18 the Heb. word for "make" is *cut*, and refers to the severing of the victims; here it is "give," "place," and implies that it was an act of grace on God's part (comp. Note on chap. ix. 9). Abram had now waited twenty-five years after leaving Ur-Chasdim, and fourteen or fifteen years since the ratification of the solemn covenant between him and Jehovah (chap. xv. 17); but the time had at length arrived for the fulfilment of the promise, and in token thereof Abram and Sarai were to change their names, and all the males be brought near to God by a solemn sacrament.

(4) **Of many nations.**—This is a feeble rendering of a remarkable phrase. Literally the word signifies a confused noise like the din of a populous city. Abram is to be the father of a thronging crowd of nations. And so in verse 5.

(5) **Abram.**—That is, *high father.*

Abraham = *Father of a multitude,* "raham" being an Arabic word, perhaps current in Hebrew in ancient times. Another interpretation of Abram is that it is equivalent to Abi-aram, Father of Aram, or Syria. This too is an Arabic form, like Abimael in chap. x. 28. By some commentators the stress is thrown upon the insertion of the letter "h," as being the representative of the name Yahveh or Yehveh. (Compare the change of Oshea into Jehoshua, Num. xiii. 16.)

(10) **Shall be circumcised.**—It is stated by Herodotus (Book ii. 104) that the Egyptians were circumcised, and that the Syrians in Palestine confessed that they learned this practice from the Egyptians. Origen, however, seems to limit circumcision to the priesthood (Epist. ad Rom., § ii. 13); and the statement of Herodotus is not only very loose, but his date is too far posterior to the time of Abram for us to be able to place implicit confidence in it. If we turn to the evidence of Egyptian monuments and of the mummies, we find proof of the rite having become general in Egypt only in quite recent times. The discussion is, however, merely of archæological importance; for circumcision was just as appropriate a sign of the covenant if borrowed from institutions already existing as if then used for the first time. It is, moreover, an acknowledged fact that the Bible is always true to the local colouring. Chaldæan influence is predominant in those early portions of Genesis which we owe to Abram, a citizen of Ur of the Chaldees; his life and surroundings subsequently are those of an Arab sheik; while Egyptian influence is strongly marked in the latter part of Genesis, and in the history of the Exodus from that country. In this fact we have a sufficient answer to the theories which would bring down the composition of the Pentateuch to a late period: for the author would certainly have written in accordance with the facts and ideas of his own times. If, however, Abram had seen circumcision in Egypt, when the famine drove him thither, and had learned the significance of the rite, and that the idea of it was connected with moral purity, there was in this even a reason why God should choose it as the outward sign of the sacrament which He was now bestowing upon the patriarch.

The fitness of circumcision to be a sign of entering into a covenant, and especially into one to which children were to be admitted, consisted in its being a representation of a new birth by the putting off of the old man, and the dedication of the new man unto holiness. The flesh was cast away that the spirit might grow strong; and the change of name in Abram and Sarai was typical of this change of condition. They had been born again, and so must again be named. And though women could not indeed be admitted directly into the covenant, yet they shared in its privileges by virtue of their consanguinity to the men, who were as sponsors for them; and thus Sarai changes her name equally with her husband.

covenant betwixt me and you. (12) And
[1] he that is eight days old [a] shall be cir-
cumcised among you, every man child
in your generations, he that is born in
the house, or bought with money of any
stranger, which *is* not of thy seed.
(13) He that is born in thy house, and he
that is bought with thy money, must
needs be circumcised: and my covenant
shall be in your flesh for an everlasting
covenant. (14) And the uncircumcised
man child whose flesh of his foreskin is
not circumcised, that soul shall be cut
off from his people; he hath broken my
covenant.
(15) And God said unto Abraham, As
for Sarai thy wife, thou shalt not call
her name Sarai, but Sarah *shall* her
name *be*. (16) And I will bless her, and
give thee a son also of her: yea, I will
bless her, and [2] she shall be *a mother* of
nations; kings of people shall be of her.
(17) Then Abraham fell upon his face,
and laughed, and said in his heart,
Shall *a child* be born unto him that is an
hundred years old? and shall Sarah,

[1] Heb., *a son of eight days.*

[a] Lev. 12. 3; Luke 2. 21; John 7. 22.

[2] Heb., *she shall become nations.*

---

(12) **Eight days old.**—That is, just one week after birth, as the day of birth was counted among the eight days.

(13) **He that is born in thy house . . .**—Two things follow from this wide extension of the rite of circumcision: the first, that all members of Abram's household, being thus sharers in the covenant, were also numbered as belonging to the nations that sprang from him. We have seen that even in early days his followers must have numbered six or seven hundred men (chap. xiv. 14), and they were growing in multitude all the rest of his life, and during the lifetime of Isaac. They were then divided between Esau and Jacob at Isaac's death (chaps. xxxv. 27, xxxvi. 6, 7), but the diminution in the number of Jacob's family thus caused must have been compensated by those whom he gathered for himself in Mesopotamia (chap. xxx. 43). All his household went down with him into Egypt, as part of his *taf*, translated "little ones" in chap. xlvi. 5, but really signifying the whole body of dependents, men, women, and children. Placed there in the fruitful Delta, they would be counted as members of that tribe to the chief of which they belonged, and would swell the numbers of the vast host which left Egypt (Exod. xii. 37). The second point is, that as all who were circumcised were regarded as Israelites, so also circumcision was confined to the Israelites. It was not a catholic ordinance, intended, like baptism, for all people and all times. Nor was it primarily a religious institution. The bought slave was circumcised first, and instructed afterwards. No profession of faith was required, but he was admitted to the privilege in right of his master. The reason of this was that it was an admission into the Jewish nation first, and by consequence only into the church. It is one of the many points which distinguish slavery, as practised among the Jews, from the degrading form of it which existed in modern times, that from the days of Abram onwards the slave by being circumcised was proclaimed to be one of the same race and nation as his master, and thereby entitled to share in his national and religious privileges.

(14) **Shall be cut off from his people.**—Jewish commentators generally consider that this penalty consisted in the offender being left to the direct interposition of God, who would punish him with childlessness and premature death (*Talmud: Tract. Yebam*, 55). Most Christian commentators suppose that the offender was to be put to death by the civil magistrate; but this view is untenable. For a distinction is constantly drawn between the penalty of death, and the being "cut off from among the people," as, for instance, in Lev. xx. So, too, the killing of a clean beast anywhere, except at the door of the tabernacle (*Ibid.*, xvii. 4), and the eating of blood (*Ibid.*, 9, 14), are to be thus dealt with, while blasphemy and murder are to be punished with death (*Ibid.*, xxiv. 16, 17). Now it became very common to kill clean beasts in all parts of the land, and the eating of blood, though regarded with horror (1 Sam. xiv. 32—34), apparently had no penalty attached to it. The Jewish commentators seem to err only in being too special, and in defining the method in which God would punish. The punishment really seems to have been that of excommunication or outlawry, to which other penalties might have been attached by custom: but the main point was that one uncircumcised (as subsequently one who violated the principles of the Mosaic law) forfeited his privileges as a member of the Jewish nation, could claim no protection from the elders for life and property, and could not take his place at the gate of the city.

(15) **Sarai.**—Probably *princely*, an adjective of the same form as *shaddai*, verse 1; while *Sarah* means *princess*. The change of name shows that she was admitted to the covenant. (Comp. verse 10.)

(16) **A son . . . of her.**—This is the first place where it was definitely promised that Abram's heir should be Sarah's own son. This must be remembered in estimating the conduct of Abram and Sarah in the matter of Hagar. They had long waited, and hoped, before taking measures of their own for the fulfilment of the promise. The rest of the verse should be translated, "she shall become (grow into) nations: kings of peoples shall become of her, that is, "shall spring from her."

(17) **Abraham . . . laughed.**—The Jewish interpreters regard Abraham's laugh as one of joy, and Sarah's (chap. xviii. 12) as one of unbelief. We may, however, well doubt whether there really was this difference between them; but our Lord confirms the view that joy was uppermost in Abraham's heart (John viii. 56). Still with belief there was surprise, and the feeling that what was promised was so strange as to be well-nigh incredible. One who was ready to sacrifice his only son at God's word (Heb. xi. 19) would not be staggered by this strangeness, and yet the thought of Sarah's bearing a child at the age of ninety might easily present itself to his mind in a ludicrous aspect. As for Sarah, there is no proof that at the time when she laughed she knew or even suspected that the three travellers were more than men. She overheard their conversation, and laughed, imagining perhaps that they did not know how old she was. Really, the idea brought out by this double laughter is that Isaac's birth was contrary to nature.

that is ninety years old, bear? (8) And
Abraham said unto God, O that Ish-
mael might live before thee! (19) And
God said, [a] Sarah thy wife shall bear
thee a son indeed; and thou shalt call
his name Isaac: and I will establish my a ch. 18. 10, & 21. 2.
covenant with him for an everlasting
covenant, *and* with his seed after him.
(20) And as for Ishmael, I have heard
thee: Behold, I have blessed him, and
will make him fruitful, and will multi-
ply him exceedingly; [b] twelve princes
shall he beget, and I will make him a b ch. 25. 12.
great nation. (21) But my covenant will
I establish with Isaac, which Sarah
shall bear unto thee at this set time in
the next year. (22) And he left off talk-
ing with him, and God went up from
Abraham. c Heb. 13. 2.
(23) And Abraham took Ishmael his
son, and all that were born in his house,
and all that were bought with his
money, every male among the men of
Abraham's house; and circumcised the
flesh of their foreskin in the selfsame
day, as God had said unto him. (24) And
Abraham *was* ninety years old and nine,
when he was circumcised in the flesh of
his foreskin. (25) And Ishmael his son
was thirteen years old, when he was
circumcised in the flesh of his foreskin.
(26) In the selfsame day was Abraham
circumcised, and Ishmael his son.
(27) And all the men of his house, born
in the house, and bought with money
of the stranger, were circumcised with
him.

CHAPTER XVIII. — (1) And the
LORD appeared unto him in the plains of
Mamre: and he sat in the tent door in
the heat of the day; (2) [c] and he lift
up his eyes and looked, and, lo, three
men stood by him: and when he saw
them, he ran to meet them from the
tent door, and bowed himself toward
the ground, (3) and said, My Lord, if now
I have found favour in thy sight, pass

(18) **O that Ishmael . . .**—For thirteen years Ishmael had been the "son of the house" (chap. xv. 3), and regarded probably as the true heir. Mingled then with Abraham's joy there was also the pain, natural to a father, of knowing that this transference of the promise to Sarah's child meant the deposition and disappointment of one who for so long had held the post of honour. Stoicism would have repressed this upright and natural feeling, but God hears and accepts the father's prayers; and while the birthright and religious pre-eminence is justly given to the son of the freewoman, there is a large earthly blessing for the handmaid's son.

(19) **Indeed.**—In the Hebrew this word comes first, and is intended to remove all doubt or desire for any other turn of affairs. It should be rendered, "And God said, For a certainty Sarah thy wife shall bear thee a son."

Thou shalt call his name Isaac.—That is, *he laughs.* The name was to be a perpetual memorial that Isaac's birth was naturally such an impossibility as to excite ridicule.

(25) **Ishmael . . . . was thirteen years old.**—Hence the Mohammedans defer circumcision to the thirteenth year.

(26) **In the selfsame day.**—Heb., *In the bone of this day*, and so in verse 23 (see chap. ii. 23). In the circumcising of the household together with Abraham and his son we see that no impassable interval separated the Hebrew slave from his master, but that he was to share all the national and religious privileges of the freeman.

XVIII.

VISIT OF ANGELS TO ABRAHAM AT MAMRE; AND OVERTHROW OF SODOM.

(1) **And the Lord** (Jehovah) **appeared unto him.**—No new section could begin in this way, but evidently this is a continuation of the narrative of the circumcision. We thus find a Jehovistic section coupled in the closest way with one which is Elohistic (comp. chap. xvii. 22, 23); and even here it is Elohim who for Abraham's sake delivers Lot (chap. xix. 29). Far more important, however, is it to notice that this familiar intercourse, and clear revelation of Jehovah to Abraham, follows upon his closer relation to God by virtue of the sacrament of circumcision. Jewish tradition adds that this visit was made to Abraham on the third day after the rite had been performed, and was for the purpose of healing him from the painful consequences of it. It was on this account, as they think, that Abraham was resting at home, instead of being with his herds in the field.

The plains (Heb., *the oaks*) **of Mamre.**—(See chaps. xiii. 18, xiv. 13.)

The tent door.—Heb., *the opening of the tent*, formed by looping back one of the curtains.

The heat of the day.—The time of noon, when Orientals rest from labour (comp. chap. iii. 8). As the air in the tent would be sultry, Abraham sits in the shade on the outside. So in verse 8 the meal is spread under a tree.

(2) **Three men.**—Jewish commentators explain the number by saying that, as no angel might execute more than one commission at a time, one of the three came to heal Abraham, the second to bear the message to Sarah, and the third to destroy Sodom. More correctly one was "the angel of Jehovah," who came as the manifestation of Deity to Abraham, and the other two were his companions, commissioned by him afterwards to execute judgment on the cities of the plain. The number three pointed also to the Trinity of Persons in the Godhead, and is therefore read by our Church as one of the lessons for Trinity Sunday. But we must be careful not to use it as a proof of this doctrine, lest the inference should be drawn of a personal appearance of the Father and of the Holy Ghost, which would savour of heretical impiety.

(3) **My lord.**—Heb. *'donai*, a term of simple respect, just as the bowing towards the earth is exactly what an

not away, I pray thee, from thy ser-
vant: (4) let a little water, I pray you,
be fetched, and wash your feet, and rest
yourselves under the tree: (5) and I will
fetch a morsel of bread, and [1] comfort
ye your hearts; after that ye shall pass
on: for therefore [2] are ye come to your
servant. And they said, So do, as thou
hast said.
(6) And Abraham hastened into the
tent unto Sarah, and said, [3] Make ready
quickly three measures of fine meal,
knead *it*, and make cakes upon the
hearth. (7) And Abraham ran unto the
herd, and fetcht a calf tender and good,
and gave *it* unto a young man; and he
hasted to dress it. (8) And he took
butter, and milk, and the calf which he
had dressed, and set *it* before them;
and he stood by them under the tree,
and they did eat.
(9) And they said unto him, Where *is*
Sarah thy wife? And he said, Behold, in
the tent. (10) And he said, I will certainly
return unto thee according to the time of
life; and, lo, [a] Sarah thy wife shall have

1 Heb., *stay.*

2 Heb., *you have passed.*

3 Heb., *Hasten.*

a ch. 17. 19, & 21. 2.

Arab sheik would do now to a passing traveller. Abraham's conduct is marked by all that stately courtesy usual among Orientals. He calls himself their slave: regards it as a favour that they should partake of his hospitality; speaks slightingly of the repast prepared as a mere morsel of bread; and treats it as a providential act that they had come into his neighbourhood. It was only afterwards that he knew that he was entertaining angels unawares (Heb. xiii. 2). While, moreover, he addresses the chief traveller first, as courtesy required, he immediately afterwards changes to the plural, lest he should seem wanting in hospitable welcome to his companions.

(4) **Wash your feet.**—This is the first necessity of Oriental hospitality (Judges xix. 21), not merely because the feet, protected only by sandals, are soiled by the dirt of the roads, but because it cools the whole body, and allays the feverishness caused by the heat of travelling. Thus refreshed they are "to rest," Heb., *to lay themselves down*, in the shade.

(5) **Comfort ye your hearts.**—Heb., *strengthen ye*, the original meaning of comfort, a word formed from the Latin *fortis* = strong, brave. The heart in Hebrew is the sum total of all the powers, mental and bodily, of the whole man.

After that ye shall pass on.—Coming at noon, the travellers after rest and refreshment would continue their journey. It is quite plain that Abraham still regarded them as passing wayfarers.

Therefore . . .—Abraham thus suggests that his tent was pitched near to the route on purpose that he might exercise that hospitality which was and continues to be the sacred duty of an Arab sheik.

(6) **Three measures.**—Heb. *three seahs*, the seah being a little more than a peck. It is still usual on the arrival of a stranger to make this hasty preparation for his entertainment, the ordinary meal even of a wealthy sheik consisting of flour and some camels' milk boiled together. Cakes such as those here described, baked amid the embers on the hot hearth-stone, are considered a delicacy (1 Kings xix. 6). Flesh is seldom eaten; but if a traveller arrives, sweet milk and rice are added to the meal, and if he be a person of distinction a lamb or kid is killed. Abraham's calf, "tender and good," shows that he regarded his visitors as persons of more than ordinary high rank; and the quantity of food cooked seems to show that the three travellers had numerous attendants. The calf would be cut into small portions, and a meal like this is, we are told, got ready in a very short time.

(8) **Butter.**—Heb. *curds*, or curdled milk. Neither the Hebrews, Greeks, nor Romans knew how to make butter, and the word itself signifies cheese made of cows' milk. This is less prized in the East than that made from the milk of sheep, or of goats, while camels' milk is regarded by the Arabs as best for drinking. In a hot climate milk is more refreshing when slightly sour; but Abraham brought both fresh milk (probably from the camels) and sour milk (from the sheep), and this with the cakes and the calf made a stately repast. With noble courtesy "he stood by them, and they did eat." The Targum of Jonathan and other Jewish authorities translate "and they made show of eating," lest it should seem as though angels ate (Judges xiii. 16). There is the same mystery as regards our risen Lord (Luke xxiv. 43).

(9) **They said.**—But in verse 10 "he said," and in verses 13, 17, 20, &c., "the Lord (Jehovah) said." The messenger speaks as one with Jehovah, or as being His representative.

Where is Sarah thy wife?—This question is contrary to Oriental manners, as the women may be referred to only in the most indirect manner. But during the meal Abraham, as he talked with the strangers, had probably begun to recognise in them something more than human.

(10) **According to the time of life.**—Heb., *according to the living time.* It is evident from verse 14, and 2 Kings iv. 16, 17, that these words denote some fixed period, but the exact rendering is in dispute. "When the season revives" = next spring, is entirely remote from Oriental thought, and the rendering of Zunz "at the living time" is poetical, but meaningless. The true rendering is probably "a year hence," as when the year is over it dies, and a new year lives in its place. Jewish tradition is strongly in favour of this view, translating "according to this time next year," and adding that the season was the Passover. The only other tenable rendering is "in course of time."

Which was behind him.—The LXX. has a preferable reading, *and she was behind it.* The door, as we have seen, was an opening made by looping back the curtain, which would effectually conceal Sarah's person.

(12) **Sarah laughed.**—See Note on chap. xvii. 17. The laughter of both husband and wife brings into prominence the inconceivable character of the fact. Sarah's conduct has been very unjustly condemned. Though Abraham may have begun to guess that his visitors were more than men, she probably had no such suspicions. Sitting inside the tent, and catching their words only occasionally, listening, perhaps, now only because she heard her own name mentioned, when she hears them talk of her having a child she naturally laughs.

a son. And Sarah heard *it* in the tent
door, which *was* behind him. (11) Now
Abraham and Sarah *were* old *and* well
stricken in age; *and* it ceased to be
with Sarah after the manner of women.
(12) Therefore Sarah laughed within her-
self, saying, After I am waxed old shall
I have pleasure, my [a] lord being old also?
(13) And the LORD said unto Abraham,
Wherefore did Sarah laugh, saying,
Shall I of a surety bear a child, which
am old? (14) Is any thing too hard for
the LORD? At the time appointed I
will return unto thee, according to the
time of life, and Sarah shall have a son.
(15) Then Sarah denied, saying, I laughed
not; for she was afraid. And he said,
Nay; but thou didst laugh.

(16) And the men rose up from thence,
and looked toward Sodom: and Abra-
ham went with them to bring them on
the way. (17) And the LORD said, Shall
I hide from Abraham that thing which
I do; (18) seeing that Abraham shall
surely become a great and mighty na-
tion, and all the nations of the earth
shall be [b] blessed in him? (19) For
I know him, that he will command
his children and his household after
him, and they shall keep the way
of the LORD, to do justice and judg-
ment; that the LORD may bring upon
Abraham that which he hath spoken of
him.

(20) And the LORD said, Because the
cry of Sodom and Gomorrah is great,
and because their sin is very grievous;
(21) I will go down now, and see whether
they have done altogether according to
the cry of it, which is come unto me;
and if not, I will know. (22) And the
men turned their faces from thence, and
went toward Sodom: but Abraham
stood yet before the LORD.

a 1 Pet. 3. 6.

b ch. 12. 3. & 22. 18; Acts 3. 25; Gal. 3. 8.

---

thinking possibly that they did not know how old she was.

After I am waxed old.—The Hebrew word is stronger and more lively. It means "to be worn out like an old garment."

(14) **Is anything too hard for the Lord?**—Heb., *Is anything too wonderful for Jehovah?* At last it is made evident that the travellers are messengers from God; but, until this declaration, there could have been, at most, only a dim feeling that the visitation was more than human. Though the angel does not claim for himself divinity, yet the narrator prefixes to his words, *And Jehovah said.* In some ineffable way there was an identity between Jehovah and the angel.

(15) **Sarah denied.**—With strange inconsistency Sarah knows that the speaker is Divine, and that He perceived the thoughts that passed "within herself" in the retirement of the tent, and yet denies; but it was the inconsistency of fright. Struck with terror at the thought that she had ridiculed the promise of Jehovah, she offers no excuse, but takes refuge, as frightened people are apt to do, in falsehood. Gently reproved, the result was the building-up of her faith, just as Mary's doubt was removed and her faith perfected by the angel's words (St. Luke i. 34—37).

(16) **The men . . . looked toward Sodom.**—This visitation of God combined mercy and love for Abraham, and through him for all mankind, with the punishment of men whose wickedness was so universal that there were none left among them to bear witness for God, and labour for a better state of things. There is a strange mingling of the human and the Divine in the narrative. Even after the fuller manifestation of themselves they are still called *men*, and Abraham continues to discharge the ordinary duties of hospitality by accompanying them as their guide. Their route would lie to the south-east, over the hill-country of Judah, and tradition represents Abraham as having gone with them as far as the village of Caphar-Barucha, whence it is possible through a deep ravine to see the Dead Sea.

(19) **For I know him, that he will.**—This translation has most of the Versions in its favour, and means that Abraham's good conduct earns for him the Divine condescension. But the Hebrew is, *For I have known him in order that he may command his sons, &c.* It gives God foreknowledge of the purpose for which He had called Abraham as the reason for thus revealing to him the method of the Divine justice. And this purpose was, that from Abraham should spring a nation whose institutions were to be fraught with Divine truth, whose prophets were to be the means of revealing God's will to man, and of whom, as concerning the flesh, the Messiah should come. What more fitting than that one appointed to fill so noble a calling should also be raised to the rank of a prophet, and be permitted to share in the Divine counsels? This rendering closely agrees with what is said in verse 18 about Abraham growing into a mighty nation; and it was the unique and high purpose for which this nation was to be called into being which brought Abraham into so close a relation to Jehovah.

(21) **I will go down.**—God examines before He punishes (see Note on chap. xi. 5) with the same care and personal inspection as the most conscientious earthly judge.

Altogether.—Some take this word, not as an adverb, but as a noun (comp. Isa. x. 23), and translate "I will see whether they have done according to the cry of it: (in which case there shall be for them) utter destruction." But the ellipse is harsh; and inquiry, the knowing and not the punishing, is the prominent thought in the words of Jehovah. Hence too the last clause, "I will know." The two angels go to Sodom to give the people a final trial. If they meet with upright treatment, then God will know that there are limits to the wickedness of its inhabitants, and it will be spared.

(22) **Abraham stood yet before the Lord** (before Jehovah).—The two angels went on their way in form as men, towards Sodom, but the one who was a manifestation of Jehovah (verses 13, 17) remained behind.

(23) And Abraham drew near, and said,
Wilt thou also destroy the righteous
with the wicked? (24) Peradventure
there be fifty righteous within the city:
wilt thou also destroy and not spare the
place for the fifty righteous that *are*
therein? (25) That be far from thee to
do after this manner, to slay the righ-
teous with the wicked: and that the
righteous should be as the wicked, that
be far from thee: Shall not the Judge
of all the earth do right? (26) And the
LORD said, If I find in Sodom fifty righ-
teous within the city, then I will spare
all the place for their sakes. (27) And
Abraham answered and said, Behold
now, I have taken upon me to speak
unto the Lord, which *am but* dust and
ashes: (28) Peradventure there shall lack
five of the fifty righteous: wilt thou
destroy all the city for *lack of* five? And
he said, If I find there forty and five, I
will not destroy *it*. (29) And he spake
unto him yet again, and said, Peradven-
ture there shall be forty found there.
And he said, I will not do *it* for forty's
sake. (30) And he said *unto him*, Oh let
not the Lord be angry, and I will speak:
Peradventure there shall thirty be found
there. And he said, I will not do *it*, if
I find thirty there. (31) And he said,
Behold now, I have taken upon me to
speak unto the Lord: Peradventure
there shall be twenty found there. And
he said, I will not destroy *it* for twenty's
sake. (32) And he said, Oh let not the
Lord be angry, and I will speak yet but
this once: Peradventure ten shall be
found there. And he said I will not
destroy *it* for ten's sake.

(33) And the LORD went his way, as
soon as he had left communing with
Abraham: and Abraham returned unto
his place.

a ch. 18. 4.

CHAPTER XIX.—(1) And there came
two angels to Sodom at even; and Lot
sat in the gate of Sodom: and Lot see-
ing *them* rose up to meet them; and he
bowed himself with his face toward the
ground; (2) and he said, Behold now,
my lords, turn in, I pray you, into your
servant's house, and tarry all night, and
[a] wash your feet, and ye shall rise up
early, and go on your ways. And they
said, Nay; but we will abide in the
street all night. (3) And he pressed
upon them greatly; and they turned in

---

(23) **Abraham drew near.**—As Jewish commentators remark, this word is especially used of prayer, and Abraham's intercession is unspeakably noble. Nor must we suppose that he thought only of Lot. Doubtless he remembered the day when he had restored the persons and spoil to the king of Sodom. He had then seen their human affection; the joy of parent meeting with child, and friend with friend; and he hoped that there were good people among them, and that so marvellous a deliverance would work in many of them a true repentance. Neither must we suppose that Abraham adroitly began with a large number, with the intention of lessening it. It was the readiness with which each prayer was heard which made him in his earnestness continue his entreaties. It thus illustrates the principle that the faith of the believer grows strong as he feels that his prayers are accepted, and he ventures finally to offer petitions, nothing wavering, which at an earlier stage would have seemed to him to ask more than he might venture to hope from the Divine goodness.

Destroy.—Heb., *sweep away;* and so in verse 24. The difference is not without force; for the verb "to sweep away" gives the idea of a more indiscriminate ruin than the usual word *destroy*, which Abraham substitutes for it in verses 28, 31, 32.

(33) **The Lord** (Jehovah) **went his way.**—Not to avoid further importunity, for Abraham had ended his entreaty, and obtained all that he had asked for; but because the purpose of the revelation was fulfilled. Besides the primary object of making known the perfect justice of God's dealings with men, it further showed that the Gentile world was both subject to Jehovah's dominion, and that there was mercy for it as well as for the covenant people. Such, in future times, was also the lesson of the Book of Jonah.

XIX.

(1) **And there came two angels.**—Heb., *And the two angels came.* It is a continuation of the preceding narrative, and takes up the history from chap. xviii. 22.

Lot sat in the gate of Sodom.—He had therefore become a citizen of Sodom, probably after the deliverance from the Elamite invasion, when, as a relative of Abraham, he would be treated with great honour. This personal respect had made him close his eyes to the sinfulness of the people, and he had consented to live inside the town, and even to let its citizens marry his daughters. Meanwhile all intercourse between him and Abraham apparently had ceased, and he had lost all share in the covenant of circumcision.

(2) **In the street.**—That is, the broad open space of the city. (Comp. Judges xix. 15, 20.) In a warm climate there is little hardship in passing the night in the open air; and as at this early date there were no caravanserais, travellers had to lodge in this way unless they found some hospitable entertainer.

(3) **He pressed upon them greatly.**—This he did as knowing the licentiousness of the people; but the angels do not readily accept his hospitality, as they had done that of Abraham, because his character had deteriorated.

Unleavened bread.—Heb., *thin cakes*, like those now eaten by the Jews at the Passover. They took little time in preparation, for which reason we find them also used by the witch of Endor (1 Sam. xxviii. 24).

unto him, and entered into his house;
and he made them a feast, and did bake
unleavened bread, and they did eat.
(4) But before they lay down, the men
of the city, *even* the men of Sodom, com-
passed the house round, both old and
young, all the people from every quarter:
(5) and they called unto Lot, and said
unto him, Where *are* the men which
came in to thee this night? bring them
out unto us, that we may know them.
(6) And Lot went out at the door unto
them, and shut the door after him,
(7) and said, I pray you, brethren, do not
so wickedly. (8) Behold now, I have two
daughters which have not known man;
let me, I pray you, bring them out unto
you, and do ye to them as *is* good in your
eyes: only unto these men do nothing;
for therefore came they under the
shadow of my roof. (9) And they said,
Stand back. And they said *again*, This
one *fellow* came in to sojourn, and he
will needs be a judge: now will we deal
worse with thee, than with them. And
they pressed sore upon the man, *even* Lot,
and came near to break the door.
(10) But the men put forth their hand,
and pulled Lot into the house to them,
and shut to the door. (11) And they smote
the men [a] that *were* at the door of the
house with blindness, both small and
great: so that they wearied themselves
to find the door.
(12) And the men said unto Lot, Hast
thou here any besides? son in law, and
thy sons, and thy daughters, and what-
soever thou hast in the city, bring *them*
out of this place: (13) for we will destroy
this place, because the [b] cry of them is
waxen great before the face of the LORD;
and the LORD hath sent us to destroy it.
(14) And Lot went out, and spake unto
his sons in law, which married his
daughters, and said, Up, get you out of
this place; for the LORD will destroy

a Wisd. 19. 17.

b ch. 18. 20.

---

(4) **From every quarter.**—Heb., *from the end.* This may mean, either, "to the last man," or "from the very end of the town." In either case it shows that there were not in Sodom the ten righteous men who would have availed to save it (chap. xviii. 32).

(8) **I have two daughters.**—It is plain from Judges xix. 24 that this proposal was not viewed in old time with the horror which it seems to deserve. Granting with St. Ambrose that it was the substitution of a smaller for a greater sin, and with St. Chrysostom that Lot was bound by the laws of hospitality to do his utmost to protect his guests, yet he was also bound as a father equally to protect his daughters to the last extremity: and if men might substitute smaller for greater sins, they would have an excuse for practising every form of wickedness. The difficulty arises from the high character given of Lot by St. Peter (2 Pet. ii. 7, 8): but Lot was righteous only relatively; and though his soul was daily vexed by what he saw, it was not vexed enough to make him quit such evil surroundings, and return to the healthy and virtuous life of the mountains. And, when finally he sought refuge in them, as it was not of his own free will, but on compulsion (verse 30), he found there no peace, but shared, even if unknowingly, in deeds of horrible lust. The warning of his fall is, that men who part with religious privileges for the sake of worldly advantage are in danger of sinking into moral degradation, and of losing, with their faith and hope, not only their self-respect and happiness, but even that earthly profit for the sake of which they sacrificed their religion.

Unto these men.—The form of the pronoun is archaic, and occurs again in verse 25. It is found in a few other places in the Pentateuch, but never elsewhere.

For therefore, &c. . . .—Comp. chap. xviii. 5.

(9) **This one fellow came in to sojourn.**—Heb. *the one came to sojourn,* as if an extraordinary concession had been made in Lot's favour in allowing him to dwell within their walls. In ancient times the rights of citizenship were most jealously guarded, and the position of a sojourner made very bitter.

He will needs be a judge.—Heb., *is ever acting as a judge.* This suggests that Lot had previously reproved the men of Sodom, and agrees with 2 Pet. ii. 8.

(11) **Blindness.**—This word occurs elsewhere only in 2 Kings vi. 18, and in both cases it is plain that actual blindness is not meant. Had the men here been struck with blindness they would not have wearied themselves with trying to find the door, but would either have gone away in terror at the visitation, or, if too hardened for that, would have groped about till they found it. So, if the Syrian army had been made actually blind, they would have surrendered themselves; nor would it have been practicable to guide an army of blind men on so long a march as that from Dothan to Samaria. In both cases the men were unaware that anything had happened to them. The people of Sodom thought they saw the door; the Syrians supposed that the locality was one well known to them, and only when the confusion was removed did they become conscious that they were at Samaria. The word really means a disturbance of vision caused by the eye not being in its proper connection with the brain. And so the men of Sodom ever seemed just upon the point of reaching the door, and pressed on, and strove and quarrelled, but always failed, they knew not how, but as they always supposed by one another's fault. It is a strange picture of men given over to unbelief and sin, and who "seeing see not," because they reject the true light.

(14) **Which married his daughters.**—Heb., *the takers of his daughters*—a present participle, for which reason Ewald, Tuch, and others translate "who were to marry his daughters." The traditional view is that given in our Version, and is confirmed by verse 15, where the words—"thy two daughters which are here," Heb., *which are found*—certainly suggest the idea that Lot had other daughters, besides the two which escaped with him.

this city. But he seemed as one that
mocked unto his sons in law.
(15) And when the morning arose, then
the angels hastened Lot, saying, Arise,
take thy wife, and thy two daughters,
which [1] are here; lest thou be con-
sumed in the [2] iniquity of the city.
(16) And [a] while he lingered, the men laid
hold upon his hand, and upon the hand
of his wife, and upon the hand of his
two daughters; the LORD being merci-
ful unto him: and they brought him
forth, and set him without the city.
(17) And it came to pass, when they had
brought them forth abroad, that he said,
Escape for thy life; look not behind
thee, neither stay thou in all the plain;
escape to the mountain, lest thou be con-
sumed. (18) And Lot said unto them,
Oh, not so, my Lord: (19) behold now,
thy servant hath found grace in thy
sight, and thou hast magnified thy
mercy, which thou hast shewed unto me
in saving my life; and I cannot escape
to the mountain, lest some evil take me,
and I die: (20) behold now, this city *is*
near to flee unto, and it *is* a little one:
Oh, let me escape thither, (*is* it not a
little one?) and my soul shall live.
(21) And he said unto him, See, I have
accepted [3] thee concerning this thing
also, that I will not overthrow this city,
for the which thou hast spoken.
(22) Haste thee, escape thither; for I
cannot do anything till thou be come
thither. Therefore the name of the city
was called Zoar. (23) The sun was [4] risen
upon the earth when Lot entered into
Zoar.

(24) Then [b] the LORD rained upon
Sodom and upon Gomorrah brimstone
and fire from the LORD out of heaven;
(25) and he overthrew those cities, and
all the plain, and all the inhabitants of
the cities, and that which grew upon the
ground. (26) But his wife looked back

[1] Heb., *are found.*
[2] Or, *punishment.*
[a] Wisd. 10. 6.
[3] Heb., *thy face.*
[4] Heb., *gone forth.*
[b] Deut. 29 23; Isa. 13. 19; Jer. 50. 40. Amos 4. 11; Luke 17. 29; Jude 7.

As one that mocked.—Heb., *as one that was laughing,* or joking, and so not in earnest.

(15) **When the morning arose.**—Lot had thus the night for making his preparations, but part of this he spent in his visits to his sons-in-law.

Consumed.—Heb., *swept away;* and so in verse 17. See chap. xviii. 23, 24, where it is rendered "destroy."

(16) **And while he lingered.**—Heb., *and he lingered.* Lot still clung to his wealth, and could not make up his mind to leave it, and so at length the angels took him by the hand and compelled him to quit the doomed city.

The Lord being merciful unto him.—Heb., *in Jehovah's pity for him.* (Comp. Isa. lxiii. 9.)

(17) **Abroad.**—Heb., *outside*—that is, of the city.

Look not behind thee.—This was not merely to prevent delay, but also showed that God demanded of them a total abandonment in heart and will of the condemned cities, and hence the severity with which the violation of the command was visited.

Plain.—The Ciccar or circle of Jordan. So also in verses 25, 28, 29; see Note on chap. xiii. 10.

(19) **Lest some evil.**—Heb., *lest the evil,* lest the threatened calamity overtake me and I die.

(21) **I have accepted thee.**—Heb., *I have lifted up thy face.* (See Note on chap. iv. 6, 7.)

(22) **Zoar.**—This town is identified by Dr. Tristram (*Land of Moab,* p. 330) with Zi'ara, at the northern end of the Dead Sea. It is described as lying upon the borders of the Moabite territory, in Isa. xv. 5; Jer. xlviii. 34. Eusebius says that a Roman garrison was posted there, but he probably accepted the current tradition which placed the five cities at the southern extremity of the lake.

(23) **The sun was risen.**—As Lot started at dawn, he had thus had about an hour for his flight.

(24) **The Lord** (Jehovah) **rained . . . from the Lord** (from Jehovah).—Many commentators, following the Council of Sirmium, see in this repetition of the name of Jehovah an indication of the Holy Trinity, as though God the Son rained down fire from God the Father. More correctly Calvin takes it as an emphatic reiteration of its being Jehovah's act. Jehovah had mysteriously manifested Himself upon earth by the visit of the three angels to Abraham, but His activity on earth is one with His willing in heaven.

Brimstone and fire.—Though God used natural agencies in the destruction of the Ciccar cities, yet what was in itself a catastrophe of nature became miraculous by the circumstances which surrounded it. It was thus made the means not merely of executing the Divine justice, of strengthening Abraham's faith, and of warning Lot, but also of giving moral and religious instruction throughout all time. Seen by its light, events of history, for which sufficient secondary causes may be discovered, are nevertheless shown to be direct manifestations of the Divine justice, and to have moral causes as their real basis. We lose the benefit of the teaching of the Bible if we suppose that the events recorded there were different in kind from those which take place now. A certain limited number of events were so; but of most it is simply the curtain that is drawn back, and we see God's presence no longer veiled, as with us, but openly revealed. As for the catastrophe itself, it was not a mere thunderstorm which set the earth, saturated with naphtha, on fire; but, in a region where earthquakes are still common, there was apparently an outburst of volcanic violence, casting forth blazing bitumen and brimstone. This falling down upon the houses, and upon the soil charged with combustible matter, caused a conflagration so sudden and widespread that few or none could escape. Sulphur and nitre are still found as natural products on the shores of the Dead Sea.

(25) **Overthrew.**—This does not mean *submerged,* and the agent in the destruction was fire and not water. "The plain" (Heb., *the Ciccar*) still existed, and when Abraham saw it, was wrapped in smoke.

(26) **His wife looked back from behind him.**—In Oriental countries it is still the rule for the wife to

from behind him, and she became a
pillar of salt.
(27) And Abraham gat up early in the
morning to the place where he stood
before the LORD: (28) and he looked
toward Sodom and Gomorrah, and to-
ward all the land of the plain, and be-
held, and, lo, the smoke of the country
went up as the smoke of a furnace.
(29) And it came to pass, when God
destroyed the cities of the plain, that
God remembered Abraham, and sent
Lot out of the midst of the overthrow,
when he overthrew the cities in the
which Lot dwelt. (30) And Lot went up
out of Zoar, and dwelt in the mountain,
and his two daughters with him; for he
feared to dwell in Zoar: and he dwelt
in a cave, he and his two daughters.
(31) And the firstborn said unto the
younger, Our father *is* old, and *there is*
not a man in the earth to come in unto
us after the manner of all the earth:
(32) come, let us make our father drink
wine, and we will lie with him, that we
may preserve seed of our father.
(33) And they made their father drink
wine that night: and the firstborn went
in, and lay with her father; and he per-
ceived not when she lay down, nor when
she arose. (34) And it came to pass on
the morrow, that the firstborn said unto
the younger, Behold, I lay yesternight
with my father: let us make him drink
wine this night also; and go thou in,
and lie with him, that we may preserve
seed of our father. (35) And they made
their father drink wine that night also:
and the younger arose, and lay with
him; and he perceived not when she lay
down, nor when she arose. (36) Thus
were both the daughters of Lot with
B.C. cir. 1897. child by their father. (37) And the
firstborn bare a son, and called his name
Moab: the same *is* the father of the
Moabites unto this day. (38) And the
younger, she also bare a son, and called
his name Ben-ammi: the same *is* the
father of the children of Ammon unto
this day.

---

walk behind her husband. As regards the method of her transformation, some think that she was stifled by sulphureous vapours, and her body subsequently encrusted with salt. More probably, the earthquake heaped up a mighty mass of the rock-salt, which lies in solid strata round the Dead Sea, and Lot's wife was entangled in the convulsion and perished, leaving the hill of salt, in which she was enclosed, as her memorial. Salt cones are not uncommon in this neighbourhood, and the American Expedition found one, about forty feet high, near Usdum (Lynch, *Report*, pp. 183 *et seq.*). Entombed in this salt pillar, she became a "monument of an unbelieving soul" (Wisdom x. 7).

(27) **Abraham gat up early in the morning.**—This was necessary, because he had a walk of some miles before he reached "the place where he stood before Jehovah" on the previous evening; and probably the mighty forces which overthrew the cities had been some hours at work when he reached the head of the ravine through which the terrible scene became visible. Naturally his anxiety to know the result of his intercession, and the fate of his brother's son, would urge him to be on foot at the early dawn.

(28) **Lo, the smoke of the country** (really, *land*) **went up as the smoke of a furnace.**—The substitution of the word *country* for *land* is confusing. It was the *land of the Ciccar*, just mentioned, which was in flames. As Abraham could see the Ciccar, it must have been at the northern end of the Dead Sea (see Note on chap. xviii. 16); and as a violent conflagration was raging throughout it, the site of the cities could not have been submerged (see Note on chap. xiv. 3). The violence of the fire is indicated by the last word, which is not the ordinary word for a *furnace*, but means a kiln, such as that used for burning chalk into lime, or for melting ores of metal.

(30) **He feared to dwell in Zoar.**—Though this little place had been granted him for an asylum, yet, terrified at the sight of the smoking valley, and remembering that he had been originally commanded to go to the mountains, he summons up his courage and proceeds thither. The limestone regions of Palestine are full of caverns; and the patriarch, whose wealth had been so great that he and Abraham could not dwell together, is now content to seek in one of these caverns a miserable home.

(31) **The firstborn said unto the Younger.**—Several modern commentators see in this recital a mark of Jewish hatred towards the Moabites and Ammonites, and an attempt to brand their origin with shame. Really we find in Deut. ii. 9—19, no trace of the existence of this hostility, but, on the contrary, the relationship of these two nations to Israel is used as a ground for kindly feelings; and in the story of Ruth the Moabitess, and the friendship which existed between the king of Moab and David, we have proof that such feelings existed.

(32) **That we may preserve seed of our father.**—This was a very strong feeling in ancient times, and affords the sole excuse for the revolting conduct of these women. The utter degradation of Lot and his family is the most painful part of his story, which thus ends in his intense shame.

(37, 38) **Moab . . . Ben-ammi.**—Both these names suggest an incestuous origin, but the latter in a less repulsive way. "Son of my people" means one born of intercourse with her own kin and family. It is a striking proof of the vigour of the race of Terah, that from this lone cavern, and after the loss of all the wealth possessed by Lot, these two children were able to reduce to obedience the aborigines dwelling on the eastern shore of the Dead Sea, and establish petty kingdoms there. Both Moabites and Ammonites have finally merged in the Arabs.

CHAPTER XX.—(1) And Abraham
journeyed from thence toward the south
country, and dwelled between Kadesh
and Shur, and sojourned in Gerar.
(2) And Abraham said of Sarah his
wife, She *is* my sister: and Abimelech
king of Gerar sent, and took Sarah.
(3) But God came to Abimelech in a
dream by night, and said to him, Be-
hold, thou *art but* a dead man, for the
woman which thou hast taken; for she
is [1] a man's wife. (4) But Abimelech had
not come near her: and he said, Lord,
wilt thou slay also a righteous nation?
(5) Said he not unto me, She *is* my
sister? and she, even she herself said,
He *is* my brother: in the [2] integrity of
my heart and innocency of my hands
have I done this. (6) And God said
unto him in a dream, Yea, I know that
thou didst this in the integrity of thy
heart; for I also withheld thee from

B.C. cir. 1898.

1 Heb., *married to an husband.*

2 Or, *simplicity,* or *sincerity.*

XX.

Abraham's Denial of his Wife at Gerar.

(1) **Abraham journeyed from thence.**—That is, from Mamre, where he had so long halted, and which seems to have continued to be one of his homes. As he had been commanded to traverse the whole land (chap. xiii. 17, 18), we need seek no reasons for his removal. It was the rule of his life to move from place to place, both on account of his cattle, and also because by so doing he was taking possession of the country. There were, nevertheless, certain places which were his head-quarters, such as Bethel, Mamre, and Beer-sheba.

The south country.—It is a proper name, the Negeb; see Note on chap. xii .9. For Kadesh, see chap. xvi. 14; for Shur, *ibid.* 7; and for Gerar, chap. x. 19.

(2) **She is my sister.**—Twenty years before, Abraham had acted in the same way in Egypt, and Pharaoh had rebuked him, but sent him away with large presents. We learn from this chapter, verse 13, that the false representation which twice brought them into trouble was habitual with the two; nor does Abraham ever seem conscious that he was acting in it wrongfully. To us it seems cowardly, in one who had so many men trained to battle, thus to expose his wife to danger; and to have recourse to deceit, at the very time when such abundant revelations were being made to him, also shows an apparent want of faith in God. But Holy Scripture neither represents its heroes as perfect, nor does it raise them disproportionately above the level of their own times. Its distinguishing feature rather is that it ever insists upon a perpetual progress upwards, and urges men onward to be better and holier than those that went before. Abraham was not on the same high spiritual level as a Christian ought to be who has the perfect example of Christ as his pattern, and the gift of the Holy Ghost for his aid; and the fact that God rescued him and Sarah from all danger in Egypt may have seemed to him a warrant that in future difficulties he would have the same Divine protection. Human conduct is ever strangely chequered, but we have a wholesome lesson in the fact, that it was Abraham's politic device which twice entangled him in actual danger.

Abimelech (called in chap. xxvi. 1, *king of the Philistines,* where see Note) . . . **took Sarah.**—She was now ninety years of age, and naturally her beauty must have faded. Some, however, think that with the promise of a son her youth had been renewed, while others suppose that the purpose uppermost in the mind of Abimelech was political, and that what he really desired was an alliance with the powerful sheik who had entered his territories.

(3) **God** (Elohim) **came . . .**—From the use of this title of the Deity it has been said that this narrative is an Elohistic form of the Jehovistic narrative in chap. xii. 10—20. But we have seen that even in the History of the Fall, where the writer in so remarkable a manner styles the Deity Jehovah-Elohim, he nevertheless restricts Eve and the serpent in their conversation to the name Elohim. With the same care in the application of the names, it is necessarily Elohim who appears to a heathen king; and had the title Jehovah been used it would have been a violation of the narrator's rule. Moreover, the sole reason for calling that narrative Jehovistic is that in chap. xii. 17 it is Jehovah who plagues Pharaoh for Sarah's sake. But equally here, verse 18, it is Jehovah who protects Sarah from Abimelech; in both cases it being the covenant-God, who saves his people from injury.

Thou art but a dead man.—Heb., *thou diest,* or *art dying.* Abimelech was already suffering from the malady spoken of in verse 17, when Elohim appeared to him and warned him that death would be the result of perseverance in retaining Sarah. It was this malady which was the cause of the abstention spoken of in verses 4 and 6.

(4) **A righteous nation.**—Knobel has pointed out that there is an allusion here to the fate of Sodom. Though the malady was confined to Abimelech and his household, yet he sees destruction threatening his whole people, who, compared with the inhabitants of the Ciccar cities, were righteous. There is indirect proof of the truth of Abimelech's assertion in the fact that death (see verse 3) is acquiesced in as the fitting punishment for adultery.

(5) **In the integrity of my heart . . .**—Not only does Abimelech assert this, but Elohim (see verse 6) admits the plea. And yet this Philistine king indulges in polygamy, and claims the right of taking the female relatives of any one passing through his territory to add them to his harem. But the words mean no more than that he was not consciously violating any of his own rules of morality, and thus illustrate the Gospel principle that men will be punished not by an absolute decree, but equitably, according to their knowledge (Luke xii. 47, 48). Abimelech was doing wrong, and was suffering punishment, but the punishment was remedial, and for his advancement in right-knowing and right-doing. It is thus by means of revelation that men have attained to a proper understanding of the moral law. Though often called "the law of Nature," yet Nature does not give it, but only acknowledges it when given. The inner light is but a faint and inconstant glimmering, but Christ is the true light; for only by Him does the law of Nature become a clear rule for human guidance (John i. 9; Rom. ii. 14, 15; Matt. vi. 23).

sinning against me: therefore suffered
I thee not to touch her. (7) Now there-
fore restore the man *his* wife; for he *is*
a prophet, and he shall pray for thee,
and thou shalt live: and if thou restore
her not, know thou that thou shalt
surely die, thou, and all that *are* thine.
(8) Therefore Abimelech rose early in
the morning, and called all his servants,
and told all these things in their ears:
and the men were sore afraid. (9) Then
Abimelech called Abraham, and said
unto him, What hast thou done unto
us? and what have I offended thee, that
thou hast brought on me and on my
kingdom a great sin? thou hast done
deeds unto me that ought not to be
done. (10) And Abimelech said unto
Abraham, What sawest thou, that thou
hast done this thing? (11) And Abraham
said, Because I thought, Surely the fear
of God *is* not in this place; and they
will slay me for my wife's sake. (12) And
yet indeed *she is* my sister; she *is* the
daughter of my father, but not the
daughter of my mother; and she be-
came my wife. (13) And it came to pass,
when God caused me to wander from
my father's house, that I said unto her,
This *is* thy kindness which thou shalt
show unto me; at every place whither
we shall come, [a] say of me, He *is* my
brother.
(14) And Abimelech took sheep, and

a ch. 12. 13.

---

(7) **He is a prophet.**—This is not said as an aggravation of Abimelech's sin, but as an encouragement to him to restore Sarah. It is therefore rightly joined with the words "He shall pray for thee." For the word prophet is used here in its old sense of *spokesman* (comp. Exod. chap. vii. 1, with chap. iv. 16), and especially of such an one as mediates between God and man. There was a true feeling that God in His own nature is beyond the reach of man (Job ix. 32, 33, xvi. 21; 1 Tim. vi. 16); and this in heathen nations led to men peopling their heavens with a multitude of minor deities. In Israel, after the founding of the prophetic schools by Samuel, the prophets became an order, whose office it was partly to enliven the services of the Temple with sacred minstrelsy (1 Chron. xxv. 1), but chiefly to be God's spokesmen, both declaring His will to Jew and Gentile (Jer. i. 5), and also maintaining religion and holiness by earnest preaching and other such means. In this way they were forerunners, and even representatives, of Christ, who is the one true and only Mediator between God and man. Not only Abraham, therefore, but the patriarchs generally are called "Christs and prophets" (Ps. cv. 15), as being speakers for God to man, and for man to God, until the true Christ and prophet came. Abimelech, moreover, is thus taught that he does not himself hold a near relation to God, but requires some one to speak for him; perhaps, too, he would gather from it that he had need of fuller instruction, and that he ought to try to attain to a higher level, and that Abraham would become a prophet to him in its other sense of being a teacher. (For the prophet as an intercessor, see Exod. viii. 28, 29; Deut. ix. 19, 20; 1 Sam. vii. 5, xii. 19, 23; 1 Kings xiii. 6; Job xlii. 8.)

(10) **What sawest thou?**—Some modern commentators explain the Hebrew as meaning, What purpose hadst thou? What didst thou look for? But the old rendering is probably right. Abimelech first denies by indignant questions that he had been guilty of any wrong towards Abraham, and then asks what he had seen in the conduct of himself and people to justify such mistrust of them. Throughout, the king speaks as a man conscious that his citizens so respected the rights of a stranger and of marriage, that Sarah would have been perfectly safe had Abraham openly said that she was his wife.

(11) **Surely the fear of God . . .**—Abraham's general condemnation of the people had some excuse in the widespread depravity of the nations in Canaan, but was nevertheless unjust. Even as regards these nations, they were not utterly corrupt (chap. xv. 16), and both in Egypt and in Gerar the standard of morality was higher than Abraham supposed. His difficulty was the result of his own imperfect faith; but the fact that this artifice was arranged between man and wife when starting on their long wanderings, proves that they rather over-rated than under-rated the risks that lay before them. The expedient was indeed a sorry one, and shows that Abraham's faith was not yet that of a martyr; but it also shows that both of them felt that Abraham might have to save his life by a means almost as bad as death. And thus, after all, it was no common-place faith, but one as firm at root as it was sorely tried and exercised.

(12) **Not the daughter of my mother.**—This disproves the notion that Sarah was the same as Iscah (chap. xi. 29); for as Iscah was Terah's granddaughter, the distinction between the identity of the father and the diversity of the mother would in her case be unmeaning. Sarah was apparently Abraham's half-sister, being Terah's daughter by another wife; and we gather from her calling her child Sarai—that is, *princely* (see chap. xvii. 15)—that she was not a concubine, but belonged to some noble race.

(13) **When God caused me to wander.**—According to rule, Elohim is construed with a verb singular for the true God, but with a verb plural for false gods. Here the verb is plural, and the same construction occurs in chap. xxxv. 7; Exod. xxii. 9; 2 Sam. vii. 22 (but singular in 1 Chron. xvii. 20); and Ps. lviii. 11: moreover, in Josh. xxiv. 19, Elohim is joined with an adjective (holy) in the plural. These exceptions may either be relics of a less strict use of the name Elohim, or they may be errors of copyists, misled by the ordinary rules of grammar. This latter view is confirmed by the fact that the Samaritan Pentateuch, both here and in chap. xxxv. 7, has the singular.

At every place.—The fact of this compact between Abraham and Sarah having been made so long before, would convince Abimelech that their conduct was not occasioned by anything which they had seen at Gerar (comp. verse 10).

(14) **Abimelech . . . gave them unto Abraham.**—Pharaoh's presents were given when he took Sarah, and though he did not exact them back,

oxen, and menservants, and women-
servants, and gave *them* unto Abraham,
and restored him Sarah his wife.
(15) And Abimelech said, Behold, my
land *is* before thee: dwell [1] where it
pleaseth thee. (16) And unto Sarah he
said, Behold, I have given thy brother
a thousand *pieces* of silver: behold, he
is to thee a covering of the eyes, unto
all that *are* with thee, and with all *other*:
thus she was reproved. (17) So Abraham
prayed unto God: and God healed
Abimelech, and his wife, and his maid-
servants; and they bare *children*.
(18) For the LORD had fast closed up all
the wombs of the house of Abimelech,
because of Sarah Abraham's wife.

1 Heb., *as is good in thine eyes.*

a ch. 17. 19. & 18. 10.

b Acts 7. 8; Gal. 4. 22; Heb. 11. 11.

B.C. cir. 1897.

c ch. 17. 12.

CHAPTER XXI.—(1) And the LORD
visited Sarah as he had said, and the
LORD did unto Sarah [a] as he had spoken.
(2) For Sarah [b] conceived, and bare Abra-
ham a son in his old age, at the set time
of which God had spoken to him.
(3) And Abraham called the name of his
son that was born unto him, whom
Sarah bare to him, Isaac. (4) And
Abraham circumcised his son Isaac
being eight days old, [c] as God had com-
manded him. (5) And Abraham was an
hundred years old, when his son Isaac
was born unto him. (6) And Sarah said,
God hath made me to laugh, *so that* all
that hear will laugh with me. (7) And
she said, Who would have said unto

yet he bade Abraham "go his way" in displeasure. More generously, the Philistine gives presents on restoring Sarah, and grants her husband permission to dwell in his land wherever it pleased him. He also acknowledges thereby that he had done Abraham a wrong.

(16) **A thousand pieces of silver.**—Heb., *a thousand of silver.* This was the total value of Abimelech's present, and not an additional gift. A thousand shekels would be about £125, a large sum at a time when silver was scarce and dear.

He is to thee a covering of the eyes.—This speech of Abimelech is full of difficulty. It begins with a touch of irony in calling Abraham "thy brother." Next, if the pronoun is translated in the masculine, *he,* the meaning would be that Abraham ought to have been Sarah's protector, but had failed in this duty; but, more probably, it is neuter, and refers to the gift. The "covering of the eyes" may mean a veil to protect her from the wanton desires of others, or to conceal her shame at the wrong done to her. Finally, the verb rendered "reproved" is equivocal, and should rather be translated *righted.* It may also be the third person singular feminine, as in our version, or the second person. in which case it is part of Abimelech's speech. The clause "and with all" must then be taken with this verb, and the whole be rendered, *and in everything thou art even righted.* The correct rendering probably is, "And unto Sarah he said, Behold, I have given thy brother (a gift worth) a thousand (pieces) of silver: behold, it shall be to thee for a covering of the eyes to all that are with thee (that is,—so large a compensation for the wrong done thee in taking thee from thy husband, will be a proof to all thy friends and attendants that thou hast not been disgraced, but treated with honour); and in respect of all that has happened thou art thus righted."

(17) **Abraham prayed . . .**—As Abimelech had now made very liberal compensation, it became the duty of Abraham to intercede for him. The malady seems to have been one confined to Abimelech, as its object was to protect Sarah; but in some way it so affected the whole household as to produce general barrenness.

Maidservants.—Not the word rendered *womenservants* in verse 14, but one specially used of concubines.

XXI.

Birth of Isaac, and Rejection of Ishmael.

(1) **And the Lord** (Jehovah) **visited Sarah as he had said.**—See chap. xvii. 19, where it is Elohim who gives the promise. So here in verse 2 the name Elohim is interchanged with Jehovah.

(3) **Abraham called the name of his son.**—Attention has been called to the fact that we have here two things contrary to subsequent usage: for, first, the father names the child, and not the mother; and, secondly, he names him at his birth, instead of waiting until his circumcision. It might be enough to answer that the child was really named by God (chap. xvii. 19), and that Abraham only acknowledges that the son born was the promised Isaac; but really, as we have seen before, there was as yet no settled rule as to either of these points.

Isaac.—This name not only recorded the fact of the laughter of the father (chap. xvii. 17) and of the mother (chap. xviii. 12), but was a standing memorial that Isaac's birth was contrary to nature, and one of which the promise was provocative of ridicule in the sight even of his parents.

(6, 7) **God hath made me to laugh.**—Sarah's laugh was one of mingled emotions. Joy was uppermost in her mind, but women do not laugh for joy at the birth of a child. Doubtless she called to mind the feelings with which she listened to the announcement of her bearing a son, made by those whom she then regarded as mere passing wayfarers (chap. xviii. 12), but whom she had now long known to be the messengers of God. And still the event seemed to her marvellous and astonishing, so that "all that hear," she said, "will laugh with me"—Heb., *for me,* or *over me*—not "will ridicule me," but will be merry at the thought of an old woman of ninety having a son. Deeper feelings would come afterwards, and the acknowledgment that that which was contrary to nature was wrought by Him whom nature must obey; but surprise is uppermost in the little poem in which Sarah gives utterance to her first feelings:—

> Who would have said unto Abraham
> Sarah suckleth sons?
> For I have borne a son to his old age.

Abraham, that Sarah should have given
children suck? for I have born *him* a
son in his old age.
(8) And the child grew, and was
weaned: and Abraham made a great
feast the *same* day that Isaac was
weaned. (9) And Sarah saw the son of
Hagar the Egyptian, which she had
born unto Abraham, mocking.
(10) Wherefore she said unto Abraham,
[a] Cast out this bondwoman and her son:
for the son of this bondwoman shall not
be heir with my son, *even* with Isaac.
(11) And the thing was very grievous in
Abraham's sight because of his son.
(12) And God said unto Abraham, Let it
not be grievous in thy sight because of
the lad, and because of thy bondwoman;
in all that Sarah hath said unto thee,
hearken unto her voice; for in Isaac
shall thy seed be called. (13) And also
of the son of the bondwoman will I make
a nation, because he *is* thy seed.
(14) And Abraham rose up early in the
morning, and took bread, and a bottle
of water, and gave *it* unto Hagar,
putting *it* on her shoulder, and the
child, and sent her away: and she de-
parted, and wandered in the wilderness
of Beer-sheba. (15) And the water was
spent in the bottle, and she cast the
child under one of the shrubs. (16) And

a Gal. 4. 30.

---

(8) **The child grew, and was weaned.**—According to tradition, Isaac was two years old when weaned. Three years is the age mentioned in 2 Chron. xxxi. 16, 2 Macc. vii. 27; and Samuel was old enough at his weaning to be left at the tabernacle with Eli (1 Sam. i. 24). In Persia and India it is still the custom to celebrate the weaning of a child by an entertainment.

(9) **Mocking.**—The verb used here is the same as that rendered *to laugh* in verse 6, but in an intensive conjugation. What exactly Ishmael was doing is not said, but we may dismiss all those interpretations which charge him with abominable wickedness; for had he been guilty of any such criminal conduct, the sending him away would not have been so "very grievous in Abraham's sight" (verse 11). On the other hand, we may feel sure that Sarah was not without good reason for her conduct; for St. Paul bears witness that Ishmael persecuted Isaac (Gal. iv. 29). The LXX. and Vulg. translate *playing, sporting*, and Gesenius thinks that he was "dancing gracefully;" but if this were all, Sarah's jealousy would have been most unjust. When, however, we consider that Ishmael had been for fourteen years the heir, and that he now fell back into an inferior position, we cannot be surprised if at this banquet in his rival's honour he gave way to spiteful feelings, and by word and gesture derided and ridiculed him. Hagar too had probably never regarded Sarah with much affection since her forced return, and now that her son was disinherited, her bitterness would grow more intense. These jealousies are the inevitable results of polygamy; and wherever it exists, the father's life is made wretched by the intrigues of the women for their children.

(10) **Bondwoman.**—Heb., *ammâh.* This word is rightly translated *handmaid* in Gal. iv. 22, &c., Revised Version. It is rendered *maid* in Gen. xxx. 3, and in the plural, *maidservants*, in chap. xx. 17, where, as we have seen, it means Abimelech's inferior wives. So also in 1 Sam. xxv. 41, Abigail professes her willingness to descend from the position of an *ammâh* to that of a maidservant in David's honour. The rendering "bondwoman" unduly depresses Hagar's condition, and with it that of the Jewish Church in the allegory contained in Gal. iv. 22—31.

(11) **The thing was very grievous in Abraham's sight.**—Heb., *the word* (or matter) *was evil exceedingly in Abraham's eyes.* It was not merely painful to him because of his natural affection for Ishmael (chap. xvii. 18), but he also thought the proposal unjust.

(12) **In Isaac shall thy seed be called.**—Heb., *in Isaac there shall be called to thee a seed:* that is, the seed that shall especially be accounted thine, and which, as such, shall inherit the promises, will be that sprung from Isaac.

(13) **The son of the bondwoman.**—Heb., *of the handmaid.* Hagar is never acknowledged as Abraham's wife, though her child, as Abraham's son, receives a noble promise for the father's sake.

(14) **And the child.**—Ishmael was now sixteen or seventeen years of age, but the word *yeled* used in this place has no reference to age, and in chap. iv. 23 is even translated "young man." It literally signifies *one born*, and is applied in chap xlii. 22 to Joseph, when he was about Ishmael's age. So the "children who mocked Elisha" (2 Kings ii. 23) were doubtless grown young men. In verse 18, Ishmael is called "a lad;" shortly afterwards he was able to maintain himself and Hagar with his bow (verse 20), and his mother took a wife for him from Egypt (verse 21). The narrative, therefore, does not represent Ishmael as a small child, and the idea has probably arisen from the supposition that Abraham placed Ishmael, as well as the supply of food, on Hagar's shoulder.

She departed, and wandered.—Her dismissal had come upon Hagar suddenly, and so she had no plan or purpose, but went hither and thither till the water in the skin was spent.

The wilderness of Beer-sheba.—As yet this region had no name (see verse 31). It lay about twenty Roman miles or more below Hebron, and was the most southerly part of Palestine, while beyond it lay the vast desert of Et-Tih, of which the wilderness of Beer-sheba formed a part. Gerar, which place Abraham had now evidently left, was situated upon the western side of Beer-sheba, but at no great distance from it. (See chaps. xxi. 22, xxvi. 26.)

(15) **She cast the child under one of the shrubs.**—The act was one of despair. Ishmael, though seventeen years of age, had not yet come to his strength, and at a time when human life was so prolonged that forty was the usual age for marriage, was probably not as capable of bearing fatigue as a young man nearly grown up would be in our days. He thus became exhausted, and apparently fainted; and his mother, after trying in vain to support him, cast him down in anguish, and abandoned herself to her grief.

(16) **Let me not see the death of the child.**—The whole story is most touching. Day after day the

she went, and sat her down over against
him a good way off, as it were a bow-
shot: for she said, Let me not see the
death of the child. And she sat over
against *him*, and lift up her voice, and
wept. (17) And God heard the voice of
the lad; and the angel of God called to
Hagar out of heaven, and said unto her,
What aileth thee, Hagar? fear not;
for God hath heard the voice of the lad
where he *is*. (18) Arise, lift up the lad,
and hold him in thine hand; for I will
make him a great nation. (19) And God
opened her eyes, and she saw a well of
water; and she went, and filled the
bottle with water, and gave the lad
drink. (20) And God was with the lad;
and he grew, and dwelt in the wilderness,
and became an archer. (21) And he
dwelt in the wilderness of Paran: and
his mother took him a wife out of the
land of Egypt.
(22) And it came to pass at that time,
that Abimelech and Phichol the chief
captain of his host spake unto Abraham,
saying, God *is* with thee in all that thou
doest: (23) now therefore swear unto me
here by God [1] that thou wilt not deal
falsely with me, nor with my son, nor
with my son's son: *but* according to the
kindness that I have done unto thee,
thou shalt do unto me, and to the land
wherein thou hast sojourned. (24) And
Abraham said, I will swear. (25) And
Abraham reproved Abimelech because
of a well of water, which Abimelech's

1 Heb., *if thou shalt lie unto me.*

---

mother, with her child, had wandered in the wilderness, using the water in the skin sparingly, ever hoping to come to some spring, but with too little knowledge of the locality to guide her steps wisely. At last the water is spent, and the young life withers first, and the mother knows that soon they both must die. They had made their last effort, and with that hopelessness which travellers have so often described as stealing over the lost wanderer in the desert, they yield themselves to their doom. The boy is entirely passive; but not so the mother. A softer nature would have remained with him to soothe him, but the agony of the wild Egyptian will grant her no rest. She casts his fainting body almost angrily under a shrub, and withdraws to a bow-shot distance, because she cannot bear to see him die. She there gives way not to tears only, but to unrestrained outcries of grief. But it is not her loud lamentation, but the mute prayer of Ishmael that is heard, and an angel of God comes to her relief.

(17) **The angel of God.**—In chap. xvi. 7 it was "the angel of Jehovah" which appeared unto Hagar; here it is the angel of Elohim. It is impossible not to be struck with this exact use of the names of Deity. Hagar was then still a member of Abraham's family; here she is so no longer; and it is Elohim, and not Jehovah, the covenant God of the chosen race, who saves her.

(18) **Hold him in thine hand.**—Literally, *strengthen thine hand in him*, hold him firmly. As Jerome remarks, the boy thus going hand in hand with his mother must have been her companion in her journey, and not a burden upon her shoulder. We must add that the words do not refer to what she was to do immediately, but to the future. She was not simply to lead him to the water, but to be his brave and faithful protector, such as we learn that she really became.

(19) **A well of water.**—Not a cistern, but a spring of living water. The mirage in the desert so wearies the traveller, that at last he turns in despair from what may be more truthful signs. But after her outburst of grief, Hagar would grow more calm, and, encouraged by the angel's voice, she renews her search, and finds. As Abravanel notices, the well already existed, and was not created for Hagar's use; for God, it is said, opened her eyes, that is, enabled her to see something that indicated the existence of water: trees probably rising round the spring, or some vegetable upgrowth.

(20) **He grew.**—Literally, *became great*, that is, grew to manhood.

And dwelt in the wilderness.—He sought no refuge in Egypt, where so large a Semitic population was gathering, nor in any Canaanite town, but took to the wandering life in the desert, such as is still usual with the Arabs.

An archer.—Heb., *a shooter of bowshots.* Another explanation, from a verb signifying *to multiply*, or *be great*, is not tenable.

(21) **A wife out of the land of Egypt.**—However natural this might be on Hagar's part, it would nevertheless strengthen the heathen element in Ishmael and his descendants. We find, nevertheless, that he was subsequently on friendly terms with Isaac (chap. xxv. 9; xxviii. 8, 9). For Paran, see chap. xiv. 6.

ABIMELECH'S COVENANT WITH ABRAHAM.

(22) **Abimelech and Phichol.**—Abimelech, that is *Father-King*, was the title not only of the king of Gerar, but of the kings of the Philistines generally (chap. xxvi. 1; 1 Sam. xxi. 10, marg.; Ps. xxxiv., tit.). In like manner Phichol, *mouth of all*, seems to have been the official designation of the prime minister, and commander-in-chief. This visit of the king and his vizier appears to have taken place some considerable time after the beginning of the sojourn of Abraham at Gerar; for the friendly feelings which then existed had evidently given way to a coolness, occasioned by the quarrels between their herdsmen. In this narrative, Abraham appears as a chieftain powerful enough for a king to wish to make an alliance with him; and thus his abandonment of Sarah, and his receiving of presents in compensation for the wrong done her, seems the more unworthy of him. Abimelech, on the other hand, acts generously as of old, and shows no signs of ill-will at the growing power of one whose expectation was that his race would possess the whole land.

(23) **Nor with my son, nor with my son's son.**—The words are not those commonly used for son and grandson, but a Hebrew phrase signifying *my kith and kin.* They might be translated, "nor with mine offshoot nor mine offspring." The words occur again in the same proverbial way in Job xviii. 19; Isa. xiv. 22.

servants had violently taken away.
(26) And Abimelech said, I wot not who
hath done this thing: neither didst thou
tell me, neither yet heard I *of it*, but to
day. (27) And Abraham took sheep and
oxen, and gave them unto Abimelech;
and both of them made a covenant.
(28) And Abraham set seven ewe lambs
of the flock by themselves. (29) And
Abimelech said unto Abraham, What
mean these seven ewe lambs which thou
hast set by themselves? (30) And he
said, For *these* seven ewe lambs shalt
thou take of my hand, that they may be
a witness unto me, that I have digged
this well. (31) Wherefore he called that
place [1] Beer-sheba; because there they
sware both of them. (32) Thus they made
a covenant at Beer-sheba: then Abime-
lech rose up, and Phichol the chief
captain of his host, and they returned
into the land of the Philistines.
(33) And *Abraham* planted a [2] grove in
Beer-sheba, and called there on the
name of the LORD, the everlasting God.
(34) And Abraham sojourned in the
Philistines' land many days.

CHAPTER XXII.—(1) And it came
to pass after these things, that [a] God

1 That is, *the well of the oath.*

2 Or, *tree.*

B.C. cir. 1892.

a Heb. 11. 17.

B.C. cir. 1872.

(26) **I wot not.**—This explains the reason of Abimelech's visit. The king's herdsmen had robbed Abraham of a well, a species of property jealously defended in the East because of its great value, and Abraham in some way had made his displeasure felt. Abimelech, ever friendly towards Abraham, by whose nobleness of character he had been greatly impressed, comes to learn the cause of the coolness, and to enter into a more close and lasting alliance with the patriarch. With Oriental indirectness, he makes no complaint, and speaks only of his wish for continued friendship, but by his allusion to his past kindness hints that this had not been received as it ought. Abraham fully understands his real meaning, and tells him what had happened; whereupon the matter is set right, and Abraham requites his previous generosity with gifts of cattle.

(28) **Seven ewe lambs.**—The word in Hebrew for *swearing* is a passive verb, literally signifying "to be sevened," that is, done or confirmed by seven. In this ancient narrative we see a covenant actually thus made binding. Seven ewe lambs are picked out and placed by themselves, and by accepting these Abimelech bound himself to acknowledge and respect Abraham's title to the well. Apparently this manner of ratifying an oath was unknown to the Philistines, as Abimelech asks, "What mean these seven ewe lambs?" but it is equally possible that this question was dictated by the rules of Oriental courtesy. When Abraham had picked out the lambs, it became Abimelech's duty to ask what was the purpose of the act, which was then explained, and as soon as the lambs were accepted, the ratification was complete.

(31) **Beer-sheba.**—That is, *the well of seven*, but with a covert allusion to the seven lambs having been used for the ratification of an oath. Robinson found the exact site in the Wady-es-Seba, with its name still preserved as Bir-es-Seba. There are there two wells of solid construction, the first twelve and a half feet in diameter; the other, situated about 200 yards to the south, much smaller, being only five feet in diameter. Both are lined with solid masonry, and reach down to never-failing springs in the rock. Around are stone troughs for watering the cattle, and the parapet of the larger well is worn into deep indentations, by the ropes used in drawing the water (Finn, *Bye-ways in Palestine*, p. 190).

(33) **And Abraham planted a grove in Beer-sheba.**—Heb., *a tamarisk tree.* Under a noble tree of this kind, which grows to a great size in hot countries, Saul held his court at Gibeah, and under another his bones were laid at Jabesh (1 Sam. xxii. 6, xxxi. 13).

And called there on the name of the Lord, the everlasting God.—Heb., *on the name of Jehovah, El 'olam* (comp. chap. iv. 26). In chap. xiv. 22, Abraham claimed for Jehovah that he was *El 'elyon*, the supreme God; in chap. xvii. 1, Jehovah reveals Himself as *El shaddai*, the almighty God; and now Abraham claims for Him the attribute of eternity. As he advanced in holiness, Abraham also grew in knowledge of the manifold nature of the Deity, and we also more clearly understand why the Hebrews called God, not El, but Elohim. In the plural appellation all the Divine attributes were combined. El might be *'elyon*, or *shaddai*, or *'olam;* Elohim was all in one.

(34) **In the Philistines' land.**—In verse 32 Abimelech on returning to Gerar is said to have gone back "into the land of the Philistines." But Beer-sheba also in a general way belonged to his dominions, and Abraham dwelt there in peace by reason of the treaty which existed between him and the Philistine king.

XXII.

THE OFFERING OF ISAAC ON MOUNT MORIAH.

(1) **God did tempt Abraham.**—Heb., *proved* him, put his faith and obedience to the proof. For twenty-five years the patriarch had wandered in Palestine, and seen the fulfilment of the promise perpetually deferred, and yet his faith failed not. At length the long-wished-for heir is born, and, excepting the grievous pain of parting with Ishmael, all went well with him, and seemed to presage a calm and happy old age. He was at peace with his neighbours, had quiet possession of ample pasture for his cattle, knew that Ishmael was prosperous, and saw Isaac fast approaching man's estate (verse 12). In the midst, nevertheless, of this tranquil evening of his days came the severest trial of all; for he was commanded to slay his son. The trial was twofold. For, first, human sacrifice was abhorrent to the nature of Jehovah, and Abraham's clear duty would be to prove the command. Could such a deed really be enjoined upon him by God? Now no subjective proof would be sufficient. In after times many an Israelite was moved by deep religious fanaticism to give his firstborn in the hope of appeasing the anger of God at his sin (Mic. vi. 7); but instead of

did tempt Abraham, and said unto him, Abraham: and he said, [1] Behold, *here* I *am.* (2) And he said, Take now thy son, thine only *son* Isaac, whom thou lovest, and get thee into the land of Moriah; and offer him there for a burnt offering upon one of the mountains which I will tell thee of.

1 Heb., *Behold me.*

(3) And Abraham rose up early in the morning, and saddled his ass, and took two of his young men with him, and Isaac his son, and clave the wood for the burnt offering, and rose up, and went unto the place of which God had told
him. (4) Then on the third day Abraham
lifted up his eyes, and saw the place

peace it brought only a deeper condemnation upon his soul. Had Abraham been moved only by an internal and subjective impulse, his conduct would have deserved and met with similar condemnation. But when, upon examination, he became convinced that the command came from outside himself, and from the same God with whom on former occasions he had so often held converse, then the antecedents of his own life required of him obedience. But even when satisfied of this, there was, secondly, the trial of his faith. A command which he had tested, not only subjectively by prayer, but objectively by comparison with the manner of previous revelations, bade him with his own hand destroy the son in whom "his seed was to be called." His love for his child, his previous faith in the promise, the religious value and worth of Isaac as the appointed means for the blessing of all mankind—this, and more besides, stood arrayed against the command. But Abraham, in spite of all, obeyed, and in proportion to the greatness of the trial was the greatness of the reward. Up to this time his faith had been proved by patience and endurance, but now he was bidden himself to destroy the fruit of so many years of patient waiting (Heb. xi. 17—19), and, assured that the command came from God, he wavered not. Thus by trial was his own faith made perfect, and for Isaac too there was blessing. Meekly, as befitted the type of Christ, he submitted to his father's will, and the life restored to him was henceforth dedicated to God. But there was a higher purpose in the command than the spiritual good of these two saints. The sacrifice had for its object the instruction of the whole Church of God. If the act had possessed no typical value, it would have been difficult for us to reconcile to our consciences a command which might have seemed, indirectly at least, to have authorised human sacrifices. But there was in it the setting forth of the mystery of the Father giving the Son to die for the sins of the world; and therein lies both the value and the justification of Abraham's conduct and of the Divine command.

(2) **Take now.**—*Now* is not an adverb of time, but an interjection of entreaty, usually coupled with requests, and intended to soften them. It thus makes the words more an exhortation than a command.

Thine only son Isaac.—The words in the original are more emphatic, being, "Take, I pray, thy son, thine only son, whom thou lovest, even Isaac." If childlessness was so unendurable in old time to Abraham (chap. xv. 2), what would it be now, after so many years of enjoyment of a son, and after giving up Ishmael for his sake (chap. xvii. 18)?

The land of Moriah.—Moriah may either mean *Jah is teacher* (see Note on chap. xii. 6), or *Jah is provider*. The first is supported by Isa. ii. 3, where the verb is rendered *will teach;* but the second agrees best with verses 8, 14. If this be the meaning, the name would be derived from this event, and would signify the place where "Jehovah will Himself provide the sacrifice." It has been suggested by many able commentators, that the place meant was Moreh in Sichem, and that the site of the sacrifice was, as the Samaritans affirmed, the natural altar upon the summit of Mount Gerizim. But as Abraham and Isaac reached the spot on the third day, and evidently at an early hour, Gerizim is too remote from Beer-sheba for this to be possible. Even Jerusalem is distant enough, as the journey from Beer-sheba takes twenty and a half hours; and travellers in those days had to cook their own food, and prepare their own sleeping accommodation. We may notice also, that Moriah is described as "a land," in some part of which Abraham was to be shown the special mountain intended for the sacrifice; Moreh, on the contrary, was a place where Abraham had lived, and which was therefore well known to him.

Offer him there for a burnt offering.—Hengstenberg and others have argued that Abraham was not to kill Isaac, but to surrender him spiritually to God, and sanctify him by a burnt offering. But this is contradicted by the narrative itself (verse 10), and by the passage in the Epistle to the Hebrews referred to above, where the victory of Abraham's faith is described as consisting in the belief, that even though Isaac were killed, nevertheless the promise would still in some Divine manner be fulfilled in him.

(3) **And Abraham . . .**—Every preparation for the sacrifice is minutely detailed, as if to show the calmness with which Abraham girded up himself for obedience. He even took the wood ready cleft, not because there was no wood there (verse 13), but in order that on arriving at the destined place there might be nothing to distract their thoughts, and that so they might proceed at once to the sacrifice.

(4) **On the third day.**—We may compare the patriarch's feelings during these two weary days of travel with those of Hagar as she wandered in the wilderness, and each day felt the death of her child growing nearer and more certain. But hers were human sorrows only, while Abraham was giving up the son on whom his spiritual hopes depended.

Afar off.—The summit called the Mountain of the House, usually identified with Mount Moriah, cannot be seen by a traveller from Beer-sheba at a greater distance than three miles (Stanley, *Sinai and Palestine*, p. 251). Hence it has been argued that some more widely conspicuous hill-top must be meant. But the phrase *afar off* is used very indefinitely, and three miles exactly agrees with what Abraham did. For he left the servants at the spot, and laid the wood on Isaac, and went the rest of the way on foot. It must have sorely taxed the strength of the lad to be compelled to carry the wood a distance of three miles; while to have carried it from the spot where Gerizim becomes visible would have been impossible.

In Isaac thus carrying the wood on which he was to be sacrificed, the Fathers discerned a type of Christ carrying his cross (John xix. 17).

afar off. (5) And Abraham said unto his
young men, Abide ye here with the ass;
and I and the lad will go yonder and
worship, and come again to you.
(6) And Abraham took the wood of the
burnt offering, and laid *it* upon Isaac his
son; and he took the fire in his hand,
and a knife; and they went both of
them together. (7) And Isaac spake
unto Abraham his father, and said, My
father: and he said, [1] Here *am* I, my
son. And he said, Behold the fire and
the wood: but where *is* the [2] lamb for a
burnt offering? (8) And Abraham said,
My son, God will provide himself a lamb
for a burnt offering: so they went both
of them together.

(9) And they came to the place which
God had told him of; and Abraham
built an altar there, and laid the wood
in order, and bound Isaac his son, and
[a] laid him on the altar upon the wood.
(10) And Abraham stretched forth his
hand, and took the knife to slay his son.
(11) And the angel of the LORD called
unto him out of heaven, and said,
Abraham, Abraham: and he said, Here
am I. (12) And he said, Lay not thine
hand upon the lad, neither do thou any
thing unto him: for now I know that
thou fearest God, seeing thou hast not
withheld thy son, thine only *son* from
me. (13) And Abraham lifted up his
eyes, and looked, and behold behind *him*
a ram caught in a thicket by his horns:
and Abraham went and took the ram,
and offered him up for a burnt offering
in the stead of his son.

(14) And Abraham called the name of
that place [3] Jehovah-jireh: as it is said

1 Heb., *Behold me.*

2 Or, *kid.*

a Jam. 2. 21.

3 That is, *The LORD will see, or, provide.*

---

(5) **I and the lad will . . . come again to you.**—In these words Abraham gives utterance to the hope ascribed to him in Heb. xi. 19. The belief in the resurrection of the body was no new thing with Abraham, as it was part of the creed both of Chaldea and Egypt (Tomkins, *Studies*, p. 127).

(8) **God will provide himself a lamb.**—Heb., *the lamb.* We learn from Heb. xi. 17—19, that Abraham expected that he was to consummate the sacrifice, but that Isaac would be restored to him from the dead, and the promise that his seed was to be born of him so fulfilled. The bestowal of Isaac had been so extraordinary, that Abraham would not feel staggered at what otherwise would have seemed incredible. Apparently, therefore, he meant Isaac by *the lamb,* thus showing that it was not he who chose the victim, but God. The few words that passed between father and son, the notice by the latter that amid such careful preparation no victim had been provided, the father's answer that that matter was left to God, the resolute faith of the one, and the trusting submission of the other, as "they went both of them together," form a picture full not merely of interest, but even of tragical pathos.

(9) **Abraham . . . bound Isaac.**—Jewish commentators agree that this was done with Isaac's consent, nor could it well have been otherwise. Thus his youthful faith was tried equally with that of his father, his future life sanctified, and himself ennobled by being made a type of Christ (1 Pet. ii. 23).

(11) **The angel of the Lord.**—Up to this point, the narrative had been Elohistic, but it is the angel of Jehovah who interferes to stop the sacrifice (see on chap. xvi. 7).

(13) **Behind.**—By a slight change in the shape of a consonant, many ancient authorities read *one ram* instead of *a ram behind* ("him" is not in the Hebrew). This correction is almost certain, as nowhere else is the word translated *behind* used as an adverb of place. The ram was probably that with four horns, still common in the East.

A burnt offering in the stead of his son.—We have here the fact of substitution, and the doctrine of a vicarious sacrifice. The ram took Isaac's place, and by its actual death completed the typical representation of the Saviour's death on Calvary. In *The Speaker's Commentary* it has been well shown, that there is no difficulty in this representation being composed of two parts, so that what was wanting in Isaac should be supplied by the ram. And while it would have been most painful for Isaac to have actually died by his father's hand, the doctrine of the possibility of a vicarious sacrifice would have been even less clearly taught thereby. He therefore rises again to life from the altar, and the ram dies in his stead, and by the two combined the whole mystery is set forth of God giving His Son to die for mankind, and of life springing from His death. Compare the mystery of the two birds, Lev. xiv. 4; and the two goats, *ibid.* xvi. 8.

(14) **Jehovah-jireh.**—That is, *Jehovah will provide.* In verse 8, Abraham had said "Elohim-jireh," *God will provide.* He now uses Jehovah as the equivalent of Elohim. It is added that hence arose a proverb, "In the mount of the Lord it shall be seen," or rather, *In the mount of Jehovah it shall be provided.*—The verb literally means *to see,* or, *to see to a thing,* and the sense of the proverb plainly is that in man's necessity God will Himself see to it, and provide due help and deliverance. The Samaritan, Syriac and Vulg. have a better reading, namely, "In the mount Jehovah will provide." This makes no change in the consonants, which alone are authoritative, but only in the vowels, which were added since the Christian era, and represent the tradition of the Jewish school of Tiberias. The LXX., without changing the vowels, translate, "In the mount Jehovah shall be seen," which would be a prophecy of the manifestation of Christ. The other two renderings, besides their general proverbial sense, point onward to the providing upon this very spot of the sacrifice that was to take away the sins of the world (comp. Isa. liii. 5).

But when and how did this grow into a proverb? and who added this note? It may have been inserted by Moses when he arranged these marvellous documents; less probably by Ezra and the men of the Great Synagogue, when they collected and revised the several books of Holy Scripture after the exile. In either case, the proverb is a national testimony to the genuineness of the record, and proves that the

to this day, In the mount of the LORD it
shall be seen.
(15) And the angel of the LORD called
unto Abraham out of heaven the second
time, (16) and said, [a] By myself have I
sworn, saith the LORD, for because thou
hast done this thing, and hast not with-
held thy son, thine only *son:* (17) that
in blessing I will bless thee, and in
multiplying I will multiply thy seed as
the stars of the heaven, and as the sand
which *is* upon the sea [1] shore; and thy
seed shall possess the gate of his
enemies; (18) [b] and in thy seed shall all
the nations of the earth be blessed; be-
cause thou hast obeyed my voice.
(19) So Abraham returned unto his
young men, and they rose up and went
together to Beer-sheba; and Abraham
dwelt at Beer-sheba.

(20) And it came to pass after these
things, that it was told Abraham,
saying, Behold, Milcah, she hath also
born children unto thy brother Nahor;
(21) Huz his firstborn, and Buz his
brother, and Kemuel the father of
Aram, (22) and Chesed, and Hazo, and
Pildash, and Jidlaph, and Bethuel.
(23) And Bethuel begat [c] Rebekah: these
eight Milcah did bear to Nahor, Abra-
ham's brother. (24) And his concubine,
whose name *was* Reumah, she bare also
Tebah, and Gaham, and Thahash, and
Maachah.

CHAPTER XXIII.—(1) And Sarah
was an hundred and seven and twenty
years old: *these were* the years of the
life of Sarah. (2) And Sarah died in
Kirjath-arba; the same *is* Hebron in

[a] Ps. 105. 9; Ecclus. 44. 21; Luke 1. 73; Heb. 6. 13.

[1] Heb., *lip.*

[b] ch. 12. 3. & 18. 18; Ecclus. 44. 22; Acts 3. 25; Gal. 3. 8.

B.C. cir. 1860.

[c] Called, Rom. 9. 10, *Rebecca.*

---

facts narrated in it were so impressed upon the memory of Abraham's descendants, as to shape their thoughts and language.

(16) **By myself have I sworn, saith the Lord** (Jehovah).—This solemn interposition of an oath (Heb. vi. 17), of which the present is the sole instance in Holy Scripture, plainly indicates that this trial of Abraham's faith was of no common kind, and that its typical teaching is of no ordinary value. Abraham might have appealed to God's own attributes, and said, Far be it from thee, Lord, to command a human sacrifice, and bid a father slay his son. He might have pleaded the promises bound up with Isaac's life. But no, as soon as he is convinced that the command comes from God, he obeys, and, against hope, still believes that the promises will all be fulfilled in the sacrificed Isaac. He is thus the highest and most perfect example of faith, and by his offering of his son the Church received the assurance that the Son of God incarnate in the flesh would upon that very mountain offer the sacrifice Divinely necessary for the pardon of man's sins.

The blessing now given to Abraham differs from those that precede it in three particulars. First, it is no longer a promise, but a solemn compact ratified by an oath. Next, it assures Abraham's seed of victory, whereby the spiritual Israel is certified of the ultimate triumph of the Gospel. Lastly, it transfers to Abraham's offspring the promise of being the means of blessedness to all mankind.

NAHOR'S POSTERITY.

(20) **Thy brother Nahor.**—Dwelling so far apart, news would seldom reach Abraham of those whom he had left at Haran. But besides the domestic interest, the knowledge thus conveyed to him was the cause probably of Abraham's determination to seek a wife for his son from among his own kindred. It has been noticed that Nahor has twelve sons, eight by his lawful wife, and four by his concubine. So Jacob has twelve sons, eight by two lawful wives, and four by two concubines. Lastly, Ishmael has twelve sons. These coincidences are curious, but afford no ground for the assertion that therefore these narratives are mythical. For coincidences quite as strange are to be found in every history, and in daily life.

(21) **Huz.**—The same name as *Uz* in chap. x. 23, xxxvi. 28, the Hebrew in all cases being 'Uz. For the various regions supposed to have been "the land of Uz," see Notes on Job i. 1; Jer. xxv. 20.

Buz.—Probably he was the ancestor of Elihu (Job xxxii. 2); but Buz, in Jer. xxv. 23, seems to have been a region in Idumea.

Kemuel, the father of Aram.—He was not the progenitor of the Aramaic race, but the ancestor of the family of Ram, to which Elihu belonged (Job xxxii. 2), Ram being the same as Aram (Keil). If so, Buz and Kemuel must have coalesced into one tribe.

(22) **Chesed.**—He was not the ancestor of the ancient Chasdim or Chaldees, but possibly of the small tribe of robbers with the same name who plundered Job (Job i. 17). Of the rest, no trace remains in history.

(24) **Maachah.**—This name appears as that of a small Aramaic people, in Deut. iii. 14; Josh. xii. 5; 2 Sam. x. 6.

XXIII.

DEATH AND BURIAL OF SARAH.

(1) **Sarah was an hundred and seven and twenty years old.**—Sarah is the only woman whose age at her death is mentioned in the Bible, an honour doubtless given her as the ancestress of the Hebrew race (Isa. li. 2). As she was ninety at Isaac's birth, he would now be thirty-seven years of age.

(2) **Kirjath-arba; the same is Hebron.**—This was a very ancient city, built seven years before Zoan in Egypt (Num. xiii. 22), probably by a tribe of Semites on their way to the Delta. It lies upon the very border of the Negeb of Judah, about twenty-two miles south of Jerusalem. Originally it was named Kirjath-arba, and though Arba is called "the father of Anak" (Josh. xv. 13), yet the literal meaning *City of Four* (arba being the Hebrew numeral *four*), coupled with the fact that Hebron means *alliance* (chap. xiii. 18), suggests that its building was the result of the union of four families; and afterwards, from the name of the city,

the land of Canaan: and Abraham
came to mourn for Sarah, and to weep
for her.
(3) And Abraham stood up from
before his dead, and spake unto the
sons of Heth, saying, (4) I *am* a stranger
and a sojourner with you: give me a
possession of a buryingplace with you,
that I may bury my dead out of my
sight.
(5) And the children of Heth answered
Abraham, saying unto him, (6) Hear us,
my lord: thou *art* [1] a mighty prince
among us: in the choice of our se-
pulchres bury thy dead; none of us
shall withhold from thee his sepulchre,
but that thou mayest bury thy dead.
(7) And Abraham stood up, and bowed
himself to the people of the land, *even*
to the children of Heth. (8) And he
communed with them, saying, If it be
your mind that I should bury my dead
out of my sight; hear me, and intreat
for me to Ephron the son of Zohar,
(9) that he may give me the cave of
Machpelah, which he hath, which *is* in
the end of his field; for [2] as much money
as it is worth he shall give it me for a
possession of a buryingplace amongst
you.
(10) And Ephron dwelt among the
children of Heth: and Ephron the
Hittite answered Abraham in the
[3] audience of the children of Heth, *even*
of all that went in at the gate of his
city, saying, (11) Nay, my lord, hear me:

1 Heb., *a prince of God.*

2 Heb., *full money.*

3 Heb., *ears.*

Arba may have been often used as a proper name. At the conquest of Palestine there were descendants of Anak still dwelling there, and apparently they had restored the old title, but were expelled by Caleb (Josh. xv. 14), who took it as his possession, and seems to have given its name to a grandchild, as a memorial of his victory (1 Chr. ii. 42). It is still an important town, with a population of 17,000 Moslems and about 600 Jews.

Abraham came to mourn.—At this period Abraham was in quiet possession of several head-quarters, and apparently was himself at Beer-sheba when Sarah died at Hebron, where probably he had left Isaac in charge of his mother and the cattle.

(3) **Abraham stood up from before his dead.**—His first care on arriving at Hebron had been to prostrate himself in Sarah's tent, and give utterance to his grief. Only after this he rises to prepare for her burial.

The sons of Heth.—Up to this time we have read only of Amorites, Mamre and his brothers, at Hebron. It now appears that it was the property of the Hittites, a race who, while the Israelites sojourned in Egypt, became so powerful as to contend for empire with the Egyptians themselves. Their capital was Emesa in Northern Syria, and their history is now being made known to us not only by means of Egyptian records, but also of inscriptions in their own language (See Note on chap. x. 15).

(4) **A possession of a buryingplace.**—While strangers might pasture their cattle upon the open downs, yet the consent of the natives seems to have been necessary before Abraham could occupy any spot permanently (chap. xv. 13; xx. 15). He now wanted even more, and for the actual appropriation of any portion of the soil a public compact and purchase was required, which must be ratified not merely by the seller but by the consent of all the tribe, convened in full assembly at the gate of the city. Thus, in spite of his power and wealth, Abraham, as regards his legal position towards the inhabitants, was but a stranger and sojourner (Heb. xi. 9), and could secure a resting-place for his dead only by their consent.

(6) **A mighty prince.**—Heb., *a prince of God.* Comp. "wind of God" (chap. i. 2); "wrestlings of God" (chap. xxx. 8); "mountains of God" (Ps. xxxvi. 6); "cedars of God" (Ps. lxxx. 10). So also "a sleep of Jehovah" for a deep sleep (1 Sam. xxvi. 12).

In the choice of our sepulchres.—The interview between Abraham and the Hittites is marked by the utmost courtesy on both sides, but it is a mistake to suppose that this acceptance of the patriarch's proposal contained the idea that he might select a sepulchre without paying for it. The payment, in true Oriental fashion, is kept in the background, but is pre-supposed on both sides. After the acceptance of his proposal, it was Abraham's turn to name the burying-place he wished, and the owner next consents, but while treating the purchase-money as a matter of small importance, he nevertheless asks a very high price, to which Abraham at once consents.

(9) **The cave of Machpelah.**—That is, *the double cave,* consisting probably of an outer and an inner compartment. As the land around is also called "the field of Machpelah" (chaps. xlix. 30; l. 13), some imagine that it was the valley that was double; but more probably it took its name from the cavern. For a description of the Haram, within which the bones of Abraham and Sarah probably still lie, see Palmer, *Desert of the Exodus,* p. 397; Stanley, *Sinai and Palestine,* p. 101; and also the Appendix to his *Sermons in the East.*

For as much money as it is worth.—Heb., *for full silver,* rendered "the full price" in 1 Chr. xxi. 22.

A buryingplace amongst you.—This translation is quite wrong. Abraham had no wish that Sarah should be buried amongst the Hittites, but required that the sale should be duly attested. The Heb. is, *Let him give it me in the midst of you* (that is, in a general assembly of the people), *for a possession and a buryingplace.*

(10) **And Ephron dwelt among . . .**—Again a mistranslation. The Heb. is, *Ephron was sitting in the midst of the Hittites.* At these assemblies held at the gate of the city every free-born citizen had a right to be present, and matters were settled by common consent. As Ephron was the owner of the cave, his approval was necessary, and this Abraham treats as a favour, and requests that Ephron's fellow-citizens will intercede in his behalf.

(11) **The field give I thee.**—Only the cave had been mentioned, but for its quiet possession the land

the field give I thee, and the cave that
is therein, I give it thee; in the presence
of the sons of my people give I it thee:
bury thy dead.
(12) And Abraham bowed down him-
self before the people of the land.
(13) And he spake unto Ephron in the
audience of the people of the land,
saying, But if thou *wilt give it*, I pray
thee, hear me: I will give thee money
for the field; take *it* of me, and I will
bury my dead there.
(14) And Ephron answered Abraham,
saying unto him, (15) My lord, hearken
unto me: the land *is worth* four hun-
dred shekels of silver; what *is* that
betwixt me and thee? bury therefore
thy dead.
(16) And Abraham hearkened unto
Ephron; and Abraham weighed to
Ephron the silver, which he had named
in the audience of the sons of Heth,
four hundred shekels of silver, current
money with the merchant. (17) And the
field of Ephron, which *was* in Machpe-
lah, which *was* before Mamre, the field,
and the cave which *was* therein, and all
the trees that *were* in the field, that
were in all the borders round about,
were made sure (18) unto Abraham for a
possession in the presence of the children
of Heth, before all that went in at the
gate of his city.
(19) And after this, Abraham buried
Sarah his wife in the cave of the field
of Machpelah before Mamre: the same
is Hebron in the land of Canaan.
(20) And the field, and the cave that *is*
therein, were made sure unto Abraham
for a possession of a buryingplace by the
sons of Heth.

1 Heb., *gone into days.*

B.C. cir. 1857.

CHAPTER XXIV.—(1) And Abraham
was old, *and* [1] well stricken in age: and
the LORD had blessed Abraham in all
things. (2) And Abraham said unto his

---

around was necessary. In the thrice repeated "give I it thee," there is the same courtly idea as in verse 6, that they were not buying and selling, but making mutual presents.

(12) **Abraham bowed down.**—This obeisance on the patriarch's part is the Oriental method of returning thanks for the granting of a request; and so in verse 7. The next step is to fix the price.

(13) **But if thou wilt give it, I pray thee, hear me.**—Heb., *But if thou wilt, I pray thee, hear me.* It expresses simply a strong desire that Ephron will listen to and grant his next request.

(15) **The land is worth . . .**—Our version misses the courtliness of Ephron's answer, who only fixes the price indirectly, saying, "Land worth four hundred shekels of silver, what is that betwixt me and thee?" The money amounts to about £50, no mean price, considering the high value of silver in those days.

(16) **Abraham weighed . . . current money with the merchant.**—Shekel literally means weight, and money was not coined until long afterwards. In the last clause, by inserting *money* our version antedates facts. According to the Hebrew, it was the silver that was current with the merchants. The metal was probably made into small bars, marked by the refiner to indicate their quality: and Abraham weighed out to Ephron about 200 ounces of silver in bars of the quality usual in trade.

(17) **Before Mamre.**—That is, opposite to it. The Haram wherein the bodies of Abraham and Sarah lie, is situated on the eastern side of the valley, so that Abraham's oak-grove must have been on its western slope. The old Christian tradition, which places it at Ramet-el-Chalil, does not agree with this description, and is, moreover, too far away. The remains pointed out there as those of Abraham's house, are the ruins of a heathen temple. But it is useless to look for any remains of the abode of a nomad dwelling in tents, especially after the site has been occupied by a great city. Moreover, Hebron itself has changed its position. For Benjamin of Tudela, who visited it nearly seven centuries ago, says that the old Hebron was on the heights, but had been abandoned, and that the new city lay in the valley.

The field, and the cave . . .—It is interesting to compare this document, so legally exact and full, with the numerous tablets of terra-cotta now in our museums, and which record with equal exactness the daily business transactions of the people of Ur-Chasdim, whence Abraham had migrated.

(20) **Were made sure unto Abraham.**—For the difficulties connected with St. Stephen's apparent confusion of this transaction with that recorded in chap. xxiii. 19, see Note on Acts vii. 16.

XXIV.

MARRIAGE OF ISAAC AND REBEKAH.

(1) **Abraham was old.**—As Isaac was thirty-seven years of age when Sarah died (chap. xxiii. 1), and forty at his marriage (chap. xxv. 20), Abraham, who was a centenarian at Isaac's birth, would now be nearly 140. As he lived to be 175 (chap. xxv. 7), he survived Isaac's marriage thirty-five years, and lived to see Esau and Jacob nearly grown up.

(2) **Unto his eldest servant of his house.**—Heb., *his servant, the elder of his house.* It is the name of an office; and though one holding so confidential a post would be a man of ripe years, yet it is not probable that Abraham would send any one who was not still vigorous on so distant a journey. Eliezer of Damascus had held a similar office fifty-five years previously (chap. xv. 2), but this was probably a younger man.

Put . . . thy hand under my thigh.—As Jacob requires that Joseph should swear to him in the same manner (chap. xlvii. 29), this form of oath was evidently regarded as a very solemn one. The meaning of it has been much discussed, but we find the thigh in chap. xlvi. 26, Exod. i. 5—in both which places it is

eldest servant of his house, that ruled
over all that he had, [a]Put, I pray thee,
thy hand under my thigh: (3) and I
will make thee swear by the LORD, the
God of heaven, and the God of the
earth, that thou shalt not take a wife
unto my son of the daughters of the
Canaanites, among whom I dwell:
(4) but thou shalt go unto my country,
and to my kindred, and take a wife
unto my son Isaac.

(5) And the servant said unto him,
Peradventure the woman will not be
willing to follow me unto this land:
must I needs bring thy son again unto
the land from whence thou camest?

(6) And Abraham said unto him, Be-
ware thou that thou bring not my son
thither again. (7) The LORD God of
heaven, which took me from my father's
house, and from the land of my kindred,
and which spake unto me, and that
sware unto me, saying, [b]Unto thy seed
will I give this land; he shall send his
angel before thee, and thou shalt take a
wife unto my son from thence. (8) And
if the woman will not be willing to
follow thee, then thou shalt be clear
from this my oath: only bring not my
son thither again. (9) And the servant
put his hand under the thigh of Abra-
ham his master, and sware to him con-
cerning that matter.

(10) And the servant took ten camels of
the camels of his master, and departed;
[1]for all the goods of his master *were* in
his hand: and he arose, and went to
Mesopotamia, unto the city of Nahor.
(11) And he made his camels to kneel
down without the city by a well of water
at the time of the evening, *even* the time
[2]that women go out to draw *water*.

a ch. 47. 29.

b ch. 12. 7, & 13. 15, & 15. 18, & 26. 4.

1 Or, *and*.

2 Heb. *that women which draw water go forth.*

---

rendered *loins*—used as the source of posterity. Probably, therefore, as Tuch argues, it is an euphemistic manner of describing the circumcised member, which was to be touched by the hand placed beneath the thigh; and thus the oath was really by the holy covenant between Abraham and God, of which circumcision was the symbol.

(6) **Beware thou that thou bring not my son thither again.**—The betrothal of Isaac and Rebekah is told with the utmost exactness of detail, because it contained two principles of primary importance to Abraham's posterity: the first, that they were not to allow themselves to be merged among the Canaanites, but remain a distinct people; for this intermarriage with women of their own race was only a means to an end, and not a binding law, to be observed for its own sake. And secondly, that under no circumstances might they return to Mesopotamia, but must cling devotedly to the land of which God had promised them the possession. We learn from verse 8 that this second point was regarded by Abraham as even more important than the first; and with reason. For the race might remain distinct even if Isaac took a woman of Palestine to wife, though there would be the risk of religious deterioration; but if they returned to Padan-aram they were certain to be absorbed, and could look for no higher lot than that attained to by Laban's descendants.

(7) **Land of my kindred.**—Rather, *of my nativity;* and so in verse 4. (See Note on chap. xii. 1.) It is a different word from that rightly translated *kindred* in verse 38. Jewish interpreters say that by his *father's house* here, and by his *country* in verse 4, Abraham meant Charran: but by his *birthplace* he meant Ur of the Chaldees. If, therefore, the servant failed in obtaining a wife at Charran, he was to continue his journey to Ur, where Abraham, doubtless, had many relatives.

(10) **And the servant.**—Why did not Isaac go himself in search of a wife? We must not conclude from his inactivity that the matter had not his full concurrence; but he was the heir, and according to Oriental manners it was fit that the choice should be left to a trusty deputy. What is peculiar in the narrative is the distance to which the servant was sent, and the limitation of his choice to a particular family; but both these peculiarities arose from the religious considerations involved. Jacob subsequently went in person on a similar errand, but we must remember that Rebekah was also seeking for him a place of safety. But for this, and had he been the sole heir, she would probably have sent an embassy to her brother's house to ask for him a wife.

For all the goods of his master were in his hand.—Rather, *with every good thing of his master's in his hand.* It was necessary not only that the servant should take with him such a convoy as would ensure his safety and that of the bride on their return, but also such rich presents as would adequately represent Abraham's wealth and power.

Mesopotamia.—Heb., *Aram-Naharaim:* that is, "Aram of the two rivers." Aram means *highland,* but it became the title of the whole Syrian race; and here Aram-Naharaim means that part of Syria which lies between the Tigris and Euphrates. It was a mountainless region, except towards the north. For Padan-aram, see Note on chap. xxv. 20.

The city of Nahor.—This was Charran (chap. xxvii. 43). Nahor had probably migrated thither from Ur when Terah was growing old, that he might occupy the pastures which Abraham was about to abandon.

(11) **He made his camels to kneel down.**—Camels rest kneeling, but the servant did not unlade them till he knew that God had heard his prayer. (See verse 32.)

By a well of water.—The well was the property of the whole city, and might be used only at a fixed hour; and the servant therefore waits till the women came to draw. This duty of fetching water is not peculiar to Oriental women, but to this day in most parts of Europe, wherever the supply comes from a public source, women may be seen thus occupied. Rebekah carried her pitcher upon her shoulder; in the south of France the Basque women, like the ancient Egyptians, carry it on their heads, and the habit of

(12) And he said, O LORD God of my
master Abraham, I pray thee, send me
good speed this day, and shew kindness
unto my master Abraham. (13) Behold,
[a]I stand *here* by the well of water; and
the daughters of the men of the city
come out to draw water: (14) and let it
come to pass, that the damsel to whom
I shall say, Let down thy pitcher, I pray
thee, that I may drink; and she shall
say, Drink, and I will give thy camels
drink also: *let the same be* she *that* thou
hast appointed for thy servant Isaac;
and thereby shall I know that thou hast
shewed kindness unto my master.

(15) And it came to pass, before he had
done speaking, that, behold, Rebekah
came out, who was born to Bethuel, son
of Milcah, the wife of Nahor, Abraham's
brother, with her pitcher upon her shoul-
der. (16) And the damsel *was* [1]very fair
to look upon, a virgin, neither had any
man known her: and she went down to
the well, and filled her pitcher, and came
up. (17) And the servant ran to meet her,
and said, Let me, I pray thee, drink a
little water of thy pitcher. (18) And she
said, Drink, my lord: and she hasted,
and let down her pitcher upon her hand,
and gave him drink. (19) And when she
had done giving him drink, she said, I
will draw *water* for thy camels also, until
they have done drinking. (20) And she
hasted, and emptied her pitcher into the
trough, and ran again unto the well to
draw *water*, and drew for all his camels.
(21) And the man wondering at her held
his peace, to wit whether the LORD had
made his journey prosperous or not.

(22) And it came to pass, as the camels
had done drinking, that the man took a
golden [2]earring of half a shekel weight,
and two bracelets for her hands of ten
shekels weight of gold; (23) and said,

B.C. cir. 1857.

a ver. 43.

1 Heb. *good of countenance.*

2 Or, *jewel for the forehead.*

thus balancing it gives them a peculiarly erect and graceful carriage.

(12–14) **O Lord God . . .**—Heb., *Jehovah, God of my lord Abraham.* The word translated "master" throughout this chapter is *'donai*, the ordinary word for *lord*, and it is so rendered in verse 18. As a circumcised member of Abraham's household, the servant prays to Jehovah, Abraham's God; and though in verse 5 he had suggested a difficulty, apparently it was from no want of faith, but that he might know whether under any circumstances Isaac might return to Aram-Naharaim. He now leaves the success of his mission to Jehovah; and while he would use his own discernment in selecting from the troop of advancing maidens one whose countenance gave promise of goodness of heart, the fulfilment of the appointed signal which was to mark God's approval would also show that she was no churlish woman, but one active, generous, and kind.

Send me good speed this day.—Heb., *cause it to meet me this day.*

I stand.—This word here, and in verse 43, is not the same as that used in verse 30, but one that means *I post myself*, or *I take my station.*

Thereby.—Rather, *by her:* by her giving the appointed sign I shall know that thou hast showed kindness to my lord.

The damsel.—This word (Heb., *Na'ar*) is of the common gender in the Pentateuch, except in Deut. xxii. 19, where it has the feminine termination. It is used of Abraham's young men in chaps. xiv. 24, xviii. 7, &c., but no less than twenty-two times of women. In the rest of the Bible the gender is always marked, and even here it is read in the feminine in the Jewish synagogues. We have herein another of the many linguistic proofs of the extreme antiquity of the Pentateuch, and it is the more interesting because found in a Jehovistic section. The same word is used again in verses 16 and 28. (See Note on chap. xliii. 8.)

(16) **She went down to the well.**—The water, therefore, was reached by a flight of steps, the usual rule wherever the well was fed by a natural spring. Cisterns, on the contrary, supplied from the rains were narrower at the top than at the bottom.

Mr. Malan (*Philosophy or Truth*, p. 93), in an interesting account of his visit to this well, says that on going out from Haran in the evening to examine it, he found "a group of women filling, no longer their pitchers, since the steps down which Rebekah went to fetch the water are now blocked up, but their water-skins by drawing water at the well's mouth. Everything around that well bears signs of age and of the wear of time; for as it is the only well of drinkable water there, it is much resorted to. Other wells are only for watering the flocks. There we find the troughs of various height for camels, for sheep and for goats, for kids and for lambs; there the women wear nose-rings and bracelets on their arms, some of gold or of silver, and others of brass, or even of glass."

(21) **And the man wondering at her . . .**—The verb is rare, and the LXX., Syr., and Vulg., followed by Gesenius and Fürst, translate, "And the man gazed attentively at her, keeping silence, that he might know," &c. The servant, we may well believe, was astonished at the exactness and quickness with which his prayer was being answered, but this is not the point to which the rest of the verse refers; rather, it sets him before us as keenly observing all she said and did, and carefully coming to the conclusion that the comely and generous maiden was the destined bride of the son of his lord.

(22) **Earring.**—Really *nose-ring*; for in verse 47 the man places it on her nose, wrongly translated *face* in our version. The word occurs again in Ezek. xvi. 12, where it is rendered *jewel*, and again is placed "on the nose;" it is also similarly translated *jewel* in Prov. xi. 22, where it is placed in "a swine's snout." It was hung not from the central cartilage of the nose, but from the left nostril, the flesh of which was pierced for the purpose; and such rings are still the usual betrothal present in Arabia, and are commonly worn both there and in Persia, made not only of gold and of silver,

Whose daughter *art* thou? tell me, I
pray thee: is there room *in* thy father's
house for us to lodge in? (24) And she
said unto him, I *am* the daughter of
Bethuel the son of Milcah, which she
bare unto Nahor. (25) She said moreover
unto him, We have both straw and pro-
vender enough, and room to lodge in.
(26) And the man bowed down his head,
and worshipped the LORD. (27) And he
said, Blessed *be* the LORD God of my
master Abraham, who hath not left
destitute my master of his mercy and
his truth: I *being* in the way, the LORD
led me to the house of my master's
brethren.

(28) And the damsel ran, and told *them*
of her mother's house these things.
(29) And Rebekah had a brother, and his
name *was* Laban: and Laban ran out
unto the man, unto the well. (30) And it
came to pass, when he saw the earring
and bracelets upon his sister's hands,
and when he heard the words of Rebe-
kah his sister, saying, Thus spake the
man unto me; that he came unto the
man; and, behold, he stood by the
camels at the well. (31) And he said,
Come in, thou blessed of the LORD;
wherefore standest thou without? for I
have prepared the house, and room for
the camels. (32) And the man came into
the house: and he ungirded his camels,
and gave straw and provender for the
camels, and water to wash his feet, and
the men's feet that *were* with him.
(33) And there was set *meat* before him to
eat: but he said, I will not eat, until I
have told mine errand. And he said,
Speak on.

(34) And he said, I *am* Abraham's ser-
vant. (35) And the LORD hath blessed
my master greatly; and he is become
great: and he hath given him flocks, and
herds, and silver, and gold, and men-
servants, and maidservants, and camels,
and asses. (36) And Sarah my master's
wife bare a son to my master when she
was old: and unto him hath he given all
that he hath. (37) And my master made

---

but of coral, mother-of-pearl, and even cheaper materials. (See Quotation in Note on verse 16.) Its weight, about a quarter of an ounce, would make it not more disfiguring than many of the personal ornaments worn at the present time.

Bracelets are profusely worn at this day by Oriental women, the whole arm to the elbow being usually covered by them.

(24) **Bethuel the son of Milcah, which she bare unto Nahor.**—Rebekah mentions her father's mother to show that she was descended from a high-born wife; but the servant would welcome it as proving that not only on the father's side, but also on the mother's, she was Isaac's cousin, Milcah being the daughter of Haran, Abraham's brother. And when thus he knew that she fulfilled all the conditions, he gave her the jewels which he was holding in his hand, and bowed the head, and gave thanks.

(28) **The damsel ran, and told (them of) her mother's house.**—The words inserted in italics are worse than useless. The wife of a sheik has a separate tent (verse 67), and the result of polygamy is to make each family hold closely together. Naturally, too, the maiden would first show her mother and the women presents of so special a meaning. We even find Laban, the brother, acting as Rebekah's representative; and it is only when the final decision has to be given that Bethuel is allowed to have any voice in the matter (verse 50).

(29) **Laban ran out unto the man.**—Not until he had seen Rebekah, as narrated in the next verse—this being a brief summary, followed by a more detailed account. Milcah had probably sent and summoned him to her tent, where his sister showed him her presents, and told him what had happened. He then hurried out to offer due hospitality to the generous stranger.

(31) **Come in, thou blessed of the Lord.**—This hospitality was in the East almost a matter of course, though Laban's earnestness may have been increased by the sight of his sister's golden ornaments. More remarkable is it that Laban addresses the servant as "blessed of Jehovah;" for we learn in Josh. xxiv. 2 that the monotheism of Nahor and his family was by no means pure. Still, neither were they idolaters, and the "other gods" whom they served were probably teraphim, as certainly were the gods of Laban mentioned in chap xxxi. 30. Even to the last these household gods seem to have retained a hold upon the affections of the nation (Hos. iii. 4); and probably most uneducated minds, even when their religion is in the main true, have nevertheless a tendency to add on to it some superstitions, especially in the way of fashioning for themselves some lower mediator.

(33) **I will not eat, until I have told mine errand.**—Two points in Oriental manners are here brought into view: the first, that hospitality, so necessary in a country where there are no inns, was, and still is, a religion to the Bedouin; the second, that consequently he will concede anything rather than have his hospitality refused. Aware of this feeling, Abraham's servant will not partake of Laban's bread and salt until he has told his request. After he had become Laban's guest, Laban would have been free to do as he liked; but he must now grant what is asked, or the stranger would decline to enter his dwelling.

Mr. Fraser (*Historical Description of Afghanistan* chap. xi. p. 424: Edinburgh, 1834) and Ferrier (*L'Afghanistan*, chap. xi., p. 119: ed. 1842) mention a remarkable custom connected with Afghan hospitality which admirably illustrates the behaviour of Abraham's servant. It is called *menawâti*, from two words signifying *I am come in.* Any one who has a favour to ask goes to the tent or house of the person from whom he expects it, but refuses to sit on his carpet or partake of his food until he has granted the required boon. And custom makes it a point of honour to concede it, if it be in the power of the person thus appealed to.

me swear, saying, Thou shalt not take a
wife to my son of the daughters of the
Canaanites, in whose land I dwell:
(38) but thou shalt go unto my father's
house, and to my kindred, and take a
wife unto my son. (39) And I said unto
my master, Peradventure the woman
will not follow me. (40) And he said
unto me, The LORD, before whom I walk,
will send his angel with thee, and pros-
per thy way; and thou shalt take a wife
for my son of my kindred, and of my
father's house: (41) then shalt thou be
clear from *this* my oath, when thou
comest to my kindred; and if they give
not thee *one*, thou shalt be clear from
my oath. (42) And I came this day unto
the well, and said, O LORD God of my
master Abraham, if now thou do pros-
per my way which I go: (43) [a] behold, I
stand by the well of water; and it shall
come to pass, that when the virgin
cometh forth to draw *water*, and I say
to her, Give me, I pray thee, a little
water of thy pitcher to drink; (44) and
she say to me, Both drink thou, and I
will also draw for thy camels: *let* the
same *be* the woman whom the LORD hath
appointed out for my master's son.
(45) And before I had done speaking in
mine heart, behold, Rebekah came forth
with her pitcher on her shoulder; and
she went down unto the well, and drew
water: and I said unto her, Let me
drink, I pray thee. (46) And she made
haste, and let down her pitcher from her
shoulder, and said, Drink, and I will
give thy camels drink also: so I drank,
and she made the camels drink also.
(47) And I asked her, and said, Whose
daughter *art* thou? And she said, The
daughter of Bethuel, Nahor's son, whom
Milcah bare unto him: and I put the
earring upon her face, and the bracelets
upon her hands. (48) And I bowed down
my head, and worshipped the LORD, and
blessed the LORD God of my master
Abraham, which had led me in the right
way to take my master's brother's
daughter unto his son. (49) And now if
ye will deal kindly and truly with my
master, tell me: and if not, tell me;
that I may turn to the right hand, or to
the left.

(50) Then Laban and Bethuel answered
and said, The thing proceedeth from the
LORD: we cannot speak unto thee bad
or good. (51) Behold, Rebekah *is* before
thee, take *her*, and go, and let her be thy
master's son's wife, as the LORD hath
spoken. (52) And it came to pass, that,
when Abraham's servant heard their
words, he worshipped the LORD, *bowing
himself* to the earth. (53) And the servant
brought forth [1] jewels of silver, and
jewels of gold, and raiment, and gave
them to Rebekah: he gave also to her
brother and to her mother precious
things.

(54) And they did eat and drink, he and
the men that *were* with him, and tarried
all night; and they rose up in the morn-

[a] ver. 13.

[1] Heb. *vessels*.

(38) **Kindred.**—Not the word so translated in verses 4, 7, but that rendered *family* in chaps. viii. 19, marg., x. 5, xii. 3, &c. Strictly, it signifies a sub-division of a tribe (Numb. i. 18).

(43) **The virgin.**—Not the word used in verse 16, nor that rendered *damsel* there and in verse 14, but *'almah*, a young woman just ripening for marriage. It is applied to Miriam in Exod. ii. 8, where it is rendered *maid*, and to the mother of the Immanuel in Isa. vii. 14.

(45) **Speaking in mine heart.**—The Heb. idiom is far more exact and true: namely, *before I had done speaking to my heart.*

(47) **Upon her face.**—Heb., *upon her nose.* This mistranslation explains the strange rendering *jewel for the forehead* in the margin of verse 22.

(50) **Laban and Bethuel.**—See Note on verse 28. Even when thus tardily mentioned, the father is placed after the brother; and of this we need look for no further explanation than that by polygamy the father was estranged from his own children, while each separate family held very closely together. Thus when Dinah was wronged, it was two of her mother's sons, Simeon and Levi, who avenged her (chap. xxxiv. 13—25); and so it was Absalom who avenged Tamar (2 Sam. xiii. 22). Still, Bethuel's consent was finally necessary; but as soon as it was given all active arrangements were left to the mother and Laban (verses 53—55), and Bethuel is mentioned no more.

(53) **Jewels of silver, and jewels of gold.**—Heb., *vessels*. In ancient times a wife had to be bought (chap. xxxiv. 12), and the presents given were not mere ornaments and jewellery, but articles of substantial use and value. Quickly indeed in a country of such ceremonial politeness the purchase took a more honourable form, but Orientals do not let their courtesy interfere with their interests, and the relatives would take care that the freewill offerings did not fall below the usual standard. These went partly to the bride, and partly to her relatives: and as they are described here as going exclusively to the brother and mother, Jewish tradition has invented the story that Bethuel was ill at the time, and died on the day of the servant's arrival. But the manner in which Isaac speaks of him in chap. xxviii. 2 does not allow us to suppose that he was either dead at the time of her departure, or that he was a person of no ability or importance. Possibly, therefore, polygamy had led to the custom of the purchase-presents going to the mother's tent.

ing, and he said, [a]Send me away unto
my master. (55) And her brother and her
mother said, Let the damsel abide with
us [1]*a few* days, at the least ten; after
that she shall go. (56) And he said unto
them, Hinder me not, seeing the LORD
hath prospered my way; send me away
that I may go to my master. (57) And
they said, We will call the damsel, and
enquire at her mouth. (58) And they
called Rebekah, and said unto her, Wilt
thou go with this man? And she said,
I will go. (59) And they sent away Re-
bekah their sister, and her nurse, and
Abraham's servant, and his men. (60) And
they blessed Rebekah, and said unto
her, Thou *art* our sister, be thou *the
mother* of thousands of millions, and let
thy seed possess the gate of those which
hate them.
(61) And Rebekah arose, and her dam-
sels, and they rode upon the camels, and
followed the man: and the servant took
Rebekah, and went his way. (62) And
Isaac came from the way of the [b]well
Lahai-roi; for he dwelt in the south
country. (63) And Isaac went out [2]to
meditate in the field at the eventide:
and he lifted up his eyes, and saw, and,
behold, the camels *were* coming. (64) And
Rebekah lifted up her eyes, and when
she saw Isaac, she lighted off the camel.
(65) For she *had* said unto the servant,
What man *is* this that walketh in the
field to meet us? And the servant *had*
said, It *is* my master: therefore she
took a vail, and covered herself. (66) And
the servant told Isaac all things that he
had done. (67) And Isaac brought her
into his mother Sarah's tent, and took
Rebekah, and she became his wife; and
he loved her: and Isaac was comforted
after his mother's *death*.

CHAPTER XXV. — (1) Then again
Abraham took a wife, and her name *was*

[a] ver. 56 & 59.

[1] Or, *a full year*, or, *ten* months.

[b] ch. 16. 14. & 25. 11.

[2] Or, *to pray*.

---

(55) **A few days, at the least ten.**—Heb., *days or a decade*, which Onkelos, Saadja, Rashi, and others translate as in the margin: "a year or ten months." But while this rendering has high Jewish authority for it, yet more probably *decade* was the name for the third part of a month. It would be curious thus to find that the family of Terah, either with or instead of weeks, measured time by periods of ten days, as was certainly the custom of the Egyptians at one period of their history.

(58) **Wilt thou go with this man?**—A woman in the East has little choice in the matter of her marriage, and here, moreover, everything was so plainly providential, that Rebekah, like her father and brother (verse 50), would have felt it wrong to make difficulties, and she expresses her readiness to go at once, though she will never see her relatives again. Of course there would be some little delay for preparation, but none for leave-taking.

(59) **Their sister.**—Bethuel may have had other sons, though Laban only is mentioned.

Her nurse.—How dear Deborah was, first to Rebekah, and afterwards to Jacob, may be seen by the lamentation at her death (chap. xxxv. 8).

(60) **Thousands of millions.**—Heb., *thousands of ten thousands*. A million was a number which at this early period the Hebrews had no means of expressing. The blessing contains two parts: the first, the hope of fruitfulness founded on the primæval command (chap. i. 28); the second, that of victory in war (see chap. xxii. 17).

(62) **The well Lahai-roi.**—Hagar's well (chap. xvi. 14), situated in the "south country," that is, the Negeb (see chap. xii. 9). The oasis round it became Isaac's favourite residence (chap. xxv. 11), and was in the neighbourhood of Beer-sheba, where Abraham was dwelling when Sarah died at Hebron (chap. xxiii. 2). The journey of the servant would take some months, and during this time Abraham's herds would be shifted from station to station, but it would be known where he was from the period of the year. As Isaac was at the station most remote from Charran, Rebekah would have visited all his homes before arriving at Beer-lahai-roi.

(63) **To meditate.**—Many Jewish commentators translate *to pray*, and derive one of the three Jewish forms of prayer from this act of Isaac. But though the verb is rare, the substantive is used in Ps. civ. 34 of religious meditation; and this sense well agrees with the whole character of the calm, peaceful Isaac, already marked out as the type of the Lamb dumb before His slayers (chap. xxii. 7).

(64) **She lighted off.**—Heb., *fell*: descended hastily from her camel. It is still the custom in the East for an inferior when meeting a superior to dismount, and advance on foot. Rebekah, therefore, would have been thought bold and disrespectful had she not acknowledged the superiority of her lord. Besides beauty, we have already seen in her kindliness of heart, activity, and courageous submission to the guidance of Providence; we now see her modesty and courtesy towards her husband.

(65) **She took a vail, and covered herself.**—Brides are usually taken to the bridegroom enveloped in a vail, which covers the whole body, and is far larger than that ordinarily worn. At the present time the bride-vail is usually red, the ordinary vail blue or white. By wrapping herself in this vail Rebekah notified that she was the bride. After marriage it was seldom worn at this early period, and so both the Egyptians and Abimelech saw Sarah's beauty.

(67) **Sarah's tent.**—So Leah and Rachel had each her own tent (chap. xxxi. 33; but see on verse 28).

XXV.

ABRAHAM'S MARRIAGE WITH KETURAH.

(1) **Then again Abraham took a wife.**—This rendering implies that Abraham's marriage with Keturah did not take place until after Sarah's death; but this, though probable, is far from certain, as the Hebrew simply says, *And Abraham added*

Keturah. (2) And [a]she bare him Zimran,
and Jokshan, and Medan, and Midian,
and Ishbak, and Shuah. (3) And Jok-
shan begat Sheba, and Dedan. And the
sons of Dedan were Asshurim, and
Letushim, and Leummim. (4) And the
sons of Midian; Ephah, and Epher,
and Hanoch, and Abidah, and El-
daah. All these *were* the children of
Keturah.

(5) And Abraham gave all that he had
unto Isaac. (6) But unto the sons of the
concubines, which Abraham had, Abra-
ham gave gifts, and sent them away
from Isaac his son, while he yet lived,
eastward, unto the east country.

(7) And these *are* the days of the years
of Abraham's life which he lived, an
hundred threescore and fifteen years.
(8) Then Abraham gave up the ghost, and
died in a good old age, an old man, and
full *of years;* and was gathered to his
people. (9) And his sons Isaac and Ish-
mael buried him in the cave of Mach-
pelah, in the field of Ephron the son of
Zohar the Hittite, which *is* before
Mamre; (10) [b]the field which Abraham
purchased of the sons of Heth: there

[a] 1 Chron. i. 32.

[b] ch. 23. 16.

---

and took a wife. This statement is altogether indefinite; but as Abraham was 137 years of age at Sarah's death, and lived to be 175, it is quite possible that, left solitary by Isaac's marriage, he took Keturah to wife, and had by her six sons. The sole objection is his own statement, in chap. xvii. 17, that it was a thing beyond nature for a man a hundred years old to have a son; how much more improbable, then, must it have become after forty more years had passed by! The argument on the other side, which would infer that the marriage took place in Sarah's lifetime, from the fact that the birth of grandchildren is mentioned in verses 3 and 4, has little weight, as their names might have been subsequently added to bring down the genealogy to a later date.

Jewish commentators cut the knot by identifying Keturah with Hagar, who in the meanwhile had, as they say, set an example of matronly virtue in the manner in which she had devoted herself to the bringing up of Ishmael. But in verse 6 there is an evident allusion to both Hagar and Keturah in the mention of Abraham's "concubines" in the plural; and in 1 Chron. i. 32 the children of Keturah are distinguished from Hagar's one son, Ishmael. To this we must add that as Ishmael was fourteen years old when Isaac was born, he would be now about fifty-four years of age, and his mother have passed the period of life when she could bear six sons.

The position, moreover, of Keturah was entirely distinct from that of Hagar. The latter was Sarah's representative; and her son, if Sarah had remained barren, would have been the heir. Keturah was a secondary wife, whose children from the first held an inferior position in the household. So Bilhah and Zilpah became the substitutes of Rachel and Leah, and therefore their children ranked side by side with Reuben and Joseph, though not altogether on the same level. They were patriarchs, and the progenitors of tribes, even if the tribes sprung from them held a lower rank.

(2) **Zimran.**—The home of Keturah's descendants is placed by Josephus and Jerome in Arabia-Felix; but the supposed traces of their names are untrustworthy.

Midian is the one son of Keturah who had a great future before him, for his race became famous traders (chap. xxxvii. 28); and as they are called *Medanites* there in the Hebrew, in verse 36, it is probable that Medan and Midian coalesced into one tribe. Jethro, the father-in-law of Moses, belonged to them (Exod. ii. 15, 16), and, enriched by commerce, they became so powerful as to be dangerous neighbours to the Israelites. (Judges vi., vii., viii.)

Shuah.—From him perhaps descended Bildad the Shuhite, Job's friend (Job. ii. 11). The name in the Hebrew is different from that also rendered "Shuah" in chap. xxxviii. 2.

(3) **Jokshan begat Sheba, and Dedan.**—But Sheba and Dedan are also described as the sons of Raamah, the son of Cush (chap. x. 7). We have here proof that these genealogies are to a certain extent geographical, and that whereas these districts at first were peopled by a Hamitic race, they were subsequently conquered by men of the Semitic stock, who claimed Abraham for their ancestor. Most probably, therefore, we ought not to regard Sheba and Dedan as the names here of men. As men they were the sons of Raamah, but when the sons of Jokshan wrested these two countries from the family of Cush, they called them sons of their progenitor, because the dominant portion of the population had sprung from him. They appear as countries in Jer. vi. 20, xlix. 8; Ezek. xxv. 13, xxvii. 15, 22, xxxviii. 13, &c.

Asshurim, and Letushim, and Leummim.—These are certainly not the names of men, but of the three tribes into which the Dedanites were divided.

(6) **The east country.**—By this is meant Arabia and Southern Mesopotamia, where, by their superior vigour and organisation, the descendants of Abraham were able to establish their supremacy over the natives. Burckhardt tells us that the Bedaween still follow Abraham's practice. When their children are grown up, they give each of the younger sons his share of their goods (Luke xv. 12), whereupon they move to a distance, and leave the eldest brother in quiet possession of the home.

(7) **An hundred threescore and fifteen years.**—As Abraham was seventy-five years of age when he left Haran (chap. xii. 4), his sojourn in Canaan lasted just a century, one quarter of which was spent in the long trial of his faith before Isaac was granted to him. As, however, Esau and Jacob were born when Isaac was sixty years of age (chap. xxv. 26), they would be fifteen at Abraham's death, and probably had often seen their grandfather, and received his blessing.

(8) **Abraham . . . was gathered to his people.**—Upon the belief in a future life implied in thes words, see Note on chap. xv. 15, and comp. Heb. xi. 16.

(9) **His sons Isaac and Ishmael.**—Isaac was now seventy-five years of age, and Ishmael eighty-nine, and the two old men, with their enmity long over, met as friends at their father's burial. While Keturah's sons were apparently sent far away into Arabia, Ishmael at Paran (chap. xxi. 21) would be at no very great

was Abraham buried, and Sarah his
wife. (11) And it came to pass after the
death of Abraham, that God blessed his
son Isaac; and Isaac dwelt by the [a]well
Lahai-roi.
(12) Now these *are* the generations of
Ishmael, Abraham's son, whom Hagar
the Egyptian, Sarah's handmaid, bare
unto Abraham: (13) and [b]these *are* the
names of the sons of Ishmael, by their
names, according to their generations:
the firstborn of Ishmael, Nebajoth; and
Kedar, and Adbeel, and Mibsam, (14) and
Mishma, and Dumah, and Massa, (15) Ha-
dar, and Tema, Jetur, Naphish, and
Kedemah: (16) these *are* the sons of Ish-
mael, and these *are* their names, by their
towns, and by their castles; twelve
princes according to their nations.
(17) And these *are* the years of the life of
Ishmael, an hundred and thirty and
seven years: and he gave up the ghost
and died; and was gathered unto his
people. (18) And they dwelt from Havi-
lah unto Shur, that *is* before Egypt,
as thou goest toward Assyria: *and*
he [1]died in the presence of all his
brethren.

a ch. 13. 14 & 24. 62.

b 1 Chron. 1. 29.

1 Heb. *fell.*

---

distance from the well Lahai-roi, which was Isaac's favourite residence.

(11) **God blessed his son Isaac.**—With this general summary the *Tôldôth Terah* concludes, and no portion of Holy Scripture is more interesting or valuable; for in it the broad foundation is laid for the fulfilment of the protevangelium contained in chap. iii. 15, the progenitor of the chosen race is selected and proved on trial, and the preparation made for the giving of the Law, and for the growing light of prophecy, by the nearness wherewith Abraham walked with God.

THE TÔLDÔTH ISHMAEL.

(12) **These are the generations of Ishmael.**—Following the usual rule of this book, Ishmael is not dismissed from the Divine presence without a short record of his history, after which he falls into the background, and the historian proceeds with his main subject, which is the preparation for the forming of that race and nation of whom, according to the flesh, Christ came. These brief notices, moreover, of personages not in the direct line of Christ's ancestry have their value in God's great purpose that the Jewish Messiah should be the Redeemer of the Gentiles also (Rom. x. 12); and consequently from the first their history was not alien from God's counsels.

(13—15) **The sons of Ishmael.**—Of the Arabian tribes sprung from Ishmael we read of Nebajoth and Kedar in Isa. lx. 7 as pastoral tribes, rich in flocks. Dumah is deemed worthy of a special prophecy (*Ib.*, xxi. 11); while the people of Tema are described there in verse 14 as generous and hospitable, and in Job vi. 19 they appear as active traders. (See also Jer. xxv. 23.) Jetur, Naphish, and other Hagarite tribes, were conquered by Reuben and his allies (1 Chron. v. 19), and Jetur became the Iturea of Luke iii. 1. For the occasional references made to these and other sons of Ishmael in classical writers, the reader may consult Smith's *Dictionary of the Bible*, or similar works. The abode of the twelve tribes sprung from Ishmael was the northern part of Arabia, whence gradually they extended their influence, and apparently soon absorbed the Joktanites (chap. x. 26—30), themselves a kindred Semitic race. These genealogies would be inexplicable if we did not remember that successive waves of people occupied these lands, and that while the old names remained, the dominant race was new. So the rapid growth of individuals into tribes (as of Midian, chap. xxv. 2) was the result of races of higher civilisation and greater energy subduing feeble and less highly-developed tribes. Hence in verse 16 the sons of Ishmael are called "princes." We gather from this that Ishmael had gathered round him a body of men of the Semitic race, of whom large numbers were constantly on the move towards Egypt (chap. xii. 15), and by their aid had established his rule in Paran, and handed it on to his sons.

(16) **By their towns, and by their castles.**—Towns and castles in the wilderness of Paran there were none, but we know for certain that the first of these words signified an unwalled village. (See Lev. xxv. 31, where it is exactly described; also Ps. x. 8; Isa. xlii. 11.) It was, however, a settled and permanent place of dwelling. The other word rendered here castle, but used as the equivalent of *tent* in Ps. lxix. 25, is really a cluster of tents, the encampment of a tribe, and movable. It occurs in Num. xxxi. 10; 1 Chron. vi. 54; Ezek. xxv. 4. As is well known, the Arabs are divided into two classes—the dwellers in tents, who are ever moving from station to station, within certain limits, nevertheless, which they seldom pass over; and the agricultural class, who have fixed habitations, are looked upon as inferiors, and probably are the remains of a conquered race. To this day they pay a sort of rent, or black-mail, to the nobler Arabs. We find, then, this distinction already existing when this *Tôldôth* was drawn up; the agricultural Arabs dwelling in unwalled villages, while the nomad tribes pitched now here, and now there, their clusters of black camels'-hair tents. And thus we have in these words proof that Ishmael and his subjects were not all upon the same level; for while he, his sons, and his noblest retainers would dwell in tents, the inhabitants of the villages would be men of inferior origin, compelled to submit themselves to him.

(18) **Havilah** was far to the south, on the Persian Gulf. (See chap. x. 29.)

Shur.—This was their western limit towards Egypt. (See chap. xvi. 7.) In 1 Sam. xv. 7 this same region is assigned to the Amalekites.

As thou goest toward Assyria.—This does not mean that Shur was on the route toward Assyria, but gives the eastern limit of the country inhabited by the descendants of Ishmael.

He died.—But the Hebrew is, *he fell*—that is, his lot fell; he settled there.

In the presence of.—This means *to the east* of all his brethren. Just as Assyria was regarded as lying to the north of Palestine, because on starting the traveller journeyed in that direction, so Arabia was considered to be on the east, for a similar reason. (But see Note on chap. xvi. 12.)

(19) And these *are* the generations of
Isaac, Abraham's son: Abraham begat
Isaac: (20) and Isaac was forty years old
when he took Rebekah to wife, the
daughter of Bethuel the Syrian of
Padan-aram, the sister to Laban the
Syrian.
(21) And Isaac intreated the LORD for
his wife, because she *was* barren: and
the LORD was intreated of him, and Re-
bekah his wife conceived. (22) And the
children struggled together within her;
and she said, If *it be* so, why *am* I thus?
And she went to enquire of the LORD.
(23) And the LORD said unto her,

Two nations *are* in thy womb, and two
manner of people shall be separated
from thy bowels;
And *the one* people shall be stronger
than *the other* people; and [a]the elder
shall serve the younger.

a Rom. 9. 12.

(24) And when her days to be delivered
were fulfilled, behold, *there were* twins
in her womb. (25) And the first came out

THE TÔLDÔTH ISAAC (chaps. xxv. 19—xxxv. 29).

THE BIRTH OF ISAAC'S SONS.

(19) **Abraham begat Isaac.**—The *Tôldôth* in its original form gave probably a complete genealogy of Isaac, tracing up his descent to Shem, and showing thereby that the right of primogeniture belonged to him; but the inspired historian uses only so much of this as is necessary for tracing the development of the Divine plan of human redemption.

(20) **The Syrian.**—Really, *the Aramean*, or descendant of Aram. (See chap. x. 22, 23.) The name of the district also correctly is "Paddan-Aram," and so far from being identical with Aram-Naharaim, in chap. xxiv. 10, it is strictly the designation of the region immediately in the neighbourhood of Charran. The assertion of Gesenius that it meant "Mesopotamia, with the desert to the west of the Euphrates, in opposition to the mountainous district towards the Mediterranean," is devoid of proof. (See Chwolsohn, *Die Ssabier*, i., p. 304.) In Syriac, the language of Charran, padana means a *plough* (1 Sam. xiii. 20), or a *yoke of oxen* (*Ibid*, xi. 7); and this also suggests that it was the cultivated district close to the town. In Hosea xii. 12 it is said that "Jacob fled to the field of Aram;" but this is a very general description of the country in which he found refuge, and affords no basis for the assertion that Padan-aram was the level region. Finally, the assertion that it is an ancient name used by the Jehovist is an assertion only. It is the name of a special district, and the knowledge of it was the result of Jacob's long-continued stay there. Chwolsohn says that traces of the name still remain in Faddân and Tel Faddân, two places close to Charran, mentioned by Yacut, the Arabian geographer, who flourished in the thirteenth century.

(21) **Isaac intreated the Lord.**—This barrenness lasted twenty years (verse 26), and must have greatly troubled Isaac; but it would also compel him to dwell much in thought upon the purpose for which he had been given to Abraham, and afterwards rescued from death upon the mount Jehovah-Jireh. And when offspring came, in answer to his earnest pleading of the promise, the delay would serve to impress upon both parents the religious significance of their existence as a separate race and family, and the necessity of training their children worthily. The derivation of the verb *to intreat*, from a noun signifying *incense*, is uncertain, but rendered probable by the natural connection of the idea of the ascending fragrance, and that of the prayer mounting heavenward (Rev. v. 8, viii. 4).

(22) **The children struggled together.**—Two dissimilar nations sprang from Abraham, but from mothers totally unlike; so, too, from the peaceful Isaac two distinct races of men were to take their origin, but from the same mother, and the contest began while they were yet unborn. And Rebekah, apparently unaware that she was pregnant with twins, but harassed with the pain of strange jostlings and thrusts, grew despondent, and exclaimed—

If it be so, why am I thus?—Literally, *If so, why am I this?* Some explain this as meaning "Why do I still live?" but more probably she meant, If I have thus conceived, in answer to my husband's prayers, why do I suffer in this strange manner? It thus prepares for what follows, namely, that Rebekah wished to have her condition explained to her, and therefore went to inquire of Jehovah.

She went to enquire of the Lord.—Not to Shem, nor Melchizedek, as many think, nor even to Abraham, who was still alive, but, as Theodoret suggests, to the family altar. Isaac had several homes, but probably the altar at Bethel, erected when Abraham first took possession of the Promised Land (chap. xii. 7), and therefore especially holy, was the place signified; and if Abraham were there, he would doubtless join his prayers to those of Rebekah.

(23) **And the Lord said unto her.**—Not by the mouth of Abraham, nor in a dream, but directly, as He spake of old to Adam and Eve. We read of no appearance, as in chap. xvii. 1, nor must we invent one. The manner in which Jehovah thus spake has not been revealed, and it is enough for us to know that Jehovah did speak of old to men. The answer is in the form of poetry:—

> "Two nations are in thy womb;
> And two peoples from thy bowels shall be separated;
> And people shall be mightier than people;
> And the great shall serve the small."

The second line shows that even in their earliest childhood her sons would be unlike in character and unfriendly in disposition; upon this follows their development into hostile nations, and the prediction that the son who started with the advantages of the birthright, the stronger physical nature, and superior strength in men and arms (chap. xxxii. 6), would, nevertheless, finally hold the inferior position. There can be no doubt that the secondary cause of the vaster development of Jacob was his being placed by Joseph in the fruitful Delta, where the Israelites were constantly joined by a stream of Semitic immigrants, whose movement towards Egypt is a perfectly authenticated fact of the history of those times. (See chap. xii. 15.)

(25) **Red.**—Heb., *admoni*, a secondary reason for the name Edom. (See verse 30.)

All over like an hairy garment.—Heb., *all of him*—that is, completely—*like a garment of hair*: words rendered "a rough garment" in Zech. xiii. 4, where it

red, all over like an hairy garment·
and they called his name Esau. (26) And
after that came his brother out, and
[a]his hand took hold on Esau's heel; and
his name was called Jacob: and Isaac
was threescore years old when she bare
them.
(27) And the boys grew: and Esau was
a cunning hunter, a man of the field;
and Jacob *was* a plain man, dwelling in
tents. (28) And Isaac loved Esau, because
[1]he did eat of *his* venison: but Rebekah
loved Jacob.
(29) And Jacob sod pottage: and Esau
came from the field, and he *was* faint:

(30) and Esau said to Jacob, Feed me, I
pray thee, [2]with that same red *pottage;*
for I *am* faint: therefore was his name
called Edom. (31) And Jacob said, Sell
me this day thy birthright. (32) And
Esau said, Behold, I *am* [3]at the point to
die: and what profit shall this birth-
right do to me? (33) And Jacob said,
Swear to me this day; and he sware
unto him: and [b]he sold his birthright
unto Jacob. (34) Then Jacob gave Esau
bread and pottage of lentiles; and he
did eat and drink, and rose up, and
went his way: thus Esau despised *his*
birthright.

a Hos. 12. 3.

B.C. cir. 1805.

1 Heb., *venison was in his mouth.*

B.C. cir. 1827

2 Heb., *with that red,* with that *red* pottage.

3 Heb., *going to die.*

b Heb. 12. 16.

---

is used of the jacket of sheepskin worn by the prophets. It appears, therefore, that Esau's body was entirely covered with red down, which developed in time into hair as coarse as that of a kid (chap. xxvii. 16), and betokened a strong and vigorous, but sensual nature.

Esau.—The Jewish commentators form this name from the verb *to make,* and render it *well-made;* but the usual explanation is *hairy,* from a word now extant only in Arabic.

(26) **His hand took hold on Esau's heel.**—Usually there is a considerable interval—an hour or more—between the birth of twins; but here Jacob appeared without delay, following immediately upon his brother. This is expressed by the metaphorical phrase that his hand had hold on Esau's heel—that is, there was absolutely no interval between them. Though very rare, yet similar cases have been chronicled from time to time.

His name was called Jacob.—The name signifies *one who follows at another's heels.* It was Esau who first put upon it a bad meaning (chap. xxvii. 36), and this bad sense has been riveted to it by Jacob's own unworthy conduct. It is constantly so used even in the Bible. Thus in Hosea xii. 3—a passage quoted in defence of a literal explanation of the metaphor in this verse by those who are acquainted only with the English Version—the Hebrew has, *he Jacobed,* literally, *heeled*—that is, overreached, got the better by cunning of—*his brother in the womb.* This is the very meaning put upon the name by Esau, and in Jer. ix. 4 and elsewhere; but it is not well rendered by our word *supplant,* which contains a different metaphor, the *planta* being the sole of the foot; whereas to be at a person's heel is to be his determined pursuer, and one who on overtaking throws him down.

DEVELOPMENT OF THE CHARACTERS OF ESAU AND JACOB. ESAU SELLS HIS BIRTHRIGHT.

(27) **The boys grew.**—With advancing years came also the formation of their characters. Esau became a skilful hunter, a "man of the field": not a husbandman, but one who roamed over the open uncultivated wilderness (see chap. iv. 8) in search of game; but "Jacob was a plain man." This is a most inadequate rendering of a word translated *perfect* in Job i. 1, 8; Ps. xxxvii. 37, &c., though this rendering is as much too strong as that in this verse is too weak. On chap. vi. 9, we have shown that the word conveys no idea of perfection or blamelessness, but only of general integrity. Both the word there and in chap. xvii. 1, and the slightly different form of it used here, should in all places be translated *upright.*

Dwelling in tents.—Esau equally had a tent for his abode, but Jacob stayed at home, following domestic occupations, and busied about the flocks and cattle. Hence he was the mother's darling, while Isaac preferred his more enterprising son. Thus the struggle between the twins led also to a divergence of feeling on the part of the parents. Throughout his history Jacob maintains this character, and appears as a man whose interests and happiness were centred in his home.

(28) **Because he did eat of his venison.**—Literally, *because the venison*—that is, the produce of Esau's hunting—*was in his mouth;* in our phrase, *was to his taste*—was what he liked. The diet of an Arab sheik is very simple (see Note on chap. xviii. 6); and Isaac, a man wanting in physical vigour and adventurousness—as is usually the case with the children of people far advanced in years—both admired the energy which Esau had inherited from Rebekah, and relished the fruits of it.

(29, 30) **Jacob sod pottage.**—The diverse occupations of the two youths led, in course of time, to an act fatal to Esau's character and well-being. Coming home one day weary, and fainting with hunger, he found Jacob preparing a pottage of lentils. No sooner did the savoury smell reach him than he cried out in haste, "Let me swallow, I pray, of the red, this red." The verb expresses extreme eagerness, and he adds no noun whatever, but points to the steaming dish. And Jacob, seeing his brother's greediness and ravenous hunger, refuses to give him food until he has parted with the high and sacred prerogative which made him the inheritor of the Divine promise.

Therefore was his name called Edom.—Esau may have been called Edom, that is, *Rufus,* the red one, before, but after this act it ceased to be a mere allusive by-name, and became his ordinary appellation.

(34) **He did eat and drink, and rose up, and went his way.**—These words graphically describe Esau's complete indifference to the spiritual privileges of which he had denuded himself. There is no regret, no sad feeling that he had prolonged his life at too high a cost. And if Jacob is cunning, and mean in the advantage he took of his brother, still he valued these privileges, and in the sequel he had his reward and his punishment. He was confirmed in the possession of the birthright, and became the progenitor of the chosen race, and of the Messiah; but henceforward his life was full of danger and difficulty. He

CHAPTER XXVI.—(1)And there was a famine in the land, beside the first famine that was in the days of Abraham. And Isaac went unto Abimelech king of the Philistines unto Gerar.

(2) And the LORD appeared unto him, and said, Go not down into Egypt; dwell in the land which I shall tell thee of: (3) sojourn in this land, and I will be with thee, and will bless thee; for unto thee, and unto thy seed, [a]I will give all these countries, and I will perform the oath which I sware unto Abraham thy father; (4) and I will make thy seed to multiply as the stars of heaven, and will give unto thy seed all these countries; and in thy seed shall all the nations of the earth be [b]blessed; (5) because that Abraham obeyed my voice, and kept my charge, my commandments, my statutes, and my laws.

(6) And Isaac dwelt in Gerar: (7) and the men of the place asked *him* of his wife; and he said, She *is* my sister: for he feared to say, *She is* my wife; lest, *said he*, the men of the place should kill me for Rebekah; because she *was* fair to look upon. (8) And it came to pass, when he had been there a long time, that Abimelech king of the Philistines looked out at a window, and saw, and, behold, Isaac *was* sporting with Rebekah his wife. (9) And Abimelech called Isaac, and said, Behold, of a surety she *is* thy wife: and how saidst thou, She *is* my sister? And Isaac said unto him, Because I said, Lest I die for her. (10)And Abimelech said, What *is* this thou hast done unto us? one of the people might lightly have lien with thy wife, and thou shouldest have brought guiltiness upon us. (11) And Abimelech charged all *his* people, saying, He that toucheth this man or his wife shall surely be put to death.

(12) Then Isaac sowed in that land, and

B.C. cir. 1804.

a ch. 13. 15 & 15. 18.

b ch. 12. 3, & 15. 18, & 22. 18.

---

had to flee from his brother's enmity, and was perpetually the victim of fraud and the most cruel deceit. But gradually his character ripened for good. He ceased to be a scheming, worldly-minded Jacob, and became an Israel, and in his pious old age we see a man full of trust and faith in God, unworldly and unselfish, and animated by tender and loving feeling. Purified from his early infirmities, and with all his better nature strengthened and sanctified by sorrow, he shows himself worthy of his second name, and becomes "a prince with God."

XXVI.

ADVENTURES OF ISAAC AT GERAR.

(1) **Isaac went . . . . unto Gerar.**—Following the stream of Semitic migration (chap. xii. 15), Isaac had originally purposed going to Egypt, but is commanded by God to abide in the land, and upon so doing he receives the assurance that he will be confirmed in the inheritance of the promises made to his father. Isaac was now dwelling at the well Lahai-Roi, and though the exact site of this place is unknown, yet it lay too far to the south for Isaac to have gone to Gerar on his direct way to Egypt.

(2) **The Lord appeared unto him.**—Only once besides does Jehovah manifest himself to Isaac (verse 24), and sixty years had now passed since the revelations recorded in chap. xxii. Excepting to Abraham, it was only at rare and distant intervals that God spake to the patriarchs. The greater part of their lives was spent under the control of the same ordinary Providence as that which governs our actions now; but on special occasions God was pleased to confirm their faith in Him in a way not necessary now that we have had made known to us the whole counsel of God.

(3, 4) **These countries.**—On the archaic form of the pronoun *these*, see Note on chap. xix. 8. The countries are enumerated in chap. xv. 19—21. For the "oath," see chap. xxii. 16; and for the metaphor, "as the stars," see chap. xv. 5.

(7) **He said, She is my sister.**—We have already seen that Abraham at Gerar showed no consciousness of having done wrong in denying his wife (chap. xx. 2); and we now find Isaac imitating his example with even less reason for his conduct. The circumstances are, however, different. It is the people who inquire about Isaac's relation to Rebekah, and though she was "fair to look upon," yet no annoyance followed upon his denial of her. The king after "a long time" detects their intimacy; but there are no presents, and no marks of respect to Rebekah, and no friendship. It is only after long quarrels, during which Isaac is obliged to withdraw to a long distance from Gerar, that finally peace is made between them.

(8) **Abimelech.**—Upon this title of the Philistine monarchs see Note on chap. xxi. 22. As eighty years had elapsed since Abraham's sojourn in Gerar, it is highly improbable that the same king was still reigning; but both king and people maintain on this occasion the good character previously deserved. The Philistines, however, at this period, were a feeble colony of strangers, and were kept in restraint by a sense of their weakness. They had received a vast accession of strength from abroad before they became formidable enemies of the Israelites at the end of the period of the Judges. (See chap. x. 14.)

(12) **Isaac sowed in that land.**—When Abraham planted a tamarisk-tree at Beer-sheba (chap. xxi. 33) it showed that he regarded the place as a permanent residence, which it was worth his while to adorn, and to provide for its increasing pleasantness. Isaac and Jacob took a still further step in advance towards a settled life when they began to cultivate plots of ground. At first, however, Isaac did no more than the Bedaween do at present; for they often sow a piece of land, wait till the crop is ripe, and then resume their roving habits. Permanently to till the soil is with them a mark of inferiority (chap. xxv. 16). But the tendency, both with Abraham and Isaac, had long been to remain in the region about Beer-sheba. Isaac had been driven thence

[1]received in the same year an hundred-
fold: and the LORD blessed him. (13)And
the man waxed great, and [2]went for-
ward, and grew until he became very
great: (14) for he had possession of
flocks, and possession of herds, and
great store of [3]servants: and the Philis-
tines envied him. (15) For all the wells
which his father's servants had digged
in the days of Abraham his father, the
Philistines had stopped them, and filled
them with earth.
(16) And Abimelech said unto Isaac, Go
from us; for thou art much mightier
than we. (17) And Isaac departed thence,
and pitched his tent in the valley of
Gerar, and dwelt there.
(18) And Isaac digged again the wells
of water, which they had digged in the
days of Abraham his father; for the
Philistines had stopped them after the
death of Abraham: and he called their
names after the names by which his
father had called them.
(19) And Isaac's servants digged in the
valley, and found there a well of [4]spring-
ing water. (20) And the herdmen of Gerar
did strive with Isaac's herdmen, saying,
The water *is* our's: and he called the
name of the well [5]Esek; because they
strove with him. (21) And they digged
another well, and strove for that also:
and he called the name of it [6]Sitnah.
(22) And he removed from thence, and
digged another well; and for that they
strove not: and he called the name of it
[7]Rehoboth; and he said, For now the
LORD hath made room for us, and we
shall be fruitful in the land.
(23) And he went up from thence to
Beer-sheba. (24) And the LORD appeared
unto him the same night, and said, I
am the God of Abraham thy father:
fear not, for I *am* with thee, and will
bless thee, and multiply thy seed for my
servant Abraham's sake. (25) And he
builded an altar there, and called upon
the name of the LORD, and pitched his

1 Heb., *found*.
2 Heb., *went going*.
3 Or, *husbandry*.
4 Heb., *living*.
5 That is, *Contention*.
6 That is, *Hatred*.
7 That is, *Room*.

by the famine, by which he had probably lost much of his cattle, and many even of his people. Apparently he was even so weakened thereby as to be no match for the Philistines of Gerar. His large harvest recouped him for his losses, and made him once more a prosperous man; and in due time Beer-sheba was again his home, and with settled habits agriculture was sure to begin.

An hundredfold.—The Heb. is, *a hundred measures*, but the word is unknown elsewhere, and the LXX. and Syriac read, *a hundred of barley*, measures being understood, as in Ruth iii. 15. Herodotus (Book i. 193) mentions two—and even three—hundredfold as possible in Babylonia; but our Lord seems to give one hundredfold as the extreme measure of productiveness in Palestine (Matt. xiii. 8). Such a return, like Isaac's, would be rare and extraordinary.

(14) **Great store of servants.**—Marg., *husbandry*. In Job i. 3 the word is rendered *household* in the text, and *husbandry* again in the margin. Literally it means *making employment*, and answers to our word *business*. But if in a man's life there is much activity and plenty to do, there must be people to do it, and profits made whereby to maintain them. And thus the translation, "great store of servants," gives the sense; but we see besides that Isaac kept them all actively employed,

(15) **The wells.**—In the East the digger of a well is regarded as a public benefactor; but the Philistines stopped those that Abraham had digged, probably because they regarded his possession of them, though confirmed by the covenant between him and Abimelech (chap. xxi. 32), as an intrusion upon their rights as the people of the country, Envious, too, at the rapid increase of an alien's wealth, they determined to drive Isaac away; and for this no expedient would be more effectual than the preventing him from procuring water for his cattle. Following upon this came an express command of the king to depart, which Isaac obeyed; for he had sought refuge there because of the famine, and had no right to continue at Gerar, if the people refused their hospitality.

(17) **The valley of Gerar.**—The word *nahal*, rendered "valley," means a narrow defile through which a summer torrent flows. In the bed of these streams water can generally be found by digging, and Isaac hoped that he was far enough from the city for the enmity to cease. But he was mistaken, though he seems for a short period to have been left in peace.

(18–22) **Isaac digged again the wells . . .**—This activity of Isaac called forth anew the opposition of the Philistines, His first well was in the wady of Gerar, and was the more valuable because it was not the mere remains of the water of the torrent, but was fed by a spring, as we learn from its being called "a well of living water." But though Isaac had a right to these wells by reason of the old covenant between his father and the king, yet when his claim was resisted he abandoned the well, but in token of displeasure called it Esek, *contention*. When compelled to resign his next well he called it by a harsher name—Sitnah, *enmity*; for their opposition was developing into bitter persecution. And now, wearied with the strife, he withdrew far away, and the Philistines, having gained their end, followed him no farther. In quiet, therefore, he again dug a well, and called it Rehoboth, *wide open spaces*. It has been identified with one in the wady Ruhaibeh, now stopped up, but originally twelve feet in diameter and cased with hewn stone. It lies to the south of Beer-sheba, at a distance of 8½ leagues, and about forty miles away from Gerar.

(23–25) **He went up from thence to Beer-sheba.**—This was a very serious act on Isaac's part. He leaves the solitudes where he had found a refuge from the enmity of the Philistines, and returns to a place scarcely five leagues distant from their city. Should the old rancour revive, it may now take the form of actual war. And next, he does not go back to the well Lahai-Roi, where he had so long resided, but to

tent there: and there Isaac's servants
digged a well.
(26) Then Abimelech went to him from
Gerar, and Ahuzzath one of his friends,
and Phichol the chief captain of his
army. (27) And Isaac said unto them,
Wherefore come ye to me, seeing ye
hate me, and have sent me away from
you? (28) And they said, [1]We saw certainly that the LORD was with thee:
and we said, Let there be now an oath
betwixt us, *even* betwixt us and thee,
and let us make a covenant with thee;
(29) [2]that thou wilt do us no hurt, as we
have not touched thee, and as we have
done unto thee nothing but good, and
have sent thee away in peace: thou *art*
now the blessed of the LORD. (30) And he
made them a feast, and they did eat and
drink. (31) And they rose up betimes in
the morning, and sware one to another:
and Isaac sent them away, and they departed from him in peace.
(32) And it came to pass the same day,
that Isaac's servants came, and told him
concerning the well which they had
digged, and said unto him, We have
found water. (33) And he called it [3]Shebah: therefore the name of the city *is*
[4]Beer-sheba unto this day.
(34) And Esau was forty years old when
he took to wife Judith the daughter of

1 Heb., *Seeing we saw.*

2 Heb., *If thou shalt, &c.*

3 That is, *An oath.*

4 That is, *The well of the oath.*

B.C. cir. 1796.

Beer-sheba, his father's favourite home. It was a claim on his part to the rights and inheritance of Abraham, and the claim was admitted. The same night Jehovah appears to him, bids him put away his fears, and renews to him the promises which were his by the right of his birth.

My servant Abraham.—A title of high honour and significance, given to Moses repeatedly, to Joshua (Josh. xxiv. 29), to Israel (Isa. xli. 8), and to the Messiah (Isa. lii. 13). It means God's prime minister and vicegerent.

He builded an altar.—In returning to Beer-sheba, Isaac had apparently faced the dangers of his position, through confidence in the promises made to his father, with whom he identified himself by taking up his abode at his home. And no sooner are the promises confirmed to him than he restores the public worship of God in the very place where Abraham had established it (chap. xxi. 33).

Digged a well.—The word is not that previously used in the chapter, but one that signifies the re-opening of the well which Abraham had dug, but which had become stopped by violence or neglect.

(26) **Abimelech went to him.**—The return of Isaac to Beer-sheba was a matter of serious importance also to Abimelech. The Philistines were themselves an alien race, and an alliance between Isaac and Ishmael, and others of the Semitic stock, might end in their expulsion from the country. Abraham had also been confederate with the Amorites (chap. xiv. 13), and on friendly terms with the Hittites (chap. xxiii. 6), the two most powerful races of Canaan, and they might be ready to aid his son. When, then, Isaac thus retraced his steps, Abimelech, uncertain of Isaac's purpose, determined to offer peace and friendship, and to propose the renewal of the old covenant which had existed between Abraham and the people of Gerar.

Ahuzzath.—This is one of several points peculiar to this narrative; but it is uncertain whether it be a proper name, or whether, with the Targum and Jerome, we are to understand by it *a company*, that is, an escort of friends. If it be a proper name, the rendering should be, *Ahuzzath, his friend*, that is, his confidant and privy counsellor.

Phichol.—See Note on chap. xxi. 22.

(27) **Wherefore come ye to me?**—Isaac's return had brought matters to a crisis, and the king must now decide whether there was to be peace or war.

(28, 29) **Let there be now an oath.**—The word literally signifies a *curse*. Each side uttered an imprecation, with the prayer that it might fall upon himself if he broke the terms of the covenant.

Let us make a covenant.—Heb., *cut*. (See Note on chap. xv. 10, 18; where also see the explanation of this use of the word *curse*.)

The Lord was with thee . . . blessed of the Lord.—This use of the word "Lord," that is, *Jehovah*, is very remarkable. In chap. xxi. 22, 23 Abimelech uses the term Elohim, *God*, in accordance with the careful discrimination in the use of the names of the Deity often previously referred to. By the long residence, first of Abraham and then of Isaac, in their territory, the Philistines would indeed have become better acquainted with the religion of the patriarchs; but as *Jehovah* was not their special title for the Deity (Exod. vi. 3), we must conclude, with Rosenmüller, that it was Moses who wrote Jehovah in the place of the word actually employed by Abimelech. We gather, however, that the king did not use any generic or heathen names of the Deity, but that whereby the patriarchs worshipped their covenant God, and his so doing was probably intended as an act of homage to Him.

(32) **We have found water.**—As there are two wells at Beer-sheba, it is uncertain whether this was Abraham's well, re-opened by Isaac (see verse 25), or a new one.

(33) **Therefore the name of the city is Beer-sheba unto this day.**—There was no city at this time at Beer-sheba, but one is mentioned at the conquest of Canaan by Joshua (Josh. xv. 28). This note, as is the case generally with those which speak of a thing existing "unto this day," was added by Ezra and the men of the Great Synagogue, after the return from Babylon (comp. chap. xxii. 14); and its meaning is that, whereas Abraham's name had been forgotten while the place lay desolate, this remarkable coincidence of the water being again found, just when the covenant had been confirmed by the customary sevenfold sacrifice, so impressed the minds of the people that the title of Beer-sheba never again passed into oblivion.

ESAU'S MARRIAGE WITH CANAANITISH WOMEN.

(34) **Esau was forty years old.**—He was therefore of exactly the same age as Isaac was when, sixty years before, he married Rebekah. But by thus intermarrying with idolaters Esau violated the great principle laid down by Abraham (chap. xxiv. 3), forfeited thereby his birthright, and, as such marriages were illegal, is even

Beeri the Hittite, and Bashemath the
daughter of Elon the Hittite: (35) which
[a]were [1]a grief of mind unto Isaac and to
Rebekah.

CHAPTER XXVII.—(1) And it came
to pass, that when Isaac was old, and
his eyes were dim, so that he could not
see, he called Esau his eldest son, and
said unto him, My son: and he said
unto him, Behold, *here am* I. (2) And he
said, Behold now, I am old, I know not
the day of my death: (3) now therefore
take, I pray thee, thy weapons, thy
quiver and thy bow, and go out to the
field, and [2]take me *some* venison; (4) and

a ch. 27. 46.

1 Heb., *bitterness of spirit.*

2 Heb., *hunt.*

B.C. cir. 1760.

---

called a fornicator in Heb. xii. 16. As his conduct was regarded by his parents with "grief of mind"—Heb., *bitterness of spirit*: that is, with mingled anger and sorrow—Esau partially repented, and took as a third wife a daughter of Ishmael (chap. xxviii. 9). In the *Tôldôth Esau* (chap. xxxvi. 2, 3) the names are different, and a fourth wife, of the inhabitants of Seir, takes the place of Judith.

Judith.—The names are remarkable, as showing that the Hittites spoke a Semitic tongue. Judith is the feminine form of Judah, and means *praised.* Beeri can scarcely be the original name of her father, as it means *well-finder*, but was probably gained by his skill in discovering water. We find it, however, in the genealogy of Hosea (Hos. i. 1). Bashemath or Basmath, the *fragrant*, was the name also of a daughter of Solomon (1 King iv. 15); and Elon, *oak-grove*, was the name of a judge (Judges xii. 11).

As this conduct of Esau prepares the mind for his final rejection and loss of the birthright, the place of these two verses would rightly be at the beginning of chap. xxvii. The Jews arrange them as a separate section.

XXVII.

Jacob by Subtilty obtains the Firstborn's Blessing.

(1) **It came to pass.**—The importance of this chapter is manifest. Just as in Abraham's life the decision had to be made which of the two sons, Ishmael and Isaac, was to be the heir of the promise, so, here again, there is the same Divine election (Rom. ix. 10—13): but while Abraham obeyed, though with heavy heart (chap. xxi. 11), Isaac even struggled against God's will, and his assent was obtained by human craft working tortuously to effect that which God would have wrought in His own better way. In this case, however, the sons are more closely allied, being twins, born of the same mother, but the younger following so closely upon the very heels of the elder as to seem, even at his birth, as if in eager pursuit. They grow up strangely unlike—the one brave, active, vigorous, but indifferent to everything save earthly things. In his skill and love of hunting, Esau is the very counterpart of Ishmael. The other is calm, sedentary, keenly alive to business, devoted to domestic pursuits, but chiefly valuing the spiritual privileges for which Abraham had left his distant home, and become a wanderer in the highlands of Canaan. Thoroughly as all honest men must disapprove of the mean way in which Jacob bought the birthright, yet, at least, he valued that which Esau so despised as to sell it for the gratification of a hungry appetite. And now again the transfer is ratified by means of another unworthy artifice, but Esau this time is grieved and distressed; for at least he loved his father, and gave proof of the possession of the same warm heart that made him afterwards fall so lovingly upon his brother's neck, and kiss him with tears of hearty affection (chap. xxxiii. 4).

For Jacob, it must be said that he sought no earthly good. It was not the elder brother's share of the father's wealth that he wanted. All that was Isaac's he resigned to Esau, and went away to push his fortunes elsewhere. Even when he returned with the substance he had gotten in Padan-aram, he was no match for Esau (chap. xxxiii. 1), though Isaac was still living. While, too, Esau violated the family law laid down by Abraham, Jacob conformed to it. By marrying Canaanitish women, Esau forfeited by his own act the birthright which previously he had sold; for his children, being illegitimate (Heb. xii. 16), could not inherit the promise. What was utterly wrong in Rebekah's and Jacob's conduct was that they used miserable artifices to do that which should have been left to God; and Isaac was equally wrong in trying to make void and annul the clear intimation of prophecy (chap. xxv. 23).

Isaac was old.—Isaac was now 117 years of age, but he lived to be 180 (chap. xxxv. 28). (See Excursus on Chronology of Jacob's Life at end of this book.) He had thus sixty-three more years to live, but not only himself (verse 2), but Esau also expected his speedy decease (verse 41). Probably, therefore, his failing eyesight was the result of some acute disorder, which so enfeebled his general health that he had grown despondent, and thought his death near. But evidently he recovered, and attained to a good old age. It seems, however, that though the lives of the patriarchs were so long extended, yet that their bodily vigour slowly decayed through the latter portion of their days. Jacob when but 130 speaks of himself as a grey-haired old man, already upon the brink of the grave (chaps. xlii. 38, xlvii. 9). Moreover, the term *old* is used in a very general sense in the Old Testament, and thus Samuel is described as old in 1 Sam. viii. 1, when we should have spoken of him as at most middle-aged.

(3) **Thy quiver.**—This word does not occur elsewhere, and is rendered in the Targum and Syriac *a sword.* As it is derived from a root signifying *to hang*, it probably means, like our word *hanger*, a sort of knife; but all that we can say for certain is that it was some sort of hunting implement.

Take me some venison.—The Heb. is *hunt me a hunting.* "*Venison,*" the Latin *venatio*, means anything taken by hunting.

(4) **Savoury meat.**—On the rare occasions on which an Arab sheik tastes flesh, it is flavoured with almonds, pistachio nuts, and raisins. It would thus not be easy for Isaac to distinguish the taste of the flesh of a kid from that of an antelope. As the Arabs always spare their own flocks and herds, the capture of a wild animal gives them the greater pleasure, and a feast thus provided seemed to the patriarch a proper occasion for the solemn decision which son should inherit the promises made to Abraham.

That my soul may bless thee.—We gather from the solemn blessing given to his sons by Jacob (chap. xlix.) that this was a prophetic act, by which

make me savoury meat, such as I love,
and bring *it* to me, that I may eat; that
my soul may bless thee before I die.
(5) And Rebekah heard when Isaac
spake to Esau his son. And Esau went
to the field to hunt *for* venison, *and* to
bring *it.* (6) And Rebekah spake unto
Jacob her son, saying, Behold, I heard
thy father speak unto Esau thy brother,
saying, (7) Bring me venison, and make
me savoury meat, that I may eat, and
bless thee before the LORD before my
death. (8) Now therefore, my son, obey
my voice according to that which I com-
mand thee. (9) Go now to the flock, and
fetch me from thence two good kids of
the goats; and I will make them savoury
meat for thy father, such as he loveth:
(10) and thou shalt bring *it* to thy father,
that he may eat, and that he may bless
thee before his death.
(11) And Jacob said to Rebekah his
mother, Behold, Esau my brother *is* a
hairy man, and I *am* a smooth man:
(12) my father peradventure will feel me,
and I shall seem to him as a deceiver;
and I shall bring a curse upon me, and
not a blessing. (13) And his mother said
unto him, Upon me *be* thy curse, my son:
only obey my voice, and go fetch me
them. (14) And he went, and fetched, and
brought *them* to his mother: and his
mother made savoury meat, such as his
father loved.
(15) And Rebekah took [1]goodly raiment
of her eldest son Esau, which *were* with
her in the house, and put them upon
Jacob her younger son: (16) and she put
the skins of the kids of the goats upon
his hands, and upon the smooth of his
neck: (17) and she gave the savoury meat
and the bread, which she had prepared,
into the hand of her son Jacob.
(18) And he came unto his father, and
said, My father: and he said, Here *am*
I; who *art* thou, my son? (19) And Jacob
said unto his father, I *am* Esau thy first-
born; I have done according as thou

1 Heb., *desirable.*

the patriarchs, under the influence of the Spirit, and in expectation of death, decided to which son should belong the birthright. Jacob when dying bestowed it on Judah (verses 8—12). But here Isaac resisted the Spirit; for the clear warning had been given that "the elder should serve the younger" (chap. xxv. 23). Isaac may have been moved to this act by indignation at the manner in which Esau had been induced to sell the birthright, and in annulling that sale he would have been within his rights; but he was not justified in disregarding the voice of prophecy, nor in his indifference to Esau's violation of the Abrahamic law in marrying heathen women. And thus he becomes the victim of craft and treachery, while Jacob is led on to a deed which was the cause of endless grief to him and Rebekah, and has stained his character for ever. But had Jacob possessed the same high standard of honour as distinguished David afterwards, he would equally have received the blessing, but without the sin of deception practised upon his own father.

(5) **Rebekah heard.**—She was possibly present when Isaac gave the order, and he may even have wished her to know his determination to give the blessing to his favourite son. But the words filled her with dismay. She had, no doubt, treasured the prophecy of Jacob's ultimate superiority, and now it seemed as if the father would reverse it. Had her faith been pure and exalted, she would have known that God would fulfil His word without her help; but all alike act from unworthy motives, and all have their meed of punishment. But here the fault began with Isaac, and Rebekah probably considered that she was preventing a grievous wrong.

(7) **Before the Lord** (*Jehovah*).—Rebekah has been accused of inserting words which Isaac had not used; but it is unreasonable to suppose that more is recorded of Isaac's address to his son than the main sense. Still, these words had a meaning to Jacob which they did not bear to Esau. The latter cared for his father's blessing, partly from natural affection, but chiefly because of the temporal benefits connected with it. To Jacob its value consisted in the covenant between Jehovah and the family of Abraham.

(9) **Two good kids.**—These would be about equal to one antelope or animal of the larger game. After Isaac had eaten of the flesh, so solemn an occasion would doubtless be marked by a feast for those, at least, in the foremost tents, if not for all the household and followers of Isaac.

(13) **Upon me be thy curse.**—No curse followed upon their conduct; but, on the contrary, Isaac acknowledged the substantial justice of the act of Rebekah and her son, and confirmed Jacob in the possession of the blessing (verse 33). It seems strange, nevertheless, that neither of them had any scruples at the immorality of the deed, but apparently thought that as the end was right they were justified in using falsehood and treachery.

(15) **Goodly raiment.**—It has been supposed that the elder son held a sort of priestly office in the household, and as Isaac's sight was growing dim, that Esau ministered for him at sacrifices. Evidently the clothing was something special, and such as was peculiar to Esau: for ordinary raiment, however handsome, would not have been kept in the mother's tent, but in that of Esau or of one of his wives.

(16) **The skins of the kids.**—In hot countries the coats of animals are far less thick and coarse than in cold climates, and some species of Oriental goats are famous for their soft, silky wool. But in those cases in which men have their bodies covered with hair, it is by no means of a delicate texture. In Cant. iv. 1 Solomon's hair is compared to that of a flock of goats.

(19) **Arise . . . sit and eat.**—The Hebrews at this time, and for centuries, sat at their meals (1 Sam. xx. 25). It was from the Romans that they learned to recline at table, as we find was their custom in the Gospels. It is a mistake, moreover, to suppose that Isaac was a bedridden old man, for Jacob bids him

badest me: arise, I pray thee, sit and
eat of my venison, that thy soul may
bless me. (20) And Isaac said unto his
son, How *is it* that thou hast found *it* so
quickly, my son? And he said, Because
the LORD thy God brought *it* [1] to me.
(21) And Isaac said unto Jacob, Come near,
I pray thee, that I may feel thee, my son,
whether thou *be* my very son Esau or
not. (22) And Jacob went near unto Isaac
his father; and he felt him, and said, The
voice *is* Jacob's voice, but the hands *are*
the hands of Esau. (23) And he discerned
him not, because his hands were hairy,
as his brother Esau's hands: so he
blessed him. (24) And he said, *Art* thou
my very son Esau? And he said, I *am*.
(25) And he said, Bring *it* near to me, and
I will eat of my son's venison, that my
soul may bless thee. And he brought *it*
near to him, and he did eat: and he
brought him wine, and he drank.
(26) And his father Isaac said unto him,
Come near now, and kiss me, my son.
(27) And he came near, and kissed him:
and he smelled the smell of his raiment,
and blessed him, and said,

See, the smell of my son *is* as the
smell of a field which the LORD hath
blessed: (28) therefore [a] God give thee of
the dew of heaven, and the fatness of
the earth, and plenty of corn and wine:
(29) let people serve thee, and nations
bow down to thee: be lord over thy
brethren, and let thy mother's sons bow
down to thee: cursed *be* every one that
curseth thee, and blessed *be* he that
blesseth thee.

(30) And it came to pass, as soon as
Isaac had made an end of blessing
Jacob, and Jacob was yet scarce gone
out from the presence of Isaac his
father, that Esau his brother came in
from his hunting. (31) And he also had
made savoury meat, and brought it unto
his father, and said unto his father, Let
my father arise, and eat of his son's
venison, that thy soul may bless me.
(32) And Isaac his father said unto him,
Who *art* thou? And he said, I *am* thy

1 Heb., *before me.*

a Heb. 11. 20.

---

arise and seat himself. Nor does he help him, though his sight was weak. It is only when commanded to draw near that he lets his father touch him.

(20) **Because the Lord thy God brought it to me.**—Jacob does not keep up his acting well here, for it was not in accordance with Esau's character to see anything providential in his success in hunting. This may have helped to arouse Isaac's suspicions, who immediately proceeds to examine him.

(21) **Come near . . . that I may feel thee.**—Besides the answer, in a style very different from Esau's way of thinking, Isaac was surprised at the short delay in bringing the savoury meat; for the game had to be sought at a distance away from the cattle-pastures. Though, too, the voices of the twins had a certain degree of similarity, yet they would also have their peculiarities, and Isaac detected the difference. But the artifice of the kid-skins fitted, no doubt, cleverly to Jacob's hands and neck saved him from detection; for after Isaac had passed his hands over him, his doubt entirely vanished.

(26) **Come near now, and kiss me, my son.**—This was the solemn preparation for the giving of the blessing. Isaac's suspicions had now quite passed away. He had eaten and drunk, and the time had now come for the decision which son was to inherit the promise.

(27) **As the smell of a field.**—From the abundance of aromatic plants, the pastures of Palestine are peculiarly fragrant; but Isaac, deceived by the scent of Esau's own garments, intended probably to contrast the pure sweetness of one whose life was spent in the open field with the less pleasant odour which Jacob would bring with him from the cattle-shed.

(28) **Therefore God give thee.**—Heb., *And the Elohim give thee.* Here, as not unfrequently is the case, the name Elohim follows immediately upon that of Jehovah. As the blessings of dew and fertile land are the gifts of the God of nature, the use of the title Elohim is in accordance with the general rule.

The fatness of the earth.—Heb., the *fatnesses:* that is, the fat places. In the countries where Esau and Jacob were to have their homes, the land varies from districts of extraordinary fertility to regions of barren rock and sterile sand. It was these rich fields which Isaac's blessing conveyed to Jacob.

Wine.—Not the word used in verse 25, but *tirosh,* the unfermented juice of the grape. It thus goes properly with corn, both being the natural produce of the field.

(29) **Let people serve thee.**—Heb., *peoples.* Up to this point the blessing had been general, but now Isaac bestows the birthright, carrying with it wide-spread dominion, precedence over all other members of the family, and special blessedness. The phrases "thy brethren" and "thy mother's sons" include all nations sprung from Abraham, and all possible offshoots from Isaac's own descendants.

Cursed . . . and blessed.—This is a special portion of the blessing given to Abraham (chap. xii. 3); but Isaac stops short with this, and does not bestow the greater privilege that "in him should all families of the earth be blessed" (chaps. xii. 3, xxii. 18, xxvi. 4). The reason for this may be that it was a blessing which God must grant, and not man; or he may have had misgivings that it was more than Esau was worthy to receive; or, finally, his whole conduct being wrong, he could see and value only the earthly and lower prerogatives of the birthright. Subsequently he bestows the Abrahamic blessing upon Jacob in general terms (chap. xxviii. 4); but this, its highest privilege, is confirmed to Jacob by Jehovah Himself (*ibid.*, verse 14).

(31) **He also had made.**—Heb., *he also made.* Esau returned just as Jacob was leaving Isaac's presence. There would still be some considerable delay before the captured game was made into savoury meat.

son, thy firstborn Esau. (33) And Isaac
[1]trembled very exceedingly, and said,
Who? where *is* he that hath [2]taken
venison, and brought *it* me, and I have
eaten of all before thou camest, and
have blessed him? yea, *and* he shall be
blessed. (34) And when Esau heard the
words of his father, he cried with a
great and exceeding bitter cry, and said
unto his father, Bless me, *even* me also,
O my father. (35) And he said, Thy bro-
ther came with subtilty, and hath taken
away thy blessing. (36) And he said, Is
not he rightly named [3]Jacob? for he
hath supplanted me these two times: he
took away my birthright; and, behold,
now he hath taken away my blessing.
And he said, Hast thou not reserved a
blessing for me?
(37) And Isaac answered and said unto
Esau, Behold, I have made him thy lord,
and all his brethren have I given to him
for servants; and with corn and wine
have I [4]sustained him: and what shall
I do now unto thee, my son?
(38) And Esau said unto his father, Hast
thou but one blessing, my father? bless
me, *even* me also, O my father. And
Esau lifted up his voice, [a]and wept.
(39) And Isaac his father answered and
said unto him,

Behold, [b]thy dwelling shall be [5]the
fatness of the earth, and of the dew of
heaven from above; (40) and by thy sword
shalt thou live, and shalt serve thy
brother; and it shall come to pass when
thou shalt have the dominion, that thou
shalt break his yoke from off thy neck.
(41) And Esau hated Jacob because of
the blessing wherewith his father blessed

[1] Heb., *trembled with a great trembling greatly.*
[2] Heb., *hunted.*
[3] That is, *A supplanter.*
[4] Or, *supported.*
[a] Heb. 12. 17.
[b] ver. 28.
[5] Or, *of the fatness.*

---

(33) **Isaac trembled very exceedingly.**—This was not from mere vexation at having been so deceived, and made to give the blessing contrary to his wishes. What Isaac felt was that he had been resisting God. In spite of the prophecy given to the mother, and Esau's own irreligious character and heathen marriages, he had determined to bestow on him the birthright by an act of his own will; and he had failed. But he persists no longer in his sin. Acknowledging the Divine purpose, he has no word of blame for Rebekah and Jacob, but confirms to him the possession of the birthright, and declares, "Yea, he shall be blessed."

(36) **Is not he rightly named Jacob?**—In thus playing upon his brother's name, Esau has had a lasting revenge; for the bad sense which he for the first time put upon the word Jacob has adhered to it, no doubt, because Jacob's own conduct made it only too appropriate. Its right meaning is "one who follows close upon another's heels." (See Note on chap. xxv. 26.)

(38) **Hast thou but one blessing?**—Only one son could inherit the spiritual prerogatives of the birthright, and the temporal lordship which accompanied it. And even lower earthly blessings would avail little if Esau's descendants were to be subject to the dominion of the other brother's race. With some mitigation, then, of his lot Esau must now be content.

(39) **Isaac his father answered.**—Unwillingly, and only after repeated entreaty and earnest expostulation, and even tears, upon Esau's side, does Isaac bring himself to the effort to lessen in any way the painful consequences to his favourite son of his brother having robbed him of the blessing. Plainly, he felt that he had endeavoured to do what was wrong, and was afraid lest he should still be found resisting God's will.

Thy dwelling shall be the fatness.—Heb., *thy dwelling shall be of the fat places of the earth.* (See Note on verse 28.) But most modern expositors consider that the preposition should not be translated "of," but *from*, that is:—

"Behold thy dwelling shall be away from the fat places of the earth,
And away from the dew of heaven from above,
And by (Heb., *upon*—depending upon) thy sword thou shalt live," &c.

By this rendering the parts of the blessing agree together. Those who have fertile lands live by agriculture, but the inhabitants of sterile regions must look to more adventurous enterprises for a living. So the Swiss, like the Greeks of old, long served as mercenaries in the armies of other states. Idumæa, though not destitute of fruitful tracts, and even famous for its orchards, was, as a whole, sterile and unproductive, and the people were restless and unquiet. Moreover, Isaac had already given the corn-land and vineyards to Jacob (verse 37), and had no second gift of them in his power. It is no answer to this to say that as the same preposition is used in verse 28, it cannot have a contrary sense in the two blessings. It there follows a verb of giving, and necessarily has a partitive signification. Here there is nothing absolutely to settle its meaning, and we are left to the general sense. Possibly, Isaac may have purposely used an ambiguous word; but the meaning as a whole is clear. Esau was to inhabit a land which by its barrenness would force him to a life of adventure, military service, and freebooting.

(40) **When thou shalt have the dominion.**—This rendering of a rare and difficult Hebrew word is scarcely more than a guess made by two or three ancient Jewish commentators. Its real meaning here, and in Jer. ii. 31, Hosea xi. 12, is *to toss the yoke*—be restless and unquiet. The prophecy of Edom's subjection to his brother was literally fulfilled, as Idumæa was for ages a mere dependency upon Judah; but in the days first of Joram, and then of Ahaz, it revolted, and recovered its freedom. It was again conquered by Hyrcanus, the nephew of Judas Maccabæus; nor was its subject condition altered by the fact that the dynasty of the Herods was of Edomite extraction. In troubled times, then, it broke the yoke from its neck; but generally Edom served his brother.

Jacob is sent away by his Father and Mother to Haran.

(41) **The days of mourning for my father are at hand.**—Esau evidently expected that his father's death was near, and such also was Isaac's own expectation (verse 2); but he recovered, and lived for more than half a century. Perhaps on

him: and Esau said in his heart, The
days of mourning for my father are at
hand; [a]then will I slay my brother
Jacob. (42) And these words of Esau her
elder son were told to Rebekah: and
she sent and called Jacob her younger
son, and said unto him, Behold, thy
brother Esau, as touching thee, doth
comfort himself, *purposing* to kill thee.
(43) Now therefore, my son, obey my
voice; and arise, flee thou to Laban my
brother to Haran; (44) and tarry with
him a few days, until thy brother's fury
turn away; (45) until thy brother's anger
turn away from thee, and he forget *that*
which thou hast done to him: then I
will send, and fetch thee from thence:
why should I be deprived also of you
both in one day?

(46) And Rebekah said to Isaac, [b]I am
weary of my life because of the daugh-
ters of Heth: if Jacob take a wife of
the daughters of Heth, such as these
which are of the daughters of the land,
what good shall my life do me?

CHAPTER XXVIII.—(1) And Isaac
called Jacob, and blessed him, and
charged him, and said unto him, Thou
shalt not take a wife of the daughters
of Canaan. (2) [c]Arise, go to Padan-
aram, to the house of Bethuel thy
mother's father; and take thee a wife
from thence of the daughters of Laban
thy mother's brother. (3) And God Al-
mighty bless thee, and make thee fruit-
ful, and multiply thee, that thou mayest
be [1]a multitude of people; (4) and give
thee the blessing of Abraham, to thee,
and to thy seed with thee; that thou
mayest inherit the land [2]wherein thou
art a stranger, which God gave unto
Abraham. (5) And Isaac sent away
Jacob: and he went to Padan-aram

a Obad. 10.

B.C. cir. 1760.

b ch. 26. 35.

c Hos. 12. 12.

1 Heb., *an assembly of people.*

2 Heb., *of thy sojournings.*

---

this account another translation has been suggested, namely, "Days of mourning for my father are at hand: for I will slay Jacob." But there is no support for this in the Hebrew, and it represents Esau as utterly inhuman; whereas, with all his faults, he had a warm, loving heart. Chap. xxviii. ought to have begun here, as the break at the end of verse 46 is very injurious to the meaning.

(42) **These words of Esau.**—Though spoken "in his heart," Esau had evidently made no secret of his evil purpose, and Rebekah therefore determines to send Jacob to her father's house, not merely for safety, but that he might take a wife from among his own kindred. He was now formally acknowledged as the heir of the birthright and of the promises made to Abraham, and must therefore conform to the principle laid down in his own father's case, and marry into the family of Nahor. "She sends, therefore, and calls him" to her tent, and takes secret counsel with him; and Jacob consents to take this distant journey. Thus the separation of mother and son, and long and painful travel, are the immediate result of their scheming.

(44) **A few days.**—Like Esau (verse 41), Rebekah expected that Isaac's end was near. Really Jacob was absent for forty years, and while Isaac lived to see him return, Rebekah saw him again no more. Yet this was better than for Esau to slay him, and then, like another Cain, to be banished far away.

(46) **Rebekah said to Isaac.**—With this begins a new act. In the previous five verses we had the general results of Rebekah's guile: we have now the special consequence of Jacob's departure for Haran. Upon Rebekah's communication to Isaac follows his decision in the next chapter. In the Hebrew there is no break from the beginning of chap. xxvii. to the end of verse 9 of chap. xxviii.

XXVIII.

(1) **Isaac called Jacob . . . .**—Though Rebekah's primary motive was her concern for Jacob's safety, yet we must not imagine that his marriage was a mere pretext. On the contrary, now that he was acknowledged as the firstborn, both he and she would have been abandoning his high position had they not arranged for the fulfilment of his duty in this respect. What is remarkable is the frankness of Isaac's conduct. There is no attempt to substitute Esau for Jacob, nor to lessen the privileges of the latter, but with hearty cheerfulness he blesses the younger son, and confirms him in the possession of the whole Abrahamic blessing.

(2) **Padan-aram.**—See Note on chap. xxv. 20. Throughout this verse Isaac shows a much more intimate acquaintance with the family at Haran than was possessed by Abraham. (Comp. chap. xxiv. 4.) And though we gather from verse 5 that Bethuel was now dead, yet it is evident that he was a person of more importance than is supposed by the Rabbins, who ascribe to his feebleness or death the prominent part taken by Laban in his sister's marriage. It was this greater knowledge which made Isaac send Jacob in person, and not a deputy. With a few trusty attendants he would journey till he reached the usual caravan route which led through Damascus to Haran, and would then attach himself to some trading company for escort and society.

(3) **God Almighty.**—Heb., *El Shaddai.* As it was Isaac's purpose in this blessing to confirm Jacob in the possession of the promises made to Abraham, he is careful to use the same title as that borne by God in the covenant whereby the land of Canaan was given to his seed, and of which the sacrament of circumcision was the seal. (See chap. xvii. 1.)

A multitude of people.—Heb., *a congregation of peoples.* This is not the word used in chap. xvii. 4, but one that signifies an assembly, especially one summoned for religious purposes. Like the Greek word for church, *ecclesia,* it comes from a root signifying "to convoke." It subsequently became the regular phrase for "the congregation of Israel" (Lev. xvi. 17), and implies even here that the nations descended from Jacob would have a religious significance.

(5) **Jacob's and Esau's mother.**—This insertion of particulars already well known is in exact accord-

unto Laban, son of Bethuel the Syrian, the brother of Rebekah, Jacob's and Esau's mother.

(6) When Esau saw that Isaac had blessed Jacob, and sent him away to Padan-aram, to take him a wife from thence; and that as he blessed him he gave him a charge, saying, Thou shalt not take a wife of the daughters of Canaan; (7) and that Jacob obeyed his father and his mother, and was gone to Padan-aram; (8) and Esau seeing that the daughters of Canaan [1] pleased not Isaac his father; (9) then went Esau unto Ishmael, and took unto the wives which he had Mahalath the daughter of Ishmael Abraham's son, the sister of Nebajoth, to be his wife.

(10) And Jacob went out from Beer-sheba, and went toward [a] Haran. (11) And he lighted upon a certain place, and tarried there all night, because the sun was set; and he took of the stones of that place, and put *them for* his pillows, and lay down in that place to sleep. (12) And he dreamed, and behold a ladder set up on the earth, and the top of it reached to heaven: and behold the angels of

1 Heb., *were evil in the eyes, &c.*

a Called, Acts 7. 2, *Charran.*

B.C. cir. 1760.

---

ance with the Oriental manner of writing, which, moreover, is very careful in impressing all matters of family relation on the mind. (Comp. chap. xxv. 12.) It is worthy of notice that as Jacob has now been confirmed in the possession of the birthright by the father as well as by the mother, his name is placed first.

Esau Marries a Daughter of Ishmael.

(6) **When Esau.**—The solemn transfer of the birthright to Jacob, and Isaac's complete assent thereto, must have been the cause of no little grief to Esau, and evidently it made him feel that he had greatly contributed to this result by his own illegitimate marriages. When, then, he sees Jacob sent away to obtain a wife, in accordance with the rule established by Abraham, he determines also to conform to it, and marries a daughter of Ishmael. She is called Bashemath in chap xxxvi. 3, and described in both places as "the sister of Nebajoth," in order to show that as Nebajoth "the firstborn" (chap. xxv. 13) was undoubtedly the son of Ishmael by his first wife, "whom Hagar took for him out of the land of Egypt" (chap. xxi. 21), so also Mahalath shared in this precedence, and was not the daughter of any of Ishmael's subsequent wives, or of a concubine.

Jacob's Dream.

(10) **And Jacob.**—Though this history is called the *Tôldôth Isaac*, yet it is really the history of Jacob, just as the *Tôldôth Terah* was the history of Abraham, and the *Tôldôth Jacob*, beginning at chap. xxxvii. 2, is the history of Joseph. Up to this time all had been preparation, but now at length Jacob is confirmed in the possession of the birthright, and made the heir of the Abrahamic blessing; and henceforward his fortunes solely occupy the inspired narrator, though Isaac had still sixty-three years to live. (See Note on chap. xi. 27.)

(11) **He lighted upon a certain place.**—Heb., *he lighted upon the place.* The article probably signifies that it was the place appointed for the revelation, though lighted upon by Jacob by chance. As it lay twelve miles north of Jerusalem, in the mountains of Ephraim, Jacob had already been at least four days on the route (see Note on chap. xxii. 4); and though we are not to suppose that Isaac would send away the son who was heir of the blessing without a few trusty servants (nor does the expression in chap. xxxii. 10 require it), yet Jacob would none the less feel the solemnity of the journey, and the difficulties which surrounded him. Well may he have asked whether *El Shaddai* would confirm him in the possession of that which he had defiled by fraud and cunning. And thus, meditating much and praying much, he had in those four days drawn near to God, and is at last accepted. The interest in Jacob's life lies in the gradual improvement and progress of his character. Religion was always a reality with him; but at first it was of a low type, and marred by duplicity and earthly scheming. His schemes succeed, but bring with them sorrow and trial; and trial purifies him, and gradually he advances into a region of unselfish and holy piety. Though to the last he was a man sagacious, and full of expedients, yet the nobler part of his character finally had the supremacy.

He took of the stones . . . .—Heb., *he took one of the stones of the place, and put it as his bolster.* Jewish commentators identify the place with Mount Moriah, and say that the stone which Jacob placed under his head was one of those which had formed the altar upon which Isaac had been bound for sacrifice. The name Beth-el signified, they add, the temple, and as *makôm*—place—is thrice used in this verse, it mysteriously foreshadowed the three temples—Solomon's, Zerubbabel's, and Herod's—which successively occupied the site. More probably Beth-el was really the town of that name, and these explanations are allegorical rather than expository.

(12) **Behold a ladder . . . .**—Isaac had confirmed Jacob in the possession of the blessing before he started on his long journey, but it was necessary that he should also have the Divine ratification of his appointment; for the chief privilege was the covenant with God previously confirmed to Isaac, his father (chap. xvii. 19—21). Day after day, then, he travels forward, anxious and oppressed, feeling as he went farther from his home the responsibilities attendant upon that birthright which he had coveted so eagerly. His lot was now a repetition of that of Abraham; but he had travelled from Haran with a noble following, and by express command. Jacob had at most but a few attendants, and no voice from God had ever as yet reached him. But faith in Him was growing strong, and the Divine ratification to him of the Abrahamic covenant was at length vouchsafed. In his sleep he sees a ladder, or staircase, rising from the ground at his side, and reaching up to heaven. It tells him that heaven and earth are united, and that there is a way from one to the other. Upon these stairs "messengers of Elohim are ascending and descending," carrying up to God men's prayers, and the tale of their wants and sorrows, of their faith and hope and trust; and bringing down to them help and comfort and blessing. At the head of the ladder Jehovah himself stands. The word is that

God ascending and descending on it.
(13) [a]And, behold, the LORD stood above it,
and said, I *am* the LORD God of Abra-
ham thy father, and the God of Isaac:
the land whereon thou liest, to thee will
I give it, and to thy seed; (14) and thy
seed shall be as the dust of the earth,
and thou shalt [1]spread abroad [b]to the
west, and to the east, and to the north,
and to the south: and in thee and [c]in
thy seed shall all the families of the
earth be blessed. (15) And, behold, I *am*
with thee, and will keep thee in all
places whither thou goest, and will bring
thee again into this land; for I will not
leave thee, until I have done *that* which
I have spoken to thee of.

(16) And Jacob awaked out of his sleep,
and he said, Surely the LORD is in this
place; and I knew *it* not. (17) And he
was afraid, and said, How dreadful *is*
this place! this *is* none other but the
house of God, and this *is* the gate of
heaven.

(18) And Jacob rose up early in the
morning, and took the stone that he
had put *for* his pillows, and set it up *for*
a pillar, and poured oil upon the top of
it. (19) And he called the name of that
place [2]Beth-el: but the name of that
city *was called* Luz at the first. (20) And
Jacob vowed a vow, saying, If God will
be with me, and will keep me in this
way that I go, and will give me bread to
eat, and raiment to put on, (21) so that
I come again to my father's house in
peace; then shall the LORD be my God:
(22) and this stone, which I have set *for* a

[a] ch. 35. 1; & 48. 3.

[1] Heb., *break forth.*

[b] Deut. 12. 20.

[c] ch. 12. 3; & 18. 18; & 22. 18; & 26. 4.

[2] That is, *The house of God.*

---

used in chap. xxiv. 13, and signifies that the Deity was not there accidentally, but that He holds there His permanent station. Finally, Jehovah from His heavenly post confirms to Jacob all the promises made from the time when Abraham left Ur of the Chaldees, and assures him of His constant presence and protection.

It has been pointed out that each of the three stages in the dream has emphasis given to it by the word *behold*, and that this rises to a climax at the third repetition, when the covenant God is seen stationed at the head of this pathway between earth and heaven. But besides this, the value of Jacob in Jehovah's sight arises now from his being the appointed ancestor of the Messiah, in whom all the families of the earth were to be blessed (verse 14). Christ, too, is the Way symbolised by this ladder (John xiv. 6), and the bridge of union between the material and the spiritual world (1 Tim. ii. 5). Our Lord, accordingly, Himself claims that "the angels of God ascend and descend upon Him" (John i. 51).

(16) **Surely the Lord** (Jehovah) **is in this place.**—Jacob was not unaware of the omnipresence of the Deity: what astonished him was that Jehovah should thus reveal Himself far away from the shrines where He was worshipped. Rebekah had gone to one of these to inquire of Jehovah (chap. xxv. 22), and probably to a shrine in the very neighbourhood of the place where Jacob was sleeping (chap. xii. 8). But first Abraham, and then Isaac, had for so long made Beer-sheba their home, that Jacob probably knew little about the sanctity of the spot, and felt himself far away from all the religious associations of his youth, and from that "presence of Jehovah" which in antediluvian times had also been supposed to be confined to certain localities (chap. iv. 16). But one great object of the dream was to show that Jehovah watches over the whole earth, and that messengers to and fro come from Him and return unto Him.

(17) **How dreadful.**—The manifestation of God must always inspire awe and dread, but not fear: for where He reveals Himself, there is "the gate of heaven"—the appointed entrance for prayer now, and for admission to the glorified life hereafter.

(18) **Jacob . . . took the stone . . . and set it up for a pillar.**—In so doing, Jacob's object was to mark the spot where so important a communication had been made to him. But besides its use as a memorial, it would enable him to identify the place upon his return, and pay there his vows. And as oil was the symbol of the dedication of a thing to holy uses, he pours oil upon the top of it.

(19) **Beth-el . . . Luz.**—In Josh. xvi. 1, 2, we find that Luz and Beth-el were distinct places, though near one another; and with this agrees the present passage. For plainly, Jacob and his attendants did not go inside the city, but slept on the open ground; and as they would carry their provisions with them, they would need no supplies from its Canaanite inhabitants. Probably at the time of Joshua's conquest Beth-el was rather a holy place than a town, and when Ephraim seized upon Luz and put the people to the sword (Judges i. 23—25), the victors transferred the name of Beth-el to it. Thus the spot where Jacob slept would not be the town of Beth-el, but some place a mile or two away from it.

(20-22) **Then shall the Lord** (Jehovah) **be my God.**—This is a false translation, and gives a wrong sense. Jacob, in his vow, which implies no doubt on his part, but is his acceptance of the terms of the covenant, says: "If Elohim will be with me, and will protect me on this journey that I go, and will give me bread to eat and clothing to wear, and if I come again in peace to my father's house, and Jehovah will be my Elohim, then this stone which I have set up as a pillar shall be Beth-Elohim; and of all that thou shalt give me I will surely pay thee tithes." Verses 20 and 21 are a recapitulation of the mercies of which he was to be the recipient, while in verse 22 Jacob states what shall be his vow of gratitude.

But what was a Beth-Elohim? It has been supposed that it was a sort of cromlech, set up to be itself an object of adoration. Attention has also been called to the Baitylia, or stones "possessed of a soul," which the Phœnicians are said by Eusebius (*Praep. Evang.* i. 10) to have worshipped; and it has been thought, with some probability, that the word is a corrupt form of the Hebrew Beth-Elohim. These Baitylia, however, were meteoric stones, and their sanctity arose from their having fallen from heaven. Stones, moreover, set up at first simply as memorials may in time have been worshipped, and hence the pro-

pillar, shall be God's house: and of all
that thou shalt give me I will surely
give the tenth unto thee.

CHAPTER XXIX.—(1) Then Jacob
[1]went on his journey, and came into the
land of the [2]people of the east. (2) And
he looked, and behold a well in the field,
and, lo, there *were* three flocks of sheep
lying by it; for out of that well they
watered the flocks: and a great stone
was upon the well's mouth. (3) And
thither were all the flocks gathered:
and they rolled the stone from the well's
mouth, and watered the sheep, and put
the stone again upon the well's mouth
in his place. (4) And Jacob said unto
them, My brethren, whence *be* ye? And
they said, Of Haran *are* we. (5) And he
said unto them, Know ye Laban the son
of Nahor? And they said, We know
him. (6) And he said unto them, [3]*Is* he
well? And they said, *He is* well: and,
behold, Rachel his daughter cometh
with the sheep. (7) And he said, Lo, [4]*it
is* yet high day, neither *is it* time that
the cattle should be gathered together:
water ye the sheep, and go *and* feed
them. (8) And they said, We cannot,
until all the flocks be gathered together,
and *till* they roll the stone from the
well's mouth; then we water the sheep.
(9) And while he yet spake with them,
Rachel came with her father's sheep:
for she kept them. (10) And it came to
pass, when Jacob saw Rachel the daugh-
ter of Laban his mother's brother, and
the sheep of Laban his mother's brother,
that Jacob went near, and rolled the
stone from the well's mouth, and watered
the flock of Laban his mother's brother.
(11) And Jacob kissed Rachel, and lifted

[1] Heb., *lift up his feet.*

[2] Heb., *children.*

[3] Heb., Is there *peace to him?*

[4] Heb., *yet the day is great.*

---

hibition in Lev. xxvi. 1, Deut. xvi. 22; but there is no trace of any such idolatrous tendency here. Jacob apparently meant by a Beth-Elohim a place where prayer and offerings would be acceptable, because God had manifested Himself there; and His vow signified that if, preserved by Jehovah's care, he was permitted to visit the place again, he would consecrate it to Jehovah's service, and spend there in sacrifice, or in some other way to His honour, the tithe of whatever property he might have acquired.

XXIX.

MARRIAGE OF JACOB WITH LEAH AND RACHEL.

(1) **Jacob went on his journey.**—Heb., *Jacob lifted up his feet,* that is, hastened forward. Confirmed in the possession of the birthright by God as well as man, and encouraged by the promise of the Divine presence, and of a safe return home, he casts no wistful glances back, but pursues his journey under the inspiriting influence of hope.

The people of the East.—Usually the Arabians are designated by this phrase, but it here signifies the tribes who inhabited northern Mesopotamia.

(2) **Behold a well in the field.**—This was not the well whence Rebekah drew the water; for it was in the field, the open pasture ground, whereas Rebekah's well was just outside the city (chap. xxiv. 11), and she obtained the water by going down the steps which led to it (*ibid.* 16).

A great stone was upon the well's mouth.—The region round Haran, though fertile, is very dry, and the chief use of the stone was to prevent the well from being choked with sand. As the proper translation is *the stone upon the well's mouth was great,* it would also serve to prevent the well from being used, except at fixed times; for it probably required the strength of two or three men (comp. Robinson, *Bibl. Res.* ii. 180) to remove it; nor does the language of verse 10 necessarily imply that Jacob rolled it away without the aid of others. Besides this, the stone may have marked that the well was private property: for, as we have seen in the account of the covenants of Abraham and Isaac with Abimelech, no possession was more valued than that of wells. And as we find the shepherds all waiting for Rachel, and that immediately on her arrival the stone is rolled away, and her sheep watered first, while the rest, though they had been there long before her, yet have to bide their time till her wants are supplied, it is probable that Laban had at least a first claim upon its enjoyment. No such courtesy was shown to the daughters of Jethro (Exod. ii. 17).

(5) **Laban the son of Nahor.**—Laban was really the son of Bethuel and grandson of Nahor; but Nahor was the founder of the family, as being the original immigrant from Ur, who came to supply Abraham's place on his departure.

(7) **Neither is it time that the cattle should be gathered together.**—Rather, *neither is it time for folding the cattle.* As there were still several hours of daylight, Jacob is surprised that they do not immediately upon their arrival give the sheep water, and drive them back to the pasture. But if the well belonged to Laban, their reason for waiting till Rachel came is plain.

(8) **And till they roll the stone . . .**—More correctly, *then they roll the stone from the well's mouth, and we water the sheep.* As soon as the flocks were all collected round the well the stone is removed, and all in their turn give their sheep water.

(9) **Rachel came with her father's sheep.**—Comp. Exod. ii. 16; and so in modern times Mr. Malan saw "the sheik's daughter, the beautiful and well-favoured Ladheefeh, drive her flock of fine patriarchal sheep" to a well for water in this very region (*Philosophy or Truth,* p. 95). As forty years at least elapsed between this meeting of Jacob and Rachel and the birth of Benjamin, she must have been a mere child at this time.

(10) **Laban his mother's brother.**—The threefold repetition of these words has no other reason than that given in the Note on chap. xxviii. 5.

(11) **Jacob kissed Rachel . . . and wept.**—Jacob first made himself useful to Rachel, and then discloses to her who he is, claims her as a cousin, and

up his voice, and wept. (12)And Jacob
told Rachel that he *was* her father's
brother, and that he *was* Rebekah's son:
and she ran and told her father. (13)And
it came to pass, when Laban heard the
[1]tidings of Jacob his sister's son, that
he ran to meet him, and embraced him,
and kissed him, and brought him to his
house. And he told Laban all these
things. (14) And Laban said to him,
Surely thou *art* my bone and my flesh.
And he abode with him [2]the space of a
month.
(15) And Laban said unto Jacob, Be-
cause thou *art* my brother, shouldest
thou therefore serve me for nought?
tell me, what *shall* thy wages *be*? (16)And
Laban had two daughters: the name of
the elder *was* Leah, and the name of the
younger *was* Rachel. (17) Leah *was* ten-
der eyed; but Rachel was beautiful and
well favoured. (18) And Jacob loved Ra-
chel; and said, I will serve thee seven
years for Rachel thy younger daughter.
(19) And Laban said, *It is* better that
I give her to thee, than that I should
give her to another man: abide with
me. (20) And Jacob served seven years
for Rachel; and they seemed unto
him *but* a few days, for the love he had
to her.
(21) And Jacob said unto Laban, Give
me my wife, for my days are fulfilled,
that I may go in unto her. (22) And La-
ban gathered together all the men of
the place, and made a feast. (23) And it

1 Heb., *hearing.*

2 Heb., *a month of days.*

B.C. cir. 1753.

---

kisses her. Then, overcome with joy at this happy termination of his long journey, and at finding himself among relatives, he can restrain his feelings no longer, but bursts into tears. In this outburst of emotion we see the commencement of his lifelong affection for the beautiful child whom he thus opportunely met.

(12) **Her father's brother.**—Really his nephew; but terms of relationship are used in a very indefinite way in Hebrew. (Comp. verses 5, 15, chap. xiii. 8, &c.)

(13) **Laban . . . ran to meet him, and embraced him.**—Rachel told her father, because it was a matter simply of the hospitable reception of a relative, and not such news as Rebekah had run to tell those of her mother's house. And to Laban the tidings must have been most welcome, as he called to mind how, seventy-seven years ago, he had seen his dear sister depart to marry the son of the distant sheik. It seems strange, however, that the daughters of this old man should be so young. Either they must have been the children of a wife of his old age, or his granddaughters, but regarded as his own because their father was dead. As Laban's sons are not mentioned till chap. xxxi. 1, probably on account of their youth, the former is the more probable explanation.

(14) **The space of a month.**—Heb., *a month of days*, that is, a full month.

(15) **What shall thy wages be?**—As Jacob had given upon his arrival a full account of himself (verse 13), Laban probably expected the very answer he received; nevertheless, the proposal was fair and upright. Doubtless he had seen, during Jacob's stay of a month, that his services would be very valuable.

(17) **Leah was tender eyed.**—Leah, whose name signifies *languor, weariness*, had dull bleared eyes. Probably she suffered, as so many do in that hot sandy region, from some form of ophthalmia. Rachel (Heb., *the ewe*) was, on the contrary, "beautiful and well favoured" (Heb., *beautiful in form and beautiful in look*). Leah's bleared eyes would be regarded in the East as a great defect, just as bright eyes were much admired. (See 1 Sam. xvi. 12, where David is described as *fair of eyes*.) Yet it was not Rachel, with her fair face and well-proportioned figure, and her husband's lasting love, that was the mother of the progenitor of the Messiah, but the weary-eyed Leah.

(18) **I will serve thee seven years for Rachel thy younger daughter.**—Heb., *thy daughter, the little one*, just as Leah, in verse 16, is called the *great one.* (See Note on chap. ix. 24.) So in chap. xliv. 20, the phrase "the little one" simply means *the youngest.* Wives had to be purchased in the East (chap. xxiv. 53), and as Jacob had brought no rich presents, such as Abraham had sent when seeking a wife for his son, he had only his personal services to offer. As the sale was usually veiled in true Oriental fashion under the specious form of freewill gifts, we shall find that both Leah and Rachel are offended at being thus openly bartered by Laban.

(19) **It is better that I give her to thee.**—It is still the custom among the Arabs to prefer a relative as the husband of a daughter, and on giving a moderate dowry the elder cousins can claim the elder daughters in marriage, and the younger the younger. Thus Jacob, as the second son, had a claim upon Rachel. The Rabbins even say that Leah's eyes were weak from weeping, because Esau had not come to marry her. This absurd idea bears witness, nevertheless, to the custom of the intermarriage of cousins being an established rule, and gives a reason for Laban's acceptance of Jacob as the husband of his younger child. As Jacob offered seven years' service for Rachel, and gave a second seven years' service for her after he had been tricked into taking Leah, we may conclude that the length of time was not unreasonable.

(20) **They seemed unto him but a few days.**—Jacob was at least fifty-seven years of age, but the late marriages hitherto of the patriarchs show that they only slowly arrived at manhood. We need not be surprised, then, at the warmth of his affection, nor was it a passing emotion, but lasted all his life through. This, however, is the last of these late marriages; for Jacob's sons married when young.

(21) **My days are fulfilled.**—That is, the appointed time of service is completed. It was undeniably at the end of the seven years that the marriage took place.

(23) **He took Leah his daughter.**—As the bride is taken to the bridegroom's house closely veiled (see Note on chap. xxiv. 65), and as probably there was some similarity in voice and form between the two sisters, this deception was quite easy. But Leah must

came to pass in the evening, that he took
Leah his daughter, and brought her to
him; and he went in unto her. (24) And
Laban gave unto his daughter Leah
Zilpah his maid *for* an handmaid. (25) And
it came to pass, that in the morning, be-
hold, it *was* Leah: and he said to Laban,
What *is* this thou hast done unto me?
did not I serve with thee for Rachel?
wherefore then hast thou beguiled me?
(26) And Laban said, It must not be so
done in our [1] country, to give the younger
before the firstborn. (27) Fulfil her week,
and we will give thee this also for the
service which thou shalt serve with me
yet seven other years. (28) And Jacob
did so, and fulfilled her week: and he
gave him Rachel his daughter to wife
also. (29) And Laban gave to Rachel
his daughter Bilhah his handmaid to be
her maid. (30) And he went in also unto
Rachel, and he loved also Rachel more
than Leah, and served with him yet
seven other years.
(31) And when the LORD saw that Leah
was hated, he opened her womb: but
Rachel *was* barren. (32) And Leah con-
ceived, and bare a son, and she called
his name [2] Reuben: for she said, Surely
the LORD hath looked upon my afflic-
tion; now therefore my husband will
love me. (33) And she conceived again,
and bare a son; and said, Because the
LORD hath heard that I *was* hated, he
hath therefore given me this *son* also:
and she called his name [3] Simeon.
(34) And she conceived again, and bare a
son; and said, Now this time will my
husband be joined unto me, because I
have borne him three sons: therefore
was his name called [4] Levi. (35) And she
conceived again, and bare a son: and

1 Heb., *place*.

B.C. cir. 1752.

2 That is, *See a son*.

B.C. cir. 1751.

3 That is, *Hearing*.

B.C. cir. 1750.

4 That is, *Joined*.

B.C. cir. 1749.

---

have been a party to the fraud, and therefore Jacob's dislike of her was not altogether without reason.

(24) **Laban gave unto his daughter Leah Zilpah . . .**—Bethuel had given Rebekah not only Deborah her nurse, but also damsels (chap. xxiv. 61); but then she had been obtained by presents of unusual costliness. Still, Laban does not seem to have acted very liberally by his daughters, and they resented his treatment of them (chap. xxxi. 15).

(26) **It must not be so done in our country.**—Heb., *It is not so done in our place, to give*, &c. We have seen that it is still customary for the elder cousin to take the elder daughter, and the younger the younger. But Laban affirms that if the elder daughter be not claimed, it was the rule in Haran for her to take precedence over her sisters. In India the practice is such as Laban describes, but we have no proof of the existence of any such custom among the Bedaween. Apparently Leah loved Jacob (chap. xxx. 15), and Laban wanted a continuance of his service, and so this unscrupulous plot was arranged between them upon a pretext which, if not false, was yet overstrained. Jacob plainly had no idea of such a custom, and would not have given seven years' service for Leah.

(27) **Fulfil her week.**—The marriage festival seems to have lasted a week, as was the custom in later times (Judges xiv. 12), and to have forsaken Leah during this period would have been to offer her an insult which her brothers must have avenged. Appeased, therefore, by the promise of Rachel as soon as the seven days are over, Jacob, rather than quarrel with the whole family, submits to the wrong. The Hebrew is remarkable, "Fulfil the week of this, and we will give to thee also the this for the service." But in Hebrew *this . . . this* means *the one* and *the other* (chap. xxxi. 38, 41), and it is a mistake to suppose that the language will allow the first *this* to be understood of any one but Leah, and the second *this* of any one but Rachel.

(28) **He gave him Rachel . . . to wife also.**—After the monogamy of Abraham, and the stricter monogamy of Isaac, how came Jacob to marry two wives? Abravanel says that as Esau ought to have married Leah, and Jacob Rachel, he acted only as his brother's substitute in taking the elder, and was still free to marry the younger sister, who was his by custom. He thinks also that Jacob, recalling the promise of a seed numerous as the dust (chap. xxviii. 14), and seeing how near the family had been to total extinction in the days of his father and grandfather, desired to place it on a more secure basis. More probably, even after Leah had been forced upon him, Jacob regarded Rachel as his own, and as polygamy was not actually forbidden, considered that he was only acting justly by her and himself in marrying her. He had seen Esau blamed, not for marrying two wives, but for taking Hittites; and his love for Rachel would make him need but little argument. The only other alternative, namely, to have divorced Leah, would have been worse, and happily divorce was not a practice as yet introduced.

BIRTH OF JACOB'S ELEVEN SONS, AND HIS DAUGHTER.

(31) **Leah was hated.**—We must not soften this down too much; for plainly Leah was not the object of love at all. It was her fruitfulness which gave her value in her husband's eyes, and when this ceased, Jacob utterly neglected her (chap. xxx. 15).

(32–35) **She called his name Reuben.**—There is something very touching in the history of these four births. When the first child is born, Leah joyfully calls him "Reuben," that is, *See, a son!* and fondly hopes that now she is a mother her husband will love her. And the mention of her "affliction" shows that, while she loved Jacob tenderly, he was to her more than unloving. Her second son she calls "Simeon," that is, *hearing*, and, disappointed in her first hope, regards the child as a gift of Jehovah to compensate her for the lack of the affection for which she so longed. Her third son she calls "Levi," that is, *joined*, still hoping that as in her tent alone there were children to play around the father, he would be more united to her. But her hope remains unfulfilled. And when her fourth son is born, she calls him "Judah," that is, *praise*. Throughout, in the midst of her melancholy, there is a tone of fervent piety, and that not merely to God, but to the covenant Jehovah. And now slowly she parts with her hope of

she said, Now will I praise the LORD:
therefore she called his name [a][1]Judah;
and [2]left bearing.

CHAPTER XXX.—(1) And when Ra-
chel saw that she bare Jacob no children,
Rachel envied her sister; and said unto
Jacob, Give me children, or else I die.
(2) And Jacob's anger was kindled against
Rachel: and he said, *Am* I in God's
stead, who hath withheld from thee the
fruit of the womb? (3) And she said,
Behold my maid Bilhah, go in unto
her; and she shall bear upon my knees,
that I may also [3]have children by her.
(4) And she gave him Bilhah her hand-
maid to wife: and Jacob went in unto
her. (5) And Bilhah conceived, and bare
Jacob a son. (6) And Rachel said, God
hath judged me, and hath also heard my
voice, and hath given me a son: there-
fore called she his name [4]Dan. (7) And
Bilhah Rachel's maid conceived again,
and bare Jacob a second son. (8) And
Rachel said, With [5]great wrestlings have
I wrestled with my sister, and I have
prevailed: and she called his name
[6][b]Naphtali.

(9) When Leah saw that she had left
bearing, she took Zilpah her maid, and
gave her Jacob to wife. (10) And Zilpah
Leah's maid bare Jacob a son. (11) And
Leah said, A troop cometh: and she
called his name [7]Gad. (12) And Zilpah
Leah's maid bare Jacob a second son.
(13) And Leah said, [8]Happy am I, for the
daughters will call me blessed: and she
called his name [9]Asher.

B.C. cir. 1747.

a Matt. 1. 2.
1 That is, *Praise*
2 Heb., *stood from bearing.*

B.C. cir. 1749.

3 Heb., *be built by her.*
4 That is, *Judging.*
5 Heb., *wrestlings of God.*

B.C. cir. 1749.

6 That is, *My wrestling.*
b Called, Matt. 4. 13, *Nephthalim.*
7 That is, *A troop, or, company.*

B.C. cir. 1748.

B.C. cir. 1747.

8 Heb., *In my happiness.*

B.C. cir. 1748.

9 That is, *Happy.*

---

human affection, and finds comfort in Jehovah alone. *This time,* she says, *I will praise Jehovah.* And it was this son of the despised one, whose birth called forth from her this hymn of simple thanksgiving, who was fore-ordained to be the ancestor of the promised seed.

XXX.

(1) **Give me children, or else I die.**—There is an Oriental proverb that a childless person is as good as dead; and this was probably Rachel's meaning, and not that she should die of vexation. Great as was the affliction to a Hebrew woman of being barren (1 Sam. i. 10), yet there is a painful petulance and peevishness about Rachel's words, in strong contrast with Hannah's patient suffering. But she was very young, and a spoiled wife; though with qualities which riveted Jacob's love to her all life through.

(3) **Behold my maid Bilhah.**—Rachel had little excuse for this action; for there was no religious hope involved, as when Sarah gave Hagar to Abraham (chap. xvi. 2), but solely vexation at her own barrenness, and envy of her sister. All that can be said in her defence is, that the custom existed, and, perhaps, because it was distasteful to the wife, was looked upon as meritorious (verse 18).

She shall bear upon my knees.—So in chap. l. 23, it is said, in the Hebrew, that "the children of Machir were born upon Joseph's knees," not *borne,* as in our margin. It appears that there was a custom of placing the new-born child upon the knees, first of the father, who, by accepting it, acknowledged the infant as his own; and secondly, upon those of the mother. In this case, as Bilhah's children were regarded as legally born of Rachel, they would be placed upon Rachel's knees. Probably, too, the children of Machir, by being placed upon Joseph's knees, were in some way adopted by him.

That I may also have children by her.—Heb., *be built by her.* (See Note on chap. xvi. 2.)

(6) **God hath judged me.**—Rachel has no misgivings herself as to the rectitude of her conduct, and by the name she gives the child, she affirms that God also had given a decision in her favour; for "Dan" means *judging.* While, too, Leah had spoken of Jehovah, Rachel speaks of Elohim, not merely because she could not expect a child of Bilhah to be the ancestor of the Messiah, but because she was herself half an idolater (chap. xxxi. 19). When, however, she has a child of her own, she, too, taught by long trial, speaks of Jehovah (verse 24).

(8) **With great wrestlings.**—Heb., *wrestlings of God,* but the Authorised Version undoubtedly gives the right sense. (See Note on chap. xxiii. 6.) By *wrestling,* some commentators understand prayer, but the connection of the two ideas of wrestling and prayer is taken from chap. xxxii. 24, where an entirely different verb is used. Rachel's was a discreditable victory, won by making use of a bad custom, and it consisted in weaning her husband still more completely from the unloved Leah. Now that Bilhah and children were added to the attractiveness of her tent, her sister, she boasts, will be thought of no more.

(9–13) **Leah . . . took Zilpah . . .**—By ceasing to bear, Leah had lost her one hold upon her husband's affection, and to regain it she follows Rachel's example. The struggle of these two women for the husband gives us a strange picture of manners and morals, but must not be judged by our standard. Leah herself regards the bestowal of her handmaid upon Jacob as a deserving act of self-sacrifice (verse 18). The names, moreover, which she gives to Zilpah's children show that the happier frame of mind to which she had attained when she called her fourth son "Judah," *praise,* remained unbroken. On the birth of the first, she says, "With good luck!" and calls his name "Gad," that is, *luck.* The Jews read, in their synagogue, *Luck cometh,* whence the rendering of the Authorised Version, "A troop cometh;" but there is no justification for the change. With regard to the meaning of the word "Gad," all the Versions render it *prosperity, good fortune.* Nor is the Samaritan, as has been alleged, an exception; for though the worthless Latin translation of it has "a troop cometh," the Samaritan itself has *with good luck.* In Isa. lxv. 11 we find Gad used as the name of an idol. Zilpah's other son is called Asher, that is, *happy,* in Latin Felix, and Leah says, "With my happiness," using just the same turn of speech as before. The first child came bringing her good luck; the second brought her happiness.

(14) And Reuben went in the days of
wheat harvest, and found mandrakes
in the field, and brought them unto
his mother Leah. Then Rachel said to
Leah, Give me, I pray thee, of thy son's
mandrakes. (15) And she said unto her,
Is it a small matter that thou hast taken
my husband? and wouldest thou take
away my son's mandrakes also? And
Rachel said, Therefore he shall lie with
thee to night for thy son's mandrakes.
(16) And Jacob came out of the field in
the evening, and Leah went out to meet
him, and said, Thou must come in unto
me; for surely I have hired thee with
my son's mandrakes. And he lay with
her that night. (17) And God hearkened
unto Leah, and she conceived, and bare
Jacob the fifth son. (18) And Leah said,
God hath given me my hire, because I
have given my maiden to my husband:
and she called his name [1]Issachar.
(19) And Leah conceived again, and bare
Jacob the sixth son. (20) And Leah said,
God hath endued me *with* a good dowry;
now will my husband dwell with me,
because I have born him six sons: and
she called his name [2][a]Zebulun. (21) And
afterwards she bare a daughter, and
called her name [3]Dinah.
(22) And God remembered Rachel, and
God hearkened to her, and opened her

B.C. cir. 1748.

B.C. cir. 1747.

1 That is, *An hire.*

2 That is, *Dwelling.*

B.C. cir. 1746.

a Called, Matt. 4. 13, *Zabulon.*

B.C. cir. 1745.

3 That is, *Judgment.*

(14) **Reuben went . . .**—When Leah ceased from bearing, there would be a considerable interval before she and Jacob gave up all expectation of further seed by her. Slowly and unwillingly she would substitute Zilpah for herself, and there would then be a further period of three or four years, to give time for the birth of Gad and Asher: and as Jacob at this time utterly neglected Leah, we do not know but that even a longer space intervened. Moreover, Jacob had other daughters besides Dinah (chap. xxxvii. 35), and probably by these handmaids. We may well believe, therefore, that Reuben at this time was from fifteen to twenty years of age, and might be trusted to wander at his will over the wild uncultivated waste.

In the days of wheat harvest.—This is mentioned to fix the time, namely, early in May. As Laban led a settled life, he may have grown wheat, as Jacob did in Canaan (chap. xxxvii. 7), but mandrakes would most assuredly not be found on tilled land.

Mandrakes.—Heb., *love-apples.* It is generally agreed that the fruit meant is that of the *Atropa mandragora,* which ripens in May, and is of the size of a small plum, round, yellow, and full of soft pulp. The plant belongs to the same family (the *Solanaceæ*) as the potato, and the egg plant, the fruit of which is largely used as a vegetable in North America.

The mandragora has a long carrot-shaped root, from which grows a mass of leaves of a greyish colour, not unlike those of the primrose, but larger, and which lie flat upon the ground, and from among them rise blossoms, singly, of a rich purple colour. Canon Tristram (*Nat. Hist. of Bible,* p. 467) says that the fruit is not unpleasant, and that he has often eaten of it without experiencing any soporific or other bad effect. But in the East it has been, and is, the subject of many superstitions, and its Hebrew name arose from the popular belief that it was a specific against barrenness. Rachel, therefore, who still hankered after children of her own, was anxious to obtain some of the fruit, and Leah consents only upon the proffered condition that Jacob shall spend the night in her tent.

(18) **Issachar.**—Heb., *there is hire.* As is so often the case in Hebrew names, there is a double play in the word: for, first, it alluded to the strange fact that Jacob had been hired of Rachel by the mandrakes; but, secondly, Leah gives it a higher meaning, "for God," she says, "hath given me my hire." In her eyes the birth of her fifth son was a Divine reward for the self-sacrifice involved in giving her maid to Jacob, and which had been followed by years of neglect of herself. As, too, it is said that "God hearkened unto Leah," we may feel sure that she had prayed for God's blessing upon her re-union with her husband; for Calvin's objection that prayer would scarcely accompany such odious courses has little weight. Leah and Rachel were uneducated and untrained country women, whose sole anxiety was to have offspring. Leah was the most religious and best disciplined of the two; and the shame really was that she should have been forced thus to buy her husband's attentions.

(20) **Zebulun.**—Leah is more than usually obscure in the reasons she gives for this name; for she plays upon two words, which probably both belonged to the Mesopotamian *patois:* and as this was a Syriac dialect, we must look to that language for their explanation. The first is *zebed;* and here there is no difficulty. It means such presents as a father gives his daughter on her marriage, over and above those enumerated in the marriage contract. Of the second, *zabal,* there is no trace. Nor do the Syro-Arabic lexicons acknowledge in the word "Zebulun" such a sense as that of *dwelling,* given it in our margin. Bar-Ali explains it as meaning "salvation of the night, or a good dowry," and Bar-Bahlul, "a dowry of the night," both deriving it from *zebed,* a dowry, and *lun,* to pass the night. The derivation is wrong as far as concerns *lun;* for the word Zebulun is formed simply from *zebed,* the final *d* of which is changed into *l* for mere reasons of euphony. The Versions take the word *zabal* as meaning, "to be with," Vulg.; "to choose," LXX.; "to cleave to," Syriac. It occurs nowhere else, but the substantive *zebul* is not uncommon, and means *dwelling, station.*

As a woman's value in the East rises with each son, Leah now hoped for more love from her husband. Nor does she seem to have been disappointed.

(21) **Dinah.**—That is, *judgment.* (See Note on verse 6.) The birth of Dinah is chronicled because it led to Simeon and Levi forfeiting the birthright. Jacob had other daughters (chaps. xxxvii. 35, xlvi. 7), but the birth of a girl is regarded in the East as a misfortune; no feast is made, and no congratulations offered to the parents.

(22—24) **God remembered Rachel.**—Rachel's long barrenness had probably humbled and disciplined her; and, cured of her former petulance, she trusts no longer to "love-apples," but looks to God for the great blessing of children. He hearkens to her prayer, and

womb. (23) And she conceived, and bare
a son; and said, God hath taken away
my reproach: (24) and she called his name
[1]Joseph; and said, The LORD shall add
to me another son.
(25) And it came to pass, when Rachel
had born Joseph, that Jacob said unto
Laban, Send me away, that I may go
unto mine own place, and to my country.
(26) Give *me* my wives and my children,
for whom I have served thee, and let me
go: for thou knowest my service which
I have done thee.
(27) And Laban said unto him, I pray
thee, if I have found favour in thine
eyes, *tarry: for* I have learned by expe-
rience that the LORD hath blessed me
for thy sake. (28) And he said, Appoint
me thy wages, and I will give *it*.
(29) And he said unto him, Thou know-
est how I have served thee, and how thy
cattle was with me. (30) For *it was* little
which thou hadst before I *came*, and it
is *now* [2]increased unto a multitude; and
the LORD hath blessed thee [3]since my
coming: and now when shall I provide
for mine own house also?
(31) And he said, What shall I give
thee? And Jacob said, Thou shalt not
give me any thing: if thou wilt do this
thing for me, I will again feed *and* keep
thy flock. (32) I will pass through all
thy flock to day, removing from thence
all the speckled and spotted cattle, and
all the brown cattle among the sheep,
and the spotted and speckled among the
goats: and *of such* shall be my hire.
(33) So shall my righteousness answer for
me [4]in time to come, when it shall come
for my hire before thy face: every one
that *is* not speckled and spotted among
the goats, and brown among the sheep,
that shall be counted stolen with me.
(34) And Laban said, Behold, I would it
might be according to thy word.
(35) And he removed that day the he

1 That is, *Adding*.

2 Heb., *broken forth*.

3 Heb., *at my foot*.

4 Heb., *to morrow*.

---

remembers her. (Comp. 1 Sam. i. 19.) In calling his name Joseph, there is again a play upon two words, for it may be formed from the verb used in verse 23, and would then mean *he takes away;* or it may signify *he adds*, which is the meaning made prominent by Rachel. And God did add to her another son, but the boon cost her her life. As Joseph was born six or seven years before Jacob left Padan-aram, Rachel had been barren for twenty-six years. We must add that in her joy at Joseph's birth there is no trace of the ungenerous triumph over Leah so marked in her rejoicing at the birth of the sons of Bilhah; and in her trust that "Jehovah would add to her another son," she evidently had in mind the covenant promises, which a son of her own womb might now inherit. As a matter of fact, the long struggle for supremacy lay between the houses of Joseph and Judah; and Judah finally prevailed.

JACOB SERVES LABAN SIX YEARS FOR WAGES.

(25) **Jacob said unto Laban, Send me away.**—After Jacob had served Laban fourteen years for his two daughters, he continued with him for twenty years without any settled hire, receiving merely maintenance for himself and family. During most of this time he would be too encumbered with pregnant wives and young children to wish to take so long a journey. (See "Excursus on Chronology of Jacob's Life.") In these thirty-four years of service there would be time for the vast increase of Laban's wealth referred to in verse 30. But at length Joseph is born, and as his other sons were most of them grown to man's estate, as soon as Rachel was fit for the journey Jacob desired to return to his father, if for no other reason, yet because now it was time to provide for his children, and at Isaac's death he was joint heir of his property.

(27) **I have learned by experience.**—Heb., *I have divined.* The verb means, *to speak between the teeth; to mutter magical formulæ.* Others wrongly suppose that it signifies "to divine by omens taken from serpents;" and some imagine that Laban had consulted his teraphim. Words of this sort lose, at a very early date, their special signification, and all that Laban means is—"I fancy," "I conjecture." His answer is, however, most Oriental. It is courtly and complimentary, but utterly inconclusive. "If now I have found favour in thine eyes, I have a feeling that God hath blessed me for thy sake." It, of course, suggests that he would be glad if Jacob would remain with him. In verse 28 Laban comes to the point, but probably this was reached by many circuitous windings.

(30) **It was little.**—The Rabbins see proof of this in Laban's sheep being kept by a young girl like Rachel (chap. xxix. 9).

It is now increased.—Heb., *broken forth*, spread itself abroad with irresistible might. (Comp. Exod. i. 12.)

Since my coming.—Heb., *at my foot.* This answers to "before I came" (Heb., *before me*) in the first clause. "It was little that thou hadst before me, and it hath broken forth into a multitude, and God hath blessed thee behind me." Wherever I have gone, prosperity has followed in my footsteps.

(32) **The speckled and spotted cattle** (sheep).—In the East sheep are generally white, and goats black or brown. Jacob, therefore, proposes that all such shall belong to Laban, but that the parti-coloured should be his hire. By "speckled" are meant those sheep and goats that had small spots upon their coats, and by "spotted," those that had large patches of another colour. Besides these, Jacob is to have all "brown cattle," that is, *sheep*, for the word "cattle" is usually now confined to kine, which was not the case 200 years ago. This translation is taken from Rashi, but the word usually signifies *black.* Philippsohn says that black sheep are seldom seen in the East, but that sheep of a blackish-red colour are common. In verse 35 we have another word, "ring-straked," that is, having the colours in stripes. This is never the case with sheep, but goats often have their coats thus definitely marked.

(35) **And he removed.**—The question has been asked whether it was Jacob or Laban who made the

goats that were ringstraked and spotted,
and all the she goats that were speckled
and spotted, *and* every one that had
some white in it, and all the brown
among the sheep, and gave *them* into
the hand of his sons. (36) And he set
three days' journey betwixt himself and
Jacob: and Jacob fed the rest of Laban's
flocks.

(37) And Jacob took him rods of green
poplar, and of the hazel and chesnut
tree; and pilled white strakes in them,
and made the white appear which *was*
in the rods. (38) And he set the rods
which he had pilled before the flocks in
the gutters in the watering troughs
when the flocks came to drink, that they
should conceive when they came to
drink. (39) And the flocks conceived be-
fore the rods, and brought forth cattle
ringstraked, speckled, and spotted.
(40) And Jacob did separate the lambs,
and set the faces of the flocks toward
the ringstraked, and all the brown in
the flock of Laban; and he put his own
flocks by themselves, and put them not
unto Laban's cattle. (41) And it came to
pass, whensoever the stronger cattle did
conceive, that Jacob laid the rods before
the eyes of the cattle in the gutters,

---

division, and whether Jacob was to have all such sheep and goats as were parti-coloured already, or such only as should be born afterwards. The authors of the Authorised Version evidently thought that Laban himself removed all speckled sheep and goats, and kept them; but the Hebrew is by no means so much in favour of this view as their own translation. Thus, in verse 32 they insert "of such" in italics; the Hebrew distinctly says, *And it shall be my hire:* that is, every one speckled or spotted shall be *mine*, the singular number being used throughout. Next, in verse 33 they translate, *in time to come:* according to this, if the parti-coloured sheep and goats at any time produced white or black lambs, as they generally would, such would revert to Laban; the Hebrew says, *My righteousness shall answer for me to-morrow.* Jacob was to make the selection at once, but the next day Laban was to look over all those put aside, and if he found among them any white sheep, or black or brown goats, he was to regard them as stolen—that is, not merely might he take them back, but require the usual fine or compensation.

And gave them into the hand of his sons.—It has been assumed that these were Laban's sons, on the ground that Jacob's sons were not old enough to undertake the charge; but as Reuben was twenty-six, this was not the case. Jacob's flocks would have fared but badly if they had been entrusted to Laban's sons, nor could he, six years later, have escaped, had his property been in their keeping, without Laban being immediately aware of it.

(36) **He set three days' journey betwixt himself and Jacob.**—This means that Laban required that there should be an interval of between thirty and forty miles between "himself," that is, his flocks, and those of Jacob. His wealth in sheep and goats must have been enormous to require so large a separate feeding-ground; and this we learn from verse 30 had been the result of Jacob's care. The words "and Jacob fed," &c., are added to correct the natural supposition that he would at least give some part of his time and care to his own flocks, whereas it was his personal duty to attend only to those of Laban. The verse, nevertheless, is awkward, and the Syriac has probably preserved the right-reading: "And he set three days' journey between himself and Laban: and Jacob fed the flock of Laban that was left." The Samaritan and LXX. read, "between them and Jacob."

(37) **And Jacob took him rods. . . .**—Jacob's plan was to place before the ewes and she-goats at breeding time objects of a speckled colour, and as he put them at their watering-place, where everything was familiar to them, they would, with the usual curiosity of these animals, gaze upon them intently, with the result, physically certain to follow, that many of them would bear speckled young.

Poplar.—Really, the storax-tree (*styrax officinalis*). "This," says Canon Tristram, "is a very beautiful perfumed shrub, which grows abundantly on the lower hills of Palestine." The word occurs elsewhere only in Hos. iv. 13, and the idea that it was the poplar arises solely from the name signifying *white;* but this epithet is even more deserved by the storax, "which in March is covered with a sheet of white blossom, and is the predominant shrub through the dells of Carmel and Galilee" (*Natural History of the Bible*, pp. 395, 396).

Hazel.—Heb., *luz* (chap. xxviii. 19), the almond-tree (*amygdalus communis*). Dr. Tristram (*Natural History of the Bible*, p. 358) says that he never observed the true hazel wild in Southern or Central Palestine, nor was it likely to occur in Mesopotamia. The almond is one of the most common trees in Palestine.

Chesnut tree.—Heb., *armon*, the plane-tree (*platanus orientalis*). "We never," says Dr. Tristram (p. 345), "saw the chesnut in Palestine, excepting planted in orchards in Lebanon; while the plane-tree, though local, is frequent by the sides of streams and in plains." The tree is mentioned again in Ezek. xxxi. 8.

(38) **In the gutters . . .**—Heb., *in the troughs at the watering-places.* So virtually all the versions; and see Exod. ii. 16, where the word rendered here "gutters" is rightly translated *troughs.* The idea that there were gutters through which to pour the water into the troughs is utterly modern, but all travellers describe the fixed troughs put for the convenience of the cattle round the wells.

(40) **Jacob . . . set the faces of the flocks toward . . .**—As the speckled lambs and kids would for some time remain with Laban's flocks, this may perhaps mean that, when driving them to water, Jacob placed all the striped kids and dark lambs together, that, by being in a mass, they might work upon the imagination of the ewes and she-goats. Finally, after these had conceived he drove the parti-coloured young away to his own flocks.

(41, 42) **The stronger cattle . . . when the cattle were feeble.**—The words for "strong" and "feeble" are literally *bound* and *covered*, so that evidently we have technical terms, which Onkelos and the Syriac

that they might conceive among the
rods. (42) But when the cattle were
feeble, he put *them* not in: so the
feebler were Laban's, and the stronger
Jacob's. (43) And the man increased ex-
ceedingly, and had much cattle, and
maidservants, and menservants, and
camels, and asses.

CHAPTER XXXI.—(1) And he heard
the words of Laban's sons, saying, Jacob
hath taken away all that *was* our
father's; and of *that* which *was* our
father's hath he gotten all this glory.
(2) And Jacob beheld the countenance
of Laban, and, behold, it *was* not toward
him [1]as before.
(3) And the LORD said unto Jacob,
Return unto the land of thy fathers,
and to thy kindred; and I will be with
thee.
(4) And Jacob sent and called Rachel
and Leah to the field unto his flock,
(5) and said unto them, I see your
father's countenance, that it *is* not
toward me as before; but the God of
my father hath been with me. (6) And
ye know that with all my power I have
served your father. (7) And your father
hath deceived me, and changed my
wages ten times; but God suffered him
not to hurt me. (8) If he said thus, The
speckled shall be thy wages; then all
the cattle bare speckled: and if he said

1 Heb., *as yesterday and the day before.*

B.C. cir. 1739.

explain of the females at the two breeding seasons. The ewes in the spring, after the cold season, are *bound,* firmly knit together, and the lambs strong and healthy. The other word, *covered,* seems to mean seeking concealment, hiding away (Job. xxiii. 9); and therefore *faint,* its meaning in Pss. lxi. 2, cii., title (Authorised Version, *overwhelmed*), and Isa. lvii. 16 (Authorised Version, *fail*). The autumn-born lambs are of no great value, and Jacob left them to the course of nature.

(43) **The man increased exceedingly.**—Heb., *broke forth,* as in verse 30. Wool, as the chief material for clothing, is a very valuable commodity in the East, and by the sale of it Jacob would obtain means for the purchase of male and female servants and camels. The latter were especially valuable for purposes of commerce, in which Jacob evidently was actively engaged, and whence probably came his chief gains.

XXXI.

JACOB'S FLIGHT.—THE PURSUIT OF HIM BY LABAN, AND THEIR RECONCILIATION.

(1) **Laban's sons.**—No mention hitherto had been made of Laban having any other children than Leah and Rachel. If his sons were by the same wife, they would be men about fifty-five or sixty years of age. In saying that Jacob had taken "all that was their father's" they were guilty of exaggeration; for Laban was still rich, and probably, upon the whole, was a gainer by the presence of one so highly gifted as Jacob. Their word "glory" suggests that, enriched by cattle and commerce, Jacob had now become a person of great importance in the eyes of the people of Haran.

(3) **The Lord said unto Jacob.**—This is probably the revelation, more exactly described in verses 10—13, as given to Jacob in a dream. It is there ascribed to Elohim, but here to Jehovah. The narrator's purpose in this, probably, is to show that while Jacob regarded the providence that watched over him as the act of Elohim, it was really in His character of Jehovah, the covenant-God, that He thus guarded him. (See Note on chap. xxvi. 29.)

Thy kindred.—Heb., *thy birthplace,* as in chaps. xii. 1, xxiv. 4, 7, &c.

(4) **Jacob sent and called Rachel and Leah . . .**—Rachel is placed first, as the chief wife. The field was probably the pasture where Laban's flocks fed, as they were specially under Jacob's charge; and there, in the open ground, the three would run no risk of having their conversation overheard. Jacob's speech to his wives consists of three parts: first, he tells them of the change in Laban's manner towards him, and his consequent fear of violence; he next justifies his own conduct towards their father, and accuses him of repeated injustice; finally, he announces to them that he had received the Divine command to return to Canaan. As regards the second point, Jacob had undoubtedly used stratagems to increase his wages, and of this his wives must have been well aware. On the other hand, we learn that Laban had openly violated the terms of the bargain; and, whereas all the parti-coloured kids and lambs were to belong to Jacob, no sooner did they increase beyond expectation, than Laban, first, would give him only the speckled, the most common kind, and finally, only the ring-straked, which were the most rare. Of course Jacob would keep all the sheep and goats which he had once made over to the charge of his sons; it would be the additions to them from Laban's flocks which were thus diminished.

As regards the vision, it has been thought that Jacob has compressed two occurrences into one narrative; but for insufficient reasons. It was at the breeding-time (verse 10) that Jacob saw the vision, with its two-fold lesson: the first, that the multiplication of his wages had been God's gift, and not the result of his own artifices; the second, that this bestowal of wealth was to enable him to return to Canaan. His wives heartily concurred in his purpose, but it was not till the time of sheep-shearing came (verse 19) that he effected his escape. But there is no difficulty in this delay. How large the household of Jacob had become we learn from the greatness of the present he selected for Esau (chap. xxxii. 13—15), and it could not be removed without preparation. The servants and camels must be gathered in from their trading expeditions, tents must be got ready, and camels' furniture and other requisites obtained; finally, they could not start until the ewes were fit for their journey, and only at a time of year when there would be herbage for the cattle on the march. We find that when they reached the Jabbok, Jacob's flocks and herds were "giving suck" (chap. xxxiii. 13 in the Heb.), but it is not easy to calculate the interval between this and the time when they commenced their journey.

(7) **Ten times.**—That is, a good many times.

thus, The ringstraked shall be thy hire;
then bare all the cattle ringstraked.
(9) Thus God hath taken away the cattle
of your father, and given *them* to me.
(10) And it came to pass at the time that
the cattle conceived, that I lifted up
mine eyes, and saw in a dream, and,
behold, the [1]rams which leaped upon
the cattle *were* ringstraked, speckled,
and grisled. (11) And the angel of God
spake unto me in a dream, *saying*,
Jacob: And I said, Here *am* I. (12) And
he said, Lift up now thine eyes, and
see, all the rams which leap upon the
cattle *are* ringstraked, speckled, and
grisled: for I have seen all that Laban
doeth unto thee. (13) I *am* the God of
Beth-el, [a]where thou anointedst the
pillar, *and* where thou vowedst a vow
unto me: now arise, get thee out from
this land, and return unto the land of
thy kindred.

(14) And Rachel and Leah answered
and said unto him, *Is there* yet any
portion or inheritance for us in our
father's house? (15) Are we not counted
of him strangers? for he hath sold us,
and hath quite devoured also our money.
(16) For all the riches which God hath
taken from our father, that *is* our's, and
our children's: now then, whatsoever
God hath said unto thee, do.

(17) Then Jacob rose up, and set his
sons and his wives upon camels; (18) and
he carried away all his cattle, and all
his goods which he had gotten, the
cattle of his getting, which he had
gotten in Padan-aram, for to go to
Isaac his father in the land of Canaan.
(19) And Laban went to shear his sheep:
and Rachel had stolen the [2]images that
were her father's. (20) And Jacob stole
away [3]unawares to Laban the Syrian,
in that he told him not that he fled.
(21) So he fled with all that he had; and
he rose up, and passed over the river,

1 Or, *he goats.*

a ch. 28. 18.

2 Heb., *teraphim.*

3 Heb., *the heart of Laban.*

---

(10) **Rams.**—Heb., *he-goats.* The Authorised Version has made the alteration, because the word rendered "cattle" is really *sheep* (and so in verses 8, 12, &c.); but, like our word *flock*, it also included goats.

(12) **Grisled.**—That is, covered with spots like hailstones, the word "grisled" being derived from the French *grêle*, hail. Others derive the word from *gris*, *grisaille*, grey.

(13) **I am the God of Beth-el.**—The angel of Elohim (verse 11) was the speaker, but the words were those of God (1 Thess. ii. 13; Heb. i. 1). With this verse compare chap. xxviii. 13.

(15) **He hath sold us.**—There is a marked asperity towards their father in the answer of Jacob's wives, and not only the petted Rachel but the neglected Leah joins in it. Now, though his sale of them to Jacob had been more open than Oriental good manners usually allowed, and though he seems to have acted meanly in giving no portion with them, yet these were old sores, long since healed and forgiven. Laban must have been stingy, grasping, and over-reaching in recent times, to have kept the memory of old wrongs so fresh in the minds of his daughters.

(17, 18) **Jacob rose up.**—This was the final result of Jacob's deliberation with his wives, but it did not take place till the time of sheep-shearing. Jacob must have prepared his plans very carefully to be able to leave none of his wealth behind; but he would be greatly helped in this by the fact that his own head-quarters were thirty or forty miles distant from Haran (chap. xxx. 36).

(19) **Laban went to shear his sheep.**—The sheep-shearing was a joyous time, when the hard toil of the shearers was relieved by feasting (1 Sam. xxv. 8). Laban's flocks, apparently, were also at some distance from Haran, and his sons and men-servants would all be with him, busily occupied in the work. Apparently, too, Laban's wealth was not seriously diminished, though it had not of late increased; and his repeated change of the hire proves that he was quite able to take care of himself. But why was not Jacob present, as he had chief charge of Laban's flocks? Possibly, he was expected there, and was missed; but, more probably, as the result of the growing estrangement between them, caused by the too rapid increase of Jacob's riches, Laban and his sons had gradually taken the management of their flocks into their own hands.

Images.—Heb., *teraphim*, called Laban's gods in verse 30, and we find that their worship continued throughout the Old Testament history. Micah sets up teraphim, as well as a molten and a graven image, and an ephod (Judges xviii. 17). Though in 1 Sam. xv. 23, where the Authorised Version has *idolatry*, teraphim are spoken of in strong terms of condemnation, yet Michal possessed them, and placed them in David's bed. We gather from this that they had a head shaped like that of a man, but, probably, a dwarf trunk, as she seems to have put more than one in the bed to represent David's body (1 Sam. xix. 13). So, too, here Rachel hides them under the camel's furniture (verse 34), which proves that they, in this case, were of no great size. In the history of the thorough reformation carried out by King Josiah we find the mention of teraphim among the things put away (2 Kings xxiii. 24). We learn, nevertheless, from Zech. x. 2, that they were still used for divination; and from Hos. iii. 4 that both pillars and teraphim had long been objects of ordinary superstition among the ten tribes. As Nebuchadnezzar divines by them (Ezek. xxi. 21) they were possibly of Chaldæan origin; and, probably, were not so much worshipped as used for consultation. Women seem to have been most given to their service, and probably regarded them as charms, and told fortunes by them; and here Rachel stole them upon the supposition that they would bring prosperity to her and her husband.

(20) **Jacob stole away unawares.**—Heb., *stole the heart.* But the heart was regarded by the Hebrews as the seat of the intellect, and so *to steal a man's understanding*, like the similar phrase in Greek, means to elude his observation.

(21) **The river.**—The Euphrates.

and set his face *toward* the mount
Gilead.
(22) And it was told Laban on the
third day that Jacob was fled. (23) And
he took his brethren with him, and
pursued after him seven days' journey;
and they overtook him in the mount
Gilead. (24) And God came to Laban
the Syrian in a dream by night, and
said unto him, Take heed that thou
speak not to Jacob [1]either good or bad.
(25) Then Laban overtook Jacob. Now
Jacob had pitched his tent in the
mount: and Laban with his brethren
pitched in the mount of Gilead.
(26) And Laban said to Jacob, What
hast thou done, that thou hast stolen
away unawares to me, and carried away
my daughters, as captives *taken* with
the sword? (27) Wherefore didst thou
flee away secretly, and [2]steal away from
me; and didst not tell me, that I might
have sent thee away with mirth, and
with songs, with tabret, and with harp?
(28) And hast not suffered me to kiss my
sons and my daughters? thou hast now
done foolishly in *so* doing. (29) It is in
the power of my hand to do you hurt:
but the God of your father spake unto
me yesternight, saying, Take thou heed
that thou speak not to Jacob either
good or bad. (30) And now, *though* thou
wouldest needs be gone, because thou
sore longedst after thy father's house,
yet wherefore hast thou stolen my
gods?
(31) And Jacob answered and said to
Laban, Because I was afraid: for I
said, Peradventure thou wouldest take
by force thy daughters from me.
(32) With whomsoever thou findest thy
gods, let him not live: before our

1 Heb., *from good to bad.*

2 Heb., *hast stolen me.*

Mount Gilead.—Gilead, *the region of rock,* was the mountainous frontier between the Aramean and Canaanite races. The form of the word is so remote from ordinary Hebrew that we have in it, probably, a very old appellation of this region; and Jacob apparently plays upon it in his name *Galeed* (verse 47).

(23) **His brethren.**—As Jacob, who had no relatives with him except his sons, applies this term in verse 46 to his followers, it is, probably, an honourable way of describing retainers, who were freemen and of a higher class than men-servants.

Seven days' journey.—The route chosen by Jacob was apparently the more easterly one, past Tadmor, and through the Hauran, leaving Damascus to the west. The hill, which subsequently was called Mount Gilead, lay to the south of the Jabbok; but as Mahanaim, reached some days after the meeting with Laban, is to the north of that river, the word Gilead was evidently applied to the whole of the region of chalk cliffs on the east of the Jordan. This is made certain by the fact that Laban overtook Jacob in seven days. But as the distance from Haran to the most northerly part of this country (afterwards assigned to the half-tribe of Manasseh) was fully three hundred miles, it would require hard riding on the part of Laban and his brethren to enable them to overtake Jacob, even on the borders of this region. There is no difficulty about Jacob's movements. His flocks were pastured at so remote a distance from Haran that it would be easy for him to send them in detachments to the ford of the Euphrates, distant about sixty or seventy miles; he would make all the arrangements with his four elder sons and trusty servants, and, probably, even see them across the ford himself, and would return to Haran to fetch his wives and younger children only when all was well advanced. Finally, when Laban goes to a distance, in another direction, for his sheep-shearing, Jacob "sets his sons and his wives upon camels," and follows with the utmost speed. They would have remained quietly at Haran to the last, to avoid suspicion, and, excepting Leah's four elder sons, the rest would have been too young to be of much use. When Jacob, with his wives, overtook the cattle, they would, probably, not travel more than ten or twelve miles a day; but three days passed before Laban learned what had taken place, and a couple of days at least must have been spent in returning to Haran and preparing for the pursuit. Thus Jacob had reached Canaanite ground—a matter of very considerable importance—before his father-in-law overtook him.

(24) **Either good or bad.**—Heb., *from good to bad:* a proverbial expression, rightly translated in the Authorised Version, but conveying the idea of a more absolute prohibition than the phrase used in chap. xxiv. 50.

(26—30) **Laban said . . .**—Laban reproaches Jacob, first, for carrying away his daughters secretly, which was an affront to them (verse 26) and an injury to his own feelings (verse 28); secondly, he tells him that he should have punished him but for the Divine warning; lastly, he accuses him of stealing his teraphim.

Captives . . .—Heb., *captives of the sword,* women carried off in war as spoil.

(28) **My sons.**—That is, my grandsons.

(29) **It is in the power of my hand.**—This is the rendering here of all the versions, and is confirmed by Deut. xxviii. 32; Neh. v. 5; Micah ii. 1; but Keil and Knobel wish to translate, "My hand is for God." This comes to the same thing in an impious way, as the sense would be, "My hand is an El, a god, for me," and enables me to do what I will.

The speech of Laban is half true and half false. He would have wished not to part with Jacob at all, but to have recovered from him as much as he could of his property. But if he was to go, he would have liked outward appearances maintained; and, probably, he had an affection for his daughters and their children, though not so strong as to counterbalance his selfishness. His character, like that of all men, is a mixture of good and evil.

(31, 32) **Jacob answered.**—Jacob gives the true reason for his flight; after which, indignant at the charge of theft, he returns, in his anger, as rash an answer about the teraphim as Joseph's brethren subsequently did about the stolen cup (chap. xliv. 9).

Let him not live.—The Rabbins regard this as a prophecy, fulfilled in Rachel's premature death. Its

brethren discern thou what *is* thine with me, and take *it* to thee. For Jacob knew not that Rachel had stolen them.

(33) And Laban went into Jacob's tent, and into Leah's tent, and into the two maidservants' tents; but he found *them* not. Then went he out of Leah's tent, and entered into Rachel's tent. (34) Now Rachel had taken the images, and put them in the camel's furniture, and sat upon them. And Laban [1] searched all the tent, but found *them* not. (35) And she said to her father, Let it not displease my lord that I cannot rise up before thee; for the custom of women *is* upon me. And he searched, but found not the images.

(36) And Jacob was wroth, and chode with Laban: and Jacob answered and said to Laban, What *is* my trespass? what *is* my sin, that thou hast so hotly pursued after me? (37) Whereas thou hast [2]searched all my stuff, what hast thou found of all thy household stuff? set *it* here before my brethren and thy brethren, that they may judge betwixt us both. (38) This twenty years *have* I *been* with thee; thy ewes and thy she goats have not cast their young, and the rams of thy flock have I not eaten. (39) That which was torn *of beasts* I brought not unto thee; I bare the loss of it; of [a]my hand didst thou require it, *whether* stolen by day, or stolen by night. (40) *Thus* I was; in the day the drought consumed me, and the frost by night; and my sleep departed from mine eyes. (41) Thus have I been twenty years in thy house; I served thee fourteen years for thy two daughters, and six years for thy cattle: and thou hast changed my wages ten times. (42) Except the God of my father, the God of Abraham, and the fear of Isaac, had been with me, surely thou hadst sent me away now empty. God hath seen mine affliction and the labour of my hands, and rebuked *thee* yesternight.

(43) And Laban answered and said unto Jacob, *These* daughters *are* my daughters, and *these* children *are* my children, and *these* cattle *are* my cattle, and all that thou seest *is* mine: and what can I do this day unto these my daughters, or unto their children which they have born? (44) Now therefore come thou, let us make a covenant, I and thou; and let it be for a witness between me and thee.

(45) And Jacob took a stone, and set it up *for* a pillar. (46) And Jacob said unto his brethren, Gather stones; and they took stones, and made an heap: and they did eat there upon the heap. (47) And Laban called it [3]Jegar-sahadutha: but Jacob called it Galeed.

(48) And Laban said, This heap *is* a

1 Heb., *felt.*

2 Heb., *felt.*

a Ex. 22. 12.

3 That is, *The heap of witness.*

---

more simple meaning is, *I yield him up to thee even to be put to death.*

(34) **The camel's furniture.**—That is, the camel's saddle. It is now made of wicker-work, and is protected by curtains and a canopy. Probably Rachel's was far simpler; and as the teraphim seem to have had heads shaped like those of a man, and dwarf bodies, they would easily be crammed under it.

(36) **Jacob was wroth.**—Naturally he regarded the accusation about the teraphim as a mere device for searching his goods, and when nothing was found gave free vent to his indignation.

(40) **The frost by night.**—From September to May the nights in the East are usually cold, and the change from great heat by day to a freezing temperature as soon as the sun sets is very trying to health.

(41) **Thus have I been . . .**—Heb., *This for me twenty years in thy house,* but taken in connection with the preceding *this,* in verse 38, the meaning is "During the one twenty years that I was with thee, thy ewes, &c.," upon which follows "During the other twenty years that were *for me* in thy house, I served thee, &c." (See Note on chap. xxix. 27, and Excursus on the Chronology of Jacob's Life.)

(42) **The fear of Isaac.**—That is, the object of Isaac's worship. The reason given by the Jewish Commentators for this remarkable way of describing the Deity whom Isaac served is that, as his father was still alive, Jacob would have been wanting in reverence, if he had spoken of God as "Isaac's God," even though Jehovah had condescended so to call Himself (chap. xxviii. 13).

(43) **Laban answered . . .**—Laban does not attempt any reply to Jacob's angry invectives, but answers affectionately. Why should he wish to injure Jacob, and send him away empty? All that he had was still Laban's in the best of senses; for were not Rachel and Leah his daughters? And were not their children his grandsons? How was it possible that he could wish to rob them? He proposes, therefore, that they should make a covenant, by which Jacob should bind himself to deal kindly with his daughters, and to take no other wife; while he promises for himself that he would do Jacob no wrong. Jacob therefore sets up a large stone, as a pillar and memorial; and Laban subsequently does the same; while, probably between the two hills on which they had severally encamped (verse 25), they collect a large mass of other stones, on which they feast together, in token of friendship (chap. xxvi. 30).

(47) **Jegar-sahadutha.**—These are two Syriac words of the same meaning as Gal-'eed, *Heap of Witness.* A Syriac (or Aramaic) dialect was most probably the ordinary language of the people in Mesopotamia, but it

witness between me and thee this day.
Therefore was the name of it called
Galeed; (49) and [1]Mizpah; for he said,
The LORD watch between me and thee,
when we are absent one from another.
(50) If thou shalt afflict my daughters, or
if thou shalt take *other* wives beside my
daughters, no man *is* with us; see, God
is witness betwixt me and thee. (51) And
Laban said to Jacob, Behold this heap,
and behold *this* pillar, which I have
cast betwixt me and thee; (52) this heap
be witness, and *this* pillar *be* witness,
that I will not pass over this heap to
thee, and that thou shalt not pass over
this heap and this pillar unto me, for
harm. (53) The God of Abraham, and
the God of Nahor, the God of their
father, judge betwixt us. And Jacob
sware by the fear of his father Isaac.
(54) Then Jacob [2]offered sacrifice upon
the mount, and called his brethren to
eat bread: and they did eat bread, and
tarried all night in the mount. (55) And
early in the morning Laban rose up,
and kissed his sons and his daughters,
and blessed them: and Laban departed,
and returned unto his place.

CHAPTER XXXII.—(1) And Jacob
went on his way, and the angels of God
met him. (2) And when Jacob saw them,
he said, This *is* God's host: and he called
the name of that place [3]Mahanaim.
(3) And Jacob sent messengers before
him to Esau his brother unto the land
of Seir, the [4]country of Edom. (4) And
he commanded them, saying, Thus shall
ye speak unto my lord Esau; Thy
servant Jacob saith thus, I have
sojourned with Laban, and stayed
there until now: (5) and I have oxen,

1 That is, *A beacon*, or, *watchtower*.

2 Or, *killed beasts*.

3 That is, *Two hosts*, or, *camps*.

4 Heb., *field*.

---

seems plain that Laban and his family also spoke Hebrew, not merely from his calling the place Mizpah, a Hebrew word, but from the names given by his daughters to their children.

(49) **Mizpah.**—That is, *Watchtower*. There is, probably, a play in this name upon the pillar which Laban proceeds to set up, and which in Hebrew is *Mazebah*. In the reason given for the name Laban calls Jacob's God *Jehovah*, an appellation which he must have learned from Jacob, and which proves not merely that he had some knowledge of Hebrew but that he and Jacob had talked together upon religious subjects, and that he was not a mere idolater, though he did call the teraphim his gods.

(53) **Judge.**—The verb is plural, "be *judges*," and as Laban thus joins the name Elohim with a verb plural, it seems as if he regarded Abraham's Elohim as different from the Elohim of Nahor. We ought, therefore, to translate *the gods of their father*. Apparently, he thought that Abraham took one of Terah's Elohim, and Nahor another. His views were thus polytheistic; and so, generally, the ancients regarded the gods as local beings, with powers limited to certain districts. Jacob swears by the one Being who was the sole object of Isaac's worship. (See Note on chap. xx. 13.)

(54) **Jacob offered sacrifice.**—The meaning is, that Jacob slaughtered cattle, and made a feast: but as animals originally were killed only for sacrifice, and flesh was eaten on no other occasion, the Hebrew language has no means of distinguishing the two acts.

XXXII.

(1) **Jacob went on his way.**—The meeting of Jacob and Laban had been on the dividing line between the Aramean and the Canaanite lands, and consequently at a spot where Laban would have found no allies in the natives, but rather the contrary. Delivered thus from danger from behind, Jacob now takes his journey through the country that was to be the heritage of his seed, and doubtless he was harassed by many anxious thoughts; for Esau might prove a fiercer foe than Laban. It was fit therefore that he should receive encouragement, and so after some days, probably after about a week's journey southward, he has a vision of "angels of God."

Angels of God.—Numberless conjectures have been hazarded as to who were these "messengers of Elohim," and how they were seen by Jacob. Some, taking the word in its lower sense, think they were prophets; others, that it was a caravan, which gave Jacob timely information about Esau's presence in Seir; others, that it was a body of men sent by Rebekah to aid Jacob in repelling Esau. More probably, as Jacob on his road to Padan-aram had been assured of God's watchful care of him by the vision of the angels ascending and descending the stairs, so now also in a dream he sees the angels encamped on each side of him, to assure him of protection against his brother.

(2) **Mahanaim.**—That is, *the two camps*, his own and that of the angels; or, possibly, two camps of angels, one on either side of him. Mahanaim was in the tribe of Gad, and became an important town. (See 2 Sam. ii. 8, xvii. 24; 1 Kings iv. 14.)

JACOB'S RECONCILIATION WITH ESAU.
(Chap. xxxii. 3—xxxiii. 16.)

(3) **Jacob sent messengers.**—As Jacob travelled homewards to Hebron the news somehow reached him that Esau, at the head of a large body of retainers, was engaged in an expedition against the Horites. These, as we have seen on chap. xiv. 6, were a miserable race of cave-men, utterly unable to cope with Esau and his trained servants. We learn from chap. xxxvi. 6 that Esau's home was still with Isaac at Hebron, and probably this was a mere marauding expedition, like that against the people of Gath, which a century later cost Ephraim the lives of so many of his sons (1 Chron. vii. 21); but it revealed to Esau the weakness of the inhabitants, and also that the land was admirably adapted for his favourite pursuit of hunting. He seems also to have taken a Horite wife (chap. xxxvi. 5), and being thus connected with the country, upon Isaac's death he willingly removed into it, and it then became "the country," Heb. *the field of Edom*. Its other name, *Seir*, *i.e.* rough, hairy, shows that it was then covered with forests, and the term *field* that it

and asses, flocks, and menservants, and
womenservants: and I have sent to tell
my lord, that I may find grace in thy
sight.
(6) And the messengers returned to
Jacob, saying, We came to thy brother
Esau, and also he cometh to meet thee,
and four hundred men with him.
(7) Then Jacob was greatly afraid and
distressed: and he divided the people
that *was* with him, and the flocks, and
herds, and the camels, into two bands;
(8) and said, If Esau come to the one
company, and smite it, then the other
company which is left shall escape.
(9) And Jacob said, O God of my father
Abraham, and God of my father Isaac,
the LORD which saidst unto me, [a]Return
unto thy country, and to thy kindred,
and I will deal well with thee: (10) [1]I am
not worthy of the least of all the mercies,
and of all the truth, which thou hast
shewed unto thy servant; for with my
staff I passed over this Jordan; and
now I am become two bands. (11) Deliver
me, I pray thee, from the hand of my
brother, from the hand of Esau: for I
fear him, lest he will come and smite
me, *and* the mother [2]with the children.
(12) And thou saidst, I will surely do
thee good, and make thy seed as the
sand of the sea, which cannot be
numbered for multitude.
(13) And he lodged there that same
night; and took of that which came to
his hand a present for Esau his brother;
(14) two hundred she goats, and twenty
he goats, two hundred ewes, and twenty
rams, (15) thirty milch camels with their
colts, forty kine, and ten bulls, twenty
she asses, and ten foals. (16) And he de-
livered *them* into the hand of his ser-

a ch. 31. 13.

1 Heb., *I am less than all, &c.*

2 Heb., *upon.*

---

was an uncultivated region. It was entirely in the spirit of the adventurous Esau to make this expedition, and on his father's death to prefer this wild land to the peaceful pastures at Hebron, where he was surrounded by powerful tribes of Amorites and Hittites. The land of Seir was a hundred miles distant from Mahanaim, but Esau apparently had been moving up through what were afterwards the countries of Moab and Ammon, and was probably, when Jacob sent his messengers, at no very great distance. At all events, Jacob remained at Mahanaim till his brother was near, when he crossed the brook Jabbok, and went to meet him.

(7) **Jacob was greatly afraid.**—Jacob's message to his brother had been very humble, for he calls Esau his lord, and himself a servant. He hopes also to "find grace in his sight," and by enumerating his wealth shows that he required no aid, nor need claim even a share of Isaac's property. But Esau had given no answer, being probably undecided as to the manner in which he would receive his brother. The "four hundred men with him" formed probably only a part of the little army with which he had invaded the Horite territory. Some would be left with the spoil which he had gathered, but he took so many with him as to place Jacob completely in his power. And Jacob's extreme distress, in spite of the Divine encouragement repeatedly given him, shows that his faith was very feeble; but it was real, and therefore he sought refuge from his terror in prayer.

(9) **Jacob said.**—Jacob's prayer, the first recorded in the Bible, is remarkable for combining great earnestness with simplicity. After addressing God as the Elohim of his fathers, he draws closer to Him as the Jehovah who had personally commanded him to return to his birthplace (chap. xxxi. 13). And next, while acknowledging his own unworthiness, he shows that already he had been the recipient of the Divine favour, and prays earnestly for deliverance, using the touching words "and smite me, mother upon children." His mind does not rest upon his own death, but upon the terrible picture of the mother, trying with all a mother's love to protect her offspring, and slain upon their bodies. In Hosea x. 14 this is spoken of as the most cruel and pitiable of the miseries of war. But finally he feels that this sad end is impossible; for he has God's promise that his seed shall be numerous as the sand of the sea. In prayer to man it may be ungenerous to remind another of promises made and favours expected, but with God each first act of grace and mercy is the pledge of continued favour.

(13) **He lodged there.**—That is, at Mahanaim. On the first news of Esau's approach in so hostile a manner, Jacob had divided his possessions into two main divisions, in the hope of saving at least one. He now, quieted by his prayer, makes more exact arrangements, selects a present for Esau of five hundred and fifty head of cattle, sends them forward with intervals between, that repeated impressions might soften his brother's fierce mood, sees all his followers safely across the Jabbok, and remains alone behind to pray. As he thus placed everything in Esau's power, faith seems to have regained the ascendancy over his fears, though he still takes every prudent measure for the safety of those whom he loved.

Of that which came to his hand.—Heb., *of that which came in his hand.* Some Jewish interpreters take the phrase literally, and suppose that it was precious stones; more truly it means "what he possessed," or what he had with him. The phrase "which came to his hand" would imply that he made no selection, but took what came first in his way.

(14, 15) **Goats—ewes—camels—kine—asses.**—As the kinds of cattle are arranged according to their value, it is remarkable that kine should be prized above camels; for the milk of cows was regarded as of little worth. This high estimation of them, therefore, must have arisen from an increased regard for agriculture, the ploughing being done in the East by oxen. Asses of course come last, as being the animal used by chieftains for riding, and therefore prized as matters of luxury. (See chaps. xii. 16; Judg. v. 10.) Jacob selected "milch camels" because their milk forms a valuable part of the daily food of the Arabs.

(16) **A space.**—Heb., *a breathing place.* These paration of the droves would be a matter of course, as each

vants, every drove by themselves; and
said unto his servants, Pass over before
me, and put a space betwixt drove and
drove. (17) And he commanded the fore-
most, saying, When Esau my brother
meeteth thee, and asketh thee, saying,
Whose *art* thou? and whither goest thou?
and whose *are* these before thee? (18) Then
thou shalt say, *They be* thy servant
Jacob's; it *is* a present sent unto my
lord Esau: and, behold, also he *is* be-
hind us. (19) And so commanded he the
second, and the third, and all that fol-
lowed the droves, saying, On this man-
ner shall ye speak unto Esau, when ye
find him. (20) And say ye moreover,
Behold, thy servant Jacob *is* behind us.
For he said, I will appease him with
the present that goeth before me, and
afterward I will see his face; perad-
venture he will accept [1]of me.
(21) So went the present over before
him: and himself lodged that night in
the company. (22) And he rose up that
night, and took his two wives, and his
two womenservants, and his eleven
sons, and passed over the ford Jabbok.
(23) And he took them, and [2]sent them
over the brook, and sent over that he
had.
(24) And Jacob was left alone; and
there wrestled a man with him until the
[3]breaking of the day. (25) And when he
saw that he prevailed not against him,
he touched the hollow of his thigh; and
the hollow of Jacob's thigh was out of
joint, as he wrestled with him. (26) And
he said, Let me go, for the day breaketh.

1 Heb., *my face.*

2 Heb., *caused to pass.*

3 Heb., *ascending of the morning.*

---

kind would travel peaceably onward only by itself. But Jacob rightly concluded that the repeated acknowledgment of Esau as his lord, added to the great value of the gift, would fill his brother's heart with friendly feelings, and perhaps therefore he put a longer space than usual between the successive droves.

(20) **I will appease him.**—The Heb. literally is, *he said I will cover his face with the offering that goeth before my face, and afterwards I will see his face; peradventure he will lift up my face.* The covering of the face of the offended person, so that he could no longer see the offence, became the usual legal word for making an atonement (Lev. ix. 7, &c.). For the "offering" (Heb., *minchah*) see Gen. iv. 3; and for "the lifting up of the face," *ibid.* 7.

(22) **The ford Jabbok.**—Heb., *the ford of the Jabbok.* This river, now called the Wady Zerba or Blue Torrent, formed afterwards the boundary between the tribes of Manasseh and Gad. It flows through a deep ravine, with so rapid a current as to make the crossing of it a matter of difficulty. Dr. Tristram (*Land of Israel*, p. 558) says that the water reached his horse's girths when he rode through the ford.

(23) **The brook.**—Really, the ravine or valley; Arab., *wady.* Jacob, whose administrative powers were of a very high character, sees his wives, children, and cattle not only through the ford, but across the valley on to the high ground beyond. Staying himself to the very last, he is left alone on the south side of the torrent, but still in the ravine, across which the rest had taken their way. The definite proof that Jacob remained on the south side lies in the fact that Peniel belonged to the tribe of Gad; but, besides this, there could be no reason why he should recross the rapid river when once he had gone through it, and probably the idea has risen from taking the word *brook* in verse 23 in too narrow a sense. Really it is the word translated *valley* in chap. xxvi. 17, but is used only of such valleys or ravines as have been formed by the action of a mountain torrent. When Jacob had seen his wives and herds safe on the top of the southern ridge, the deep valley would be the very place for this solitary struggle. This ravine, we are told, has a width of from four to six miles.

(24) **There wrestled.**—This verb, *abak*, occurs only here, and without doubt it was chosen because of its resemblance to the name Jabbok. Its probable derivation is from a word signifying *dust*, because wrestlers were quickly involved in a cloud of dust, or because, as was the custom in Greece, they rubbed their bodies with it.

A man.—Such he seemed to be to Jacob; but Hosea (chap. xii. 4) calls him an angel; and, in verse 30, Jacob recognises in him a manifestation of the Deity, as Hagar had done before, when an angel appeared to her (chap. xvi. 13). There is no warrant for regarding the angel as an incarnation of Deity, any more than in the case of Manoah (Judges xiii. 22); but it was a manifestation of God mediately by His messenger, and was one of the many signs indicative of a more complete manifestation by the coming of the Word in the flesh. The opposite idea of many modern commentators, that the narrative is an allegory, is contradicted by the attendant circumstances, especially by the change of Jacob's name, and his subsequent lameness, to which national testimony was borne by the customs of the Jews.

(25) **The hollow of Jacob's thigh was out of joint.**—The hollow is in the Hebrew the pan or socket into which the end of the thigh bone is inserted, and the verb more probably signifies that it was sprained from the over-tension of the muscles in the wrestling. But, in spite of his sprained tendons, Jacob still resisted, and could not be thrown down, and the angel, unable to gain any further advantage, at last acknowledges Jacob's superiority, and at sunrise craves permission to depart.

(26) **Let me go . . .**—Heb., *send me away, for the gleam of morning has gone up.* The asking of permission to depart was the acknowledgment of defeat. The struggle must end at daybreak, because Jacob must now go to do his duty; and the wrestling had been for the purpose of giving him courage, and enabling him to meet danger and difficulty in the power of faith. A curious Jewish idea is that the angel was that one whose duty it was to defend and protect Esau. By the aid of his own protecting angel Jacob, they say, had overpowered him, and had won the birthright and the precedence as "Israel, a prince with God and man."

And he said, [a]I will not let thee go, ex-
cept thou bless me. (27) And he said
unto him, What *is* thy name? And he
said, Jacob. (28) And he said, [b]Thy
name shall be called no more Jacob, but
Israel: for as a prince hast thou power
with God and with men, and hast pre-
vailed. (29) And Jacob asked *him*, and
said, Tell *me*, I pray thee, thy name.
And he said, Wherefore *is* it *that* thou
dost ask after my name? And he
blessed him there. (30) And Jacob called
the name of the place [1]Peniel: for I
have seen God face to face, and my life
is preserved.

(31) And as he passed over Penuel the
sun rose upon him, and he halted upon
his thigh. (32) Therefore the children
of Israel eat not *of* the sinew which
shrank, which *is* upon the hollow of the
thigh, unto this day: because he touched
the hollow of Jacob's thigh in the sinew
that shrank.

CHAPTER XXXIII.—(1) And Jacob
lifted up his eyes, and looked, and, be-
hold, Esau came, and with him four
hundred men. And he divided the
children unto Leah, and unto Rachel,
and unto the two handmaids. (2) And
he put the handmaids and their children
foremost, and Leah and her children
after, and Rachel and Joseph hinder-
most. (3) And he passed over before
them, and bowed himself to the ground
seven times, until he came near to his
brother. (4) And Esau ran to meet him,
and embraced him, and fell on his neck,
and kissed him: and they wept. (5) And
he lifted up his eyes, and saw the women
and the children; and said, Who *are*
those [2]with thee? And he said, The
children which God hath graciously
given thy servant. (6) Then the hand-
maidens came near, they and their chil-
dren, and they bowed themselves. (7) And
Leah also with her children came near,
and bowed themselves: and after came
Joseph near and Rachel, and they
bowed themselves.

a Hos. 12. 4.

b ch. 35. 10.

1 That is, *The face of God.*

2 Heb., *to thee.*

Except thou bless me.—The vanquished must yield the spoil to the victor; and Jacob, who had gradually become aware that the being who was wrestling with him was something more than man, asks of him, as his ransom, a blessing.

(28) **Israel.**—That is, *a prince of God*, or, *one powerful with God.* (See Note on chap. xvii. 15.) Esau had given a bad meaning to the name of Jacob, nor had it been undeserved. But a change has now come over Jacob's character, and he is henceforth no longer the crafty schemer who was ever plotting for his own advantage, but one humble and penitent, who can trust himself and all he has in God's hands. The last words signify, *for thou art a prince with God and men;* or possibly, *for thou hast striven with God and men.*

(29) **Wherefore . . .**—In much the same manner the angel refuses to tell Manoah his name (Judges xiii. 18). Probably, however, in the blessing which followed there was a clear proof that Jacob's opponent was a Divine personage.

(30) **Peniel.**—Elsewhere *Penuel,* and so probably it should be read here. It means, "the face of God." For the rest of the verse see Note on chap. xvi. 13.

(31) **As he passed over Penuel.**—Rather, *as he passed Penuel.* It was the place where he had wrestled, and as soon as the angel left him he proceeded onwards to rejoin his wives. It appears, from what is here said, that it was not till he tried to walk that he found out that he was lame. As his sinews grew cool, the injury to his hip-joint showed itself.

(32) **The sinew which shrank.**—This translation has much authority in its favour, as the LXX. render *the sinew that became numb,* and the Vulgate *the sinew that withered.* More probably, however, it is the proper name for the large tendon which takes its origin from the spinal cord, and extends down the thigh unto the ankle. Technically it is called *nervus ischiaticus,* and by the Greeks was named *tendo Achillis,* because it reaches to the heel. Jewish commentators notice that this was the second special ordinance imposed upon the race of Abraham, circumcision having been enjoined upon them by God, while this grew out of an historical event in the life of their progenitor, to the reality of which it bears remarkable testimony.

XXXIII.

(3) **He passed over before them.**—While providing some small chance of escape for his wives and children, arranged according to their rank, Jacob manfully went first and placed himself entirely in Esau's power. He endeavoured, nevertheless, by his sevenfold obeisance in acknowledgment of Esau's superiority, to propitiate him; for the cause of the quarrel had been Jacob's usurpation of Esau's right of precedence as the first born. This bowing in the East is made by bending the body forward with the arms crossed, and the right hand held over the heart.

(4) **Esau ran to meet him.**—Whatever may have been Esau's intention when he started, no sooner does he see his brother than the old times of their childhood return to his heart, and he is overcome with love; nor does he ever seem afterwards to have wavered in his fraternal affection. We have had a proof before (in chap. xxvii. 38) of Esau being a man of warm feelings, and similarly now he is again overmastered by his loving impulses. It is curious that the Hebrew word for "he kissed him" has had what are called extraordinary vowels attached to it, and the Masorites are supposed to signify thereby that Esau's kiss was not a sign of genuine love. For such an ill-natured supposition there is no warrant whatsoever.

(5) **Who are those with thee?**—Heb., *to thee,* that is, Who are these belonging to thee? Esau noticed that they were Jacob's family, and asked for fuller information concerning them.

(8) And he said, [1] What *meanest* thou
by all this drove which I met? And he
said, *These are* to find grace in the sight
of my lord. (9) And Esau said, I have
enough, my brother; [2] keep that thou
hast unto thyself. (10) And Jacob said,
Nay, I pray thee, if now I have found
grace in thy sight, then receive my pre-
sent at my hand: for therefore I have
seen thy face, as though I had seen the
face of God, and thou wast pleased with
me. (11) Take, I pray thee, my blessing
that is brought to thee; because God
hath dealt graciously with me, and
because I have enough. And he urged
him, and he took *it*.
(12) And he said, Let us take our jour-
ney, and let us go, and I will go before
thee. (13) And he said unto him, My
lord knoweth that the children *are* ten-
der, and the flocks and herds with
young *are* with me: and if men should
overdrive them one day, all the flock
will die. (14) Let my lord, I pray thee,
pass over before his servant: and I will
lead on softly, [3]according as the cattle
that goeth before me and the children
be able to endure, until I come unto my
lord unto Seir. (15) And Esau said, Let
me now [4]leave with thee *some* of the
folk that *are* with me. And he said,
[5]What needeth it? let me find grace
in the sight of my lord. (16) So Esau
returned that day on his way unto
Seir.
(17) And Jacob journeyed to Succoth,

1 Heb., *What is all this band to thee?*

2 Heb., *be that to thee that is thine.*

3 Heb., *according to the foot of the work, &c. and according to the foot of the children.*

4 Heb., *set*, or, *place.*

5 Heb., *Wherefore is this?*

---

(8) **What meanest thou by all this drove . . . ?** Heb., *What is all this camp of thine that I met?* From the time of Jacob's coming to Mahanaim, the word *mahaneh*, "camp," is used in a very remarkable way. It is the word translated *bands* in chap. xxxii. 7, and *company* in verses 8, 21. It is the proper word for an encampment of pastoral people with their flocks, and might be used not unnaturally of the five droves; for they would remind Esau of the cattle driven in at evening to the place where they were to pass the night.

(10) **For therefore I have seen thy face.**—The latter half of the verse would more correctly be translated, *inasmuch as I have seen thy face as one seeth the face of Elohim, and thou hast received me graciously.* To the Hebrew the thought of God was not terrifying, and so the vision of God's face was the sight of something good and glorious. There is much of Oriental hyperbole in comparing the sight of Esau to the beholding of the face of Deity, but it clearly conveyed the idea that Esau was using his power as generously and lovingly as is the wont of God; and God was so much nearer to the Hebrew in those simple days than he is to men now that science has revealed to them the immensity of His attributes, that there was no irreverence in the comparison.

The behaviour of Esau is very generous. He wished to spare his brother so large a present, and therefore leads the conversation to it, knowing, of course, what was the meaning of the five herds, as their drivers had delivered to him Jacob's message. To have refused it, however, would have been a mark of hostility, especially as Jacob represented it as the gift of an inferior for the purpose of obtaining the favour of one from whom he had feared danger. But Esau expostulates with his brother. He too was rich, and Jacob should keep what was his own. But Jacob still urges its acceptance as the proof of goodwill, magnifies the value of Esau's favour, and declares that by God's goodness he has still abundance, even after giving his brother so princely a present. It is called a "blessing" because it was considered lucky to receive a gift, and of all good-luck God was the giver. (Comp. 1 Sam. xxv. 27, xxx. 26.)

(13) **Flocks and herds with young.**—Heb., *that give suck.* Thompson (*Land and Book*, p. 205) infers from this that it was now winter, and thinks that this is confirmed by Jacob making folds for his cattle at Succoth. If so, more than six months would have elapsed since Jacob's flight from Haran; but the conclusion is uncertain, and Jacob probably halted at Succoth because of his lameness.

(14) **According as the cattle . . .**—Rather, *according to the pace*—Heb., *foot*—*of the cattle that is before me, and according to the pace of the children.* Joseph was only six or seven years old; and Leah's two younger sons, and probably Zilpah's, were too tender to endure much fatigue.

Unto Seir.—This implies a purpose of visiting Esau in his new acquisition, not carried out probably because Esau did not as yet settle there, but returned to Hebron to his father.

Jacob's Settlement in Canaan.—Dinah's Wrong, and the Fierce Vengeance of Simeon and Levi (chap. xxxiii. 17—xxxiv.).

(17) **Succoth.**—That is, *booths.* There are two claimants for identification with Jacob's Succoth, of which the one is in the tribe of Gad, on the east of the Jordan, in the corner formed by that river and the Jabbok; the other is the place still called Sakût, on the west of the Jordan, but as it lies ten miles to the north of the junction of the Jordan and Jabbok, it is not likely that Jacob would go so far out of his way.

Jacob . . . built him an house, and made booths for his cattle.—This is something quite unusual, as the cattle in Palestine remain in the open air all the year round, and the fact that the place retained the name of the booths shows that it was noticed as remarkable. But the fact, coupled with the right translation of verse 18, is a strong but undesigned testimony to the truth of the narrative. Jacob had been pursued by Laban, and suffered much from anxiety and the labour attendant upon the hurried removal of so large a household. Delivered from danger in the rear, he has to face a greater danger in front, and passes many days and nights in terror. At last Esau is close at hand, and having done all that man could do, he stays behind to recover himself, and prepare for the dreaded meeting next day. But instead of a few calm restful hours he has to wrestle fiercely all night, and when at sunrise he moves forward he finds that he has sprained his hip. He gets through the interview with Esau with much feeling, agitated alternately by fear, and

and built him an house, and made booths for his cattle: therefore the name of the place is called [1] Succoth.
(18) And Jacob came to Shalem, a city of [2] Shechem, which *is* in the land of Canaan, when he came from Padan-aram; and pitched his tent before the city.
(19) And he bought a parcel of a field, where he had spread his tent, at the hand of the children of [3] Hamor, Shechem's father, for an hundred [4] pieces of money.
(20) And he erected there an altar, and called it [5] El-elohe-Israel.

CHAPTER XXXIV.—(1) And Dinah the daughter of Leah, which she bare unto Jacob, went out to see the daughters of the land.
(2) And when Shechem the son of Hamor the Hivite, prince of the country, saw her, he took her, and lay with her, and [6] defiled her.
(3) And his soul clave unto Dinah the daughter

1 That is, *Booths.*
2 Called, Acts 7. 16, *Sychem.*
B.C. cir. 1732.
3 Called, Acts 7. 16, *Emmor.*
4 Or, *lambs.*
5 That is, *God the God of Israel.*
6 Heb., *humbled her.*

---

hope, and joy, enduring all the while his bodily pain as best he can, and then, delivered from all danger, he breaks down. The word "journeyed" simply means that he broke up his camp from the high ground where he had met his brother, and went into the corner close by, where the two rivers would both protect him and provide his cattle with water and herbage. And there he not only put up some protection, probably wattled enclosures made with branches of trees, for his cattle, but built a house for himself—something, that is, more solid than a tent; and there he lay until he was healed of his lameness. The strained sinew would require some months of perfect rest before Jacob could move about; but it was healed, for "Jacob came whole and sound to the city of Shechem." (See next verse.)

(18) **Jacob came to Shalem, a city of Shechem.**—The Sam. Pent. has *shalom*, "safe"; but *shalem* is right, and means *whole, sound.* Onkelos, however, followed by most modern commentators, renders it *in peace*, but this too would not mean *peaceably*, but that his troubles were now at an end, and his lameness cured. Philippsohn's rendering, however, is more exact, namely, *wohlbehalten*, in good condition. Rashi also, no mean authority, sees in it an allusion to the cure of Jacob's lameness. As Shechem was a man, his city would not be Shalem, but that called after his own name. In chap. xii. 6 it is called "Sichem," where see Note. Sichem was probably the old name, but after the cruel fate brought upon it by Shechem's misconduct the spelling was modified to suit the history.

In the land of Canaan. — Jacob therefore had now crossed the river Jordan, and so far completed his homeward journey. Probably as soon as he had recovered from his lameness he visited his father, but as his possessions were large, and Esau was the chief at Hebron, there was no room at present for him to dwell there, nor in fact was this possible until Isaac's death. But as we find Deborah with them soon afterwards, it is plain that he had gone to visit Isaac, and, finding his mother dead, had brought away with him her beloved nurse.

(19) **He bought . . .**—Abraham had been obliged to buy land for a burial-place, and we find even then that the field he wanted had an owner who could give him a title to its possession. Jacob a century later finds it necessary to buy even the ground on which to pitch his tent, though his cattle might still roam freely about for pasture. This, however, would certainly not have been required except in the immediate neighbourhood of a town. As he had now recovered from his sprain, he returns to his habits as a nomad, and dwells in a tent. In this, the first parcel of ground possessed by Jacob, the embalmed body of Joseph was buried (Josh. xxiv. 32; see also John iv. 5); and it is remarkable that the possession of it was secure, even when the owners were far away in Egypt.

An hundred pieces of money.—Heb., *a hundred kesitas.* It is plain that the kesita was an ingot of metal of some considerable value, from what is said in the Book of Job (chap. xlii. 11), that each of his friends gave the patriarch "one kesita and a nose-ring of gold." The etymology of the word is uncertain, and apparently all knowledge of its meaning had at an early period passed away, inasmuch as Onkelos and some of the versions translate it *lambs*, for which rendering there is no support.

(20) **He erected there an altar.**—Abraham had already built an altar in this neighbourhood (chap. xii. 7), and Jacob now followed his example—partly as a thanksoffering for his safe return, partly also as taking possession of the country; but chiefly as a profession of faith, and public recognition of the new relation in which he stood to God. This especially appears in his calling the altar "El, the Elohim of Israel." Of course the title of Jehovah could not be used here, as the altar had a special reference to the change of Jacob's name, and was an acknowledgment on his own part of his now being Israel, a prince with El, that is, with God.

XXXIV.

(1) **Dinah . . . went out to see the daughters of the land.**—Those commentators who imagine that Jacob sojourned only twenty years at Haran are obliged to suppose that he remained two or more years at Succoth, and some eight years at Shechem, before this event happened, leaving only one more year for the interval between Dinah's dishonour and the sale of Joseph to the Ishmaelites. But even so, if Dinah was now not more than fourteen, there would be left a period of only nine years, in which Leah has to bear six sons and a daughter, with a long interval of barrenness, during which Zilpah was given to Jacob and bears two sons. But besides this impossibility, Jacob evidently remained at Succoth only until he was *shalem*, sound and whole from his sprain, and Dinah's visit was one of curiosity, for she went "to see the daughters of the land," that is, she wanted, as Abravanel says, to see what the native women were like, and how they dressed themselves. Josephus says that she took the opportunity of a festival at Shechem; but as neither her father nor brothers knew of her going, but were with their cattle as usual, it is probable that with one or two women only she slipped away from her father's camp and paid the penalty of her girlish curiosity. But she would feel no such curiosity after being a year or two at Shechem, so that it is probable that her dishonour took place within a few weeks after Jacob's arrival there. So, too, Hamor's words in verses 21 and 22 plainly

of Jacob, and he loved the damsel, and spake [1]kindly unto the damsel. (4) And Shechem spake unto his father Hamor, saying, Get me this damsel to wife. (5) And Jacob heard that he had defiled Dinah his daughter: now his sons were with his cattle in the field: and Jacob held his peace until they were come.

(6) And Hamor the father of Shechem went out unto Jacob to commune with him. (7) And the sons of Jacob came out of the field when they heard *it:* and the men were grieved, and they were very wroth, because he had wrought folly in Israel in lying with Jacob's daughter; which thing ought not to be done. (8) And Hamor communed with them, saying, The soul of my son Shechem longeth for your daughter: I pray you give her him to wife. (9) And make ye marriages with us, *and* give your daughters unto us, and take our daughters unto you. (10) And ye shall dwell with us: and the land shall be before you; dwell and trade ye therein, and get you possessions therein. (11) And Shechem said unto her father and unto her brethren, Let me find grace in your eyes, and what ye shall say unto me I will give. (12) Ask me never so much dowry and gift, and I will give according as ye shall say unto me: but give me the damsel to wife.

(13) And the sons of Jacob answered Shechem and Hamor his father deceitfully, and said, because he had defiled Dinah their sister: (14) and they said unto them, We cannot do this thing, to give our sister to one that is uncircumcised; for that *were* a reproach unto us: (15) but in this will we consent unto you: If ye will be as we *be,* that every male of you be circumcised; (16) then will we give our daughters unto you, and we will take your daughters to us, and we will dwell with you, and we will become one people. (17) But if ye will not hearken unto us, to be circumcised; then will we take our daughter, and we will be gone.

(18) And their words pleased Hamor, and Shechem Hamor's son. (19) And the young man deferred not to do the thing, because he had delight in Jacob's daughter: and he *was* more honourable than all the house of his father. (20) And Hamor and Shechem his son came unto the gate of their city, and communed with the men of their city, saying, (21) These men *are* peaceable with us; therefore let them dwell in the land, and trade therein; for the land, behold, *it is* large

1 Heb., *to her heart.*

---

show that Jacob was a new comer; for he proposes that the people should "let them dwell in the land," and therefore consent to the condition required by them that the Hivites should be circumcised. It would have been absurd thus to speak if Jacob had already dwelt there eight years with no apparent intention of going away.

(5) **Jacob heard.**—As Dinah did not return home (verse 26), her father probably learned her dishonour from the maidservants who had gone out with her. But "he held his peace," chiefly from his usual cautiousness, as being no match for the Hivites, but partly because Leah's sons had the right to be the upholders of their sister's honour.

(7) **He had wrought folly in Israel.**—The great anger of Jacob's sons agrees as completely with the general harshness of their characters as the silence of the father with his habitual thoughtfulness; but it was aroused by a great wrong. The use, however, of the term *Israel* to signify the family of Jacob as distinguished from his person belongs to the age of Moses, and is one of the proofs of the arrangement of these records having been his work. In selecting them, and weaving them together into one history, he would add whatever was necessary, and in the latter half of this verse we apparently have one such addition.

(10) **Ye shall dwell with us.**—Hamor proposes that Jacob's family shall abandon their nomad life, and settle among the Hivites. and trade with them, and get possessions, not merely of cattle and movable goods, but of immovable property. He wished the two clans to coalesce into one community.

(12) **Dowry and gift.**—The word rendered *dowry* (mohar) is the price paid to the parents and relatives of the bride, though taking the form of a present. The *gift* (matthan) was the present made by the bridegroom to the bride herself. Besides this, her relatives were expected to give her presents, and with some tribes of Arabs it is usual even to make over to her the dowry.

(13, 14) **And said . . . and they said.**—These are two different verbs in the Hebrew, and should be translated *and spake (because he had defiled Dinah their sister), and said.* The intermediate words are parenthetical, and there is no reason for translating *spake* by *plotted, laid a snare,* as Gesenius and others have done.

(18) **Their words pleased Hamor.**—We gather from this that circumcision was a rite not only well known, but regarded as something honourable; for otherwise they would not so readily have submitted to a thing so painful.

(21) **Let us take their daughters . . .**—In a young community, such as this of the Hivites at Shechem appears to have been, the addition of a large number of women was a valuable increase of their strength, and one that brought the promise also of future extension. Jacob's men were also chiefly of the Semitic stock, and therefore possessed of high physical and mental endowments; and as they were rich in cattle

enough for them; let us take their
daughters to us for wives, and let us
give them our daughters. (22) Only here-
in will the men consent unto us for to
dwell with us, to be one people, if every
male among us be circumcised, as they
are circumcised. (23) *Shall* not their
cattle and their substance and every
beast of their's *be* our's? only let us
consent unto them, and they will dwell
with us. (24) And unto Hamor and unto
Shechem his son hearkened all that went
out of the gate of his city; and every
male was circumcised, all that went out
of the gate of his city.

(25) And it came to pass on the third
day, when they were sore, that two of
the sons of Jacob, Simeon and Levi,
Dinah's brethren, took each man his
sword, and came upon the city boldly,
and [a] slew all the males. (26) And they slew
Hamor and Shechem his son with the
[1] edge of the sword, and took Dinah out
of Shechem's house, and went out.
(27) The sons of Jacob came upon the

a ch. 49. 6.

1 Heb., *mouth*.

b ch. 27. 43.

slain, and spoiled the city, because they
had defiled their sister. (28) They took
their sheep, and their oxen, and their
asses, and that which *was* in the city,
and that which *was* in the field, (29) and
all their wealth, and all their little
ones, and their wives took they captive,
and spoiled even all that *was* in the
house.

(30) And Jacob said to Simeon and Levi,
Ye have troubled me to make me to stink
among the inhabitants of the land,
among the Canaanites and the Periz-
zites: and I *being* few in number, they
shall gather themselves together against
me, and slay me; and I shall be destroy-
ed, I and my house. (31) And they said,
Should he deal with our sister as with
an harlot?

CHAPTER XXXV.—(1) And God
said unto Jacob, Arise, go up to Beth-
el, and dwell there: and make there an
altar unto God, that appeared unto thee
[b] when thou fleddest from the face of

---

and other wealth, their incorporation with the people of Shechem would raise it to a high rank among the petty states of Canaan. There was much plausibility, therefore, in Hamor's proposal and arguments.

(25) **Simeon and Levi, Dinah's brethren.**—As born of the same mother, they, with Reuben and Judah, were especially bound to espouse their sister's cause, but the method they took was cruel in the extreme. And it seems that these two were the leaders in the plot, having probably excluded Reuben from it, as a man of feeble character and opposed to bloodshed (chap. xxxvii. 22); and Judah, as one too honourable to take part in so nefarious a transaction. Long afterwards Jacob speaks of it in terms of the strongest reprobation (chap. xlix. 5—7). In executing their cruel deed, they would command the services of the more active and fierce portion of Jacob's servants; but they must have been not boys, but men of ripe manhood, before they could have had influence or power enough for so terrible an exploit.

(27) **The sons of Jacob.**—After slaying Hamor and Shechem, the two brothers "took Dinah and went out." It was after this that Jacob's sons generally—though not without exceptions, for several of them were still very young—joined in seizing the spoil.

(29) **Their little ones.**—Heb., *their taf.* (See Note on chap. xvii. 13.) How erroneous is the translation "little ones" may be seen from Num. xxxi. 17, 18, which in the Heb. is, "Now, therefore, kill every male in the *taf* . . . and all the *taf* of women that are unmarried." It would be monstrous to suppose that boys were to be put to death, and men escape, nor would little girls be likely to be married. In 2 Chron. xxxi. 18 the *taf* is distinguished both from the sons and daughters; and so also in chap. xx. 13, where we read "their *tafs* and their children. The LXX. have altered the order here, but otherwise translate correctly *their persons,* that is, their property in men-servants and maid-servants, as opposed to their cattle and their wealth in goods. In chap. l. 8 the LXX. translate *clan,* and in verse 21 *household.* The slaves thus seized would form the most valuable part probably of the spoil.

(30) **Ye have troubled me.**—Jacob's timidity led him to think first of the danger that would result from the conduct of his sons, and only afterwards of the cruelty and treacherousness of their deed. He commented upon this on his dying bed in words of fitting reprobation, but his reproof now is singularly weak, and the retort of his sons just. If the danger were all, this could have no weight when a shameful wrong had been done; but in avenging this wrong they had committed a crime of a deeper dye

XXXV.

JACOB RETURNS TO BETH-EL AND HEBRON.—DEATH OF ISAAC.

(1) **Arise, go up to Beth-el.**—The position of Jacob at Shechem had become dangerous; for though the first result of the high-handed proceeding of Simeon and Levi was to strike the natives with terror (verse 5), yet reprisals might follow if they had time to learn the comparatively small number of Jacob's followers. It was necessary, therefore, to remove; but besides this, Beth-el was the goal of the patriarch's journeyings. He had made a solemn vow there on his journey to Padan-aram, and though forty-two years had elapsed, it had not been forgotten (see chap. xxxi. 13); and the Divine command to go thither was the outward authorisation of what his own conscience dictated. On this account we cannot believe that he had remained long at Shechem. Nomads are singularly leisurely in their movements. There is nothing of the rush and hurry of city life in their doings or purposes. They are capable of a great effort occasionally, but then relapse into their usual slowness. And so, when Jacob found good pasture and

Esau thy brother. (2) Then Jacob said
unto his household, and to all that *were*
with him, Put away the strange gods
that *are* among you, and be clean, and
change your garments: (3) and let us
arise, and go up to Beth-el; and I will
make there an altar unto God, who
answered me in the day of my distress,
and was with me in the way which I
went. (4) And they gave unto Jacob all
the strange gods which *were* in their
hand, and *all their* earrings which *were*
in their ears; and Jacob hid them under
the oak which *was* by Shechem. (5) And
they journeyed: and the terror of God
was upon the cities that *were* round
about them, and they did not pursue
after the sons of Jacob.

(6) So Jacob came to Luz, which *is*
in the land of Canaan, that *is*, Beth-el,
he and all the people that *were* with
him. (7) And he built there an altar,
and [a] called the place [1] El-beth-el:
because there God appeared unto him,
when he fled from the face of his
brother.

(8) But Deborah Rebekah's nurse died,
and she was buried beneath Beth-el
under an oak: and the name of it was
called [2] Allon-bachuth.

(9) And God appeared unto Jacob
again, when he came out of Padan-aram,
and blessed him. (10) And God said unto
him, Thy name *is* Jacob: thy name shall
not be called any more Jacob, [b] but
Israel shall be thy name: and he called

a ch. 28. 19.

1 That is, *The God of Beth-el.*

2 That is, *The oak of weeping.*

b ch. 32. 28.

---

plenty of room for his cattle at Shechem, he remained there for awhile; but he did not abandon his purpose of going first to Beth-el, and finally to Hebron.

(2) **Strange gods.**—Besides Rachel's teraphim, many, probably, of the persons acquired by Jacob at Haran were idolaters, and had brought their gods with them. Besides these, the numerous men and women who formed the "*tafs*" of the Shechemites were certainly worshippers of false deities. The object, then, of this reformation was not merely to raise Jacob's own family to a higher spiritual state, but also to initiate the many heathen belonging to their households into the true religion. Outward rites of purification and changes of garment were to accompany the religious teaching given, because of their symbolical value; and we can well believe that much deep and earnest religious feeling would be evoked by the solemnities which accompanied this drawing near of the whole tribe to God. This reformation is also interesting as being the first of a long series of such acts constantly recurring in the history of Israel; and especially it is parallel to the sanctification of the people at Sinai. There, also, there was the initiation not merely of the lineal Israel, but also of the mixed multitude, into the true religion—for Jacob's family had then grown into a nation; and there, also, symbolical washings were enjoined (Exod. xix. 10—14). These subsequently were still practised under the Law, and grew into the baptism by which we are now admitted into the Church of Christ.

(3) **Who answered me . . .**—The narrative of Jacob's life, and the detail of God's providential care of him, would doubtless affect strongly the minds of his followers, and make them ready to abandon their idols, "and worship the God that was Israel's God" (chap. xxxiii. 20).

(4) **Earrings.**—Earrings seem to have been worn not so much for ornament as for superstitious purposes, being regarded as talismans or amulets. Hence it was from their earrings that Aaron made the golden calf (Exod. xxxii. 2—4).

The oak.—Not Abraham's oak-grove (chap. xii. 6), referred to probably in Judges ix. 6, 37—the Hebrew word in these three places being *êlôn*—but that under which Joshua set up his pillar of witness (Josh. xxiv. 26), the tree being in both these places called *allâh*, or *êlâh*, a terebinth.

(5) **The terror . . .**—Heb., *a terror of God,* that is, a very great terror (see chaps. xxiii. 6, xxx. 8). But to the deeply religious mind of the Hebrew everything that was great and wonderful was the result of the direct working of the Deity. (But see Note on chap. xlviii. 22.)

(7) **El-beth-el.**—That is, *the God of the house of God:* the God into whose house he had been admitted, and seen there the wonders of His providence.

God appeared.—The verb here, contrary to rule, is plural (see Note on chap. xx. 13), but the Samaritan Pentateuch has the singular. No argument can be drawn either way from the versions, as the word for God is singular in them all, and the verb necessarily singular also. In no other language but Hebrew is the name of God plural, but joined with verbs and adjectives in the singular.

(8) **Deborah.**—As she was at Hebron with Rebekah when Jacob journeyed to Haran, he must have somehow gone thither before this, have seen his father, and told him of his fortunes. Apparently Rebekah was then dead, and Jacob brought back Deborah with him. (See Note on chap. xxxiii. 18.) How dear she was to them is shown by their calling the tree under which she was buried *the oak of weeping.* This oak was "beneath Beth-el," that is, in the valley below it. Deborah must have died at a great age, for she gave Rebekah suck, and must therefore have been grown up at her birth. Now Jacob, when he returned from Padan-aram, was ninety-seven years of age; and as he was born twenty years after his mother's marriage—if we allow the shortest possible space for the interval spent at Succoth and Shechem—Deborah must have been nearly one hundred and sixty years of age. This again confirms the conclusion that Dinah's dishonour occurred very soon after the arrival of Jacob at Shechem. (See Note on chap. xxxiv. 1.)

(9) **When he came out of Padan-aram.**—The word "out" is not in the Hebrew, which says, *on his coming from*—that is, on his arrival at Beth-el from Padan-aram. The insertion of the word "out" leads to a confusion with the revelation recorded in chap. xxxi. 3. At Beth-el Jacob, when going forth, had seen the dream which assured him of Divine protection; at Beth-el, on his return, God renews the covenant, confirms to him the name of Israel, and transfers to him the

his name Israel. (11) And God said unto
him, I *am* God Almighty: be fruitful
and multiply; a nation and a company
of nations shall be of thee, and kings
shall come out of thy loins; (12) and the
land which I gave Abraham and Isaac,
to thee I will give it, and to thy seed
after thee will I give the land.
(13) And God went up from him in the
place where he talked with him. (14) And
Jacob set up a pillar in the place where
he talked with him, *even* a pillar of
stone: and he poured a drink offering
thereon, and he poured oil thereon.
(15) And Jacob called the name of the
place where God spake with him, Beth-el.
(16) And they journeyed from Beth-el;
and there was but [1]a little way to come
to Ephrath: and Rachel travailed, and
she had hard labour. (17) And it came
to pass, when she was in hard labour,
that the midwife said unto her, Fear
not; thou shalt have this son also.
(18) And it came to pass, as her soul
was in departing, (for she died) that
she called his name [2]Ben-oni: but his
father called him [3]Benjamin. (19) And
Rachel died, and was buried in the way
to Ephrath, which *is* Beth-lehem. (20) And
Jacob set a pillar upon her grave: that *is*
the pillar of Rachel's grave unto this day.
(21) And Israel journeyed, and spread
his tent beyond the tower of Edar.
(22) And it came to pass, when Israel

1 Heb., *a little piece of ground.*

2 That is, *The son of my sorrow.*

B.C. cir. 1729.

3 That is, *The son of the right hand.*

---

promises of a numerous seed and of the possession of the land. It was the ratification to him of the inheritance of all the hopes and assurances given to Abraham.

(11) **God Almighty.**—Heb., *El-shaddai*, the name by which God had entered into the covenant with Abraham (chap. xvii. 1).

A company.— Heb., *a congregation of nations.* (See chap. xxviii. 3, where it is "a congregation," or church, "of peoples.")

(13) **God went up from him.**—This formula, used before in chaps. xvii. 22, xviii. 33, shows that this manifestation of God's presence was more solemn than any of those previous occasions upon which the Deity had revealed Himself to Jacob. It was, in fact, the acknowledgment of the patriarch as the heir of the Abrahamic covenant.

(14) **Jacob set up a pillar.**—In doing this Jacob was imitating his previous action when God manifested Himself to him in his journey to Haran, chap. xxviii. 18. This consecration of it by pouring on it oil, and offering to God a drink-offering, was in itself natural and right. But as these memorial pillars were subsequently worshipped, they were expressly forbidden by the Mosaic Law, the word correctly rendered "pillar" in this place being translated *standing image* in Lev. xxvi. 1, and *image* in Deut. xvi. 22.

(15) **Jacob called . . .**—See chap. xxviii. 19. The name had, of course, remained unknown and unused, as what then passed had been confined to Jacob's own inward consciousness. He now teaches the name to his family, explains the reason why he first gave it, and requires them to employ it. But with so grand a beginning the town was debased to unholy uses, and from being Beth-el, *the house of God*, it became Beth-aven, *the house of iniquity* (Hos. x. 5).

(16) **But a little way.**—Heb., *and there was still a "chibrath" of land to come to Ephrath.* This word occurs four times in the Old Testament: here, in chap. xlviii. 7, in 2 Kings v. 19, and in Amos ix. 9, where it is used in the sense of a *sieve.* Many of the Rabbins, therefore, translate "in the spring-time," because the earth is then riddled by the plough like a sieve; and the Targum and Vulgate adopt this rendering. The real meaning of the word is lost, but probably it was a measure of distance; and the Jewish interpreters generally think that it meant a mile, because Rachel's traditional tomb was about that distance from Bethlehem. **Ephrath** (the fruitful) and **Beth-lehem** (the house of bread) have virtually the same meaning, but the latter name would be given to the town only when its pastures had given place to arable lands, where corn was sown for bread.

(18) **Ben-oni . . . Benjamin.**— Rachel, in her dying moments, names her child *the son of my sorrow;* for though *ón* has a double meaning, and is translated *strength* in chap. xlix. 3, yet, doubtless, her feeling was that the life of her offspring was purchased by her own pain and death. Jacob's name, "son of the right hand," was probably given not merely that the child might bear no ill-omened title, but to mark his sense of the value and preciousness of his last born son. Abravanel well remarks that earthly happiness is never perfect, and that the receiving of Divine revelations made no difference to Jacob's earthly lot. God had just solemnly appeared to him, and he is on his last journey, within two days' easy march of Hebron, when he loses the wife whom he so loved. For more than forty years he had been an exile from his home; he was now close to it, but may never welcome there the one for whom he had so deep and lasting an affection.

(20) **That is the pillar of Rachel's grave unto this day.**— This is a later addition, but whether inserted by Moses or Ezra we cannot tell. Its site was known in the days of Samuel (1 Sam. x. 2); and as the pillar would be a mass of unwrought stone, with which the natives would have no object in interfering, its identification upon the conquest of Canaan would not be difficult.

(21) **The tower of Edar.**— Heb., *Eder.* Micah (chap. iv. 8) calls it "the hill of the daughter of Zion;" but the word used often means a beacon-hill, a hill on which a tower for observation is erected, wrongly translated in the Authorised Version *a stronghold.* The tower may, therefore, have been a few miles south of Jerusalem; and as the word "beyond" includes the idea of *up to, as far as*, the meaning is that Jacob now occupied this region permanently with his cattle. Until Esau, with his possessions, withdrew to Seir, there would be no room for Jacob and his flocks and herds at Hebron, but he would at Eder be so near his father as to be able often to visit him. And thus his exile was now over, and he was at last at home.

(22) **Reuben.**—Again another grief for Jacob to mar his return home, and this time it arises from the

dwelt in that land, that Reuben went a ch. 49. 4.
and [a]lay with Bilhah his father's con-
cubine: and Israel heard *it*. Now the
sons of Jacob were twelve:
(23) The sons of Leah; Reuben, Jacob's
first-born, and Simeon, and Levi, and B.C. 1716.
Judah, and Issachar, and Zebulun: (24) The
sons of Rachel; Joseph, and Benjamin: b ch. 25. 8
(25) and the sons of Bilhah, Rachel's hand-
maid; Dan, and Naphtali: (26) and the
sons of Zilpah, Leah's handmaid; Gad,
and Asher: these *are* the sons of Jacob, B.C. cir. 1796.
which were born to him in Padan-aram.

(27) And Jacob came unto Isaac his
father unto Mamre, unto the city of
Arbah, which *is* Hebron, where Abra-
ham and Isaac sojourned. (28) And the
days of Isaac were an hundred and four-
score years. (29) And Isaac gave up the
ghost, and died, and [b]was gathered unto
his people, *being* old and full of days:
and his sons Esau and Jacob buried
him.

CHAPTER XXXVI.—(1) Now these
are the generations of Esau, who *is*

---

sin of his first-born, who thereby forfeits the birthright. It was the thought of these miseries, following upon his long years of exile, which made Jacob speak so sorrowfully of his experience of life before Pharaoh (chap. xlvii. 9).

And Israel heard it.—The Masora notes that some words have here fallen out of the text, which the LXX. fill up by adding, "And it was evil in his sight."

(26) **In Padan-aram.**—The words are to be taken only generally, as Benjamin was born in Canaan.

(27) **The city of Arbah, which is Hebron.**—Better rendered *Kirjath-arba* in chap. xxiii. 2, where see Note.

(28) **The days of Isaac were an hundred and fourscore years.**—As Isaac was sixty when his sons were born, Jacob was one hundred and twenty years of age at his father's death, and one hundred and thirty when he appeared before Pharaoh (chap. xlvii. 9). Now, as Joseph was seventeen when sold into Egypt (chap. xxxvii. 2), and thirty when raised to power (chap. xli. 46), and as the seven years of plenty and two of the years of famine had passed before Jacob went down into Egypt, it follows that the cruel deed, whereby he was robbed of his favourite child, was committed about twelve years before the death of Isaac.

(29) **Esau and Jacob buried him.**—Esau, who apparently still dwelt at Hebron until his father's death, takes here the precedence as his natural right. But having in previous expeditions learnt the physical advantages of the land of Seir, and the powerlessness of the Horites to resist him, he gives up Hebron to his brother, and migrates with his large wealth to that country.

XXXVI.

The Tôldôth Esau.

(1) **The generations of Esau.** — This *tôldôth*, consisting of chaps. xxxvi.—xxxvii. 1, is very remarkable, if it were only for the difficulties with which it abounds, and which have too often been aggravated by the determination of commentators to make Holy Scripture bend to their pre-conceived ideas as to what it ought to be, instead of dutifully accepting it as it is. It begins with an enumeration of Esau's wives, in which the names are different from those given in chaps. xxvi. 34, xxviii. 9. Next we have the genealogy of Esau, upon the same principle as that whereby the *tôldôth* Ishmael was inserted immediately after the history of Abraham's death (chap. xxv. 12—18); but this is followed, in verses 20—30, by a genealogy of the Horite inhabitants of Mount Seir. Among these Esau dwelt as the predominant power, but nevertheless on friendly terms, for a reason which we shall see hereafter. We next have a list of kings who are said to have reigned in Edom "before there reigned any king over the children of Israel." This is not a prophetical portion of the Bible, but a dry genealogical table, and the attempts made to evade the plain meaning of the words, namely, that at the time when this list of kings was written there were kings in Israel, are painful to read, and can have no other effect than to harden sceptics in unbelief. Of these Edomite kings, it is remarkable that they do not succeed one another by hereditary succession, nor have they the same capital, but seem to belong to a time of anarchy, like that which existed in Israel under the Judges. During this period the Edomites and Horites were fused together, chiefly by conquest (Deut. ii. 12, 22), but partly also by the gradual dying out of the inferior race, just as the red man is fading away in North America, and the Maori in New Zealand. Finally, we have a list of the eleven dukes of Edom, "after their places." As these dukes represented tribes or clans, this catalogue is geographical, and as such it is described in verse 43, and was intended to give the political arrangement of the land at the later date when this addition was made, and when considerable changes had taken place since the time of the first settlement.

These last two documents, forming verses 31—43, were probably added at the time when the Books of Samuel were composed; but as we find the list of the kings given also in 1 Chron. i. 43—50, and as at that date great activity existed in completing the canon of Holy Scripture, some suppose that the lists in both places are by the same hand. It is entirely wrong to describe them as interpolations; for it was the rule to add to and complete genealogies; and besides there existed in the Jewish Church a living authority in the prophets who had the right and power to make necessary additions to the Divine record. It is to the "schools of the prophets" that we owe, under God's providence, the existence of most of the Old Testament Scriptures, and the preservation of all of them; and they did not preserve them for the sake of the authors, but for the sake of what was written. And there is nothing derogatory to the authority or inspiration of Holy Scripture in believing that the prophets were from time to time moved by the Spirit to add to what had been written. The contents of the Old Testament bear witness everywhere to the scrupulous fidelity with which men guarded in the prophetic schools the sacred deposit entrusted to their care; but it is equally certain that we find notes inserted from time to time, as in chap. xxxv. 20,

Edom. (2) Esau took his wives of the daughters of Canaan; Adah the daughter of Elon the Hittite, and Aholibamah the daughter of Anah the daughter of Zibeon the Hivite; (3) and Bashemath Ishmael's daughter, sister of Nebajoth. (4) And [a]Adah bare to Esau Eliphaz; and Bashemath bare Reuel; (5) and Aholibamah bare Jeush, and Jaalam, and Korah: these *are* the sons of Esau, which were born unto him in the land of Canaan.

(6) And Esau took his wives, and his sons, and his daughters, and all the [1]persons of his house, and his cattle, and all his beasts, and all his substance which he had got in the land of Canaan; and went into the country from the face of his brother Jacob. (7) For their riches were more than that they might

B.C. cir. 1760.

B.C. cir. 1740.

a 1 Chron. 1. 35.

1 Heb., *souls.*

No one can doubt but that the remark that the pillar standing on Rachel's grave "unto this day" was the same stone which Jacob had set up, was inserted at a later date, and apparently after the conquest of Canaan. So in chap. xiv. 17 we have a note inserted subsequently to the establishment of the kingly office. Why should there be any difficulty in believing that these two lists of kings and dukes, added to complete a genealogy, belonged also to a time when there were kings in Israel?

It is probable, however, that the list of kings given here is of an earlier date than that in the first chapter of Chronicles, for Hadar (more correctly, in Chronicles, Hadad) seems to have been living when this document was composed, and hence the full information about his wife. In Chronicles (chap i. 51) there is added "Hadad died also." And if he really were alive when this catalogue was written, he had by that time been dead for centuries; for its date would then be one comparatively early.

(2) **Adah the daughter of Elon the Hittite.**—In chap. xxvi. 34, she is called "Bashemath the daughter of Elon the Hittite," and is placed second. Here she is everywhere placed first. We do not often elsewhere find women possessed of two names, but it has not been sufficiently borne in mind that she was a Hittite, and her own name in her own language neither Adah nor Bashemath. As Adah means *ornament*, and Bashemath *sweet-scented*, both may possibly have been terms of endearment, arising from modifications of her Hittite name.

Aholibamah the daughter of Anah the daughter of Zibeon the Hivite.—She is supposed to answer to Judith the daughter of "Beeri the Hittite," in chap. xxvi. 34. But in verses 24, 25, we find her genealogy given again, and Zibeon, the father of Anah, the father of Aholibamah, is there described as a Horite. Now, as *Hivi* (Hivite) and *Hori* (Horite) differ in Hebrew only in the length of the top of the middle letter, and as mistakes in the transcription of Biblical names are of constant occurrence, it seems certain that Aholibamah was a Horite, and therefore, entirely distinct from Judith. Judith, the first wife, apparently had no children, and hence arose the temptation to Esau to marry some one besides. Hence, too, Adah comes in her proper order, as being the first wife who had sons; and Eliphaz as the son of the first wife who had children, has the right of primogeniture. Hence, too, Aholibamah in the genealogy is always placed third. She was the fourth and last wife taken, and her children are placed after those of Bashemath. And this was a matter of far too great importance in a genealogy for there to be any mistake made in it. And now we see the reason for giving the genealogy of the Horites, and also why Esau took the Horite land for a possession. In some expedition into the country of Seir, Esau had married the daughter of one of the dukes there, and through her had acquired a right to ducal rank. Through her family, moreover, he had friendly relations with one portion at least of the Horite people. Our knowledge of the princely Hittites has of late been too largely increased for us to be able to connect a Horite race with them, and Rebekah distinctly calls Judith and Adah-Bashemath daughters of Heth. Excepting the Semites, no race in Palestine stands so high as the Hittites, and no race so low as the Horites. But their rulers were probably of a higher breed; and Esau's invasions of their country, his final settlement there, and the introduction of the genealogy of "Seir the Horite," together with Aholibamah's place as the last of Esau's wives, all are facts which strongly confirm the supposition of his having contracted a Horite marriage during Jacob's absence in Padan-aram.

The meanness of the Horites is not a deduction merely from their having dwelt in caves, for the country is so admirably adapted to this mode of living that it still exists there; but they are omitted from the table of nations in chap. x., and seem generally to have been a feeble aboriginal race.

(3) **Bashemath Ishmael's daughter, sister of Nebajoth.**—The Samaritan text reads Mahalath here, and in verses 4, 10, 17, as in chap. xxviii. 9. There can be little doubt that Mahalath is the right reading, but the versions, nevertheless, agree with the Masoretic Hebrew text, so that the error must have been of very ancient date. As Mahalath was of a Semitic stock, she would have her own Semitic name, and there would be no double translation of it, as in the case of the daughter of Elon.

(5) **In the land of Canaan.**—We find Esau with a band of armed men in Seir on Jacob's return from Padan-aram, but he still had his home at Hebron with his father until Isaac's death, twenty-two years afterwards. Evidently he had taken Aholibamah home thither, and she had borne him three sons. After Isaac's death the land of Seir had so great attractions for him that he migrated thither with his share of Isaac's wealth, and left Hebron to Jacob, who now moved down thither from the town of Eder, and took possession of the homestead of his fathers. And thus the inheritance of the birthright came finally to Jacob by Esau's own act, and would doubtless have so come to him; only his father's blessing and the transference to him of the Abrahamic promises would have been given him, not at the time of Isaac's temporary illness, but on his deathbed.

(6) **Into the country from the face.**—Heb. *into a land away from the face, &c.*

(7) **The land wherein they were strangers.**—The large growth of their wealth made the separation of Esau and Jacob as inevitable as had been that of Abraham and Lot. It is a usual incident in the life of nomads, and a tribe can multiply only to the extent of

dwell together; and the land wherein
they were strangers could not bear them
because of their cattle. (8) Thus dwelt
Esau in [a]mount Seir: Esau *is* Edom.
(9) And these *are* the generations of
Esau the father of [1]the Edomites in
mount Seir: (10) these *are* the names of
Esau's sons; [b]Eliphaz the son of Adah
the wife of Esau, Reuel the son of
Bashemath the wife of Esau. (11) And
the sons of Eliphaz were Teman, Omar,
Zepho, and Gatam, and Kenaz. (12) And
Timna was concubine to Eliphaz Esau's
son; and she bare to Eliphaz Amalek:
these *were* the sons of Adah Esau's wife.
(13) And these *are* the sons of Reuel;
Nahath, and Zerah, Shammah, and
Mizzah: these were the sons of Bashe-
math Esau's wife. (14) And these were
the sons of Aholibamah, the daughter
of Anah the daughter of Zibeon, Esau's
wife: and she bare to Esau Jeush, and
Jaalam, and Korah.

B.C. cir. 1715.

a Josh. 24. 4.

1 Heb., *Edom.*

b 1 Chron. 1. 35, &c.

B.C. cir. 1840.

c 1 Chron. 1. 38.

(15) These *were* dukes of the sons of
Esau: the sons of Eliphaz the firstborn
son of Esau; duke Teman, duke Omar,
duke Zepho, duke Kenaz, (16) duke
Korah, duke Gatam, *and* duke Amalek:
these *are* the dukes *that came* of Eliphaz
in the land of Edom; these *were* the
sons of Adah. (17) And these *are* the
sons of Reuel Esau's son; duke Nahath,
duke Zerah, duke Shammah, duke
Mizzah: these *are* the dukes *that came*
of Reuel in the land of Edom; these
are the sons of Bashemath Esau's wife.
(18) And these *are* the sons of Aholi-
bamah Esau's wife; duke Jeush, duke
Jaalam, duke Korah: these *were* the
dukes *that came* of Aholibamah the
daughter of Anah, Esau's wife. (19) These
are the sons of Esau, who *is* Edom, and
these *are* their dukes.
(20) [c]These *are* the sons of Seir the
Horite, who inhabited the land; Lotan,
and Shobal, and Zibeon, and Anah,

---

the capabilities of their district to support them. When this is reached, one portion of the tribe must seek a new home. This necessity was in the present case aggravated by Esau and Jacob being only sojourners in Canaan, surrounded by tribes who claimed to be owners of the soil: and this may have helped in determining Esau's choice; for in right of Aholibamah, he was in her country a duke. Maimonides also observes, that though Esau had gone on hunting expeditions to Seir, and even possibly for plunder, yet that he was not sufficiently powerful to take possession of the country until by Isaac's death the number of his retainers was largely multiplied.

(8) **Mount Seir.**—The land of Idumea extends from the southern extremity of the Dead Sea to the Gulf of Elath, and consists of a chain of mountains running parallel to the Akaba, or continuation of the deep depression through which the Jordan flows till it loses itself in the Dead Sea. The hills are of limestone, with masses here and there of basalt; and though large portions are so covered with stones as to be barren, the rest is moderately fertile, not indeed in corn, but in figs, pomegranates, and other fruits. The climate is pleasant, the heat in summer being moderated by cool winds, but the winters are cold. The border of it was distant only some fifty or sixty miles from Hebron, so that Esau's transference of himself thither was an easy matter. (Comp. Note on chap. xxvii. 39.)

(9) **The father of the Edomites.** — Heb., *the father of Edom.* He was himself the man Edom, but the word here means the country of which he was the colonizer.

(12) **Amalek.**—We have already read of the "field of the Amalekite" in chap. xiv. 7. As Balaam describes Amalek as "the beginning of nations" (so the Heb., Num. xxiv. 20), the race can scarcely have had so ignoble an origin as to have sprung from a concubine of Eliphaz; for we gather from Amos vi. 1 that the phrase used by Balaam implied precedence and nobility. It was, moreover, one of the most widely spread races of antiquity, occupying the whole country from Shur, on the borders of Egypt, to Havilah, in Arabia Felix. But probably there was a fusion of some of the Horites with the Amalekites, just as the Kenezites, under Caleb, were fused into the tribe of Judah. For in 1 Chron. iv. 42, 43, we find the Simeonites invading Mount Seir, and smiting Amalekites there. Of these Amalekites in Seir, Amalek, the grandson of Esau, was probably the founder; for in verse 16 he is called *a duke,* and therefore one district of the country would belong to his descendants, in the same manner as each son of Jacob had a territory called after his name. In this district the chiefs would be Semites of the race of Esau; the mass of the people a blended race of Horites and Amalekites. There is no difficulty in the absence of their names from chap. x. Though Balaam magnified them, they were regarded by Israel, not as a nation, but as a hateful horde of plunderers.

(15) **Dukes.**—Duke is the Latin word *dux,* a leader; but the Hebrew word *alluph* signifies *a tribal prince.* It is derived from *eleph,* a thousand, used in much the same way as the word *hundred* with us for a division of the country. Probably it was one large enough to have in it a thousand grown men, whereas a hundred in Saxon times was a district in which there were a hundred homesteads. For this use of it, see Micah v. 2. Each *alluph,* therefore, would be the prince of one of these districts, assigned to him as the possession of himself and his seed.

(16) **Duke Korah.**—The Samaritan Pentateuch rightly omits this name. He was a son of the Horite wife, Aholibamah.

(18) **Duke Jeush . . .**—Aholibamah's three sons are dukes, but only the grandsons of the other wives. The reason of this probably is that she belonged to the dominant family of Seir, and her sons took the command of districts and tribes of the Horite people in her right.

(20) **The sons of Seir the Horite.**—This genealogy is given partly because it contains that of Aholibamah,

(21) and Dishon, and Ezer, and Dishan:
these *are* the dukes of the Horites, the
children of Seir in the land of Edom.
(22) And the children of Lotan were Hori
and Hemam; and Lotan's sister *was*
Timna. (23) And the children of Shobal
were these; Alvan, and Manahath, and
Ebal, Shepho, and Onam. (24) And
these *are* the children of Zibeon; both
Ajah, and Anah: this *was that* Anah
that found the mules in the wilderness,
as he fed the asses of Zibeon his father.
(25) And the children of Anah *were* these;
Dishon, and Aholibamah the daughter
of Anah. (26) And these *are* the children
of Dishon; Hemdan, and Eshban, and
Ithran, and Cheran. (27) The children of
Ezer *are* these; Bilhan, and Zaavan,
and Akan. (28) The children of Dishan
are these; Uz, and Aran. (29) These *are*
the dukes *that came* of the Horites;
duke Lotan, duke Shobal, duke Zibeon,
duke Anah, (30) duke Dishon, duke Ezer,
duke Dishan: these *are* the dukes *that*
came of Hori, among their dukes in the
land of Seir.

(31) And these *are* the kings that
reigned in the land of Edom, before
there reigned any king over the children
of Israel. (32) And Bela the son of Beor
reigned in Edom: and the name of his
city *was* Dinhabah. (33) And Bela died,
and Jobab the son of Zerah of Bozrah
reigned in his stead. (34) And Jobab
died, and Husham of the land of Temani
reigned in his stead. (35) And Husham
died, and Hadad the son of Bedad, who
smote Midian in the field of Moab,
reigned in his stead: and the name of
his city *was* Avith. (36) And Hadad died,
and Samlah of Masrekah reigned in his
stead. (37) And Samlah died, and Saul
of Rehoboth *by* the river reigned in his
stead. (38) And Saul died, and Baal-
hanan the son of Achbor reigned in his
stead. (39) And Baal-hanan the son of
Achbor died, and Hadar reigned in his
stead: and the name of his city *was*
Pau; and his wife's name *was* Mehet-
abel, the daughter of Matred, the
daughter of Mezahab.

B.C. cir. 1780.

(40) And these *are* the names of the
dukes *that came* of Esau, according to
their families, after their places, by
their names; duke Timnah, duke
Alvah, duke Jetheth, (41) duke Aholi-

---

but chiefly because the Horites were in time fused with the descendants of Esau, and together formed the Edomites.

(22) **Timna.**—Not the Timna mentioned in verse 12; for she is here described as sister of Lotan the brother of Zibeon, who was grandfather of Aholibamah, Esau's wife. But the Timna mentioned there was the concubine of Esau's grandson, and junior by four generations.

(24) **Anah that found the mules.**—Mules is the traditional rendering of the Jews; but as horses were at this date unknown in Palestine, Anah could not have discovered the art of crossing them with asses, and so producing mules. Jerome, moreover, says that "the word in Punic, a language allied to Hebrew, means hot springs;" and this translation is now generally adopted. Lange gives a list of hot springs in the Edomite region, of which those of Calirrhoe, "the stream of beauty," in the Wady Zerka Maion, are probably those found by Anah.

(31) **The kings.**—In the triumphal song of Moses on the Red Sea we still read of "dukes of Edom" (Exod. xv. 15; but when Israel had reached the borders of their land, we find that Edom had then a king (Num. xx. 14). But in the list given here, no king succeeds his father, and probably these were petty monarchs, who sprang up in various parts of the country during a long period of civil war, in which the Horites were finally as completely conquered as were the Canaanites in Palestine under the heavy hands of Saul and Solomon. In the time of the dukes, there were also Horite dukes of the race of Seir, ruling districts mixed up apparently with those governed by the descendants of Esau. But all these now disappear.

(33) **Jobab.**—The LXX. identify him with Job, but on no probable grounds.

(35) **Who smote Midian . . .**—All memory of this exploit has passed away, and the complete silence of the Bible regarding every one of these kings, makes it probable that they belonged to an early date prior to the time in Israel when historical events were carefully recorded.

(37) **Rehoboth by the river.**—Heb., *Rehoboth hannahar*, Rehoboth-of-the-river, so called, perhaps, to distinguish it from Rehoboth-ir (chap. x. 11). If the river is the Euphrates, this city was not on Edomite ground, and Saul probably reigned in Idumea by right of conquest.

(39) **Hadar.**—He is more correctly called Hadad in the Samaritan text here, and in the Hebrew also in 1 Chron. i. 50. The two letters *r* and *d* are in Hebrew so much alike, that they are repeatedly confused with one another. As we have already observed (see Note on verse 1) he was probably alive when this catalogue of kings was drawn up.

(40) **According to their families, after their places.**—The final list of the dukes is said, both here and in verse 43, to be territorial, by which is meant, not that the persons mentioned were not real men, but that Edom finally settled down into eleven "thousands" named after these chieftains. So in Canaan the names of the sons of Jacob became those also of territorial divisions, two of which, however, were given to Joseph and his sons, while no district was called after Levi. What is remarkable here is the vast amount of change. No Horite duke gives his name to any of these divisions of the land of Edom. Omitting Korah from verse 16, there were originally thirteen of these tribal princes,

bamah, duke Elah, duke Pinon, (42) duke
Kenaz, duke Teman, duke Mibzar,
(43) duke Magdiel, duke Iram: these *be*
the dukes of Edom, according to their
habitations in the land of their posses-
sion: he *is* Esau the father of [1]the
Edomites.

CHAPTER XXXVII.—(1) And Jacob
dwelt in the land [2]wherein his father
was a stranger, in the land of Canaan.
(2) These *are* the generations of Jacob.
Joseph, *being* seventeen years old, was
feeding the flock with his brethren; and
the lad *was* with the sons of Bilhah,
and with the sons of Zilpah, his father's
wives: and Joseph brought unto his
father their evil report. (3) Now Israel
loved Joseph more than all his children,
because he *was* the son of his old ages
and he made him a coat of *many*
[3]colours. (4) And when his brethren
saw that their father loved him more
than all his brethren, they hated him,
and could not speak peaceably unto
him.

1 Heb., *Edom.*

B.C. cir. 1496.

2 Heb., *of his father's sojournings.*

3 Or, *pieces.*

B.C. 1729.

---

each with his own territory, but with no central government; just as the children of Israel dwelt for centuries in Canaan, each tribe independently in its own district, and with nothing to bind them together except their religion. In verses 40—43 we find eleven tribes, of which only two, those of Teman and Kenaz, retain the names of the sons of Esau, while of the rest we know nothing. We may, however, safely conclude that these nine persons, who gave their names to districts of Edom, were all men who rose to power during the troubled times when king after king seized the crown only to be displaced by some one else. Probably many such men arose, but these were all who consolidated their power sufficiently to leave their names behind them. Amidst this anarchy, the two districts of Teman and Kenaz alone remained unbroken, and continued to be ruled by princes of the same family. This word "family" has in Hebrew a meaning different from that which it has with us; for it signifies one of the larger divisions of a tribe, of which the subdivisions are called "fathers' houses," which again are subdivided into households (Num. i. 2, &c.). In verse 43 "habitations" would be better rendered *settlements.*

XXXVII.

(1) **And Jacob . . .**—This verse is not the beginning of a new section, but the conclusion of the *Tôldôth Esau.* In chap. xxxvi. 6, we read that Esau went into a land away from Jacob. Upon this follows in verse 8, "And Esau dwelt in Mount Seir;" and now the necessary information concerning the other brother is given to us, "And Jacob dwelt in the land . . . of Canaan." In the Hebrew the conjunctions are the same.

The Tôldôth Jacob.

Joseph is Sold by his Brethren into Egypt.

(2) **The generations of Jacob.**—This *Tôldôth*, according to the undeviating rule, is the history of Jacob's descendants, and specially of Joseph. So the *Tôldôth* of the heaven and earth (chap. ii. 4) gives the history of the creation and fall of man. So the *Tôldôth Adam* was the history of the flood; and, not to multiply instances, that of Terah was the history of Abraham. (See Note on chap. xxviii. 10.) This *Tôldôth*, therefore, extends to the end of Genesis, and is the history of the removal, through Joseph's instrumentality, of the family of Jacob from Canaan into Egypt, as a step preparatory to its growth into a nation.

Joseph being seventeen years old.—He was born about seven years before Jacob left Haran, and as the journey home probably occupied two full years, he would have dwelt in Isaac's neighbourhood for seven or eight years. Isaac's life, as we have seen, was prolonged for about twelve years after the sale of Joseph by his brethren.

And the lad was with the sons of Bilhah, and with the sons of Zilpah.—Heb., *And he was lad with the sons of Bilhah,* &c. The probable meaning of this is, that as the youngest son it was his duty to wait upon his brothers, just as David had to look after the sheep, while his brothers went to the festival; and was also sent to the camp to attend to them (1 Sam. xvi. 11, xvii. 17, 18). The sons of Jacob were dispersed in detachments over the large extent of country occupied by Jacob's cattle, and Joseph probably after his mother's death, when he was about nine years' old, would be brought up in the tent of Bilhah, his mother's handmaid. He would naturally, therefore, go with her sons, with whom were also the sons of the other handmaid. They do not seem to have taken any special part in Joseph's sale.

Joseph brought unto his father their evil report.—Heb., *Joseph brought an evil report of them unto their father.*

(3) **He was the son of his old age.**—Jacob was ninety-one when Joseph was born; but at Benjamin's birth he was eight or nine years older; and according to the common belief that Jacob was only twenty years in Padan-aram, the four sons of the handmaids must have been about Joseph's age, and Leah's last two sons even younger. But the epithet is intelligible if Jacob had waited twenty-seven years after his marriage with Rachel, before Joseph was born. There would then be a considerable interval between him and the other sons; and though Rachel had a second son some years afterwards, yet Joseph would continue to be the son long looked for, whose birth had given him so great happiness; whereas his joy at Benjamin's coming was bought at the terrible price of the mother's death.

A coat of many colours.—Two explanations are given of this phrase; the first, that it was a long garment with sleeves or fringes; the other, that it was composed of patchwork of various colours. The latter is the more probable interpretation; for from the tomb at Beni-Hassan we learn that such dresses were worn in Palestine, as a train of captive Jebusites is represented upon it clad in rich robes, the patterns of which seem to have been produced by sewing together small pieces of different colours. So also in India beautiful dresses are made by sewing together strips of crimson, purple, and other colours. (Roberts' *Oriental Illustrations,* p. 43.) Some have thought that Jacob by this

(5) And Joseph dreamed a dream, and
he told *it* his brethren: and they hated
him yet the more. (6) And he said unto
them, Hear, I pray you, this dream
which I have dreamed: (7) for, behold,
we *were* binding sheaves in the field,
and, lo, my sheaf arose, and also stood
upright; and, behold, your sheaves
stood round about, and made obeisance
to my sheaf. (8) And his brethren said
to him, Shalt thou indeed reign over
us? or shalt thou indeed have dominion
over us? And they hated him yet the
more for his dreams, and for his words.
(9) And he dreamed yet another dream,
and told it his brethren, and said, Behold,
I have dreamed a dream more;
and, behold, the sun and the moon and
the eleven stars made obeisance to me.
(10) And he told *it* to his father, and to
his brethren: and his father rebuked
him, and said unto him, What *is* this
dream that thou hast dreamed? Shall
I and thy mother and thy brethren
indeed come to bow down ourselves to
thee to the earth? (11) And his brethren
envied him; but his father observed
the saying.

(12) And his brethren went to feed
their father's flock in Shechem. (13) And
Israel said unto Joseph, Do not thy
brethren feed *the flock* in Shechem?
come, and I will send thee unto them.
And he said to him, Here *am I.* (14) And
he said to him, Go, I pray thee, [1] see
whether it be well with thy brethren,
and well with the flocks; and bring me
word again. So he sent him out of the
vale of Hebron, and he came to Shechem.

(15) And a certain man found him, and,
behold, *he was* wandering in the field:
and the man asked him, saying, What
seekest thou? (16) And he said, I seek
my brethren: tell me, I pray thee,
where they feed *their flocks.* (17) And
the man said, They are departed hence;

[1] Heb., *see the peace of thy brethren, &c.*

---

dress marked out Joseph as the future head of the family, in the place of Reuben, supposing it to indicate the priestly office borne by the firstborn; but this is doubtful, and it was Judah to whom Jacob gave the right of primogeniture.

(5) **Joseph dreamed a dream.**—Though dreams as a rule do but arise from the mind being wearied with overmuch business (Eccles. v. 3), or other trivial causes; yet as being from time to time used by God for providential purposes, they are occasionally described as a lower kind of prophecy (Num. xii. 6—8; Deut. xiii. 1; 1 Sam. xxviii. 15). In the life of Joseph they form the turning point in his history, and it is to be noticed that while revelations were frequently made to Jacob, we have henceforward no record of any such direct communication from God to man until the time of Moses. The utmost granted to Joseph was to dream dreams; and after this the children of Israel in Egypt were left entirely to natural laws and influences. (Comp. Note on chap. xxvi. 2.)

(7) **Stood upright.**—Heb., *took its station.* It is the verb used in chap. xxiv. 13, where see Note. It implies that the sheaf took the position of chief. We gather from this dream that Jacob practised agriculture, not occasionally, as had been the case with Isaac (chap. xxvi. 12), but regularly, as seems to have been usual also at Haran (chap. xxx. 14).

(9) **He dreamed yet another dream.**—In Joseph's history the dreams are always double, though in the case of those of the chief butler and baker, the interpretation was diverse.

(10) **His father rebuked him.**—In making the sun and moon bow down before him. Joseph's dream seemed to violate the respect due to parents. As Jacob probably regarded his son's dreams as the result of his letting his fancy dwell upon ideas of self-exaltation, he rightly rebuked him; while, nevertheless, "observing his saying." (Comp. Luke ii. 51.)

Thy mother.—Rachel was certainly dead, as Joseph had at this time eleven brethren. Nor did Leah ever bow down before him; for she died at Hebron (chap. xlix. 31). The enumeration of "sun, moon, and stars," means Jacob, his wives, and his children, that is, the whole family, elders and juniors, were to make obeisance to Joseph. It is a general phrase, like that in chap. xxxv, 26, and is not to be too literally interpreted. But as the handmaids were both of them younger than either Rachel or Leah, they may have gone down with Jacob into Egypt; and probably Bilhah had done a mother's part by Joseph after Rachel's death.

(12) **Shechem.**—Jacob's sons seem to have retained Shechem, by right of their high-handed proceedings related in chap. xxxiv. 27—29. By seizing the "*tafs*" of the Shechemites, Simeon and Levi must have added large numbers of grown men to the roll of their retainers; and after accustoming them to their service, they would have become powerful enough to resist any attacks of the natives. (See chap. xxxiv. 29, and Note on chap. xvii. 13). But it gives us a great idea of Jacob's wealth and power, that while dwelling a little to the north of Hebron, he should send part of his cattle so far away as to Shechem, a distance of sixty miles.

(14) **Whether it be well with thy brethren.**—Jacob might well fear lest the natives should form a confederacy against his sons, and take vengeance upon them for their cruelty. They were too fierce themselves to have any such alarm, but Jacob was of a far more timid disposition.

The vale of Hebron.—The flocks and herds which formed the portion of Jacob's cattle which pastured nearest home, occupied the country immediately to the north of Hebron as far as the tower of Eder; but he would no doubt pitch his own tent as near as possible to that of his father

(17) **Dothan.**—This town was twelve miles north of Shechem, and is famous as being the place where Elisha struck the Syrian army with blindness (2 Kings vi 13—23) It is situated in a small but fertile valley, and

for I heard them say, Let us go to
Dothan. And Joseph went after his
brethren, and found them in Dothan.
(18) And when they saw him afar off,
even before he came near unto them,
they conspired against him to slay him.
(19) And they said one to another, Be-
hold, this [1]dreamer cometh. (20) Come
now therefore, and let us slay him, and
cast him into some pit, and we will
say, Some evil beast hath devoured
him: and we shall see what will become
of his dreams. (21) And [a]Reuben heard
it, and he delivered him out of their
hands; and said, Let us not kill him.
(22) And Reuben said unto them, Shed
no blood, *but* cast him into this pit that
is in the wilderness, and lay no hand
upon him; that he might rid him out
of their hands, to deliver him to his
father again.
(23) And it came to pass, when Joseph
was come unto his brethren, that they
stript Joseph out of his coat, *his* coat
of *many* [2]colours that *was* on him;
(24) and they took him, and cast him
into a pit: and the pit *was* empty,
there was no water in it. (25) And they
sat down to eat bread: and they lifted
up their eyes and looked, and, behold,
a company of Ishmeelites came from
Gilead with their camels bearing spicery
and balm and myrrh, going to carry *it*
down to Egypt. (26) And Judah said
unto his brethren, What profit *is it* if
we slay our brother, and conceal his

1 Heb., *master of dreams.*

a ch. 42. 22.

2 Or, *pieces.*

Jacob's sons, having exhausted the produce of the larger plain round Shechem, had moved northward thither. Not having found them at Shechem, Joseph did not know where to go, but wandered about "in the field"—the open downs—till he met some one who could give him information. Had he been a practised hunter, like Esau, he would have followed them by the tracks of the cattle.

(19) **This dreamer.**—Heb., *this lord of dreams*, a phrase expressive of contempt.

(20) **Into some pit.**—Heb., *into one of the pits*, that is, cisterns dug to catch and preserve the rain water. In summer they are dry, and a man thrown into one of them would have very little chance of escape, as they are not only deep, but narrow at the top. The Jewish interpreters accuse Simeon of being the prime mover in the plot, and say that this was the reason why Joseph cast him into prison (chap. xlii. 24).

(22) **Into this pit that is in the wilderness.**—Reuben apparently pointed to some cistern in the desolate region which girds the little valley of Dothan around. We learn from chap. xlii. 21 that Joseph begged hard for mercy, and to be spared so painful a death, but that his brothers would not hear.

Though never represented in the Scriptures as a type of Christ, yet the whole of the Old Testament is so full of events and histories, which reappear in the Gospel narrative, that the Fathers have never hesitated in regarding Joseph, the innocent delivered to death, but raised thence to glory, as especially typifying to us our Lord. Pascal (*Pensées*, ii. 9. 2) sums up the points of resemblance—in his father's love for him, his being sent to see after the peace of his brethren, their conspiring against him, his being sold for twenty pieces of silver, his rising from his humiliation to be the lord and saviour of those who had wronged him; and with them the saviour also of the world. As too, he was in prison with two malefactors, so was our Lord crucified between two thieves; and as one of these was saved and one left to his condemnation, so Joseph gave deliverance to the chief butler, but to the chief baker punishment. It would be easy to point out other resemblances, but, leaving these, it is important also to notice that Joseph's history is likewise a vindication of God's providential dealings with men. He is innocent, and pure in life, but wronged again and again; yet every wrong was but a step in the pathway of his exaltation. And like the histories of all great lives, Joseph's adventures do not begin and end in himself. Upon him depended a great future. Noble minds care little for personal suffering, if from their pain springs amelioration for the world. Now Joseph's descent into Egypt was not only for the good and preservation of the people there, but was also an essential condition for the formation of the Jewish Church. In Egypt alone could Israel have multiplied into a nation fit to be the depositaries of God's law, and to grow into a church of prophets.

(25) **A company of Ishmeelites.**—Dothan was situated on the great caravan line by which the products of India and Western Asia were brought to Egypt. As the eastern side of Canaan is covered by the great Arabian desert, the caravans had to travel in a north-westernly direction until, having forded the Euphrates, they could strike across from Tadmor to Gilead. The route thence led them over the Jordan at Beisân, and so southward to Egypt. For "Ishmeelites," we have "Midianites," Heb., *Medyanim*, in verse 28, and Medanites, Heb., *Medanim*, in verse 36; but the Targum and the Syriac, instead of Ishmeelites, read *Arabs*. Midian was a son of Abraham by Keturah, and Ishmael was his son by Hagar. But probably these merchants were descended from neither by blood, but belonged to some branch of the Canaanites, who were the great traders of ancient times, and which Ishmael and Midian had compelled to submit to their sway. (But see Note on chap. xxv. 2.) The Jewish interpreters are reduced to great straits in reconciling these names, and even assert that Joseph was sold three times. Really Ishmeelites, Midianites, and Medanites are all one and the same, if we regard them as bearing the names only politically.

It is remarkable that the Egyptians never took part in the carrying trade. Even the navigation of the Red Sea they left to the Phœnicians, Israelites, and Syrians, though Psammetichus, Pharaoh-Necho, and Apries tried to induce the Egyptians to take to maritime pursuits. Their products were corn, stuffs of byssus and other materials, and carpets; but the exportation of these goods they left to foreign traders.

Spicery, and balm, and myrrh.—The first was probably gum tragacanth, though some think that it was storax, the gum of the styrax tree (see chap. xxx. 37).

blood? (27) Come, and let us sell him
to the Ishmeelites, and let not our hand
be upon him; for he *is* our brother *and*
our flesh. And his brethren [1]were
content. (28) Then there passed by
Midianites merchantmen; and they
drew and lifted up Joseph out of the
pit, [a]and sold Joseph to the Ishmeelites
for twenty *pieces* of silver: and they
brought Joseph into Egypt.
(29) And Reuben returned unto the
pit; and, behold, Joseph *was* not in
the pit; and he rent his clothes. (30) And
he returned unto his brethren, and
said, The child *is* not; and I, whither
shall I go?
(31) And they took Joseph's coat, and
killed a kid of the goats, and dipped
the coat in the blood; (32) and they sent
the coat of *many* colours, and they
brought *it* to their father; and said,
This have we found: know now whether
it *be* thy son's coat or no. (33) And he
knew it, and said, *It is* my son's coat;
an [b]evil beast hath devoured him;
Joseph is without doubt rent in pieces.
(34) And Jacob rent his clothes, and put
sackcloth upon his loins, and mourned
for his son many days. (35) And all his
sons and all his daughters rose up to
comfort him; but he refused to be
comforted; and he said, For I will go
down into the grave unto my son
mourning. Thus his father wept for
him.
(36) And the Midianites sold him into
Egypt unto Potiphar, an [2]officer of
Pharaoh's, *and* [3][4]captain of the guard.

1 Heb., *hearkened.*

a Ps. 105. 17; Wisd. 10. 13; Acts 7. 9.

B.C. cir. 1729.

b ch. 44. 28.

2 Heb., *eunuch*: but the word doth signify not only *eunuchs*, but also *chamberlains*, *courtiers*, and *officers*.

3 Heb., *chief of the slaughtermen*, or, *executioners*.

4 Or, *chief marshal.*

"Balm," that is, balsam, was probably the resin of the *balsamodendron Gileadense*, a tree which grows abundantly in Gilead, and of which the gum was greatly in use for healing wounds. "Myrrh" was certainly *ladanum*, the gum of the cistus rose (*cistus creticus*). As all these were products of Palestine valued in Egypt, Jacob included them in his present to the governor there (chap. xliii. 11).

(28) **Twenty pieces of silver.**—Twenty shekels of silver were computed, in Lev. xxvii. 5, as the average worth of a male slave under twenty. It would be about £2 10s. of our money, but silver was of far greater value then than it is now.

(29) **Reuben returned.**—Evidently he was not present when Joseph was sold to the Midianites. This has been made into a difficulty, but really it confirms the truth of the narrative. For the difficulty arises solely from the supposition that Joseph's brethren immediately after casting him into the pit "sat down to eat bread," an act well described as most cold-blooded. But they were not actually guilty of it; for what the narrative says is that they were having their evening meal when the caravan came in sight. Reuben, between the casting of Joseph into the pit and the evening meal, had apparently gone a long round to fetch in the more distant cattle, and probably had remained away as long as possible, in order to feel sure that his brethren would on his return be at their dinner. He hoped thus to be able to go alone to the cistern, and rescue Joseph, and send him away home before the rest could interfere. Thus rightly understood, it is a proof of the trustworthiness of the history.

(31) **A kid of the goats.**—Heb., *a full grown he-goat.* Maimonides thinks that the reason why he-goats were so often used as sin-offerings under the Levitical law was to remind the Israelites of this great sin committed by their patriarchs.

(32) **They brought it.**—Heb., *they caused it to go*, that is, sent it by the hand of a messenger. They were unwilling to see the first burst of their father's agony.

And said.—These were the words that were to be spoken by the messenger who was charged to bear the coat to Jacob.

(34) **Many days.**—Jacob mourned for Joseph not merely during the usual period, but so long as to move even the hearts of those who had wronged him. For not only his daughters, but "all his sons rose up to comfort him." Probably he had several daughters by Leah and the two handmaidens, Dinah alone having been mentioned by name, because two of her brothers forfeited the birthright by the cruelty with which they avenged her wrong. We learn how long and intense Jacob's sorrow was from chap. xlv. 26—28. His daughters are mentioned also in chap. xlvi. 7.

(35) **Into the grave.**—Heb., *Sheol*, which, like Hades in Greek, means the place of departed spirits. Jacob supposed that Joseph had been devoured by wild beasts, and as he was not buried, the father could not have "gone down into the grave unto his son." (Comp. Note on chap. xv. 15.)

(36) **Midianites.**—Heb., *Medanites.* (See Note on verse 25.)

Potiphar.—Three chief interpretations are given of this name. The first explains it by two Coptic words, according to which it would signify "father of the king." This would make it an official name equivalent to prime minister or vizier. Gesenius considers it to be the same name as Potipherah (chap. xli. 50), and explains it as meaning "consecrated to Ra," that is, the sun-god. Thirdly, Canon Cook, in the "Excursus on Egyptian Words," at the end of Vol. I. of *The Speaker's Commentary*, argues with much cogency, that it means "father of the palace." This again would be an official name.

An officer.—Though this word literally in Hebrew signifies an eunuch, yet either, as seems probable from other places, it had come to mean any officer of the palace, or Potiphar was chief of the eunuchs, and therefore is himself numbered among them.

Captain of the guard.—Heb., *chief of the slaughterers*, by which the LXX. understand the slaughterers of animals for food, and translate "chief cook." The other versions understand by it the commander of the king's body-guard, whose business it would be to execute condemned criminals. A comparison with 2 Kings xxv. 8, where the same title is given to Nebuzar-adan, proves that this interpretation is correct.

CHAPTER XXXVIII. — (1) And it
came to pass at that time, that Judah
went down from his brethren, and
turned in to a certain Adullamite,
whose name *was* Hirah. (2) And Judah
saw there a daughter of a certain
Canaanite, whose name *was* [a]Shuah;
and he took her, and went in unto her.
(3) And she conceived, and bare a son;
and he called his name Er. (4) [b]And
she conceived again, and bare a son;
and she called his name Onan. (5) And
she yet again conceived, and bare a son;
and called his name Shelah: and he
was at Chezib, when she bare him.
(6) And Judah took a wife for Er his
firstborn, whose name *was* Tamar.
(7) And [c]Er, Judah's firstborn, was
wicked in the sight of the LORD; and
the LORD slew him. (8) And Judah said
unto Onan, Go in unto thy brother's
wife, and marry her, and raise up seed
to thy brother. (9) And Onan knew
that the seed should not be his; and it
came to pass, when he went in unto his
brother's wife, that he spilled *it* on the
ground, lest that he should give seed to
his brother. (10) And the thing which
he did [1]displeased the LORD: wherefore
he slew him also. (11) Then said Judah
to Tamar his daughter in law, Remain
a widow at thy father's house, till
Shelah my son be grown: for he said,
Lest peradventure he die also, as his

a 1 Chron. 2. 3.

b Num. 26. 19.

c Num. 26. 19.

B.C. cir. 1727.

1 Heb., *was evil in the eyes of the* LORD.

XXXVIII.

FAMILY HISTORY OF JUDAH.

This episode is no interruption of the narrative, for, as we have seen, the *Tôldôth Jacob* is the history generally of Jacob's posterity, and especially of the next great event in their development into a nation, namely the descent into Egypt. Two main reasons may be assigned therefore for giving this history of Judah's life; the first, that it shows the great risk of utter contamination incurred by the patriarchs in living among the Canaanites; the second, and more important, that Judah was invested by his father with the rights of primogeniture, and therefore that this history belongs to the genealogy of the Messiah.

(1) **At that time.**—This does not mean at the time of Joseph's sale; for as there was only an interval of twenty-two years between that event and the descent into Egypt, this period is scarcely long enough for the events recorded in this chapter. According to the usual chronology, Judah, Leah's fourth son, would not have been more than eight years old when he left Padan-aram, and only one year at most older than Joseph, the son of Jacob's old age. But the more true chronology which we have followed, gives time for him to have been Joseph's senior by twenty years, and the events recorded here probably began soon after his father's arrival at the tower of Eder.

Adullamite.—The town of Adullam, near which was David's famous cave, has been clearly identified by Lieut. Conder (*Tent-work*, ii. 158). It lay in the great valley of Elah, which formed the highway from Hebron to the country of the Philistines, some two or three miles south of Shochoh, and fifteen or sixteen miles west by north from Hebron. Judah "went down" thither, not as Abenezra and others have supposed, because it was to the south, but because it was towards the sea, and the road is an actual descent from the hill country of Judah into the Shephelah, or lowland, in which Adullam was situated. The sons of Jacob often, probably, with a few retainers, made expeditions in search of pastures for their cattle; and Hirah, apparently, had shown Judah hospitality on some such journey, and finally a friendship had grown up between them. "Turned in to," however, literally means *pitched* (his tent) *close by*; and the friendship between Judah and Hirah, thus accidentally formed, seems to have ended in Hirah taking the charge of Judah's cattle.

(2) **Canaanite.**—This is rendered in the Targum *merchant*, and so the Authorised Version translates Canaanite in Prov. xxxi. 24. In favour of this view is the fact, that the marriage of Simeon with a Canaanitish woman is regarded as an act so exceptional, as to be worth recording (chap. xlvi. 10). But we may well doubt whether, at so early an age, the terms Canaanite and merchant had become synonymous. "Shuah" was the name of the woman's father, as appears plainly in the Hebrew. (See also verse 12.)

(5) **Chezib.**—Mr. Conder has found traces of this place at *Ain Kezbeh*, near Beit Nettif, a little to the north of Adullam (*Handbook*, p. 408). In Micah i. 14, 15, it is called Achzib, and is there also placed near Adullam.

(8) **Go in unto thy brother's wife.**—We learn from this that the law of the Levirate, by which the brother of the dead husband was required to marry the widow, was of far more ancient date than the law of Moses. Its object, first of all, was to prevent the extinction of any line of descent, a matter of great importance in those genealogical days; and, secondly, it was an obstacle to the accumulation of landed property in few hands, as the son first born after the Levirate marriage inherited the property of his deceased uncle, while the second son was the representative of the real father. A similar custom existed in parts of India, Persia, &c., and prevails now among the Mongols. The Mosaic Law did not institute, but regulated the custom, confining such marriages to cases where the deceased brother had died without children, and permitting the brother to refuse to marry the widow, under a penalty, nevertheless, of disgrace. Onan, by refusing to take Tamar, may have been actuated by the selfish motive of obtaining for himself the rights of primogeniture, which would otherwise have gone to his eldest son, as the heir of his uncle 'Er.

(11) **For he said, lest he also die.**—It is evident from this that Judah, for reasons which, in verse 26, he acknowledged to be insufficient, wished to evade the duty of giving a third son to Tamar. It does not follow that he blamed her for their deaths; for the loss of two sons in succession might well frighten him. Philippsohn says that it became the rule, that if a woman lost two husbands, the third brother was not bound to marry her, and she was even called *Katlannith*,

brethren *did*. And Tamar went and
dwelt in her father's house.
(12) And [1]in process of time the
daughter of Shuah Judah's wife died;
and Judah was comforted, and went up
unto his sheepshearers to Timnath, he
and his friend Hirah the Adullamite.
(13) And it was told Tamar, saying, Be-
hold thy father in law goeth up to
Timnath to shear his sheep. (14) And
she put her widow's garments off from
her, and covered her with a vail, and
wrapped herself, and sat in an [2]open
place, which *is* by the way to Timnath;
for she saw that Shelah was grown, and
she was not given unto him to wife.
(15) When Judah saw her, he thought
her *to be* an harlot; because she had
covered her face. (16) And he turned
unto her by the way, and said, Go to,
I pray thee, let me come in unto thee;
(for he knew not that she *was* his
daughter in law). And she said, What
wilt thou give me, that thou mayest
come in unto me? (17) And he said, I
will send *thee* [3]a kid from the flock.
And she said, Wilt thou give *me* a
pledge, till thou send *it?* (18) And he
said, What pledge shall I give thee?
And she said, Thy signet, and thy
bracelets, and thy staff that *is* in thine
hand. And he gave *it* her, and came
in unto her, and she conceived by him.
(19) And she arose, and went away, and
laid by her vail from her, and put on
the garments of her widowhood. (20) And
Judah sent the kid by the hand of his
friend the Adullamite, to receive *his*
pledge from the woman's hand: but he
found her not. (21) Then he asked the
men of that place, saying, Where *is* the
harlot, that *was* [4]openly by the way
side? And they said, There was no
harlot in this *place*. (22) And he returned
to Judah, and said, I cannot find her;
and also the men of the place said, *that*
there was no harlot in this *place*. (23) And
Judah said, Let her take *it* to her, lest we
[5]be shamed: behold, I sent this kid,
and thou hast not found her.

1 Heb., *the days were multiplied.*

2 Heb., *the door of eyes,* or, *of Enajim.*

3 Heb., *a kid of the goats.*

4 Or, *in Enajim.*

5 Heb., *become a contempt.*

---

the murderess. (But see St. Matth. xxii. 25, 26, where no such custom is acknowledged.)

(12) **Timnath.**—There were two places of this name (Josh. xv. 10, 57). One was a little to the west of Bethlehem, the other upon the Philistine border, beyond Bethshemesh. As it lay, however, only about seven miles beyond Adullam, and as the flocks there were Judah's private property (verse 13), and under the charge of Hirah, this remoter place, now called Tibneh, is probably the Timnath meant, as at Bethlehem the pastures were occupied by his father. (See also verse 14.) For the sheep-shearing, see chap. xxxi. 19. Instead of "his friend Hirah," the LXX. and Vulg. render *his shepherd Hirah.* This would require no change in the consonants, but only in the vowels. Most of the other authorities agree with the Authorised Version; but even so, there was most probably some partnership between Judah and Hirah in these flocks, and they would be under Hirah's charge whenever Judah was absent, tending the flocks of his father.

(14) **In an open place.**—Heb., *in the gate of Enajim.* Enajim means "the two fountains," and we learn from verse 21 that it was the town where Tamar's father dwelt, and where Tamar was living with him in her widowhood. In the exploration of Palestine, Enajim has been identified with a place called Allin, Anin, or Anaim, three miles east of Tibneh, and situated upon an ancient road coming from Adullam. This makes the conclusion come to for other reasons certain, that the Timnath on the Philistine border was the town meant.

(15) **Because she had covered her face.**—The Jewish commentators all agree that this was not the custom of harlots; and as Judah, in verse 21, calls her *kedeshah,* one consecrated, he probably thought that she was a woman performing the vow required of every female votary of the Phœnician Venus (Astarte), once in her lifetime (Herod. i 199). Hence the hire was a kid to be sacrificed to the goddess. As for Tamar, her object was to assert her claim to the inheritance of 'Er. Lange considers that the wickedness of 'Er had caused him, equally with Onan, to neglect her, and that consequently there was no real incest. This is made probable by her immediate conception.

(18) **Thy bracelets.**—Heb., *thy cord.* The art of engraving was probably not advanced enough among these nomads to permit them to engrave gems small enough to wear in a ring. Judah evidently suspended his signet round his neck by a cord; and this custom still exists among the Arabs, of whom some wear signet rings, while others hang them round their necks. Probably each man of distinction had his emblem, and in chap. xlix. Jacob seems to refer to them. Thus Judah's emblem was a lion, Zebulun's a ship, Issachar's an ass, &c.

Thy staff.—The staff in ancient times was elaborately adorned. Herodotus (i. 195) describes the staves carried by the Babylonians, as having on them carvings of fruit, or of some flower or bird; and Homer perpetually makes mention of the "sceptres," that is, walking-sticks, of the kings, as carved so magnificently as to be worthy of being ascribed to Hephaestus, and handed down as emblems of authority from father to son. (See *Iliad,* ii. 101—107.) It is from these staves that the sceptres of kings, and the batons of field-marshals, &c., are derived.

(21) **Where is the harlot . . .?**—Heb., *Where is the kedeshah* (see verse 15) *that was at Enajim by the wayside?* "Enajim (the two founts) by-the-wayside," seems to have been the full name of the village. (See verse 14.)

(23) **Lest we be shamed.**—Maimonides asserts that Judah had committed no breach of the Law, the utmost therein commanded being that no Jewish woman should become a *kedeshah* (Deut. xxiii. 17). But Judah evidently regards what he had done as shameful, and

(24) And it came to pass about three
months after, that it was told Judah,
saying, Tamar thy daughter in law hath
played the harlot; and also, behold, she
is with child by whoredom. And Judah
said, Bring her forth, and let her be
burnt. (25) When she *was* brought forth,
she sent to her father in law, saying,
By the man, whose these *are*, *am* I with
child: and she said, Discern, I pray
thee, whose *are* these, the signet, and
bracelets, and staff. (26) And Judah
acknowledged *them*, and said, She hath
been more righteous than I; because
that I gave her not to Shelah my son.
And he knew her again no more.
(27) And it came to pass in the time
of her travail, that, behold, twins *were*
in her womb. (28) And it came to pass,
when she travailed, that *the one* put out
his hand: and the midwife took and
bound upon his hand a scarlet thread,
saying, This came out first. (29) And it
came to pass, as he drew back his hand,
that, behold, his brother came out: and
she said, [1]How hast thou broken forth?
this breach *be* upon thee: therefore his
name was called [2][a]Pharez. (30) And
afterward came out his brother, that
had the scarlet thread upon his hand:
and his name was called Zarah.

1 Or, *Wherefore hast thou made this breach against thee?*

2 That is, *A breach.*

a 1 Chron. 2. 4; Matt. 1. 3.

B. C. 1729.

CHAPTER XXXIX.—(1) And Joseph
was brought down to Egypt; and
Potiphar, an officer of Pharaoh, captain
of the guard, an Egyptian, bought him
of the hands of the Ishmeelites, which
had brought him down thither. (2) And
the LORD was with Joseph, and he was
a prosperous man; and he was in the
house of his master the Egyptian.
(3) And his master saw that the LORD
was with him, and that the LORD made
all that he did to prosper in his hand.
(4) And Joseph found grace in his sight,
and he served him: and he made him

---

having his friend's testimony, if needed, to prove that he had performed what he promised, he bears with the loss of his signet and staff, rather than let the people know that he had been guilty of an act which they too would condemn.

(24) **Let her be burnt.**—As being by law the wife of Shelah, Tamar was condemned by Judah in right of his position, as head of the family, to the punishment usual for adultery. In subsequent times, this penalty was limited to one who had married mother and daughter (Lev. xx. 14); or to the daughter of a priest guilty of unchastity (ibid. xxi. 9). On this account, the Jewish expositors argue that Tamar belonged to a priestly family, and some even think that she was descended from Melchisedek.

(25, 26) **She sent . . .**—The Talmud praises Tamar for so acting, as to bring no public disgrace upon Judah; and he acknowledges that he was most to blame, because the cause of her crime was his own failure to act justly by her.

(30) **Zarah.**—Heb., *the rising*, especially of the sun. There is in the name an allusion to the red streak placed upon the child's hand.

XXXIX.

JOSEPH'S FORTUNES IN THE HOUSE OF POTIPHAR.

(1) **Potiphar . . . bought him.** — Having given the genealogy of Judah's house, which, owing to the sins of Reuben, Simeon, and Levi, was now to be the Messianic line, and invested with the inheritance of the Abrahamic promises, the history reverts to Joseph, because it was through him that Israel was to be transplanted into Egypt. His life there is divided into two main portions, during the first of which, for thirteen years, he was a slave; while during the second, for seventy years, he was governor over all the land of Egypt. In his former capacity he is falsely accused by his mistress, and cast into prison. But this unjust treatment was the necessary pathway to his elevation, because it was in the prison that he interpreted the dreams of Pharaoh's two officers, and so, in the king's emergency, was summoned, upon the testimony of the chief butler, to appear before him.

(2) **The Lord.**—Heb., *Jehovah.* In the history of Joseph there is the greatest possible precision in the use of the divine names. Wherever, as here, the writer speaks in his own person, he uses the name Jehovah, which is a strong argument for the Mosaic authorship of this narrative, as while the whole colour of this *Tôldôth* is strongly Egyptian, the word Jehovah was not specifically the name, in the family of Abraham, for God in covenant with man until the time of the Exodus (Exod. vi. 3). Once Jacob uses it in the blessing of Dan (chap. xlix. 18), in an ejaculation marked by deep religious feeling, but the passage referred to in Exodus does not mean that the patriarchs did not use the name of Jehovah at all, but that it was a name with no particular fulness of meaning. Excepting this one place, the name of the Deity everywhere is either El or Elohim, with the article prefixed only on special occasions (see Notes on chaps. xlv. 8, xlvi. 3). Very probably Joseph had left memorials of his life behind him, in which naturally he used only the general term God. In framing these into a history, the writer carefully shows that it was the covenant Jehovah who guarded and kept His innocent worshipper.

Prosperous.—Heb., *causing to prosper.* Joseph brought a blessing with him to his master's house. (See verse 3, where the same word is translated *made to prosper.*)

In the house.—Slaves generally were bought for the hard work of the field, but Potiphar assigned to Joseph the lighter home service, because perhaps of his youth and comeliness.

(4) **He served him.**—Rather, *he ministered to him* (Num. iii. 6), as the word is used not so much of work as of office. So in chap. xl. 4, it is used of the attendance of Joseph upon the chief butler and baker in prison. His office is explained more exactly in the next

overseer over his house, and all *that* he had he put into his hand. (5) And it came to pass from the time *that* he had made him overseer in his house, and over all that he had, that the LORD blessed the Egyptian's house for Joseph's sake; and the blessing of the LORD was upon all that he had in the house, and in the field. (6) And he left all that he had in Joseph's hand; and he knew not ought he had, save the bread which he did eat. And Joseph was *a* goodly *person*, and well favoured.

(7) And it came to pass after these things, that his master's wife cast her eyes upon Joseph; and she said, Lie with me. (8) But he refused, and said unto his master's wife, Behold, my master wotteth not what *is* with me in the house, and he hath committed all that he hath to my hand; (9) *there is* none greater in this house than I; neither hath he kept back any thing from me but thee, because thou *art* his wife: how then can I do this great wickedness, and sin against God? (10) And it came to pass, as she spake to Joseph day by day, that he hearkened not unto her, to lie by her, *or* to be with her.

(11) And it came to pass about this time, that *Joseph* went into the house to do his business; and *there was* none of the men of the house there within. (12) And she caught him by his garment, saying, Lie with me: and he left his garment in her hand, and fled, and got him out. (13) And it came to pass, when she saw that he had left his garment in her hand, and was fled forth, (14) that she called unto the men of her house, and spake unto them, saying, See, he hath brought in an Hebrew unto us to mock us; he came in unto me to lie with me, and I cried with a [1]loud voice: (15) and it came to pass, when he heard that I lifted up my voice and cried, that he left his garment with me, and fled, and got him out. (16) And she laid up his garment by her, until his lord came home. (17) And she spake unto him according to these words, saying, The Hebrew servant, which thou hast brought unto us, came in unto me to mock me. (18) And it came to pass, as I lifted up my voice and cried, that he left his garment with me, and fled out. (19) And it came to pass, when his master heard the words of his wife, which she spake unto him, saying, After this manner did thy servant to me; that his wrath was kindled. (20) And Joseph's master took him, and put him into the prison, a place where the king's prisoners *were* bound: and he was there in the prison.

(21) But the LORD was with Joseph, and [2]shewed him mercy, and gave him favour in the sight of the keeper of the prison. (22) And the keeper of the prison

1 Heb., *great.*

2 Heb., *extended kindness unto him.*

---

verse, where we read that "he made him overseer," or his deputy. In the Egyptian monuments we often find an overseer with writing materials keeping an account of all expenditure and of the labour done.

(6) **Save the bread . . .**—Aben Ezra connects this with the first clause in the verse, and says that Potiphar did not leave his food in Joseph's hand, because as an Egyptian he could not eat victuals prepared by a Hebrew. (See chap. xliii. 32.) But in any case the meaning would be, that Potiphar did not care to know about anything except the food prepared for his own use.

A goodly person and well favoured.—These are the words used of Rachel in chap. xxix. 17, where see Note.

(7) **His master's wife.**—Egyptian women did not live in seclusion, nor did they go veiled. (See chap. xii. 13; Rawlinson, *Hist. Ancient Egypt*, i. 552.) The story of an innocent youth calumniated by an unchaste woman whom he has repulsed, became a favourite subject with classical authors, as in the myths of Bellerophon and Anteia, Hippolytus and Phaedra, and others. The Egyptians had a favourite popular romance of this kind, called "The Two Brothers," in which the wife of the elder brother Anpu behaves towards Bata, the younger, in exactly the same way as Potiphar's wife towards Joseph. See *Records of the Past*, ii. 139—152.

(11) **To do his business.**—That is, to attend to his ordinary duties as steward. The absence of all men from the house is explained by the supposition that it was a festival; but as she called to them (verse 14) it seems as if they were engaged in their several departments close by.

(14) **He hath brought in.**—The wife ascribes it as a fault to Potiphar, that, by buying a foreign slave, he had exposed her to insult. And so in verse 17.

(20) **Prison.**—Heb., *sohar*. This word occurs in the Bible only in this and the next chapter, but in the Talmud it is used for a walled prison. It is supposed to mean a round or arched tower. As the king's prisoners were confined there, it was a portion of Potiphar's official residence, as he was captain of the royal body-guard (see chap. xl. 3); but we learn that it had its own keeper, though Potiphar was the chief in command (chap. xl. 4). The Jewish commentators consider that Potiphar did not really believe the accusation, or he would certainly have put Joseph to death. We learn, however, from Ps. cv. 18, that his treatment in the prison at first was very severe; but as Potiphar, in chap. xl. 4, is said to have entrusted Joseph with the

committed to Joseph's hand all the
prisoners that *were* in the prison; and
whatsoever they did there, he was the
doer *of it.* (23) The keeper of the prison
looked not to any thing *that was* under
his hand; because the LORD was with
him, and *that* which he did, the LORD
made *it* to prosper.

CHAPTER XL.—(1) And it came to
pass after these things, *that* the butler
of the king of Egypt and *his* baker had
offended their lord the king of Egypt.
(2) And Pharaoh was wroth against two
of his officers, against the chief of the
butlers, and against the chief of the
bakers. (3) And he put them in ward in
the house of the captain of the guard,
into the prison, the place where Joseph
was bound. (4) And the captain of the
guard charged Joseph with them, and
he served them: and they continued
a season in ward.
(5) And they dreamed a dream both of
them, each man his dream in one night,
each man according to the interpretation
of his dream, the butler and the baker
of the king of Egypt, which *were* bound
in the prison. (6) And Joseph came in
unto them in the morning, and looked
upon them, and, behold, they *were* sad.
(7) And he asked Pharaoh's officers that
were with him in the ward of his lord's
house, saying, Wherefore [1]look ye *so*
sadly to day? (8) And they said unto
him, We have dreamed a dream, and
there is no interpreter of it. And Joseph
said unto them, *Do* not interpretations
belong to God? tell me *them,* I pray
you.
(9) And the chief butler told his dream
to Joseph, and said to him, In my
dream, behold, a vine *was* before me;
(10) and in the vine *were* three branches:
and it *was* as though it budded, *and* her
blossoms shot forth; and the clusters
thereof brought forth ripe grapes:
(11) and Pharaoh's cup *was* in my hand:
and I took the grapes, and pressed them
into Pharaoh's cup, and I gave the cup

B.C. cir. 1720.

[1] Heb., *are your faces evil.*

B.C. cir. 1718.

---

charge of the chief butler and baker, he must soon have been convinced of his innocence.

XL.

JOSEPH INTERPRETS THE DREAMS OF THE CHIEF BUTLER AND BAKER.

(1) **Butler.**—Heb., *one who gives to drink,* cup-bearer. As we learn in verse 11 that it was grape-wine which he gave the king to drink, this chapter has been the main dependence of the new critics for their proof that the Book of Genesis was not written by Moses. For Herod. (ii. 77) says, "The Egyptians make use of wine prepared from barley, because there are no vineyards in their country." As Herodotus was thirteen centuries later than the time of Joseph, they argue not only that the vine could not have been introduced into Egypt at so early a date, but that the records of Joseph's life could not have been put together by any-one acquainted with Egypt, in spite of their exact knowledge in all other respects of Egyptian customs. But when we turn to Herodotus himself, we find the most complete refutation of the previous statement. For, in Book ii. 37, speaking of the liberal treatment of the priests, he says, that they had an allowance of "grape-wine." Again, in chap. 39, he tells us that it was the custom to pour wine on a victim about to be sacrificed. To one used to the extensive vineyards of Greece and Asia Minor, the comparative scarcity of the vine, and the use of another ordinary drink in its place, would be striking; but that he was guilty of gross exaggeration in his statement is proved by evidence far more trustworthy than his own writings. For, on the tombs at Beni-hassan, which are anterior to the time of Joseph, on those at Thebes, and on the Pyramids, are representations of vines grown in every way, except that usual in Italy, festooned on trees; there is every process of the vintage, grapes in baskets, men trampling them in vats, various forms of presses for squeezing out the juice, jars for storing it, and various processes, even of the fermentation, noticed. Numerous engravings of the sculptures and paintings on these ancient monuments may be seen in Wilkinson's *Egypt;* and most abundant evidence of the culture of the vine in ancient Egypt has been collected, and an account of the vines grown there given in Malan's *Philosophy or Truth,* pp. 31—39. It neither is nor ever was a great wine-producing country, but the vine existed from one end of the country to the other, as it does at this day.

Baker.—Wilkinson, *Ancient Egyptians,* ii. 38, 39, gives proof from the monuments, that they had carried the art of making confectionery to very great perfection.

(3, 4) **In the house of the captain of the guard.**—That is, of Potiphar. As he is said to have charged Joseph with the care of these two high officials, he must, ere this, have become aware of his innocence. But as the wife in ancient times in Egypt was endowed with all the husband's property, and was a formidable person, as we learn from many of the records now being translated and published, Potiphar may not have wished to offend her.

He served them.—Used only of light service. (See Note on chap. xxxix. 4.)

(8) **There is no interpreter.**—In Egypt it was the business of men trained for the purpose, called in chap. xli. 8, *magicians* and *wise men,* to interpret dreams, and to such the butler and baker could have no access from their prison. But Joseph denies that art and training can really avail, and claims that the interpretation belongs to God.

(11) **And pressed them.**—Plutarch, *Is. et Osir.* § 6, says that before the time of Psammetichus the Egyptians did not drink wine, nor make libations of it to the gods. This statement has been abundantly disproved, and probably arose from the writer supposing that the

into Pharaoh's hand. (12) And Joseph
said unto him, This *is* the interpretation
of it: The three branches *are* three
days: (13) Yet within three days shall
Pharaoh [1]lift up thine head, and restore
thee unto thy place: and thou shalt
deliver Pharaoh's cup into his hand,
after the former manner when thou
wast his butler. (14) But [2]think on me
when it shall be well with thee, and
shew kindness, I pray thee, unto me,
and make mention of me unto Pharaoh,
and bring me out of this house. (15) For
indeed I was stolen away out of the
land of the Hebrews: and here also
have I done nothing that they should
put me into the dungeon.
(16) When the chief baker saw that
the interpretation was good, he said
unto Joseph, I also *was* in my dream,
and, behold, *I had* three [3]white baskets
on my head: (17) and in the uppermost
basket *there was* of all manner [4]of bake-
meats for Pharaoh; and the birds did
eat them out of the basket upon my
head. (18) And Joseph answered and
said, This *is* the interpretation thereof:
The three baskets *are* three days:
(19) Yet within three days shall Pharaoh
[5]lift up thy head from off thee, and
shall hang thee on a tree; and the birds
shall eat thy flesh from off thee.
(20) And it came to pass the third day,
which was Pharaoh's birthday, that he
made a feast unto all his servants: and
he [6]lifted up the head of the chief
butler and of the chief baker among
his servants. (21) And he restored the
chief butler unto his butlership again;
and he gave the cup into Pharaoh's
hand: (22) but he hanged the chief
baker: as Joseph had interpreted to
them. (23) Yet did not the chief butler
remember Joseph, but forgat him.

CHAPTER XLI.—(1) And it came to
pass at the end of two full years, that
Pharaoh dreamed: and, behold, he

1 Or, *reckon.*

2 Heb., *remember me with thee.*

3 Or, *full of holes.*

4 Heb., *meat of Pharaoh, the work of a baker, or, cook.*

5 Or, *reckon thee, and take thy office from thee.*

B.C. cir. 1715.

6 Or, *reckoned.*

---

custom of, possibly, one district was the universal rule. Nevertheless, the king's drink here does not seem to have been fermented wine, but a sort of sherbet made of fresh grape-juice and water. It is a pleasant beverage, still much used in the East, but sometimes the grape juice is left till fermentation has just begun when it acquires a pleasant briskness, and is less cloying.

Into Pharaoh's hand.—Heb., *I placed the cup upon Pharaoh's palm.* The word is used in chap. xxxii. 25 of the *hollow* of Jacob's thigh (see Note there). Here it means the hollow produced by bending the fingers inwards. Now the Hebrews always spoke of placing the cup in a person's hand (Ezek. xxiii. 31, and see Ps. lxxv. 8; Jer. li. 7); and even here Joseph, though probably speaking the Egyptian language, nevertheless used the Hebrew idiom, saying, *thou wilt give Pharaoh's cup into his hand.* It is the Egyptian cup-bearer, who, using the idiom of his own country, speaks of placing the cup upon Pharaoh's palm, the reason being that Egyptian cups had no stems, but were flat bowls or saucers, held in the very way which the cup-bearer describes.

(15) **I was stolen.**—Joseph here speaks only generally, as his purpose was to arouse the sympathy of the Egyptian by making him know that he was free born, and reduced to slavery by fraud. It would have done harm rather than good to have said that his sale was owing to family feuds; and, moreover, noble-minded men do not willingly reveal that which is to the discredit of their relatives.

Land of the Hebrews.—Jacob and his race had settled possessions in Canaan at Hebron, Shechem, Beer-sheba, &c. The term Hebrew, moreover, was an old one; for in the ancient record of the invasion of Palestine by Chedorlaomer, we saw that Abram was described as "the Hebrew" (chap. xiv. 13). But Joseph did not mean that the land of Canaan belonged to them, but that he was stolen from the settlements of these "immigrants," and from the land wherein they sojourned.

(16, 17) **Three white baskets.**—Rashi explains the phrase of baskets of wicker-work, but most commentators agree in rendering it "baskets of white bread." The "bakemeats" were all preparations of pastry and confectionery, as throughout the Bible *meat* does not mean flesh, but food. (Comp. Luke xxiv. 41; John xxi. 5.)

On my head.—The Egyptian men carried burdens on their heads; the women on their shoulders (Herod. ii. 35).

Bakemeats.—Heb., *All sorts of work for Pharaoh the work of a baker.*

(19) **Shall Pharaoh lift up thy head from off thee.**—In verse 13 the lifting up of the butler's head meant his elevation to his former rank. Here there is the significant addition "from off thee," implying that he would be beheaded, and his body publicly exposed to ignominy.

(20) **He lifted up the head.**—From its use in this verse some have supposed that the phrase must mean "to put them on their trial," or "take account of them" (whence the margin *reckon*). More probably the words are used to point out the exact fulfilment of Joseph's interpretation of their dreams.

XLI.

JOSEPH INTERPRETS PHARAOH'S DREAMS; HE IS MADE GOVERNOR OF EGYPT, AND MARRIES THERE.

(1) **Pharaoh dreamed.**—After two years spent in the prison, the time has now come for Joseph's elevation to power; and it is to be noticed that this was not brought about by those arts by which men usually attain to greatness, such as statesmanship, or military skill; nor was it by accident, but according to the Biblical rule, by the direct intervention of Providence.

stood by the river. (2) And, behold,
there came up out of the river seven
well favoured kine and fatfleshed; and
they fed in a meadow. (3) And, behold,
seven other kine came up after them
out of the river, ill favoured and lean-
fleshed; and stood by the *other* kine
upon the brink of the river. (4) And the
ill favoured and leanfleshed kine did
eat up the seven well favoured and fat
kine. So Pharaoh awoke. (5) And he
slept and dreamed the second time:
and, behold, seven ears of corn came
up upon one stalk, [1]rank and good.
(6) And, behold, seven thin ears and
blasted with the east wind sprung up
after them. (7) And the seven thin ears
devoured the seven rank and full ears.
And Pharaoh awoke, and, behold, *it was*
a dream.
(8) And it came to pass in the morning
that his spirit was troubled; and he sent
and called for all the magicians of Egypt,
and all the wise men thereof: and Pha-
raoh told them his dream; but *there was*
none that could interpret them unto
Pharaoh.
(9) Then spake the chief butler unto
Pharaoh, saying, I do remember my
faults this day: (10) Pharaoh was wroth
with his servants, and put me in ward
in the captain of the guard's house, *both*
me and the chief baker: (11) and we
dreamed a dream in one night, I and he;
we dreamed each man according to the
interpretation of his dream. (12) And
there was there with us a young man, an
Hebrew, servant to the captain of the
guard; and we told him, and he [a]inter-
preted to us our dreams; to each man
according to his dream he did interpret.
(13) And it came to pass, as he interpret-
ed to us, so it was; me he restored unto
mine office, and him he hanged.
(14) [b]Then Pharaoh sent and called
Joseph, and they [2]brought him hastily

1 Heb., *fat.*

a ch. 40. 12, &c.

b Ps. 105. 20.

2 Heb., *made him run.*

Just as centuries afterwards, Daniel rose to high office at Babylon by God making known to him the dream of Nebuchadnezzar; so here, the transplantation of Israel into Egypt is brought about by the revelation to Joseph of "what was to be hereafter."

The river.—Heb., *Yeor*, the Egyptian word for "great river." It is the usual name in the Bible for the Nile, but is used for the Tigris in Dan. xii. 5, 6, and for any large river in Job xxviii. 10. The Pharaoh in whose reign Joseph became governor of Egypt, is generally supposed to have been Apophis, the most famous of the shepherd kings. But Canon Cook, in his Essay, *On the bearings of Egyptian History upon the Pentateuch*, after carefully reviewing the whole subject, decides in favour of King Amenemha III., the greatest monarch of the noble twelfth dynasty, and the last king of all Egypt.

(2) **Kine.**—The cow was regarded by the Egyptians as the symbol of the earth, and of agriculture; and naturally both the kine and the ears of wheat rose out of the river, because as no rain falls in Egypt, its fertility entirely depends upon the overflow of the Nile. The cows sacred to Isis were seven in number, and in a copy of the *Ritual of the Dead*, Mr. Malan (p. 192) found a picture of the seven sacred cows with the divine bull.

In a meadow.—Heb., *in the marsh-grass.* The word occurs only in this chapter and in Job viii. 11, where it is translated *flag.* It is the name of the rank herbage which grows luxuriantly along the banks of the Nile; or, as some think, of one special kind of marsh-grass, called by botanists *cyperus esculentus.*

(5) **Seven ears . . . upon one stalk.**—The wheat cultivated in Egypt is called *triticum compositum*, because it produces several ears upon the same stalk. The statement of Herodotus (ii. 36), that the Egyptians regarded it as disgraceful to feed upon wheat or barley, is disproved by the paintings in the temples, especially in the district of Thebes, which show that it was the main crop there, and its cultivation held in high honour. Maspero, *Hist. Ancienne*, p. 9, says, "In spite of Herodotus, the usual food of the people was wheat and other cereals, which the soil of Egypt produces in abundance."

(6) **East wind.**—In Palestine the prevalent winds are those which blow from the west or east, and the latter, coming across arid deserts, is injurious to vegetation. In Egypt the winds generally are from the north or south, but the south-east wind, called Chamsin, blowing from the deserts of Arabia, has even more disastrous effects upon plants than the east wind in Palestine, and from the small dust with which it is laden is baleful also to human life. As there are no words in Hebrew for any except the four principal winds, this south-eastern wind may be meant; or as *kĕdim*, east wind, became the usual name of every wind that burned up vegetation, the term may be employed in a general sense.

(8) **Magicians.**—The word used here probably means the "sacred scribes," who were skilled in writing and reading hieroglyphics. But in ancient times the possession of real knowledge was generally accompanied by a claim to an occult and mysterious acquaintance with the secrets of the gods and of nature. And as the people regarded the knowledge which such scribes really possessed as more than human, the claim was easily maintained, or, rather, grew naturally out of the superstition of the multitude. So, too, the "wise men" were men educated and trained, but probably the profession of magic, of divination, and astrology was that which gained for them wealth and honour, and not the possession of whatever real science existed at that time in Egypt. We find, subsequently, even Joseph claiming the power of divination.

There was none that could interpret . . .—Probably many of the wise men made the attempt, but in such an imperfect manner as not to be able to satisfy Pharaoh's mind, or allay the excitement of his spirit.

(14) **He shaved himself.**—Herodotus (ii. 36) mentions that the Egyptians suffered their hair and beards

out of the dungeon: and he shaved *him-*
self, and changed his raiment, and came
in unto Pharaoh. (15) And Pharaoh said
unto Joseph, I have dreamed a dream,
and *there is* none that can interpret it:
and I have heard say of thee, *that* [1]thou
canst understand a dream to interpret
it.

(16) And Joseph answered Pharaoh,
saying, *It is* not in me: God shall give
Pharaoh an answer of peace.

(17) And Pharaoh said unto Joseph, In
my dream, behold, I stood upon the
bank of the river: (18) and, behold, there
came up out of the river seven kine, fat-
fleshed and well favoured; and they fed
in a meadow: (19) and, behold, seven
other kine came up after them, poor and
very ill favoured and leanfleshed, such
as I never saw in all the land of Egypt
for badness: (20) and the lean and the
ill favoured kine did eat up the first
seven fat kine: (21) and when they had
[2]eaten them up, it could not be known
that they had eaten them; but they
were still ill favoured, as at the begin-
ning. So I awoke. (22) And I saw in
my dream, and, behold, seven ears came
up in one stalk, full and good: (23) and,
behold, seven ears, [3]withered, thin, *and*
blasted with the east wind, sprung up
after them: (24) and the thin ears devour-
ed the seven good ears: and I told *this*
unto the magicians; but *there was* none
that could declare *it* to me.

(25) And Joseph said unto Pharaoh,
The dream of Pharaoh *is* one: God hath
shewed Pharaoh what he *is* about to do.
(26) The seven good kine *are* seven years;
and the seven good ears *are* seven years:
the dream *is* one. (27) And the seven thin
and ill favoured kine that came up after
them *are* seven years; and the seven
empty ears blasted with the east wind
shall be seven years of famine. (28) This
is the thing which I have spoken unto
Pharaoh: What God *is* about to do he
sheweth unto Pharaoh. (29) Behold,
there come seven years of great plenty
throughout all the land of Egypt:
(30) and there shall arise after them seven
years of famine; and all the plenty
shall be forgotten in the land of Egypt;
and the famine shall consume the land;
(31) and the plenty shall not be known in
the land by reason of that famine follow-
ing; for it *shall be* very [4]grievous.
(32) And for that the dream was doubled
unto Pharaoh twice; *it is* because the
thing *is* [5]established by God, and God
will shortly bring it to pass. (33) Now
therefore let Pharaoh look out a man
discreet and wise, and set him over the
land of Egypt. (34) Let Pharaoh do *this*,
and let him appoint [6]officers over the
land, and take up the fifth part of the
land of Egypt in the seven plenteous
years. (35) And let them gather all the
food of those good years that come, and
lay up corn under the hand of Pharaoh,
and let them keep food in the cities.
(36) And that food shall be for store to
the land against the seven years of
famine, which shall be in the land of
Egypt; that the land [7]perish not through
the famine.

(37) And the thing was good in the
eyes of Pharaoh, and in the eyes of all

1 Or, *when thou hearest a dream, thou canst interpret it.*

2 Heb., *come to the inward parts of them.*

3 Or, *small.*

4 Heb., *heavy.*

5 Or, *prepared of God.*

6 Or, *overseers.*

7 Heb., *be not cut off.*

---

to grow only when in mourning; whereas in Palestine the beard was regarded as a manly ornament. On Egyptian monuments only captives and men of low condition are represented with beards. In the prison, therefore, Joseph would leave his beard untrimmed, but when summoned into the king's presence, he would shave it off. Abravanel notices that for each suffering of Joseph there was an exact recompense. It was for dreams that his brethren hated him, and by help of dreams he was exalted in Egypt. They stripped him of his many-coloured coat; the Egyptians clothed him in byssus. They cast him into a pit, and from the pit of the prison he was drawn forth by Pharaoh. They sold him into slavery; in Egypt he was made lord.

(18) **In a meadow.**—Heb., *in the marsh-grass*, as in verse 2.

(19) **Poor and very ill-favoured and leanfleshed.**—Pharaoh, in his recital, describes his dreams at greater length than is the case in the narrative (verses 2—7), and also mentions the impressions made upon his imagination by what he had seen, as, for instance, that he had never beheld such lean cattle, and that they were as wretched in look after eating up the fat kine as before. There is also a slight difference in his description of the kine. In verse 3 they are called "evil in appearance, and lean of flesh;" but the words here are "lean, and evil in shape, and thin of flesh."

(23) **Withered.**—This word occurs only in this place. Its meaning is *stony*, that is, the grains were shrivelled and hard like bits of grit.

(34) **Take up the fifth part of the land.**—Heb., *let him fifth the land*, that is, exact a fifth part of the produce. It has been supposed that it had been usual in Egypt to pay to the king a tithe of the crop, and the doubling of the impost would not press very heavily on the people in these years of extraordinary abundance. As the reason of the enactment would be made known, it would also induce all careful people to store up a portion of their own superabundance for future need

his servants. (38) And Pharaoh said
unto his servants, Can we find *such a one*
as this *is*, a man in whom the Spirit of
God *is?* (39) And Pharaoh said unto
Joseph, Forasmuch as God hath shewed
thee all this, *there is* none so discreet
and wise as thou *art:* (40) [a]thou shalt
be over my house, and according unto
thy word shall all my people [1]be ruled:
only in the throne will I be greater than
thou. (41) And Pharaoh said unto Joseph,
See, I have set thee over all the land of
Egypt. (42) And Pharaoh took off his
ring from his hand, and put it upon
Joseph's hand, and arrayed him in ves-
tures of [2]fine linen, and put a gold chain
about his neck; (43) and he made him
to ride in the second chariot which he
had; and they cried before him, [3][4]Bow
the knee: and he made him *ruler* over
all the land of Egypt. (44) And Pharaoh
said unto Joseph, I *am* Pharaoh, and
without thee shall no man lift up his
hand or foot in all the land of Egypt.
(45) And Pharaoh called Joseph's name
Zaphnath-paaneah; and he gave him to
wife Asenath the daughter of Poti-pherah
[5]priest of On. And Joseph went out
over *all* the land of Egypt.
(46) And Joseph *was* thirty years old

a Ps. 105. 21; 1 Mac. 2. 53; Acts 7. 10.

1 Heb., *be armed*, or, *kiss*.

2 Or, *silk*.

3 Or, *Tender father*.

4 Heb., *Abrech*.

5 Or, *prince*.

Subsequently, a fifth of the produce was fixed by Joseph permanently as the king's rent.

(38) **In whom the Spirit of God is.**—Joseph from the first declared that he neither claimed for himself, nor possessed any art of divination, but that "Elohim would answer (that which would be for) the peace of Pharaoh" (verse 16). And not only does Pharaoh now recognise the truth of Joseph's words, but sees also in him the instrument by which Elohim had spoken. But besides the interpretation of the dreams, Joseph had given the king wise and prudent advice, and he justly felt that one so gifted by God, and so intelligent in counsel, was the person best fitted to carry Egypt through the years of trouble in store for her.

(40) **Over my house.**—The chief over the palace was in ancient times next in power to the sovereign, and under the Frankish kings the "major domi," or mayor of the palace, first usurped the whole royal power, and finally Pepin, the son of Charles Martel, took the name of king as well as the reality.

According unto thy word shall all my people be ruled.—The general sense is easy, namely that all the people of Egypt should obey Joseph's orders, but the translation of the phrase is difficult. The ordinary meaning of the verb is *to kiss*, and the translation would then be *And on thy mouth shall all my people kiss*, that is, they shall do thee homage (1 Sam. x. 1; Ps. ii. 12). The versions seem to have taken this sense, though they translate very loosely "shall obey thee;" or "shall receive judgment at thy mouth;" or "shall be governed by thee." As however in 1 Chron. xii. 2; 2 Chron. xvii. 17; Ps. lxxviii. 9, the verb is used of bearing arms, Aben-Ezra translates "shall arm themselves," and supposes that Joseph was made commander-in-chief. Others, again, form the verb used here from the same root as that which would give *meshek* in chap. xv. 2 the meaning of "running about," and translate *at thy mouth*, that is, *according to thy command, shall all my people busy themselves*. The first is the most natural and probable rendering.

In the throne.—Heb., *as to the throne*, in all that concerns my royal rank, dignity, and rights.

(42) **His ring.**—Heb., *his signet ring*. As decrees became law when stamped with the royal signet, it was naturally the symbol of authority; and so with us, at the formation of a ministry the great seal is formally delivered into the hands of the highest legal personage in the realm, who is thus invested with power.

Vestures of fine linen.—The word used here is Egyptian, *shesh*, and signifies a kind of flax from which linen of great fineness and whiteness was made. Much of the dress of the Levitical priests was to be made of this flax, called in Hebrew byssus (Exod. xxxix. 28, &c.). In the East it is usual on all occasions of showing the royal favour, to give changes of raiment: but there is here the further signification, that as this fine white linen was the special dress of the king and the priests, the bestowal of it indicated Joseph's admission into the ruling classes of Egypt. Probably, as he married a priest's daughter, he was himself also previously enrolled among the ranks of the priesthood.

A gold chain.—This also appears upon the monuments as one of the royal insignia. Ancient necklaces of such exquisite workmanship have been discovered in Egypt, that patterns copied from them are common now at the chief jewellers.

(43) **In the second chariot.**—The object of this procession was to display Joseph to the people as their new governor. The Pharaoh, probably, took the chief part in this parade, riding in the first chariot of state.

Bow the knee.—Heb., *abrech*. Canon Cook explains this as meaning *rejoice, be happy*. It is in the imperative singular, and is addressed by the people to Joseph; for it is said "they cried before him," that is, the multitude, and not a herald. Naturally, therefore, it is in the singular, as the *vivat rex* of the Middle Ages, or *vive le roi* now. The similarity of sound with *habrech*, bow the knee, is a mere chance, and as this word also is singular, it must be addressed to Joseph, and not to the people.

(45) **Zaphnath-paaneah.**—This word also is Egyptian, and, fortunately, there is no Hebrew word of similar sound to suggest a false meaning. Canon Cook shows that it means "food of life," or "food of the living." The LXX. have *Psonthom-phanek*, which Jerome, on the authority of the Jews in Egypt, translates "saviour of the world." By "the world," would be meant the living, as in Canon Cook's explanation, which, in the sense of "he who feeds the world," or "the living," is the best exposition yet given. There is no authority for the supposition that the name means "revealer of secrets."

Asenath.—An Egyptian word signifying the "favourite of Neith," the Egyptian Minerva.

Potipherah.—See Note on chap. xxxix. 1.

On.—This is also an Egyptian word, signifying the sun, whence in Hebrew the name of this city was Beth-shemesh, *house of the sun*; in Greek, Heliopolis; and in Latin, Oppidum Solis. It was famous for its temple of Ra, the sun, destroyed at an early period by the

when he stood before Pharaoh king of
Egypt. And Joseph went out from
the presence of Pharaoh, and went
throughout all the land of Egypt.
(47) And in the seven plenteous years
the earth brought forth by handfuls.
(48) And he gathered up all the food of
the seven years, which were in the land
of Egypt, and laid up the food in the
cities: the food of the field, which *was*
round about every city, laid he up in the
same. (49) And Joseph gathered corn as
the sand of the sea, very much, until he
left numbering; for *it was* without
number.
(50) [a]And unto Joseph were born two
sons before the years of famine came,
which Asenath the daughter of Poti-
pherah [1]priest of On bare unto him.
(51) And Joseph called the name of the
firstborn [2]Manasseh: For God, *said he*,
hath made me forget all my toil, and all
my father's house. (52) And the name of
the second called he [3]Ephraim: For God
hath caused me to be fruitful in the
land of my affliction.
(53) And the seven years of plenteous-
ness, that was in the land of Egypt,
were ended. (54) [b]And the seven years
of dearth began to come, according as
Joseph had said: and the dearth was in
all lands; but in all the land of Egypt
there was bread. (55) And when all the
land of Egypt was famished, the people
cried to Pharaoh for bread: and Pharaoh
said unto all the Egyptians, Go unto
Joseph; what he saith to you, do.
(55) And the famine was over all the face
of the earth: And Joseph opened [4]all
the storehouses, and sold unto the
Egyptians; and the famine waxed sore
in the land of Egypt. (57) And all

a ch. 46. 20. & 48. 5.

B.C. cir. 1711.

1 Or, *prince*.

B.C. cir. 1708.

2 That is, *forgetting*.

3 That is, *fruitful*.

b Ps. 105. 16.

B.C. cir. 1712.

4 Heb., *all wherein was*.

Persians, but still remarkable for its ruins, among which is an obelisk covered with hieroglyphics of extreme antiquity. Several of the obelisks now at Rome were brought by the emperor Caligula from this spot. It is situated about six miles north-east of Cairo.

A difficulty has been felt by some in a Hebrew shepherd being thus described as marrying the daughter of a priest of the sun; and also that Joseph, a worshipper of the One God, should ally himself with an idolater. But the elevation of a slave to high rank is not an uncommon occurrence in the East, especially as he might be of as good birth and education as his owner, slaves being obtained either by kidnapping, or by war. And a slave so raised to power, would not be likely to oppose his benefactor, nor would even a high priest refuse a daughter to the king's favourite, especially if, as appears to have been the case, he had first been raised to the priesthood. Joseph too, would rightly regard the whole matter as providential, and though he might not know for what exact purpose, as regards his race, he was thus exalted, there was noble work for him to do in saving Egypt from perishing by famine. The narrative throughout represents him as remaining true to the religion of his family (chaps. xli. 51, 52; xlii. 18; xliii. 29; xlv. 5, 7, 8, 9; xlviii. 9; l. 19, 20, 24), but probably, on public occasions he would be required to attend at the religious solemnities of the Egyptian gods. We must remember, however, that their worship had not degenerated as yet into the miserable idolatry of later times, and that the Egyptian creed contained much primæval truth, though in a corrupted form. Pharaoh himself, in verses 38, 39, speaks as one that acknowledged a supreme God, and Joseph throughout freely used to him the name of Elohim. As for Asenath, no doubt Joseph would teach her higher views of the Deity, and make her acquainted with the religious hopes and destinies of the Abrahamic race.

The possibility, however, of a foreigner attaining to high rank in Egypt, is demonstrated by the story of Saneha, translated in *Records of the Past*, vol. vi., pp. 131—150. It belongs to the reign of Amenemha I., a king of the twelfth dynasty, and represents Saneha as entering Egypt in the dress of a herbseller, but in time he marries there the eldest daughter of a local king, has a large landed estate given him, "which abounded in wines more than in water," and, finally, is sent for by King Amenemha, and raised to such high rank, as to be clad in "garments of kingly attire," and on his going to the royal palace "the king's children attend him, proceeding even unto the great gates." This curious evidence, which is even a little older than the time of Joseph, proves that there is nothing unusual or improbable in his exaltation.

(48) **All the food.**—Probably besides the fifth paid as tax to the king, and out of which all the current expenses of the realm would have to be provided, Joseph bought corn largely during these years when it was at its cheapest.

(51) **Manasseh.**—That is, *causing to forget*. Joseph has been blamed for forgetting "his father's house," but the phrase means that now that he was married and had a child, he ceased to suffer from home sickness, and became contented with his lot. He pined no longer for the open downs of Canaan as he had done in the prison; but his love for his father was as warm as ever.

(52) **Ephraim.**—That is, *fruitfulness*. The dual ending probably intensifies the meaning.

(54) **The dearth.**—As the Nile at this early period was not assisted and regulated in its overflow by dams and canals, famines were much more common in Egypt than when subsequently the kings had done so much to provide against this danger. As, too, this dearth was "in all lands," in Arabia, Palestine, Ethiopia, &c., there was evidently a long period of excessive drought. Still Egypt is always liable to famine, and Bar-Hebræus (*Chronicon*, p. 260) gives terrible details of the sufferings of Egypt in the year of the Hej'ra 462, when so great was the loss of life, that whereas in the city of Tanis (Zoan) 300,000 men paid poll-tax in the previous year, there remained in it less than a hundred souls at the end of the dearth.

One argument adduced by Canon Cook, *Excursus on the Bearings of Egyptian History on the Pentateuch*, p. 451, for placing the descent of the Israelites into Egypt in the reign of Amenemha III., is that it

countries came into Egypt to Joseph for
to buy *corn;* because that the famine
was *so* sore in all lands.

CHAPTER XLII. — (1) Now when
[a]Jacob saw that there was corn in Egypt,
Jacob said unto his sons, Why do ye
look one upon another? (2) And he said,
Behold, I have heard that there is
corn in Egypt: get you down thither,
and buy for us from thence; that we
may live, and not die. (3) And Joseph's
ten brethren went down to buy corn in
Egypt. (4) But Benjamin, Joseph's bro-
ther, Jacob sent not with his brethren;
for he said, Lest peradventure mischief
befall him.

a Acts 7. 12.

B.C. cir. 1707.

1 Heb., *hard things with them.*

b ch. 37. 5.

(5) And the sons of Israel came to buy
corn among those that came: for the
famine was in the land of Canaan.
(6) And Joseph *was* the governor over the
land, *and* he *it was* that sold to all the
people of the land: and Joseph's bre-
thren came, and bowed down themselves
before him *with* their faces to the earth.
(7) And Joseph saw his brethren, and he
knew them, but made himself strange
unto them, and spake[1] roughly unto them;
and he said unto them, Whence come ye?
And they said, From the land of Canaan
to buy food. (8) And Joseph knew his
brethren, but they knew not him. (9) And
Joseph [b]remembered the dreams which
he dreamed of them, and said unto

---

was this monarch who "first established a complete system of dykes, canals, locks, and reservoirs, by which the inundations of the Nile were henceforth regulated." The artificial lake of Moeris was also made by his orders, and other works of extraordinary vastness. Now not only would such works be suggested by a dearth of unusually long continuance, but the measures taken by Joseph during the seven years of famine would place the whole resources of the country at the Pharaoh's disposal.

XLII.

First Visit of Joseph's Brethren to Egypt.

(1) **When Jacob saw.**—That is, learned, understood, that there was corn in Egypt. As we have seen (chap. xxxvii. 25), there was a large caravan trade between Palestine and Egypt, and the report would gradually get abroad that food might be purchased there.

Why do ye look . . .—In the second rainless season not only would the flocks and herds begin to languish, but the numerous retainers of Jacob and his sons would also become enfeebled from insufficient nourishment, and begin to die of low fever and those other diseases which follow in the train of famine. Jacob's words, therefore, mean, Why are you irresolute, and uncertain what to do? And then he encourages them to take this journey as a possible means of providing for the wants of their households.

(3) **Joseph's ten brethren.**—Either their cattle and households had been already greatly reduced by the mortality caused by the famine, or each patriarch must have taken a number of servants with him, if the corn carried home was to be enough to be of any real use. We learn, however, that they still possessed flocks and herds when they went down into Egypt (chap. xlvii. 1), and also households of servants (chap. xlvi. 5, where see Note). Joseph, moreover, besides the wagons and their contents, sends twenty loads of provisions for the use of his father by the way (chap. xlv. 21—23), showing thereby that there were very many mouths to feed. Probably, therefore, there was some small amount of rain in Palestine, though not enough for the support of crops of corn. There would be, however, supplies of milk and flesh, but not much more.

(6) **Joseph's brethren came and bowed down themselves before him.**—Throughout the land of Egypt Joseph would sell by deputy, and only give general directions; but the arrival of so large a party as Joseph's ten brethren, each probably with several attendants, would be reported to the governor in person, as certainly was the case with Abraham when he went into Egypt (chap. xii. 14, 15). Such visits would happen only occasionally, and the arrival of foreigners was always a matter looked upon with suspicion, especially upon the Arabian frontier.

(7) **Joseph . . . spake roughly unto them.**—Joseph has been accused of harshness in his treatment of his brethren, and still more so of his father in forcing him to send away Benjamin. The latter was, no doubt, the result of his great longing to see his only brother, and he may not have known how dear he was to Jacob, or have reflected upon the pain which his father would feel in parting with him. Still it was but a temporary separation, to prepare for a happy re-union. As regards his half-brethren, Joseph was obliged to prove them, and he did nothing to them which they did not richly deserve. From the first he probably wished to have his father and Benjamin to dwell with him, and share his good fortune; but if his brethren were still the cruel and heartless wretches which they had shown themselves to have been in their conduct to him twenty years before, we may well suppose that he would justly have left them to their fate. Possibly his first emotion towards them was one of indignation, but it melted away, when, even in but one of them, he saw proof that they were not entirely destitute of better feeling (see verses 22, 24).

(8) **Joseph knew.**—As this is twice repeated, some suppose that Joseph (in verse 7) had only a suspicion, from their dress and appearance, that these Canaanites were his brethren; but that when they spake the Hebrew tongue (comp. verse 23), every doubt was removed. They would not recognize him, as he used the Egyptian language, was clad in a white linen dress, and being but seventeen when sold, had during the twenty years of separation changed in appearance much more than they had.

(9) **Ye are spies.**— This is the suspicion under which every traveller labours in the East; but in those days the whole Semitic race was especially looked upon in Egypt with distrust, and, as we saw in chap. xii. 15,

them, Ye *are* spies; to see the naked-
ness of the land ye are come. (10) And
they said unto him, Nay, my lord, but
to buy food are thy servants come.
(11) We *are* all one man's sons; we *are*
true *men*, thy servants are no spies.
(12) And he said unto them, Nay, but to
see the nakedness of the land ye are
come. (13) And they said, Thy servants
are twelve brethren, the sons of one man
in the land of Canaan; and, behold, the
youngest *is* this day with our father,
and one *is* not. (14) And Joseph said unto
them, That *is it* that I spake unto you,
saying, Ye *are* spies: (15) hereby ye shall
be proved: By the life of Pharaoh ye
shall not go forth hence, except your
youngest brother come hither. (16) Send
one of you, and let him fetch your bro-
ther, and ye shall be [1]kept in prison,
that your words may be proved, whether
there be any truth in you: or else by the
life of Pharaoh surely ye *are* spies.
(17) And he [2] put them all together into
ward three days. (18) And Joseph said
unto them the third day, This do, and
live; *for* I fear God: (19) if ye *be* true
men, let one of your brethren be bound
in the house of your prison: go ye, carry
corn for the famine of your houses:
(20) but [a]bring your youngest brother
unto me; so shall your words be veri-
fied, and ye shall not die. And they
did so.

(21) And they said one to another, We
are verily guilty concerning our brother,
in that we saw the anguish of his soul,
when he besought us, and we would not
hear; therefore is this distress come
upon us. (22) And Reuben answered
them, saying, [b]Spake I not unto you,
saying, Do not sin against the child;
and ye would not hear? therefore, be-
hold, also his blood is required. (23) And
they knew not that Joseph understood
them; for [3]he spake unto them by an
interpreter. (24) And he turned himself
about from them, and wept; and re-

1 Heb., *bound.*
2 Heb., *gathered.*
a ch. 43. 5.
b ch. 37. 21.
3 Heb., *an interpreter was between them.*

---

a chain of fortresses had been built to protect the land from their incursions. Such an arrival, therefore, as that of Joseph's brethren would be a matter of state, worthy of the attention of the highest officials; and probably they had themselves come prepared to be assailed with the accusation of having political objects in view in their visit.

The nakedness of the land.—That is, its defenceless condition, from the want of fortresses and garrisons. Egypt was chiefly assailable on the side of Palestine, and was often at war with the Hittites there. So also the Hyksos, who subdued Egypt, were Semites from Palestine, and thus there was reason for looking closely at visitors from that quarter.

(11) **We are all one man's sons.**— Joseph's brethren had probably expected this accusation, and their answer, as Abravanel points out, is a sound one: for no man would send his whole family on so dangerous an errand. And thus they press their family relations as a proof of their being *true*, that is, honest, just men, with no evil designs; and Joseph, who was glad in this way to obtain intelligence of his father and Benjamin, finally, after persisting in the accusation until he had learned all he wished to know, accepts their argument as valid.

(14) **That is it . . .**—Joseph persists in his charge, because, besides the information which he gained, he also wished to get Benjamin into his power, that he might have him with him. As for his brethren, he had probably as yet no settled purpose, but naturally he would feel great indignation at the treatment he had experienced at their hands, and might not be unwilling to give them some degree of punishment.

(15) **By the life of Pharaoh.**—It was common in ancient times to swear by the king's life (see 1 Sam. xvii. 55; 2 Sam. xiv. 19), and even by the life of Jehovah (*ibid.* xv. 21; 2 Kings ii. 2, 4, 6). It is only in the stricter morality of the Gospel that such oaths are forbidden (Matt. v. 33—37).

(18) **I fear God** (Elohim).—By the use of the name Elohim they would understand that he worshipped the same God as they did. For though he may himself have used the Egyptian word for the supreme Deity, yet doubtless he would take care that the interpreter used the word Elohim.

(20) **Bring your youngest brother.**—Besides his desire to be re-united to his brother, Joseph reasonably felt that the possession of Benjamin would be the best means of inducing his father also to come to him. While substituting a much milder proposal for his former one, that nine should remain in prison, and the tenth go to fetch Benjamin, Joseph nevertheless takes care to make his brethren feel that he was in earnest.

(21) **We are verily guilty.**— They had evidently expected that whatever suspicions might be aroused by their first appearance, all such ideas would disappear upon their explanation of themselves and their purpose. Instead of this they are thrown into prison, abandoned to their reflections for three days, and dismissed only upon the condition of their leaving one brother as a hostage for their coming again accompanied by Benjamin: and as they knew no reason for this, it would fill their minds with fear. But though they were now suffering unjustly, it brought back to their mind their former sin; and the fact that it was so fresh in their memories is a sign of the reality of their repentance.

(22) **His blood.**—Evidently they thought that Joseph was dead, so that the accusation brought against them of falsehood for saying in verse 13 "one is not" is groundless. Moreover, Jacob uses the same words of Simeon (chap. xlii. 36), meaning by it only that he was lost to him.

(24) **He turned. . .and wept.**—There was no bitterness in Joseph's heart, and at their first word of regret he melted. But lest he should lose Benjamin he overcame his feelings, and commanded that Simeon should be bound, choosing him, probably, as the one chiefly

turned to them again, and communed
with them, and took from them Simeon,
and bound him before their eyes.
(25) Then Joseph commanded to fill
their sacks with corn, and to restore
every man's money into his sack, and to
give them provision for the way: and
thus did he unto them. (26) And they
laded their asses with the corn, and
departed thence. (27) And as one of them
opened his sack to give his ass pro-
vender in the inn, he espied his money;
for, behold, it *was* in his sack's mouth.
(28) And he said unto his brethren, My
money is restored; and, lo, *it is* even in
my sack: and their heart [1]failed *them*,
and they were afraid, saying one to
another, What *is* this *that* God hath
done unto us?
(29) And they came unto Jacob their
father unto the land of Canaan, and
told him all that befell unto them;
saying, (30) The man, *who is* the lord of
the land, spake [2]roughly to us, and took
us for spies of the country. (31) And we
said unto him, We *are* true *men;* we
are no spies: (32) we *be* twelve brethren,
sons of our father; one *is* not, and the
youngest *is* this day with our father in
the land of Canaan. (33) And the man,
the lord of the country, said unto us,
Hereby shall I know that ye *are* true
men; leave one of your brethren *here*
with me, and take *food for* the famine
of your households, and be gone: (34) and
bring your youngest brother unto me:
then shall I know that ye *are* no spies,
but *that* ye *are* true *men:* *so* will I de-
liver you your brother, and ye shall
traffick in the land.
(35) And it came to pass as they emptied
their sacks, that, behold, every man's
bundle of money *was* in his sack: and
when *both* they and their father saw the
bundles of money, they were afraid.
(36) And Jacob their father said unto
them, Me have ye bereaved *of my
children:* Joseph *is* not, and Simeon *is*

1 Heb., *went forth.*

2 Heb., *with us hard things.*

---

guilty of the wrong done him. As soon as the rest had departed, he would probably make his imprisonment as easy as possible, especially as he was detained, not as an evil-doer, but as a hostage.

(25) **To fill their sacks.**—Heb., *their vessels.* The word includes all their means of transport, and probably they had come with materials sufficient for the removal of a large quantity of corn. They had sacks as well. So in verse 19, Joseph had commanded them to "carry corn for the famine of their houses." And as their households were numerous, what would nine sacks of corn avail for their maintenance?

To restore every man's money into his sack.—It is evident that each one had made his own separate purchase for his own household. The restoration of the money frightened Joseph's brethren, as they saw in it a pretext for their detention on their next visit. But Joseph could not have meant thus to alarm them, as their fear would act as an obstacle to their coming again accompanied by Benjamin. It is more likely that he intended it as an encouragement, and sign of secret good will.

(27) **In the inn.**—Heb., *lodging-place,* literally, place to pass the night. It is quite possible that on a route frequented by numerous caravans there were places where a certain amount of protection for the beasts of burden and their attendants had been provided, either by the rulers, or by benevolent people. But Joseph's brethren would find there at most only walls and water. "The one" who opened his sack is said by tradition to have been Levi. At the end of the verse this sack is called by another name, signifying a travelling-bag, or wallet for forage. The translation of these three different words, vessel, wallet, and sack, indifferently by the last of them, has led to the absurd view, common among commentators, that Joseph's brethren went down into Egypt, each with one ass and one sack. Hence their astonishment that such an insignificant knot of men should be brought before the governor of Egypt. But the word used in verse 25 signifies everything into which corn could be put; and the word at the end of this verse is the travelling-bag, which each of the patriarchs carried behind him on his riding ass. Their men would go on foot at the side of the beasts of burden laden with the corn.

It is said here that one only found his money at the lodging-place, and that the rest did not find their money until they emptied their sacks on reaching home. The sacks mentioned here (in verse 35) were the same as the travelling-bags, for they are expressly so called in chap. xliii. 21, 22, 23. In chap. xliii. 21, however, they tell Joseph's steward that they all found their money in the mouth of their sacks on opening them at the lodging-place. This was not strictly accurate, but it would have been wearisome and useless to enter into such details. Two things it was necessary to show: the first, that all had found their money; the second, that they had gone too far on their journey homewards to be able to return and give the money back. Probably what is said in chap. xliii. 21 was literally true only of one, and he found his money because it had been put in last, and was therefore at the mouth of the wallet. In all the other sacks it had been put in first, under the corn, and so they did not find it until "they had emptied their sacks."

(28) **Their heart failed them.**—This verse is far more poetical in the Hebrew, where, literally it is *And their heart went forth, and they trembled each to his brother.* Their courage left them, and they stood looking at one another in terror.

(33) **Leave one of your brethren.**—While acknowledging that the lord of Egypt had spoken "hard things" with them, they do not mention that Simeon was left in bonds, nor even the harsher part of the treatment which they had met with, lest Jacob should be afraid to send Benjamin on their next visit.

(36) **All these things are against me.**—Heb., *are upon me,* are burdens which I have to bear.

not, and ye will take Benjamin *away:*
all these things are against me. (37) And
Reuben spake unto his father, saying,
Slay my two sons, if I bring him not to
thee: deliver him into my hand, and I
will bring him to thee again. (38) And
he said, My son shall not go down with
you; for his brother is dead, and he is
left alone: if mischief befall him by the
way in the which ye go, then shall ye
bring down my gray hairs with sorrow
to the grave.

CHAPTER XLIII.—(1) And the famine
was sore in the land. (2) And it came to
pass, when they had eaten up the corn
which they had brought out of Egypt,
their father said unto them, Go again,
buy us a little food. (3) And Judah
spake unto him, saying, The man [1] did
solemnly protest unto us, saying, Ye
shall not see my face, except your [a] bro-
ther *be* with you. (4) If thou wilt send
our brother with us, we will go down
and buy thee food: (5) but if thou wilt
not send *him*, we will not go down: for
the man said unto us, Ye shall not see
my face, except your brother *be* with you.
(6) And Israel said, Wherefore dealt ye
so ill with me, *as* to tell the man whether
ye had yet a brother? (7) And they said,
The man [2] asked us straitly of our state,
and of our kindred, saying, *Is* your father
yet alive? have ye *another* brother? and
we told him according to the [3] tenor of
these words: [4] could we certainly know
that he would say, Bring your brother
down?
(8) And Judah said unto Israel his
father, Send the lad with me, and we
will arise and go; that we may live, and
not die, both we, and thou, *and* also our
little ones. (9) I will be surety for him;
of my hand shalt thou require him: [b] if
I bring him not unto thee, and set him
before thee, then let me bear the blame
for ever: (10) for except we had lingered,
surely now we had returned [5] this second
time.
(11) And their father Israel said unto

[1] Heb., *protesting he protested.*
[a] ch. 42. 20.
[2] Heb., *asking he asked us.*
[3] Heb., *mouth*
[4] Heb., *knowing could we know.*
[b] ch. 44. 32.
[5] Or, *twice by this.*

---

(37) **Slay my two sons.**—Reuben does not suppose that Jacob would really put his grandchildren to death, but simply means to offer his father a strong assurance that Benjamin would run no danger. He regarded the risk as so slight that he was willing to stake the lives of two of his children, perhaps all he then had, upon Benjamin's safe return. To take such a proposal as meant literally is irrational. But it was but feeble talk, in agreement with the general weakness of Reuben's character.

(38) **Then shall ye bring down my gray hairs with sorrow to the grave.**—Heb., *to Sheol* (See Note on chap. xxxvii. 35). Jacob, both here and in chap. xlvii. 9, speaks as one on whom sorrow had pressed very heavily. Always of a timid and affectionate disposition, he looks onward now without hope, and sees in the future only dangers and ill-fortune. Probably by this time he had lost Leah as well as Rachel, but the blow that had struck him utterly down had evidently been the loss of Joseph, in whom Rachel had still seemed to live on for him. And therefore now he clung the more warmly to Benjamin, and it is plain that the father's deep sorrow for the loss of the petted son had softened the hearts of his brethren. They have no grudge against Benjamin because he has taken Joseph's place, but rather seem to share in their father's feelings, and their hearts were in accordance with what Judah says in chap. xliv. 18—34, that any personal suffering would be cheerfully borne by them, rather than to have to undergo the sight of the repetition of such grief as they previously had themselves inflicted.

XLIII.

The Second Visit to Egypt.

(7) **The man asked us straitly.**—In chap. xlii. 13 they appear rather as volunteering a statement of their family relations than as having it wrung from them by cross-examination. But really this history must be taken as explaining and supplementing the former. Accused of being spies, they would naturally give an account of themselves, and Joseph, anxious to know about his father and brother, would certainly put numerous questions to them concerning their home and family. And they would answer them fully and frankly, little suspecting who was the questioner, and what was his real reason for exacting Benjamin's presence in proof of their trustworthiness.

Of our state and of our kindred.—Heb., *concerning ourselves and our birthplace* (see chaps. xii. 1, xxiv. 4, 7, xxxi. 3), that is, our home. Questions about ourselves would be such as those given: "Is your father yet alive? Have ye a brother?" And besides these, Joseph would interrogate them closely concerning the place whence they came, and the state of things there.

(8) **The lad.**—Benjamin was now between twenty and thirty years of age. The term "lad" in Judah's mouth is one of affection, but even in itself it suits very well to a youth of this age. Rebekah (in chap. xxiv. 16) is called in the Hebrew *a lad* (see Note there), and so is Shechem in chap. xxxiv. 19. The assertion, therefore, that Benjamin is here represented as a mere boy, is disproved by the use of the word in the Hebrew.

Our little ones.—Heb., *our "tafs,"* that is, our households. (See Note on chap. xxxiv. 29.)

(9) **Then let me bear the blame for ever.**—This is much more manly and therefore more persuasive than Reuben's talk about pledging the lives of his children. For it was real, nor would it be a slight matter to stand in his father's presence all the rest of his life as one guilty of a grievous crime.

(11) **The best fruits.**—Heb., *the song*, that is, whatever in the land is most celebrated in song.

In your vessels.—The word used in chap. xlii. 25, where see Note. Concerning this present two remarks must be made; the first, that it proves that

them, If *it must be* so now, do this; take of the best fruits in the land in your vessels, and carry down the man a present, a little balm, and a little honey, spices, and myrrh, nuts, and almonds: (12) and take double money in your hand; and the money that was brought again in the mouth of your sacks, carry *it* again in your hand; peradventure it *was* an oversight: (13) take also your brother, and arise, go again unto the man: (14) and God Almighty give you mercy before the man, that he may send away your other brother, and Benjamin. [1] If I be bereaved *of my children*, I am bereaved.

(15) And the men took that present, and they took double money in their hand, and Benjamin; and rose up, and went down to Egypt, and stood before Joseph. (16) And when Joseph saw Benjamin with them, he said to the ruler of his house, Bring *these* men home, and [2] slay, and make ready; for *these* men shall [3] dine with me at noon. (17) And the man did as Joseph bade; and the man brought the men into Joseph's house. (18) And the men were afraid, because they were brought into Joseph's house; and they said, Because of the money that was returned in our sacks at the first time are we brought in; that he may [4] seek occasion against us, and fall upon us, and take us for bondmen, and our asses. (19) And they came near to the steward of Joseph's house, and they communed with him at the door of the house, (20) and said, O sir, [a][5] we came indeed down at the first time to buy food: (21) and it came to pass, when we came to the inn, that we opened our sacks, and, behold, *every* man's money *was* in the mouth of his sack, our money in full weight: and we have brought it again in our hand. (22) And other money have we brought down in our hands to buy food: we cannot tell who put our money in our sacks. (23) And he said, Peace *be* to you, fear not: your God, and the God

1 Or, *And I, as I have been, &c.*

2 Heb., *kill a killing.*

3 Heb., *eat.*

4 Heb., *roll himself upon us.*

a ch. 42. 3.

5 Heb., *coming down we came down.*

---

though there was not rain enough in Palestine to bring the corn to perfection, yet that there was some small supply, sufficient to maintain a certain amount of vegetation; and but for this Jacob could not have kept his cattle alive (chap. xlvii. 1). And next, the smallness of the present does not so much show that Jacob had very simple ideas respecting the greatness of the king of Egypt, as that there was a scarcity even of these fruits. Probably the trade in them had ceased, and therefore even a moderate quantity would be welcome. For the words rendered balm, spices and myrrh (really balsam, gum-tragacanth and ladanum), see Note on chap. xxxvii. 25.

Honey.—As both the honey made by bees and date honey were common in Egypt, many suppose that this was grape-honey, prepared by boiling down the juice of ripe grapes to a third of its original quantity. Hebron is famous for its preparation, and even in modern times three hundred camel loads used to be exported thence annually into Egypt. Diluted with water it forms a very grateful drink, and it is also largely eaten with bread, as we eat butter.

Nuts.—That is, *pistachio nuts*, the fruit of the *pistachia vera.* As the tree delights in dry, rocky situations, it will not grow in Egypt. It has an oily kernel, both palatable in itself and also much used for making savoury meats. These and the almonds, which also do not grow well in Egypt, would be acceptable gifts.

(12) **Double money.**—So Rashi; but others render it literally, *second money*, that is, a second sum of money. This agrees with the phrase "other money" in verse 22.

(14) **God Almighty.**—Heb., *El Shaddai*, the name by which Abraham's covenant (chap. xvii. 1) was renewed to Jacob (chap. xxxv. 11).

If I be bereaved . . .—An expression of pious resignation, united with heartfelt anguish. The inserted words *of my children* lessen the pathos of the patriarch's ejaculation, which literally is "and I, if I am bereaved, I am bereaved."

(16) **Slay.**—The charge of inaccuracy brought against the narrator, upon the supposition that the higher classes in Egypt, especially the priests, did not eat flesh, has been abundantly disproved, as the representations of feasts belonging to this period show that an abundance of animal food was consumed. Animals, moreover, sacred in one district were freely eaten in another. Generally the priests might eat the flesh of oxen and geese, but not mutton, pork or fish. (Rawlinson's *Egypt*, i. 438.)

(19) **At the door of the house.**—Alarmed at a thing so unexpected as being taken to the house of the governor, they can see nothing but danger, and will not enter until they receive the assurance of safety from the officer "who was over Joseph's house." (See Note on verse 25.)

(21) **The inn.**—The *lodging-place.* (See Note on chap. xlii. 27.)

Our sacks.—Heb., *our travelling* or *forage bags.* It is the word used at the end of chap. xlii. 27. So immediately afterwards the silver was found "in the mouth of the travelling-bag." And so again in verses 22 and 23. This is accurate, as the silver was placed in the private bag of each one, and not in the corn sacks; but as we have seen in chap. xlii 27, 35, only one of them found his money at the lodging-place. This, however, was a matter of no importance, while it was necessary to show that they were a full day's journey on the route homewards before the mistake was discovered.

(23) **Your God . . .**—Either Joseph had instructed his steward what to say, or he had trained his household generally in the truths of his religion. (See Note on chap. xlii. 18.) The word for "treasure" means *hidden treasure*, or as we call it a "windfall."

of your father, hath given you treasure
in your sacks: [1] I had your money. And
he brought Simeon out unto them.
(24) And the man brought the men
into Joseph's house, and [a] gave *them*
water, and they washed their feet; and
he gave their asses provender. (25) And
they made ready the present against
Joseph came at noon: for they heard
that they should eat bread there.
(26) And when Joseph came home, they
brought him the present which *was* in
their hand into the house, and bowed
themselves to him to the earth. (27) And
he asked them of *their* [2] welfare, and said,
[3] *Is* your father well, the old man of whom
ye spake? *Is* he yet alive? (28) And they
answered, Thy servant our father *is* in
good health, he *is* yet alive. And they
bowed down their heads, and made
obeisance. (29) And he lifted up his
eyes, and saw his brother Benjamin,
his mother's son, and said, *Is* this your
younger brother, of whom ye spake
unto me? And he said, God be gracious
unto thee, my son. (30) And Joseph
made haste; for his bowels did yearn
upon his brother: and he sought *where*
to weep; and he entered into *his* cham-
ber, and wept there. (31) And he washed
his face, and went out, and refrained
himself, and said, Set on bread. (32) And
they set on for him by himself, and
for them by themselves, and for the
Egyptians, which did eat with him, by
themselves: because the Egyptians
might not eat bread with the Hebrews;
for that *is* an abomination unto the
Egyptians. (33) And they sat before
him, the firstborn according to his
birthright, and the youngest according
to his youth: and the men marvelled
one at another. (34) And he took *and
sent* messes unto them from before him:
but Benjamin's mess was five times so
much as any of their's. And they
drank, and [4] were merry with him.

CHAPTER XLIV.—(1) And he com-
manded [5] the steward of his house,
saying, Fill the men's sacks *with* food,
as much as they can carry, and put
every man's money in his sack's mouth.
(2) And put my cup, the silver cup, in
the sack's mouth of the youngest,
and his corn money. And he did ac-
cording to the word that Joseph had
spoken.

1 Heb., *your money came to me.*

a ch. 18. 4. & 24. 32.

2 Heb., *peace.*

3 Heb., Is there *peace to your father?*

4 Heb., *they drank largely.*

5 Heb., him *that* was *over his house.*

By bringing out Simeon he would remove their worst fears, and so at last they consent to go in.

(25) **For they heard . . .**—As Joseph in verse 16 gives his orders in the Egyptian language, his brethren would not understand why they were taken to the governor's palace; but probably the steward now tells them that they were to feast with the governor, in order to allay their fears, as the rights of hospitality were too sacred to permit of perfidy to a guest.

(28) **They bowed down.**—This was the literal fulfilment of the first dream concerning the eleven sheaves making obeisance. As their business in Egypt was to buy corn, there was a fitness also in their being represented as sheaves.

(29) **Is this your younger brother?**—Rather, *your youngest brother.* Joseph's question was one of surprise. Can this young man, now nearly thirty, be the little Benjamin, who was but a child of eight or nine when last I saw him!

(31) **He washed his face.**—This was done to remove all traces of his tears.

(32) **By himself . . . by themselves.**—These caste distinctions were common in ancient times, and still exist in India. Joseph probably had his food served separately because of his high rank; but the word "abomination" shows that eating with foreigners was shunned by the Egyptians for religious considerations. Herodotus (ii. 41) says that the Greeks were equally the objects of their dislike, and that the use even of a Greek knife would render food, otherwise clean, polluted in the eyes of the Egyptians.

(33) **They sat.**—The Egyptians are always represented on the monuments as sitting at their meals. For the Hebrew custom see Note on chap. xxvii. 19. The brethren, on finding themselves placed according to their age, must have supposed that Joseph possessed powers of divination, especially as the giving of due precedence was and is looked upon in the East as a matter of high importance.

(34) **Messes.**—A portion of food from that prepared for the chief is regarded in the East as a mark both of honour and friendship, and the largeness of Benjamin's mess marked him out as the especial object of Joseph's regard. The words literally are, "And the portion of Benjamin was great above the portions of all of them five hands," that is, five times. It has been supposed that Joseph intended to try his brethren by this preference, and see if they were still envious. More probably it was dictated simply by his love.

They drank and were merry with him.—Heb., *They drank and were drunken with him.* The verb is that used of Noah in chap. ix. 21, but probably the rendering in Haggai i. 6, "and were filled with drink," would give the right meaning. They lost all fear and suspicion, and gave themselves up to enjoyment.

XLIV.

The Cup is placed in Benjamin's Riding-Bag.

(2) **Put my cup . . .**—Rather *bowl,* as it signifies a large round vessel from which the wine was poured into the drinking cups. Joseph's purpose apparently was to detain no one but Benjamin, and it was only when Judah spake so very nobly, and pointed out that Jacob's heart would be broken with grief if he lost the one remaining son of Rachel, made more dear

(3) As soon as the morning was light,
the men were sent away, they and their
asses. (4) *And* when they were gone out
of the city, *and* not *yet* far off, Joseph
said unto his steward, Up, follow after
the men; and when thou dost overtake
them, say unto them, Wherefore have
ye rewarded evil for good? (5) *Is* not
this *it* in which my lord drinketh, and
whereby indeed he [1]divineth? ye have
done evil in so doing. (6) And he over-
took them, and he spake unto them
these same words. (7) And they said
unto him, Wherefore saith my lord
these words? God forbid that thy
servants should do according to this
thing: (8) behold, the money, which we
found in our sacks' mouths, we brought
again unto thee out of the land of
Canaan: how then should we steal out
of thy lord's house silver or gold?
(9) With whomsoever of thy servants it
be found, both let him die, and we also
will be my lord's bondmen. (10) And he
said, Now also *let it be* according unto
your words: he with whom it is found
shall be my servant; and ye shall be
blameless. (11) Then they speedily took
down every man his sack to the ground,
and opened every man his sack. (12) And
he searched, *and* began at the eldest,
and left at the youngest: and the cup
was found in Benjamin's sack.

(13) Then they rent their clothes, and
laded every man his ass, and returned
to the city. (14) And Judah and his
brethren came to Joseph's house; for
he *was* yet there: and they fell before
him on the ground. (15) And Joseph
said unto them, What deed *is* this that
ye have done? wot ye not that such a
man as I can certainly [2]divine? (16) And
Judah said, What shall we say unto my
lord? what shall we speak? or how
shall we clear ourselves? God hath
found out the iniquity of thy servants:
behold, we *are* my lord's servants, both
we, and *he* also with whom the cup is
found. (17) And he said, God forbid that
I should do so: *but* the man in whose
hand the cup is found, he shall be my
servant; and as for you, get you up in
peace unto your father.

(18) Then Judah came near unto him,
and said, Oh, my lord, let thy servant, I
pray thee, speak a word in my lord's

[1] Or, *maketh trial.*

[2] Or, *make trial.*

---

to him by his brother's fate, that he determined to give a home to them all. He naturally supposed that his father had long since ceased to grieve for himself, and probably even hoped to prevail upon him subsequently to join him in Egypt. But when Judah offered himself for slavery rather than that his father should suffer the grief of seeing them return without Benjamin, Joseph understood that Jacob's anguish would be great beyond endurance, and he also became aware that his brethren were no longer as heartless as they had shown themselves of old.

(5) **Whereby he divineth.**—Cup divination was common in Egypt in ancient times, and was a kind of clairvoyance, the bowl being partly filled with water, and the eye of the diviner fixed upon some one point in it till, wearied with gazing, a state of half stupor was induced, during which the mind, freed from the control of reason, acted in a manner parallel to its operation in dreams. The same effect can be produced by gazing intently on a globe of glass, and other such things. In verse 15, Joseph asserts that he practised this art, and innocently. Though used now generally for imposture, there is in clairvoyance a real physical basis, which would be inexplicable in an unscientific age; and the genuine piety and goodness of Joseph would not raise him above the reach of the superstitions of his time.

(7) **God forbid.**—Heb., *far be it from thy servants to do, &c.*

(8–13) **Let him die.**—Joseph's brethren, conscious of their innocence, deny the theft, and, like Jacob when accused of stealing the teraphim (chap. xxxi. 32), declare that the guilty person shall die, and the rest be made slaves; readily too they consent to be searched, and take their travelling-bags from off the asses on which they were riding. The steward, who knew where the bowl was, answers that only the man in whose bag it is found shall be punished, and that not by death but by slavery. Beginning with Reuben's bag, the money is found, but this the steward makes light of; he then takes the next, and as each brother sees that he has with him more than he knew of, their minds must have been filled with confusion and terror. They would be liable to slavery for taking the money, but when the bowl is found in Benjamin's possession all hope was gone, and they rent their clothes in uncontrollable grief.

(17) **God forbid.**—Heb., *far be it from me to do so.* Joseph passes over the money found in their sacks, and which he had intended as a gift to help them in the remaining years of famine, but expresses his determination to keep Benjamin as a slave. Had they been as hardhearted as when they sold him into slavery, they would readily have gone away, leaving their brother to his fate. But they had changed, and therefore they earnestly exert themselves for his deliverance, though they must have felt it to be an almost hopeless task. They would feel sure of Benjamin's innocence, but they would also remember that the previous day Joseph had shown him the utmost honour; and this would be a proof to them that for some reason or other the Egyptian governor had taken a fancy to him, and determined to have him in his service; and that therefore he had contrived this wicked scheme.

(18) **Then Judah came near.**—The power of Judah's speech lies in the facts themselves, which gain in pathos from being simply told; but the ending is grand because of the speaker's magnanimity. He offers to give up all that a man holds dearest in order that

ears, and let not thine anger burn against thy servant: for thou *art* even as Pharaoh. (19) My lord asked his servants, saying, Have ye a father, or a brother? (20) And we said unto my lord, We have a father, an old man, and a child of his old age, a little one; and his brother is dead, and he alone is left of his mother, and his father loveth him. (21) And thou saidst unto thy servants, Bring him down unto me, that I may set mine eyes upon him. (22) And we said unto my lord, The lad cannot leave his father: for *if* he should leave his father, *his father* would die. (23) And thou saidst unto thy servants, [a]Except your youngest brother come down with you, ye shall see my face no more. (24) And it came to pass when we came up unto thy servant my father, we told him the words of my lord. (25) And our father said, Go again, *and* buy us a little food. (26) And we said, We cannot go down: if our youngest brother be with us, then will we go down: for we may not see the man's face, except our youngest brother *be* with us. (27) And thy servant my father said unto us, Ye know that my wife bare me two *sons:* (28) and the one went out from me, and I said, [b]Surely he is torn in pieces; and I saw him not since: (29) and if ye take this also from me, and mischief befall him, ye shall bring down my gray hairs with sorrow to the grave. (30) Now therefore when I come to thy servant my father, and the lad *be* not with us; seeing that his life is bound up in the lad's life; (31) it shall come to pass, when he seeth that the lad *is* not *with us*, that he will die: and thy servants shall bring down the gray hairs of thy servant our father with sorrow to the grave. (32) For thy servant became surety for the lad unto my father, saying, [c]If I bring him not unto thee, then I shall bear the blame to my father for ever. (33) Now therefore, I pray thee, let thy servant abide instead of the lad a bondman to my lord; and let the lad go up with his brethren. (34) For how shall I go up to my father, and the lad *be* not with me? lest peradventure I see the evil that shall [1]come on my father.

CHAPTER XLV.—(1) Then Joseph could not refrain himself before all them that stood by him; and he cried, Cause every man to go out from me. And there stood no man with him, while Joseph made himself known unto his brethren. (2) And he [2]wept aloud: and the Egyptians and the house of Pharaoh heard. (3) And Joseph said unto his brethren, [d]I *am* Joseph; doth my father yet live? And his brethren could not answer him; for they were [3]troubled at his presence.

(4) And Joseph said unto his brethren, Come near to me, I pray you. And they

[a] ch. 43. 3.
[b] ch. 37. 33.
[c] ch. 43. 9.
[1] Heb., *find my father.*
[2] Heb., *gave forth his voice in weeping.*
[d] Acts 7. 13.
[3] Or, *terrified.*

---

his father may be spared a grief too heavy to bear. There is, however, very considerable skill in the manner in which Judah shows that it was at Joseph's repeated urgency that they had brought Benjamin with them, while omitting all mention of the fact that they had been falsely charged by him with being spies.

(28) **The one went out . . .**—The mention of the disappearance of the one son, which Jacob could account for only by supposing him to be dead, is made in order to give the reason for the intense love of the father to the son still remaining. The allusion also to his mother would move Joseph's feelings, though of this Judah would not be aware.

(29) **To the grave.**—Heb., *to Sheol.* (See Note on chap. xxxvii. 35.)

(32—34) **Thy servant became surety.**—Judah first gives the reason why he was especially bound to see to Benjamin's welfare, but he adds to it the more affecting argument that he could not bear to look upon his father's anguish. And with these moving words he ends his appeal, which to Joseph's mind had carried the conviction, first, that to separate Benjamin, even for a time from Jacob, would be an act of extreme unkindness; and secondly, that his brethren were deserving not only of pardon, but of love.

XLV.

Joseph is Reconciled to his Brethren, and encourages them and his Father to make Egypt their home.

(1) **Joseph could not refrain himself.**—The picture which Judah had drawn of his father's love for Benjamin, the thought that by separating them he might have made his father die of grief, and the sight of his brethren, and especially of Judah offering to endure a life of slavery in order that Benjamin might go free, overpowered Joseph's feelings, and he commanded all his attendants to quit the apartment in order that there might be no restraint upon himself or his brethren when he made known to them that he was the brother whom they had so cruelly years ago condemned to be a slave.

(2) **And the Egyptians and the house of Pharaoh heard.**—Not the sound of Joseph's weeping, but the news that his brethren had come, as in verse 16.

(4) **I am Joseph your brother.**—There is much force in the assurance that he was still their brother. For they stood speechless in terrified surprise at finding

came near. And he said, I *am* Joseph
your brother, whom ye sold into Egypt.
(5) Now therefore be not grieved, [1] nor
angry with yourselves, that ye sold me
hither: [a] for God did send me before you
to preserve life. (6) For these two years
hath the famine *been* in the land: and
yet *there are* five years, in the which
there shall neither *be* earing nor harvest.
(7) And God sent me before you [2] to pre-
serve you a posterity in the earth, and
to save your lives by a great deliverance.
(8) So now *it was* not you *that* sent me
hither, but God: and he hath made me
a father to Pharaoh, and lord of all his
house, and a ruler throughout all the
land of Egypt. (9) Haste ye, and go up
to my father, and say unto him, Thus
saith thy son Joseph, God hath made
me lord of all Egypt: come down unto
me, tarry not: (10) and thou shalt dwell
in the land of Goshen, and thou shalt
be near unto me, thou, and thy children,
and thy children's children, and thy
flocks, and thy herds, and all that thou
hast: (11) And there will I nourish thee;
for yet *there are* five years of famine;
lest thou, and thy household, and all
that thou hast, come to poverty. (12) And,
behold, your eyes see, and the eyes of
my brother Benjamin, that *it is* my
mouth that speaketh unto you. (13) And
ye shall tell my father of all my glory
in Egypt, and of all that ye have seen;
and ye shall haste and bring down my
father hither.

(14) And he fell upon his brother Ben-
jamin's neck, and wept; and Benjamin
wept upon his neck. (15) Moreover he
kissed all his brethren, and wept upon
them: and after that his brethren talked
with him.

(16) And the fame thereof was heard
in Pharaoh's house, saying, Joseph's
brethren are come: and it [3] pleased
Pharaoh well, and his servants. (17) And
Pharaoh said unto Joseph, Say unto thy
brethren, This do ye; lade your beasts,
and go, get you unto the land of
Canaan; (18) and take your father and

1 Heb., *neither let there be anger in your eyes.*

B.C. cir. 1706.

a ch. 50. 20.

2 Heb., *to put for you a remnant.*

3 Heb., *was good in the eyes of Pharaoh.*

---

that the hated dreamer, upon the anguish of whose soul they had looked unmoved, was now the ruler of a mighty empire. But with magnanimous gentleness he bids them neither to grieve nor be angry with themselves; for behind their acts there had been a watchful Providence guiding all things for good.

(6) **Earing.**—An old English word for ploughing, derived from the Latin *arare*, Anglo-Saxon *erian*, to plough.

(7) **To preserve you a posterity in the earth.**—Heb., *To put for you a remnant in the land,* that is, to preserve a remainder for you, as the word is translated in 2 Sam. xiv. 7. During the seven years' famine many races probably dwindled away, and the Hebrews, as mere sojourners in Canaan, would have been in danger of total extinction.

By a great deliverance.—That is, by a signal interference on your behalf. But the word rendered "deliverance," more exactly signifies *that which escapes* (see 2 Kings xix. 31, where, as here, it is joined with the word *remnant*, and verse 30, where it is itself rendered *remnant*). The two nouns really signify the same thing; but whereas in the first clause the words seem to forebode that only few would escape, in the second there is the assurance of their surviving in such numbers as to be able to grow into a great nation.

(8) **But God.**—Heb., *but the God.* The article is rarely found with Elohim in the history of Joseph, but wherever it is added it is a sign of deep feeling on the speaker's part. (Comp. chap. xlviii. 15.) It was *the Elohim,* who had been the object of the worship of their race, that had now interposed to save them.

A father.—This was a not uncommon title of the chief minister or vizier of Oriental kings.

(10) **The land of Goshen.**—This land, also called "the land of Rameses" (chap. xlvii. 11), probably from the city "Raamses," which the Israelites were compelled to build there (Exod. i. 11), was situated on the eastern bank of the Nile, and apparently commencing a little to the north of Memphis extended to the Mediterranean, and to the borders of the Philistines' land (Exod. xiii. 17). In Ps. lxxviii. 12, 43, it is called the "field of Zoan," or Tanis. It probably was an unsettled district, but rich in pastures, and belonged in a very loose way to Egypt. In the LXX. it is called "Gesem of Arabia," to which country both Herodotus and Strabo reckoned all the district on the east of the Nile towards the Isthmus of Suez as belonging. And here the Israelites were constantly joined by large numbers of Semitic immigrants, who were enrolled in their "tafs," and swelled the rapidly increasing number of their dependants. For, as we have seen before, not merely the lineal descendants of Abraham were circumcised, but all his household and his slaves; and being thus admitted into the covenant became members of the Jewish church and nation (chap. xvii. 23).

(11) **Thy household.**—As the famine had lasted only two years, and as Jacob had preserved his flocks and herds, so probably he had lost few or none of the large number of men-servants and women-servants who belonged to him. He would thus go down to Egypt as head of a large tribe, who would be called Israelites after him, just as the Ishmaelites, to whom Joseph was sold (chap. xxxvii. 25), bore Ishmael's name, not because they were lineally descended from him, but because he had made them subject to his authority and that of his race. In verse 18 Joseph speaks of "their households," showing that each of the patriarchs had now his own body of dependants, besides the still larger clan which belonged to Jacob.

(16) **It pleased Pharaoh . . .**—It was of great importance, as regards the future position of the Israelites in Egypt, that they should go thither, not as men who had forced themselves on the country, but as invited guests. Hence the information that

your households, and come unto me:
and I will give you the good of the
land of Egypt, and ye shall eat the fat
of the land. (19) Now thou art com-
manded, this do ye; take you wagons
out of the land of Egypt for your little
ones, and for your wives, and bring
your father, and come. (20) Also [1]regard
not your stuff; for the good of all the
land of Egypt *is* your's.

(21) And the children of Israel did so:
and Joseph gave them wagons, accord-
ing to the [2]commandment of Pharaoh,
and gave them provision for the way.
(22) To all of them he gave each man
changes of raiment; but to Benjamin
he gave three hundred *pieces* of silver,
and five changes of raiment. (23) And
to his father he sent after this *manner;*
ten asses [3]laden with the good things of
Egypt, and ten she asses laden with
corn and bread and meat for his father
by the way. (24) So he sent his brethren
away, and they departed: and he said
unto them, See that ye fall not out by
the way.

(25) And they went up out of Egypt,
and came into the land of Canaan unto
Jacob their father, (26) and told him,
saying, Joseph *is* yet alive, and he *is*
governor over all the land of Egypt.
And [4]Jacob's heart fainted, for he
believed them not. (27) And they told
him all the words of Joseph, which he
had said unto them: and when he saw
the wagons which Joseph had sent to
carry him, the spirit of Jacob their
father revived: (28) and Israel said, *It is*
enough; Joseph my son *is* yet alive: I
will go and see him before I die.

CHAPTER XLVI. — (1) And Israel
took his journey with all that he had,
and came to Beer-sheba, and offered
sacrifices unto the God of his father
Isaac. (2) And God spake unto Israel
in the visions of the night, and said,
Jacob, Jacob. And he said, Here *am* I.

1 Heb., *let not your eye spare, &c.*
2 Heb., *mouth.*
3 Heb., *carrying.*
4 Heb., *his.*

---

the arrival of Joseph's brethren was a thing pleasing to Pharaoh, and hence also the fulness with which his commands are recorded.

(19) **Wagons.**—Egypt being a flat country and carefully cultivated was adapted for the use of vehicles, and consequently they were brought into use there at an early period. Those depicted on the monuments had two wheels, and were drawn by oxen. The chariots of Pharaoh and Joseph were probably drawn by horses, which had about this time been introduced into Egypt.

Your little ones.—Heb., *your "taf."* (See Note on chap. xxxiv. 29.) The "taf" included the whole mass of dependants; and while "the household" (verse 18) would have reference chiefly to the men, the "taf," in opposition to it, would consist of the female slaves and the children.

(20) **Regard not your stuff.**—Heb., *and let not your eye have pity* (Jonah iv. 10) *upon your vessels,* that is, upon your implements and household furniture.

(22) **Changes of raiment.** — Gifts of clothing were marks of special favour in the East (chap. xli. 42). Joseph's brethren would thus show by their very apparel how honourable had been their treatment.

(23) **Meat.**—Heb., *food, victual,* the usual meaning of *meat* in our version.

(24) **See that ye fall not out by the way.**—Heb., *do not get angry on the journey.* Joseph feared that they might reproach one another for their treatment of him, and try to throw the blame on the one or two chiefly guilty, and that so quarrels might ensue. This is the meaning given to the passage in all the versions, and agrees with Joseph's efforts to quiet their fears, and convince them of his good intentions. Several modern commentators, however, translate "Be not afraid of the journey," but on insufficient grounds.

(26) **Jacob's heart fainted.**—Heb., *grew cold.* This was not the effect of incredulity or suspicion, but of surprise. Jacob, crushed by the loss of the child who had taken the place of his beloved Rachel in his heart, had nothing left to interest him except Benjamin. When, therefore, the news come that Joseph still lives, his mind cannot open itself to receive the joyful tidings, and their first effect is to chill him with a renewed sense of his loss. It is only when he sees the wagons, and other clear proofs of the fact, that life returns to his benumbed faculties, and he becomes capable of joy.

(28) **And Israel said.**—We must not lay too much stress upon this change of name, as though it were a title appropriate to the patriarch only in his happier and triumphant hours; for in chap. xlv. 6 it is given him in the midst of his distress. It rather shows that the names were long both in use as regards the patriarch personally, but as the title of Israel was alone given to Jacob's family, it is plain that a high significance was attached to it, and that the inheritance of the Abrahamic promises was at an early date connected therewith.

XLVI.

Emigration of Israel and his Sons into Egypt.

(1) **Israel . . . came to Beer-sheba.**—Though Jacob, in the first tumult of his joy, had determined upon hastening to Egypt, yet many second thoughts must have made him hesitate. He would call up to mind the boding prophecy in chap. xv. 13, that the descendants of Abraham were to be reduced to slavery, and suffer affliction in a foreign land for four hundred years. It might even be a sin, involving the loss of the Abrahamic covenant, to quit the land of Canaan, which Abraham had expressly forbidden Isaac to abandon (chap. xxiv. 8). Isaac, too, when going into Egypt, had been commanded to remain in Palestine (chap. xxvi. 2). Jacob therefore determines solemnly to consult God before finally taking so important a step, and no place could be more suitable than Beer-

(3) And he said, I *am* God, the God of
thy father: fear not to go down into
Egypt; for I will there make of thee a
great nation: (4) I will go down with
thee into Egypt; and I will also surely
bring thee up *again*: and Joseph shall
put his hand upon thine eyes. (5) And
Jacob rose up from Beer-sheba: and
the sons of Israel carried Jacob their
father, and their little ones, and their
wives, in the wagons which Pharaoh
had sent to carry him. (6) And they
took their cattle, and their goods, which
they had gotten in the land of Canaan,
and came into Egypt, [a]Jacob, and all
his seed with him: (7) his sons, and his
sons' sons with him, his daughters, and
his sons' daughters, and all his seed
brought he with him into Egypt.
(8) And [b]these *are* the names of the
children of Israel, which came into
Egypt, Jacob and his sons: [c]Reuben,
Jacob's firstborn. (9) And the sons of
Reuben; Hanoch, and Phallu, and
Hezron, and Carmi. (10) And [d]the sons
of Simeon; Jemuel, and Jamin, and
Ohad, and Jachin, and Zohar, and
Shaul the son of a Canaanitish woman.
(11) And the sons of [e]Levi; Gershon,
Kohath, and Merari. (12) And the sons
of [f]Judah; Er, and Onan, and Shelah,
and Pharez, and Zarah: but Er and

a Josh. 24. 4; Ps. 105. 23; Isai. 52. 4.

b Ex. 1. 1. & 6. 14; Num. 26. 8; 1 Chr. 5. 1.

c Num. 26. 5.

d Ex. 6. 15; 1 Chr. 4. 24.

e 1 Chr. 6. 1.

f 1 Chr. 2. 3. & 4. 21; ch. 38. 3.

---

sheba, as both Abraham and Isaac had built altars there for Jehovah's worship (chap. xxi. 33, xxvi. 25), and, moreover, it lay upon the route from Hebron to Egypt.

(3) **I am God, the God of thy father.**—Heb., *I am the El, the Elohim of thy father.* This is the last revelation given to Jacob, nor is any other supernatural event recorded until the vision of the burning bush (Exod. iii. 4). It is brief, clear, and decisive, and every clause is weighty. Jacob is to migrate into Egypt, his race is to grow there into a nation, so that the stay there would be long; God's presence and blessing will accompany and remain with them, and finally will bring them back to the promised land. For himself, too, there is the promise that Joseph will tend his sick bed and be with him at his death.

(4) **Joseph shall put his hand upon thine eyes.**—Both among the Jews and Greeks it was the duty of those nearest in blood to close the eyes of a deceased relative. The promise conveyed the assurance that Jacob would die peacefully, surrounded by his friends. For the fulfilment see chap. l. 1.

(6) **Their goods.**—These are not *the vessels* spoken of contemptuously by Pharaoh (chap. xlv. 20), but their personal property, of which they would naturally have much which they would not be willing to leave behind. Abraham had brought large wealth with him from Haran (chap. xii. 5), some of which may have even come from Ur-Chasdim, and much had been gathered since. The patriarchs would leave their household stuff behind, but all valuables, and the records of their house, and their *tôldôth*, they would carefully carry with them.

They . . . came into Egypt.—For a full account of the scene depicted on the tomb of Khnum-hotep at Beni-hassan, and which at one time was identified with the arrival of the sons of Jacob, see Tomkins, *Times of Abraham*, 110—114.

(7) **His daughters.**—See Note on chap. xxxvii. 35.

GENEALOGICAL TABLE OF THE ISRAELITES.

(8) **These are the names of the children of Israel which came into Egypt.**—This document, consisting of verses 8—27, is one that would be of the highest importance to the Israelites, when taking possession of Canaan, being as it were their title-deed to the land. Accordingly we find that it is drawn up in a legal manner, representing as sons some who were really grandsons, but who took as heads of families the place usually held by sons. We next find that it represents them as all born in Canaan, not in a natural sense, but as the rightful heirs of the country. Technically every head of a family was born in Canaan, and thus the danger was obviated of an objection to the possession of this rank being accorded to one born in Egypt. As a matter of fact Pharez (verse 12) was an infant when taken down into Egypt. (See chap. xxxviii. 29, and Excursus on Chronology of Jacob's life.) It is difficult enough to find time sufficient for his birth in the interval between the return from Padan-Aram, and the descent into Egypt; for the birth of his two sons, Hezron and Hamul, there is no space whatsoever. In verse 21 Benjamin has ten sons assigned him, but he was at most about thirty years of age when he went into Egypt, and some of these sons are expressly said elsewhere to have been his grandsons. Commentators have indeed endeavoured to show that Benjamin might have been a few years older, but they do this by upsetting their own conclusions previously arrived at; and there is no process which so legitimately produces scepticism as the re-statement by commentators of the facts so marshalled on each occasion as to suit the apparent exigencies of the passage before them, but in a manner irreconcilable with previous difficulties.

The genealogical table of the twelve patriarchs is thrice given in Holy Scripture: here, in Num. xxvi., and in 1 Chron. i.—viii. See also Exod. vi. 14—16, where only Reuben, Simeon, and Levi are given.

(9) **Reuben** has four sons: Hanoch, Phallu, Hezron, Carmi. In these the genealogies all agree.

(10) **Simeon** has six sons, namely

	Num. xxvi. 12, 13.	1 Chron. iv. 24.
Jemuel,	*Nemuel,*	*Nemuel,*
Jamin,	Jamin,	Jamin,
Ohad,	(omitted)	(omitted)
Jachin,	Jachin,	*Jarib,*
Zohar,	*Zerah,*	*Zerah,*
Shaul.	Shaul.	Shaul.

Jewish tradition represents Shaul as being really the son of Dinah by a Canaanite father, Shechem, but as adopted by Simeon to save his sister's honour, yet with a note that he was of half Canaanitish blood.

(11) **Levi** has three sons: Gershon, Kohath, and Merari.

(12) **Judah** has five sons, of whom Er and Onan die prematurely. The names of the other three are Shelah,

Onan died in the land of Canaan. And
the sons of Pharez were Hezron and
Hamul. (13) [a]And the sons of Issachar;
Tola, and Phuvah, and Job, and
Shimron. (14) And the sons of Zebu-
lun; Sered, and Elon, and Jahleel.
(15) These *be* the sons of Leah, which
she bare unto Jacob in Padan-aram,
with his daughter Dinah: all the souls
of his sons and his daughters *were* thirty
and three. (16) And the sons of Gad;
Ziphion, and Haggi, Shuni, and Ezbon,
Eri, and Arodi, and Areli. (17) [b]And
the sons of Asher; Jimnah, and Ishuah,
and Isui, and Beriah, and Serah their
sister: and the sons of Beriah; Heber,
and Malchiel. (18) These *are* the sons of
Zilpah, whom Laban gave to Leah his
daughter, and these she bare unto
Jacob, *even* sixteen souls. (19) The sons
of Rachel Jacob's wife; Joseph, and
Benjamin. (20) And unto Joseph in the
land of Egypt were born Manasseh and
Ephraim, [c]which Asenath the daughter
of Poti-pherah [1]priest of On bare unto
him. (21) [d]And the sons of Benjamin
were Belah, and Becher, and Ashbel,
Gera, and Naaman, Ehi, and Rosh,
Muppim, and Huppim, and Ard.
(22) These *are* the sons of Rachel, which
were born to Jacob: all the souls *were*
fourteen. (23) And the sons of Dan;
Hushim. (24) And the sons of Naphtali;
Jahzeel, and Guni, and Jezer, and
Shillem. (25) These *are* the sons of
Bilhah, which Laban gave unto Rachel

a 1 Chr. 7. 1.
b 1 Chr. 7. 30.
c ch. 41. 50.
1 Or, *prince.*
d 1 Chr. 7. 6. & 8. 1.

Pharez, and Zarah (spelt correctly Zerah in Num. xxvi. 20; 1 Chron. ii. 4). So also the right spelling is Pherez, and not Pharez. In 1 Chron. iv. 1 Judah has five sons: Pharez, Hezron, Carmi, Hur, and Shobal, and Shelah is also mentioned there in verse 21, but see Note there.

(13) **Issachar** has four sons:

	Num. xxvi. 23, 24.	1 Chron. vii. 1.
Tola,	Tola,	Tola,
Phuvah,	*Pua,*	*Puah,*
Job,	*Jashub,*	*Jashub,*
Shimron.	Shimron.	*Shimrom.*

(14) **Zebulun** has three sons:

	Num. xxvi. 26.
Sered,	Sered,
Elon,	Elon,
Jahleel.	Jahleel.

No genealogy of the tribe of Zebulun is given in the Book of Chronicles.

(15) **All the souls . . . were thirty and three.**—That is, six sons, twenty-three grandsons, two great-grandsons, Dinah, and Jacob himself. The other daughters and granddaughters are omitted.

(16) **Gad,** the eldest of the sons of Zilpah, has seven sons:

	Num. xxvi. 15—17.
Ziphion,	*Zephon,*
Haggi,	Haggi,
Shuni,	Shuni,
Ezbon,	*Ozni,*
Eri,	Eri.
Arodi,	*Arod,*
Areli.	Areli.

In 1 Chron. v. 11—15 only the registration of the Gadites is given in the time of King Jotham.

(17) **Asher** has four sons:

	Num. xxvi. 44, 45.	1 Chron. vii. 30.
Jimnah,	*Jimna,*	*Imnah,*
Ishuah,	(omitted)	Isuah,
Isui,	*Jesui,*	*Ishuai,*
Beriah.	Beriah.	Beriah.

The sister is everywhere Serach, though called Serah here, and Sarah in Numbers. The three documents all agree in the names of Heber and Malchiel, sons of Beriah.

(18) **Sixteen souls.**—That is, Gad and his seven sons, Asher and his four sons, the two grandsons and Serach.

(20) **Manasseh and Ephraim.**—In these names all the documents agree.

(21) **Benjamin** has ten sons:

	Num. xxvi. 38—40.	1 Chron. vii. 6.	1 Chron. viii. 1—5.
Belah,	Bela,	Bela,	Bela,
Becher,	(omitted)	Becher,	(omitted)
Ashbel,	Ashbel,	*Jediael.*	Ashbel,
Gera,	(omitted)		(given as grandson)
Naaman,	(given as grandson)		do.
Ehi,	*Ahiram,*		*Aharah, Nohah,*
Rosh,	(omitted)		*Rapha* (?)
Muppim,	*Shupham,*		(given as grandson)
Huppim,	*Hupham,*		do.
Ard,	(given as grandson)		do.

Thus in Numbers Benjamin has only five sons, but Naaman and Ard are also heads of families, and are described as sons of Bela. In Chronicles Benjamin is first described as having three sons, among whom appears Becher with numerous descendants, though omitted elsewhere, and then as having five sons, one of whom, Nohah, has a name completely different from any of those in the other three documents. And not only is Bela described as the father of Gera, Naaman, Muppim (called Shephuphan), Huppim (called Huram), and Ard (called Addar); but also of Abihud, Abishua, Ahoah, and another Gera.

(22) **All the souls were fourteen.**—Made up of Joseph and two sons, and Benjamin and ten sons.

(23) **Dan** has one son, Hushim, called Shuham in Num. xxvi. 42. No genealogy of this tribe is given in Chronicles.

(24) **Naphtali** has four sons:

	Num. xxvi. 48, 49.	1 Chron. vii. 13.
Jahzeel,	Jahzeel,	*Jahziel,*
Guni,	Guni,	Guni,
Jezer,	Jezer,	Jezer,
Shillem.	Shillem.	*Shallum.*

(25) **All the souls were seven.**—Made up of Dan and one son, and Naphtali and four sons.

Excepting Benjamin, the other genealogies do not offer any great difficulties; for variations in the spelling of names are too common to cause surprise, and names would be omitted whenever in later times the family had ceased to have a representative. Thus, probably, no member of the tribe of Dan returned from the Captivity with an authenticated genealogy, and therefore

his daughter, and she bare these unto
Jacob: all the souls *were* seven. (26) [a] All
the souls that came with Jacob into
Egypt, which came out of his [1] loins,
besides Jacob's sons' wives, all the souls
were threescore and six; (27) and the
sons of Joseph, which were born him
in Egypt, *were* two souls: all the
souls of the house of Jacob, which
came into Egypt, *were* threescore and
ten.
(28) And he sent Judah before him
unto Joseph, to direct his face unto
Goshen; and they came into the land
of Goshen. (29) And Joseph made ready
his chariot, and went up to meet Israel
his father, to Goshen, and presented
himself unto him; and he fell on his
neck, and wept on his neck a good
while. (30) And Israel said unto Joseph,
Now let me die, since I have seen thy
face, because thou *art* yet alive. (31) And
Joseph said unto his brethren, and unto
his father's house, I will go up, and
shew Pharaoh, and say unto him, My
brethren, and my father's house, which
were in the land of Canaan, are come
unto me; (32) and the men *are* shepherds,
for [2] their trade hath been to feed cattle;
and they have brought their flocks, and
their herds, and all that they have.
(33) And it shall come to pass, when
Pharaoh shall call you, and shall say,
What *is* your occupation? (34) That ye
shall say, Thy servants' trade hath been
about cattle from our youth even until
now, both we, *and* also our fathers:
that ye may dwell in the land of
Goshen; for every shepherd *is* an
abomination unto the Egyptians.

a Deut. 10. 22.

1 Heb., *thigh.*

2 Heb., *they are men of cattle.*

---

no mention of them is made in the book of Chronicles. The utter confusion in the genealogy of Benjamin is the natural result of the ruinous war narrated in Judges xx., xxi.; but when that tribe produced a king, the utmost care would be taken to remedy, as far as possible, the destruction of documents caused by that struggle; and the genealogy in 1 Chron. viii. is the royal pedigree of King Saul.

(26) **All the souls were threescore and six.**—This total is obtained by omitting Jacob, Joseph, and Joseph's two sons. If we include these, the whole number becomes threescore and ten, as in verse 27. In the LXX. the names of five grandsons are added to verse 20, and thus the total is made seventy-five, as quoted by St. Stephen in Acts vii. 14.

Arrival of Jacob in Egypt.

(28) **To direct his face unto Goshen.**—Joseph does not bring his brethren into the narrow and populous Nile Valley which formed Egypt proper, because they could not have maintained there an isolated mode of life. But this was indispensable for them if they were to multiply into a nation fit to be the guardians and depositories of a growing revelation, until the fulness of the time should come, when the world would be ready to receive the perfect knowledge of God's will. As the Egyptians were an agricultural people, and hated sheep and shepherds (verse 34), the Israelites would run no danger of being absorbed by them so long as they continued to devote themselves to their old pursuits. As Goshen was admirably suited for a pastoral life, they would remain there as distinct and separate from the rest of mankind as they had been in Canaan.

(29) **He fell on his neck.**—Most of the versions and commentators understand this of Joseph throwing himself on Jacob's neck, but Maimonides says that a son would not take so great a liberty with his father. The Authorised Version seems to understand it of Jacob, and this gives the best and most natural sense. The preceding words literally are, *and he appeared unto him:* that is, came into his presence; whereupon Jacob fell on his neck, and wept there "again and again."

(30) **Now let me die.**—Heb., *I would die this time* (chap. ii. 23), *after I have seen thy face,* &c. Calmly will Jacob wait for death now that the great longing of his soul has been satisfied.

(32) **The men are shepherds.**—As Joseph's object was to keep his brethren isolated in Goshen, he instructs them not to conceal their occupation, because Pharaoh on knowing it would not wish them to dwell in Egypt itself.

(34) **For every shepherd is an abomination unto the Egyptians.**—This is probably a remark of the narrator, and it is confirmed by the monuments, which generally represent shepherds as unshaven and ill-dressed. Necessarily the Egyptians had sheep and cattle (chap. xlvii. 16, 17), and even Pharaoh had herds (chap. xlvii. 6); but the care of them was probably left by the peasantry to the women and children, while the men busied themselves with the cultivation of their fields. We need not go far to seek for the cause of this dislike. The word "abomination," first of all, suggests a religious ground of difference; and not only did shepherds probably kill animals worshipped in different Egyptian districts, but their religion generally was diverse from that of the fixed population. But next, men who lead a settled life always dislike wandering clans, whose cattle are too likely to prey upon their enclosed land (see Note on chap. iv. 8), and who, moving from place to place, are usually not very scrupulous as to the rights of property. Such nomades, too, are generally lower in civilisation, and more rude and rough, than men who have fixed homes. The subjugation of Egypt by the Hyksos was possibly subsequent to the era of Joseph; but we now know from Egyptian sources that there was perpetual war between Egypt and the Hittites, and probably raids were often made upon the rich fields on the banks of the Nile by other Semitic tribes dwelling upon its eastern frontier; and as all these were regarded as shepherds, there was ground enough for the dislike of all nomades as a class, even though the Egyptians did not disdain to have cattle themselves. But as the land in the Nile Valley was arable, the cattle kept would only be such as were useful for agriculture, whereas they formed the main wealth of the Israelites.

CHAPTER XLVII.—(1) Then Joseph
came and told Pharaoh, and said, My
father and my brethren, and their
flocks, and their herds, and all that
they have, are come out of the land of
Canaan; and, behold, they *are* in the
land of Goshen. (2) And he took some
of his brethren, *even* five men, and
presented them unto Pharaoh. (3) And
Pharaoh said unto his brethren, What
is your occupation? And they said unto
Pharaoh, Thy servants *are* shepherds,
both we, *and* also our fathers. (4) They
said moreover unto Pharaoh, For to
sojourn in the land are we come; for
thy servants have no pasture for their
flocks; for the famine *is* sore in the
land of Canaan: now therefore, we
pray thee, let thy servants dwell in
the land of Goshen.
(5) And Pharaoh spake unto Joseph,
saying, Thy father and thy brethren
are come unto thee: (6) the land of
Egypt *is* before thee; in the best of
the land make thy father and brethren
to dwell; in the land of Goshen let
them dwell: and if thou knowest *any*
men of activity among them, then make
them rulers over my cattle.
(7) And Joseph brought in Jacob his
father, and set him before Pharaoh:
and Jacob blessed Pharaoh. (8) And
Pharaoh said unto Jacob, [1]How old *art*
thou? (9) And Jacob said unto Pharaoh,
[a]The days of the years of my pilgrimage
are an hundred and thirty years: few
and evil have the days of the years of
my life been, and have not attained
unto the days of the years of the life of
my fathers in the days of their pilgrim-
age. (10) And Jacob blessed Pharaoh,
and went out from before Pharaoh.
(11) And Joseph placed his father and
his brethren, and gave them a posses-

1 Heb., *how many are the days of the years of thy life?*

a Heb. 11. 9, 13.

XLVII.

JOSEPH PRESENTS HIS FATHER AND BRETHREN TO PHARAOH.

(1) **Behold, they are in the land of Goshen.**—Though Joseph had all along wished this to be the dwelling-place of his brethren, yet it was necessary to obtain Pharaoh's permission; and at present Joseph only mentions that they had halted there. In verse 4 they ask for the necessary consent.

(2) **Even five men.**—As the number "five" appears again and again in this narrative (chaps. xliii. 34, xlv. 22), it may have had some special importance among the Egyptians, like the number seven among the Jews.

(3) **Also our fathers.**—Joseph had instructed them to add this (chap. xlvi. 34), because occupations were hereditary among the Egyptians, and thus Pharaoh would conclude that in their case also no change was possible in their mode of life.

(4) **To sojourn.**—Joseph's brethren ask for permission only for a temporary stay. Apparently, too, in spite of the famine, there was pasture for cattle in Goshen. They had been able hitherto to keep them alive even in Canaan; and probably the Nile, though it did not overflow, yet on reaching the delta lost itself in swamps, which produced a great quantity of the marsh grass described in chap. xli. 2. We find in this chapter that not only were Pharaoh's herds intact, but also those of the people.

(7) **Jacob blessed Pharaoh.**—The presentation of Jacob to Pharaoh seems to have been a much more solemn matter than that of Joseph's brethren. Pharaoh looks upon them with interest as the brothers of his vizier, grants their request for leave to dwell in Goshen, and even empowers Joseph to make the ablest of them chief herdsmen over the royal cattle. But Jacob had attained to an age which gave him great dignity: for to an Egyptian 120 was the utmost limit of longevity. Jacob was now 130, and Pharaoh treats him with the greatest honour, and twice accepts his blessing. More must be meant by this than the usual salutation, in which each one presented to the king prayed for the prolongation of his life. Pharaoh probably bowed before Jacob as a saintly personage, and received a formal benediction.

(9) **My pilgrimage.**—Heb., *my sojournings;* and so at end of verse. The idea of a pilgrimage is a modern one. Even in 1 Peter ii. 11 "pilgrim" means in the Greek a stranger who has settled in a country of which he is not a native. So, too, here Jacob was not a pilgrim, for he was no traveller bound for religious motives to some distant shrine, but he was a sojourner, because Canaan was not the native land of his race.

Few and evil.—Evil certainly: for from the time when he deceived his father, Jacob's life had been one of great anxiety and care, in addition to his many sorrows. If he had gained wealth in Haran, it had been by great industry and personal toil, aggravated by Laban's injustice. On his return, there was the double terror of Laban's pursuit behind and Esau's menacing attitude in front. He had then long lain ill at Succoth, waiting till time healed his sprained hip. His entry into the promised land had been made miserable by his daughter's dishonour and the fierce conduct of his sons. And when his home was in sight, he had lost his beloved Rachel; and finally, been compelled to remain at a distance from his father, because Esau was there chief and paramount. His father dies, and Esau goes away; but the ten years between Isaac's death and the descent into Egypt had been years of mourning for Joseph's loss. All these troubles had fallen upon him, and made his days evil; but they were few only in comparison with those of his father and grandfather. In Pharaoh's eyes Jacob had lived beyond the usual span of human existence; but to himself he seemed prematurely old. His end came after seventeen years of peaceful decay spent under Joseph's loving care.

The land of Rameses.—See Note on chap. xlv. 10. Though the LXX. take "land of Ramesés" as equivalent to Goshen, it was more probably some special

sion in the land of Egypt, in the best
of the land, in the land of Rameses, as
Pharaoh had commanded. (12) And
Joseph nourished his father, and his
brethren, and all his father's household,
with bread, [1] [2]according to *their* families.
(13) And *there was* no bread in all the
land; for the famine *was* very sore, so
that the land of Egypt and *all* the land
of Canaan fainted by reason of the
famine. (14) And Joseph gathered up
all the money that was found in the
land of Egypt, and in the land of Ca-
naan, for the corn which they bought:
and Joseph brought the money into
Pharaoh's house. (15) And when money
failed in the land of Egypt, and in the
land of Canaan, all the Egyptians came
unto Joseph, and said, Give us bread:
for why should we die in thy presence?
for the money faileth. (16) And Joseph
said, Give your cattle; and I will give
you for your cattle, if money fail.
(17) And they brought their cattle
unto Joseph: and Joseph gave them
bread *in exchange* for horses, and for
the flocks, and for the cattle of the
herds, and for the asses: and he [3]fed
them with bread for all their cattle for
that year.
(18) When that year was ended, they
came unto him the second year, and
said unto him, We will not hide *it* from
my lord, how that our money is spent;
my lord also hath our herds of cattle;
there is not ought left in the sight of
my lord, but our bodies, and our lands:
(19) wherefore shall we die before thine
eyes, both we and our land? buy us and
our land for bread, and we and our land
will be servants unto Pharaoh: and
give *us* seed, that we may live, and not
die, that the land be not desolate.
(20) And Joseph bought all the land of
Egypt for Pharaoh; for the Egyptians
sold every man his field, because the
famine prevailed over them: so the land
became Pharaoh's. (21) And as for the

1 Or, *as a little child is nourished.*

2 Heb., *according to the little ones.*

3 Heb., *led them.*

---

district of it, for, as we have seen, Goshen was a territory of vast extent. Raamses (Exod. i. 11) is the same word, though the Masorites have given it different vowels; but whether such a town already existed, or whether when built it took its name from the district, we cannot tell. If there were such a place, it would at this period be a poor village, consisting of a few shepherds' huts; but long afterwards, in the days of King Rameses II., "it was the centre of a rich, fertile, and beautiful land, described as the abode of happiness, where all alike, rich and poor, lived in peace and plenty."—Canon Cook, *Excursus on Egyptian Words*, p. 487. It deserved therefore its description as "the best of the land."

(12) **According to their families.**—Heb., *according to the "taf."* This, as we have seen above, means "according to the clan or body of dependants possessed by each one." Dan, with his one child, would have been starved to death if the allowance for himself and his household had depended upon the number of his "little ones," which is the usual translation of this word in the Authorised Version. (See margin.)

JOSEPH'S POLICY IN EGYPT.

(16) **Give your cattle.**—As the people were in want of food, and their land incapable of cultivation as long as the Nile ceased to overflow, this was a merciful arrangement, by which the owners were delivered from a burden, and also a portion of the cattle saved for the time when they would be needed again for agricultural purposes. As the charge of so many cattle in time of dearth would be a very serious matter (1 Kings xviii. 5, 6), we now see the reason why Pharaoh wished the ablest of Joseph's brethren to be employed in the task; and probably while there was no food for them in the Nile Valley, there would still be grass in the alluvial soil of the delta, which men used to move about with cattle would be able to find.

(17) **Horses . . . flocks . . . herds . . . asses.**—The mention of horses is a most important fact in settling the much-debated question as to the dynasty under which Joseph became governor of Egypt. When Abram went there, horses do not seem as yet to have been known (see Note on chap. xii. 16), but oxen and asses were common, and the former indigenous in the country (Maspero, *Histoire Ancienne*, pp. 11, 12). The horse was introduced by the Hyksos, according to Lenormant, *Les Prem. Civilisations*, i., 306 ff.; Rawlinson, *Egypt*, i., 74; and the first representation of one is drawing the war-chariot of the king who expelled them. The "flocks" are expressly said in the Hebrew to be *sheep*. This, too, is important; for while goats were indigenous in Egypt, sheep do not appear in the most ancient monuments, though they were introduced at an earlier date than horses.

(18) **The second year.**—Not the second year of the famine, but the year following that in which they had given up their cattle.

(20) **So the land became Pharaoh's.**—Joseph has been accused of reducing a free people to slavery by his policy. Undoubtedly he did vastly increase the royal power; but from what we read of the vassalage under which the Egyptians lived to a multitude of petty sovereigns, and also to their wives, their priests, and their embalmers, an increase in the power of the king, so as to make it predominant, would be to their advantage. The statement made here that the land in Egypt belonged entirely to the king is confirmed by Herodotus and other Greek authorities. The same is the case in India at this day; only, instead of the rent being a fifth part of the produce, it is in India a fixed annual sum, which is settled at comparatively distant intervals. In Burmah the agriculturists hold their land directly from the Crown.

(21) **He removed them to cities.**—Joseph's object in this measure was most merciful. As the corn was stored up in the cities, the people would be

people, he removed them to cities from
one end of the borders of Egypt even
to the *other* end thereof. (22) Only the
land of the [1]priests bought he not; for
the priests had a portion *assigned them*
of Pharaoh, and did eat their portion
which Pharaoh gave them: wherefore
they sold not their lands.
(23) Then Joseph said unto the people,
Behold, I have bought you this day and
your land for Pharaoh: lo, *here is* seed
for you, and ye shall sow the land.
(24) And it shall come to pass in the
increase, that ye shall give the fifth
part unto Pharaoh, and four parts shall
be your own, for seed of the field, and
for your food, and for them of your
households, and for food for your little
ones. (25) And they said, Thou hast
saved our lives: let us find grace in the
sight of my lord, and we will be Pha-
raoh's servants. (26) And Joseph made
it a law over the land of Egypt unto
this day, *that* Pharaoh should have the
fifth *part;* except the land of the
[2]priests only, *which* became not
Pharaoh's.
(27) And Israel dwelt in the land of
Egypt, in the country of Goshen; and
they had possessions therein, and grew,
and multiplied exceedingly. (28) And
Jacob lived in the land of Egypt seven-
teen years: so [3]the whole age of Jacob
was an hundred forty and seven years.
(29) And the time drew nigh that Israel
must die: and he called his son Joseph,
and said unto him, If now I have found
grace in thy sight, [a]put, I pray thee,
thy hand under my thigh, and deal
kindly and truly with me; bury me
not, I pray thee, in Egypt: (30) but I
will lie with my fathers, and thou shalt
carry me out of Egypt, and bury me
in their burying-place. And he said, I
will do as thou hast said. (31) And he
said, Swear unto me. And he sware

1 Or, *princes.*

2 Or, *princes.*

3 Heb., *the days of the years of his life.*

a ch. 24. 2.

---

sure of nourishment only if they were in the immediate neighbourhood of the food. As a consequence, possibly, of Joseph's policy, the number of cities in the Valley of the Nile became so enormous that Herodotus computes them at 20,000. Thus the people would not dwell at any distance from their lands, while it would be impossible for them to reside actually on their plots of ground, as these every year are overflowed by the Nile.

(22) **The priests had a portion assigned to them of Pharaoh.**—Herodotus (ii. 37) mentions that it was still the custom in Egypt for the priests to have a daily allowance of cooked food. Very probably this usage began in Joseph's time; but it is not here ascribed to him, but to the king himself. Being thus supplied with food, they did not sell their lands; and with this, again, the Greek accounts tally, as they represent the king, the priests, and the warriors as the only landholders in Egypt. The last class, however, held their land from the king.

(23) **Lo, here is seed for you.**—As Joseph would give them seed wherewith to sow their fields only when the famine was nearly over, these arrangements seem to have been completed shortly before the end of the seventh year; and then, with seed it would be necessary also to supply them with oxen to plough the soil, and swine wherewith to trample in the seed (Rawlinson, *Egypt*, i. 76). A fifth part of the produce would be a very moderate rent, especially as there were no rates or taxes to be paid. The whole expenses of the State had to be defrayed from this rent.

(25) **Thou hast saved our lives.**—The people were more than satisfied with Joseph's regulations; and if he had made them dependent upon the Pharaoh, apparently he had broken the yoke of the smaller lords, the hereditary princes of the districts into which Egypt was parcelled out; and they were more likely to be well-treated by the ruler of the whole land than by men of inferior rank. On these hereditary principalities at the period of the twelfth dynasty, see Maspero, *Hist. Anc.*, p. 121.

ISRAEL IN EGYPT.

(29) **The time drew nigh that Israel must die.**—For seventeen years Jacob lived in Egypt, and saw the growing prosperity of his race under the fostering hand of Joseph. Placed at the entrance of Egypt, on the side of Arabia and Palestine, the clans of his sons would daily grow in number by the addition of Semitic immigrants, by whose aid they would make the vast and fertile region assigned them, and which had previously had but a scanty population, a well-cultivated and thriving land. But at last Jacob feels his end approaching, though apparently he was not as yet in immediate danger of death. But there was a wish over which he had long pondered; and desiring to have his mind set at rest, he sends for Joseph, and makes him promise that he will bury him in the cave at Machpelah. We find him again charging all his sons to grant him this request (chap. xlix. 29—32); nor need we seek for any remote reason for it. Jacob's whole nature was a loving one, and strongly influenced by home and domestic feelings; and at Machpelah his nearest relatives were buried. In the next chapter he dwells upon Rachel's death, and his burial of her apart from the rest at Ephrath; and this seems to have increased his grief at her loss. At Machpelah, Abraham, whom he had known as a boy, his beloved father and mother, and Leah, who had evidently at last won his affections, all lay; and there, naturally, he too wished to lie among his own.

Put . . . thy hand under my thigh.—See Note on chap. xxiv. 2.

(31) **Israel bowed himself upon the bed's head.**—The LXX., followed by the Epistle to the Hebrews (chap. xi. 21) and the Syriac, read, "on the top of his staff." The word in the Hebrew, without vowels, may mean either *bed* or *staff*, and as we have mentioned above (chap. xxii. 14), the points indicating the vowels were added in later times, and while valuable as representing a very ancient tradition, are neverthe-

unto him. And [a]Israel bowed himself
upon the bed's head.

CHAPTER XLVIII.—(1) And it came
to pass after these things, that *one* told
Joseph, Behold, thy father *is* sick: and
he took with him his two sons, Manasseh
and Ephraim. (2) And *one* told Jacob,
and said, Behold, thy son Joseph cometh
unto thee: and Israel strengthened
himself, and sat upon the bed.
(3) And Jacob said unto Joseph, God
Almighty appeared unto me at [b]Luz in
the land of Canaan, and blessed me,
(4) and said unto me, Behold, I will make
thee fruitful, and multiply thee, and I
will make of thee a multitude of people;
and will give this land to thy seed after
thee *for* an everlasting possession.
(5) And now thy [c]two sons, Ephraim and
Manasseh, which were born unto thee in
the land of Egypt before I came unto
thee into Egypt, *are* mine; as Reuben
and Simeon, they shall be mine. (6) And
thy issue, which thou begettest after
them, shall be thine, *and* shall be called
after the name of their brethren in their
inheritance. (7) And as for me, when I
came from Padan, [d]Rachel died by me
in the land of Canaan in the way, when
yet *there was* but a little way to come
unto Ephrath: and I buried her there in

B.C. 1689.

a Heb., 11. 21.

b ch. 28. 13 & 35. 6.

c ch. 41. 50; Josh. 13. 7.

d ch. 35. 19.

less not of final authority. The rendering, however, of the Authorised Version is the most satisfactory. It was scarcely worth mentioning that Jacob bowed before Joseph, leaning on his staff; but the picture of the aged patriarch leaning back upon his bed, content and happy in his son's promise, and giving thanks to God for the peace of his approaching end, is one full of pathos and dignity.

XLVIII.

The Blessing of Manasseh and Ephraim, and the Recognition of them by Jacob as Heads of Tribes.

(1) **His two sons.**—We have already seen that the purpose of the genealogy given in chap. xlvi. was not the enumeration of Jacob's children and grandchildren, but the recognition of those of his descendants who were to hold the high position of heads of "families." In this chapter a still more important matter is settled; for Jacob, exercising to the full his rights as the father and head of the Israelite race, and moved thereto both by his love for Rachel, the high rank of Joseph, and also by the spirit of prophecy, bestows upon Joseph two tribes. No authority less than that of Jacob would have sufficed for this, and therefore the grant is carefully recorded, and holds its right place immediately before the solemn blessing given by the dying patriarch to his sons. The occasion of Joseph's visit was the sickness of his father, who not merely felt generally that his death was near, as in chap. xlvii. 29, but was now suffering from some malady; and Joseph naturally took with him his two sons, that they might see and be blessed by their grandfather before his death.

(2) **Strengthened himself.**—Jacob thus prepared himself, not merely because he wished to receive Joseph in a manner suitable to his rank, but chiefly because he was about himself to perform a sacred act, under the influence of the Divine Spirit.

Sat upon the bed.—We learn that he left his bed, and placed himself upon it in a sitting posture, from what is recorded in verse 12.

(3) **God Almighty.**—Heb., *El Shaddai.* The act recorded in this chapter is grounded by Jacob upon the promise made to him at Bethel on his return from Padan-aram; and it was under the old covenant name by which God had revealed Himself to Abram (chap. xvii. 1) that he was there made the heir of the Abrahamic promises. (See Note on chap. xxxv. 11.)

Luz.—This use of the old name shows how very slowly the new titles of places, derived from incidents in the history of a small tribe, took the place of their native and original appellations. In a similar manner, in the recent exploration of Palestine, it has been found that the high-sounding titles given by the Seleucidæ and Romans to towns there have never been adopted by the peasantry, who still call them by their old names.

(4) **A multitude of people.**—In chap. xxxv. 11 the words are "a congregation (or church) of nations;" here "a congregation (same word) of peoples." (See Note there.)

(5) **As Reuben and Simeon, they shall be mine.**—That is, Ephraim shall be regarded as my firstborn, and Manasseh as my second son. This was undoubtedly the case; for though "Judah prevailed above his brethren, and of him came the prince (and of him the Messiah), yet the birthright was Joseph's" (1 Chron. v. 2). The legal right of the firstborn was a double share of the father's goods. This was bestowed upon Joseph in giving him two tribes, and to the other sons but one. It was in a spiritual sense, and with reference to the promise that all mankind should be blessed in Jacob's seed, that the birthright was Judah's. As Joseph was the son of the chief and best-beloved wife, he had a sort of claim to the birthright; but in agreement with the law afterwards specially enacted (Deut. xxi. 15—17), Jacob acknowledges that the right had belonged to Reuben, but excludes him from the possession of it as the penalty of his great and terrible sin. Simeon and Levi are next passed over, because of their cruelty, and so Judah takes Reuben's place.

(6) **Thy issue, which thou begettest after them.**—We gather from chap. l. 23 that Joseph probably had no other sons. But if such were born to him, they were not to count as heads of tribes, but be regarded as the children of Ephraim and Manasseh, and take rank only as heads of families.

(7) **Rachel died by me.**—Heb., *died upon me*, or, as we should say, "died in my arms." The mention of Rachel is to account for an act so authoritative as the bestowal of the double portion of the firstborn upon Joseph. Jacob grounds the justification of his act, not upon her being the chief wife, but upon her untimely death, which prevented her bearing other sons. Even now Leah, if we count Levi, had six tribes, each handmaid two, and Rachel three.

The same is Beth-lehem.—A note added subsequently, when the place was famous as the birthplace

the way of Ephrath; the same *is* Beth-
lehem.
(8) And Israel beheld Joseph's sons,
and said, Who *are* these? (9) And
Joseph said unto his father, They *are*
my sons, whom God hath given me in
this *place*. And he said, Bring them, I
pray thee, unto me, and I will bless them.
(10) Now the eyes of Israel were [1]dim for
age, *so that* he could not see. And he
brought them near unto him; and he
kissed them, and embraced them.
(11) And Israel said unto Joseph, I had
not thought to see thy face: and, lo,
God hath shewed me also thy seed.
(12) And Joseph brought them out from
between his knees, and he bowed himself
with his face to the earth. (13) And
Joseph took them both, Ephraim in his
right hand toward Israel's left hand,
and Manasseh in his left hand toward
Israel's right hand, and brought *them*
near unto him. (14) And Israel stretched
out his right hand, and laid *it* upon
Ephraim's head, who *was* the younger,
and his left hand upon Manasseh's head,
guiding his hands wittingly; for Ma-
nasseh *was* the firstborn.
(15) And [a]he blessed Joseph, and said,
God, before whom my fathers Abraham
and Isaac did walk, the God which fed
me all my life long unto this day, (16) the
Angel which redeemed me from all evil,
bless the lads; and let my name be
named on them, and the name of my
fathers Abraham and Isaac; and let
them [2]grow into a multitude in the midst
of the earth.
(17) And when Joseph saw that his
father laid his right hand upon the head
of Ephraim, it displeased him: and he
held up his father's hand, to remove it
from Ephraim's head unto Manasseh's
head. (18) And Joseph said unto his
father, Not so, my father: for this *is*
the firstborn; put thy right hand upon
his head. (19) And his father refused,
and said, I know *it*, my son, I know *it*:
he also shall become a people, and he also
shall be great: but truly his younger
brother shall be greater than he, and
his seed shall become a [3]multitude of

1 Heb., *heavy*.

a Heb. 11. 21.

2 Heb., *as fishes do increase*.

3 Heb., *fulness*.

---

of David. It would not be called Beth-lehem until corn was cultivated there.

(8) **Who are these?**—This question is asked as the solemn turning of the discourse to the young men who were now to be invested with the patriarchal rank. They were at this time about eighteen or twenty years of age.

(12) **He bowed himself.**—The Samaritan, Syriac, and LXX. Versions regard the Hebrew verb as a contracted plural, and many modern commentators adopt this view. It would thus be Manasseh and Ephraim who stood before Jacob with faces bent towards the ground. The pronoun, however, is in favour of the verb being singular, and the sense it gives is equally satisfactory.

(14) **Guiding his hands wittingly.**—The LXX., Syriac, and Vulg. translate, "placing his hands cross-wise;" but the Targum of Onkelos favours the translation of our version. There is some amount of philological support for the rendering of the three chief versions; but it must mainly rest upon their own authority, which is, however, very great.

(15, 16) **He blessed Joseph, and said.**—In Jacob's blessing there is a threefold appellation of the Deity, and a threefold blessing given to Joseph's sons. God is, first, the Elohim before whom his fathers had walked. Next, He is the Elohim who, as a shepherd, had watched over Jacob all his life long. But, thirdly, He is that Divine Presence which had been, and still was, Jacob's "goël," redeeming and rescuing him from all evil. The blessing is first general, the verb "bless" being singular, which, following the threefold repetition of God's name in the plural, is rightly used by Luther as a proof of a Trinity in Unity in the Godhead. Secondly, Ephraim and Manasseh are to bear the names, and be the representatives of Abraham, Isaac, and Jacob. Lastly, they are to grow into a multitude with extraordinary rapidity, the word used signifying that they were to increase with a prolificness as great as that of fishes.

The word "goël" is here used for the first time. It subsequently became the term for the nearest blood relative, whose duty it was to avenge a murder; but it is here used in its wider sense of a Saviour and a Deliverer. (Comp. Exod. vi. 6; Isa. lix. 20, &c.) The angel who wrestled with Jacob cannot accurately be described as having appeared to him in the character of a deliverer (chap. xxxii. 24—30). He appeared as an adversary; and Jacob learned in the struggle, by overcoming him, that he had power with God and man, and would prevail over all the difficulties and foes that still stood in his way. Moreover, the verb is present, "the angel that redeemeth me from all evil." Jacob recognised a Divine Presence which constantly guarded him, and which was ever his Redeemer and Saviour.

(19) **His younger brother shall be greater.**—In the final numbering of the tribes on the plains of Moab, the tribe of Manasseh had 52,700 souls, and that of Ephraim only 32,500 (Num. xxvi. 34, 37). It was the division of the tribe of Manasseh into two portions which made it politically insignificant, while Ephraim obtained a commanding position in the land of Canaan; and as Joshua was an Ephraimite, it naturally held the rank of foremost tribe during his days, and claimed it always afterwards. For Joshua, after the conquest of Canaan, must have held a position similar to that of General Washington after the independence of the United States had been secured, and all Israel would regard him as their ruler and chief. The influence also of the tribe would be strengthened by the ark being placed in one of its towns.

nations. (20) And he blessed them that
day, saying, In thee shall Israel bless,
saying, God make thee as Ephraim and
as Manasseh: and he set Ephraim before
Manasseh. (21) And Israel said unto
Joseph, Behold, I die: but God shall be
with you, and bring you again unto the
land of your fathers. (22) Moreover I
have given to thee one portion above thy
brethren, which I took out of the hand of
the Amorite with my sword and with my
bow.

CHAPTER XLIX. — (1) And Jacob
called unto his sons, and said,

Gather yourselves together, that I may
tell you *that* which shall befall you in
the last days. (2) Gather yourselves
together, and hear, ye sons of Jacob; and
hearken unto Israel your father.

---

(20) **In thee shall Israel bless.**—In conformity with these words, the Israelites to this day use Jacob's formula in blessing their children.

(22) **One portion.**—Heb., *one Shechem.* In favour of this being the town of Shechem is the fact that it did belong to Jacob (chap. xxxvii. 12, where see Note); also that Joseph's embalmed body was deposited there (see Josh. xxiv. 32, where the land is said to have been bought for a hundred kesitas); and, lastly, the testimony of John iv. 5, where a parcel of ground at Sychar, close to Shechem, is identified with the ground given by Jacob to Joseph. On the other hand, *one Shechem* is an unnatural way of describing a town. Shechem also means, as we have seen (chap. xii. 6), the *shoulder*, and Abulwalid, in his Lexicon, quoting this place, says that both the Hebrews and Arabs gave this name to any elevated strip of ground. This is confirmed by Num. xxxiv. 11, &c., though the word actually used, *chatef*, is different. Probably, therefore, there was a play upon words in calling this plot of hill-ground Shechem, and not *chatef*, but made with the intention of showing that the town of Shechem was the portion really signified. But what is meant by "Jacob having taken it out of the hand of the Amorite by his sword and his bow"? Shechem was strictly a town of the Hivites, but as they were but a feeble tribe, the term Amorite may be used to give greater glory to the exploit. In chap xv. 16, the Amorites, literally *mountaineers*, are described as owners of the whole country, and probably it was a term loosely applied to all the inhabitants of the uplands, though occasionally used with a more definite meaning (chap. xv. 21). As Jacob so strongly condemns the conduct of Simeon and Levi (chap. xlix. 5—7), he can scarcely refer to their exploit, and therefore commentators generally suppose that he used the words prophetically, meaning, "which my descendants will, centuries hence, conquer for themselves with their swords and bows." But this is to take the words of Holy Scripture in a non-natural sense. Jacob was the owner of a strip of this "shoulder-land" in a way in which he was not the owner of any other portion of land in Canaan, except the cave of Machpelah; and we find him sending his cattle to pasture there when he was himself dwelling far away (chap. xxxvii. 12). And it is quite possible that, after the inhuman treatment of the Hivites at Shechem, the Amorites did gather themselves together to avenge the wrong, but were deterred by the threatening position taken up by Jacob, or even repulsed in an attack. The latter supposition would best harmonise with the fact that "a mighty terror fell upon all the cities round about" (chap. xxxv. 5), and also with the exultant spirit in which Jacob, a pre-eminently peaceful and timid man, here alludes to the one military exploit of his life.

XLIX.

The Blessing of the Twelve Tribes.

(1) **That which shall befall you.**—This dying song of Jacob has been regarded alike by Jews and Christians as a prophetic hymn spoken by the patriarch under the influence of the Holy Spirit. By many modern commentators, however, it has been placed in David's time, and even ascribed to Nathan, partly on the ground that it is too spirited to have been the composition of one lying in the last decrepitude of old age, but chiefly because, in the description given of Judah, it is supposed to refer to the elevation of David to the royal dignity. But if it was thus written by a member of David's court, we should reasonably expect an exact knowledge of the state of things in David's time. For this, in fact, is the argument upon which these critics depend, that the internal evidence shows that it belongs to David's reign. Now, so far is this from being true, that not only is the whole exceedingly general, containing scarcely more than faint and dim hopes and anticipations, but, except in the matter of Judah's pre-eminence, there is no knowledge whatsoever of the arrangements of David's time. Thus, for instance, there is no word about Levi's priestly functions, and his dispersion in Israel is described as a punishment, and put upon exactly the same level as that of Simeon It is said in answer that it was David who established the priesthood, and set the Levites apart for their duties. If so, this was the very reason why Nathan, a seer of his court, should have put into Jacob's mouth some allusion to so important an event, in order to justify so strong a proceeding as the depriving of a tribe of its lands and political importance, the seizure of towns in every other tribe for the abode of its members, and the bestowal upon them of priestly functions. If however David, by an act of despotic power, was able to effect so violent a subversion of all tribal rights, it is strange that no reference is ever made to it: and, moreover, both the Pentateuch and the Books of Joshua (chaps. iii. 3; viii. 33, &c.), of Judges (chap. xvii. 9—13), and of Samuel (1 Sam. ii. 13, 27, 28; vi. 15, &c.) must be of a date so modern as for all remembrance of David's act to have passed away, and for the national traditions to have created for themselves a setting modelled upon a state of things that never existed, and which was contradictory to the most glorious age of the nation's history. But national traditions precede the historical period of a people's annals, and from the time of David careful records of all events in Judah and Israel were kept, and the history of Judah and Israel was one of the chief subjects of instruction given to the youth of the nation in the prophetic schools. But let us take another instance. At the settlement of the tribes in Canaan, it was Asher and not Zebulun to which the sea-coast

(3) Reuben, thou *art* my firstborn, my
might, and the beginning of my strength,
the excellency of dignity, and the excel-
lency of power: (4) unstable as water,
[1] thou shalt not excel; because thou
[a] wentest up to thy father's bed; then de-
filedst thou *it:* [2] he went up to my couch.

(5) Simeon and Levi *are* brethren; [3] in-
struments of cruelty *are in* their habita-
tions. (6) O my soul, come not thou into
their secret; unto their assembly, mine
honour, be not thou united: for in their
anger they slew a man, and in their self-
will they [4] digged down a wall. (7) Cursed
be their anger, for *it was* fierce; and
their wrath, for it was cruel: I will
divide them in Jacob, and scatter them
in Israel.

1 Heb., *do not thou excel.*

a ch. 35. 22; 1 Chr. 5. 1.

2 Or, *my couch is gone.*

3 Or, *their swords are weapons of violence.*

4 Or, *houghed oxen.*

---

upon the north fell by lot; south of Asher was the half-tribe of Manasseh, and south of this was Dan. (Comp. Judges v. 17.) Zebulun was an inland tribe, and did not "dwell at the haven of the sea." It is unnecessary to continue this examination, but generally we may affirm that the sole argument for Jacob's blessing having been written in historic times is the position given to Judah. Everything besides negatives this view; and we may reasonably ascribe the high rank of Judah to the fact that after the setting aside of Reuben, Simeon and Levi, he became the firstborn.

In the last days.—Heb., *in the after part of days.* The phrase is often opposed to "the beginning of days," and is constantly used of the times of the Messiah. Here these "after days" apparently commence with the conquest of Canaan, but look onward to the advent of Christ.

(3) **The beginning of my strength.**—In chap. xxxv. 18, the word *oni* means "my sorrow," and it is so translated here by the Vulg., Aquila, and Symmachus. But in this verse Jacob magnifies the prerogatives of the firstborn, and our version is undoubtedly right in deriving *oni* from a different and not uncommon word signifying strength. It occurs in Deut. xxi. 17; Job xl. 16; Pss. lxxviii. 51, cv. 36, &c.

The excellency . . .—We must here supply, "And therefore to thee as the firstborn belonged," first, *the excellency of dignity,* that is, the priesthood; and secondly, *the excellency of power,* that is, the kingly office. As a matter of history no king, judge, or prophet is recorded as having sprung from the tribe of Reuben.

(4) **Unstable.**—This translation is shown to be right by the use of the word in Judges ix. 4; Zeph. iii. 4, in both which places it is translated *light.* Out of this sense of lightness and frivolity naturally arose the meaning which the word has in Syriac of wantonness. In Arabic it means *boastful,* another side of feebleness. With this sense the comparison with water well agrees; for it is its nature to seek a dull level, and while yielding to every impression to retain none. The other meaning given to it by many able critics is "boiling over like water," a description of the unrestrained violence of Reuben's passions.

Thou shalt not excel.—That is, thou shalt not have that excellency which was thine by right of birth.

(5) **Simeon and Levi are brethren.**—That is, they are alike in character and disposition. Despising the feeble Reuben, they seem to have been close friends and allies, and probably tried to exercise a tyrannical authority over their younger brethren, Judah being the only one near them in age.

Their habitations.—This translation is universally abandoned, but there is much difference of opinion as to the real meaning of the word. The most probable explanation is that given by Jerome and Rashi, who render it *swords.* Apparently it is the Greek word *machaera,* a knife; and as neither the Hebrews nor the Canaanites were metallurgists, such articles were imported by merchants from Ionia. Long before the days of Jacob, caravans of traders traversed the whole country, and the goods which they brought would carry with them their own foreign names. The sentence, therefore, should be translated, "weapons of violence are their knives." The other meaning given by some competent critics, namely, *compacts,* if the word could be formed at all from the supposed root, would mean *marriage contracts,* and this gives no intelligible sense.

(6) **Their secret.**—The word *sôd* used here is literally the little carpet, or cushion, upon which an Oriental sits. Consequently, for two persons to sit upon the same carpet marks a high degree of friendship and familiarity. It would therefore be more exactly translated *alliance,* or *intimacy.*

Unto their assembly, mine honour, be not thou united.—For *assembly* (Heb. *congregation*), see chaps. xxviii. 3, xxxv. 11. It means here their union, or confederacy. In the first clause Jacob bids his *soul,* his true self, not to enter their alliance; here, after the manner of the parallelism of Hebrew poetry, he intensifies the meaning. For by *mine honour,* he signifies all that gave him dignity and worth in the sight of God and man. And this nobleness would be degraded and lost by union with men banded together for evil.

In their self-will they digged down a wall.—Self-will is worse than anger, and signifies that arrogant temper which leads on to wanton cruelty. The last words mean, *they houghed an ox.* The Vulg. and Syriac took it as our version does, and understood it of making a breach in the walls of Shechem; but they had a different reading, *shur,* whereas the word in the Hebrew is *shor,* an ox, and it is so rendered by the LXX. The ox was in old times the symbol of majesty, and thus *bulls* are put for *princes* in Pss. xxii. 12, lxviii. 30. Thus, then, the meaning is, "In their anger at the wrong done to their sister they slew Hamor, prince of Shechem, with his people; and from wanton cruelty, without any just cause for indignation, they hamstrung the noblest of their brethren, not killing Joseph outright, but disabling him by selling him into slavery, that he might there perish."

(7) **Cursed . . .**—Jacob condemns Simeon and Levi, not because they were angry, but because they vented their anger in a perfidious and violent manner. The next sentence literally is, *And their rage, for it was hard.* The indignation at Joseph's dreams, told them by him innocently, led them to an act harsh and inhuman (see chap. xlii. 21).

I will divide them . . .—This prediction was equally fulfilled in the fact that neither of the tribes

(8) Judah, thou *art he* whom thy brethren shall praise: thy hand *shall be* in the neck of thine enemies; thy father's children shall bow down before thee.
(9) Judah *is* a lion's whelp: from the prey, my son, thou art gone up: he stooped down, he couched as a lion, and as an old lion; who shall rouse him up?
(10) The sceptre shall not depart from Judah, nor a lawgiver from between his feet, until Shiloh come; and unto him *shall* the gathering of the people *be.*

---

of Simeon and Levi possessed any political importance in Israel. The brothers had banded together to oppress their kindred; their descendants were powerless. But in every other respect the fulfilment was utterly diverse. In the wilderness the Simeonites dwindled from 59,300 to 22,200 men (Num. i. 23, xxvi. 14); and after the conquest of Canaan, were so feeble as to have only fifteen towns assigned them, scattered about in the territory of Judah. And there they melted away, being either absorbed into the tribe among whom they dwelt, or withdrawing to wander as nomads in the wilderness of Paran. In Levi's case the curse was changed into a blessing by the faithfulness of the tribe upon a very trying occasion (Exod. xxxii. 26—28); and we learn from it the great lesson that the Divine rewards and punishments, even when specified in prophecy, are nevertheless conditional upon human conduct. Of this diversity of fulfilment there is not the slightest indication in Jacob's blessing, while in that of Moses the lot of Levi is described in terms of the highest praise, and that of Simeon is passed over in inglorious silence.

(8) **Judah, thou art he whom thy brethren shall praise.**—Judah had received his name, Praise, because at his birth Leah had praised Jehovah (chap. xxix. 35). It is now to have another justification in the noble history of his race, which, taking the foremost place by reason of the disqualification of Reuben, Simeon, and Levi, finally was destined to win freedom and empire for Israel. We have seen that "the excellency of power" ought to have belonged to Reuben; it now falls to Judah's lot, is to be attained by exploits that shall deserve the praise of all the tribes, and is to be exercised over not only the descendants of Leah, but all Jacob's children.

(9) **Judah is a lion's whelp.**—We have seen that the sons of Jacob had each his signet, and that Judah's was so large as to be worn by him attached to a cord fastened round his neck (chap. xxxviii. 18). Probably his emblem was a lion; that of Zebulun a ship; that of Issachar an ass; that of Dan an adder, and so on. Using then his self-chosen emblem, Jacob compares him, first, to a "lion's whelp," full of activity and enterprise, and which, after feasting upon its prey, *goes up* to its mountain lair, calm and fearless in the consciousness of its strength. But as Judah is a young lion in his activity and fearlessness, so is he "a lion" full-grown and majestic in his repose, which Jacob's words literally describe. For the "stooping down" is the bending of the limbs together before the lion *couches*, that is, lies down in his den.

As an old lion.—Heb., *as a lioness*, the female being said to be more fierce than the male, and to resent more angrily any disturbance of its rest.

(10) **The sceptre shall not depart from Judah.**—Heb., *a sceptre.* The staff, adorned with carvings, and handed down from father to son, soon became the emblem of authority (see Note on chap. xxxviii. 18). It probably indicates here tribal rather than royal rank, and means that Judah would continue, until the time indicated, to be a self-governed and legally-constituted tribe.

Nor a lawgiver from between his feet.—Most modern critics translate *ruler's staff*, but "lawgiver" has the support of all the ancient versions, the Targums paraphrasing it by *scribe*, and the Syriac in a similar way by *expounder—i.e.*, of the law. *Ruler's staff* has the parallelism in its favour, but the ancient versions must not be lightly disregarded, and, besides, everywhere else the word means law-giver (see Deut. xxxiii. 21; Judges v. 14; Isa. xxxiii. 22). "From between his feet" means, "from among his descendants." The Targum of Onkelos renders, "from his children's children."

Until Shiloh come.—Many modern critics translate, "until he come to Shiloh," but this is to be rejected, first, as being contrary to all the ancient versions; and, secondly, as turning sense into nonsense. The town of Shiloh was in the tribe of Ephraim, and we know of no way in which Judah ever went thither. The ark was for a time at Shiloh, but the place lost all importance and sank into utter obscurity after its destruction by the Philistines, long before Judah took the leading part in the commonwealth of Israel.

Shiloh.—There are several interpretations of this word, depending upon different ways of spelling it. First, Jerome, in the Vulg., translates it, "He who shall be sent." He read, therefore, *Shalu'ch*, which differs from the reading in the Hebrew text by omitting the *yod*, and putting the guttural ח for *h* (Heb., ה) as the final letter. We have, secondly, *Shiloh*, the reading of the present Hebrew text. This would mean, *Peaceful*, or *Peace-maker*, and agrees with the title given to the Messiah by Isaiah (chap. ix. 6). But, thirdly, all the versions excepting the Vulg. read *Sheloh.* Thus, the LXX. has, "He for whom it is laid up" (or, according to other MSS., "the things laid up for him."). With the former reading, Aquila and Symmachus agree; with the latter, Theodotion, Epiphanius, and others, showing that Sheloh was the reading in the centuries immediately after the Nativity of our Lord. The Samaritan transcript of the Hebrew text into Samaritan letters reads Sheloh, and the translation into Aramaic treats the word as a proper name, and renders, "Until Sheloh come." Onkelos boldly paraphrases, "Until Messiah come, whose is the kingdom;" and, finally, the Syriac has, "Until he come, whose it is." There is thus overwhelming evidence in favour of the reading Sheloh, and to this we must add that Sheloh is the reading even of several Hebrew MSS. We may, in fact, sum up the evidence by saying that the reading *Shiloh*, even in the Hebrew text, has only modern authority in its favour, and that all ancient authorities are in favour of Sheloh; for even Jerome omits the *yod*, though he changes the aspirate at the end into a guttural.

Sheloh literally means, *Whose it is*, and is an Aramaic form, such as that in chap. vi. 3, where we have observed that these Aramaisms are a proof either of extreme antiquity, or of a very late date. We find another in Judges v. 7, in the song of Deborah, confessedly a very ancient composition; and the form is

(11) Binding his foal unto the vine, and his ass's colt unto the choice vine; he washed his garments in wine, and his clothes in the blood of grapes: (12) his eyes *shall be* red with wine, and his teeth white with milk.

(13) Zebulun shall dwell at the haven of the sea; and he *shall be* for an haven of ships; and his border *shall be* unto Zidon.

(14) Issachar *is* a strong ass couching down between two burdens: (15) and he saw that rest *was* good, and the land that *it was* pleasant; and bowed his shoulder to bear, and became a servant unto tribute.

---

quite in its place here in the elevated phraseology of this blessing, and in the mouth of Jacob, who had lived so long in a land where an Aramaic dialect was spoken.

Finally, Ezekiel, chap. xxi. 27 (Heb., 32), quotes Jacob's words, using however the Hebrew idiom, "Until he come, whose is the right." And St. Paul (Gal. iii. 19) refers to it in the words, "Until the seed come to whom it is promised," where the latter words seem to be a free rendering of the phrase in the LXX., "for whom it is laid up."

The passage has always been regarded as Messianic, not merely by Christians, but by the Jews, all whose ancient writers, including the Talmud, explain the name Shiloh, or Sheloh, of the Messiah. But the Targum of Onkelos would of itself be a sufficient proof, as we have there not the opinions or knowledge of one man, but the traditional explanation of the Pentateuch, handed down orally from the time of Ezra, and committed to writing probably in the first century of the Christian era. The objection has, indeed, been made in modern times that the patriarchs had no Messianic expectations. With those who believe in prophecy such an objection can have no weight; but independently of this, the promise made to Abraham, and solemnly confirmed to Jacob, that in his seed all the kindreds of the earth should be blessed, was pre-eminently Messianic: as was also the name Jehovah; for that name was the embodiment of the promise made to Eve, and beginning with her cry of hope that she had gotten the Coming One, had become by the time of Enoch the symbol of the expectation of mankind that God would appear on earth in human nature to save them.

Unto him shall the gathering of the people be.—The word used here is rare, and the translation "gathering" was a guess of Rashi. Really it means *obedience*, as is proved by the one other place where it occurs (Prov. xxx. 17). For "people" the Heb. has *peoples*. Not Israel only, "the people," but all nations are to obey Him "whose is the kingdom." This is the rendering of Onkelos, "and him shall the peoples obey;" and of the Samaritan Version, "and at his hand shall the peoples be led." The LXX., Syriac, and Vulg. agree in rendering, "and he shall be the expectation of the nations."

(11) **Binding his foal . . .**—Having declared the spiritual prerogative of Judah, the patriarch now foretells that his land would be so rich in vineyards that the traveller would tie his ass to the vine, as the tree abundant everywhere.

Choice vine is, literally, *the vine of Sorek*, a kind much valued, as bearing a purple berry, small but luscious, and destitute of stones. The abundance of grapes is next hyperbolically described as so great that their juice would be used like water for the commonest purposes.

Blood of grapes especially refers to the juice of the red kinds, which were more valued in the East than white.

(12) **His eyes shall be red with wine.**—The word rendered *red* occurs only here, and is rendered in the Versions, *bright, sparkling*, and in the Vulg., *beautiful*. They also give the word rendered in our Version *with* a comparative force, which seems to be right: "His eyes shall be brighter than wine, and his teeth whiter than milk." The words do not refer to Judah's person, but describe the prosperity of his descendants, whose temporal welfare will show itself in their bright and healthy countenances.

(13) **Zebulun . . .**—"Sea" is plural in the Heb., and is rightly so rendered in the Syriac. The territory of the tribe lay upon the inland sea of Gennesaret, but did not extend to the shore of the Mediterranean. We do not know of any literal fulfilment of the prediction, but Moses also speaks of Zebulun and Issachar as tribes that would "suck of the abundance of the seas." It is very possible that, living in the neighbourhood of the Phœnicians, they took part in maritime pursuits; and thus the general meaning of the blessing may be that Zebulun would be a tribe, not of agriculturists, but of traders. It is also remarkable that Tyre, which was much nearer the tribe of Zebulun, and was the leading city in David's time, is not mentioned, but only the more ancient town of Sidon.

(14) **Issachar.**—The description of Issachar's lot is derived partly from the cognizance he had chosen for his signet, and partly from his personal character. He had taken for his symbol the ass—a very noble, active, spirited, and enduring animal in the East. (See chap. xvi. 12, where Ishmael is compared to the wild ass, which adds to these qualities the love of freedom.) His real character was slothful, inactive, and commonplace. Jacob therefore likens him to a "strong ass;" Heb., *an ass of bone*, that is, one coarsely bred, as animals of high parentage have small bones. He is thus fit only to be a drudge, and with the laziness of a cart-horse lies down "between two burdens." The word occurs again in Judges v. 16, and is there more correctly rendered *sheepfolds*. More exactly it means the pens in which the cattle were folded during the nights of summer; and it is in the dual form, because these pens were divided into two parts for the larger and smaller cattle. Thus Issachar, stretched at ease between his cattle-pens, gives us the idea of a tribe occupied with pastoral pursuits, and destitute of all higher aspirations.

(15) **A servant unto tribute.**—Heb., *task-work*. It means service paid in actual labour, such as was exacted by Solomon of the descendants of the Canaanites (1 Kings ix. 21, where the phrase used here is translated "a tribute of bondservice;" and 2 Chron. viii. 8). In the Middle Ages this forced labour—called "service without wages" in Jer. xxii. 13—was one of the wrongs most deeply felt by the peasantry, as they had to neglect their own plots of ground to labour for their seigneurs. The picture, then, is that of a race settled in a rich agricultural country, and content to endure a great deal of injustice because their condition as a whole was prosperous.

(16) Dan shall judge his people, as one
of the tribes of Israel. (17) Dan shall be
a serpent by the way, [1]an adder in the
path, that biteth the horse heels, so that
his rider shall fall backward. (18) I have
waited for thy salvation, O LORD.

(19) Gad, a troop shall overcome him:
but he shall overcome at the last.

(20) Out of Asher his bread *shall be* fat,
and he shall yield royal dainties.

(21) Naphtali *is* a hind let loose: he
giveth goodly words.

(22) Joseph *is* a fruitful bough, *even* a
fruitful bough by a well; *whose* [2]branches
run over the wall: (23) the archers have
sorely grieved him, and shot *at him*, and
hated him: (24) but his bow abode in
strength, and the arms of his hands
were made strong by the hands of the
mighty *God* of Jacob; (from thence *is*

1 Heb., *an arrow-snake.*

2 Heb., *daughters.*

(16, 17) **Dan.**—In passing on to the sons of the handmaids it was necessary to assure them of an independent rank among their brethren. The four tribes descended from them did always hold an inferior position, but Jacob by his words to Dan prevented their ever becoming subject states. Playing, then, upon the name Dan (a *judge*), he says that he shall judge his people as a distinct and separate tribe, possessed of all those rights of selfgovernment and tribal independence which this rank implied. It seems also that Dan's symbol was a serpent, and from this Jacob prophesies that though too weak a tribe to take the foremost place in war, yet that Dan should not be without military importance; and this was especially the case in the days of Samson. The word rendered *adder* is more exactly the *arrow-snake*, which lies in wait in the "path," a narrow track, and springs upon its prey as it passes. A horse bitten in this way would rear and throw its rider, who would then be in the power of his assailant.

(18) **I have waited for thy salvation, O Lord** (Jehovah).—Among the many explanations hazarded of this ejaculation the most probable is that given in the *Speaker's Commentary*, that the thought of the serpent wounding his prey in the heel carried the mind of the patriarch back to the fall of man, and the promise made to Eve. And thus it is a profession of faith, naturally called out by this chain of ideas, in the advent in due time of the promised Deliverer, and of which the accomplishment had become united in thought with the name of Jehovah.

(19) **Gad.**—The word Gad, as we have seen (chap. xxx. 11), means *good fortune*, but Jacob connects it with the root *gâdad*, "to gather in troops." Thus, then, "A troop" or "throng of plunderers shall throng upon him, but he shall throng upon their heel." Settling upon the east of the Jordan he shall be exposed to many a sudden incursion of plunderers, but, though ever unready, he shall gather his forces and repel them, and follow with avenging energy upon their rear.

(20) **Asher.**—The territory of this tribe, extending along the coast from Mount Carmel to Lebanon, was very productive. Zebulun, the trading tribe, could reach the sea only through their possessions.

(21) **Naphtali.**—Gad had been described as moving slowly in war, and allowing himself to be surprised by hordes of plunderers, whom, nevertheless, as soon as he has collected his forces, he repels and pursues with vigour. Naphtali, on the contrary, is light and active, moving rapidly like "a hind let loose;" or, literally, *sent forth*, like the scouts or van of an army. And thus he brings back "goodly words"—Heb., *words of pleasure*—that is, trustworthy intelligence to guide the army in its motions. Another translation has been proposed, which has the support of the LXX.: "Naphtali is a spreading terebinth, which shoots forth goodly branches." It retains the consonants of the Hebrew text, but gives them different vowels.

(22—26) **Joseph.**—The blessing of Joseph is, in many particulars, the most remarkable of them all. Jacob throughout it seems struggling with himself, and anxious to bestow more than was in his power. Joseph was his dearest son, the child of his chief and most beloved wife; he was, too, the saviour of Israel's family, and the actual ruler of Egypt; and his father had even bestowed upon him the portion of the first-born in giving him two tribes, and to the rest but one. Nevertheless, he cannot bestow upon him the sovereignty. In clear terms he had described Judah as the lion, whose lordly strength should give Israel victory and dominion, and the sceptre must remain his until He whose right it is to rule should come. And thus Jacob magnifies again and again, but in obscure terms, his blessing upon Joseph, which, when analyzed, amounts simply to excessive fruitfulness, with no Messianic or spiritual prerogative. Beginning with this, Jacob next dwells upon Joseph's trials, and upon the manliness with which he had borne and overcome them; and then magnifies the blessedness of the earthly lot of his race, won for them by the personal worth of Joseph, with a description of which Jacob ends his words.

(22) **A fruitful bough.**—Literally the words are, "Son of a fruitful tree is Joseph; son of a fruitful tree by a fountain: the daughters spread over the wall." That is, Joseph is like a fruitful tree planted near a fountain of living water, and of which the branches, or suckers, springing from it overtop the wall built round the spring for its protection. This fruitfulness of Joseph was shown by the vast number of his descendants.

(23) **The archers.**—Naturally Jacob next describes the sorrows of Joseph's youth, but in poetical terms, so as not to wound the feelings of his bretnren, or rouse up thoughts of vengeance in Joseph's own mind. Thus he compares him to a warrior, too mighty for his enemies to close with in open conflict, but whom they harass from a distance. "Hated him" would be better translated, *laid snares for him*, were guilty of treachery and deceit.

(24) **His bow abode in strength.**—The word for strength is highly poetical. It means that which goes on for ever, like the flowing streams or the eternal hills. In spite of all the machinations of his enemies, the bow of Joseph remained constant and enduring in its might.

Were made strong.—The Hebrew word is difficult, but more probably means, *were pliant, supple*, such as the arms of an archer ought to be.

From thence is the shepherd, the stone of Israel.—The Jewish commentators understand "from

the shepherd, the stone of Israel:)
(25) *Even* by the God of thy father, who
shall help thee; and by the Almighty,
who shall bless thee with blessings of
heaven above, blessings of the deep that
lieth under, blessings of the breasts,
and of the womb: (26) the blessings of
thy father have prevailed above the
blessings of my progenitors unto the
utmost bound of the everlasting hills:
they shall be on the head of Joseph, and
on the crown of the head of him that was
separate from his brethren.

(27) Benjamin shall ravin *as* a wolf: in
the morning he shall devour the prey,
and at night he shall divide the
spoil.

(28) All these *are* the twelve tribes of
Israel: and this *is it* that their father
spake unto them, and blessed them;
every one according to his blessing he

a ch. 47. 30.

b ch. 23. 16.

blessed them. (29) And he charged them,
and said unto them, I am to be gathered
unto my people: [a] bury me with my
fathers in the cave that *is* in the field
of Ephron the Hittite, (30) in the cave
that *is* in the field of Machpelah, which
is before Mamre, in the land of Canaan,
[b] which Abraham bought with the field
of Ephron the Hittite for a possession
of a buryingplace. (31) There they buried
Abraham and Sarah his wife; there they
buried Isaac and Rebekah his wife;
and there I buried Leah. (32) The
purchase of the field and of the cave
that *is* therein *was* from the children of
Heth.

(33) And when Jacob had made an end
of commanding his sons, he gathered
up his feet into the bed, and yielded up
the ghost, and was gathered unto his
people.

---

thence" of Joseph, who had become the ruler and protector of Israel. But "from thence" answers in the parallelism to *from the hands of.* Fully it would be, *from thence where dwells the Shepherd,* &c., that is,—Joseph's triumph came from God, who is the Shepherd (or Ruler) and the Rock of Israel.

(25) **Even by the God of thy father.**—In the Hebrew this follows directly upon the preceding clause: "from the Shepherd, the Stone of Israel; from the God of thy father, who shall help thee; and from the Almighty," &c.

Blessings of heaven above are the rains and dew; those of "the deep" beneath are lakes, rivers, and springs; and those of "the breasts and womb" mean an abundant offspring both of men and cattle. (For the opposite curse see Hosea ix. 14.)

(26) **The blessings of thy father.**—As the passage now stands, it means that the blessings which Jacob bestows upon Joseph are greater than those which he had himself received from his ancestors, Abraham and Isaac. This was scarcely the case, as the chief spiritual blessing was bestowed upon Judah, while for Joseph there was only earthly prosperity. For this reason most modern commentators adopt the reading of the Samaritan Pentateuch, supported by the Samaritan Targum and the LXX., "The blessings of thy father are mightier than the blessings of the ancient mountains, than the desire (or beauty) of the everlasting hills." Not only is the parallelism of the poetry thus preserved, but the rendering is easy and natural, while the other translation is full of difficulties, especially as to the words, "my progenitors," and "the utmost bound." The sense thus given to them cannot be obtained by any ordinary philological process.

Him that was separate from his brethren.—This scarcely gives the force of the verb, which means, *set apart, consecrated.* Hence the Vulg. renders "Nazarite," the Hebrew word being *nezir.* The Syriac and Samaritan Targum translate, "him that is the crown of his brethren;" and the LXX., "him who was the leader of his brethren." Many see in this an allusion to the sovereignty over the ten tribes being finally attained to by Ephraim, but probably the meaning is that Joseph was the noblest and highest in rank among Jacob's children.

(27) **Benjamin.**—With this description of their ancestor agrees the character of his race, which was the most spirited and warlike of all the tribes of Israel.

It would be interesting to compare the notices of the several tribes in the subsequent history with Jacob's blessing of their progenitors, and with that also given by Moses. The fathers, moreover, found in the words of the patriarch faint foreshadowings of the spiritual truths of Christianity. But such discussions exceed the limits of a commentary, and it has seemed best to give only the primary explanation of Jacob's words, in accordance, as far as possible, with the standpoint of the patriarch himself.

(28) **These are the twelve tribes.**—As we have seen in the case of Dan, Jacob had the further object of forming his descendants into twelve separate communities, which were, like the States in America, each to be independent, and have its own tribal government. From this position Levi naturally was excluded, when selected for the priesthood, and room was thus made for the bestowal of two of these communities upon the descendants of Joseph. Only in case of war they were to combine under the chieftainship of Judah. In the Book of Judges, however, we find the tribes as separate in matters of war as of peace, and by the time of Saul the need of a closer union had been felt, and tribal independence had been found to lead only to anarchy.

(33) **He gathered up his feet into the bed.**—This seems to indicate that the events recorded in chaps. xlviii. and xlix. all took place at the same time. In chap. xlviii. 2 we read that Jacob strengthened himself for this great final effort, seating himself upon the bed and placing his feet upon the ground. (See verse 12.) And now that all was over, wearied with what must have sorely exercised both his feelings and his physical powers, he gathered himself together upon the bed, and probably soon afterwards peaceably passed away to his eternal rest.

CHAPTER L.—(1) And Joseph fell
upon his father's face, and wept upon
him, and kissed him. (2) And Joseph
commanded his servants the physicians
to embalm his father: and the physicians
embalmed Israel. (3) And forty days
were fulfilled for him; for so are fulfilled
the days of those which are embalmed:
and the Egyptians [1]mourned for him
threescore and ten days. (4) And when
the days of his mourning were past,
Joseph spake unto the house of Pharaoh,
saying, If now I have found grace in
your eyes, speak, I pray you, in the ears
of Pharaoh, saying, (5) [a]My father made
me swear, saying, Lo, I die: in my grave
which I have digged for me in the land
of Canaan, there shalt thou bury me.
Now therefore let me go up, I pray thee,

1 Heb., *wept.*

a ch. 47. 29.

and bury my father, and I will come
again. (6) And Pharaoh said, Go up, and
bury thy father, according as he made
thee swear.

(7) And Joseph went up to bury his
father: and with him went up all the
servants of Pharaoh, the elders of his
house, and all the elders of the land of
Egypt, (8) and all the house of Joseph,
and his brethren, and his father's house:
only their little ones, and their flocks,
and their herds, they left in the land of
Goshen. (9) And there went up with
him both chariots and horsemen: and
it was a very great company. (10) And
they came to the threshing-floor of Atad,
which *is* beyond Jordan, and there they
mourned with a great and very sore
lamentation: and he made a mourning

L.

BURIAL OF JACOB, AND HAPPY OLD AGE OF JOSEPH.

(2) **The physicians embalmed Israel.**—The command given first by Jacob to Joseph (chap. xlvii. 29, 30), and then urged earnestly upon all his sons, and with the reminder that the cave of Machpelah had been purchased and belonged to him by right (chap. xlix. 29—32), made it specially necessary that the patriarch's body should be prepared for so long a journey. It was also usual at that period to embalm the dead; and during the many centuries while the custom lasted, from B.C. 2000 to A.D. 700, it is calculated that no less than 420,000,000 bodies were thus preserved. For the process, which was very expensive if done in the best manner, see Rawlinson, *Egypt*, i. 511 ff. The embalmers are not generally called physicians, but probably what is meant is that the embalming of Jacob's body was superintended by the physicians attached to Joseph's household. Egypt was famous for its physicians, who were in advance of those of other countries, and were subdivided into classes, which had each the charge of some special disease. (See Rawlinson as above, i. 305 ff.) Maspero thinks that their real knowledge was inconsiderable, and that there were specialists only for the eyes, and one or two similar diseases (*Hist. Anc.* 82). Ophthalmia continues to be one of the most common diseases of Egypt.

(3) **Forty days.**—Herodotus (ii. 86) describes the process of embalming as occupying seventy days, but he was speaking of what he saw at Thebes, whereas Memphis was the Egyptian capital in Joseph's time; and the mummies of Thebes are, we are told, far more perfectly preserved than those of Memphis. Diodorus agrees very nearly with the periods mentioned here, saying (i. 91) that the embalming took somewhat more than thirty days, and the mourning for a king seventy-two. The usual period of mourning among the Israelites was thirty days (Num. xx. 29; Deut. xxxiv. 8). Probably, therefore, the forty days spent in the embalming were included in the "threescore and ten days," during which the Egyptians mourned for Jacob.

(4) **Joseph spake unto the house of Pharaoh.**—It may seem at first sight strange that Joseph should make his request through mediators, but probably no one in the attire of mourning might enter the royal presence. (Comp. Esth. iv. 2.) The dress of a mourner was squalid, his beard unshorn, his hair in disorder, and while these outward signs of grief were maintained, he was also expected to confine himself to his own house.

(9) **A very great company.**—Heb., *camp*, the word following immediately upon the mention of the chariots and horsemen which went as the escort of the elders. These were the chief officers of Pharaoh's household, and also of the districts into which Egypt was divided, of which each had its separate governor. Of the Israelites only the men of rank, Jacob's own sons, and the officers of his house took part in the funeral procession, while their *little ones*—Heb., *their "tafs,"* translated here in the LXX. *their clans*, and signifying the great body of their dependents—remained with their cattle in the land of Goshen.

(10) **Threshingfloor of Atad.**—Atad means "a thorn-bush," the *rhamnus paliurus* of Linnæus, translated "bramble" in Judges ix. 14. As agriculture was only beginning to be practised in Canaan, this threshing-floor would be common property, situated in some place easy of access, and probably a village would grow up near it.

Beyond Jordan.—It is disputed whether this means on the east or on the west of the Jordan. It is certain that the route taken by Joseph lay to the east of the Dead Sea; for Goren-Atad is placed by Jerome at Beth-Hoglah, which lay between the Jordan and Jericho, and Joseph could have gone thither only by travelling through the territories of Moab and Ammon. This may seem a long detour, but, as may be seen in the Excursus on the Expedition of Chedorlaomer, the route through the wilderness of Judah was very difficult; and though the western shore of the Dead Sea was practicable as far as Engedi, it was necessary there to ascend a mountain-path so steep that a few Amorites might have guarded it against any number of invaders; and probably it was absolutely impracticable for chariots. It would have been easy, however, to reach Hebron through the Philistine country; but it is re-

for his father seven days. (11) And when
the inhabitants of the land, the Canaan-
ites, saw the mourning in the floor of
Atad, they said, This *is* a grievous mourn-
ing to the Egyptians: wherefore the
name of it was called [1]Abel-mizraim,
which *is* beyond Jordan. (12) And his
sons did unto him according as he com-
manded them: (13) for [a]his sons carried
him into the land of Canaan, and buried
him in the cave of the field of Mach-
pelah, which Abraham [b]bought with the
field for a possession of a buryingplace
of Ephron the Hittite, before Mamre.
(14) And Joseph returned into Egypt, he,
and his brethren, and all that went up
with him to bury his father, after he had
buried his father.

(15) And when Joseph's brethren saw
that their father was dead, they said,
Joseph will peradventure hate us, and
will certainly requite us all the evil
which we did unto him. (16) And they
[2]sent a messenger unto Joseph, saying,
Thy father did command before he died,
saying, (17) So shall ye say unto Joseph,
Forgive, I pray thee now, the trespass
of thy brethren, and their sin; for they
did unto thee evil: and now, we pray
thee, forgive the trespass of the servants
of the God of thy father. And Joseph
wept when they spake unto him. (18) And
his brethren also went and fell down be-
fore his face; and they said, Behold, we
be thy servants. (19) And Joseph said
unto them, [c]Fear not: for *am* I in the
place of God? (20) But as for you, ye
thought evil against me; *but* God meant
it unto good, to bring to pass, as *it is*
this day, to save much people alive.
(21) Now therefore fear ye not: I will
nourish you, and your little ones. And
he comforted them, and spake [3]kindly
unto them.

(22) And Joseph dwelt in Egypt, he,
and his father's house: and Joseph lived
an hundred and ten years. (23) And
Joseph saw Ephraim's children of the

1 That is, *The mourning of the Egyptians.*

a Acts 7. 16.

b ch. 23. 16.

2 Heb., *charged.*

c ch. 45. 5.

3 Heb., *to their hearts.*

---

markable that we find hostilities going on between the descendants of Joseph and the Philistines (1 Chron. vii. 21); and if raids were of common occurrence between the Semitic clans in Goshen and the Philistines, Joseph would not expose his father's remains to the danger of an attack. Possibly they may even have refused their consent, and hence the attack upon them by Ephraim's sons. On the other hand, the sons of Esau would show great respect to the body of their uncle—(Jewish tradition makes even the sons of Ishmael and of Keturah take part in the mourning)—and moreover they had not yet attained to any great power; and we gather from Esau's march through the lands on the west of the Dead Sea (chap. xxxii. 6) that the natives there were too few and feeble to resist the chariots and horsemen which formed the escort. While therefore "beyond Jordan" would naturally mean "on the east of Jordan," it may here express the fact that Joseph had just crossed the Jordan when the lamentation was made. The only other tenable explanation is that Goren-Atad was really on the eastern bank of the Jordan, and that though Beth-Hoglah was the nearest village, the two were not identical. It would be natural to make the solemn seven days' mourning, either when just about to enter the Canaanite territory or at the tomb.

(11) **Abel-mizraim.**—There is here an example of that play upon words that is always dear to Orientals. The word for "mourning" is *êbel*, while *abel* means a meadow, and is often found prefixed to the names of towns. When the Versions were made no vowel points were as yet affixed to the Hebrew consonants, and they all read Ebel-mizraim, *the mourning of Egypt.* The Hebrew text alone, as at present pointed, has Abel-mizraim, *the meadow of Egypt.*

(15) **Joseph will peradventure . . .**—Heb., *What if Joseph should hate us, &c.* They had not seen any change in his treatment of him, but if it were the case that he cherished feelings of revenge, they felt that they were now in his power.

(16, 17) **Thy father did command . . .**—Many Jewish expositors consider that this was untrue, and that Jacob was never made aware of the fact that his brethren had sold Joseph into slavery. It is, however, probable, from chap. xlix. 6, that Jacob not only knew of it, but saw in Simeon and Levi the chief offenders. But besides the father's authority the message brings a twofold influence to bear upon Joseph: for first it reminds him that they were his brethren, and next, that they shared the same religious faith—no slight band of union in a country where the religion was so unlike their own.

(19) **Am I in the place of God?**—That is, *am I to act as judge, and punish?* Judges are sometimes in Hebrew even called God (as in Exod. xxi. 6, xxii. 8, 9; 1 Sam. ii. 25), as exercising His authority.

(20) **Ye thought . . . God meant.**—The verb in the Heb. is the same, and contrasts man's purpose with God's purpose. In chap. xlv. 7 Joseph had already pointed out that the Divine providence had overruled the evil intentions of his brethren for good. At the end of the verse "much people," or *a great people,* means the Egyptians.

(21) **Your little ones.**—Heb., *your "tafs:"* rendered in the LXX., "your households," and in the Syriac, "your families," your dependents—its usual translation in that Version.

(23) **The third generation.**—These would be Joseph's great-grandchildren. Thus Eran, son of Shuthelah, son of Ephraim, was to be born in Joseph's lifetime (Num. xxvi. 35, 36).

Were brought up . . .—Heb., *were born upon Joseph's knees,* that is, were adopted by him. (See Note on chap. xxx. 3.) They would not form tribes, as this prerogative was reserved for the sons of Jacob (chap. xlviii. 5), but they would count as Joseph's sons (chap. xlviii. 6), and form "families."

third *generation:* [a] the children also of
Machir the son of Manasseh were
[1] brought up upon Joseph's knees.
(24) And Joseph said unto his brethren,
I die: and [b] God will surely visit you, and
bring you out of this land unto the land
which he sware to Abraham, to Isaac,
and to Jacob. (25) And [c] Joseph took an
oath of the children of Israel, saying,
God will surely visit you, and ye shall
carry up my bones from hence. (26) So
Joseph died, *being* an hundred and ten
years old: and they embalmed him, and
he was put in a coffin in Egypt.

a Num. 32. 39.

1 Heb., *borne.*

b Heb. 11. 22.

c Ex. 13. 19.

(24) **God will . . . bring you out of this land.**—This is, first, a proof of Joseph's faith, commended in Heb. xi. 22; and, secondly, it is a preparation for the next book (Exodus). Joseph's faith thus unites the two books together.

(26) **A coffin.**—The word means a case or chest of wood. The mummy-cases were generally of sycamore-wood. As it would not be possible for the Israelites, now that their great protector was no more, to go with a military escort to Hebron to bury him, Joseph orders that his embalmed body should be placed in some part of Goshen, whence it would be easy to remove it when the time of deliverance had arrived. And his wish was fulfilled; for "Moses took the bones of Joseph with him" (Exod. xiii. 19), and Joshua buried them in Shechem, in the piece of ground which Jacob had given to him (Josh. xxiv. 32).

With the death of Joseph ends the preparation for the formation of a chosen race. Summoned from a remote city upon the Persian Gulf to Palestine, Abraham had wandered there as a stranger, and Isaac and Jacob had followed in his steps. But in Palestine the race could never have multiplied largely; for there were races already there too powerful to permit of their rapid increase. Abraham and Lot, Esau and Jacob had been compelled to separate; but now, under Joseph, they had been placed in a large, fertile, and well-nigh uninhabited region. The few who dwelt there were, as far as we can judge, of the Semitic stock, and whatever immigrants came from time to time were also of the same race, and were soon enrolled in the "*taf*" of some noble or chief. And thus all was ready for their growth into a nation; and when we next read of them they had multiplied into a people so vast that Egypt was afraid of them.

EXCURSUS ON NOTES TO GENESIS

EXCURSUS A: UPON THE PROBATION OF ADAM (Chap. ii. 16).

The great object for which the world is constituted such as we actually find it to be is evidently the trial and probation of man's moral nature. We cannot wonder, therefore, at finding Adam subject to a probation; and even if he had remained innocent we have no right to suppose that his posterity would always have withstood temptation, or that the world would not finally have become such in the main as it is now. But the manner of Adam's probation was different. In Paradise he had unlimited freedom, except in one small particular, and no promptings of his own nature urged him to take delight in disobedience and sin. But if thus he was free from passion, on the other hand his conscience was undeveloped, even if it could be said to exist at all in one who did not know the difference between good and evil. He was devoid, too, of experience, and his reason must have been in a state as rudimentary as his conscience. For as there was no struggle between passion and conscience, man had not then learned to choose between opposing ends and purposes, as he has now. Nevertheless, Adam was an intellectual being. He must have had a deep knowledge of natural history; for doubtless he called the animals after their natures. In verse 23 he calls his wife *Ishah*, and himself *Ish*. Now, this name signifies a *being*, and in so calling himself Adam seems to claim for man that he is the one creature upon earth conscious of his own existence. And when Eve appears he simply adds a feminine termination to the name, recognising her thereby as the female counterpart of himself; but in so doing he shows a mastery of language, and the power of inflecting words according to the rules of grammar. There is proof, after the fall, of even increased insight into the nature of things; for in the name Eve, *life*, Adam plainly recognised in her difference of sex the Divinely-appointed means for the maintenance of human life upon earth. But man now, to balance the corruption of his nature, has, in addition to intellect, the help of conscience, of increased knowledge and experience of the effects of sin, and of largely-developed reason. Devoid of such assistance, a difficult probation, such as is the lot of mankind now, would apparently have been beyond the power of Adam to sustain; whereas, had he not been tempted from without, he might easily, with his passions as yet unstirred, and most of his intellectual gifts still dormant, have endured the simple trial to which he was subjected. But temptation from without was permitted, and Adam fell.

It would be easy to lose ourselves in reasoning upon the possibilities involved in Adam's trial; but there are points upon which there can be no doubt. First, if probation is the normal law of our condition now, it would be just as right and equitable to make Adam subject to a probation. And alike for Adam then and for men now, probation seems to be a necessary condition of the existence of beings endowed with free will. Secondly, the fall was not all loss; St. Paul affirms this with reference to the gift of a Saviour (Rom. v. 17—19). And besides this, higher qualities are called into existence now than were possible in the case of one who had no experimental knowledge of evil. We may even say that in giving this command Jehovah was appealing to qualities still dormant in Adam; and this exercise of the Divine attribute of foreknowledge makes us sure that the Divine purpose was to develop these qualities: not necessarily, however, by the fall, for they would have been to some extent exercised by resisting temptation. Thirdly, Adam, had he remained innocent, could nevertheless have attained to no higher happiness than such as was possible for a being in a rudimentary and passionless state of existence. He would have attained to the perfection of innocence, of pure physical enjoyment, and of even large scientific knowledge; but his moral nature would have developed very slowly, and its profounder depths would have remained unstirred. He would have been a happy grown-up child, not a proved and perfected man. The sufferings of this fallen world are intense (Rom. viii. 22), but the product in those who use their probation aright, is probably higher than any product of Paradise could have been. The holiness attained to by Enoch, the seventh from Adam, was of a different and higher kind than the most perfect innocence of a being who had been called to make no earnest struggle; for it was as the gold tried in the fire (1 Pet. i. 7).

EXCURSUS B: ON THE NAMES ELOHIM AND JEHOVAH-ELOHIM

Throughout the first account of creation (Gen. i. 1—ii. 3) the Deity is simply called *Elohim.* This word is strictly a plural of *Eloah,* which is used as the name of God only in poetry, or in late books like those of Nehemiah and Daniel. It is there an Aramaism, God in Syriac being *Aloho,* in Chaldee *Ellah,* and in Arabic *Allahu*—all of which are merely dialectic varieties of the Hebrew Eloah, and are used constantly in the singular number. In poetry Eloah is sometimes employed with great emphasis, as, for instance, in Ps. xviii. 31: "Who is Eloah except Jehovah?" But while thus the sister dialects used the singular both in poetry and prose, the Hebrews used the plural Elohim as the ordinary name of God, the difference being that to the one God was simply *power, strength* (the root-meaning of Eloah); to the other He was the union of all powers, the Almighty. The plural thus intensified the idea of the majesty and greatness of God; but besides this, it was the germ of the doctrine of a plurality of persons in the Divine unity.

In the second narrative (chaps. ii. 4—iii. 24), which is an account of the fall of man, with only such introductory matter regarding creation as was necessary for making the history complete, the Deity is styled *Jehovah-Elohim.* The spelling of the word Jehovah is debatable, as only the consonants (J, h, v, h) are certain, the vowels being those of the word *Adonai* (Lord) substituted for it by the Jews when reading it in the synagogue, the first vowel being a mere apology for a sound, and pronounced *a* or *e*, according to the nature of the consonant to which it is attached. It is generally represented now by a light breathing, thus—*Y'hovah, 'donai.* As regards the spelling, Ewald, Gesenius, and others argue for Yahveh; Fürst for Yehveh, or Yeheveh; and Stier, Meyer, &c., for Yehovah. The former has the analogy of several other proper names in its favour; the second the authority of Exod. iii. 14; the last, those numerous names like Yehoshaphat, where the word is written Yeho. At the end of proper names the form it takes is Yahu, whence also Yah. We ought also to notice that the first consonant is really *y;* but two or three centuries ago *j* seems to have had the sound which we give to *y* now, as is still the case in German.

But this is not a matter of mere pronunciation; there is a difference of meaning as well. Yahveh signifies "He who brings into existence;" Yehveh "He who shall be, or shall become;" what Jehovah may signify I do not know. We must further notice that the name is undoubtedly earlier than the time of Moses. At the date of the Exodus the *v* of the verb had been changed into *y*. Thus, in Exod. iii. 14, the name of God is *Ehyeh,* "I shall become," not Ehveh. Had the name, therefore, come into existence in the days of Moses, it would have been Yahyeh, Yehyeh, or Yehoyah, not Yahveh, &c.

The next fact is that the union of these two names—Jehovah-Elohim—is very unusual. In this short narrative it occurs twenty times, in the rest of the Pentateuch only once (Exod. ix. 30); in the whole remainder of the Bible about nine times. Once, moreover, in Ps. l. 1, there is the reversed form, Elohim-Jehovah. There must, therefore, be some reason why in this narrative this peculiar junction of the two names is so predominant.

The usual answer is that in this section God appears in covenant with man, whereas in chaps. i.—ii. 3 He was the Creator, the God of nature and not of grace, having, indeed, a closer relation to man, as being the most perfect of His creatures (chap. i. 26), but a relation different only in degree and not in kind. This is true, but insufficient; nor does it explain how Jehovah became the covenant name of God, and Elohim His generic title. Whatever be the right answer, we must expect to find it in the narrative itself. The facts are so remarkable, and the connection of the name Jehovah with this section so intimate, that if Holy Scripture is to command the assent of our reason we must expect to find the explanation of such peculiarities in the section wherein they occur.

What, then, do we find? We find this. The first section gives us the history of man's formation, with the solemn verdict that he was very good. Nature without man was simply good; with man, creation had reached its goal. In this, the succeeding section, man ceases to be very good. He is represented in it as the object of his Maker's special care, and, above all, as one put under law. Inferior creatures work by instinct, that is, practically by compulsion, and in subjection to rules and forces which control them. Man, as a free agent, attains a higher rank. He is put under law, with the power of obeying or disobeying it. God, who is the infinitely high and self-contained, works also by law, but it comes from within, from the perfectness of His own nature, and not from without, as must be the case with an imperfect being like man, whose duty is to strive after that which is better and more perfect. Add that, even in the first section, man was described as created "in God's image, after His likeness." But as law is essential to God's nature—for without it He would be the author of confusion—so is it to man's. But as this likeness is a gift conferred upon him, and not inherent, the law must come with the gift, from outside, and not from himself; and it can come only from God. Thus, then, man was necessarily, by the terms of his creation, made subject to law, and without it there could have been no progress upward. But he broke the law, and fell. Was he, then, to remain for ever a fallen being, hiding himself away from his Maker, and with the bonds of duty and love, which erewhile bound him to his Creator, broken irremediably? No. God is love; and the purpose of this narrative is not so much to give us the history of man's fall as to show that a means of restoration had been appointed. Scarcely has the breach been made before One steps in to fill it. The breach had been caused by a subtle foe, who had beguiled our first parents in the simplicity of their innocence; but in the very hour of their condemnation they are promised an avenger, who, after a struggle, shall crush the head of their enemy (chap. iii. 15).

Now this name, *Y-h-v-h,* in its simplest form Yehveh, means "He shall be," or "shall become." With the substitution of *y* for *v*, according to a change which had taken place generally in the Hebrew language, this is the actual spelling which we find in Exod. iii. 14: namely, *Ehyeh 'sher Ehyeh,* "I shall be that I shall be." Now, in the New Testament we find that the received name for the Messiah was "the coming One" (Matt. xxi. 9, xxiii. 39; Mark xi. 9; Luke vii. 19, 20, xiii. 35, xix. 38; John i. 15, 27, iii. 31, vi. 14, xi. 27, xii. 13; Acts xix. 4; Heb. x. 37); and in the Revelation of St. John the name of the Triune God is, "He who is and who was, and the coming One" (chaps. i. 4, 8, xi. 17). But St. Paul tells us of a notable change in the language of the early Christians. Their solemn formula was Maran-atha, "Our Lord is come" (1 Cor. xvi. 22). The Deliverer was no longer future, no longer "He who shall become," nor "He who shall be what He shall be." It is not now an indefinite hope: no longer the sighing of the creature waiting for the manifestation of Him who shall crush the head of his enemy. The faint ray of light which dawned in Gen. iii. 15 has become the risen Sun of Righteousness; the Jehovah of the Old Testament has become the Jesus of the New, of whom the Church joyfully exclaims, "We praise Thee as God: we acknowledge Thee to be Jehovah."

But whence arose this name Jehovah? Distinctly from the words of Eve, so miserably disappointed in their primary application: "I have gotten a man, even Jehovah," or Yehveh (chap. iv. i.). She, poor fallen creature, did not know the meaning of the words she uttered, but she had believed the promise, and for her faith's sake the spirit of prophecy rested upon her, and she gave him on whom her hopes were fixed the title which was to grow and swell onward till all inspired truth gathered round it and into it; and at length Elohim, the Almighty, set to it His seal by calling Himself "I shall be that I shall be" (Exod. iii. 14). Eve's word is simply the third person of the verb of which *Ehyeh* is the first, and the correct translation of her speech is, "I have gotten a man, even he that shall be," or "the future one." But when God called Himself by this appellation, the word, so indefinite in her mouth, became the personal name of Israel's covenant God.

Thus, then, in this title of the Deity, formed from the verb of existence in what is known as the future or indefinite tense, we have the symbol of that onward longing look for the return of the golden age, or age of paradise, which elsewhere in the Bible is described as the reign of the Branch that shall grow out of Jesse's root (Isa. xi. 4—9). The hope was at first dim, distant, indistinct, but it was the foundation of all that was to follow. Prophets and psalmists were to tend and foster that hope, and make it clear and definite. But the germ of all their teaching was contained in that mystic four-lettered word, the tetragrammaton, Y-h-v-h. The name may have been popularly called Yahveh, though of this we have no proof; the Jews certainly understood by it Yehveh—"the coming One." After all, these vowels are not of so much importance as the fact that the name has the pre-formative *yod.* The force of this letter prefixed to the root form of a Hebrew verb is to give it a future or indefinite sense; and I can find nothing whatsoever to justify the assertion that Jehovah—to adopt the ordinary spelling—means "the existent One," and still less to attach to it a causal force, and explain it as signifying "He who calls into being."

Finally, the pre-Mosaical form of the name is most instructive, as showing that the expectation of the Messiah was older than the time of the Exodus. The name is really man's answer to and acceptance of the promise made to him in chap. iii. 15; and why should not Eve, to whom the assurance was given, be the first to profess her faith in it? But in this section, in which the name occurs twenty times in the course of forty-six verses, there is a far deeper truth than Eve supposed. Jehovah (*Yehveh*) is simply "the coming One," and Eve probably attached no very definite idea to the words she was led to use. But here He is called Jehovah-Elohim, and the double name teaches us that the coming One, the future deliverer, is God, the very Elohim who at first created man. The unity, therefore, and connection between these two narratives is of the closest kind and the prefixing in this second section of Jehovah to Elohim, the Creator's name in the first section, was the laying of the foundation-stone for the doctrine that man's promised Saviour, though the woman's seed, was an Emmanuel, God as well as man.

EXCURSUS C: ON THE DURATION OF THE PARADISIACAL STATE OF INNOCENCE

The *Bereshit Rabba* argues that Adam and Eve remained in their original state of innocence for six hours only. Others have supposed that the events recorded in chaps. ii. 4—iii. 24 took place in the course of twenty-four hours, and suppose that this is proved by what is said in chap. ii. 4, that the earth and heavens, with Adam and the garden, were all made in one day, before the end of which they suppose that he fell. This view, like that which in chap. i. interprets each creative day of a similar period, really amounts to this: that the narrative of Holy Scripture is to be forced to bend to an arbitrary meaning put upon a single word, and drawn not from its meaning in Hebrew, but from its ordinary use in English. More correctly, we might venture to say that the use of the word *day* in chap. ii. 4 is a Divine warning against so wilful a method of exposition.

Read intelligently, the progress of time is carefully marked. In verse 6 the earth is watered by a mist: in paradise there are mighty rivers. Now, mist would not produce rivers; and if there were mist in the morning, and rain in the afternoon, a long period of time would still be necessary before the falling rains would form for themselves definite channels. A vast space must have elapsed between the mist period and that in which the Tigris and Euphrates rolled along their mighty floods.

And with this the narrative agrees. All is slow and gradual. God does not summon the Garden of Eden into existence by a sudden command, but He "planted" it, and "out of the ground He made to grow" such trees as were most remarkable for beauty, and whose fruit was most suitable for human food. In some favoured spot, in soil fertile and fit for their development, God, by a special providence, caused such plants to germinate as would best supply the needs of a creature so feeble as man, until, by the aid of his reason, he has invented those aids and helps which the animals possess in their own bodily organisation. The creation of full-grown trees belongs to the region of magic. A book which gravely recorded such an act would justly be relegated to the Apocrypha; for the God of revelation works by law, and with such long ages of preparation that human eagerness is often tempted to cry, "How long?" and to pray that God would hasten His work.

And next, as regards Adam. Placed in a garden, two of the rivers of which—the Tigris and the Euphrates—seem to show that the earth at his creation had already settled down into nearly its present shape, he is commanded "to dress and keep it." The inspired narrator would scarcely have spoken in this way if Adam's continuance in the garden had been but a few hours or days. We find him living there so long that his solitude becomes wearisome to him, and the Creator at length affirms that it is not good for him to be alone. Meanwhile, Adam is himself searching for a partner, and in the hope of finding one, he studies all the animals around him, observes their ways, gives them names, discovers many valuable qualities in them, makes several of them useful to him, but still finds none among them that answers to his wants. But when we read that "Adam gave names to all cattle, and to the fowls of the air, and to every beast of the field," we cannot but see that this careful study of the creatures round him must have continued through a long period before it could have resulted in their being thus generally classified and named in Adam's mind. At length Eve is brought, and his words express the lively pleasure of one who, after repeated disappointments, had at length found that of which he was in search. "This," he says, "this time is bone of my bone."

How long Adam and Eve enjoyed their simple happiness after their marriage is left untold; but this naming of the animals at least suggests that some time elapsed before the fall. Though Adam had observed their habits, yet he would scarcely have given many of them names before he had a rational companion with whom to hold discourse. For some, indeed, he would have found names when trying to call them to him, but only for such as seemed fit for domestication. The rest he would pass by till there was some one to whom to describe them. Thus Eve seems to have known something of the sagacity of the serpent. She, too, as well as Adam, recognised the voice of Jehovah walking in the garden (chap. iii. 8); and the girdles spoken of in verse 7 seem also to indicate, by their elaboration, that the guilty pair remained in Paradise some time after the fall. The indications of time are, however, less numerous and definite after the creation of Eve than before; but certainly Adam was for some considerable period a denizen of Paradise, and probably there was a longer time than is generally supposed spent in innocence by him and his wife, and also some delay between the fall and their expulsion from their happy home.

EXCURSUS D: ON THE BOOKS OF GENERATIONS

The most cursory reader must be struck by the manner in which this phrase frequently occurs in the Book of Genesis, and never again till the beginning of St. Matthew's Gospel. After the magnificent and Divine opening of chap. i. 1—ii. 3, the rest of the book is a series of "generations," in each of which there are peculiarities of diction and style, but also plain marks of a master-hand, which has moulded them into a continuous narrative. These generations, or *tôldôth*, are ten in number, namely:—

Chap.	ii. 4—	iv 26,	the tôldôth	of	heaven and earth.
——	v. 1—	vi. 8,	,,	,,	Adam.
——	vi. 9—	ix. 29,	,,	,,	Noah.
——	x. 1—	xi. 9,	,,	,,	the sons of Noah.
——	xi. 10—	xi. 26,	,,	,,	Shem.
——	xi. 27—	xxv. 11,	,,	,,	Terah.
——	xxv. 12—	xxv. 18,	,,	,,	Ishmael.
——	xxv. 19—	xxxv. 29,	,,	,,	Isaac.
——	xxxvi. 1—	xxxvii. 1,	,,	,,	Esau.
——	xxxvii. 2—	l. 26,	,,	,,	Jacob.

Now, first, modern discoveries have shown that there is no difficulty, as some have supposed, in believing that the patriarchs could read and write. Ur of the Chaldees, whence Terah emigrated, proves to have been a famous seat of learning, and Mr. Sayce (*Chald. Gen.*, p. 24) says that the earliest inscriptions of any importance which we now possess belong to the time of a king of Ur, supposed to have lived three thousand years before the Christian era. These inscriptions, he adds, consist of texts on bricks and on signet cylinders, and some of these latter may be, he thinks, of even greater antiquity. Even the daily transactions of business were in Abram's time perpetuated with the utmost punctuality and decorum by means of those contract, and sale, and even loan tablets of terra cotta which are still existing; and it is now known that in Chaldea among the Accadians, as in Egypt, papyrus was used as a writing material as well as clay, and more rarely, stone (Tomkins, *Studies on the Times of Abraham*, p. 45). So far from losing, the Book of Genesis gains infinitely in value and importance, if not on its divine, yet on its human side, if we find reason for believing that we may have in it the contents of bricks and cylinders carried by Abraham from Ur to Haran first, and thence to Canaan.

Next, the only reverent way of interpreting Holy Scripture is, not to make it bend to human theories, but to make our views bend to what it says of itself. Here, then, it represents the Book of Genesis as composed out of documents already existing. We have no right to assume that these documents were less inspired because pre-Mosaic. Enoch, Noah, Abraham are all represented as men very near unto God. Others, such as Shem, Jacob, Joseph, were scarcely less so; and there are peculiarities in the *tôldôth* of Jacob which suggest that a narrative written by Joseph was at least the basis of that history. Now, had Genesis been the work of one inspired pen, surely it would have proceeded onward with steady purpose, and, as is the invariable rule of Holy Scripture, the writer would have preserved his own style and individuality throughout. As it is, the narrative which begins at chap. ii. 4 is as diverse from the history of creation as it could possibly be; and apparently that history (chap. i. 1—ii. 3), which is not a *tôldôth*, was given in order to guard against the errors which might easily have arisen from misunderstanding the account given in the second narrative. Now, the history of creation must have been directly inspired. We cannot, indeed, tell how the knowledge it contains was communicated, whether by a series of visions in a trance or by ideas impressed upon the writer's mind; but obviously it was intended to represent creation as developed in an orderly progression by the promulgation of Divine laws, following at successive intervals, one upon another, and culminating in the Sabbath of Elohim. In the second narrative creation is but a secondary subject, and is described simply in contrast with the Garden of Eden.

But the author of the Book of Genesis—and we know of no one whose claims stand on such strong grounds as those of Moses—also shows his individuality, and arranges his materials on a settled plan. Divinely inspired, as we believe, he would nevertheless make no unnecessary change or alteration in the documents before him; nay, he does not even care for verbal accuracy (witness chap. xxviii. 9, compared with chap. xxxvi. 3). In the *Chaldean Genesis* we have a document far older than the time of Moses; and in the account of the flood, in the sending out of the raven and dove from the ark, in the sacrifice offered by Noah, and the choice of the rainbow as a sign of reconciliation, there is much that is common to the inspired and uninspired narratives. But the perusal and comparison of the two is most instructive, and leaves the mind impressed with the infinite superiority of the Bible narrative.

The writer's plan was this. After giving us an account of creation, in which man appears as God's master work, and then of the Paradise, in which man is shown to be the especial object of Jehovah's love, henceforward his one purpose is man's restoration, and the selection successively of Seth, Shem, Abraham, and Jacob as the persons through whom the promise of a Deliverer was to be fulfilled. He does not actually exclude all such portions of the patriarchal records as had no direct bearing upon his subject, but after a passing notice omits the mention of them for the future. Thus in the second narrative he gives the temptation, the fall, its outcome in Cain's sin, and then a brief history of Cain's family, with particulars of their advance in the arts of civilisation, in refinement, in luxury, and in pride; and then he drops them for ever. We know nothing more about the Cainites, but henceforward the narrative is occupied with Seth and his posterity.

The same rule is followed again and again; and thus, while the Book of Genesis is full of most interesting information about the ancient world, we nevertheless feel that its one main purpose was to show that the redemption of mankind by the bestowal of a Saviour was no after-thought, but the very starting point of God's revealed message of love to His fallen creatures.

EXCURSUS E: UPON ELAM AND THE CONQUESTS AND ROUTE OF CHEDORLAOMER (Chap. xiv.).

Of Elam we lately knew nothing more than that it was a country called after a son of Shem, and this narrative, containing an account of a conquest of Canaan by Elamites, was a puzzle to thoughtful Bible readers, and a mark for the derision of such critics as imagine that everything of which a clear explanation cannot be given must necessarily be unhistorical. Within the last few years our knowledge has so grown that the narrative fits exactly into its place, although neither the name of Chedorlaomer nor the history itself has been found in the cuneiform texts.

The country of Elam itself is a vast highland on the eastern side of the Tigris, with broad plains lying between mountains which sometimes attain an elevation of eight or ten thousand feet. It is easily defensible, rich, and well watered, and its inhabitants were dreaded neighbours of the Babylonians, upon whose fertile plains they constantly poured down in sudden inroads, and returned to their hills laden with booty. It was from Elam that the Accadians descended and conquered Babylonia, and we thus gather that its earlier inhabitants were Turanians, sprung from Japheth. The names of the towns in that part of the country of which Susa is the capital still bear witness to the supremacy there of this race, while the names of the rest of the Elamite towns are said by M. Oppert (*Records of the Past*, ix. 5) to be Semitic. Elamitic Semites appear also among the Assyrian sculptures, where "their keen and refined features are set off to great advantage by the blunt outline and thick protruding lips, which have been identified with the Kissians, or Cossaeans, of classic authors, the Kassi of the monuments, the sons of Cush of the Bible" (Rawlinson's *Anc. Mon.*, ii. 500). Thus in Elam, as on the Tigris and Euphrates, we find the families of the three sons of Noah distinct in lineament and language, but dwelling near one another, and coming in successive waves of population to struggle for the possession of the land.

The first great event recorded concerning Elam is found in the Annals of Assurbanipal, son of Esarhaddon, king of Assyria. He asserts that he conquered Elam, and took the city of Susa in B.C. 645, and that he then brought back an image of Nana which Kudur Nakhunté had carried away from Babylonia 1,635 years before; that is, in B.C. 2280. As Nana and Nakhunté seem to be names of the same goddess, while Kudur means "servant," we thus find this Elamite king calling himself, perhaps from this exploit, "the servant of Nakhunté." La'omar, or Lagomar, is the name of another Elamite god, and thus Chedorlaomer means "servant of Lagomar."

Nearer to the time of Abram we find an Elamite king named Kudur-Mabuk, who claims the title of *adda Martu*, that is, *lord of Phœnicia*, showing that he too, like Chedorlaomer, had conquered Syria. His son was named Eriaku, and being associated with his father in the government, received Larsa as his capital. The names Eriaku and Larsa are the same as those of Arioch and of Ellasar, and this further suggests the idea that Kudur-lagomar and Kudur-Mabuk may have been the same person. Canon Rawlinson gives the probable date of Kudur-Mabuk's reign as about B.C. 2100, Mr. Sayce about a century later, and M. Lenormant somewhere about the epoch of Abraham (Tomkins's *Studies*, p. 180).

Now the Elamite king, fourteen years before, had subdued the Jordan valley (verse 5), and as this second expedition was prior to Abram's taking Hagar to wife, which happened in the tenth year after his migration to Palestine (see chap. xvi. 3), it follows that Abram and Terah were still at Kharran when Chedorlaomer passed through it, as he must have done, on his march. Himself a Turanian, he would look with ill-will on powerful Semitic chiefs such as were Abraham and Lot, and his visit may have had something to do in urging them on their further route as soon as Terah's death set them free. We see also that, besides the caravan road, there was a war track to Canaan, and thus, with troubles from Elamite invasions at home to urge him on, Abram was but following the great current of population in going to Palestine first, and thence onward to Egypt. So many took this route and remained in Egypt that, under the name of the Hyksos, they took possession, first of the Delta, and then of Egypt generally. And in this stream of human migration there was one whose going and purpose was Divine.

For twelve years Chedorlaomer's tribute was regularly paid, but in the thirteenth year the five kings who possessed the wealthiest portion of the Jordan valley rebelled. A twelvemonth is spent in gathering Elam's forces; but in the next spring, attended by three subject monarchs, the king starts on his march to punish the revolters. On his arrival at Damascus, probably by the same route which Abram had followed, we find him taking a wide circuit, so as to sweep the whole country and fall upon the rebels last, and from the side where they least expected an attack. For, moving southwards through Bashan, he smites the Rephaim and other tribes along the plateau on the east of Jordan, until he reaches the wild mountains inhabited by the cave-dwelling Horites, and which extend from the Dead Sea to the gulf of Akaba. The most southerly spot reached by him was El-Paran, *the oak-forest of Paran*, situated on the edge of the great desert of Et-Tih. Turning hence to the north and north-west, he smites on his way the Amalekites, whose wandering tribes occupied this vast desert, and thus reaches the Dead Sea, along the western shore of which he marches till he reaches Hazezon-Tamar, better known as En-gedi. This ravine is, as Dr. Tristram has shown, of the utmost strategical importance. For it is easy to march along the shore of the lake as far as this point, while inland the route lies across a rough and almost waterless wilderness. But north of En-gedi the shore-line is impracticable even for footmen. We gather that the Amorites held the pass, but were not reinforced by their countrymen, and probably were surprised—for a handful of men could defend the zigzag path which mounts up the side of the precipice to a height of 1,800 feet. At the head of this ravine Chedorlaomer was less than twenty miles distant from Abram at Mamre, but with a difficult country between; and, moreover, his object was to smite and plunder the rich cities of the plain. As he had now traversed two-thirds of the length of the Dead Sea, it again becomes manifest that Sodom and the other cities were at its northern end. In the vale of Siddim the battle is fought, and the five kings, entangled among the bitumen pits, are defeated with so great slaughter that a remnant only escapes. Fleeing, not to the mountains of Moab, as commentators assume, but to those of Judea, they carry the news to Abram, telling him that, with other captives, Lot and his goods are carried away. He draws out at once 318 men, all trained to arms, and all born in his house, and therefore of sure fidelity, as those bought or lately acquired would not be, and, reinforced by bodies of Amorites under Mamre, Aner, and Eshcol, starts in rapid pursuit. Encumbered with goods and prisoners and cattle, Chedorlaomer marched but slowly, and when, after four or five days' pursuit, Abram overtook the Elamites, they would probably be as little prepared for an attack as the Amalekites whom David found, after they had sacked Ziklag, "spread abroad upon all the earth, eating and drinking and dancing" (1 Sam. xxx. 16). Still they were numerous, and most of them veteran warriors, and so Abram waits till night, and then, dividing his little army into three divisions, he makes his attack, throws them into confusion, and pursuing them almost to the gates of Damascus, recovers all the persons and spoil which they had gathered in their long route downwards and upwards throughout the whole length of Palestine.

EXCURSUS F: ON THE ANGEL, [HEB., "MESSENGER OF JEHOVAH"] (Chap. xvi.).

It is in chapter xvi. that we first meet with this term, and as in several places there is an apparent identification of Jehovah's messenger with Jehovah Himself, and even with Elohim, it becomes necessary to say a few words upon the much debated question, whether it was a created angel that was the means of communication between Jehovah and His ancient people; or whether it was an anticipation of the Incarnation of Christ, and even a manifestation in human form of the Second Person of the Divine Trinity.

God in His absolute and perfect nature is, as we are clearly taught, beyond the reach of human sense, and even of human reason. "No man hath seen God" (John i. 18, vi. 46), "for He is the King invisible, Who dwells in the unapproachable light" (1 Tim. i. 17, vi. 16); but we are taught with equal clearness that it was the office of Christ to reveal Him to us (John xii. 45, xiv. 9); and that Christ is not merely "the effulgence of His glory, but the very image and impress of His substance" (Heb. i. 3). In his own nature, then, incomprehensible and exalted far above the reach of our mental powers, God is nevertheless made intelligible to man, and brought near to our hearts and minds in Christ, so that we can conceive of Him as a Person, and as such love and worship Him. Yet was this Incarnation of God the Son the most sublime and awful mystery ever displayed upon earth; and to suppose that it was a mystery often repeated, so far from being a help to our faith, would be the reverse. We may well believe that God prepared men's minds for so Divine a fact as "the emptying Himself of His glory, that He might be made in the likeness of men" (Phil. ii. 7); but that He became Man except at Bethlehem should have for its proof nothing less than the express warrant of Holy Writ.

In three cases there is an apparent identification of the angel with God. Thus of Hagar it is said, "She called the name of Jehovah that speaketh to her *El Roï*" (*a God of seeing*); and as a reason for the name she adds, "Do not I see after my seeing?" (chap. xvi. 13). Similarly, after Jacob had wrestled with "a man" until the breaking of the day, he "called the name of the place Peni-el (*the face of God*): for I have seen God face to face, and my life is preserved" (chap. xxxii. 30). Finally, after "the angel of Jehovah" had gone up in the flame from off the altar, Manoah said, "We shall surely die, because we have seen Elohim (Judges xiii. 22).

In these and any similar cases the utmost that we can venture to affirm is that they had seen God representatively by the appearance to them of His angel; by whom also "Jehovah spake to Hagar." Upon this latter point there is a valuable note of Bar-Hebræus in his Scholia on Acts vii. 30, "He that was visible was an angel: He that spake was God." Nor is there any difficulty in the fact that in verse 10 the angel says to Hagar, "I will multiply thy seed." For it is the rule in Holy Scripture to ascribe to the agent the deeds which he executes by God's commission. Thus Ezekiel speaks of himself destroying Jerusalem (Ezek. xliii. 3), the sense being that rightly put in our margin—that "he prophesied that the city should be destroyed." Sent by Jehovah to execute His will, angel and prophet alike are described as themselves the doers of the task assigned to them. This rule should be remembered in the exposition of chap. xix., where the two angels speak of themselves as destroying Sodom.

In the case, however, of the "three men who stood by" Abraham at Mamre, there is a very close identification of one of the angels with Jehovah. In the first verse we read that "Jehovah appeared unto Abraham." This might well be by the mission of the angels, but after a sudden change to the singular number in verse 10, the speaker is both henceforward called Jehovah, and speaks as not only himself the doer and judge, but as if it rested with him to save or destroy at his own will. There is also a marked distinction between him and the two angels who visit Lot, and who describe themselves as sent by Jehovah (chap. xix. 13), though even here, in verses 17—22, there is an approximation to a higher personification. In the case of the angel who visits Gideon there is again an apparent identification between him and Jehovah (Judges vi. 14, 16—23); nevertheless, Gideon still calls him an angel of Jehovah in verse 22, and he is called an angel of Elohim in verse 20.

In this case, and in that of the angel who appeared to Manoah, they refuse to partake of food, whereas the three angels who appeared to Abraham at Mamre ate of the food prepared for them. They are also called men, and behave in a very human manner, whereas the angels who appeared to Gideon and Manoah both display supernatural powers, and "do wondrously." Nevertheless, nowhere else is there so close an identification between the angel and Jehovah as in this appearance at Mamre, and in the history of the intercession for Sodom both the angel and Abraham speak as if Jehovah was there present in person.

In the case of the revelation to Abraham after the sacrifice of Isaac, the "angel of Jehovah" calls to him from heaven, and we have no account of any appearance in human form.

If, however, we turn to other passages of Holy Scripture the explanation seems plain. In the passage of God's ancient people through the wilderness, an angel was especially entrusted with their guidance and protection. He is called "the angel of Elohim," and his symbol was the pillar of fire and of the cloud (Exod. xiv. 19). Once, however, he appears in human form to Joshua, and claims the office of captain of Jehovah's host (Josh. v. 13—15). In the full description of him in Exod. xxiii. 20—25, we read in verse 21 "my Name is in him." Now this angel is called in Isa. lxiii. 9 "the angel of God's presence," literally, *of His Face*; and in this there is an evident allusion to Exod. xxxiii. 14, 15, where Moses says, "If Thy Face go not, carry us not up hence;" and Jehovah says, "My Face shall go, that I may give thee rest."

It seems, therefore, that under the Old Covenant, while generally it was created angels who were the medium of communication between God and man, yet that there was one kind of manifestation of Deity so high as that God's Name was in him, and God's Face shown by him. As all revelation was by God the Son (John i. 18) we may fearlessly connect this angel with our blessed Lord, called "the angel of the covenant" in Mal. iii. 1; but it would be rash and presumptuous to attempt to define the exact nature of these appearances. The union of matter and spirit in any way is beyond our powers of understanding; how much more when that Spirit is God! But this we may reverently say, that these personal manifestations were an anticipation in the Old Testament of that which is the cardinal doctrine in the New—that God has taken upon Him human nature, and appeared in fashion as a man. The saints of old knew of their Redeemer at first only as "the woman's seed:" they learned next to unite the thought of Him with the name Jehovah; and, finally, they knew that Jehovah was also God. So was the broad foundation laid for the prophetic teaching that He was Emmanuel, in one person God and Man; and for the feeling so necessary for all true personal piety that God vouchsafes His presence on earth. He who now walks in the midst of the golden candlesticks (Rev. i. 13) from time to time manifested His Face visibly to the saints of the Church of old. And not only was the father of the faithful thus visited, but even a runaway handmaid was neither disregarded, nor deemed unworthy of heavenly care. We might lose ourselves in profitless speculations as to the manner of events so mysterious, but the practical lesson is plain, that though "the heaven and the heaven of heavens cannot contain God, yet He deigns to dwell upon earth" (1 Kings viii. 27), and that His presence now vouchsafed by the spiritual indwelling of the Holy Ghost, is as efficacious for guidance, help, and comfort as were these visible manifestations in early times, when there was not as yet that full knowledge of God and of His ways, which has been given us in His Holy Word.

EXCURSUS G: UPON THE CHRONOLOGY OF JACOB'S LIFE (Chap. xxvii.)

The elaborate calculations of Lightfoot, and most Jewish and Christian commentators, intended to show that when Jacob set out upon his journey to Haran, he and Esau were each about 77 years of age, and Isaac their father about 137, though based apparently upon the letter of Scripture, are so contrary to its facts that evidently there must be some error in them. Fortunately there are several dates which are open to no doubt, and if we start with these, it may prove not impossible to arrive at more trustworthy conclusions.

When, then, Jacob went down into Egypt, he was 130 years of age (chap xlvii. 9), and as Joseph when he "stood before Pharaoh" was 30 (chap. xli. 46), and as his first years of power were the seven years of plenty, and there had been already two years of famine when he made himself known to his brethren, he was plainly about 14 years of age when his father joined him. Now he was a lad of 17 when sold into Egypt (xxxvii. 2), and as he was born before the contract to serve Laban for the speckled cattle (xxx. 25), which lasted for six years (xxxi. 41), he was about 7 when Jacob returned to Canaan. It follows, therefore, that Jacob was 91 when Joseph was born. Now the usual calculations allow only twenty years for Jacob's sojourn in Padan-aram, of which the first seven were spent in service before Leah and Rachel were given him in marriage. If from the twenty, we subtract these seven years and the seven years of Joseph's age, there remain only six years for the birth of Leah's six sons and the interval of her barrenness; and undeniably the narrative would be guilty of very remarkable exaggeration in its account of Rachel's childlessness, and Rachel herself of excessive impatience, considering that at the end of six years she gave birth herself to a son, and in the interval had given her maid Bilhah to Jacob, who had by her two sons; and as the birth of these was the occasion to Rachel of very unseemly exultation over her sister (xxx. 6, 8), her conduct can only be accounted for by the fact that Leah had already a numerous offspring when Rachel gave Bilhah to her husband.

The case of Leah is still plainer. She bears four sons, after which she "left bearing" (xxix. 35), and this barrenness continued so long that she gave Zilpah as her substitute to Jacob, who bare him two sons, Gad and Asher. Now neither Rachel nor Leah would have resorted to this expedient until they utterly despaired of having children themselves; and Leah herself describes it as an act of great self-sacrifice (xxx. 18). Zilpah's sons both seem to have been born in this period of Leah's barrenness; for we find that Jacob had entirely discarded Leah, and it was only at Rachel's request that he visited her again. Zilpah had taken Leah's place plainly because she had no expectation of having more offspring, and from chap. xxx. 15 it is evident that Jacob shared in this view, and had long ceased to pay any visits to Leah's tent. Moreover, this interval lasted so long that Reuben was old enough to be allowed to ramble in the field—that is, the uncultivated pasture land where the flocks fed; and he had sufficient self-control to bring the mandrake-berries which he had found home to his mother. According to the usual calculations, he was between three and four years old at this time: for it is necessary to arrange for the births of Issachar and Zebulun within the six years. He is therefore described as carried by the reapers to the wheatfield, and somewhere there he finds the mandrakes; but the wheat harvest is mentioned only to fix the time, and Reuben had evidently gone a long ramble to places not often visited. For it is plain that the mandrakes were rarities, and that their discovery was unusual; and this would not have been the case had they been found near the tents, nor is it likely that a young child would have been the discoverer. On the other hand, if Reuben were an active young man, nothing was more probable than for him to wander away into distant quarters, looking, perhaps, for game; and the kind heart which made him bring the berries to his mother is in agreement with the brotherly affection which made him determine to save the life even of the hated Joseph (xxxvii. 21, 22, 29, 30). "Unstable" he was, with no great qualities, but not destitute of generosity or of sympathy; and to Leah her sons must have been her one comfort under her many trials, and no doubt she treated them lovingly. Now if we put all these things together—the birth of Leah's four sons; Rachel's jealousy at her sister's fruitfulness, and her gift of Bilhah to her husband; Leah's interval of barrenness, and her gift of Zilpah to take her place; the complete estrangement of Jacob from Leah, upon the supposition that she would never again conceive; and the fact that she had to purchase of Rachel the visit of Jacob to her tent, which was followed by the birth of two more sons,—if we bear all this in mind, few persons could probably be found capable of believing that so much could have taken place in six years. If we add the further consideration that Hebrew women suckled their children for two or more years (note on xxi. 8), the supposition that Leah had four sons in four years becomes very unlikely. The patriarchal women are described as the reverse of fruitful. Even Leah, the one exception, has only seven children; and where any patriarch has a large family, he obtained it by having more than one wife.

After the six sons, Dinah was born, for so it is distinctly said in verse 21. But even if we interpolate Dinah among the sons, so far from making the difficulty less, we only land ourselves in an impossibility: for we have now to cram seven births, and a period of barrenness into six years. We must, then, accept what Holy Scripture says as a literal fact—that she was born after Zebulun. Now if we bear in mind that Jacob was seven years unmarried, that Dinah was Leah's seventh child, and that her mother had an interval of barrenness, it is plain that, if Jacob's sojourn at Padan-aram lasted only twenty years, Dinah could not have been more than two or three years old when Jacob returned to Canaan. Now in the ten years which elapsed between Jacob's return, bringing with him Joseph, then seven years old, and the sale of Joseph to the Midianites, at the age of seventeen, Jacob dwelt first at Shechem (xxxiii. 18), then at Beth-el (xxxv. 1), and finally near Hebron (xxxvii. 14). But not only is Dinah marriageable at Shechem, but her brothers, Simeon and Levi, about whose age there can be no doubt, as they were Leah's second and third sons,—these lads, then, aged one eleven and the other ten, on their arrival at Shechem, are so precociously powerful as to take "each one his sword, and come upon the city, and slay all the males" (xxxiv. 25). Jacob, a peaceful man, is horrified at what they do, but dares only to expostulate with these boys; and they, acting upon the usual law, that where there are several wives, the women look not to the father, but to those of their mother's tent, for protection, give him a fiery answer. Really we find in verse 13 that the sons of Jacob were grown men, who took the management of the matter into their own hands.

If, too, Jacob was seventy-seven when he went to Haran, then, as his mother was barren for twenty years, and Laban was a grown man when he made the arrangements for his sister Rebekah's marriage, Laban must by this time have been nearly 120. Yet evidently all his children are very young. The difficulty is not, indeed, removed by subtracting twenty years; but it is lessened.

Moreover, as Joseph was born seven years before Jacob left Padan-aram, and Reuben in the eighth year of his sojourn there, he would be Joseph's senior by only five years. Yet Reuben calls him a "child" (xxxvii. 30), and all the rest treat him as one far younger than themselves, though really he was of much the same age as Issachar and Zebulon, and Zilpah's two sons, Gad and Asher. Judah, Leah's fourth son, would at most be only four years older than Joseph, yet he seems to have had a flock of his own at Timnath (xxxviii. 12), marries, and has three sons. The first, Er, grows up, and Judah takes for him a wife; but he was wicked, and died a premature death. Tamar is then given in marriage to the second son, and he also dies prematurely; whereupon Judah sends Tamar back to her father's house, with a promise that when Shelah, his third son, is grown up, he shall be given her as a husband. While she is dwelling in her father's house, Judah's wife dies, and there were the days of mourning; and as Tamar had long waited in vain, she has recourse, when Judah was comforted after the loss of his wife, to an abominable artifice, and bears twin sons to her father-in-law. Now there were at most twenty-three years between the sale of Joseph and the going down of Jacob's family into Egypt, and if it was really the case that Judah was only twenty-one at Joseph's sale, all these events could not have happened within so short a period. The phrase "at that time," at the beginning of chap. xxxviii., by no means implies that the marriage of Judah with Shuah's daughter was contemporaneous with the sale of Joseph. It is quite indefinite, and intended to show that the episode about Judah and his family happened about the same general period; but really it could not have taken place many years previously, for, as we have seen, only ten years elapsed between Jacob's return and the cruel treatment of Joseph by his brethren. Judah's marriage, then, must have happened soon after the return to Canaan, when, nevertheless, according to these calculations, he was a boy only eleven years of age.

It is quite plain, therefore, that Jacob's sojourn in Padan-aram lasted more than twenty years. What, then, is the explanation? It was long ago given by Dr. Kennicott, and, as stated in the *Speaker's Commentary*, Bishop Horsley considered that the reasons he gave for his conclusions were unanswerable. All really depends upon the translation of verses 38 and 41 of chap. xxxi., and in the Authorised Version the two periods of twenty years are made to be identical, the second statement being taken as a mere amplification of the first. But if we turn to the Hebrew, it clearly distinguishes the two periods. In verse 38 it is literally, "This twenty years I was with thee; thy ewes, and thy she goats, did not cast their young," &c.; and in verse 41, "This twenty years was for me in thy house: I served thee fourteen years for thy two daughters, and six years for thy sheep." But in Hebrew the phrase *this . . . this,* means *the one* and *the other*, or, in our language, *this* and *that.* (See Note on chap. xxix. 27.) Thus, then, there were two periods of service, each about twenty years in duration, of which one was for settled wages, and the other for no stipulated hire. They would not necessarily be continuous, and Dr. Kennicott arranges them as follows:—First, Jacob served Laban fourteen years for his two daughters; next, there was a long period of twenty years, during which he took care of Laban's flocks, receiving from them maintenance for himself and family, but acquiring no separate wealth; finally, after Joseph's birth, Jacob rebelled at this treatment, and determined to go back to his father, but was prevailed upon to remain, on the promise of receiving for himself all the speckled sheep and goats.

This explanation is confirmed by the curious phrase in verse 41: "This (second) twenty years was *for me* in thy house." The other twenty years were for Laban's sole good, and made him a wealthy man; but the fourteen years for the two maidens, and the six for the cattle, were, Jacob says, "for me." They were mine, spent in attaining to the fulfilment of my own purposes.

In the *Speaker's Commentary*, the following table is given as a probable arrangement of the chief events in Jacob's life:—

	Years of Jacob's life.	
	0	Jacob and Esau born.
	40	Esau marries two Hittite wives, chap. xxvi. 34.
Fourteen years' service.	57	Jacob goes to Padan-Aram, Isaac being 117.
	58	Esau marries a daughter of Ishmael, chap. xxviii. 9.
	63	Ishmael dies, aged 137, chap. xxv. 17.
	64	Jacob marries Leah and Rachel, chap. xxix. 20, 21, 27, 28.
		Reuben, Simeon, Levi, and Judah born of Leah.
		Dan and Naphtali born of Bilhah.
	71	End of fourteen years' service.
Twenty years' unpaid service.	72	Beginning of twenty years mentioned in chap. xxxi. 38.
		Gad and Asher born of Zilpah.
		Issachar and Zebulun born of Leah.
		Dinah born.
	91	Joseph born of Rachel.
Six years' service for cattle.	92	Agreement made, chap. xxx. 25—34.
	97	Flight from Padan-aram.
	98	Benjamin born; Rachel dies.
	108	Joseph, at seventeen, is carried to Egypt, chap. xxxvii. 2.
	120	Isaac dies, aged 180, chap. xxxv. 28.
	121	Joseph, aged 30, governor of Egypt.
	130	Jacob goes down to Egypt, chap. xlvi. 1.
	147	Jacob dies, chap. xlvii. 28.

In this table there are only two dates to which I should venture to take exception. First, it is not probable that Dan and Naphtali were born during the seven years which followed upon Jacob's marriages. Rachel would resort to an expedient so painful to a wife only in despair at her own barrenness, and in envy of her sister's fruitfulness. The giving of Bilhah must have taken place during the twenty years of unpaid service. Next, Benjamin could scarcely have been born in the very year following the return from Padan-aram; for after the interview with Esau, Jacob goes to Succoth, and thence to Shechem, where he buys a plot of ground. We learn, nevertheless, that Jacob, when Dinah was wronged, had not been there long, from what Hamor and Shechem said to the citizens (chap. xxxiv. 21, 22). From Shechem, Jacob next goes to Beth-el, and "dwells there" (xxxv. 1), but after some little stay, moves southward, towards the home of his father; and it was near Bethlehem that Benjamin was born. Most certainly Jacob would keep steadily in view his return to Isaac; but the events between the flight from Haran and Rachel's death at Bethlehem, are too many to be crowded into a year. On the other hand, Rachel's age warns us that Benjamin's birth could not have happened long after her arrival in Canaan. If, then, we place it in the hundredth year of Jacob's life, and the thirty-fourth of his marriage, two things follow—the first, that Rachel was very young at her marriage, and a mere child when Jacob first met her; the second, that Jacob must have spent about twenty years with Isaac at Hebron before the latter's death.

THE SECOND BOOK OF MOSES, CALLED
EXODUS

INTRODUCTION

TO

THE SECOND BOOK OF MOSES, CALLED

EXODUS

I. Title.—The Hebrews knew the five books of the Pentateuch by their initial word or words, *Berêshith, Ve-êleh shemôth, Vay-yikra,* &c.; but as this kind of nomenclature was unknown to the Greeks, the Alexandrian translators had to devise new titles, which should be intelligible to those for whom their translation was made. Following a method which was at once natural and familiar to the Hellenic world by its very early application to the *Iliad* of Homer,[1] they named the several parts of the work from their contents, and gave to the second book, very happily, the title it still bears of "Exodos," "departure," "outgoing," or "setting forth," since a main subject of the narrative is the "outgoing" of the Israelites from Egypt. Jerome, in his translation of the Bible, preserved the word, merely Latinising it into "Exodus"; and the acceptance of his version by the Western Church has led to the general adoption of the name used by him among the nations of Western Europe.

II. Contents, Design, and General Plan of the Book.—Although the outgoing of the Israelites from Egypt is one of the principal matters treated of in the Book of Exodus, yet it was not the sole, nor even the main, purpose of the writer to give an account of that remarkable passage of history. His purpose was a wider and grander one. It embraced a space of time anterior to even the first preparations for departure, and another subsequent to the completion of the journey and escape. It was theocratic rather than historic. It was to "give an account of the first stage in the fulfilment of the promises made by God to the patriarchs with reference to the growth of the children of Israel,"[2] by tracing their development from a family into a tribe, and from a tribe into a nation. Genesis left Israel in Egypt a family or "house" (Gen. l. 22); Exodus leaves them a nation of above two millions of souls, organised under chiefs (Exod. xviii. 21—24), with a settled form of worship, a priesthood, a code of laws, and a judicature. It finds them still a family (chap. i. 1—6); it leaves them the people of God (chap. xxxiii. 13). By the entrance of "the glory of the Lord" into the tabernacle (chap. xl. 34) the theocracy is completed—God locally dwells with His people as their Ruler, Director, and Guide. The nation receives its Head, and becomes "a kingdom" (chap. xix. 6). It is still nomadic—it has no settled country—but it is an organised whole.

In tracing the steps of this change, the author of the book pursues the ordinary historical and chronological method. Having recapitulated (from Gen. xlvi.) the family of Jacob, and mentioned the death of Joseph (chap. i. 1—6), he sketches rapidly the condition of the descendants of Jacob during the period which intervened between Joseph's decease and the birth of Moses, dwelling especially on the rapid increase of the Israelites (verses 7, 12, 20), and relating incidentally the steps in the "affliction" to which they were subjected by the Egyptians, according to God's prophecy to Abraham (Gen. xv. 13). From this he passes to the birth, providential escape, and bringing up of Moses, their pre-destined deliverer, and to the circumstances which compelled him to quit Egypt, and become an exile in the land of Midian. The call and mission of Moses are next related, together with the circumstances of his return from Midian to Egypt, the consent of Jethro to his departure (chap. iv. 18), the circumcision of Eliezer (*ib.* 24—26), the meeting with Aaron (*ib.* 27, 28), and the acceptance of Moses for their leader by the people (*ib.* 29—31). The account of Moses' first application to Pharaoh follows, and its result—the increase of the people's burthens, with their consequent despair, and the despondency of Moses (chaps. v., vi. 1—13). After a genealogical parenthesis (chap. vi. 14—27), the narrative of the struggle between Moses and Pharaoh is resumed, and carried on through five chapters (chaps. vii.—xi.), which contain the account of all the "plagues of Egypt," except the last, and exhibit in a strong light the tergiversation and final obduracy of Pharaoh. The crisis now approaches, and in preparation for it the Passover is instituted, with full directions for its continued observance (chap. xii. 1—28). The blow then falls—the firstborn are slain—and the Israelites are not only allowed to depart, but are sent out of Egypt "in haste" (chap. xii. 33), laden with presents from those who wished to expedite their departure (*ib.* 35, 36). The account of the "Exodus" itself is then given, and the journey traced from Rameses, by way of Succoth and Etham, to Pi-hahiroth, on the western shore of the Red Sea (chaps. xii. 37—xiv. 4). Upon this follows an account of the pursuit made by Pharaoh, of the miraculous passage of the sea by the host of Israel, and the destruction in the returning waters of the entire Egyptian chariot and cavalry force (chap. xiv. 5—31). This portion of the narrative is appropriately concluded by the song of triumph sung by Moses and Miriam (chap. xv. 1—21).

Israel being now in safety, the account of their journey is resumed. Their line of march is traced through the wilderness of Shur to Marah (chap. xv. 22—26); from Marah to Elim (*ib.* 27); thence through the wilderness of Sin to Rephidim (chap. xvii. 1); and from Rephidim to Sinai (chap. xix. 42). On the march occur the murmuring and miracle at Marah (chap. xv. 23—25); the giving of the quails and of manna (chap. xvi. 4—36); the great battle with the Amalekites at

[1] See Herod. ii. 116; and compare Heyne, *Excurs. ad Hom. Iliad.* xxiv. § 2, p. 787.

[2] Keil, *Commentary on the Old Testament,* Vol. I., p. 415.

Rephidim (chap. xvii. 8—13); and the visit of Jethro to Moses, with his advice, and the consequent organisation of the people (chap. xviii. 1—27).

The scene of the rest of Exodus is Sinai and the plain at its northern base. In chap. xix. the author describes the preparations made for the giving of the fundamental law, which is then explicitly stated in four chapters (chaps. xx.—xxiii.), and consists of the Decalogue (chap. xx. 1—17) and the "Book of the Covenant" (chaps. xx. 22—xxiii.). In chap. xxiv. he tells of the acceptance of the covenant by Israel (verses 3—8), and of the first ascent of Moses into the mount (verses 9—18). After this, seven chapters (chaps. xxv.—xxxi.) relate the directions there given to Moses by God with respect to the mode in which He would be worshipped, and the "house" which He would have constructed for Him. In chap. xxxii. Israel's apostacy is related, together with its immediate punishment; and in chap. xxxiii. we have an account of the steps taken by Moses to obtain from God a renewal of the forfeited covenant. In chap. xxxiv. the writer relates the circumstances of Moses' second ascent into the mount, and declares the terms upon which the covenant was renewed. The construction of the various parts of the tabernacle and of the priestly garments is then given in five chapters (chaps. xxxv.—xxxix.); and the work concludes with an account in one chapter (chap. xl.) of the setting up of the tabernacle, and the entrance of the "Glory of God" into it.

III. Divisions.—Primarily, the work divides itself into two portions:—1. An historical narrative of the fortunes of Israel from the death of Joseph to the arrival of the nation in front of Sinai (chaps. i.—xix.). 2. A didactic portion, containing all the most essential points of the Law and of the worship (chaps. xx.—xl.). This didactic portion is, however, historical in its setting, and is intermixed with some purely historical sections, as especially chap. xxiv. and chaps. xxxii., xxxiii.

Part I. may be sub-divided as follows:—

Section.	Chap.	
1.	i.	The oppression of Israel in Egypt.
2.	ii.	The birth, escape from death, and bringing up of Moses. His first attempt to deliver his people, and flight to Midian.
3.	iii., iv.	The call and mission of Moses, and his return to Egypt.
4.	v., vi. 1—13.	The first interview between Moses and Pharaoh, with its result—the increase of the people's burthens, their despair, and the despondency of Moses.
5.	vi. 14—27.	The genealogy of Moses and Aaron.
	vii.—xi.	The efforts made by Moses, under Divine guidance, to overcome the obstinacy of Pharaoh. The first nine "plagues of Egypt."
7.	xii. 1—28.	The institution of the Passover.
8.	xii. 29—36.	The tenth plague, and its consequences.
9.	xii. 37—xiv. 4.	The departure from Egypt, and the journey to Pi-hahiroth.
10.	xiv. 5—31.	The pursuit of Pharaoh. The passage of the Red Sea. Great destruction of the Egyptians.
11.	xv. 1—21.	The song of triumph sung by Moses and Miriam.
12.	xv. 22—xvii.	The journey of the Israelites from the Red Sea to Rephidim. The victory over the Amalekites.
13.	xviii.	Jethro's visit to Moses.
14.	xix.	Arrival of Israel before Mount Sinai, and preparations made for the giving of the Law.

Part II. contains the following sub-divisions:

Section.	Chap.	
1.	xx. 1—21.	Delivery of the Decalogue.
2.	xx. 22—xxiii.	Words of the "Book of the Covenant."
3.	xxiv.	Acceptance of the covenant, and ascent of Moses into the mount.
4.	xxv.—xxxi.	Instructions given to Moses with respect to the structure of the tabernacle, and the consecration and attire of the priests.
5.	xxxii.—xxxiv.	Infraction of the covenant by the idolatry of the calf, and renewal of it through the intercession of Moses.
6.	xxxv.—xxxix.	Construction of the tabernacle and its furniture. Making of the "holy garments."
7.	xl.	Erection of the tabernacle, and entrance of the "Glory of God" into it.

IV. Date of the Composition.—The antiquity of the Book of Exodus is evidenced by the simplicity of its constructions, and the occurrence in it of a certain number of extremely archaic forms. Its composition by an eye-witness of most of the events which it relates is indicated by the vividness with which they are portrayed, and the details and unnecessary *minutiæ* into which the writer enters. The descriptions of the effect of the hail upon the Egyptian standing crops (chap. ix. 31, 32), of the character and appearance of the manna (chap. xvi. 14—31), and of the descent of Jehovah upon Mount Sinai (chaps. xix. 16—19, xx. 18) have all the appearance of being by an eye-witness. Who but an eye-witness would note the exact number of the wells at Elim, and of the palm-trees that grew about them (chap. xv. 27)? Or the fact that the first tables of stone were "written on the one side, and on the other" (chap. xxxii. 15)? Or the circumstance that Moses and Joshua heard the sound of the idol feast in honour of the golden calf before they got sight of it (*ibid.* 17—19)? What Israelite of later times would have presumed to fix the exact date of the setting forth from Elim as "the fifteenth day of the second month after their departing out of the land of Egypt" (chap. xvi. 1)? Or to state that Miriam and the Israelite women accompanied their song of triumph "with timbrels" (chap. xv. 20)? Or to give the precise position of Pi-hahiroth as "between Migdol and the sea, over against Baal-zephon" (chap. xiv. 2)? Who but an eye-witness would have noticed that the locusts were taken away by "a strong west wind," or would have ventured to state that "there remained not one locust in all the coasts of Egypt" (chap. x. 19)? Little graphic touches strongly indicative of the eye-witness are such as the following:—"Zipporah cut off the foreskin of her son, *and cast it at his feet*" (chap. iv. 25). "Aaron met Moses in the mount of God, *and kissed* *him*" (*ibid.* 27). The officers of the Israelites "met Moses and Aaron, *who stood in the way*, as they came forth from Pharaoh" (chap. v. 20). "The frogs died out of the houses, out of the villages, and out of the fields; *and they gathered them together in heaps*" (chap. viii. 13, 14). "The Lord sent thunder and hail, *and the fire ran along upon the ground*" (chap. ix 23). "The locusts covered the face of the earth, so that *the land was darkened*" (chap. x. 15). "Darkness over the land of Egypt, *even darkness which may be felt*" (*ib.* 21). "And Pharaoh rose up in the night, he and all his servants, and all the Egyptians; *and there was a great cry in Egypt*" (chap. xii. 30). "The people took their dough before it was leavened, *their kneading troughs being bound up in their clothes upon their shoulders*" (*ib.* 34). "The Lord caused the sea to go back *by a strong east wind all that night*" (chap. xiv. 21). "Thus the Lord saved Israel that day out of the hand of the Egyptians; *and Israel saw the Egyptians dead upon the sea shore*" (*ib.* 30). The Egyptians "sank into the bottom *as a stone*; they *sank as lead* in the mighty waters" (chap. xv. 5—10). "The quails came up *and covered the camp*; and in the morning the dew *lay round about the host*" (chap. xvi. 13). "They did mete the manna *with an omer*" (*ib.* 18). "When the sun waxed hot, the manna *melted*" (*ib.* 21). "Moses went out to meet his father-in-law, *and did obeisance, and kissed him*" (chap. xviii. 7). "The whole mount (Sinai) *quaked greatly*" (chap. xix. 18). "All the people answered *with one voice*, and said: All the words which the Lord hath said we will do" (chap. xxiv. 3). The subject need not be further pursued. It is evident that the style of narration is exactly that of an eye-witness, and we must either suppose intentional fraud, or the composition of Exodus by one of those who quitted Egypt at this time under the circumstances narrated. The date of the final completion of the work will therefore be, *at the latest*, some twenty or thirty years after the entrance into Canaan.

V. Author.—If the Book of Exodus be granted to have been written by a contemporary—an Israelite present at the greater part of the scenes recorded in it—the question of its exact author becomes one of mere literary curiosity. The credibility of the Biblical history is established, as even Strauss admits,[1] if it can be shown that it was written by eye-witnesses. And the author of Exodus can have been no ordinary Israelite, no uneducated person, no mere member of the rank and file; he must have been among the foremost of his nation, highly gifted, possessed of rare culture, a man of mark, one of the chief leaders. It would not detract from the value of the work as an historical record if it could be shown to have been written by Aaron or Hur, by Joshua or Caleb; but the interest is increased, no doubt, if it can justly be regarded as the work of Moses.

What ground, then, is there for this belief, which, notwithstanding all that has been urged against it, is still the prevalent one? In the first place, there is the unanimous tradition. "The Book of the Law" is ascribed to Moses by Joshua,[2] by the author of Kings,[3] by the author of Chronicles,[4] by Ezra,[5] by Nehemiah,[6] by Malachi,[7] by our blessed Lord,[8] by St. John the Baptist,[9] by Philip the Apostle,[10] by St. Peter,[11] by St. Paul repeatedly, and by all the Jewish Targums, Rabbis, and commentators generally. A work which there is every reason to regard as the same is assigned to him by Hecatæus of Abdera, by Manetho, by Eupolemus, by Nicolas of Damascus, by Juvenal, and by Longinus. There is no counter-tradition. No writer of antiquity, of either great or small authority, has ever suggested any other author of Exodus, or (if we take the word author in its wider sense) of the entire Pentateuch, but Moses.

Secondly, there is a large mass of internal evidence pointing to the Mosaic authorship of Exodus. Not only was the author familiar with Egypt, but he had a large acquaintance with the Egyptian language, laws, art, and literature. The number of Egyptian words and phrases which occur in Exodus is considerable.[12] The Mosaic legislation has Egyptian features. The ornamentation of the tabernacle, and the fabrics used for curtains and for garments, betray an acquaintance with the resources and methods of Egyptian industrial skill. Acquaintance with Egyptian literature is shown in the more elevated parts of the work, especially in the "Song of Moses." As there is no reason to believe that any other Israelite of the time had enjoyed the advantage of being bred up in the Egyptian learning, and familiarised with the highest specimens of Egyptian artistic and literary genius, it is unlikely that any other member of the community could have produced Exodus. But Moses was fully competent for the task. Moses, brought up at the court, as the son of a princess, "learned in all the wisdom of the Egyptians" (Acts vii. 22)—or, at any rate, in all that was not of a recondite character—familiar with artists and literary men, accustomed to the splendour and magnificence of the Pharaonic palaces and temples, might naturally have at once the literary skill, the legislative ability, and power of artistic conception which the work displays. Further, many of the little turns noticed in the preceding section, and others similar to them, which betray the hand of an eye-witness, are of such a nature that the eye-witness could only be Moses. Who but Moses could know that before he "slew the Egyptian" he "*looked this way and that*" (chap. ii. 12)? Who but he would remember that he "buried him *in the sand*" (*ib.*)? Who but he could know that he *turned aside* to see the great sight of the burning bush (chap. iii. 3), or that he "fled from before" the serpent into which his rod was turned (chap. iv. 3), or that when he quitted Midian, he set his wife and child *upon an ass* (*ib.* 20), or that Zipporah cut off her son's foreskin "with a *stone*" (*ib.* 25), or that when she had cut it off, she *cast it at Moses' feet* (*ib.*)? Who but he could tell us that at Marah "he cried unto the Lord, and *the Lord showed him a tree*" (chap. xv. 25), or that at Rephidim his "hands were *heavy*" (chap. xvii. 12), or the exact reasons for which he gave his two sons their names (chap. xviii. 3, 4), or that when he came down from the mount he "wist not that his face shone" (chap. xxxiv. 29), or that when he saw the glory of God, he "*made haste*, and bowed his head toward the earth, and worshipped" (*ib.* 8)? Not only the actions of Moses, but his thoughts and feelings, the very words of his prayers breathed inwardly to God (chaps. xxxii. 31, 32, xxxiii. 12—16, &c.), are declared to us with openness, simplicity, and an unmistakable stamp of truth. Who but Moses could dare to lay bare to us the secret thoughts of Moses, to expose to us the very recesses of his heart?

1 *Leben Jesu*, § 13, p. 55, E.T.
2 Josh. viii. 31.
3 2 Kings xiv. 6.
4 2 Chron. xxv. 4.
5 Ezra vi. 18.
6 Nehem. xiii. 1.
7 Mal. iv. 4.
8 John vii. 19, &c.
9 John i. 17.
10 *Ib.* 45.
11 Acts iv. 22.

12 See Canon Cook's "Essay" in the *Speaker's Commentary*, Vol. I., pp. 476—492

Again, a strong argument for the Mosaic authorship may be drawn from the entire manner in which Moses is portrayed and spoken of. Whereas to the Hebrew nation—who owed him so much—Moses had always been the first and greatest of men, the writer of Exodus is unconscious of his possessing any personal greatness at all. The points in the personality of Moses which have impressed him the most, and on which he lays the greatest stress, are his deficiencies in natural gifts, and his numerous imperfections of temper and character. Rash and impetuous, beginning his public life with a crime (chap. ii. 12), and following up his crime with an assumption of authority that was unwise (*ib.* 13), he next shows a timid spirit, when he finds that his crime is known (*ib.* 14, 15), and betaking himself to exile, relinquishes all patriotic effort. Called by God, and entrusted with the mission of delivering Israel, he holds back, hesitates, pleads his personal defects, until he angers God, and loses half his leadership (chap. iv. 1—14). Unsuccessful in his first application to Pharaoh, he utters a remonstrance which verges on irreverence (chap. v. 22, 23). Encouraged by fresh promises, and bidden to make a second application, he responds by a fresh disparagement of his natural powers (chap. vi. 12). When at last he makes up his mind to carry out his struggle with Pharaoh to the bitter end, he shows, no doubt, courage and confidence in God; but still he is never praised: no single word is uttered in commendation of his moral qualities; once only is he said to have been "very great in the sight of Pharaoh's servants and of the people" (chap. xi. 3). It has been urged that he would not have spoken of himself in this tone—and it is just possible that the words are a later addition to his work—but still they contain no praise; they do but note a fact, and a fact of importance to the narrative, since it accounts for the gifts lavished upon Israel at their departure. In the later portion of Exodus, it is absence of all words of praise rather than any record of faults that we note; nothing calls forth from the writer a single sentence of approval; even when the offer is made to be blotted out of God's book for the sake of his people (chap. xxxii. 32), the same reticence is observed: no comment follows; there is no apparent recognition that the offer was anything but a small matter. Nor is any notice taken of the courage, faith, and wisdom exhibited by Moses in the performance of his mission from the time of his second appearance before Pharaoh (chap. vii. 10). Contrast with this silence what later writers say of him, as the son of Sirach (Ecclus. xlv. 1—5), the author of the Epistle to the Hebrews (chap. xi. 24—28; comp. chap. iii. 5), and the completer of Deuteronomy (chap. xxxiv. 10—12). It will be sufficient to quote the last-named passage to show what his countrymen generally thought of their deliverer. "And there arose not a prophet since in Israel like unto Moses, whom the Lord knew face to face, in all the signs and the wonders, which the Lord sent him to do in the land of Egypt to Pharaoh," &c. The humble estimate formed of the deliverer, and the general reticence, are quite intelligible, and in harmony with the rest of the Scripture, if the author was Moses. They are wholly unintelligible on any other hypothesis.

VI. Credibility.—Strauss observes, as has already been stated (see above, § v.), that "it would, *most unquestionably*, be an argument of *decisive* weight in favour of the credibility of the Biblical history could it indeed be shown that it was written by eye-witnesses."[1] And, again, "Moses, being the leader of the Israelites on their departure from Egypt, would undoubtedly give *a faithful history* of the occurrences, unless" (which no one supposes) "he intended to deceive."[2] These admissions show that the credibility of Exodus is involved in the Mosaic authorship, and is proved if that be proved, as we conceive that it is. Still, as all men are not logically-minded, the following remarks on the credibility of the narrative itself, whoever was the writer, may not be superfluous.

The narrative contains an account of Egypt, touching in numerous points its history, geography, productions, climatic peculiarities, manners and customs, &c., with much definiteness and exactness. A writer who ventures on such *minutiæ*, unless a contemporary, and familiar with the scene which he describes, is liable to trip at every turn, and is certain to be caught tripping if subjected to a close scrutiny by those who, with all the aids of modern historical research, have made the country and the period their special study. But the more closely Exodus is scrutinised by learned Egyptologists, the more triumphantly does it emerge from the ordeal; and it is not too much to say that, for the future, no sceptical critic is likely to repeat the attack of Von Bohlen, which called forth so crushing a reply from Hengstenberg.[3] The narrative of Exodus, though at present it receives no direct confirmation from the Egyptian monuments, is indirectly confirmed on so many and such minute points, that its historical character must be admitted, unless we tax the writer with conscious imposture. He is familiar with the Egypt of the early Rameside period, and must have known the circumstances of the departure of Israel. If he has misrepresented them, he must have done so intentionally, and have sought to give his fiction an air of reality by observing, in all his details, the utmost truthfulness and accuracy.

Though the general narrative is unconfirmed by the Egyptian monuments, which would not be likely to notice an inglorious episode in Egyptian history, yet it receives a certain amount of confirmation from an Egyptian writer of repute, as well as from several of the classical historians. Manetho, an Egyptian priest, who wrote a history of Egypt, in the time of the first Ptolemy (B.C. 323—283), declared that, in the reign of an Amenophis, who was the son of a Rameses, and the father of a Sethos, a man named Moses led out of Egypt a colony of unclean persons, and conducted them to Syria.[4] Hecatæus, of Abdera, who lived about the same time, told a similar story, adding that the colony consisted of foreigners, and settled in Judæa.[5] Artapanus, Chæremon, Eupolemus, Lysimachus, Tacitus, and others gave accounts which were not very different. It was generally accepted as historic truth in the ancient world, that the nation known as Jews or Israelites had at one time dwelt in Egypt, had quitted that country under circumstances of hostility, and had passed through the desert to Palestine. Most writers agreed that the leader of the migration had been Moses. Some mentioned both Moses and Aruas, *i.e.*, Aaron.[6] The passage of the Red Sea was admitted by the Egyptians themselves, who only differed

[1] *Leben Jesu*, § 13, p. 55, E.T. [2] *Ib.*, p. 56, E.T.

[3] See the important work of this writer, entitled *Œgypten und Mose*, published in 1840, and translated into English for Clark's Theological Library in 1845. Some additions have been made to the proof furnished by Hengstenberg in the following work of the present writer—*Historical Illustrations of the Old and New Testament*, pp. 67—79.

[4] Ap. Joseph. *Contra Apion.* i. 26, 27.

[5] Ap. Phot. *Bibliothec.*, p. 1152.

[6] Trog. Pompeius in the Epitome of Justin (xxxiv. 2).

as to the question whether it had been miraculous or not. While the priests of Memphis maintained that Moses had merely taken advantage of a low tide to lead the Israelites across, those of Heliopolis, more honest or better informed, freely declared that, "on the Egyptian king, at the head of a large force, pursuing after the Jews, because they were carrying away with them the riches which they had borrowed of the Egyptians, the voice of God commanded Moses to smite the sea with his rod, and divide it. Moses, therefore, when he was thus admonished, touched the water with his rod, and so the sea *parted asunder*, and the host marched through on dry ground."[1] The march by way of Mount Sinai is witnessed to by one classical writer,[2] and there is a general agreement that the laws which marked off the Jews from all other nations were given them by Moses.

At the present day, the credibility of Exodus is assailed on two principal grounds:—1. The miraculous character of a large portion of the narrative. 2. The exaggeration, which is thought to be apparent, in the numbers. A school of foreign critics denies the possibility of a miracle; and among ourselves there are many who accept the view of Hume, that it is more probable that the witnesses to miracles should have been deceived, than that the miracles should have happened. It is impossible, within the limits of an "Introduction," to discuss these large questions. Every Christian, every believer in the Apostles' Creed, must accept miracles. And when the Resurrection and Ascension of our Lord are once accepted, any other minor miracles cease to be felt as difficulties. In the present case, it is observable:—(1) that the miracles were needed; (2) that they were peculiarly suitable and appropriate to the circumstances; and (3) that they were of such a nature that it was impossible for eye-witnesses to be deceived with regard to them. Moses especially, whom we have shown to have been almost certainly the writer of Exodus, could not have been deceived as to the miracles. He must have known whether he performed them or not. Even if the writer be a companion of Moses (Joshua or Caleb), and not Moses himself, deception is inconceivable. Either the plagues of Egypt happened, or they did not. Either the Red Sea was *divided*, or it was not. Either the pillar of fire and of the cloud guided the movements of the host for forty years, or there was no such thing. Either there was manna each morning round about the camp, or there was none. The facts were too plain, too simple, too obvious to sense for there to be any doubt about them. The record is either a true account, or a tissue of lies. We cannot imagine the writer an eye-witness, and reject the main features of his tale, without looking on him as an impudent impostor. No "enthusiasm," no "poetic temperament," could account for such a record, if the Exodus was accomplished without miracles. The writer either related the truth, or was guilty of conscious dishonesty.

With respect to the numerical difficulties, it is to be borne in mind, in the first place, that numbers are peculiarly liable to corruption in ancient works, from the fact that they were not fully expressed, but written in a sort of cipher.[3] It is quite possible that the numbers in our present copies of Exodus are in excess, and express the ideas of a reviser, such as Ezra, rather than those of the original author. The males of full age who quitted Egypt *may have been* 100,000, or 60,000, instead of 600,000, and the migration one of 400,000 or 200,000 souls, instead of two millions. But, on the whole, judicious criticism inclines to uphold the numbers of the existing text. Alarm would not have been felt by the Egyptian kings until the people had *greatly* multiplied, and become formidable from a military point of view,[4] which they could not have been until the fully-grown men numbered some hundreds of thousands. For the population of Egypt was probably from seven to eight millions,[5] and the military class, at a far less flourishing time than that of the Exodus, was reckoned at above 400,000.[6] Nor could Canaan well have been conquered by an emigrant body which did not amount to some millions, since the country was well peopled at the time, and its occupants were brave and warlike. The difficulty of subsistence for two millions of persons in the desert is entirely met by the continuous miracle of the manna, and that of sufficient pasture for their numerous flocks and herds, by the far greater fertility of the Sinaitic peninsula in ancient than in modern times, of which abundant indications have been observed by recent travellers.[7] Ewald, Kalisch, Kurtz, and Keil accept the numbers of the present text of Exodus, and believe the migration to have been successfully accomplished by a body of about two millions of persons.

VII. **Condition of the Text.**—The condition of the text of Exodus is extremely good. Variant readings of any importance are few, and passages which require emendation almost non-existent. There are one or two short sentences[8] which may be interpolations by a later hand, perhaps Joshua's: and there is one long insertion (chap. vi. 14—27) which seems not to be from the pen of Moses, but which he may have sanctioned. Some critics, grounding themselves upon the LXX. or Samaritan Version, or both, maintain that a considerable number of passages have fallen out of the text, which were originally part of it;[9] but the predominant voice of scholars pronounces the passages in question to be unauthorised additions, foisted into the work by the Greek or the Samaritan translators. Even the supposed transposition of the passage concerning the altar of incense from chap. xxvi. to chap. xxx., the place where it stands in the Hebrew copies, which at first sight seems highly probable, is condemned by the spirit of the rule, *Proclivi lectioni præstat ardua*, and is rejected by all recent commentators. Thus Exodus would seem to have come down to us almost in the condition in which it was left by Moses, who was regarded with so much veneration by succeeding prophets, that the greatest care was taken to hand down his works unaltered.

[1] *Frag. Hist. Gr.*, Vol. III., pp. 223, 224.

[2] Justin, *l.s.c.*

[3] Wilkinson, in Rawlinson's *Herodotus*, Vol. II., p. 51, 2nd edition; Rawlinson, *Ancient Monarchies*, Vol. I., p. 131.

[4] See Exod. i. 9, 10.

[5] Diod. Sic. i. 31; Joseph., *Bell. Jud.* ii. 16.

[6] Herod. ii. 165–6.

[7] See *Our Work in Palestine* (chap. xiii., p. 270). The writer says:—"Objections have been made, based on the present barrenness of the peninsula, to the narrative of the Bible. *They vanish before the results of the survey.* The barrenness of the peninsula is due to neglect. In former times it was more richly wooded; the wadies were protected by walls stretching across, which served as dams to resist the force of the rushing waters; the mountains were terraced, and clothed with gardens and groves."

[8] As especially the second clause of verse 3 in chap. xi.

[9] The most important of these passages are chap. i. 11, where the LXX. add "On" to "Pithom and Raamses"; and xii. 40, where the LXX. insert "and in the land of Canaan" after "Egypt"; and the Samaritan, adopting this change, adds further, "and their fathers" after "the children of Israel." Other places, where comparatively unimportant additions occur, are chap. vii., between verses 18 and 19; viii., between 19 and 20; ix., between 5 and 6, and between 19 and 20; x., between 2 and 3; xi., between 2 and 4; and xx., between 17 and 18.

THE SECOND BOOK OF MOSES, CALLED

EXODUS

(1) CHAPTER I.—Now [a] these *are* the
names of the children of Israel, which
came into Egypt; every man and his
household came with Jacob. (2) Reuben,
Simeon, Levi, and Judah, (3) Issachar,
Zebulun, and Benjamin, (4) Dan, and
Naphtali, Gad, and Asher. (5) And all
the souls that came out of the [1] loins of
Jacob were [b] seventy souls: for Joseph
was in Egypt *already*.

(6) And Joseph died, and all his breth-
ren, and all that generation. (7) [c] And
the children of Israel were fruitful, and
increased abundantly, and multiplied,
and waxed exceeding mighty; and the
land was filled with them.

(8) Now there arose up a new king
over Egypt, which knew not Joseph.
(9) And he said unto his people, Behold,
the people of the children of Israel *are*

B.C. cir. 1706.

B.C. cir. 1635.

a Gen. 46. 8; ch. 6. 14.

1 Heb., *thigh*.

b Gen. 46. 27; Deut. 10. 22.

c Acts 7. 17.

THE MULTIPLICATION OF THE ISRAELITES IN EGYPT, AND THEIR OPPRESSION BY A NEW KING.

(1) **Now these are the names.**—The divisions between the "books" of the Pentateuch are not arbitrary. Genesis ends naturally and Exodus begins at the point where the history of the individuals who founded the Israelite nation ceases and that of the nation itself is entered on. That history commences properly with verse 7. Verses 1—6 form the connecting link between the two books, and would not have been needed unless Exodus had been introduced as a distinct work, since they are little more than a recapitulation of what had been already stated and stated more fully in Genesis. Compare verses 1—5 with Gen. xlvi. 8—27, and verse 6 with Gen. l. 26.

Every man and his household.—"A household," in the language of the East, includes not only children and grand-children, but retainers also—"servants born in the house"—like those of Abraham (Gen. xiv. 14). The number of each "household" may thus have been very considerable.

(3–4) **Reuben . . .**—The sons of the legitimate wives are placed first, then those of the concubines. Leah has precedence over Rachel; Bilhah over Zilpah. The children of each wife and concubine are given in order of seniority. The omission of Joseph from the list is explained in the last clause of verse 5.

(5) **All the souls . . . were seventy souls.** Comp. Gen. xlvi. 8—27. The number is made up as follows:—Jacob himself, 1; his sons, 12; his daughter, Dinah, 1; his grandsons, 51; his grand-daughter Serah, 1; his great-grandsons, 4—Total, 70. His daughters, except Dinah, and his sons' daughters, except Serah, spoken of in Gen. xlvi. 7, are not included. If his female descendants were, at the time of his descent into Egypt, as numerous as the males, the entire number of those who "came out of his loins" must have been 132. To form a calculation of the number of persons who entered Egypt with him, we must add the wives of his sons and grandsons, and the husbands of his daughters and granddaughters. A further liberal allowance must be also made for retainers. (See the comment on verse 1.) It is not perhaps surprising that Kurtz, taking all these classes into account, should calculate that those who entered Egypt with Jacob amounted to "several thousands" (*History of The Old Covenant*, vol. ii. p. 149, E.T.).

(7) **The children of Israel were fruitful.**—A *great* multiplication is evidently intended. Egypt was a particularly healthy country, and both men and animals were abnormally prolific there. Grain was so plentiful that want, which is the ordinary check on population, was almost unknown. The Egyptian kings for many years would look favourably on the growth of the Hebrew people, which strengthened their eastern frontier, the quarter on which they were most open to attack. God's blessing was, moreover, upon the people, which he had promised to make "as the stars of the heaven, and as the sand which is upon the sea-shore, for multitude" (see Gen. xxii. 17). On the actual extent of the multiplication and the time that it occupied, see the comment on chap. xii. 37—41.

The land—*i.e.*, where they dwelt—Goshen (Gen. xlvii. 4—6)—which seems to have been the more eastern portion of the Delta.

(8) **There arose up a new king.**—A king of a new dynasty might seem to be intended. Some suppose him to be Aahmes I., the founder of the eighteenth dynasty of Manetho; others suggest Rameses II., one of the greatest monarchs of the nineteenth. The present writer inclines to regard him as Seti I., the father of this Rameses, and the son of Rameses I. Seti, though not the actual founder of the nineteenth dynasty, was the originator of its greatness. (See Excursus I. "On Egyptian History, as connected with the Book of Exodus," at the end of this Book.)

Which knew not Joseph.—It seems to be implied that, for some considerable time after his death, the memory of the benefits conferred by Joseph upon Egypt had protected his kinsfolk. But, in the shifts and changes incident to politics—especially to Oriental politics—this condition of things had passed away. The "new king" felt under no obligation to him, perhaps was even ignorant of his name. He viewed the political situation apart from all personal predilections, and saw a danger in it.

(9) **He said unto his people.**—It is not intended to represent the Egyptian monarch as summoning a popular assembly, and addressing it. "His people" is

more and mightier than we: (10) Come
on, let us deal wisely with them; lest
they multiply, and it come to pass, that,
when there falleth out any war, they
join also unto our enemies, and fight
against us, and *so* get them up out of
the land. (11) Therefore they did set
over them taskmasters to afflict them
with their burdens. And they built for
Pharaoh treasure cities, Pithom and
Raamses. (12) [1] But the more they
afflicted them, the more they multiplied
and grew. And they were grieved be-
cause of the children of Israel. (13) And
the Egyptians made the children of
Israel to serve with rigour: (14) and they
made their lives bitter with hard bond-
age, in morter, and in brick, and in all

1 Heb., *And as they afflicted them, so they multiplied,* &c.

---

antithetical to "the people of the children of Israel," and simply marks that those whom he addressed were of his own nation. No doubt they were his nobles, or, at any rate, his courtiers.

More and mightier than we.—Heb., *great and mighty in comparison with us.* The more to impress his counsellors, and gain their consent to his designs, the king exaggerates. Ancient Egypt must have had a population of seven or eight millions, which would imply nearly two millions of adult males, whereas the adult male Israelites, near a century later, were no more than six hundred thousand (chap. xii. 37). Wicked men do not scruple at misrepresentation when they have an end to gain.

(10) **Let us deal wisely.**—Instead of open force, the king proposes stratagem. He thinks that he has hit upon a *wise* scheme—a clever plan—by which the numbers of the Israelites will be kept down, and they will cease to be formidable. The nature of the plan appears in verse 11.

When there falleth out any war.—The Egyptians were in general an aggressive people—a terror to their neighbours, and seldom the object of attack. But about the beginning of the nineteenth dynasty a change took place. "A great nation grew up beyond the frontier on the north-east to an importance and power which began to endanger the Egyptian supremacy in Western Asia" (Brugsch, *History of Egypt*, vol. ii. p. 2). War threatened them from this quarter, and the impending danger was felt to be great.

They join also.—Rather, *they too join.* It was not likely that the Hebrews would have any real sympathy with the attacking nation, whether Arabs, Philistines, Syrians, or Hittites; but they might regard an invasion as affording them a good opportunity of striking a blow for freedom, and, therefore, attack the Egyptians simultaneously with their other foes. The Egyptians themselves would perhaps suppose a closer connection between them and the other Eastern races than really existed.

Get them up out of the land.—The Pharaohs of the nineteenth dynasty were excessively jealous of the withdrawal from Egypt of any of their subjects, and endeavoured both to hinder and to recover them. Immigration was encouraged, emigration sternly checked. The loss of the entire nation of the Hebrews could not be contemplated without extreme alarm.

(11) **Task-masters.**—Heb., *chiefs of tributes.* The Egyptian system of forced labour, which it was now resolved to extend to the Israelites, involved the appointment of two sets of officers—a lower class, who personally overlooked the labourers, and forced them to perform their tasks, and a higher class of superintendents, who directed the distribution of the labour, and assigned to all the tasks which they were to execute. The "task-masters" of the present passage are these high officials.

To afflict them.—This was the object of the whole proceeding. It was hoped that severe labour under the lash would produce so much suffering that the number of the Israelites would be thinned, and their multiplication stopped. Humanly speaking, the scheme was a "wise" one—*i.e.*, one likely to be successful.

They built for Pharaoh treasure-cities.—By "treasure-cities" we are to understand "magazines" —*i.e.*, strongholds, where munitions of war could be laid up for use in case of an invasion. (In 1 Kings ix. 19, and 2 Chron. viii. 4, the same expression is translated "cities of store.") The Pharaohs of the nineteenth dynasty gave great attention to the guarding of the north-eastern frontier in this way.

Pithom.—This city is reasonably identified with the "Patumus" of Herodotus (ii. 158), which was in Lower Egypt, not far from Bubastis (*Tel Basta*). It is mentioned in the inscriptions of the nineteenth dynasty under the name of Pi-Tum (Brugsch, *History of Egypt*, vol. ii. p. 128). It was, as the name implies, a city of the sun-god, and was probably not very far from Heliopolis, the main seat of the sun-god's worship.

Raamses.—Pi-Ramesu, the city of Rameses, was the ordinary seat of the Court during the earlier part of the nineteenth dynasty. It appears to have been a new name for Tanis, or for a suburb of Tanis, which overshadowed the old city. Rameses II. claims to have built the greater part of it; but it was probably commenced by his father, Seti, who made the defence of the north-eastern frontier one of his main cares. The name must be considered as a mere variant rendering of the Egyptian Ramessu or Ramesu. The site is marked by the mounds at San.

(12) **The more they afflicted them, the more they multiplied and grew.**—This result was not natural. It can only be ascribed to God's superintending Providence, whereby "the fierceness of man" was made to "turn to his praise." Naturally, severe and constant labour exhausts a nation, and causes its numbers to diminish.

They were grieved.—This is scarcely strong enough. Translate, "They were sore distressed."

(13) **With rigour.**—Forced labour in Egypt was of a very severe character. Those condemned to it worked from morning to night under the rod of a task-master, which was freely applied to their legs or backs, if they rested their weary limbs for a moment. (See *Records of the Past*, vol. viii. p. 149; Chabas, *Mélanges Egyptologiques*, vol. ii. p. 121). The heat of the sun was great; the burthens which the labourers had to carry were heavy, and the toil was incessant. Death often resulted from the excessive work. According to Herodotus, a single monarch, Neco, destroyed in this way 120,000 of his subjects (*Herod.* ii. 158).

(14) **In morter and in brick.**—It has been questioned whether the Egyptians used brick as a material

manner of service in the field: all their
service, wherein they made them serve,
was with rigour.
(15) And the king of Egypt spake to
the Hebrew midwives, of which the
name of the one *was* Shiphrah, and the
name of the other Puah: (16) and he
said, When ye do the office of a midwife
to the Hebrew women, and see *them*
upon the stools; if it *be* a son, then
ye shall kill him: but if it *be* a daugh-
ter, then she shall live. (17) But the
midwives feared God, and did not as
the king of Egypt commanded them,
but saved the men children alive.
(18) And the king of Egypt called for the
midwives, and said unto them, Why
have ye done this thing, and have saved
the men children alive? (19) And the
midwives said unto Pharaoh, Because
the Hebrew women *are* not as the
Egyptian women; for they *are* lively,
and are delivered ere the midwives
come in unto them. (20)Therefore God
dealt well with the midwives: and the
people multiplied, and waxed very
mighty. (21) And it came to pass, be-
cause the midwives feared God, that he
made them houses.
(22) And Pharaoh charged all his

---

for building. No doubt temples, palaces, and pyramids were ordinarily of stone; but the employment of brick for walls, fortresses, and houses, especially in the Delta, is well attested. (See the *Quarterly Statement of the Palestine Exploration Fund* for July, 1880, pp. 137, 139, 143, &c.) Pyramids, too, were sometimes of brick (*Herod.* ii. 136). The manufacture of bricks by foreigners, employed (like the Israelites) as public slaves, is represented by the kings upon their monuments.

All manner of service in the field.—Josephus speaks of their being employed to dig canals (*Ant. Jud.* ii. 9, § 1), and there is a trace in Deut. xi. 10 of other labours connected with irrigation having been devolved on them. Such labours, under the hot sun of Egypt, are exhausting and dangerous to health.

And all their service . . was with rigour. Rather, *besides all their other service, which they made them serve with rigour.*

(15) **The Hebrew midwives.**—Or *the midwives of the Hebrew women* (ταῖς μαίαις τῶν Ἑβραίων, LXX.). The Hebrew construction admits of either rendering. In favour of the midwives being Egyptians is the consideration that the Pharaoh would scarcely have expected Hebrew women to help him in the extirpation of the Hebrew race (Kalisch); against it is the Semitic character of the names—Shiphrah, "beautiful;" Puah, "one who cries out;" and also the likelihood that a numerous and peculiar people, like the Hebrews, would have accoucheuses of their own race.

(16) **Upon the stools.**—Literally, *upon the two stones.* It has been suggested that a seat corresponding to the modern *kursee elwilâdeh* is meant. This is a "chair of a peculiar form," upon which in modern Egypt the woman is seated during parturition. (See Lane, *Modern Egyptians,* vol. iii. p. 142.) But it does not appear that this seat is composed of "two stones;" nor is there any distinct evidence of its employment at the time of child-birth in Ancient Egypt. The emendation of Hirsch—*banim* for *âbnaim,* is very tempting. This will give the sense, "When ye look upon the children."

(17) **The midwives feared God.**—The midwives, whether Hebrews or Egyptians, believed in a God who would punish wrong-doing, and therefore resolved not to obey the Pharaoh.

(19) **The Hebrew women are not as the Egyptian women.**—This was probably true; but it was not the whole truth. Though the midwives had the courage to disobey the king, they had not "the courage of their convictions," and were afraid to confess their real motive. So they took refuge in a half truth, and pretended that what really occurred in some cases only was a general occurrence. It *is* a fact, that in the East parturition is often so short a process that the attendance of a midwife is dispensed with.

(20) **Therefore God dealt well with the midwives.**—Heb., *and God dealt well, &c.* The reason is stated in verse 21. It was not because they equivocated and deceived the king, but because they feared God sufficiently to disobey the king, and run the risk of discovery. If they had been discovered, their life would have paid the forfeit.

(21) **He made them houses.**—God rewarded those who had showed tenderness to young children, by giving them children of their own, who grew up, and became in their turn fathers and mothers of families. There is no indication that the "houses" spoken of were Hebrew ones.

(22) **Every son that is born.**—The LXX. add "to the Hebrews," but without any necessity, since the context shows that only Hebrew children are meant.

Ye shall cast into the river.—Infanticide, so shocking to Christians, has prevailed widely at different times and places, and been regarded as a trivial matter. In Sparta, the State decided which children should live and which should die. At Athens a law of Solon left the decision to the parent. At Rome, the rule was that infants were made away with, unless the father interposed, and declared it to be his wish that a particular child should be brought up. The Syrians offered unwelcome children in sacrifice to Moloch; the Carthaginians to Melkarth. In China infanticide is said to be a common practice at the present day. Heathen nations do not generally regard human life as sacred. On the contrary, they hold that considerations of expediency justify the sweeping away of any life that inconveniences the State. Hence infanticide is introduced by Plato into his model republic (*Rep.* v. 9). Almost all ancient nations viewed the massacre of prisoners taken in war as allowable. The Spartan *crypteia* was a system of licensed murder. The condemnation to death of all male Hebrew children by Pharaoh is thus in no respect improbable. On the other hand, the mode of the death presents difficulties. For, first, the Nile was viewed as a god; and to fill it with corpses would, one might have supposed, have been regarded as a pollution. Secondly, the Nile water was the only water drunk; and sanitary considerations might thus have been expected to have pre-

people, saying, Every son that is born
ye shall cast into the river, and every
daughter ye shall save alive.

CHAPTER II.—(1) And there went *a* a
man of the house of Levi, and took *to*
wife a daughter of Levi. (2) And the
woman conceived, and bare a son: and
when she saw him that he *was a* goodly
child, she *b* hid him three months.
(3) And when she could not longer hide
him, she took for him an ark of bul-
rushes, and daubed it with slime and
with pitch, and put the child therein;
and she laid *it* in the flags by the river's
brink. (4) And his sister stood afar off,
to wit what would be done to him.
(5) And the daughter of Pharaoh came
down to wash *herself* at the river; and
her maidens walked along by the river's
side; and when she saw the ark among
the flags, she sent her maid to fetch it.
(6) And when she had opened *it,* she saw
the child: and, behold, the babe wept.
And she had compassion on him, and
said, This *is one* of the Hebrews' chil-

a ch. 6. 20; Num. 26. 59.

B.C. cir. 1573.

B.C. 1571.

b Acts 7. 20; Heb. 11. 23.

vented the edict. Perhaps, however, the children were viewed as offerings to the Nile, or to Savak, the crocodile-headed god, of whom each crocodile was an emblem. At any rate, as the Nile swarmed with crocodiles throughout its whole course, the bodies were tolerably sure to be devoured before they became putrescent.

II.

THE BIRTH, EDUCATION, AND EARLY LIFE OF MOSES.

(1) **There went.**—Comp. Gen. xxxv. 22; Hosea i. 3. The expression is idiomatic, and has no special force.

A man of the house of Levi.—Note the extreme simplicity of this announcement; and compare it with the elaborate legends wherewith Oriental religions commonly surrounded the birth of those who were considered their founders, as Thoth, Zoroaster, Orpheus. Even the name of the man is here omitted as unimportant. It is difficult to conceive any one but Moses making such an omission.

A daughter of Levi—*i.e.,* a woman of the same tribe as himself, a descendant of Levi—not a daughter in the literal sense, which the chronology makes impossible.

(2) **When she saw him that he was a goodly child.**—St. Stephen says, that Moses was "comely before God"—ἀστεῖος τῷ θεῷ (Acts vii. 28). Trogus Pompeius spoke of him as recommended by the beauty of his personal appearance (*ap.* Justin, *Hist. Philipp.* xxxvi. 2). His infantine "goodliness" intensified the desire of his mother to save his life, but must not be regarded as the main cause of her anxiety.

She hid him three months.—As long as she could hope to conceal him effectually. It must be remembered that Egyptians were mixed up with Israelites in Goshen, and that each Hebrew household would be subjected to espionage from the time of the issue of the edict.

(3) **An ark of bulrushes.**—Literally, *a chest of the papyrus plant.* The words used are both of Egyptian origin. *Teb, teba,* or *tebat,* is a "box" or chest in Egyptian, and is well Hebraised by *têbah,* or, as it is here vocalised, *têybah.* The papyrus plant was in Egyptian *kam,* as in modern Coptic, whence probably the Hebrew *gôme.* It was a material frequently used by the Egyptians for boats and even larger vessels (Isa. xviii. 2; Theophrast. *Hist. Plant.* iv. 8, § 4; Plin. *H. N.* xiii. 11).

Slime and pitch.—By "slime" seems to be meant bitumen, or mineral pitch, as in Gen. xi. 3; by "pitch" (*zaphath*), the ordinary vegetable pitch of commerce. Mineral pitch, though not a product of Egypt, was imported into the country from Mesopotamia, and was largely used for embalming (Brugsch, *History of Egypt,* vol. i. p. 361).

In the flags.—A rank aquatic vegetation abounds on the Lower Nile, and in all the back-waters and marshy tracts connected with it. Jochebed placed her child "in the flags," that the ark might not float away down the river, and so be lost to her sight. The word used for "flag"—*sûph*—seems to be a Hebraised form of *tufi,* a common Egyptian word, having this sense.

(4) **His sister.**—Presumably Miriam, the only sister of Moses mentioned elsewhere (chap. xv. 20, 21; Num. xxvi. 59). To have taken the part which is assigned her in this chapter, she must have been a girl of some fourteen or fifteen years of age, and possessed of much quickness and intelligence.

(5) **The daughter of Pharaoh came down to wash herself.**—This would be quite in accordance with Egyptian ideas. Women were allowed great liberty in Egypt, and moved about much as they pleased. Cleanliness was especially regarded; and the Nile water was considered healthy and fructifying (Strab. xv. p. 695). The princess would, of course, seek a part of the river which was reserved for females. Probably Jochebed knew where she was accustomed to bathe.

Her maidens.—As a princess, she was, of course, accompanied by a number of female attendants (*na'arôth*). Even ordinary Egyptian ladies seem to have been attended at the bath by four or five such persons. One of them was, however, more especially her waiting-woman (*âmah*), and to her the princess addressed herself.

(6) **When she had opened it.**—The princess opened the ark herself, perhaps suspecting what was inside, perhaps out of mere curiosity.

The babe (rather, *the boy*) **wept.** Through hunger, or cold, or perhaps general discomfort. An ark of bulrushes could not have been a very pleasant cradle.

She had compassion on him.—The babe's tears moved her to pity; and her pity prompted her to save it. She must have shown some sign of her intention—perhaps by taking the child from the ark and fondling it—before Miriam could have ventured to make her suggestion. (See the next verse.)

This is one of the Hebrews' children.—The circumstances spoke for themselves. No mother would have exposed such a "goodly child" (verse 2) to so sad a death but one with whom it was a necessity.

dren. (7) Then said his sister to Pharaoh's
daughter, Shall I go and call to thee a
nurse of the Hebrew women, that she
may nurse the child for thee? (8) And
Pharaoh's daughter said to her, Go.
And the maid went and called the child's
mother. (9) And Pharaoh's daughter
said unto her, Take this child away, and
nurse it for me, and I will give *thee* thy
wages. And the woman took the child,
and nursed it. (10) And the child grew,
and she brought him unto Pharaoh's
daughter, and he became her son. And
she called his name[1] Moses: and she
said, Because I drew him out of the
water.

(11) And it came to pass in those days,
when Moses was grown, that he went
out unto his brethren, and looked on
their burdens: and he spied an Egyp-
tian smiting an Hebrew, one of his
brethren. (12) And he looked this way
and that way, and when he saw that
there was no man, he slew the Egyptian,

[1] That is, *Drawn out.*

B. C. 1531.

---

(7) **Then said his sister.**—Miriam had bided her time. She had still kept in the background, but had approached within hearing distance; and when the princess observed that the babe must be "one of the Hebrews' children," was prompt with the rejoinder, "Shall I not fetch thee then a Hebrew mother to nurse him?" If the child was to be nursed at all—if he was to be brought up—a Hebrew nurse would be the fittest.

That she may nurse the child for thee.—"For thee." Miriam divines the thought of the princess, or half divines, half anticipates it, and helps to make it take a fixed shape. She assumes that the child is to be brought up, and *for the princess*, as her *protegé*, at any rate, if not something more.

(8) **The maid went and called the child's mother.**—Jochebed must have been waiting near, eagerly expecting—perhaps, while concealed from sight, watching the result, and ready to appear the moment that she was summoned. Miriam knew where to find her, and brought her quickly to the princess.

(9) **Nurse it for me.**—The princess adopts Miriam's suggestion; the child is to be nursed *for her*—is to be hers. She will place it out to nurse, and pay the customary wages.

(10) **The child grew.**—Josephus regards these words as implying a growth that was strange and abnormal (*Ant. Jud.* ii. 9, § 6). But nothing more seems to be intended than nature's ordinary course. The child grew and reached the time when it was usual in Egypt that children should be weaned. We have no means of determining what this time was. It may have been the completion of the first year; but more probably it was the completion of the second (2 Macc. vii. 27).

She brought him unto Pharaoh's daughter.—Jochebed carried out the terms of her engagement faithfully, and gave up her son to the princess at the time agreed upon.

He became her son.—Possibly by a formal act of adoption; but we have at present no evidence that adoption was an Egyptian custom. Perhaps the writer means simply that she brought him up as if he had been her son, gave him a son's education, and a son's privileges. (On the education of Moses, see Excursus II. at the end of this Book.)

She called his name Moses.—In Egyptian probably "Mesu," which is found as a name in the monuments of the nineteenth dynasty, and which is common as the latter half of a name—*e.g.*, Ra-mesu, Aah-mesu, Amen-mesu, &c. In ordinary use this word meant "born" and "son." (Comp. the Latin *natus.*) It was, however, derived from an Egyptian verb, meaning "to produce," "to draw forth;" and the princess justified her imposition of the name by a reference to this etymology. Owing to the existence of a cognate verb in Hebrew, it was possible to transfer her explanation into the Hebrew language exactly and literally. The play upon words cannot be rendered in English.

(11) **In those days.**—Notes of time are used with considerable latitude by the sacred writers. (Comp. Gen. xxxviii.; 2 Kings xx. 1.) According to the tradition followed by St. Stephen (Acts vii. 23), Moses was "full forty years old" when he took the step here indicated. We might have expected him to have come forward sooner; but there may have been difficulties in his so doing. It is remarkable that he does not tell us anything of his life during youth or early manhood. Later tradition was full of details (Stanley, *Lectures on the Jewish Church*, pp. 107—9), which, however, are worthless.

He went out unto his brethren.—It is probable that Pharaoh's daughter had never concealed from Moses that he was not her own child, but one of the oppressed race. She may even have allowed him to hold communication with his family. It is not, however, a mere visit that is here spoken of, but a complete withdrawal from the palace, and renunciation of his position at the court. "By faith, Moses, when he was come to years, refused to be called the son of Pharaoh's daughter, choosing rather to suffer affliction with the people of God than to enjoy the pleasures of sin for a season" (Heb. xi. 24—25). It is the first sign of that strong sympathy and tender affection for his people which characterises him throughout the narrative, and culminates in the pathetic cry, "Forgive them; and if not, blot me out of thy book" (chap. xxxii. 32).

Looked on their burthens—*i.e*, examined into their condition, watched their treatment, made himself acquainted with it by personal inspection.

He spied an Egyptian smiting a Hebrew.—Probably a taskmaster chastising one of the labourers, whom he accused of idling. St. Stephen regards the act as one of "oppression" and "wrong-doing" (Acts vii. 24). Moses must certainly have viewed it in this light, or he would not have been so moved to indignation as to kill the Egyptian. Though not a cruel nation, the Egyptians, no doubt, like other slave-drivers, occasionally abused their power, and treated the unfortunate labourers with cruelty.

(12) **He looked this way and that way.**—To see that no one observed him.

He slew the Egyptian.—Jewish commentators gloss over the act, or even eulogise it as patriotic and heroical. But it was clearly the deed of a hasty and undisciplined spirit. The offence did not deserve death, and if it had, Moses had neither legal office nor Divine call, justifying him in making himself an executioner. The result was, that, by his one wrong act, Moses put

and hid him in the sand. (13) And when
he went out the second day, behold, two
men of the Hebrews strove together:
and he said to him that did the wrong,
Wherefore smitest thou thy fellow?
(14) And he said, Who made thee [1] a
prince and a judge over us? intendest
thou to kill me, as thou killedst the
Egyptian? And Moses feared, and said,
Surely this thing is known.
(15) Now when Pharaoh heard this
thing, he sought to slay Moses. But
Moses fled from the face of Pharaoh, and
dwelt in the land of Midian: and he sat
down by a well. (16) Now the [2] priest
of Midian had seven daughters: and
they came and drew *water*, and filled the
troughs to water their father's flock.
(17) And the shepherds came and drove
them away: but Moses stood up and
helped them, and watered their flock.
(18) And when they came to Reuel their
father, he said, How *is it that* ye are
come so soon to day? (19) And they said,
An Egyptian delivered us out of the
hand of the shepherds, and also drew
water enough for us, and watered the
flock. (20) And he said unto his daugh-
ters, And where *is* he? why *is* it *that* ye
have left the man? call him, that he

1 Heb., *a man, a prince.*

2 Or, *prince.*

---

it out of his power to do anything towards alleviating the sufferings of his brethren for forty years.

Hid him in the sand.—To the east of the Delta the sand creeps up close to the cultivated grounds. There are even patches of it within the Delta itself. Moses naturally remembered that he dug the grave "in the sand." Any other writer would probably have said "in the ground."

(13) **The second day**—*i.e.*, the next day.

Him that did the wrong.—Heb., *the wicked one.* Our version follows the LXX.

Wherefore smitest thou thy fellow?—Comp. Acts vii. 26, where the words of Moses are reported somewhat differently, "Sirs, ye are brethren; why do ye wrong one to another?" In either case there was no offensive assumption of authority. But the wrong-doer took offence, nevertheless.

(14) **Who made thee a prince and a judge over us?**—As the reputed son of a princess, Moses would be in some sort a "prince." But no one had given him jurisdiction over the Hebrews. He had not really interfered as one who claimed authority, but as any man of position and education naturally interferes to stop a quarrel.

Intendest thou to kill me?—Here is the sting of the rejoinder; here was the assumption of authority—not in the interposition of to-day, but in the blow of yesterday. That fatal error laid Moses open to attack, and deprived him of the influence as a peacemaker which he might otherwise have exercised over his countrymen.

Surely this thing is known.—We are not told how the "thing" came to be known. "Murder will out," says the English proverb. Perhaps, though Moses thought himself unnoticed, some Egyptian had seen the deed. Perhaps the man whom he had avenged had told the tale.

(15) **When Pharaoh heard . . . he sought to slay Moses.**—Naturally. The administration of justice was one of the chief duties of the royal office; and the crime committed by Moses was one to be punished by death. There was nothing to reduce it from murder to manslaughter. And the motives which extenuate it in the eyes of moderns—patriotic zeal and hatred of oppression—would not have commanded the sympathies of a Pharaoh.

Moses fled.—Or, *had fled.* Moses would fly as soon as he found his act was known. He fled "at the saying" of the Israelite (Acts vii. 29). When Pharaoh sought for him, he was gone.

Dwelt in the land of Midian—*i.e.*, "Was led to make Midian his home," under circumstances about to be related. The Midian of this book seems to be the south-eastern portion of the Sinaitic peninsula, not the opposite Arabian coast, where were the main settlements of the nation.

Sat down by a well.—Rather, *the well.* There must have been one principal well in these parts, copious, and so generally resorted to. Moses fixed his temporary abode in its neighbourhood.

(16) **The priest of Midian.**—Reuel may have been both "priest" and "prince," like Melchizedek (Gen. xiv. 18); but there is no reason to doubt that he is here called "priest." In chap. xviii. 12, Jethro is represented as exercising priestly functions. The Midianites, descendants of Abraham by Keturah, worshipped the true God, and seem to have been at this time a religious people. The name Reuel, or Raguel, means "friend of God." Jethro's sacrifices were "for God," and Aaron and the elders eat bread with him "before God."

They came and drew water.—Comp. Gen. xxix. 9. According to Oriental ideas, there is nothing derogatory in the daughters of a chief so acting.

(17) **The shepherds came.**—Those of the neighbourhood. The rule of the desert is that those who come to a well take their turns in the use of the water in the order of their arrival. But these rude shepherds declined to wait for their turn. It appears later on, by the question of Reuel, "How is it that ye are come so soon to-day?" that this rude and unfair conduct of the shepherds was habitual.

Moses stood up and helped them.—Moses is again the champion of the oppressed, but has learnt wisdom by the past, and uses no unnecessary violence. His air and manner intimidated the wrong-doers, and they allowed the maidens' sheep to be watered first.

(19) **An Egyptian.**—So they concluded from his dress and appearance, perhaps even from his speech. It would be natural for them to make the mistake, and for Moses to remember it. Any other author would probably have said, "a man," or "a stranger."

And also drew water enough.—The shepherds had consumed some of the maidens' water before Moses's interference, so that he had to draw more for them.—another "little trait," which speaks for the Mosaic authorship.

(20) **That he may eat bread.**—Arab hospitality was offended that the stranger had not been invited into the tent to partake of the evening meal. The feeling of the modern Bedouin would be the same.

may eat bread. (21) And Moses was con-
tent to dwell with the man: and he
gave Moses Zipporah his daughter.
(22) And she bare *him* a son, and he
called his name [a] Gershom: for he said,
I have been a stranger in a strange land.
(23) And it came to pass in process of
time, that the king of Egypt died: and
the children of Israel sighed by reason
of the bondage, and they cried, and their
cry came up unto God by reason of the
bondage. (24) And God heard their
groaning, and God remembered his
[b] covenant with Abraham, with Isaac,
and with Jacob. (25) And God looked
upon the children of Israel, and God
[1] had respect unto *them*.

B.C. 1491.

a ch. 18. 3.

b Gen. 15. 14 & 46. 4.

1 Heb., *knew*.

c Acts 7. 30.

CHAPTER III.—(1) Now Moses kept
the flock of Jethro his father in law, the
priest of Midian: and he led the flock
to the backside of the desert, and came
to the mountain of God, *even* to Horeb.
(2) And the angel of the LORD appeared
unto him in a [c] flame of fire out of the
midst of a bush: and he looked, and,
behold, the bush burned with fire, and
the bush *was* not consumed. (3) And
Moses said, I will now turn aside, and
see this great sight, why the bush is not
burnt. (4) And when the LORD saw that
he turned aside to see, God called unto
him out of the midst of the bush, and
said, Moses, Moses. And he said, Here
am I. (5) And he said, Draw not nigh

---

(21) **Moses was content to dwell with the man.**—Reuel must have been so pleased with the manner and appearance of Moses that he invited him to take service with him—perhaps to share his tent. Moses consented, and in course of time took to wife Zipporah, one of Reuel's daughters. Marriage with the Midianites was allowed, even under the Law. It has been conjectured that Reuel might have communicated to Moses traditions or even documents concerning their common ancestor, Abraham, and his family. But there is nothing to indicate the use of letters at this early date by the Midianites.

(22) **Gershom.**—Almost certainly from *ger*, "a stranger," and *shâm*, "there." So Jerome, who translates it *advena ibi*. (Comp. Josephus and the LXX., who write the name Gers*am*.)

(23) **In process of time.**—Heb., *in those many days*. As Moses was now eighty years old (chap. vii. 7), and only forty when he quitted Egypt, the Pharaoh from whom he fled must have reigned above forty years. Between the commencement of the eighteenth and the close of the nineteenth dynasty, two kings only seem to have reigned so long as this—Thothmes III. and Rameses II. Our choice of the Pharaoh from whom Moses fled thus lies between these two.

The children of Israel sighed.—Or, "groaned." They had perhaps expected that a new king would initiate a new policy, or, at any rate, signalise his accession by a remission of burthens. But the new monarch did neither.

Their cry came up unto God.—"Exceeding bitter cries" always find their way to the ears of God. The existing oppression was such that Israel cried to God as they had never cried before, and so moved Him to have compassion on them. The miraculous action, begun in chap. iii., is the result of the cries and groans here mentioned.

III.

(1) **Moses kept the flock.**—The natural occupation of one who had thrown in his lot with the Midianites.

Jethro, his father-in-law.—Rather, *his relation by marriage*. The word is one of very wide use, corresponding with the Latin *affinis*. It is even applied to a husband, as in chap. iv. 25. The supposition that it means "father-in-law" has led to the identification of Jethro with Reuel, which is very unlikely. He was more probably Reuel's son, and Moses's brother-in-law. His father having died, he had succeeded to his father's position, and was at once priest and sheikh of the tribe.

To the backside of the desert.—Heb., *behind the desert*—*i.e.*, to the fertile tract which lay behind the sandy plain stretching from the Sinaitic range to the shore of the Elanitic gulf.

The mountain of God—*i.e.*, Sinai. See chap. xviii. 5; xix. 2—23, &c.

Even Horeb.—Rather, *towards Horeb*, or *Horeb way*. Horeb seems to have been the name of the entire mountain region; Sinai of the group or mass known now as Jebel Musa.

(2) **The angel of the Lord.**—Heb., *an angel of Jehovah*. In verse 4 the angel is called both "Jehovah" and "Elohim," whence it is concluded, with reason, that it was the Second Person of the Trinity who appeared to Moses.

Out of the midst of a bush.—Literally, *out of the midst of the acacia*. As the *seneh*, or acacia, is very common in the Sinaitic region, we can scarcely suppose that a special tree, growing alone, is intended. Probably the article is one of reference, and the meaning is, "the bush of which you have all heard." (Comp. John iii. 24.)

(3) **I will now turn aside.**—A minute touch, indicating that Moses is the writer. He remembers that the bush did not grow on the track which he was pursuing, but lay off it, and that he had to "turn aside," in order to make his inspection.

This great sight.—The phenomenon was strange and unusual—worthy of note, whatever might be the cause.

(4) **When the Lord saw . . . God called.**—Heb., *When Jehovah saw, Elohim called*. The German theory of two authors of Exodus, one Jehovistic and the other Elohistic, is completely refuted by this passage; for it is impossible to ascribe one clause of a sentence to one author, and the next to another. If originally the same term had been used in both places, a reviser would not have altered one without altering both.

Moses, Moses.—Comp. Gen. xxvi. 11; 1 Sam. iii. 10; and Acts ix. 4. The repetition marks extreme urgency.

(5) **Put off thy shoes.**—Rather, *thy sandals*. It is doubtful whether shoes were known at this early

hither: [a] put off thy shoes from off thy
feet, for the place whereon thou standest
is holy ground. (6) Moreover he said, [b] I
am the God of thy father, the God of
Abraham, the God of Isaac, and the
God of Jacob. And Moses hid his
face; for he was afraid to look upon
God.

(7) And the LORD said, I have surely
seen the affliction of my people which
are in Egypt, and have heard their cry
by reason of their taskmasters; for I
know their sorrows; (8) and I am come
down to deliver them out of the hand of
the Egyptians, and to bring them up out
of that land unto a good land and a large,
unto a land flowing with milk and
honey; unto the place of the Canaanites,
and the Hittites, and the Amorites, and
the Perizzites, and the Hivites, and the
Jebusites. (9) Now therefore, behold, the
cry of the children of Israel is come
unto me: and I have also seen the
oppression wherewith the Egyptians
oppress them. (10) Come now therefore,
and I will send thee unto Pharaoh, that
thou mayest bring forth my people the
children of Israel out of Egypt.

(11) And Moses said unto God, Who
am I, that I should go unto Pharaoh,
and that I should bring forth the chil-
dren of Israel out of Egypt? (12) And
he said, Certainly I will be with thee;
and this *shall be* a token unto thee, that
I have sent thee: When thou hast
brought forth the people out of Egypt,
ye shall serve God upon this moun-
tain.

a Josh. 5. 15; Acts 7. 33.

b Matt. 22. 32; Acts 7. 32.

---

date. They would certainly not have been worn in Midian. Egyptians before the time of Moses, and Orientals generally, in ancient (as in modern) times, removed their sandals (or their shoes) from their feet on entering any place to which respect was due, as a temple, a palace, and even the private house of a great man. It is worthy of notice that God Himself orders this mark of respect to be shown to the place which His Presence has hallowed. On the reverence due to holy places, see the Note on Gen. xxviii. 16, 17.

(6) **The God of thy father.**—It is generally agreed that "father" is put collectively here for "forefathers." (Comp. Gen. xxxi. 42.) Hence St. Stephen, quoting the passage, renders it, "I am the God of thy fathers" (Acts vii. 32).

The God of Abraham.—Primarily, no doubt, the meaning was, *the God who was worshipped by Abraham, Isaac, and Jacob;* but the form of the expression, "the God of Abraham," &c., indicated the continued existence of the patriarchs after death, since He can only be the God of existent, and not of non-existent things. (See Matt. xxii. 32.)

Moses hid his face, with the same feeling which made Jacob exclaim, "How dreadful is this place" (Gen. xxviii. 17). Though nothing was to be seen but an appearance as of material fire, the knowledge that God was there rendered the fire awful.

(7) **The Lord said.**—Heb., *Jehovah said.* The "God" of verse 6 is "Jehovah" here, and again "God" in verse 11. (See the Note on verse 4.)

I have surely seen.—Heb., *seeing I have seen.* It is not so much certainty as continued looking that is implied. (Comp. chap. ii. 25.)

Taskmasters.—A different word from that similarly translated in chap. i. 11, and one that implies cruel usage. It is sometimes rendered "oppressors" (Zech. ix. 8).

(8) **I am come down.**—By condescension to human infirmity, which conceives of all things under the limitations of time and space, God is spoken of as dwelling ordinarily in heaven, or "the heaven of heavens," whence sometimes He "comes down" to manifest Himself to men. That this was not understood literally, even by the Jews, appears from such passages as 1 Kings viii. 27; Ps. cxxxvii. 7—16; Prov. xv. 3, &c.

A good land and a large.—The land promised to Abraham (Gen. xv. 18) well deserves this description. Besides Philistia, and Palestine on both sides of the Jordan, it included almost the whole of Syria from Galilee on the south, to Amanus, Taurus, and the Euphrates on the north and north-east. This tract of country is 450 miles long, and from sixty to a hundred and twenty miles broad. Its area is not much less than 50,000 square miles. Although some parts are unproductive, it is, on the whole, a region of great fertility, quite capable of forming the seat of a powerful empire.

A land flowing with milk and honey.—This expression, here used for the first time, was already, it is probable, a proverbial one, denoting generally, richness and fertility. (See Num. xiii. 27.)

The Canaanites . . . .—See the comment on Gen. (chap. x. 15—17; chap. xiii. 7).

(11) **Who am I, that I should go?**—The men most fit for great missions are apt to deem themselves unfit. When God called Jeremiah to be a prophet, his reply was, "O Lord God! Behold, I cannot speak, for I am a child" (Jer. i. 6). St. Ambrose fought hard to escape being made Archbishop of Milan. Augustine was loth to undertake the mission to England. Anselm was with difficulty persuaded to accept the headship of our Church in the evil days of Rufus. The first impression of a fit man selected for a high post generally is, "Who am I?" In Moses's case, though there were some manifest grounds of fitness—*e.g.*, his Egyptian training and learning, his familiarity with the court, his knowledge of both nations and both languages—yet, on the other hand, there were certain very marked (apparent) disqualifications. Forty years of exile, and of a shepherd's life had at once unfitted him for dealing with a court, and made him a stranger to his brethren. Want of eloquence seemed to be a fatal defect in one who must work mainly by persuasion. Even his age (eighty) might well have seemed to him unsuitable.

(12) **Certainly I will be with thee.**—Heb., *since I will be with thee.* An answer addressed not to the thing said, but to the thing meant. Moses meant to urge that he was unfit for the mission. God's reply is, "Not unfit, *since* I will be with thee." I will supply all thy defects, make good all thy shortcomings. "My strength is made perfect in weakness."

(13) And Moses said unto God, Behold, *when* I come unto the children of Israel, and shall say unto them, The God of your fathers hath sent me unto you; and they shall say to me, What *is* his name? what shall I say unto them?

(14) And God said unto Moses, I AM THAT I AM: and he said, Thus shalt thou say unto the children of Israel, I AM hath sent me unto you.

(15) And God said moreover unto Moses, Thus shalt thou say unto the children of Israel, The LORD God of your fathers, the God of Abraham, the God of Isaac, and the God of Jacob, hath sent me unto you: this *is* my name for ever, and this *is* my memorial unto all generations. (16) Go, and gather the elders of Israel together, and say unto them, The LORD God of your fathers, the God of Abraham, of Isaac, and of Jacob, appeared unto me, saying, I have surely visited you, and *seen* that which is done to you in Egypt: (17) and I have said, I will bring you up out of the affliction of Egypt unto the land of the Canaanites, and the Hittites, and the Amorites, and the Perizzites, and the Hivites, and the Jebusites, unto a land flowing with milk and honey. (18) And they shall hearken to thy voice: and thou shalt come, thou and the elders of Israel, unto the king of Egypt, and ye shall say unto him, The LORD God of the Hebrews hath met with us: and now let us go, we beseech thee, three days' journey into the wilderness, that we may sacrifice to the LORD our God.

This shall be a token unto thee.—It is in accordance with the Divine economy to give men "tokens," which are future, and appeal to faith only. (Comp. 1 Sam. ii. 34; 2 Kings xix. 27.)

(13) **What is his name?**—In Egypt, and wherever polytheism prevailed, every god had, as a matter of course, a name. Among the Israelites hitherto God had been known only by titles, as *El* or *Elohim*, "the Lofty One;" *Shaddai*, "the Powerful;" *Jahveh*, or *Jehovah*, "the Existent." These titles were used with some perception of their meaning; no one of them had as yet passed into a proper name. Moses, imagining that the people might have become so far Egyptianised as to be no longer content with this state of things, asks God by what name he shall speak of Him to them. Who shall he say has appeared to him?

(14) **I AM THAT I AM.**—It is generally assumed that this is given to Moses as the full name of God. But perhaps it is rather a deep and mysterious statement of His nature. "I am that which I am." My nature, *i.e.*, cannot be declared in words, cannot be conceived of by human thought. I exist in such sort that my whole inscrutable nature is implied in my existence. I exist, as nothing else does—necessarily, eternally, really. If I am to give myself a name expressive of my nature, so far as language can be, let me be called "I AM."

Tell them I AM hath sent me unto you.—I AM, assumed as a name, implies (1) an existence different from all other existence. "I am, and there is none beside me" (Isa. xlv. 6); (2) an existence out of time, with which time has nothing to do (John viii. 58); (3), an existence that is real, all other being shadowy; (4) an independent and unconditioned existence, from which all other is derived, and on which it is dependent.

(15) **The Lord God of your fathers.**—Heb., *Jehovah, God of your fathers.* The "I AM" of the preceding verse (*'ehyeh*) is modified here into *Jahveh*, or Jehovah, by a substitution of the third person for the first. The meaning of the name remains the same.

This is my name for ever.—Jehovah is the predominant name of God throughout the rest of the Old Testament. (On the meaning of the name see Note on Gen. ii. 4.) Rendered by the LXX. *κύριος*, ["Lord,"] the name appears under that form everywhere throughout the Authorised Version printed in capitals. It does not occur in the New Testament, since "Lord" takes its place. An equivalent of the name occurs, however, frequently in the Revelation of St. John, where God appears as "He which is, and which was, and which is to come" (Rev. i. 4, 8, iv. 8, xi. 17, xvi. 5). Necessary, self-sustained, independent, eternal existence, must always be of his essence.

My memorial—*i.e.*, the designation by which I shall be remembered.

(16) **The elders of Israel.**—Not so much the old men generally, as the rulers—those who bore authority over the rest—men of considerable age, no doubt, for the most part. Rosenmüller reasonably concludes from this direction that the Hebrews, even during the oppression, enjoyed some kind of internal organisation and native government (*Schol. in Exod.* p. 58).

I have surely visited.—Heb., *Visiting, I have visited.* (Comp. Gen. l. 24.)

(17) **I have said.**—See verse 8. Perhaps there is also a reference to the promise made to Abraham (Gen. xv. 14).

The affliction of Egypt.—Comp. Gen. xv. 13; Exod. i. 11, 12; iii. 7.

(18) **They shall hearken.**—The pronoun "they" refers to "the elders" of verse 16. For the fulfilment of the promise, see chap. iv. 29—31. The elders appear to have been persuaded easily, and at once.

Thou and the elders.—We are not told in chap. v. that the elders did present themselves before Pharaoh; but it is possible that they may have done so. Or Moses and Aaron, who spoke in their name, and by their authority, may have been regarded as sufficiently representing them.

The Lord God of the Hebrews hath met with us.—Heb., *Jehovah, the God of the Hebrews.* Pharaoh would readily comprehend this statement. He would quite understand that the Hebrews, being of a different race from the Egyptians, had a God of their own, and that this God would from time to time give intimations to them of His will. Such intimations were supposed to be given to the Egyptian kings occasionally by their gods.

Three days' journey.—The necessity for withdrawing to so great a distance arose from that remark-

(19) And I am sure that the king of
Egypt will not let you go, [1] no, not by a
mighty hand. (20) And I will stretch
out my hand, and smite Egypt with all
my wonders which I will do in the
midst thereof: and after that he will
let you go. (21) And I will give this
people favour in the sight of the Egyp-
tians: and it shall come to pass, that,
when ye go, ye shall not go empty:
(22) [a] But every woman shall borrow of
her neighbour, and of her that sojourn-
neth in her house, jewels of silver, and
jewels of gold, and raiment: and ye
shall put *them* upon your sons, and upon
your daughters; and ye shall spoil [2] the
Egyptians.

[1] Or, *but by strong hand.*

[a] ch. 11. 2 & 12. 35.

[2] Or, *Egypt.*

CHAPTER IV. — (1) And Moses
answered and said, But, behold, they
will not believe me, nor hearken unto
my voice: for they will say, The LORD
hath not appeared unto thee. (2) And
the LORD said unto him, What *is* that
in thine hand? And he said, A rod.
(3) And he said, Cast it on the ground.
And he cast it on the ground, and it
became a serpent; and Moses fled from

able peculiarity in the Egyptian religion, the worship of animals. Cows, or at any rate, white cows, were sacred throughout the whole of Egypt, and to kill them was regarded as a crime of the deepest dye. Sheep were sacred to the inhabitants of one nome or canton, goats to those of another (Herod. ii. 42). Unless the Hebrews retired to a place where there were no Egyptians, they would be unable to perform their sacred rites without danger of disturbance, and even bloodshed. (See below, chap. viii. 26.)

The wilderness.—"*The* wilderness" to those who dwelt in Goshen was the broad sandy and rocky tract which intervened between Egypt and Palestine—the modern *El-Tih*—a desert reckoned at three days' journey across (Herod. iii. 5). It is "a vast limestone plateau of irregular surface, projecting wedge-fashion into the peninsula of Sinai, just as Sinai itself projects into the Red Sea. It terminates in a long cliff or encampment, steep and abrupt on the south-western side, gradually falling away towards the south-east."—(*Our Work in Palestine*, p. 275.)

That we may sacrifice.—It is idle to speculate whether, if Pharaoh had granted the request, the Israelites would have returned to Egypt after sacrificing. God knew that he would not grant it.

(19) **I am sure.**—Heb., *I know*, which is more suitable, since it is God who speaks, and to Him the future is known with as absolute a certainty as the past.

No, not by a mighty hand.—Rather, *not even under a mighty hand* (*ne quidem valida manu castigatus*, Rosenmüller). Pharaoh, even when chastised by My mighty hand, will not voluntarily permit of your departure (see chap. xiv. 5—23).

(20) **I will stretch out my hand.**—Hands are stretched out to help and save. God promises here more than He had promised before (verse 12). He shows *how* He will "be with" Moses. He will lend him miraculous aid, performing in his behalf "all his wonders," and with them "smiting the Egyptians."

(22) **Every woman shall borrow.**—Rather, *shall ask* (*αἰτήσει*, LXX.; *postulabit*, Vulg.). That there was really no pretence of "borrowing," appears from chap. xii. 33—36, where we find that the "jewels" were not asked for until the very moment of departure, when the Israelites were being "thrust forth," and the people were urgent on them to be gone, certainly neither expecting nor wishing to see them again. Asking for presents is a common practice in the East, and persons who were quitting their homes to set out on a long journey through a strange country would have abundant excuse, if any had been needed, for soliciting aid from their rich neighbours.

Of her neighbour.—Egyptians were mingled with the Israelites in Goshen, as we see by chap. ii. 3.

Of her that sojourneth in her house.—Rosenmüller supposes that Egyptians who rented houses which belonged to the Hebrews are intended; but the expression used is more suitable to lodgers or visitors. (Comp. Job xix. 15.)

Upon your sons.—The Egyptian men of the Rameside period wore gold and silver ornaments almost as freely as the women. Their ornaments included armlets, bracelets, anklets, and collars.

Ye shall spoil, *i.e.*, It shall be as if ye had conquered the Egyptians, and spoiled them. Compare the promise made to Abraham (Gen. xv., 14); and for the fulfilment, see below (chap. xii. 35, 36).

IV.

(1) **Behold.**—Some render the word here used by "perhaps" (LXX., Aben-Ezra, Saadia, &c.); but it does not appear to have anywhere this meaning. Moses meant to express a positive conviction that he would not be listened to. His faith was weak.

They will say, The Lord hath not appeared.—It is very probable that the people would have said this if Moses had not had any credentials to produce. It is even possible that they did say it. There had been no appearance of Jehovah to any one for above four hundred years, and they might well think that the age of miracles was past. Miracles cluster around certain crises in God's dealings with man, ceasing altogether between one crisis and another. They were suspended for above 500 years between the time of Daniel and the appearance of the angel to Zacharias.

(2) **A rod.**—Most commentators regard the "rod" of Moses as his shepherd's crook, and this is certainly possible; but the etymology of the word employed seems rather to point to an ordinary staff, or walking-stick. Egyptians of rank usually carried long *bâtons;* and one suggestion is, that the rod of Moses was "that which he had been accustomed to carry as the son of Pharaoh's daughter." But even if this was still in his possession after forty years of exile, he is not likely to have taken it with him when he went a-shepherding. Probably the "rod" was a common staff, such as a shepherd of eighty years old might need for a support.

(3) **A serpent.**—The word here used (*nakhash*) is a generic one for a snake of any kind, and tells us nothing as to the species. A different word (*tannin*) is

before it. (4) And the LORD said unto
Moses, Put forth thine hand, and take
it by the tail. And he put forth his
hand, and caught it, and it became a
rod in his hand: (5) that they may be-
lieve that the LORD God of their fathers,
the God of Abraham, the God of Isaac,
and the God of Jacob, hath appeared
unto thee.
(6) And the LORD said furthermore
unto him, Put now thine hand into
thy bosom. And he put his hand into
his bosom: and when he took it out,
behold, his hand *was* leprous as snow.
(7) And he said, Put thine hand into thy
bosom again. And he put his hand
into his bosom again; and plucked it
out of his bosom, and, behold, it was
turned again as his *other* flesh. (8) And
it shall come to pass, if they will not
believe thee, neither hearken to the
voice of the first sign, that they will
believe the voice of the latter sign.
(9) And it shall come to pass, if they
will not believe also these two signs,
neither hearken unto thy voice, that
thou shalt take of the water of the
river, and pour *it* upon the dry *land:*
and the water which thou takest out
of the river [1]shall become blood upon
the dry *land.*
(10) And Moses said unto the LORD,
O my Lord, I *am* not [2]eloquent, neither
[3]heretofore, nor since thou hast spoken
unto thy servant: but I *am* slow of
speech, and of a slow tongue.
(11) And the LORD said unto him, Who
hath made man's mouth? or who

1 Heb., *shall be and shall be.*

2 Heb., *a man of words.*

3 Heb., *since yesterday, nor since the third day.*

used in chap. vii. 10, while *nakhash* recurs in chap. vii. 15. *Tannin* is, like *nakhash*, a generic term.

And Moses fled from before it.—It was natural for Moses to remember his alarm, and record it. Any later writer would have passed over so *small* a circumstance. (See the Introduction, p. 3.)

(4) **Take it by the tail.**—Those who venture to handle poisonous snakes, like the modern Egyptians and the inhabitants of the coast of Barbary, generally take hold of them by the neck, in which case they are unable to bite. To test the faith and courage of Moses, the command is given him to lay hold of *this* serpent "by the tail."

He put forth his hand.—Faith triumphed over instinct. Moses had "fled from" the snake when first he saw it (verse 3). Now he is daring enough to stoop down, put his hand on the creature's tail, and so lift it up.

It became a rod.—Its real nature returned to it. Once more it was, not a stiffened serpent, but an actual staff, or walking-stick.

(5) **That they may believe . . .**—These are God's words to Moses, in continuation of those which form the first portion of the preceding verse. The clause describing the action of Moses in verse 4 is parenthetic. The words give Divine sanction to the view, so strangely combatted of late, that the power of working miracles is given to men, primarily and mainly, for its evidential value, to accredit them as God's messengers. Without the gift of miracles neither would Moses have persuaded the Israelites, nor would the Apostles have converted the world.

(6) **His hand was leprous as snow.**—The worst form of leprosy was called by the Greeks λεύκη, "the white disease." When it is fully developed, the whole skin appears glossy white, and every hair is "white like wool" (Celsus, *De Re Medica*, v. 28, § 12). This form is said to be absolutely incurable. It was probably from the fact of Moses exhibiting a leprous hand that the Egyptians called the Israelites "the lepers," as related by Manetho (*ap.* Joseph. *contra Ap.* i. 26), Chæremon (*ibid.*, i. 32), and others.

(8) **The voice of the first sign.**—Not "the voice of Moses witnessed to by the first sign" (Rosenmüller), but the voice, which the sign itself might be regarded as uttering. (Comp. Ps. cv. 27, where Moses and Aaron are said to have proclaimed "the *words* of God's signs.") A miracle speaks to men.

They will believe, *i.e.*, most of them. Accustomed to the tricks of the serpent charmers (see chap. vii. 11 and comment *ad loc.*), the Israelites might be unmoved by the sight of the first miracle. They were then to be shown the second, which would be much more astonishing to them, having no parallel in their experience. This would persuade the greater number. As some, however, might still doubt, a third sign was provided. God is patient with all reasonable doubt.

(9) **Shall become blood.**—The verb is repeated in the Hebrew, which intensifies the assertion. The English equivalent of the phrase used would be, "shall assuredly become." The signs were, no doubt, selected primarily for facility of exhibition; but they may also have been intended to be significant. The change of a rod into a serpent showed that a feeble implement might become a power to chastise and to destroy. That of a healthy into a leprous hand, and the reverse, indicated that Moses's mission was both to punish and to save; while the change of water into blood suggested—albeit vaguely—the conversion of that peace and prosperity, which Egypt was enjoying, into calamity, suffering, and bloodshed.

(10) **I am not eloquent.**—Heb., *No man of words am I.* Moses, still reluctant, raises a new objection. He is not gifted with facility of speech. Words do not come readily to him; *perhaps*, when they come, he has a difficulty in uttering them. According to a Jewish tradition, he was unable to pronounce the labials, *b, f, m, p, v.* According to his own expressions at the end of the verse, he was "heavy" or "slow of speech," and "heavy" or "slow of tongue."

Neither heretofore.—Heb., *neither yesterday, nor the day before.* It is a Hebrew idiom to make these words cover past time generally. (See below, chap. v. 7, 8, 14; and comp. Gen. xxxi. 2, 5, and 2 Sam. iii. 17.)

Nor since thou hast spoken.—Converse with God had not cured his defect of utterance, whatever it was. He remained "slow of speech and slow of tongue"—unready, *i.e.*, and hesitating.

(11) **Who maketh.**—Rather, *hath made.*

maketh the dumb, or deaf, or the seeing, or the blind? have not I the LORD?
(12) Now therefore go, and I will be [a] with thy mouth, and teach thee what thou shalt say.
(13) And he said, O my Lord, send, I pray thee, by the hand *of him whom* thou [1] wilt send.
(14) And the anger of the LORD was kindled against Moses, and he said, *Is* not Aaron the Levite thy brother? I know that he can speak well. And also, behold, he cometh forth to meet thee: and when he seeth thee, he will be glad in his heart.
(15) And thou shalt speak unto him, and put words in his mouth: and I will be with thy mouth, and with his mouth, and will teach you what ye shall do.
(16) And he shall be thy spokesman unto the people: and he shall be, *even* he shall be to thee instead of a mouth, and [b] thou shalt be to him instead of God.
(17) And thou shalt take this rod in thine hand, wherewith thou shalt do signs.
(18) And Moses went and returned to Jethro his father in law, and said unto him, Let me go, I pray thee, and return unto my brethren which *are* in Egypt, and see whether they be yet alive. And Jethro said to Moses, Go in peace.
(19) And the LORD said unto Moses in Midian, Go, return into Egypt: for all the men are dead which sought thy

a Matt. 10. 19; Mark 13. 11; Luke 12. 11.

1 Or, *shouldest.*

b ch. 7. 1.

(12) **I will be with thy mouth.**—To suggest words (see Matt. x. 19, 20), and assist utterance. Comp. the reluctance of Jeremiah (Jer. i. 6), and God's dealings with him (*ibid.*, 7—9).

(13) **Send, I pray thee, by the hand of him whom thou wilt send.**—Rather, *pray send by whom thou wilt.* A curt, impatient, and scarcely reverent speech. Moses means that he will undertake the task if God insists; but that God would do far better to send another. Hence the "anger of the Lord" against him (verse 14), which led to Aaron's association with him as joint leader of the people.

(14) **The Levite.**—Aben-Ezra and Rosenmüller think that this was the usual designation of the brother of Moses among the Israelites, who thus distinguished him from other Aarons. But as a distinguishing mark, the term would be superfluous here, since "thy brother" prevented the possibility of any other Aaron being thought of. Probably, the term is a title of honour, the priestly character already attaching to the tribe in God's counsels.

I know that he can speak well.—Heb., *I know that speaking he can speak.* Facility of utterance, rather than excellence of speech, is intended.

And also, *i.e.*, not only does his ready speech make him a suitable person to appoint, but he is coming to join thee, so that he and thou may arrange your respective parts at once.

(15) **Thou shalt . . . put words in his mouth,** *i.e.*, Tell him what he is to say—furnish the matter of his speeches, which he will then clothe with appropriate language.

With thy mouth.—Suggesting the matter to thee.

With his mouth.—Suggesting the language to him.

(16) **He shall be thy spokesman.**—Heb., *He shall speak for thee.*

He shall be, even he shall be.—Rather, *it shall come to pass that he shall be, &c.*

Instead of God.—God did not speak to Aaron directly, but only through Moses. Aaron was to recognise in Moses God's mouthpiece, and to consider what Moses told him as coming from God. Moses had still, therefore, the higher position.

(17) **This rod,** *i.e.*, "the rod that had been changed into a serpent," as the LXX. paraphrase.

(18) **Signs.**—Rather, "*the* signs" (τὰ σημεῖα, LXX.); *i.e.*, the signs which thou wilt have to perform, as already implied in chap. iii. 20.

Moses . . . returned to Jethro.—Heb., *to Jether.* When Moses married Zipporah, he was probably adopted into the tribe, of which Reuel, and after him Jethro, was the head. The tribal tie was close, and would make the asking of permission for even a temporary absence the proper, if not even the necessary, course. Apart from this, Moses would have had to "return," in order to restore the flock, which he was tending, to its owner. (See chap. iii. 1.)

My brethren.—Not "my nation," for Moses could not doubt that some survived; nor "my actual brothers," for he had but one brother; but, "my relations," or "my family," my kith and kin. Let me go and see whether my relatives survive, or whether they have succumbed to the tyranny of the Pharaoh. It is certain that this was not Moses' sole motive, not even his main motive for wishing to return to Egypt; but, as it was among his motives, he was within his right in putting it forward, and omitting to mention others.

Jethro said, Go in peace.—Jethro's character is altogether one of which kindness and peacefulness are the main elements. If he be identified with Reuel, the pleasing picture drawn in chap. ii. 18—21 will furnish traits towards his portraiture. Even without this, the present passage and the notice in chap. xviii. sufficiently delineate him. He is a sort of second Melchizedek, both priest and king, a worshipper of the true God, and one in whose presence both Moses and Aaron are content to play a secondary part (chap. xviii 9, 12). But he never asserts himself; he is always kind, gentle, acquiescent, helpful. He might easily have made a difficulty at the present point of the narrative, have demurred to the weakening of the tribe by the withdrawal of an important member from it, have positively refused to allow of the departure of Zipporah and her children. But his words are simply "Go in peace." He consents, and does not mar the grace of his act by any show of reluctance. He lets Moses take his wife and children. He afterwards receives them back, and protects them (chap. xviii. 2); and, finally, when his protection is no more needed, he restores them to their natural guardian, by a spontaneous act, as it would seem.

(19) **In Midian.**—Moses appears to have delayed his departure after he obtained permission to go from Jethro. Hence the address "Go, return," which is peremptory.

life. (20) And Moses took his wife and
his sons, and set them upon an ass, and
he returned to the land of Egypt: and
Moses took the rod of God in his hand.
(21) And the LORD said unto Moses,
When thou goest to return into Egypt,
see that thou do all those wonders
before Pharaoh, which I have put in
thine hand: but I will harden his heart,
that he shall not let the people go.
(22) And thou shalt say unto Pharaoh,
Thus saith the LORD, Israel *is* my son,
even my firstborn: (23) and I say unto
thee, Let my son go, that he may serve
me: and if thou refuse to let him go,
behold, I will slay thy son, *even* thy
firstborn.
(24) And it came to pass by the way in
the inn, that the LORD met him, and
sought to kill him. (25) Then Zipporah
took a sharp [1]stone, and cut off the
foreskin of her son, and [2]cast *it* at his
feet, and said, Surely a bloody husband
art thou to me. (26) So he let him go:
then she said, A bloody husband *thou
art*, because of the circumcision.

1 Or, *knife.*

2 Heb., *made it touch.*

All the men which sought thy life.—Not only the Pharaoh (chap. ii. 23), but the kindred of the murdered man, and the officials empowered by the Pharaoh to arrest Moses. As forty years had elapsed since the homicide, this is readily conceivable.

(20) **His sons.**—Only one had been mentioned previously, viz., Gershom (chap. ii. 22), unless we accept the Vulgate addition to that place. But another had been recently born to him.

Set them upon an ass.—Heb., *upon the ass, i.e.*, either "upon *his* ass," or, according to some, "upon asses." The singular of a substantive with the article is sometimes used for the genus (Gen. xv. 11).

He returned.—Rather, *set out to return* (ἐπέστρεψε, LXX.).

The rod of God.—An emphatic phrase. God's endowment of the rod with miraculous power had made it "the rod of God." It was the instrument by means of which most of the plagues and the other miracles were wrought (chap. vii. 20; viii. 6, 17; ix. 23; x. 13; xiv. 16; xvii. 5; Num. xx. 9; &c.).

(21) **All those wonders.**—Not the "three signs" of chap. iii. 3—9, but the "portents" or "wonders" which were to be done before Pharaoh, and which had been alluded to in chap. iii. 20. These were, in the counsel of God, already "put into Moses' hand," though their exact nature was as yet unknown to Moses himself.

I will harden his heart.—The hardening of Pharaoh's heart has been the subject of much controversy. It is ascribed to God in this place, and again in chap. vii. 3; ix. 12; x. 1, 20, 27; xiv. 4, 8; to Pharaoh in chap. viii. 15, 32; and ix. 34; to the action of the heart itself in chap. vii. 13, 22; ix. 7 and 35. It is conceivable that these may be simply three forms of speech, and that the actual operation was one and the same in every case. Or, three different modes of operation may be meant. It is in favour of the latter view, that each term has a period during which it is predominant. In the narrative of what happened, the action of the heart is itself predominant in the first period; that of Pharaoh on his heart in the second; that of God in the third. We may suppose that, at first, Pharaoh's nature was simply not impressed, and that then his heart is said to have "hardened itself," or "remained hard;" that after a while, he began to be impressed; but by an effort of his will controlled himself, and determined that he would not yield: thus "hardening his own heart;" finally, that after he had done this twice (chap. viii. 15, 32), God stepped in and "smote him with a spirit of blindness and infatuation," as a judgment upon him (chap. ix. 12), thus, finally, "hardening" him (comp. Rom. ix. 18). This divine action was repeated on three subsequent occasions (chap. x. 20, 27; xiv. 8), Pharaoh's time of probation being past, and God using him as a mere means of showing forth His glory. There is nothing in this contrary to the general teaching of the Scriptures, or to the Divine Perfection.

(22) **Israel is my son.**—Compare Hosea xi. 1. This tender relation, now first revealed, is not a mere metaphor, meaning "as dear to me as a son," but a reality. The Israel of God enjoys the sonship of adoption by being taken into the True Son, and made one with Him (Rom. viii. 14—17).

My first-born.—Admitted to sonship in the Messiah before the other nations of the earth.

(23) **I will slay thy son, even thy first-born.**—The threat was not made until immediately before the tenth plague (chap. xi. 5). It is not recorded in the words which Moses is here directed to use; but the speech of Moses in chap. xi. is no doubt much abbreviated.

(24) **In the inn.**—There would not be any "inn," as we understand the word, in the Sinaitic peninsula. Probably there would not even be a caravanserai. Nothing more is meant by *mâlon* than a recognised resting-place.

The Lord met him.—The LXX. have ἄγγελος Κυρίου, "an angel of the Lord;" and so the Targum of Onkelos and the Arabic versions. But the existing Hebrew text is probably correct. God met Moses, *i.e.*, visited him with a sharp attack of illness, which threatened to be fatal. Both he and his wife seem at once to have concluded that the visitation was a punishment, on account of their having neglected to circumcise their new-born son. Perhaps Moses had an intimation from God to that effect.

(25) **A sharp stone.**—On the use of stone knives by the Egyptian *paraschistæ* see Herod. ii. 86. They were regarded as more pure than metal knives. From Josh. v. ii. it would seem that stone knives were in the early ages commonly employed for circumcision by the Israelites.

At his feet.—Moses' feet, undoubtedly. The action was petulant and reproachful. Zipporah regarded the bloody rites of her husband's religion as cruel and barbarous, and cast the foreskin of her son at his feet, as though he were a Moloch requiring a bloody offering.

A bloody husband.—Heb., *a husband of bloods.* A husband, *i.e.*, who causes the blood of his children to be shed unnecessarily for some unintelligible reason.

(26) **So he let him go.**—God let Moses go, *i.e.*, allowed him to recover—accepted Zipporah's act as sufficient, albeit tardy, reparation, and spared the life of her husband.

(27) And the LORD said to Aaron, Go
into the wilderness to meet Moses.
And he went, and met him in the
mount of God, and kissed him. (28) And
Moses told Aaron all the words of the
LORD who had sent him, and all the
signs which he had commanded him.
(29) And Moses and Aaron went and a ch. 3. 18.
gathered together all the elders of the
children of Israel: (30) and Aaron spake
all the words which the LORD had
spoken unto Moses, and did the signs
in the sight of the people. (31) And the
people believed: and when they heard
that the LORD had visited the children
of Israel, and that he had looked upon
their affliction, then they bowed their
heads and worshipped.

CHAPTER V.—(1) And afterward Moses
and Aaron went in, and told Pharaoh,
Thus saith the LORD God of Israel, Let
my people go, that they may hold a
feast unto me in the wilderness. (2) And
Pharaoh said, Who *is* the LORD, that I
should obey his voice to let Israel go?
I know not the LORD, neither will I let
Israel go. (3) And they said, [a]The God

Then she said.—When Moses was sufficiently recovered, Zipporah explained to him why she had called him "a bloody husband;" it was "on account of the circumcisions," *i.e.*, the two circumcisions—of Gershom in Midian, many years previously, and now of Eliezer. We learn from chap. xviii. 2, 3, that Zipporah and her boys were sent back to Jethro by Moses, probably at this time. Moses was in haste, and the child could not have travelled conveniently for some days.

(27) **Go into the wilderness.**—Either the directions given to Aaron were more definite than this, or they were supplemented by Divine guidance. He went and *met* Moses on "the mount of God," *i.e.*, in the Sinaitic region. Without Divine guidance, he would naturally have sought him in Midian.

Kissed him.—Comp. Gen. xxxiii. 4; xlv. 14, 15. In the East, men closely related still kiss on meeting, as they did in Moses' time, and in the days of Herodotus (i. 134).

(28) **Who had sent him.**—Rather, "which he had laid upon him," *τοὺς λόγους Κυρίου, οὓς ἀπέστειλε*, LXX.

All the signs, *i.e.*, the three miracles of verses 3—9.

THE RETURN TO EGYPT.

(29) **Moses and Aaron went.**—The two brothers returned together from the Sinaitic region to Egypt. No particulars of the journey are narrated, nor can we even tell what was the route which they followed. On their arrival, they at once set themselves to carry out the charge committed to them (chap. iii. 16). The Israelites in Egypt, though suffering under severe oppression, had an organisation of their own, jurisdiction attaching probably to the heads of tribes, or of chief families. (Comp. Num. i. 4—16.) These persons are here called "elders," which the LXX. render *τὴν γερουσίαν*, "the senate." Moses and Aaron could have no power to convoke them; but they invited them to a conference, and the elders came.

(30) **Aaron spake.**—According to the Divine command (verse 16).

And did the signs.—So, generally, afterwards (chap. vii. 10, 19; viii. 6, 17, &c.), not, however, universally (see chap. ix. 10, 23; x. 13; xiv. 21; &c.).

The people believed.—The narrative is very much compressed. The elders heard the words, and saw the signs first. Then they must have summoned an assembly of the people, after working hours, and the people must have been addressed and shown the signs. The effect was to convince them also, and to induce them to accept Moses and Aaron for the national leaders.

Worshipped.—Some think that Moses was the object of the worship; but it is better to regard it as offered to "the Lord," who had "visited" them.

V.

FIRST APPLICATION OF MOSES TO PHARAOH, AND INCREASE OF THE OPPRESSION.

(1) **Went in.**—Heb., *went*—*i.e.*, left their usual residence, and approached the Court, which, according to the Psalms (Ps. lxxviii. 12, 43), was held at Zoan (*i.e.*, Tanis). This was the ordinary residence of Rameses II. and his son Menephthah.

Thus saith the Lord God of Israel.—Heb., *Thus has said Jehovah, God of Israel.* The Pharaohs claimed to hold direct communications with the Egyptian deities, and could not deny the possibility of the Hebrew leaders holding communications with their God. Menepthah himself—the probable "Pharaoh of the Exodus"—gave out that he had received a warning from Phthah in the fifth year of his reign (Brugsch, *History of Egypt*, vol. ii., p. 119; 1st ed.).

That they may hold a feast unto me.—God's entire purpose is not at once revealed to Pharaoh. He is tried with a moderate demand, which he might well have granted. By refusing it he showed himself harsh, unkind, and inconsiderate, so tempting God to lay upon him a greater burthen.

In the wilderness—*i.e.*, beyond the frontier, or, at any rate, beyond inhabited Egypt—that the Egyptians might not be driven to fury by seeing animals sacrificed which they regarded as sacred. (See chap. viii. 26, and the comment *ad loc.*)

(2) **Who is the Lord?**—Heb., *Who is Jehovah?* If Jehovah was a name, the use of which had been laid aside, as would seem to have been the case by the later chapters of Genesis, and which was revived by the scene at the burning bush, Pharaoh may very probably not have heard of it.

That I should obey his voice.—The king means to say, that, whoever Jehovah is, He can have no authority over *him*, as He is not one of *his* gods. The Egyptians were accustomed to the idea of local gods, and quite expected every nation to have a deity or several deities of its own; but they regarded the power of each as circumscribed, certainly not extending beyond the race or nation to which the god belonged.

(3) **The God of the Hebrews.**—Moses accepts Pharaoh's view, and does not insist on the authority of Jehovah over Egyptians, but makes an appeal *ad misericordiam.* He has, at any rate, authority over

of the Hebrews hath met with us: let
us go, we pray thee, three days' journey
into the desert, and sacrifice unto the
LORD our God; lest he fall upon us
with pestilence, or with the sword.
(4) And the king of Egypt said unto
them, Wherefore do ye, Moses and
Aaron, let the people from their works?
get you unto your burdens.
(5) And Pharaoh said, Behold, the
people of the land now *are* many, and
ye make them rest from their burdens.
(6) And Pharaoh commanded the same
day the taskmasters of the people, and
their officers, saying, (7) Ye shall no
more give the people straw to make
brick, as heretofore: let them go and
gather straw for themselves. (8) And
the tale of the bricks, which they did
make heretofore, ye shall lay upon
them; ye shall not diminish *ought*
thereof: for they *be* idle; therefore
they cry, saying, Let us go *and* sacrifice
to our God. (9) [1]Let there more work
be laid upon the men, that they may
labour therein; and let them not regard
vain words.
(10) And the taskmasters of the people
went out, and their officers, and they
spake to the people, saying, Thus saith
Pharaoh, I will not give you straw.
(11) Go ye, get you straw where ye can
find it: yet not ought of your work
shall be diminished. (12) So the people
were scattered abroad throughout all
the land of Egypt to gather stubble
instead of straw. (13) And the task-
masters hasted *them*, saying, Fulfil your
works, *your* [2]daily tasks, as when there
was straw. (14) And the officers of the

[1] Heb., *Let the work be heavy upon the men.*

[2] Heb., *a matter of a day in his day.*

Hebrews; and, having made a requirement, He will be angered if they neglect it. Will not Pharaoh allow them to escape His anger?

With the sword.—Egypt was very open to invasion on its eastern frontier; and the brunt of an invasion in this quarter would fall upon the Hebrews. In the time of the nineteenth dynasty, Hittite incursions were especially feared.

(5) **And Pharaoh said.**—Moses and Aaron having retired, *re infectâ*, Pharaoh turns to the officers of his court and reproaches them with allowing the Hebrews to be idle. They have time to hold meetings (chap. iv. 30, 31), and listen to inflammatory harangues, and depute leaders to make very inconvenient proposals—why are they not kept closer to their tasks? Some change of system is requisite.

Make them rest.—Rather, "*let them rest.*"

(6) **Taskmasters . . . officers.**—Three grades of officials are mentioned as employed in superintending the forced labours of the Hebrews—(1) "lords of service" (*sarey massim*), in chap. i. 11; (2) "taskmasters" (*nogĕshim*), here and in verses 10, 13, 14; and (3) "officers"—literally, *scribes* (*shotĕrim*), here and in verses 11—21. The "lords of service" were probably a small body who exercised a general superintendence, and determined the works in which the Hebrews should be employed. They were, no doubt, native Egyptians. The *nogĕshim*, or "taskmasters," were their subordinates — Egyptians like themselves — comparatively numerous, and serving as intermediaries between the "lords" and the "officers." These last were Hebrews, and engaged mainly in keeping the tale of the bricks, and seeing that the proper number was reached. Such an organisation is consonant with all that we know of the Egyptian governmental system, which was bureaucratic and complex, involving in every department the employment of several grades of officials.

(7) **Straw to make brick.**—"The use of crude brick was general in Egypt for dwelling-houses, tombs, and ordinary buildings, the walls of towns, fortresses, and the sacred enclosures of temples, and for all purposes where stone was not required, which last was nearly confined to temples, quays, and reservoirs" (Wilkinson, in Rawlinson's *Herodotus*, vol. ii. p. 213). These crude bricks were always made of the mud of the Nile, mixed with chopped straw, which served to bind them together (Rosellini, *Monumenti Civili*, vol. ii. p. 252).

Let them go and gather straw.—It has been estimated that this requirement would "more than double" the people's toils (Canon Cook). They would have to disperse themselves over the harvest fields, often lying at a considerable distance from the brick-fields, to detach the straw from the soil, gather it into bundles, and convey it to the scene of their ordinary labours. Having done this they were then required to complete the ordinary "tale."

(9) **Let them not regard vain words.**—Or, *false words.* The reference is to the promises of deliverance wherewith Moses and Aaron had raised the people's hopes (chap. iv. 30). Pharaoh supposed these to be "vain words," as Sennacherib did those spoken by Hezekiah (2 Kings xviii. 20).

(12) **Stubble instead of straw.**— Heb., *stubble for the straw.* Reaping in Egypt was effected by cutting off the ears only from the stalks, and thus a very tall stubble was left in the fields. This appears not to have been valued by the cultivators, and whoever wished was allowed to collect it. After collecting it, and bringing it to the brick-fields in bundles, they would have to chop it small before it would be fit for use.

(13) **The taskmasters hasted them.**—The Egyptian monuments show us foreign labourers engaged in brick-making under Egyptian overseers, or "taskmasters," who are armed with sticks, and "haste" the labourers whenever they cease work for the purpose of resting themselves. The overseers are represented as continually saying to the workpeople, "Work without faintness." (See Wilkinson, in Rawlinson's *Herodotus*, vol. ii. p. 214.)

As when there was straw.—Heb., *as when there was the straw—i.e.*, as when the straw was furnished to you.

(14) **The officers . . were beaten.**—This is the usual practice in the East. When any requisition is made on a town or a village, or any body of persons, the procuring of it is left to the "head men," who are alone

children of Israel, which Pharaoh's
taskmasters had set over them, were
beaten, *and* demanded, Wherefore have
ye not fulfilled your task in making
brick both yesterday and to day, as
heretofore?
(15) Then the officers of the children
of Israel came and cried unto Pharaoh,
saying, Wherefore dealest thou thus
with thy servants? (16) There is no
straw given unto thy servants, and
they say to us, Make brick: and, be-
hold, thy servants *are* beaten; but the
fault *is* in thine own people. (17) But
he said, Ye *are* idle, *ye are* idle: there-
fore ye say, Let us go *and* do sacrifice
to the LORD. (18) Go therefore now, *and*
work; for there shall no straw be given
you, yet shall ye deliver the tale of
bricks. (19) And the officers of the
children of Israel did see *that* they *were*
in evil *case*, after it was said, Ye shall
not minish *ought* from your bricks of
your daily task.
(20) And they met Moses and Aaron,
who stood in the way, as they came
forth from Pharaoh: (21) And they said
unto them, The LORD look upon you,
and judge; because ye have made our
savour [1]to be abhorred in the eyes of
Pharaoh, and in the eyes of his servants,
to put a sword in their hand to slay us.
(22) And Moses returned unto the
LORD, and said, Lord, wherefore hast
thou *so* evil entreated this people? why
is it *that* thou hast sent me? (23) For
since I came to Pharaoh to speak in thy
name, he hath done evil to this people;
[2]neither hast thou delivered thy people
at all.

CHAPTER VI.—(1) Then the LORD
said unto Moses, Now shalt thou see
what I will do to Pharaoh: for with a
strong hand shall he let them go, and
with a strong hand shall he drive them
out of his land. (2) And God spake
unto Moses, and said unto him, I *am*

1 Heb., *to stink.*

2 Heb., *delivering thou hast not delivered.*

---

responsible to the Government, and are punished in case they fail to exact the full amount.

And demanded.—Rather, *and asked,* or (as Kalisch renders it) "with the words."

(15) **The officers . . . came and cried unto Pharaoh.**—The Egyptian monarchs were accessible to all. It was a part of their duty to hear complaints personally; and they, for the most part, devoted to this employment the earlier hours of each day (see Herod. ii. 173). Those who came to them generally *cried* to them for justice, as is the Oriental wont.

(16) **The fault is in thine own people.**—Heb., *thy people is in fault.* There can be no reasonable doubt that this clause is antithetical to the preceding one, and means that, though the Hebrews are punished, the people really in fault are the Egyptians.

(17) **Ye are idle.**—Idleness was regarded by the Egyptians as one of the worst sins. It had to be specially disclaimed in the final judgment before Osiris (Birch, in Bunsen's *Egypt*, vol. v. p. 254). Men sometimes disclaimed it in the epitaphs which they placed upon their tombs (*Records of the Past*, vol. vi. p. 137). Pharaoh had already made the charge, by implication, against Moses and Aaron (verse 4). No doubt, among the Egyptians themselves, a good deal of idleness resulted from the frequent attendance upon religious festivals (Herod. ii. 59—64). Hence the charge might seem plausible.

(20) **Who stood in the way.**—Heb., *in their way.* The meaning is, that Moses and Aaron were "standing"—*i.e.*, waiting to meet them, and know the result of their interview with the monarch.

(21) **Ye have made our savour to be abhorred.**—Heb., *to stink.* An idiom common to the Hebrews with the Egyptians (Comp. Gen. xxxiv. 30; 1 Sam. xiii. 4; 2 Sam. x. 6, &c., with *Papyr. Anastas.* i. 27, 7), and very expressive. The English idiom, "to be in bad odour with a person," is similar, but lacks the force of the Hebrew phrase.

In the eyes.—Mixed metaphors occur in all languages, and may generally be accounted for by the literal meaning of some familiar expression having come to be forgotten. In Heb., *liphney*, "in the face of," and *bĕ'eyney*, "in the eyes of," were mere prepositions, having the force of "before," "with," "in regard to."

A sword . . . to slay us.—This was not, perhaps, mere Oriental hyperbole. The officers may have feared that their inability to enforce the Pharaoh's impracticable demands would ultimately lead to their execution.

(22) **Moses returned unto the Lord.**—He could find nothing to say to the officers. The course of events had as much disappointed him as it had them. All that he could do was to complain to God, with a freedom which seems to us almost to border on irreverence, but which God excused in him, since it had its root in his tender love for his people. Moses might perhaps have borne with patience a mere negative result—the postponement of any open manifestation of the Divine power—but the thought that he had increased the burthens and aggravated the misery of his countrymen was more than he could bear without complaining.

VI.

GOD'S RENEWAL AND ENLARGEMENT OF HIS PROMISES.

(1) **Now shalt thou see.**—Moses' complaint was that God delayed, and "was slack as concerning His promise." Hitherto He had not "delivered His people at all." The answer, "*Now* shalt thou see," is an assurance that there will be no more delay; the work is just about to begin, and Moses will behold it. He will then cease to doubt.

With a strong hand shall he let them go.—Rather, *through a strong hand: i.e.*, through the compulsion which my strong hand will exert on him.

the Lord: (3) and I appeared unto
Abraham, unto Isaac, and unto Jacob,
by *the name of* God Almighty, but by
my name JEHOVAH was I not known
to them. (4) And I have also established
my covenant with them, to give them
the land of Canaan, the land of their
pilgrimage, wherein they were strangers.
(5) And I have also heard the groaning
of the children of Israel, whom the
Egyptians keep in bondage; and I have
remembered my covenant. (6) Where-
fore say unto the children of Israel,
I *am* the Lord, and I will bring you
out from under the burdens of the
Egyptians, and I will rid you out of
their bondage, and I will redeem you
with a stretched out arm, and with
great judgments: (7) and I will take
you to me for a people, and I will be to
you a God: and ye shall know that I
am the Lord your God, which bringeth
you out from under the burdens of the
Egyptians. (8) And I will bring you in
unto the land, concerning the which I
did [1] swear to give it to Abraham, to
Isaac, and to Jacob; and I will give
it you for an heritage: I *am* the
Lord.
(9) And Moses spake so unto the chil-

[1] Heb., *lift up my hand.*

Drive them.—Comp. chap. xii. 31—33.

(3) **I appeared . . . by the name of God Almighty.**—This name, "El Shaddai," is first found in the revelation made of Himself by God to Abraham (Gen. xvii. 1). It is used by Isaac (Gen. xxviii. 3), and repeated in the revelation made to Jacob (Gen. xxxv. 11). Its primary idea is, no doubt, that of "overpowering strength." (See the comment on Gen. xvii. 1.) The primary idea of "Jehovah" is, on the contrary, that of absolute, eternal, unconditional, independent existence. Both names were probably of a great antiquity, and widely spread among Semitic races; but, at different times and in different places, special stress was laid on the one or on the other. To the early patriarchs God revealed Himself as "El Shaddai," because He desired to impress upon them His ability to fulfil the promises which He had made to them; to Moses and Israel generally, at the date of the Exodus, He insisted on His name Jehovah, because they were in the closest contact with polytheism, and had themselves, in many cases, fallen into polytheism (Josh. xxiv. 14), against which this Name was a standing protest, since "the Existent" must mean "the Self-Existent," and so "the Only Existent." (See Deut. iv. 39: "Jehovah, he is God in heaven above, and upon the earth beneath: *there is none else.*")

By my name Jehovah was I not known to them.—Rather, *was I not made manifest to them.* The antiquity of the name itself appears—(1) from its derivation, which is from the obsolete *havah*, a form already in the time of Moses superseded by *hayah;* (2) from its occurrence in some of the most ancient documents inserted by Moses into the Book of Genesis, *e.g.*, chaps. ii. 4, iii., iv., xi. 1—9, &c.; (3) from its employment by Abraham as an element in a name (Gen. xxii. 14). But though the name was ancient, and known to the patriarchs, its full meaning was not known to them, and so God was not manifested to them by it.

(4) **My covenant.**—See Gen. xv. 18—21, xvii. 7, 8, xxvi. 3, 4, xxxv. 12, &c.

The land of Canaan.—Canaan proper was the tract between Sidon and Gaza (Gen. x. 19), which is now counted as "Palestine"; but the region promised to Abraham, and included in a larger sense of the word "Canaan," was very much more extensive, reaching as it did from the Nile to the Euphrates (Gen. xv. 18). This vast territory was actually possessed by Israel under David and Solomon (1 Kings iv. 21—24).

The land of their pilgrimage, wherein they were strangers.—Heb., *The land of their sojournings, wherein they sojourned.* (Comp. Gen. xvii. 8, xxiii. 4, xxviii. 4.) Abraham, Isaac, and Jacob were occupants of Canaan merely by sufferance: they were allowed to dwell in it because it was not half peopled; but the ownership was recognised as belonging to the Canaanite nations, Hittites and others (Gen. xx. 15, xxiii. 3—20, &c.).

(6) **I will redeem you.**—The idea of God purchasing, or redeeming, Israel is here brought forward for the first time. Later on we learn that the redemption was accomplished in a twofold way—(1) by the long series of wonders, culminating in the tenth plague, whereby they were taken out of Pharaoh's hand, and ceased to be his slaves, becoming instead the servants of God; and (2) by being led through the Red Sea, and thus delivered, one and all, from impending death, and so purchased anew. (See chap. xv. 13—16.) The delivery from Pharaoh typified *our* deliverance from the power of Satan; the bringing forth from Egypt *our* deliverance from the power of sin.

With a stretched out arm.—See the comment on chap. iii. 20.

With great judgments.—That the "wonders" to be performed would also be "judgments" is here first declared plainly, though previously hinted at (chap. iii. 20, iv. 23). In Genesis God had said that he would "judge" the nation which should afflict Israel (Gen. xv. 14), but not that he would do so miraculously.

(7) **I will take you to me for a people.**—Comp. chap. xix. 5, 6; Deut. vii. 6. The selection of Israel as a "peculiar people" did not involve the abandonment of all other nations, as we see by the instances of Balaam, Ruth, Job, Nebuchadnezzar, Darius the Mede, Cyrus, and others. God always continued to "govern all the nations upon the earth" (Ps. lxvii. 4); and "in every nation those that feared him and worked righteousness" were accepted with him (Acts x. 35). The centurion of the Gospels (Matt. viii. 5—13, Luke vii. 2—10) and Cornelius in the Acts (Acts x. 1—33) carry the same principle into Gospel times.

I will be to you a God.—See Gen. xvii. 8.

(8) **I will give it you for an heritage: I am the Lord.**—Heb., *I will give it to you for an heritage, I Jehovah.* The whole is one sentence, and implies that, as being Immutable and Eternal, He would assuredly give it them.

(9) **They hearkened not.**—The second message was received in quite a different spirit from the first.

dren of Israel: but they hearkened not
unto Moses for [1]anguish of spirit, and
for cruel bondage.
(10) And the LORD spake unto Moses,
saying, (11) Go in, speak unto Pharaoh
king of Egypt, that he let the children
of Israel go out of his land. (12) And
Moses spake before the LORD, saying,
Behold, the children of Israel have not
hearkened unto me; how then shall
Pharaoh hear me, who *am* of uncircum-
cised lips? (13) And the LORD spake
unto Moses and unto Aaron, and gave
them a charge unto the children of
Israel, and unto Pharaoh king of Egypt,
to bring the children of Israel out of
the land of Egypt.
(14) These *be* the heads of their fathers'
houses: [a]The sons of Reuben the first-
born of Israel; Hanoch, and Pallu,
Hezron, and Carmi: these *be* the
families of Reuben. (15) [b]And the sons
of Simeon; Jemuel, and Jamin, and
Ohad, and Jachin, and Zohar, and
Shaul the son of a Canaanitish woman:
these *are* the families of Simeon.
(16) And these *are* the names of [c]the
sons of Levi according to their gene-
rations; Gershon, and Kohath, and
Merari: and the years of the life of

1 Heb., *shortness*, or, *straitness*.

a Gen. 46. 9; 1 Chron. 5. 3.

b 1 Chron. 4. 24.

B.C. 1619.

c Num. 3. 17; 1 Chron. 6. 1.

Then "the people believed, and bowed their knees and worshipped" (chap. iv. 31). Now they could not even be induced to listen. But there is nothing strange in this. The reason is obvious. The first announcement of coming deliverance elated them with a hope to which they had been long strangers. Their spirits sprang to the message, and readily accepted it. But now they had been chilled by disappointment. The only result of their leader's interference hitherto had been to increase their misery (chap. iv. 7—23). They had therefore lost heart, and could trust him no longer.

Anguish of spirit.—Heb., *shortness of breath.* (Comp. Job xxi. 4.) The expression points to extreme lassitude and depression.

THE SECOND MESSAGE TO PHARAOH.

(11) **Speak unto Pharaoh.**—The second message was an advance upon the first. The first asked only for permission to enter the wilderness, much of which was within the limits of Egypt; the second was a demand that the Israelites should be allowed "to go out of the land." Such is the way of Providence generally. If we refuse a light cross, a heavier cross is laid on us. If we will not close with the Sybil on the first occasion, she offers us a worse bargain on the second.

(12) **How then shall Pharaoh hear me?**—This time the objection comes from Moses. His double rejection, by Pharaoh (chap. v. 1—4) and by Israel (chap. vi. 9), had thrown him back into utter despondency. All that diffidence and distrust of himself which he had shown in his earlier communications with Jehovah (chaps. iii. 11, iv. 1, 10, 13) revived, and he despaired of success in his mission. Was it of any use his making a second appeal to the foreign monarch when he had failed with his own countrymen?

Uncircumcised lips.—Rosenmüller argues from this expression that Moses was "tongue-tied;" but it is not clear that more is meant here than in chap. iv. 10, where Moses says that he is "slow of speech and of a slow tongue." He had some difficulty of utterance; but whether or not it was a physical impediment remains uncertain. "Uncircumcised" is used, according to the Hebrew idiom, for any imperfection which interferes with efficiency. An "uncircumcised ear," is explained in Jer. vi. to be an ear that "cannot hearken;" and an "uncircumcised heart" (Lev. xxvi. 41) is a heart that fails to understand.

(13) **The Lord . . . gave them a charge.**—The reluctance and opposition of Moses led to an express "charge" being laid upon himself and Aaron, the details of which are given in chap. vii. 1—9. Verse 1 of chap. vii. probably followed originally on verse 12 of this chapter. When the genealogy was inserted at this point, the present verse, which summarises chap. vii. 1—9, was added, as also verses 28—30 at the end of the chapter.

THE FAMILY OF MOSES.

(14) **These be the heads of their fathers' houses.**—Genealogies have always had a special interest for the Semitic races. They occupy quite as prominent a position in Arabian as in Jewish history. The descent of a man who aspired to be a leader would be a subject of curiosity, with a Semitic people, to all those who submitted themselves to his guidance; and Moses naturally inserts his at the point where, fully accepting the post of leader, he came forward and commenced his struggle with Pharaoh for the emancipation of his nation. A "father's house" is a family. (See Num. i. 2, 18.)

(14, 15) **Reuben . . . Simeon.**—It fixes the position of the family of Levi in the house of Jacob to commence the genealogy with a mention of the two elder brothers. As, however, the writer is really concerned only with the Levites, the families of Reuben and Simeon are dismissed with the briefest possible notice. Nothing new is recorded of them. (See Gen. xlvi. 9, 10.)

(16) **Gershon, Kohath, and Merari** were all born before Levi went into Egypt (Gen. xlvi. 8, 11, 27), which was when he was about forty or fifty years of age. It is not unlikely that they were at that time all grown up. If Levi lived to be "an hundred thirty and seven years" old, he would probably before he died have seen his descendants of the fifth generation. Attempts have been made to show that the present genealogy is complete, and that Moses was Levi's great-grandson. But in Joshua's case there were ten generations (at least) between him and Jacob (1 Chron. vii. 23—27); so that three generations only between Jacob and Moses are scarcely possible. The Israelites were in the habit of constructing their genealogies by omitting some of the links, as we see plainly in the genealogy of Ezra (Ezra vii. 1—5) and in St. Matthew's genealogy of our Lord (Matt. i. 8). In this present genealogy four or five (perhaps more) names are probably omitted between Amram, the son of Kohath, and Amram, the father of

Levi *were* an hundred thirty and seven
years. (17) The sons of Gershon; Libni,
and Shimi, according to their families.
(18) And [a]the sons of Kohath; Amram,
and Izhar, and Hebron, and Uzziel:
and the years of the life of Kohath *were*
an hundred thirty and three years.
(19) And the sons of Merari; Mahali
and Mushi: these *are* the families of
Levi according to their generations.
(20) And [b]Amram took him Jochebed his
father's sister to wife; and she bare
him Aaron and Moses: and the years
of the life of Amram *were* an hundred
and thirty and seven years. (21) And
the sons of Izhar; Korah, and Nepheg,
and Zithri. (22) And the sons of
Uzziel; Mishael, and Elzaphan, and
Zithri. (23) And Aaron took him
Elisheba, daughter of Amminadab,
sister of Naashon, to wife; and she
bare him Nadab, and Abihu, Eleazar,
and Ithamar. (24) And the sons of
Korah; Assir, and Elkanah, and Abi-
asaph: these *are* the families of the
Korhites. (25) And Eleazar Aaron's son
took him *one* of the daughters of Putiel
to wife; and [c]she bare him Phinehas:
these *are* the heads of the fathers
of the Levites according to their
families.

(26) These *are* that Aaron and Moses,
to whom the LORD said, Bring out the
children of Israel from the land of
Egypt according to their armies.
(27) These *are* they which spake to
Pharaoh king of Egypt, to bring out
the children of Israel from Egypt:
these *are* that Moses and Aaron.

(28) And it came to pass on the day
when the LORD spake unto Moses in the
land of Egypt, (29) that the LORD spake
unto Moses, saying, I *am* the LORD:
speak thou unto Pharaoh king of Egypt
all that I say unto thee. (30) And Moses
said before the LORD, Behold, I *am* of
uncircumcised lips, and how shall Pha-
raoh hearken unto me?

a Num. 26. 57; 1 Chron. 6. 2.

b ch. 2. 1; Num. 26. 59.

B. C. cir. 1530.

c Num. 25. 11.

Moses, as will appear if we model the genealogy of Moses upon that of Joshua.

Jacob.

Levi.	Joseph.
Kohath	Ephraim.
Amram	Beriah.
———	Rephah.
———	Telah.
———	Tahan.
———	Laadan.
———	Ammihud.
———	Elishama.
Amram.	Nun.
Moses.	Joshua.

(17) **The sons of Gershon.**—From this point the genealogy is no longer a recapitulation, but an original historical document of first-rate importance, which is confirmed by Numbers (Num. iii. 18—33) and Chronicles (1 Chron. vi. 17—19). It is remarkable that Gershon had but two sons, Kohath but four, and Merari but two. Yet the Levites in the year after the Exodus numbered 22,300 males (Num. iii. 22, 28, 34). This increase could only have taken place, at the rate indicated, in the course of some ten or eleven generations.

(20) **Amram took him Jochebed his father's sister to wife.**—Marriages with aunts and nieces were not unlawful before the giving of the Law. They were common throughout the East, and at Sparta (Herod. vi. 71, vii. 239).

The years of the life of Amram.—The long lives of Levi, Kohath, and Amram, the father of Moses, are not recorded for any chronological purpose, but to show that the blessing of God rested in an especial way on the house of Levi, even before it became the priestly tribe. Life in Egypt at the time not unfrequently reached 120 years; but the 137 of Levi, the 133 of Kohath, and the 137 of Amram, the father of Moses, would, even in Egypt, have been abnormal.

(23) **Elisheba, daughter of Amminadab, sister of Naashon.**—Amminadab and Naashon were among the ancestors of David (Ruth iv. 19, 20; 1 Chron. ii. 10—15), and their names are consequently found in the genealogies of our Lord (Matt. i. 4; Luke iii. 32, 33). Naashon was "prince of Judah" at the time of the Exodus (Num. i. 7, 16).

(24) **The sons of Korah** did not partake in his sin, and therefore "died not" (Num. xxvi. 11), but became the heads of important families.

(25) **According to their families.**—The genealogy proper here ends. But the author appends to it an emphatic statement that the Moses and Aaron mentioned in it (verses 20, 23) are the very Moses and Aaron appointed by God to lead the Israelites out of Egypt—the very Moses and Aaron who delivered God's message to Pharaoh (verses 26, 27).

(26) **Their armies.**—This expression is here used of the Israelites for the first time. It seems to refer to that organisation, of a quasi-military character, which was given to the people by the order of Moses during the long struggle with Pharaoh, and which enabled them at last to quit Egypt, not a disorderly mob, but "harnessed," or "in military array" (chap. xiii. 18). The expression is repeated in chaps. vii. 4 and xii. 17, 51.

THE SECOND MESSAGE TO PHARAOH (*resumed*).

(28-30) These verses are most closely connected with chap. vii. They are a recapitulation of main points in chap. vi., rendered necessary by the long parenthesis (verses 14—27), and serve to unite chap. vii. with the previous narrative. They contain no new information.

CHAPTER VII.—(1) And the LORD
said unto Moses, See, I have made thee
a god to Pharaoh: and Aaron thy
brother shall be thy prophet. (2) Thou
shalt speak all that I command thee:
and Aaron thy brother shall speak unto
Pharaoh, that he send the children of
Israel out of his land. (3) And I will
harden Pharaoh's heart, and multiply
my signs and my wonders in the land
of Egypt. (4) But Pharaoh shall not
hearken unto you, that I may lay my
hand upon Egypt, and bring forth mine
armies, *and* my people the children of
Israel, out of the land of Egypt by great
judgments. (5) And the Egyptians shall
know that I *am* the LORD, when I
stretch forth my hand upon Egypt, and
bring out the children of Israel from
among them.

B.C. 1491.

(6) And Moses and Aaron did as the
LORD commanded them, so did they.
(7) And Moses *was* fourscore years old,
and Aaron fourscore and three years
old, when they spake unto Pharaoh.

(8) And the LORD spake unto Moses
and unto Aaron, saying, (9) When Pha-
raoh shall speak unto you, saying, Shew
a miracle for you: then thou shalt
say unto Aaron, Take thy rod, and cast
it before Pharaoh, *and* it shall become
a serpent. (10) And Moses and Aaron
went in unto Pharaoh, and they did so
as the LORD had commanded: and Aaron
cast down his rod before Pharaoh, and
before his servants, and it became a
serpent. (11) Then Pharaoh also called
the wise men and the sorcerers: now
the magicians of Egypt, they also did
in like manner with their enchantments.

VII.

(1) **See, I have made thee a god to Pharaoh . . .**—This is God's answer to the objection of Moses that his lips were uncircumcised (chap. vi. 12), and probably followed it immediately. The force of it would seem to be: "Thou art not called on to speak, but to act. In action thou wilt be to Pharaoh as a god —powerful, wonder-working, irresistible; it is Aaron who will have to speak to him, and *he* is eloquent" (chap. iv. 14).

Thy prophet.—Or *spokesman*—the declarer of thy mind, which is the primary sense of "prophet."

(3) **I will harden Pharaoh's heart.**—See the comment on chap. iv. 21.

My signs and my wonders.—"Signs" (*'ôthôth*) were miracles done as credentials, to prove a mission (chap. iv. 8, 9, 30). "Wonders" (*môphôth*) were miracles generally; *niphlĕ'ôth*, also translated "wonders" (chap. iii. 20), were miracles, wrought in the way of punishment. These last are called also *shôphĕtim*, "judgments." (See verse 4.)

(4) **Pharaoh shall not hearken unto you, that I may lay.**—Heb., *Pharaoh will not hearken unto you, and I will lay.* No relation of effect and cause is here asserted as existing between the two clauses, which are co-ordinate.

Mine armies, and my people. Rather, *my armies, my people.* The two expressions are in apposition—the second exegetical of the first.

Great judgments.—See the comment on chap. vi. 6.

(5) **The Egyptians shall know that I am the Lord.**—Heb., *that I am Jehovah: i.e.,* that I answer to my name—that I am the only really existing God, their so-called gods being "vapour, smoke, nothingness." No doubt this was one of the main lessons intended to be taught by the whole series of miraculous events connected with the Exodus. Egypt was the greatest monarchy in the whole world. She was now at the height of her glory. Among existent polytheisms, hers was the most famous; and her gods must have seemed, not only to herself, but to all the surrounding nations, the most powerful. To discredit them was to throw discredit upon polytheism generally, and to exalt the name of Jehovah above that of all the deities of the nations. (Comp. chap. xiv. 11—16.)

(6) **Moses and Aaron did as the Lord commanded them.**—The reluctance and resistance of Moses from this time ceased. He subdued his own will to God's, and gained the praise of being "faithful as a servant in all his house" (Heb. iii. 5). Aaron's obedience continued until Sinai was reached, but there failed before the frenzy of the people (chap. xxxii 1—6).

(7) **Moses was fourscore years old.**—Compare Deut. xxxiv. 7; Acts vii. 23, 30. The air of Egypt, and, probably, still more that of the desert, was favourable to longevity; and the Egyptian monuments show many cases of officials actively employed after they were a hundred years old.

(9) **Shew a miracle for you.**—Pharaoh had perhaps heard of the miracles wrought by Aaron before the people of Israel (chap. iv. 30), and was curious to be an eye-witness of one, as was Herod Antipas (Luke xxiii. 8). Or he may have thought that if Moses and Aaron "shewed a miracle," his own magicians would be able to show greater ones, and he would then dismiss the brothers as charlatans and impostors. He certainly did not intend to be influenced by any miracle which they might show, or to accept it as evidence that their message to him was a command from God.

Thy rod.—The rod is now called Aaron's, because Moses had entrusted him with it. (Comp. verse 19, and chap. viii. 5, 16, 17.)

A serpent.—Or, *a snake.* The word is not the same as that used in chap. iv. 3, but appears to be a synonym.

(11) **The magicians of Egypt.**—These persons are called indifferently *khăkâmim*, "wise men," *mĕkashshĕphim*, "mutterers of charms," and *khartummim*, "scribes," perhaps "writers of charms." Magic was very widely practised in Egypt, and consisted mainly in the composition and employment of charms, which were believed to exert a powerful effect, both over man and over the brute creation. A large part of the "Ritual of the Dead" consists of charms, which were to be uttered by the soul in Hades, in order to enable it

(12) For they cast down every man his rod, and they became serpents: but Aaron's rod swallowed up their rods.
(13) And he hardened Pharaoh's heart, that he hearkened not unto them; as the LORD had said.

(14) And the LORD said unto Moses, Pharaoh's heart *is* hardened, he refuseth to let the people go.
(15) Get thee unto Pharaoh in the morning; lo, he goeth out unto the water; and thou shalt stand by the river's brink against he come; and the rod which was turned to a serpent shalt thou take in thine hand.
(16) And thou shalt say unto him, The LORD God of the Hebrews hath sent me unto thee, saying, Let my people go, that they may serve me in the

---

to pass the various monsters which it would encounter there. Charms were also regarded as potent in this life to produce or remove disease, and avert the attacks of noxious animals. Some Egyptian works are mere collections of magical receipts, and supply strange prescriptions which are to be used, and mystic words which are to be uttered. A Jewish tradition, accepted by the Apostle Paul (2 Tim. iii. 6), spoke of two magicians as the special opponents of Moses, and called them "Jannes and Jambres." (See the Targums of Jerusalem and of Jonathan, and comp. Numen. *ap.* Euseb. *Præp. Ev.* ix. 8.) The former of these, Jannes, obtained fame as a magician among the classical writers, and is mentioned by Pliny (*H. N.* xxx. 1) and Apuleius (*Apolog.* p. 108). It has been supposed by some that the magicians were really in possession of supernatural powers, obtained by a connection with evil spirits; but, on the whole, it is perhaps most probable that they were merely persons acquainted with many secrets of nature not generally known, and trained in tricks of sleight-of-hand and conjuring.

They also did in like manner.—The magicians had entered into the royal presence with, apparently, rods in their hands, such as almost all Egyptians carried. These they cast down upon the ground, when they were seen to be serpents. This was, perhaps, the mere exhibition of a trick, well known to Egyptian serpent-charmers in all ages (*Description de l'Egypte*, vol. i. p. 159), by which a charmed serpent is made to look like a stick for a time, and then disenchanted. Or it may have been effected by sleight-of-hand, which seems to be the true meaning of the word *lĕhâtim*, translated "enchantments." (Rosenmüller, *Scholia in Exodum*, p. 110.)

(13) **He hardened Pharaoh's heart.**—This is a mis-translation. The verb is intransitive, and "Pharaoh's heart" is its nominative case. Translate, "Pharaoh's heart hardened itself." It is essential to the idea of a final *penal* hardening that in the earlier stages Pharaoh should have been left to himself.

That he hearkened not.—Heb., *and he hearkened not.*

As the Lord had said.—See above, chaps. iii. 19, vii. 4.

THE FIRST PLAGUE.

(14—21) *The water turned to blood.*—Moses had already been empowered to turn water into blood on a small scale (chap. iv. 9), and had exhibited his power before his own people (*ib.* ver. 30). But the present miracle is different. (1) It is to be done on the largest possible scale; (2) in the sight of all the Egyptians; and (3) not as a sign, but as a "judgment." All the Nile water—whether in the main river, or its branches, or the canals derived from it, or the pools formed by its inundation or by percolation through its banks, or in artificial reservoirs, including the tanks of wood or stone attached to houses (verse 19)—is to be "turned to blood:" *i.e.*, not merely turned of a red colour, either by admixture of earthy matter or of *Infusoriae*, but made to have all the qualities and appearance of blood, so as to become offensive, horrible, loathsome (verse 18). The judgment strikes the Egyptians two several blows. (1) It involves an insult to their religion, and brings it into discredit, since the Nile-god, Hapi, was a main object of worship, closely connected with Osiris, and even with Ammon, celebrated in hymns with the most extravagant titles of honour (*Records of the Past*, vol. iv. pp. 108—110), and a frequent object of public adoration in festivals. (2) It is a great physical affliction. They are accustomed to use the Nile water for drinking, for ablutions, for the washing of their clothes, and for culinary purposes; they have great difficulty in procuring any other; they delight in the Nile water, regard it as the best in the world, are in the habit of drinking deep draughts of it continually. This is all put a stop to. They suffer from thirst, from enforced uncleanliness, from the horror of blood all about them, even in their cisterns. Again, their fish are killed. Fish was one of their principal foods, perhaps the main food of the common people; and the river was the chief source whence the fish supply was obtained, for even the Lake Moeris was an off-shoot from the river (Herod. ii. 149). Their fish supply is stopped. The punishment is retaliatory: for as they had made the Nile the means of destroying Hebrew infants (chap. i. 22), so that Hebrew parents had loathed to drink of it, as though stained with the blood of their children, so is it now made by means of blood undrinkable for themselves. The plague lasts seven days (verse 25), a longer time than any other; and if not so destructive as the later ones, was perhaps of all the most nauseous and disgusting.

(15) **He goeth out unto the water.**—Perhaps to bathe, like the princess who saved Moses (chap. ii. 5), perhaps to inaugurate some festival in the river's honour. Of these the Egyptian calendar contained several.

The river's brink.—Heb., *the lip of the river.* (Comp. chap. ii. 3.)

(16) **The Lord God of the Hebrews.**—Heb., *Jehovah, the God of the Hebrews.* On the first application made to him by Moses and Aaron, Pharaoh had professed not to know who Jehovah was (chap. v. 2). To prevent his again doing so, Moses is ordered to give both name and title.

Hath sent me.—Rather, *sent me.*

Let my people go.—Comp. chap. v. 1. The reference is to Moses' first appearance before Pharaoh, and the message then delivered.

Thou wouldest not hear.—Rather, *thou hast not heard: i.e.*, thou hast not obeyed.

wilderness: and, behold, hitherto thou
wouldest not hear. (17) Thus saith the
LORD, In this thou shalt know that I
am the LORD: behold, I will smite with
the rod that *is* in mine hand upon the
waters which *are* in the river, and they
shall be turned to blood. (18) And the
fish that *is* in the river shall die, and
the river shall stink; and the Egyptians
shall lothe to drink of the water
of the river.

(19) And the LORD spake unto Moses,
Say unto Aaron, Take thy rod, and
stretch out thine hand upon the waters
of Egypt, upon their streams, upon their
rivers, and upon their ponds, and upon
all their [1] pools of water, that they may
become blood; and *that* there may be
blood throughout all the land of Egypt,
both in *vessels of* wood, and in *vessels of*
stone. (20) And Moses and Aaron did so,
as the LORD commanded; and he [a] lifted
up the rod, and smote the waters that
were in the river, in the sight of Pharaoh,
and in the sight of his servants;
and all the [b] waters that *were* in the
river were turned to blood. (21) And the
fish that *was* in the river died; and the
river stank, and the Egyptians could not
drink of the water of the river; and
there was blood throughout all the land
of Egypt. (22) [c] And the magicians of
Egypt did so with their enchantments:
and Pharaoh's heart was hardened,
neither did he hearken unto them; as
the LORD had said. (23) And Pharaoh

1 Heb., *gathering of their waters.*

a ch. 17. 5.

b Ps. 78. 44.

c Wis. 17. 7.

---

(17) **In this thou shalt know that I am the Lord.**—See the comment on verse 5.

The rod that is in my hand, *i.e.*, "in the hand of my servant." God is here represented as about to do that which was actually done by Aaron (verse 20). "*Qui facit per alium, facit per se.*"

(18) **The fish that is in the river shall die.**—The natural discoloration of the Nile, whether by red earth or by *Cryptogams* and *Infusoriæ*, has no pernicious effect at all upon the fish, nor is the water rendered by these discolorations at all unfit for use. The Nile naturally abounds with fish of various kinds; and though to Europeans they have, most of them, an insipid taste, yet, both in ancient and in modern times, the subsistence of the natives has been largely drawn from this source. It was a severe punishment to the Egyptians to be deprived of their fish supply. It was also implied contempt in regard of their religious worship, since at least three species of the Nile fish were sacred—the oxyrhincus, the lepidotus, and the phagrus, or eel. (Herod. ii. 72; Plut. *De Isid. et Osir.* vii. 18, 22.)

The river shall stink.—The Nile is said to have sometimes an offensive odour naturally; but the phenomenon is not marked, and can scarcely be that which is here alluded to, when the blood-like waters, laden with the bodies of putrid fish, caused a disgust and horror that were unspeakable.

(19) **The waters of Egypt** consist of the main stream of the Nile; its branches; canals derived from it; natural lakes, pools, or ponds, either left by the inundation or anticipative of it, being derived by percolation from the main stream; and artificial reservoirs of a larger or smaller size in gardens, courts, and houses. There is no other stream but the Nile in the whole country; and there are no natural springs, fountains, or brooks. Water may, however, at all times, and in all parts of the Nile Valley, be obtained by digging wells; but, as the soil is impregnated with nitre, the well water is highly unpalatable. It is generally allowed that the author of Exodus shows in the present verse, coupled with verse 24, a very exact knowledge of the Egyptian water system.

Vessels of wood, and vessels of stone.—It was usual to store the Nile water in tanks or cisterns within the houses, in order that it might deposit its sediment. These tanks or cisterns, which existed in all the houses of the better class, were either of wood or stone.

(20) **He lifted up the rod.**—"He" is, undoubtedly, Aaron. (See verse 19.)

In the sight of Pharaoh, and in the sight of his servants.—If the occasion was one of a Nile festival, Pharaoh would have "gone out to the water" (verse 15) accompanied by all the great officers of the Court, by a large body of the priests, and vast numbers of the people. If it was a mere occasion of bodily ablution, he would have had with him a pretty numerous train of attendants. In either case considerable publicity was given to the miracle, which was certainly not "done in a corner."

(21) **The Egyptians could not drink.**—Previously they had "lothed to drink" (verse 18), but apparently had drunk. Now they could do so no longer—the draught was too nauseous.

(22) **The magicians . . . did so with their enchantments.**—The act of the magicians must have been a very poor imitation of the action of Moses and Aaron. The two brothers had turned into blood all the waters of the river, the canals, the pools or lakes, and the reservoirs. The magicians could not act on this large scale. They could only operate, or seem to operate, on some small quantity of water, obtained probably in the way noticed in verse 24. On this they succeeded, so far as to satisfy Pharaoh, who was probably easy to satisfy, and perhaps so far as to satisfy the courtiers. They turned the liquid of a red colour, or by sleight-of-hand substituted blood for it. The result was subjected to no test, and was perhaps not even done in the presence of any hostile witness. But it enabled the king to harden himself, and refuse the request of the brothers.

(23) **Neither did he set his heart to this also.**—Heb., *Neither did he set his heart* (*i.e.*, pay attention) *even to this.* Pharaoh did not lay even this to heart. He passed it over as a slight matter, unworthy of much thought, and "turned, and went into his house." Probably care was taken to keep him constantly supplied with the well water, which, however brackish, would be sufficient for his customary ablutions. He drank, no doubt, a more generous liquid.

turned and went into his house, neither
did he set his heart to this also. (24) And
all the Egyptians digged round about
the river for water to drink; for they
could not drink of the water of the
river. (25) And seven days were ful-
filled, after that the LORD had smitten
the river.

CHAPTER VIII.—(1) And the LORD
spake unto Moses, Go unto Pharaoh,
and say unto him, Thus saith the LORD,
Let my people go, that they may serve
me. (2) And if thou refuse to let *them*
go, behold, I will smite all thy borders
with frogs: (3) and the river shall bring
forth frogs abundantly, which shall go
up and come into thine house, and into
thy bedchamber, and upon thy bed, and
into the house of thy servants, and upon
thy people, and into thine ovens, and
into thy [1] kneadingtroughs: (4) and the
frogs shall come up both on thee, and
upon thy people, and upon all thy ser-
vants.

(5) And the LORD spake unto Moses,
Say unto Aaron, Stretch forth thine
hand with thy rod over the streams,
over the rivers, and over the ponds, and
cause frogs to come up upon the land of
Egypt. (6) And Aaron stretched out his
hand over the waters of Egypt; and the
frogs came up, and covered the land of
Egypt.

[1] Or, *dough*.

---

(24) **All the Egyptians digged round about the river.**—Wells may be sunk in any part of the alluvium, and will always yield water, which is, however, brackish and unpalatable. This water is, no doubt, derived by percolation from the river; but the percolation is a slow process, and blood would scarcely percolate far. The water obtained was probably in the ground before the miracle took place, and was not made subject to it.

(25) **And seven days were fulfilled.**—These words seem to mark the duration of the first plague, which was the longer because Pharaoh made no submission at all in consequence of it. Obtaining sufficient water for his own purposes (see the comment on verse 23), he thought little of its continuance.

VIII.

THE SECOND PLAGUE.

(1–4) It is generally allowed that the second plague was one of frogs. All the ancient versions agree in the interpretation; and the only rival rendering—"crocodiles"—is too absurd to be argued against. We may take it, therefore, as certain that the second infliction upon Egypt was an innumerable multitude of frogs, which came up out of the river, and infested the cities, the houses, the sleeping apartments, the beds, the ovens, and the kneading-troughs. There was no escaping them. They entered the royal palace no less than the peasant's cottage; they penetrated to the inner chambers; they leaped upon the couches and beds; they polluted the baking utensils, and defiled the water and the food. Here, again, the infliction was double. (1) Frogs were sacred animals to the Egyptians, who regarded them as symbols of procreative power, and associated them especially with the goddess Heka (a wife of Kneph, or Num), whom they represented as frog-headed. Sacred animals might not be intentionally killed; and even their involuntary slaughter was not unfrequently punished with death. To be plagued with a multitude of reptiles which might not be put to death, yet on which it was scarcely possible not to tread, and which, whenever a door was opened were crushed, was a severe trial to the religious feelings of the people, and tended to bring the religion itself into contempt. (2) The visitation was horrible to the senses—nauseous, disgusting. The frogs were hideous to the eye, grating to the ear, repulsive to the touch. Their constant presence everywhere rendered them a continual torment. If other later plagues were more injurious, the plague of frogs was perhaps of all the most loathsome. We read without surprise in Eustathius (*Comment. in Hom. Il.*, p. 35) that the people of Pæonia and Dardania on one occasion, were so plagued by a multitude of frogs, which filled the houses and the streets, infected the water, invaded the cooking utensils, and made all the food uneatable, that after a time, being unable to bear the pest any longer, they "fled from that region altogether."

(1) **Let my people go.**—The usual demand, which it was determined to reiterate until Pharaoh yielded. (See chaps. v. 1, vii. 16, viii. 20, ix. 1—13, x. 3.)

(2) **With frogs.**—The particular species intended is thought to be the modern *dofka* (Rana Mosaica), which is a large kind, resembling our toad, which crawls more than it leaps, and croaks perpetually.

(3) **The river shall bring forth frogs.**—The frogs do not now come up directly out of the river, but rather out of the ponds and marshes which are left by the inundation. (See verse 5.) These, however, may be viewed as detached portions of the river. Frogs in Egypt are, even at the present day, an occasional annoyance and inconvenience.

Thy bedchamber . . . thy bed.—No nation of antiquity set such a value on cleanliness as the Egyptians. Priests were required to dress entirely in linen, and to wash their entire bodies in cold water twice every day and twice every night (Herod. ii. 37). With other classes ablutions were frequent, and the utmost care was taken to avoid contact with whatever was uncleanly. It is difficult to conceive a greater annoyance to an Egyptian than frogs in the bedchamber and on the bed.

Ovens.—Or, *baking-pans*—earthenware vessels commonly heated by having a fire lighted inside them, and the dough attached by pressure after the fire had been withdrawn.

Kneading troughs.—Comp. below, chap. xii. 34, which fixes the sense; and for representations of both kneading-troughs and ovens, see Rosellini, *Monumenti Civili*, pls. 84, 85.

(6) **The frogs came up.**—Hebrew, *the frog.* The term designates the species.

(7) [a]And the magicians did so with their
enchantments, and brought up frogs
upon the land of Egypt.
(8) Then Pharaoh called for Moses and
Aaron, and said, Intreat the LORD, that
he may take away the frogs from me,
and from my people; and I will let the
people go, that they may do sacrifice
unto the LORD. (9) And Moses said unto
Pharaoh, [1]Glory over me: [2]when shall
I entreat for thee, and for thy servants,
and for thy people, [3]to destroy the frogs
from thee and thy houses, *that* they may
remain in the river only? (10) And he said,
[4]To morrow. And he said, *Be it* accord-
ing to thy word: that thou mayest
know that *there is* none like unto the
LORD our God. (11) And the frogs shall
depart from thee, and from thy houses,
and from thy servants, and from thy
people; they shall remain in the river
only.
(12) And Moses and Aaron went out
from Pharaoh: and Moses cried unto
the LORD because of the frogs which he
had brought against Pharaoh. (13) And
the LORD did according to the word of
Moses; and the frogs died out of the
houses, out of the villages, and out of
the fields. (14) And they gathered them
together upon heaps: and the land
stank. (15) But when Pharaoh saw that
there was respite, he hardened his heart,
and hearkened not unto them; as the
LORD had said.
(16) And the LORD said unto Moses,
Say unto Aaron, Stretch out thy rod,
and smite the dust of the land, that it

a Wis. 17. 7.

1 Or, *Have this honour over me, &c.*

2 Or, *against when.*

3 Heb., *to cut off.*

4 Or, *Against to-morrow.*

---

(7) **The magicians did so.**—It cannot be concluded from this that the magicians had the power of creating frogs. All that the writer means to express is, that they *seemed* to Pharaoh and to the Court to do on a small scale what Moses and Aaron had done on the largest possible scale. The means which they employed was probably sleight-of-hand. It has been well observed that they would have shown their own power and the power of their gods far more satisfactorily had they succeeded in taking the frogs away.

(8) **Pharaoh called for Moses.**—This was the first sign of yielding. Pharaoh had borne the infliction of the water turned to blood without flinching, probably because individually he had suffered but little from it. (See the comment on chap. vii. 23.) But he suffered from the frogs as much as any one else (verses 3, 4); and the personal inconvenience drove him to make a concession. As far as words could go, the concession was complete. (1) He acknowledged the power of Jehovah ("Intreat the Lord, that *He* may take away, &c."); (2) he acknowledged the power of righteous men's prayers; (3) he made an absolute unreserved promise to "let the people go."

(9) **And Moses said . . . Glory over me.**—This phrase seems equivalent to—"I submit to thy will," "I am content to do thy bidding." It was probably an ordinary expression of courtesy in Egypt on the part of an inferior to a superior; but it was not a Hebrew idiom, and so does not occur elsewhere.

When shall I intreat?—Rather, as in the margin, *against when?* or *for when?*—*i.e.*, what date shall I fix in my prayer to God as that at which the plague shall be removed? And so, in the next verse, for "to-morrow" translate *against to-morrow.* It seems strange that Pharaoh did not say, "To-day, this very instant;" but perhaps he thought even Jehovah could not do so great a thing at once.

(10) **That thou mayest know.**—Comp. chap. vii. 5, 17. Moses is not content that Pharaoh should simply acknowledge Jehovah as he had done (verse 8), but wishes him to be convinced that no other god can compare with Him.

(13, 14) **The frogs died.**—God, who knew the heart of Pharaoh, and its insincerity, or at any rate its changefulness, took the plague of frogs away in a manner that made its removal almost as bad as its continuance. The frogs did not return into the river; neither were they devoured by flights of cranes or ibises. They simply died—died where they were—in thousands and tens of thousands, so that they had to be "gathered upon heaps." And "the land stank." In the great plague of frogs mentioned by Eustathius (see the comment on verses 1—4) it was the stench of the frogs after they were dead which caused the people to quit their country.

(15) **When Pharaoh saw that there was respite.**—Hebrew, *a breathing space.*

He hardened his heart.—Hitherto Pharaoh's nature had not been impressed; his heart had remained dull, callous, hard. Now an impression had been made (verse 8), and he must have yielded, if he had not called in his own will to efface it. Herein was his great guilt. (See the comment on chap. iv. 21.)

THE THIRD PLAGUE.

(16, 17) It is disputed whether this plague was one of lice or of mosquitoes. Josephus and the Jewish commentators generally take the former view, while the latter is supported by the LXX. and Vulgate, by the authorities of Philo, Artapanus, Origen, and St. Augustine in ancient, and by those of Rosenmüller, Michaelis, Œdmann, Gesenius, Keil, and Kalisch in modern times. The word used (*kinnim*) seems connected with the Greek κίνιψ, or κώνωψ, and is reasonably regarded as formed by *onomatopœia*, from the sharp tingling sound given out by the insect when on the wing.* The trouble caused to the Egyptians of the Delta by mosquitoes is noticed by Herodotus (ii. 95); while moderns, as Forskal (*Descript. Anim.* p. 85), declare that they amount to an absolute pest at certain seasons. They are most troublesome towards October, and are said to attack not only the exposed parts of the skin, but especially the ears, the nostrils, and the eyes, where they do great damage. Some have thought that mosquitoes do not molest cattle (verse 17); but Kalisch says, "They molest *especially* beasts, as oxen and horses, flying into their eyes and nostrils, driving them to madness

* In Egyptian the word for "mosquito" is *Khnemms* (Brugsch, *Dict. Hierogl.* p. 1103).

may become lice throughout all the land
of Egypt. (17) And they did so; for
Aaron stretched out his hand with his
rod, and smote the dust of the earth,
and it became lice in man, and in beast;
all the dust of the land became lice
throughout all the land of Egypt.
(18) And the magicians did so with their
enchantments to bring forth lice, but
they could not: so there were lice upon
man, and upon beast. (19) Then the
magicians said unto Pharaoh, This *is*
the finger of God: and Pharaoh's heart
was hardened, and he hearkened not
unto them; as the LORD had said.
(20) And the LORD said unto Moses,
Rise up early in the morning, and stand
before Pharaoh; lo, he cometh forth to
the water; and say unto him, Thus saith
the LORD, Let my people go, that they
may serve me. (21) Else, if thou wilt not
let my people go, behold, I will send
[1]swarms *of flies* upon thee, and upon thy
servants, and upon thy people, and into
thy houses: and the houses of the Egyptians shall be full of swarms *of flies*, and
also the ground whereon they *are*.
(22) And I will sever in that day the land
of Goshen, in which my people dwell,
that no swarms *of flies* shall be there;
to the end thou mayest know that I *am*
the LORD in the midst of the earth.

[1] Or, *a mixture of noisome beasts, &c.*

---

and fury, and sometimes even torturing them to death."

It is to be noticed that the third plague, whatever it was, came without warning. It was God's judgment on Pharaoh for hardening his heart and breaking his promise (verse 15); and he was not given the option of avoiding it by submission to God's will.

(16) **Smite the dust of the land.**—Dust prevails in Egypt to an extent that is highly inconvenient. "We travelled to Ashmim," says one writer, "through clouds of dust, raised by a high wind, which intercepted our view as much as if we had been travelling in a fog." "There is one great source of discomfort," says another, "arising from the dryness of the atmosphere, namely, an excessive quantity of dust." When "all the dust of the land became mosquitoes" (verse 17), the plague must indeed have been great.

(18) **The magicians did so**—*i.e.*, tried to do so—took moist earth, and dried it, and pulverised it, and tried the effect of their magic charms upon it, but failed to produce mosquitoes, as Aaron had done. Mosquitoes were things too delicate to be caught, and manipulated, and produced at a given moment by sleight-of-hand. The magicians tried to produce a counterfeit of the miracle, but could not. Then they excused themselves to their master with the words, "This is the finger of a god."

(19) **The finger of God.**—Rather, *of a god.* The magicians meant to say, "This is beyond the power of man: it is supernatural; some god must be helping Moses and Aaron." They did not mean to profess a belief in One God.

Pharaoh's heart was hardened.—The mosquitoes did not impress Pharaoh as the frogs had done (verses 8—15). His heart remained hard. He had no need to harden it by an act of his will. Probably the visitation affected him but little, since he would possess mosquito curtains, and could inhabit the loftier parts of his palace, which would be above the height whereto the mosquito ascends (Herod. ii. 95).

THE FOURTH PLAGUE.

(20, 21) There is, again, a doubt as to the nature of the fourth plague. In the original it is called the plague of "the *'arôb*," which is used throughout in the singular number. The LXX. translate *ha-'arob* by "the dog-fly" (ἡ κυνόμυια). The Jewish commentators connect the word with the root *'ereb* or *'arab*, and suppose it to designate either a mixed multitude of all kinds of wild beasts (Josephus and Jonathan), or a mixture of all sorts of insects (Aquila, &c.). Moderns generally agree with the LXX. that a definite species of animal—probably an insect—is meant, but doubt about the particular creature. The dog-fly, it is said (*Musca canina*), is not a pest in houses, as the *'arôb* was (verses 21, 24), nor does it do any damage to the land (verse 24). It is therefore suggested that the plague was really one of the kakerlaque, a kind of beetle, which is injurious both to the persons of men, to the furniture and fittings of houses, and to the crops in the fields. It is in favour of the kakerlaque that, like all beetles, it was sacred, and might not be destroyed, being emblematic of the sun-god, Ra, especially in his form of Khepra, or "the creator." Egyptians were obliged to submit to such a plague without attempting to diminish it, and would naturally view the infliction as a sign that the sun-god was angry with them. They would also suffer grievously in person, for the kakerlaque "inflicts very painful bites with its jaws" (Kalisch); and they would begin for the first time to suffer in their property, which neither the frogs nor the mosquitoes had damaged. The plague was thus—if one of the kakerlaque—an advance on previous plagues, and if less disgusting than some others, was far more injurious.

(20) **Early in the morning.**—Comp. chap. vii. 15; and on the early habits of an Egyptian king, see Herod. ii. 172.

He cometh forth to the water.—It is conjectured that this was on the occasion of the great autumn festival, when, after the retirement of the Nile within its banks, and the scattering of the grain upon the fresh deposit of mud, the first blades of corn began to appear. It is not improbable that Khepra, "the creator," was then especially worshipped.

(21) **Swarms of flies.**—Heb., *the 'arôb.* Comp. "the frog" (verse 13), and "the mosquito" (*ha-kinnim*) in verse 17. On the species intended, see the comment on verses 20, 21.

(22) **I will sever in that day the land of Goshen.**—This was a new feature, and one calculated to make a deep impression both on king and people. The "land of Goshen" can only have been some portion of the Eastern Delta, a tract in nowise different from the rest of Egypt—low, flat, well-watered, fertile. Nature had put no severance between it and the regions where the Egyptians dwelt; so the severance to be made would be a manifest miracle.

(23) And I will put [1] a division between
my people and thy people: [2] to morrow
shall this sign be. (24) And the LORD
did so; and [a] there came a grievous
swarm *of flies* into the house of Pha-
raoh, and *into* his servants' houses, and
into all the land of Egypt: the land was
[3] corrupted by reason of the swarm *of*
flies.

(25) And Pharaoh called for Moses and
for Aaron, and said, Go ye, sacrifice to
your God in the land. (26) And Moses
said, It is not meet so to do; for we
shall sacrifice the abomination of the
Egyptians to the LORD our God: lo,
shall we sacrifice the abomination of
the Egyptians before their eyes, and
will they not stone us? (27) We will go
three days' journey into the wilderness,
and sacrifice to the LORD our God, as
[b] he shall command us. (28) And Pha-
raoh said, I will let you go, that ye may
sacrifice to the LORD your God in the
wilderness; only ye shall not go very
far away: intreat for me. (29) And
Moses said, Behold, I go out from thee,
and I will intreat the LORD that the
swarms *of flies* may depart from Pha-
raoh, from his servants, and from his
people, to morrow: but let not Pharaoh
deal deceitfully any more in not letting
the people go to sacrifice to the LORD.

(30) And Moses went out from Pha-
raoh, and intreated the LORD. (31) And
the LORD did according to the word of
Moses; and he removed the swarms *of*
flies from Pharaoh, from his servants,
and from his people; there remained

1 Heb., *a redemption.*
2 Or, *by to morrow.*
a Wis. 16. 9.
3 Or, *destroyed.*
b ch. 3. 18.

(24) **The land was corrupted.**—Rather, as in the margin, *destroyed.* Kalisch observes, "These insects"—*i.e.,* the kakerlaque (*Blatta Orientalis*), "really fill the land, and molest men and beasts; they consume all sorts of materials, *devastate the country,* and are in so far more detrimental than the gnats, as they destroy also the property of the Egyptians."

(25) **Pharaoh called for Moses.**—Pharaoh suffered from the kakerlaque equally with his subjects, or rather, *more* than his subjects. It was "upon him," inflicting its painful bites (verse 21); it was "upon his palaces" (verse 21), destroying his rich and magnificent furniture; it was upon his lands, ravaging and devastating them (verse 24). He therefore gave way before this plague almost at once, and without waiting for any remonstrance on the part of the magicians or others, "called for Moses."

In the land.—Pretending to grant the request made of him, Pharaoh mars all by this little clause. A three days' journey into the wilderness had been demanded from the first (chap. v. 3), and no less could be accepted.

(26) **It is not meet so to do.**—Pressed to remain "in the land," and sacrifice, Moses deemed it right to explain to the king why this was impossible. The Israelites would have to "sacrifice the abomination of the Egyptians"—*i.e.,* animals of which the Egyptians abominated the killing; and if they did this in the presence of Egyptians, a riot would be certain to break out—perhaps a civil war would ensue. The animal-worship of the Egyptians is a certain, and generally recognised, fact. It seemed to the Greeks and Romans the most striking characteristic of the Egyptian religion. (See Herod. ii. 65—76; Diod. Sic. i. 82—84; Cic. *De Nat. Deor.* i. 36; &c.) The sacrificial animals of the Hebrews—sheep, goats, and cattle—were all of them sacred animals, either to the Egyptians generally, or to the inhabitants of certain districts. A Theban could not endure the sacrifice of a sheep, nor a Mendesian that of a goat (Herod. ii. 42). White cows and heifers—perhaps cows and heifers generally—were sacred to Isis-Athor. Any bull-calf might be an Apis; and it could not be known whether he was Apis or not till the priests had examined him (Herod. iii. 28). The extent to which the Egyptians carried their rage when a sacred animal was killed in their presence is illustrated by many facts in history. On one occasion a Roman ambassador, who had accidentally killed a cat, was torn to pieces by the populace (Diod. Sic. i. 83). On another, war broke out between the Oxyrinchites and the Cynopolites, because the latter had eaten one of the fish considered sacred by the former (Plutarch, *De Isid. et Osir.* § 44). The fear of Moses was thus not at all groundless.

Will they not stone us?—This is the first mention of "stoning" in Scripture or elsewhere. It was not a legalised Egyptian punishment; but probably it was everywhere one of the earliest, as it would be one of the simplest, modes of wreaking popular vengeance. Æschylus mentions it (*Sept. c. Th.* 183), also Herodotus (v. 38). It was known in ancient Persia (Ctes. *Fr.* 50).

(27) **As he shall command us.**—Comp. chap. x. 26—"We know not with what we must serve the Lord, until we come thither."

(29) **And Moses said, Behold . . . I will intreat the Lord.**—Moses accepted Pharaoh's second promise, and took no special exception to its condition—"only ye shall not go very far away." He had distinctly stated his own demand, which was for "a three days' journey into the wilderness" (chaps. v. 3, viii. 27). It was for Pharaoh to settle with himself whether he considered that distance "very far" or not. As he made no clear objection to the distance, Moses was bound to suppose that he allowed it.

Let not Pharaoh deal deceitfully any more.—God's servants must rebuke even kings when they openly break the moral law (1 Sam. xiii. 13, xv. 16—23; 2 Sam. xii. 7—12; 1 Kings xxi. 20—22; Matt. xiv. 4, &c.). Pharaoh had promised unconditionally to let the people go if the frogs were removed (verse 8), and had then flagrantly broken his word. Moses was right to rebuke his "deceit."

(31) **There remained not one.**—The sudden and entire removal of a plague like this at the word of Moses was almost as great a miracle as its sudden coming at his word, and is therefore, when it happened, carefully recorded. (See chap. x. 19.) It seems not to have happened with the frogs (verses 11—13) or with the mosquitoes.

not one. (32) And Pharaoh hardened
his heart at this time also, neither would
he let the people go.

CHAPTER IX.—(1) Then the LORD
said unto Moses, Go in unto Pharaoh,
and tell him, Thus saith the LORD God
of the Hebrews, Let my people go, that
they may serve me. (2) For if thou re-
fuse to let *them* go, and wilt hold them
still, (3) behold, the hand of the LORD
is upon thy cattle which *is* in the field,
upon the horses, upon the asses, upon
the camels, upon the oxen, and upon
the sheep: *there shall be* a very grievous
murrain. (4) And the LORD shall sever
between the cattle of Israel and the
cattle of Egypt: and there shall nothing
die of all *that is* the children's of Israel.
(5) And the LORD appointed a set time,
saying, To morrow the LORD shall do
this thing in the land. (6) And the
LORD did that thing on the morrow,
and all the cattle of Egypt died: but
of the cattle of the children of Israel
died not one. (7) And Pharaoh sent,
and, behold, there was not one of the
cattle of the Israelites dead. And the
heart of Pharaoh was hardened, and he
did not let the people go.

(8) And the LORD said unto Moses and
unto Aaron, Take to you handfuls of
ashes of the furnace, and let Moses
sprinkle it toward the heaven in the

---

(32) **Pharaoh hardened his heart at this time also.**—Comp. verse 15. Again, it is after being impressed, and partially relenting, that Pharaoh hardens his own heart.

IX.

THE FIFTH PLAGUE.

(1—3) The nature of the fifth plague is manifest, and admits of no dispute. It was a *rinderpest*, or murrain upon cattle; which, however, unlike most similar disorders, attacked *the greater number* of the domesticated animals—horses, asses, camels, oxen, and sheep. Thus it was "very grievous" (verse 3). Horses were highly prized by the Egyptians, and were a comparatively recent importation, having been unknown before the time of the seventeenth, or "Shepherd" Dynasty. They were at first used only in war; then by rich men, in peace, to draw their chariots. They had now, however, it would seem, come to be employed also in agriculture. (Note the words "in the field.") Asses were the ordinary beasts of burthen, and abounded in Egypt anciently—as indeed they do at the present day. The Egyptian monuments mention cases where a single landowner owned as many as seven or eight hundred of them. Camels are not represented by the Egyptian sculptors, but are mentioned in the inscriptions (Chabas, *Etudes sur l'Antiquité Historique*, pp. 400—413), and must have been employed in the trade between Egypt and the Sinaitic peninsula. Both oxen and sheep were numerous, and constituted a great part of the wealth of individuals. The plague fell upon such animals as were "in the field" at the time—*i.e.*, in the open air, and not confined in stables or sheds. It was the Egyptian practice to house a considerable portion of their cattle; but at the probable season of this plague—December or January—the majority would be in the pastures. Thus the Egyptian losses were very heavy, and the king, no doubt, suffered with the rest, for the Egyptian monarchs were large cattle-owners (Gen. xlvii. 6, 17). The Pharaoh was, however, less impressed by this plague than by the fourth, and made no sign of submission.

(4) **The Lord shall sever.**—Comp. chap. viii. 22. Apparently Israel had been subjected to the first, second, and third plagues, which caused annoyance only, and not loss. Their exemption began with the fourth plague, and then probably continued without intermission, though it is not always mentioned.

(5) **The Lord appointed a set time.**—As murrain is not uncommon in Egypt, especially in the Delta, and the coming affliction might therefore be ascribed by the Egyptians to natural causes, God took care to mark its miraculous character (1) by appointing a time; (2) by exempting the cattle of Israel; (3) by making the disease fatal to *all* the cattle of the Egyptians that were left "in the field."

To morrow.—The delay allowed any Egyptians who believed Moses to save their cattle by housing them.

(7) **Pharaoh sent.**—The Pharaoh evidently did not believe it possible that there should be such a widespread destruction of the Egyptian cattle without the Hebrew cattle suffering at all. He therefore sent persons to inquire and report on the facts. These persons found the announcement of Moses fulfilled to the letter. This was the more surprising, as Goshen consisted mainly of the low flat tract bordering on the Menzaleh marshes.

The heart of Pharaoh was hardened.—Even the exact correspondence of the result with the announcement did not soften the heart of the king. It remained dull and unimpressed—literally, "heavy" (*kâbêd*). Loss of property would not much distress an absolute monarch, who could easily exact the value of what he had lost from his subjects.

THE SIXTH PLAGUE.

(8—10) Here, again, there is little question of what the plague was. Doubts may be entertained as to its exact character, and its proper medical designation, but all agree, and cannot but agree, that it was a visitation of the bodies of men with a severe cutaneous disorder, accompanied by pustules or ulcers. It was not announced beforehand to the Egyptians, nor were they allowed the opportunity of escaping it. Like the third plague, it was altogether of the nature of a judgment; and the judgment was a severe one. Now, for the first time, was acute suffering inflicted on the persons of men; now, for the first time, was it shown how Jehovah could smite with a terrible disease; and if with a disease, why not with death? No doubt those stricken suffered unequally; but with some the affliction may have resembled the final affliction of Job, when he was

sight of Pharaoh. (9) And it shall be-
come small dust in all the land of Egypt,
and shall be a boil breaking forth *with*
blains upon man, and upon beast,
throughout all the land of Egypt.
(10) And they took ashes of the furnace,
and stood before Pharaoh; and Moses
sprinkled it up toward heaven; and it
became a boil breaking forth *with* blains
upon man, and upon beast. (11) And the
magicians could not stand before Moses
because of the boils; for the boil was
upon the magicians, and upon all the
Egyptians. (12) And the LORD hardened
the heart of Pharaoh, and he hearkened
not unto them; [a] as the LORD had spoken
unto Moses.
(13) And the LORD said unto Moses,
Rise up early in the morning, and stand
before Pharaoh, and say unto him, Thus
saith the LORD God of the Hebrews,
Let my people go, that they may serve
me. (14) For I will at this time send all
my plagues upon thine heart, and upon
thy servants, and upon thy people; that
thou mayest know that *there is* none

[a] ch. 4. 21.

smitten with "sore boils from the sole of his foot unto his crown" (Job ii. 7). Its severity is marked by the statement that "the magicians could not stand before Moses because of the boils" (verse 11). And it was universal, or quasi-universal (verse 11). Moreover, it was not confined to men; it was also "upon the beasts"—*i.e.*, upon such of the domesticated animals as had escaped the preceding plague. It does not, however, seem to have been fatal; and it wrought no change upon the Pharaoh, whose heart God is now, for the first time, said to have hardened (verse 12), as He had declared to Moses (chaps. iv. 21, vii. 3).

(8) **Ashes of the furnace.**—Furnaces in Egypt were either for the melting of metal, the preparing of lime, or the baking of bricks. It was probably from a furnace of this last kind that the ashes were now taken. Much of Goshen had been converted into a brick-field (chaps. i. 14, v. 7—13); and though most of the bricks made would be simply dried in the sun, a portion would be subjected to artificial heat in brick-kilns. When ashes from one of these kilns were made the germs of a disease that was a sore infliction, their own wrong-doing became to the Egyptians a whip wherewith God scourged them.

(10) **Moses sprinkled it up toward heaven.**—Presenting it, as it were, to God, in evidence of His people's wrongs.

A boil breaking forth with blains.—Heb., *an inflammation, producing pustules.* Diseases of this character are not uncommon in Egypt (comp. Deut. xxviii. 27), but they are not often very severe; nor do they attack indifferently man and beast. The miraculous character of the plague was shown (1) by its being announced beforehand; (2) by its severity (verse 11); (3) by its universality (verse 11); and 4) by its extension to animals.

(11) **The magicians could not stand before Moses.**—It is uncertain whether the magicians were present accidentally, or had come for the express purpose of "withstanding Moses" (2 Tim. iii. 8). The latter may be suspected, as the plague was made to fall with special violence upon them.

(12) **The Lord hardened the heart of Pharaoh.**—The judicial punitive hardening of Pharaoh's heart by God Himself now began. As with the heathen in later times, "because they did not like to retain God in their knowledge, God gave them over to a reprobate mind" (Rom. i. 28), so now with Pharaoh: because he had twice hardened himself—*i.e.*, resisted an impression made upon him, and crushed his inclination to yield to it (chap. viii. 15, 32), God hardened him. (See the comment on chap. iv. 21.)

THE SEVENTH PLAGUE.

(13-19) The plagues fall into triads, or groups of three. This is the first plague of the third group, and presents to us several new features. (1) It is ushered in with an unusually long and exceeding awful message (verses 13—19), in which Pharaoh is warned that God is now about to "send *all* His plagues *upon his heart,*" and that he has been raised up simply that God may show forth His power in his person. (2) It is the first plague that attacks human life; and this it does upon a large scale: all those exposed to it perish (verse 19). (3) It is more destructive than any previous plague to property. It not only slays cattle, like the murrain, but destroys plants and trees (verse 25), and ruins half the harvest (verse 31). (4) It is accompanied with terrible demonstrations—"mighty thunderings," huge hailstones, rain, and fire that "runs along upon the ground" (verse 23). (5) It is made to test the degree of faith to which the Egyptians have attained, by means of a revelation of the way whereby it may be escaped (verse 20). Though the plagues do not form a regularly ascending series, each transcending the last, yet there is a certain progression observable. The earlier ones cause annoyance rather than injury; those which follow cause loss of property; then God's hand is laid on men's persons, so as to hurt, but not to kill; lastly, life itself is attacked. The seventh plague was peculiarly astonishing and alarming to the Egyptians, because hail and thunder, even rain, were rare phenomena in their country; and a thunderstorm accompanied by such features as characterised this one was absolutely unknown. The hailstones must have been of an enormous size and weight to kill men and cattle. The "fire infolding itself amid the hail" must indicate a very unusual form of the electric fluid. It is not surprising that the visitation brought down the pride of Pharaoh more than any preceding one, and made him for the time consent unconditionally to the people's departure (verse 28).

(13) **Early in the morning.**—Comp. chaps. vii. 15, viii. 20.

(14) **I will . . . send all my plagues upon thine heart.**—The naturally obdurate heart of Pharaoh, which he had further indurated by his own voluntary action (chap. viii. 15, 32), and which God had begun to harden penally (verse 12), was now to be softened by a repetition of blow after blow, until it should finally succumb, and yield, and humble itself under the mighty hand of God, and consent to the departure of the whole people, with flocks, and herds, and "little ones."

like me in all the earth. (15) For now I
will stretch out my hand, that I may
smite thee and thy people with pesti-
lence; and thou shalt be cut off from
the earth. (16) And in very deed for
[a]this *cause* have I [1]raised thee up, for
to shew *in* thee my power; and that
my name may be declared throughout
all the earth. (17) As yet exaltest thou
thyself against my people, that thou
wilt not let them go? (18) Behold, to
morrow about this time I will cause it
to rain a very grievous hail, such as
hath not been in Egypt since the foun-
dation thereof even until now. (19) Send
therefore now, *and* gather thy cattle,
and all that thou hast in the field; *for*
upon every man and beast which shall
be found in the field, and shall not be
brought home, the hail shall come down
upon them, and they shall die.
(20) He that feared the word of the
LORD among the servants of Pharaoh
made his servants and his cattle flee
into the houses: (21) and he that [2]re-
garded not the word of the LORD left
his servants and his cattle in the field.
(22) And the LORD said unto Moses,
Stretch forth thine hand toward heaven,
that there may be hail in all the land of
Egypt, upon man, and upon beast, and
upon every herb of the field, throughout
the land of Egypt. (23) And Moses
stretched forth his rod toward heaven:
and the LORD sent thunder and hail, and
the fire ran along upon the ground;
and the LORD rained hail upon the land
of Egypt. (24) So there was hail, and
fire mingled with the hail, very grievous,
such as there was none like it in all the
land of Egypt since it became a nation.
(25) And the hail smote throughout all the
land of Egypt all that *was* in the field,
both man and beast; and the hail smote
every herb of the field, and brake every
tree of the field. (26) Only in the land of

a Rom. 9. 17.

1 Heb., *made thee stand.*

2 Heb., *set not his heart unto.*

---

(15) **For now I will stretch out my hand.**—The words admit of this translation, but the context will not allow it. Translate—*And now I might have stretched out mine hand, and smitten both thee and thy people with pestilence; and then thou hadst been cut off from the earth; but, &c.*

(16) **And in very deed for this cause have I raised thee up.**—Rather, *but truly on this account have I made thee stand—i.e.*, kept thee alive, not for thy deserts, not even in pity, but only "for to show in thee My power." Thou hast provoked Me so that long since thou wouldst have been "cut off from the earth," only that My glory will be the more shown forth by thy continuance in life, and by the further plagues and punishments whereto thou wilt be subjected.

That my name may be declared.—Comp. chaps. xiv. 17, xv. 14—16, &c.

(17) **As yet exaltest thou thyself?**—Heb., *Dost thou still exalt*, or *oppose, thyself against My people?* —*i.e.*, Art thou not tired of the contest? Dost thou still, in thy folly, continue it?

(18) **Such as hath not been in Egypt since the foundation thereof.**—Rain, and even hail, are not unknown at the present day in Lower Egypt, though they are, comparatively speaking, rare phenomena. Thunderstorms are especially uncommon, and when they occur are for the most part mild and harmless. A thunderstorm which killed a man in Thevenot's time (*Voyages*, vol. i., p. 344) was regarded as most extraordinary, and "spread universal consternation." There is hail from time to time between November and March; but it very seldom does any considerable damage.

(19) **Gather thy cattle.**—The peculiar circumstances of Egypt, where the whole country was overflowed by the Nile during some months of each year, caused the provision of shelter for cattle to be abnormally great. Every year, at the time of the inundation, all the cattle had to be "gathered" into sheds and cattle-yards in the immediate vicinity of the villages and towns, which were protected from the inundation by high mounds. Thus it would have been easy to house all the cattle that remained to the Egyptians after the murrain, if the warning here given had been attended to generally.

(20, 21) **He that feared . . .**—*Some* impression, we see, had been made by the preceding plagues, and the warning was taken to some extent; but it was otherwise with many. So in Gospel times, "Some believed the things which were spoken, and some believed not" (Acts xxviii. 24). The result was death, both to the cattle and their keepers (verse 19). (Comp. Josh. x. 11.)

(22) **Upon every herb of the field.**—The damage that hail can do to crops is well known, and has given rise among ourselves to a special form of insurance. Such a storm as that here described would necessarily have destroyed all vegetation that was more than a few inches high, and must have greatly injured shrubs and fruit-trees. (See verses 25, 31.)

(23) **The fire ran along upon the ground.**—Heb., *fire walked earthwards.* Kalisch and Knobel understand by this mere ordinary lightning, but Aben-Ezra, Canon Cook, and others think that the phenomenon was such as our Version well expresses. There is no doubt that the electric fluid occasionally takes a form which has something of permanency, continuing several seconds, or even minutes, either stationary or with a slow motion. Appearances of this kind have been called "fire-balls," and indicate an excessive electrical disturbance, involving great peril to life and property. If the expression "fire walked earthwards" does not imply anything of this kind, yet the peculiar phrase of verse 24 would seem to do so.

(24) **Fire mingled with the hail.**—Heb., *a fire infolding itself in the midst of the hail.* (Comp. Ezek. i. 4; and see the comment on verse 23.)

(25) **The hail . . . brake every tree of the field.**—What is meant is, not that the hail "brake the mightiest trees to fragments" (Millington, *Plagues of Egypt*, p. 135), but that it broke off the small boughs

Goshen, where the children of Israel
were, was there no hail.
(27) And Pharaoh sent, and called for
Moses and Aaron, and said unto them,
I have sinned this time: the LORD *is*
righteous, and I and my people *are*
wicked. (28) Intreat the LORD (for *it is*
enough) that there be no *more* [1]mighty
thunderings and hail; and I will let you
go, and ye shall stay no longer. (29) And
Moses said unto him, As soon as I am
gone out of the city, I will spread abroad
my hands unto the LORD; *and* the thun-
der shall cease, neither shall there be any
more hail; that thou mayest know how
that the [a]earth *is* the LORD'S. (30) But
as for thee and thy servants, I know
that ye will not yet fear the LORD God.
(31) And the flax and the barley was
smitten: for the barley *was* in the ear,
and the flax *was* bolled. (32) But the
wheat and the rie were not smitten: for
they *were* [2]not grown up.
(33) And Moses went out of the city
from Pharaoh, and spread abroad his
hands unto the LORD: and the thunders
and hail ceased, and the rain was not
poured upon the earth. (34) And when
Pharaoh saw that the rain and the hail
and the thunders were ceased, he sinned
yet more, and hardened his heart, he
and his servants. (35) And the heart of
Pharaoh was hardened, neither would
he let the children of Israel go; as the
LORD had spoken [3]by Moses.

CHAPTER X.—(1) And the LORD said
unto Moses, Go in unto Pharaoh: [b]for

1 Heb., *voices of God.*

a Ps. 24. 1.

2 Heb., *hidden*, or, *dark.*

3 Heb., *by the hand of Moses.*

b ch. 4.

---

and twigs, so damaging the trees and, if they were fruit-trees, destroying the prospect of fruit.

(27) **Pharaoh sent.**—It is evident that the Pharaoh was more impressed by this plague than by any preceding one. This may have been partly because it caused destruction of human life, partly on account of its extraordinary and awful character. It must be borne in mind that the storm was still continuing, and gave no sign of coming to a natural end (verses 29, 33).

I have sinned this time—*i.e.*, This time I confess that I have sinned in resisting Jehovah; I do not any more maintain that I have acted right.

The Lord is righteous.—Heb., *Jehovah is the Just One*—a form of speech implying that Jehovah, *and He alone*, was just.

Wicked.—Heb., *the sinners*. "I and my people" stand in contrast with God and His people. Previously Pharaoh had denounced the Israelites as idlers and hypocrites (chap. v. 8, 17); now he admits that it is only he and his people that are to blame. The confession is satisfactory, except in so far as it divides between Pharaoh and the Egyptians the blame which was almost wholly his.

(29) **That thou mayest know how that the earth is the Lord's.**—Comp. verse 15. It was the general belief of the Egyptians, as of most ancient nations, that each country had its own god or gods. Pharaoh had already admitted Jehovah's power (chap. viii. 8), and now regarded Him as the God of the Hebrews (chap. viii. 28). God desired to have it generally acknowledged that He was the God of the whole earth.

(31) **The flax and the barley was smitten.**—Flax was grown largely in Egypt, since linen garments were very generally worn by the people, and were the necessary attire of the priests (Herod. ii. 37). Mummies also were swathed in linen bandages (Herod. ii. 86); and soldiers wore linen corselets (Herod. ii. 182, iii. 47). Barley was grown as food for horses, as an element in the manufacture of beer, and as a material for an inferior kind of bread. The flax is "bolled"—*i.e.*, forms its seed-vessel—towards the end of January or beginning of February, and the barley comes into ear about the same time. These facts fix the date of this plague, and help to fix the dates both of the earlier and the later ones.

(32) **The wheat and the rie.**—"Rie," or rye, is a wrong translation. It is a grain which has never been grown in Egypt. The only three kinds of grain cultivated were wheat, barley, and the *holcus sorghum*, or *doora*. There is no doubt that this last is intended by the Hebrew *cussemêth*, which is a word derived from the Egyptian. The wheat is a full month later than the barley in Egypt, and does not come into ear till March. The *holcus sorghum* may be grown at any time, except during the inundation. If sown with the wheat, it would ripen about the same period.

They were not grown up.—Heb., *they were late*, or *dark*. The ear was undeveloped, and lay hid in the low tufts that grew like grass.

(33) **Moses went out of the city . . . and spread abroad his hands.**—Moses did not fear the storm. Though it still raged, he quitted the shelter of the city, and went out into the midst of it, and spread out his hands to God, when lo! at once the rain, and hail, and thunder ceased at his bidding, and soon "there was a great calm." As Millington observes—"Moses knew that he was safe, though all around might be destroyed; the very hairs of his head were all numbered, not one of them could perish. Standing there under the tempestuous canopy of heaven, bareheaded, in the attitude of prayer, he spread abroad his hands unto the Lord, and the thunder and hail ceased, and the rain was not poured upon the earth" (*Plagues of Egypt*, p. 135).

(34) **Pharaoh . . . sinned yet more, and hardened his heart.**—As Pharaoh had never been so much moved previously, so it now required a greater effort of his will to "harden his heart" than it had ever done before; and thus he now "sinned yet more" than he had as yet sinned. It seems strange that the mercy of God should still have allowed him one other chance (chap. x. 3—6).

X.

THE EIGHTH PLAGUE.

(1—4) The eighth plague, like the third and fourth, was one where insect life was called in to serve God's purposes, and chastise the presumption of His enemies. The nature of the visitation is uncontested and incon-

I have hardened his heart, and the heart of his servants, that I might shew these my signs before him: (2) and that thou mayest tell in the ears of thy son, and of thy son's son, what things I have wrought in Egypt, and my signs which I have done among them; that ye may know how that I *am* the LORD.

(3) And Moses and Aaron came in unto Pharaoh, and said unto him, Thus saith the LORD God of the Hebrews, How long wilt thou refuse to humble thyself before me? let my people go, that they may serve me. (4) Else, if thou refuse to let my people go, behold, to morrow will I bring the [a]locusts into thy coast: (5) and they shall cover the [1]face of the earth, that one cannot be able to see the earth: and they shall eat the residue of that which is escaped, which remaineth unto you from the hail, and shall eat every tree which groweth for you out of the field: (6) and they shall fill thy houses, and the houses of all thy servants, and the houses of all the Egyptians; which neither thy fathers, nor thy fathers'

a Wis. 16. 9.

1 Heb., *eye.*

---

testable—it was a terrible invasion of locusts. Locusts are an occasional, though not a frequent, scourge in Egypt. They are not bred there, and necessarily arrive from some foreign country. When they descend, their ravages are as severe as elsewhere. "In the present day," says Mr. Stuart Poole, "locusts suddenly appear in the cultivated land, coming from the desert in a column of great length. They fly across the country, darkening the air with their compact ranks, which are undisturbed by the constant attacks of kites, crows, and vultures, and making a strange whizzing sound, like that of fire, or many distant wheels. Where they alight they devour every green thing, even stripping the trees of their leaves. Rewards are offered for their destruction; but no labour can seriously reduce their numbers" (*Dict. of the Bible*, vol. ii., p. 887). C. Niebuhr witnessed two invasions—in 1761 and 1762; Denon witnessed another about the year 1800; and Tischendorf saw one recently. They always enter Egypt either from the south or from the east, and necessarily come with a wind, since they cannot possibly fly any considerable distance without one. It is probable that at different times different varieties of the locust visit the country; but all varieties are almost equally destructive. After the loss of their cattle by murrain and hail, and the ruin of the flax and barley crops by the latter agency, nothing was wanting to complete the desolation of the country and the impoverishment of its inhabitants but the ruin of the wheat and *doora* crops, which the locusts speedily effected.

(1) **I have hardened . . . the heart of his servants.**—They, too, had first hardened their own hearts (chap. ix. 34), and so deserved a penal hardening. A certain amount of responsibility rested on *them.* Had they allowed the miracles to have their full natural effect upon their minds, they would have been convinced that resistance was useless, and would have impressed their views upon the Pharaoh. Even in the most absolute governments public opinion has weight, and the general sentiment of the Court almost always carries the sovereign with it.

That I might shew these my signs.—There is nothing derogatory to the Divine Nature in a penal hardening being, as it were, utilised to increase the glory of God, and affect for good future generations of His people. The accumulation of plague upon plague, which the obduracy of Pharaoh and his subjects brought about, was of vast importance in presenting to Israel, and even to the surrounding nations, a manifestation of the tremendous power of God, calculated to impress them as nothing else would have done.

(2) **That thou mayest tell.**—Those who experience God's mercies are bound to hand on the memory of what He has done for them to future generations. Natural gratitude would prompt such action. But, lest the duty should be neglected, the Israelites had it at this time constantly enjoined upon them (chaps. xii. 26, 27, xiii. 14, 15; Deut. xxxii. 7; Josh. iv. 6, &c.).

(4) **To morrow will I bring the locusts into thy coast.**—Locusts, as already observed, are not indigenous to Egypt, but only occasional visitants. Consequently they always enter the country from some other, as Nubia, Abyssinia, Syria, or Arabia. On the quarter from which the present plague came, see the comment on verse 13.

(5) **They shall cover the face of the earth, that one cannot be able to see the earth.**—This is the case almost invariably with all the severer visitations of locusts. "The plain was covered with them," says Denon (*Travels*, p. 286), speaking of Egypt. "The ground is covered with them for several leagues," declares Volney (*Travels*, vol. i., p. 285). "Over an area of 1,600 or 1,800 square miles," observes Barrow, "the whole surface might literally be said to be covered with them." The Hebrew name, which means "multitudinous," is thus very appropriate.

They shall eat the residue of that which is escaped . . . every tree.—Comp. chap. ix. 32. The description of Joel has never been surpassed: "A fire devoureth before them, and behind them a flame burneth: the land is as the garden of Eden before them, and behind them a desolate wilderness; yea, and *nothing shall escape them*" (Joel ii. 3). Comp. Volney (*l.s.c.*): "When their swarms appear, everything green vanishes instantaneously from the fields, as if a curtain were rolled up; the trees and plants stand leafless, and nothing is seen but naked boughs and stalks." Very graphic is Joel again in respect of this last feature: "He hath laid my vine waste, and barked my fig-tree: he hath made it clean bare, and cast it away; the branches thereof are made white" (Joel i. 7). Nor is it only shrubs, but even trees, that suffer. "They are particularly injurious to the palm-trees," says Burckhardt; "these they strip of every leaf and green particle, the trees remaining like skeletons, with bare branches."

(6) **They shall fill thy houses.**—"They shall run to and fro in the city," says the prophet Joel; "they shall run upon the wall, they shall climb up upon the houses; they shall enter in at the windows, like a thief." Modern travellers bear abundant witness to the same effect; as Burckhardt: "They overwhelm the province of Nedjd sometimes to such a degree that, having

fathers have seen, since the day that
they were upon the earth unto this day.
And he turned himself, and went out
from Pharaoh.
(7) And Pharaoh's servants said unto
him, How long shall this man be a snare
unto us? let the men go, that they may
serve the LORD their God: knowest thou
not yet that Egypt is destroyed? (8) And
Moses and Aaron were brought again
unto Pharaoh: and he said unto them,
Go, serve the LORD your God: *but* [1] who
are they that shall go? (9) And Moses
said, We will go with our young and
with our old, with our sons and with our
daughters, with our flocks and with our
herds will we go; for we *must hold* a feast
unto the LORD. (10) And he said unto
them, Let the LORD be so with you, as I
will let you go, and your little ones:
look *to it;* for evil *is* before you. (11) Not
so: go now, ye *that are* men, and serve
the LORD; for that ye did desire. And
they were driven out from Pharaoh's
presence.
(12) And the LORD said unto Moses,
Stretch out thine hand over the land of
Egypt for the locusts, that they may
come up upon the land of Egypt, and
eat every herb of the land, *even* all that
the hail hath left. (13) And Moses
stretched forth his rod over the land of
Egypt, and the LORD brought an east
wind upon the land all that day, and all
that night; *and* when it was morning,
the east wind brought the locusts.
(14) And the locusts went up over all the
land of Egypt, and rested in all the

1 Heb., *who and who, &c.*

destroyed the harvest, they penetrate by thousands into the private dwellings, and devour whatsoever they can find, even the leather of the water vessels" (*Notes*, vol. ii., p. 90). And Morier: "They entered the inmost recesses of the houses, were found in every corner, stuck to our clothes, and infected our food" (*Second Journey*, p. 100). Kalisch is quite correct when he says: "Sometimes they penetrate into the houses; they fly into the mouths of the inmates; they throw themselves on the food; they gnaw leather, and even wood" (*Commentary*, p. 123).

Which neither thy fathers, nor thy fathers' fathers have seen.—Only one notice of locusts has been found in the native records.

He turned himself, and went out.—It seems to be meant that Moses did not on this occasion wait to see what effect his menace would have on Pharaoh. He "*knew* that Pharaoh would not yet fear the Lord" (chap. ix. 30).

(7) **Let the men go.**—Though the heart of Pharaoh remained hard, the plagues had a certain effect on the minds of the Egyptians. First, the magicians were impressed, and said, "This is the finger of God" (chap. viii. 19). Then a certain number of the people "feared the word of the Lord, and made their servants and their cattle flee into the houses" (chap. ix. 20). Now the very officers of the Court, those who were in the closest contact with the king, believed that the words of Moses would come true, and counselled the king to yield, and "let the men go." It has been supposed that they meant "the men only" (Knobel, Cook); but this is pure conjecture. The word used, which is not that of verse 11, would cover women and children. The officers of the Court—rich landowners mostly—would dread impending ruin if the wheat and *doora* crops were destroyed, and would intend to counsel entire submission.

(8) **Moses and Aaron were brought again unto Pharaoh.**—Moses and Aaron had uttered their threat, and had straightway left his presence. The courtiers "brought them again to Pharaoh." The courtiers, no doubt, supposed that the king would yield; and the king was prepared to yield *to a certain extent.* But he had conceived of a compromise in his own mind, and this he hoped to impose upon Moses; hence his insidious question—

Who are they that shall go?—Pharaoh had not hitherto raised this question. He had known well enough that the demand extended to *all* the people (chap. viii. 8); but now he pretends that there had been an ambiguity, and requires that it shall be cleared up. Moses gives him an answer (verse 9) which takes away all further pretence of doubt.

(9) **With our sons and with our daughters . . . for we must hold a feast.**—It was customary in Egypt for children to join in festivals (Herod. ii. 60).

With our flocks and with our herds.—The family of Jacob brought numerous flocks and herds into Egypt (Gen. xlvii. 1). These had, no doubt, increased, notwithstanding the oppression, and at the time of the Exodus must have been very numerous. The requirement to "take a lamb for an house" (chap. xii. 2) on the institution of the Passover involved the killing, on a single day, of 200,000 lambs. Even after this the flocks and herds which went out with them (chap. xii. 38) were "very much cattle."

(10) **Little ones.**—Heb., *families.* These would include the children and the dependents. (See comment on chap. i. 1.)

Evil is before you.—Heb., *evil is before your faces—i.e.,* you contemplate doing me a mischief, by depriving me of the services of so large a body of labourers.

(11) **Ye that are men.**—Heb., *haggĕbarim—i.e.,* the full-grown males.

That ye did desire.—There was no ground for this reproach. Moses and Aaron had always demanded the release of the entire nation ("let my *people* go"); and nations are composed of women and children as much and as essentially as they are of adult males.

(13) **An east wind.**—The LXX. translate by *νότον*, "a south wind," probably because locusts most commonly enter Egypt from the south, being bred in Nubia or Abyssinia; but the Hebrew (*ruakh kâdim*) is undoubtedly an east wind; and modern travellers tell us that this is a quarter from which locusts arrive in Egypt occasionally (Denon, *Voyages en Egypte*, p. 286). In such cases they are bred in Northern Arabia.

(14) **The locusts went up over all the land of Egypt.**—It is not, perhaps, certain that this is intended literally, since universal expressions are con-

coasts of Egypt: very grievous *were*
they; before them there were no such
locusts as they, neither after them shall
be such. (15) For they covered the face
of the whole earth, so that the land was
darkened; and they did eat every herb
of the land, and all the fruit of the trees
which the hail had left: and there re-
mained not any green thing in the trees,
or in the herbs of the field, through all
the land of Egypt.
(16) Then Pharaoh [1]called for Moses
and Aaron in haste; and he said, I have
sinned against the LORD your God, and
against you. (17) Now therefore forgive,
I pray thee, my sin only this once, and
intreat the LORD your God, that he may
take away from me this death only.
(18) And he went out from Pharaoh, and
intreated the LORD. (19) And the LORD
turned a mighty strong west wind,
which took away the locusts, and [2]cast
them into the Red sea; there remained
not one locust in all the coasts of Egypt.
(20) But the LORD hardened Pharaoh's
heart, so that he would not let the
children of Israel go.
(21) And the LORD said unto Moses,
Stretch out thine hand toward heaven,
that there may be darkness over the

1 Heb., *hastened to call.*

2 Heb., *fastened.*

---

tinually used by the sacred writers where something less than universality is meant. But, strengthened as the clause is by the succeeding one, we must suppose a very general visitation to be spoken of. Now Egypt extends, from north to south, a distance of above 500 miles, and the Delta has a width of 150 miles. No column of locusts having nearly such dimensions is recorded in history. Perhaps the visitation was confined to the Delta and the vicinity of Memphis. Even so, it would have covered an area of 7,000 square miles, or one nearly equal to that of Wales.

(15) **They covered the face of the whole earth, so that the land was darkened.**—See the comment on verse 5, and compare also Clarke's *Travels in Russia*, p. 445:—"The steppes were literally covered with the bodies of these insects. . . . The whole face of nature seemed to be concealed as by a living veil."

They did eat every herb of the land.—"When these animals arrive in swarms," says Clarke, "the whole vegetable produce disappears. Nothing escapes them, from the leaves of the forest to the herbs of the plain" (*Travels*, pp. 446, 447). "It is sufficient," observes a traveller in Spain, "if these terrible columns stop half an hour on a spot, for everything growing on it—vines, olive-trees, and corn—to be entirely destroyed. After they have passed, nothing remains but the large branches and the roots, which, being underground, have escaped their voracity."

All the fruit of the trees.—Egypt was famous for its fruits, which consisted of figs, grapes, olives, mulberries, pomegranates, dates, pears, plums, apples, peaches, and the produce of the *persea* and the *nebk*, or *sidr*. The fruit of the *nebk* would be ripe in March, and the blossom-buds of the other fruit-trees would be formed, or even opening. On the damage which locusts do to fruit-trees, see the comment on verse 5, and add the following:—"When the weeds in the vineyards do not supply them with sufficient nutriment, they completely strip the bark and buds off the young twigs, so that these shoots remain throughout the summer as white as chalk, without producing fresh foliage" (Pallas, *Travels*, vol. ii., p. 425).

Which the hail had left.—See chap. ix. 25, and comp. Ps. cv. 32, 33:—"He gave them hail for rain, and flaming fire in their land; he smote their vines also, and their fig trees, and brake the trees of their coasts."

(16) **Pharaoh called for Moses and Aaron in haste.**—Heb., *hasted to call for Moses and Aaron.* The expression "hasted to call" is new, and marks extreme urgency. The visitation of the locusts was felt as far more severe than any previous one. It entirely destroyed all the remaining harvest, both of grain and fruit, and must have produced a terrible famine, had it not been for the Egyptian institution of granaries (Gen. xli. 35, 48, &c.).

I have sinned . . .—Comp. chap. ix. 27. This confession is an improvement upon the former one: (1) as acknowledging a double fault—"against the Lord and against you;" and (2) as free from any attempt to put the blame, either wholly or in part, upon others. It was probably sincere at the time; but the feeling from which it sprang was short-lived.

(17) **This death.**—Comp. verse 7. The entire destruction of the harvest threatened death to large numbers of the poorer class of persons.

(19) **The Lord turned a mighty strong west wind . . .**—As locusts come, so they commonly go, with a wind. They cannot fly far without one. It often happens that a wind blows them into the sea. Pallas says, speaking of Crimean locusts in the year 1799:—"Great numbers of them were carried [from the Crimea] by northerly winds into the sea, where they perished, and were afterwards washed on shore in heaps" (*Travels*, vol. ii., p. 424).

The Red sea.—Heb., *the sea of weeds*, or *of rushes.* The Red Sea probably acquired this name among the Hebrews from the fact that in the time of Moses its north-western recess communicated with a marshy tract, extending as far as the Bitter Lakes, and abounding in aquatic plants of a luxuriant growth. (Comp. chap. ii. 3, where the same term designates the water-plants of the Nile.)

There remained not one locust . . .—Niebuhr says of locusts in Arabia:—"Souvent il en reste beaucoup après le départ général" (*Description de l'Arabie*, p. 153). But, on the other hand, there are times when the whole swarm takes its departure at once. "A wind from the south-west," says Morier, "which had brought them, so completely drove them forwards that not a vestige of them was to be seen two hours afterwards" (*Second Journey*, p. 98).

(20) **The Lord hardened Pharaoh's heart.**—Comp. above, chap. ix. 12.

THE NINTH PLAGUE.

(21–23) The ninth plague, like the third and sixth, was sent without any previous warning. It consisted in a "thick darkness," which may have been brought about by means of the *Khamsîn*, or "Wind of the

land of Egypt, [1]even darkness *which*
may be felt. (22) And Moses stretched
forth his hand toward heaven; and
there was a thick darkness in all the
land of Egypt three days: (23) they saw
not one another, neither rose any from
his place for three days: [a]but all the
children of Israel had light in their
dwellings.

(24) And Pharaoh called unto Moses,
and said, Go ye, serve the LORD; only
let your flocks and your herds be stayed:
let your little ones also go with you.
(25) And Moses said, Thou must give [2]us
also sacrifices and burnt offerings, that
we may sacrifice unto the LORD our God.
(26) Our cattle also shall go with us;
there shall not an hoof be left behind;
for thereof must we take to serve the
LORD our God; and we know not with
what we must serve the LORD, until we
come thither.

(27) But the LORD hardened Pharaoh's
heart, and he would not let them go.
(28) And Pharaoh said unto him, Get
thee from me, take heed to thyself, see
my face no more; for in *that* day thou
seest my face thou shalt die. (29) And
Moses said, Thou hast spoken well, I
will see thy face again no more.

1 Heb., *that one may feel darkness.*

a Wisd. 18. 1.

2 Heb., *into our hands.*

Desert," which frequently blows about the time of the vernal equinox, and brings with it such clouds of a fine impalpable sand that the light of the sun is obscured, and an effect produced which some travellers have compared to "the most gloomy night." Or it may have been a shutting out of the sun's rays by dense fog and cloud of a more ordinary character; though in that case there must have been something in the visitation very much exceeding any known instance of such darkness. "They saw not one another," we are told, "for three days" (verse 23). The darkness was one which "might be felt" (verse 21). Such a preternatural continuance of absolutely impenetrable "blackness of darkness" would cause to any man a feeling of intense alarm and horror. To the Egyptians it would be peculiarly painful and terrible. Ra, the sun-god, was among the principal objects of their worship, especially in the Delta, where Heliopolis and Pithom were cities dedicated to him. Darkness was a creation of Set—the Evil Principle, the destroyer of Osiris—and of Apophis, the Great Serpent, the impeder of souls in the lower world. It would have seemed to the Egyptians that Ra was dead, that Set had triumphed over his brother, that Apophis had encircled the world with his dark folds, and plunged it in eternal night. Hence Pharaoh's early call for Moses, and permission that the people should depart, *with their families* (verse 24): a concession which, however, was marred by the proviso, "Only let your flocks and herds be stayed."

(21) **Darkness which may be felt.**—Heb., *one shall grasp darkness.* The Authorised Version seems to give the true meaning, which is found also in the LXX. and the Vulg. The idea is an exaggeration of that instinctive feeling which makes us speak of "*thick* darkness." The general voice of mankind confirms the use of the phrase.

(23) **They saw not one another.**—Heb., *man did not see his brother.* The darkness was absolute, equal to that of the darkest night.

Neither rose any from his place.—Comp. chap. xvi. 29. No one quitted his house. Mr. Millington imagines that they all sat "glued to their seats" (*Plagues of Egypt*, p. 159), but this savours of over-literalism. It is not necessary to suppose that they had no artificial light, or that they ceased to move from chamber to chamber. What the writer intends to note is that all business and all intercourse with neighbours was suspended. No one quitted the house in which he was when the darkness began.

All the children of Israel had light in their dwellings.—The visitation, whatever it was, did not extend to the land of Goshen. (Comp. chaps. viii. 22—24, ix. 4—7, 26.)

(24) **Let your little ones also go with you.**—Rather, *your families.* Pharaoh yields another point, but he will not yield all. He has not yet made up his mind really to "let the people go." He must still keep some hold on them, and the cattle will serve his purpose equally with the "little ones." If the Israelites depart without their cattle, they will be sure to return for them.

(26) **Our cattle also shall go with us.**—Once more Moses rejects the proffered compromise—rejects it absolutely and altogether. The cattle shall *all* go with the people; "not an hoof shall be left behind." And why? First, because it is theirs ("*our* cattle," "*our* flocks," "*our* herds"), and not Pharaoh's; secondly, because it is God's—*all*, to the last head, if He requires it; and He has not said as yet how much of it He will require. The festival to be held in the wilderness is altogether a new thing; its ritual has not at present been laid down. The people will only be told "with what they must serve the Lord" when they are come to the place where they are to serve Him: *i.e.*, to Sinai (chap. iii. 12).

(28) **Get thee from me.**—This address is rude, fierce, uncourteous. That a Pharaoh of the nineteenth (or eighteenth?) dynasty should have so spoken implies extreme and very uncommon excitement. Generally the Pharaohs of this polished period were as imperturbable as Chinese mandarins. We must suppose that up to this time the king had persuaded himself that he would be able to bring Moses to a compromise, but that now at last he despaired of so doing; hence his anger and rudeness.

Thou shalt die.—Egyptian kings had the power of life and death, but rarely exercised it arbitrarily, or without trial. Very long and elaborate judicial processes have been found among the Egyptian remains. Still, no doubt, a monarch could put to death whomsoever he pleased; and so Egyptian courtiers were wont to acknowledge that they had lived to old age "by the favour of the king" (Brugsch, *History of Egypt*, vol. i., p. 92).

(29) The division between chap. x. and chap. xi. is unfortunate. The interview between Pharaoh and Moses was not yet over. It is continued in verses 4—8 of the next chapter, and only terminates when the prophet "went out from Pharaoh in a great anger." Verses 1—3 of chap. xi. are parenthetic.

CHAPTER XI.—(1) And the LORD
said unto Moses, Yet will I bring one
plague *more* upon Pharaoh, and upon
Egypt; afterwards he will let you go
hence: when he shall let *you* go, he
shall surely thrust you out hence alto-
gether. (2) Speak now in the ears of
the people, and let every man borrow of
his neighbour, and every woman of her
neighbour, [a]jewels of silver, and jewels
of gold. (3) And the LORD gave the
people favour in the sight of the Egyp-
tians. Moreover the man [b]Moses *was*
very great in the land of Egypt, in the
sight of Pharaoh's servants, and in the
sight of the people.
(4) And Moses said, Thus saith the
LORD, [c]About midnight will I go out
into the midst of Egypt: (5) and all the
firstborn in the land of Egypt shall die,
from the firstborn of Pharaoh that
sitteth upon his throne, even unto the
firstborn of the maidservant that *is* be-
hind the mill; and all the firstborn of

a ch. 3. 22 & 12. 35.

b Ecclus. 45. 1.

c ch. 12. 29.

XI.

ANNOUNCEMENT OF THE TENTH PLAGUE.

(1) **And the Lord said.**—Rather, *Now the Lord had said.* The passage (verses 1—3) is parenthetic, and refers to a revelation made to Moses before his present interview with Pharaoh began. The insertion is needed in order to explain the confidence of Moses in regard to the last plague (verse 5), and the effect it would have on the Egyptians (verse 8).

When he shall let you go, he shall surely thrust you out hence altogether.—The word rendered "altogether" belongs to the first clause. Translate, *when he shall let you go altogether, he shall assuredly thrust you out hence.*

(2) **Let every man borrow.**—See the comment on chap. iii. 22. The directions to "ask" the Egyptians for presents is extended here from the women alone to both women and men. Egyptian obduracy and Israelitish loss through some of the plagues may have caused the enlargement of the original instruction.

(3) **The Lord gave the people favour**—*i.e.*, when the time arrived. (See below, chap. xii. 36.)

The man Moses.—At first sight there seems a difficulty in supposing Moses to have written thus of himself. "The man" is not a title by which writers of any time or country are in the habit of speaking of themselves; but it is far more difficult to imagine any one but Moses giving him so bald and poor a designation. To other writers he is a "prophet" (Deut. xxxiv. 10; Luke xxiv. 27; Acts iii. 22, vii. 37), or "a man of God" (Deut. xxxiii. 1; Josh. xiv. 6; Ps. xc., Title; Ezra iii. 2), or "the servant of the Lord" (Josh. i. 1; Heb. iii. 5); never simply "the man."

Very great.—It has been said that this expression does not comport well with the "meekness" of Moses. But it is the mere statement of a fact, and of one necessary to be stated for the proper understanding of the narrative. Moses, in the course of his long contention as an equal with Pharaoh, had come to be regarded, not only by the courtiers, but by the Egyptians generally, as a great personage—a personage almost on a par with the Pharaoh, whom they revered as a god upon earth. The position to which he had thus attained exerted an important influence on the entire Egyptian people at this time, causing them to be well-inclined towards his countrymen, and willing to make sacrifices in order to help them and obtain their good-will.

(4) **And Moses said.**—In continuation of the speech recorded in chap. x. 29, face to face with Pharaoh, Moses makes his last appeal—utters his last threats. The Pharaoh has bidden him "see his face no more" (chap. x. 28), and he has accepted the warning, and declared "I will see thy face again no more" (chap. x. 29). It is the last interview—the last interchange of speech. Moses had to deliver himself of a message. Hardened as his heart is, Pharaoh is yet to be allowed "a place for repentance." God announces to him, by the mouth of Moses, the coming destruction of the firstborn—emphasizes the terrible nature of the impending calamity by the announcement that through all Egypt there would be "a great cry"—contrasts with their despair the absolute immunity of the Israelites—and finally warns the Pharaoh that he and his people will shortly urge the departure which they now refuse to permit. If Pharaoh had even now relented, it was not too late—the great blows might have been escaped, the death of the firstborn and the destruction of the armed force in the Red Sea. But he had "hardened himself," and then "been hardened," until, practically, the time for relenting was gone by. He remained obdurate, and "would not let the children of Israel go out of his land" (verse 10).

About midnight.—The particular night was not specified; and the torment of suspense was thus added to the pain of an unintermittent fear. But the dreadful visitation was to come at the dreadest hour of the twenty-four—midnight. Thus much was placed beyond doubt.

(5) **All the firstborn . . . shall die.**—The Heb. word translated *firstborn* is applied only to males; and thus the announcement was that in every family the eldest *son* should be cut off. In Egypt, as in most other countries, the law of primogeniture prevailed—the eldest son was the hope, stay, and support of the household, his father's companion, his mother's joy, the object of his brothers' and sisters' reverence. The firstborn of the Pharaoh bore the title of *erpa suten sa*, or "hereditary crown prince," and succeeded his father, unless he died or was formally set aside during his father's lifetime. Among the nobles, estates were inherited, and sometimes titles descended to the firstborn. No greater affliction can be conceived, short of the general destruction of the people, than the sudden death in every family of him round whom the highest interests and fondest hopes clustered.

The maidservant that is behind the mill marks the lowest grade in the social scale, as the king that sits upon his throne marks the highest. All alike were to suffer. In every family there was to be one dead (chap. xii. 30).

All the firstborn of beasts.—The aggravation of the calamity by its extension to beasts is very remarkable, and is probably to be connected with the Egyptian animal-worship. At all times there were in Egypt four animals regarded as actual incarnations of deity, and the objects of profound veneration. Three of these were bulls, while one was a white cow. It is

beasts. (6) And there shall be a great
cry throughout all the land of Egypt,
such as there was none like it, nor shall
be like it any more. (7) But against any
of the children of Israel shall not a dog
move his tongue, against man or beast:
that ye may know how that the LORD
doth put a difference between the Egyp-
tians and Israel. (8) And all these thy
servants shall come down unto me, and
bow down themselves unto me, saying,
Get thee out, and all the people [1]that
follow thee: and after that I will go
out. And he went out from Pharaoh
in [2]a great anger.
(9) And the LORD said unto Moses,
Pharaoh shall not hearken unto you;
that my wonders may be multiplied in
the land of Egypt. (10) And Moses and
Aaron did all these wonders before
Pharaoh: and the LORD hardened Pha-
raoh's heart, so that he would not let
the children of Israel go out of his
land.

CHAPTER XII.—(1) And the LORD
spake unto Moses and Aaron in the land
of Egypt, saying, (2) This month *shall be*
unto you the beginning of months: it
shall be the first month of the year to
you.
(3) Speak ye unto all the congregation
of Israel, saying, In the tenth *day* of
this month they shall take to them
every man a [3]lamb, according to the
house of *their* fathers, a lamb for an

1 Heb., *that is at thy feet.*

2 Heb., *heat of anger.*

3 Or, *kid.*

---

not unlikely that all were required to be "firstborns;" in which case the whole of Egypt would have been plunged into a religious mourning on account of their deaths, in addition to the domestic mourning that must have prevailed in each house. The deaths of other sacred animals, and of many pet animals in houses, would have increased the general consternation.

(6) **There shall be a great cry.**—The shrill cries uttered by mourners in the East are well known to travellers. Mr. Stuart Poole heard those of the Egyptian women at Cairo, in the great cholera of 1848, at a distance of two miles (Smith's *Dictionary of the Bible*, vol. ii., p. 888). Herodotus, describing the lamentations of the Persian soldiers at the funeral of Masistius, says that "all Bœotia resounded with their clamour" (ix. 24). The Egyptian monuments represent mourners as tearing their hair, putting dust upon their heads, and beating their breasts (Wilkinson, in Rawlinson's *Herodotus*, vol. ii., p. 138).

(7) **Shall not a dog move his tongue.**—Compare Josh. x. 21. The expression is evidently proverbial.

(8) **All these thy servants**—*i.e.*, the high officers of the Court who were standing about Pharaoh. These grandees would come to Moses when the blow fell, and prostrate themselves before him as if he were their king, and beseech him to take his departure with all his nation. The details are given more fully and more graphically in this place than in the subsequent narrative (chap. xii. 31).

In a great anger.—Heb., *in heat of anger: i.e.*, burning with indignation. Moses had not shown this in his speech, which had been calm and dignified; but he here records what he had felt. For once his acquired "meekness" failed, and the hot natural temper of his youth blazed up. His life had been threatened—he had been ignominiously dismissed—he had been deprived of his right of audience for the future (chap. x. 28). Under such circumstances, he "did well to be angry."

(9, 10) **And the Lord said . . .**—The series of the nine wonders wrought by Moses and Aaron is terminated by this short summary, of which the main points are—(1) God had said (chap. iv. 21) that the miracles would fail to move Pharaoh; (2) He had assigned as the reason for this failure His own will that the wonders should be multiplied (chap. vii. 3); (3) the miracles had now been wrought; (4) Pharaoh had not been moved by them; (5) God had hardened his heart, as a judgment upon him, after he had first himself hardened it. The result had been a series of manifestations calculated to impress the Israelites with a sense of God's protecting care, the Egyptians and the neighbouring nations with a sense of His power to punish.

XII.

INSTITUTION OF THE PASSOVER.

(1) **In the land of Egypt.**—This section (verses 1—28) has the appearance of having been written independently of the previous narrative—earlier, probably, and as a part of the Law rather than of the history. It throws together instructions on the subject of the Passover which must have been given at different times (comp. verses 3, 12, 17), some before the tenth of Abib, some on the day preceding the departure from Egypt, some on the day following. As far as verse 20 it is wholly legal, and would suit Leviticus as well as Exodus. From verse 20 it has a more historical character, since it relates the action taken by Moses.

(2) **The beginning of months.**—Hitherto the Hebrews had commenced the year with Tisri, at or near the autumnal equinox. (See chap. xxiii. 16.) In thus doing, they followed neither the Egyptian nor the Babylonian custom. The Egyptians began the year in June, with the first rise of the Nile; the Babylonians in Nisannu, at the vernal equinox. It was this month which was now made, by God's command, the first month of the Hebrew year; but as yet it had not the name Nisan: it was called Abib (chap. xiii. 4), the month of "greenness." Henceforth the Hebrews had two years, a civil and a sacred one (Joseph., *Ant. Jud.*, i. 3, § 3). The civil year began with Tisri, in the autumn, at the close of the harvest; the sacred year began with Abib (called afterwards Nisan), six months earlier. It followed that the first civil was the seventh sacred month, and *vice versâ.*

(3) **In the tenth day.**—It is evident that this direction must have been given before the tenth day had arrived, probably some days before. The object of the direction was to allow ample time for the careful inspection of the animal, so that its entire freedom from

house: (4) and if the household be too little for the lamb, let him and his neighbour next unto his house take *it* according to the number of the souls; every man according to his eating shall make your count for the lamb. (5) Your lamb shall be without blemish, a male [1]of the first year: ye shall take *it* out from the sheep, or from the goats: (6) and ye shall keep it up until the fourteenth day of the same month: and the whole assembly of the congregation of Israel shall kill it [2]in the evening. (7) And they shall take of the blood, and strike *it* on the two side posts and on the upper door post of the houses, wherein they shall eat it. (8) And they shall eat the flesh in that night, roast with fire, and unleavened bread; *and* with bitter *herbs* they shall eat it.

[1] Heb., *son of a year.*

[2] Heb., *between the two evenings.*

---

all blemish might be ascertained. The animal was not to be killed till four days later (verse 6).

A lamb.—The word used (*seh*) is a vague one, applied equally to sheep and goats, of any age and of either sex. Sex and age were fixed subsequently (verse 5), but the other ambiguity remained; and it is curious that practically only lambs seem to have been ever offered. The requirement indicates a social condition in which there was no extreme poverty. All Israelites are supposed either to possess a lamb or to be able to purchase one.

According to the house of their fathers.—Rather, *for the house of their fathers*: *i.e.*, for their family.

(4) **If the household be too little for the lamb.**—There would be cases where the family would not be large enough to consume an entire lamb at a sitting. Where this was so, men were to club with their neighbours, either two small families joining together, or a large family drafting off some of its members to bring up the numbers of a small one. According to Josephus (*Bell. Jud.*, vi. 9, § 3), ten was the least number regarded as sufficient, while twenty was not considered too many.

Every man according to his eating shall make your count for the lamb.—Rather, *shall ye count.* In determining the number for any given Paschal meal, ye shall "count men according to their eating," admitting more or fewer, as they are likely to consume less or more.

(5) **Without blemish.**—Natural piety teaches that we must not "offer the blind, the lame, or the sick for sacrifice" (Mal. i. 8). We must give to God of our best. The Law emphasized this teaching, and here, on the first occasion when a sacrifice was formally appointed, required it to be absolutely without blemish of any kind. Afterwards the requirement was made general (Lev. xxii. 19—25). It was peculiarly fitting that the Paschal offering should be without defect of any kind, as especially typifying "the Lamb of God," who is "holy, harmless, undefiled"—a "lamb without spot."

A male.—Males were reckoned superior to females, and were especially appropriate here, since the victim represented the firstborn male in each house.

Of the first year—*i.e.*, not above a year old. As children are most innocent when young, so even animals were thought to be.

(6) **Ye shall keep it up.**—Heb., *ye shall have it in custody*: separate it, *i.e.*, from the flock, and keep it in or near your house for four days. During this time it could be carefully and thoroughly inspected. (Comp. verse 3.)

The whole assembly of the congregation . . . shall kill it.—Every head of a family belonging to the "congregation" was to make the necessary arrangements, to have the victim ready, and to kill it on the fourteenth day, the day of the full moon, at a time described as that "between the two evenings." There is some doubt as to the meaning of this phrase. According to Onkelos and Aben Ezra, the first evening was at sunset, the second about an hour later, when the twilight ended and the stars came out. With this view agrees the direction in Deut. xvi. 6:—"Thou shalt sacrifice the passover at even, *at the going down of the sun.*" It is objected that, according to Josephus (*Bell. Jud.*, vi. 9, § 3), the actual time of the sacrifice was "from the ninth to the eleventh hour"—*i.e.*, from three o'clock to five—and that there would not have been time for the customary ceremonies during the short twilight of Palestine. The ceremonies consisted in the slaughter of the lambs at the tabernacle door, and the conveyance of the blood in basins to the altar, in order that it might be sprinkled upon it. For this operation a period of several hours' duration would seem to have been necessary: hence the time came gradually to be extended; and when this had been done, a new interpretation of the phrase "between the evenings" grew up. The first evening was explained to begin with the decline of the sun from the zenith, and the second with the sunset; but this can scarcely have been the original idea.

(7) **Strike it.**—With a bunch of hyssop. (See verse 22.)

The two side posts and on the upper door post.—The idea seems to have been that the destroying influence, whatever it was, would enter the house by the door. The sight of the bloody stains above the door and on either side would prevent its entering. The word translated "upper door post" appears to be derived from *shâcaph*, "to look out," and to signify properly the latticed window above the door, through which persons reconnoitred those who knocked before admitting them. Such windows are frequently represented in the early Egyptian monuments. The blood thus rendered conspicuous would show that atonement had been made for the house, *i.e.*, for its inmates.

(8) **Roast with fire.**—Roasting is the simplest, the easiest, and the most primitive mode of cooking meat. It was also the only mode open to all the Hebrews, since the generality would not possess cauldrons large enough to receive an entire lamb. Further, the requirement put a difference between this and other victims, which were generally cut up and boiled (1 Sam. ii. 14, 15).

Unleavened bread . . . bitter herbs.—As partaking of the lamb typified feeding on Christ, so the putting away of leaven and eating unleavened bread signified the putting away of all defilement and corruption ere we approach Christ to feed on Him (1 Cor. v. 8). As for the bitter herbs, they probably represented "self-denial" or "repentance"—fitting concomitants

(9) Eat not of it raw, nor sodden at all
with water, but roast *with* fire; his
head with his legs, and with the pur-
tenance thereof. (10) And ye shall let
nothing of it remain until the morning;
and that which remaineth of it until the
morning ye shall burn with fire. (11) And
thus shall ye eat it; *with* your loins
girded, your shoes on your feet, and
your staff in your hand; and ye shall
eat it in haste: it *is* the LORD's pass-
over.
(12) For I will pass through the land
of Egypt this night, and will smite all
the firstborn in the land of Egypt, both
man and beast; and against all the
[1] gods of Egypt I will execute judgment:
I *am* the LORD. (13) And the blood shall
be to you for a token upon the houses
where ye *are*: and when I see the blood,
I will pass over you, and the plague
shall not be upon you [2] to destroy *you*,
when I smite the land of Egypt.
(14) And this day shall be unto you for
a memorial; and ye shall keep it a feast
to the LORD throughout your genera-
tions; ye shall keep it a feast by an
ordinance for ever. (15) Seven days shall
ye eat unleavened bread; even the first
day ye shall put away leaven out of
your houses: for whosoever eateth
leavened bread from the first day until

1 Or, *princes.*

2 Heb., *for a destruction.*

---

of the holy feast, where the Lamb of God is our food. At any rate, they were a protest against that animalism which turns a sacred banquet into a means of gratifying the appetite (1 Cor. xi. 20—22).

(9) **His head with his legs . . .**—The lamb was to be roasted whole: "not a bone of it was to be broken" (verse 46). Justin Martyr says that it was prepared for roasting by means of two wooden spits, one perpendicular and the other transverse, which extended it on a sort of cross, and made it aptly typify the Crucified One.

The purtenance thereof.—Heb., *its inside.* The entrails were taken out, carefully cleansed, and then replaced.

(10) **Ye shall let nothing of it remain.**—That there might be neither profanation nor superstitious use of what was left. (Comp. the requirement of the Church of England with respect to the Eucharistic elements.)

That which remaineth—*i.e.*, the bones and such particles of flesh as necessarily adhered to them. These were to be at once totally consumed by fire. Thus only could they be, as it were, annihilated, and so secured from profanation.

(11) **Thus shall ye eat it.**—The injunctions which follow are not repeated in any later part of the Law, and were not generally regarded as binding at any Passover after the first. They all had reference to the impending departure of the Israelites, who were to eat the Passover prepared as for a journey. The long robe (*beged*), usually allowed to flow loosely around the person, was to be gathered together, and fastened about the loins with a girdle; sandals, not commonly worn inside the house, were to be put on the feet, and a walking-stick was to be held in one hand. The meal was to be eaten "in haste," as liable to be interrupted at any moment by a summons to quit Egypt and set out for Canaan. Some such attitude befits Christians at all times, since they know not when the summons may come to them requiring them to quit the Egypt of this world and start for the heavenly country.

It is the Lord's passover.—The word "passover" (*pesakh*) is here used for the first time. It is supposed by some to be of Egyptian origin, and to signify primarily "a spreading out of wings, so as to protect." But the meaning "pass over" is still regarded by many of the best Hebraists as the primary and most proper sense, and the word itself as Semitic. It occurs in the geographic name Tiphsach (Thapsacus), borne by the place where it was usual to cross, or "pass over," the Euphrates.

(12) **For I will pass through.**—Rather, *go through,* since the word used is entirely unconnected with *pesakh.*

Against all the gods of Egypt I will execute judgment.—The translation "gods" is far preferable to that of "princes," given in the margin. The death of all the firstborn beasts would have been felt by the Egyptians as a heavy judgment upon their gods. Some of their sacred animals were regarded as actual incarnations of deity; and if any of these perished, as is likely, the threat would have been executed to the letter. But even apart from this, as cows, sheep, goats, cats, dogs, jackals, crocodiles, hippopotami, apes, ibises, frogs, &c., were sacred, either throughout Egypt or in parts of it, a general destruction of all firstborn animals would have been felt as a blow dealt to the gods almost equally.

I am the Lord.—Heb., *I, Jehovah.* The construction is, "I, Jehovah, will execute judgment."

(13) **The blood shall be to you for a token.**—Rather, *the blood shall be for a token for you*: *i.e.*, it shall be a token to Me on your behalf. (See the comment on verse 7, and compare verse 23.)

(14) **Ye shall keep it a feast . . . by an ordinance for ever.**—The Passover is continued in the Eucharist (1 Cor. v. 7, 8); and the Easter celebration, which the Church makes binding on all her members, exactly corresponds in time to the Paschal ceremony, and takes its place. In this way the Passover may be regarded as still continuing under Christianity, and as intended to continue, "even to the end of the world."

(15) **Seven days.**—The division of time into periods of seven days each was unknown to the more ancient Egyptians, but is thought to have existed in Babylonia as early as B.C. 2000. That it was recognised in the family of Abraham appears from Gen. xxix. 27. According to some, God established the division by an express command to our first parents in Paradise that they should keep the seventh day holy (see Gen. ii. 3); but this is greatly questioned by others, who regard Gen. ii. 3 as *anticipatory,* and think the Sabbath was not instituted until the giving of the manna (Exod. xvi. 23). However this may have been, it is generally allowed that the Israelites had not observed the seventh day in Egypt, where, indeed, they were held to labour continually, and that the Sabbath as an actual observance dates from the Exodus. The injunction here given, if it belongs to

the seventh day, that soul shall be cut
off from Israel. (16) And in the first day
there shall be an holy convocation, and in
the seventh day there shall be an holy
convocation to you; no manner of
work shall be done in them, save *that*
which every [1] man must eat, that only
may be done of you. (17) And ye
shall observe *the feast of* unleavened
bread; for in this selfsame day have
I brought your armies out of the
land of Egypt: therefore shall ye
observe this day in your generations by
an ordinance for ever. (18) [a] In the first
month, on the fourteenth day of the
month at even, ye shall eat unleavened
bread, until the one and twentieth day
of the month at even. (19) Seven days
shall there be no leaven found in your
houses: for whosoever eateth that which
is leavened, even that soul shall be
cut off from the congregation of Israel,
whether he be a stranger, or born in the
land. (20) Ye shall eat nothing leavened;
in all your habitations shall ye eat un-
leavened bread.

(21) Then Moses called for all the elders
of Israel, and said unto them, Draw out
and take you a [2] lamb according to your
families, and kill the passover. (22) [b] And
ye shall take a bunch of hyssop, and dip
it in the blood that *is* in the bason, and
strike the lintel and the two side posts
with the blood that *is* in the bason; and

1 Heb. *soul.*

a Lev. 23. 5; Num. 28. 16.

2 Or, *kid.*

b Heb. 11. 28.

---

the time of the tenth plague, would be the first preliminary note of warning with respect to the Sabbath, raising an expectation of it, and preparing the way for it, leading up to the subsequent revelations in the wilderness of Sin and at Sinai.

Ye shall put away leaven out of your houses.—There was to be no compromise, nothing resembling half measures. Leaven, taken as typical of corruption, was to be wholly put away, not allowed by any householder to lurk anywhere within his house—a solemn warning that we are to make no compromise with sin.

That soul shall be cut off from Israel.—See the Note on Gen. xvii. 14.

(16) **In the first day there shall be an holy convocation.**—The Passover was to be kept on the fourteenth day of Abib, at even. The seven following days were to be "days of unleavened bread." On the first of these, the fifteenth of Abib (Lev. xxiii. 6), there was to be a "holy convocation," *i.e.*, a general gathering of the people to the door of the sanctuary for sacrifice, worship, and perhaps instruction. (Comp. Neh. viii. 1.) The term "convocation" implies that the people were summoned to attend; and the actual summons appears to have been made by the blowing of the silver trumpets (Num. x. 2). On the seventh day, the twenty-first of Abib, was to be another similar meeting. "No manner of work" was to be done on either of these two days; or rather, as explained in Lev. xxiii. 7, 8, "no servile work."

(17) **In this selfsame day have I brought your armies out of the land of Egypt.**—On the application of the word "armies" to the people of Israel, see above (chap. vi. 26). The expression "have I brought" indicates either that these directions were not given until after the Exodus, or at any rate that they were not reduced to writing until then.

(18) **In the first month.**—The Hebrew omits "month" by a not unusual ellipse. (Comp. Ezek. i. 1.)

At even.—The evening intended is not that with which the fourteenth day began, but that with which it closed, the end of the fourteenth and beginning of the fifteenth day. (See Lev. xxiii. 5, 6.)

(19) **A stranger**—*i.e.*, a foreigner in blood, who has been adopted into the nation, received circumcision, and become a full proselyte. It is not improbable that many of the "six hundred thousand" reckoned to "Israel" (verse 37) were of this class—persons who had joined themselves to the nation during the sojourn in Egypt, or even earlier. (See Note on Gen. xvii. 13.) When the "exclusiveness" of the Hebrews is made a charge against them, justice requires us to remember that from the first it was open to those who were not of Hebrew blood to share in the Hebrew privileges by accepting the covenant of circumcision, and joining themselves to the nation. It was in this way that the Kenites, and even the Gibeonites, became reckoned to Israel.

Born in the land.—Heb., *natives of the land*: *i.e.*, of Canaan. Canaan was regarded as belonging to Abraham and his descendants from the time of the first promise (Gen. xii. 7). Thenceforth it was their true home: they were its expatriated inhabitants.

The First Passover kept.

(21) **Moses called for all the elders.**—He had been directed to "speak unto all the congregation" (verse 3) but understood the direction as allowing him to do so *mediately*, through the elders.

Draw out.—Some understand this intransitively—"Withdraw, and take," *i.e.*, go, and take; others transitively—"Withdraw a lamb from the flock."

According to your families—*i.e.*, with reference to the number of your families, but not necessarily one for each. (See verse 4.)

(22) **A bunch of hyssop.**—The "hyssop" (*êzob*) of the Old Testament is probably the caper plant, called now *asaf*, or *asuf*, by the Arabs, which grows plentifully in the Sinaitic region (Stanley: *Sinai and Palestine*, p. 21), and is well adapted for the purpose here spoken of. It was regarded as having purifying properties (Lev. xiv. 4, 49—52; Num. xix. 6; Ps. li. 7), and was therefore suitable for sprinkling the blood of expiation.

In the bason.—The word translated "bason" has another meaning also, viz., "threshold;" and this meaning was preferred in the present place both by the LXX. and by Jerome. Whichever translation we adopt, there is a difficulty in the occurrence of the article, since neither the threshold nor any bason had been mentioned previously. Perhaps Moses assumed that whenever a victim was offered, the blood had to be caught in a bason, and therefore spoke of "*the* bason" as something familiar to his hearers in this connection. If the lamb had been sacrificed *on the threshold*, it would scarcely

none of you shall go out at the door of
his house until the morning. (23) For the
LORD will pass through to smite the
Egyptians; and when he seeth the blood
upon the lintel, and on the two side
posts, the LORD will pass over the door,
and will not suffer the destroyer to come
in unto your houses to smite *you.* (24) And
ye shall observe this thing for an ordinance
to thee and to thy sons for ever.
(25) And it shall come to pass, when ye be
come to the land which the LORD will
give you, according as he hath promised,
that ye shall keep this service. (26) [a] And
it shall come to pass, when your children
shall say unto you, What mean ye by
this service? (27) That ye shall say, It *is*
the sacrifice of the LORD's passover, who
passed over the houses of the children
of Israel in Egypt, when he smote the
Egyptians, and delivered our houses.
And the people bowed the head and
worshipped.
(28) And the children of Israel went
away, and did as the LORD had commanded
Moses and Aaron, so did they.
(29) [b] And it came to pass, that at midnight
the LORD smote all the firstborn
in the land of Egypt, [c] from the firstborn
of Pharaoh that sat on his throne unto
the firstborn of the captive that *was* in
the [1] dungeon; and all the firstborn of
cattle. (30) And Pharaoh rose up in the
night, he, and all his servants, and all

a Josh. 4. 6.

b ch. 11. 4.

c Wisd. 18. 11.

1 Heb., *house of the pit.*

---

have been necessary to put the blood on the lintel and doorposts also.

None of you shall go out.—Moses seems to have given this command by his own authority, without any positive Divine direction. He understood that the atoning blood was the sole protection from the destroying angel, and that outside the portal sprinkled with it was no safety.

(23) **The destroyer.**—The "plague" of verse 13 is here called "the destroyer" (τὸν ὀλεθρεύοντα, LXX.), as again in Heb. xii. 28. Jehovah seems to have employed an angel, or "angels" (Ps. lxxix. 48) as His agents to effect the actual slaying of the firstborn. (Comp. 2 Sam. xxiv. 16; 1 Chron. xxi. 15; 2 Kings xix. 35.) There is no struggle or opposition (as Bishop Lowth and Redslob think) between Jehovah and "the destroyer," who is simply His minister (Heb. i. 14), bidden to enter some houses and to "pass over" others.

(24) **This thing.**—Not the sprinkling of the blood, which was never repeated after the first occasion, but the sacrifice of the lamb, commanded in verse 21.

(27) **It is the sacrifice of the Lord's passover.**—Heb., *This is a passover-sacrifice to Jehovah.* The emphatic word is "Passover;" and it was the meaning of this term which was especially to be explained. The explanation would involve an historical account of the circumstances of the institution, such as would be apt to call forth feelings of gratitude and devotion.

THE TENTH PLAGUE.

(29, 30) The nature of the tenth plague is indubitable, but as to the exact agency which was employed there may be different views. In every family in which the firstborn child had been a male, that child was stricken with death. Pharaoh's firstborn son—the *erpa suten sa*—the heir to his throne, was taken; and so in all other families. Nobles, priests, tradesmen, artisans, peasants, fishermen—all alike suffered. In the hyperbolic language of the narrator, "there was not a house where there was not one dead." And the deaths took place "at midnight," in the weirdest hour, at the most silent time, in the deepest darkness. So it had been prophesied (chap. xi. 4); but the particular night had not been announced. As several days had elapsed since the announcement, the Egyptians may have been wrapt in fancied security. Suddenly the calamity fell upon them, and "there was a great cry." Death did not come, as upon the host of Sennacherib, noiselessly, unperceivedly, but "with observation." Those who were seized woke up and aroused their relatives. There was a cry for help, a general alarm, a short, sharp struggle—and then a death.

The visitation is ordinarily ascribed to God Himself (chaps. iv. 23, xi. 4, xii. 12, 27, 29, xiii. 15, &c.), but in verse 23 to "the destroyer." It has been already shown that this expression points to angelic agency. That agency, however, does not exclude a further natural one. As in 2 Sam. xxiv. the seventy thousand whom the destroying angel killed (verse 16) are said to have been slain by a pestilence (verse 15), so it may have been here. Pestilence often rages in Egypt in the spring of the year, and carries off thousands in a very short space. As with so many of the other plagues, God may here too have employed a natural agency. None the less would the plague have been miraculous—(1) in its intensity; (2) in its coming at the time prophesied, viz., midnight; (3) in its selection of victims, viz., the firstborn males only, and all of them; (4) in its avoidance of the Israelites; and (5) in its extension, as prophesied, to the firstborn of animals.

(29) **All the firstborn.**—The Hebrew word used applies only to males.

The firstborn of Pharaoh.—The law of primogeniture prevailed in Egypt, as elsewhere generally. The Pharaoh's eldest son was recognised as "hereditary crown prince," and sometimes associated in the kingdom during his father's lifetime. This had been the case with Rameses II., probably the Pharaoh from whom Moses fled (chap. ii. 15); but the practice was not common. In any case, however, the eldest son of the reigning monarch occupied a most important position, and his loss would be felt as a national calamity.

The firstborn of the captive.—The variation of phrase between this verse and chap. xi. 5 is curious, but appears not to be of any significance. The writer simply means, in both places, "all, from the highest to the lowest."

All the firstborn of cattle.—Rather, *of beasts,* as in chap. xi. 5. (On the reasons for beasts being included in the calamity, see the Note on that passage.)

(30) **A great cry.**—See the comment on chap. xi. 6. The combination of public calamity, private grief, and

the Egyptians; and there was a great
cry in Egypt; for *there was* not a house
where *there was* not one dead.
(31) And he called for Moses and Aaron
by night, and said, Rise up, *and* get you
forth from among my people, both ye
and the children of Israel; and go, serve
the LORD, as ye have said. (32) Also take
your flocks and your herds, as ye have
said, and be gone; and bless me also.
(33) And the Egyptians were urgent upon
the people, that they might send them
out of the land in haste; for they said,
We *be* all dead *men*. (34) And the people
took their dough before it was leavened,
their [1]kneadingtroughs being bound up
in their clothes upon their shoulders.
(35) And the children of Israel did according
to the word of Moses; and they
borrowed of the Egyptians [a]jewels of
silver, and jewels of gold, and raiment:
(36) and the LORD gave the people
favour in the sight of the Egyptians,
so that they lent unto them *such things
as they required*. And they spoiled the
Egyptians.
(37) And [b]the children of Israel journeyed
from Rameses to Succoth, about six

1 Or, *dough*.

a ch. 3. 22 & 11. 2.

b Num. 33. 3.

---

shocked religious fanaticism might well produce a cry "such as there was none like it, neither shall be like it any more" (chap. xi. 6).

Not a house where there was not one dead.—This cannot have been literally true. In half the families a daughter would have "opened the womb;" in others, the firstborn son would have been absent, or dead previously. To judge Scripture fairly, we must make allowance for the hyperbole of Oriental thought and expression, which causes the substitution of universal terms for general ones, and the absence of qualifying clauses. The meaning is that in the great majority of houses there was one dead. This may well have been so, if we include the dependants and the *animals*. Pet animals—dogs, cats, gazelles, and monkeys—abounded in Egyptian homes.

THE DISMISSAL OF THE ISRAELITES.

(31) **He called for Moses and Aaron.**—This does not mean that Pharaoh summoned them to his presence, but only that he sent a message to them. (See above, chap. xi. 8.) The messengers were undoubtedly chief officials; they "bowed themselves down" before Moses, who was now recognised as "very great" (chap. xi. 3), and delivered their master's message, which granted in express terms all that Moses had ever demanded. Pharaoh's spirit was, for the time, thoroughly broken.

(32) **And bless me also.**—Here Pharaoh's humiliation reaches its extreme point. He is reduced by the terrible calamity of the last plague not only to grant all the demands made of him freely, and without restriction, but to crave the favour of a blessing from those whom he had despised, rebuked (chap. v. 4), thwarted, and finally driven from his presence under the threat of death (chap. x. 28). Those with whom were the issues of life and death must, he felt, have the power to bless or curse effectually.

(33) **The Egyptians were urgent.**—Not only Pharaoh, but the Egyptian nation generally was anxious for the immediate departure of the Israelites, and expedited it in every way. This must greatly have facilitated their all setting forth at once. It also accounts for the readiness of the Egyptians to part with their "jewels" and "raiment" (verse 35).

(34) **Kneadingtroughs.**—Light, portable wooden bowls, such as are now used by the Arabs.

(35) **They borrowed.**—See the comment on chap. iii. 22.

(36) **They lent.**—Rather, "they *gave*." It is that the Egyptians neither expected nor wished the Israelites to return.

THE DEPARTURE OF ISRAEL, THEIR NUMBERS, AND THE TIME OF THE EGYPTIAN SOJOURN.

(37—41) The two principal statements of this passage are—(1) that the sojourn of the Israelites in Egypt lasted four hundred and thirty years; and (2) that at the time of the departure the number of the "men" (*gĕbârim*) was six hundred thousand. This latter statement is evidently a rough one, but it is confirmed, and even enlarged, by the more accurate estimate of Numbers i. and ii., which goes into particulars with respect to the several tribes, and makes the exact amount of the adult male population, exclusive of the Levites, to be 625,540 (chap. ii. 32). It would follow that the nation, at the time of its departure, was one of above two millions of souls.

Two difficulties are raised with respect to this estimate:—(1) Could the Israelites possibly have increased during their sojourn in Egypt from the "seventy souls" who went down with Jacob to two millions? (2) Is it conceivable that such a multitude, with their flocks and herds, could have quitted Egypt on one day, and marched in a body through the narrow *wadys* of the Sinaitic region to the plain in front of Sinai? Could even that plain have contained them? With regard to the first point, before it can be decided we must ascertain what are the exact data. What is to be taken as the original number of those who "went down into Egypt?" what as the duration of the sojourn? It has been already shown (see the comment on chap. i. 5) that the descendants of Jacob who entered Egypt were probably a hundred and thirty-two rather than seventy; that they were accompanied by their wives and husbands; that they took with them also their "households," which were very numerous (see Note on Gen. xvii. 13); and that the entire number is fairly estimated at "several thousands." Let us then place it at 3,000.

The duration of the sojourn in Egypt, stated in the Hebrew text at 430 years, is reduced by the LXX. and Samaritan Versions to half the time: *i.e.*, to 215 years. If we accept Mr. Malthus's statement, that in the absence of artificial checks population will double itself every twenty years, we shall find that 3,000 persons might, in the space of two centuries, increase to above 3,000,000; so that even the 215 years of the Greek and Samaritan Versions would admit of such a multiplication as that required. But as there is no sufficient reason for preferring the Versions to the Original, or the period of 215 to that of 430 years, we are entitled to regard the latter term as the real duration of the sojourn, in which case a doubling of the population

hundred thousand on foot *that were* men,
beside children. (38) And [1]a mixed mul-
titude went up also with them; and
flocks, and herds, *even* very much cattle.
(39) And they baked unleavened cakes of
the dough which they brought forth out
of Egypt, for it was not leavened; be-
cause they were thrust out of Egypt,
and could not tarry, neither had they
prepared for themselves any victual.
(40) Now the sojourning of the children
of Israel, who dwelt in Egypt, *was* [a]four
hundred and thirty years. (41) And it
came to pass at the end of the four hun-
dred and thirty years, even the selfsame
day it came to pass, that all the hosts
of the LORD went out from the land of
Egypt. (42) It *is* [2]a night to be much
observed unto the LORD for bringing
them out from the land of Egypt: this
is that night of the LORD to be observed
of all the children of Israel in their
generations.
(43) And the LORD said unto Moses and
Aaron, This *is* the ordinance of the pass-
over: There shall no stranger eat thereof:
(44) but every man's servant that is bought
for money, when thou hast circumcised
him, then shall he eat thereof. (45) A
foreigner and an hired servant shall not

1 Heb., *a great mixture.*

a Gen. 15. 13; Acts 7. 6; Gal. 3. 17.

2 Heb., *a night of observations.*

---

every forty-five years would have produced the result indicated. Such a result under the circumstances, in the rich soil of Egypt, in the extensive territory granted to the Israelites, and with God's special blessing on the people, is in no way surprising.

The difficulty of handling so vast a body, and marching them from Goshen to the Red Sea, and from the Red Sea to Sinai, remains, and, no doubt, is considerable. But we must remember that as far as Marah the country was perfectly open, and allowed of any extension of the line of march on either flank. After this, the *wadys* were entered, and the real difficulties of the journey began. Probably the host spread itself out, and proceeded to the rendezvous in front of the Ras Sufsafeh by several routes, of which Moses traces only the one which he himself followed. The plain Er-Rahah, according to the calculations of the best engineers, would have contained the entire multitude; but it is unnecessary to suppose that all were at any one time present in it. The whole Sinaitic district was probably occupied by the flocks and herds, and the herdsmen who tended them. Many of the tents may have been pitched in the Wady-ed-Deir and the Seil Leja. All that the narrative requires is that the *main body* of the people should have been encamped in front of Sinai, have heard the Decalogue delivered, and consented to the covenant.

(37) **From Rameses to Succoth.**—The difference between the Raamses of chap. i. 11 and the Rameses of this passage is merely one of "pointing;" nor is there the least ground for supposing that a different place is intended. Pi-Ramesu was the main capital of the kings of the nineteenth dynasty, having superseded Tanis, of which it was a suburb. (See Note on chap. i. 11.) Succoth has been identified by Dr. Brugsch with an Egyptian town called Thukot; but it is probably a Semitic word, signifying "tents" or "booths." The district south-east of Tanis is one in which clusters of "booths" have been at all times common. Some one of these—situated, perhaps, near the modern Tel-Dafneh, fifteen miles south-east of Tanis—was the first halt of the Israelites.

(38) **A mixed multitude went up also with them.**—Nothing is told us of the component elements of this "mixed multitude." We hear of them as "murmuring" in Num. xi. 4, so that they seem to have remained with Israel. Some may have been Egyptians, impressed by the recent miracles; some foreigners held to servitude, like the Israelites, and glad to escape from their masters. It is noticeable that the Egyptian writers, in their perverted accounts of the Exodus, made a multitude of foreigners (Hyksôs) take part with the Hebrews.

(39) **Unleavened cakes.**—Such are commonly eaten by the Arabs, who make them by mixing flour with water, and attaching round pieces of the dough to the insides of their ovens after they have heated them.

(40) **The sojourning of the children of Israel, who dwelt in Egypt.**—Heb., *which they sojourned in Egypt.*

Was four hundred and thirty years.—Comp. the prophecy:—"Thy seed shall be a stranger in *a land* that is not theirs [Egypt, not Canaan], and shall serve them; and they shall afflict them *four hundred years*: and also *that nation* whom they shall serve will I judge" (Gen. xv. 13, 14). The genealogy of Joshua (1 Chron. vii. 22—27), which places him in the eleventh generation from Jacob, accords well with this term of years. The other genealogies are more or less abbreviated.

(41) **The selfsame day . . . all the hosts . . . went out.**—*All started, i.e.,* on one and the same day—the fifteenth of the month Abib. Some would start during the night, some in the morning, others at different periods of the day. They had different distances to traverse in order to reach the appointed halt, Succoth.

FURTHER DIRECTIONS RESPECTING THE PASSOVER.

(43—51) **This is the ordinance.**—These directions, together with those which follow with respect to the sanctification of the firstborn (chap. xiii. 1—16), seem to have been given to Moses *at Succoth,* and were consequently recorded at this point of the narrative. They comprise three principal points:—(1) The exclusion of all uncircumcised persons from the Passover (verse 43); (2) the admission of all full proselytes (verses 48, 49); and (3) the injunction that no bone of the lamb should be broken (verse 46).

(43) **No stranger.**—Comp. verse 48 for limitations. If a stranger wished to join, and would accept circumcision for himself and the males of his family, he might partake in the rite.

(44) **Every man's servant.**—Slaves born in the house were required to be circumcised on the eighth day, like Israelites (Gen. xvii. 13). Bought slaves were allowed their choice. It is noticeable that the circumcised slave was to be admitted to full religious equality with his master.

(45) **An hired servant.**—It is assumed that the hired servant will be a foreigner; otherwise, of course, he would participate.

eat thereof. (46) In one house shall it be
eaten; thou shalt not carry forth ought
of the flesh abroad out of the house;
[a]neither shall ye break a bone thereof.
(47) All the congregation of Israel shall
[1]keep it. (48) And when a stranger shall
sojourn with thee, and will keep the
passover to the LORD, let all his males
be circumcised, and then let him come
near and keep it; and he shall be as one
that is born in the land: for no uncir-
cumcised person shall eat thereof. (49) One
law shall be to him that is homeborn,
and unto the stranger that sojourneth
among you.

(50) Thus did all the children of Israel;
as the LORD commanded Moses and
Aaron, so did they.

(51) And it came to pass the selfsame
day, *that* the LORD did bring the children
of Israel out of the land of Egypt by
their armies.

CHAPTER XIII.—(1) And the LORD
spake unto Moses, saying, (2) [b] Sanctify
unto me all the firstborn, whatsoever
openeth the womb among the children
of Israel, *both* of man and of beast: it
is mine.

(3) And Moses said unto the people,
Remember this day, in which ye came
out from Egypt, out of the house of
[2]bondage; for by strength of hand the
LORD brought you out from this *place*:
there shall no leavened bread be eaten.
(4) This day came ye out in the month
Abib. (5) And it shall be when the LORD
shall bring thee into the land of the
Canaanites, and the Hittites, and the
Amorites, and the Hivites, and the Jebu-
sites, which he sware unto thy fathers to
give thee, a land flowing with milk and
honey, that thou shalt keep this service
in this month. (6) Seven days thou shalt
eat unleavened bread, and in the seventh
day *shall be* a feast to the LORD. (7) Un-
leavened bread shall be eaten seven
days; and there shall no leavened bread

a Num. 9. 12; John 19. 36.

1 Heb., *do it.*

b ch. 22. 29 & 34. 19; Lev. 27. 26; Num. 3. 13 & 8. 16; Luke 2. 23.

2 Heb., *servants.*

---

(46) **Neither shall ye break a bone thereof.**—In the case of all other victims, the limbs were to be separated from the body. Here the victim was to be roasted whole, and to remain whole, as a symbol of unity, and a type of Him through whom men are brought into unity with each other and with God. (See John xix. 33—36.)

(51) This last verse of the chapter would more appropriately commence chap. xiii., with which it is to be united. Translate—"And it came to pass, on the selfsame day that the Lord brought the children of Israel out of the land of Egypt by their armies, that the Lord spake unto Moses, saying," &c.

By their armies.—See Note 2 on chap. xiii. 18.

XIII.

SANCTIFICATION OF THE FIRSTBORN, AND LAW OF REDEMPTION.

(2) **Sanctify unto me all the firstborn.**—It was a reasonable demand that the existing firstborn of Israel, spared by God when the Egyptian firstborn were destroyed, should be regarded thenceforth as His, and set apart for His service. The extension of the demand to existing beasts was also reasonable, since they too had been spared. God's further requirement, that henceforth all the future firstborn should also be His, was intended to perpetuate the memory of the recent deliverance, and to help to fix it in the mind of the nation. The substitution of a redemption in the case of unclean beasts was necessitated by the circumstances of the case, since they could not be sacrificed; and the redemption of the firstborn sons naturally followed when the Levitical priesthood was established, and their services were no longer necessary. (See Num. iii. 40—51, xviii. 16.) The Jews still observe the ordinance, so far as the children are concerned, and redeem the son which has "opened the womb" on the thirtieth day after the birth.

(3) **Remember this day.**—Remembrance was secured in four ways:—(1) By the month being made to commence the ecclesiastical year; (2) by the institution of the Passover; (3) by the seven days of unleavened bread; and (4) by the redemption, and the inquiries it would necessitate (verses 14, 15).

(4) **The month Abib.**—Abib means "green ears of corn," or "greenness;" and the month of Abib was that in which the wheat came into ear, and the earth generally renewed its verdure. It was a "vague," or shifting month, since it properly began with the day of the full moon that followed next after the vernal equinox. It retained its name until the Babylonian captivity, when the Babylonian name Nisan superseded the original one (Neh. ii. 1; Esther iii. 7).

(5) **The Canaanites, and the Hittites . . .** The full number of the Canaanitish nations was seven, five of which are here enumerated. The other two were the Perizzites and the Girgashites, which seem to have been the least important. The most important were the Canaanites, Hittites, and Amorites; and these are consequently almost always placed first. At the time of the Exodus, and for many centuries afterwards, the actually most powerful nation would seem to have been that of the Hittites. (See Josh. i. 4; 1 Kings x. 29; 2 Kings vii. 6; and compare the Egyptian and Assyrian remains *passim.*)

A land flowing with milk and honey.—See Note on chap. iii. 8.

Thou shalt keep this service.—Kalisch concludes from this verse, and from chap. xii. 25, that there was no obligation upon the Israelites to keep the Passover until they obtained possession of Canaan. He holds that two Passovers only were celebrated before that event—one by Moses in the wilderness of Sinai (Num. ix. 1—5), and the other by Joshua at Gilgal, in the plain of Jericho (Josh. v. 10, 11).

(6) **A feast to the Lord.**—Comp. chap. xii. 16, where a "holy convocation" is ordered for the seventh

be seen with thee, neither shall there be
leaven seen with thee in all thy quarters.
(8) And thou shalt shew thy son in that
day, saying, *This is done* because of that
which the LORD did unto me when I came
forth out of Egypt. (9) And it shall be
for a sign unto thee upon thine hand,
and for a memorial between thine eyes,
that the LORD's law may be in thy
mouth: for with a strong hand hath
the LORD brought thee out of Egypt.
(10) Thou shalt therefore keep this
ordinance in his season from year to
year.

(11) And it shall be when the LORD shall
bring thee into the land of the Canaan-
ites, as he sware unto thee and to thy
fathers, and shall give it thee, (12) [a] that
thou shalt [1] set apart unto the LORD all
that openeth the matrix, and every
firstling that cometh of a beast which
thou hast; the males *shall be* the LORD's.
(13) And every firstling of an ass thou
shalt redeem with a [2] lamb; and if thou
wilt not redeem it, then thou shalt break
his neck: and all the firstborn of man
among thy children shalt thou redeem.
(14) And it shall be when thy son asketh
thee [3] in time to come, saying, What *is*
this? that thou shalt say unto him, By
strength of hand the LORD brought us
out from Egypt, from the house of bond-
age: (15) and it came to pass, when
Pharaoh would hardly let us go, that the
LORD slew all the firstborn in the land
of Egypt, both the firstborn of man, and
the firstborn of beast: therefore I sacri-
fice to the LORD all that openeth the
matrix, being males; but all the firstborn
of my children I redeem. (16) And it shall
be for a token upon thine hand, and for
frontlets between thine eyes: for by
strength of hand the LORD brought us
forth out of Egypt.

a ch. 22. 29 & 34. 19; Ezek. 44. 30.

1 Heb., *cause to pass over.*

2 Or, *kid.*

3 Heb., *to morrow.*

---

day. The Jews regard this day—the twenty-first of Abib—as the anniversary of the passage of the Red Sea.

(9) **It shall be for a sign unto thee upon thine hand, and for a memorial between thine eyes.**—The practice of wearing *tĕphillin,* or "phylacteries," is referred by the Jews themselves to the time of the Exodus, and regarded by them as resting on the present passage, together with Deut. vi. 8 and xi. 18. These phylacteries consist of small strips of parchment, on which are written certain passages from the Law—viz., Exod. xiii. 2—10; Deut. vi. 4—9, and Deut. xi. 13—21—and which are then folded tight, placed in small boxes, and attached by bands to the left wrist and the forehead at the hours of prayer. It is well known that a similar custom prevailed in Egypt (Wilkinson, *Ancient Egyptians,* vol. iii., p. 364); and this has been made an objection to the Mosaic institution of phylacteries, since Moses, it has been thought, would not have encouraged an Egyptian superstition. But the adoption of Egyptian customs, *purged from their superstition,* is quite in the spirit of the Mosaic institutions, and in no way reprehensible. If the Israelites were addicted to wearing amulets, like the Egyptians, it would have been a wise proviso to substitute for the magic charms of sorcerers the solemn words of the Law, and in this way to turn a current superstition to a good account. The Law was thereby honoured, and the special passages selected would come to be generally known to those who wore them, and to be "in their mouth" and "in their heart" (Deut. xi. 18). [Dean Plumptre notices, in his *Commentary on the Temptation* (St. Matt.), that our Blessed Lord used against the adversary quotations from the Scriptures forming these very Tephillin.]

(11) **The land of the Canaanites.**—Either their superior importance or their genealogical position (Gen. x. 15) caused the term "Canaanites" to be used inclusively of all the Palestinian nations. The land is always "the land of Canaan" (Gen. xi. 31, xii. 5, xiii. 12, &c.).

(12) **Thou shalt set apart**—*i.e.,* separate off from the rest of the flock or herd, that it might not be mixed up with those which were not "sanctified."

(13) **Every firstling of an ass.**—It is observable that nothing is said of the Israelites possessing horses. Horses were well known in Egypt at the time, but were kept only by the kings and the great men. The Hebrews had not been in a position ever to have possessed any. Asses, on the contrary, were exceedingly common, and formed the ordinary beasts of burden in the country. In default of camels, which they seem not to have owned, the Israelites must have carried their tents and other baggage on asses.

Thou shalt redeem.—Since the ass was unclean. In Egypt he is said to have been "Typhonian;" and Set, the Evil Principle, is represented with long ears, which may be those of an ass, cropped towards the upper extremity. The redeeming of an ass with a lamb (or kid) was favourable to the owner, since the ass colt must have been of considerably more value.

If thou wilt not redeem it, then thou shalt break his neck.—There will always be in every nation those who grudge to make any offering to God, and who will seek to evade every requisition for a gift. To check such niggardliness, the present law was made. It would be effectual without requiring to be put in force.

All the firstborn of man among thy children shalt thou redeem.—This was declared in anticipation of the arrangement afterwards to be made, whereby the tribe of Levi was taken in lieu of the firstborn for the service of the sanctuary (Num. iii. 40—45), and an obligation was imposed on Israelites of other tribes to "redeem" their sons by a payment of five shekels for each to the priests (Num. xviii. 15, 16).

(16) **It shall be for a token.**—See the comment on verse 9. The "frontlets" (*totaphôth*) of this passage, and of Deut. vi. 8, were called *tĕphillin* in Chaldee, both words signifying properly "bands" or "circlets." The injunctions on the subject which are here given might undoubtedly be explained as meta-

(17) And it came to pass, when Pharaoh
had let the people go, that God led them
not *through* the way of the land of the
Philistines, although that *was* near; for
God said, Lest peradventure the people
repent when they see war, and they re-
turn to Egypt: (18) but God led the
people about, *through* the way of the
wilderness of the Red sea: and the
children of Israel went up [1]harnessed
out of the land of Egypt.

(19) And Moses took the bones of Joseph
with him: for he had straitly sworn the
children of Israel, saying, [a]God will
surely visit you; and ye shall carry up
my bones away hence with you.
(20) And [b]they took their journey from
Succoth, and encamped in Etham, in the
edge of the wilderness. (21) And [c]the
LORD went before them by day in a pillar
of a cloud, to lead them the way; and
by night in a pillar of fire, to give them

1 Or, *by five in a rank.*

a Gen. 50. 25; Josh. 24. 32.

b Num. 33. 6.

c Num. 14. 14; Deut. 1. 33; Ps. 78. 14; 1 Cor. 10. 1.

---

phorical; but those in Deut. vi. 6—9 seem to have been intended, and were certainly understood, literally.

THE DIRECTION OF THE MARCH.

(17) **God led them not through the way of the land of the Philistines.**—In verses 17—19 the writer interposes some parenthetic remarks, which are not a continuation of the narrative interrupted (chap. xii. 42), but rather reflections that occur to him. The starting point of the journey being Tanis or Rameses, in the Eastern Delta, not far from the sea, he sees that the shortest, and apparently the easiest, route for the Israelites to have pursued would have been that which led along the coast, from Tanis to Pelusium, thence to Rhinocolura, and from Rhinocolura to Gaza, Ascalon, and Ashdod, the chief towns of the Philistines. The distance along this line was not more than about 200 miles, and might have been accomplished in a fortnight. He anticipates an inquiry, Why did they not pursue this route? The reply is, that such was not the will of God; and the reason why it was not His will is further given—"The people would probably have repented when they saw war, and would have returned to Egypt." It is implied that the Philistines were already a strong and warlike people, which they may well have been, though not mentioned in the contemporary Egyptian monuments. The Egyptians mention by name very few of the nations of Syria, and the few names which they put on record can seldom be identified.

Although that was near.—Rather, *because that was near.* God did not, because it was near, lead them that way, but another.

When they see war.—If the Philistines are to be regarded as identical with the "Purusata" of the Egyptian remains, they must be viewed as one of the most warlike people of the time. Even leaving aside this identification—which is very uncertain—we must view them as one of the most important of the tribes inhabiting the lower Syrian region. In Joshua's time they already possessed their five strong fortresses—Gaza, Ascalon, Ashdod, Gath, and Ekron (Josh. xiii. 3); and during the period of the Judges they raised themselves to the leading position in the Palestinian region. Palestine derives its name from them, and would not have obtained the name unless they had been a very remarkable race. We can well understand that the Israelites after four centuries of slavery would have been an ill match for the Philistines, and that, if defeated or intimidated, they might have felt that no course was open to them but a return to Egypt.

(18) **But God led the people about.**—Or, *led the people a circuit*—took them, not by the direct route, through Pelusium, past Lake Serbônis, to Rhinocolura and Gaza, but led them by the most circuitous route possible—the way of the Red Sea and the wilderness of Sinai to the Transjordanic region, the land of the Amorites, and so across Jordan to Canaan proper. The passage seems to dispose altogether of Dr. Brugsch's theory, that the "Red Sea" of the writer of Exodus was the Lake Serbônis, and that it was not until after this lake was passed that their journey was deflected to the south.

The children of Israel went up harnessed out of the land of Egypt.—It is generally agreed that this is a wrong translation. Very few of the Israelites can have possessed suits of armour until after the passage of the Red Sea, when they may have stripped the bodies of the slain Egyptians. Nor has the word used ever the force of "harnessed." It might mean "with their loins girded," but such an exposition would deprive the statement made of any force. Loins were always girded in preparation for a journey, and there would be no need to mention the fact. The best explanation is, that the word here means "organised," "in military order" (Saadia, Gesenius, Lee, Knobel, Cook). It was clearly necessary, to prevent confusion, that a military order should have been adopted, and there are not wanting indications that during the year of contention with Pharaoh such an organisation was introduced and proceeded with. (See chaps. iv. 29, 31, vi. 26, xii. 3, 21, 51.) It must have been brought to a high pitch of perfection for the Exodus to have taken place, as it seems to have done, without serious confusion or entanglement.

(19) **Moses took the bones of Joseph.**—Joseph's body had been embalmed according to the Egyptian fashion (Gen. l. 26). He had ordered it to be conveyed to Canaan when the Israelites went there (Gen. l. 25).

THE JOURNEY RESUMED.

(20) **They took their journey from Succoth, and encamped in Etham.**—The exact positions of both Succoth and Etham are uncertain, and can only be conjectured; but they probably lay to the south-east of Tanis, between that city and the Bitter Lakes. Succoth may have been at or near Tel Dafneh, about fifteen miles from Tanis, and Etham near the modern Ismailia, on the verge of the desert. Dr. Brugsch's identification of Etham with the Egyptian *Khetam* is highly improbable, since the Hebrew *aleph* never replaces the Egyptian *kh*, which is a very strong guttural. E-tham would mean "the house of Tum," and point to a temple of the Sun-god, who was specially worshipped in the Eastern Delta, at Heliopolis, Patumus, and elsewhere.

(21) **The Lord went before them.**—In verses 17, 18, the writer has declared that "God led the people;" he now explains how. From Succoth certainly, probably from Rameses, He moved in front of the host in the form of a pillar, which had the appearance of smoke

light; to go by day and night: (22) he
took not away the pillar of the cloud by
day, [a]nor the pillar of fire by night, *from*
before the people.

CHAPTER XIV.—(1) And the LORD
spake unto Moses, saying, (2) Speak unto
the children of Israel, that they turn and
encamp before [b]Pi-hahiroth, between
Migdol and the sea, over against Baal-zephon:
before it shall ye encamp by
the sea. (3) For Pharaoh will say of the
children of Israel, They *are* entangled in
the land, the wilderness hath shut them
in. (4) And I will harden Pharaoh's
heart, that he shall follow after them;
and I will be honoured upon Pharaoh,
and upon all his host; that the Egyptians
may know that I *am* the LORD. And
they did so.
(5) And it was told the king of Egypt
that the people fled: and the heart of
Pharaoh and of his servants was turned
against the people, and they said, Why
have we done this, that we have let
Israel go from serving us? (6) And he
made ready his chariot, and took his
people with him: (7) and he took six

a Neh. 9. 19.

b Num. 33. 7.

by day and of fire by night. The Israelites marched, it is implied, some part of each day and some part of each night, which would be in accordance with modern practice, and is an arrangement introduced to get the march accomplished before the sun attains his full power. The pillar was at once a signal and a guide. When it moved, the people moved; when it stopped, they encamped (chap. xl. 36—38); where it went, they followed. It bore some resemblance to the fire and smoke signals which generals used when at the head of their armies (Lepsius, *Denkmäler*, vol. ii., pl. 150, 2; *Papyr. Anastas*, 1; Q. Curt, *Vit. Alex.* v. 2, &c.), and indicated that God had constituted Himself the generalissimo of the host; but it was altogether of a miraculous and abnormal character.

To go by day and night.—The night journeys of the people are mentioned again in Num. ix. 21.

(22) **He took not away.**—Comp. chap. xl. 38; Num. ix. 16, x. 34. The cloud probably disappeared at Abel-shittim (Num. xxxiii. 49).

XIV.

THE PURSUIT BY PHARAOH AND THE PASSAGE OF THE RED SEA.

(2) **Speak unto the children of Israel, that they turn.**—The march of the Israelites had been hitherto almost due south-east. They had reached the edge of the desert (chap. xiii. 20), near the head of the Bitter Lakes. If this direction had been maintained, their next day's march would have taken them out of Egypt into the "wilderness of Etham"—a desolate tract, in which there was no water, and probably scarcely any herbage. The Bitter Lakes would have been upon their right hand, and, so far as the Egyptians were concerned, they would have been in safety. But at this point an express command was given them to "turn." Kalisch, Rosenmüller, and others understand this as a command to "return," or "retrace their steps;" but this is clearly not what was intended, since their march was to bring them to "the sea," which they had not reached previously. The question arises, What sea? Brugsch suggests the Mediterranean; but it is against this that the Mediterranean has not yet been mentioned in Exodus, and that, when mentioned, it is not as "the sea," but as "the sea of the Philistines" (chap. xxiii. 31). "The sea" of this verse can scarcely be different from "the Red Sea" of chap. xiii. 18, the only sea previously mentioned by the writer. To reach this sea it was necessary that they should deflect their course to the right, from south-east to south, so keeping within the limits of Egypt, and placing the Bitter Lakes on their left hand.

Pi-hahiroth . . . Migdol . . . Baal-zephon.—These places cannot be identified. They were Egyptian towns or villages of no importance, near the head of the Gulf of Suez, situated on its western shores. The names nearest to Pi-hahiroth in Egyptian geography are Pehir and Pehuret. Migdol would, in Egyptian, be Maktal; and there was an Egyptian town of that name near Pelusium, which, however, cannot be intended in this place. Baal-zephon was probably a Semitic settlement, which had received its name from some worshippers of the god Baal. Eastern Egypt contained many such settlements. The accumulation of names indicates an accurate acquaintance with Egyptian topography, such as no Israelite but one who had accompanied the expedition is likely to have possessed.

(3) **Entangled in the land.**—Literally, *confused, perplexed.* (Comp. Esther iii. 15.) Pharaoh, seeing that the Israelites had placed the Bitter Lakes on their left, and were marching southward, in a direction which would soon put the Red Sea on one side of them and a desert region—that about the Jebel Atakah—on the other, thought that they must be quite ignorant of the geography, and have, as it were, "lost their way." He observed, moreover, that "the wilderness had shut them in." The desert tract between the Nile Valley and the Red Sea lay upon their left and in their front: they would soon be unable to proceed, and would not know which way to turn.

(5) **The heart of Pharaoh and of his servants was turned against the people.**—No doubt the change began as soon as Israel commenced its march. The emigration left Eastern Egypt a solitude, suspended all the royal works that were in progress, threw the whole course of commerce and business into disorder. Beforehand, neither the king nor the people had understood what the loss of six hundred thousand labourers—some of them highly skilled—would be. When Israel was gone they realised it; consequently both king and people regretted what they had done.

(6) **He made ready his chariot.**—Egyptian monarchs of the Rameside period almost always led their armies out to battle, and when they did so, uniformly rode with a single attendant, who acted as charioteer, in a two-horse chariot. "Made ready" means, of course, *ordered to be made ready.*

(7) **Six hundred chosen chariots.**—The chariot force was that on which the Egyptians chiefly relied for victory from the beginning of the eighteenth

hundred chosen chariots, and all the chariots of Egypt, and captains over every one of them.
(8) And the LORD hardened the heart of Pharaoh king of Egypt, and he pursued after the children of Israel: and the children of Israel went out with an high hand.
(9) But the [a]Egyptians pursued after them, all the horses *and* chariots of Pharaoh, and his horsemen, and his army, and overtook them encamping by the sea, beside Pi-hahiroth, before Baal-zephon.
(10) And when Pharaoh drew nigh, the children of Israel lifted up their eyes, and, behold, the Egyptians marched after them; and they were sore afraid: and the children of Israel cried out unto the LORD.
(11) And they said unto Moses, Because *there were* no graves in Egypt, hast thou taken us away to die in the wilderness? wherefore hast thou dealt thus with us, to carry us forth out of Egypt?
(12) [b]*Is* not this the word that we did tell thee in Egypt, saying, Let us alone, that we may serve the Egyptians? For *it had been* better for us to serve the Egyptians, than that we should die in the wilderness.

a Josh. 24. 6; 1 Mac. 4. 9.

b ch. 6. 9.

---

dynasty. Diodorus Siculus assigns to his Sesostris (probably Rameses II.) a force of 27,000 chariots; but this is, no doubt, an exaggeration. The largest number of chariots brought together on any one occasion that is *sufficiently attested*, is believed by the present writer to be 3,940, which were collected by various confederates against an Assyrian king (*Ancient Monarchies*, vol. ii., p. 103, Note). In 1 Sam. xiii. 5, 30,000 chariots are mentioned, no doubt by some numerical error. A force of 2,500 is said by Rameses II. to have been brought against him in his great Hittite campaign (*Records of the Past*, vol. ii., pp. 69, 71). Sheshonk I. (Shishak) invaded Judæa with 1,200 (2 Chron. xii. 3). The "six hundred *chosen* chariots" of the present passage are thus quite within the limits of probability. Most likely they constituted a division of the royal guard, and were thus always at the king's disposal.

And all the chariots of Egypt.—The word "all" must not be pressed. The writer means "all that were available—that could be readily summoned." These could only be the chariots of Lower Egypt—*those* stationed at Memphis, Heliopolis, Bubastis, Pithom, Sebennytus perhaps, and Pelusium. They would probably amount to several hundreds.

Captains over every one of them.—Rather, *over the whole of them.* These "captains" are again mentioned in chap. xv. 4. The word in the original—a derivative from the numeral three—is supposed to have meant, primarily, "persons occupying the third rank below the king."

(8) **The children of Israel went out.**—Rather, *were going out.*

With an high hand—*i.e.*, confidently, boldly, perhaps somewhat proudly, as having brought the Egyptians to entreat them to take their departure (chap. xii. 33).

(9) **All the horses and chariots of Pharaoh.**—Heb., *all the chariot-horses of Pharaoh.*

And his horsemen.—It is questioned whether "horsemen" are really intended here, and suggested that the word used may apply to the "riders" *in the chariots.* But it certainly means "horsemen" in the later books of Scripture, and, indeed, is the only Hebrew word having exactly that signification. Though the Egyptians do not represent cavalry in any of their battle pieces, yet there is abundant testimony that they employed them. Diodorus Siculus gives his Sesostris 24,000 cavalry to 27,000 chariots (Book i. 54, § 4). Shishak invaded Judæa with 60,000 (2 Chron. xii. 3). Herodotus makes Amasis lead an army on horseback (ii. 162). The Egyptian monuments appear to make frequent mention of cavalry as forming a portion of the armed force. (*Records of the Past*, vol. ii., pp. 68, 70, 72, 83, &c., vol. iv., 41, 44, 45, &c.) It is suspected that some conventional rules of art prevented the representation of cavalry in the sculptures, which never show us an Egyptian, and but rarely a foreigner, on horseback.

And his army—*i.e., his infantry.* The host of this Pharaoh, like that of Shishak (2 Chron. xii. 3), consisted apparently of the three arms, cavalry, infantry, and chariots.

(10) **The children of Israel . . . were sore afraid.**—It has been objected that 600,000 men above twenty years of age had no need to be afraid of such an army as the Pharaoh could have hastily gathered. The entire armed force of Egypt is reckoned by Herodotus (ii. 166—168) at 410,000, and it is tolerably clear that not one-half of these could have been mustered. It would imply, indeed, more facility of mobilisation than we should have expected in this early age, if Pharaoh was able to bring 100,000 men into the field upon a sudden emergency. Why, then, it is asked, should the Israelites have been "sore afraid" of a force but one-sixth of their number? Were they "arrant cowards?" The answer is that the Egyptian army, whatever its number, was composed of trained soldiers, well-armed and used to war; the 600,000 Israelites were, in the main, unarmed, ignorant of warfare, and trained very imperfectly. Above a million Persian *soldiers* were defeated and slaughtered like sheep by 47,000 Græco-Macedonians at Arbela. A similar result would, humanly speaking, have followed on a conflict between the Israelites and the Egyptians at Pi-hahiroth. The fear of the former was therefore perfectly legitimate.

The children of Israel cried out unto the Lord.—If Israel had been unduly timid—which we have shown not to have been the case—at any rate they knew where to make their appeal for succour. There is no help like that of Jehovah.

(11) **Because there were no graves in Egypt.**—Spoken in bitter irony, doubtless, but scarcely with any conscious reference to Egypt as "a land of tombs." They meant simply to say: "Might we not as well have died there as here?"

(12) **Is not this the word that we did tell thee . . .?**—At one time they had refused to listen to Moses (chap. vi. 9); but in the main they had acquiesced in his proceedings, and allowed him to act in their name. The reproach was therefore unjust and undeserved; but it is in human nature to make such reproaches in times of danger and difficulty.

(13) And Moses said unto the people,
Fear ye not, stand still, and see the sal-
vation of the LORD, which he will shew
to you to day: [1]for the Egyptians whom
ye have seen to day, ye shall see them
again no more for ever. (14) The LORD
shall fight for you, and ye shall hold
your peace.

(15) And the LORD said unto Moses,
Wherefore criest thou unto me? speak
unto the children of Israel, that they go
forward: (16) but lift thou up thy rod, and
stretch out thine hand over the sea, and
divide it: and the children of Israel shall
go on dry *ground* through the midst of
the sea. (17) And I, behold, I will harden
the hearts of the Egyptians, and they
shall follow them: and I will get me
honour upon Pharaoh, and upon all his
host, upon his chariots, and upon his
horsemen. (18) And the Egyptians shall
know that I *am* the LORD, when I have
gotten me honour upon Pharaoh, upon
his chariots, and upon his horsemen.

(19) And the angel of God, which went
before the camp of Israel, removed and
went behind them; and the pillar of the
cloud went from before their face, and
stood behind them: (20) and it came be-
tween the camp of the Egyptians and
the camp of Israel; and it was a cloud
and darkness *to them*, but it gave light
by night *to these:* so that the one came
not near the other all the night.

(21) And Moses stretched out his hand
over the sea; and the LORD caused the
sea to go *back* by a strong east wind all
that night, and made the sea dry *land*,
and the waters were [a]divided. (22) And
[b]the children of Israel went into the

1 Or, *for whereas ye have seen the Egyptians to day, &c.*

a Josh. 4. 23; Ps. 114. 3.

b Ps. 78. 13; 1 Cor. 10. 1; Heb. 11. 29.

(13, 14) **Fear ye not, stand still.**—There are times when all our strength must be "in quietness and confidence" (Isa. xxx. 15). So long as we have means of resistance put in our power, with a reasonable prospect of success, it is our duty to use them—to exert ourselves to the uttermost, to make all possible efforts. God, for the most part, "helps those who help themselves." But there are occasions when we can do nothing—when all must be left to Him. (Comp. 2 Chron. xx. 17.) Under these circumstances, our duty and our true wisdom is to wait patiently, quietly, courageously. Moses, probably, did not yet know how God would effect Israel's deliverance, but he was confident that, in one way or another, it would be effected.

The Egyptians whom ye have seen . . .—Heb., *As ye have seen the Egyptians to-day, ye shall see them no more for ever: i.e.*, never again shall ye see them in the pride of power, haughty, menacing, terrible. When next you behold them they will be stiff and lifeless—pale corpses strewing the Red Sea shore (see verse 30). The reference is to the present time only, not to the future relations of the two peoples.

(15–18) **Wherefore criest thou unto me?**—Like the people (verse 10), Moses had cried to Jehovah, though he tells us of his cry only thus indirectly. God made answer that it was not a time to cry, but to act: "Speak unto the children of Israel, that they go forward," &c. The Israelites were to strike their tents at once, and prepare for a forward movement. Moses was to descend to the edge of the sea, with his rod in his hand, and to stretch it out over the sea, and then await the consequences, which would be a "division" of the waters—the sea-bed would for a certain space become dry, and Israel would be able to cross to the other side (verse 16); the Egyptians would follow, and then destruction would come upon them, and God would "get himself honour upon Pharaoh, and upon all his host" (verses 17, 18). The exact mode of the destruction was not announced.

(19, 20) **The angel of God, which went before the camp of Israel**—The "Jehovah" of chap. xiii. 21 becomes here "the angel of God," as "the angel of Jehovah" in the burning bush (chap. iii. 2) becomes "God" (verse 4), and "Jehovah" (verse 7). The angel is distinguished from the cloud, and represented as antedating its movements and directing them. It is clear that the object of the movement now made was double: (1) to check and trouble the Egyptians by involving them in "cloud and darkness;" and (2) to cheer and assist the Israelites by affording them abundant light for all their necessary arrangements. Although there is nothing in the original corresponding to our translators' expressions, "to them," "to these," yet those expressions seem to do no more than to bring out the true sense. (Comp. the Targums of Onkelos and Jonathan, the Syriac Version, and the *Commentaries* of Rosenmüller, Maurer, Knobel, and Kalisch.)

(21) **The Lord caused the sea to go back by a strong east wind.**—By "a strong east wind" we are at liberty to understand one blowing from any point between N.E. and S.E. If we imagine the Bitter Lakes joined to the Red Sea by a narrow and shallow channel, and a south-east wind blowing strongly up this channel, we can easily conceive that the water in the Bitter Lakes might be driven northward, and held there, while the natural action of the ebb tide withdrew the Red Sea water to the southward. A portion of the channel might in this way have been left dry, and have so continued until the wind changed and the tide began to flow. It is true that Scripture does not speak of the ebb and flow of the tide, since in them there was nothing unusual; but an Egyptian tradition distinctly stated that "Moses waited for the ebb tide in order to lead the Israelites across." (Artipanus, ap. Euseb. *Præp. Ev.*, ix. 27.) Whether the whole effect was purely natural, or whether (as in so many other cases) God used the force of nature so far as it could go, and further supernaturally increased its force, we are not told, and may form what opinion we please.

The waters were divided.—The waters of the Bitter Lakes were for a time separated completely from those of the Red Sea. By gradual elevation and desiccation the channel over which the Israelites passed has probably now become dry land.

(22) **The waters were a wall unto them.**—Any protection is in Scripture called "a wall," or "a rampart" (1 Sam. xxv. 16; Prov. xviii. 11; Isa. xxvi. 1; Jer. i. 18; Nahum iii. 8). In the present case, the waters protected Israel on either flank—the Red Sea

midst of the sea upon the dry *ground:*
and the waters *were* a wall unto them on
their right hand, and on their left.
(23) And the Egyptians pursued, and
went in after them to the midst of the
sea, *even* all Pharaoh's horses, his
chariots, and his horsemen. (24) And it
came to pass, that in the morning watch
the LORD looked unto the host of the
Egyptians through the pillar of fire
and of the cloud, and troubled the host
of the Egyptians, (25) and took off their
chariot wheels, [1]that they drave them
heavily: so that the Egyptians said,
Let us flee from the face of Israel; for
the LORD fighteth for them against the
Egyptians. (26) And the LORD said unto
Moses, Stretch out thine hand over the
sea, that the waters may come again
upon the Egyptians, upon their chariots,
and upon their horsemen. (27) And
Moses stretched forth his hand over the
sea, and the sea returned to his strength
when the morning appeared; and the
Egyptians fled against it; and the LORD
[2]overthrew the Egyptians in the midst
of the sea. (28) And the waters returned,
and covered the chariots, and the horse-
men, *and* all the host of Pharaoh that
came into the sea after them; there

1 Or, *and made them to go heavily.*

2 Heb., *shook off.*

---

upon the right, the Bitter Lakes upon the left. Poetical writers, as was natural, used language still more highly metaphorical (Ps. lxxviii. 13; chap. xv. 8), and spoke of the waters as "standing on an heap." Hence, some moderns have gone so far as to maintain that on this occasion the water "gave up its nature, formed with its waves a strong wall, and instead of streaming like a fluid, congealed into a hard substance" (Kalisch). But this is to turn poetry into prose, and enslave oneself to a narrow literalism.

(23–28) **The Egyptians pursued.**—All the Israelites having entered the bed of the sea, the pillar of the cloud, it would seem, withdrew after them, and the Egyptians, who, if they could not see, could at any rate hear the sound of the departure, began to advance, following on the track of the fugitives. What they thought concerning the miracle, or what they expected, it is difficult to say. They can scarcely have entered on the bed of the sea without knowing it. Probably they assumed that, as the bed had somehow become dry, it would continue dry long enough for their chariots and horsemen to get across. The distance may not have been so much as a mile, which they may have expected to accomplish in ten minutes; but when once they were entered, their troubles began. "The Lord looked unto the host of the Egyptians through the pillar . . . and troubled the host of the Egyptians" (verse 24). By some terrible manifestation of His presence and of His anger, proceeding from the pillar of the cloud in their front, God threw the Egyptian troops into consternation and confusion. A panic terror seized them. Some probably stopped, some fled; but there were others who persevered. Then followed a second difficulty. The progress of the chariots was obstructed. According to the present reading of the Hebrew text, the wheels parted from the axles, which would naturally bring the vehicles to a stand. According to the LXX. and a reading found in the Samaritan Pentateuch, the wheels "became entangled," as they would if they sank up to the axles in the soft ooze. Hereby the advance was rendered slow and difficult: "they drave them heavily." To the Egyptians the obstruction seemed more than could be accounted for by natural causes, and they became convinced that Jehovah was fighting for Israel and against them (verse 25). Hereupon they turned and fled. But the flight was even harder than the advance. A confused mass of horses and chariots filled the channel—they impeded each other—could make no progress—could scarcely move. Then came the final catastrophe. At God's command, Moses once more stretched his hand over the sea, and the waters returned on either side—a north-west wind brought back those of the Bitter Lakes (chap. xiv. 10), the flood tide those of the Red Sea—and the whole of the force that had entered on the sea-bed in pursuit of the Israelites was destroyed.

(23) **All Pharaoh's horses, his chariots, and his horsemen.**—The chariot and cavalry force alone entered the sea, not the infantry. (Comp. verse 28 and chap. xv. 1.) The point is of importance as connected with the question whether the Pharaoh himself perished. If all his force entered, he could not well have stayed behind; if only a portion, he might have elected to remain with the others. Menephthah, the probable Pharaoh of the Exodus, was apt to consult his own safety. (*Records of the Past*, vol. iv., pp. 44, 45.)

(24) **In the morning watch.**—Between 2 a.m. and 6.

(26) **And the Lord said.**—Or, *The Lord had said.* Probably the command was given as soon as the Israelites were safe across. It would take some hours for the north-west wind to bring back the waters of the Bitter Lakes.

(27) **When the morning appeared.**—This would be about five o'clock. The light showed the Egyptians their danger. The white-crested waves were seen advancing on either side, and threatening to fill up the channel. The Egyptians had to race against them; but in vain. Their chariot wheels clogged, themselves and their horses encumbered with heavy armour, they made but slow way over the soft and slimy ground; and while they were still far from shore, the floods were upon them, and overwhelmed them. In this way God "overthrew the Egyptians in the midst of the sea."

(28) **The chariots, and the horsemen, and all the host . . .**—This translation is misleading. The Heb. runs thus: "The chariots and the horsemen (who were) all the host of Pharaoh that came into the sea." It is implied that his footmen did not enter the sea.

There remained not so much as one of them.—The armour of an Egyptian warrior would make it impossible for him to escape by swimming from such a catastrophe. All who were caught by the tide would certainly be drowned. The question whether the Pharaoh was drowned or no cannot be ruled by the expression here used, nor by any parallel one in the Psalms (Pss. lxxviii. 53, cvi. 11); it depends on more general considerations. In the first place, is it likely

remained not so much as [a]one of them.
(29) But the children of Israel walked
upon dry *land* in the midst of the sea;
and the waters *were* a wall unto them
on their right hand, and on their left.
(30) Thus the LORD saved Israel that
day out of the hand of the Egyptians;
and Israel saw the Egyptians dead upon
the sea shore. (31) And Israel saw that
great [1]work which the LORD did upon
the Egyptians: and the people feared
the LORD, and believed the LORD, and
his servant Moses.

CHAPTER XV. — (1) Then sang
[b]Moses and the children of Israel this
song unto the LORD, and spake, saying,
I will sing unto the LORD, for he hath

a Ps. 106. 11.

1 Heb., *hand.*

b Wisd. 10. 20.

that if the Pharaoh had been killed there would have been no explicit mention of it? Would the point have remained one open to question? Secondly, if the Pharaoh had been killed, would the Egyptian annals have retained no trace of it? Must we not have had some account of a great king cut off in the flower of his age, after a reign of two, or at the most three, years? (Comp. chaps. ii. 23, iv. 19, &c.) But Menephthah, to whom all the indications point, reigned at least eight years. The latter part of his reign was inglorious, and he left the empire a prey to pretenders; but he was not suddenly cut off after reigning a year or two. Thirdly, was an Egyptian king sure to lead an attack, and place himself in the position of most peril? This has been asserted, and it is so far true, that *most* Egyptian kings, according to the records which they have left of themselves, so acted. But it happens that Menephthah records it of himself that on one great occasion, at any rate, he kept himself out of danger. His country was invaded by a vast army of Libyans and others from the north-west in the fifth year of his reign; the assailants menaced his chief cities, and the peril was great. Menephthah collected all his forces to meet the danger, but declined to lead them out in person, pretending that one of the Egyptian gods, Phthah, had forbidden him to quit Memphis (Brugsch, *History of Egypt*, vol. ii., p. 119). It is thus quite probable that he would remain with the reserve of footmen when the chariots and horsemen entered the bed of the sea.

(30) **Israel saw the Egyptians dead upon the sea shore.**—On one who saw this sight it would be likely to make a great impression; to after generations it was nothing, since it had no further consequences. That it is recorded indicates the pen of an eye-witness.

(31) **Israel saw that great work.**—The destruction of the Pharaoh's chariot force and cavalry in the Red Sea secured the retreat of Israel, and saved them from any further molestation at the hands of the Egyptians. The spirit of the nation was effectually broken for the time; and it was not till after several reigns, and an interval of anarchy, that there was a revival. The king himself probably despaired of effecting anything against a foe that was supernaturally protected; and the army, having lost the flower of the chariot force, on which it mainly depended for success, desired no further contest. The Israelites, as will be seen further on, in their rapid march to Sinai avoided the Egyptian settlements, and having once reached the Sinaitic region, they were beyond the dominion of Egypt, and for forty years quite out of the path of Egyptian conquest. The episode in the life of the nation begun by the descent of Jacob into Egypt now terminated, and a fresh beginning was made. In the open air of the desert, cut off from all other races, admitted to close communion with Jehovah, the people entered upon that new and higher existence which culminated in the teaching of the prophets, in the noble struggles of Ezra and Nehemiah, and in the memorable stand on behalf of religious truth and national independence which was made by the Maccabees.

XV.

THE SONG OF MOSES.

(1) **Then sang Moses and the children of Israel.**—With his usual modesty, Moses does not say that he composed the magnificent ode which follows; but it is scarcely conceivable that it can have had any other author. It bears a close resemblance to the Egyptian religious poetry, with which Moses—and probably no other Israelite of the time—would have been familiar from his early training; and it breathes the elevated tone of religious sentiment that was scarcely shared with Moses by any contemporary. The prophetic statements in the latter verses of the hymn have led some to assign to it a date later than Joshua; but the vagueness of these statements stands in a remarkable contrast with the definiteness and graphic power of the descriptive portion, and points to the time of Moses for the composition. The poetic genius shown in the composition is, no doubt, very considerable; but the statement that it transcends all later Hebrew poesy would not have been made by any critic whose judgment was not biassed by his theories. The ode is distinguished from later similar compositions by greater simplicity in the language, and greater freedom in the rhythmical arrangement. There is the usual "parallelism of clauses," with its three varieties of "antithetic, synthetic, and synonymous;" but the regular cadence is interrupted with unusual frequency by triplet stanzas, and the parallelism is less exact than that of later times.

The ode divides itself into two portions (verses 1—12 and verses 13—18): the first retrospective, the second prospective. Part II. has no sub-divisions; but Part I. consists of three, or perhaps we should say of four, portions. First comes the burden, or refrain (verse 1), which was repeated at the close of each sub-division by Miriam and her choir of women (verse 21). Then we have the first stanza, or strophe, reaching from verse 2 to verse 5. Next we have stanza or strophe 2, extending from verse 6 to verse 10. After this, stanza or strophe 3, comprising verses 11 and 12. These shorter, and as it were tentative, efforts are followed by the grand burst of prophetic song which constitutes Part II., and extends from verse 13 to verse 18, terminating with the sublime utterance, beyond which no thought of man can go, "The Lord shall reign for ever and ever."

I will sing.—It may convey to the ordinary reader some idea of the rhythm of the ode to transcribe into Roman characters and accentuate this opening passage, which is as follows:—

Ashírah layhováh ki gaóh gaáh,
Sús v'rokebó ramáh bayyám.

triumphed gloriously: the horse and his rider hath he thrown into the sea. (2) The LORD *is* my strength and song, and he is become my salvation: he *is* my God, and I will prepare him an habitation; my father's God, and I will exalt him. (3) The LORD *is* a man of war: the LORD *is* his name. (4) Pharaoh's chariots and his host hath he cast into the sea: his chosen captains also are drowned in the Red sea. (5) The depths have covered them: they sank into the bottom as a stone. (6) Thy right hand, O LORD, is become glorious in power: thy right hand, O LORD, hath dashed in pieces the enemy. (7) And in the greatness of thine excellency thou hast overthrown them that rose up against thee: thou sentest forth thy wrath, *which* consumed them as stubble. (8) And with the blast of thy nostrils the waters were gathered together, the floods stood upright as an heap, *and* the depths were congealed in the heart of the sea. (9) The enemy said, I will pursue, I will overtake, I will divide the spoil; my

---

He hath triumphed gloriously.—Heb., *he hath glorified himself gloriously* (ἐνδόξως δεδόξασται, LXX.). The main idea implied in the verb *gââh* is exaltation.

(2) **The Lord is my strength and song.**—Heb., *My strength and song is Jah.* The contracted form of Jehovah, Jah, is here used for the first time; but its existence in the current speech has already been indicated by the name Moriah, which occurs in Gen. xxii. 1. It is here used on account of the rhythm.

He is become my salvation.—Heb., *he has been to me for salvation: i.e.,* "he has saved me out of the hand of Pharaoh." The beauty and force of the passage causes Isaiah to adopt it into one of his most glorious poems, the "joyful thanksgiving of the faithful for the mercies of God," contained in his twelfth chapter. (See verse 2.)

I will prepare him an habitation.—So Onkelos and Aben-Ezra; but Jarchi, the Targums of Jerusalem and Jonathan, the LXX., and Vulg., with most moderns, translate, "I will glorify him." It is a strong objection to the rendering of the Authorised Version that Moses is not likely to have had the idea of preparing God a habitation until the revelation of God's will on the subject was made to him on Sinai (chaps. xxv.—xxvii.). The law of parallelism also requires such a meaning as "glorify" to correspond with the "exalt" of the next clause.

My father's God.—"Father" here, by a common Hebrew idiom, stands for "forefathers" generally. (Comp. Note on chap. iii. 6.)

(3) **The Lord is a man of war.**—The directness and boldness of the anthropomorphism is markedly archaic, and is wisely retained by our translators. How turgid and yet weak are the Samaritan, "mighty in battle," and the LXX., "crusher of wars," in comparison!

The Lord is his name.—In the very name, Jehovah, is implied all might, all power, and so necessarily the strength to prevail in battle. The name, meaning "the Existent," implies that nothing else has any real existence independently of Him; and if no existence, then necessarily no strength.

(4) **His chosen captains.**—Comp. chap. xiv. 7, where the same word is used.

Are drowned.—Rather, *were drowned.*

(5) **The depths have covered them.**—Rather, *covered them.* The first stanza, or strophe, here terminates—the first historical review is completed. In it attention is concentrated on the one great fact of the deliverance by the destruction of the Egyptians in the Red Sea. At the close it is probable that Miriam, with her chorus of women, took up the refrain of verse 1, and slightly modifying it, sang, as recorded in verse 21, "Sing ye to the Lord, for he hath glorified himself gloriously; the horse and his rider hath he thrown into the sea."

(6—10) The second stanza, or strophe, expands the subject-matter of the first. It begins, like the first, with some general expressions, setting forth the glory and power of Jehovah (verses 6, 7), as shown in the recent catastrophe. From this it proceeds to the catastrophe itself, which it describes in considerable detail, noting (1) the sudden rise of the wind (verse 8); (2) the gathering together of the waters into separate masses (*ibid.*); (3) the boastful and vindictive temper of the Egyptians (*ibid.*); (4) the rise of a second wind (verse 9); (5) the consequent return of the waters; and (6) the submerging of the host by them. The second stanza is considerably longer than the first, consisting of twelve, whereas the first consists of only seven, lines.

(6) **Thy right hand.**—Here is a second anthropomorphism, following naturally on the first, and occurring in the later Scriptures frequently, though now used for the first time.

Hath dashed in pieces.—Rather, *dashes in pieces.* The verb is in the future, but is a future of continuance.

(7) **Thou hast overthrown . . .**—Heb., *thou overthrowest them that rise up against thee; thou sendest forth thy wrath: it consumeth them like stubble.*

(8) **The blast of thy nostrils.**—The "east wind" of chap. xiv. 21. (Comp. Ps. xviii. 15.) As a physical effect, the gathering together of the waters, is ascribed to the "blast," we must understand a physical cause. Otherwise, God's wrath might be meant, as in Job iv. 9.

The floods stood upright as an heap, and the depths were congealed.—The literalism which, taking its stand on these phrases, maintains that the water "gave up its nature (Kalisch) indicates an inability to distinguish poetry from prose, and fact from imagery. As well might it be held that the east wind was actually the breath of God's nostrils. (See the Note on chap. xiv. 22.)

(9) **The enemy said.**—Pharaoh's soldiers were as anxious as their master to come to blows. (See above, verse 7.) They hoped to acquire the rich spoil which the Israelites had carried off from Egypt in the shape of gold and silver ornaments and goodly apparel (chap. xii. 35, 36), as well as their flocks and herds (*ibid.* verse 38).

My lust.—Heb., *my soul.* The particular passion to be gratified was cupidity, or desire of riches.

lust shall be satisfied upon them; I will
draw my sword, my hand shall [1]destroy
them. (10) Thou didst blow with thy
wind, the sea covered them: they sank
as lead in the mighty waters. (11) Who
is like unto thee, O LORD, among the
[2]gods? who *is* like thee, glorious in
holiness, fearful *in* praises, doing won-
ders? (12) Thou stretchedst out thy
right hand, the earth swallowed them.
(13) Thou in thy mercy hast led forth
the people *which* thou hast redeemed:
thou hast guided *them* in thy strength
unto thy holy habitation. (14) [a]The
people shall hear, *and* be afraid: sorrow
shall take hold on the inhabitants of

1 Or, *repossess.*

2 Or, *mighty ones?*

a Deut. 2. 25; Josh. 2. 9.

Destroy them.—So the Vulg., Onkelos, Rosenmüller, Knobel, Kalisch, and others. The meaning "re-possess," given in the margin, rests upon the rendering of the LXX., which is κυριεύσει, but is otherwise unsupported.

(10) **Thou didst blow with thy wind.**—A new fact, additional to the narrative in chap. xiv., but in complete harmony with it. As a strong east (south-east) wind had driven the waters of the Bitter Lakes to the north-westward, so (it would seem) their return was aided and hastened by a wind from the opposite direction, which caused the sea to "cover" the Egyptians.

They sank as lead.—Compare verse 5. To an eye-witness, it would seem, the sudden submersion and disappearance of each warrior, as the waters closed around him, was peculiarly impressive. Each seemed to be swallowed up at once, without a struggle. This would be a natural result of the heavy armour worn by the picked warriors.

In the mighty waters.—With these words the second stanza, or strophe, closes. Miriam and her maidens, it is probable, again interposed with the magnificent refrain, "Sing ye to the Lord, for he hath glorified himself gloriously; the horse and his rider hath he thrown into the sea."

(11, 12) Stanza 3 is a short one, entering into no details—simply summing up the entire result in two sentences: one, parallel to verses 2, 3 and 6, 7, setting forth the glory of God, as shown in the occurrences; the other emphasising the great fact of the occasion, and stating it in the briefest possible terms: "Thou stretchedst out thy right hand; the earth swallowed them." This second clause is parallel to verses 4, 5 and 8—10. It concentrates into four words the gist of those two passages.

(11) **Who is like unto thee . . . among the gods?**—This is undoubtedly the true meaning. It had been a main object of the entire series of miraculous visitations to show that Jehovah was "exalted far above all other gods." (See chaps. vii. 5, xiv. 4, 18.) Moses now emphasises the contrast by adducing three points on which Jehovah is unapproachable—holiness, awefulness, and miraculous power. God is (1) "glorious in holiness," exalted in this respect far, far above all other beings; (2) "fearful in praises"—the proper object of the profoundest awe, even to those who approach Him with praise and thanksgiving; and (3) one who "doeth wonders," who both through nature, and on occasions overruling nature, accomplishes the most astonishing results, causing all men to marvel at His Almighty power. The gods of the heathen were, in fact, either nonentities or evil spirits. So far as they were the former, they could come into no comparison at all with Jehovah; so far as they were the latter, they fell infinitely short of Him in every respect. Of holiness they possessed no remnant; in awfulness they were immeasurably inferior; in the ability to work wonders they did not deserve to be mentioned in the same breath. "Among the gods," as the Psalmist says, "there is none like unto thee, O Lord; there is none that can do as thou doest" (Ps. lxxxvi. 8).

(12) **The earth swallowed them.**—The sea, which actually "swallowed them," was a part of the earth. Literalism might argue that the statement contravened former ones (verses 4, 5, 10); but the fact is otherwise. If we only allow our common sense fair play, and permit sacred writers the same latitude as profane ones, we shall find wonderfully few discrepancies, or even difficulties, in the Biblical narrative.

(13—18) The concluding stanza of the ode involves a change of attitude, and deals with new matters. The poet's eye fixes itself upon the future. First, he speaks of the guidance of God, lately begun, and about to continue until Canaan is reached (verse 13). Then his glance turns to the enemies of Israel, and he considers the effect which the miraculous deliverance of Israel from Egypt will have upon them (verses 14—16). Finally, he sees the people brought into the "land of their inheritance," and securely established there under the ordering of Divine Providence. Then, with an ascription of glory which may be compared with the Doxology attached to the Lord's Prayer in St. Matthew (chap. vi. 13), and to that attached in the Liturgies of the Church to the Psalms and Canticles, he terminates his composition.

(13) **Hast led forth . . . hast guided.**—Or, *leadest forth . . . guidest.* The guidance was not over; rather, it was just begun. The want of a present tense in Hebrew causes the preterite and future to have, both of them, under certain circumstances, the force of the present.

Thy holy habitation.—It might be supposed that Canaan was the "habitation" intended; but the words of verse 17 imply something more. Moses certainly knew that when Canaan was reached God would select a place to "put His name there" (Deut. xii. 5, 11, 14, xiv. 23, 24, xvi. 6, 11, &c.), and possibly knew by revelation what place would be ultimately selected.

(14) **The people.**—Heb., *The peoples: i.e.,* all the various tribes and nations of the desert and of Palestine—the Amalekites, Edomites, Philistines, Moabites, Amorites, &c.

Shall hear, and be afraid.—On the fear which was actually felt, see Num. xxii. 3; Josh. ii. 11, v. 1, ix. 3—15, &c.

The inhabitants of Palestina are the Philistines, from whom the Holy Land derived the name which it still retains in most of the languages of modern Europe. The Hebrew word is *Phělâsheth,* of which the nearest English equivalent would be "Philistia."

Palestina. (15) Then the dukes of Edom
shall be amazed; the mighty men of
Moab, trembling shall take hold upon
them; all the inhabitants of Canaan
shall melt away. (16) [a] Fear and dread
shall fall upon them; by the greatness
of thine arm they shall be *as* still as a
stone; till thy people pass over, O LORD,
till the people pass over, *which* thou
hast purchased. (17) Thou shalt bring
them in, and plant them in the moun-
tain of thine inheritance, *in* the place,
O LORD, *which* thou hast made for
thee to dwell in, *in* the Sanctuary, O
Lord, *which* thy hands have established.
(18) The LORD shall reign for ever and
ever.
(19) For the horse of Pharaoh went in
with his chariots and with his horse-
men into the sea, and the LORD brought
again the waters of the sea upon them;
but the children of Israel went on dry
land in the midst of the sea.
(20) And Miriam the prophetess, the
sister of Aaron, took a timbrel in her
hand; and all the women went out after

[a] Deut. 2. 25; Josh. 2. 9.

---

(15) **The dukes of Edom.**—Comp. Gen. xxxvi. 15, where the same title is found. Apparently in the course of the thirty-eight years between the Exodus and the approach to Canaan, the oligarchy of "dukes" had been replaced by a monarchy. (See Num. xx. 14.) The fear of Israel had also passed away; and the Edomites "came out against Moses with much people, and with a strong hand," laying a foundation for that prolonged hatred of which we have traces in 2 Sam. viii. 14; 1 Kings xi. 14—22; 2 Kings viii. 20—22; 2 Chron. xx. 16; Ps. cxxxvii. 7, &c.

The mighty men of Moab.—On the terror of the Moabites, when Israel approached their borders, see Num. xxii. 3, 4. The efforts made by Balak to procure Balaam's curse upon them were indications of the alarm felt.

All the inhabitants of Canaan shall melt away.—Compare Josh. ii. 11: "As soon as we had heard these things, *our hearts did melt*;" and chap. v. 1: "It came to pass . . . when all the kings of the Canaanites heard that the Lord had dried up the waters of Jordan, that *their hearts melted*, neither was there any spirit in them any more."

(16) **Fear and dread shall fall upon them.**—A portion of the Edomites felt so much fear of Israel that they allowed them to pass through their coasts (Deut. ii. 4). The Moabites of Ar acted similarly (Deut. ii. 29).

Till thy people pass over—*i.e.*, cross the frontier of the Canaanites, and enter their country. There is no need to suppose that Moses had as yet any distinct idea of the place where the frontier would be crossed.

(17) **In the mountain of thine inheritance.**—Some suppose Mount Moriah to be especially intended; but it is better to understand Canaan generally, which is a country consisting almost entirely of mountains, with only two plains of any extent—those of Sharon and Esdraelon.

The Sanctuary can only mean the place where God was "to put his name." (See the comment on verse 13.) This is spoken of as already "made" and "established," because it was so in the Divine counsels, as Moses very well knew. (See Deut. xii. 5, 11, 14, xiv. 23, 24, &c.)

(18) **The Lord shall reign for ever and ever.**—Compare Pss. x. 16, xxix. 10, cxlv. 13, cxlvi. 10. In simplicity and consequent force the expression of the idea by Moses transcends all later ones.

(19) This verse is parenthetic. It forms no part of the "Song of Moses." Originally, perhaps, when that song was a separate document, it was appended as an historical comment, showing the occasion on which the poem was composed. When the records of Moses were collected—either by himself, towards the close of his life, or by Joshua—the addition was kept, although it had become unnecessary for the original purpose. As it stands, it emphasises the great fact of Israel's final deliverance—the nucleus around which Exodus gathers itself.

(20) **Miriam the prophetess.**—In Miriam we have the first of that long series of religious women presented to us in Holy Scripture who are not merely pious and God-fearing, but exercise a quasi-ministerial office. Examples of other "prophetesses" will be found in Judg. iv. 4; 2 Kings xxii. 14; Isa. viii. 3; Luke ii. 36. In the early Christian Church there was an order of "deaconesses" (Rom. xvi. 1; *Apost. Const.*, vi. 17). The office of "prophetess" seems to have been permitted to women in Egypt, though that of "priestess" was, until Ptolemaic times, forbidden them.

The sister of Aaron.—She is called "sister of Aaron," rather than of Moses, because Aaron was the head of the family (chaps. vi. 20, vii. 7). There is no reasonable doubt that she was the sister who kept watch on Moses when he was in the ark of bulrushes (chap. ii. 3—8). On her later history, see Num. xii. 1—15. The prophet Micah regarded her as having had a part in the work of Israel's deliverance (Micah vi. 4).

Timbrels and with dances.—By "timbrels" are meant tambours, or tambourines, favourite instruments in Egypt, and usually played by women there (Wilkinson: *Ancient Egyptians*, vol. i., p. 93). The combination of music with song in religious worship, here for the first time brought before us, became the fixed rule of the Tabernacle service from the time of David (2 Sam. vi. 15; 1 Chron. xxiii. 5, xxv. 1—6), and was adopted into the Temple service from its first establishment (2 Chron. v. 12). Sanctioned under the new covenant by the general praise of psalmody, and by the representations given in the Apocalypse of the Church triumphant in heaven (Rev. v. 8, xiv. 2, 3), it has always maintained itself in the Christian Church, and still holds its ground firmly. Dancing, on the contrary, though adopted into religious worship by many nations, sanctioned by the present passage, by the example of David (2 Sam. vi. 16), and by expressions in the Psalms (cxlix. 3, cl. 4), has never found an entrance into Christian ceremonial, unless among a few fanatic sects. The reason of this is to be found in the abuses which, through human infirmity, became by degrees connected with the practice, causing it to become unfit for a religious purpose. In the primitive times, however, solemn

her with timbrels and with dances.
(21) And Miriam answered them,

Sing ye to the LORD, for he hath
triumphed gloriously; the horse and
his rider hath he thrown into the sea.

(22) So Moses brought Israel from the
Red sea, and they went out into the
wilderness of Shur; and they went three
days in the wilderness, and found no
water. (23) And when they came to
Marah, they could not drink of the
waters of Marah, for they *were* bitter:
therefore the name of it was called
[1]Marah. (24) And the people murmured
against Moses, saying, What shall we
drink? (25) And he cried unto the
LORD; and the LORD shewed him a
[a]tree, *which* when he had cast into the
waters, the waters were made sweet:
there he made for them a statute and
an ordinance, and there he proved them,
(26) and said, If thou wilt diligently hear-
ken to the voice of the LORD thy God,
and wilt do that which is right in his
sight, and wilt give ear to his command-
ments, and keep all his statutes, I will
put none of these diseases upon thee,
which I have brought upon the Egyp-
tians: for I *am* the LORD that healeth
thee.

(27) [b]And they came to Elim, where
were twelve wells of water, and three-
score and ten palm trees: and they
encamped there by the waters.

1 That is, *Bitterness.*

a Ecclus. 38. 5.

b Num. 33. 9.

---

and stately dances were deemed appropriate to festival periods and religious rejoicings, and among the more moral tribes and nations had nothing unseemly about them.

The arrangement of the choir on this occasion into two bands—one of males, the other of females—and the combined employment of music, song, and dancing by the female band, are in close accord with Egyptian customs.

(21) **Miriam answered them.**—Miriam and her maidens at the close of each portion of the "Song"—*i.e.,* at the end of verses 5, 10, 12, and 18—sang the refrain which is here given—a refrain very slightly altered from the opening verse of the "Song" itself, marking, no doubt, the time with their timbrels, and moving gracefully through a stately and solemn dance.

THE JOURNEY FROM THE RED SEA TO ELIM.

(22) **So Moses brought Israel.**— Rather, *And Moses brought Israel.* The regular narrative is here resumed from chap. xiv. 31, and the Israelites are brought two stages upon their journey towards Sinai (chap. iii. 12)—first to Marah (verse 23), and next to Elim (verse 27). It is uncertain at what exact point of the coast they emerged from the sea-bed, but it can scarcely have been at any great distance from the modern Suez. The "springs of Moses," Ayun Musa, which are about seven miles from Suez, may well have been the halting-place where the "Song" was composed and sung. At this spot there is considerable vegetation, and a number of wells, variously reckoned at seven, seventeen, and nineteen.

The wilderness of Shur is the arid tract extending from Lake Serbônis on the north to Ain Howarah towards the south. It seems to have been called also "the wilderness of Etham" (Num. xxxiii. 8). The Israelites traversed only the southern portion, which is an actual desert, treeless, waterless, and, except in the early spring, destitute of herbage.

They went three days.—From Ayun Musa to Ain Howarah is a distance of about thirty-six miles, so that, if Howarah is Marah, the average of a march can have been no more than twelve miles. This, however, is quite likely with so large a multitude, and when there was no reason for haste.

(23) **The waters of Marah . . . were bitter.**—The extreme bitterness of the springs at the southern extremity of the wilderness of Shur is witnessed to by all travellers. (Burckhardt: *Travels in Syria,* p. 777; Robinson: *Palestine,* vol. i., p. 106; Wellsted, *Arabia,* vol. ii., p. 38, &c.) There are several such springs, that called Ain Howarah being the most copious, but scarcely so bitter as some others.

Therefore the name of it was called Marah.—"Marah" means "bitterness" both in Hebrew and in Arabic. It appears to be a form of the root which we find also in *mare* and *amarus.*

(25) **The Lord shewed him a tree.**—There are trees which have the power of sweetening bitter water; but none of them is at present found in the Sinaitic peninsula, and the Arabs are not now acquainted with any means of rendering the bitter waters of Howarah and the neighbouring springs palatable. Perhaps in ancient times there were forms of vegetable life in the peninsula which do not now exist there. Moses would scarcely have been "shown a tree" unless the tree had some virtue of its own; but, on the other hand, the tree alone is scarcely to be credited with the entire effect. As in so many other instances, God seems to have made use of nature, as far as nature could go, and then to have superadded His own omnipotent energy in order to produce the required effect. (Compare our blessed Lord's method in working His miracles.)

He made for them a statute and an ordinance.—God took advantage of the occasion to draw a lesson from it. He promised that, as He had healed the waters, so, if the Israelites would henceforth faithfully keep His commandments, He would "heal" *them* (verse 26), keeping them free from all the diseases of Egypt, and from the far greater evil involved in their own corrupted nature and infirmity.

(27) **Elim**—the next stage to Marah, where there were "twelve wells of water, and threescore and ten palm trees"—seems to be rightly identified with the Wady Ghurundel in which "abundant grass grows thick and high," where acacias and tamarisks are plentiful, and in which, notwithstanding the ruthless denudation of the country by the Arabs, there are still a certain number of palm-trees. These are not now "seventy" in number, neither are they the ideal palm-trees of pictures, or even such as grow in the Valley of the Nile and in Upper Egypt generally. They are "either dwarf—that is, trunkless—or else with savage hairy trunks, and branches all dishevelled" (Stanley: *Sinai and*

CHAPTER XVI.—(1) And they took
their journey from Elim, and all the
congregation of the children of Israel
came unto the wilderness of Sin, which
is between Elim and Sinai, on the
fifteenth day of the second month after
their departing out of the land of
Egypt. (2) And the whole congregation
of the children of Israel murmured
against Moses and Aaron in the wilder-
ness: (3) and the children of Israel said
unto them, Would to God we had
died by the hand of the LORD in the
land of Egypt, when we sat by the flesh
pots, *and* when we did eat bread to the
full; for ye have brought us forth into
this wilderness, to kill this whole as-
sembly with hunger.
(4) Then said the LORD unto Moses,
Behold, I will rain bread from heaven
for you; and the people shall go out
and gather [1]a certain rate every day,

[1] Heb., *the portion of a day in his day.*

Palestine, p. 68)—specimens of the palm-tree growing under difficulties. The exact number of "twelve wells," which is mentioned in the text, cannot now be traced with any distinctness; but there is a perennial brook which supports the vegetation through the whole of the year, and in the winter-time there is a large stream which flows down to the sea through the wady.—(Niebuhr: *Description de l'Arabie*, p. 347.)

They encamped there.—The head-quarters of the camp were at Elim (Wady Ghurundel); probably the mass of the people filled all the neighbouring wadys, as those of Useit, Ethal, and Tayibeh, or Shuweikah, which are all fertile, and have good pasturage.

XVI.

THE JOURNEY FROM ELIM.—THE MANNA GIVEN.

(1) **They took their journey from Elim.**—The stay at Elim was probably for some days. "Sin" was reached exactly one month after the departure from Egypt, yet there had been only five camping-places between Sin and Rameses, and one journey of three days through a wilderness (chap. xv. 22). Long rests are thus clearly indicated, and probably occurred at Ayun Musa, at Marah, and at Elim. The places named were the head-quarters of the camp on each occasion, but the entire host must have always covered a vast tract, and the flocks and herds must have been driven into all the neighbouring valleys where there was pasture. Wadys Useit, Ethal, and Tayibeh are likely to have been occupied at the same time with Wady Ghurundel.

All the congregation . . . came unto the wilderness of Sin.—"All the congregation" could only be united in certain favourable positions, where there happened to be a large open space. Such an open space is offered by the tract now called El Markha, which extends from north to south a distance of twenty miles, and is from three to four miles wide in its more northern half. To reach this tract, the Israelites must have descended by Wady Useit or Wady Tayibeh to the coast near Ras Abu Zenimeh, and have then continued along the coast until they crossed the twenty-ninth parallel. This line of march is indicated in Num. xxxiii. 10, 11, where we are told that "they removed from Elim, *and encamped by the Red Sea;* and they removed from the Red Sea, and encamped in the wilderness of Sin."

(2) **The whole congregration . . . murmured.**—This is the third "murmuring." The first was at Pi-hahiroth, on the appearance of the host of Pharaoh (chap. xiv. 11, 12); the second was at Marah, when the water proved undrinkable (chap. xv. 24); the third, in the wilderness of Sin, was brought about by no special occurrence—unless it were the exhaustion of the supplies of grain which had been brought out of Egypt—but seems to have resulted from a general dissatisfaction with the conditions of life in the wilderness, and with the prospects which lay before them.

(3) **Would to God we had died.**—Heb., *Would that we had died.* There is no mention of "God."

By the hand of the Lord.—There is, perhaps, an allusion to the last of the plagues, "Would that we had not been spared, but had been smitten, as the Egyptians were! A sudden death would have been far better than a long and lingering one." (Comp. Lam. iv. 9.)

When we did eat bread to the full.—The Israelites had been well fed in Egypt. They had been nourished upon flesh, fish, bread, and abundant vegetables, especially cucumbers, melons, leeks, onions, and garlick (Num. xi. 5). It was the habit of the Egyptians to feed well those whom they employed in forced labours (Herod. ii. 125), just as slave-owners commonly do their slaves. The remembrance of the past abundance intensified the pain felt at the present want.

To kill this whole assembly with hunger.—It is difficult to imagine that there could have been as yet any real danger of starvation. The cattle may have suffered considerably in the passage through the wilderness of Shur, but the bulk of it survived (chap. xvii. 3), and there were lambs enough for the whole nation to observe a Passover a few months later at Sinai (Num. ix. 1—5). But it may well be that a considerable number of the Israelites had had no cattle; others may have lost what they had, or have consumed them. Want may have stared some in the face, and the nation generally may have come to see that the prospect before them was a dismal one. Even supposing that the desert was anciently four or five times as productive as it is now, it could not possibly have afforded sufficient pasturage to maintain such flocks and herds as would have been requisite to support on their milk and flesh a population of two millions. It may have been brought home to the people that their flocks and herds were rapidly diminishing, and they may have realised the danger that impended of ultimate starvation after the cattle was all gone.

(4) **I will rain bread from heaven for you.**—This first announcement at once suggests that the supply is to be supernatural. "Bread from heaven" was not simply "food out of the air" (Rosenmüller), but a celestial, that is, a Divine supply of their daily needs.

A certain rate every day.—Heb., *a day's meal each day*—sufficient, that is, for the wants of himself and family for a day.

That I may prove them.—Human life is a probation. God proves and tries those *most* whom He takes to Himself for His "peculiar people," and the trial is often by means of positive precepts, which are especially

that I may prove them, whether they
will walk in my law, or no. (5) And it
shall come to pass, that on the sixth
day they shall prepare *that* which they
bring in; and it shall be twice as much
as they gather daily.

And Moses and Aaron said unto
all the children of Israel, At even, then
ye shall know that the LORD hath
brought you out from the land of Egypt:
(7) and in the morning, then ye shall see
the glory of the LORD; for that he
heareth your murmurings against the
LORD: and what *are* we, that ye murmur against us? (8) And Moses said,
This shall be, when the LORD shall give
you in the evening flesh to eat, and in
the morning bread to the full; for that
the LORD heareth your murmurings
which ye murmur against him: and
what *are* we? your murmurings *are*
not against us, but against the LORD.

a ch. 13. 21.

b Num. 11. 31.

c Num. 11. 7; Ps. 78. 24; Wisd. 16. 20.

(9) And Moses spake unto Aaron, Say
unto all the congregation of the children
of Israel, Come near before the LORD:
for he hath heard your murmurings.

(10) And it came to pass, as Aaron
spake unto the whole congregation of
the children of Israel, that they looked
toward the wilderness, and, behold, the
glory of the LORD [a]appeared in the
cloud. (11) And the LORD spake unto
Moses, saying, (12) I have heard the murmurings of the children of Israel: speak
unto them, saying, At even ye shall eat
flesh, and in the morning ye shall be
filled with bread; and ye shall know
that I *am* the LORD your God.

(13) And it came to pass, that at even
[b]the quails came up, and covered the
camp: and in the morning the dew lay
round about the host. (14) And when
[c]the dew that lay was gone up, behold,
upon the face of the wilderness *there lay*

---

calculated to test the presence or absence of a spirit of humble and unquestioning obedience. Our first parents were tested by a positive precept in Paradise; the family of Abraham were tested by a positive precept—circumcision on the eighth day; the Israelites were tested, both in the wilderness and afterwards throughout their career as a nation, by a number of positive precepts, whereof this concerning the manna was one. Christians are tested by positive precepts with respect to common worship, prayer, and sacraments—the object being in all cases to see whether men "will walk in God's law or no." Men are very apt to prefer their own inventions to the simple rule of following at once the letter and the spirit of God's commandments.

(5) **On the sixth day**—*i.e., the sixth day after the first giving of the manna* (Kalisch). Although in Babylonia, from a time certainly earlier than the Exodus, a Sabbath was observed on the seventh, fourteenth, twenty-first, and twenty-eighth day of each month (Sayce: *Records of the Past*, vol. vii., pp. 157—167), yet we have no evidence that the year was divided into weeks, much less that the several days of the week were known as the first, second, third, fourth, &c. In Egypt, the week of seven days was at this time unknown.

They shall prepare.—On the method of preparation see Num. xi. 8.

It shall be twice as much.—Some suppose this to be a command—"Ye shall gather twice as much;" but it is more natural to take it as an announcement of a fact—"You will find that what you have gathered turns out to be twice as much." (So Kurtz, Kalisch, and Knobel.) A miraculous doubling of the quantity seems to be intended. (Comp. verse 22.)

(6) **At even, then ye shall know . . . .**—The allusion is to the quails, which came up "at even," and covered the camp. (See verses 12, 13.)

(7) **And in the morning, then ye shall see the glory of the Lord.**—The reference here is to the manna, which "in the morning lay round about the host" (verse 13), not to the "appearance" of verse 10, which preceded the coming of the quails, and was not —as far as we are told—"in the morning." The "glory of God" was strikingly revealed in a gift which was not transient, but secured permanently the subsistence of the people so long as it might be necessary for them to continue in the wilderness. (Comp. the parallelism of verses 8 and 12.)

(10) **The glory of the Lord appeared in the cloud.**—The Hebrew, as at present pointed, has "in *a* cloud," but there can be no reasonable doubt that the "pillar of *the* cloud" is meant. It was before this that they had been required to appear (verse 9), and from this almost certainly that some bright radiance was now made to stream forth. The object was at once to rebuke their murmurings, and to uphold the authority of Moses and Aaron.

(13) **At even the quails came up.**—The common quail (*Tetrao coturnix*) is very abundant in the East, and regularly migrates from Syria and Arabia in the autumn of the year for the purpose of wintering in Central Africa, whence it returns in immense masses in the spring (Schubert: *Reise*, vol. ii., p. 361). Exhausted after a long flight over the Red Sea, the flocks drop to the ground as soon as they reach the coast, and it is then easy either to take the birds with the hand or to kill them with sticks. Diodorus says that "the inhabitants of Arabia Petræa were wont to prepare long nets, and spread them near the coast for many furlongs, by which means they caught a great quantity of quails, which were in the habit of coming in from the sea" (ii. 60). The flesh of the quail is regarded as a delicacy throughout the East, though if too many are eaten it is said to be unwholesome.

The dew lay.—Literally, *there was a lying of dew.* A heavy fall seems to be meant.

(14) **Was gone up**—*i.e., was drawn up by the heat of the sun.*

A small round thing, as small as the hoar frost.—What the manna was has been much disputed. There are two natural substances, quite distinct, with which it has been compared, and by some persons identified. One is a deposit from the air, which falls

a small round thing, *as* small as the
hoar frost on the ground. (15) And when
the children of Israel saw *it*, they said
one to another, [1]It *is* manna: for they
wist not what it *was*. And Moses said
unto them, [a]This *is* the bread which the
LORD hath given you to eat. (16) This
is the thing which the LORD hath com-
manded, Gather of it every man accord-
ing to his eating, an omer [2]for every
man, *according to* the number of your
[3]persons; take ye every man for *them*
which *are* in his tents. (17) And the
children of Israel did so, and gathered,
some more, some less. (18) And when
they did mete *it* with an omer, [b]he that
gathered much had nothing over, and
he that gathered little had no lack;
they gathered every man according to
his eating. (19) And Moses said, Let no
man leave of it till the morning.
(20) Notwithstanding they hearkened not
unto Moses; but some of them left of
it until the morning, and it bred worms,
and stank: and Moses was wroth with
them. (21) And they gathered it every
morning, every man according to his
eating: and when the sun waxed hot,
it melted.
(22) And it came to pass, *that* on the

1 Or, *What is this?* or, *It is a portion.*

a John 6. 31; 1 Cor. 10. 3.

2 Heb., *by the poll*, or, *head.*

3 Heb., *souls.*

b 2 Cor. 8. 15.

---

indifferently on trees, stones, grass, &c., and is generally thick and sticky, like honey, but under certain circumstances is "concreted into small granular masses." This has been described by Aristotle (*Hist. An.*, v. 22), Pliny (*H. N.*, xi. 12), Avicenna (p. 212), Ælian (*Hist. An.*, xv. 7), Shaw, Forskal, and others. It has been called ἀερόμελι, or "air-honey" (Athen. *Deipn*, xi., p. 500). It is collected by the Arabs, and eaten with their unleavened cakes as a condiment. It so far resembles the manna that it comes with the dew, is spread upon the ground generally, and melts when the sun's rays attain a certain power (Œdmann: *Misc. Collect.*, vol. iv., p. 7). But it is never found in large quantities; it does not fall for more than two months in the year; and it is wholly unfit to serve as man's principal food, being more like honey than anything else. The other substance is a gum which exudes from certain trees at certain seasons of the year, in consequence of the punctures made in their leaves by a small insect, the *Coccus manniparus*. It has been described at length by C. Niebuhr in his *Description de l'Arabie* (pp. 128, 129); by Rauwolf (*Travels*, vol. i., p 94); Gmelin (*Travels through Russia to Persia*, Part III., p. 28), and others. It is comparatively a dry substance, is readily shaken from the leaves, and consists of small yellowish-white grains, which are hard, and have been compared to coriander seed by moderns (Rauwolf, *l.s.c.*). The name "manna" attaches in the East to this latter substance, which is employed both as a condiment, like the "air-honey," and also as a laxative. The special points in which it differs from the manna of Scripture are its confinement to certain trees or bushes; its comparative permanency, for it "accumulates on the leaves" (Niebuhr, p. 129), and its unfitness for food. It has also, like the "air-honey," only a short season—the months of July and August.

The manna of Scripture in certain respects resembles the one, and in certain other respects the other of these substances, but in its most important characteristics resembles neither, and is altogether *sui generis*. For (1) it was adapted to be men's principal nourishment, and served the Israelites as such for forty years; (2) it was supplied in quantities far exceeding anything that is recorded of the natural substances compared with it; (3) it continued through the whole of the year; (4) for forty years it fell regularly for six nights following, and ceased upon the seventh night; (5) it "bred worms" if kept to a second day, when gathered on five days out of the six, but when gathered on the sixth day continued good throughout the seventh, and bred no worms. The manna of Scripture must therefore be regarded as a miraculous substance, created *ad hoc*, and not as a natural product. It pleased the Creator, however, to proceed *on the lines* of Nature, so to speak, and to assimilate His new to certain of His old creations.

(15) **It is manna**.—This is certainly a wrong translation. The words of the original, *man hu*, must either be rendered, as in the LXX. and the Vulg., "What is this?" or, as by Kimchi, Knobel, Gesenius, Kurtz, and others, "This is a gift." It is against the former rendering that *man* does not mean "what" in Hebrew, but only in Chaldee, and that "what is this" would be a very strange name to give to a substance. Against the latter it may be said that neither is *man* found elsewhere in Hebrew in the sense of "a gift;" but it has that sense in Arabic; and in Hebrew *mânan* is "to give."

This is the bread—*i.e., the promised bread.* (See verse 4.)

(16) **Every man according to his eating.**—Comp. chap. xii. 4. Each man was to gather according to his immediate need and that of his family. No one was to seek to accumulate a store.

An omer.—About three pints English.

For every man.—Literally, *for every head.* As families would average four members, each man would have to gather, on an average, six quarts. If even 500,000 men gathered this amount, the daily supply must have been 93,500 bushels.

His tents.—Heb., *his tent.*

(18) **When they did mete it with an omer.**—Each Israelite gathered what he supposed would be about an omer for each member of his family. Some naturally made an over, some an under estimate; but whatever the quantity collected, when it came to be measured in the camp, the result was always the same—there was found to be just an omer for each. This result can only have been miraculous.

(19) **Let no man leave of it.**—Moses must have been divinely instructed to issue this command. It was doubtless given in order that the Israelites might realise their absolute dependence upon God for food from day to day, and might so be habituated to complete trust and confidence in Him.

(20) **It bred worms.**—On the Sabbath it bred no worms (verse 24), so that we must view the result spoken of as a punishment for disobedience, not as produced naturally. Neither of the natural mannas is subject to any very rapid decomposition.

(22) **On the sixth day they gathered twice as much.**—See the third Note on verse 5.

sixth day they gathered twice as much
bread, two omers for one *man*: and all
the rulers of the congregation came and
told Moses. (23) And he said unto them,
This *is that* which the LORD hath said,
To morrow *is* the rest of the holy sab-
bath unto the LORD: bake *that* which
ye will bake *to day*, and seethe that ye
will seethe; and that which remaineth
over lay up for you to be kept until the
morning. (24) And they laid it up till
the morning, as Moses bade: and it did
not stink, neither was there any worm
therein. (25) And Moses said, Eat that
to day; for to day *is* a sabbath unto the
LORD: to day ye shall not find it in the
field. (26) Six days ye shall gather it;
but on the seventh day, *which is* the
sabbath, in it there shall be none.
(27) And it came to pass, *that* there went
out *some* of the people on the seventh
day for to gather, and they found none.
(28) And the LORD said unto Moses, How
long refuse ye to keep my command-
ments and my laws? (29) See, for that
the LORD hath given you the sabbath,
therefore he giveth you on the sixth day
the bread of two days; abide ye every
man in his place, let no man go out of
his place on the seventh day. (30) So the
people rested on the seventh day.
(31) And the house of Israel called the
name thereof Manna: and it *was* like
coriander seed, white; and the taste of
it *was* like wafers *made* with honey.

(32) And Moses said, This *is* the thing
which the LORD commandeth, Fill an
omer of it to be kept for your genera-
tions; that they may see the bread
wherewith I have fed you in the wilder-

The rulers . . . came and told Moses.—They were evidently surprised, and came to Moses for an explanation. Either he had not communicated to them the Divine announcement of verse 5, or they had failed to comprehend it.

(23) **To morrow is the rest of the holy sabbath unto the Lord.**—Heb., *to morrow is a rest of a holy Sabbath to Jehovah.* If the translation of the Authorised Version were correct, the previous institution of the Sabbath, and the knowledge, if not the observance, of it by the Israelites would be necessarily implied, since no otherwise would the double use of the article be intelligible. But *in the Hebrew there is no article* either here or in verse 25. The absence of the article indicates that it is a new thing which is announced—if not absolutely, at any rate to those to whom the announcement is made. Much, no doubt, may be said in favour of a primæval institution of the Sabbath (see the comment on Gen. ii. 2, 3); and its observance in a certain sense by the Babylonians (see the first Note on verse 5) is in favour of its having been known to the family of Abraham; but during the Egyptian oppression the continued observance would have been impossible, and the surprise of the elders, as well as the words of Moses, show that at this time the idea was, to the Israelites, practically a novelty.

Bake . . . seethe.—These directions imply a very different substance from any of the natural forms of manna. The heavenly "gift" could be either made into a paste and baked, or converted into a porridge.

(25) **To day is a sabbath.**—That is to say, *a rest.* By these words the Sabbath was either instituted, or re-instituted, and became thenceforth binding on the Israelites. Its essential character of a weekly "rest" was at once assigned to it—(1) by its name; (2) by God's resting on it from His self-imposed task of giving the manna; and (3) by the rest which the absence of manna on the seventh day imposed on the people. Thus the way was prepared for the stringent law of Sabbath observance laid down in the fourth commandment.

(28) **How long refuse ye to keep my commandments?**—The people had already broken one of the positive precepts with respect to the manna (see verse 20); now they broke another—in the spirit, at any rate—since they would have gathered had they found anything to gather. Thus they provoked God a second time; yet was He "so merciful, that He destroyed them not," but "turned His anger away, and did not stir up all His wrath" (Ps. lxxviii. 38). Apparently He made allowance for the ordinance being a new one, to which they were not yet accustomed.

(29) **Abide ye every man in his place.**—Some Jews took this direction absolutely literally, and remained all the Sabbath Day in the position in which they found themselves at waking; but this slavish adherence to the letter was in general repudiated, and the command understood as having forbidden persons to leave the camp on the Sabbath. Hence the "Sabbath Day's journey," which was fixed at six stadia, because that was (traditionally) the extreme distance from the centre of the camp to its furthest boundary.

(31) **Manna.**—Rather, *man.* (See Note on verse 15.) "Manna" is a Greek form, first used by the LXX. translator of Numbers (chap. xi. 6, 7, 9).

It was like coriander seed.—The appearance of the manna is compared above to hoar frost (verse 14); here, and in Num. xi. 7, to coriander seed. The former account describes its look as it lay on the ground, the latter its appearance after it was collected and brought in. The coriander seed is "a small round grain, of a whitish or yellowish grey." In Numbers it is further said that the colour was that of *bdellium,* which is a whitish resin.

The taste of it was like wafers made with honey.—In Numbers the taste is compared to that of fresh oil (Num. xi. 8). The wafers or cakes used by the Egyptians, Greeks, and other ancient nations as offerings, were ordinarily composed of fine wheaten flour, oil, and honey. According to a Jewish tradition, which finds a place in the Book of Wisdom (chap. xvi. 20, 21), the taste of the manna varied according to the wish of the eater, and "tempered itself to every man's liking."

(32—35) **And Moses said . . . Fill an omer.**—This narrative, which must belong to a later date than any other part of Exodus, since it assumes that the Tabernacle is set up (verse 34), seems to have been placed here on account of its subject-matter. The

ness, when I brought you forth from
the land of Egypt. (33) And Moses said
unto Aaron, Take a pot, and put an
omer full of manna therein, and lay it
up before the LORD, to be kept for your
generations. (34) As the LORD com-
manded Moses, so Aaron laid it up be-
fore the Testimony, to be kept. (35) And
the children of Israel did eat manna
forty years, [a]until they came to a land
inhabited; they did eat manna, until
they came unto the borders of the land
of Canaan. (36) Now an omer *is* the
tenth *part* of an ephah.

CHAPTER XVII.—(1) And all the
congregation of the children of Israel
journeyed from the wilderness of Sin,
after their journeys, according to the
commandment of the LORD, and pitched
in Rephidim: and *there was* no water
for the people to drink. (2) Wherefore
[b]the people did chide with Moses, and
said, Give us water that we may drink.
And Moses said unto them, Why chide
ye with me? wherefore do ye tempt the
LORD? (3) And the people thirsted there
for water; and the people murmured
against Moses, and said, Wherefore *is*
this *that* thou hast brought us up out of
Egypt, to kill us and our children and
our cattle with thirst?

a Josh. 5. 12; Neh. 9. 15.

b Num. 20. 4.

---

writer wishes to conclude the history of the manna, and has two further points to note concerning it: (1) the preservation of an omer of it as a perpetual memorial (verses 32—34); and (2) the fact of its continuance until the Israelites reached the borders of Canaan. The passage is probably an addition to the original "Book," but contains nothing that may not have been written by Moses.

(33) **Lay it up before the Lord.**—Comp. verse 33, where Aaron is said to have "laid it up before the Testimony," *i.e.*, the Two Tables. According to the writer of the Epistle to the Hebrews, the Ark of the Covenant contained three things only—the tables, the pot of manna, and Aaron's rod that budded (Heb. ix. 4). The deposit of the manna in so sacred a place may be accounted for by its typifying "the true bread from heaven" (John vi. 32).

(35) **The children of Israel did eat manna forty years.**—Moses may have added this verse to the present chapter shortly before his death, when the manna had continued for thirty-nine years and nine months. He does not say that it had ceased to be given. We know that in fact it did not cease till the Jordan was crossed by the Israelites under Joshua, and Canaan was actually reached (Josh. v. 10—12).

(36) **Now an omer.**—The "omer" and the "ephah" were both of them Egyptian measures. One—the latter—continued in use among the Hebrews, at any rate, until the captivity (Ezek. xlv., xlvi.); the other—the omer—fell out of use very early. Hence this parenthetic verse, which is exegetical of the word "omer," and may have been added by the completer of Deuteronomy, or by some later editor—perhaps Ezra.

XVII.

THE MURMURING AT REPHIDIM AND THE FIGHT WITH AMALEK.

(1) **The children of Israel journeyed from the wilderness of Sin.**—The route by which Rephidim was reached is very uncertain. From El Markha there are three modes of reaching the Wady Feiran, where Rephidim is placed by most critics. One route (the shortest) is from the northern part of El Markha by Wady Shellal and Wady Magharah, where there was an important Egyptian settlement. This the Israelites would probably have avoided. Another, from the central part of El Markha, leads through the Wady Seih Sidreh to Magharah, and would, therefore, have been equally inconvenient. The third is circuitous, but has the advantage of being very open, and therefore suitable for a vast host. It passes through the whole of El Markha, and then, skirting the mountain, enters Wady Feiran at its south-western extremity. The probability seems on the whole to be that the Israelites pursued this last route.

After their journeys.—We find from Num. xxxiii. 12, 13, that Rephidim was reached from the wilderness of Sin by three journeys—from Sin to Dophkah, from Dophkah to Alush, and from Alush to Rephidim. The distance by the route which we have supposed the Israelites to have taken is about fifty miles.

Rephidim means *rests*, or *resting-places*, and is an appropriate name for the central part of the Wady Feiran—the most fertile spot in the whole peninsula, where there is usually abundant water, rich vegetation, and numerous palm-trees. (Lepsius, *Tour from Thebes to Sinai*, pp. 21, 37; Stanley, *Sinai and Palestine*, pp. 40, 41.) According to Dean Stanley, "the oldest known tradition of the peninsula" identifies Rephidim with Paran—the seat of an early bishopric—undoubtedly the same word with Feiran.

There was no water.—Though Feiran is usually watered by a copious stream, there have been occasions when the brook has been dried up. Graul found it dry in March, 1858. (Stanley, p. 40, Note 3.)

(2) **The people did chide.**—Water is scanty along the route by which we have supposed Rephidim to have been reached. Such a supply as the people may have brought with them from Elim would have been exhausted. They would have looked forward to Rephidim both for their immediate necessity and for replenishing their water-skins. They would be suffering both from thirst and disappointment. The needs of their children and their cattle (verse 3) would be an aggravation of their pain. They would see no hope in the future. Under the circumstances we cannot be surprised at their "chiding." Nothing but a very lively faith, or an utter resignation to the will of God, could have made a people patient and submissive in such an extremity.

Give us water.—It was not faith that spoke in these words, but wrath. They had no belief that Moses could give them water, and "were almost ready to stone" him (verse 4).

(3) **To kill us.**—This was no exaggeration. Thirst kills as surely as hunger, and more quickly. Whole armies have died of it. (Herod. iii. 26.) Ships' crews

(4) And Moses cried unto the LORD,
saying, What shall I do unto this
people? they be almost ready to stone
me. (5) And the LORD said unto Moses,
Go on before the people, and take with
thee of the elders of Israel; and thy
rod, wherewith [a]thou smotest the river,
take in thine hand, and go. (6) [b]Behold,
I will stand before thee there upon the
rock in Horeb; and thou shalt smite
the rock, and there shall come water
out of it, that the people may drink.
And Moses did so in the sight of the
elders of Israel. (7) And he called the
name of the place [1]Massah, and [2]Meribah,
because of the chiding of the
children of Israel, and because they
tempted the LORD, saying, Is the LORD
among us, or not?

(8) [c]Then came Amalek, and fought
with Israel in Rephidim. (9) And Moses
said unto [d]Joshua, Choose us out men,
and go out, fight with Amalek: to
morrow I will stand on the top of the
hill with the rod of God in mine hand.
(10) So Joshua did as Moses had said to

a ch. 7. 20.

b Num. 20. 9; Ps. 78. 15 & 105. 41; Wis. 11. 4; 1 Cor. 10. 4.

1 That is, *Tentation.*

2 That is, *Chiding*, or, *Strife.*

c Deut 25. 17; Wis. 11. 3.

d Called *Jesus*, Acts 7. 45.

---

have perished of it on the ocean, with "water, water everywhere, and not a drop to drink." Unless a supply could somehow or other have been provided speedily, the whole people must have been exterminated.

(4) **They be almost ready to stone me.**—Heb., *Yet a little and they will stone me.* On tumultuary stoning, see the second Note on chap. viii. 26.

(5) **Go on before the people.**—The people were probably in no condition to move. They were exhausted with a long day's march—weary, faint, nerveless. Moses and the elders, who probably journeyed on asses, would have more strength.

Take with thee of the elders—as witnesses. Each miracle had an educational value, and was designed to call forth, exercise, and so strengthen the faith of the people.

(6) **The rock in Horeb** must necessarily designate some particular rock of the Horeb region already known to Moses during his previous stay in these parts. It cannot possibly, however, have been the traditional "rock of Moses" in the Seil Leja, under Ras Sufsafeh, since that rock is a long day's journey from the site of Rephidim, near which the miracle must have been performed. (See Stanley, *Sinai and Palestine*, pp. 46—48.)

(7) **Massah** means *trial*, or *temptation*, being formed from the root used in verse 2 ("Wherefore do ye *tempt* the Lord?") It is the word translated by "trial" in Job ix. 23, and by "temptation" in Deut. iv. 34, vii. 19, xxix. 3, and Ps. xcv. 8.

Meribah means *chiding*, or *quarrel*, and is from the root *rûb*, or *rîb*, translated "chide" in verse 2, and rendered elsewhere generally by "strive," or "contend." The name Meribah was given also to the place where water was again produced miraculously by Moses striking the rock (Num. xx. 13.) It is this latter "Meribah" to which reference is made in Deut. xxxiii. 8, and Ps. lxxxi. 7, and which is called by way of distinction in Deut. xxxii. 51, "Meribah-Kadesh."

(8) **Then came Amalek.**—The Amalekites had not been previously (except in the anticipatory notice of Gen. xiv. 7) mentioned as a nation. Their name marks them for descendants of Amalek, the grandson of Esau (Gen. xxxvi. 12, 16); and it would seem that they early became the predominant people in the Sinaitic peninsula. Balaam speaks of them as "the first of the nations" (Num. xxiv. 20); and though we do not meet with the name in the Egyptian records, yet it is probable that they were among the hostile nations whom we find constantly contending with the Egyptians upon their north-eastern frontier. Though Edomites, they are always regarded as a distinct race, and one especially hostile to Israel (verse 16). Their present hostility was not altogether unprovoked. No doubt they regarded the Sinaitic region as their own, and as the most valuable portion of their territory, since it contained their summer and autumn pastures. During their absence in its more northern portion, where there was pasture for their flocks after the spring rains, a swarm of emigrants had occupied some of their best lands, and threatened to seize the remainder. Naturally, they would resent the occupation. They would not understand that it was only temporary. They would regard the Israelites as intruders, robbers, persons entitled to scant favour at their hands. Accordingly, they swooped upon them without mercy, attacked their rear as they were upon the march, cut off their stragglers, and slew many that were "feeble, faint, and weary" (Deut. xxv. 17, 18). They then encamped in their neighbourhood, with the design of renewing the struggle on the next day. It was under these circumstances that Moses had to make his arrangements.

(9) **Moses said unto Joshua.**—This is the first mention of Joshua. He was an Ephraimite, the son of a man called Nun, and the tenth in descent from Joseph (see Note on chap. vi. 16), in the prime of life—about 45 years old—and probably known as possessing military capacity. His actual name at the time was Hoshea, which might have been viewed as a good omen, since the word meant "Saviour." Moses afterwards changed his name to Jehoshua (Num. xiii. 16), which became by contraction Joshua. We find him, later in Exodus, acting as Moses' personal attendant, or "minister" (xxiv. 13, xxxii. 17, xxxiii. 11), accompanying him to the top of Sinai, and placed by him in charge of the first "Tabernacle." Afterwards he, with Caleb, was the only one of the spies who brought back a true report of Canaan. (Num. xiv. 6—9.) His choice as leader to succeed Moses resulted naturally from his antecedents, and is related in Num. xxvii. 18—23.

Choose us out men.—The weakness of Israel was in its unwieldy numbers. Moses saw this, and, after deciding that he was himself unfit for battle, and passing the command on to Joshua, made the one suggestion that a select body of troops should be employed against the assailants. The advice was good, and "Joshua did as Moses had said to him" (verse 10).

I will stand on the top of the hill.—A particular "hill" was no doubt meant—a "hill," and not a mountain. But the *exact* scene of the battle is too uncertain to make it possible to fix on any one particular eminence.

(10) **Moses, Aaron, and Hur went up.**—Moses, we know, was eighty years of age (chap. vii. 7);

him, and fought with Amalek: and
Moses, Aaron, and Hur went up to the
top of the hill. (11) And it came to pass,
when Moses held up his hand, that
Israel prevailed: and when he let down
his hand, Amalek prevailed. (12) But
Moses' hands *were* heavy; and they
took a stone, and put *it* under him, and
he sat thereon; and Aaron and Hur
stayed up his hands, the one on the one
side, and the other on the other side;
and his hands were steady until the go-
ing down of the sun. (13) And Joshua
discomfited Amalek and his people with
the edge of the sword. (14) And the
LORD said unto Moses, Write this *for* a
memorial in a book, and rehearse *it* in the
ears of Joshua: for [a] I will utterly put out
the remembrance of Amalek from under
heaven. (15) And Moses built an altar,
and called the name of it [1] Jehovah-nissi:
(16) for he said, [2] Because [3] the LORD hath
sworn *that* the LORD *will have* war with
Amalek from generation to generation.

a Num. 24. 20; 1 Sam. 15. 3.

1 That is, *The LORD my banner.*

2 Or, *Because the hand* of Amalek is *against the throne of the LORD,* therefore, &c.

3 Heb., *the hand upon the throne of the LORD.*

Aaron was eighty-three; Hur, the *grandfather* of Bezaleel (chap. xxxi. 2), the architect of the Tabernacle, can scarcely have been less. Unfit for battle themselves, they felt it was by prayer and intercession that they could best help forward a good result, and so withdrew themselves from the actual conflict to a place where they could command it.

Hur.—According to Jewish tradition (Joseph., *Ant. Jud.*, iii. 2, § 4) Hur was the husband of Miriam, and so the brother-in-law of Moses and Aaron. He was a descendant of Judah through Pharez and Hezron. (1 Chron. ii. 3—20.) Moses left him joint regent with Aaron when he ascended up into Sinai (chap. xxiv. 14).

(11) **When Moses held up his hand . . . Israel prevailed,** &c.—In order to teach the lesson of the value of intercessory prayer, God made the fortunes of the fight to vary according as Moses "held up his hand," or allowed it to sink down. It is not probable that the Israelites were *directly* affected by the bodily movements of Moses, or indeed could discern them, but Moses, Aaron, and Hur were struck by the fact that the fluctuations in the battle coincided with the motions of Moses' hands.

(12) **Moses' hands were heavy.**—Moses writes with a clear remembrance of his feelings at the time. His hands, long stretched to heaven, grew weary, "heavy," feeble; he could no longer raise them up, much less stretch them out, by his own muscular energy. They sank down, and dropped by his sides. If the battle was not to be lost, it was necessary to find some remedy. Apparently, Aaron and Hur bethought themselves of an effective remedy, none being suggested by Moses.

They took a stone.—Partly to give him a certain amount of rest, but, perhaps, mainly to enable them the better to sustain his hands. The fact is one of those "little" ones, which none but one engaged in the transactions would have been likely to have been acquainted with. (See "Introduction," § v.)

Aaron and Hur stayed up his hands.—Left to himself, Moses had become exhausted both mentally and bodily, and when his hands dropped, had ceased to pray. Sustained physically by his two companions, his mind recovered itself, and was able to renew its supplications and continue them. The result was the victory.

(14) **Write this for a memorial in a book.**—Heb., *in the book.* That "books" existed long prior to Moses is implied in his quotation of them (Gen. v. 1; Num. xxi. 14), and has of late years been abundantly proved by the discoveries made of Egyptian papyruses dating from a time long anterior to the Jewish lawgiver. The expression used in the present place, if it may be trusted,* "*the* book," is remarkable, and seems to imply that a book already existed at the date of the engagement, in which God's dealings with His people were entered from time to time. (See Introduction to *Speaker's Commentary*, vol. i., p. 1.) This book was probably the germ of the existing Pentateuch, which was composed in many portions, and at intervals, as occasion arose.

I will utterly put out the remembrance of Amalek.—The extermination of Amalek, here prophesied, was afterwards laid as a positive command upon the Israelites (Deut. xxv. 19), and was accomplished in part by Saul and David (1 Sam. xiv. 48, xv. 7, xxvii. 8, xxx. 17; 2 Sam. viii. 12), but finally and completely in the reign of Hezekiah (1 Chron. iv. 43). Amalek's sin was, that after all the signs and wonders which had shown the Israelites to be God's peculiar people, he braved God's displeasure by attacking them (Deut. xxv. 18). To this audacity and contempt of Jehovah's power he added a cruel pitilessness, when he fell upon the rear of an almost unarmed host, at a time when they were "faint and weary."

(15) **Moses built an altar.**—Primarily, no doubt, to sacrifice thank-offerings upon it, as an acknowledgment of the Divine mercy in giving Israel the victory. But secondarily as a memorial—a monument to commemorate Israel's triumph.

And called the name of it Jehovah-nissi.—Jacob had named an altar "El-Elohe-Israel" (Gen. xxxiii. 20); but otherwise we do not find altars given special names. When an altar was built as a memorial, the purpose would be helped by a name, which would tend to keep the event commemorated in remembrance. Jehovah-nissi—"the Lord is my banner"—would tell to all who heard the word that here there had been a struggle, and that a people which worshipped Jehovah had been victorious. It is not clear that there is any reference to "the rod of God" (verse 9) as in any sense the "banner" under which Israel had fought. The banner is Jehovah Himself, under whose protection Israel had fought and conquered.

(16) **Because the Lord hath sworn that the Lord will have war with Amalek.**—Heb., *because (his) hand is against the throne of Jehovah, (there shall be) war to Jehovah with Amalek,* &c. The Hebrew can scarcely be said to be "obscure." It gives plainly enough the sense which our translators have placed in the margin. Amalek, by attacking Israel, had lifted up his hand against the throne of God, therefore would God war against him from generation to generation.

* *Bĕsēpher,* "in a book," and *bassēpher,* "in the book," differ only in the pointing, which, resting solely on tradition, cannot be entirely depended on. The LXX. omit the article.

CHAPTER XVIII.—(1) When [a] Jethro,
the priest of Midian, Moses' father in
law, heard of all that God had done for
Moses, and for Israel his people, *and*
that the LORD had brought Israel out of
Egypt; (2) then Jethro, Moses' father in
law, took Zipporah, Moses' wife, after
he had sent her back, (3) and her two
sons; of which the [b] name of the one *was*
[1] Gershom; for he said, I have been an
alien in a strange land: (4) and the
name of the other *was* [2] Eliezer; for
the God of my father, *said he, was* mine
help, and delivered me from the sword
of Pharaoh: (5) and Jethro, Moses' father
in law, came with his sons and his wife
unto Moses into the wilderness, where
he encamped at the mount of God:
(6) and he said unto Moses, I thy father
in law Jethro am come unto thee, and
thy wife, and her two sons with her.
(7) And Moses went out to meet his father in law, and did obeisance, and
kissed him; and they asked each other
of *their* [3] welfare; and they came into
the tent.
(8) And Moses told his father in law
all that the LORD had done unto Pharaoh and to the Egyptians for Israel's
sake, *and* all the travail that had [4] come
upon them by the way, and *how* the
LORD delivered them. (9) And Jethro
rejoiced for all the goodness which the
LORD had done to Israel, whom he had
delivered out of the hand of the Egyptians. (10) And Jethro said, Blessed *be*
the LORD, who hath delivered you out
of the hand of the Egyptians, and out of

a ch. 2. 16.

b ch. 2. 22.

1 That is, *A stranger there.*

2 That is, *My God is an help.*

3 Heb., *peace.*

4 Heb., *found them.*

XVIII.

THE VISIT OF JETHRO.

(1) **Jethro, the priest of Midian, Moses' father in law.**—On Jethro's probable relationship to Moses, see the second Note on chap. iii. 1. On the priesthood of Reuel, which Jethro seems to have inherited, see Note on chap. ii. 16. It has been very unnecessarily supposed that the chronological order of the narrative is here deranged, Jethro's visit having been really paid after the legislation of Sinai and the setting up of the Tabernacle (Aben Ezra, Ranke, Kurtz). Both the position of the chapter and its contents are against this theory.

And that the Lord had brought Israel out.—Rather, *in that the Lord had brought Israel out.* It was this fact especially which Jethro had heard, and which induced him to set out on his journey.

(2) **After he had sent her back.**—Heb., *after her dismissal.* The fact had not been previously stated, but is in harmony with the general narrative, which has been absolutely silent concerning Zipporah since chap. iv. 26. Moses had sent Zipporah back to her own relations, either in anger, on account of the scene described in chap. iv. 24—26, or simply that he might not be encumbered with wife and children during the dangers and troubles which he anticipated in Egypt. Jethro assumed that, as the main troubles were now over, he would be glad to have his wife and children restored to him.

(3) **Gershom.**—See Note on chap. ii. 22.

(4) **Eliezer.**—Eliezer is supposed to have been the boy whom Zipporah circumcised in the wilderness (chap. iv. 25). He grew to manhood, and had a son, Rehabiah (1 Chron. xxiii. 17), whose descendants were in the time of David very numerous (1 Chron. xxiii. 17; and comp. 1 Chron. xxvi. 25, 26). It is uncertain whether Moses gave him his name before parting from him, in allusion to his escape from the Pharaoh who "sought to slay him" (chap. ii. 15), or first named him on occasion of receiving him back, in allusion to his recent escape from the host which had been destroyed in the Red Sea.

(5) **Where he encamped at the mount of God.**—It is quite possible that "the mount of God" may be here used, in a broad sense, of the entire Sinaitic mountain-region, as "wilderness" is just before used in the broad sense of the infertile region between Egypt and Palestine. Or the movement described in chap. xix. 1, 2 may have taken place before Jethro's arrival, though not related until after it. We must bear in mind that Exodus was probably composed in detached portions, and arranged afterwards. The present chapter has every appearance of being one such detached portion.

(7) **Moses went out . . . and did obeisance.**—Oriental etiquette required the going forth to meet an honoured guest (Gen. xviii. 2, xix. 1, &c.). The obeisance was wholly voluntary, and marks the humility of Moses, who, now that he was the prince of his nation, might well have required Jethro to bow down to him.

And kissed him.—Kissing is a common form of salutation in the East, even between persons who are in no way related. Herodotus says of the Persians: "When they meet each other in the streets, you may know if the persons meeting are of equal rank by the following token: if they are, instead of speaking they kiss each other on the lips. In the case where one is a little inferior to the other, the kiss is given on the cheek" (Book i. 134). (Comp. 2 Sam. xv. 5, xix. 39, xx. 9; Matt. xxvi. 48, 49; Acts xx. 37, &c.; and for the continuance of the custom to the present day, see the collection of instances given in the article KISS, in Smith's *Dictionary of the Bible*, vol. ii., p. 46.)

They asked each other of their welfare.—Heb., *wished peace to each other*—exchanged, that is, the customary salutation, "Peace be with you."

(8) **Moses told . . . all.**—Jethro had only heard previously a very imperfect account of the transactions. (See Note 2 on verse 1.) Moses now told him all the particulars.

(10, 11) **Jethro said, Blessed be the Lord.**—Heb., *Jehovah.* The Midianites, descendants of Abraham by Keturah, acknowledged the true God, and the Israelites could rightfully join with them in acts of worship. But it is scarcely likely that they knew God among themselves as "Jehovah." Jethro, however, understanding Moses to speak of the supreme God under that designation, adopted it from him,

the hand of Pharaoh, who hath de-
livered the people from under the hand
of the Egyptians. (11) Now I know that
the LORD *is* greater than all gods: [a]for
in the thing wherein they dealt proudly
he was above them. (12) And Jethro,
Moses' father in law, took a burnt offer-
ing and sacrifices for God: and Aaron
came, and all the elders of Israel, to eat
bread with Moses' father in law before
God.

(13) And it came to pass on the mor-
row, that Moses sat to judge the people:
and the people stood by Moses from the
morning unto the evening. (14) And
when Moses' father in law saw all that
he did to the people, he said, What *is*
this thing that thou doest to the peo-
ple? why sittest thou thyself alone,
and all the people stand by thee from
morning unto even? (15) And Moses
said unto his father in law, Because the
people come unto me to enquire of God:
(16) when they have a matter, they come
unto me; and I judge between [1]one
and another, and I do make *them* know
the statutes of God and his laws.

(17) And Moses' father in law said
unto him, The thing that thou doest *is*
not good. (18) [2]Thou wilt surely wear
away, both thou, and this people that *is*
with thee: for this thing *is* too heavy
for thee; [b]thou art not able to perform
it thyself alone. (19) Hearken now unto

a ch. 1. 10, 16, 22, & 5. 7, & 14. 18.

1 Heb., *a man and his fellow.*

2 Heb., *Fading thou wilt fade.*

b Deut. 1. 9.

---

blessed His name, and expressed his conviction that Jehovah was exalted above all other gods. The pure monotheism of later times scarcely existed as yet. The gods of the nations were supposed to be spiritual beings, really existent, and possessed of considerable power, though very far from omnipotent. (See Deut. xxxii. 16, 17.)

(11) **For in the thing . . .**—Heb., *even in the matter in which they dealt proudly against them.* Jehovah's superior power had been shown especially in the matter in which the Egyptians had dealt most proudly —viz., in pursuing the Israelites with an army when they had given them leave to depart, and attempting to re-capture or destroy them.

(12) **Jethro . . . took a burnt offering and sacrifices for God.**—Jethro had brought sacrifices with him, and now offered them in token of his thankfulness for God's mercies towards himself and towards his kinsman. He occupied a position similar to that of Melchizedek (Gen. xiv. 18), holding a priesthood of the most primitive character, probably as patriarch of his tribe, its head by right of primogeniture. As Abraham acknowledged rightly the priesthood of Melchizedek (Gen. xiv. 19; Heb. vii. 2—9), so Moses and Aaron rightly acknowledged that of Jethro. They markedly indicated their acceptance of his priestly character by participation in the sacrificial meal, which, as a matter of course, followed his sacrifice. They "ate bread with Moses' father in law" (or rather, *brother-in-law*) "before God."

(13) **On the morrow.**—The day following Jethro's arrival.

Moses sat to judge the people.—The office of prince, or ruler, was in early times regarded as including within it that of judge. Rulers in these ages were sometimes even called "judges," as were those of Israel from Joshua to Samuel, and those of Carthage at a later date (*suffetes*). Ability to judge was thought to mark out a person as qualified for the kingly office (Herod. i. 97). Moses, it would seem, had, from the time that he became chief of his nation, undertaken the hearing of all complaints and the decision of all causes. He held court days from time to time, when the host was stationary, and judged all the cases that were brought before him. No causes were decided by any one else. Either it had not occurred to him that the duty might be discharged by deputy, or he had seen reasons against the adoption of such an arrangement. Perhaps he had thought his countrymen unfit as yet for the difficult task. At any rate, he had acted as sole judge, and had, no doubt, to discharge the duty pretty frequently. Knowing that there was much business on hand, he did not allow the visit of his near connection to interfere with his usual habits, but held his court just as if Jethro had not been there.

The people stood by Moses from the morning unto the evening.—So great was the number of causes, or so difficult were they of decision, that Moses was occupied the whole day in deciding them. Following the usual Oriental practice, he began early in the morning, and found himself compelled to continue until nightfall. It is not clear whether his "sessions" were always of this length, or whether on this occasion the ordinary time was exceeded. Some have suggested that the division of the Amalekite spoil would naturally have led to disputes, and so to complaints.

(14) **Why sittest thou thyself alone?**—The emphatic word is "alone." Why dost thou not, Jethro means, devolve a part of the duty upon others?

(15, 16) Moses assigns two reasons for his conduct. (1) The people want decisions which they can feel to have Divine sanction—they "come to him to enquire of God"—and the ruling of inferior judges would not be regarded by them as equally authoritative. (2) He does not simply judge—*i.e.*, decide the particular question brought before him; but he takes the opportunity to educate and instruct the people in delivering his judgments—he "makes them know the statutes of God and His laws"—he expounds principles and teaches morality. Both reasons were clearly of great weight, and constituted strong arguments in favour of his practice.

(17) **The thing that thou doest is not good.**—Weighty as the arguments were, they failed to convince Jethro. He brought forward counter-arguments. By continuing to act as hitherto, Moses would, in the first place, exhaust his own strength, and, secondly, exhaust the patience of the people. His practice was unadvisable, both on his own account and on theirs. To keep suitors waiting all day, and perhaps finally dismiss them without their turn having come, was not fair upon *them.*

(19) **God shall be with thee.**—Rather, *may God be with thee.* May He give thee wisdom to direct thy course aright.

my voice, I will give thee counsel, and
God shall be with thee: Be thou for
the people to God-ward, that thou
mayest bring the causes unto God:
(20) and thou shalt teach them ordin-
ances and laws, and shalt shew them the
way wherein they must walk, and the
work that they must do. (21) Moreover
thou shalt provide out of all the people
able men, such as fear God, men of
truth, hating covetousness; and place
such over them, *to be* rulers of thousands,
and rulers of hundreds, rulers of fifties,
and rulers of tens: (22) and let them
judge the people at all seasons: and it
shall be, *that* every great matter they
shall bring unto thee, but every small
matter they shall judge: so shall it be
easier for thyself, and they shall bear
the burden with thee. (23) If thou shalt
do this thing, and God command thee
so, then thou shalt be able to endure,
and all this people shall also go to their
place in peace.
(24) So Moses hearkened to the voice
of his father in law, and did all that he
had said. (25) And Moses chose able
men out of all Israel, and made them
heads over the people, rulers of thou-
sands, rulers of hundreds, rulers of fifties,
and rulers of tens. (26) And they judged
the people at all seasons: the hard causes
they brought unto Moses, but every
small matter they judged themselves.
(27) And Moses let his father in law depart;
and he went his way into his own land.

Be thou for the people to God-ward.—Be the person, *i.e.*, to bring before God whatever needs to be brought before Him. Continue both to act as representative of the people towards God, and as representative of God towards the people. Take all difficult causes to Him, and pronounce to the people His decision upon them. Be also the expounder to the people of God's laws and ordinances; be their moral instructor, and the guide of their individual actions (verse 20). All this is quite compatible with the change which I am about to recommend to thee.

(21) **Provide out of all the people able men.**—This was the gist of Jethro's advice. It seems somewhat surprising that it should have been needed. In Egypt, as in all other settled governments, while the king was the fountain of justice, it was customary for him to delegate the duty of hearing causes to officials of different ranks, who decided in this or that class of complaints. In Arabia a similar practice no doubt prevailed. Jethro himself had his subordinates, the head men of the various clans or families, who discharged judicial functions in "small matters," and thereby greatly lightened the burthen which would otherwise have rested upon his shoulders. His advice to Moses was simply that he should adopt this generally established system—one which belongs to a very early period in the history of nations.

Jethro's definition of "able men"—men, *i.e.*, fitted to exercise the judicial office—is interesting. He requires them to be (1) God-fearing, (2) truthful, and (3) men of integrity. The second and third requirements would approve themselves to men of all times and countries. The first would generally be deemed superfluous. But it really lies at the root of all excellence of character, and is the point of greatest importance.

Rulers of thousands, and rulers of hundreds . . .—An organisation of the entire people on a decimal system is implied in the arrangement suggested. Such an organisation may not improbably have existed at the time in connection with the march and the encamping. (See the Comment on chap. xiii. 18.) Jethro thought that it might be utilised for judicial purposes. One man out of ten might be competent to judge in "small matters." If either party were dissatisfied, there might be an appeal to the "ruler of fifty"—from him to the "ruler of an hundred," and then to the "ruler of a thousand." In all ordinary disputes this would suffice, and the contest would not require to be carried further.

(22) **At all seasons.**—Not on occasional court days, as had been the custom of Moses, but day by day continually.

Every great matter they shall bring unto thee.—It must have been left to the judges themselves to decide what were "great" and what were "small matters." Under ordinary circumstances, courts would be inclined to extend their jurisdiction, and take enlarged views of their competency; but the difficulties of desert life were such as to counteract this inclination, and induce men to contract, rather than widen, their responsibilities. When the wilderness life was ended, the judicial system of Jethro came to an end also, and a system at once simpler and more elastic was adopted.

(23) **If thou shalt do this thing, and God command thee so.**—A reference of the entire matter to God, before any final decision was made, is plainly indicated. Moses must have already had some mode of consulting God on any point which required to be settled, and obtaining an answer. Was it by the "Urim and Thummim"?

Thou shalt be able to endure.—Comp. verse 18, where the inability of Moses to endure, unless he made some change, was strongly asserted.

And all this people shall also go to their place in peace.—The people, *i.e.*, will go on their way to Canaan peacefully and contentedly, without suffering the inconvenience to which they are now subject.

(24, 25) **Moses hearkened.**—The appointment of judges, according to Jethro's advice, was not made until after the giving of the Law and the setting up of the Tabernacle. (See Deut. i. 9—15.) In one particular Moses departed from the counsel given to him. Instead of directly choosing the "able men" himself, he left the selection to the people (Deut. i. 13), and contented himself with investing the men chosen with their authority. Comp. the course taken by the apostolic college with respect to the first deacons (Acts vi. 3—6).

(27) **Moses let his father in law depart.**—Heb., *Moses dismissed his connection.* The supposed identity of Hobab (Num. x. 29; Jud. iv. 11) with Jethro seems

CHAPTER XIX.—(1) In the third
month, when the children of Israel were
gone forth out of the land of Egypt,
the same day came they *into* the wilder-
ness of Sinai. (2) For they were de-
parted from Rephidim, and were come *to*
the desert of Sinai, and had pitched in
the wilderness; and there Israel camped
before the mount. (3) And [a]Moses went
up unto God, and the LORD called unto
him out of the mountain, saying, Thus
shalt thou say to the house of Jacob,
and tell the children of Israel; (4) [b]Ye
have seen what I did unto the Egyptians,
and *how* I bare you on eagles' wings,
and brought you unto myself. (5) Now
[c]therefore, if ye will obey my voice
indeed, and keep my covenant, then ye
shall be a peculiar treasure unto me
above all people: for [d]all the earth *is*
mine: (6) and ye shall be unto me a
[e]kingdom of priests, and an holy nation.
These *are* the words which thou shalt
speak unto the children of Israel.

(7) And Moses came and called for the
elders of the people, and laid before

a Acts 7. 38.
b Deut. 29. 2.
c Deut. 5. 2.
d Deut. 10. 14; Ps. 24. 1.
e 1 Pet. 2. 9; Rev. 1. 6.

---

precluded by this statement, for Hobab clearly remained with Moses till the close of the stay at Sinai, and Moses, instead of "dismissing" him, was most unwilling that he should depart.

XIX.

THE MANIFESTATION OF GOD TO THE PEOPLE ON MOUNT SINAI.

(2) **They were departed from Rephidim.**—If Rephidim was where we have placed it, in the Wady Feiran, the march to "the wilderness of Sinai" (*Er Rahah*) must have been by the Wady Solaf, or the Wady esh Sheikh, or possibly by both. The distance by Wady Solaf is about eighteen, by Wady esh Sheikh about twenty-five miles. The wilderness of Sinai, now generally identified with Er Rahah, is a plain two miles long by half a mile wide, "enclosed between two precipitous mountain ranges of black and yellow granite, and having at its end the prodigious mountain block of Ras Sufsafeh" (Stanley, *Sinai and Palestine*, p. 74). It is nearly flat, and covered at present with stunted tamarisk bushes. "No spot in the whole peninsula is so well supplied with water" (*Our Work in Palestine*, p. 268).

Israel camped before the mount.—On the capacity of the plain Er Rahah to receive the entire multitude, see Stanley (*Sinai and Palestine*, p. 42), and comp. the comment on chap. xii. 37—41. The Ras Sufsafeh is visible from every part of the plain.

(3) **Moses went up unto God**—*i.e.*, ascended Sinai, where he expected that God would speak with him.

The Lord called unto him out of the mountain.—While he was still on his way, as it would seem, so that he was spared the toil of the ascent. God meets us half-way when we "arise and go" to Him.

(4) **I bare you on eagles' wings.**—Comp. Deut. xxxii. 11, "As an eagle stirreth up her nest, fluttereth over her young, spreadeth abroad her wings, taketh them, *beareth them upon her wings.*" When its young are first fledged, the eagle is said to assist them in their flight by flying beneath them, so that they may settle upon its wings or back, if necessary. God means that He has bestowed upon His people the same tender and powerful care, has borne them up mightily when they might have fallen, supported their first flight as fledglings, and so saved them from disaster.

Brought you unto myself.—Not so much "brought you to my presence here on Sinai," as "brought you out of Egypt and its corrupting influences (Josh. xxiv. 14), and led you back to my pure worship and true religion." That is spoken of as accomplished, whereof God had begun the accomplishment.

(5) **A peculiar treasure.**—The Hebrew *sĕgullah* is from a root, found in Chaldee, signifying "to earn," or "acquire," and means primarily some valuable possession, which the owner has got by his own exertions. (Comp. 1 Chron. xxix 3, where the English Version translates it by "mine own proper good.") God views the Israelites as made His own by the long series of mighty works done for their deliverance, whereby He is sometimes said to have "redeemed" (chap. vi. 6, xv. 13), or "purchased" them (chap. xv. 16). The word *sĕgullah* is here used for the first time. Later it becomes an *epitheton usitatum* of Israel. (See Deut. vii. 6, xiv. 2, xxvi. 18; Ps. cxxxv. 4; Mal. iii. 17; and comp. also Titus ii. 14; 1 Pet. ii. 9.)

Above all people: for all the earth is mine.—While claiming a peculiar right in Israel, God does not mean to separate Himself from the other nations, to cease to care for them, or give them up to their own devices. He is always "the Most High *over all the earth*" (Ps. lxxxiii. 18), "a light to lighten *the Gentiles*," one who "judges *the people* righteously, and *governs all the nations upon earth*" (Ps. lxvii. 4). Israel's prerogative does not rob them of their birthright. He is the favoured son; but they, too, "are, all of them, children of the Most High" (Ps. lxxxii. 6).

(6) **A kingdom of priests.**—All of them both "kings and priests unto God"—kings as lords over themselves, equals one to another, owing allegiance to God only—priests, as entitled to draw near to God in prayer without an intermediary, to bring Him their offerings, pay Him their vows, and hold communion with Him in heart and soul. The same privileges are declared by St. Peter (1 Pet. ii. 9) and St. John (Rev. i. 6) to belong to all Christians, who in this respect, as in so many others, are now "the Israel of God" (Gal. vi. 16).

An holy nation.—It is not the duty of personal, but the privilege of official, holiness that is here intended. Each Israelite was to be as near to God, as fully entitled to approach Him, as the priests of other nations either were or thought themselves. Personal holiness was the natural and fitting outcome from this official holiness; but it is not here spoken of. God has, however, previously required it of Israel by the words "If ye will obey my voice indeed, and keep my covenant" (verse 5).

(7) **Moses . . . . called for the elders.**—The "elders" formed the usual channel of communication between Moses and the people, reporting his words to them, and theirs to him. (See chap. iv. 29, xii. 21, xvii. 5, 6, xviii. 2, xxiv. 14, &c.) On their position and authority, see Note on chap. iii. 16.

their faces all these words which the
LORD commanded him. (8) And [a]all the
people answered together, and said, All
that the LORD hath spoken we will do.
And Moses returned the words of the
people unto the LORD. (9) And the
LORD said unto Moses, Lo, I come unto
thee in a thick cloud, that the people
may hear when I speak with thee, and
believe thee for ever. And Moses told
the words of the people unto the LORD.

(10) And the LORD said unto Moses,
Go unto the people, and sanctify them
to day and to morrow, and let them
wash their clothes, (11) and be ready
against the third day: for the third day
the LORD will come down in the sight
of all the people upon mount Sinai.
(12) And thou shalt set bounds unto the
people round about, saying, Take heed
to yourselves, *that ye* go *not* up into the
mount, or touch the border of it: [b]who-

a ch. 24. 3, 7; Deut. 5. 27 & 26. 17.

b Heb. 12. 20.

Before their faces.—This translation is a curious piece of literalism. *Liphney*, in the time of Moses, was a mere preposition, signifying "before."

(8) **All the people answered together.**—There was no hesitation, no diversity of opinion, no self-distrust. In view of the great privileges offered to them, all were willing, nay, eager, to promise for themselves that "they would obey God's voice indeed, and keep his covenant." In the glow and warmth of their feelings the difficulty of perfect obedience did not occur to them.

Moses returned the words—*i.e.*, "took them back," "reported them."

(9) **And the Lord said . . . .**—The first step in the great event of the formation of a covenant between God and Israel was completed by the people's acceptance of God's offer. The second step was now to be taken. The terms of the covenant must be declared, and it pleased God to declare them, or, at any rate, the most important and fundamental of them, in the hearing of the people. He therefore makes the announcement of His approaching manifestation of Himself, and proceeds to give directions connected with it to Moses.

Lo, I come unto thee in a thick cloud.—Heb., *in the denseness of a cloud.* Though God is light—nay, because He is light, clouds and darkness are round about Him (Ps. xcvii. 2). Even when He reveals Himself, He still "dwells in the thick darkness" (2 Chron. vi. 1). It is absolutely necessary that He should be closely veiled when He draws near to men, for otherwise they could not endure for a moment "the brightness of His presence." (See chap. xl. 35; 2 Chron. v. 14, vii. 2.) If even the light that remained on Moses' face after converse with God required him thenceforth ordinarily to wear a veil before the people (chap. xxxiv. 33—35), how much more needful must it be that God should cover His face when He condescends to converse with men! In the present case, it would seem to have been "the pillar of the cloud" that had guided Israel, which served Him for a covering, and out of which He spake to Moses and the people.

That the people may hear . . . . and believe thee for ever.—God's purpose in manifesting Himself to the people was twofold:—(1) To impress them with the awful sense of His presence, and through them, their descendants; (2) to make them more ready to submit to Moses, and "believe him for ever." On the whole, it must be said that the purpose was accomplished. God has remained to the Israelites, for more than three millennia, an awful power, real, personal, tremendous. The Law of Moses, under whatever false interpretations, has remained the guide of their life. Though the living Moses was often resisted and contemned, the dead Moses has been reverenced and obeyed from his death to the present time. His laws are still accepted and professedly obeyed by the entire Jewish community.

(10) **Go unto the people, and sanctify them.**—The approaching manifestation required, above all things, that the people should be "sanctified." Sanctification is twofold—outward and inward. The real essential preparation for approach to God is inward sanctification; but no external command can secure this. Moses was therefore instructed to issue directions for outward purification; and it was left to the spiritual insight of the people to perceive and recognise that such purity symbolised and required internal purification as its counterpart. The external purification was to consist in three things—(1) Ablution, or washing of the person; (2) washing of clothes; and (3) abstinence from sexual intercourse (verse 15).

Let them wash their clothes.—The Levitical law required the washing of clothes on many occasions (Lev. xi. 25, 28, 40, xiii. 6, 34, 58, xiv. 8, 9, 47, xv. 5—22, &c.) in connection with purification. The same idea prevailed in Egypt (Herod., ii. 37), in Greece (Hom. *Od.*, iv. l. 759), and in Rome (Dollinger, *Jew and Gentile*, vol. ii., p. 82). It is a natural extension of the idea that ablution of the person cleanses, not from physical only, but from moral defilement.

(11) **Against the third day.**—There is no special "significance" in this mention of "the third day." The important point is, that the purification was to continue through two entire days—one day not being sufficient. This taught the lesson that man's defilement is, in the sight of God, very great.

The Lord will come down in the sight of all the people.—See the comment on verse 9.

(12) **Thou shalt set bounds.**—Here was another formal and mechanical direction, having for its object to deepen and intensify the lesson of God's unapproachable majesty and holiness. Moses was required to "set bounds to the people," *i.e.*, to make a substantial fence between the camp and the base of Sinai, which should prevent both animals and men from coming in contact with the mountain. Modern travellers generally observe how abruptly the rocky precipice of Ras Sufsafeh rises from the plain in front of it, so that in many places it is quite possible to stand on the plain and yet touch the mountain. The idea that a line of natural mounds now to be seen near the base of Sinai represents the "bounds" of Moses (Stanley, *Sinai and Palestine*, p. 43) is unsatisfactory, since the "bounds" of Moses were most certainly artificial ones. It is, however, possible that his "bounds" may have followed the line of the natural barrier.

That ye go not up into the mount.—Unless it had been forbidden, there might have seemed to be no reason why pious Israelites might not have ascended the height, to draw near to God in prayer. It is a

soever toucheth the mount shall be
surely put to death: (13) there shall not
an hand touch it, but he shall surely be
stoned, or shot through; whether *it be*
beast or man, it shall not live: when
the [1] trumpet soundeth long, they shall
come up to the mount.
(14) And Moses went down from the
mount unto the people, and sanctified
the people; and they washed their
clothes. (15) And he said unto the peo-
ple, Be ready against the third day:
come not at *your* wives.
(16) And it came to pass on the third
day in the morning, that there were
thunders and lightnings, and a thick
cloud upon the mount, and the voice of
the trumpet exceeding loud; so that all
the people that *was* in the camp trem-
bled. (17) And Moses brought forth the
people out of the camp to meet with
God; and they stood at the nether part
of the mount. (18) And [a] mount Sinai
was altogether on a smoke, because the
LORD descended upon it in fire: and
the smoke thereof ascended as the
smoke of a furnace, and the whole
mount quaked greatly. (19) And when
the voice of the trumpet sounded long,
and waxed louder and louder, Moses
spake, and God answered him by a
voice. (20) And the LORD came down
upon mount Sinai, on the top of the
mount: and the LORD called Moses up

1 Or, *cornet.*

a Deut. 4. 11.

---

praiseworthy feeling which breathes in the words, "Nearer, my God, to thee;" but the nation was not fit for close approach.

(13) **There shall not an hand touch it.**—This translation gives an entirely wrong sense. The meaning is, beyond all doubt, "There shall not a hand touch *him,*" *i.e.*, the transgressor. To stop him and seize him, another person must have transgressed the bounds, and so have repeated the act which was forbidden. This course was to be avoided, and punishment was to be inflicted on the transgressor by stoning him, or transfixing him with arrows, from within the barrier.

Whether it be beast or man.—Though beasts are innocent of wrong-doing, and are thus no proper objects of punishment, yet the law of God requires their slaughter in certain cases—*e.g.* (1) when they are dangerous (chap. xxi. 28); (2) when they have become polluted (Lev. xx. 15); (3) When their owner's sin is appropriately punished through their loss (chap. xiii. 13). In the present case, it could only be through the culpable carelessness of an owner that a beast could get inside the barrier.

When the trumpet soundeth long.—Comp. verse 19.

They shall come up to the mount.—Rather, *into the mount.* The expression used is identical with that of the preceding verse, and there rendered "go up into the mount." Thus the act forbidden in verse 12 is allowed in verse 13; it is not, however, allowed to the same persons. The word "they" (*hêmah*) in this present place is emphatic, and refers to certain privileged persons, as Moses and Aaron (verse 24), not to the people generally.

(15) **Come not at your wives.**—Comp. 1 Sam. xxi. 4, 5; 1 Cor. vii. 5. It was the general sentiment of antiquity that a ceremonial uncleanness attached even to the chastest sexual connection. (Herod. i. 189, ii. 64; Hesiod. *Op. et D.*, ll. 733—4: Tibull, *Carm.* ii. 1. ll. 11, 12; Porphyr., *De Abstinentia,* iv. 7.) The Levitical law took the same view (Lev. xv. 18), as did the Indian law (*Menu,* v. 63), the Persian (*Zendavesta,* quoted by Bähr, *Symbolik,* vol. ii., p. 466), and the Mahometan (*Koran,* iv. 5).

(16—20) **Thunders and lightnings, and a thick cloud.**—Compare with this description that of Deut. (iv. 11, 12), which is fuller in some respects:—"Ye came near and stood under the mountain; and the mountain *burned with fire unto the midst of heaven,* with darkness, clouds, and *thick darkness.* And the Lord spake unto you out of the fire: ye heard the voice of the words, but saw no similitude; only ye heard a voice." The phenomena accumulated to impress the people seem to have been loud thunder, fierce flashes of lightning, a fire that streamed up from the mountain to the middle of the sky, dense volumes of smoke producing an awful and weird darkness, a trembling of the mountain as by a continuous earthquake, a sound like the blare of a trumpet loud and prolonged, and then finally a clear penetrating voice. So awful a manifestation has never been made at any other place or time, nor will be until the consummation of all things. To regard it as a mere "storm of thunder and lightning," or as "an earthquake with volcanic eruptions," is to miss altogether the meaning of the author, and to empty his narrative of all its natural significance.

The voice of the trumpet.—Heb., *a voice of a trumpet.* The trumpet's blare is the signal of a herald calling attention to a proclamation about to be made. At the last day the coming of Christ is to be announced by "the trump of God" (1 Thess. iv. 16). In the Apocalypse angels are often represented as sounding with trumpets (Rev. viii. 7, 8, 10, 12, ix. 1, 14, &c.) when some great event is about to occur.

(17) **Out of the camp.**—An open space must have intervened between the camp and the "bounds." Into this Moses led the representatives of the people, so bringing them as near to God as was permitted.

At the nether part of the mount.—In the plain directly in front of the Ras Sufsafeh, and almost under it.

(18) **Mount Sinai was altogether on a smoke.**—Heb., *smoked, all of it.* Some understand by this, "dense clouds, having the *appearance* of smoke." But if "the mountain burned with fire," as asserted (Deut. iv. 11), the smoke would be real.

The whole mount quaked greatly.—Comp. Ps. lxviii. 8, "The earth shook, the heavens also dropped at the presence of God: even Sinai itself was moved at the presence of God." The expression is more suitable to an earthquake than to the vibration sometimes produced by very violent thunder.

(20) **On the top of the mount.**—On the summit of the Ras Sufsafeh, not on the Jebel Musa, which is out of sight from the plain of Er Rahah.

to the top of the mount; and Moses went up.
(21) And the LORD said unto Moses,
Go down, [1] charge the people, lest they break through unto the LORD to gaze, and many of them perish.
(22) And let the priests also, which come near to the LORD, sanctify themselves, lest the LORD break forth upon them.
(23) And Moses said unto the LORD, The people cannot come up to mount Sinai: for thou chargedst us, saying, Set bounds about the mount, and sanctify it.
(24) And the LORD said unto him, Away, get thee down, and thou shalt come up, thou, and Aaron with thee: but let not the priests and the people break through to come up unto the LORD, lest he break forth upon them.
(25) So Moses went down unto the people, and spake unto them.

[1] Heb., *contest.*

CHAPTER XX.—(1) And God spake all these words, saying,

GOD'S WARNING TO THE PEOPLE AGAINST A TOO NEAR APPROACH.

(21–25) Warning was given, as soon as God announced His intention of descending upon Sinai, that the people must not approach too near. "Bounds" were set, and the people required to keep within them. Actual contact with the mountain was forbidden under penalty of death (verse 12). It is evident from verse 23 that the command to "set bounds" had been obeyed, and a fence erected which it would have required some force to "break through;" nor can there be any doubt that Moses had promulgated the directions, which he had received from God, forbidding any approach to the mount, and threatening death to those who should "touch" it. Yet still it is evident from this concluding paragraph of the chapter (verses 21—25) that the first warning was insufficient. An intention to "break through, to gaze," must have been entertained by many. To this intention the existing priesthood, whatever it was, were parties (verse 22). It always grates upon men's feelings to be told that they are less holy than others; and we can easily understand that those who had hitherto acted as priests to the nation would resent their exclusion from "holy ground" to which the sons of Amram were about to be admitted. Even of the people there may have been many who participated in the feeling, and thought that Moses and Aaron were "taking too much upon them, seeing that the whole congregation" was holy. Hence, a further very stringent command was requisite, and Moses, having reached the summit, was sent down again from the top to the bottom in order to enjoin upon priests and people alike, in the most solemn possible way, the necessity of their observing the bounds set.

(21) **Lest they break through**—*i.e., force their way through the barrier which Moses had erected.*

To gaze, and many of them perish.—Some might have perished by the execution of the orders given in verse 13. But the allusion is perhaps rather to such a heaven-sent plague as destroyed the men of Beth-shemesh to the number of 50,070 (1 Sam. vi. 19).

(22) **The priests.**—This has been called an anachronism, since the Levitical priesthood was not as yet instituted. But the Israelites, like all other ancient tribes or races, must have had priests long ere this, appointed upon one principle or another. It is a reasonable conjecture that hitherto the heads of families had exercised sacerdotal functions.

Break forth—*i.e., punish in some open and manifest way.* Compare the "breach" upon Uzzah (2 Sam. vi. 8).

(23) **The people cannot come up.**—Moses probably means that they cannot do so unwittingly; he does not contemplate the case of an intentional trespass. But it was this which God knew to be contemplated, and was desirous of preventing.

(24) **Away, get thee down.**—He "with whom is no variableness, neither shadow of turning" (James i. 17) overrules the objection of Moses, and persists. The warning is required, and is to be given. Moses, submissive as usual, yields, and "goes down unto the people and speaks unto them." The result is that no attempt to break through the barrier is made.

XX.

THE TEN COMMANDMENTS.

(1) **God spake.**—It is distinctly stated in Deuteronomy that the Ten Commandments were spoken to "all the assembly of Israel," by God, "out of the midst of the fire, of the cloud, and of the thick darkness, with a great voice" (Deut. v. 22). It was not till after their delivery that the people entreated to be spared further communications of so awful a character. How the sounds were produced is a mystery unrevealed, and on which it is idle to speculate. Jehovah alone appears as the speaker in the Old Testament; in the New, we hear of the instrumentality of angels (Acts vii. 53; Gal. iii. 19; Heb. ii. 2).

All these words.—In Scripture the phrase used to designate the Ten Commandments is "the *Ten Words*" (chap. xxxiv. 28; Deut. iv. 13, x. 4). It has been universally recognised, both by the Jewish and Christian Churches, that they occupy an unique position among the utterances which constitute God's revelation to man. Alone uttered publicly by God in the ears of the people, alone inscribed on stone by the finger of God Himself, alone, of all commands, deposited in the *penetrale* of worship—the Ark—they formed the germ and basis, the very pith and kernel of the covenant which God, through Moses, made with man, and which was to continue for above thirteen hundred years the exposition of His will to the human race. They enunciate a morality infinitely above that of all the then existing nations of the earth—nay, above that of the wisest of mankind to whom revelation was unknown. There is no compendium of morality in Confucianism, in Buddhism, in the religion of Zoroaster, or of Egypt, or of Greece or Rome, which can be put in competition with the Decalogue. Broad exceedingly (Ps. cxix. 96), yet searching and minute in its requirements; embracing the whole range of human duty, yet never vague or indeterminate; systematic, yet free from the hardness and narrowness commonly attaching to systems: the Decalogue has maintained and will always maintain itself, if not as an absolutely complete summary of human duty, yet as a summary

(2) *a*I *am* the LORD thy God, which
have brought thee out of the land of
Egypt, out of the house of [1]bondage.
(3) Thou shalt have no other gods before
me.
(4) *b*Thou shalt not make unto thee
any graven image, or any likeness *of*

a Deut. 5. 6; Ps. 81. 10.

1 Heb., *servants.*

b Lev. 26. 1; Ps. 97. 7.

any thing that *is* in heaven above, or
that *is* in the earth beneath, or that *is*
in the water under the earth: (5) thou
shalt not bow down thyself to them, nor
serve them: for I the LORD thy God *am*
a jealous God, visiting the iniquity of
the fathers upon the children unto the

---

which has never been superseded. When our Lord was asked what a man must do to inherit eternal life, He replied by a reference to the Decalogue: "Thou knowest the commandments" (Mark x. 19). When the Church would impress on her children their complete duty both to God and man, she requires them to be taught the "Ten Words." When adult Christians are to be reminded, before coming to Holy Communion, of the necessity of self-examination and repentance, the same summary is read to them. It is an extraordinary testimony to the excellence of the compendium that, originating in Judaism, it has been maintained unchanged in a religious system so different from Judaism as Christianity.

(2) **I am the Lord thy God.**—The binding nature of commands upon the conscience depends upon the authority of the person who issues them. That there might be no dispute as to what the authority was in the case of the Decalogue, God prefaced the commands themselves by this distinct statement. By whomsoever they were communicated (see the first Note on verse 1), they were the commands of Jehovah Himself.

Which have brought thee out of the land of Egypt.—Thus exhibiting at once Almighty power and the tenderest compassion and care. God desires the obedience which springs from love, not fear.

(3) **Thou shalt have no other gods before me.**—Heb., *There shalt be to thee no other god before me.* The result is the same, whether we translate *Elohim* by "god" or "gods;" but the singular verb shows that the plural form of the name is a mere plural of dignity.

Before me—literally, *before my face*—means strictly, "side by side with me"—*i.e.*, "in addition to me." God does not suppose that the Israelites, after all that He had done for them, would discard Him, and substitute other gods in His place, but fears the syncretism which would unite His worship with that of other deities. All polytheisms were syncretic, and readily enlarged their pantheons, since, when once the principle of unity is departed from, whether the plurality be a little greater or a little less cannot much signify. The Egyptian religion seems to have adopted Ammon at a comparatively late period from Arabia; it took Bar, or Baal, Anta, or Anaïtis, Astaret, or Astarte, Reshpu, or Reseph, &c., from Syria, and it admitted Totun from Ethiopia. Israel, in after-times, fell into the same error, and, without intending to apostatise from Jehovah, added on the worship of Baal, Ashtoreth, Moloch, Chemosh, Remphan, &c. It is this form of polytheism against which the first commandment is directed. It asserts the *sole* claim of Jehovah to our religious regards.

(4) **Thou shalt not make unto thee any graven image.**—The two main clauses of the second commandment are to be read together, so as to form one sentence: "Thou shalt not make to thee any graven image, &c., so as to worship it." (See the explanation of Josephus, *Ant. Jud.*, iii. 5, § 5: Ὁ δεύτερος λόγος κελεύει μηδένος εἰκόνα ζώου ποιήσαντας προσκυνεῖν.) It was not until the days of Hebrew decline and degeneracy that a narrow literalism pressed the words into an absolute prohibition of the arts of painting and sculpture (Philo, *De Oraculis,* § 29). Moses himself sanctioned the cherubic forms above the mercy-seat, the brazen serpent, and the lilies and pomegranates of the golden candlestick. Solomon had lions on the steps of his throne, oxen under his "molten sea," and palm-trees, flowers, and cherubim on the walls of the Temple, "within and without" (1 Kings vi. 29). What the second commandment forbade was the worship of God under a material form. It asserted the spirituality of Jehovah. While in the rest of the ancient world there was scarcely a single nation or tribe which did not "make to itself" images of the gods, and regard the images themselves with superstitious veneration, in Judaism alone was this seductive practice disallowed. God would have no likeness made of Him, no representation that might cloud the conception of His entire separation from matter, His purely spiritual essence.

In heaven above . . . in the earth beneath . . . in the water under the earth.—Comp. Gen. i. 1—7. The triple division is regarded as embracing the whole material universe. In the Egyptian idolatry images of all three kinds were included.

(5) **Nor serve them.**—The idolatry of the ancient world was, practically, not a mere worship of celestial beings through material representations of them, but an actual culture of the images themselves, which were regarded as possessed of miraculous powers. "I myself," says Arnobius, "not so very long ago, worshipped gods just taken out of the furnace, fresh from the anvil of the smith, ivory, paintings, stumps of trees swathed in bandages; and if I happened to cast my eyes on a polished stone smeared with olive oil, I made reverence to it, *as if a power were present therein,* and addressed myself in supplication for blessings to the senseless block" (*Advers. Gentes,* i. 29). "People pray," says Seneca, "to the images of the gods, implore them on bended knees, sit or stand long days before them, throw them money, and sacrifice beasts to them, so treating them with deep respect" (*Ap. Lactant.*, ii. 2).

A jealous God.—Not in the sense in which He was regarded as "jealous" by some of the Greeks, who supposed that success or eminence of any kind provoked Him (Herod. iii. 40, 125), but jealous of His own honour, one who will not see "His glory given to another" (Isa. xlii. 8, xlviii. 11), or allow rivals to dispute His sole and absolute sovereignty. (Comp. chap. xxxiv. 14; Deut. iv. 24, v. 9, vi. 15; Josh. xxiv. 19.)

Visiting the iniquity of the fathers upon the children.—It is a fact that, under God's natural government of the world, the iniquity of fathers *is* visited upon their children. Diseases caused by vicious courses are transmitted. The parents' extravagance leaves their children beggars. To be the son of a felon is to be heavily handicapped in the race of life. That

third and fourth *generation* of them that
hate me; (6) and shewing mercy unto
thousands of them that love me, and
keep my commandments.
(7) [a] Thou shalt not take the name of
the LORD thy God in vain; for the
LORD will not hold him guiltless that
taketh his name in vain.
(8) Remember the sabbath day, to keep
it holy. (9) [b] Six days shalt thou labour,
and do all thy work: (10) but the seventh
day *is* the sabbath of the LORD thy

a Lev. 19.12, Deut. 5.11; Matt. 5.33.

b ch. 23.12; Ezek. 20.12; Luke 13.14.

---

this should be so is perhaps involved in "the nature of things"—at any rate, it is part of the scheme of Divine government by which the world is ordered. We all inherit countless disadvantages on account of our first parents' sin. We each individually inherit special tendencies to this or that form of evil from the misconduct of our several progenitors. The knowledge that their sins will put their children at a disadvantage is calculated to check men in their evil courses more than almost anything else; and this check could not be removed without a sensible diminution of the restraints which withhold men from vice. Still, the penalty upon the children is not final or irreversible. Under whatever disadvantages they are born, they may struggle against them, and lead good lives, and place themselves, even in this world, on a level with those who were born under every favourable circumstance. It is needless to say that, as respects another world, their parents' iniquities will not be visited on them. "Each man will bear his own burthen." The soul that sinneth, it shall die. "The son shall not bear the iniquity of the father, neither shall the father bear the iniquity of the son; the righteousness of the righteous shall be upon him, and the wickedness of the wicked shall be upon him" (Ezek. xviii. 20).

(6) **Shewing mercy unto thousands.**—Rather, *to the thousandth generation*, as is distinctly expressed in Deut. vii. 9. God's mercy infinitely transcends His righteous anger. Sin is visited on three, or at most four, generations. Righteousness is remembered, and advantages descendants, for ever.

(7) **Thou shalt not take the name of the Lord thy God in vain.**—The Hebrew is ambiguous, as is to some extent the English translation. Most modern critics regard the phrase used as forbidding *false* swearing only; but some think that it forbids also "profane" or "vain swearing." Our Lord's comment in the Sermon on the Mount favours the view that false swearing alone was actually forbidden by the Law, since He proceeds to condemn profane swearing on His own authority: "But I say unto you" (Matt. v. 34). False swearing is among the greatest insults that man can offer to God, and, as being such, is naturally forbidden in the first table, which teaches us our duty to God. It is also destructive of civil society; and hence it is again forbidden in the second table (verse 16), which defines our duties to our neighbour. The laws of all organised States necessarily forbid it, and generally under a very severe penalty. The Jewish Law condemned the false witness to suffer the punishment which his evidence was calculated to inflict (Deut. xix. 19). The Egyptians visited perjury with death or mutilation. The Greeks were content to punish it with a heavy fine, and ultimately with the loss of civil rights. The Romans, in the more ancient times, inflicted the death penalty. It was generally believed, alike in Egypt, in Greece, and in Rome, that the anger of the gods was especially provoked by this crime, and that a Divine Nemesis pursued those who committed it, and made them suffer for their sin, either in their own person or in that of their posterity.

The Lord will not hold him guiltless.—Punishment will assuredly overtake the perjured man, if not in this life, then in another. Jehovah will vindicate His own honour.

(8) **Remember the sabbath day.**—It is pertinent to remark that this command is introduced differently from any other by the word "remember." But we cannot, therefore, conclude that the Sabbath was a primitive institution, which the Israelites were bound to have held in perpetual remembrance, since the reference may be merely to the injunction recently given in connection with the gathering of the manna (chap. xvi. 23). The Sabbath had certainly been at that time solemnly instituted, if no earlier. (See Note on chap. xvi. 25.)

To keep it holy.—It had been already noted that the rest of the Sabbath was to be a "holy rest" (chap. xvi. 23); but it is not quite clear what was intended by this. For the most part, the Law insists on abstinence from labour as the main element of Sabbath observance (chaps. xvi. 23—30, xx. 9—11, xxiii. 12, xxxiv. 21, xxxv. 2, 3; Deut. v. 12—15, &c.); and it can scarcely be said to prescribe anything positive with respect to the religious employment of the day. That the morning and evening sacrifice were to be doubled might indeed suggest to a religiously-minded Israelite that his own religious exercises and devotions should also be augmented; but the Law made no such requirement. His attendance at the morning and evening sacrifice was not required nor expected. No provision was made for his receiving religious teaching on the day; no special offerings were required from him upon it. The day became one of "languid bodily ease, relaxation, and luxury" to the bulk of the later Jews (Augustin. *Enarr. in Ps.* xci.); but probably there were always some whom natural piety taught that, in the absence of their ordinary employments, it was intended they should devote themselves to prayer and communion with God—to meditation on "high and holy themes," such as His mercies in past time, His character, attributes, revelations of Himself, government of the world, dealings with men and nations. Thus only could the day be really "kept holy," with a positive, and not a mere negative, holiness.

(9) **Six days shalt thou labour.**—The form is certainly imperative; and it has been held that the fourth commandment is "not limited to a mere enactment respecting one day, but prescribes the due distribution of a week, and *enforces the six days' work as much as the seventh day's rest*" (Garden in Smith's *Dictionary of the Bible*, vol. iii., p. 1068). But the work on the six days is really rather assumed as what will be than required as what must be; and the intention of the clause is prohibitory rather than mandatory —"thou shalt not work more than six days out of the seven."

(10) **But the seventh day is the sabbath of the Lord thy God.**—Heb., *But the seventh day (shall be) a sabbath to the Lord thy God*—*i.e.*, it shall be a day of holy rest from things worldly, and of devotion to things heavenly. (See Note 2 on verse 8.)

God: *in it* thou shalt not do any work,
thou, nor thy son, nor thy daughter,
thy manservant, nor thy maidservant,
nor thy cattle, nor thy stranger that *is*
within thy gates: (11) for [a] *in* six days
the LORD made heaven and earth, the
sea, and all that in them *is*, and rested
the seventh day: wherefore the LORD
blessed the sabbath day, and hallowed
it.
(12) [b] Honour thy father and thy mother: that thy days may be long upon
the land which the LORD thy God giveth
thee.

a Gen. 2. 2.

b Deut. 5. 16: Matt. 15. 4; Eph. 6. 2.

In it thou shalt not do any work.—This negative aspect of the Sabbath is further emphasised by particular prohibitions:—(1) The prohibition against gathering the manna on the Sabbath (chap. xvi. 26); (2) the prohibition against lighting a fire (chap. xxxv. 3); (3) against gathering sticks (Num. xv. 35). Some exceptions were allowed, as the work of the Priests and Levites in the Temple on the Sabbath, attendance on and care of the sick, rescue of a beast that was in peril of its life, &c. (See Matt. xii. 5, 11.) But the tendency was to press the negative aspect to an extreme, and to ignore the positive one. By the time of the Maccabees it had come to be considered unlawful to defend oneself against the attack of an enemy on the Sabbath (1 Macc. ii. 32—38; 2 Macc. v. 25, 26, vi. 11, xv. 1); and, though this extravagant view did not maintain its ground, yet at the time of our Lord's ministry a rigour of observance was in vogue upon other points which exceeded the limits of reasonable exegesis. Our Lord's practice was pointedly directed against the overstrained theory of Sabbath observance which was current in His day, and was clearly intended to vindicate for His disciples a liberty which ecclesiastical authority was disposed to deny them. There are parts of Christendom in which, even at the present day, a similar spirit prevails, and a similar vindication is needed.

Nor thy son, nor thy daughter.—The whole family was to partake in the Sabbatical rest. Labour was to cease, not to be devolved by the stronger on weaker members.

Thy manservant, nor thy maidservant.—The rest was to extend also to the domestics, who specially required it, since the heavier labours of the household had to be performed by them.

Thy cattle.—Labour can scarcely be exacted from cattle without man being also called upon to work. God, however, "careth for cattle," even for their own sakes, and wills that the Sabbath rest be extended to them. "His mercy is over all His works," and embraces the dumb unreasoning animals no less than His human creatures. (Comp. Gen. viii. 1, ix. 9—11; Exod. ix. 19; Deut. xxv. 4; Jonah iv. 11.)

(11) **For in six days the Lord made heaven and earth.**—Comp. Gen. ii. 2, 3, and Exod. xxxi. 17. It is not improbable that the work of creation was made to occupy six days because one day in seven is the appropriate proportion of rest to labour for such a being as man. God might have created all things on one day had He so pleased; but, having the institution of the Sabbath in view, He prefigured it by spreading His work over six days, and then resting on the seventh. His law of the Sabbath established a conformity between the method of His own working and that of His reasonable creatures, and taught men to look on work, not as an aimless, indefinite, incessant, weary round, but as leading on to an end, a rest, a fruition, a time for looking back, and seeing the result and rejoicing in it. Each Sabbath is such a time, and is a type and foretaste of that eternal "sabbatising" in another world which "remaineth for the people of God" (Heb. iv. 9). The secondary object of the institution of the Sabbath, assigned in Deut. v. 15, is in no way incompatible with this primary one. The thought of God's works in creation might well be associated in the mind of an Israelite with the thought of His "wondrous works" in Egypt, and the recollection of the blessed peace and rest in which creation resulted, with the memory of the glad time of repose and refreshment which supervened upon the weary task-work of the Egyptian bondage.

(12) **Honour thy father and thy mother.**—It is not a matter of much importance how we divide the commandments; nor is it historically certain how they were originally distributed between the two tables. But, practically, the view that the fifth commandment begins the second table, which lays down our duty towards our neighbours, is to be preferred for its convenience, though it trenches upon symmetrical arrangement. Of all our duties to our fellow-men, the first and most fundamental is our duty towards our parents, which lies at the root of all our social relations, and is the first of which we naturally become conscious. Honour, reverence, and obedience are due to parents from the position in which they stand to their children:—(1) As, in a certain sense, the authors of their being; (2) as their shelterers and nourishers; (3) as their protectors and educators, from whom they derive the foundation of their moral training and the first elements of their knowledge. Even among savages the obligations of children towards their parents are felt and acknowledged to a greater or a less extent; and there has never been a civilised community of whose moral code they have not formed an important part. In Egypt the duty of filial piety was strictly inculcated from a very early date (Lenormant, *Histoire Ancienne*, vol. i., pp. 342, 343), and a bad son forfeited the prospect of happiness in another life (*ibid.*, pp. 513, 514). Confucianism bases all morality upon the parental and filial relation, and requires the most complete subjection, even of the grown-up son, to his father and mother. Greek ethics taught that the relation of children to their parents was parallel to that of men to God (Aristot. *Eth. Nic.* viii. 12, § 5); and Rome made the absolute authority of the father the basis of its entire State system. The Divine legislation of Sinai is in full accord, here as elsewhere, with the voice of reason and conscience, affirming broadly the principles of parental authority and filial submission, but leaving the mode in which the principles should be carried out to the discretion of individuals or communities.

That thy days may be long upon the land.—The fifth commandment (as all allow) is "the first commandment *with promise*" (Eph. vi. 2); but the promise may be understood in two quite different senses. (1) It may be taken as guaranteeing national permanence to the people among whom filial respect

(13) [a]Thou shalt not kill.
(14) Thou shalt not commit adultery.
(15) Thou shalt not steal.
(16) Thou shalt not bear false witness against thy neighbour.
(17) [b]Thou shalt not covet thy neighbour's house, thou shalt not covet thy neighbour's wife, nor his manservant, nor his maidservant, nor his ox, nor his ass, nor any thing that *is* thy neighbour's.

a Matt. 5. 21.

b Rom. 7. 7.

and obedience is generally practised; or (2) it may be understood in the simpler and more literal sense of a pledge that obedient children shall, as a general rule, receive for their reward the blessing of long life. In favour of the former view have been urged the facts of Roman and Chinese permanence, together with the probability that Israel forfeited its possession of Canaan in consequence of persisting in the breach of this commandment. In favour of the latter may be adduced the application of the text by St. Paul (Eph. vi. 3), which is purely personal and not ethnic; and the exegesis of the Son of Sirach (Wisd. iii. 6), which is similar. It is also worthy of note that an Egyptian sage, who wrote long before Moses, declared it as the result of his experience that obedient sons did attain to a good old age in Egypt, and laid down the principle broadly, that "the son who attends to the words of his father will grow old in consequence" (Lenormant, *Histoire Ancienne*, vol. i., p. 342).

(13) **Thou shalt not kill.**—From the peculiar duties owed by children to their parents, the Divine legislator went on to lay down those general duties which men owe to their fellow-men. And of these the first is that of respecting their life. The security of life is the primary object of government; and it has been well said that men originally coalesced into States with a view to self-preservation (Arist., *Pol.* i. 1). All written codes forbid murder; and in communities which are without written codes an unwritten law condemns it. When God "set a mark upon Cain" (Gen. iv. 15), He marked thereby His abhorrence of the murderer. The "seven precepts of Noah" included one which distinctly forbade the taking of human life (Gen. ix. 6). In all countries and among all peoples, a natural instinct or an unwritten tradition placed murder among the worst of crimes, and made its penalty death. The Mosaic legislation on the point was differenced from others principally by the care it took to distinguish between actual murder, manslaughter (chap. xxi. 13), death by misadventure (Num. xxxv. 23), and justifiable homicide (chap. xxii. 2). Before, however, it made these distinctions, the great principle of the sanctity of human life required to be broadly laid down; and so the law was given in the widest possible terms—"Thou shalt not kill." Exceptions were reserved till later.

(14) **Thou shalt not commit adultery.**—Next to the duty of respecting a man's life is placed that of respecting his domestic peace and honour. Adultery is an invasion of the household, a destruction of the bond which unites the family, a dissolution of that contract which is the main basis of social order. It was forbidden by all civilised communities, and in uncivilised ones frequently punished with death. The Mosaic enactments on the subject are peculiar chiefly in the absolute equality on which they place the man and the woman. Adulterers are as hateful as adulteresses, and are as surely to be put to death (Lev. xx. 10; Deut. xxii. 22—24, &c.). The man who acts treacherously against "the wife of his covenant" is as great a sinner as the woman who breaks the marriage bond (Mal. ii. 14—16). There is "no respect of persons" and no respect of sexes with God.

(15) **Thou shalt not steal.**—Our third duty towards our neighbour is to respect his right to his property. The framers of Utopias, both ancient and modern, have imagined communities in which private property should not exist. But such a condition of things has never yet been realised in practice. In the laws of all known States private property has been recognised, and social order has been, in a great measure, based upon it. Here, again, law has but embodied natural instinct. The savage who hammers out a flint knife by repeated blows with a pebble, labouring long, and undergoing pain in the process, feels that the implement which he has made is his own, and that his right to it is indisputable. If he is deprived of it by force or fraud, he is wronged. The eighth commandment forbids this wrong, and requires us to respect the property of others no less than their person and their domestic peace and honour.

(16) **Thou shalt not bear false witness against thy neighbour.**—Our fourth duty to our neighbour is not to injure his character. Our great poet has said—

> "Who steals my purse, steals trash,
> But he who filches from me my good name,
> Robs me of that which not enriches him,
> Yet leaves me poor indeed,"—

thus indicating the fact that calumny may injure a man more than robbery. False witness is, of course, worst when given in a court of justice; and this offence has generally been made punishable by law. It was peculiar to the Hebrew legislation that it not only forbade and punished (Deut. xix. 16—20) false testimony of this extreme kind, but denounced also the far commoner, yet scarcely less injurious, practice of spreading untrue reports about others, thus injuring them in men's esteem. The ninth commandment is broad enough in its terms to cover both forms of the sin, though pointing especially to the form which is of the more heinous character. Lest its wider bearing should be overlooked, the Divine legislator added later a distinct prohibition of calumny in the words, "Thou shalt not raise a false report" (chap. xxiii. 1).

(17) **Thou shalt not covet.**—This command seems to have been added in order to teach the general principle that the Law of God is concerned, not with acts and words only, but with the thoughts of the heart. Rightly understood, the seventh and eighth commandments contain the tenth, which strikes at covetousness and lustful desire. (Comp. Matt. v. 27, 28.) But ancient moralists did not usually recognise this; thought, unless carried out into acts, was regarded as "free;" no responsibility was considered to attach to it, and consequently no one felt it needful to control his thoughts or regulate them. It was therefore of importance that the Divine Law should distinctly assert a control over men's thoughts and feelings, since they are the source of all that is evil in word and act; and true godliness consists in bringing "every thought into captivity to Christ" (2 Cor. x. 5).

(18) And [a] all the people saw the thun-
derings, and the lightnings, and the
noise of the trumpet, and the mountain
smoking: and when the people saw *it*,
they removed, and stood afar off. (19) And
they said unto Moses, [b] Speak thou with
us, and we will hear: but let not God
speak with us, lest we die. (20) And
Moses said unto the people, Fear not:
for God is come to prove you, and that
his fear may be before your faces, that
ye sin not.
(21) And the people stood afar off, and
Moses drew near unto the thick darkness
where God *was*.
(22) And the LORD said unto Moses,
Thus thou shalt say unto the children
of Israel, Ye have seen that I have talked
with you from heaven. (23) Ye shall not
make with me gods of silver, neither

a Heb. 12. 18

b Deut. 5. 27 & 18. 16.

AT THE PEOPLE'S REQUEST, MOSES BECOMES THEIR INTERMEDIARY.

(18—21) The delivery of the Ten Commandments by a voice manifestly superhuman impressed the people with an awful fear. They felt the near contact with God to be more than they could bear. Even Moses was so deeply moved that he exclaimed, "I exceedingly fear and quake" (Heb. xii. 21). The people were still more afraid, and felt compelled to withdraw to a distance, beyond the sound of the terrible voice. From Deuteronomy we learn that they retired within their tents (Deut. v. 30), having first sent a deputation to Moses, with a request that he would thenceforth act as their intermediary. It pleased God to assent to this proposal; and the remainder of the Law was communicated by God to Moses, and by Moses to the Israelites.

(18) **And all the people saw the thunderings** —*i.e.*, perceived them. On the true character of the Sinaitic manifestation, see Note on chap. xix. 16—20.

They removed.—Moses had brought the representatives of the people as near to Sinai as possible—close to the foot of the great precipice of Ras Sufsâfeh (chap. xix. 17). The wide plain of Er-Rahah allowed of a removal to a considerable distance.

(19) **Speak thou with us.**—Comp. Deut. v. 24—27, where the words of the people are reported at greater length:—"Behold, the Lord our God hath shewed us his glory and his greatness, and we have heard his voice out of the midst of the fire: we have seen this day that God doth talk with man, and he liveth. Now therefore why should we die? for this great fire will consume us: if we hear the voice of the Lord our God any more, then we shall die. For who is there of all flesh, that hath heard the voice of the living God speaking out of the midst of the fire, as we have, and lived? Go thou near, and hear all that the Lord our God shall say: and speak thou unto us all that the Lord our God shall speak unto thee; and we will hear it, and do it."

(20) **Moses said unto the people, Fear not.**—God approved the people's proposal, and directed that they should withdraw to their tents (Deut. v. 28—30). Moses then "drew near" to Him, and entered into "the thick darkness where God was" (verse 21). It is worthy of notice that the same manifestation which repelled the people attracted Moses.

THE BOOK OF THE COVENANT.

(22—26) In the remainder of chap. xx., and in the three chapters which follow, we have a series of laws delivered by God to Moses, immediately after the delivery of the Decalogue, which constituted the second stage of the revelation, and stood midway between the first great enunciation of abstract principles in the Ten Commandments and the ultimate minute and complicated elaboration of rules to meet all cases which fills the three Books of Leviticus, Numbers, and Deuteronomy. This intermediate revelation appears to have been at once committed to writing, and in its written shape was known as "the Book of the Covenant" (chap. xxiv. 7), and regarded with special veneration.

"The Book of the Covenant" is wanting in system and arrangement, but is not wholly unsystematic. It commences with some laws concerning the worship of God (chap. xx. 22—26), proceeds from the Divine to the human, and treats in its second section (chap. xxi. 1—32) of "the rights of persons," then concerns itself with "the rights of property" (chap. xxi. 33 to xxii. 15), and, finally, winds up with "miscellaneous laws" (chap. xxii. 16 to xxiii. 19), partly on things Divine, partly on things human—the things Divine being reserved to the last, so that the end of the legislation is in close harmony with the beginning. Altogether, the enactments contained in the short space of three chapters are some seventy; and the "Book of the Covenant" is thus no mere tentative sketch; but a very wonderful condensation of the essence of all the more important matters which Moses afterwards put forth by Divine inspiration in the long space of nearly forty years.

LAWS CONCERNING RELIGION.

(22) **Ye have seen that I have talked with you from heaven.**—It was important to identify the giver of the Book of the Covenant with the deliverer of the Ten Commandments, and accordingly this was done in the opening words of the Book.

(23) **Ye shall not make with me gods of silver.**—The expression "make with me" is unusual, but does not seem to have any peculiar force. Gods of silver and gods of gold are specially forbidden, because it was to idolatry of this kind that the Israelites were specially inclined. The golden calf is no isolated phenomenon. Molten images of gods, generally of silver, sometimes of gold, were objects of worship to Israel throughout the ages which preceded the Captivity. Jeroboam set up molten images at Dan and Bethel (1 Kings xiv. 9; 2 Kings xvii. 16). Baal was worshipped under the semblance of a molten image (2 Chron. xxviii. 2) as were probably Ashtaroth, Chemosh, and Moloch. The animal worship of the Egyptians had no attractions for the Hebrews; they did not offer to images of stone or marble, like the Assyrians or the Greeks; much less was it their habit to "bow down to stocks," like so many of the heathen nations around them. The "molten image," generally completed by a certain amount of graving, was the form of idol which had most charms for them, and the more precious the material the more satisfied were they to worship it. (Comp. Isa. xxx. 22, xlii. 17; Jer. x. 14; Hosea xiii. 2, &c.). Occasionally indeed they overlaid wood or stone with plates of gold or silver, to produce an idol

shall ye make unto you gods of gold.
(24) An altar of earth thou shalt make
unto me, and shalt sacrifice thereon thy
burnt offerings, and thy peace offerings,
thy sheep, and thine oxen: in all places
where I record my name I will come
unto thee, and I will bless thee. (25) And
[a]if thou wilt make me an altar of stone,
thou shalt not [1]build it of hewn stone:
for if thou lift up thy tool upon it, thou
hast polluted it. (26) Neither shalt thou
go up by steps unto mine altar, that thy
nakedness be not discovered thereon.

[a] Deut. 27. 5, Josh. 8. 31.

[1] Heb., *build them with hewing.*

[b] Lev. 25. 41; Deut. 15. 12; Jer. 34. 14.

[2] Heb., *with his body.*

CHAPTER XXI.—(1) Now these *are*
the judgments which thou shalt set
before them.
(2) [b]If thou buy an Hebrew servant, six
years he shall serve: and in the seventh
he shall go out free for nothing. (3) If
he came in [2]by himself, he shall go out
by himself: if he were married, then his
wife shall go out with him. (4) If his
master have given him a wife, and she
have born him sons or daughters; the
wife and her children shall be her
master's, and he shall go out by himself.

(Hab. x. 19); but such images were at once less common and held in less account.

(24) **An altar of earth thou shalt make unto me.**—The earliest altars were, naturally, either of earth, or of unhewn stones, gathered into a heap, since these could be constructed with little labour, and without tools. But, as civilisation advanced, more elaborate structures took the place of the primitive ones. It became usual to erect altars of hewn stone, adorned with carvings more or less rich, among which might often be introduced human and animal forms. We must understand the command here given, and that of verse 25, as intended to forbid structures of this latter kind, which, if allowed, might have led on to idolatry.

Thy burnt offerings and thy peace offerings.—Sacrifice began soon after Paradise was quitted (Gen. iv. 3, 4), and shortly became a universal practice. Noah offered sacrifice on leaving the ark (Gen. viii. 20); and in the family of Abraham the rite was an established one (Gen. xii. 7, xv. 9, xxii. 7, xxvi. 25, xxxi. 54, &c.). Egyptians, Assyrians, Babylonians, Persians, Phœnicians, Greeks, Romans, Scythians, Celts, Germans, all equally regarded sacrifice as a main element of their religion; and if the Hebrews had not offered actual sacrifices during their oppression in Egypt, they had, at any rate, maintained the wish to offer them, and it was (primarily) for the purpose of sacrificing that they had quitted Egypt. The legislation assumes that they are acquainted with the difference between "burnt offerings" and "peace offerings," and desirous of offering both kinds.

(25) **If thou wilt make me an altar of stone.**—Among civilised nations altars were almost always of stone, which superseded earth, as more durable. God does not absolutely prohibit the employment of stone altars by the Israelites, who are found to use them upon certain occasions (Josh. viii. 31; 1 Kings xviii. 32). He is content to forbid the shaping of the stones by an implement, that so they may not give rise to idolatry. (See Note on verse 24.)

Thou hast polluted it.—Nature is God's handiwork, and, therefore, pure and holy. Man, by contact with it, imparts to it of his impurity. The altar, whereby sin was to be expiated, required to be free from all taint of human corruption. For the construction of the altar afterwards sanctioned, see the comment on chap. xxvii. 1.

(26) **Neither shalt thou go up by steps unto mine altar.**—When the dress of the priests had been so arranged that no exposure of the person was possible (ch. xxvii. 42, 43), this precept became unnecessary. Thus it would seem that Solomon's altar had steps. (Compare 2 Chr. iv. 1 with Ezek. xliii. 17.)

XXI.

Laws concerning the Rights of Persons.

(1) **These are the judgments.**—"The laws" (Knobel), "the rights" (Keil), "the rules which shall guide judicial decisions" (Pool). The paraphrase alone gives the full meaning.

(2) **If thou buy an Hebrew servant.**—Ancient society was founded upon slavery. "The ultimate elements of the household," says Aristotle, "are the master and his slave, the husband and his wife, the father and his children" (*Pol.* i. 2, § 1). In any consideration of the rights of persons, those of the slave class naturally presented themselves first of all, since they were the most liable to infraction. Slaves might be either natives or foreigners. A Hebrew could become a slave—(1) through crime (chap. xxii. 3); (2) through indebtedness (Lev. xxv. 39); (3) through his father's right to sell him (Neh. v. 5). Foreign slaves might be either prisoners taken in war, or persons bought of their owners (Lev. xxv. 45). The rights of Hebrew slaves are here specially considered.

Six years shall he serve.—The Hebrew was not to be retained in slavery for a longer space than six years. If a jubilee year occurred before the end of the six years, then he regained his freedom earlier (Lev. xxv. 39—41); but in no case could he be retained more than six years in the slave condition, except by his own consent, formally given (verse 5). This law was an enormous advance upon anything previously known in the slave legislation of the most civilised country, and stamps the Mosaic code at once as sympathising with the slave, and bent on ameliorating his lot. It has been thought strange by some that slavery was not now abrogated; but even Christianity, fifteen hundred years later, did not venture on so complete a social revolution.

(3) **His wife shall go out with him.**—The privilege of the married Hebrew slave was to attach also to his wife, if he was married when he became a slave. It further, no doubt, attached to his children.

(4) **If his master have given him a wife.**—If, however, the Hebrew slave, being previously unmarried, had been allowed by his master to take to wife one of his female slaves, then, when the husband claimed his freedom the wife could not claim hers. Both she and her children remained in the slave condition.

(5) And if the servant [1] shall plainly say,
I love my master, my wife, and my
children; I will not go out free: (6) then
his master shall bring him unto the
judges; he shall also bring him to the
door, or unto the door-post; and his
master shall bore his ear through with
an aul; and he shall serve him for ever.
(7) And if a man sell his daughter to
be a maidservant, she shall not go out
as the menservants do. (8) If she [2] please
not her master, who hath betrothed her
to himself, then shall he let her be re-
deemed: to sell her unto a strange nation
he shall have no power, seeing he hath
dealt deceitfully with her. (9) And if he
have betrothed her unto his son, he shall
deal with her after the manner of
daughters. (10) If he take him another
wife; her food, her raiment, and her
duty of marriage, shall he not diminish.
(11) And if he do not these three unto her,
then shall she go out free without money.
(12) [a] He that smiteth a man, so that he

1 Heb., *saying shall say.*

2 Heb., *be evil in the eyes of, &c.*

a Lev. 24. 17.

---

(5) **And if.**—Better, *But if.*

I love my master.—Under every system of slavery affection grows up between the slaves and a master who is indulgent to them. At Rome it was common for slaves to endure the severest torture rather than betray or accuse their owners. If a man has no rights, he is thankful for small mercies, and responds with warm feeling to those who treat him kindly. As the Hebrew form of slavery was of a mild type, masters being admonished to treat their slaves "not as bondservants, but as hired servants" (Lev. xxv. 39, 40), and, again, "not to rule over them with rigour" (verse 46), there would naturally be frequent cases where the slave would not wish to "go out." He might actually "love his master;" or he might value the security from want which attaches to the slave condition; or he might be unwilling to break up the family which, by his master's favour, he had been allowed to create. For such cases some provision was necessary. It was made by the law here formulated (verses 5, 6), which allowed the Hebrew slave, if he liked, to forfeit all claim to freedom, and take upon him permanently the condition of a bondman.

(6) **His master shall bring him unto the judges.**—A formal act was necessary. The State must sanction the passing of a citizen into the slave condition, and so the "judges" were called in. The change was to be made by a significant ceremony. In order to mark that henceforth the volunteer bondman became attached to the household, he was to be physically attached to the house by having an awl forced through his ear, and then driven into the door or door-post. Hence "opening the ear" became a synonym for assigning a man to the slave condition in perpetuity (Ps. xl. 6). The word used for "judges" is *ha-Elohim,* "the gods," or "the exalted ones," which has the same sense in chap. xxii. 8, 9.

(7) **If a man sell his daughter to be a maidservant.**—The right of selling their children into slavery was regarded in ancient times as inherent in the *patria potestas,* and was practised largely by many nations (Herod. v. 6; Heyne, *Opusc.*, vol. iv., p. 125). Among the Hebrews such sales were, comparatively speaking, rare; but still they occasionally took place, in consequence of extreme poverty (Neh. v. 5). Women sold in this way might claim their freedom at the end of six years if they chose (Deut. xv. 17); but if purchased to be wives, they received a further protection. If the intention were carried out, they were to be entitled to the status of wives during their whole lifetime, even though their husbands contracted further marriages (verse 10). If, instead of becoming the wife of her purchaser, a woman was made over by him to his son, she was to enjoy all the rights of a daughter (verse 9). If the purchaser declined to act in either of these two ways, he was compelled to take one of two other courses. Either he must get another Hebrew to discharge his obligation of marriage (verse 8), or he must return the maid intact to her father, without making any demand for the restitution of the purchase-money (verse 11). These provisoes afforded a considerable protection to the slave-concubine, who might otherwise have been liable to grievous wrong and oppression.

(8) **Who hath betrothed her to himself.**—The reading is to be preferred which gives the opposite sense—"who hath *not* betrothed her;" and the meaning is, "If the man, after purchasing the woman to be his wife, finds that he does not like her, and *refuses* to go through the ceremony of betrothal"—

Then shall he let her be redeemed.—Heb., *then let him cause her to be redeemed: i.e.*, let him provide some one to take his place, and carry out his contract, only taking care that the substitute be a Hebrew, and not one of "a strange nation," since her father did not intend to have her wed a foreigner.

(10) **If he take him another wife.**—Polygamy is viewed as lawful in this passage, as elsewhere generally in the Mosaic Law, which did not venture to forbid, though to some extent discouraging it. The legislator was forced to allow many things to the Hebrews, "for the hardness of their hearts" (Matt. xix. 8).

Her duty of marriage.—Rather, *her right of cohabitation.*

(11) **These three**—*i.e., one of these three things:* (1) Espouse her himself; (2) marry her to his son; or (3) transfer her, on the terms on which he received her, to another Hebrew.

(12—14) **He that smiteth a man, so that he die.**—Homicide had been broadly and generally forbidden in the sixth commandment. But something more was necessary. Laws are for the most part inoperative unless they are enforced by penalties; and for every case of homicide the same penalty would not be fitting. Accordingly we have here, first, the assignment of the death penalty for homicide of the first degree, *i.e.*, murder; and secondly, the provision of a refuge for homicide of the second degree, *i.e.*, manslaughter, or death by misadventure. The death penalty for murder had already received Divine sanction in the injunctions given to Noah (Gen. ix. 6). Tradition, backed up by conscience, had made it an almost universal law. The Sinaitic legislation adopted the law into the national code, and lent it additional force by the proviso, which we know to have been carried out in practice (1 Kings ii. 28—34), that the

die, shall be surely put to death. (13) And
if a man lie not in wait, but God deliver
him into his hand; then [a]I will appoint
thee a place whither he shall flee. (14) But
if a man come presumptuously upon his
neighbour, to slay him with guile; thou
shalt take him from mine altar, that he
may die. (15) And he that smiteth his
father, or his mother, shall be surely
put to death.
(16) And he that stealeth a man, and
selleth him, or if he be found in his
hand, he shall surely be put to death.
(17) And [b]he that [1]curseth his father,
or his mother, shall surely be put to death.
(18) And if men strive together, and one
smite [2]another with a stone, or with *his*
fist, and he die not, but keepeth *his* bed:
(19) if he rise again, and walk abroad
upon his staff, then shall he that smote
him be quit: only he shall pay *for* [3]the
loss of his time, and shall cause *him* to
be thoroughly healed.
(20) And if a man smite his servant, or
his maid, with a rod, and he die under
his hand; he shall be surely [4]punished.

a Deut. 19. 3.

b Lev. 20. 9; Prov. 20. 20; Matt. 15. 4; Mark 7. 10.

1 Or, *reviteth.*

2 Or, *his neighbour.*

3 Heb., *his ceasing.*

4 Heb., *avenged.*

---

murderer was even to be torn from God's altar, if he took refuge there.

(13) **If a man lie not in wait, but God deliver him into his hand.**—If, that is, without malice aforethought, a man happen upon his enemy, God's providence bringing the two into contact without man's contrivance, and the result is that one slay the other, then the law of the refuge or asylum shall come in. A place is to be provided whither the man-slayer may flee, and where he may be safe, at any rate until the cause is inquired into. Hitherto, throughout the East, it had been regarded as the duty of the next of kin to avenge homicide of whatever kind, and blood had been exacted for blood, however sudden, however provoked, however excusable had been the homicide. No right of asylum, so far as we know, had ever been established before. The Sinaitic legislation for the first time interposed the "city of refuge," between the "avenger of blood" and his victim. It was for the elders of the city to see that the privilege was not abused. Where the case was doubtful, the man-slayer had to be remitted for trial to the elders of his own town (Num. xxxv. 22—25); where the elders considered his claim made out, he was entitled to protection.

(14) **If a man come presumptuously.**—Rather, *if a man come maliciously*, or *with premeditation.* (Vulg., *de industria.*)

Thou shalt take him from mine altar.—Comp. 1 Kings ii. 28—34. In most parts of the ancient world a scruple was felt about putting criminals to death when once they had taken sanctuary, and those who did so were regarded as accursed (Herod. v. 71, 72; Thucyd. i. 126; Plut. *Vit. Sol.*, § 12). The Mosaic Law regarded this scruple as a superstition, and refused to sanction it.

(15—17) **And he that smiteth his father . . .**—With homicide are conjoined some other offences, regarded as of a heinous character, and made punishable by death: viz. (1), striking a parent; (2) kidnapping; and (3) cursing a parent. The immediate sequence of these crimes upon murder, and their punishment by the same penalty, marks strongly God's abhorrence of them. The parent is viewed as God's representative, and to smite him is to offer God an insult in his person. To curse him implies, if possible, a greater want of reverence; and, since curses can only be effectual as appeals to God, it is an attempt to enlist God on our side against His representative. Kidnapping is a crime against the person only a very little short of murder, since it is to deprive a man of that which gives life its chief value—liberty. Many a man would prefer death to slavery; and to almost all the passing into the slave condition would be a calamity of the most terrible kind, involving life-long misery. Its suddenness and unexpectedness, when the result of kidnapping, would augment its grievousness, and render it the most crushing of all misfortunes. Joseph's history shows us how easy it was to sell a free man as a slave, and obtain his immediate removal into a distant country (Gen. xxxvii. 25—28). The Egyptian annals tell us of bloody wars carried on for kidnapping purposes (Lenormant, *Histoire Ancienne*, vol. i., pp. 423, 424). In the classical times and countries, the slaves offered for sale in the markets had usually been obtained in this way. The stringent law of the Mosaic code (verse 16) was greatly needed to check an atrocious crime very widely committed.

(18, 19) Severe assault, endangering life, but not actually taking it, is placed under the same head with homicide, as approaching to it, but is not to be punished in the same way. If death ensues in such a case, the crime is, of course, murder or manslaughter, according to the attendant circumstances; but if death does not ensue, it is aggravated assault only. In such cases punishment could not be inflicted by retaliation—the usual penalty under the Mosaic Law (verses 24, 25)—without a risk of killing the man, which would have been an excessive punishment. The law therefore imposed a fine, which was to be fixed at such an amount as would at once compensate the sufferer for the loss of his time (verse 19), and defray the cost of his cure.

(18) **With a stone, or with his fist.**—Comp. the difference made under the English law between wounding with a sharp or a blunt instrument.

(19) **If he rise again, and walk abroad upon his staff.**—The charge of murder was not to be kept hanging over a man indefinitely. If the injured person recovered sufficiently to leave his bed, and get about by the help of a stick, the injurer was to pay his fine and be quit of his offence, whatever might happen afterwards.

(20) **And if a man smite his servant.**—The homicide hitherto considered has been that of freemen; but the Mosaic Law was not content to stop at this point. Unlike most other codes, it proceeded to forbid the homicide of slaves. Hitherto, throughout the East, and also in many parts of the West, slaves had been regarded as so absolutely their master's property that he was entitled to do as he pleased with them. Now, for the first time—so far as we know—was the life of the slave protected. The exact extent of the protection is uncertain. According to the Talmud, the master who killed his slave was put to death; according to some modern Jews, as Kalisch, he had merely to pay a fine. In any case, the killing was an offence of which

(21) Notwithstanding, if he continue a day or two, he shall not be punished: for he *is* his money.
(22) If men strive, and hurt a woman with child, so that her fruit depart *from her*, and yet no mischief follow: he shall be surely punished, according as the woman's husband will lay upon him; and he shall pay as the judges *determine*.
(23) And if *any* mischief follow, then thou shalt give life for life, (24) [a]eye for eye, tooth for tooth, hand for hand, foot for foot, (25) burning for burning, wound for wound, stripe for stripe.

(26) And if a man smite the eye of his servant, or the eye of his maid, that it perish; he shall let him go free for his eye's sake. (27) And if he smite out his manservant's tooth, or his maidservant's tooth; he shall let him go free for his tooth's sake.
(28) If an ox gore a man or a woman, that they die: then [b]the ox shall be surely stoned, and his flesh shall not be eaten; but the owner of the ox *shall be* quit. (29) But if the ox were wont to push with his horn in time past, and it hath been testified to his owner, and he

a Lev. 24. 20; Deut. 19. 21; Matt. 5. 38.

b Gen. 9. 5.

---

the law took cognisance. Later on it appears that even assaults on slaves, if they reached a certain intensity, were unlawful, and involved the slave's compulsory emancipation (verses 26, 27).

With a rod.—The usual instrument of punishment. It would follow, as a matter of course, that if a more dangerous implement was used the master was punished with equal, or greater, severity.

(21) **If he continue a day or two, he shall not be punished.**—Comp. the proviso with respect to freemen (verse 19). The notion is, that unless the death follows speedily it must be presumed not to have been intended; and this might be especially presumed in the case of a man killing his slave, since thereby he inflicted on himself a pecuniary loss.

(22–25) A personal injury peculiar to women—a hurt producing miscarriage—is here considered. The miscarriage might cost the woman her life, in which case the man who caused it was to suffer death (verse 23); or it might have no further ill result than the loss of the child. In this latter case the penalty was to be a fine, assessed by the husband with the consent of the judge (verse 22). The death penalty, where the woman died, is clearly excessive, and probably belongs to the pre-Mosaic legislation, which required "life for life" in every case.

(22) **If men strive, and hurt a woman with child.**—It is assumed that this hurt would probably take place through the interference of a pregnant wife in some strife wherein her husband was engaged. It would almost certainly be accidental.

And yet no mischief follow—*i.e.*, no further mischief—nothing beyond the loss of the child.

(22, 23) **Life for life, eye for eye.**—It is a reasonable conjecture that the law of retaliation was much older than Moses, and accepted by him as tolerable rather than devised as rightful. The law itself was very widely spread. Traces of it are found in India, in Egypt, among the Greeks, and in the laws of the Twelve Tables. Aristotle says that the Pythagoreans approved it, and that it was believed to be the rule by which Rhadamanthus administered justice in the other world. There is, *primâ facie*, a semblance of exact rectitude and equality about it which captivates rude minds, and causes the adoption of the rule generally in an early condition of society. Theoretically, retaliation is the exactest and strictest justice; but in practice difficulties arise. How is the force of a blow to be measured? How are exactly similar burns and wounds to be inflicted? Is eye to be given for eye when the injurer is a one-eyed man? And, again, is it expedient for law to multiply the number of mutilated citizens in a community? Considerations of these kinds cause the rule to be discarded as soon as civilisation reaches a certain point, and tend generally to the substitution of a money compensation, to be paid to the injured party by the injurer. The present passage sanctioned the law of retaliation in principle, but authorised its enforcement in a single case only. In a later part of the Mosaic code the application was made universal (Lev. xxiv. 17—21; Deut. xix. 21).

(26, 27) **The eye . . . tooth.**—An exception to the law of retaliation is here made. If the injurer is a free man and the injured person a slave, the marked social inequality of the parties would make exact retaliation an injustice. Is the slave, then, to be left without protection? By no means. As the legislation had already protected his life (verse 20), so it now protects him from permanent damage to his person. The master who inflicts any such permanent damage—from the least to the greatest—loses all property in his slave, and is bound at once to emancipate him. The loss of an eye is viewed as the greatest permanent injury to the person; the loss of a tooth as the least.

(28–32) Injuries to the person might arise either from man or from animals. Protection from both was needed. The law given to Noah (Gen. ix. 5) had already laid it down that whenever a beast killed a man his life was to be forfeit. This law was now re-enacted, but with a further and very important proviso. If the animal had an owner, and the owner had reason to know that it was dangerous, then not only the beast, but the owner also was to be held guilty. He was to be liable to a process for murder (verse 29); but, with the consent of the aggrieved family, might pay a sum of money as compensation instead (verse 30). In the case of a slave, the sum was fixed at what was regarded as the standard price of a slave (Lev. xxv. 44—46, xxvii. 3), viz., thirty silver shekels.

(28) **The ox shall be surely stoned**—*i.e.*, he shall die the death of a murderer.

His flesh shall not be eaten.—An ox killed by stoning would not be bled in the usual way, and would be "unclean" food for Hebrews. According to the Rabbis, the flesh might not even be disposed of to the Gentiles, but had to be buried. If this were so, the object must have been to mark strongly that whatever creature took human life was accursed.

(29) **His owner also shall be put to death.**—It seems clear that under this law the representatives

hath not kept him in, but that he hath
killed a man or a woman; the ox shall
be stoned, and his owner also shall be
put to death. (30) If there be laid on him
a sum of money, then he shall give for
the ransom of his life whatsoever is laid
upon him. (31) Whether he have gored
a son, or have gored a daughter, accord-
ing to this judgment shall it be done
unto him. (32) If the ox shall push a
manservant or a maidservant; he shall
give unto their master thirty shekels of
silver, and the ox shall be stoned.
(33) And if a man shall open a pit, or
if a man shall dig a pit, and not cover
it, and an ox or an ass fall therein;
(34) the owner of the pit shall make *it*
good, *and* give money unto the owner of
them; and the dead *beast* shall be his.
(35) And if one man's ox hurt another's,
that he die; then they shall sell the live
ox, and divide the money of it; and the
dead *ox* also they shall divide. (36) Or if
it be known that the ox hath used to
push in time past, and his owner hath
not kept him in; he shall surely pay ox
for ox; and the dead shall be his own.

CHAPTER XXII.—(1) If a man shall
steal an ox, or a [1]sheep, and kill it, or
sell it; he shall restore five oxen for an
ox, and [a]four sheep for a sheep.
(2) If a thief be found breaking up, and
be smitten that he die, *there shall* no
blood *be shed* for him. (3) If the sun be
risen upon him, *there shall be* blood *shed*
for him; *for* he should make full resti-
tution; if he have nothing, then he shall
be sold for his theft. (4) If the theft be
certainly found in his hand alive, whether

1 Or, *goat.*

a 2 Sam. 12. 6.

---

of the slain person might have exacted life for life; but probably they would in almost all cases have been ready to accept a compensation.

(30) **Whatsoever is laid upon him.**—Primarily, by the aggrieved relatives; but in the case of an exorbitant demand there was, no doubt, an appeal to the judges, who would then fix the amount.

LAWS CONCERNING THE RIGHTS OF PROPERTY.

(33–36) The legislation slides from rights of persons to rights of property easily and without effort, by passing from the injuries which cattle cause to those which they suffer. They are injured (1) by the culpable *laches* of persons leaving their pits uncovered; (2) by hurts which one man's cattle inflict upon another's. Both kinds of loss have to be made good.

(33) **If a man shall open a pit.**— Rather, *uncover a well.* The wells in the East commonly have covers, which are removed when water is drawn, and then replaced. If a man neglected to replace a cover, he was rightly answerable for any damage that might ensue. The case was the same if he dug a new well, and neglected to cover it over.

(34) **The dead beast shall be his.**—Having paid the full value of the live animal, the owner of the well was entitled to make what he could by the carcase.

(35–36) **If one man's ox hurt another's.**—Where no blame attached to the owner, the loss was to be equally shared. Where the dangerous character of the animal was, or ought to have been, known, the man whose ox was killed received its full value.

XXII.

(1–4) Theft is here treated of with great brevity, only three kinds being distinguished—(1) Housebreaking; (2) stealing without conversion of the property; (3) stealing with conversion. The main principle of punishment laid down is the exaction from the offender of *double* (verse 4). When, however, there has been conversion of the property, the penalty is heavier, the return of four-fold in the case of a sheep, of five-fold in that of an ox (verse 1). Incidentally it is enacted that the burglar may be resisted by force (verse 2), and that to kill him shall be justifiable homicide; and further, it is laid down that a thief unable to make the legal restitution shall become a slave in order to pay his debt (verse 3).

(1) **If a man shall steal an ox, or a sheep.**—The flocks and herds of the Israelites constituted their principal property, and hence cattle-stealing is taken as the representative of theft in general.

And kill it, or sell it.—Plainly showing persistence and determination.

Five oxen . . . four sheep.—The principle of the variation is not clear. Perhaps the theft of an ox was regarded as involving more audacity, and so more guilt, in the thief.

(2) **If a thief be found breaking up.**—Rather, *breaking in: i.e.,* making forcible entry into a dwelling-house. Most codes agree with the Mosaic in allowing the inmates of the house to resist such an attempt if made at night, and to shed the blood of the burglar, if necessary. He may be considered as having dissolved the "social compact," and converted himself from a fellow-citizen into a public enemy. A murderous intent on his part may be suspected.

(3) **If the sun be risen upon him.**—In the daytime no violence is to be feared. The housebreaker seeks to avoid observation, and decamps if discovered. Moreover, assistance is readily obtainable, and thus there is no need of resorting to extreme measures. The English law makes exactly the same distinction as the Mosaic.

For he should make full restitution.—Heb., *restoring, he shall restore.* It is not quite clear whether he is to restore *double;* but so most commentators understand the passage.

If he have nothing.—Rather, *if he have not enough.* If he cannot make the *full* restitution of the preceding verse, then "he shall be sold for his theft." He shall become the slave for the term of six years of the man whom he has robbed, and in that way pay his debt.

(4) **If the theft be certainly found in his hand.**—If he had not converted it, consumed it, or, if it were an animal, killed it, then, instead of the four-

it be ox, or ass, or sheep; he shall
restore double.
(5) If a man shall cause a field or vine-
yard to be eaten, and shall put in his
beast, and shall feed in another man's
field; of the best of his own field, and
of the best of his own vineyard, shall he
make restitution.
(6) If fire break out, and catch in thorns,
so that the stacks of corn, or the standing
corn, or the field, be consumed *therewith;*
he that kindled the fire shall surely make
restitution.
(7) If a man shall deliver unto his
neighbour money or stuff to keep, and it
be stolen out of the man's house; if the
thief be found, let him pay double. (8) If
the thief be not found, then the master
of the house shall be brought unto the
judges, *to see* whether he have put his
hand unto his neighbour's goods. (9) For
all manner of trespass, *whether it be* for
ox, for ass, for sheep, for raiment, *or* for
any manner of lost thing, which *another*
challengeth to be his, the cause of both
parties shall come before the judges;
and whom the judges shall condemn, he
shall pay double unto his neighbour.
(10) If a man deliver unto his neighbour
an ass, or an ox, or a sheep, or any beast,
to keep; and it die, or be hurt, or driven
away, no man seeing *it:* (11) *then* shall an
oath of the LORD be between them both,
that he hath not put his hand unto his
neighbour's goods; and the owner of it
shall accept *thereof,* and he shall not
make *it* good. (12) And [a] if it be stolen
from him, he shall make restitution unto

a Gen. 31. 39.

---

fold or five-fold restitution of verse 1, a restoration of double was to suffice.

(5) **If a man shall cause a field . . . to be eaten.**—On theft follows trespass, another injury to property. Two kinds of trespass alone are mentioned; but from these the principles to be followed in punishing trespass generally can be sufficiently made out. Accidental injury, such as that caused by fire extending from one man's field into another's, was to be simply compensated up to the amount of damage done; but voluntary injury, such as followed on the turning of beasts into a neighbour's ground, was to be more than compensated. The amount of produce destroyed was to be exactly calculated, and then the injurer was to make good the full amount of his neighbour's loss out of *the best* of his own produce.

(6) **If fire break out, and catch in thorns.**—In the East, as elsewhere—*e.g.,* Italy (Virg. *Georg.,* i. 84) and England—it is customary at certain seasons to burn the weeds and other refuse of a farm, which is collected for the purpose into heaps, and then set on fire. Such fires may spread, especially in the dry East, if care be not taken, and cause extensive damage to the crops, or even the corn-heaps of a neighbour. The loss in such cases was to fall on the man who lit the fire.

(7–13) Property deposited in the hands of another for safe keeping might be so easily embezzled by the trustee, or lost through his negligence, that some special laws were needed for its protection. Conversely the trustee required to be safe-guarded against incurring loss if the property intrusted to his care suffered damage or disappeared without fault of his. The Mosaic legislation provided for both cases. On the one hand, it required the trustee to exercise proper care, and made him answerable for the loss if a thing intrusted to him was stolen and the thief not found. Embezzlement it punished by requiring the trustee guilty of it to "pay double." On the other hand, in doubtful cases it allowed the trustee to clear himself by an oath (verse 10), and in clear cases to give proof that the loss had happened through unavoidable accident (verse 12).

(7) **If a man shall deliver unto his neighbour money or stuff to keep.**—The practice of making deposits of this kind was widespread among ancient communities, where there were no professional bankers or keepers of warehouses. The Greeks called such a deposit παρακαταθήκη. It was usually made in money, or at any rate in the precious metals. A refusal to restore the thing deposited was very rare, since a special nemesis was considered to punish such conduct (Herod. vii. 86). However, at Athens it was found necessary to have a peculiar form of action for the recovery of deposits (παρακαταθήκης δίκη).

(8) **To see whether he have put his hand.**—Kalisch translates, *to swear that he has not put his hand,* and so the LXX. (καὶ ὀμεῖται) and Vulg. (*et jurabit quod non extenderit manum*).

(9) **For all manner of trespass.**—Rather, *in every case of fraud.* The context limits the expression to cases of fraud, or alleged fraud, *in connection with a deposit.*

For ox, for ass, for sheep.—The deposit of animals is unknown in classical antiquity, but might well be the custom of a people whose wealth consisted in flocks and herds. In the wilderness small proprietors might have been glad to intrust their few animals to the herdsmen who guarded the flocks and herds of their wealthier neighbours.

Which another challengeth to be his.—The case is supposed of the trustee saying a thing is lost which the depositor declares he can identify, and show to be still in his (the trustee's) possession.

The cause of both parties shall come before the judges.—This seems to mean that the challenge was to be made at the challenger's risk. If he proved his point to the satisfaction of the judges, he was to recover double; if he failed, he was to forfeit double of what he had claimed.

(10) **And it die, or be hurt, or driven away.**—The animal might "die" naturally, or "be hurt" by a wild beast or a fall down the rocks, or "be driven away" by the marauding tribes of the desert. Both parties might be agreed on the fact of its disappearance; the dispute would be as to the mode of the disappearance. Here the trustee might bring proof, if he could (verse 13); if not, he might clear himself by an "oath of the Lord" (verse 11).

(12) **If it be stolen from him, he shall make restitution.**—It seems to have been considered that

the owner thereof. (13) If it be torn in
pieces, *then* let him bring it *for* witness,
and he shall not make good that which
was torn.

(14) And if a man borrow *ought* of his
neighbour, and it be hurt, or die, the
owner thereof *being* not with it, he shall
surely make *it* good. (15) *But* if the owner
thereof *be* with it, he shall not make *it*
good: if it *be* an hired *thing*, it came for
his hire.

(16) And [a]if a man entice a maid that
is not betrothed, and lie with her, he
shall surely endow her to be his wife.
(17) If her father utterly refuse to give
her unto him, he shall [1]pay money according to the dowry of virgins.

(18) Thou shalt not suffer a witch to live.

(19) Whosoever lieth with a beast shall
surely be put to death.

(20) [b]He that sacrificeth unto *any* god,
save unto the LORD only, he shall be
utterly destroyed.

(21) [c]Thou shalt neither vex a stranger,
nor oppress him: for ye were strangers
in the land of Egypt.

[a] Deut. 22. 28.

[1] Heb., *weigh.*

[b] Deut. 13. 13, 14, 15; 1 Mac. 2. 24.

[c] Lev. 19. 33.

---

theft could have been prevented by proper care, but that hurts from wild beasts or accidents were not preventible.

(13) **Let him bring it for witness.**—This would not always be possible. Where it was not, the trustee could fall back on the oath.

(14, 15) Lending is a species of deposit; but for the benefit, not of the depositor, but of the man with whom the deposit is made. The obligation of the latter to keep intact and to return is therefore even more stringent than in the preceding case. Consequently, if the thing lent were lost or injured, however the loss was brought about, the borrower was justly called upon to make it good. The only exception was, when the lender was still in charge of what he lent, present with it, and able to keep guard over it.

(15) **If it be a hired thing.**—Letting out for hire is akin to lending; but still quite a different transaction. Damage to a thing hired was not to be made good by the hirer, since the risk of it might be considered to have formed part of the calculation upon which the amount of the hire was fixed.

MISCELLANEOUS LAWS.

(16–31) The remainder of the chapter contains laws which it is impossible to bring under any general head or heads, and which can, therefore, only be regarded as miscellaneous. Moses may have recorded them in the order in which they were delivered to him; or have committed them to writing as they afterwards occurred to his memory.

(16) **If a man entice a maid.**—The seduction of a maiden is regarded more seriously in primitive than in more advanced communities. The father looked to receive a handsome sum (ἕδνα) from the man to whom he consented to betroth his virgin daughter; and required compensation if his daughter's eligibility as a wife was diminished. If the seducer were a person to whom he felt it a degradation to marry his daughter, he might exact from him such a sum as would be likely to induce another to wed her; if he was one whom he could accept as a son-in-law, he might compel him to re-establish his daughter's status by marriage. It might be well if modern societies would imitate the Mosaic code on this point by some similar proviso.

He shall surely endow her—*i.e.*, pay the customary sum to the father. See Deut. xxii. 29, where the sum is fixed at fifty shekels of silver.

(17) **He shall pay money according to the dowry of virgins.**—It is not stated what the amount was to be in this case; but probably it was more than in the other.

(18) **Thou shalt not suffer a witch to live.**—The word translated "witch" in this passage is the feminine singular of that rendered by "sorcerers" in chap. vii. 11, and means "a mutterer of charms." The use of the feminine form can only be accounted for by supposing that, practically, withcraft was at the time mainly professed by females. Whether "witches" had actual help from evil spirits, or only professed to work magical effects by their aid, the sin against God was the same. Jehovah was renounced, and a power other than His invoked and upheld. Witchcraft was as much rebellion against God as idolatry or blasphemy, and deserved the same punishment.

(19) The sin here denounced was common among the Canaanitish nations (Lev. xviii. 24), and not unknown in Egypt (Herod. ii. 46). It was therefore necessary that God's abhorrence of it should be distinctly declared to Israel.

(20) **He that sacrificeth.**—Sacrifice in this place represents worship generally, being its most essential act. Elsewhere the death-penalty is affixed to any acknowledgment of false gods (Deut. xiii. 1—16).

Shall be utterly destroyed.—Heb., *Shall be devoted, i.e.*, devoted to destruction.

(21–24) The juxtaposition of laws against oppression with three crimes of the deepest dye seems intended to indicate that oppression is among the sins which are most hateful in God's sight. The lawgiver, however, does not say that it is to be punished capitally, nor, indeed, does he affix to it any legal penalty. Instead of so doing, he declares that God Himself will punish it "with the sword" (verse 24). Three classes of persons particularly liable to be oppressed are selected for mention—(1) Strangers, *i.e.*, foreigners; (2) widows; and (3) orphans. Strangers have seldom been protected by any legislation, unless, indeed, they formed a class of permanent residents, like the Metœci at Athens. The law of civilised communities has generally afforded some protection to the orphan and the widow, particularly in respect of rights of property. The protection given is, however, very generally insufficient; and it is of the highest importance that it should be supplemented by an assured belief that, beyond all legal penalties there lies the Divine sentence of wrath and punishment, certain to fall upon every one who, careless of law and right, makes the stranger, the widow, or the orphan to suffer wrong at his hands.

(21) **For ye were strangers.**—Ye should, therefore, sympathise with "strangers;" not "vex them," not

(22) [a]Ye shall not afflict any widow, or
fatherless child. (23) If thou afflict them
in any wise, and they cry at all unto me,
I will surely hear their cry; (24) and my
wrath shall wax hot, and I will kill you
with the sword; and your wives shall
be widows, and your children fatherless.
(25) [b]If thou lend money to *any of* my
people *that is* poor by thee, thou shalt
not be to him as an usurer, neither shalt
thou lay upon him usury. (26) If thou at
all take thy neighbour's raiment to
pledge, thou shalt deliver it unto him by
that the sun goeth down: (27) For that
is his covering only, it *is* his raiment for
his skin: wherein shall he sleep? and
it shall come to pass, when he crieth
unto me, that I will hear; for I *am*
gracious.
(28) [c]Thou shalt not revile the [1]gods,
nor curse the ruler of thy people.
(29) Thou shalt not delay *to offer* [2]the
first of thy ripe fruits, and of thy
[3]liquors: [d]the firstborn of thy sons shalt
thou give unto me. (30) Likewise shalt
thou do with thine oxen, *and* with thy
sheep: seven days it shall be with his
dam; on the eighth day thou shalt give
it me.
(31) And ye shall be holy men unto me:

a Zech. 7. 10.

b Lev. 25. 37; Deut. 23. 19; Ps. 15. 5.

c Acts 23. 5.

1 Or, *judges*.

2 Heb., *thy fulness*.

3 Heb., *tear*

d ch. 13. 2, 12 & 34. 19.

"oppress them," but "love them as yourselves" (Lev. xix. 34). The condition of foreigners in Israel is shown to have been more than tolerable by the examples of the Kenites (Judg. i. 16; iv. 11); of Araunah the Jebusite (2 Sam. xxiv. 18—24); of Uriah the Hittite (2 Sam. xxiii. 39), Zelek the Ammonite (2 Sam. xxiii. 37), and others.

(23) **If thou afflict them in any wise, and they cry at all unto me.**—Rather, *If thou afflict them sore, and they cry earnestly unto me.* On the transgression of the laws against oppression by the later Israelites, see Jer. v. 28; vii. 6; xxii. 3, 17; Zech. vii. 20; Mal. iii. 5; Matt. xxiii. 14, &c. The sword of the Babylonians and the sword of the Romans avenged the sufferers, according to the prophecy of verse 24.

(25—27) The Mosaic law of borrowing and lending was strange and peculiar. It was absolutely forbidden to exact any interest from those borrowers who were Israelites. The wording of the present passage, and of some others (Lev. xxv. 35; Deut. xv. 7), construed strictly, prohibits interest only on loans to the poor; but, as in a primitive state of society only the poor wish to borrow, the qualifying expression lost its force, and to exact any interest of any Israelite was regarded as wrong. (See Ps. xv. 5; Prov. xxviii. 8; Neh. v. 7, 11; Ezek. xviii. 13; xxii. 12.) And some prohibitions, as Deut. xxiii. 19, were expressed in the most general terms. On the other hand, the lending of money upon interest to foreigners was distinctly allowed (Deut. xxiii. 20), and no limit placed upon the amount of interest that might be taken.

(25) **Usurer. . . . usury.**—The Hebrew *nôsheh* and *nĕshek* have no sense of "excess" attached to them. They mean simply "interest," and "the man who lends upon interest."

(26, 27) **Thy neighbour's raiment.**—The *simlah*, or *salmah*, here translated "raiment," was the large flowing outer raiment, elsewhere called *beged*, which was commonly of woollen, and corresponded to the *abba* of the modern Arabs. It was a warm wrapper, and has sometimes been compared to a Scotch plaid. The poor Israelite did not much want it by day; but needed it as a blanket by night—a practice known to many modern tribes of Arabs. The present passage forbids the retention of this garment as a pledge during the night, and seems to imply a continuous practice of pledging the *simlah* by day, and being allowed to enjoy the use of it, nevertheless, as a nocturnal covering.

(28) **Thou shalt not revile the gods.**—The LXX. and Vulgate give the passage this sense; and so it was understood, or at any rate expounded, by Philo (*De Vit. Mos.* iii. 26) and Josephus (*Ant. Jud.* iv. 8, § 10), who boasted that the Jews abstained from reviling the gods of the nations. But the practice of the most pious Israelites in the best times was different (1 Kings xviii. 27; Ps. cxv. 4—8, cxxxv. 15—18; Isa. xli. 29, xliv. 9—20; Jer. x. 11—15, &c.). The gods of the heathen were uniformly, and with the utmost scorn, "reviled." It has been suggested that the true meaning of *elohim* in this place is "judges" (Rosenmüller, Zunz, Herxheimer); but to have that sense, the word requires the article. It is best, therefore, to translate by "God," as is done by De Wette, Knobel, Keil, Kalisch, Canon Cook, &c., and to understand the entire passage as intended to connect the sin of cursing a ruler with that of reviling God, the ruler being regarded as God's representative.

(29) **The first of thy ripe fruits.**—Heb., *of thy fulness.* "Firstfruits" were the spontaneous tribute of natural piety among almost all nations. They were called by the Greeks ἀπαρχαί, by the Romans *primitiæ*. Abel's offering (Gen. iv. 4) was one of the "firstlings of his flock," and Cain's probably one of firstfruits. In the present passage it is assumed that firstfruits are due, and the stress is laid upon offering them promptly, without "delay." Delay would show a grudging spirit.

Of thy liquors.—As wine and oil. (Compare Neh. x. 37, 39.)

The firstborn of thy sons.—See the Note on chap. xiii. 2; and on the means of redeeming firstborn sons, see chap. xiii. 13, and Num. xvii. 15, 16.

(30) **Thine oxen.**—Rather, *thy beeves.* The word used is applied to horned cattle of either sex.

Seven days it shall be with his dam.—Compare Lev. xxii. 27. The main object of forbidding sacrifice before the eighth day would appear to have been regard for the health and comfort of the mother, which needed the relief obtained by suckling its offspring. There may also have underlain the prohibition some reference to birth as an impure process. Compare the circumcision of the male child on the eighth day.

(31) **Ye shall be holy men unto me.**—Compare chap. xix. 6. The holiness really desired was holiness of heart and spirit. Outward ordinances could not effect this; but, to keep the thought perpetually before men's minds, a network of external obligations was

[a]neither shall ye eat *any* flesh *that is* torn of beasts in the field; ye shall cast it to the dogs.

CHAPTER XXIII. — (1) Thou shalt not [1]raise a false report: put not thine hand with the wicked to be an unrighteous witness. (2) Thou shalt not follow a multitude to *do* evil; neither shalt thou [2]speak in a cause to decline after many to wrest *judgment:* (3) neither shalt thou countenance a poor man in his cause.

(4) If thou meet thine enemy's ox or his ass going astray, thou shalt surely bring it back to him again. (5) [b]If thou see the ass of him that hateth thee lying under his burden, [3]and wouldest forbear to help him, thou shalt surely help with him.

(6) Thou shalt not wrest the judgment of thy poor in his cause. (7) Keep thee far from a false matter; and the innocent and righteous slay thou not: for I will not justify the wicked. (8) And [c]thou shalt take no gift: for the gift blindeth

a Lev. 22. 8; Ezek. 44. 31.

1 Or, *receive.*

2 Heb., *answer.*

b Deut. 22. 4.

3 Or, *wilt thou cease to help him? or, and wouldest cease to leave thy business for him: thou shalt surely leave it to join with him.*

c Deut. 16. 19; Ecclus. 20. 29.

devised, whereof a specimen is given in the law which follows. The flesh of an animal torn by a carnivorous beast would be doubly unclean: (1) By contact with the unclean carnivorous beast; and (2) through not having all the blood properly drained from it. It was therefore not to be eaten by a Hebrew.

Ye shall cast it to the dogs—*i.e.*, ye shall do this rather than eat it. The flesh might probably be given, or even sold, to an alien. (Compare Deut. xiv. 21.)

XXIII.

(1–19) The "miscellaneous laws" are here continued. From verse 1 to verse 9 no kind of sequence in the laws can be traced; from verse 10 to the first clause of verse 19 there is, on the contrary, a certain connection, since the laws enunciated are concerned with ceremonial observance. The closing law, however, is not ceremonial, but the prohibition of a practice considered to be cruel. On the whole, it may be said that The Book of the Covenant maintains its unsystematic character to the close. (See Note on chap. xx. 22—26.)

(1) **Thou shalt not raise a false report.**—The LXX. and Vulg. translate, "Thou shalt not *receive* a false report"—*i.e.*, give it credit, accept it as true, and act upon it. This meaning accords well with the succeeding clause, which forbids our giving support to the false testimony of others. In both clauses the principle of the ninth commandment is extended from principals to accessories.

(2) **Thou shalt not follow a multitude to do evil . . .**—It is perhaps true that the offence especially condemned is joining with a majority in an unrighteous judgment; but the words of the precept extend much further than this, and forbid our being carried away by numbers or popularity in any case. *Vox populi vox Dei* is a favourite maxim with many, but Scripture nowhere sanctions it. Job boasts that he did not fear a great multitude (Job xxxi. 34). David says that the "ten thousands of the people set themselves against him round about" (Ps. iii. 6). The prophets had always the multitude against them. "Strait is the gate, and narrow is the way," said our blessed Lord, "which leadeth unto life, and few there be that find it." But "wide is the gate, and broad is the way, that leadeth to destruction, and many there be which go in thereat" (Matt. vii. 13, 14). We must be prepared to face unpopularity if we would walk in accordance with the law of God.

(3) **Neither shalt thou countenance a poor man in his cause.**—We must not "pervert judgment" either in favour of the rich or of the poor. Justice must hold her scales even, and be proof equally against a paltry fear of the rich and a weak compassion for the indigent. The cause alone is to be considered, not the persons. (Comp. Lev. xix. 15.)

(4) **Thine enemy's ox.**—The general duty of stopping stray animals and restoring them to friendly owners, expressly taught in Deut. xxii. 1—3, is here implied as if admitted on all hands. The legislator extends this duty to cases where the owner is our personal enemy. It was not generally recognised in antiquity that men's enemies had any claims upon them. Cicero, indeed, says—"Sunt autem quædam officia etiam adversus eos servanda, a quibus injuriam acceperis" (*De Off.* i. 11); but he stops short of enjoining active benevolence. Here and in verse 5 we have a sort of anticipation of Christianity—active kindness to an enemy being required, even when it costs us some trouble. The principle of friendliness is involved—the germ which in Christianity blossoms out into the precept, "Love your enemies."

(5) **If thou see the ass of him that hateth thee . . .**—The sense is clear, but the words are greatly disputed. If a man sees his enemy's ass prostrate under its burthen, he is to help to raise it up. In this case he owes a double duty—(1) to his enemy, and (2) to the suffering animal. Geddes' emendation of *'azar* for *'azab*, in all the three places where the verb occurs, is the simplest and best of those suggested. The passage would then run: "If thou see the ass of him that hateth thee lying under his burthen, and wouldest forbear to help it, thou shalt surely help with him"—*i.e.*, the owner.

(6) **Thou shalt not wrest the judgment of thy poor.**—If we are not to favour the poor man in a court of justice on account of his poverty (verse 3), much less are we to treat him with disfavour. (Comp. Deut. xxiv. 17, xxvii. 19; Jer. v. 28, &c.)

(7) **Keep thee far from a false matter.**—A false *accusation* seems to be intended. If we make one it may result in an innocent man's death, and we shall be murderers; God will then assuredly hold us guilty.

(8) **Thou shalt take no gift**—*i.e.*, no bribe. Corruption has been always rife in the East, and the pure administration of justice is almost unknown there. Signal punishments by wise rulers have sometimes checked the inveterate evil (Herod. v. 25), but it recurs again and again—"Naturam expellas furca, tamen usque recurret." According to Josephus (*contr. Ap.* ii. 27), the Jewish law punished with death the judge who took a bribe. But Hebrew judges seem practically to have been no better than Oriental judges generally. (See 1 Sam. viii. 3; Ps. xxvi. 10; Prov. xvii. 23; Isa. i. 23, v. 23; Micah iii. 9—11, &c.) The corrupt

[1]the wise, and perverteth the words of
the righteous. (9) Also thou shalt not
oppress a stranger: for ye know the
[2]heart of a stranger, seeing ye were
strangers in the land of Egypt.
(10) And [a]six years thou shalt sow thy
land, and shalt gather in the fruits
thereof: (11) but the seventh *year* thou
shalt let it rest and lie still; that the
poor of thy people may eat: and what
they leave the beasts of the field shall
eat. In like manner thou shalt deal
with thy vineyard, *and* with thy [3]olive-
yard.
(12) [b]Six days thou shalt do thy work,
and on the seventh day thou shalt
rest: that thine ox and thine ass may
rest, and the son of thy handmaid, and
the stranger, may be refreshed.
(13) And in all *things* that I have said
unto you be circumspect: and make no
mention of the name of other gods,
neither let it be heard out of thy mouth.
(14) [c]Three times thou shalt keep a feast

1 Heb., *the seeing.*
2 Heb., *soul.*
a Lev. 25. 3.
3 Or, *olive trees.*
b ch. 20. 8; Deut. 5. 13; Luke 13. 14.
c Deut. 16. 16.

---

administration of justice was one of the crying evils which provoked God's judgments against His people, and led, in the first instance, to the Babylonian captivity, and afterwards to the Roman conquest.

(9) **Thou shalt not oppress a stranger.**—See Note on chap. xxii. 21. The repetition of the law indicates the strong inclination of the Hebrew people to ill-use strangers, and the anxiety of the legislator to check their inclination.

CEREMONIAL LAWS.

(10, 11) **Six years . . . the seventh year.**—The Sabbatical year which is here commanded was an institution wholly unknown to any nation but the Hebrews. It is most extraordinary that any legislator should have been able to induce a people to accept such a law. *Prima facie*, it seemed, by forbidding productive industry during one year in seven, to diminish the wealth of the nation by one-seventh. But it is questionable whether, under a primitive agricultural system, when rotation of crops was unknown, the lying of the land fallow during one year in seven would not have been an economical benefit. There was no prohibition on labour other than in cultivation. The clearing away of weeds and thorns and stones was allowed, and may have been practised. After an early harvest of the self-sown crop, the greater part of the year may have been spent in this kind of industry. Still the enactment was no doubt unpopular: it checked the regular course of agriculture, and seemed to rob landowners of one-seventh of their natural gains. Accordingly, we find that it was very irregularly observed. Between the Exodus and the Captivity it had apparently been neglected seventy times (2 Chron. xxxvi. 21), or more often than it had been kept. After the Captivity, however, the observance became regular, and classical writers notice the custom as one existing in their day (Tacit. *Hist.* v. 4). Julius Cæsar permitted it, and excused the Jews from paying tribute in the seventh year on its account (Joseph., *Ant. Jud.* xiv. 10, § 6). The object of the law was threefold—(1) to test obedience; (2) to give an advantage to the poor and needy, to whom the crop of the seventh year belonged (verse 11); and (3) to allow an opportunity, once in seven years, for prolonged communion with God and increased religious observances. (See Deut. xxxi. 10—13.)

(11) **That the poor of thy people may eat.**—For fuller particulars see Lev. xxv. 1—7. The owner was to have no larger part of the seventh year's produce than any one else. He was to take his share with the hireling, the stranger, and even the cattle, which during this year were to browse where they pleased.

Thy vineyard . . . thy oliveyard.—These would bear a full average produce, and the boon to the poor man would in these respects have been very considerable. Corn, wine, and oil were the staple commodities of Palestine (Deut. viii. 8; 2 Kings xviii. 32, &c.).

(12) The law of the weekly Sabbath is here repeated in conjunction with that of the Sabbatical year, to mark the intimate connection between the two, which were parts of one and the same system—a system which culminated in the Jubilee year (Lev. xxv. 8—13). Nothing is added to the requirements of the fourth commandment; but the merciful intention of the Sabbath day is more fully brought out—it is to be kept *in order that* the cattle may rest, and the slave and stranger may be refreshed.

(13) **Be circumspect.**—Rather, *take heed.* The verb used is a very common one.

Make no mention of the name of other gods.—The Jewish commentators understand *swearing* by the name of other gods to be the thing here forbidden, and so the Vulg., "*per nomen exterorum deorum non jurabitis.*" But the words used reach far beyond this. Contempt for the "gods of the nations" was to be shown by ignoring their very names. They were not to be spoken of, unless by preachers in the way of warning, or by historians when the facts of history could not be otherwise set forth. Moses himself mentions Baal (Num. xxii. 41), Baal-peor (*ib.* xxv. 3, 5), Chemosh (*ib.* xxi. 29), and Moloch (Levit. xx. 2—5, xxiii. 21).

(14—17) The first great festival—the Passover festival—had been already instituted (chaps. xii. 3—20, xiii. 3—10). It pleased the Divine Legislator at this time to add to that festival two others, and to make all three equally obligatory. There is some reason to suppose that, in germ, the "feast of harvest" and the "feast of ingathering" already existed. All nations, from the earliest time to which history reaches back, had festival-seasons of a religious character; and no seasons are more suitable for such festivities than the conclusion of the grain-harvest, and the final completion of the entire harvest of the year. At any rate, whatever the previous practice, these three festival-seasons were now laid down as essential parts of the Law, and continued—supplemented by two others—*the* national festivals so long as Israel was a nation. In other countries such seasons were more common. Herodotus says that the Egyptians had six great yearly festival-times (ii. 59); and in Greece and Rome there was never a month without some notable religious festivity. Such institutions exerted a political as well as a religious influence, and helped towards national unity. This was more especially the case when, as in the present instance, they were expressly made gatherings of the whole nation to a single

unto me in the year. (15) [a]Thou shalt
keep the feast of unleavened bread:
(thou shalt eat unleavened bread seven
days, as I commanded thee, in the time
appointed of the month Abib; for in it
thou camest out from Egypt: [b]and none
shall appear before me empty:) (16) and
the feast of harvest, the firstfruits of thy
labours, which thou hast sown in the
field: and the feast of ingathering,
which is in the end of the year, when
thou hast gathered in thy labours out of
the field. (17) Three times in the year all thy
males shall appear before the Lord GOD.

(18) Thou shalt not offer the blood of
my sacrifice with leavened bread; neither
shall the fat of my [1]sacrifice remain until
the morning.

(19) [c]The first of the firstfruits of thy
land thou shalt bring into the house of
the LORD thy God.

[d]Thou shalt not seethe a kid in his
mother's milk.

(20) [e]Behold, I send an Angel before

a ch. 13. 3. & 34. 18.

b Deut. 16. 16; Ecclus. 35. 4.

1 Or, *feast.*

c ch. 34. 23.

d Deut. 14. 21.

e ch. 33. 2.

---

centre. What the great Greek panegyries, Olympic, Pythian, &c., were to Hellas, that the three great annual gatherings to the place where God had fixed His name were to Israel—a means of drawing closer the national bond, and counteracting those separatist tendencies which a nation split into tribes almost necessarily developed.

(15) **The feast of unleavened bread.**—See the Notes on chap. xii. 15—20.

In the time appointed of the month Abib.—From the 14th day of the month Abib (or Nisan) to the 21st day. (See chaps. xii. 18, xiii. 4—7.)

None shall appear before me empty.—Viewed religiously, the festivals were annual national thanksgivings for mercies received, both natural and miraculous—the first for the commencement of harvest and the deliverance out of Egypt; the second for the completion of the grain-harvest and the passage of the Red Sea; the third for the final gathering in of the fruits and the many mercies of the wilderness. At such seasons we must not "appear before God empty," we must give Him not only "the salves of our lips," but some substantial acknowledgment of His goodness towards us. The law here laid down with respect to the first feast is afterwards extended to the other two (Deut. xvi. 16).

(16) **The feast of harvest.**—It was calculated that the grain-harvest would be completed fifty days after it had begun. On this fiftieth day (Pentecost) the second festival was to commence by the offering of two loaves made of the new wheat just gathered in. On the other offerings commanded, see Levit. xxiii. 18—20. The Law limited the feast to a single day—the "day of Pentecost"—but in practice it was early extended to two days, in order to cover a possible miscalculation as to the exact time.

The feast of ingathering.—Elsewhere commonly called "the feast of tabernacles" (Levit. xxiii. 34; Deut. xvi. 13, 16, xxxi. 10; 2 Chron. viii. 13; Ezra iii. 4; Zech. xiv. 16—19, &c.). Like the feast of unleavened bread, this lasted for a week. It corresponded to a certain extent with modern "harvest-homes," but was more prolonged and of a more distinctly religious character. The time fixed for it was the week commencing with the fifteenth and terminating with the twenty-first of the month Tisri, corresponding to our October. The vintage and the olive-harvest had by that time been completed, and thanks were given for God's bounties through the whole year. At the same time the sojourn in the wilderness was commemorated; and as a memorial of that time those who attended the feast dwelt during its continuance in booths made of branches of trees. (See Levit. xxiii. 40; Neh. viii. 14—17.)

(17) **Three times in the year.**—The terms of this verse, as compared with verse 14, limit the observance of the three festivals to the males, but add the important requirement of personal attendance at a given place. By "all thy males" we must understand all of full age and not incapacitated by infirmity or illness.

(18) **Thou shalt not offer the blood of my sacrifice with leavened bread.**—Some regard this prohibition as extending to all sacrifices; but the majority of commentators limit it to the sacrifice of the Paschal lamb, which was the only sacrifice as yet expressly instituted by Jehovah. According to modern Jewish notions, leavened bread is permissible at the other feasts; at Pentecost it was commanded (Levit. xxiii. 17).

The fat of my sacrifice.—Rather (as in the Margin), *the fat of my feast.* The fat of the Paschal lambs was burnt on the altar with incense the same evening. Thus the whole lamb was consumed before the morning. As the Paschal lamb is *κατ' ἐξοχήν*, "*my* sacrifice," so the Passover is "*my* feast."

(19) **The first of the firstfruits**—*i.e.*, the *very* first that ripen. There was a natural tendency to "delay" the offering (chap. xxii. 29) until a considerable part of the harvest had been got in. True gratitude makes a return for benefits received as soon as it can. "*Bis dat qui cito dat.*"

The house of the Lord.—Comp. chap. xxxiv. 26 and Deut. xxiii. 18. It is known to Moses that the "place which God will choose to put his name there" is to be a "house," or "temple."

Thou shalt not seethe a kid.—A fanciful exegesis connects the four precepts of verses 18 and 19 with the three feasts—the two of verse 18 with the Paschal festival, that concerning firstfruits in verse 19 with the feast of ingathering, and this concerning kids with the feast of tabernacles. To support this theory it is suggested that the command has reference to a superstitious practice customary at the close of the harvest—a kid being then boiled in its mother's milk with magic rites, and the milk used to sprinkle plantations, fields, and gardens, in order to render them more productive the next year. But Deut. xiv. 21, which attaches the precept to a list of unclean meats, is sufficient to show that the kid spoken of was boiled to be eaten. The best explanation of the passage is that of Bochart (*Hierozoic.* pt. i., bk. ii., chap. 52), that there was a sort of cruelty in making the milk of the mother, intended for the kid's sustenance, the means of its destruction.

THE PROMISES OF GOD TO ISRAEL, IF THE COVENANT IS KEPT.

(20—33) The Book of the Covenant terminates, very appropriately, with a series of promises. God is "the rewarder of them that diligently seek him." He chooses

thee, to keep thee in the way, and to bring thee into the place which I have prepared.
(21) Beware of him, and obey his voice, provoke him not; for he will not pardon your transgressions: for my name *is* in him.
(22) But if thou shalt indeed obey his voice, and do all that I speak; then I will be an enemy unto thine enemies, and an [1] adversary unto thine adversaries.
(23) [a] For mine Angel shall go before thee, and [b] bring thee in unto the Amorites, and the Hittites, and the Perizzites, and the Canaanites, the Hivites, and the Jebusites: and I will cut them off.
(24) Thou shalt not bow down to their gods, nor serve them, nor do after their works: [c] but thou shalt utterly overthrow them, and quite break down their images.
(25) And ye shall serve the LORD your God, and he shall bless thy bread, and thy water; and I will take sickness away from the midst of thee.
(26) [d] There shall nothing cast their young, nor be barren, in thy land: the number of thy days I will fulfil.
(27) I will send my fear before thee, and will destroy all the people to whom thou shalt come, and I will make all thine enemies turn their [2] backs unto thee.
(28) And [e] I will send hornets before thee, which shall drive out the Hivite, the Canaanite, and the Hittite, from before

1 Or, *I will afflict them that afflict thee.*
a ch. 33. 2.
b Josh. 24. 11.
c Deut. 7. 25.
d Deut. 7. 14.
2 Heb., *neck.*
e Josh. 24. 12.

---

to "reward men after their works," and to set before them "the recompense of the reward." He "knows whereof we are made," and by what motives we are influenced. Self-interest, the desire of our own good, is one of the strongest of them. If Israel will keep His covenant, they will enjoy the following blessings:—(1) The guidance and protection of His angel till Canaan is reached; (2) God's help against their adversaries, who will, little by little, be driven out; (3) the ultimate possession of the entire country between the Mediterranean and the Red Sea on the one hand, the Desert and the Euphrates on the other; (4) a blessing upon their flocks and herds, which shall neither be barren nor cast their young; and (5) a blessing upon themselves, whereby they will escape sickness and enjoy a long term of life. All these advantages, however, are conditional upon obedience, and may be forfeited.

(20) **I send an Angel before thee.**—Kalisch considers Moses to have been the "angel" or "messenger;" others understand one of the created angelic host. But most commentators see in the promise the first mention of the "Angel of the Covenant," who is reasonably identified with the Second Person of the Holy Trinity, the Eternal Son and Word of God. When the promise is retracted on account of the sin of the golden calf, it is in the words, "*I* will not go up with thee" (chap. xxxiii. 3).

(21) **My name is in him.**—God and His Name are in Scripture almost convertible terms. He is never said to set His Name in a man.

(22) **An adversary unto thine adversaries.**—Rather, *an afflictor of thy afflictors.*

(23) **I will cut them off.**—Or, *cut them down*—*i.e.*, make them cease to be nations, not exterminate them utterly. Jebusites, Hittites, and others continued to inhabit Canaan, and were probably absorbed ultimately into the Hebrew population, having become full proselytes.

(24) **Nor do after their works.**—The Canaanitish nations were not merely idolaters, they were corrupt, profligate, and depraved. All the abominations mentioned in Lev. xviii. 6—23 were practised widely among them before they were dispossessed of their territory (Lev. xviii. 24—30). No doubt the idolatry and the profligacy were closely connected, as among idolatrous nations generally; but it was for their profligacy rather than their idolatry that they were driven out. Thus it was necessary to warn Israel against both.

Thou shalt . . . quite break down their images.—Conquerors generally preserved the idols of the conquered nations as trophies of victory; to do so was forbidden to the Israelites. Idolatry had such a powerful and subtle attraction for them, that there was danger of their being seduced into it unless the entire apparatus of the idol-worship were destroyed and made away with. Hence the present injunctions, and others similar to them. (Comp. chap. xxxiv. 13; Deut. vii. 5; &c.)

(25) **He shall bless thy bread, and thy water**—*i.e.*, all the food, whether meat or drink, on which they subsisted. It is God's blessing which makes food healthful to us.

Take sickness away.—Half the sicknesses from which men suffer are directly caused by sin, and would disappear if men led godly, righteous, and sober lives. Others, as plague and pestilence, are scourges sent by God to punish those who have offended Him. If Israel had walked in God's ways, He would have preserved them from sicknesses of *all* kinds by a miraculous interposition. (Comp. Deut. vii. 15.)

(26) **There shall nothing cast their young, nor be barren.**—Abortions, untimely births, and barrenness, when they exceeded a certain average amount, were always reckoned in the ancient world among the signs of God's disfavour, and special expiatory rites were devised for checking them. Conversely, when such misfortunes fell short of the ordinary average, God's favour was presumed. The promises here made confirm man's instinctive feeling.

The number of thy days I will fulfil.—Comp. chap. xx. 12. Long life is always regarded in Scripture as a blessing. (Comp. Pss. lv. 23, xc. 10; Job v. 26, xlii. 16, 17; 1 Kings iii. 11; Isa. lxv. 20; Eph. vi. 3, &c.)

(28) **I will send hornets.**—Heb., *the hornet.* Comp. Josh. xxiv. 12, where "the hornet" is said to have been sent. No doubt hornets might be so numerous as to become an intolerable plague, and induce a nation to quit its country and seek another (see Bochart, *Hierozoic.* iv. 13). But as we have no historical account of the kind in connection with the Canaanite races, the expression here used is scarcely to be taken literally. Probably the Egyptians are the hornets intended. It was they who, under Rameses III., broke the power of the Hittites and other nations of Palestine, while the Israelites were sojourners in the wilderness. Possibly the term was chosen in reference to the

thee. (29) I will not drive them out from
before thee in one year; lest the land
become desolate, and the beast of the
field multiply against thee. (30) By little
and little I will drive them out from
before thee, until thou be increased, and
inherit the land. (31) And I will set thy
bounds from the Red sea even unto the
sea of the Philistines, and from the
desert unto the river: for I will deliver
the inhabitants of the land into your
hand; and thou shalt drive them out
before thee. (32) [a] Thou shalt make no
covenant with them, nor with their
gods. (33) They shall not dwell in thy
land, lest they make thee sin against me:
for if thou serve their gods, [b] it will
surely be a snare unto thee.

[a] ch. 34. 15; Deut. 7. 2.

[b] Deut. 7. 16; Josh. 23. 13; Judg. 2. 3.

[c] ch. 19. 8. & 24. 3. 7; Deut. 5. 27.

CHAPTER XXIV.—(1) And he said
unto Moses, Come up unto the LORD,
thou, and Aaron, Nadab, and Abihu,
and seventy of the elders of Israel; and
worship ye afar off. (2) And Moses alone
shall come near the LORD: but they
shall not come nigh; neither shall the
people go up with him.

(3) And Moses came and told the people
all the words of the LORD, and all the
judgments: and all the people answered
with one voice, and said, [c] All the words
which the LORD hath said will we
do.

(4) And Moses wrote all the words of
the LORD, and rose up early in the
morning, and builded an altar under the
hill, and twelve pillars, according to the

---

hieroglyphic sign for "king" in Egypt, which was the figure of a bee or wasp. The author of the Book of Wisdom seems, however, to have understood the expression literally (Wisd. xii. 8, 9).

(29) **The beast of the field.**—Comp. 2 Kings xvii. 25, 26, where we find that this result followed the deportation of the Samaritans by the Assyrians.

(31) **Thy bounds.**—Those whose highest notion of prophecy identifies it with advanced human foresight naturally object to Moses having foretold the vast extent of empire which did not take place till the days of David and Solomon. It is impossible, however, to understand this passage in any other way than as an assignment to Israel of the entire tract between the Desert, or "Wilderness of the Wanderings," and the Euphrates on the one hand, the Mediterranean and the Red Sea on the other. "The River" (*han-nahar*) has no other meaning in the Pentateuch than "the Euphrates." And this was exactly the extent to which the dominions of Israel reached under Solomon, as we see from the description in Kings and Chronicles (1 Kings iv. 21, 24; 2 Chron. ix. 26). It had, according to Moses (Gen. xv. 18), been already indicated with tolerable precision in the original promise made to Abraham.

(32) **Thou shalt make no covenant with them**—*i.e.*, no treaty of peace; no arrangement by which one part of the land shall be thine and another theirs. (Comp. chap. xxxiv. 12.)

Nor with their gods.—It was customary at the time for treaties between nations to contain an acknowledgment by each of the other's gods. (See the treaty between Rameses II. and the Hittites in the *Records of the Past*, vol. iv., pp. 27—32.) Thus a treaty with a nation was a sort of treaty with its gods.

(33) **They shall not dwell in thy land.**—Individuals might remain if they became proselytes, as Urijah the Hittite, Araunah the Jebusite, &c.; and the Gibeonites remained *en masse*, but in a servile condition. What was forbidden was the co-existence of friendly but independent heathen communities with Israel within the limits of Canaan. This would have been a perpetual "snare" to the Israelites, and would have continually led them into idolatry; as we find that it did during the period of the early Judges. (See Judges i. 27—36; ii. 11—13; iii. 5—7.)

XXIV.

THE RATIFICATION OF THE COVENANT.

(1) **And he said.**—We should have expected "And God said," or "And Jehovah said." The omission of the nominative is probably to be accounted for by the insertion into Exodus at this point of "the Book of the Covenant," which was originally a distinct document. Verse 1 of chap. xxiv. probably followed originally on verse 21 of chap. xx. The sequence of the words was then as follows: "And Moses drew near unto the thick darkness where God was. And he said unto Moses," &c.

Come up.—The ascent of Aaron, Nadab, Abihu, and the seventy elders seems to have been commanded in order to give greater solemnity to the ratification of the covenant between God and Israel, which is the main subject of this section. Moses received instructions on the subject before descending, and no doubt was divinely guided in the steps which he took previously to ascending with them.

Nadab, and Abihu.—Aaron's two elder sons. (See chap. vi. 23.)

Seventy of the elders.—These are not the "judges" of chap. xviii. 21—26, who were not yet appointed (see Note on chap. xviii. 24, 25), but rather the heads of tribes and families who had exercised authority over the Israelites in Egypt, and through whom Moses had always communicated with the people. (See chaps. iii. 16, iv. 29, xii. 21, xvii. 5, 6.)

(3) **Moses . . . told the people all the words of the Lord.**—Moses gave them an outline of the legislation which he subsequently committed to writing (verse 4) and formed into "the Book of the Covenant" (verse 7). Its general purport and main heads were communicated, but probably not all its details. Otherwise it would scarcely have been necessary to read the contents of the book to them. The people willingly gave in their adhesion, feeling the laws to be "holy, just, and good," and not yet knowing how difficult they would find it to render a perfect obedience.

(4) **Moses wrote.**—Comp. chap. xvii. 14. The familiarity of Moses with writing is throughout presumed in the Pentateuch. One "learned in all the wisdom of the Egyptians" under the nineteenth

twelve tribes of Israel. (5) And he sent
young men of the children of Israel,
which offered burnt offerings, and sacri-
ficed peace offerings of oxen unto the
LORD. (6) And Moses took half of the
blood, and put *it* in basons; and half of
the blood he sprinkled on the altar.
(7) And he took the book of the covenant,
and read in the audience of the people:
and they said, [a]All that the LORD hath
said will we do, and be obedient.

(8) And Moses took the blood, and
sprinkled *it* on the people, and said,
Behold [b]the blood of the covenant, which
the LORD hath made with you concern-
ing all these words.
(9) Then went up Moses, and Aaron,
Nadab, and Abihu, and seventy of the
elders of Israel: (10) and they saw the
God of Israel: and *there was* under his
feet as it were a paved work of a sapphire
stone, and as it were the body of heaven

a ver. 3.

b 1 Pet. 1. 2; Heb. 9. 20.

---

dynasty could not well be ignorant of this ordinary Egyptian accomplishment.

Under the hill.—Heb., *the mountain.* The Ras Sufsafeh is intended.

Twelve pillars.—As the altar symbolised and indicated the presence of Jehovah, one party to the Covenant, so the twelve pillars—probably long stones set up on end (Gen. xxviii. 18)—symbolised the presence of the twelve tribes, the other party. (For another instance of the employment of such symbolism see Josh. iv. 3, 9, 20.)

(5) **Young men . . . which offered burnt offerings.**—It is to be noted that, even subsequently to the appointment of the Levitical priesthood, the acts of slaughtering the victims and arranging the flesh upon the altar were regarded as appropriately performed by any Israelite (Lev. i. 5, 6, 11, 12, &c.). The sprinkling of the blood and the lighting of the fire were the special sacrificial acts reserved to the priest (Lev. i. 5, 7, 11, 13). At this time, before the Levitical priesthood had been instituted, the sprinkling of the blood would seem to have been the sole act reserved. *Young* men were employed to slay the animals as best qualified by their strength to deal with them.

Burnt offerings . . . peace offerings.—Burnt offerings were at once expiatory and signs of self-dedication. Peace offerings were indications of man's gratitude for mercies received. Both were now offered together, to mark (1) Israel's thankfulness for being taken into covenant, and (2) Israel's determination to consecrate itself wholly to the service of God.

(6) **Put it in basons.**—Reserving it for the purpose stated in verse 8.

Half of the blood he sprinkled on the altar.—This was the most essential part of every sacrifice—the act by which the victim, the representative of the offerer, was made over and delivered up to God. Usually all the blood was thus devoted; here there was need of some for another purpose.

(7) **The book of the covenant**—*i.e.*, the book which he had written overnight, the collection of laws and promises which we have in chaps. xx. 22—xxiii. 33.

In the audience of the people.—Heb., *in the ears of the people.*

And they said.—Having heard the *ipsissima verba* spoken by God to Moses, they repeated their previous acceptance (see verse 3), adding a general promise of obedience.

(8) **And Moses took the blood, and sprinkled it . . .**—Half of the blood had been sprinkled upon the altar, which symbolised Jehovah; the other half was now sprinkled upon the people, or, rather upon their representatives—the elders and others who stood nearest to Moses. Thus the two parties to the covenant, sprinkled with the blood of the same sacrifices, were brought into sacramental union. Rites somewhat similar, involving blood communion, were common throughout the East in connection with covenants (Hom. *Il.* iii. 298, xix. 252; Herod. i. 74, iii. 8, iv. 70; Xen. *Anab.* ii. 2, § 9; Lucian. *Toxar.* 37; Pomp. *Mel.* ii. 1; Tac. *Ann.* xii. 47; &c.), and were regarded as adding to their force and sacredness.

On the people.—It has been suggested (Abarbarnel) that the blood was really sprinkled on the twelve pillars which represented the people; but the words used scarcely seem to admit of such an interpretation. The writer of the Epistle to the Hebrews understood the passage as declaring that the people were sprinkled (Heb. ix. 19).

(9) **Then went up.**—According to the ordinary ideas of the time, the ratification of the covenant was now complete, and nothing more was needed. It pleased God, however, to terminate the whole transaction by a closing scene of extraordinary grandeur, beauty, and spiritual significance. A sacrifice implied a sacrificial meal (chap. xviii. 12). Moses understood that God, by summoning Aaron, Nadab, Abihu, and seventy of the elders into the mount (verse 1), had intended the sacrificial meal to be held there; and accordingly, as soon as he had sprinkled the people, ascended Sinai with the persons summoned, and had the feast prepared. A sacrificial meal was always regarded as a religious act—an act done "before God" (chap. xviii. 12), involving communion with Him. God willed now to signalise this sacrificial feast above all others by making His presence not only felt but *seen.* As Moses, Aaron with his two sons, and the elders were engaged in the feast (verse 11), a vision of marvellous splendour broke upon them. "They saw the God of Israel" (verse 10). God showed Himself to them—not, as before, amid thunders and lightnings, and a thick cloud, and fire, and smoke, and earthquake (chap. xix. 16, 18), but in His loveliness (Cant. v. 16) and His beauty, standing on pellucid sapphire, blue as the blue of heaven. They "saw God," and were neither hurt nor even terrified; they could, while seeing Him, still eat and drink—they felt themselves like guests at His board, as if He were banqueting with them. So was impressed upon them the mild and sweet relation into which they were brought towards God by covenant—a covenant made, and not yet infringed. The gentle, lovely, attractive side of God's character was shewn to them, instead of the awful and alarming one; and they were taught to look forward to a final state of bliss, in which God's covenanted servants would dwell in His presence continually.

(10) **They saw the God of Israel.**—Probably, in human form, as Isaiah saw Him (Isa. vi. 1—5), and Ezekiel (Ezek. i. 26), and even Nebuchadnezzar (Dan. iii. 25). It is not of this appearance that Moses

in *his* clearness. (11) And upon the nobles
of the children of Israel he laid not his
hand: also they saw God, and did eat
and drink.
(12) And the LORD said unto Moses,
Come up to me into the mount, and be
there: and I will give thee tables of
stone, and a law, and commandments
which I have written; that thou mayest
teach them. (13) And Moses rose up, and
his minister Joshua: and Moses went
up into the mount of God. (14) And he
said unto the elders, Tarry ye here for
us, until we come again unto you: and,
behold, Aaron and Hur *are* with you:
if any man have any matters to do, let
him come unto them.
(15) And Moses went up into the mount,

---

says: "Ye saw no similitude" (Deut. iv. 12). The appearance which they saw had "feet."

A paved work of a sapphire stone.—Heb., *a work of the clearness of sapphire.* The "sapphire" (*sappir*) of the Pentateuch is probably *lapis lazuli.*

The body of heaven—*i.e.,* "the very heaven," or "the heaven itself."

(11) **The nobles.**—The word used is an unusual one, but seems to designate the "elders" of verses 1 and 9. It implies nobility of birth.

He laid not his hand—*i.e.,* He in nowise hurt or injured them. The belief was general that a man could not see God and live (Gen. xxxii. 30; Exod. xxxii. 20; Judg. vi. 22, 23, &c.). In one sense it was true—"No man hath seen the Father." But the Son could reveal Himself under the Old Dispensation, as under the New, and not even cause terror by His presence. (See the last clause of the verse.)

Also they saw God.—Rather, *they both saw God, and also did eat and drink.* It is intended to express in the clearest way that the two facts were concurrent. As they feasted on the sacrificial meal, the vision of God was made manifest to them. It is impossible to doubt that we have here a precious forecast of the Christian's highest privilege—the realisation of the presence of God in the sacred feast of the Holy Communion.

THE SECOND ASCENT OF MOSES INTO MOUNT SINAI.

(12—18) The great work still remained to be done. A series of laws had been laid down for the nation and accepted with unanimity (verses 3, 7). But "*quid prosunt leges sine moribus?*" It was necessary for the sustentation of the religious life of the people that a sacred polity should be instituted, a form of worship set up, and regulations established with regard to all the externals of religion—holy persons, holy places, rites, ceremonies, vestments, incense, consecration. Moses was directed to ascend into the mount, and hold prolonged communion with God, in order that he might learn the mind of God with respect to all these things. His prolonged stay for "forty days and forty nights" (verse 18) was necessary to give him a full and complete knowledge of all the details so elaborately set forth in chaps. xxv.—xxx., and again in chaps. xxxv.—xl., which thenceforth constituted the essentials of the external worship of Israel, whereby the minds and habits of the people were moulded and impressed in a far more efficacious way than could ever have been done by a mere set of abstract propositions, appealing only to the intellect. "*Segnius irritant animum demissa per aures, Quam quæ sunt oculis subjecta fidelibus.*" The Decalogue and the Book of the Covenant had no doubt a considerable share in forming the character of the Hebrew nation; but a larger share must be assigned to the ritual and ceremonial which Moses was now instructed to set up, and which forms the main subject of the remainder of the Book.

(12) **Come up to me into the mount, and be there.**—After the sacrificial meal, the seventy-four persons engaged in it had descended into the plain of Er-Rahah, and possibly spent some time there, before a second summons came to Moses. This time he was directed to ascend accompanied only by his minister, Joshua (verse 13), and was warned that his stay was to be a prolonged one in the words, "And *be there.*"

And I will give thee tables of stone . . .—It is remarkable that these are not expressly said, either here or in chap. xxxi. 18, to have contained the ten commandments. The fact, however, is distinctly stated in Deut. v. 22; and with respect to the second tables, the same is affirmed in chap. xxxiv. 28. The fiction of a double decalogue is thus precluded.

(13) **Moses rose up, and his minister Joshua.**—The close connection of Joshua with Moses is here, for the first time, indicated. His employment as a general against Amalek (chap. xvii. 9—13) might have simply marked his military capacity; but from this point in the history it becomes apparent that he was Moses' most trusted friend and assistant in all matters where there was need of confidential relations between the leader and his subordinates, and thus that he was to be his successor (see chaps. xxxii. 17, xxxiii. 11; Num. xiii. 8, 16, xxvii. 18—23; Deut. xxxiv. 9), since no other person stood in any such close association.

Moses went up into the mount of God.—Ascended, *i.e.,* to the highest point of the mountain, whereof mention has been previously made; not, probably, to the Jebel Musa, but to the highest summit of the Ras Sufsafeh, upon which the cloud rested.

(14) **He said unto the elders.**—Moses understood that his stay in the mount was about to be a prolonged one (see verse 12). He therefore prudently determined to make arrangements for the government and direction of the people during his absence. Aaron his brother, and Hur, the father of Bezaleel, perhaps his brother-in-law, seemed to him the fittest persons to exercise authority over the people during his absence; and accordingly he named them as the persons to whom application was to be made under any circumstances of difficulty.

Here.—In the plain below the mountain. The injunction was that the camp should not be moved until Moses came down, however long he might be detained by the Divine colloquy.

(15) **A cloud covered the mount.**—Heb., *the cloud—i.e.,* the cloud which had accompanied them from Succoth (chap. xiii. 21—23).

and a cloud covered the mount. (16) And
the glory of the LORD abode upon mount
Sinai, and the cloud covered it six days:
and the seventh day he called unto Moses
out of the midst of the cloud. (17) And
the sight of the glory of the LORD *was*
like devouring fire on the top of the
mount in the eyes of the children of
Israel. (18) And Moses went into the
midst of the cloud, and gat him up into
the mount: and [a]Moses was in the mount
forty days and forty nights.

CHAPTER XXV.—(1) And the LORD
spake unto Moses, saying, (2) Speak
unto the children of Israel, that they
[1]bring me an [2]offering: [b]of every
man that giveth it willingly with his
heart ye shall take my offering. (3) And
this *is* the offering which ye shall
take of them; gold, and silver, and
brass, (4) and blue, and purple, and
scarlet, and [3]fine linen, and goats'
hair, (5) and rams' skins dyed red,
and badgers' skins, and shittim wood,

[a] ch. 34. 28; Deut. 9. 9.

[1] Heb., *take for me.*

[2] Or, *heave offering.*

[b] ch. 35. 5.

[3] Or, *silk.*

---

(16) **The seventh day he called unto Moses out of the midst of the cloud.**—Moses, it is evident, would not enter the cloud without a positive summons. It pleased God to put off the summons for six days. Moses doubtless employed the time in such prayer and meditation as rendered him fit for near contact with Deity.

(17) **The sight of the glory of the Lord.**—To the Israelites in the plain below, the appearance on the top of the Ras Sufsafeh was "like devouring fire." A light like that of a conflagration rested on the top of the Ras Sufsafeh all the time that Moses was away.

(18) **Moses was in the mount forty days and forty nights.**—During the whole of this time he took no food (Deut. ix. 9). Comp. the fast of Elijah (1 Kings xix. 8), and that of our blessed Lord (Matt. iii. 2). Modern imitations are in all probability impostures.

XXV.

THE GIFTS WHICH MIGHT BE GIVEN FOR THE TABERNACLE AND THE PRIESTS' DRESSES.

(2) **Speak unto the children of Israel that they bring me an offering.**—God, being about to command the construction of a dwelling for Himself, such as the circumstances of the case allowed, prefaced His directions concerning its materials and form by instructing Moses to invite the people to contribute from their stores, as an offering to Himself, the various substances which were suitable for the dwelling and its appurtenances. The erection of sanctuaries is one of the fittest occasions for man to shew his gratitude to God by giving to Him of His own, largely and liberally.

Of every man that giveth it willingly with his heart.—Heb., *of every man whose heart impels him.* Unless gifts come from the heart, they are an offence to God. He "loveth a cheerful giver." When the time came, a noble and liberal spirit was not wanting. (See chaps. xxxv. 21—29, xxxvi. 3—7.)

My offering.—Literally, *my heave-offering.* But the word seems to be intended in a generic sense.

(3) **Gold, and silver, and brass.**—The Israelites had brought out of Egypt (1) their ancestral wealth—the possessions of Abraham and the accumulations of Joseph, and (2) the rich gifts received from the Egyptians at the moment of their departure. They had added to their wealth by the plunder of the Amalekites. Thus they possessed a considerable store of the precious metals; and there is no difficulty in supposing that they furnished the gold needed for the tabernacle without seriously impoverishing themselves. The silver, which was of small amount comparatively, appears ultimately to have been furnished in another way (chaps. xxx. 12—16, xxxviii. 25—28) The brass, or rather bronze, for brass seems to have been unknown at this time, was small in amount (chap. xxxviii. 29), and of no great value. It would have constituted no serious drain on the resources of the people.

(4) **And blue, and purple, and scarlet.**—The colours intended are probably a dark blue produced from indigo, which was the only blue known to the Egyptians, a purplish crimson derived from the *murex trunculus,* the main source of the "Tyrian dye" of the ancients, and a scarlet furnished by the *coccus ilicis,* or cochineal insect of the holm oak, which was largely employed in antiquity, though now superseded by the brighter tint obtained from the *coccus cacti* of Mexico. Linen yarn of the three colours mentioned seems to have been what the people were asked to furnish (chaps. xxxv. 25, xxxix. 1).

Fine linen—*i.e.,* white thread spun from flax, which is found to be the material of almost all the Egyptian dresses, mummy cloths, and other undyed fabrics. It is of a yellowish white, soft, and wonderfully fine and delicate. (See Wilkinson in Rawlinson's *Herodotus,* vol. ii., p. 233).

Goats' hair.—The covering of an Arab tent is to this day almost always of goats'-hair. An excellent fabric is woven from the soft inner hair of the Syrian goat, and a coarse one from the outer coat of the animal. Yarn of goats'-hair was to be offered, that from it might be produced the first of the three outer coverings of the Tabernacle (chap. xxvi. 7—14).

(5) **Rams' skins dyed red.**—North Africa has always been celebrated for the production of the best possible leather. Herodotus describes the manufacture of his own times (*Hist.* iv. 189). Even at the present day, we bind our best books in *morocco.* Brilliant colours always were, and still are, affected by the North African races, and their "red skins" have been famous in all ages. It is probable that the Israelites had brought with them many skins of this kind out of Egypt.

Badgers' skins.—The badger is not a native of North Africa, nor of the Arabian desert; and the translation of the Hebrew *takhash* by "badger" is a very improbable conjecture. In Arabic, *tukhash* or *dukhash* is the name of a marine animal resembling the seal; or, perhaps it should rather be said, is applied with some vagueness to a number of sea-animals, as seals, dugongs, dolphins, sharks, and dog-fish. The skins here spoken of are probably those of some one or more of these animals. They formed the outer covering of the Tabernacle (chap. xxvi. 14).

Shittim wood.—That the *shittah* (plural, *shittim*) was a species of Acacia is now generally admitted.

(6) oil for the light, spices for anointing
oil, and for sweet incense, (7) onyx stones,
and stones to be set in the [a] ephod, and
in the [b] breastplate.
(8) And let them make me a sanctuary;
that I may dwell among them. (9) Ac-
cording to all that I shew thee, *after*
the pattern of the tabernacle, and the
pattern of all the instruments thereof,
even so shall ye make *it*.
(10) [c] And they shall make an ark *of*
shittim wood: two cubits and a half
shall be the length thereof, and a cubit
and a half the breadth thereof, and a
cubit and a half the height thereof.
(11) And thou shalt overlay it with pure

a ch. 28. 4.

b ch. 28. 15.

c ch. 37. 1.

It was certainly not the palm; and there are no trees in the Sinaitic region from which boards could be cut (see chap. xxvi. 15) except the palm and the acacia. The Sinaitic acacia (*A. seyal*) is a "gnarled and thorny tree, somewhat like a solitary hawthorn in its habit and manner of growth, but much larger" (Tristram). At present it does not, in the Sinaitic region, grow to such a size as would admit of planks, ten cubits long by one and a half wide, being cut from it; but, according to Canon Tristram (*Nat. Hist. of the Bible*, p. 392), it attains such a size in Palestine, and therefore may formerly have done so in Arabia. The wood is "hard and close-grained, of an orange colour with a darker heart, well adapted for cabinet-work."

(6) **Oil for the light.**—It is assumed that the "sanctuary," which is to be built (verse 8), will need to be lighted. Oil therefore is to be provided for the lighting. Later on (chap. xxvii. 20) it is laid down that the oil must be "pure olive oil beaten."

Spices for anointing oil.—Rather, *for the anointing oil.* Here, again, there is an assumption that anointing oil will be needed, and that spices will be a necessary ingredient in such oil. We find afterwards that the Tabernacle itself, all its vessels, and the priests appointed to serve in it, had to be consecrated by anointing (chaps. xxix. 7, 36, xxx. 26—30). The particular spices to be mixed with the "anointing oil" are enumerated in chap. xxx. 23, 24.

And for sweet incense.—Rather, *for the sweet incense*—the incense, *i.e.*, which would have to be burnt. (See chap. xxx. 1—8; and for the composition of the incense, chap. xxx. 34.)

(7) **Onyx stones.**—The Hebrew *shoham* is rendered here by "sard" (LXX.), "sardonyx" (Vulg. and Josephus), and "beryl" (Rosenmüller and others). In Job xxviii. 16, the same word is rendered by the LXX. "onyx." There is thus considerable doubt what stone is meant. Only three such stones seem to have been required as offerings, one for the high priest's breast-plate (chap. xxviii. 20), and two for the shoulder-pieces of the ephod (chap. xxviii. 9—12).

Stones to be set in the ephod and in the breastplate.—Heb., *stones of insertion for the ephod and for the breast-plate.* The stones of the ephod were two only, both probably either onyx or sardonyx; those of the breast-plate were twelve in number, all different (chap. xxviii. 17—20).

The Sanctuary and its Contents.

(8) **Let them make me a sanctuary.**—The enumeration of the gifts (verses 3—7) has been subordinate to this. Hitherto Israel had had no place of worship, no structure dedicated to God. God now brings this state of things to an end, by requiring them to "make him a sanctuary." In Egypt they had seen structures of vast size and extraordinary magnificence erected in every city for the worship of the Egyptian gods. They are now to have their own structure, their "holy place," their "house of God." As, however, they are still in a nomadic condition, without fixed abode, continually shifting their quarters, a building, in the ordinary sense of the word, would have been unsuitable. They must soon have quitted it or have foregone their hopes of Palestine. God therefore devised for them a structure in harmony with their condition—a "tent-temple"—modelled on the ordinary form of the better Oriental tents, but of the best materials and of an unusual size—yet still portable. It is this structure, with its contents and its adjuncts, which forms the main subject of the rest of the book of Exodus, and which is now minutely and elaborately described in six consecutive chapters (chaps. xxv.—xxx.)

That I may dwell among them.—Compare chaps. xxix. 42—46, xl. 34—38. Though God "dwelleth not in temples made with hands" (Acts vii. 48), is not confined to them, cannot be comprehended within them, yet since it pleases Him to manifest Himself especially in such abodes, He may be well said to "dwell there" in a peculiar manner. His dwelling with Israel was not purely spiritual. From time to time He manifested Himself sensibly in the Holy of Holies, where He dwelt continually, and might be consulted by the temporal ruler of the nation.

(9) **The pattern.**—It has been maintained that God shewed to Moses (1) a material structure, furnished with material objects, as the model which he was to follow in making the Tabernacle and its appurtenances; (2) a pictorial representation of the whole; (3) a series of visions in which the forms were represented to the eye of the mind. The entire analogy of the Divine dealings is in favour of the last-mentioned view.

The Ark.

(10) **They shall make an ark.**—*Arôn*, the word here rendered "ark," is an entirely different word from that previously so translated in Gen. vi. 14; Exod. ii. 3, which is *têbah. Arôn* is properly a chest or coffer of small dimensions, used to contain money or other valuables (2 Kings xii. 9, 10; 2 Chron. xxv. 8—11, &c.). In one place it is applied to a mummy-case (Gen. l. 26). Here it designates a wooden chest three feet nine inches long, two feet three inches broad, and two feet three inches deep. The primary object of the ark was to contain the two tables of stone, written with the finger of God, which Moses was to receive before he came down from the mount. (See chap. xxiv. 12, and comp. chap. xx. 16.) Sacred coffers were important parts of the furniture of temples in Egypt. They usually contained the image or emblem of some deity, and were constructed so as to be readily carried in processions.

(11) **Thou shalt overlay it with pure gold.**—It is possible, but scarcely probable, that gilding is intended. Gilding was well known in Egypt long before the time of Moses, and may have been within the artistic powers of some of the Hebrews. But it is a

gold, within and without shalt thou
overlay it, and shalt make upon it a
crown of gold round about. (12) And
thou shalt cast four rings of gold for it,
and put *them* in the four corners thereof;
and two rings *shall be* in the one side of
it, and two rings in the other side of it.
(13) And thou shalt make staves *of* shittim
wood, and overlay them with gold.
(14) And thou shalt put the staves into the
rings by the sides of the ark, that the
ark may be borne with them. (15) The
staves shall be in the rings of the ark:
they shall not be taken from it. (16) And
thou shalt put into the ark the testimony
which I shall give thee.

(17) And thou shalt make a mercy seat
of pure gold: two cubits and a half
shall be the length thereof, and a cubit
and a half the breadth thereof. (18) And
thou shalt make two cherubims *of* gold,
of beaten work shalt thou make them,
in the two ends of the mercy seat.
(19) And make one cherub on the one end,
and the other cherub on the other end:
even [1]of the mercy seat shall ye make

1 Or, *of the matter of the mercy seat.*

---

process requiring much apparatus, and less likely to have been practised in the desert than the far simpler one of overlaying with gold plates. Gold plates would also have been regarded as more suitable, because more valuable. It is the Jewish tradition that gold plates were employed.

A crown of gold—*i.e.*, a rim or border of gold, carried round the edge of the chest at the top. The object was probably to keep the *kapporeth*, or mercy-seat, in place.

(12) **Four rings of gold.**—Though the ark was not to be carried in procession, like Egyptian arks, yet it would have to be carried when the Israelites resumed their journeyings. The four rings were made to receive the two "staves" or poles by which the ark was to be borne at such times on the shoulders of the priests (verses 13, 14).

In the four corners thereof.—Literally, *at the four feet thereof.* The rings were to be affixed, not at the four upper corners of the chest, but at the four bottom corners, in order that the ark, when carried on men's shoulders, might be elevated above them, and so be in no danger of coming in contact with the bearers' persons. The arrangement might seem to endanger the equilibrium of the ark when carried; but as Kalisch observes, "the smallness of the dimensions of the ark rendered its safe transportation, even with the rings at its feet, not impossible."

(15) **The staves . . . shall not be taken from it.**—The staves were to remain always in the rings, whether the ark was in motion or at rest, that there might never at any time be a necessity for touching the ark itself, or even the rings. He who touched the ark imperilled his life. (See 2 Sam. vi. 6, 7.)

(16) **The testimony which I shall give thee.**—The two tables of stone were called "the Testimony" (comp. chap. xvi. 34), as being God's witness against sin (Deut. xxxi. 26). As containing them, the ark was called "the ark of the testimony" (chap. xxv. 22, xxvi. 34, xxx. 6, 26, &c.; Num. iv. 5, vii. 89; Josh. iv. 16).

THE MERCY SEAT.

(17) **A mercy seat.**—Those critics to whom the idea of expiation is unsatisfactory, as Knobel and Gesenius, render *kapporeth*, the word here used, by "lid" or "cover." *Kaphar*, it may be admitted, has the physical meaning of "to cover" (Gen. vi. 14); but *kipper*, the Piel form of the same verb, has never any other meaning than that of "covering," or "expiating *sins*." And *kapporeth* is not formed from *kaphar*, but from *kipper*. Hence the ἱλαστήριον of the LXX., the *propitiatorium* of the Vulg., and the "mercy seat" of the Authorised Version are correct translations. (Comp. 1 Chron. xxviii. 11, where the Holy of Holies is called *beyth-hak-kapporeth*, which is certainly not "the house of the cover," but "the house of expiation.")

Of pure gold.—Not of shittim wood, overlaid with a plating of gold, but a solid mass of the pure metal. It has been calculated that the weight would be 750 lbs. Troy, and the value above £25,000 of our money. It was intended to show by this lavish outlay, that the "mercy seat" was that object in which the accessories of worship culminated, the crowning glory of the material tabernacle.

(18) **Two cherubims.**—"Cherubims," or rather *cherubim*, had been known previously in one connection only—they had been the guardians of Eden when Adam and Eve were driven forth from it (Gen. iii. 24). It is generally allowed that in that passage, as in most others where the word occurs, living beings, angels of God, are intended. But not all angels are cherubim. The cherubim constitute a select class, very near to God, very powerful, very resolute, highly fitted to act as guards. It is probably with this special reference that the cherubic figures were selected to be placed upon the mercy seat—they guarded the precious deposit of the two tables, towards which they looked (verse 20). The question as to the exact form of the figures is not very important; but it is one which has been discussed with great ingenuity and at great length. Some hold that the proper figure of a cherub is that of a bull or ox, and think that the cherubim of the tabernacle were winged bulls, not unlike the Assyrian. Others regard them as figures still more composite, like the Egyptian sphinxes or the chimæræ of the Greeks. But the predominant opinion seems to be that they were simply human figures with the addition of a pair of wings. (So Kalisch, Keil, Bishop Harold Browne, Canon Cook, and others.) In this case they would bear a considerable resemblance to the figures of Ma, or Truth, so often seen inside Egyptian arks, sheltering with their wings the scarabæus or some other emblem of deity.

Of beaten work—*i.e.*, not cast, but brought into shape by the hammer. In the Egyptian language *karabu* was "to hammer," whence, according to some, the word "cherub."

In the two ends.—Literally, *from the two ends*—rising, that is, from either end of the mercy seat.

(19) **Of the mercy seat shall ye make the cherubims.**—The meaning seems to be that the cherubims were not to be detached images, made separately, and then fastened to the mercy seat, but to be formed out of the same mass of gold with the mercy seat, and so to be part and parcel of it.

the cherubims on the two ends thereof.
(20) And the cherubims shall stretch forth
their wings on high, covering the mercy
seat with their wings, and their faces
shall look one to another; toward the
mercy seat shall the faces of the che-
rubims be. (21) And thou shalt put the
mercy seat above upon the ark; and in
the ark thou shalt put the testimony
that I shall give thee. (22) And there I
will meet with thee, and I will commune
with thee from above the mercy seat,
from [a] between the two cherubims which
are upon the ark of the testimony, of all
things which I will give thee in com-
mandment unto the children of Israel.
(23) [b] Thou shalt also make a table *of*
shittim wood: two cubits *shall be* the
length thereof, and a cubit the breadth
thereof, and a cubit and a half the
height thereof. (24) And thou shalt over-
lay it with pure gold, and make thereto
a crown of gold round about. (25) And
thou shalt make unto it a border of an
hand breadth round about, and thou
shalt make a golden crown to the border
thereof round about. (26) And thou shalt
make for it four rings of gold, and put
the rings in the four corners that *are* on
the four feet thereof. (27) Over against
the border shall the rings be for places
of the staves to bear the table. (28) And
thou shalt make the staves *of* shittim
wood, and overlay them with gold, that
the table may be borne with them.
(29) And thou shalt make the dishes
thereof, and spoons thereof, and covers
thereof, and bowls thereof, [1] to cover

a Num. 7. 89.

b ch. 37. 10.

1 Or, *to pour out withal.*

(20) **The cherubims shall stretch forth their wings on high.**—The two wings of both cherubs were to be elevated and advanced so as to overshadow the mercy seat, and, as it were, protect it. In the Egyptian figures of Ma, one wing only has this position, the other being depressed and falling behind the figure.

Towards the mercy seat.—Bent downwards, *i.e.*, as though gazing on the mercy seat. (Compare chap. xxxvii. 9).

(22) **There will I meet with thee.**—The place of the *Shechinah*, or visible manifestation of God's presence, was to be between the two cherubim over the mercy seat. There God would meet His people, "to speak there unto them" (chap. xxix. 42), either literally, as when He answered inquiries of the high priest by Urim and Thummim, or spiritually, as when He accepted incense, and the blood of offerings, and prayers, offered to Him by the people through their appointed representatives, the priests. It was for the purpose of thus "meeting" His people that the entire tabernacle was designed, and hence its ordinary name was "the Tent of Meeting," unhappily rendered in the Authorised Version by the "tabernacle of the congregation." (See Note on chap. xxvii. 21.)

THE TABLE OF SHEWBREAD.

(23–30) **Thou shalt also make a table.**—The ark and mercy seat, which covered it, constituted the entire furniture of the inner sanctuary, or "Holy of Holies" (chap. xl. 20, 21). When this had been shown to Moses the next thing to be done was to set before him the furniture of the outer sanctuary, or holy place. This consisted of three articles—(1) The table of shewbread, described in the present passage; (2) the golden candlestick, described in verses 31—40; and (3) the altar of incense, described in chap. xxx. 1—10. The "table of shewbread" was a receptacle for the twelve loaves, which were to be "set continually before the Lord" (Lev. xxiv. 8) as a thank-offering on the part of His people—a perpetual acknowledgment of His perpetual protection and favour. It was to be just large enough to contain the twelve loaves, set in two rows, being a yard long, and a foot and a-half broad. The vessels belonging to the table (verse 29) were not placed on it.

(23) **Of shittim wood.**—See the last Note on verse 5. No other wood was to be employed, either for the sanctuary itself, or for its furniture.

(24) **Thou shalt overlay it . . .**—Like the ark (verse 11), and the altar of incense (chap. xxx. 3), the table was to be overlaid with plates of gold. It was a species of altar, on which lay offerings to God, and, being close to the Divine Presence, required to be made of the best materials.

A crown of gold round about.—Rather, *a border*, or *edging of gold*, something to prevent what was placed on the table from readily falling off.

(25) **A border of a hand-breadth.**—Rather, *a band*, or *framing*. The representation of the table of shewbread on the Arch of Titus at Rome gives the best idea of this "band" or framing. It was a flat bar about midway between the top of the table and its feet, connecting the four legs together, and so keeping them in place. Its "golden crown," or "edging," can have been only for ornament.

(26) **Four rings.**—Compare verse 12. The table, like the ark, would have to be carried from place to place. Though it was less sacred than the ark, still provision was made for carrying it by means of staves and rings.

The four corners that are on the four feet.—Rather, *that are at the four feet*. Not the top corners of the table, *i.e.*, but the bottom corners. The table, like the ark, was, when carried, to be elevated above the shoulders of the bearers. So we see it borne on the Arch of Titus.

(27) **Over against the border shall the rings be.**—Rather, *opposite the band*, or *framing*. The meaning is not very clear. If the framing had been at the bottom of the legs, we might have understood that the rings were attached to the table opposite the places where the "framing" was inserted into the legs. But the "framing" appears to have been halfway up the legs (see Note on verse 25), while the rings were at the bottom. They could therefore have only been "opposite the framing" in a loose and vague sense.

For places of the staves.—Rather, *for places for staves*.

(29) **The dishes thereof . . .**—The "dishes" of the shewbread table were probably large bowls in which

withal: *of* pure gold shalt thou make
them. (30) And thou shalt set upon the
table shewbread before me alway.
(31) [a] And thou shalt make a candle-
stick *of* pure gold: *of* beaten work shall
the candlestick be made: his shaft, and
his branches, his bowls, his knops, and
his flowers, shall be of the same. (32) And
six branches shall come out of the sides
of it; three branches of the candlestick
out of the one side, and three branches
of the candlestick out of the other side:
(33) three bowls made like unto almonds,
with a knop and a flower in one branch;
and three bowls made like almonds in
the other branch, *with* a knop and a
flower: so in the six branches that come
out of the candlestick. (34) And in the
candlestick *shall be* four bowls made like
unto almonds, *with* their knops and
their flowers. (35) And *there shall be* a
knop under two branches of the same,
and a knop under two branches of the
same, and a knop under two branches of
the same, according to the six branches
that proceed out of the candlestick.
(36) Their knops and their branches shall
be of the same: all it *shall be* one beaten
work *of* pure gold. (37) And thou shalt
make the seven lamps thereof: and they
shall [1] light the lamps thereof, that they
may give light over against [2] it. (38) And
the tongs thereof, and the snuffdishes
thereof, *shall be of* pure gold. (39) *Of* a
talent of pure gold shall he make it,
with all these vessels. (40) And [b] look
that thou make *them* after their pattern,
[3] which was shewed thee in the mount.

[a] ch. 37. 17.

[1] Or, *cause to ascend.*

[2] Heb., *the face of it.*

[b] Acts 7. 44; Heb. 8. 5.

[3] Heb., *which thou wast caused to see.*

---

the loaves or "cakes" were brought to the table. Such bowls are common in the Egyptian wall decorations. The so-called "spoons" were small pots in which the incense was put (Levit. xxiv. 7) and burnt. Two such appeared upon the table on the Arch of Titus. The "covers" and "bowls" are flagons and chalices to contain the drink offerings which were necessary accompaniments of every meat offering.

To cover withal.—Rather (as in the margin), *to pour out withal.* Drink offerings were poured out in libation.

(30) **Thou shalt set upon the table shewbread before me alway.**—For a detailed account of the arrangement of the shewbread see Levit. xxiv. 5—9. The Hebrew expression translated "shewbread" is literally, "bread of face," or "bread of presence"—bread, that is, which was set forth always before the presence of God.

THE GOLDEN CANDLESTICK.

(31—39) The golden candlestick, like the table of shewbread, was represented on the Arch of Titus, and the careful copy made under the direction of Reland in 1710, and published in his work, *De Spoliis Templi*, gives probably the best idea that can be formed of it. It was composed of a straight stem, rising perpendicularly from a base, and having on either side of it three curved arms or branches, all of them in the same plane, and all rising to the same level. The stem and arms were ornamented with representations of almond flowers, pomegranates, and lily blossoms, repeated as there was room for them, the top ornament being in every case a lily blossom, which held a hemispherical lamp. The form and ornamentation of the base are unknown, since the representation of the base upon the Arch of Titus is manifestly from some Roman work which had superseded the original pedestal. The special object of the candlestick seems to have been to give light by night. Its lamps were to be lighted at even (chap. xxx. 8) by the High Priest, and were to burn from evening to morning (chap. xxvii. 21), when they were to be "dressed," or trimmed (chap. xxx. 7), and "extinguished" (Kalisch, *Comment. on Exodus*, p. 370). The Holy Place had sufficient light during the day from the entrance, where the curtain would let the light through, if indeed it were not also partially looped up.

(31) **Of beaten work.**—Like the cherubim. (See Note on verse 18.)

His bowls, his knops, and his flowers.—Rather, *its cups, its pomegranates, and its blossoms.* The "cups" are afterwards said to be "like almonds" (verse 33), *i.e.*, almond blossoms.

Shall be of the same—*i.e.*, "of one piece with the stem and branches;" not separate ornaments put together.

(33) **Three bowls made like unto almonds.**—Or, *three cups like almond blossoms.* It is not quite clear if these were consecutive, or if each cup held a "knop" (pomegranate), on which followed a (lily) blossom. On the whole Reland's representation accords best with the latter view.

In the other branch.—Rather, *in another branch.* The ornamentation was the same in the first, the second, and all the other branches; but in the longer branches the triple series was probably repeated oftener.

(34) **In the candlestick.**—By "the candlestick" in this place must be meant the central shaft or stem, which is viewed as that whereto all the rest is accessory. Here the triple series was to be repeated four times.

(37) **Thou shalt make the seven lamps thereof.**—Literally, *thou shalt make its lamps seven.* Each branch, as well as the stem, was to have its own lamp. The Arch of Titus shows them to us as hemispherical bowls.

They shall light.—See Note on verses 31—39, and comp. chaps. xxvii. 31, xxx. 8; Levit. xxiv. 3.

(38) **Tongs . . . snuffdishes.** — "Tongs," or pincers, were required for trimming the wicks of the lamps, and removing loose portions; "snuffdishes" for receiving the fragments thus removed.

(39) **Of a talent of pure gold.**—There are various estimates of the value and weight of the Hebrew gold talent, but none of them places it much below £4,000 of our money. Some carry the estimate as high as £10,000 or £11,000.

Shall he make it.—"He" refers to the artificer by whom the candlestick would be constructed.

(40) **After their pattern.**—Comp. verse 9.

CHAPTER XXVI.—(1) Moreover thou
shalt make the tabernacle *with* ten cur-
tains *of* fine twined linen, and blue, and
purple, and scarlet: *with* cherubims [1] of
cunning work shalt thou make them.
(2) The length of one curtain *shall be* eight
and twenty cubits, and the breadth of
one curtain four cubits: and every one
of the curtains shall have one measure.
(3) The five curtains shall be coupled
together one to another; and *other* five
curtains *shall be* coupled one to another.
(4) And thou shalt make loops of blue
upon the edge of the one curtain from
the selvedge in the coupling; and like-
wise shalt thou make in the uttermost
edge of *another* curtain, in the coupling
of the second. (5) Fifty loops shalt thou
make in the one curtain, and fifty loops
shalt thou make in the edge of the cur-
tain that *is* in the coupling of the second;
that the loops may take hold one of
another. (6) And thou shalt make fifty
taches of gold, and couple the curtains
together with the taches: and it shall
be one tabernacle.

[1] Heb., *the work of a cunning workman*, or, *embroiderer.*

XXVI.

The Tabernacle.

(1—37) The sacred tent which was to form the "House of God," or temple, for Israel during the continuance of the people in the wilderness, and which in point of fact served them for a national sanctuary until the construction of the first temple by Solomon, is described in this chapter with a minuteness which leaves little to be desired. It is called *ham-mishkân*, "the dwelling," and *ha-'ohel*, "the tent" (verse 36)—the former from its purpose, as being the place where God "dwelt" in a peculiar manner (chap. xxv. 22); the latter from its shape and general construction, which resembled those of other tents of the period. The necessary foundation was a framework of wood. This consisted of five "pillars," or tent-poles, in front (verse 37), graduated in height to suit the slope of the roof, and doubtless five similar ones at the back, though these are not mentioned. A ridge-pole must have connected the two central tent-poles, and over this ridge-pole the covering of the tent, which was of goats'-hair (verse 7), was no doubt strained in the ordinary way by means of cords and "pins," or tent-pegs (chap. xxxv. 18). Thus an oblong square space was roofed over, which seems to have been sixty feet long by thirty broad. Within this "tent" ('*ohel*) was placed the "dwelling" (*mishkân*). The "dwelling" was a space forty-five feet long by fifteen broad, enclosed on three sides by walls of boards (verses 18—25), and opening in front into a sort of porch formed by the projection of the "tent" beyond the "dwelling." Towards the open air this porch was closed, wholly or partially, by a curtain (verse 36). The "dwelling" was roofed over by another "curtain," or "hanging," of bright colours and rich materials (verses 1—6). It was divided into two portions, called respectively "the Holy Place," and "the Holy of Holies"—the former towards the porch, the latter away from it. These two places were separated by a "vail" hung upon four pillars (verses 31, 32). Their relative size is uncertain; but it may be suspected that the Holy of Holies was the smaller of the two, and conjectured that the proportion was as one to two, the Holy of Holies being a square of fifteen feet, and the Holy Place an oblong, thirty feet long by fifteen. The whole structure was placed within an area called "the Court of the Tabernacle," which is described in the next chapter.

1. The Fine Linen Covering.

(1) **The tabernacle.**—Literally, *the dwelling* (see chap. xxv. 9, where *mishkân* first occurs). It is a derivative from *shâkan*, translated by "dwell" in the preceding verse.

Ten curtains.—The same word (*yĕri'ah*) is used for the constituent parts of the covering, and for the entire covering, or, at any rate, for each of the two halves into which it was divided (verses 4, 5). In the first use, it corresponds to what we should call "a breadth."

Fine twined linen—*i.e.*, linen thread formed by twisting several distinct strands together. Egyptian thread was ordinarily of this character.

Blue, and purple, and scarlet.—See the Notes on chap. xxv. 4.

Cherubims of cunning work.—Rather, *cherubim, the work of a cunning weaver. Ma'asêh khoshêb* and *ma'asêh rokêm* (verse 36) seem to be contrasted one with the other, the former signifying work where the patterning was inwoven, the latter where it was embroidered with the needle. The inweaving of patterns or figures was well understood in Egypt (Herod. iii. 47; Plin. *H. N.*, viii. 48).

(2) **The length . . . eight and twenty cubits.**—Mr. Fergusson has shown that to cover over a space twenty cubits wide with a roof, the two sides of which should meet at a right angle, a tent-cloth almost exactly twenty-eight cubits long would be required.

(3) **The five curtains.**—It is anomalous that the article should be used here. Probably it has crept in from "the curtains" of the preceding verse. The meaning is that five "breadths" should be sewn together to form one curtain, and five other "breadths" to form another, and then that the two curtains so formed should be joined into one by means of "loops" and "taches." The object of making two curtains instead of one was clearly portability. The entire covering would have been too heavy and too bulky to be conveniently carried in one piece.

(4) **From the selvedge in the coupling.**—Rather, *at the coupling*. The selvedge, *i.e.*, nearest to the place where the two curtains were to be coupled together.

(5) **That the loops may take hold one of another.**—Rather, *correspond one to another*. They were not to "take hold," but to be attached by golden links.

(6) **Taches,** or *clasps*. These might be split-rings, or links like modern sleeve-links.

And it shall be one tabernacle.—Rather, *and* (so) *the tabernacle shall be one*. The division of the curtain which formed the roof into two portions tended to make a division in the tabernacle itself. To prevent this, the two curtains were to be so looped together as

(7) And thou shalt make curtains *of*
goats' *hair* to be a covering upon the
tabernacle : eleven curtains shalt thou
make. (8) The length of one curtain *shall*
be thirty cubits, and the breadth of one
curtain four cubits : and the eleven cur-
tains *shall be all* of one measure. (9) And
thou shalt couple five curtains by them-
selves, and six curtains by themselves,
and shalt double the sixth curtain in the
forefront of the tabernacle. (10) And
thou shalt make fifty loops on the edge
of the one curtain *that is* outmost in the
coupling, and fifty loops in the edge of
the curtain which coupleth the second.
(11) And thou shalt make fifty taches of
brass, and put the taches into the loops,
and couple the [1]tent together, that it
may be one. (12) And the remnant that
remaineth of the curtains of the tent,
the half curtain that remaineth, shall
hang over the backside of the tabernacle.
(13) And a cubit on the one side, and a
cubit on the other side [2]of that which
remaineth in the length of the curtains
of the tent, it shall hang over the sides
of the tabernacle on this side and on
that side, to cover it.
(14) And thou shalt make a covering
for the tent *of* rams' skins dyed red, and
a covering above *of* badgers' skins.
(15) And thou shalt make boards for
the tabernacle *of* shittim wood standing
up. (16) Ten cubits *shall be* the length of
a board, and a cubit and a half *shall be*
the breadth of one board. (17) Two [3]tenons
shall there be in one board, set in order
one against another : thus shalt thou
make for all the boards of the tabernacle.
(18) And thou shalt make the boards for
the tabernacle, twenty boards on the
south side southward. (19) And thou
shalt make forty sockets of silver under
the twenty boards ; two sockets under

1 Or, *covering.*

2 Heb., *in the remainder*, or, *surplusage.*

3 Heb., *hands.*

---

to be practically one. Thus the tabernacle itself became one.

2. THE GOATS'-HAIR TENT-CLOTH.

(7–13) An awning such as that described in verses 1—6 would have neither kept out sun nor rain. For this purpose an ordinary cloth of goats'-hair was requisite, and accordingly Moses was instructed to make a second covering, which was to be of this material, and to extend over the whole of the first, thus externally concealing it. This second covering was, like the first, to be in two portions (verses 9—11), each of them made up of several "breadths," but the two portions were not to be of the same size. Both were to be thirty cubits in length, but the hinder portion was to contain five "breadths," while the portion in front was to contain six. Thus the outer covering was six feet broader than the inner one: The object was the protection of the inner covering, which was overlapped at both ends by the outer one (verses 9, 12).

(7) **To be a covering.**—Literally, *to be a tent.* (See the first Note on the chapter.)

Eleven curtains—*i.e.*, eleven breadths. (See Note 2 on verse 1.)

(8) **Thirty cubits.**—The additional cubit on either side (comp. verse 2) would hang down and form a "valance" along the sides of the tent. (See verse 13.)

(9) **Thou . . . shalt double the sixth curtain in the forefront of the tabernacle.**—The additional "breadth" was to be doubled back upon itself, so giving a sort of finish to the roof in the front of the structure.

(12) **The remnant that remaineth.**—Even after the doubling back, the goats'-hair covering would be half a breadth wider than the linen one. This half-breadth was to be allowed to hang down at the back of the tent.

3. THE TWO OUTER COVERINGS.

(14) As the object of the two outer coverings must have been to keep out rain, we must suppose them to have protected not only the ridge of the roof, but, at any rate, the whole of the *mishkân*. Their length must, therefore, have been at least thirty cubits, and their breadth fourteen.

4. THE WALLS OF THE TABERNACLE.

(15—30) The various coverings which have been described had it for their object to roof over and protect an oblong chamber or "dwelling," within which God was to manifest Himself and to be worshipped. The directions which follow (verses 15—33) are for the construction of this chamber. It was to be enclosed by boards of shittim wood, fifteen feet high by two feet three inches wide, which were to be plated with gold, and made to stand upright by being inserted into solid sockets of silver. The two sides were to contain, each of them, twenty such boards, and thus to be forty-five feet long, while the connecting wall was to be composed of six such boards, together with two corner posts (verse 23), giving it a length, probably, of ten cubits, or fifteen feet.

(15) **Boards . . . of shittim wood.**—On the possibility of boards fifteen feet long by two feet three inches wide being cut from the *Acacia seyal*, see the last Note on chap. xxv. 5.

(17) **Two tenons.**—By "tenons" here are meant projections, probably round, from the end of each plank, made to fit into holes prepared for them in the "sockets." They were to be "set in order one against another": *i.e.*, placed regularly at certain intervals, so that each corresponded in position to its fellow.

(18) **On the south side southward.**—Rather, *on the south side to the right.* The tabernacle faced the east, and was regarded as looking in that direction. Thus its south wall was on the right.

(19) **Forty sockets.**—Each "socket" was to receive one of the "tenons." As there were twenty boards (verse 18), and two tenons to each board (verse 17), the sockets had to be forty.

one board for his two tenons, and two sockets under another board for his two tenons. (20) And for the second side of the tabernacle on the north side *there shall be* twenty boards: (21) and their forty sockets *of* silver; two sockets under one board, and two sockets under another board. (22) And for the sides of the tabernacle westward thou shalt make six boards. (23) And two boards shalt thou make for the corners of the tabernacle in the two sides. (24) And they shall be [1]coupled together beneath, and they shall be coupled together above the head of it unto one ring: thus shall it be for them both; they shall be for the two corners. (25) And they shall be eight boards, and their sockets *of* silver, sixteen sockets; two sockets under one board, and two sockets under another board.

(26) And thou shalt make bars *of* shittim wood; five for the boards of the one side of the tabernacle, (27) and five bars for the boards of the other side of the tabernacle, and five bars for the boards of the side of the tabernacle, for the two sides westward. (28) And the middle bar in the midst of the boards shall reach from end to end. (29) And thou shalt overlay the boards with gold, and make their rings *of* gold *for* places for the bars: and thou shalt overlay the bars with gold.

(30) And thou shalt rear up the tabernacle [a]according to the fashion thereof which was shewed thee in the mount.

(31) And thou shalt make a vail *of* blue, and purple, and scarlet, and fine twined linen of cunning work: with cherubims shall it be made: (32) and thou shalt hang it upon four pillars of shittim *wood* overlaid with gold: their hooks *shall be of* gold, upon the four sockets of silver. (33) And thou shalt hang up the vail under the taches, that thou mayest bring in thither within the vail the ark of the testimony: and the vail shall divide

1 Heb., *twinned.*

a ch. 25. 9. 40; Acts 7. 44; Heb. 8. 5.

---

(22) **For the sides of the tabernacle westward.**—Rather, *for the back of the tabernacle* (LXX., τὰ ὀπίσω). (See Note on verse 18.) The west is always regarded as "behind" by the Orientals.

Six boards.—Six boards, presumably of the same width with the others (verse 16), would extend a length of nine cubits only, or thirteen and a half feet. The tenth cubit seems to have been made up by the corner boards, or posts, which are counted with the "six". boards as forming the back of the tabernacle in verse 25.

(24) **They shall be coupled together beneath.**—The corner boards were to be coupled to the others in two places, below and above, in each place by means of one ring. Rings, through which passed the ends of the bars mentioned in verses 26—29, are supposed to be meant.

(25) **Sixteen sockets.**—Two for each corner board, and twelve for the six boards between them.

(26) **Bars of shittim wood.**—The object of the "bars" was to hold the "boards" together, and prevent there being any aperture between one board and another. They were fifteen in number, five for each of the three sides of the boarded space. The "middle bar" on each side was to extend from end to end of the tabernacle (verse 28), the four bars above and below being shorter, each coupling together probably one-half of the boards of its side. The bars were passed through "rings" attached to the boards (verse 29), each board having at least one such ring. It is probable that they were placed *outside* the tabernacle walls.

(27) **For the boards of the side of the tabernacle, for the two sides westward.**—This is quite unintelligible. Translate, *for the boards of the side of the tabernacle, which is at the back westward.*

(28) **In the midst of the boards.**—Rather, *midway in the boards*—equi-distant, *i.e.*, from the bottom and the top.

(30) **According to the fashion thereof which was shewed thee.**—See chap. xxv. 9, 40. However minute—even tediously minute—the description, there would necessarily have been a multitude of particulars, not to be described in words, where Moses would have to be guided by the pattern that he had seen.

5. The Vail, and the Position which it was to Occupy.

(31) **Thou shalt make a vail.**—It was of the essence of the *mishkân* that it should have an outer and an inner sanctuary, a place for the daily ministrations of the priests, and an *adytum* or *penetrale* of extreme holiness, in which was to be the Divine Presence, and into which the high priest alone was to be privileged to enter, and he but once in the year. (See chap. xxx. 10; Lev. xvi. 2—34; Heb. ix. 7.) The separation between these two chambers was to be made by a vail of the same materials and workmanship as the inner covering of the *mishkân* (verse 1).

(32) **Four pillars.**—These seem to have been true pillars or columns, and not tent-poles. They were probably of equal height, and equally spaced, and were perhaps connected at the top by a cornice or beam. Together with the vail they formed a screen, which shut off the "Holy of Holies" from the outer chamber. They were, doubtless, of the same height as the boards, *i.e.*, fifteen feet (verse 16).

Their hooks.—Each pillar was to have a hook near the top, whereto the vail was to be attached.

Upon the four sockets.—Heb., *upon four sockets.*—Each pillar was to have its "socket," into which it was to be inserted, and which was itself probably to be sunk into the ground.

(33) **Thou shall hang up the vail under the taches.**—The "taches" meant are the links whereby the two portions of the inner covering were connected together (verse 6). If "under the taches" means *directly* under them, we must regard the *mishkân* as divided into two chambers of equal size. It is possible, however, that "under" may be used with some vague-

unto you between the holy *place* and the
most holy. (34) And thou shalt put the
mercy seat upon the ark of the testimony in the most holy *place*. (35) And
thou shalt set the table without the vail,
and the candlestick over against the
table on the side of the tabernacle toward
the south: and thou shalt put the table
on the north side.

(36) And thou shalt make an hanging
for the door of the tent, *of* blue, and
purple, and scarlet, and fine twined linen,
wrought with needlework. (37) And thou
shalt make for the hanging five pillars *of*
shittim *wood*, and overlay them with gold,
and their hooks *shall be of* gold: and thou
shalt cast five sockets of brass for them.

CHAPTER XXVII.—(1) And thou
shalt make an altar *of* shittim wood,
five cubits long, and five cubits broad;
the altar shall be foursquare: and the
height thereof *shall be* three cubits.
(2) And thou shalt make the horns of it
upon the four corners thereof: his horns
shall be of the same: and thou shalt
overlay it with brass. (3) And thou shalt
make his pans to receive his ashes, and

---

ness, and that the "Holy of Holies" may in the tabernacle, as well as in the Temple, have been only half the size of the outer chamber.

That thou mayest bring in.—Heb., *and thou shalt bring in.*

6. The Position of the Furniture.

(34, 35) The sole furniture of the most holy place, or "Holy of Holies," was to be the ark, with its covering of the mercy-seat. In the "Holy Place" without the vail were to be the "table of shewbread" against the north wall, and the "golden candlestick" opposite to it, against the south wall. Intermediate between them, but advanced nearer the vail, was to be the "golden altar of incense" (chaps. xxx. 6, xl. 26), which, however, is not here mentioned.

7. The Hanging for the Door.

(36, 37) It is essential in the East to shut out light and heat, whence tents have always doors. These are usually made of a piece of cloth, which is raised for a man to enter, and falls behind him. But for a tent of the size described, which seems to have been above twenty-two feet high in the centre, something more was required. The "hanging" spoken of appears to have been a beautifully embroidered curtain, which could be either drawn up or let down, and which was attached by golden "hooks" to five pillars plated with gold, thus dividing the entrance into four equal spaces.

(37) **Five pillars.**—The odd number is surprising, especially compared with the "four pillars" of the interior (verse 32), until we remember that a tent such as that described must have a pillar, or tent-pole, in the middle of its gable-end, and an equal number of supports on either side. It is, in fact, this fifth pillar which, together with the use of the word *'ohel*, gives to the tent theory of Mr. Fergusson, now generally adopted, its solid basis.

Their hooks.—The hooks from which the hanging was to be suspended. (Comp. verse 32.)

Sockets of brass.—Rather, "of bronze." (See Note on chap. xxv. 3.)

XXVII.

The Altar of Burnt Offering.

(1) **Thou shalt make an altar.**—Heb., *the altar.* It is assumed that a sanctuary must have an altar, worship without sacrifice being unknown. (See chaps. v. 1—3, viii. 25—28, xii. 27, xviii. 12, xx. 24—26, &c.)

Of shittim wood.—This direction seems at first sight to conflict with those given in chap. xx. 24, 25, where altars were required to be either of earth or of unhewn stone. But the explanation of the Jewish commentators is probably correct, that what was here directed to be made was rather an "altar-case" than an altar, and that the true altar was the earth with which, at each halt in the wilderness, the "case" of shittim wood covered with bronze was filled. (So Jarchi, Kalisch, and others.)

Foursquare.—Ancient altars were either rectangular or circular, the square and the circle being regarded as perfect figures. A triangular altar was discovered by Mr. Layard in Mesopotamia, but even this had a circular top. In Hebrew architecture and furniture curved lines were for the most part avoided, probably as presenting greater difficulties than straight ones.

The height thereof . . . three cubits.—A greater height would have made it difficult to arrange the victims upon the altar. Otherwise the notion of perfection in form would probably have led to the altar being a cube.

(2) **The horns of it.**—It is not true to say, as Kalisch does, that "the altars of almost all ancient nations were frequently provided with horns." On the contrary, horns were, so far as is known, peculiar to Israelite altars. Originally, they would seem to have been mere ornaments at the four upper corners, but ultimately they came to be regarded as essential to an altar, and the virtue of the altar was thought to lie especially in them. The victims were bound to them (Ps. cxviii. 27); criminals clung to them (1 Kings i. 50, ii. 28); and the blood of sin offerings was smeared upon them for purposes of expiation (chap. xxix. 12; Lev. viii. 15, ix. 9, &c.).

His horns shall be of the same—*i.e.*, of one piece with the rest of the altar, not separate portions attached by nails or soldering. (Comp. chap. xxv. 19.)

Thou shalt overlay it with brass—*i.e.*, with bronze. All the woodwork of the tabernacle was overlaid with one metal or another. Here a metallic coating was especially necessary, to prevent the wood from being burnt.

(3) **His pans to receive his ashes.**— Scuttles, in which the ashes were placed for removal from the sanctuary, are intended. The word translated "to receive his ashes" is a rare one, and implies a mixture with the ashes of unburnt fat.

His shovels.—A right rendering. The "shovels" would be used in clearing away the ashes from off the altar.

his shovels, and his basons, and his flesh-
hooks, and his firepans: all the vessels
thereof thou shalt make *of* brass. (4) And
thou shalt make for it a grate of net-
work *of* brass; and upon the net shalt
thou make four brasen rings in the four
corners thereof. (5) And thou shalt put
it under the compass of the altar be-
neath, that the net may be even to the
midst of the altar. (6) And thou shalt
make staves for the altar, staves *of*
shittim wood, and overlay them with
brass. (7) And the staves shall be put
into the rings, and the staves shall be
upon the two sides of the altar, to bear
it. (8) Hollow with boards shalt thou
make it: as [1] it was shewed thee in the
mount, so shall they make *it*.

(9) And thou shalt make the court of
the tabernacle: for the south side south-
ward *there shall be* hangings for the court
of fine twined linen of an hundred cubits
long for one side: (10) and the twenty
pillars thereof and their twenty sockets
shall be of brass; the hooks of the pillars
and their fillets *shall be of* silver. (11) And
likewise for the north side in length
there shall be hangings of an hundred
cubits long, and his twenty pillars and
their twenty sockets *of* brass; the hooks
of the pillars and their fillets *of* silver.
(12) And *for* the breadth of the court on
the west side *shall be* hangings of fifty
cubits: their pillars ten, and their
sockets ten. (13) And the breadth of the
court on the east side eastward *shall be*

1 Heb., *he shewed.*

His basons.—Basins were needed to receive the blood of the victims (chap. xxiv. 6), which was cast from basins upon the foot of the altar.

His fleshhooks.—Implements with three prongs, used for arranging the pieces of the victim upon the altar. The priests' servants sometimes applied them to a different purpose (1 Sam. ii. 13).

His firepans.—The word here used is elsewhere translated either "snuffdishes," or "censers." Probably vessels employed in carrying embers from the brazen altar to the altar of incense (Levit. xvi. 12) are intended.

(4) **A grate of network.**—Rather, *a grating of network.* The position of the grating is doubtful. According to one view, it reached from the middle of the altar to its base, and protected the sides of the altar from the feet of the ministering priests. According to another, it surrounded the upper part of the altar, and was intended to catch any portions of the victims that accidentally fell off. There are no sufficient data to enable us to determine between these views.

Upon the net shalt thou make four brasen rings.—The brazen altar, like the ark and the table of shewbread, was to be carried by the priests when the Israelites changed their camping-ground. It therefore required "rings," like them (chap. xxv. 12, 26). These were, in the case of the altar, to be attached to the network, which must have been of a very solid and substantial character.

(5) **Under the compass of the altar beneath.**—The position of the network depends upon this expression. Was "the compass of the altar" its circumference at the top, or was it a belt or step encircling the altar half-way up? The low height of the altar—four feet six inches—would seem to make a "step" unnecessary; but the altar may undoubtedly have been surrounded by a "belt" for ornament.

(6) **Staves for the altar.**—See Note 2 on verse 4.

(8) **Hollow with boards.**—Compare the second Note on verse 1.

The Court of the Tabernacle.

(9–18) Almost every ancient temple stood within a sacred enclosure, which isolated it from the common working world, and rendered its religious character more distinctly apparent. Such enclosures were particularly affected by the Egyptians, and were usually oblong squares, surrounded by walls, with, for the most part, a single entrance. An open space of this kind, always desirable, was absolutely necessary where the sanctuary itself was covered in, since it would have been intolerable to kill and burn victims in a confined and covered space. The altar which has been described (verses 1—8) was necessarily placed outside the tabernacle, and formed the chief furniture of the court, for which directions are now given.

(9) **For the south side southward.**—Rather, *for the south side upon the right.* (See Note on chap. xxvi. 18.)

Hangings.—The word used is new and rare. It is rendered ἱστία, "sails," by the LXX., and seems to designate a coarse sail-cloth, woven with interstices, through which what went on inside the court might be seen. The court, it must be remembered, was open to all Israelites (Levit. i. 3, &c.).

Of fine twined linen.—Made of linen thread, *i.e.*, each thread having several strands; not "fine linen" in the modern sense.

(10) **And the twenty pillars thereof . . .**—Heb., *and its pillars, twenty* (in number), *and their bases, also twenty* (shall be) *of bronze.* Kalisch says that the pillars of the court were "of wood, not plated with metal" (*Comment.*, p. 371); but the present passage, and also chap. xxxviii. 10, rightly translated, contradict this view.

The hooks of the pillars.—Comp. chap. xxvi. 37. As the pillars were for the support of the "hangings," they required "hooks," whereto the "hangings" might be attached.

Their fillets.—Rather, *their connecting-rods.* The pillars of the court were to be united by rods, which would help to support the "hangings."

(11, 12) **The north side . . .** This side of the court was to be in exact correspondence with the south. The western side was to be of only half the length (fifty cubits), and required therefore only half the number of pillars and sockets.

(13) **On the east side eastward.**—Rather, *in front, towards the east.* Both the tabernacle and the Temple faced to the east, which was regarded as "the front of the world" by the Orientals generally. The

fifty cubits. (14) The hangings of one
side *of the gate shall be* fifteen cubits:
their pillars three, and their sockets
three. (15) And on the other side *shall be*
hangings fifteen *cubits:* their pillars
three, and their sockets three. (16) And
for the gate of the court *shall be* an
hanging of twenty cubits, *of* blue, and
purple, and scarlet, and fine twined
linen, wrought with needlework: *and*
their pillars *shall be* four, and their
sockets four. (17) All the pillars round
about the court *shall be* filleted with
silver; their hooks *shall be of* silver, and
their sockets *of* brass. (18) The length
of the court *shall be* an hundred cubits,
and the breadth [1]fifty every where, and
the height five cubits *of* fine twined
linen, and their sockets *of* brass. (19) All
the vessels of the tabernacle in all the
service thereof, and all the pins thereof,
and all the pins of the court, *shall be of*
brass.

(20) And thou shalt command the chil-
dren of Israel, that they bring thee pure
oil olive beaten for the light, to cause
the lamp [2]to burn always. (21) In the
tabernacle of the congregation without
the vail, which *is* before the testimony,
Aaron and his sons shall order it from
evening to morning before the LORD:
it shall be a statute for ever unto their
generations on the behalf of the children
of Israel.

1 Heb., *fifty by fifty.*

2 Heb., *to ascend up.*

---

belief was probably connected with the sun's rising, towards which men in early times looked anxiously. It was, however, a belief quite separate from sun-worship.

(14) **The hangings of one side.**—Rather, *at one side.* On three sides of the court—the south, the west, and the north—there was to be no interruption in the hangings—no entrance or gateway. But it was otherwise on the fourth side, towards the east. Here was to be the entrance to the court, and here consequently the line of hangings was to be broken in the middle. A curtain, similar to that at the east end of the tabernacle (chap. xxvi. 36), but hung on four pillars instead of five, and capable of being drawn up or down, was to give admission to the court on this side, and was to occupy twenty cubits out of the fifty which formed the entire width of the court. On either side would remain a space of fifteen cubits, which was to be occupied by "hangings," similar to those on the other three sides of the court. Each of these lengths of fifteen cubits required three pillars for its support. Thus the pillars on the east side were ten, as on the west.

(16) **For the gate of the court**—*i.e.,* the entrance.

An hanging.—The word is the same as that similarly translated in verses 36 and 37 of chap. xxvi.; and the description of the "hanging" is also, word for word, the same. It would contrast strongly with the plain white "sail-cloth" round the rest of the enclosure, and would clearly point out to all the place of entrance.

(17) **Filleted with silver.**—Rather, *united by silver rods.* (See the last Note on verse 10.)

(18) **The length . . . an hundred cubits.**—Comp. verse 9, where this is given as the length of the hangings.

The breadth fifty.—Comp. verse 12.

The height five cubits.—This had not been previously either stated or implied. It has been noted that, with one exception, all the measurements of the tabernacle and the court, as distinct from the furniture, are either five cubits or some multiple of five. The one exception is the length of the inner covering (chap. xxvi. 2), which was determined by the pitch of the roof.

THE VESSELS AND PINS.

(19) **All the vessels of the tabernacle**—*i.e.,* all those which had not already been appointed to be of a richer material. (Comp. chap. xxv. 38.) Bronze was the most convenient material for vessels, and maintained its place even in the magnificent Temple of Solomon (1 Kings vii. 15—45; 2 Kings xxv. 13, 14).

All the pins thereof.—These had not been previously mentioned; but the writer assumes it as known that every tent (*'ohel*), such as he has described, can only be erected by means of cords and tent-pegs, or "pins."

All the pins of the court.—The "pins of the court" seem to be pegs employed internally and externally to keep the pillars of the court in place. Their employment implies that of cords.

THE OIL FOR THE LAMP.

(20) **Thou shalt command the children of Israel that they bring thee pure olive oil.**—This instruction had been already given (chap. xxv. 2, 6), only not with such particularity. "Oil" had been required, but not "pure olive oil beaten." By this is meant the best possible olive oil—that which was obtained by "beating," or pounding in a mortar; which was free from various impurities that belonged to the oil crushed out, after the ordinary fashion, in a mill.

To cause the lamp to burn always—*i.e.,* every night without intermission. Josephus says that three lights were kept burning both night and day (*Ant. Jud.*, iii. 7, § 7); but there is nothing in Scripture to confirm this. The tabernacle would have received sufficient light during the daytime through the entrance curtain, which was of linen (chap. xxvi. 36), not to mention that the curtain may, when necessary, have been looped up. The lighting of the lamps every evening is distinctly asserted in chap. xxx. 8; their extinction in the morning appears from 1 Sam. iii. 3.

(21) **In the tabernacle of the congregation.**—Heb., *in the tent of meeting*—*i.e.,* the place where God met the earthly ruler of His people. (See chap. xxv. 22.)

Before the testimony—*i.e.,* in front of the Ark which contained "the Testimony," or "Two Tables." (See Note on chap. xvi. 34.)

Aaron and his sons.—The priestly character of Aaron and his descendants, laid down in the next chapter, is here anticipated.

From evening to morning.—See the second Note on verse 20.

CHAPTER XXVIII. — (1) And take thou unto thee Aaron thy brother, and his sons with him, from among the children of Israel, that he may minister unto me in the priest's office, *even* Aaron, Nadab and Abihu, Eleazar and Ithamar, Aaron's sons. (2) And thou shalt make holy garments for Aaron thy brother for glory and for beauty. (3) And thou shalt speak unto all *that are* wise hearted, whom I have filled with the spirit of wisdom, that they may make Aaron's garments to consecrate him, that he may minister unto me in the priest's office. (4) And these *are* the garments which they shall make; a breastplate, and an ephod, and a robe, and a broidered coat, a mitre, and a girdle: and they

XXVIII.

THE DESIGNATION OF AARON AND HIS SONS FOR THE PRIESTLY OFFICE, WITH DIRECTIONS FOR THEIR MINISTERIAL APPAREL.

(1) **Take thou unto thee Aaron thy brother.**—Heb., *make to draw near to thee Aaron thy brother.* Hitherto the position of Moses had been absolutely unique. He had been, from the time that Egypt was quitted, the one and only intermediary between God and the people—the one and only priest of the nation. Now this was to be changed. Perhaps in consequence of his original reluctance and want of faith (chaps. iii. 11, iv. 10—13), perhaps on account of Aaron's elder birth (chap. vii. 7), it pleased God to commit the office of ministering to Him in the tabernacle, not to Moses and his descendants, but to Aaron and those sprung from his loins. In this way Aaron and his sons were "drawn near" to Moses in respect of rank, position, and dignity.

That he may minister to me in the priest's office.—Or, "that he may be priest to me." The actual investiture of Aaron with the priestly office did not take place until some time after the tabernacle was completed. It is related in Lev. viii.; and his first priestly acts are recorded in the following chapter (Lev. ix. 8—22).

Nadab and Abihu.—On Nadab and Abihu, the two eldest sons of Aaron, see chaps. vi. 23, and xxiv. 1.

Eleazar and Ithamar.—The priestly office was, in fact, continued in the families of these two. Eleazar became high priest at the death of Aaron (Num. xx. 28), and was succeeded by his son Phinehas, whom we find high priest in the time of Joshua (Josh. xxii. 13) and afterwards (Judges xx. 28). At a later date, but under what circumstances is unknown, the high priesthood passed to the line of Ithamar, to which Eli belonged.

(2) **Holy garments.**—Though holiness is, strictly speaking, a personal quality, yet all nations have felt it right to regard as "holy," in a certain modified sense, all those material objects which are connected with religion and employed in the worship of God. Hence we hear, both in Scripture and elsewhere, of "holy places," "holy vessels," "holy books," "holy garments." These last are required especially for the ministrants in holy places, who need to be marked out by some evident signs from the body of the worshippers. In Egypt the ministering priests in temples always wore peculiar dresses; and probably there was no nation in the time of Moses which, if it possessed a class of priests, did not distinguish them by some special costume, at any rate when they were officiating. The natural instinct which thus exhibited itself, received Divine sanction by the communications which were made to Moses in Sinai, whereby special dresses were appointed both for the high priest and for the ordinary priests.

For glory and for beauty.—These words have great force. God would have His priests richly, as well as decently, apparelled, for two objects—(1) For glory—to glorify them—to give them an exalted position in the eyes of the nation, to cause them to be respected, and their office to be highly regarded; (2) for beauty—to make the worship of the sanctuary more beautiful than it would otherwise have been, to establish a harmony between the richly-adorned tabernacle and those who ministered in it; to give to the service of the sanctuary the highest artistic, as well as the highest spiritual, perfection. The relation of art to religion is a subject on which volumes have been written, and which cannot be discussed here; but God's regard for "beauty" is here brought prominently before us, and no honest exegesis can ignore the pregnant fact that when God was pleased to give directions for His worship upon earth, they were made subservient, not only to utility and convenience, but to beauty. Beauty, it would seem, is not a thing despised by the Creator of the universe.

(3) **Thou shalt speak unto all that are wise hearted.**—By "all that are wise hearted" we must understand all that had the special knowledge which would enable them to give effectual aid in the production of such garments as were about to be commanded. The Hebrews regarded the heart as the seat of knowledge, with perhaps neither more nor less scientific accuracy than underlies our own current modes of speech whereby the heart is made the seat of the affections.

Whom I have filled with the spirit of wisdom.—Few passages in the Bible are more antagonistic than this to the general current of modern thought. God speaks of Himself as having infused His Spirit into the hearts of men, in order to enable them to produce satisfactory priestly garments. Moderns suppose such things to be quite beneath the notice of the Creator of the universe. But it has to be remembered, on the other hand, (1) that God is the fountain whence all knowledge is derived; (2) that He alone knows what is beneath Him and what is not beneath Him; and (3) that dress is not a wholly insignificant matter, or so much would not have been said in Scripture about it (Gen. iii. 21, xxxvii. 3, xli. 42; Lev. viii. 7—9, xvi. 4; Num. xv. 38, &c.). Garments intended "for glory and for beauty" (verse 2) required artistic power in those who were to make them; and artistic power, like all other intellectual excellence, is the gift of God.

To consecrate him.—Investiture in the holy garments was a part of the ceremony of consecration. (See Lev. viii. 7—9 and 13.)

(4) **These are the garments.**—The garments peculiar to the high priest are taken first, and described with great elaboration in thirty-six verses (4—39). The most conspicuous was the breastplate, described in verses 13—30, and here mentioned first of all. Next

shall make holy garments for Aaron
thy brother, and his sons, that he may
minister unto me in the priest's office.
(5) And they shall take gold, and blue,
and purple, and scarlet, and fine linen.
(6) And they shall make the ephod *of*
gold, *of* blue, and *of* purple, *of* scarlet,
and fine twined linen, with cunning
work. (7) It shall have the two shoulder-
pieces thereof joined at the two edges
thereof; and *so* it shall be joined to-
gether. (8) And the [1] curious girdle of
the ephod, which *is* upon it, shall be of
the same, according to the work thereof;
even of gold, *of* blue, and purple, and
scarlet, and fine twined linen. (9) And
thou shalt take two onyx stones, and
grave on them the names of the children
of Israel: (10) six of their names on one
stone, and *the other* six names of the rest
on the other stone, according to their
birth. (11) [a] With the work of an en-
graver in stone, *like* the engravings of a
signet, shalt thou engrave the two stones
with the names of the children of Israel:
thou shalt make them to be set in ouches
of gold. (12) And thou shalt put the two
stones upon the shoulders of the ephod

1 Or, *embroidered.*

a Wis. 18. 24.

---

to this came the peculiar vestment called the "ephod," a sort of jerkin or waistcoat, upon which the breastplate was worn (described in verses 6—12). Under the ephod was the long robe of blue, called "the robe of the ephod," which may be considered as the main garment, and which is described in verses 31—35. Upon his head the high priest wore a "mitre" or turban (described in verses 36—38); and inside his "robe" he wore a linen shirt or tunic, secured by a girdle (verse 39). Underneath the tunic he wore linen drawers (verses 42, 43). Nothing is said as to any covering for his feet; but it is probable that they were protected by sandals.

(5) **They shall take gold, and blue.**—Heb., *the gold and the blue, &c.*—*i.e.*, they (the wise-hearted men of verse 3) shall receive (from Moses) the (necessary) gold, blue, &c., for the construction of the vestments. It is to be noted that the materials are the same as those employed for the vail and curtains of the sanctuary (chap. xxvi. 1, 31, 36), but with the further addition of gold and precious stones (verses 9, 17—21).

1. THE EPHOD.

(6—12) The ephod was, as already observed (Note on verse 4), a sort of jerkin or waistcoat. It was made in two pieces, a front piece and a back piece, which were joined together at the shoulders, apparently by a seam (verse 7). The pieces descended to the waist; and there one or other of them was expanded into a band, called "the curious girdle of the ephod," which being passed round the waist and fastened, kept both front and back pieces in place (verse 8). On either shoulder was an onyx stone set in gold (verses 9—11), and engraved with the names of six of the tribes.

(6) **With cunning work.**—On this phrase, see Note on chap. xxvi. 1.

(7) **The two shoulder pieces thereof.**—Rather, *two shoulder pieces.*

(8) **The curious girdle.**—The word *khêsheb*, which is thus translated, means properly "device," "ornamental work," and has not in itself the sense of "belt" or "girdle." Still, there is no reason to doubt that the *khêsheb* of the ephod was in fact a girdle, as Josephus calls it (*Ant. Jud.*, iii. 7, § 4), though named from the peculiar skill displayed in its patterning. Josephus says it was "a girdle dyed of many hues, with gold interwoven in it."

Shall be of the same.—Not sewn on, but woven continuously with the front or back piece.

(9) **Two onyx stones.**—The *shôham* of the Hebrews has been regarded by some as the emerald, by others as the beryl; but it is probably either the stone usually called the onyx, or that variety which is known as the sardonyx—a stone of three layers—black, white, and red. (See Joseph., *Ant. Jud.*, iii. 7, § 5.) Emeralds could not have been cut by any process known at the time. Onyx and sardonyx were used from a very early period, as stones for signets, both in Egypt and elsewhere.

And grave on them the names of the children of Israel.—That gem-engraving was practised from a remote antiquity both in Egypt and in Babylonia appears from the remains found in those countries. The signet cylinders of Chaldæan kings are regarded by the best Assyriologists as going back, at least, to B.C. 2,000. The signets of Egyptian monarchs reach, at any rate, to the twelfth dynasty, which is perhaps nearly as early. The hardest kinds of stone—diamond, ruby, emerald, sapphire, topaz—defied the art of the time; but stones of the second class—sard, carnelian, onyx, beryl, jasper, lapis lazuli—readily yielded to the engraver's tools. There is no difficulty in supposing that among the Israelites were to be found persons who had been engaged in Egyptian workshops during the servitude, and were acquainted with Egyptian art in all its principal departments. The "names" to be engraved were doubtless the "tribe" names, as explained by Josephus.

(10) **The other six names of the rest.**—Heb., *the remaining six names.* Either Levi was omitted, or Joseph's name took the place of Ephraim's and Manasseh's.

According to their birth—*i.e.*, in the order of their seniority.

(11) **The engravings of a signet.**—Compare Note 2 on verse 9. Signets had been already mentioned in Gen. xxxviii. 18, 25, xli. 42. Those of Egypt were for the most part rings, with cylindrical bezels turning upon an axis. Those of Babylonia were cylinders, which were commonly worn by a string round the wrist. The engraving of the Babylonian cylinders is frequently of a very fine quality.

Thou shalt make them to be set in ouches of gold.—The setting intended seems to have been a sort of open or filigree work, such as is very common in Egyptian ornaments of the time. The term "ouche" —more properly "nouch"—is derived from the old French "nouche," a buckle or clasp (see Skeat's *Etymol. Dict.*, § 5).

(12) **For stones of memorial unto the children of Israel.**—Rather, *for the children of Israel.* The intention was that the stones should be "stones of memorial" *to* God, on behalf of Israel; should remind

for stones of memorial unto the children
of Israel: and Aaron shall bear their
names before the LORD upon his two
shoulders for a memorial. (13) And thou
shalt make ouches *of* gold; (14) and two
chains *of* pure gold at the ends; *of*
wreathen work shalt thou make them,
and fasten the wreathen chains to the
ouches.
(15) And thou shalt make the breast-
plate of judgment with cunning work;
after the work of the ephod thou shalt
make it; *of* gold, *of* blue, and *of* purple,
and *of* scarlet, and *of* fine twined linen,
shalt thou make it. (16) Foursquare it
shall be *being* doubled; a span *shall be*
the length thereof, and a span *shall be*
the breadth thereof. (17) And thou shalt
[1]set in it settings of stones, *even* four
rows of stones: *the first* row *shall be* a

1 Heb., *fill in it fillings of stone.*

God that the high priest represented all the tribes, and pleaded before Him on their behalf, and in their name. The tribes were represented doubly in the costume of the high priest, by the onyx stones and by the stones of the breastplate.

2. THE BREASTPLATE.

(13—30) The space devoted to the "breastplate" is indicative of its high importance. It was the most costly, most magnificent, and most conspicuous of the high priest's garments, while at the same time it was the most mysterious. Externally it was a blaze of gold and jewels; internally it held those strange and precious objects known as "the Urim and the Thummim" (verse 30), by means of which the Divine will was made known to the high priest, and through him to the people. The basis of the garment was a linen fabric of similar materials and workmanship with the ephod (verse 15), square in shape, about nine inches each way, and "doubled," so as to form internally a bag or pocket. Upon this linen groundwork were fastened twelve "stones," or jewels, set in an open-work of gold, and arranged in four rows, three in each (verses 17—21). These stones covered probably the greater portion of the external surface of the breastplate. To its two upper corners were attached two rings of gold, which were made fast by means of gold chains to buttons ("ouches") on the upper part of the ephod; and to its two lower corners were attached similar rings, which were fastened by a lace to rings of the same material on the lower part of the ephod (verses 13, 14, 22—28).

(13) **Ouches of gold.**—"Buttons" or "rosettes" of similar open-work to that which formed the setting of the onyx stones upon the shoulders of the ephod (verse 11). These "buttons" must have been sewn on to the ephod.

(14) **Chains . . . at the ends.**—Rather, *chains of equal length*, or, perhaps, *of wreathen work.*

Of wreathen work.—Heb., *after the manner of a rope.* Such chains are often seen round the necks of Persian officials in the Persepolitan sculptures, and appear also to have been used by the grandees of Egypt. They were composed of a number of gold wires twisted together. The chains spoken of in this place are the same as those mentioned in verses 22—25. Their object was to attach the two upper corners of the breastplate to the upper part of the ephod.

(15) **The breastplate of judgment.**—The word *khoshen* does not really signify "breastplate," but "ornament." It was the main ornament of the priestly attire. It was called "the ornament *of judgment*" on account of its containing the Urim and Thummim, whereby God's "judgments" were made known to His people. (See Note on verse 30.)

With cunning work.—Rather, *of the work of the weaver.* (Comp. chaps. xxvi. 1, 31, xxviii. 6.)

(16) **Foursquare it shall be.**—On the idea of perfection connected with the square, see Note on chap. xxvii. 1. But for this, twelve gems would probably have been arranged in the shape of an oblong.

Doubled.—Symmachus translates *khoshen* by δόχιον, "a receptacle" or "bag;" and if the Urim and the Thummim, being material objects, were to be "put in" it (verse 30), such a construction would seem to have been absolutely necessary. Hence the "doubling," which would not have been needed merely for strength, since linen corselets, stout enough to resist the blow of a sword, were among the manufactures of Egypt, and could no doubt have been produced by the Hebrews.

A span.—The "span" was reckoned at half a cubit, or about nine inches.

(17—19) **Set in it settings of stones . . .** There is always considerable difficulty in identifying ancient with modern gems, the etymologies of the words being frequently uncertain, the names (where they have survived) having sometimes changed their meaning, and the opinions of early commentators, who might seem to speak with some authority, being discrepant. In the present case, scarcely one of the twelve stones can be said to be determined with certainty. 1. The *ôdem*, identified by the LXX. and the Vulg. with the "sard," has been regarded as the ruby, the carbuncle, and the carnelian. Etymologically the word means "red," or "the red stone." The ruby is certainly wrong, since ancient engravers could not cut it. Either "sard" or "carnelian" is probably intended, both being common in Egypt. 2. The *pitdah* is certainly not the topaz, which could no more be cut than the ruby. If the word is derived, as supposed, from a root meaning "pale," the chrysolite, which resembles a pale topaz, but is far softer, may be meant. 3. The *bâreketh* is rendered *smaragdus*, "emerald," by the LXX. and Vulg.; but neither could the emerald be cut by the ancient engravers. The word means "brightly flashing," which tells us next to nothing. "Beryl" and "a kind of corundum" have been suggested; but neither is particularly sparkling. 4. The *nôphek*, translated ἄνθραξ by the LXX. and Josephus, may well be the "carbuncle," as is now generally supposed. It cannot, any more than the *ôdem*, be the ruby. 5. The *sappir* one might have supposed by its name to be certainly the "sapphire;" but this, again, is a gem which ancient engravers could not cut. It would seem that here we have one of the cases where the name has been transferred from one stone to another, the modern "lapis lazuli" being the gem which was called "sapphire" by the ancients. 6. The *yahălôm* is certainly not the "diamond," which is the hardest of all gems. The LXX. and Vulg. translate by "jasper" (ἴασπις, *jaspis*); but this seems really to have been the twelfth stone. Other renderings are mere conjectures, and the *yahălôm* must be regarded as unknown. 7. The

[1]sardius, a topaz, and a carbuncle: *this*
shall be the first row. (18) And the second
row *shall be* an emerald, a sapphire, and
a diamond. (19) And the third row a
ligure, an agate, and an amethyst.
(20) And the fourth row a beryl, and an
onyx, and a jasper: they shall be set in
gold in their [2]inclosings. (21) And the
stones shall be with the names of the
children of Israel, twelve, according to
their names, *like* the engravings of a
signet; every one with his name shall
they be according to the twelve tribes.
(22) And thou shalt make upon the breast-
plate chains at the ends *of* wreathen
work *of* pure gold. (23) And thou shalt
make upon the breastplate two rings of
gold, and shalt put the two rings on the
two ends of the breastplate. (24) And
thou shalt put the two wreathen *chains*
of gold in the two rings *which are* on the
ends of the breastplate. (25) And *the*
other two ends of the two wreathen
chains thou shalt fasten in the two
ouches, and put *them* on the shoulder-
pieces of the ephod before it. (26) And
thou shalt make two rings of gold, and
thou shalt put them upon the two ends
of the breastplate in the border thereof,
which *is* in the side of the ephod inward.
(27) And two *other* rings of gold thou shalt
make, and shalt put them on the two
sides of the ephod underneath, toward
the forepart thereof, over against the
other coupling thereof, above the curious
girdle of the ephod. (28) And they shall
bind the breastplate by the rings thereof
unto the rings of the ephod with a lace
of blue, that *it* may be above the curious
girdle of the ephod, and that the breast-
plate be not loosed from the ephod.
(29) And Aaron shall bear the names of

1 Or, *ruby.*

2 Heb., *fillings.*

---

leshem, rendered "ligure" by the LXX., the Vulgate, Josephus, and our translators, is probably the stone known to the ancients as *lapis ligurius*, but what that stone was is a matter of great uncertainty. It has been regarded as amber, as jacinth, and as tourmaline; but amber does not admit of engraving, while jacinth and tourmaline are pure conjectures. This stone, then, must also be regarded as unknown. 8. The *shevo*, rendered *achates*, "agate," by the LXX. and the Vulg., is generally allowed to have been that stone, which was well known to the ancients, and widely used for engraving. 9. The *akhlâmâh* was regarded as the amethyst by the LXX., the Vulgate, and Josephus; but it has been suggested that it may have been "malachite" (Knobel); and there is no disproving the suggestion. Still the amethyst, which is easily engraved, and was well known in Egypt, should find a place in the present list, and may well have been intended by the *akhlâmâh*. 10. The *tarshish*, by its name, should be a stone brought from Tarshish, which is either Tarsus or Tartessus. Some suppose it to have been the beryl, some the chrysolite, others the turquoise. There are really no sufficient grounds for identifying it with any known gem. 11. The *shôham* has been already discussed (see Note on verse 9), and identified with the onyx, or the sardonyx. 12. The *yâsh'peh* should, by its name, be the "jasper," which was one of the stones most used in Egypt, and which could scarcely have been absent from the present list. The LXX., however, translate "onyx," Josephus and the Vulgate "beryl;" so that here again there is uncertainty. The views of the present writer may be best presented to the reader by means of a table:—

1st Row of Gems . .	Odem (the Sard)	Pitdah (the Chrysolite)	Barĕketh (uncertain)
2nd Row .	Nôphek (the Carbuncle)	Sappir (the Lapis Lazuli)	Yahălôm (uncertain)
3rd Row . .	Leshem (uncertain)	Shevo (the Agate)	Akhlâmâh (the Amethyst)
4th Row . .	Tarshish (uncertain)	Shôham (the Onyx or the Sardonyx)	Yâsh'peh (the Jasper)

(20) **They shall be set in gold in their inclosings.**—Or, *in their settings.* Every gem was to be enclosed in its own setting of gold.

(21) **The stones shall be with the names of the children of Israel.**—Rather, *the stones shall be according to the names*, &c.—twelve, neither more nor fewer.

Every one with his name . . .—Rather, *each stone, according to its name* (*i.e.*, the name engraved upon it), *shall be* (or, *stand*) *for one of the twelve tribes.*

(22) **Chains at the ends.**—Rather, *chains of equal length*; or, *chains of wreathen work.* (See Note on verse 14.)

Of wreathen work.—Heb., *after the manner of ropes.*

(23) **Two rings on the two ends**—*i.e.*, on the two upper corners of the breastplate. The chains were to be passed through the two rings, which they were then to unite with the "ouches" of the ephod. (See verses 13, 14.)

(26) **Thou shalt make two rings**— *i.e.*, "two other rings." These were to be put on the two lower corners of the breastplate, "in the border thereof," or at its extreme edge.

(27, 28) Two gold rings were also to be sewn on to the ephod, low down and in front, so as just to appear above the "curious girdle of the ephod," and the lower rings of the breastplate were to be laced to these rings by a "lace of blue." The breastplate was thus securely attached to the ephod, and showed above the "curious girdle" without covering it.

(29) **Aaron shall bear the names . . . upon his heart.**—Comp. verse 12. The high priest was to be wholly identified with the people; to be one with them in affection no less than in action; to bear their names on his shoulders, as supporting them and wrestling for them, while he also bore their names on his heart, as loving them and feeling for them. Thus he was continually to present before God a two-fold "memorial" of His people, and to make a sort of double appeal, on the one hand, to God's power, and, on the other hand, to His mercy and loving-kindness.

the children of Israel in the breastplate
of judgment upon his heart, when he
goeth in unto the holy *place*, for a me-
morial before the LORD continually.
(30) And thou shalt put in the breast-
plate of judgment the Urim and the
Thummim; and they shall be upon
Aaron's heart, when he goeth in before
the LORD: and Aaron shall bear the
judgment of the children of Israel upon
his heart before the LORD continually.
(31) And thou shalt make the robe of
the ephod all *of* blue. (32) And there
shall be an hole in the top of it, in the
midst thereof: it shall have a binding
of woven work round about the hole of
it, as it were the hole of an habergeon,
that it be not rent. (33) And *beneath* up-
on the [1] hem of it thou shalt make pome-
granates *of* blue, and *of* purple, and *of*
scarlet, round about the hem thereof;
and bells of gold between them round
about: (34) a golden bell and a pome-
granate, a golden bell and a pomegran-
ate, upon the hem of the robe round
about. (35) [a] And it shall be upon Aaron
to minister: and his sound shall be
heard when he goeth in unto the holy
place before the LORD, and when he
cometh out, that he die not.

1 Or, *skirts.*

a Ecclus. 45. 9.

---

(30) **Thou shalt put in the breastplate of judgment the Urim and the Thummim.**—Comp. Levit. viii. 8. The expression used is identical with that employed in chap. xxv. 15, 21 with respect to putting the Two Tables into the Ark of the Covenant, and can scarcely have any other meaning than the literal placing of one thing inside another. It has been already shown (see Note on verse 16) that the breastplate was a bag, and so capable of being used as a receptacle. The words "Urim and Thummim" mean literally, "lights and perfections," or, if the plural be one of dignity, "light and perfection" (Aquila and Symmachus translate by φωτισμοὶ καὶ τελειότητες; the LXX., by ἡ δήλωσις καὶ ἡ ἀλήθεια; the Vulg. by *doctrina et veritas*). The question arises, what do these two words, as here used, designate? Do they designate material objects; if so, what objects? In favour of their designating material objects are (1) the expressions, "thou shalt put in the breastplate the Urim and the Thummim," "they shall be upon Aaron's heart," "he put in the breastplate the Urim and the Thummim" (Levit. viii. 8); (2) the fact that the words are accompanied by the article, on this, the first mention of them, as if they were familiar objects, well known at the time to the people generally; and (3) the explanations of Philo and Josephus, which, while they differ in all other respects, agree in this, that material objects are intended. But, if so, what objects? The two sides of the breastplate, says Philo (*De Monarch.*, ii. 5). But these were not "put in" the breastplate after it was complete, as implied in chap. xxviii. 30; Levit. viii. 8. The twelve jewels, says Josephus; but the present passage, taken in conjunction with verses 17—21, distinguishes the Urim and Thummim from them. Some small objects which the bag of the breastplate could hold, and with which the people had long been familiar, can alone answer the requirements of the case. Most modern critics are thus far agreed; but when the further question is asked, what were these objects? the greatest difference appears. Diamonds, cut and uncut; slips of metal, marked with "yes" and "no"; lots, of some kind or other; and small images, like the *teraphim* (Gen. xxxi. 19), are among the suggestions. A very slight examination of the arguments by which these various views are supported is sufficient to show that certainty on the subject is unattainable. Probability, however, seems on the whole to be in favour of a connection between divination by *teraphim* and consultation of God by Urim and Thummim (Judges xvii. 5; xviii. 14, 17, 20; Hosea iii. 4), whence it is reasonable to conclude that the Urim and Thummim were small images, by which God had been consulted in the past, and by which Moses was now authorised to state that He would be consulted in the future. How the consultation was made, and the decision given, is a question still more obscure than that which has been just considered, and one which seems to the present writer to admit of no solution. The reader who is curious upon the point may be referred to Dean Plumptre's article on "Urim and Thummim," in Dr. W. Smith's *Dictionary of the Bible*, where the views propounded are ingenious, if not altogether satisfactory.

3. THE ROBE OF THE EPHOD.

(31—35) The "robe of the ephod" was a frock or tunic, reaching from the neck to below the knees. It was put on over the head, for which a hole was left (verse 32). Josephus says that it had no sleeves; and it would seem that the upper portion, above the waist, was wholly, or almost wholly, concealed by the ephod and breastplate; but the lower portion, from the waist downwards, formed the outer dress of the high priest, and was conspicuous. The plain blue contrasted well with the variegated ephod and the sparkling breastplate. The robe had no ornament excepting round the bottom, where it was fringed with alternate bells and pomegranates. The pomegranates were a decoration, and nothing more; but the bells served a purpose, which is explained in verse 35.

(32) **As it were the hole of a habergeon.**—Linen corselets, or "habergeons," were common in Egypt, and were shaped as is here indicated. The word used for "habergeon," *takhărah*, is thought to be Egyptian.

(33) **Pomegranates.** — The pomegranate was a favourite ornament in Assyria, but not in Egypt. It appears from Josh. vii. 21 that the fabrics of Babylon were carried by the merchants into Syria at a date not much later than this, whence we may conclude that they circulated also in Arabia and Egypt.

Bells of gold.—The bell is also more Assyrian than Egyptian. Its use as an article of priestly costume has no direct parallel, nor are bells known to have been employed in the religious services of any ancient nation. The statement that Persian kings wore bells rests upon no sufficient authority. We seem to have here the introduction of an entirely new religious usage.

(35) **And his sound shall be heard.**—Rather, *that its sound may be heard.* The great object of the

(36) And thou shalt make a plate *of* pure gold, and grave upon it, *like* the engravings of a signet, HOLINESS TO THE LORD.
(37) And thou shalt put it on a blue lace, that it may be upon the mitre; upon the forefront of the mitre it shall be.
(38) And it shall be upon Aaron's forehead, that Aaron may bear the iniquity of the holy things, which the children of Israel shall hallow in all their holy gifts; and it shall be always upon his forehead, that they may be accepted before the LORD.
(39) And thou shalt embroider the coat of fine linen, and thou shalt make the mitre *of* fine linen, and thou shalt make the girdle *of* needlework.
(40) And for Aaron's sons thou shalt make coats, and thou shalt make for them girdles, and bonnets shalt thou

---

bells was to make known to the people, by a sensible manifestation, every movement of their representative, every act that he performed on their behalf. The bells enabled them to follow in their thoughts the entire service that he was engaged in, to join their prayers and praises with his, and offer to God a common worship. So important was this union of priest and people in the worship of God regarded, that death was denounced on the high priest who should minister in the sanctuary without this essential garment.

4. The Mitre.

(36—39) The head-dress of the high priest was to be of fine white linen (*shêsh*) and appears by the description of Josephus (*Ant. Jud.* iii. 7, § 3) to have been a turban, made of several thick swathes or folds in the usual way. It was to be adorned in front with a plate of pure gold bearing the inscription "Holiness to Jehovah," which was to be attached to the linen fabric by a ribbon or "lace" of blue.

(36) **Thou shalt make a plate.**—The plate is so much of the essence of the mitre that it is put forward first, as that whereto all the rest is subordinate. It was to be "of pure gold," and "fastened on high upon the mitre" (chap. xxxix. 31); so catching the eye even more than the breastplate, and drawing men's special attention. But the plate itself was only the vehicle for an inscription, and thus men's attention would be especially directed to that. It taught the great truth that religion culminates in "Holiness to Jehovah," without which all else is worthless—forms, ceremonies, priestly attire, sacrifice, prayer, are mockeries. It required primarily the high priest himself to be holy; but it was a call also to the whole nation, whose representative the high priest was, that they should be "a holy nation," "a kingdom of priests" (chap. xix. 6), and should consecrate themselves heart and soul to Jehovah.

(37) **Thou shalt put it on a blue lace.**—Compare chap. xxxix. 31, where we read "they tied unto it a lace of blue." Probably the two ends of the plate were perforated, and a blue lace or cord passed through the holes and tied to the plate, which was then put in front of the turban and kept in place by the two cords being tied together at the back of the head.

(38) **That Aaron may bear the iniquity of the holy things.**—The "holy things" are the offerings brought by the people. These would always have some "iniquity" attaching to them, some imperfection, owing to the imperfection of human nature and the mixed character of human motives. The high priest's official holiness enabled him to present to God offerings thus imperfect without offending Him. It was accepted as purging the offerings from their impurity.

It shall be always upon his forehead—that is to say, during his ministrations.

5. The Inner Tunic or "Coat."

(39) The garments hitherto described have been the outer garments. To these are now added the inner ones, of which there was but little to be said. They consisted of linen drawers (verses 42, 43), a linen tunic or shirt, woven in a peculiar way, and, to confine the tunic, a girdle, which was to be of many colours (chap. xxxix. 29), and ornamented with embroidery.

Thou shalt embroider.—It is generally agreed that this is a wrong rendering. Kalisch translates, "thou shalt weave." Gesenius, "thou shalt work in chequer." Canon Cook, "thou shalt weave in diaper work." The word used, which is a rare one, probably designates some peculiar kind of weaving.

The coat.—"Coat" is an unfortunate translation. The *ketôneth* (comp. Gr. χιτών) was a long white linen tunic or shirt, having tight-fitting sleeves, and reaching nearly to the feet. The sleeves must certainly have shown, as they were the only covering of the priest's arms; and the lower part of the tunic probably showed below the "robe of the ephod."

6. The Inner Girdle.

It appears from chap. xxxix. 29 that the girdle was to be "of fine twined linen, and blue, and purple, and scarlet," like the ephod (verse 6). It was not, however, to be woven of these colours, but to have them worked into it with the needle. As it was worn immediately above the tunic and underneath the robe of the ephod (Lev. viii. 7), little, if any, of it could have been seen. Perhaps, however, the ends may have depended below the robe of the ephod.

7. The Ministerial Attire of the Priests.

(40) **For Aaron's sons thou shalt make coats**—*i.e.*, linen tunics like that of the high priest already described (see the last Note on verse 39), but not woven in any peculiar fashion.

Girdles.—Perhaps similar to the inner girdle of the high priest, but nowhere described particularly.

Bonnets.—Rather, *caps.* Plain, close-fitting caps, like those so commonly worn in Egypt, seem to be intended. The word used, *migbâ'ah*, is derived from *gâbia'*, "a cup" or "basin."

For glory and for beauty.—It is certainly remarkable that so plain a dress as that of the ordinary priests—a white tunic, a girdle, which may or may not have been embroidered, and a plain white close-fitting cap—should be regarded as sufficing "for glory and for beauty." White robes, however, are in Scripture constantly represented as eminently glorious (Dan. vii. 9; Mark ix. 3; John xx. 12; Acts i. 10; Rev. iv. 4, vi. 11, vii. 9—14, xv. 6, &c.).

make for them, for glory and for beauty.
(41) And thou shalt put them upon Aaron
thy brother, and his sons with him;
and shalt anoint them, and [1] consecrate
them, and sanctify them, that they
may minister unto me in the priest's
office. (42) And thou shalt make them
linen breeches to cover [2] their naked-
ness; from the loins even unto the
thighs they shall [3] reach: (43) and they
shall be upon Aaron, and upon his sons,
when they come in unto the tabernacle
of the congregation, or when they come
near unto the altar to minister in the
holy *place*; that they bear not iniquity,
and die: *it shall be* a statute for ever
unto him and his seed after him.

CHAPTER XXIX.—(1) And this *is*
the thing that thou shalt do unto them
to hallow them, to minister unto me in
the priest's office: [a] Take one young
bullock, and two rams without blemish,
(2) and unleavened bread, and cakes un-
leavened tempered with oil, and wafers
unleavened anointed with oil: *of* wheaten
flour shalt thou make them. (3) And
thou shalt put them into one basket,
and bring them in the basket, with the
bullock and the two rams. (4) And Aaron
and his sons thou shalt bring unto the
door of the tabernacle of the congrega-
tion, and shalt wash them with water.
(5) And thou shalt take the garments,
and put upon Aaron the coat, and the

1 Heb., *fill their hand.*

2 Heb., *flesh of their nakedness.*

3 Heb., *be.*

a Lev. 8. 2.

---

(41) **Thou shalt put them upon Aaron . . . and his sons.**—Moses was by these words commanded to take the part in the consecration of Aaron and his sons which he is related to have taken in Lev. viii. 6—30.

And shalt anoint them.—See the comment on chap. xxix. 7—9.

(42) **Thou shalt make them linen breeches.**—Rather, *linen drawers.* Drawers reaching from the waist to a little above the knee were the sole garment of many in Egypt, a necessary garment of all. Their object was as here stated.

(43) **The tabernacle of the congregation.**—Heb., *the tent of meeting.*

The holy place seems to be here the court of the tabernacle, within which the altar was to be set up (chap. xl. 6, 29).

That they bear not iniquity, and die.—The death penalty is threatened against the sin of ministering without the garments needed for decency, as against the sin of neglecting to wear the robe of the ephod (verse 35). In both cases a Divine vengeance, rather than a legal punishment, is probably intended.

XXIX.

The Form of Consecration for the Priests.

(1) **This is the thing that thou shalt do unto them to hallow them.**—The consecration of the priests had been commanded in the preceding chapter (chap. xxviii. 41). The method of it is now laid down. It consists of five things:—(1) Ablution (verse 4); (2) Investiture (verses 5—9); (3) Chrism, or anointing (verse 7); (4) Sacrifice (verses 10—23); and (5) Filling the hand (verse 24). All of these were symbolical acts, typical of things spiritual—ablution, of the putting away of impurity; investiture, of being clothed with holiness; unction, of the giving of Divine grace, &c.; the entire consecration forming an acted parable, very suggestive and full of instruction to such as understood its meaning.

Take one young bullock.—The *first* thing to be done was to prepare the victims which would be needed, and to have them ready against the time when they would be required for sacrifice.

Without blemish.—Heb., *perfect.* (See Note 1 on chap. xii. 5.)

(2) **Unleavened bread.**—Unleavened bread seems to have been required as purer than leavened, since fermentation was viewed as a species of corruption.

Cakes . . . tempered with oil.—Rather, *cakes that have had oil poured over them.* A tolerably thick cake is intended.

Wafers.—These were cakes, or biscuits, extremely thin and unsubstantial, as is implied by the etymology of the term used. Oil is commonly eaten with cakes of both kinds by the Orientals.

(4) **Aaron and his sons thou shalt bring unto the door . . .**—The place of the laver, not yet mentioned, but designed in God's counsels, was between the brazen altar and the Tabernacle (chap. xxx. 18), and consequently near the door of the latter. Rabbinical tradition says that it was not placed exactly opposite the door, but a little towards the south side of the court.

And shalt wash them.—This is the first mention in Scripture of a religious ablution. Water is so natural a symbol of purity, and ablution so apt a representative of the purging from sin, that we can feel surprise neither at the widespread use of the symbolism in religions of very different characters, nor at its adoption into the system at this time imposed by Divine Providence upon the Hebrews. As it was to maintain its place even in the Divinely-appointed ceremonial of Christianity, it must have been *à fortiori* suitable for the earlier and less spiritual dispensation. The widespread employment of it in other religions—*e.g.,* in Egypt (Herod. ii. 37); in Persia (*Zendavesta,* viii. p. 271, Spiegel's translation); in Greece (Döllinger, *Jew and Gentile,* vol. i., p. 220); in Italy (*Dict. of Greek and Rom. Antiq.,* p. 719), and elsewhere—was no argument against its adoption into the Mosaic ceremonial, since the Divine legislation of Sinai was not intended to annul or supersede natural religion, but only to improve and expand it.

(5) **Thou shalt take the garments**—*i.e.,* those described in the preceding chapter.

The coat—*i.e.,* the linen tunic (chap. xxviii. 39). As the inner garment, this had to be put on first. Comp. Lev. viii. 7—9, where the investiture is more fully described, and is seen to have comprised nine acts:—(1) The putting on of the tunic; (2) The girding of the tunic with the under-girdle; (3) The putting on of the robe of the ephod; (4) The putting on of the ephod; (5) Girding with the curious girdle of the

robe of the ephod, and the ephod, and
the breastplate, and gird him with the
curious girdle of the ephod: (6) and thou
shalt put the mitre upon his head, and
put the holy crown upon the mitre.
(7) Then shalt thou take the anointing
[a] oil, and pour *it* upon his head, and
anoint him.

(8) And thou shalt bring his sons, and
put coats upon them. (9) And thou
shalt gird them with girdles, Aaron and
his sons, and [1] put the bonnets on them:
and the priest's office shall be their's for
a perpetual statute: and thou shalt
[2] [b] consecrate Aaron and his sons.
(10) And thou shalt cause a bullock to be
brought before the tabernacle of the
congregation: and [c] Aaron and his sons
shall put their hands upon the head of
the bullock. (11) And thou shalt kill the
bullock before the LORD, *by* the door of
the tabernacle of the congregation.
(12) And thou shalt take of the blood of
the bullock, and put *it* upon the horns
of the altar with thy finger, and pour
all the blood beside the bottom of the
altar. (13) And [d] thou shalt take all the
fat that covereth the inwards, and [3] the
caul *that is* above the liver, and the two
kidneys, and the fat that *is* upon them,
and burn *them* upon the altar. (14) But
the flesh of the bullock, and his skin,
and his dung, shalt thou burn with fire
without the camp: it *is* a sin offering.

(15) Thou shalt also take one ram; and
Aaron and his sons shall put their hands

a ch. 30. 25.

1 Heb., *bind.*

2 Heb., *fill the hand of.*

b ch. 28. 41.

c Lev. 1. 4.

d Lev. 3. 3.

3 It seemeth by anatomy, and the Hebrew doctors, to be *the midriff.*

---

ephod; (6) The putting on of the breastplate; (7) The putting of the Urim and Thummim into the bag of the breastplate; (8) The putting on of the mitre; and (9) The attachment of the golden plate to the front of the mitre. These minute directions may well be regarded as justifying those given in our own Ordinal with respect to the vesting of bishops at the time of their consecration.

(6) **The holy crown.**—The golden plate, inscribed with "Holiness to the Lord," and attached to the mitre by a lace or riband, resembled the "diadems" worn in the East by monarchs, and regarded as the main emblem of their sovereignty. In Egypt, such a diadem is found first in the reign of Amenôphis IV. (Khuenaten), the ninth king of the eighteenth dynasty. The assignment of a crown to the high priest gave him that quasi-royal dignity which marked him as a type of our Lord in His threefold office of Prophet, Priest, and King.

(7) **The anointing oil**—*i.e.,* the oil mentioned in chap. xxv. 6, and recently glanced at in chap. xxviii. 41. On its composition see chap. xxx. 23—25.

Pour it upon his head.—As the ablution typified cleansing from sin, so the anointing was emblematic of the outpouring of Divine grace upon the person anointed. The *pouring* of the oil on Aaron's head was perhaps to indicate the freeness and abundance with which God gives His grace to His servants. (Comp. Ps. cxxxiii. 2.)

(8) **Coats**—*i.e.,* tunics. (See Note 1 on chap. xxviii. 40.)

(9) **The bonnets.**—Rather, *caps.* (See Note 3 on chap. xxviii. 40.)

The priest's office shall be their's for a perpetual statute.—That is, not only shall they individually be priests, but the office shall descend to their posterity, and so be theirs perpetually.

Thou shalt consecrate Aaron and his sons.—Heb., *Thou shalt fill the hand of Aaron and the hand of his sons.* Induction into an office was usually effected in the East by placing its insignia in the hand of the person appointed to it. Aaron and his sons were to be inducted by having a portion of the sacrifices placed in their hands (verse 24).

(10) **Thou shalt cause a bullock to be brought.**—Rather, *the bullock: i.e.,* the bullock mentioned in verse 1, which was to be kept in readiness for the consecration sacrifice.

Aaron and his sons shall put their hands upon the head of the bullock.—By this symbolical action, which was commanded in the case of every sin offering (Lev. iv. 4, 15, 24, 29, 33, xvi. 21, &c.), the offerer identified himself with the animal, and transferred to it the guilt of his own sins and imperfections. The animal thereby became accursed, and its death paid the penalty due to the sins laid upon it, and set free those who had committed them. Similarly, Christ, our sin offering, was "made a curse for us" (Gal. iii. 13).

(12) **Thou shalt take of the blood . . . and put it upon the horns of the altar.**—It has been already noticed that the virtue of the altar was considered to reside especially in its horns; hence fugitives clung to them (1 Kings i. 50, ii. 28). In all sin offerings it was required (1) That some of the victim's blood should be smeared upon the altar's horns; and (2) That the remainder should be poured at its base (Lev. iv. 7, 18, 30, 34).

(13) **Thou shalt take all the fat that covereth the inwards.**—Whole burnt offerings were, comparatively speaking, of rare occurrence in the ancient world. Usually, parts only of the victims were consumed by fire upon the altar; the greater portion was either eaten by the priests and the worshippers, or burnt elsewhere than on the altar. Among the parts regarded as most fitting to be consumed on the altar, the fat always held a high place. This is to be accounted for either by its being considered a delicacy, or by the readiness with which it caught fire and kindled into a clear bright blaze.

The caul that is above the liver—*i.e.,* the membrane which covers the upper portion of the liver, sometimes called "the little omentum."

(14) **The flesh . . . shalt thou burn . . . without the camp.**—Comp. Lev. iv. 11, 12, 21; Heb. xiii. 11—13. This was the general rule with sin offerings. The whole animal was reckoned too impure for any portion of it to be suitable for human food.

His dung.—That which the intestines contained at the time of death.

(15) **One ram.**—Heb., *the one ram: i.e.,* one of the two rams already mentioned in verse 1.

upon the head of the ram. (16) And thou
shalt slay the ram, and thou shalt take
his blood, and sprinkle *it* round about
upon the altar. (17) And thou shalt cut
the ram in pieces, and wash the inwards
of him, and his legs, and put *them* unto
his pieces, and [1] unto his head. (18) And
thou shalt burn the whole ram upon the
altar: it *is* a burnt offering unto the
LORD: it *is* a sweet savour, an offering
made by fire unto the LORD.

(19) And thou shalt take the other
ram; and Aaron and his sons shall put
their hands upon the head of the ram.
(20) Then shalt thou kill the ram, and
take of his blood, and put *it* upon the
tip of the right ear of Aaron, and upon
the tip of the right ear of his sons, and
upon the thumb of their right hand, and
upon the great toe of their right foot,
and sprinkle the blood upon the altar
round about. (21) And thou shalt take
of the blood that *is* upon the altar, and of
the anointing oil, and sprinkle *it* upon
Aaron, and upon his garments, and up-
on his sons, and upon the garments of
his sons with him: and he shall be hal-
lowed, and his garments, and his sons,
and his sons' garments with him.
(22) Also thou shalt take of the ram the
fat and the rump, and the fat that
covereth the inwards, and the caul *above*
the liver, and the two kidneys, and the
fat that *is* upon them, and the right
shoulder; for it *is* a ram of consecra-
tion: (23) and one loaf of bread, and one
cake of oiled bread, and one wafer out
of the basket of the unleavened bread

[1] Or, *upon.*

Put their hands upon the head of the ram.—Again identifying themselves with the animal, as in verse 10, but with a different purpose from their former one. Then they transferred their sins to the victim; now they claimed a part in the victim's dedication to God, offering themselves with it, and becoming, themselves, "a sweet savour, an offering made by fire unto the Lord" (verse 18).

(16) **Thou shalt take his blood, and sprinkle it.**—Rather, *scatter it.* The act of throwing the blood from a basin against the lower part of the altar is intended. The verb is a different one from that rightly translated "sprinkle" in verse 21. The LXX. render it by προσχεῖν, and the Vulg. by *fundere.*

Round about upon the altar.—Practically, this was done by casting it on two of the corners of the altar—the north-east and the south-west—thus moistening all the four sides (*Middoth,* iii. 2).

(17) **Thou shalt cut the ram in pieces.**—This was the ordinary practice, not only among the Hebrews, but also among other nations, as the Egyptians (Herod. ii. 40), the Greeks, the Romans, and others. It was probably found to facilitate the burning of the animal, which was with difficulty consumed entire. The shoulder, thigh, head, ribs, rump, heart, and kidneys appear separate in the representations of sacrifices on Egyptian altars.

(18) **Thou shalt burn the whole ram upon the altar.**—A burnt offering, as representing self-sacrifice, was *entirely* acceptable to God; the whole might be consumed upon the altar. It was otherwise with sin offerings, of which only certain parts could be thus offered. (Comp. above, verse 14; and see Lev. iv. 12, 21, &c.)

A sweet savour.—Comp. Gen. viii. 21 and Note *ad loc.* It was a general heathen notion that the gods were actually delighted with the odour of the sacrifices offered to them; but there are no just grounds for taxing the Hebrews with such coarse and materialistic ideas. The expression, as used in this place, in Gen. viii. 21, and in Leviticus and Numbers repeatedly, is metaphorical. (Comp. chap. v. 21.)

(19) **The other ram.**—Comp. verses 1 and 15. This ram is called in Leviticus (chap. viii. 22) "the ram of consecration." It formed, as has been observed (*Speaker's Commentary,* vol. i. pt. 2, p. 535), "by far the most peculiar part of the whole ceremony." Consecrated to God by the act of sacrifice, its blood was used, together with the holy oil, for the consecration of Aaron and his sons (verses 20, 21); while at the same time its most sacred parts were placed on their hands by Moses, that with them they might perform their first sacerdotal act, and so be inaugurated into their office (verses 22—24). This last was not only the crowning act of the ceremony, but also its most essential feature—the act which imparted to Aaron and his sons the priestly character.

(20) **Take of his blood.**—The blood was regarded as the life (Gen. ix. 4). The life consecrated to God and accepted by Him was given back by Him to His ministers, that it might consecrate them wholly to His service, and so fit them for it. Placed upon the tip of the right ear, it reminded them that their ears were to be ever open and attentive to the whispers of the Divine voice; placed on the thumb of the right hand, it taught that they should take in hand nothing but what was sanctified; placed upon the great toe of the right foot, it was a warning that they were to walk thenceforth in the paths of holiness.

(21) **Take of the blood . . . and of the anointing oil.**—The twofold sprinkling, with blood and with oil, denoted the necessity of a twofold holiness—that of justification by the atoning blood of Christ, and that of sanctification by the outpouring of the Holy Spirit. The anointing which is here spoken of seems to have been the only anointing received by the sons of Aaron. (See Lev. viii. 30.)

(22) **Thou shalt take of the ram the fat . . .**—These were the portions commonly burnt upon the altar in the case of peace offerings. (See Lev. iii. 9—11.) By "the rump" is meant the broad fat tail which characterises Oriental sheep, and which is said to weigh from six to twenty pounds. (Fellows, *Asia Minor,* p. 10. Comp. Herod. iii. 113; Leo African. ix. p. 293A.)

The caul above the liver.—See Note 2 on verse 13.

(23) **The basket . . . that is before the Lord.**—Comp. verse 3. The objects mentioned formed the "meat offering," which always accompanied a peace offering.

that *is* before the LORD: (24) and thou
shalt put all in the hands of Aaron, and
in the hands of his sons; and shalt
[1] wave them *for* a wave offering before
the LORD. (25) And thou shalt receive
them of their hands, and burn *them* up-
on the altar for a burnt offering, for a
sweet savour before the LORD: it *is* an
offering made by fire unto the LORD.
(26) And thou shalt take the breast of
the ram of Aaron's consecration, and
wave it *for* a wave offering before the
LORD: and it shall be thy part. (27) And
thou shalt sanctify the breast of the wave
offering, and the shoulder of the heave
offering, which is waved, and which is
heaved up, of the ram of the consecration,
even of *that* which *is* for Aaron, and of
that which is for his sons: (28) and it shall
be Aaron's and his sons' by a statute for
ever from the children of Israel: for it
is an heave offering: and it shall be an
heave offering from the children of Israel
of the sacrifice of their peace offerings,
even their heave offering unto the LORD.

1 Or, *shake to and fro.*

2 Heb., he *of his sons.*

a Lev. 8. 31; Matt. 12. 4.

(29) And the holy garments of Aaron
shall be his sons' after him, to be an-
ointed therein, and to be consecrated
in them. (30) *And* [2] that son that is
priest in his stead shall put them on
seven days, when he cometh into the
tabernacle of the congregation to min-
ister in the holy *place.*
(31) And thou shalt take the ram of the
consecration, and seethe his flesh in the
holy place. (32) And Aaron and his sons
shall eat the flesh of the ram, and the
[a] bread that *is* in the basket, *by* the door
of the tabernacle of the congregation.
(33) And they shall eat those things
wherewith the atonement was made, to
consecrate *and* to sanctify them: but a
stranger shall not eat *thereof,* because
they *are* holy. (34) And if ought of the
flesh of the consecrations, or of the
bread, remain unto the morning, then
thou shalt burn the remainder with
fire: it shall not be eaten, because it *is*
holy.
(35) And thus shalt thou do unto

---

(24) **Thou shalt put all in the hands of Aaron, and in the hands of his sons.**—Rather, *on the hands.* Having placed the offerings on the hands of his brother and his brother's sons, Moses was to put his own hands beneath theirs, and to make a waving motion towards the four quarters of the sky, thus presenting the offerings to the ubiquitous God. Aaron and his sons thus performed their first priestly act, as passive instruments in Moses' hands, by his muscular energy. Their priestly character was by these means made complete. (On "wave offerings," see Note upon Lev. vii. 30.)

(25) **Thou shalt receive them . . . and burn them.**—On communicating his priestly functions to his brother and his brother's sons, Moses was not immediately to lay them aside; but, as he had begun the consecration ceremony, so he was to complete it. (Comp. verses 31—37, and Lev. viii. 28—36.)

(26) **Thou shalt take the breast.**—It was the general law that in "wave offerings" the breast should be the officiating priest's (Lev. vii. 29—31); hence, on this occasion, it was assigned to Moses.

THE LAW OF THE WAVE AND HEAVE OFFERINGS, AND OF THE CONSECRATION GARMENTS.

(27, 28) **The wave offering.**—For the future, in every case of offerings made at a consecration, both the breast and the right shoulder (Lev. vii. 32) were to be given to the officiating priest, who was to "wave" the one and "heave" the other before the Lord. "Heaving" was a single movement, an uplifting of the thing heaved; "waving" was a repeated movement, a swaying of the thing waved backwards and forwards horizontally. Both were modes of presenting the thing to God.

(29) **The holy garments of Aaron shall be his sons' after him.**—That Eleazar was consecrated in his father's holy garments we learn from Num. xx. 28; but nothing is recorded as to the investiture of later high priests. Still, it is reasonable to suppose that the injunctions here given were carried out so long as the garments worn by Aaron held together.

To be anointed therein.—The anointing of each successive high priest is here commanded by implication. Jewish tradition affirms the practice to have been in conformity.

THE FEAST UPON THE CONSECRATION OFFERINGS.

(31—34) The writer having digressed in verse 27 from his main subject (the consecration of Aaron and his sons) to the consideration of certain permanent laws which arose out of the occasion, returns to his main subject at this point, and records the directions which he received with respect to the feast that followed, as a matter of course, on the consecration sacrifice. The parts of the victim neither consumed on the altar nor assigned to the officiating priest, were to be boiled at the door of the Tabernacle (Lev. viii. 31), and there consumed by Aaron and his sons, together with the loaf of unleavened bread, the oiled cake, and the wafer, which still remained in the "basket of consecrations" (Lev. viii. 31) mentioned in verses 3 and 23. No "stranger"—*i.e.,* no layman—was to join with them in the feast (verse 33); and, if they were unable to consume the whole, what remained was to be burnt. (Comp. the injunctions with respect to the paschal lamb, given in chap. xii. 10, xxiii. 18.) Christian ritualism draws from these injunctions the propriety of an entire consumption of the elements on each occasion of the celebration of the Eucharist.

THE SEVENFOLD REPETITION OF THE CONSECRATION CEREMONIAL.

(35) **Seven days shalt thou consecrate them.**—The number seven possessed an ideal completeness, resting on the primeval facts of creation (Gen. i., ii.). It is the number almost exclusively used under the old

Aaron, and to his sons, according to all
things which I have commanded thee:
seven days shalt thou consecrate them.
(36) And thou shalt offer every day a
bullock *for* a sin offering for atonement:
and thou shalt cleanse the altar, when
thou hast made an atonement for it,
and thou shalt anoint it, to sanctify it.
(37) Seven days thou shalt make an
atonement for the altar, and sanctify it;
and it shall be an altar most holy:
whatsoever toucheth the altar shall be
holy.
(38) Now this *is that* which thou shalt
offer upon the altar; [a] two lambs of the
first year day by day continually.
(39) The one lamb thou shalt offer in the
morning; and the other lamb thou
shalt offer at even: (40) and with the one
lamb a tenth deal of flour mingled with
the fourth part of an hin of beaten oil;
and the fourth part of an hin of wine
for a drink offering. (41) And the other
lamb thou shalt offer at even, and shalt
do thereto according to the meat offering
of the morning, and according to
the drink offering thereof, for a sweet
savour, an offering made by fire unto
the LORD. (42) *This shall be* a continual
burnt offering throughout your generations
at the door of the tabernacle of
the congregation before the LORD:
where I will meet you, to speak there
unto thee. (43) And there I will meet
with the children of Israel, and [1] *the
tabernacle* shall be sanctified by my
glory. (44) And I will sanctify the tabernacle
of the congregation, and the

a Num. 28. 3.

1 Or, Israel.

covenant, when acts are to attain their result by repetition. (See Lev. iv. 6, 17, viii. 11, xiv. 7, xvi. 14; Num. xix. 4; Josh vi. 4; 1 Kings xviii. 43; 2 Kings v. 10; Ps. cxix. 164; &c.) Here we are to understand a sevenfold repetition of the entire ceremonial of consecration. (See Lev. viii. 33, 34.)

(36) **Thou shalt cleanse the altar, when thou hast made an atonement for it.**—Rather, *by making an atonement for it.* The atonement was made by smearing the blood of the bullock upon the horns of the altar (verse 12, compared with Lev. viii. 15).

And thou shalt anoint it.—Comp. Lev. viii. 11, where we find that the altar was anointed by having the holy oil sprinkled upon it seven times. It is not quite clear at what period in the ceremonial this was done.

(37) **An altar most holy.**—Heb., *an altar, holiness of holinesses.*

Whatsoever toucheth the altar shall be holy.—Rather, *must be holy;* nothing which is not holy must touch it. The future has the force of an imperative, as in the Ten Commandments.

THE LAW OF THE DAILY SACRIFICE, AND THE PROMISE OF GOD'S PRESENCE.

(38—42) The consecration of the altar, which took place during the consecration of the priests, was to be followed immediately by the establishment of the daily sacrifice. Two lambs were to be offered every day, one in the morning, the other "between the evenings" (verse 39); partly in expiation of the daily sins of the nation, but mainly as a sign that the nation daily renewed its self-dedication to Jehovah, and offered itself afresh to be "a reasonable, holy, and lively sacrifice" to Him. Meat and drink offerings were to accompany the burnt sacrifice—signs of the gratitude due to God for His perpetual mercies, and acknowledgments of His protecting care and lovingkindness. At the same time incense was to be burnt upon the golden altar before the vail, as a figure of the perpetual prayer that it behoved the nation to send up to the Throne of Grace for a continuance of the Divine favour. (See chap. xxx. 7, 8.)

(38) **Two lambs of the first year.**—See Note on chap. xii. 5. The LXX. insert ἀμώμους, "without blemish;" but this general requirement (Lev. xxii. 22, 24, 25), relaxed only in the case of free-will offerings (Lev. xxii. 23), does not need to be perpetually repeated.

(39) **At even.**—Heb., *between the two evenings.* (On the meaning of the phrase, see Note 2 on chap. xii. 6.)

(40) **A tenth deal.**—Heb., *a tenth.* A tenth of what measure is not said, but we may presume an ephah to be intended. The tenth part of an ephah was an omer (chap. xvi. 36). The omer is reckoned at rather less than half a gallon.

An hin.—The hin was, like the omer and the ephah, an Egyptian measure. It is estimated at about three-quarters of a gallon.

Beaten oil.—See Note 1 on chap. xxvii. 20.

(41) **The meat offering . . . the drink offering.**—A "handful" of each meat offering was thrown upon the altar and burnt (Lev. ii. 2); the remainder belonged to the priests (Lev. ii. 3). Scripture says nothing of the disposal of the drink offering. According to Josephus (*Ant. Jud.* iii. 9, § 4), it was poured out in libation upon the altar. According to others, a portion only was thus disposed of, while the rest was the priests'. The latter view seems the more probable.

(42) **The tabernacle of the congregation.**—Rather, *the tent of meeting.*

Where I will meet you.—This passage determines the meaning of the expression, "tent of meeting." It was not the place where the congregation met together, for the congregation were forbidden to enter it, but the place where God met His people through their mediator and representative, the high priest, who could there commune with God and obtain replies from Him on all practical matters that were of national importance. (See chap. xxv. 22 and Note *ad loc.*) The fact that all communication was to be through the high priest is indicated by the change of person: "Where I will meet *you*, to speak there unto *thee.*"

(43) **The tabernacle shall be sanctified by my glory.**—See chap. xl. 34, 35; and comp. Lev. ix. 24; 1 Kings viii. 10, 11; 2 Chron. v. 13, 14, vii. 2.

(44) **I will sanctify also both Aaron and his sons.**—Something beyond the formal consecration seems to be intended. God will continually sanctify the Levitical priesthood by the presence of His Holy

altar: I will sanctify also both Aaron
and his sons, to minister to me in the
priest's office. (45) And [a] I will dwell
among the children of Israel, and will
be their God. (46) And they shall know
that I *am* the LORD their God, that
brought them forth out of the land of
Egypt, that I may dwell among them:
I *am* the LORD their God.

CHAPTER XXX.—(1) And thou
shalt make an altar to burn incense up-
on: *of* shittim wood shalt thou make it.
(2) A cubit *shall be* the length thereof,
and a cubit the breadth thereof; four-
square shall it be: and two cubits *shall*
be the height thereof: the horns thereof
shall be of the same. (3) And thou shalt
overlay it with pure gold, the [1] top there-
of, and the [2] sides thereof round about,
and the horns thereof; and thou shalt
make unto it a crown of gold round
about. (4) And two golden rings shalt
thou make to it under the crown of it,
by the two [3] corners thereof, upon the
two sides of it shalt thou make *it;* and
they shall be for places for the staves to
bear it withal. (5) And thou shalt make
the staves *of* shittim wood, and overlay
them with gold. (6) And thou shalt put
it before the vail that *is* by the ark of
the testimony, before the mercy seat

a Lev. 26. 12; 2 Cor. 6. 16.

1 Heb., *the roof and the walls.*

2 Heb., *walls.*

3 Heb., *ribs.*

Spirit with them, in their ministerial acts, and even in their daily walk, if they will seek to serve Him.

(45) **I will dwell among the children of Israel.**—It must not be supposed that the fulfilment of this promise was effected by the mere presence of the Shechinah within the Tabernacle. It pledged God to a perpetual supervision, care, and tender protection of His people, such as we find actually exercised in the history of the nation.

(46) **They shall know . . .** —*i.e.*, My after care of them will prove me the same loving and all-powerful God whose help effected their deliverance from the bondage of Egypt.

XXX.

THE ALTAR OF INCENSE.

(1) **Thou shalt make an altar to burn incense upon.**—Why the directions concerning the altar of incense were delayed until this place, instead of being given when the rest of the furniture of the holy place was described (chap. xxv.), it is impossible to say. But there is certainly no reason to suspect a dislocation of the text. The mode in which Aaron is spoken of in verses 7—10 implies a previous mention of his consecration to the high priesthood.

That incense would be among the offerings which God would require to be offered to Him had appeared already in chap. xxv. 6. Its preciousness, its fragrance, and its seeming to mount in cloud after cloud to heaven, gave it a natural place in the symbolism of worship, and led to its employment in the religious rites of a variety of nations. Egyptian priests continually appear on the monuments with censers in their hands, in which presumably incense is being offered, and the inscriptions mention that it was imported from Arabia, and used largely in the festivals of Ammon (*Records of the Past*, vol. x., pp. 14—19). Herodotus tells us that the Babylonians consumed annually a thousand talents' weight of it at the feast of Belus (i. 183). The employment of it by the Greeks and Romans in their sacrifices is well known. Here again, as so often in the Mosaical dispensation, God sanctioned in His worship an innocent rite, which natural reason had pointed out to man as fitting and appropriate, not regarding its employment in false religions as debarring it from adoption into the true.

Of shittim wood shalt thou make it.—Of the same main material as "the brazen altar" (chap. xxvii. 1), but covered differently.

(2) **Foursquare shall it be.**—Of the same shape with "the brazen altar" (chap. xxvii. 1), but much smaller—two cubits high instead of three cubits, and a cubit square at top instead of five cubits. This small space was ample for the burning of so precious a material, which could only be offered in small quantities.

The horns thereof.—Comp. chap. xxvii. 2, and Note 1, *ad loc.*

Shall be of the same — *i.e.*, of one piece with the altar, not made separately, and then attached to it.

(3) **Thou shalt overlay it with pure gold.**—Next to the Ark of the Covenant the most holy article of furniture contained either in the sanctuary or in its court was the altar of incense. It symbolised prayer in its general use (Ps. cxli. 2; Luke i. 10), and it symbolised expiation in the purpose whereto it was to be applied on certain occasions, as when the high priest had sinned in his official capacity (Lev. iv. 3—12), or when the whole congregation had sinned through inadvertence (*ib.* verses 13—21). It was, therefore, "most holy to the Lord." Hence, its materials were to be the same with those of the ark of the covenant, and its place was to be directly opposite the ark, near to it, but on the outer side of the vail (chap. xl. 5).

A crown of gold round about.—Comp. what is said of the table of shewbread (chap. xxv. 24). In both cases a raised rim or edging is meant, which would prevent what was on the top from falling off.

(4) **Two golden rings.**—The golden altar was so much smaller and lighter than the brazen one that two rings only were required for carrying it, instead of the "four rings" needed by the brazen altar (chap. xxvii. 4).

By the two corners thereof.—Rather, *on the two sides thereof.* The word used means, literally, "ribs," and is explained in the clause which follows.

(6) **Before the vail.**—The ark was *behind* the vail (chaps. xxvi. 33, xl. 3), the altar of incense directly in front of it, nearer to the vail than either the golden candlestick or the table of shewbread. Hence the writer of the Epistle to the Hebrews speaks of it as belonging, in a certain sense, to the Holy of Holies (Heb. ix. 4; see Kay, in *Speaker's Commentary*). The "vail that is by the ark of the testimony" is distinguished here from the vail, or curtain, at the entrance to the holy place.

Before the mercy seat.—The altar bore a close relation to the mercy seat. It was the instrument by

that *is* over the testimony, where I will
meet with thee. (7) And Aaron shall
burn thereon [1] sweet incense every
morning: when he dresseth the lamps,
he shall burn incense upon it. (8) And
when Aaron [2] [3] lighteth the lamps [4] at
even, he shall burn incense upon it, a
perpetual incense before the LORD
throughout your generations. (9) Ye
shall offer no strange incense thereon,
nor burnt sacrifice, nor meat offering;
neither shall ye pour drink offering
thereon. (10) And Aaron shall make an
atonement upon the horns of it once in
a year with the blood of the sin offering
of atonements: once in the year shall
he make atonement upon it throughout
your generations: it *is* most holy unto
the LORD.
(11) And the LORD spake unto Moses,
saying, (12) [a] When thou takest the sum
of the children of Israel after [5] their
number, then shall they give every man
a ransom for his soul unto the LORD,
when thou numberest them; that there
be no plague among them, when *thou*
numberest them. (13) This they shall
give, every one that passeth among
them that are numbered, half a shekel
after the shekel of the sanctuary: ([b] a
shekel *is* twenty gerahs:) an half shekel
shall be the offering of the LORD.
(14) Every one that passeth among them
that are numbered, from twenty years

1 Heb., *incense of spices.*

2 Or, *setteth up.*

3 Heb., *causeth to ascend.*

4 Heb., *between the two evens.*

a Num. 1. 2, 5.

5 Heb., *them that are to be numbered.*

b Lev. 27. 25; Num. 3. 47; Ezek. 45. 12.

---

which the "mercy" there enthroned was made available to the penitent sinner.

Where I will meet with thee.—Comp. chaps. xxv. 22, xxix. 42, 43.

(7) **Aaron shall burn thereon sweet incense** (Heb., *incense of spices*) **every morning.**—On the composition of the incense, see verses 34, 35. That the offering of incense regularly accompanied both the morning and evening sacrifice appears from Ps. cxli. 2; Luke i. 10. That it was symbolical of prayer may be gathered both from those passages and also from Rev. v. 8, viii. 3, 4.

When he dresseth the lamps.—Comp. chap. xxvii. 31.

(9) **Ye shall offer no strange incense.**—By "*strange* incense" is meant any that was composed differently from that of which the composition is laid down in verses 34, 35.

Nor burnt sacrifice, nor meat offering; neither . . . drink offering.—All these were to be offered on the brazen altar, not on the altar of incense, which was in no way suited for them.

(10) **Aaron shall make an atonement upon the horns of it once in a year.**—This passage seems to determine the sense of Lev. xvi. 18, where some have supposed that "the altar that is before the Lord" is the brazen altar. Once in the year, on the great day of atonement, the high priest, after entering within the vail and sprinkling the blood of the offerings upon the mercy seat (Lev. xvi. 14, 15), was to "go out unto the altar that was before the Lord, and put of the blood of the bullock, and of the blood of the goat, upon the horns of the altar round about, and sprinkle of the blood upon it with his finger seven times," and so "cleanse it, and hallow it," and "make an atonement for it" (*ib.* verses 18, 19).

THE RANSOM OF SOULS.

(12) **When thou takest the sum of the children of Israel.**—A formal enrolment and registration seems to be intended. Hitherto, nothing but a rough estimate of the number had been attempted (chap. xii. 37); now that a covenant had been made with God, an exact account of those who were within the covenant was needed. Moses, apparently, was contemplating such an exact enumeration when the command contained in this text was given him. It would be natural for one trained in Egyptian habits to desire such exact statistical knowledge. (For the minuteness and fulness of the Egyptian statistics of the time, see *Records of the Past,* vol. ii., pp. 19—28; vol. iv. pp. 46, 47; vol. vi. pp. 35—69, &c.)

Then shall they give every man a ransom for his soul.—On being formally enrolled among the people of God, it would be brought home to every man how unworthy he was of such favour, how necessary it was that atonement should in some way or other be made for him. God therefore appointed a way—the same way for all—in order to teach strongly that all souls were of equal value in His sight, and that unworthiness, whatever its degree, required the same expiation.

That there be no plague among them.—If a man did not feel his need of "ransom," and gladly pay the small sum at which the ransom was fixed, he would show himself so proud and presumptuous that he might well provoke a Divine "plague," or punishment.

(13) **Half a shekel.**—When shekels came to be coined, they were round pieces of silver, about the circumference of a shilling, but considerably thicker, and worth about 2s. 7d. of our money. Their average weight was about 220 grains troy. In Moses's time coins were unknown, and a half-shekel was a small lump of silver, unstamped, weighing probably about 110 grains. The ransom of a soul was doubtless made thus light in order that the payment might not be felt practically as a burthen by any.

After the shekel of the sanctuary.—Without a standard laid up somewhere, weights and measures will always fluctuate largely. Even with a standard, they will practically vary considerably. The "shekel of the sanctuary" probably designates a standard weight kept carefully by the priests with the vessels of the sanctuary. All offerings were to be estimated by this shekel (Lev. xxvii. 25).

A shekel is twenty gerahs.—Rather, *the shekel, i.e.,* the shekel of the sanctuary is of this weight. A "gerah" was, literally, *a bean,* probably the bean of the carob or locust tree (*Ceratonia siliqua*), but became the name of a weight, just as our own "grain" did. It must have equalled about eleven grains troy.

(14) **From twenty years old and above.**—A Hebrew was not reckoned full grown till twenty. At twenty the liability to military service began (Num. i. 3;

old and above, shall give an offering un-
to the LORD. (15) The rich shall not
[1] give more, and the poor shall not [2] give
less than half a shekel, when *they* give
an offering unto the LORD, to make an
atonement for your souls. (16) And thou
shalt take the atonement money of the
children of Israel, and shalt appoint it
for the service of the tabernacle of the
congregation; that it may be a me-
morial unto the children of Israel before
the LORD, to make an atonement for
your souls.

(17) And the LORD spake unto Moses,
saying, (18) Thou shalt also make a laver
of brass, and his foot *also of* brass, to
wash *withal*: and thou shalt put it be-
tween the tabernacle of the congrega-
tion and the altar, and thou shalt put
water therein. (19) For Aaron and his
sons shall wash their hands and their
feet thereat: (20) when they go into the
tabernacle of the congregation, they
shall wash with water, that they die not,
or when they come near to the altar to
minister, to burn offering made by fire
unto the LORD: (21) so they shall wash
their hands and their feet, that they die
not: and it shall be a statute for ever to
them, *even* to him and to his seed
throughout their generations.

(22) Moreover the LORD spake unto
Moses, saying, (23) Take thou also unto
thee principal spices, of pure myrrh five
hundred *shekels*, and of sweet cinnamon
half so much, *even* two hundred and

1 Heb., *multiply*.

2 Heb., *diminish*.

2 Chron. xxv. 5). At twenty the Levites commenced their service in the sanctuary (1 Chron. xxiii. 24—27; 2 Chron xxxi. 17; Ezra iii. 8).

(15) **The rich shall not give more, and the poor shall not give less.**—See Note 2 on verse 12.

(16) **Thou shalt . . . appoint it for the service of the tabernacle.**—It appears, by chap. xxxviii. 27, 28, that the silver collected by this tax, which amounted to above a hundred talents, was employed for making the sockets which supported the boards of the tabernacle (chap. xxvi. 19—25), and those of the pillars of the vail (*ib.* verse 32), together with the hooks for the pillars of the court, their capitals, and connecting rods. Thus, so long as the tabernacle stood, the precious metal paid as ransom remained in the sight of the people, and was a continual "memorial," or reminder, to them of the position into which they were brought by covenant with God.

THE BRAZEN LAVER.

(18) **Thou shalt also make a laver of brass.**—Rather, *of bronze.* (See Note on chap. xxv. 3.) Water was required for the ablutions of the priests (verses 19—21), for the washing of certain parts of the victim, (chap. xxix. 27; Lev. i. 9, 13, &c.), and probably for the cleansing of the altar itself and the ground whereon it stood from blood stains and other defilements.

His foot.—The laver was probably in the shape of a large urn or vase, supported upon a comparatively slender stem, which rose from a pedestal. Vases of this kind are represented in the Assyrian bas-reliefs. (See *Ancient Monarchies*, vol. i., p. 481.)

Thou shalt put it between the tabernacle of the congregation and the altar.—It was essential that the laver should be near the altar, since on every occasion of their ministering at the altar the priests had to wash at it (verse 20). It was also essential that it should be near the entrance into the tabernacle, since they had likewise to wash before they entered into the holy place. Jewish tradition says that its place was between the entrance and the brazen altar, not, however, exactly between them, but a little to the south.

(19) **Aaron and his sons shall wash their hands and their feet.**—Washing the hands symbolised purity in act; washing the feet, holiness in all their walk and conversation.

(20) **That they die not.**—Comp. chap. xxviii. 35, 43. It is not altogether easy to see why the death-penalty was threatened against neglect of certain ceremonial observances, and not of others. Ablution, however, was so easy, and probably so long-established a practice, that to omit it would imply intentional disrespect towards God.

(21) **A statute for ever.**—Comp. chap. xxvii. 21; xxviii. 43; xxix. 9. The external act was to continue so long as the dispensation lasted; the internal purity, which it symbolised, would be required of those who entered the Divine Presence for ever. (See Heb. xii. 14.)

THE COMPOSITION OF THE HOLY OIL.

(23) **Principal spices.**—The East is productive of a great variety of spices; but of these some few have always been regarded with especial favour. Herodotus (iii. 107—112) mentions five "principal spices" as furnished by Arabia to other countries, whereof two at least appear to be identical with those here spoken of.

Pure myrrh.—Heb., *myrrh of freedom.* The shrub which produces myrrh is the *balsamodendron myrrha.* The spice is obtained from it in two ways. That which is purest and best exudes from it naturally (Theophrast. *De Odoribus*, § 29; Plin., *H. N.*, xii. 35), and is here called "myrrh of freedom," or "freely flowing myrrh." The other and inferior form is obtained from incisions made in the bark. Myrrh was very largely used in ancient times. The Egyptians employed it as a main element in their best method of embalming (Herod. ii. 86), and also burnt it in some of their sacrifices (*ib.* 40). In Persia it was highly esteemed as an odour (Athen., *Deipn.* xii., p. 514A); the Greeks used it in unguents and as incense; Roman courtesans scented their hair with it (Hor. *Od.*, iii. 14, l. 22); the later Jews applied it as an antiseptic to corpses (John xix. 39). This is the first mention of myrrh (Heb., *môr*) in the Bible, the word translated "myrrh" in Gen. xxxvii. 25 and xliii. 11 being *lôt*, which is properly, not myrrh, but ladanum.

Sweet cinnamon.—While myrrh was one of the commonest of spices in the ancient world, cinnamon was one of the rarest. It is the produce of the *laurus cinnamomum*, or *cinnamomum zeylanicum*, a tree allied to the laurel, which now grows only in Ceylon, Borneo, Sumatra, China, Cochin China, and in India on the

fifty *shekels*, and of sweet calamus two
hundred and fifty *shekels*, (24) and of
cassia five hundred *shekels*, after the
shekel of the sanctuary, and of oil olive
an [a] hin: (25) and thou shalt make it an
oil of holy ointment, an ointment com-
pound after the art of the [1] apothecary:
it shall be an holy anointing oil. (26) And
thou shalt anoint the tabernacle of the
congregation therewith, and the ark of
the testimony, (27) and the table and all
his vessels, and the candlestick and
his vessels, and the altar of incense,
(28) and the altar of burnt offering with
all his vessels, and the laver and his
foot. (29) And thou shalt sanctify them,
that they may be most holy: whatso-
ever toucheth them shall be holy.

a ch. 29. 40.

1 Or, *perfumer*.

(30) And thou shalt anoint Aaron and his
sons, and consecrate them, that *they*
may minister unto me in the priest's
office. (31) And thou shalt speak unto
the children of Israel, saying, This shall
be an holy anointing oil unto me
throughout your generations. (32) Upon
man's flesh shall it not be poured,
neither shall ye make *any other* like it,
after the composition of it: it *is* holy,
and it shall be holy unto you. (33) Who-
soever compoundeth *any* like it, or who-
soever putteth *any* of it upon a stranger,
shall even be cut off from his people.

(34) And the LORD said unto Moses,
Take unto thee sweet spices, stacte, and
onycha, and galbanum; *these* sweet
spices with pure frankincense: of each

---

coast of Malabar. According to Herodotus (iii. 111) and Strabo (xvi., p. 535), it grew anciently in Arabia; but this is doubted, and the Arabians are believed to have imported it from India or Ceylon, and passed it on to the Phœnicians, who conveyed it to Egypt and Greece. The present passage of Scripture is the first in which it is mentioned, and in the rest of the Old Testament it obtains notice only twice (Prov. vii. 16; Cant. iv. 14). The word used, which is *kinnĕmôn*, makes it tolerably certain that the true cinnamon is meant.

Sweet calamus.—There are several distinct kinds of aromatic reed in the East. One sort, according to Pliny (*H. N.*, xii. 22), grew in Syria, near Mount Lebanon; others were found in India and Arabia. It is quite uncertain what particular species is intended, either here or in the other passages of Scripture where "sweet cane" is spoken of. (See Cant. iv. 14; Isa. xliii. 24; Jer. vi. 20; Ezek. xxvii. 17.)

(24) **Cassia.**—In the original, *kiddâh*, not *kĕtsiôth*, which is the exact equivalent of the Greek and Latin *cassia*. According to the best Hebrew authorities, however, cassia is intended by both words, which are derived from roots signifying "to split," or "to peel off." Cassia is the inner bark of a tree called by botanists *cinnamomum cassia*, which is a native of India, Java, and the Malay peninsula. It has nearly the same flavour as cinnamon, but is more pungent, and of a coarser texture. The word *kiddâh* occurs in Scripture only here and in Ezek. xxvii. 19.

An hin.—See Note on chap. xxix. 40.

(25) **After the art of the apothecary.** — Skill was to be called in. The spices were not to be pounded and mixed with the oil in a rude and unscientific way, but the best art of the time was to be employed in effecting the composition. Jewish tradition says that its essence was first extracted from each of the spices, and then the oil mingled with the essences.

(26) **Thou shalt anoint the tabernacle.**—The tabernacle and its contents were to be first consecrated, then the priests. In the tabernacle itself, the consecration was to begin with the ark of the testimony in the Holy of Holies, then to proceed to the Holy place, where the table of shewbread with its "vessels," the golden candlestick, and the altar of incense were to be anointed; and finally to pass the vail to the outer court, where the holy oil was to be sprinkled upon the brazen altar, and upon the laver, to sanctify them. (See verses 26—29; and comp. Lev. viii. 10, 11.)

(30) **Thou shalt anoint Aaron.** — Comp. chap. xxix. 7; Lev. viii. 12.

And his sons.—See chap. xxix. 21.

That they may minister unto me.—As Aaron and his sons were unfit to minister until the holy oil had been poured on them, so Christian priests can be no otherwise fitted to discharge their office than by their receiving that effluence of the Holy Spirit which the holy oil typified.

(32) **Upon man's flesh shall it not be poured**—*i.e.*, it shall not be in ordinary use as an unguent—a mere "man," who is not a priest, shall not apply it to his private use. It shall be reserved altogether for holy purposes.

Neither shall ye make any other like it, after the composition of it—*i.e.*, after the recipe given in verses 23—25. The ingredients might be used in unguents separately—they might even be so used when united in some different proportions from those laid down for the "holy ointment"—but in the proportions fixed for the holy oil they must have no secular employment.

THE COMPOSITION OF THE HOLY INCENSE.

(34) **Take unto thee sweet spices.** — Rather, *Take unto thee spices.* The word translated "spices" has no epithet. Incense, as commonly used in the ancient world, was not a composition, but some single spice, most frequently frankincense. That, however, employed by the Hebrews was always a compound. According to Josephus (*Bell. Jud.*, v. 5, § 5), the incense burnt in the later temple contained thirteen ingredients.

Stacte is probably the gum storax, which is the produce of the *styrax officinalis*, a tree common in Syria and Palestine. It burns readily, and emits much smoke (Herod. iii. 107).

Onycha is thought to be the "claw" or *operculum* of the *unguis odoratus*, or *blatta Byzantina*, a sort of shell-fish common in the Red Sea. This "claw" produces, when burnt, a strong odour.

Galbanum is a gum well known to modern chemists. It may be procured from various plants, as the *opoidia galbanifera*, the *galbanum Persicum*, and others. When

shall there be a like *weight:* (35) and
thou shalt make it a perfume, a confection after the art of the apothecary,
[1] tempered together, pure *and* holy:
(36) and thou shalt beat *some* of it very small, and put of it before the testimony in the tabernacle of the congregation, where I will meet with thee: it shall be unto you most holy.
(37) And *as for* the perfume which thou shalt make, ye shall not make to yourselves according to the composition thereof: it shall be unto thee holy for the LORD.
(38) Whosoever shall make like unto that, to smell thereto, shall even be cut off from his people.

[1] Heb., *salted.*

[a] 1 Chron. 2. 20.

CHAPTER XXXI.—(1) And the
LORD spake unto Moses, saying, (2) See,
I have called by name Bezaleel the [a] son of Uri, the son of Hur, of the tribe of
Judah: (3) and I have filled him with the spirit of God, in wisdom, and in understanding, and in knowledge, and in

---

burnt, this gum has a strong pungent odour, which is said to be disagreeable in itself, but to bring out and prolong the scent of other spices (Plin. *H. N.*, xii. 54).

Frankincense was probably the main element of the "holy incense," as it is of such incense as is burnt in modern times. It is a gum or resin obtained from incisions in the bark of the *arbor thuris*, or frankincense-tree, which grows abundantly in India, and in the islands of the Indian archipelago. Anciently, the tree appears to have grown also in Arabia, whence the Egyptians (*Records of the Past*, vol. x., pp. 14—17), the Phœnicians, the Hebrews (Isa. lx. 6; Jer. vi. 20), and the Greeks obtained it in large quantities. The odour is very peculiar, and to most persons very agreeable. In England it is best known as the scent given out by the pastilles which are burnt in sick rooms.

(35) **A confection after the art of the apothecary.**—See Note on verse 25. Bezaleel's art was called in, both for the composition of the holy oil and of the holy incense (chap. xxxvii. 29).

Tempered together.—So the LXX., the Vulg., and the Targums of Onkelos and Jonathan. But most moderns render "salted," or "mixed with salt." (See Buxtorf, Gesenius, Lee, Rosenmüller, De Wette, Kalisch, Keil, &c.). The word used is capable of either meaning.

(36) **Thou shalt . . . put it before the testimony.**—Some pieces of the incense were to be continually before the ark of the covenant, either on the golden altar, or perhaps at its base ready for offering. This would symbolise the need of the perpetual offering of prayer.

(37, 38) These instructions are similar to those given with respect to the holy oil (verses 32, 33). Neither of the two holy compounds were to be applied to any profane use.

XXXI.

THE APPOINTMENT OF BEZALEEL AND AHOLIAB.

(1—11) The instructions needed for the making of the tabernacle, its furniture, and the priests' dresses, were now complete. Moses was sufficiently informed, by what he had heard and seen, both as to the "Tent of Meeting" itself, and as to all its appurtenances and paraphernalia. But Moses was not himself an artist. Among the branches of knowledge comprised in his Egyptian education the skill of the artistic constructor had not been included. (See *Excursus* **B.** at the end of the Book.) It was therefore necessary that the manual work of carrying out the instructions given him should be entrusted to others. We might have expected that it would have been left to Moses to select the individuals from among the thousands of artificers who had accompanied him out of Egypt. But God saw fit to mark the importance of the work by taking the direct appointment of the persons to be employed upon Himself. He knew what was in man. He knew to whom he had given the highest artistic power, and who at the same time that they possessed it would work in the most religious spirit. He accordingly named two persons, Bezaleel and Aholiab, as those to whom the superintendence of the whole business should be given. Bezaleel was to be leader and chief, Aholiab assistant. Bezaleel's task was to be general, Aholiab's, apparently, special (chap. xxxviii. 23). Both, however, were to receive the special assistance of God's Holy Spirit for the due execution of their respective tasks (verses 3—6), and both, as chosen instruments of God, and faithful workers in His service, had their names equally commemorated in His Holy Book, and were thus upheld as examples to future ages.

(2) **I have called by name.**—It is a high honour to be called of God *by name.* He thus calls only those whom He appoints to some great work, as Moses (chaps. iii. 4, xxxiii. 12), Samuel (1 Sam. iii. 10), and Cyrus (Isa. xlv. 3, 4).

Bezaleel the son of Uri, the son of Hur.—Hur, the grandfather of Bezaleel, is generally supposed to be identical with the Hur who supported Moses's hands (chap. xvii. 12), and was left joint regent with Aaron when Moses went up into Mount Sinai (chap. xxiv. 14). There is, however, no evidence of this beyond the identity of the name.

Of the tribe of Judah.—Descended from Judah through Pharez, Hezron, and Caleb (1 Chron. ii. 5, 18—20).

(3—4) **I have filled him with the spirit of God . . . to devise cunning works.**—"Every good gift and every perfect gift (intellectual power no less than others) is from above, and cometh down from the Father of lights" (James i. 17). Artistic ability is a Divine gift, a very precious gift, best employed in God's direct service, and always to be employed in subordination to His will, as an improving, elevating, and refining—not as a corrupting—influence.

In wisdom, and in understanding, and in knowledge.—By "wisdom" is probably meant the power to invent and originate artistic forms; by "understanding," the ability to appreciate artistic suggestions received from others; by "knowledge," acquaintance with the methods and processes of art. Bezaleel was to possess all these gifts.

In all manner of workmanship.—He was also to possess that wonderful dexterity of hand on which the power of artistic execution mainly depends.

all manner of workmanship, (4) to devise
cunning works, to work in gold, and in
silver, and in brass, (5) and in cutting of
stones, to set *them*, and in carving of tim-
ber, to work in all manner of workman-
ship. (6) And I, behold, I have given with
him Aholiab, the son of Ahisamach, of
the tribe of Dan: and in the hearts of all
that are wise hearted I have put wis-
dom, that they may make all that I
have commanded thee; (7) the tabernacle
of the congregation, and the ark of the
testimony, and the mercy seat that *is*
thereupon, and all the [1] furniture of the
tabernacle, (8) and the table and his
furniture, and the pure candlestick with
all his furniture, and the altar of in-
cense, (9) and the altar of burnt offering
with all his furniture, and the laver and
his foot, (10) and the cloths of service,
and the holy garments for Aaron the
priest, and the garments of his sons, to
minister in the priest's office, (11) and
the anointing oil, and sweet incense for
the holy *place*: according to all that I
have commanded thee shall they do.

(12) And the LORD spake unto Moses,
saying, (13) Speak thou also unto the
children of Israel, saying, Verily my
sabbaths ye shall keep: for it *is* a sign

1 Heb., *vessels*.

(4—5) **Cunning works . . . in gold, and in silver, and in brass, and in cutting of stones . . .**—It is a characteristic of early art that it eschews specialism, and it is as nearly universal as possible. Theodore of Samos (ab. B.C. 600 – 560) was an architect, a worker in bronze, and an engraver of hard stones. Michael Angelo was an architect, painter, and sculptor. Giotto was the same, and also a worker in mosaic. It is some time before, in each particular people or country, the imitative arts become separated, and each artist aspires to eminence in one branch only. (Comp. the multiform artistic powers ascribed to Hiram of Tyre in 2 Chron. ii. 14.)

In cutting of stones, to set them—*i.e.*, in gem-engraving. This branch of art was needed for engraving the names of the tribes upon the two onyxes of the ephod (chap. xxviii. 9), and upon the twelve precious stones of the breastplate (*ib.* verses 17—21). It was an art very early practised both in Chaldæa and in Egypt. (See Note 2 on chap. xxviii. 8.)

In carving of timber.—Rather, *cutting of timber*. The woodwork of the sanctuary was not "carved," but plain.

(6) **Aholiab, the son of Ahisamach.**—It has been observed above (see the first Note on the chapter) that Bezaleel's work was general, Aholiab's, special. Our version, indeed, styles the latter "an engraver, and a cunning workman, and an embroiderer" (chap. xxxviii. 23), from which it might be supposed that, like Bezaleel, he cultivated various branches of art. In the original, however, nothing is said of engraving, and the true meaning seems to be that Aholiab had the charge of the textile fabrics needed for the sanctuary, and directed both the weaving and the embroidery, but did not intermeddle in other matters. (See Note on chap. xxxviii. 23).

Of the tribe of Dan.—The tribe of Dan is among the most undistinguished; but it produced two great artists—Aholiab, the skilful maker of the textile fabrics of the tabernacle, and Hiram, the master workman employed in the ornamentation of Solomon's temple (2 Chron. ii. 14).

All that are wise hearted.—On the expression "wise hearted," see Note 1 on chap. xxviii. 3.

(7—11) The enumeration of the holy objects follows the order of the instructions given concerning them (chaps. xxv.—xxx.), except that the tabernacle itself is placed first, and the altar of incense mentioned in its natural position, together with the table of shewbread and the golden candlestick (verse 8).

(10) **The cloths of service.**—Modern critics generally suppose the state robes of the high priest to be meant (Keil, Knobel, De Wette, Kalisch, Cook); but the Rabbinical interpreters understand the cloths in which the ark and other vessels of the sanctuary were wrapped when the camp was moved from place to place (see Num. iv. 6—13). These, like the cloths here spoken of (chap. xxxix. 1), were to be of blue, and purple, and scarlet; and it would be natural to distinguish them from the "holy garments," as is done both here and also in chaps. xxxv. 19, and xxxix. 1, 41. They had, however, not been previously mentioned in the directions. Perhaps the true explanation is, that under the words "cloths of service" (*bigdey sĕrâd*, or *bigdeh hassĕrâd*) are included both the garments of Aaron and also those of his sons, the two later clauses of the verse being exegetical of the first clause. In that case, we should translate: *The robes of service, both the holy garments for Aaron the priest, and also the garments of his sons.* Chap. xxxix. 41 is decidedly favourable to this interpretation.

THE LAW OF THE SABBATH DECLARED ANEW UNDER A PENAL SANCTION.

(12—17) The worship of the tabernacle was so closely connected with Sabbatical observance (Lev. xix. 30), that no surprise can be felt at a recurrence to the subject in the present place. It was not only that there might be a danger of zealous men breaking the Sabbatical rest in their eagerness to hasten forward the work of construction now required of them. The re-enactment of the Law might serve to check this tendency if it existed; but clearly the present passage is not specially directed to so narrow an object. It is altogether general in its aim and teaching. It re-enacts the law of the Sabbath (1) under a new sanction; and (2) with new light in its intention and value. Hitherto the Sabbath had been, in the main, a positive enactment intended to test obedience (chap. xvi. 4); now it was elevated into a sacramental sign between God and His people (verse 13). Having become such a sign, it required to be guarded by a new sanction, and this was done by assigning the death-penalty to any infraction of the law of Sabbath observance (verses 14, 15).

(13) **It is a sign between me and you.**—Circumcision had been given as a covenant sign to Abraham and his descendants (Gen. xvii. 9—13); but its adoption by many of the heathen nations had rendered it no longer a distinguishing mark by which God's people

between me and you throughout your
generations; that *ye* may know that I
am the LORD that doth sanctify you.
(14) [a] Ye shall keep the sabbath therefore;
for it *is* holy unto you: every one that
defileth it shall surely be put to death:
for whosoever doeth *any* work therein,
that soul shall be cut off from among
his people. (15) Six days may work be
done; but in the seventh *is* the sabbath
of rest, [1] holy to the LORD: whosoever
doeth *any* work in the sabbath day, he
shall surely be put to death. (16) Where-
fore the children of Israel shall keep
the sabbath, to observe the sabbath
throughout their generations, *for* a per-
petual covenant. (17) It *is* a sign be-
tween me and the children of Israel for
ever: for [b] *in* six days the LORD made
heaven and earth, and on the seventh
day he rested, and was refreshed.
(18) And he gave unto Moses, when he
had made an end of communing with
him upon mount Sinai, [c] two tables of
testimony, tables of stone, written with
the finger of God.

CHAPTER XXXII.

—(1) And when
the people saw that Moses delayed to
come down out of the mount, the people
gathered themselves together unto
Aaron, and said unto him, [d] Up, make us
gods, which shall go before us; for *as
for* this Moses, the man that brought us

a ch. 20. 8; Deut. 5. 12; Ezek. 20. 12.

1 Heb., *holiness*.

b Gen. 1. 31 & 2. 2.

c Deut. 9. 10.

d Acts 7. 40.

---

could be certainly known from others. Thus a new "sign" was needed. The observance of one day in seven as a day of holy rest became henceforth the distinguishing sign, and proved effectual. It was not likely to be adopted, and in point of fact was not adopted, by any of the heathen. We find it in the latest time of the Jewish nation still regarded as the special mark and badge of a Jew (Juv. *Sat.* vi. 159, xiv. 96; Mart. *Epig.* iv. 4, l. 7, &c.).

(14) **Every one that defileth it shall surely be put to death.**—This is a new enactment, and must be regarded in conjunction with the new dignity attached to Sabbath observance by its having become the special covenant sign between God and His people. The Sabbath-breaker now threw himself out of covenant with God, and not only so, but did what in him lay to throw the whole people out of covenant. His guilt was therefore great, and the assignment to it of the death-penalty is in no way surprising; rather, it is in accordance with the general spirit of the code (see chaps. xxi. 16, 17, 29, xxii. 18—20, &c.). When the occasion arose, there was no hesitation in carrying the law out (Num. xv. 32—35).

Cut off.—Or, *separated, set apart from.* His act at once cast him out from the number of God's people, made him an outlaw, *ipso facto* excommunicated him.

(15) **Six days.**—Comp. chap. xx. 9.

The sabbath of rest.—Rather, *a sabbath of rest*, or *a complete rest.* The repetition (*sabbath sabbâthôn*) gives an idea of completeness.

(17) **For in six days the Lord made heaven and earth.**—Whatever other grounds there were for Sabbath observance, this idea always lay at its root. Man was through it to be made like unto his Maker—to have from time to time a rest from his labours, as God had had (Gen. ii. 2, 3)—and thereby to realise the blessedness of that final rest which he may be sure "remaineth for the people of God."

THE TWO TABLES GIVEN.

(18) The termination and crown of the entire conference which Moses had held with God on Mount Sinai for forty days and forty nights (chap. xxiv. 18) was the committal to his hands of the two tables of testimony which had been promised before the ascent into the mount was made (*ib.* verse 12), and which were pre-supposed in the entire arrangement of the sanctuary. The Court pre-supposed the tabernacle; the outer chamber of the tabernacle, or holy place, was a mere vestibule to the inner chamber, or holy of holies: the inner chamber was a receptacle for the ark; and the ark was a chest or coffer constructed to contain the Two Tables. The entire design having been laid down, it was a first step towards the carrying out of the design to put into the hands of Moses that treasure with a view to which all the directions concerning the tabernacle had been given.

Two tables of testimony. — Rather, *the two tables.* The treasure which had been glanced at in chap. xxv. 21, and distinctly promised in chap. xxiv. 12.

Written with the finger of God.—Comp. chap. xxiv. 12, where God speaks of "commandments which *He* has written." We must understand that the tables were inscribed by some supernatural process, and not by any human hand. The exact nature of the supernatural process is not revealed to us.

XXXII.

THE IDOLATRY OF THE GOLDEN CALF.

(1) **When the people saw that Moses delayed to come down.**—After seven chapters of directions, which belong to the Mosaic or Levitical Law, the writer here resumes his historical narrative. Leaving Moses still in the mount, he returns to the plain at its base in order to relate the events which had there occurred during Moses' absence. It has been suggested that chap. xxxi. was originally followed by chap. xxxv., and that chaps. xxxii. — xxxiv. form a "distinct composition," which was subsequently inserted at this point (Cook). But this supposition is improbable. Chap. xxxv. does not cohere with chap. xxxi. Passing from one to other, we should be sensible of a gap which required filling up. Neither does chap. xxxii. commence like an independent narrative. It rests on the fact of the long delay of Moses in Sinai, which requires chaps. xxv.—xxxi. to explain it; and its mention of "*the* people," and "*the* mount," without further designation, implies reference to something that has gone before. Chaps. xxxii.—xxxiv. occur really in their natural, their proper, and, no doubt, in their original place.

The people gathered themselves together unto Aaron.—Moses, before his departure, had left

up out of the land of Egypt, we wot not
what is become of him. (2) And Aaron
said unto them, Break off the golden
earrings, which *are* in the ears of your
wives, of your sons, and of your daugh-
ters, and bring *them* unto me. (3) And
all the people brake off the golden ear-
rings which *were* in their ears, and
brought *them* unto Aaron. (4) [a] And
he received *them* at their hand, and
fashioned it with a graving tool, after
he had made it a molten calf: and they
said, These *be* thy gods, O Israel, which
brought thee up out of the land of
Egypt. (5) And when Aaron saw *it*, he
built an altar before it; and Aaron

[a] Ps. 106. 19; 1 Kings 12. 28.

---

directions that the people should in any difficulty take the advice of Aaron *and Hur* (chap. xxiv. 14). It is not surprising, however, that, when the difficulty arose, Aaron alone was consulted. Aaron had been joint-leader with Moses from the first (see chaps. iv. 29, 30, v. 1, 4, 20, &c.); Hur had only very recently been advanced into a position of authority (chaps. xvii. 10, xxiv. 14). He was, at the most, the Lepidus of the Triumvirate.

Up, make us gods.—Rather, *make us a god.* The religious condition of the Israelites during the sojourn in Egypt has been so entirely passed over in the previous narrative, that this request comes upon us as a surprise and a shock. True, there have been warnings against idolatry, reiterated warnings (chaps. xx. 4, 5, 23, xxiii. 32, 33), but no tendency towards it has manifested itself, no hint has been given that it was an immediate and pressing danger. When, however, we carefully scrutinise the rest of Scripture, we find reason to believe that a leaning towards idolatry had, in point of fact, shown itself among the people while they were in Egypt, and had even attained some considerable development. (See Lev. xvii. 7; Josh. xxiv. 14; Ezek. xx. 8, xxiii. 3.) This tendency had been checked by the series of extraordinary manifestations which had accompanied the exodus. Now, however, in the absence of Moses, in the uncertainty which prevailed as to whether he still lived or not, and in the withdrawal from the camp of that Divine Presence which had hitherto gone before them, the idolatrous instinct once more came to the front. The cry was raised, "make us a god"—make us something to take the place of the pillar of the cloud, something visible, tangible, on which we can believe the Divine Presence to rest, and which may "go before us" and conduct us.

This Moses, the man that brought us up . . .—Contemptuous words, showing how shortlived is human gratitude, and even human respect. An absence of less than six weeks, and a belief that he was no more, had sufficed to change the great deliverer into "*this Moses, the man* who brought us up."

(2) **And Aaron said . . . Break off the golden earrings.**—It is a reasonable conjecture that Aaron thought to prevent the projected idolatry by this requirement. Not having the courage to meet the demand of the people with a direct negative, he may have aimed at diverting them from their purpose by requiring a sacrifice which they would be unwilling to make, viz., the personal ornaments of their wives and children. The women might reasonably have been expected to resist, and the men to yield before such resistance; but the event proved otherwise.

Your sons.—Earrings are worn in the East almost as much by men as by women. Most Assyrian and some Egyptian monarchs are represented with them.

(3) **All the people brake off the golden earrings.**—Aaron had miscalculated the strength of the people's fanaticism. Not the slightest resistance was offered to his requirement, not the slightest objection made. "*All* the people," with one accord, surrendered their earrings. Some measure is hereby afforded of the intensity of the feeling which was moving the people and urging them to substitute an idolatrous worship for the abstract and purely spiritual religion which had reigned supreme since their departure from Egypt.

(4) **And he received them at their hand, and fashioned it with a graving tool.**—Rather, *and he received it* (*i.e.*, the gold) *at their hand, and bound it in a bag.* So Gesenius, Rosenmüller, Fürst, Knobel, Kurtz, Maurer, Scröder, Cook, &c. "Fashioned it with a graving tool" is a possible rendering of the Hebrew words, but will not suit here, since the next clause tells us that the image was a molten one, and if it had been intended to say that the image was first molten and then finished with a graving tool, the order of the two clauses would have been inverted. A similar phrase to that here used has the sense of "bound in a bag" in 2 Kings v. 23.

After he had made it a molten calf.— This is a quite impossible rendering. The original gives "and," not "after." The action of this clause must either be simultaneous with that of the last or subsequent. Translate, *and made it into a molten calf.*

A molten calf.—It has been usual to regard the selection of the "calf" form for the image as due to Egyptian influences. But the Egyptian calf-worship, or, rather, bull-worship, was not a worship of images, but of living animals. A sacred bull, called Apis, was worshipped at Memphis, and another, called Mnevis, at Heliopolis, both being regarded as actual incarnate deities. Had Egyptian ideas been in the ascendant, it would have been natural to select a living bull, which might have "gone before" the people literally. The "molten calf," which had no very exact counterpart in Egypt, perhaps points back to an older idolatry, such as is glanced at in Josh. xxiv. 14, where the Israelites are warned to "put away the gods which their fathers served on the other side of the flood," *i.e.*, of the Euphrates. Certainly the bull form was more distinctive of the Babylonian and Assyrian than of the Egyptian worship, and it may he suspected that the emigrants from Chaldæa had clung through all their wanderings to the mystic symbolism which had been elaborated in that primæval land, and which they would contrast favourably with the coarse animal worship of Egypt. In Chaldæa, the bull, generally winged and human-headed, represented the combination of wisdom, strength, and omnipresence, which characterises divinity; and this combination might well have seemed to carnal minds no unapt symbol of Jehovah.

These be thy gods.—Rather, *This is thy god.*

(5) **Aaron . . . built an altar before it.**—Having once yielded to the popular cry, Aaron was carried on from one compliance to another. He caused the mould to be made for the idol, and the gold to be melted and run into it; and now he constructed, perhaps with his own hands, an altar of rough stones or turf (chap. xx. 24, 25), and placed it directly in front of the

made proclamation, and said, To morrow
is a feast to the LORD. (6) And they rose
up early on the morrow, and offered
burnt offerings, and brought peace offer-
ings; and the [a] people sat down to eat
and to drink, and rose up to play.
(7) And the LORD said unto Moses,
[b] Go, get thee down; for thy people,
which thou broughtest out of the land
of Egypt, have corrupted *themselves:*
(8) [c] they have turned aside quickly out
of the way which I commanded them:
they have made them a molten calf, and
have worshipped it, and have sacrificed
thereunto, and said, These *be* thy gods, O
Israel, which have brought thee up out
of the land of Egypt. (9) And the LORD
said unto Moses, [d] I have seen this
people, and, behold, it *is* a stiffnecked
people: (10) now therefore let me alone,
that my wrath may wax hot against
them, and that I may consume them:
and I will make of thee a great nation.
(11) [e] And Moses besought [1] the LORD
his God, and said, LORD, why doth thy
wrath wax hot against thy people, which
thou hast brought forth out of the land
of Egypt with great power, and with a
mighty hand? (12) [f] Wherefore should
the Egyptians speak, and say, For mis-
chief did he bring them out, to slay
them in the mountains, and to consume
them from the face of the earth? Turn
from thy fierce wrath, and repent of
this evil against thy people. (13) Re-
member Abraham, Isaac, and Israel,
thy servants, to whom thou swarest by
thine own self, and saidst unto them,
[g] I will multiply your seed as the stars
of heaven, and all this land that I have

a 1 Cor. 10. 7.

b Deut. 9. 12.

c Deut. 9. 8.

d ch. 33. 3; Deut. 9. 13.

e Ps. 106. 23.

1 Heb., *the face of the LORD.*

f Num. 14. 13.

g Gen. 12. 7 & 15. 7 & 48. 16.

---

image, thus encouraging the offering of sacrifice to it. Perhaps he flattered himself that by heading the movement he could control it, and hinder it from becoming downright apostacy from Jehovah. In his view no doubt the calf was an emblem of Jehovah, and the worship paid it was the worship of Jehovah. Hence the festival which he proclaimed was to be "a feast to Jehovah." But how little able he was to guide events, or to hinder the worst evils of idolatry from speedily manifesting themselves, appears from verses 6 and 25.

(6) **They rose up early.**—Impatient to begin the new worship, the people rose with the dawn, and brought offerings, and offered sacrifice. Whether Aaron took part in these acts—which constituted the actual worship of the idol—is left doubtful.

Burnt offerings, and . . . peace offerings.—Sacrifices of both kinds were pre-Mosaical, not first originated by the Law, though deriving confirmation from it. Offerings of both kinds are noticed in Gen. iv. 3, 4; Exod. xviii. 12.

The people sat down to eat and to drink, and rose up to play.—A feast always followed a sacrifice (see chaps. xviii. 12, xxiv. 5, 11). In feasting therefore upon what they had offered, the Israelites did no wrong; but probably they indulged themselves in a license of feasting unsuited to a religious act, though common enough in the idol-festivals of the heathen. They "fed without fear" (Jude 12), transgressed the bounds of moderation, and turned what should have been a religious rite into an orgy. Then, having gratified their appetites and stimulated their passions, they ceased to eat and drink, and "rose up to play." The "play" included dancing of an indecent kind (verses 19, 25), and would probably have terminated, as the heathen orgies too often did, in the grossest sensualism, had not the descent of Moses from Sinai, and his appearance on the scene, put a stop to the unhallowed doings.

GOD'S OFFER TO MOSES.

(7) **The Lord said unto Moses, Go, get thee down.**—Moses was, of course, wholly ignorant of all that had occurred in the camp. The thick cloud which covered the top of Sinai had prevented his seeing what occurred in the plain below (chap. xxiv. 18). The phrase, "Go, get thee down," is emphatic, and implies urgency.

Thy people.—"Thine," not any longer "mine," since they have broken the covenant that united us; yet still "thine," however much they sin. The tie of blood-relationship cannot be broken.

Have corrupted themselves.—The form of the verb used (*shikhêth*) is active. We must supply "their way," or some similar phrase, after it. (Comp. Gen. vi. 12: "All flesh had corrupted *his way* upon the earth.")

(8) **These be thy gods.**—Rather, *This is thy god,* as in verse 4.

(9) **It is a stiff-necked people.**—This phrase, afterwards so common (chaps. xxxiii. 3, 5, xxxiv. 5; Deut. ix. 6, 13, x. 16; 2 Chron. xxx. 8, xxxvi. 13; Ps. lxxv. 5; Jer. xvii. 23; Acts vii. 51), occurs here for the first time. It is generally explained as "obstinate," but rather means "perverse," the metaphor being taken from the horse that stiffens his neck against the pull of the rein, and will not be guided by the rider. The LXX. omit the verse, for no intelligible reason.

(10) **Let me alone.**—This was not a command to abstain from deprecation, but rather an intimation that deprecation might have power to change God's purpose. Moses was tried by an offer which would have exalted him at the expense of the people. He was allowed to see that he might either sacrifice the people and obtain his own aggrandisement, or deny himself and save them. That he chose the better part redounds to his undying glory.

I will make of thee a great nation—*i.e.*, I will put thee in the place of Abraham, make thee the father of the faithful, destroy all existing Israelites but thee and thine, and proceed *de novo* to raise up a "great nation" out of thy loins.

MOSES' REPLY, AND GOD'S "REPENTANCE."

(11—13) Moses has three arguments: (1) God has done so much for His people, that surely He will not now make all of none effect (verse 11); (2) their destruction will give a triumph to the Egyptians (verse 12); (3) it will nullify the promises made to Abraham,

spoken of will I give unto your seed, and they shall inherit *it* for ever.
(14) And the LORD repented of the evil which he thought to do unto his people.
(15) And Moses turned, and went down from the mount, and the two tables of the testimony *were* in his hand: the tables *were* written on both their sides; on the one side and on the other *were* they written.
(16) And the [a] tables *were* the work of God, and the writing *was* the writing of God, graven upon the tables.
(17) And when Joshua heard the noise of the people as they shouted, he said unto Moses, *There is* a noise of war in the camp.
(18) And he said, *It is* not the voice of *them that* shout for mastery, neither *is it* the voice of *them that* cry for [1] being overcome: *but* the noise of *them that* sing do I hear.
(19) And it came to pass, as soon as he came nigh unto the camp, that he saw the calf, and the dancing: and Moses' anger waxed hot, and he cast the tables out of his hands, and brake them beneath the mount.
(20) [b] And he took the calf which they had made, and burnt *it* in the fire, and ground *it* to powder, and strawed *it* upon the water, and made the children of Israel drink *of it.*

a ch. 31. 18.

1 Heb., *weakness.*

b Deut. 9. 21.

Isaac, and Jacob (Gen. xv. 5, xvii. 2—6, xxvi. 1, xxviii. 12, xxxv. 11), causing Moses to eclipse their glory, and to be looked upon as the true patriarch and progenitor of the "peculiar people" (verse 13). To these arguments he adds entreaties that God will be merciful, and change His purpose (verse 12).

(14) **The Lord repented of the evil.**—Moses' intercession was effectual. God spared the people at his desire. He is, therefore, said to have "repented"; not that He had really changed His purpose, for He had known from the beginning that Moses would intercede and that He would spare, but because He first announced a (conditional) purpose, and then announced a different one. The mode of speech is, as so frequently, anthropomorphic.

THE DESCENT OF MOSES FROM SINAI, AND THE SUPPRESSION OF THE IDOLATRY.

(15) **And Moses turned**—*i.e.,* "returned," or "set out on his return," apparently without making any communication to Joshua, who was waiting for him not far off (see verse 17).

The two tables . . . were in his hand.—In Deut. ix. 15 we read that the two tables were in his "two hands," which is more exact, and more as we should have expected.

The tables were written on both their sides.—Babylonian tablets and Assyrian monoliths have usually writing on both sides, Egyptian monoliths rarely. It has been calculated that the 172 words of the Decalogue could easily have been inscribed in letters of a fair size on the four surfaces indicated, if the tablets were 27 inches long by 18 inches broad, and that two tablets of this size could readily have been conveyed in a man's two hands (Keil).

(16) **The tables were the work of God.**—Rosenmüller supposes this to mean merely that the size and shape of the stones was prescribed to Moses by God; but the natural meaning of the words is that God Himself fashioned them. This was not the case with the second tables (chap. xxxiv. 1, 4).

The writing was the writing of God.—See Note 3 on chap. xxxi. 18.

(17) **When Joshua heard.**—Joshua's presence with Moses in the mount has not been indicated since chap. xxiv. 13. But it would seem that when Moses was summoned up into the cloud (chap. xxiv. 16) his faithful "minister" remained where he was, waiting for his master. He may have found shelter in some "cleft of the rock;" and the manna may have fallen about him, and sufficed for his sustenance during the forty days and nights of his master's absence.

The noise of the people as they shouted.—"Shouting" was a feature of idolatrous rites (1 Kings xviii. 28; Acts xix. 34; Herod. ii. 60, &c.), and was in part a cause, in part a result, of the physical excitement which prevailed during such orgies. Joshua, unsuspicious of the real nature of the shouting, supposed, naturally enough, that the camp was attacked by an enemy, and that the noise was "a noise of war." But Moses, forewarned of the actual state of affairs (verses 7, 8), had probably a shrewd suspicion of the real nature of the sounds. He contented himself, however, with negativing his minister's conjecture.

(18) **Shout . . . cry . . . sing.**—The Hebrew verb is the same in all three clauses. Translate: *It is not the voice of them that cry for victory, nor is it the voice of them that cry for defeat; the voice of them that cry do I hear.* Moses' sense of hearing conveys to him no positive result. We must remember that the camp was still distant, and that the sound was conveyed circuitously, since the descent from the Ras Sufsafeh is by a side valley, from which the sight of the plain is shut out (Stanley, *Sinai and Palestine,* p. 44).

(19) **And the dancing.**—Heb., *and dances.* What Moses saw was "*the* calf" which had already been mentioned, and "dances" which had not been mentioned, but which were now going on after the usual fashion of idolatrous festivity. Such dancing among Oriental nations was uniformly of a lascivious character. (Comp. verse 25.)

He cast the tables out of his hands.—Comp. Deut. ix. 17. In righteous indignation, but perhaps with some revival of the hot temper which had led him astray in his younger days (chap. ii. 12).

(20) **He took the calf.**—To suppress the idolatry, the first step was to destroy the idol. Moses, who must have rallied to his side at once a certain number of the people, laid hold of the calf, and ordered its immediate destruction. He had it submitted to the action of fire, whereby its form was destroyed, and the material, as it would seem, calcined. This calcined material he reduced to a fine powder by rubbing or pounding, and then had the powder sprinkled on the surface of the stream which supplied the camp with water, that so the people might *seem,* at any rate, to swallow their own sin. Compare the action of Josiah (2 Kings xxiii. 6, 12). No doubt, the process of destruction took some time. It is not meant that it

(21) And Moses said unto Aaron, What
did this people unto thee, that thou
hast brought so great a sin upon them?
(22) And Aaron said, Let not the anger
of my lord wax hot: thou knowest the
people, that they *are set* on mischief.
(23) For they said unto me, Make us
gods, which shall go before us: for *as for*
this Moses, the man that brought us up
out of the land of Egypt, we wot not
what is become of him. (24) And I said
unto them, Whosoever hath any gold,
let them break *it* off. So they gave *it*
me: then I cast it into the fire, and
there came out this calf.
(25) And when Moses saw that the
people *were* naked; (for Aaron had made
them naked unto *their* shame among
[1] their enemies:) (26) Then Moses stood
in the gate of the camp, and said, Who
is on the LORD's side? *let him come* unto
me. And all the sons of Levi gathered
themselves together unto him. (27) And
he said unto them, Thus saith the LORD
God of Israel, Put every man his sword
by his side, *and* go in and out from gate
to gate throughout the camp, and slay
every man his brother, and every man
his companion, and every man his
neighbour. (28) And the children of Levi
did according to the word of Moses:
and there fell of the people that day
about three thousand men. (29) [2] For
Moses had said, [3] Consecrate yourselves
to day to the LORD, even every man up-
on his son, and upon his brother; that he
may bestow upon you a blessing this day.
(30) And it came to pass on the mor-

1 Heb., *those that rose up against them.*

3 Or, *And Moses said, Consecrate yourselves to day to the LORD, because every man* hath been *against his son, and against his brother,* &c.

3 Heb., *Fill your hands.*

---

was completed, but only that it was commenced, before Moses turned to other matters.

(21) **Moses said unto Aaron, What did this people unto thee?**—The second step was to inquire how the idolatry came about; and here Moses very reasonably addressed himself to Aaron. Aaron had been left in charge of the people (chap. xxiv. 14), to advise them, direct them, control them, if necessary. How had he acquitted himself of this charge? He had allowed the people to commit a great sin. What excuse could he offer for his conduct? Had the people injured him in any way? The question is asked ironically.

(22–24) Aaron's conduct was really without excuse; but he attempts two pleas—the first insufficient, the second false and fatuous. (1) The people compelled him; they were "set on mischief;" they made the proposal—they would have it so. (2) He threw the gold into the furnace, and "it came out a calf," as if he had not ordered the construction of the mould. In Deuteronomy, Moses informs us that Aaron's whole conduct so angered God that God would have destroyed him but for his own intercession (Deut. ix. 20).

(25) **When Moses saw that the people were naked.**—Most modern commentators prefer to translate "that the people were licentious," or "unruly." But the rendering of the Authorised Version may be defended. In the lewd and excited dancing of idolatrous orgies, garments were frequently cast aside, and the person exposed indecently. Egyptian dancers are represented on the monuments with scarcely any clothing.

Among their enemies.—Amalekites may have held many fastnesses among the hills, from which they may have been able to see what was going on in the camp.

(26) **Then Moses stood in the gate of the camp.**—The third and crowning step was now to be taken. Though the idol had been seized and its destruction commenced, though Aaron had been rebuked and put to shame, yet the revel continued. Once launched on an evil course, the bulk of the people persisted in it. Moses felt that God was openly insulted by such conduct, against which death was denounced by the Law (chap. xxii. 20), and which might at any moment provoke God to destroy the whole people (verse 10). He therefore proceeded to suppress the idolatry by a stern act of judicial severity—an execution on a large scale of those taken *flagrante delicto*. Standing in the gate—*i.e.*, the principal gate—of the camp, he summoned to his aid those who were on the Lord's side, and gave them orders to go through the camp from end to end, and put to death all whom they found still engaged in the mad revel.

All the sons of Levi.—This must not be understood literally. *All* the Levites would not have heard the summons of Moses, and some were evidently among those who persisted in idolatry (verses 27—29). In the language of the sacred writers, "all" constantly means "the greater part."

(27) **Thus saith the Lord God.**—Moses felt that he was divinely commissioned to perform this act of severity. The lives of all who had committed the idolatry were justly forfeit. Trial was unnecessary where the offence was being openly committed before the eyes of all. Such dancing and such shouting could not possibly be Jehovah-worship. It was by its very character idolatrous.

Go in and out from gate to gate . . .—*i.e.*, "pass through the whole camp from end to end, visit all parts of it, and wherever you see the rites continuing, smite with the sword—smite, and spare not."

Slay every man his brother.—Comp. verse 26. The Levites who had rallied to the call of Moses might find their own brothers or their own sons among the idolaters. If they did, they were still to smite, though the offender was their near relative.

(29) **For Moses had said, Consecrate yourselves.**—Moses had explained to them that a brave behaviour under existing circumstances would be accepted as a "consecration," and would win for the tribe a semi-priestly character. His announcement was made good when the Levites were appointed to the service of the sanctuary in lieu of the firstborn (Numb. iii. 6—13).

MOSES' INTERCESSION ON BEHALF OF THE PEOPLE.

(30–35) When Moses had, on first hearing of God's intention to destroy the people, interceded for them (verses 11—13), his prayers had received no direct

row, that Moses said unto the people,
Ye have sinned a great sin: and now I
will go up unto the LORD; peradventure
I shall make an atonement for your sin.
(31) And Moses returned unto the LORD,
and said, Oh, this people have sinned a
great sin, and have made them gods of
gold. (32) Yet now, if thou wilt forgive
their sin—; and if not, blot me, I pray
thee, out of thy book which thou hast
written. (33) And the LORD said unto
Moses, Whosoever hath sinned against
me, him will I blot out of my book.
(34) Therefore now go, lead the people
unto *the place* of which I have spoken
unto thee: behold, mine Angel shall go
before thee: nevertheless in the day when
I visit I will visit their sin upon them.
(35) And the LORD plagued the people,
because they made the calf, which
Aaron made.

CHAPTER XXXIII.—(1) And the
LORD said unto Moses, Depart, *and* go

---

answer—he had been left in doubt whether they were granted or no. Having now put an end to the offence, and to some extent punished it, he is bent on renewing his supplications, and obtaining a favourable reply. Once more he ascends into the mount to be quite alone, and so best able to wrestle with God in prayer; and this time he not merely intercedes, but offers himself as an atonement for the people, and is willing to be "blotted out of God's book," if on this condition they may be spared. God refuses the offer, but makes known to Moses that He relents—that He will spare the people, and allow them to continue their journey to the promised land; only He will send an angel to lead them instead of leading them Himself, and He will punish the sinners by a different punishment from that originally threatened (verse 10).

(31) **Moses returned unto the Lord**—*i.e.*, re-ascended Sinai, to the place where he had passed the forty days and nights.

Gods of gold.—Rather, *a god of gold.* (Comp. Note 3 on verse 1.) The plural is one of dignity.

(32) **If thou wilt forgive their sin.**—Supply after the word "sin," "well and good," "I am content," or some such phrase. Similar instances of *aposiopesis* will be found in Dan. iii. 15; Luke xiii. 9, xix. 42; John vi. 62; Rom. ix. 22. The usage is common among Orientals.

Blot me, I pray thee, out of thy book.—Comp. Rom. ix. 1—3. Moses seems to have risen to the same height of self-abnegation as St. Paul, and to have willed to be "accursed from God for his brethren, his kinsmen according to the flesh." As his sacrifice could not have redeemed them (Ps. xlix. 7), God did not accept it in the literal sense; but the offer may have availed much towards the pardon of the people, and towards lightening the chastisement which they received (verses 34, 35).

(33) **Whosoever hath sinned against me, him will I blot out.**—Comp. Ezek. xviii. 4: "The soul that sinneth, it shall die." A mere man cannot take other men's sins on him, cannot relieve them of the penalties attached to sin, the worst of which is the depravation of the soul itself. Sin persisted in blots out from God's book by the absolute contradiction that there is between evil and good. Even Christ's merits cannot avail the sinner who does not put away his sin, detest it, abhor it, revolt from it. Only One who can implant a principle of life in man can save from death.

(34) **Lead the people unto the place of which I have spoken**—*i.e.*, continue their leader until Palestine is reached. (See chaps. iii. 8, 17, vi. 4—8, &c.)

Mine Angel shall go before thee.—So far as the form of the expression goes, the promise is, as nearly as possible, a repetition of the original one, "Behold, I send an angel before thee, to keep thee in the way, and to bring thee into the place which I have prepared" (chap. xxiii. 20). But the meaning of the promise is wholly changed, as we learn from the opening paragraph of the ensuing chapter (chap. xxxiii. 1—3). The "angel" now promised as a guide is not to be God Himself ("I will not go up in the midst of thee"), but a creature, between whom and God the distance is immeasurable.

In the day when I visit I will visit their sin upon them.—All sin is followed by suffering; the sequence is inevitable. God had now consented to spare His people, and to take them back into favour; but they were not to expect that matters would be with them as if their sin had not taken place. It would still be "visited upon them"—not, indeed, by instant death, but still in some way or other. The weary waiting in the wilderness for forty years may have been a part of the punishment (Num. xiv. 33); but it may also have been inflicted on different persons in many different ways.

(35) **The Lord plagued the people.**—We are not to understand by this (with Kalisch) that a pestilence was sent, but only that sufferings of various kinds befell those who had worshipped the calf, and were, in fact, punishments inflicted on them for that transgression.

XXXIII.

THE HUMILIATION OF THE PEOPLE AT THE THREAT OF GOD'S WITHDRAWAL.

(1–6) If God consented at all to renew His covenant with the people, after they had so flagrantly broken it, the terms on which He would renew it were, in strict justice, purely optional. In the "Book of the Covenant" He had promised to go up with them by an Angel, in whom was His Name (chap. xxiii. 20—23): *i.e.*, by His Son, the Second Person in the Holy Trinity. He now, to mark His displeasure, withdrew this promise, and substituted for the Divine presence that of a mere angel. "I will send an angel before thee" (verse 2); "I will not go up in the midst of thee" (verse 3). Dimly the people felt the importance of the change, the vast difference between the angelic and the Divine, and "mourned" their loss (verse 4): mourned with some touch of real godly sorrow, and, as was the custom of the Orientals in mourning (Terent. *Heaut.* ii. 3, 47; Herodian. iv. 2, &c.), "put off their ornaments."

(1) **The Lord said unto Moses.**—In continuation and explanation of the words recorded in chap.

**up hence, thou and the people which
thou hast brought up out of the land of
Egypt, unto the land which I sware un-
to Abraham, to Isaac, and to Jacob,
saying, [a] Unto thy seed will I give it:
(2) [b] And I will send an angel before thee;
and I will drive out the Canaanite, the
Amorite, and the Hittite, and the Periz-
zite, the Hivite, and the Jebusite:
(3) unto a land flowing with milk and
honey: for I will not go up in the midst
of thee; for thou *art* a [c] stiffnecked
people: lest I consume thee in the way.
(4) And when the people heard these
evil tidings, they mourned: and no man
did put on him his ornaments. (5) For
the LORD had said unto Moses, Say un-
to the children of Israel, Ye *are* a stiff-
necked people: I will come up into the
midst of thee in a moment, and consume
thee: therefore now put off thy orna-
ments from thee, that I may know
what to do unto thee. (6) And the chil-
dren of Israel stripped themselves of
their ornaments by the mount Horeb.
(7) And Moses took the tabernacle,
and pitched it without the camp, afar
off from the camp, and called it the**

a Gen. 12. 7.

b Deut. 7. 22; Josh. 24. 11.

c ch. 32. 9; Deut. 9. 13.

---

xxxii. 33, 34, but probably at another time, after Moses had once more descended from the Ras Sufsafeh to the plain at its base.

The land which I sware unto Abraham . . .—The misconduct of Israel in their worship of the calf would not annul the promises of God to the patriarchs. These He was bound to make good. "The Lord sware, and will not repent" (Ps. cx. 4).

(2) **I will send an angel before thee.**—"An angel" is ambiguous. It might designate the Angel of the Covenant, the Angel of God's presence, as in chap. xxiii. 20; or it might mean a mere ordinary angel, on a par with those who presided over the destinies of other nations besides the Hebrews (Dan. x. 13, 20). That here the expression is used in this latter sense is made manifest by the declaration of the next verse: "I will not go up in the midst of thee."

(3) **A land flowing with milk and honey.**—See Note on chap. iii. 8.

Lest I consume thee.—Comp. chap. xxxii. 10; Lev. x. 2; Ps. lxxxviii. 21, 31, &c. "God is a consuming fire" (Heb. xii. 29). His near presence, if it does not cleanse and purify, scorches and withers. The conduct of Israel in the wilderness was such as continually to provoke Him to destroy them; and but for His amazing compassion and forbearance, the result here glanced at would assuredly have followed.

(4) **When the people heard these evil tidings, they mourned.**—It was something that the people felt the tidings to be "evil." It is natural for sinful men to shrink from the near presence of God (Matt. viii. 34; Luke v. 8); and so the Israelites had shrunk from it a short time previously (chap. xx. 19). Even now they would probably have feared a too near contact; but still, they were unwilling that God should cease to be the leader and guide of the host: they set a value on His presence and protection, which they felt that that of an angel would ill replace. Accordingly, when Moses communicated to them what God had said (verses 1—3), they "mourned," *i.e.*, not only grieved inwardly, but showed the outward tokens of grief—made a public and, as it were, national lamentation.

No man did put on him his ornaments.—The Orientals, both men and women, have always affected ornament, and taken an extreme delight in it. Herodotus tells us that the Persians who accompanied Xerxes into Greece wore generally collars and bracelets of gold (*Hist.* ix. 80). Xenophon says that the Medes indulged a similar taste (*Cyropæd.* i. 3, § 2). In Egypt, at the time of the exodus, men of station wore generally collars, armlets, and bracelets, occasionally anklets. The Assyrians wore armlets, bracelets, and ear-rings. To strip himself of his ornaments was a great act of self-denial on the part of an Oriental; but it was done commonly in the case of mourning on account of a family bereavement, and sometimes in the case of national misfortunes. (See Note on verses 1—6.)

(5) **For the Lord had said unto Moses.**—Rather, *And the Lord said unto Moses.* The message did not precede the repentance of the people, but followed it.

I will come up into the midst of thee in a moment, and consume thee.—Rather, *were I to go up in the midst of thee, even for a moment* (a brief space), *I should consume thee.* The people learnt by this the reason of God's proposed withdrawal. It was in mercy, that they might not be consumed, as there was danger of their being unless they repented and turned to God.

Put off thy ornaments.—Rather, *leave off thy ornaments, i.e.*, put them aside altogether; show thy penitence by giving up the use of them; then shall I know what to do with thee; then shall I be able to deal with thee in a way which otherwise were impossible.

(6) **And the children of Israel stripped themselves of their ornaments**—*i.e.*, left off their ornaments, ceased to wear them altogether.

By the mount Horeb.—Rather, *from mount Horeb, i.e.*, from the time of their first discarding them in Horeb (= Sinai).

MOSES ESTABLISHES A TEMPORARY TABERNACLE.

(7—11) Moses, having experienced the blessedness of solitary communion with God during the forty days spent on Sinai, felt now, as he had never felt before, the want of a "house of God," whither he might retire for prayer and meditation, secure of being undisturbed. Months would necessarily elapse before the Tabernacle could be constructed according to the pattern which he had seen in the mount. During this interval he determined to make use of one of the existing tents as a "house of prayer," severing it from the others and giving it the name "Tent of Meeting," which was afterwards appropriated to the Tabernacle. It would seem that he selected his own tent for the purpose—probably because it was the best that the camp afforded—and contented himself with another. God deigned to approve his design, and descended in the cloudy pillar on the tent each time that Moses entered it.

(7) **Moses took the tabernacle.**—Rather, *Moses took his tent.* The Hebrew article, like the Greek, has

Tabernacle of the congregation. And it
came to pass, *that* every one which
sought the LORD went out unto the
tabernacle of the congregation, which
was without the camp. (8) And it came
to pass, when Moses went out unto the
tabernacle, *that* all the people rose up,
and stood every man *at* his tent door,
and looked after Moses, until he was
gone into the tabernacle.

(9) And it came to pass, as Moses en-
tered into the tabernacle, the cloudy
pillar descended, and stood *at* the door
of the tabernacle, and *the LORD* talked
with Moses. (10) And all the people saw
the cloudy pillar stand *at* the tabernacle
door: and all the people rose up and
worshipped, every man *in* his tent door.
(11) And the LORD spake unto Moses face
to face, as a man speaketh unto his
friend. And he turned again into the
camp: but his servant Joshua, the son
of Nun, a young man, departed not out
of the tabernacle.

(12) And Moses said unto the LORD,
See, thou sayest unto me, Bring up this
people: and thou hast not let me know
whom thou wilt send with me. Yet
thou hast said, I know thee by name,
and thou hast also found grace in my
sight. (13) Now therefore, I pray thee,
if I have found grace in thy sight,
shew me now thy way, that I may know
thee, that I may find grace in thy
sight: and consider that this nation *is*
thy people. (14) And he said, My pre-
sence shall go *with thee*, and I will give
thee rest. (15) And he said unto him, If
thy presence go not *with me*, carry us
not up hence. (16) For wherein shall it
be known here that I and thy people
have found grace in thy sight? *is it* not
in that thou goest with us? so shall we
be separated, I and thy people, from all

---

often the force of the possessive pronoun. The LXX. translate λαβὼν Μωϋσῆς τὴν σκηνὴν αὐτοῦ; and so Jarchi, Aben-Ezra, Kurtz, Kalisch, Keil, Cook, &c.

And pitched it without the camp.—Heb., *and pitched it for himself without the camp.* "For himself" means *for his own use*, that he might resort to it. This was his special object.

The Tabernacle of the congregation.—Rather, *the tent of meeting.* (See Note on chap. xxv. 22.) He gave it—*i.e.*, by anticipation—the identical name by which the "Tabernacle" was afterwards commonly known. It was, in fact, a temporary substitute for the Tabernacle.

Every one . . . went out unto the tabernacle.—Though he had designed it for his own special use, Moses allowed all Israel to make use of it also.

(8) **When Moses went out . . . all the people rose up.**—As a mark of respect and reverence. (Comp. Esther v. 9.)

(9) **The cloudy pillar descended.**—During the stay of the Israelites in the plain at the foot of Sinai, the ordinary place occupied by the pillar of the cloud was the summit of the mount (chaps. xix. 16, 20, xx. 21, xxiv. 15—18, xxxiv. 5). At this time, whenever Moses entered the temporary tabernacle, the cloud came down from Sinai, ascending again when he quitted it.

And the Lord talked with Moses.—Heb., *and talked with Moses.* The "cloudy pillar" is the subject of the verb "talked." It is here identified with God, who manifested Himself through it.

(11) **Face to face.**—Comp. Num. xii. 8; Deut. xxxiv. 10. This is clearly spoken of as a privilege peculiar to Moses; but in what exactly the peculiarity consisted is not apparent. Some special closeness of approach is no doubt meant—some nearness such as had been enjoyed by no mortal previously. In later times, Isaiah (Isa. vi. 1—5) and Ezekiel (Ezek. i. 28) were perhaps equally favoured.

His servant Joshua.—Comp. chap. xxiv. 13, where Joshua is called Moses' "minister," the word employed in the Hebrew being the same.

MOSES OBTAINS A RENEWAL OF GOD'S PROMISE TO GO UP WITH THE PEOPLE.

(12—17) The self-humiliation of the people (verses 4—6) had appeased God's anger. He was now ready to be entreated. Moses therefore renews his supplications on their behalf, and especially prays for a revocation of the threatened withdrawal of the Divine Presence, and substitution for it of a mere angel. Taking advantage of his privilege to speak to God as friend with friend (verse 11), he ventures to expostulate, uses familiar terms, and persists until he at last obtains a distinct declaration that his request is granted (verse 17).

(12) **Thou hast not let me know whom thou wilt send.**—Moses finds the promises of chaps. xxxii. 34 and xxxiii. 2 ambiguous. What is meant by "mine angel" and "an angel?" Is it the "Angel" of chap. xxiii. 20—23, or no? If not, who is it?

I know thee by name.—God had shown this knowledge when He called on Moses out of the burning bush (chap. iii. 4), and again, probably, when he "called unto him out of the midst of the cloud" (chap. xxiv. 16); but the exact phrase had not been used previously. It implies a very high degree of Divine favour. God "knows by name" only those whom He greatly regards. (See Note on chap. xxxi. 2.)

(13) **Shew me now thy way**—*i.e.*, Thy course—Thy intention. Let me know if Thou really intendest to withdraw Thyself from us, and put a created being in Thy place or no.

Consider that this nation is thy people.—Moses glances back at God's words recorded in chap. xxxii. 7, and reminds God that the Israelites are not merely his (Moses') people, but also, in a higher sense, God's people. As such, God had acknowledged them (chaps. iii. 7, 10, v. 1, vi. 7, vii. 4, &c.).

(14) **My presence shall go with thee.**—There is no "with thee" in the original, and consequently the phrase is ambiguous. Moses could not tell whether it was a personal promise to himself, or a renewal of the old engagement to go with the people. He conse-

the people that *are* upon the face of the
earth.
(17) And the LORD said unto Moses, I
will do this thing also that thou hast
spoken: for thou hast found grace in
my sight, and I know thee by name.
(18) And he said, I beseech thee, shew
me thy glory. (19) And he said, I will
make all my goodness pass before thee,
and I will proclaim the name of the
LORD before thee; [a]and will be gracious
to whom I will be gracious, and will
shew mercy on whom I will shew mercy.
(20) And he said, Thou canst not see my
face: for there shall no man see me,
and live. (21) And the LORD said, Behold,
there is a place by me, and thou
shalt stand upon a rock: (22) and it shall
come to pass, while my glory passeth
by, that I will put thee in a clift of the
rock, and will cover thee with my hand
while I pass by: (23) and I will take
away mine hand, and thou shalt see my
back parts: but my face shall not be
seen.

CHAPTER XXXIV.—(1) And the
LORD said unto Moses, [b]Hew thee two
tables of stone like unto the first: and
I will write upon *these* tables the words

a Rom. 9. 15.

b Deut. 10. 1.

---

quently requires something more explicit. Will God go, not merely with him, but with the people? (verses 15, 16).

(17) **I will do this thing also that thou hast spoken.**—At length the promise is unambiguously given. Moses is rewarded for his importunity. God's people have found grace in His sight. He will "go up" with them, and so "separate them," or distinguish them, from "all the people that are on the face of the earth." Now at last Moses is satisfied.

MOSES' REQUEST TO SEE GOD'S GLORY, AND GOD'S REPLY TO IT.

(18–23) Not till he had received full assurance of the people's restoration to favour did Moses prefer any request for himself. Then, however, he made use of the privilege granted him to speak with God, "as a man speaketh unto his friend," in order to obtain a blessing for which his spiritual nature craved, and than which he could conceive nothing more desirable. "Shew me," he said, "I beseech thee, thy glory." All that he had yet seen of God was insufficient—only raised his desire, only sharpened his appetite to see more. He craved for that "beatific vision" which is the final reward of them that are perfected in another world. God could not grant his request in full, for it is impossible so long as we are in the flesh that we should look on God and live. "No man hath seen God at any time" (John i. 18). But He granted all that could be granted. He made "all his goodness pass before" Moses; He gave him a fresh revelation of His name (chap. xxxiv. 6, 7); and He even let him see some actual portion of His "glory"—as much as mortal man could possibly behold—more than any son of man had ever beheld before—more, probably, than any other son of man will ever behold until the consummation of all things (verses 22, 23).

(19) **I will make all my goodness pass before thee.**—It is not clear how this was fulfilled. Perhaps, as God announced His name—"the Lord, the Lord God, merciful and gracious, long-suffering, and abundant in goodness and truth," &c. (chap. xxxiv. 6, 7)—a revelation of God's ineffable goodness was miraculously flashed into his inmost soul, and the thousand instances of it which he had known brought distinctly to his recollection, so as to "pass before him."

And will be gracious to whom I will be gracious.—It is not meant that God's favour is bestowed arbitrarily, but only that it is in any case *favour*—a free gift, not earned nor merited.

(21) **There is a place by me.**—A place on the summit of Sinai, where God had been manifesting Himself, is clearly intended; but it is impossible to fix the place with any certainty. Speculations like those of Dr. Robinson (*Biblical Researches*, Vol. i., p. 153) are of little value.

(22) **And will cover thee with my hand.**—Kalisch observes with justice that the mysteriousness of this obscure section "attains its highest climax in the three last verses" (verses 21—23). Human language is, by its very nature, unfit for the expression of sublime spiritual truths, and necessarily clothes them in a materialistic garment which is alien to their ethereal nature. All that we can legitimately gather from this verse and the next is that Moses was directed to a certain retired position, where God miraculously both protected him and shrouded him, while a manifestation of His glory passed by of a transcendent character, and that Moses was allowed to see, not the full manifestation, but the sort of after-glow which it left behind, which was as much as human nature could endure.

XXXIV.

PREPARATIONS FOR A RENEWAL OF THE COVENANT.

(1–4) Before the covenant could be formally re-established, before Israel could be replaced in the position forfeited by the idolatry of the golden calf, it was necessary that the conditions on which God consented to establish His covenant with them should be set forth afresh. Moses had asked for the return of God's favour, but had said nothing of these conditions. It is God who insists on them. "Hew thee two tables." The moral law must be delivered afresh—delivered in its completeness—exactly as at the first (verse 1), and even the ceremonial law must be re-imposed in its main items (verses 12—26), or no return to favour is possible. Hence Moses is summoned once more to the top of Sinai, where the Law is to be delivered afresh to him, and is ordered to bring with him tables of stone like the former ones, to receive their written contents from God's hand.

(1) **Hew thee two tables.**—Something is always lost by sin, even when it is forgiven. The first tables were "the work of God" (chap. xxxii. 16), the second were hewn by the hand of Moses.

Of stone.—Literally, *of stones*—hewn, *i.e.*, out of two separate stones, which could not be said of the first tables, since none knew how God had fashioned them.

that were in the first tables, which thou
brakest. (2) And be ready in the morn-
ing, and come up in the morning unto
mount Sinai, and present thyself there
to me in the top of the mount. (3) And
no man shall [a] come up with thee, nei-
ther let any man be seen throughout all
the mount; neither let the flocks nor
herds feed before that mount.

(4) And he hewed two tables of stone
like unto the first; and Moses rose up
early in the morning, and went up unto
mount Sinai, as the LORD had com-
manded him, and took in his hand the
two tables of stone. (5) And the LORD
descended in the cloud, and stood with
him there, and proclaimed the name of
the LORD. (6) And the LORD passed by
before him, and proclaimed, The LORD,
The LORD God, merciful and gracious,
longsuffering, and abundant in goodness
and truth, (7) keeping mercy for thou-
sands, forgiving iniquity and transgres-
sion and sin, and that will by no means
clear *the guilty;* [b] visiting the iniquity of
the fathers upon the children, and upon
the children's children, unto the third
and to the fourth *generation.* (8) And
Moses made haste, and bowed his head
toward the earth, and worshipped.
(9) And he said, If now I have found grace
in thy sight, O Lord, let my Lord, I pray

a ch. 19. 12.

b ch. 20. 5; Deut. 5. 9; Jer. 32. 18.

I will write.—It is quite clear, though some have maintained the contrary, that the second tables, equally with the first, were inscribed "with the finger of God." (Comp. Deut. iv. 13, x. 2, 4.) It is also quite clear that exactly the same words were written on each.

Upon these tables.—Heb., *upon the tables.*

(2) **Be ready in the morning.**—It was necessary to allow an interval for the hewing of the stones.

In the top of the mount—*i.e.*, in the same place as before. (Comp. chaps. xix. 20, xxiv. 12, 18.)

(3) **No man shall come up with thee . . .**—These stringent commands were new. On the previous occasion, Aaron, Hur, and the elders had ascended the mount part of the way (chap. xxiv. 9—11); and Joshua had accompanied his master almost to the summit (chap. xxiv. 13), and had apparently remained in some part of the mountain during the whole time of Moses' stay (chap. xxxii. 17). Now Moses was to be quite alone, and no one was to be seen in any part of the mount. The stringency of the new orders must be connected with the promised revelation to Moses of God's glory (chap. xxxiii. 21—23).

MOSES ALLOWED TO SEE GOD'S GLORY.

(5—8) The present ascent of Moses to the top of Sinai had two objects:—(1) The repair of the loss occasioned by his breaking the first tables; and (2) the accomplishment of the promise made to him that (under certain restrictions) he should "see God's glory." Combined with this promise were two minor ones—that God would make His "goodness" pass before him, and that He would reveal to him afresh His name. The revelation of the name is recorded in verses 6, 7, the manifestation of the glory in verse 5. How Moses was enabled to see God's goodness pass before him is not stated. (Comp. Note on chap. xxxiii. 19.)

(5) **The Lord descended in the cloud.**—When Moses ceased to commune with God, the cloud removed from the door of the "Tent of Meeting," and, as it would seem, disappeared. On Moses reaching the summit of Sinai it once more became visible, "descended" on the spot where Moses was, and "stood with him there."

And proclaimed the name of the Lord.—Comp. chap. xxxiii. 19; and for the terms of the proclamation see verses 6 and 7.

(6) **The Lord passed by before him.**—In this brief phrase we have the entire historical narrative of the manifestation to Moses of God's glory. For details we must refer to the terms of the promise (chap. xxxiii. 21—23), which are also characterised by brevity, but still add something to the bare statements of the present passage. Moses was, no doubt, hidden and protected by God's hand in a "clift of the rock" while God's glory passed by. He was only allowed to look out from his hiding-place after the glory had passed, when he saw the remains of it—the "back parts;" even this was, however, so brilliant a vision that it left a permanent light upon his countenance, which he was fain ordinarily to conceal from the people by means of a veil (verses 29—35).

The Lord, The Lord God . . .—The new "name" of God is not a "name," as we understand the expression; it is rather a description of His nature by means of a series of epithets. At the bush He had revealed His eternal, self-existent character; in the descent on Sinai (chaps. xix. 16—19, xx. 18—21) He had shown His terribleness; now, in the act of pardoning His people and taking them once more into favour, He made known His attribute of mercy. The more to impress this feature of His character on Israel, He accumulated epithet on epithet, calling Himself *Rakhum,* "the tender or pitiful one;" *Khannun,* "the kind or gracious one," who bestows His benefits out of mere favour; *Erek appayim,* "the long-suffering one;" *Rab khesed,* "the great in mercy;" *Notser khesed,* "the keeper of mercy;" and *Nose 'avon,* "the forgiver of iniquity." Still, to prevent the fatal misapprehension that He is a Being of pure and mere benevolence (Butler, *Analogy,* Part I., chap. ii., p. 41), He added, to complete the description, a reference to His justice. He "will by no means clear the guilty" (comp. Nahum i. 3), and will "visit iniquity to the third and fourth generation." (Comp. chap. xx. 5.)

(8) **Moses made haste, and bowed his head.**—As the Divine glory passed before him, Moses bowed his head in adoration, worshipping God, and not daring to look until the glory had gone by. It is thus seen that with his ardent desire to look into the things of God he combined the highest and deepest reverence.

THE COVENANT RENEWED, AND THE DECALOGUE A SECOND TIME GIVEN.

(9) **If now I have found grace in thy sight.**—Rather, *Since now, &c.* The evidences of God's favour towards him—which Moses had now experienced, emboldened him to prefer fresh requests on behalf

thee, go among us; for it *is* a stiffnecked
people; and pardon our iniquity and
our sin, and take us for thine inherit-
ance.
(10) And he said, Behold, [a] I make a
covenant: before all thy people I will
do marvels, such as have not been done
in all the earth, nor in any nation: and
all the people among which thou *art*
shall see the work of the LORD: for it *is*
a terrible thing that I will do with
thee. (11) Observe thou that which I
command thee this day: behold, I drive
out before thee the Amorite, and the
Canaanite, and the Hittite, and the
Perizzite, and the Hivite, and the Jebu-
site. (12) [b] Take heed to thyself, lest
thou make a covenant with the inhabi-
tants of the land whither thou goest,
lest it be for a snare in the midst of
thee: (13) but ye shall destroy their
altars, break their [1] images, and cut
down their groves: (14) for thou shalt
worship no other God: for the LORD,
whose name *is* Jealous, *is* a [c] jealous
God: (15) lest thou make a covenant
with the inhabitants of the land, and
they go a whoring after their gods, and
do sacrifice unto their gods, and *one*
call thee, and thou eat of his sacrifice;
(16) and thou take of [d] their daughters
unto thy sons, and their daughters go a
whoring after their gods, and make thy
sons go a whoring after their gods.

a Deut. 5. 2.

b ch. 23. 32; Deut. 7. 2.

1 Heb., *statues.*

c ch. 20. 5.

d 1 Kings 11. 2.

---

of the people. God has promised to go up in the midst of them; will He not also promise to forgive their iniquity and sin if they offend Him in the way, and permanently to attach them to Himself by making them "His inheritance?" God does not directly answer these prayers, but indirectly accepts them by renewing His covenant with Israel (verses 10, 27).

(10) **I make a covenant**—*i.e.*, "I lay down afresh the terms of the covenant which I am content to make with Israel. I will go with them, and drive out the nations before them (verse 11), and work miracles on their behalf (verse 10), and enlarge their borders (verse 24), and prevent their enemies from desiring their land at the festival seasons (verse 24); they, on their part, must 'observe that which I command them this day.'" The "command" given included the moral law, as laid down in the Ten Commandments (verse 28), and a summary of the chief points contained in the "Book of the Covenant," which must be regarded as a re-publication and re-authorisation of that book.

Marvels, such as have not been done in all the earth—*e.g.*, the drying up of Jordan (Josh. iii. 16, 17), the falling down of the walls of Jericho (Josh. vi. 20), the destruction of the army of the five kings by hailstones (Josh. x. 11), and the like.

A terrible thing.—Comp. Deut. x. 21; Pss. cvi. 22, cxlv. 6. God is "terrible" to the enemies of His people.

(11) **The Amorite, and the Canaanite . . .**—The same six nations are particularised in chap. iii. 8, 17, in chap. xxiii. 23, and also in chap. xxxiii. 2. In Deut. vii. 1, and Josh. iii. 10, xxiv. 11, the Girgashites are added, and the number of the nations made seven.

(12–16) This passage may be compared with chap. xxiii. 24, 25, 32, 33. It repeats, with some enlargements, the enactments there made, and traces in detail the evil consequences which would follow from a neglect of the enactments.

(12) **A snare.**—Comp. chap. xxiii. 33; and for the nature of the snare, see verses 15, 16 of the present chapter.

(13) **Ye shall destroy their altars, break their images, and cut down their groves.**—In the "Book of the Covenant" the command had been simply to "quite break down their images" (chap. xxiii. 24). Now, after the Israelites had displayed their idolatrous leanings, it is added that they are likewise to destroy the "altars" and the "groves." Altars were common among all the idolatrous nations, sometimes attached to temples (1 Kings xvi. 32; 2 Kings xxi. 4, 5), sometimes separate from them (Num. xxiii. 1, 29; 2 Kings xvi. 10, 11), and were used for much the same purposes as the Hebrew altars: *i.e.*, for sacrifices, bloody and unbloody, and for burning incense. "Groves"—here mentioned for the first time—were peculiar to a limited number of nations, as the Assyrians, Babylonians, Phœnicians, Syrians, and a few others. They appear to have been artificial constructions, either of wood or stone, or both, imitative of vegetable forms, and probably emblematic of the productive powers of nature. The worship connected with the "groves" was of a peculiarly gross and licentious character. The very name, *ashêrah*, was a modification of Ashtoreth, or Astarte. It is remarkable that nothing is said of destroying Canaannite temples—an indication that as yet they did not exist, and a mark of the high antiquity of the book.

(14) **For thou shalt worship no other god.**—The images, altars, and groves would, if retained, lead on to the worship of the gods to whom they were dedicated—indeed, they could be retained for no other purpose. Thus their destruction followed, as a corollary, from the second commandment.

Whose name is Jealous.—Comp. chap. xx. 5, and see Note 2 on that passage. Many attempts have been made to show that jealousy is unworthy of the Divine Nature; but that the one Only God, if there be but one Only God, should claim and exact under severe penalties an undivided allegiance is natural, reasonable, and in harmony with the most exalted conceptions of the Divine essence. If God looked with indifference upon idolatry, it would imply that He cared little for His human creatures: that, like the Deity of Epicurus, having once created man and the world, He thenceforth paid no attention to them.

(15, 16) **Lest thou make a covenant with the inhabitants.**—If a covenant were made with the idolatrous nations of Canaan, and they were allowed to dwell in the land together with the Israelites (chap. xxiii. 33), the danger would be, in the first place, that

(17) Thou shalt make thee no molten
gods.
(18) The feast of [a] unleavened bread
shalt thou keep. Seven days thou shalt
eat unleavened bread, as I commanded
thee, in the time of the month Abib:
for in the [b] month Abib thou camest out
from Egypt.
(19) [c] All that openeth the matrix *is*
mine; and every firstling among thy
cattle, *whether* ox or sheep, *that is male.*
(20) But the firstling of an ass thou shalt
redeem with a [1] lamb: and if thou re-
deem *him* not, then shalt thou break
his neck. All the firstborn of thy sons
thou shalt redeem. And none shall
appear before me [d] empty.
(21) [e] Six days thou shalt work, but on
the seventh day thou shalt rest: in ear-
ing time and in harvest thou shalt rest.
(22) [f] And thou shalt observe the feast
of weeks, of the firstfruits of wheat
harvest, and the feast of ingathering at
the [2] year's end.
(23) [g] Thrice in the year shall all your
menchildren appear before the Lord
GOD, the God of Israel. (24) For I will
cast out the nations before thee, and
enlarge thy borders: neither shall any
man desire thy land, when thou shalt go
up to appear before the LORD thy God
thrice in the year.
(25) [h] Thou shalt not offer the blood of
my sacrifice with leaven; neither shall
the sacrifice of the feast of the passover
be left unto the morning.

a ch. 23. 15.
b ch. 13. 4.
c ch. 22. 29; Ezek. 44. 30.
1 Or, *kid.*
d ch. 23. 15.
e ch. 23. 12; Deut. 5. 12; Luke 13. 14.
f ch. 23. 16.
2 Heb., *revolution of the year.*
g ch. 23. 14, 17; Deut. 16. 16.
h ch. 23. 18.

Israel would be induced to partake in the idol-feasts; secondly, that intermarriages would take place; and thirdly, that such Israelites as married idolatrous wives would be persuaded by them to join in their worship, and would thus be seduced into actual idolatry. Solomon's example shows the reality of the peril. (See 1 Kings xi. 1—8.)

(17) **Thou shalt make thee no molten gods.** —It is just possible that the Israelites when they worshipped the golden calf may have conceived that they were not breaking the second commandment, which forbade the adoration of any "graven image." An express law was therefore made against "molten images."

(18) **The feast of unleavened bread shalt thou keep.**—Comp. chaps. xii. 15—20, xiii. 3—10, xxiii. 15.

The month Abib.—See Note on chap. xiii. 4.

(19) **All that openeth the matrix is mine.**—Comp. chap. xiii. 12, where the sanctification of the firstborn and the law of redemption had already been declared. For the exact mode of redemption sanctioned, see Num. xviii. 15, 16.

(20) **The firstling of an ass.**—See Notes 1—3 on chap. xiii. 13.

(21) The law of the Sabbath meets us at every turn in Exodus. It was so fundamental to the entire polity, that it naturally held a place in every section of the legislation. We have already found it (1) propounded at the giving of the manna (chap. xvi. 22—30); (2) reasserted in the fourth commandment (chap. xx. 8—11); (3) introduced into the "Book of the Covenant" (chap. xxiii. 12); and (4) appended to the directions given for the construction of the Tabernacle (chap. xxxi. 13—17).

In earing time and in harvest thou shalt rest.—"Earing-time" is ploughing time, "to ear" being an old English verb, etymologically connected with the Greek ἀρόω and the Latin *aro*. (Comp. Gen. xlv. 6; Deut. xxi. 4; 1 Sam. viii. 12; Isa. xxx. 24.) There was a special temptation to trench on the Sabbatical rest at the times most critical in respect to agricultural operations.

(22) **The feast of weeks.**—Called in chap. xxiii. 16, "the feast of harvest," and in the New Testament "the day of Pentecost"—seven weeks after the first day of unleavened bread. (See Note 1 on chap. xxiii. 16.) The special offering to be made at the feast consisted of "two wave loaves of fine flour, baken with leaven" (Lev. xxiii. 17), which were "the first-fruits of the wheat harvest."

And the feast of ingathering.—Called also "the feast of tabernacles" (Lev. xxiii. 34; Deut. xvi. 13, 16, xxxi. 10, &c.), on account of the command to "dwell in booths seven days" during its continuance (Lev. xxiii. 42). On the character of the festival see Note 2 on chap. xxiii. 16.

(23) **Thrice in the year shall all your menchildren appear before the Lord.**—On this requirement, and the political value of the three great festivals, see Note on chap. xxiii. 14—17.

(24) **I will . . . enlarge thy borders.**—The promise of "a land" for his posterity made by God to Abraham was twofold. At first it was the "land of Canaan" alone which they were to receive (Gen. xii. 5—7); but subsequently the promise was extended, and made to include the entire tract of territory between "the river of Egypt" (the Nile) and "the great river, the river Euphrates" (Gen. xv. 18). In remarkable parallelism with this double promise was the double fulfilment. At first Canaan alone was occupied, but under David and Solomon the borders were greatly enlarged; and "Solomon reigned over all kingdoms from the river (Euphrates) unto the land of the Philistines, and unto the border of Egypt" (1 Kings iv. 21). The rebellion of Jeroboam, and the establishment of the "kingdom of Israel," caused a contraction of the land to its original limits; but Menahem seems once more to have carried the dominion of Israel to the Euphrates (2 Kings xv. 16).

Neither shall any man desire thy land.—It was a part of the unwritten law of the Greeks that free passage should be given to all who were on their way to or from any of the great Pan-Hellenic festivals. But the present promise went beyond any such understanding. It secured the territory of Israel from all attack at such seasons, and must have been enforced miraculously by that providential government which God exercises over "all the nations upon the earth" (Ps. lxvii. 4).

(25) **Thou shalt not offer the blood of my sacrifice with leaven.**—Comp. chap. xxiii. 18, and the Notes *ad loc.*

(26) The first of the firstfruits of thy
land thou shalt bring unto the house of
the LORD thy God.

Thou shalt not seethe a [a] kid in his
mother's milk.

(27) And the LORD said unto Moses,
Write thou [b] these words: for after the
tenor of these words I have made a
covenant with thee and with Israel.
(28) [c] And he was there with the LORD
forty days and forty nights; he did
neither eat bread, nor drink water.
And he wrote upon the tables the
words of the covenant, the ten [1] com-
mandments.

(29) And it came to pass, when Moses
came down from mount Sinai with the
two tables of testimony in Moses' hand,
when he came down from the mount,
that Moses wist not that the skin of
his face shone while he talked with
him. (30) And when Aaron and all the
children of Israel saw Moses, behold,
the skin of his face shone; and they
were afraid to come nigh him. (31) And
Moses called unto them; and Aaron and
all the rulers of the congregation re-
turned unto him: and Moses talked
with them. (32) And afterward all the
children of Israel came nigh: and he
gave them in commandment all that
the LORD had spoken with him in
mount Sinai. (33) And *till* Moses had
done speaking with them, he put [d] a
vail on his face. (34) But when Moses
went in before the LORD to speak with

a ch. 23. 19; Deut. 14. 21.

b Deut. 4. 13.

c ch. 24. 18; Deut. 9. 9.

1 Heb., *words.*

d 2 Cor. 3. 13.

---

(26) **The first of the firstfruits.**—Comp. chap. xxiii. 19.

Thou shalt not seethe a kid.—See Note 3 on chap. xxiii. 19.

(27) **Write thou these words.**—Heb., *Write for thee these words, i.e.,* put them in writing for thine own use and the use of thy people. This express command accounts for the assignment of so much space to what is mainly repetition. The requirement of the repetition can only be explained by the importance of the laws laid down under the circumstances of the Hebrew nation, and the power of repetition to enforce upon the conscience what is pressed upon it by reiteration.

After the tenor of these words.—The summary of positive laws contained in this chapter (verses 12—26) was not intended to supersede the "Book of the Covenant," but rather to confirm and reinforce it. The covenant was renewed not upon these words only, but "after the tenor," *i.e.,* after their general aspect or bearing.

(28) **He was there with the Lord forty days and forty nights.**—As on his former ascent (chap. xxiv. 18). The long time is, at first sight, surprising, since there were now no instructions to be given. But we learn from Deuteronomy (chap. ix. 18, 19) that it was required for an earnest and prolonged intercession by Moses on behalf of his nation, which ultimately prevailed with God, and induced Him to put away His "anger and hot displeasure."

He did neither eat bread, nor drink water.—A similar fast had been kept on the previous occasion (Deut. ix. 9), though it is not mentioned in Exodus. Fasts of this extraordinary duration are only recorded of Moses, of Elijah (1 Kings xix. 8), and of our Lord (Matt. iv. 2). They are absolutely miraculous, and modern attempts to rival them are viewed by scientific men as deriving such apparent success as may have attended them from imposture.

He wrote upon the tables.—It has been concluded from this statement that Moses engraved the words upon the second tables; and the passage, if it stood alone, would certainly admit, and, indeed, naturally suggest, this meaning. But the Hebrew idiom allows us to regard Jehovah as the nominative to the verb "wrote;" and it is necessary so to do in order to bring the passage into agreement with chap. xxxiv. 1, and with Deut. x. 2, 4. Thus the second tables are to be viewed as "written with the finger of God" no less than the first (chaps. xxxi. 18, xxxii. 16).

THE DESCENT OF MOSES FROM MOUNT SINAI WITH THE SECOND TABLES.

(29) **The skin of his face shone.**—That an actual physical phenomenon is intended appears from the entire narrative, as well as from St. Paul's comment upon it in 2 Cor. iii. 7—18. According to some commentators, a radiance like that here described was a part of man's original heritage, a feature of that "image of God" wherein he was created (Gen. i. 27). The gift was forfeited by the fall, and will not be restored generally until the time of the restitution of all things. But meanwhile, from time to time, it pleases God to restore to certain of His saints the physical glory, which is the symbol of internal purity and holiness, as to Moses on this occasion and afterwards to Elijah on the mount of transfiguration (Luke ix. 31), and to St. Stephen when he pleaded before the Sanhedrin (Acts vi. 15). A glory of the kind, but of surpassing brilliancy, belonged to the human nature of our blessed Lord, who concealed it ordinarily, but allowed it to appear temporarily at the transfiguration, and permanently after His ascension (Rev. i. 16, x. 1, xxi. 23, xxii. 5). The grant of the privilege to Moses was perhaps necessary to support his authority among a people of such materialistic leanings as the Israelites.

While he talked with him.—Rather, *through his talking with him.* The brightness of Moses' face was the reflex of that eternal glory which Moses had been given to witness on this last occasion, though in a veiled and modified manner (chaps. xxxiii. 23, xxxiv. 5, 6), and which he had not seen previously. It remained henceforth a property of his countenance. Painters represent it by rays, or sometimes—but improperly—by horns, this latter usage originating in a mistaken rendering of the Vulgate (*quod cornuta esset facies sua,* instead of *quod splenderet facies sua*).

(30) **They were afraid.**—The supernatural appearance terrified them. Compare the feelings of Ezekiel (Ezek. i. 18) and St. John (Rev. i. 17).

(33) **Till Moses had done speaking with them, he put a vail on his face.**—This translation exactly inverts the meaning, which is that "*when* Moses had

him, he took the vail off, until he came out. And he came out, and spake unto the children of Israel *that* which he was commanded. (35) And the children of Israel saw the face of Moses, that the skin of Moses' face shone: and Moses put the vail upon his face again, until he went in to speak with him.

CHAPTER XXXV.—(1) And Moses gathered all the congregation of the children of Israel together, and said unto them, These *are* the words which the LORD hath commanded, that *ye* should do them. (2) [a] Six days shall work be done, but on the seventh day there shall be to you [1] an holy day, a sabbath of rest to the LORD: whosoever doeth work therein shall be put to death. (3) Ye shall kindle no fire throughout your habitations upon the sabbath day.

(4) And Moses spake unto all the congregation of the children of Israel, saying, This *is* the thing which the LORD commanded, saying, (5) Take ye from among you an offering unto the LORD: [b] whosoever *is* of a willing heart, let him bring it, an offering of the LORD; gold, and silver, and brass, (6) and blue, and purple, and scarlet, and fine linen, and goats' *hair*, (7) and rams' skins dyed red, and badgers' skins, and shittim wood, (8) and oil for the light, and spices for anointing oil, and for the sweet incense, (9) and onyx stones, and stones to be set for the ephod, and for the breastplate. (10) And every wise hearted among you shall come, and make all that the LORD hath commanded; (11) [c] the tabernacle, his tent, and his covering, his taches, and his boards, his bars, his pillars, and his sockets, (12) the ark, and the staves thereof, *with* the mercy seat, and the vail of the covering, (13) the table, and his staves, and all his vessels, and the shewbread, (14) the candlestick also for the light, and his furniture, and his lamps, with the oil for the light, (15) [d] and the incense altar, and his staves, and the anointing oil, and the sweet incense, and the hanging for the

a ch. 20. 9; Lev. 23. 3; Deut. 5. 12; Luke 13. 14.

1 Heb., *holiness*.

b ch. 25. 2.

c ch. 26. 31.

d ch. 30. 1.

---

done speaking with them, he put a vail on his face." The vail became part of his ordinary costume, and was worn excepting upon occasions of two kinds: (1) When Moses was alone with God, either in the temporary "tent of meeting" or in the permanent Tabernacle, he ceased to wear the vail, and spoke with God face to face; (2) when he had a message to the people from God, and spoke to them as God's representative, he authenticated his message by uncovering himself, and allowing the glory of his face to be seen. Otherwise, in his ordinary dealings with the people he went about veiled.

XXXV.

ITERATION OF THE LAW CONCERNING THE SABBATH.

(1–3) Moses, being about to require the people to engage in the work, first, of constructing the materials for the Tabernacle, and then of uprearing the Tabernacle itself, prefaced his requirements by a renewed promulgation of the law of the Sabbath, with additional particularity, and with a new sanction. The necessity of such a re-promulgation had been indicated to him in the last injunctions received before his first descent from Sinai (chap. xxxi. 12—17), and in acting as he now did, he must be viewed as carrying out those injunctions. The words here put on record are probably not the whole that he said to the people on the subject, but only some main points of his speech. He can scarcely have omitted to tell them that the Sabbath was to be henceforth "a sign" between God and His people (chap. xxxi. 17).

(1) **These are the words.**—Verse 2 is, in the main, a repetition of chap. xxxi. 15, but verse 3 is new, or, at any rate, only contained by implication in any previous legislation. Kindling fire was in early times a hard piece of manual work, being effected by the friction of two pieces of dry wood.

THE PEOPLE INVITED TO OFFER THE MATERIALS OF THE TABERNACLE, AND TO ASSIST IN THE WORK.

(4–9) **And Moses spake.**—This passage is the sequence and counterpart of chap. xxv. 1—7, and follows exactly the same order in the enumeration of the required offerings. Both passages equally declare the *sine quâ non* of an acceptable offering to be "a willing heart" (chaps. xxv. 2, xxxv. 5).

(10–19) **And every wise hearted among you.**—The first appeal is to all; all may contribute something towards the *materials* of the sacred structure. But the second appeal is to some only. The "wise-hearted" alone can take part in the actual construction, and "make all that the Lord hath commanded." On the expression "wise-hearted," see Note on chap. xxviii. 3. It includes skill of various kinds and degrees, even that of poor women, who "did spin with their hands, and brought that which they had spun, both of blue, and of purple, and of scarlet, and of fine linen" (verse 25). In enumerating the things to be constructed, Moses follows, not the order of the revelations made to him, but what may be called the natural order: first, the Tabernacle as a whole; then its various parts (verse 11); after this, its contents—those of the Holy of Holies (verse 12), of the Holy Place (verses 13—15), and of the Court (verses 16—18); finally, the dress to be worn by those who conducted the services (verse 19). On the Tabernacle and its parts, see chap. xxvi. 1—37; on the Ark, the staves, and the mercy-seat, chap. xxv. 10—15; on the "veil of the covering," chap. xxvi. 31; on the table and the candle-

door at the entering in of the taber-
nacle, (16) [a] the altar of burnt offering,
with his brasen grate, his staves, and all
his vessels, the laver and his foot,
(17) the hangings of the court, his pillars,
and their sockets, and the hanging for
the door of the court, (18) the pins of the
tabernacle, and the pins of the court,
and their cords, (19) the cloths of service,
to do service in the holy *place*, the holy
garments for Aaron the priest, and the
garments of his sons, to minister in the a ch. 27. 1.
priest's office.
(20) And all the congregation of the
children of Israel departed from the
presence of Moses. (21) And they came,
every one whose heart stirred him up,
and every one whom his spirit made
willing, *and* they brought the LORD's
offering to the work of the tabernacle
of the congregation, and for all his ser-
vice, and for the holy garments. (22) And
they came, both men and women, as
many as were willing hearted, *and*
brought bracelets, and earrings, and
rings, and tablets, all jewels of gold:
and every man that offered *offered* an
offering of gold unto the LORD. (23) And
every man, with whom was found blue,
and purple, and scarlet, and fine linen,
and goats' *hair*, and red skins of rams,
and badgers' skins, brought *them*.
(24) Every one that did offer an offering
of silver and brass brought the LORD's
offering: and every man, with whom
was found shittim wood for any work of
the service, brought *it*. (25) And all the
women that were wise hearted did spin
with their hands, and brought that
which they had spun, *both* of blue, and
of purple, *and* of scarlet, and of fine
linen. (26) And all the women whose
heart stirred them up in wisdom spun
goats' *hair*. (27) And the rulers brought
onyx stones, and stones to be set, for
the ephod, and for the breastplate;

---

stick, chap. xxv. 23—30; on the incense altar, chap. xxx. 1—10; on the anointing oil, chap. xxx. 23—25; on the sweet incense, chap. xxx. 34, 35; on the hanging for the door, chap. xxvi. 36; on the altar of burnt offering, chap. xxvii. 1—8; on the laver and its foot, chap. xxx. 17—21; on the hangings of the Court, its pillars, sockets, pins, &c., chap. xxvii. 9—19; and on "the cloths of service," chap. xxviii. 2—42. (On the true meaning of the expression, "cloths of service," see Note on chap. xxxi. 10.)

THE ZEAL OF THE PEOPLE IN OFFERING AND ASSISTING IN THE WORK.

(21) **They came, every one whose heart stirred him up.**—All classes came, "men and women" (verse 22), rich and poor, "rulers" (verse 27), and those whose only skill was to "spin with their hands" (verse 25). And the great majority gave freely—to the utmost of their power. Still it is implied, both here and in verses 22, 29, that there were some whose hearts did not stir them up. Enough and to spare, was, however, contributed, and at last the people had to be "restrained from bringing" (chap. xxxvi. 8).

The Lord's offering—*i.e.*, "their offering to Jehovah."

(22) **Both men and women . . . brought bracelets . . .**—It is not quite certain what the personal ornaments here mentioned are. The LXX. render *σφραγίδας, καὶ ἐνώτια, καὶ δακτυλίους, καὶ ἐμπλόκια, καὶ περιδέξια*, "signets, and earrings, and rings, and chains, and armlets," substituting five terms for four. Rosenmüller thinks the *khâkh* was a "nose ring;" others make it a "brooch" or "buckle." The last word of the four, *kumâz*, cannot possibly mean "tablets." It comes from a root signifying "rounded," and designates probably a bead necklace, such as was often worn by the Egyptians. On the use of personal ornaments by the Hebrew *men*, as well as women, see Note on chap. xxxii. 2.

Jewels of gold.—Literally, *articles of gold.*

And every man that offered, offered an offering of gold.—By repeating the word "offered," our translators have spoiled the sense. Moses is enumerating those who came. There came those who offered bracelets, earrings, rings, &c.; there came also those who offered any (other) offering of gold to the Lord.

(23) **Red skins of rams.**—Rather, *rams' skins dyed red*, as the same words are translated in chaps. xxv. 5, xxxv. 7.

Badgers' skins.—See Note 2 on chap. xxv. 5.

(24) **An offering of silver.**—Silver had been enumerated among the offerings which would be accepted (chaps. xxv. 3, xxxv. 5), and it was therefore brought; but it is difficult to say what was done with it. All the silver actually employed in the sanctuary came from the half-shekels paid when the people were numbered. (See chap. xxxviii. 25—28.) Perhaps the silver free-will offerings were returned to the donors.

(25) **All the women that were wise-hearted**—*i.e.*, "all who had sufficient skill." Spinning was probably a very general accomplishment of the Hebrew women. It was effected in early times by means of a wheel and spindle, with or without a distaff. The only materials used for the fabrics of the sanctuary appear to have been flax and goats' hair. The flax was dyed before it was spun into thread, as sometimes by the Greeks (Hom. *Od.* iv. 135).

Of fine linen.—Rather, *of white.* Most of the Egyptian linen is of a yellowish white, being made from flax imperfectly blanched.

(26) **All the women whose heart stirred them up in wisdom spun goats' hair.**—It would seem to have been more difficult to produce a thread from goats' hair than from flax. Only the most skilful undertook the more difficult task.

(27) **The rulers brought onyx stones, and stones to be set.**—The "rulers" here intended are probably the "princes of the tribes" of Israel (Num. i. 16, iii. 3, 5, &c.). The twelve stones required for the

(28) and [a] spice, and oil for the light, and
for the anointing oil, and for the sweet
incense. (29) The children of Israel
brought a willing offering unto the
LORD, every man and woman, whose
heart made them willing to bring for all
manner of work, which the LORD had
commanded to be made by the hand of
Moses.
(30) And Moses said unto the children
of Israel, See, [b] the LORD hath called by
name Bezaleel the son of Uri, the son of
Hur, of the tribe of Judah; (31) and he
hath filled him with the spirit of God,
in wisdom, in understanding, and in
knowledge, and in all manner of work-
manship; (32) and to devise curious
works, to work in gold, and in silver,
and in brass, (33) and in the cutting of
stones, to set *them*, and in carving of
wood, to make any manner of cunning
work. (34) And he hath put in his heart
that he may teach, *both* he, and Aholiab,
the son of Ahisamach, of the tribe of
Dan. (35) Them hath he filled with wis-
dom of heart, to work all manner of
work, of the engraver, and of the cun-
ning workman, and of the embroiderer,
in blue, and in purple, in scarlet, and in
fine linen, and of the weaver, *even* of
them that do any work, and of those
that devise cunning work.

a ch. 30. 23.

b ch. 31. 2.

CHAPTER XXXVI. — (1) Then
wrought Bezaleel and Aholiab, and
every wise hearted man, in whom the
LORD put wisdom and understanding to
know how to work all manner of work
for the service of the sanctuary, ac-
cording to all that the LORD had com-
manded.
(2) And Moses called Bezaleel and
Aholiab, and every wise hearted man,
in whose heart the LORD had put wis-
dom, *even* every one whose heart stirred
him up to come unto the work to do it:
(3) and they received of Moses all the
offering, which the children of Israel
had brought for the work of the service
of the sanctuary, to make it *withal*.

---

breastplate would naturally be contributed by the twelve chiefs of the tribes whose names they were to bear (chap. xxviii. 21). The two onyx stones for the ephod (chap. xxviii. 9—12), may have been the further gift of two of the number, who happened to possess stones of the large size needed.

(28) **Spice.**—See chap. xxx. 23, 24, 34.

BEZALEEL AND AHOLIAB SET OVER THE WORK.

(30—35) This passage is the sequel to chap. xxxi. 1—6, where Bezaleel and Aholiab were designated for their respective offices, and follows closely the order, and even the wording, of that passage. The verbal resemblance is even greater in the original than in the Authorised Version. The only additions made are in verses 34 and 35.

(34) **He hath put in his heart that he may teach.**—It was essential that the two master-craftsmen should be able to instruct their subordinates, to whom the actual accomplishment of the works which they designed had to be committed. God specially qualified them to act as instructors.

Both he and Aholiab.—Aholiab, though subordinate to Bezaleel, was the director of his own department, that of weaving and embroidery (chap. xxxviii. 23), and had to instruct in it as Bezaleel had in his.

(35) **Them hath he filled with wisdom of heart.**—See Notes 1 and 2 on chap. xxviii. 3; and comp. chap. xxxi. 3.

Of the engraver.—Rather, *of the artificer*. The word used is a generic one, equally applicable to workers in stone, wood, and metal.

Of the cunning workman.—Rather, *of the skilful weaver*. (See the last Note on chap. xxvi. 1.) The "skilful weaver" (*khoshêb*) was the man who wove a patterned fabric. The ordinary "weaver" (*'orêg*) wove a plain one. The "embroiderer" (*rokêm*) adorned a fabric of either kind with the needle.

XXXVI.

THE WORK COMMENCED AND THE LIBERALITY OF THE PEOPLE RESTRAINED.

(1) This verse is introductory to the entire section, which may be viewed as extending from the present point to the close of chap. xxxix. It states, in brief, that Bezaleel and Aholiab, with the skilled workmen at their disposal, proceeded to the accomplishment of the work which Moses had committed to them, and effected it "according to all that the Lord had commanded," *i.e.*, according to the instructions given to Moses in Mount Sinai, and recorded in chaps. xxv.—xxx. The entire section is little more than a repetition of those chapters, differing from them merely in recording as done that which had in them been ordered to be done. The minute exactness of the repetition is very remarkable, and seems intended to teach the important lesson, that acceptable obedience consists in a complete and exact observance of God's commandments in all respects down to the minutest point.

(2) **Moses called Bezaleel**—*i.e.*, Moses summoned Bezaleel, Aholiab, and their chief assistants, into his presence, and committed to them the offerings which he had received from the people (verse 3)—the gold, the silver, the bronze, the shittim wood, the thread, the goats' hair, the rams' skins, the seals' skins, the precious stones, the oil, the spices, &c. "They received of Moses all the offering" that had been hitherto brought.

(3) **They brought yet unto him free offerings.**—The liberality of the people continued. After the work was taken in hand, and making progress, they kept still bringing in fresh offerings morning after morning, until the workmen found that they had more than enough. Compare the liberality shown when

And they brought yet unto him free
offerings every morning.
(4) And all the wise men, that wrought
all the work of the sanctuary, came
every man from his work which they
made; (5) and they spake unto Moses,
saying, The people bring much more
than enough for the service of the work,
which the LORD commanded to make.
(6) And Moses gave commandment, and
they caused it to be proclaimed through-
out the camp, saying, Let neither man
nor woman make any more work for
the offering of the sanctuary. So the
people were restrained from bringing.
(7) For the stuff they had was sufficient
for all the work to make it, and too
much.
(8) [a] And every wise hearted man
among them that wrought the work of
the tabernacle, made ten curtains *of* fine
twined linen, and blue, and purple, and
scarlet: *with* cherubims of cunning work
made he them. (9) The length of one
curtain *was* twenty and eight cubits,
and the breadth of one curtain four
cubits: the curtains *were* all of one size.
(10) And he coupled the five curtains one
unto another: and *the other* five curtains
he coupled one unto another. (11) And
he made loops of blue on the edge of
one curtain from the selvedge in the
coupling: likewise he made in the utter-
most side of *another* curtain, in the
coupling of the second. (12) [b] Fifty loops
made he in one curtain, and fifty loops
made he in the edge of the curtain
which *was* in the coupling of the second:
the loops held one *curtain* to another.
(13) And he made fifty taches of gold,
and coupled the curtains one unto an-
other with the taches: so it became one
tabernacle.

a ch. 26. 1.

b ch. 26. 10.

1 Heb., *twinned.*

(14) And he made curtains *of* goats'
hair for the tent over the tabernacle:
eleven curtains he made them. (15) The
length of one curtain *was* thirty cubits,
and four cubits *was* the breadth of one
curtain: the eleven curtains *were* of one
size. (16) And he coupled five curtains
by themselves, and six curtains by
themselves. (17) And he made fifty loops
upon the uttermost edge of the curtain
in the coupling, and fifty loops made he
upon the edge of the curtain which
coupleth the second. (18) And he made
fifty taches *of* brass to couple the tent
together, that it might be one.
(19) And he made a covering for the
tent *of* rams' skins dyed red, and a
covering *of* badgers' skins above *that.*
(20) And he made boards for the taber-
nacle *of* shittim wood, standing up.
(21) The length of a board *was* ten
cubits, and the breadth of a board one
cubit and a half. (22) One board had two
tenons, equally distant one from an-
other: thus did he make for all the
boards of the tabernacle. (23) And he
made boards for the tabernacle; twenty
boards for the south side southward:
(24) and forty sockets of silver he made
under the twenty boards; two sockets
under one board for his two tenons, and
two sockets under another board for his
two tenons. (25) And for the other side
of the tabernacle, *which is* toward the
north corner, he made twenty boards,
(26) and their forty sockets of silver;
two sockets under one board, and two
sockets under another board. (27) And
for the sides of the tabernacle westward
he made six boards. (28) And two boards
made he for the corners of the taber-
nacle in the two sides. (29) And they
were [1] coupled beneath, and coupled to-

David was collecting materials for the Temple (1 Chron. xxix. 6—9); and, again, when Zerubbabel was about to rear up the second Temple on the return from the Captivity (Ezra ii. 68—70; Neh. vii. 70—72).

(6) **So the people were restrained from giving.**—Moses felt it necessary to interfere, and forbid further offerings. By the expression, "Let neither man nor woman *make any more work,*" it would seem that the superfluous offerings were chiefly such things as were produced by labour—thread, goats' hair yarn, and the like. (See chap. xxxv. 25, 26.) The humblest class of contributors would thus appear to have shown itself the most zealous. When will Christian liberality be so excessive as to require to be "restrained"?

THE CONSTRUCTION OF THE TABERNACLE.

(8—13) This passage follows exactly chap. xxvi. 1—6, the tenses of the verbs alone being changed. It relates the construction of the inner covering.

(14—18) The construction of the outer covering of goats' hair follows, and is expressed in terms nearly identical with those used in chap. xxvi. 7—11. Verse 14 is better rendered than that to which it corresponds in the previous passage (verse 7). There are two omissions of short clauses for the sake of brevity.

(19) This verse corresponds exactly to chap. xxvi. 14, and relates the construction of the two outer coverings.

(20—34) After the construction of the roof, that of the walls is described, the order of chap. xxvi. being

gether at the head thereof, to one ring: thus he did to both of them in both the corners. (30) And there were eight boards; and their sockets *were* sixteen sockets of silver, [1] under every board two sockets.

(31) And he made [a] bars of shittim wood; five for the boards of the one side of the tabernacle, (32) and five bars for the boards of the other side of the tabernacle, and five bars for the boards of the tabernacle for the sides westward. (33) And he made the middle bar to shoot through the boards from the one end to the other. (34) And he overlaid the boards with gold, and made their rings *of* gold *to be* places for the bars, and overlaid the bars with gold.

(35) And he made a vail *of* blue, and purple, and scarlet, and fine twined linen: *with* cherubims made he it of cunning work. (36) And he made thereunto four pillars *of* shittim *wood*, and overlaid them with gold: their hooks *were of* gold; and he cast for them four sockets of silver.

(37) And he made an hanging for the tabernacle door *of* blue, and purple, and scarlet, and fine twined linen, [2] of needlework; (38) and the five pillars of it with their hooks: and he overlaid their chapiters and their fillets with gold: but their five sockets *were of* brass.

CHAPTER XXXVII.—(1) And Bezaleel [b] made the ark *of* shittim wood: two cubits and a half *was* the length of it, and a cubit and a half the breadth of it, and a cubit and a half the height of it: (2) and he overlaid it with pure gold within and without, and made a crown of gold to it round about. (3) And he cast for it four rings of gold, *to be set* by the four corners of it; even two rings upon the one side of it, and two rings upon the other side of it. (4) And he made staves *of* shittim wood, and overlaid them with gold. (5) And he put the staves into the rings by the sides of the ark, to bear the ark.

(6) And he made the [c] mercy seat *of* pure gold: two cubits and a half *was* the length thereof, and one cubit and a half the breadth thereof. (7) And he made two cherubims *of* gold, beaten out of one piece made he them, on the two ends of the mercy seat; (8) one cherub [3] on the end on this side, and another cherub [4] on the *other* end on that side: out of the mercy seat made he the cherubims on the two ends thereof. (9) And the cherubims spread out *their* wings on high, *and* covered with their wings over the mercy seat, with their faces one to another; *even* to the mercy seatward were the faces of the cherubims.

(10) And he made the table *of* shittim wood: two cubits *was* the length thereof, and a cubit the breadth thereof, and a cubit and a half the height thereof: (11) and he overlaid it with pure gold, and made thereunto a crown of gold round about. (12) Also he made thereunto a border of an handbreath round about; and made a crown of gold for

1 Heb., *two sockets, two sockets under one board.*

a ch. 25. 28 & 30. 5.

2 Heb., *the work of a needleworker,* or, *embroiderer.*

b ch. 25. 10.

c ch. 25. 17.

3 Or, *out of,* &c.

4 Or, *out of,* &c.

---

still followed. Verses 20—34 correspond to verses 15—29 of chap. xxvi. The correspondence is closer than would appear from the Authorised Version.

(30) **Under every board two sockets.**—This is undoubtedly the true meaning; but it can scarcely be elicited from the present text. The words, *takhath hak-keresh ha-ekhâd,* which ought to have been repeated twice, as they are in chap. xxvi. 25, have accidentally fallen out here in one place.

(32) **For the sides westward.**—Rather, *for the back* (of the tabernacle) *westward.* (Comp. the Note on chap. xxvi. 27.)

(35, 36) The order of chap. xxvi is still followed. From the walls which enclosed the Tabernacle the transition is easy to the vail which divided it into two parts. Verses 35, 36 correspond to verses 31, 32 of chap. xxvi.

(37, 38) These verses correspond in the main to verses 36, 37 of chap. xxvi., which they pre-suppose and confirm, adding, however, one new fact, viz., that the capitals of the five pillars were overlaid with gold. Either God had given no order on this point, or Moses had omitted to record it.

XXXVII.

(1—24) This passage corresponds with verses 10—39 of chap. xxv., and contains an account of the construction of the holy furniture: (1) That of the Holy of Holies: viz., the ark (verses 1—5), the mercy-seat (verses 6—9); (2) that of the Holy Place, viz., the table of shewbread (verses 10—16) and the golden candlestick (verses 17—24).

Verses 1—5	correspond to verses	10—14	of chap. xxv.
,, 6—9	,, ,,	17—20	,, ,,
,, 10—16	,, ,,	23—29	,, ,,
,, 17—24	,, ,,	31—39	,, ,,

(1) **Bezaleel made.**—Aholiab had no part in the construction of the furniture of the Tabernacle, but only in the coverings, the veil, the curtains, and the priests' dresses. (See chap. xxxviii. 23.)

(7) **Beaten out of one piece.**—Rather, *of beaten work,* as the word is translated in chap. xxvi. 18.

the border thereof round about. (13) And he cast for it four rings of gold, and put the rings upon the four corners that *were* in the four feet thereof. (14) Over against the border were the rings, the places for the staves to bear the table. (15) And he made the staves *of* shittim wood, and overlaid them with gold, to bear the table. (16) And he made the vessels which *were* upon the table, his [a] dishes, and his spoons, and his bowls, and his covers [1] to cover withal, *of* pure gold.

(17) And he made the [b] candlestick *of* pure gold: *of* beaten work made he the candlestick; his shaft, and his branch, his bowls, his knops, and his flowers, were of the same: (18) and six branches going out of the sides thereof; three branches of the candlestick out of the one side thereof, and three branches of the candlestick out of the other side thereof: (19) three bowls made after the fashion of almonds in one branch, a knop and a flower; and three bowls made like almonds in another branch, a knop and a flower: so throughout the six branches going out of the candlestick. (20) And in the candlestick *were* four bowls made like almonds, his knops, and his flowers: (21) and a knop under two branches of the same, and a knop under two branches of the same, and a knop under two branches of the same, according to the six branches going out of it. (22) Their knops and their branches were of the same: all of it *was* one beaten work *of* pure gold. (23) And he made his seven lamps, and his snuffers, and his snuffdishes, *of* pure gold. (24) *Of* a talent of pure gold made he it, and all the vessels thereof.

(25) [c] And he made the incense altar *of* shittim wood: the length of it *was* a cubit, and the breadth of it a cubit; *it was* foursquare; and two cubits *was* the height of it; the horns thereof were of the same. (26) And he overlaid it with pure gold, *both* the top of it, and the sides thereof round about, and the horns of it: also he made unto it a crown of gold round about. (27) And he made two rings of gold for it under the crown thereof, by the two corners of it, upon the two sides thereof, to be places for the staves to bear it withal. (28) And he made the staves *of* shittim wood, and overlaid them with gold.

(29) And he made [d] the holy anointing oil, and the pure incense of sweet spices, according to the work of the apothecary.

CHAPTER XXXVIII.—(1) And [e] he made the altar of burnt offering *of* shittim wood: five cubits *was* the length thereof, and five cubits the breadth thereof; *it was* foursquare; and three cubits the height thereof. (2) And he made the horns thereof on the four corners of it; the horns thereof were of the same: and he overlaid it with brass. (3) And he made all the vessels of the altar, the pots, and the shovels, and the basons, *and* the fleshhooks, and the firepans: all the vessels thereof made he *of* brass. (4) And he made for the altar a brasen grate of network under the compass thereof beneath unto the midst of it. (5) And he cast four rings

a ch. 25. 29

1 Or, *to pour out withal.*

b ch. 25. 31.

c ch. 30. 1.

d ch. 30. 35.

e ch. 27. 1.

---

(16) **Which were upon the table.**—Or, *which belonged to the table* (*τὰ σκεύη τῆς τραπέζης.*—LXX.).

(19) **Another branch.**—A right translation—an improvement on "*the* other branch" of chap. xxv. 33. The meaning is that there was the same style of ornamentation in all the branches.

(25-28) **And he made . . .**—The order of the instructions given on Mount Sinai is here departed from. In them the directions for the altar of incense were separated off from those concerning the table of shewbread and the golden candlestick. Here the construction of the three pieces of furniture belonging to the Holy Place is given consecutively. The present passage corresponds with verses 1—5 of chap. xxx., with which it is in the closest agreement.

(29) In this verse we have the composition by Bezaleel of the holy oil and the incense, described in chap. xxx. 22—25 and 34, 35, related with the utmost brevity.

XXXVIII.

(1) **He made the altar.**—From the furniture of the sanctuary, the transition is natural to the furniture of the court in which it stood. This is now described. It consisted of the brazen altar, or altar of burnt-offering, and the great brazen laver. The construction of the former is related in verses 1—7; that of the latter in verse 8.

(1–9) This passage corresponds to verses 1—8 of chap. xxvii. in all main particulars, but is somewhat differently worded. The order of the clauses in verses 4, 5 is changed, and a distinct statement is made, which was not contained in the instructions, that the rings were "for places for the staves."

(3) **The pots.**—Chap. xxvii. has "his pans"; but the word used in the original is the same. It designates probably the scuttles in which the ashes were

for the four ends of the grate of brass,
to be places for the staves. (6) And he
made the staves *of* shittim wood, and
overlaid them with brass. (7) And he
put the staves into the rings on the
sides of the altar, to bear it withal; he
made the altar hollow with boards.

(8) And he made the laver *of* brass,
and the foot of it *of* brass, of the [1] look-
ingglasses of *the women* [2] assembling,
which assembled *at* the door of the tab-
ernacle of the congregation.

(9) And he made the court: on the
south side southward the hangings of
the court *were of* fine twined linen, an
hundred cubits: (10) Their pillars *were*
twenty, and their brasen sockets
twenty; the hooks of the pillars and
their fillets *were of* silver. (11) And for
the north side *the hangings were* an hun-
dred cubits, their pillars *were* twenty,
and their sockets of brass twenty; the
hooks of the pillars and their fillets *of*
silver. (12) And for the west side *were*
hangings of fifty cubits, their pillars
ten, and their sockets ten; the hooks of
the pillars and their fillets *of* silver.
(13) And for the east side eastward fifty
cubits. (14) The hangings of the one
side *of the gate were* fifteen cubits; their
pillars three, and their sockets three.
(15) And for the other side of the court
gate, on this hand and that hand, *were*
hangings of fifteen cubits; their pillars
three, and their sockets three. (16) All
the hangings of the court round about
were of fine twined linen. (17) And the
sockets for the pillars *were of* brass; the
hooks of the pillars and their fillets
of silver; and the overlaying of their
chapiters *of* silver; and all the pillars
of the court *were* filleted with silver.
(18) And the hanging for the gate of the
court *was* needlework, *of* blue, and pur-
ple, and scarlet, and fine twined linen:
and twenty cubits *was* the length, and
the height in the breadth *was* five
cubits, answerable to the hangings of the
court. (19) And their pillars *were* four,
and their sockets *of* brass four; their
hooks *of* silver, and the overlaying of
their chapiters and their fillets *of* silver.
(20) And all the [a] pins of the tabernacle,
and of the court round about, *were of* brass.

(21) This is the sum of the tabernacle,
even of the tabernacle of testimony, as
it was counted, according to the com-
mandment of Moses, *for* the service of
the Levites, by the hand of Ithamar,
son to Aaron the priest. (22) And Beza-
leel the son of Uri, the son of Hur, of
the tribe of Judah, made all that the
LORD commanded Moses. (23) And with
him *was* Aholiab, son of Ahisamach, of

[1] Or, *brasen glasses.*

[2] Heb., *assembling by troops.*

[a] ch. 27. 19.

---

placed for removal from the sanctuary. (See Note 1 on chap. xxvii. 3.)

(8) **He made the laver of brass.**—Comp. chap. xxx. 18—21, where the laver is commanded, and the uses whereto it was to be applied are laid down. By "brass" we must understand "bronze" in this place, as in others.

Of the lookingglasses.—Rather, *mirrors.* The mirrors used in ancient times were not of glass, but of burnished metal. Bronze was the metal ordinarily employed for the purpose, and was in common use in Egypt, where mirrors were bronze plates, round or oval, with a handle, like our fire-screens. The Etruscan women employed similar articles in their toilets, and had them often delicately chased with engravings.

Of the women assembling.—It would seem that these women—the women wont to frequent the "tent of meeting" which Moses had recently set up (chap. xxxiii. 7), and to flock thither in troops—offered voluntarily for the service of God the mirrors, which were among the most highly prized of their possessions. Moses, to mark his approval of their devotion, formed their offerings into the most honourable of all the brazen vessels, and recorded the fact to the women's credit.

(9—20) The construction of the court follows upon that of the furniture which it contained. The passage runs parallel with chap. xxvii. 9—19.

(17) **The overlaying of their chapiters of silver.**—Just as in chap. xxxvi. 38, we are informed that Moses, travelling beyond the letter of his instructions, overlaid the capitals of the pillars at the door of the Tabernacle itself with gold, so now we find that, without any express orders, he overlaid those at the door of the court with silver. In each case he was probably following his remembrance of the pattern seen in the mount (chap. xxv. 9, 40).

THE SUM OF THE GOLD, SILVER, AND BRONZE EMPLOYED IN THE TABERNACLE.

(21) **This is the sum.**—Kalisch translates, "These are the accounts"; Canon Cook, "This is the reckoning." The expression recurs in Numb. xxvi. 63.

The tabernacle of testimony—*i.e.,* the dwelling which was to contain God's "testimony" against sin—the Ten Commandments.

For the service of the Levites.—Rather, *a service of the Levites: i.e.,* a service which they rendered "by the hand," or through the instrumentality of Ithamar. Ithamar was the youngest of the sons of Aaron (chap. vi. 23).

(23) **Aholiab . . . an engraver.**—This is a mistranslation. *Khârâsh* means a worker in any material whatsoever. It should be rendered *artificer,* as it is in 1 Chron. xxix. 5; 2 Chron. xxxiv. 11.

A cunning workman.—Literally, *a deviser;* but the root is used especially of the devising of textile

the tribe of Dan, an engraver, and a
cunning workman, and an embroiderer
in blue, and in purple, and in scarlet,
and fine linen.
(24) All the gold that was occupied for
the work in all the work of the holy
place, even the gold of the offering, was
twenty and nine talents, and seven
hundred and thirty shekels, after the
shekel of the sanctuary.
(25) And the silver of them that were
numbered of the congregation *was* an
hundred talents, and a thousand seven
hundred and threescore and fifteen she-
kels, after the shekel of the sanctuary:
(26) a bekah for [1] every man, *that is*, half
a shekel, after the shekel of the sanc-
tuary, for every one that went to be
numbered, from twenty years old and
upward, for six hundred thousand and
three thousand and five hundred and
fifty *men*. (27) And of the hundred ta-
lents of silver were cast the sockets of
the sanctuary, and the sockets of the
vail; an hundred sockets of the hun-
dred talents, a talent for a socket.
(28) And of the thousand seven hundred
seventy and five *shekels* he made hooks
for the pillars, and overlaid their chap-
iters, and filleted them.
(29) And the brass of the offering *was*
seventy talents, and two thousand and
four hundred shekels. (30) And there-
with he made the sockets to the door
of the tabernacle of the congregation,
and the brasen altar, and the brasen

[1] Heb., *a poll.*

fabrics. (See chaps. xxvi. 1, 31, xxviii. 6, 15, xxxvi. 8, 35, xxxix. 3, &c.)

(24) **All the gold that was occupied for the work.**—Rather, *that was made use of for the work.*

The gold of the offering, was twenty and nine talents.—The gold talent is estimated by Poole as = 10,000 shekels, and the gold shekel as worth about £1 2s. of our money. In this case the gold employed in the Tabernacle would have been worth nearly £320,000. Some, however, reduce the estimate to £175,000 (Cook), and others to £132,000 (Thenius). In any case the amount was remarkable, and indicated at once the liberal spirit which animated the people and the general feeling that a lavish expenditure was required by the occasion. There is no difficulty in supposing that the Israelites possessed at the time gold to the (highest) value estimated, since they had carried with them out of Egypt, besides their ancestral wealth, a vast amount of gold and silver ornaments, freely given to them by the Egyptians (chaps. iii. 22, xii. 35, 36).

(25) **The silver . . . was an hundred talents.**—The silver talent contained 3,000 shekels, as all allow, and as appears from the present passage. If the "shekel of the sanctuary" weighed, as is generally supposed, about 220 grains troy, the value of the silver contributed would have been £40,000, or a little under. It was contributed by "them that were numbered of the congregation," each of whom paid a bekah, or half a shekel. (See above, chap. xxx. 12—16.)

(26) **A bekah for every man.**—The word "bekah" means simply *a half*, but appears to have been restricted in its use to the half-shekel. (Comp. Gen. xxiv. 22.) The exegetical clause, "half a shekel," is probably a later addition to the text, inserted to clear the sense.

For every one that went to be numbered.—It is remarkable that the principle of compulsory payment towards the fabric of the sanctuary should have received a sanction at the very time when the greatest stress was laid upon the greater acceptableness of voluntary offerings. (See chaps. xxv. 2, xxxv. 5, 21—29.) Whatever may be thought of the expediency of levying church-rates, they are clearly defensible in principle, both from the standpoint of the Old Testament and of the New (Matt. xvii. 24—27).

From twenty years old and upward.—See Note on chap. xxx. 14.

Six hundred thousand and three thousand and five hundred and fifty.—The identity of this number with that which is given in Numb. i. 46, as arrived at "in the second year, on the first day of the second month" (Numb. i. 1), is best explained by regarding both passages as having reference to the same transaction. The taking of the census occupied several months, during which the money was gradually collected, the sockets, &c., made, and the Tabernacle set up. The registration was deferred, and took place on a single day, when Moses and Aaron went round the tribes, received the results from their hands, and entered them in a book. It appears from Numb. i. 47 that the Levites were not counted in the sum total, no atonement money being taken from them. (See Birks' *Exodus of Israel*, pp. 118—120.)

(27) **The sockets of the sanctuary.**—On these, see chap. xxvi. 19, 21, 25. They consisted of forty for each side, and sixteen for the western end—total, ninety-six.

The sockets of the vail.—On these, see chap. xxvi. 32. They were four in number, and supported the four pillars on which the vail was hung. Thus the total number of the silver sockets was, as the text expresses, one hundred.

(28) **Hooks for the pillars.**—The pillars of the court had hooks of silver, to which the hangings were attached (chaps. xxvii. 10, 17, xxxviii. 10—12).

Their chapiters.—Comp. verses 17 and 19.

(29) **The brass of the offering**—*i.e.*, the bronze which the people had offered in consequence of the invitation addressed to them by Moses (chap. xxx. 5, 24).

Seventy talents.—No great quantity was needed, since bronze was only required for the laver, for the altar of burnt offering and its vessels, for the sockets of the Tabernacle gate, for those of the court, and for the "pins," or pegs, both of the court and the Tabernacle.

(30) **The sockets to the door of the tabernacle.**—See chap. xxvi. 37.

The brasen altar . . . the brasen grate.—Comp. chap. xxvii. 2—6.

The vessels of the altar.—See chaps. xxvii 3, xxxviii. 3.

grate for it, and all the vessels of the altar, (31) and the sockets of the court round about, and the sockets of the court gate, and all the pins of the tabernacle, and all the pins of the court round about.

CHAPTER XXXIX.—(1) And of the blue, and purple, and scarlet, they made cloths of service, to do service in the holy *place*, and [a] made the holy garments for Aaron; as the LORD commanded Moses. (2) And he made the ephod *of* gold, blue, and purple, and scarlet, and fine twined linen. (3) And they did beat the gold into thin plates, and cut *it into* wires, to work *it* in the blue, and in the purple, and in the scarlet, and in the fine linen, *with* cunning work. (4) They made shoulderpieces for it, to couple *it* together: by the two edges was it coupled together. (5) And the curious girdle of his ephod, that *was* upon it, *was* of the same, according to the work thereof; *of* gold, blue, and purple, and scarlet, and fine twined linen; as the LORD commanded Moses.

(6) [b] And they wrought onyx stones inclosed in ouches of gold, graven, as signets are graven, with the names of the children of Israel. (7) And he put them on the shoulders of the ephod, *that they should be* stones for a [c] memorial to the children of Israel; as the LORD commanded Moses.

(8) And he made the breastplate *of* cunning work, like the work of the ephod; *of* gold, blue, and purple, and scarlet, and fine twined linen. (9) It was foursquare; they made the breastplate double: a span *was* the length thereof, and a span the breadth thereof, *being* doubled. (10) And they set in it four rows of stones: *the first* row *was* a [1] sardius, a topaz, and a carbuncle: this *was* the first row. (11) And the second row, an emerald, a sapphire, and a diamond. (12) And the third row, a ligure, an agate, and an amethyst. (13) And the fourth row, a beryl, an onyx, and a jasper: *they were* inclosed in ouches of gold in their inclosings. (14) And the stones *were* according to the names of the children of Israel, twelve, according to their names, *like* the engravings of a signet, every one with his name, according to the twelve tribes. (15) And they made upon the breastplate chains at the ends, *of* wreathen work *of* pure gold. (16) And they made two ouches *of* gold, and two gold rings; and put the two rings in the two ends of the breastplate. (17) And they put the two wreathen chains of gold in the two rings on the ends of the breastplate. (18) And the two ends of the two wreathen chains they fastened in the two ouches, and put them on the shoulderpieces of the ephod, before it. (19) And they made two rings of gold, and put *them* on the two ends of the breastplate, upon the border of it, which *was* on the side of the ephod inward. (20) And they made two *other* golden rings, and put them on the two sides of the ephod underneath, toward the forepart of it, over against the *other* coupling thereof, above the curious girdle of the ephod. (21) And they did bind the breastplate by his rings unto the rings of the ephod with a lace of blue, that it might be above the curious girdle of the ephod, and that the breast-

a ch. 31. 10 & 35. 19.

b ch. 28. 9.

c ch. 28. 12.

1 Or, *ruby.*

---

(31) **The sockets of the court.**—See chap. xxvii. 10—12, 15—18.

The pins of the tabernacle.—Comp. chaps. xxvii. 19, xxxviii. 20; and see Note on the former passage.

The pins of the court.—See chap. xxvii. 19.

XXXIX.

THE MAKING OF THE HOLY GARMENTS.

(1–31) This section corresponds to chap. xxviii. 5—40, but does not follow exactly the same order. Verses 2—7 correspond to verses 5—12 of chap. xxviii.; verses 8—21 to verses 13—28; verses 22—26 to verses 31—35; but after this a dislocation occurs. Verses 27—29 correspond to verses 39—42 of chap. xxviii., and verses 30, 31 to verses 36—38. It is not clear why any change was made. The order observed in chap. xxviii. seems preferable.

(1) **Cloths of service.**—See Note on chap. xxxi. 10.

(3) **They did beat the gold into thin plates and cut it into wires.**—This very primitive method of forming gold thread is nowhere else mentioned. It implies a ruder state of the art of metallurgy than we should have expected.

To work it in the blue.—The blue, the purple, the scarlet, and the white linen thread were woven into a patterned fabric. The gold was inserted afterwards in the way of embroidery. A similar practice prevailed in Egypt (Wilkinson, *Ancient Egyptians*, vol. iii., p. 128).

(7) **Stones for a memorial.**—See Note on chap. xxviii. 12.

plate might not be loosed from the
ephod as the LORD commanded Moses.
(22) And he made the robe of the
ephod *of* woven work, all *of* blue.
(23) And *there was* an hole in the midst
of the robe, as the hole of an habergeon,
with a band round about the hole, that
it should not rend. (24) And they made
upon the hems of the robe pomegranates
of blue, and purple, and scarlet, *and*
twined *linen*. (25) And they made [a] bells
of pure gold, and put the bells between
the pomegranates upon the hem of the
robe, round about between the pome-
granates; (26) a bell and a pomegranate,
a bell and a pomegranate, round about
the hem of the robe to minister *in;* as
the LORD commanded Moses.
(27) And they made coats *of* fine linen
of woven work for Aaron, and for his sons,
(28) and a mitre *of* fine linen, and goodly
bonnets *of* fine linen, and [b] linen breeches
of fine twined linen, (29) and a girdle *of*
fine twined linen, and blue, and purple,
and scarlet, *of* needlework; as the LORD
commanded Moses.
(30) And they made the plate of the
holy crown *of* pure gold, and wrote
upon it a writing, *like to* the engravings
of a signet, [c] HOLINESS TO THE
LORD. (31) And they tied unto it a lace
of blue, to fasten *it* on high upon the
mitre; as the LORD commanded Moses.
(32) Thus was all the work of the tab-
ernacle of the tent of the congregation
finished: and the children of Israel did
according to all that the LORD com-
manded Moses, so did they.
(33) And they brought the tabernacle
unto Moses, the tent, and all his furni-
ture, his taches, his boards, his bars,
and his pillars, and his sockets, (34) and
the covering of rams' skins dyed red,
and the covering of badgers' skins, and
the vail of the covering, (35) the ark of
the testimony, and the staves thereof,
and the mercy seat, (36) the table, *and*
all the vessels thereof, and the shew-
bread, (37) the pure candlestick, *with* the
lamps thereof, *even with* the lamps to be
set in order, and all the vessels thereof,
and the oil for light, (38) and the golden
altar, and the anointing oil, and [1] the
sweet incense, and the hanging for the
tabernacle door, (39) the brasen altar,
and his grate of brass, his staves, and
all his vessels, the laver and his foot,
(40) the hangings of the court, his pillars,
and his sockets, and the hanging for
the court gate, his cords, and his pins,
and all the vessels of the service of the
tabernacle, for the tent of the congrega-
tion, (41) the cloths of service to do
service in the holy *place*, and the holy
garments for Aaron the priest, and his
sons' garments, to minister in the
priest's office. (42) According to all that
the LORD commanded Moses, so the

a ch. 28. 33.

b ch. 28. 42.

c ch. 28. 36.

1 Heb., *the incense of sweet spices.*

---

(24) **Pomegranates of blue . . . and twined linen.**—Rather, *of blue, and purple, and scarlet, twisted together.* (Comp. chap. xxviii. 33.)

(25) **Bells of pure gold.**—On the object of the bells, see Note on chap. xxviii. 35.

(27) **They made coats.**—Rather, *tunics* or *shirts.* See Note on chap. xxviii. 40.

(28) **A mitre . . . and goodly bonnets.**—The "mitre," or rather "turban," was for Aaron, the "goodly bonnets," or rather "caps," for his sons. (See the Notes on chap. xxviii. 36—40.)

Linen breeches.—Rather, *linen drawers.* These were to be made both for Aaron and for his sons. (See chap. xxviii. 42, 43.)

(29) **A girdle.**—The girdle was for Aaron. It is described much more fully here than in the "instructions," where it is called simply a "girdle of needlework" (chap. xxviii. 39).

(30) **The plate of the holy crown.**—See Note on chap. xxix. 6.

THE PRESENTATION OF THE WORK TO MOSES, AND HIS APPROVAL OF IT.

(33—43) It is probable that the various parts of the work were presented to Moses for inspection as they were completed; that if they did not satisfy him, they might be altered and amended *at once.* Moses alone had seen "the pattern in the mount," and Moses alone could say if the work came up to the required standard. We are not told that anything was rejected; and it is quite possible that all the portions of the work were satisfactorily rendered at their first essay by the several workmen; for the workmen, it must be remembered, besides receiving instructions from Moses, were divinely assisted in the production of their several works (chap. xxxvi. 42).

(34) **The vail of the covering**—*i.e.*, the vail which separated between the Holy place and the Holy of Holies, covering the latter from the sight of man. (Comp. chap. xl. 21.)

(37) **The lamps to be set in order.**—Heb., *the lamps of arrangement.* The reference is probably to the arrangement of the lamps in a single line or row. (Comp. Lev. xxiv. 6.)

(41) **The cloths of service . . . and the holy garments.**—There is no "and" in the original. Translate, *the cloths of service to do service in the holy place—the holy garments for Aaron the priest, and his sons' garments.* The second and third clauses are exegetical of the first. (See Note on chap. xxxi. 10.)

(43) **Moses did look upon all the work**—*i.e.*, inspected it, examined it, to see if it was "according to the pattern" shown him. Being satisfied,

children of Israel made all the work.
(43) And Moses did look upon all the
work, and, behold, they had done it as
the LORD had commanded, even so had
they done it: and Moses blessed them.

CHAPTER XL.—(1) And the LORD
spake unto Moses, saying, (2) On the
first day of the first month shalt thou
set up the tabernacle of the tent of the
congregation. (3) And thou shalt put
therein the ark of the testimony, and
cover the ark with the vail. (4) And
[a] thou shalt bring in the table, and set
in order [1] the things that are to be set
in order upon it; and thou shalt bring
in the candlestick, and light the lamps
thereof. (5) And thou shalt set the altar
of gold for the incense before the ark of
the testimony, and put the hanging of
the door to the tabernacle. (6) And
thou shalt set the altar of the burnt
offering before the door of the taber-
nacle of the tent of the congregation.
(7) And thou shalt set the laver between
the tent of the congregation and the
altar, and shalt put water therein.
(8) And thou shalt set up the court round
about, and hang up the hanging at the
court gate. (9) And thou shalt take the
anointing oil, and anoint the taber-
nacle, and all that *is* therein, and shalt

[a] ch. 26. 35.

[1] Heb., *the order thereof.*

---

he expressed his own and God's approval by blessing those who had worked so faithfully.

XL.

THE INSTRUCTIONS FOR THE UPREARING OF THE TABERNACLE.

(1–8) Though the work was now complete, and all the parts of the Tabernacle made ready, Moses did not at once proceed to erect it. As when he first went up into Sinai (chap. xxiv. 16), so now, he waited for a Divine summons, a distinct command fixing the time for him to do that which he knew that he had to do. There is an importance and a fitness in "times and seasons," which the Great Father often reserves it to Himself to determine (Acts i. 7). Moses felt this, and waited, till after a time the summons came. God fixed for the erection "the first day of the first month" (verse 2)—*i.e.*, the New Year's Day of the first year of freedom. At the same time He gave directions fixing the order in which all should be done, and determining the position of the various articles of furniture which the Tabernacle and its court were to contain (verses 4–8).

(2) **On the first day of the first month.**—The Israelites had quitted Egypt on the fourteenth day of the first month, Abib (chap. xii. 6). They had reached the wilderness of Sinai in the course of the third month, Sivan, and encamped in front of Sinai shortly after (chap. xix. 1, 2). The two long absences of Moses in the Mount had occupied nearly three months, and were separated by an interval probably of several days. It must have been the sixth or seventh month before the work was commenced, and very late in the year—the eleventh or twelfth month—before it was accomplished. Hence, the new year was now approaching, and, as it was approaching, its first day was naturally chosen as most fit for the inauguration of the new structure.

The tabernacle of the tent of the congregation.—Rather, *the tabernacle, the tent of meeting.* The words *mishkan* and *'ohel* are in apposition, not in regimen. (So also in verse 6.)

(3) **Thou shalt put therein the ark of the testimony.**—The most precious of the objects which the tabernacle was to contain was to be placed in it first. Then immediately it was to be covered up with the vail.

(4) **The table.**—The "table of shewbread" is thus commonly designated. (See chaps. xxxv. 13, xxxvii. 10, xxxix. 36, xl. 22.)

And set in order the things . . .—The twelve loaves are the "things" specially intended (see verse 23). Whether the frankincense also is glanced at (Lev. xxiv. 7) may be doubted. It was perhaps an addition to the earliest ritual.

The candlestick.—See chap. xxv. 31—37.

And light the lamps.—Not necessarily at once, but at the close of the day. (See chap. xxx. 8.)

(5) **Thou shalt set the altar of gold . . . before the ark.**—Not inside the vail, but outside, in the Holy Place; nearer, however, to the vail than either the table or the candlestick. (See Note 1 on chap. xxx. 6.)

The hanging of the door—*i.e.*, the curtain at the entrance to the Tabernacle (chaps. xxvi. 36, xxxvi. 37, &c.).

(6) **The altar of the burnt-offering.**—See chap. xxvii. 1—8.

(7) **The laver.**—Comp. chap. xxx. 18. Its proper place was close to the door of the Tabernacle, since the priests had to wash their hands and feet at it every time that they set foot within the Tabernacle (chap. xxx. 19, 20).

(8) **The court . . . the hanging.**—See chap. xxvii. 9—18.

THE INSTRUCTIONS FOR THE CONSECRATION OF THE TABERNACLE AND THE PRIESTS.

(9–15) Instructions for the consecration of the Tabernacle, its furniture and its vessels, by anointing, and for the consecration of Aaron and his sons by ablution, anointing, and investiture, were attached to those given concerning the setting up of the Tabernacle, and are here recorded, although their execution appears to have been delayed to a later date. (See Lev. viii. 1—13.) Moses perhaps found that there was not time for the completion of the ceremony on the day of the erection of the Tabernacle, and therefore deferred a part of it.

(9) **The anointing oil.**—Directions for the composition of the oil had been already given (chap. xxx. 23—25); and at the same time it had been ordered that the Tabernacle, the ark, the table, the candlestick, the two altars, the laver, and the various vessels of the sanctuary, should be consecrated by anointing them (chap. xxx. 26—29).

hallow it, and all the vessels thereof:
and it shall be holy. (10) And thou shalt
anoint the altar of the burnt offering,
and all his vessels, and sanctify the
altar: and it shall be an altar [1] most
holy. (11) And thou shalt anoint the
laver and his foot, and sanctify it.
(12) And thou shalt bring Aaron and his
sons unto the door of the tabernacle of
the congregation, and wash them with
water. (13) And thou shalt put upon
Aaron the holy garments, and anoint
him, and sanctify him; that he may
minister unto me in the priest's office.
(14) And thou shalt bring his sons, and
clothe them with coats: (15) and thou
shalt anoint them, as thou didst anoint
their father, that they may minister un-
to me in the priest's office: for their
anointing shall surely be an everlasting
priesthood throughout their generations.
(16) Thus did Moses: according to all
that the LORD commanded him, so did he.
(17) And it came to pass in the first
month in the second year, on the first
day of the month, *that* the [a] tabernacle
was reared up. (18) And Moses reared
up the tabernacle, and fastened his
sockets, and set up the boards thereof,
and put in the bars thereof, and reared
up his pillars. (19) And he spread abroad
the tent over the tabernacle, and put
the covering of the tent above upon it;
as the LORD commanded Moses.
(20) And he took and put the testi-
mony into the ark, and set the staves on
the ark, and put the mercy seat above
upon the ark: (21) and he brought the
ark into the tabernacle, and [b] set up the
vail of the covering, and covered the
ark of the testimony; as the LORD com-
manded Moses.

B.C. 1490.

1 Heb., *holiness of holinesses.*

a Num. 7. 1.

b ch. 35. 12.

---

(12) **Thou shalt bring Aaron and his sons . . . and wash them.**—See Note on chap. xxix. 4. Ablution, investiture, and anointing had all of them been previously appointed to be parts of the consecration service (chap. xxix. 4, 5, 7, &c.).

(14) **Thou shalt bring his sons, and clothe them with coats.**—Rather, *with tunics.* (Comp. chap. xxix. 8.)

(15) **Thou shalt anoint them, as thou didst anoint their father.**—By the narrative of Lev. viii., it would seem that Aaron's sons were not anointed in the same way as himself. He had the oil poured over his head (Lev. viii. 12; Ps. cxxxiii. 2). They were merely sprinkled with a mixture of oil and blood (Lev. viii. 30). The difference implied a lower degree of official holiness.

Their anointing shall surely be an everlasting priesthood.—The Jewish commentators maintain that the one anointing of the sons of Aaron sufficed for all time, and was not repeated in the case of any subsequent priests, who became fully possessed of the sacerdotal office without it. Each high priest was, on the contrary, inducted into his office by anointing, whence the high priest came to be spoken of as "the anointed priest" (Lev. iv. 3, 5, 16, xxi. 12, &c.).

(16) **Thus did Moses.**—This verse states generally the fact that Moses carried out the entire series of instructions given him in verses 2—15, but tells us nothing as to the time at which he carried them out. The passage which follows (verses 17—33) fixes the performance of the first set of instructions (verses 2—8) to "the first day of the second year." The narrative of Lev. viii. shows that the remainder (verses 9—15) were not put into execution till later.

THE UPREARING OF THE TABERNACLE.

(17) **On the first day of the month . . . the tabernacle was reared up.**—The Tabernacle was so constructed as to be capable of being rapidly both put together and taken to pieces. The erection of the framework, and the stretching upon it of the fine linen and goats'-hair coverings, must have been the main difficulty. But the family of Abraham had been familiar with tent life from the time of its quitting Ur of the Chaldees to the descent into Egypt, and its location in Egypt on the borders of the desert, in close neighbourhood to various nomadic races, had kept up its familiarity with tents, their structure, and the most approved methods of pitching and striking them. Thus it is not surprising that the first erection was completed in less than a day.

(18) **Moses . . . fastened his sockets.**—The stability of the Tabernacle must have depended almost entirely upon the sockets. These were of some considerable weight (chap. xxxviii. 27), but they cannot by their mere weight have sustained the fabric in an upright position. It is reasonable to suppose that they were let into the ground to a depth of some feet. The erection necessarily commenced with this operation.

Set up the boards.—When the sockets had been firmly fixed, the upright boards and the pillars were inserted into them by means of the "tenons" in which they terminated, and so stood erect. The coupling by "bars" rivetted the three walls into one firm and compact structure.

(19) **He spread abroad the tent over the tabernacle.**—Erected, *i.e.,* the wooden framework, with the covering of goats'-hair, which formed the true tent (*'ohel*), and so roofed in the Tabernacle (*mishkan*).

Put the covering . . . above upon it.—"The covering" (*miksêh*) is the outer protection of rams' skins and seals' skins. (See chap. xxvi. 14.)

(20) **He took and put the testimony into the ark.**—By "the testimony" we must understand the two tables of stone, written with the finger of God, which Moses had brought down with him from the top of Sinai on his last visit (chap. xxxiv. 29). On the use of the word "testimony" in this sense, see Note to chap. xxv. 16. It is not proved by this passage that the Ark held nothing but "the testimony."

Set the staves on the ark—*i.e.,* placed them in the rings, ready for use. (See chap. xxv. 14.)

(21) **The vail of the covering.**—See Note on chap. xxxix. 34, and comp. above, verse 3.

(22) And he put the table in the tent
of the congregation, upon the side of
the tabernacle northward, without the
vail. (23) And he set the bread in order
upon it before the LORD; as the LORD
had commanded Moses.
(24) And he put the candlestick in the
tent of the congregation, over against
the table, on the side of the tabernacle
southward. (25) And he lighted the
lamps before the LORD; as the LORD
commanded Moses.
(26) And he put the golden altar in
the tent of the congregation before the
vail: (27) and he burnt sweet incense
thereon; as the LORD commanded
Moses.
(28) And he set up the hanging *at* the
door of the tabernacle. (29) And he put
the altar of burnt offering *by* the door
of the tabernacle of the tent of the con-
gregation, and offered upon it the burnt
offering and the meat offering; as the
[a]LORD commanded Moses.
(30) And he set the laver between the
tent of the congregation and the altar,
and put water there, to wash *withal.*
(31) And Moses and Aaron and his sons
washed their hands and their feet
thereat: (32) when they went into the
tent of the congregation, and when they
came near unto the altar, they washed;
as the LORD commanded Moses.
(33) And he reared up the court round
about the tabernacle and the altar, and
set up the hanging of the court gate.
So Moses finished the work.
(34) [b]Then a cloud covered the tent of
the congregation, and the glory of the
LORD filled the tabernacle. (35) And
Moses was not able to enter into the
tent of the congregation, because the
cloud abode thereon, and the glory of
the LORD filled the tabernacle. (36) And
when the cloud was taken up from over
the tabernacle, the children of Israel
[1]went onward in all their journeys:
(37) but if the cloud were not taken up,
then they journeyed not till the day that
it was taken up. (38) For the cloud of
the LORD *was* upon the tabernacle by
day, and fire was on it by night, in the
sight of all the house of Israel, through-
out all their journeys.

[a] ch. 30. 9.

[b] Num. 9. 15; 1 Kings 8. 10.

[1] Heb., *journeyed.*

---

(22) **Put the table . . . upon the side of the tabernacle northward.**—On the right hand to one facing towards the vail. Moses may have known the right position from the pattern which was shewed him in the mount (chap. xxv. 40).

(23) **He set the bread in order upon it.**—Arranged, *i.e.*, the twelve loaves in two rows, as was afterwards commanded to be done (Lev. xxiv. 6).

(24) **He put the candlestick . . . over against the table.**—Directly opposite to it, on the left hand, as one faced the vail. The light would thus be thrown on the table of shewbread. (See chap. xxv. 37.)

(25) **He lighted the lamps.**—When the proper time came, *i.e.*, at even. (Comp. chap. xxx. 8; Lev. xxiv. 3.)

(26) **He put the golden altar . . . before the vail.**—In front of the Ark, the mercy-seat, and the place assigned to the Shechinah (chap. xxv. 22), but separated from them by the vail. (Comp. chap. xxx. 6.)

(27) **He burnt sweet incense thereon.**—At even, when he lighted the lamps, he also, according to the instructions given him (chap. xxx. 8) burnt incense.

(28) **The hanging at the door.**—See above, verse 5, and comp. chap. xxvi. 36.

(29) **He put the altar of burnt offering by the door of the tabernacle.**—On the altar of burnt offering, see chaps. xxvii. 1—8, xxxviii. 1—7. Some preposition has fallen out before the word "door." Our translators suppose an omission of *'al*, "at," but it is more probable that *liphney*, which occurs in verse 6, is the word omitted. The altar was not "*at* the door," but "before" or "in front of the door."

And offered upon it the burnt offering and the meat offering.—Offered upon it, *i.e.*, the first evening sacrifice—a lamb for a burnt offering, together with the prescribed meat offering. (See chap. xxix. 40.)

(30) **And he set the laver between the tent . . . and the altar.**—On the bronze laver and its position in the Tabernacle, see the Notes on chap. xxx. 18.

(31, 32) These verses are parenthetic. They interrupt the narrative of what Moses did "on the first day of the first month," informing us of the use whereto the laver was applied subsequently. (Comp. chap. xxx. 19—21.)

(33) **He reared up the court . . . and set up the hanging.**—On the court, see chap. xxvii. 9—18 For "the hanging" see chap. xxvii. 16.

THE DESCENT OF THE GLORY OF GOD UPON THE TABERNACLE.

(34) **Then a cloud.**—Heb., *the cloud, i.e.*, the same cloud that had accompanied the host and directed their journeys from Succoth (chap. xiii. 20—22).

Covered the tent.—The cloud rested on the tent outside; the "glory of God,"—some ineffably brilliant appearance—entered inside, and "filled" the entire dwelling. It pleased God thus to manifest His intention of making good His promise to go with the people in person (chap. xxxiii. 17).

(35) **Moses was not able to enter into the tent.**—Apparently, Moses, seeing the cloud descend, as it had been wont to do upon the temporary "tent of meeting" (chap. xxxiii. 9), endeavoured to re-enter the Tabernacle which he had quitted, but was unable; the "glory" forbade approach. (Comp. the effect of the "glory" when it descended on Solomon's Temple, 1 Kings viii. 11; 2 Chron. v. 14, vii. 2.)

(36—38) The cloud was henceforth, in a peculiar way, attached to the Tabernacle. As a cloud it rested upon it by day; as a pillar of fire by night. Only in one case was it removed, viz., when it was the Divine will that Israel should march. (See Num. ix. 15—22.)

ADDITIONAL NOTES TO EXODUS

EXCURSUS A: ON EGYPTIAN HISTORY, AS CONNECTED WITH THE BOOK OF EXODUS.

THE question of the exact time in Egyptian history to which the circumstances related in the Book of Exodus belong is one rather of secular interest than of importance for Biblical exegesis. Vital to the Jewish nation as was the struggle in which Moses engaged with the Pharaoh of the time, to Egypt and its people the matter was one of comparatively slight moment—an episode in the history of the sons of Mizraim which might well have left no trace in their annals. Subject races, held as bondmen by the monarchs, were common in the country; and the loss of one such race would not have made any great difference in the general prosperity of Egypt; nor would the destruction of such a chariot and cavalry force as appears to have perished in the Red Sea have seriously crippled the Egyptian military power. The phenomena of the plagues—aggravations mostly of ordinary Egyptian scourges—would not necessarily have attracted the attention of any writers, while they would, no doubt, have been studiously concealed by the historiographers of the kings. As M. Chabas observes—"Des événements de ce genre n'ont pas dû être inscrits sur les monuments publics, où l'on n'enregistrait que des succès et des gloires."* No one, therefore, has the right to require of the Biblical apologist that he should confirm the historical narrative of Exodus by producing references to it in the Egyptian records. The events themselves may never have been put on record in Egypt, or, if recorded, the record of them may have been lost. It is not, perhaps, generally known what large *lacunæ* there are in the Egyptian annals, nor how scanty are the memorials even of the best known times. The argument *a silentio*, always weak, has absolutely no value in a case where the materials on which the history is based are at once so limited and so fragmentary.

Still, an interest will always attach to the connection of sacred history with profane, and speculation will always be rife as to the identity of Pharaohs mentioned in the Bible with monarchs known to us from the Egyptian remains. Readers will naturally expect the writer of such a comment as the present to have some view, more or less distinct, as to the period in Egyptian history whereto the events recorded in Exodus belong, and may fairly claim to have such view put before them for their consideration.

Egyptian history divides itself into three main periods, which are generally distinguished as the times of the Old, the Middle, and the New Empires. The "Old Empire" was certainly anterior to Abraham, and probably lasted from about B.C. 2500 to B.C. 1900. The Middle Empire was the result of a conquest of Egypt by Asiatic invaders, and is known as the period of the Hyksôs, or "Shepherd Kings." Its duration, in the opinion of the present writer, did not exceed two hundred years† (B.C. 1900—1700). The New Empire was established by a revolt of the native Egyptians against the Hyksôs (about B.C. 1700),* and is reckoned to have lasted from that time to the Persian conquest under Cambyses (B.C. 527).

It is generally allowed that the exodus belongs to the time of the New Empire.† All the characteristics of the period, as set forth in the Biblical narrative, are so thoroughly Egyptian, that we cannot imagine Egypt at the time crushed under the iron yoke of a hated race of foreigners, and a smouldering spirit of discontent everywhere pervading the masses, and ready to burst out into insurrection. If the "Middle Empire" is thus eliminated, and our choice shown to lie between the Old Empire and the New, we cannot hesitate to prefer the latter. Under the Old Empire Egypt had no chariot force;‡ and there is every reason to believe that the horse itself was unknown in the country.§ Chronological considerations, moreover, make it impossible to throw the exodus back to a time anterior to B.C. 1900. The result is that modern critics universally, or all but universally, assign the exodus to the time of the New Empire, and that what remains to be determined is, under which dynasty, and after that, under which king, the great migration took place.

The synchronism of the twenty-second dynasty of Manetho with Solomon, which must be regarded as sufficiently established by the identity of the name Shishak with Sheshonk, and the record of Sheshonk I.'s expedition against Palestine engraved on the walls of the Temple of Karnak,‖ determines the time of the exodus to the *earlier* portion of the New Empire, and may even be said to leave us a choice between two dynasties only—the first and second of the new *régime* (Manetho's eighteenth and nineteenth). The twenty-first dynasty, which did not hold the throne for more than a hundred and thirty years,¶ is manifestly excluded, since its commencement could not be anterior to the judgeship of Samuel; while the space assigned to the twentieth, which is at the utmost a hundred and eighty years,** is certainly not more than sufficient for the time of the other judges. Hence it is now regarded by almost all commentators and critical historians as certain that the exodus took place under one or other of the two great dynasties which stand at the head of the New Empire lists, and are the most important in the whole range of Egyptian history.

In favour of the eighteenth dynasty, it is urged that the interval of time between the death of Solomon and

* Chabas, *Recherches pour servir à l'Histoire de l'Egypte aux temps de l'Exode*, p. 152.

† See the writer's *History of Egypt*, vol. ii., p.17; and compare Canon Cook's Essay in the *Speaker's Commentary*, vol. i., p. 447, who enlarges the time to "between two and three centuries."

* So Brugsch, *History of Egypt*, vol. ii., p. 314. Mariette makes the date B.C. 1703; Birch, B.C. 1600; Stuart Poole, B.C. 1525.

† This is the view of Birch, Brugsch, Lenormant, Chabas, Kalisch, Canon Cook, Ebers, Eisenlohr, and most others.

‡ It is not till the time of the eighteenth dynasty that we have any representation or any mention of chariots. The probability, however, is that they were introduced under the seventeenth.

§ Birch, *History of Ancient Egypt*, p. 82.

‖ See Rosellini, *Monumenti Storici*, pl. 148; Lepsius, *Denkmäler*, pt. iii., pl. 252.

¶ Lenormant, *Manuel d'Histoire Ancienne*, vol. i., p. 321.

** *Ibid.* Manetho said 173 or 135.

the exodus, whether taken as fixed by the date given in the First Book of Kings (chap. vi. 1) at somewhat more than five hundred years,* or, as might fairly be gathered from the scattered notices in the Books of Samuel and Judges, at about six hundred and fifty years,† brings us to the time of the eighteenth, and not of the nineteenth, dynasty, according to the computations which those most familiar with the subject have drawn from purely Egyptian sources. This argument must be allowed to have some weight; but its importance is greatly diminished by two facts. These are, the extreme uncertainty of the Egyptian, and the general inexactness of the Biblical, chronology. Egyptologists are not agreed as to the date for the accession of the eighteenth dynasty within two centuries,‡ nor as to its duration within a century.§ The chronological notices in Judges and Samuel are mostly in round numbers,|| and do not claim exactness. The Biblical chronology, moreover, is not continuous, but presents several gaps.¶ The single text on which an exact chronology could be based (1 Kings vi. 1) is with reason suspected,** and cannot be regarded as determining an otherwise insoluble problem.

A supposed agreement between the general course of events in Egyptian history at the beginning of the eighteenth dynasty and the inferences suggested by the brief narrative of Exodus has been also urged in favour of the view that the exodus is to be assigned to this period.†† But this argument is too unsubstantial and shadowy to have much force. The facts of Egyptian history obtainable from Exodus are too few, and of too ordinary a character, the inferences too uncertain, to justify the conclusion which has been drawn from them. Indeed, they are capable of being read in a directly opposite sense. A writer, second to few in his knowledge of the Egyptian records, observes that the facts mentioned "point to a divided country and a weak kingdom, and cannot apply to the time of the eighteenth dynasty."‡‡ The only definite facts seem to be (1) the building of Pithom and Raamses as store-cities by the Pharaoh who began the oppression (Exod. i. 11); (2) his employment of forced labour; (3) the existence at the time of a formidable enemy which threatened Egypt, and which the Israelites might be expected to join (*ib.* 10); and (4) the long reign of the Pharaoh from whom Moses fled, which cannot have been much less, and may have been considerably more, than forty years.§§

* The 480 years of this passage date from the fourth year of Solomon. Add 36, the remaining years of his life, and the result is 516 years.

† See Clinton, *Fasti Hellenici*, vol. i., p. 312, where the sum of the years between the exodus and the fourth year of Solomon is estimated at a minimum of 600, and a maximum of 628.

‡ Mariette makes it B.C. 1703; Brugsch, B.C. 1700; Birch, B.C. 1600; Stuart Poole, B.C. 1525; Wilkinson, B.C. 1520.

§ Brugsch assigns to it 300 years; Mariette, 241; Bunsen, 221; Wilkinson, 196 years.

|| Twenty years (Judges v. 3, xvi. 31; 1 Sam. vii. 2); forty years (Judges iii. 11, v. 31, viii. 28, xiii. 1; 1 Sam. iv. 18); eighty years (Judges iii. 30); three hundred years (Judges xi. 26).

¶ *E.g.*, the judgeships of Joshua, Shamgar, and Samuel; the space between Joshua's death and the accession of Othniel, &c.

** See the writer's "Additional Note" on the passage in the *Speaker's Commentary*, vol. ii., pp. 515, 516. Hales says on the passage, "The period of 480 years is a forgery, foisted into the text" (*Chronology*, vol. ii., p. 287).

†† Canon Cook in the *Speaker's Commentary*, vol. i., pp. 455—461.

‡‡ R. Stuart Poole in Dr. Smith's *Dictionary of the Bible*, vol. i., p. 510.

§§ Moses is eighty at his return from Midian (Exod. vii. 7), which must have followed closely upon the death of the Pharaoh from whom he fled soon after he was grown up (Exod. ii. 11—15). St. Stephen regarded him as forty at the time of his flight (Acts vii. 23); but from Exodus alone we should have supposed him younger.

Of these facts there is one—the building of Raamses—which points strongly to the nineteenth dynasty as occupying the throne. The name Raamses first appears in the dynastic lists at this time, and though it may be true that the name, or one like it, was previously known in Egypt, and had even been borne by a prince,* yet, until it had been borne by a king it was not likely to become the name of a town.† Moreover, it is exactly at this period of Egyptian history that we first hear of a city called Pi-Ramesu, "the city of Rameses," and that the kings are found to be engaged in the construction of it. They employ in its construction forced labour, and denominate the labourers *Aperu*, which is a fair Egyptian equivalent of the word Hebrew.‡ Further, Rameses is their capital, and is a sort of suburb of Tanis, which agrees well with the statement of the Psalmist that the miracles of Moses were wrought "in the field of Zoan."§ There is no other period in Egyptian history when Tanis was the capital, excepting under the Middle Empire, under which the exodus would scarcely now be placed by any one.

The existence at the time of a formidable enemy, which the Hebrews might have been expected to join, suits also the early portion of the nineteenth dynasty. It was just then that, as Dr. Brugsch says, "a great nation grew up beyond the frontier on the north-east to an importance and power which began to endanger the Egyptian supremacy in Western Asia."|| The Hittite power was a real peril to Egypt during the reigns of Rameses I., Seti I., and Rameses II., the first three kings of the dynasty, who were engaged in constant wars against these formidable neighbours. They were induced under the circumstances greatly to strengthen their north-eastern frontier by means of walls and fortresses, and evidently feared invasion from this quarter. Invasion came in the time of Rameses III., though not from the Hittites, but from a people who had temporarily subjected them. As the Israelites were Asiatics, who had immigrated into Egypt from Syria, it might easily be supposed that they would readily join a Syrian invader. No such fears or perils beset the Egypt of the eighteenth dynasty, when the country was at the height of its military glory, and accustomed to carry its arms deep into Asia.

The long reign of the Pharaoh from whom Moses fled agrees well with what we know of Rameses II. Not only did Manetho assign him a reign of above sixty years, according to all the accounts that have come down to us,¶ but his sixty-seventh year is noted upon his monuments.** Very few Egyptian kings reigned so much as forty years, and it is a noticeable circumstance that, exactly at the period of Egyptian history to which the oppression and the exodus would on other grounds have been referred, there occurs a reign of the unusual duration which is required by the facts of the narrative.

* Aahmes, the first king of the eighteenth dynasty, is said to have had a son called Rames (Cook in the *Speaker's Commentary*, vol. i., p. 454).

† No Egyptian king would have given a town the name of a mere subject. Pi-Ramesu, probably begun by Seti I., was named after Rameses II., whom he had associated.

‡ See Chabas, *Recherches pour servir à l'Histoire de l'Egypte*, pp. 142, 143. M. Chabas regards *Aperu* as "the exact Egyptian translation of the Hebrew עברי" (Hebrews). It is objected that there is no reason for the change of *b* into *p*, and that the proper transcript would have been *Aberu* (Cook in *Speaker's Commentary*, vol. i., p. 466, note 114). But the sounds of *p* and *b* in Egyptian must have been very near, or Pi-Bast would not have become Bubastis, Pi-Hesar Busiris, and the like.

§ Ps. lxxviii. 12, 43.

|| *History of Egypt*, vol. ii., p. 2, E.T.

¶ Syncell, *Chronograph.*, pp. 72B, 73A, B; Euseb., *Chron. Can.* i., 20, p. 102.

** Brugsch, *History of Egypt*, vol. ii., p. 110.

Confirmation is given to the view, that the events related in Exodus belong to the nineteenth dynasty, by the statement of George the Syncellus that the synchronism of Joseph with Apepi, the last Shepherd King, was "universally admitted."* In this case the "new king who knew not Joseph"† could not be Aahmes, the founder of the eighteenth dynasty, who immediately succeeded Apepi, and with whom Joseph must have been in part contemporary, but must rather have been the founder of the next dynasty, the nineteenth—either Rameses I., or Seti I., his son and successor. Four hundred and thirty years‡ after Apepi will bring us to the nineteenth dynasty at any rate, if not even to the twentieth, since no one now assigns to the eighteenth dynasty more than three hundred, or to the nineteenth more than a hundred and sixty years.

Again, the distorted account of the exodus which was given by Manetho,§ inaccurate as it may be in its details, preserves undoubtedly the Egyptian tradition, which placed the events in the reign of an Amenôphis, who was the son of a Rampses (Rameses) and the father of a Sethos. No other king in the Egyptian lists answers to these particulars except Menephthah, who was the son and successor of Rameses II., and the father of Seti II., or Seti-Menephthah. The name Menephthah is, indeed, inaccurately represented by Amenôphis, which is the true Greek equivalent of Amenhotep; but Manetho himself probably called the king Ammenephthes,|| which Josephus turned into Amenôphis.

Altogether, the arguments in favour of the nineteenth dynasty being that which held the throne at the time of the events recorded in Exodus seem to preponderate considerably over those which can be adduced in favour of the eighteenth. The eighteenth was too powerful and warlike to have feared invasion, or to have regarded Israel as a danger. It built no "store-cities." It was unacquainted with the name Rameses. It did not hold its court at Tanis. It contained neither king nor prince of the name of Sethos (Seti). The nineteenth was differently situated. It combined the various particulars to which the eighteenth was a stranger. Moreover, it terminated in such a time of weakness as might have been expected to follow the calamities recorded in Exodus;¶ while the eighteenth was glorious to its very close, and gave no indication of diminished greatness.

On the whole, it would seem to be most probable that the Israelites, having come into Egypt in the reign of Apôphis (Apepi), the last Shepherd King, who was a thoroughly Egyptianised Asiatic,** remained there as peaceable subjects under the great and warlike eighteenth dynasty for some three hundred years, gradually, as the memory of Joseph's benefits faded, suffering more and more oppression, but multiplying in spite of it, till at length a change of dynasty occurred, and with it a change of policy in respect of them. Moderate ill-usage was succeeded by the harshest possible treatment; their "lives were made bitter with hard bondage."* The "new king who knew not Joseph" (Exod. i. 8) is perhaps, in the mind of the writer, rather Sethos I. than Rameses I., who reigned but a year and four months.† Sethos, threatened on his north-eastern frontier by the Hittites, and fearing lest the Hebrews should join them, devised the plans ascribed to the "new king" in Exod. i.—set them to build "store-cities, Pithom and Raamses," the latter named probably after his son;‡ when this had no effect, sought to check their increase by means of the midwives; and finally required that all their male offspring should be thrown into the Nile. There is nothing in the character of Seti I., as represented upon his monuments, to render these severities improbable. He was a good son and a good father, but an implacable enemy and a harsh ruler. His treatment of prisoners taken in war was cruel beyond the wont of his time, his campaigns were sanguinary, and his temper fierce and resentful.§

If Moses was born under Seti I., and bred up by his daughter, the king under whom he found himself when he grew to manhood, and from whom he fled to the land of Midian,|| must have been Rameses II. Seti associated his son Rameses when he was about twelve years of age, and shortly afterwards he practically transferred to him the reins of power. Rameses II. claims to have held the throne for at least sixty-seven years, and was assigned sixty-six by Manetho. His reign is the longest of all the Egyptian reigns, except that of Phiops. He was a king likely to have continued the "hard bondage" of the Israelites, for he was the most indefatigable of builders, and effected the greater number of his constructions by the instrumentality of forced labour. Lenormant says that "during his reign thousands of captives must have died under the rod of the task-master, or have fallen victims to over-work or privations of every description;" and that "in all his monuments there was not, so to speak, a single stone which had not cost a human life."¶ It was the sight of oppression such as this which provoked the indignation of Moses, and led to the rash act which caused him to quit Egypt and fly to Midian.

So long as Rameses II. lived, the exile felt that he could not return. It must have been weary waiting for the space of forty years or more, while the great Pharaoh made his expeditions, excavated his canal,** and erected his numerous buildings. The weariness of prolonged exile shows itself in the name given by Moses to his eldest son: "He called his name Gershom: for he said, I have been a stranger in a strange land" (Exod. ii. 22, xviii. 3). At length, "in process of time"—after a reign which exceeded sixty-six years—"the king of Egypt died" (Exod. ii. 23); and Moses, divinely informed of the fact (Exod. iii. 19), returned to Egypt to his brethren.

If Seti I. be the king who commenced the oppression, and Rameses II. the monarch from whom Moses fled, the Pharaoh whom he found seated on the throne upon his return must have been Menephthah. The character of this king, as depicted in the Egyptian monuments, bears a considerable resemblance to that of the adver-

* Syncell, *Chronograph.*, p. 62B. There are no grounds for limiting the statement, as is done by Bunsen, to "all Christian chronographers" (*Egypt's Place*, vol. ii., p. 438); or, as is done by Canon Cook, to "Josephus and those who drew their information from him" (*Speaker's Commentary*, vol. i., p. 447).

† Exod. i. 8: "Now there arose up a new king over Egypt." The phrase naturally points to the founder of a new dynasty.

‡ See Exod. xii. 40. The authority of the Hebrew text far outweighs that of the LXX. and Samaritan Versions, which, moreover, are discordant.

§ Ap. Joseph. *contr. Ap.* i. 26, 27.

|| See Syncell, *Chronograph.*, pp. 72B and 73B.

¶ See the *Transactions of the Society of Biblical Archæology*, vol. i., pp. 274, 275; Birch, *History of Ancient Egypt*, pp. 136, 137.

** Chabas, *Les Pasteurs en Egypte*, p. 31.

* Exod. i. 14.

† Joseph. *contr. Ap.* i. 15.

‡ Seti I. associated his son Rameses on the throne early in his reign, and the two ruled conjointly for a period of (probably) twenty years.

§ See Birch, *History of Ancient Egypt*, pp. 114—118; Rawlinson, *History of Egypt*, vol. ii., pp. 299—301.

|| Exod. ii. 15.

¶ See his *Manuel d'Histoire Ancienne*, vol. i., p. 423.

** The first canal, carried from the Nile to the Red Sea, was begun by Seti I., and completed by Rameses II.

sary of Moses. He was proud, vain-glorious, disinclined to expose his own person in war, yet ready enough to send his soldiers into positions of peril.* The cruelties that he sanctioned in his Libyan war† are worthy of the monarch who, when a subject people complained of their burthens, met the complaint by making their burthens heavier.‡ He appears in Egyptian history as the weak successor of two great and powerful monarchs; he has one military success, due not to himself, but to his generals, after which his reign is inglorious, and closes in disaster.§

Menephthah held the throne for eight years. During the first four of these his annals are almost a blank. If the Biblical numbers are taken as exact,|| it is into this space that the plagues and the exodus must fall. If, on the contrary, we regard the Biblical periods of forty years as intended to be inexact, we may conjecture (1) that Moses returned to Egypt in Menephthah's second or third year;¶ and (2) that there was some further delay before he made his demands. In that case the great war of Menephthah with the Libyans and their allies, which belongs to his fifth year,** may have been over before the troubles with Israel began. Moses may have come forward shortly after its close to deliver the message with which he was charged; and the struggle between him and Menephthah may have fallen into the latter's fifth and sixth years. Menephthah, like his father, commonly held his court at Tanis. It would be there, "in the field of Zoan," that Moses and Aaron confronted him and wrought their "wonders." The struggle, the departure, the pursuit, the disaster in the Red Sea, may belong to the king's sixth year; and two years afterwards he may have succumbed to revolutionary movements consequent upon the losses which he suffered in the Red Sea catastrophe. His reign certainly ended amid clouds and darkness, and was followed by a period of civil disturbance, terminating in bloodshed and anarchy.

The troubles of this period, described in the "Great Harris Papyrus,"* together with the remarkable successes of Rameses III., second monarch of the twentieth dynasty, would fall into the period passed by Israel in the "Wilderness of the Wanderings,"† and would thus naturally obtain no direct mention in the sacred narrative. Rameses may, however, have been the "hornet" which God sent before Israel to break the power of the Canaanites and Hittites (Exod. xxiii. 28), and render the conquest of Palestine more easy.‡ He seems certainly to have made at least one great expedition into Asia, and to have reduced under his sway the whole tract between "the river of Egypt" and the Euphrates.§ Had the Israelites been in possession of Palestine at the time, he must have come into contact with them, and have seriously interfered with their independence. As it was, his Syrian wars, by weakening the Canaanite nations, paved the way for the victories of Joshua and the Israelite occupation of the "Land of Promise."

The depressed state of Egypt between the death of Rameses III. and the accession of the first Sheshonk|| accounts for the absence of all mention of the Egyptians from the Books of Joshua, Judges, and Samuel. If the exodus had taken place under the eighteenth dynasty, and the Syrian wars of Seti I., Rameses II., and Rameses III. had belonged to the period of the Judges¶ (as in that case they must), it is inconceivable that neither should the Hebrew records of the time have contained any notice of the Egyptians nor the Egyptian records of the Hebrews.

EXCURSUS B: ON THE EDUCATION OF MOSES (chap. ii. 10).

Moses would be educated like the sons of princesses generally, not like those of priests, or of persons destined for the literary life. St. Stephen, when he says that Moses was "learned in all the wisdom of the Egyptians," does not (probably) mean more than this. The question then is, In what did the education of princes and young nobles at the time of the exodus consist?

It would consist, in the first place, of orthography and grammar. Moses would be taught to speak the Egyptian language, and to write it, correctly. He would probably not be taught the hieroglyphic character, the knowledge of which was reserved to the priests, but would be familiarised with the ordinary cursive writing—the hieratic, as it was called in later times—which was the common character for books, and even for official documents, in his day. Care would be taken to instruct him in the graces of style, so far as they were understood at the time; and he would be especially practised in epistolary correspondence, which was regarded as one of the most necessary of all gentlemanlike accomplishments. Whether his attention would be turned to poetry, might perhaps be doubtful;** but he would certainly be taught a clear and perspicuous prose style, such as was required for official reports and other communications between members of the governing class.

The next branch of his education would be arithmetic and geometry. The Egyptians had made considerable progress in the former, and their calculations ran up to billions. In the latter they are said to have been exact and minute, but not to have pushed their investigations very far. It was sufficient for a youth of the upper classes to be able to keep correct accounts; and a speculative knowledge of the intricacies of numbers, or of geometrical problems, scarcely formed a part of the established curriculum.

He would be further instructed in morality, and in the Egyptian views on the subjects of the Divine

* Lenormant, *Manuel d'Histoire Ancienne*, vol. i., p. 430.
† Chabas, *Recherches pour servir, &c.*, pp. 88—91.
‡ Exod. v. 6—18.
§ Lenormant, *Manuel*, vol. i., pp. 432—434.
|| Moses is forty at his flight into Midian (Acts vii. 23), remains there forty years (Acts vii. 30), is eighty when he works his first miracle before Pharaoh (Exod. vii. 7), passes forty years in the wilderness (Deut. xxix. 5), and is a hundred and twenty at his death (Deut. xxiv. 7).
¶ There is some indication of delay on the part of Moses in Exod. iv. 19.
** Brugsch, *History of Egypt*, vol. ii., p. 123.

* See the *Records of the Past*, vol. viii., p. 46; and compare Chabas, *Recherches*, pp. 6—26.
† Menephthah does not seem to have reigned more than eight years, or two after the exodus. Amon-mes reigned, perhaps five years; Seti II., two; Siphthah, seven; Setnekht, two or three; and Rameses III. employed, perhaps, fifteen or twenty years in his warlike expeditions. This space of time is amply covered by the "forty years" of the wanderings.
‡ See the Note on chap. xxiii. 28.
§ Brugsch, *History of Egypt*, vol. ii., p. 152.
|| Birch, *History of Ancient Egypt*, pp. 147—156; Lenormant, *Manuel d'Histoire Ancienne*, vol. i., pp. 445—452.
¶ So Canon Cook, *Speaker's Commentary*, vol. i., pp. 474, 475.
** The poetry of Moses, his "songs" (Exod. xv. 1—19; Deut. xxxii. 1—43), his "blessing" (Deut. xxxiii.), and his "prayer" (Ps. xc.), indicate an actual study of Egyptian poetry, whether it was a part of his education or not.

Nature, of the relations subsisting between God and man, of a future life, and of a judgment to come. Egyptian morality was, for the most part, correct so far as it went, and was expressed in terse gnomic phrases, resembling those of the Proverbs of Solomon. The points especially inculcated were obedience to parents and to authorities generally, courtesy to inferiors, and kindness to the poor and the afflicted. The mysteries of religion were the exclusive property of the priests; but life beyond the grave, judgment, reward and punishment, probably metempsychosis, were generally inculcated; and the mystic volume, known as the "Ritual of the Dead," must have been pressed on the attention of all the educated.

It is not to be supposed that one brought up as the son of a princess would attain to the scientific knowledge possessed by Egyptian professionals of different kinds. Moses would not be an astronomer, nor an engineer, nor a physician, nor a theologian, nor even an historian; but would have that general acquaintance with such subjects which belongs to those who have enjoyed a good general education in a highly civilised community. He would also, no doubt, have a knowledge of the main principles of Egyptian jurisprudence. But here, again, his knowledge would be general, not close or intimate; and it would be a mistake to expect, in the Mosaical legislation, reproductions, to any extent, or adaptations, of the Egyptian judicial system.

THE THIRD BOOK OF MOSES, CALLED

LEVITICUS

INTRODUCTION

TO

LEVITICUS

I. Name and Signification.—The name Leviticus, by which the third book is called, is taken from the Greek Version (LXX) of the Old Testament. It properly denotes the Levitical book, or the volume treating on Levitical matters. In Hebrew it is called "the Book *Vayikra*," or simply "*Vayikra*," from the word with which it commences, and which denotes *and he called.* It is by this name that the Book is always quoted in Jewish writings. In the Hebrew manuscripts of the Old Testament, Leviticus is not only always a book by itself marked off from the rest both at the beginning and at the end by the space of four vacant lines, but like the other four books of the Pentateuch it begins a new column, whilst the other books of the Old Testament, though having the same vacant space to separate them from each other, do not begin at the top of a new column.

II. **Division.**—In accordance with the practice which obtained from time immemorial, the Book is divided, both in the most ancient MSS. and in the earliest printed editions of the Hebrew Scriptures, into the following ten sections:—

(1)	chaps.	i. 1—v. 26.
(2)	„	vi. 1—viii. 36.
(3)	„	ix. 1—xi. 47.
(4)	„	xii. 1—xiii. 59.
(5)	„	xiv. 1—xv. 33.
(6)	„	xvi. 1—xviii. 30.
(7)	„	xix. 1—xx. 27.
(8)	„	xxi. 1—xxiv. 23.
(9)	„	xxv. 1—xxvi. 2.
(10)	„	xxvi. 3—xxvii. 34.

These are ten of the fifty-four sections into which the whole Pentateuch is divided in order to furnish a lesson for each Sabbath of those years which, according to Jewish chronology, have fifty-four Sabbaths, so that the whole Law of Moses should be read through once every year. This division and the reading through of the Law in the manner here indicated are observed by the Jews to this day, and it is to these weekly lessons, in conjunction with portions from the Prophets, that reference is made in the New Testament (Acts xiii. 15, &c.). Besides this division, which is designed for the weekly lessons, the Book of Leviticus is also divided into twenty-three larger sections, which correspond more nearly to our modern chapters, and which are as follows:—

(1)	chaps.	i. 1—iii. 17.
(2)	„	iv. 1—vi. 11.
(3)	„	vi. 12—vii. 38.
(4)	„	viii. 1—x. 7.
(5)	„	x. 8—20.
(6)	„	xi. 1—47.
(7)	„	xii. 1—xiii. 28.
(8)	„	xiii. 29—59.
(9)	chaps.	xiv. 1—32.
(10)	„	xiv. 33—57.
(11)	„	xv. 1—24.
(12)	„	xv. 25—xvi. 34.
(13)	„	xvii. 1—16.
(14)	„	xviii. 1—30.
(15)	„	xix. 1—22.
(16)	„	xix. 23—xx. 27.
(17)	„	xxi. 1—xxii. 16.
(18)	„	xxii. 17—xxiii. 14.
(19)	„	xxiii. 15—xxv. 13.
(20)	„	xxv. 14—38.
(21)	„	xxv. 39—xxvi. 2.
(22)	„	xxvi. 3—46.
(23)	„	xxvii. 1—34.

These sections are called *Sedarim*, and are indicated in all the correct manuscripts of the Hebrew Scriptures.*

There is a third division, or rather subdivision, of this Book, which consists of 98 smaller sections or paragraphs, 52 of which are open sections and 46 closed sections. These minor sections are so minutely indicated by a vacant space, either at the beginning or end of the line, and are so sacredly guarded that a manuscript of the Pentateuch in which one of the open sections has, by mistake, been made into a closed section, or *vice versâ*, is ritually illegal.†

III. **Design and Contents.**—The design of the Book has been aptly described as "the spiritual statute-book of Israel as the congregation of God." By the laws therein enacted, God designed to train Israel as His peculiar people, to keep them from defilements, and to sanctify them for holy fellowship with their covenant Jehovah, who has deigned to erect His sanctuary in their midst. To effect this purpose enactments are in the first place laid down to regulate the access of the Israelites to the Divine Being, as follows: The sacrifices which obtained from time immemorial are more minutely defined and systematised (chaps. i. 1—vii. 38); the priesthood whose duty it is to offer up these sacrifices are consecrated and installed (chaps. viii. 1—x. 20); the uncleanness of animals (chap. xi. 1—47), and the impurities of men (chaps. xii. 1—xv. 33), which cause defilement and debar access to God, are described; and, finally, the Day of Atonement is instituted, which is to expiate at the end of every year the neglect of any of the above-named regulations (chap. xvi. 1—34), thus appropriately concluding the enactments which are designed to fit God's people for fellowship with Him. This group of laws is followed by sundry enactments which have for their object the holiness of the people in their

* See Ginsburg, The Massorah, Vol. ii., Letter *Samech*, § 77, p. 330.

† For a complete list of these sections see Ginsburg, The Massorah, Vol. ii., Letter *Pê*, § 407, p. 482.

every-day life, in their domestic relations, and in their intercourse with one another (chaps. xvii. 1—xx. 27); the holiness of the priesthood, and their purity in their sacred ministrations (chaps. xxi. 1—xxii. 33); the sanctification of the festivals (chaps. xxiii. 1—xxiv. 12) and of the whole land (chaps. xxv. 1—xxvi. 2); with directions about collateral questions arising from this part of legislation. The logical sequence of these different regulations, however, is not always apparent.

IV. Authorship.—As I do not believe that the Book of Leviticus, *in its present form*, was written by Moses, and as it is against the plan of this commentary to enter at this place into a discussion on this question, which has nothing whatever to do with the inspiration of the Book, I thought that I should best serve the student of Holy Writ by showing him how the laws here enacted were administered during the second Temple. I have therefore endeavoured to depict the Temple service in the time of Christ as conducted according to the laws laid down in the Book before us.

V. Literature.—The most important aids are (1) the Septuagint, an English translation of which has been published by Bagster. (2) The two Chaldee versions of the Pentateuch, one under the name of Onkelos, and the other under the name of Jonathan b. Uzziel, both of which have been translated into English, but not altogether satisfactorily, by Etheridge (Longman, 1865). The latter of the two is especially important, since, though in its present form it is a late compilation, it embodies the ancient development of the Mosaic Law as administered during the second Temple. (3) The Midrach Rabboth, which is a traditional explanation of the Mosaic Law, containing many expositions which obtained in the time of Christ. A German translation of this work by Dr. Wünsche has been published at Leipzig. Modern commentaries are too well known to require description.

THE THIRD BOOK OF MOSES, CALLED

LEVITICUS

CHAPTER I.—(1) And the LORD called
unto Moses, and spake unto him out of
the tabernacle of the congregation, say-
ing, (2) Speak unto the children of Israel,
and say unto them, If any man of you
bring an offering unto the LORD, ye shall
bring your offering of the cattle, *even* of
the herd, and of the flock.

B. C. 1490.

(3) If his offering *be* a burnt sacrifice
of the herd, let him offer a male without
blemish: he shall offer it of his own
voluntary will at the door of the taber-
nacle of the congregation before the
LORD. (4) [a]And he shall put his hand
upon the head of the burnt offering; and
it shall be accepted for him to make

a Ex 29. 10.

THE name Leviticus, that is, the Levitical book, as this portion of the Pentateuch is called in our Bibles, is taken from the Greek (LXX.) Version of the Old Testament, where it is so called because it treats of the sacrificial ordinances and the services performed by the Levites.

(1) **And the Lord called . . . and spake.**—Rather, *And he called unto Moses, and the Lord spake, &c.* (See chap. viii. 15.) At the end of the previous book we are told that when the tent of meeting was completed, the Lord showed His approbation of it by covering the outside of the edifice with a heaven-sent cloud, and by filling the inside with His glory (Exod. xl. 34—38). *He* therefore, who had filled the sanctuary with his glory now "called unto Moses," thus indicating by "And he called," which are one word in the original, the intimate connection between the two books. The ancient Jewish synagogue already pointed out the fact that this unusual phrase, "And he called unto Moses," is used as an introductory formula on the three different occasions when the Lord made a special communication to this great law-giver. Thus when the Lord first communicated to Moses that He was about to deliver the Israelites from Egypt, "He called unto him" from the burning bush (Exod. iii. 4). When the Lord was about to give to Moses the Ten Commandments for the people of Israel, "He called unto him" from the top of Sinai (Exod. xix. 3, 20); and now when the Lord is about to give to His chosen people, through His servant Moses, the laws by which their Divine worship is to be regulated, "He called unto him" from the tent of meeting (Lev. i. 1).

(2) **Speak unto the children of Israel.**—The directions for the different sacrifices specified in chaps. i. 2; iii. 17, are not in the first instance communicated to the priests who should teach them to the people, but are directly addressed to the people themselves.

Ye shall bring your offering . . .—Or, *from the cattle ye shall bring your offering, from the oxen and from the flock*, that is, if the offering be of quadrupeds in contradistinction to the "fowl" mentioned in verse 14, they are to be of oxen and small cattle (*tzōn*), *i.e.*, sheep and goats.

(3) **If his offering be a burnt sacrifice.**—Having stated what is meant by animals, the directions now treat upon the different kinds of the offerings themselves. First in order comes the burnt offering, which is divided into burnt offering from the beeves (verses 3—9), and burnt offering from the flock (verses 10—13). The ox takes precedence because it is the more costly and more important sacrifice. It had to be without disease or blemish of any kind. To offer a defective sacrifice was an insult and a deception. Hence the exclamation of the prophet, "cursed be the deceiver which hath in his flock a male and voweth and sacrificeth unto the Lord a corrupt thing" (*i.e.*, an animal with a blemish), Mal. i. 14. The offerer is to bring the animal to *the entrance of the tent of meeting*, as it should be rendered, that is, to the front of the Tabernacle where the brazen altar stood (Exod. xl. 6).

Of his own voluntary will.—The whole passage is better rendered, *at the entrance of the tent of meeting shall he offer it, that he may be accepted before the Lord.* (Comp. Exod. xxviii. 38; Lev. xix. 5, xxii. 19, 20, 29; xxiii. 11.) This meaning is unmistakably set forth in Lev. xxii. 19, 20, 21, where it is explicitly declared, "ye shall offer for your acceptance a male without blemish of the beeves, of the sheep or of the goats, but whatsoever hath a blemish that ye shall not offer, for it shall not be acceptable for you." It is to be remarked that the phrase "for your acceptance," or "acceptable for you," is only used in connection with burnt offerings and peace offerings, but never with sin offerings.

(4) **And he shall put his hand.**—Or, *lay his hand*, as the same phrase is rendered in chap. iii. 2, 3, 17, &c. The laying on of hands by the offerer on the victim was enjoined not only in the case of burnt offerings, but also in peace offerings (Lev. iii. 2, 7, 13; viii. 22, &c.) and in sin offerings (chap. iv. 4, 15, 24, 29, 33; viii. 14, &c.). The offerer indicated thereby both the surrender of his ownership of the victim, and the transfer to it of the feelings by which he was influenced in performing this act of dedication to the Lord. From the practice which obtained during the second Temple, we know that the offerer himself laid both his hands between the two horns of the animal whilst alive, and that no proxy could do it. If several offered one sacrifice, each one laid his hand separately on the victim, confessing his sins and saying, "I have sinned, I have committed iniquity, I have transgressed and I have done this and this, but I repent before Thee, and this is my atonement."

atonement for him. (5) And he shall
kill the bullock before the LORD: and
the priests, Aaron's sons, shall bring the
blood, and sprinkle the blood round
about upon the altar that *is by* the door
of the tabernacle of the congregation.
(6) And he shall flay the burnt offering,
and cut it into his pieces. (7) And the
sons of Aaron the priest shall put fire
upon the altar, and lay the wood in order
upon the fire: (8) and the priests, Aaron's
sons, shall lay the parts, the head, and
the fat, in order upon the wood that *is*
on the fire which *is* upon the altar:
(9) But his inwards and his legs shall he
wash in water: and the priest shall burn
all on the altar, *to be* a burnt sacrifice,
an offering made by fire, of a sweet
savour unto the LORD.
(10) And if his offering *be* of the flocks,
namely, of the sheep, or of the goats, for
a burnt sacrifice; he shall bring it a male
without blemish. (11) And he shall kill
it on the side of the altar northward be-
fore the LORD: and the priests, Aaron's
sons, shall sprinkle his blood round about
upon the altar. (12) And he shall cut it
into his pieces, with his head and his

Accepted for him.—That is, his offer will be acceptable before the Lord, when the offerer thus complies with the prescribed sacrificial regulations. (Comp. verse 3.)

To make atonement for him.—As the imposition of hands, confession, repentance, and prayer accompanied this sacrifice, and, moreover, as these acts secure for the offerer acceptance with God, hence expiatory virtue is here and elsewhere ascribed to this burnt offering (chaps. xiv. 20; xvii. 24: Micah vi. 6; Job i. 5; xlii. 8), which belongs more especially to sin and trespass offerings (Lev. iv. 20, 26, 31, 35; v. 16, 18; vii. 7, &c.).

(5) **And he shall kill the bullock.**—The sacrificer himself slaughtered the victim on the north side of the altar, by cutting its throat, while a priest or an assistant held a bowl under the neck to receive the blood.

Before the Lord.—That is, before the door of the tent of meeting (comp. verse 11). The two phrases constantly interchange in the directions about the sacrifices. (Comp. chaps. iii. 2, 8, 12; iv. 4, 15, 24; vi. 18, &c.)

The priests, Aaron's sons.—Better, *the sons of Aaron, the priests*, as the Authorised Version renders this phrase in Numb. x. 8. Besides the passage in Joshua xxi. 19, this phrase only occurs six times, once in Numbers, where it is properly rendered, and five times in this book, where it is translated three times "the priests Aaron's sons" (chap. i. 5, 8, 11), and twice "Aaron's sons the priests" (chaps. ii. 2; iii. 2). (See chap. xxi. 1.)

And sprinkle.—Better, *throw the blood.* The priestly functions, which began with the catching of the blood in the bowl, are now to continue also in this instance. The priest threw the blood upon the walls of the altar in two portions. He first stepped to the north-eastern corner, and from that corner diffused the blood on the northern and eastern walls; he then placed himself at the south-western corner, whence he diffused the second portion of the blood on the south and western walls. The rest of the blood he poured out at the southern side of the altar, which was furnished with two holes; these holes communicated with a drain which conducted the blood into the Kedron.

By the door of the tabernacle.—Better, *at the entrance of the tent of meeting.* (See verse 3.)

(6) **And he shall flay.**—After the priest threw the blood on the walls of the altar, the sacrificer himself had to skin and cut up the sacrifice into its natural limbs (comp. verse 12; chap. viii. 20; Exod. xxix. 17), as head, breast, legs, &c., and not mangle it. The skin was the perquisite of the officiating priest (Lev. viii).

(7) **And the sons of Aaron.**—The priests are to put the fire upon the altar, because they offered the sacrifice upon the altar. This applies to the first burnt offering which was offered upon the newly-erected altar, since afterwards the fire was always burning, and was never allowed to go out (Lev. vi. 13).

And lay the wood.—No other fuel but wood was allowed for the altar, and no one was allowed to bring it from his own house, but it had to be the wood of the congregation. (Comp. Neh. x. 34; xiii. 31.) It had to be of the best kind; worm-eaten wood or timber from pulled-down buildings was not allowed.

(8) **Shall lay the parts.**—Better, *shall lay the pieces in order*, as in verse 12. The word here rendered by *parts* is the same which is more properly translated *pieces* in verse 6. Here again the priests are not to lay the pieces upon the altar anyhow, but are to arrange them systematically. In consequence of the *order* expressed in this verse, the rule obtained during the second Temple that the parts of the victim should as much as possible be arranged in the same order which they occupied in the animal when alive.

(9) **But his inwards.**—Before, however, the cut-up victim was thus arranged to be burnt, the stomach, the bowels, and the feet had to be thoroughly cleansed. In the time of the second Temple, the washing had to be repeated three times before the ablution was deemed complete.

And the priest shall burn.—The word here used is not the one generally used to denote *consuming by fire*, but it originally signifies *to make a fume* or *vapour by incense.* It is used in connection with all sacrifices (chaps. ii. 2, 9; iii. 5, 11; iv. 10, 19; vi. 8; vii. 5, &c.) and the idea intended to be conveyed thereby is, that man upon earth fitly brought his gift to God in heaven, by causing the odour emitted from the burning sacrifice to ascend in a sweet-smelling savour to heaven.

(10) **Of the flocks.**—Bullocks of course could only be offered by the wealthy. Hence the law now provides for those who could not afford so costly a sacrifice. They are to bring a lamb of the first year, which was the ordinary burnt offering in the time of Christ, and not a goat. The directions given with regard to the burnt offering from bullocks, equally apply to the burnt offering from the flock (verses 10—13). They are therefore not repeated.

(11) **On the side of the altar northward.**—As the place for the refuse was on the east side (see verse 16), as the laver stood on the west side, and as the ascent to the altar was on the south side, the north side was the most convenient for slaughtering the victims. This also applies to the sin and trespass offerings (chaps. iv. 24, 29, 33; vi. 25; vii. 2; xiv. 13, &c.).

fat: and the priest shall lay them in
order on the wood that *is* on the fire
which *is* upon the altar: (13) but he shall
wash the inwards and the legs with
water: and the priest shall bring *it* all,
and burn *it* upon the altar: it *is* a burnt
sacrifice, an offering made by fire, of a
sweet savour unto the LORD.

(14) And if the burnt sacrifice for his
offering to the LORD *be* of fowls, then he
shall bring his offering of turtledoves, or
of young pigeons. (15) And the priest
shall bring it unto the altar, and [1] wring
off his head, and burn *it* on the altar;
and the blood thereof shall be wrung
out at the side of the altar: (16) and he
shall pluck away his crop with [2] his
feathers, and cast it beside the altar on
the east part, by the place of the ashes:
(17) and he shall cleave it with the wings
thereof, *but* shall not divide *it* asunder:
and the priest shall burn it upon the
altar, upon the wood that *is* upon the
fire: it *is* a burnt sacrifice, an offering
made by fire, of a sweet savour unto the
LORD.

CHAPTER II.—(1) And when any will
offer a meat offering unto the LORD, his
offering shall be *of* fine flour; and he
shall pour oil upon it, and put frankin-
cense thereon: (2) and he shall bring it
to Aaron's sons the priests: and he shall
take thereout his handful of the flour

1 Or, *pinch off the head with the nail.*

2 Or, *the filth thereof.*

---

(12) **With his head and his fat.**—That is, "he shall cut it into its pieces, and *sever* or *cut off* its head and its fat." By a figure of speech not uncommon in Hebrew, one verb is connected with two substantives, though it only applies to one of the two, and a kindred verb has to be supplied for the second substantive to obtain the proper sense.

(14) **Be of fowls.**—The fowls here are in contrast to the cattle in verse 2. And as the quadrupeds there are immediately defined to consist of bullocks, sheep and goats, so the generic term *winged creature* is here restricted to the dove and pigeon. It will thus be seen that five different kinds are allowed for the burnt offering, viz., the bullock, lamb, goat, dove and pigeon, the same that Abram was commanded to offer (Gen. xv. 9).

Of turtledoves.—Though in the case of the burnt offering, as well as of the sin offering, pigeons were permitted to those who were too poor to offer quadrupeds, yet in certain other cases birds were prescribed for all irrespective of their circumstances. Not only did turtledoves regularly come in large flocks (Cant. ii. 11, 12; Jer. viii. 7) into Palestine at certain periods, but owing to these sacrifices the Jews have always kept dove-cots and reared pigeons (2 Kings vi. 25; Isa. lx. 8; Joseph. *Wars*, v. 4, 4). To supply the demand for them, dealers in these birds sat about with them in cages on stalls in the Temple court (Matt. xxi. 2; John xi. 16, &c.).

(15) **And the priest.**—It was probably out of consideration for the feelings of the poor offerer, and to increase the importance of the otherwise small offering, that the priest himself brought the victim to the altar and slew it instead of the worshipper performing these acts, as in the case of quadrupeds. The imposition of hands upon the victim was dispensed with, both because the bird was too small for this ceremony, and because the offerer brought it in his hands to the place of sacrifice, thus conveying by this act the idea involved in the imposition of hands.

And wring off his head.—When the bird is handed to him, the priest is not to use any knife, but is to nip off its head with his nails, throw the severed head on the altar fire, and thus cause it to ascend in the sweet-smelling savour. As the small quantity of blood could not be caught in a bowl, and would not suffice for throwing it or pouring it on the four walls, as was the case in the offering of quadrupeds, he pressed it out from the headless body, and let it run on the walls.

(16) **His crop with his feathers.**—Just as in the case of quadrupeds the skin was flayed off the victim before it was put on the altar fire, so the feathers were removed from the bird before its body was placed on the altar. This is the natural sense which is to be expected from the context, since it can hardly be imagined that the victims would be burnt with the feathers, and thus cause an intolerable smell. The rendering, however, given in the margin, "*with the filth thereof*," is now adopted by the greater number of expositors. As the two words respectively denoting *filth* and *feathers* resemble each other in Hebrew, it is probable that one of them has dropped out of the text. The maw, therefore, with its contents, as well as the feathers, were removed to the eastern side of the altar, where the ashes from the altar were thrown (chap. vi. 3).

(17) **And he shall cleave it with the wings thereof.**—Before placing it on the altar fire the priest made an incision in the wings, without, however, separating them wholly from the body, thus corresponding in some degree to the limbing of the quadruped. (See verse 6.)

II.

(1) **A meat offering.**—Better, *an oblation of a meat offering*, as the same two words are rendered in verses 4 and 13. The meat offerings which come next in the legal enumeration, and which occupy the whole of the present chapter, consisted of three kinds. The first is fine flour with oil and frankincense (verses 1—3). The flour was of wheat (Exod. xxix. 2), and was double the value of the ordinary barley flour (2 Kings vii. 1, 16, 18), and because of its use at the sacrifices formed part of the Temple stores (1 Chron. ix. 29; xxiii. 29).

Shall pour oil upon it.—Oil being to the food of the Israelites what butter is to ours, the offerer is here commanded to put some of it into this preparation in order to make it more palatable to the priests who were to eat part of it. (See verse 3.) The frankincense was designed to counteract the offensive smell arising from the quantity of the flesh burnt there, as is evident from the following verse, where it is stated that it is wholly to be burnt.

(2) **And he shall take.**—Better, *And the priest shall take from it a handful of its flour and of its oil with all its frankincense, and this shall he burn as its memorial upon the altar*, &c.

thereof, and of the oil thereof, with all
the frankincense thereof; and the priest
shall burn the memorial of it upon the
altar, *to be* an offering made by fire, of a
sweet savour unto the LORD: (3) and
[a] the remnant of the meat offering *shall*
be Aaron's and his sons': *it is* a thing
most holy of the offerings of the LORD
made by fire.

(4) And if thou bring an oblation of a
meat offering baken in the oven, *it shall*
be unleavened cakes of fine flour mingled
with oil, or unleavened wafers anointed
with oil.

(5) And if thy oblation *be* a meat offer-
ing *baken* [1] in a pan, it shall be *of* fine
flour unleavened, mingled with oil.
(6) Thou shalt part it in pieces, and pour
oil thereon: it *is* a meat offering.

(7) And if thy oblation *be* a meat offer-
ing *baken* in the fryingpan, it shall be
made *of* fine flour with oil. (8) And thou
shalt bring the meat offering that is
made of these things unto the LORD:
and when it is presented unto the priest,
he shall bring it unto the altar. (9) And
the priest shall take from the meat offer-
ing [b] a memorial thereof, and shall burn
it upon the altar: *it is* an [c] offering made
by fire, of a sweet savour unto the
LORD. (10) And that which is left of
the meat offering *shall be* Aaron's and
his sons': *it is* a thing most holy of
the offerings of the LORD made by
fire.

(11) No meat offering, which ye shall
bring unto the LORD, shall be made with
leaven: for ye shall burn no leaven, nor
any honey, in any offering of the LORD
made by fire.

(12) As for the oblation of the firstfruits,
ye shall offer them unto the LORD: but
they shall not [2] be burnt on the altar for
a sweet savour.

a Ecclus. 7. 31.

1 Or, *on a flat plate*, or, *slice*.

b ver. 2.

c Ex. 29. 18.

2 Heb., *ascend*.

Memorial.—So called because it was designed to bring the worshipper into the grateful remembrance of God, and to remind him, as it were, of His promise to accept the service of His people rendered to Him in accordance with his command. Hence the declaration of the Psalmist, "the Lord *remember* all thine offerings, and accept thy burnt sacrifice" (Ps. xx. 4), and of the angel to Cornelius, "thy prayers and thy alms are come up for a memorial before God" (Acts x. 4).

(3) **And the remnant.**—With the exception of the memorial or the handful of flour and oil, and of all the frankincense, this meat offering belonged to the priests, who divided it among them, and by whom alone it was to be consumed in the court of the sanctuary.

A thing most holy.—The offerings consisted of two classes, *less holy* and *most holy*. The thank offerings (Lev. xxiii. 20; Num. vi. 20), the firstborn of clean sacrificed animals (Num. xviii. 17), the firstlings of oil, wine, and corn, and the paschal sacrifices, belonged to the less holy, and might be eaten entirely or partially in any clean place within the holy city by the officiating priests and their families (Lev. x. 12—14). The incense offering, the shew-bread (Exod. xxx. 26; Lev. xxiv. 9), the sin and trespass offerings (Lev. vi. 25—28; vii. 1, 6; xiv. 13, &c.), and the meat offerings here described, belonged to the most holy class. They could only be eaten in the court of the sanctuary by the priests alone.

(4) **A meat offering baken in the oven.**—The second kind of meat offering consisted of preparations baked with oil in the oven, or in the pan, or cooked in a pot (verses 4—10). The oven is probably the portable pot, open at the top, about three feet high and liable to be broken (Lev. xi. 35), which is still used in the East for making bread and cakes. After the vessel is thoroughly heated, the dough, which is made into large, thin, oval cakes resembling pancakes or Scotch oatcakes, is dexterously thrown against the sides, the aperture above is covered, and the bread is completely baked in a few minutes. Though the bread when first taken out is soft, and can be rolled up like paper, it hardens and becomes crisp when it is kept.

(5) **Baken in a pan.**—Better, *a flat plate.* This is probably the iron fire-plate (Ezek. v. 3), with a convex surface, which is placed horizontally upon stones about nine inches from the ground, and underneath which the fire is kindled, used by the Arabs to this day. The large thin cakes, and the thin wafer bread, are laid upon the convex surface, where they are baked in comparatively few minutes. These baking operations took place in the court of the sanctuary, where the vessels of ministration were kept (Ezek. xlvi. 20; 1 Chron. xxiii. 28, 29).

(6) **Thou shalt part it in pieces.**—The cake thus baked was not to be offered as a whole, but broken up in pieces and mingled with oil. Bread, broken in pieces and steeped in oil, butter, milk, or sweet juices, still constitutes a favourite dish among the Bedouin Arabs.

(7) **Baken in the frying-pan.**—Better, *boiled in a pan.* This is a deeper vessel than the frying-pan, and corresponds more to our stew-pan or pot. In this deep vessel the cakes were boiled in oil.

(8) **And thou shalt bring.**—Whichever of the three cereal preparations is preferred, the offerer is to present it to the priest, who is to take it to the altar. During the second Temple, the pieces were put into a ministering vessel, oil and frankincense were then put on them, and the vessel was carried by the offerer to the priest, and the priest carried it to the altar and brought it to the south-west.

(9, 10) **And the priest.**—Verses 9 and 10, which conclude the law about the bloodless offerings, resume and expand the directions given in verses 1 and 2.

(11) **No meat offering.**—Verses 11—13 add some general rules respecting meat offerings. As honey was used in olden times to produce fermentation, it is excluded, like fermented dough, from these offerings. (See chap. xi. 20.)

(12) **As for the oblation.**—Better, *as an oblation of firstfruits ye may offer them.* This verse mentions an exception to the rule laid down in the previous one, *i.e.*, leaven and honey, which are excluded from the meat offerings, may be used with firstfruits. Hence they are mentioned with firstfruits (Lev. xxiii. 17; 2 Chron. xxxi. 5).

(13) And every oblation of thy meat
offering [a]shalt thou season with salt;
neither shalt thou suffer the salt of the
covenant of thy God to be lacking from
thy meat offering: with all thine offer-
ings thou shalt offer salt.
(14) And if thou offer a meat offering of
thy firstfruits unto the LORD, thou shalt
offer for the meat offering of thy first-
fruits green ears of corn dried by the
fire, *even* corn beaten out of full ears.
(15) And thou shalt put oil upon it, and
lay frankincense thereon: it *is* a meat
offering. (16) And the priest shall burn
the memorial of it, *part* of the beaten
corn thereof, and *part* of the oil thereof,
with all the frankincense thereof: *it is*
an offering made by fire unto the LORD.

CHAPTER III.—(1) And if his oblation
be a sacrifice of peace offering, if he offer
it of the herd; whether *it be* a male or
female, he shall offer it without blemish
before the LORD. (2) And he shall lay
his hand upon the head of his offering,
and kill it *at* the door of the tabernacle
of the congregation: and Aaron's sons
the priests shall sprinkle the blood upon
the altar round about. (3) And he shall
offer of the sacrifice of the peace offering
an offering made by fire unto the LORD;
[b]the [1]fat that covereth the inwards, and
all the fat that *is* upon the inwards,
(4) and the two kidneys, and the fat that
is on them, which *is* by the flanks, and
the [2]caul above the liver, with the kid-
neys, it shall he take away. (5) And
Aaron's sons shall burn it on the altar
upon the burnt sacrifice, which *is* upon
the wood that *is* on the fire: *it is* an
offering made by fire, of a sweet savour
unto the Lord.
(6) And if his offering for a sacrifice of
peace offering unto the LORD *be* of the

a Mark 9. 49.

b Ex. 29. 22.

1 Or, *suet.*

2 Or, *midriff over the liver, and over the kidneys.*

---

(13) **And every oblation.**—But salt, which is the contrary to leaven, and which preserves from putrefaction and corruption, was to be an ingredient, not only of bloodless, but of all animal sacrifices (Ezek. xliii. 24).

The salt of the covenant of thy God.—From its antiseptic and savoury qualities, salt became the symbol of hospitality, friendship, durability, fidelity. "To eat bread and salt together" is, in the East, an expression for a league of mutual amity (Russell, *Aleppo*, i. 232). When the Arabs make a covenant together, they put salt on the blade of a sword, from whence every one puts a little into his mouth. This constitutes them blood relations, and they remain faithful to each other even when in danger of life (Ritter, Erd. xiv. 960). Hence the expression "a covenant of salt," which also occurs in Num. xviii. 19, and 2 Chron. xiii. 5, denotes an indissoluble alliance, an everlasting covenant. Hence, too, the phrase "salted with the salt of the palace" (Ezra iv. 14) means bound by sacred obligations of fidelity to the king.

(14) **And if thou offer.**—The third kind of meat offering (verses 14—16) is of the firstfruits. These verses should properly come immediately after verse 12, since verse 13 concludes the directions about the different kinds of *minchas* or bloodless offerings, with general remarks applying to all animal sacrifices. Such transpositions are not uncommon in the Hebrew Scriptures. Parched or roasted corn, as here described, was, and still is, a favourite article of food in the East (Lev. xxiii. 14; Josh. v. 11; 1 Sam. xvii. 17; xxv. 18; 2 Sam. xvii. 28; Ruth ii. 14). It was, therefore, an appropriate meat offering. Hence the regulations about it, verses 14—16, are the same as those given with regard to the other two kinds of bloodless offerings.

III.

(1) **A sacrifice of peace offering.**—The peace offering of which this chapter treats, consisted of two kinds, the peace offering from the herd (verses 1—5), and the peace offering from the flock (verses 6—15). As in the case of the burnt offering (chap. i. 3), the ox is mentioned first, because it is most costly and more important.

Whether it be a male.—Whilst in the case of the burnt offering (chap. i. 3, 10) the male only was legal, there is no distinction of sex here, nor is there any limitation of age. All that was required was that it should be without any organic defect.

(2) **And he shall lay his hand.**—Unlike the laying of hands on the burnt offering, there was no confession of sin here, but the utterance of words of praise to God, and this might be done in any place of the court-yard which was most convenient for the offerer to kill the sacrifice.

At the door of the tabernacle.—Better, *at the entrance of the tent of meeting.* (See chap. i. 3.)

Aaron's sons the priests.—Better, *the sons of Aaron, the priests.* (See chap. i. 5.)

Shall sprinkle.—Better, *throw* (see chap. i. 5).

(3) **And he shall offer.**—That is, he who brings the sacrifices, not the priest.

The fat.—That is, the best or choicest part. Hence the expression is also used for the best produce of the ground (Gen. xlv. 18; Num. xviii. 12). As the most valuable part of the animal, the fat belonged to God, and hence had a peculiar sanctity, for which reason it was not allowed to be eaten (Lev. iii. 17; vii. 23).

(5) **And Aaron's sons.**—After the offerer has killed the victim, taken out the choice parts and offered them to the officiating priest, the latter shall burn *it*, that is, the whole collection of the fat pieces described in verses 3 and 4, upon the ashes of the continual burnt offering, which was the daily offering of the lamb. It had always the precedence, and was burning the whole day (Lev. vi. 12). Besides these choice pieces which had thus to be burnt, the breast and the right shoulder were reserved for the priest, whilst the remainder of the peace offering was eaten by the offerer, his family and his friends (Lev. vii. 15, 16).

(6) **Of the flock.**—That is, of sheep or goats; they too might be either male or female, provided only that they were without organic defects.

flock; male or female, he shall offer it
without blemish. (7) If he offer a lamb
for his offering, then shall he offer it
before the LORD. (8) And he shall lay
his hand upon the head of his offering,
and kill it before the tabernacle of the
congregation: and Aaron's sons shall
sprinkle the blood thereof round about
upon the altar. (9) And he shall offer of
the sacrifice of the peace offering an
offering made by fire unto the LORD;
the fat thereof, *and* the whole rump, it
shall he take off hard by the backbone;
and the fat that covereth the inwards,
and all the fat that *is* upon the inwards,
(10) and the two kidneys, and the fat that
is upon them, which *is* by the flanks,
and the caul above the liver, with the
kidneys, it shall he take away. (11) And
the priest shall burn it upon the altar:
it is the food of the offering made by
fire unto the LORD.

(12) And if his offering *be* a goat, then
he shall offer it before the LORD. (13) And
he shall lay his hand upon the head of
it, and kill it before the tabernacle of
the congregation: and the sons of Aaron
shall sprinkle the blood thereof upon the
altar round about. (14) And he shall offer
thereof his offering, *even* an offering
made by fire unto the LORD; the fat
that covereth the inwards, and all the
fat that *is* upon the inwards, (15) and the
two kidneys, and the fat that *is* upon
them, which *is* by the flanks, and the
caul above the liver, with the kidneys,
it shall he take away. (16) And the priest
shall burn them upon the altar: *it is* the
food of the offering made by fire for a
sweet savour: [a]all the fat *is* the LORD'S.
(17) *It shall be* a perpetual statute for
your generations throughout all your
dwellings, that ye eat neither fat nor
[b]blood.

a ch. 7. 25.

b Gen. 9. 4; ch. 7. 26 & 17. 14.

CHAPTER IV.—(1) And the LORD
spake unto Moses, saying, (2) Speak unto
the children of Israel, saying, If a soul
shall sin through ignorance against any
of the commandments of the LORD *con-*
cerning things which ought not to be
done, and shall do against any of them:

---

(7) **A lamb.**—Better, *a sheep*, as it is rendered in Lev. i. 10; vii. 23; xxii. 19, 27, &c., since the word denotes a full-grown sheep.

(8) **Before the tabernacle of the congregation.**—Better, *before the tent of meeting.* (See verse 2.)

(9) **The whole rump.**—Better, *the whole fat tail* (so also Exod. xxix. 22; Lev. vii. 3; viii. 25; ix. 19). The sheep of Syria and Palestine were, and still are, the broad-tailed species, the broad part often weighing fifteen pounds and upwards. In young animals, the substance of the tail, which consists of marrow and fat, tastes like marrow, and it is used by the Arabs for cooking instead of butter. It is often so large that it trails on the ground, and to save the animal from the pain occasioned by dragging it on the ground, a small wheeled truck is attached to it, on which it draws it along. It is only the tail of sheep which is here included among the fat parts that are to be offered upon the altar. It is, however, not regarded as the ordinary fat of other quadrupeds (Lev. ix. 19), and hence, according to Jewish tradition, is not included in the prohibition of verse 3.

(10) **And the two kidneys.**—The ritual enjoined in these two verses is the same as in verses 4 and 5.

(11) **The food,** or *bread,* that is, which the fire upon the altar was to consume for God, or the sacrifice. Hence that which was burnt unto God was called His bread (Num. xxviii. 2; Ezek. xliv. 7), and the priests who burnt it are described as offering "the bread of their God" (Lev. xxi. 6, 8, 17).

(12–15) **And if his offering be a goat.**—The directions about the goat as a peace offering are the same as those about an ox. No mention of male or female is here made, because this point is already stated in verse 6. Unlike the burnt offering (Lev. i. 10), the goat is here separated from the sheep because of the difference in the oblation, arising from the broad tail of the sheep, which does not exist in the goat.

(16) **Shall burn them.**—That is, the fat pieces which have thus been specified (see chap. iv. 35), because they constitute the bread of Jehovah; they are to ascend in a sweet-smelling savour to heaven. (See chap. i. 9).

All the fat is the Lord's.—This part of the verse is intimately connected with the following verse. As the fat belongs to the Lord, it is therefore enacted as a perpetual statute that it must never be eaten.

(17) **A perpetual statute for your generations throughout all your dwellings.**—Better, *a statute for ever throughout your generations in all your dwellings;* so the Authorised Version in the only three other passages in which it occurs. (Comp. Lev. xxiii. 14, 21, where it is inverted; and 31.) That is, the law not to eat fat of beeves, sheep, or goats, is to be binding upon the Israelites throughout all their future generations, and is applicable to any place wherever they may dwell. As the full legislative formula only occurs four times in the Pentateuch, and is restricted to this book, it is important to render it uniformly in all the four passages. For the import of this statute see chap. vii. 23—25.

IV.

(2) **If a soul shall sin.**—It will be seen that whilst the three previous kinds of offerings, viz., the burnt offering (chap. i. 1—17), the meat offering (chap. ii. 1—16), and the peace offering (chap. iii. 1—17), are spoken of as familiarly known and practised among the Israelites before the giving of the Law, the sin offering and the trespass offering are here introduced as a new injunction. We have here no more the voluntary formula, "If any man of you bring," &c.

(3) If the priest that is anointed do sin
according to the sin of the people; then
let him bring for his sin, which he hath
sinned, a young bullock without blemish
unto the LORD for a sin offering. (4) And
he shall bring the bullock unto the door
of the tabernacle of the congregation
before the LORD; and shall lay his hand
upon the bullock's head, and kill the
bullock before the LORD. (5) And the
priest that is anointed shall take of the
bullock's blood, and bring it to the taber-
nacle of the congregation: (6) and the
priest shall dip his finger in the blood,
and sprinkle of the blood seven times
before the LORD, before the vail of the

(chaps. i. 2, ii. 1, iii. 1), as you are in the habit of bringing; but "if a soul shall sin . . . *let him* bring for his sin offering a young bullock," &c.

Through ignorance.—He did it inadvertently, and at the time of its committal did not know that it was a transgression; but recognised it as a sin after he did it. (Comp. verses 13, 22, 27; chap. v. 18; chap. xxii. 14.) According to the practice which obtained during the second Temple, the sin here spoken of, for which the sin offering was brought, was (1) a sin committed through ignorance, or involuntarily, as opposed to a sin committed with a set purpose (comp. Numb. xv. 30); (2) a sin against *a negative* command; (3) a sin consisted in acts, not in words or thoughts, as is deduced from the expression "and shall *do* against any of them;" and (4) of acts of such a nature, that if committed intentionally they would subject the sinner to the awful punishment of excision. (See Numb. xv. 29, 30.)

(3) **The priest that is anointed.**—To illustrate this law, the conduct of the high priest is adduced as the first instance, to show when and how this exalted functionary is to bring the sin offering in question. By this the Levitical law indicates that even the chief of the priesthood was but a frail being like the rest of the people, and was exposed to the same infirmities as the laity, thus precluding the assumption of spiritual superiority. Hence the remark of the Apostle, "the law made those high priests who had infirmity, and who needed daily to offer up sacrifices, first for their own sins, and then for the people's; but our high priest, Christ Jesus, was holy, harmless, undefiled, and separate from sinners, and made higher than the heavens" (Heb. vi. 27, 28). The phrase "the priest that is anointed" for "the high priest" is restricted to this book, where it occurs four times (Lev. iv. 3, 5, 16; vi. 15 in Heb.; 22 in the English). "The great priest," or high priest, is the appellation used in the other portions of the Pentateuch (Lev. xxi. 10; Numb. xxxv. 25, 28), and in Joshua (chap. xx. 6); whilst in the later books of the Old Testament this functionary is called chief priest (2 Kings xxv. 18; 2 Chron. xix. 11; xxiv. 11; xxvi. 20; xxxi. 10; Ezra vii. 5). He is called "the anointed priest," because, like Aaron, he alone was anointed when he succeeded to the high office, whilst the ordinary priests were simply consecrated. Their anointing descended with them to all futurity by virtue of being the descendants of Aaron. (See chap. viii. 12.)

According to the sin of the people.—That is, he having in ignorance committed the same sin as the common people, to which he is as liable as they. From the phrase "against any commandments of the Lord" in the preceding verse, as well as from chaps. x. 6; xxi. 10—15, it is evident that the sin of ignorance here alluded to does not refer to the inadvertent neglect of his official duty, which devolves upon the high priest as the spiritual head of the people, but to any offence whatsoever ignorantly committed. According to the marginal reading, *to make the people guilty*, or more literally, *to the guilt of the people*, which is equally admissible, the meaning of the passage is, that he by committing a sin causes the people to transgress, inasmuch as his example is followed by them; or that, in virtue of the intimate connection which subsisted between the representative of the nation and the people, the sin of the one was the sin of the other. (Comp. chap. x. 6; 1 Chron. xxi. 3.)

A young bullock.—Literally, *a steer, the son of a bull.* The sacrificial rules which obtained at the time of Christ minutely defined the respective ages of the bullock: the steer, the son of a bull, and the calf. The bullock or ox which was brought as a sacrifice had to be three years old: "the steer the son of a bull" rendered in the passage before us, and in the Authorised Version generally, by "a young bullock" (Exod. xxix. 1; Lev. iv. 14; xvi. 3; xxiii. 8, &c.), had to be two years old; whilst the calf had to be of the first year.

(4) **Unto the door of the Tabernacle of the Congregation.**—Better, *unto the entrance of the tent of meeting.* (See chap. i. 3.) The regulations about the bringing of the sin offering up to the sprinkling of the blood are the same as those about the other sacrifices.

(5) **And bring it.**—That is, after the high priest had received the blood into the bowl (see chap. i. 5), he is to bring it out of the court where the victim was slain *into the tent of meeting.*

(6) **And the priest shall dip his finger.**—The different treatment of the blood is here to be noticed. Whilst in the case of the other sacrifices the priest threw the blood upon the walls of the altar of burnt offering (see chap. i. 5), in the sin offering before us the high priest is first of all to dip his finger seven times in the blood, and sprinkle it before the Lord. The finger, according to the rules which obtained during the second Temple, was that of the right hand, as the blood was always taken and sprinkled with the right hand. Seven, being a complete number, is used for the perfect finishing of a work. Hence the seven days of creation (Gen. ii. 2, 3); seven branches were in the golden candlestick (Exod. xxv. 37; xxxvii. 23); seven times the blood was sprinkled on the day of atonement (Lev. xvi. 14); seven times was the oil sprinkled upon the altar when it was consecrated (Lev. viii. 11); seven days were required for consecrating the priests (Lev. viii. 35); seven days were necessary for purifying the defiled (Lev. xii. 2; Numb. xix. 19); seven times Naaman washed in the Jordan (2 Kings v. 10, 14); seven days Jericho was besieged, and seven priests with seven trumpets blew when the walls fell down (Josh. vi.); the lamb had seven horns and seven eyes, which are the seven spirits of God (Rev. v. 6); seven seals are on God's book (Rev. i. 5), &c., &c.

Before the Lord.—As the Lord was enthroned on the mercy-seat between the cherubim (Exod. xxv. 22) in the holy of holies, the phrase "before the Lord" is used for the place in front of the holy of holies,

sanctuary. (7) And the priest shall put
some of the blood upon the horns of the
altar of sweet incense before the LORD,
which *is* in the tabernacle of the congre-
gation; and shall pour [a]all the blood of
the bullock at the bottom of the altar
of the burnt offering, which *is at* the
door of the tabernacle of the congrega-
tion. (8) And he shall take off from it
all the fat of the bullock for the sin
offering; the fat that covereth the in-
wards, and all the fat that *is* upon the
inwards, (9) and the two kidneys, and the
fat that *is* upon them, which *is* by the
flanks, and the caul above the liver, with
the kidneys, it shall he take away, (10) as
it was taken off from the bullock of the
sacrifice of peace offerings: and the
priest shall burn them upon the altar of
the burnt offering. (11) [b]And the skin of
the bullock, and all his flesh, with his
head, and with his legs, and his inwards,
and his dung, (12) even the whole bullock
shall he carry forth [1]without the camp
unto a clean place, where the ashes are
poured out, and [c]burn him on the wood
with fire: [2]where the ashes are poured
out shall he be burnt.

(13) And if the whole congregation of
Israel sin through ignorance, [d]and the

a ch. 5. 9.

b Ex. 29. 14; Num.

1 Heb., *to without the camp.*

c Heb. 13. 11.

2 Heb., *at the pouring out of the ashes.*

d ch. 5. 2, 3, 4.

where the altar of incense, the shewbread, and the golden candlestick stood (Exod. xxvii. 21; xxviii. 35; xxx. 8; xxxiv. 34, &c.), and towards which the blood was sprinkled.

Before the vail of the sanctuary.—This phrase is simply explanatory of the former phrase. As the vail separated the holy of holies, where the shechinah dwelt, from the holy place, the words are simply used as another expression for "before the Lord." This clause has, however, been variously interpreted from time immemorial. As *before* is not in the original, but is supplied in the translation, some have maintained that the vail itself was sprinkled; whilst others, who, with the Authorised Version, regard the whole phrase to mean "before the vail," declare that the blood was sprinkled on the floor of the sanctuary in front of the vail.

(7) **And the priest shall put.**—That is, the high priest. With the finger thus dipped into it, he is to put some of the blood on each of the four horns of the golden altar on which the incense was offered.

This process, too, was peculiar to the sacrifice of the sin offering. The altar was placed in the holy place before the vail which separated off the holy of holies (Exod. xxx. 1—6). According to the practice which obtained in the time of Christ, the priest began by putting the blood first on the north-east horn, then on the north-west, then on the south-west, and, lastly, on the south-east horn. He dipped his finger in the blood of the bowl at the sprinkling of each horn, and wiped his finger on the edge of the bowl between the separate sprinklings, as the blood which remained on his finger from one horn was not deemed fit to be put on the other.

And shall pour all the blood.—That is, all the remaining blood. The bulk of the blood which remained, after expending the small quantity on the horns of the incense altar inside the sanctuary, the priest poured out at the bottom of the altar of burnt offering, which stood outside the holy place. At the time of the second Temple, there were at the south-west horn of this altar two holes, like two nostrils, through which the blood ran into a drain conveying it into the brook of Kedron.

(8) **And he shall take off from it all the fat.**—That is, the best or choicest part. (See chap. iii. 3.) At the time of Christ the sin offering was cut open, the fat and inwards were taken out, put into a vessel, salted, stewed on the fire, and burnt upon the altar as a sweet savour unto the Lord.

(9) **And the two kidneys.**—The regulations prescribed in these two verses are the same as those in connection with the peace offering in chap. iii. 4, 5.

(11) **And the skin of the bullock.**—Unlike other burnt offerings, the skins of which were taken off, and became the perquisite of the priests (chap. vii. 8), this sin offering was not flayed at all, but was cut to pieces with its skin.

(12) **Even the whole bullock shall he carry forth.**—This does not mean that the high priest himself had to carry the whole bullock all that distance, but in accordance with the idiom so common in Hebrew, where the singular is used for the plural, or the indefinite or impersonal form, denotes that those who assisted in doing the rough work of the altar shall carry the victim. Hence the ancient Greek Version (LXX.) and the Samaritan rightly render it by "and they shall carry," in the plural: *i.e.*, the whole bullock *shall be* carried forth. In verse 24 of this very chapter the Authorised Version properly translates the same idiom into "in the place where *they* kill the burnt offering," though the verb, as in the verse before us, is in the singular. (See also verse 14.)

Without the camp.—During the time of the second Temple there were three places for burning: one place was in the court of the sanctuary, where they burnt the sacrifices which were unfit and rejected; the second place was in the mountain of the house called *Birah*, where were buried those sacrifices which met with an accident after they had been carried out of the court; and the third place was without Jerusalem, called the place of ashes. It is this place to which the Apostle refers when he says, "for the bodies of those beasts whose blood is brought into the holy place by the high priest as *an offering* for sin are burned without the camp. Wherefore Jesus also, that he might sanctify the people through his own blood, suffered without the gate" (Heb. xiii. 11, 12).

And burn him on the wood with fire.—Whilst special wood was required for the burning of those victims which were consumed in the court of the sanctuary (see chap. i. 7), the sacrifices which were taken outside the city could be burnt with any wood, or even straw or stubble. All that was insisted on was that it should be burned *with fire*, as the text before us has it, but not with cinder, coals, or lime.

(13) **And if the whole congregation.**—As the whole Church, in its corporate body, is no more exempt from human frailty than its highest spiritual chief, the law now prescribes the sin offering for the congrega-

thing be hid from the eyes of the as-
sembly, and they have done *somewhat*
against any of the commandments of
the Lord *concerning things* which should
not be done, and are guilty; (14) when
the sin, which they have sinned
against it, is known, then the con-
gregation shall offer a young bullock
for the sin, and bring him before the
tabernacle of the congregation. (15) And
the elders of the congregation shall lay
their hands upon the head of the bullock
before the Lord: and the bullock shall
be killed before the Lord. (16) And the
priest that is anointed shall bring of
the bullock's blood to the tabernacle of
the congregation: (17) and the priest
shall dip his finger *in some* of the blood,
and sprinkle *it* seven times before the
Lord, *even* before the vail. (18) And he
shall put *some* of the blood upon the
horns of the altar which *is* before the
Lord, that *is* in the tabernacle of the
congregation, and shall pour out all the
blood at the bottom of the altar of the
burnt offering, which *is at* the door of
the tabernacle of the congregation.
(19) And he shall take all his fat from
him, and burn *it* upon the altar.
(20) And he shall do with the bullock as
he did with the bullock for a sin offer-
ing, so shall he do with this: and the
priest shall make an atonement for
them, and it shall be forgiven them.
(21) And he shall carry forth the bullock
without the camp, and burn him as he
burned the first bullock: it *is* a sin offer-
ing for the congregation.

(22) When a ruler hath sinned, and
done *somewhat* through ignorance *against*
any of the commandments of the Lord
his God *concerning things* which should

---

tion (verses 13—21). The case here assumed is that of the whole congregation having ignorantly committed some act which at the time of its committal they believed to be lawful, but which they afterwards discovered to be sinful. The two terms respectively rendered in the Authorised Version by *congregation* and *assembly* denote the same body of people, and are used interchangeably, so that the same congregation or assembly which inadvertently committed the sin afterwards recognised it. (Comp. Num. xv. 24—26.) An instance of such a national and congregational sin is recorded in 1 Sam. xiv. 32, where we are told that the Israelites, after smiting the Philistines, "flew upon the spoil, and took sheep, and oxen, and calves, and slew them on the ground, and the people did eat them with the blood." According to the ancient interpretation, however, which obtained at the time of Christ, "the whole congregation of Israel" and "the assembly" here spoken of denote the great Sanhedrin, the representatives of the people, who, through error, might proclaim a decree calculated to mislead the nation, thus accounting for the apparent discrepancy between this passage and Num. xv. 22—26.

(14) **Offer a young bullock.**—The same sacrifice which is prescribed for the sin of the high priest (comp. verse 3), and though not expressed here, it must be without blemish.

And bring him before the tabernacle of the congregation.—Better, *before the tent of meeting.* (See chap. i. 3.) This no more means that the whole congregation or the thousands of Israelites are all to lay hold of the victim, and carry it to the appointed place of slaughter, than the phrase in verse 12 signifies that the high priest is himself to carry the bullock. It is the regular Hebrew idiom, which denotes that the people are to cause the sacrifice to be carried. We should have deemed it superfluous to explain this well-known mode of expression had it not been that mistaken arguments have been deduced from it.

(15) **And the elders of the congregation shall lay their hands.**—As the whole congregation could not lay their hands on the victim, their representatives had to perform this act. (See verse 4.) But as the elders also were far too many to do it, since they were seventy in number, it was ordained during the second Temple that three of their members should lay their hands upon the sacrifice. Besides this sin offering there was only one other congregational offering upon which there was this laying of hands: *i.e.*, the scape-goat (Lev. xvi. 21).

(16—21) The rest of the regulations are exactly the same as those prescribed in the sin offering for the high priest himself in verses 5—12.

(22) **When a ruler hath sinned.**—The third instance adduced is that of a ruler sinning inadvertently (verses 22—26). As the word here translated "ruler" is used for a king (1 Kings xi. 34; Ezek. xxxiv. 24, xlvi. 2), the head of a tribe (Num. i. 4—16) or of the division of a tribe (Num. xxxiv. 18), opinions differ as to the exact position of the personage here meant. Now, in comparing the phrase used with regard to the sin of ignorance in the case of the high priest, the congregation, and any one of the people, it will be seen that in all the three instances it is simply described as a sin "against any commandments of the Lord" (comp. verses 2, 13, 27), whereas in the case of the ruler, we have the exceptional phrase, "against any of the commandments of the Lord *his God.*" Hence the interpretation obtained during the second Temple that the addition of the phrase *his God,* which shows a peculiar relationship to his God, denotes here one over whom God alone is exalted—the sovereign who is only responsible to *his God.*

And is guilty.—Rather, *and acknowledges his guilt,* as the Authorised Version rightly translates it in Hos. v. 15. (Comp. also Zech. xi. 5.) This sense is not only required by the disjunctive particle *or,* with which the next verse begins, but by the fact that the declaration in the present rendering, "When men sin they are guilty," is a truism. The sinner is guilty whether he sins advertently or inadvertently. The case here supposed is that the prince had himself come to the knowledge that what he had done was a sin, and had acknowledged it as such.

not be done, and is guilty; (23) or if his
sin, wherein he hath sinned, come to
his knowledge; he shall bring his offer-
ing, a kid of the goats, a male without
blemish: (24) and he shall lay his hand
upon the head of the goat, and kill it
in the place where they kill the burnt
offering before the LORD: it *is* a sin
offering. (25) And the priest shall take
of the blood of the sin offering with his
finger, and put *it* upon the horns of the
altar of burnt offering, and shall pour
out his blood at the bottom of the altar
of burnt offering. (26) And he shall burn
all his fat upon the altar, as the fat of
the sacrifice of peace offerings: and the
priest shall make an atonement for him
as concerning his sin, and it shall be
forgiven him.

(27) And if [1]any one of the [2]common
people sin through ignorance, while he
doeth *somewhat against* any of the com-
mandments of the LORD *concerning
things* which ought not to be done, and
be guilty; (28) or if his sin, which he
hath sinned, come to his knowledge:
then he shall bring his offering, a kid of
the goats, a female without blemish, for
his sin which he hath sinned. (29) And
he shall lay his hand upon the head of
the sin offering, and slay the sin offering
in the place of the burnt offering.
(30) And the priest shall take of the
blood thereof with his finger, and put
it upon the horns of the altar of burnt
offering, and shall pour out all the blood
thereof at the bottom of the altar.
(31) And [a]he shall take away all the fat
thereof, as the fat is taken away from
off the sacrifice of peace offerings; and
the priest shall burn *it* upon the altar
for a [b]sweet savour unto the LORD; and
the priest shall make an atonement for
him, and it shall be forgiven him.
(32) And if he bring a lamb for a sin
offering, he shall bring it a female
without blemish. (33) And he shall lay
his hand upon the head of the sin offer-
ing, and slay it for a sin offering in the
place where they kill the burnt offering.
(34) And the priest shall take of the blood
of the sin offering with his finger, and

1 Heb., *any soul.*
2 Heb., *people of the land.*
a ch. 3. 14.
b Ex. 29. 18.

(23) **Or if his sin.**—That is, if on his failing to see it himself, his sin is shown to him by another person.

A kid of the goats.—The expression here used (*sāêr*) properly denotes the rough, shaggy-haired he-goat, and is distinguished from *athud* (literally, *ready, vigorous*), which occurs in conjunction with it (Num. vii. 16, 17, 22, 23), and which is also translated goat in point of age. The *sāêr*, or the shaggy or longer-haired he-goat, here used is the older buck of the goat, whose hair has become long with age; whilst the *athud* is the same animal, younger and more vigorous. Hence the former was never killed for food, or used for burnt or thank offerings at the festivals (Lev. xvi. 9, 15, xxiii. 19; Num. xxviii. 15, 22, 30, xxix. 5, 11, 16), and at the consecration of the priests and sanctuary (Lev. ix. 3, 15, x. 16), whilst the latter was killed for food (Deut. xxxii. 14; Jer. li. 40), and hence, like the bull, the ram, and the lamb, was regularly presented as burnt and thank offerings (Num. vii. 17, 23, 29, &c.; Isa. i. 11, xxxiv. 6; Ezek. xxxix. 18; Pss. l. 9, 13, lxvi. 15). It will be seen that the first difference in the sin offering of a prince is that he is to bring a long-haired he-goat, and not a bull.

(24) **And kill it in the place where they kill the burnt offering.**—See chap. i. 5.

(25) **And the priest shall take.**—Here, again, the difference in the ritual is to be observed. In case of his own sin offering and in that of the congregation, the high priest himself performed the principal ceremony (verses 5—17), whilst at the sin offering of the prince the common priest officiated. The blood of the victim was not sprinkled before the vail of the Holy of Holies, nor on the incense altar which stood in the Holy, but on the brazen altar which was placed outside in the court.

(27) **And if any one of the common people.**—The fourth instance adduced (verses 27—35) is that of *any one of the people of the land,* as this phrase is rendered in Lev. xx. 2, 4; 2 Kings ix. 18, 19, xvi. 15. That is, any member of the congregation, whether he be a private Israelite, ordinary priest, or Levite, in contradistinction to the afore-mentioned high priest and ruler.

And be guilty.—Rather, *and acknowledges his guilt.* (See verse 22.)

(28) **Or if his sin . . . come to his knowledge.**—That is, is shown to him by another person. (See verse 23.)

A kid of the goats.—Better, *a shaggy-haired she-goat without blemish.* The expression is feminine in the Hebrew. The female was of less value than the male, and was therefore more suitable to the circumstances of the ordinary people.

(29–31) **And he shall lay.**—The ritual prescribed in these verses is the same as that ordained in the case of the sin offering of the prince (verses 24—26). In verse 31, however, the phrase, "for a sweet savour unto the Lord," is added to the burning of the fat pieces of the victim, which does not occur at the sin offering of the high priest, the congregation, or the prince (comp. verses 10, 19, 26), but is used at burnt offerings (chap. i. 9, 13) and peace offerings (chap. iii. 5, 16). It is supposed by some that these words are designedly used in connection with the least costly sin offering, to indicate that the humblest gift of the humblest person, if sincerely offered, is as acceptable to God as the most costly offering of the most exalted in the land.

(32) **And if he bring a lamb.**—Better, *a sheep.* (See chap. iii. 7.) Those who were unable to bring a goat might offer a female sheep as the less valuable animal, provided it was without blemish. Though the ritual is the same as with the goat (see verses 29—31), yet the sheep is treated separately, because of the fat tail, which had to be burned. (See chap. iii. 12.)

put *it* upon the horns of the altar of burnt offering, and shall pour out all the blood thereof at the bottom of the altar: (35) and he shall take away all the fat thereof, as the fat of the lamb is taken away from the sacrifice of the peace offerings; and the priest shall burn them upon the altar, according to the offerings made by fire unto the LORD: and the priest shall make an atonement for his sin that he hath committed, and it shall be forgiven him.

CHAPTER V.—(1) And if a soul sin, and hear the voice of swearing, and *is* a witness, whether he hath seen or known *of it;* if he do not utter *it,* then he shall bear his iniquity. (2) Or if a soul touch any unclean thing, whether *it be* a carcase of an unclean beast, or a carcase of unclean cattle, or the carcase of unclean creeping things, and *if* it be hidden from him; he also shall be unclean, and guilty. (3) Or if he touch the uncleanness of man, whatsoever uncleanness *it be* that a man shall be defiled withal, and it be hid from him; when he knoweth *of it,* then he shall be guilty.

---

(35) **According to the offerings made by fire.**—Better, *upon the offerings made by fire.* As the daily morning sacrifice was offered first every day, and as it continued burning on the altar all the forenoon, no fresh or special fire was to be kindled for it, but it was to be upon the fire sacrifices which had already been placed there before. (See chaps. iii. 5, v. 12.) The flesh of the sin offering, both for the prince and for the individual members of the community, was not burnt without the camp, as was the case with the flesh of the sacrifice for the high priest and for the whole congregation, but was the perquisite of the priests, and was eaten by them (Lev. vi. 26—30). This is in harmony with the law. The sinner who brought the sin offering could not partake of it. Hence the priest was not permitted to eat of the flesh of the sin offering which he offered for himself, or of the flesh of the congregational sin offering, because he was a member of the congregation.

V.

(1) **And hear the voice of swearing.**—Better, *because he heard the voice of adjuration, and might be a witness, whether he hath seen the offence or known of it, if he doth not tell it.* Having laid down in the former chapter the regulations about the sin offering, and having shown how these regulations are to be carried out when the offence against the Divine law is inadvertently committed by the spiritual head of the people, by the whole congregation, by the sovereign ruler of the nation, and by the individual members of the community, the lawgiver now proceeds to set forth in verses 1—13 of this chapter the trespass offering which every Israelite is to bring when he has violated certain precepts here specified. The first instance adduced is that of failing to come forward as witness after the judicial adjuration has been uttered. It was the duty of every member of the community to aid the authorities in maintaining the integrity of the Divine law. Hence, when an offence was committed which the constituted tribunals were unable to bring home to the offender for want of evidence, a solemn adjuration was addressed by the judge to individual members, to a district, or to the whole community. If after such an adjuration, anyone who was cognizant of the offence failed to come forward to testify what he knew, he was considered in the sight of God as participating in the transgression which he had thus concealed. It is with reference to this law that we are told, "whoso is partner with a thief, hateth his own soul, he heareth cursing and bewrayeth it not," *i.e.,* he hears the adjuration of the judges, and yet stifles his evidence, and thus becomes a partner with the culprit. An instance of this adjuration is recorded in Matt. xxvi. 63, where the high priest said to Jesus, "I adjure thee by the living God that thou tell us whether thou be the Christ, the son of God," and it was in recognition of the solemn obligation of this adjuration that Jesus answered the question.

Then he shall bear his iniquity.—Better, *and he beareth his iniquity;* that is, he is sensible that he bears the load of this guilt, he has become conscious of his sin, without which he could not bring the sacrifice here prescribed. The phrase, "and he beareth his guilt," has the same meaning as and "he," or "they are guilty" in chap. iv. 13, 22, &c. Unlike the sins committed inadvertently, spoken of in the preceding chapter, where the sin offering is prescribed, the guilt here described is that of designed and culpable silence, and of deliberately concealing a crime.

(2) **Or if a soul touch any unclean thing.**—The second instance adduced which requires this sacrifice is the case of any one touching the dead body of a clean animal, or the living or dead body of an unclean animal or reptile.

And if it be hidden from him.—That is, if he, through carelessness, forgot all about it that he had contracted this defilement; as the Vulgate rightly paraphrases it, "and forgetteth his uncleanness." The touching of a carcase simply entailed uncleanness till evening, which the washing of the person and his garments thus defiled sufficed to remove (Lev. xi. 24, 31). It was only when thoughtlessness made him forget his duty, and when reflection brought to his mind and conscience the violation of the law, that he was required to confess his sin, and bring a trespass offering.

He also shall be unclean, and guilty.—Better, *and he is unclean, and acknowledgeth that he is guilty.* (See chap. iv. 13, 22.) The Greek Version, called the Septuagint, which is the most ancient translation of the Hebrew Scriptures, omits altogether the latter part of this verse, which is represented in the Authorised Version by "and if it be hidden from him, he also shall be unclean and guilty," thus showing that the Hebrew manuscript, or manuscripts, from which this old version was made, had not this clause. This is, moreover, supported by the fact that it needlessly anticipates the summary formula of the next verse, which continues the subject, and where it appears in its proper place.

(3) **Or if he touch the uncleanness of man.**—The sundry classes of defilement which a human being might contract and impart to others by contact, are set forth in Lev. xii.—xv.

(4) Or if a soul swear, pronouncing with *his* lips to do evil, or to do good, whatsoever *it be* that a man shall pronounce with an oath, and it be hid from him; when he knoweth *of it*, then he shall be guilty in one of these. (5) And it shall be, when he shall be guilty in one of these *things*, that he shall confess that he hath sinned in that *thing*: (6) and he shall bring his trespass offering unto the LORD for his sin which he hath sinned, a female from the flock, a lamb or a kid of the goats, for a sin offering; and the priest shall make an atonement for him concerning his sin.

(7) And if [1]he be not able to bring a lamb, then he shall bring for his trespass, which he hath committed, two turtledoves, or two young pigeons, unto the LORD; one for a sin offering, and the other for a burnt offering. (8) And he shall bring them unto the priest, who shall offer *that* which *is* for the sin offering first, and [a]wring off his head from his neck, but shall not divide *it* asunder: (9) and he shall sprinkle of the blood of the sin offering upon the side of the altar; and the rest of the blood shall be wrung out at the bottom of the altar: it *is* a sin offering.

1 Heb., *his hand cannot reach to the sufficiency of a lamb.*

a ch. 1. 15.

When he knoweth of it, then he shall be guilty.—Better, *and he knoweth it, and feeleth that he is guilty.* That is, he afterwards becomes conscious that he has contracted the defilement, and feels his guilt. (See verse 2.)

(4) **Pronouncing with his lips.**—Better, *speaking heedlessly with his lips.* That is, if he uttered an oath in thoughtlessness or in passion, without his heart realising it, that he will do this or that.

To do evil, or to do good.—That is, anything whatsoever which is comprehended under the name good and evil, as these two categories are idiomatically used to embrace all human action. (Comp. Gen. xxiv. 50, xxxi. 24; Num. xxiv. 13; Isa. li. 23.)

Whatsoever it be that a man shall pronounce with an oath.—Better, *that a man heedlessly utters with an oath.* That is, anything that a man may rashly or thoughtlessly undertake to do, or to abstain from doing, with an oath.

And it be hid from him.—That is, if through this careless way in which it was done, he forgot all about it. (See verse 2.)

When he knoweth of it . . .—Better, *and he then considereth it, and acknowledgeth that he is guilty* (see chaps. iv. 13, 22, v. 2, &c.), in one of these things with regard to which a man may rashly swear that he will do or not do them, and contract guilt.

(5) **And it shall be, when . . .**—When he feels that he has been guilty of one of these sins specified in verses 1—4, he must confess the offence which he has committed. For the form of confession which obtained during the second Temple, see chap. i. 4.

(6) **And he shall bring his trespass offering . . . a lamb or a kid of the goats.**—Better, *a sheep, or a shaggy she-goat* (see chap. iv. 23, 32). The first thing to be noticed is that the sacrifice is here called (*āshām*) "trespass offering," which is the right rendering of the word, and is so translated in thirty-five out of the thirty-six passages in which it is used for a sacrifice. In the verse before us, and in the rest of this section, viz., verses 7—13, which treat of this sacrifice, no distinction is made between the ranks of the offenders. There is no special legislation for the high priest, the whole congregation, or the prince, as in the case with the (*chātāth*) sin offering, which is described in the former chapter. The spiritual officer and temporal sovereign are here on a level with the ordinary layman. There is no scale in the sacrifices corresponding to the position of the sinner. They are all alike to bring the same victim, either sheep or she-goat. Though nothing is here said about the sacrificial rites which were to be performed in connection with the victim, in this case it is implied that, apart from the minor deviations here specified, they were to be the same as those in connection with the sin offering. The rule which obtained during the second Temple, is as follows: the trespass offerings were killed, and their blood sprinkled, as is before described in chap. iv.; they were then flayed, the fat and the inwards taken out and salted, and strewed on the fire upon the altar. The residue of this flesh was eaten by the priests in the court, like the sin offerings.

(7) **And if he be not able to bring.**—The only exception to this general rule was poverty. The poor man who was unable to bring a sheep or she-goat, might bring two turtle-doves, as these were plentiful and cheap in Palestine. (See chap. i. 14.) We have seen in the preceding verse that in the case of the trespass offering, as in that of the sin offering, the fat parts, or the choicest portion, had to be consumed on the altar, being "the bread of Jehovah," and that the residue was the perquisite of the priests. As the fat parts of the dove, or the portion for the altar, could not be separated from the bird, and as the burning of it wholly would destroy the character of the trespass offering, and make it into a whole burnt offering, two doves were brought. One represented the portion for the Lord, and hence was burnt on the altar, whilst the flesh of the other became the perquisite of the officiating priest.

(8) **And wring off his head.**—For the manner in which this was performed see chap. i. 15. It will be seen that it is here distinctly ordered that in this operation the head of the bird is not to be severed from its body. Herein it differed from the burnt offering in chap. i. 15. At the time of the second Temple, the priest went to the south-west horn of the altar, held the two feet of the bird between two fingers, and the two wings between two fingers, stretched out the neck of the victim to the breadth of his two fingers, and cut it with the nail of his thumb, breaking open the great blood-vessel at the neck.

(9) **And he shall sprinkle.**—Here again there is a striking difference between the ritual in the sacrifice before us and that in the case of the regular sin offering described in the previous chapters. The blood is simply to be thrown on the walls of the altar, whilst in the ordinary sin offering, the priest had not only to dip his finger seven times in the blood of the victim, but had to put it on *the horns* of the altar (chap. iv. 6, 7, 17, 18, 25, 30, 34).

(10) And he shall offer the second *for* a
burnt offering, according to the [1]manner:
and the priest shall make an atonement
for him for his sin which he hath sinned,
and it shall be forgiven him.
(11) But if he be not able to bring two
turtledoves, or two young pigeons, then
he that sinned shall bring for his offer-
ing the tenth part of an ephah of fine
flour for a sin offering; he shall put
no oil upon it, neither shall he put *any*
frankincense thereon: for it *is* a sin
offering. (12) Then shall he bring it to
the priest, and the priest shall take his
handful of it, [a] *even* a memorial thereof,
and burn *it* on the altar, [b]according to
the offerings made by fire unto the
LORD: it *is* a sin offering. (13) And the
priest shall make an atonement for him

1 Or, *ordinance.*

a ch. 2. 2.

b ch. 4. 35.

as touching his sin that he hath sinned
in one of these, and it shall be forgiven
him: and *the remnant* shall be the
priest's, as a meat offering.
(14) And the LORD spake unto Moses,
saying, (15) If a soul commit a trespass,
and sin through ignorance, in the holy
things of the LORD; then he shall bring
for his trespass unto the LORD a ram
without blemish out of the flocks, with
thy estimation by shekels of silver, after
the shekel of the sanctuary, for a tres-
pass offering: (16) and he shall make
amends for the harm that he hath done
in the holy thing, and shall add the fifth
part thereto, and give it unto the priest:
and the priest shall make an atonement
for him with the ram of the trespass
offering, and it shall be forgiven him.

---

(10) **According to the manner.**—That is, according to the rites prescribed in chap. i. 14, &c.

(11) **But if he be not able.**—The benign consideration for the poor, and the desire not to mulct them too heavily for their frailties, are here still more evinced in the statute before us. If anyone is so impoverished that the offering of two birds would press too heavily upon him, he might bring the tenth part of an ephah of fine flour, a little less than half a gallon.

For it is a sin offering.—That is, because it is a sin offering, and not a *Minchah* or meat offering (see chap. ii. 1), therefore it shall have no oil or frankincense, otherwise its distinguishing features as such would be destroyed.

(12) **And the priest shall take.**—After he separated a handful of the flour, which was burnt on the altar as a memorial to the Lord (see chap. ii. 12), the officiating priest consumed the rest.

According to the offering made by fire.—Better, *upon the offering made by fire.* (See chap. iv. 35.)

(13) **As touching his sin that he had sinned in one of these.**—That is, in one of the three sins specified in verses 1—4 of this chapter. (See verse 5.)

And the remnant shall be the priest's.—Better, *and it shall belong to the priest.* The word *remnant* is not in the original, and is better left out, since with the exception of the handful which he took out to burn upon the altar, the whole tenth part of the ephah of fine flour belonged to the priest. At the time of Christ, this only took place when the offerer was a layman. But when a priest committed the offence and brought the offering in question, the whole tenth part of the ephah of flour was burnt on the altar, as was done in the case of the meat offering.

(14) **And the Lord spake unto Moses.**—As the introductory formula implies, this is another communication made to the lawgiver at a different time, and sets forth a further development of the laws respecting the trespass offering.

(15) **If a soul commit a trespass.**—The word used here for trespass is not the same which is so rendered in verse 19, and from which the noun rendered in this very chapter by trespass offering (chap. v. 6, 7, 15, 16, 19), is derived. It literally denotes to cover, then to act covertly, to be faithless, especially in matters of a sacred covenant made either with God (Lev. xxvi. 40; Num. xxxi. 16; Deut. xxxii. 51, &c.), or between husband and wife (Num. v. 12, 27).

And sin through ignorance.—If at the time of its committal he did not know that it was a transgression. (See chap. iv. 2.)

In the holy things of the Lord.—That is, inadvertently keeping back the things which belong to the sanctuary, and to the service of the Lord, as, for instance, the tithes, the firstfruits, or not consecrating or redeeming his firstborn (Exod. xxviii. 38; Num. v. 6—8).

A ram without blemish.—For committing any of these transgressions presumptuously, the transgressor incurred the punishment of excision (Num. xv. 30; Heb. x. 28); but when they were done unawares, he was to bring a ram as a sacrifice. According to the rules which obtained during the second Temple, it must be over thirty-one days in the second year of its age. It was of greater value than the female sheep. The sacrifice for a trespass in holy things, though ignorantly committed, was therefore more costly than for the sin of ignorance mentioned in verse 6.

With thy estimation by shekels of silver.—That is, according to the valuation of Moses, to whom this was primarily addressed, the ram is to be so grown up as to be worth several, or at least two shekels. The act of valuing was transferred by Moses to the officiating priests. (See chap. xxvii. 8, 12; Num. xviii. 16.) For the shekels of the sanctuary see Exod. xxx. 13.

(16) **And he shall make amends.**—As the sacrifice was simply to atone for the transgression, the offender was in the first place to make restitution of the full value of the principal which he had inadvertently appropriated.

And shall add the fifth part thereto.—Besides paying the principal, the fifth part of the value of the holy property thus restored is to be added to the original amount. According to the rules which obtained in the time of Christ, the principal was estimated as four-fifths of the whole, and the lacking one-fifth was added. Thus, for instance, if the offender had consumed holy things to the value of four shekels, he had to pay five shekels, the fifth being added to

(17) And if a [a] soul sin, and commit any
of these things which are forbidden to
be done by the commandments of the
LORD; though he wist *it* not, yet is he
guilty, and shall bear his iniquity.
(18) And he shall bring a ram without
blemish out of the flock, with thy esti-
mation, for a trespass offering, unto the
priest: and the priest shall make an
atonement for him concerning his ig-
norance wherein he erred and wist *it*
not, and it shall be forgiven him. (19) It
is a trespass offering: he hath certainly
trespassed against the LORD.

CHAPTER VI.—(1) And the LORD
spake unto Moses, saying, (2) If a soul
sin, and commit a trespass against the
LORD, and lie unto his neighbour in
that which was delivered him to keep,
or in [1] fellowship, or in a thing taken
away by [2] violence, or hath deceived his

[a] ch. 4. 2.

[1] Or, *in dealing.*

[2] Heb., *putting of the hand.*

the four. This, according to our mode of reckoning, is one-fourth. No distinction is here made whether the offender be the high priest, a prince, or a private individual.

(17) **And if a soul sin.**—To guard the Israelites most effectually against making profane use of anything dedicated to the sanctuary and its service, it is here further enacted in verses 17—19, that a trespass offering is to be brought when a man only suspects that he had used things which belonged to the Lord, though he can no longer remember what particular holy property it was, which he used for his own purpose. In the canonical exposition, which obtained during the second Temple, of these sacrificial laws, the trespass offering enacted here is called "The Doubtful Offering," in contradistinction to the one enacted in verses 14—16, which is called "The Certain Offering."

These things.—That is, the holy things of the Lord specified in verse 15.

Though he wist it not, *i.e.*, is uncertain about it. Thus, for instance, he might be in doubt whether or not his transgression consisted in not delivering the first-fruit to the sanctuary, or in having used some other sacred property. (Comp. Gen. xx. 5, &c., 2 Sam. xx. 1, &c.)

Yet is he guilty, and shall bear his iniquity.—Still, he feels that he may be guilty of the transgression, and consequently is burdened with the weight of his iniquity. (See chap. v. 1.)

(18) **And he shall bring a ram.**—Under such circumstances of suspense and feelings of guilt, he is to bring the same victim as in the former instance.

With thy estimation.—That is, according to thy *i.e.*, Moses' valuation, the ram is to be worth two shekels. (See verse 15.)

And wist it not.—Better, *though he wist* or *knew not*, the precise sacred thing which he used, as the same phrase is rendered in the preceding verse. That is, to be on the right side, the priest shall make an atonement for him concerning this error of inadvertence, though the offender is uncertain whether he actually committed the offence or not. Still, as the case is a doubtful one, he is exempt from the additional fifth part which the transgressor had to pay who indisputably committed this offence in ignorance. (See verse 16.)

(19) **It is a trespass offering.**—That is, though the prescribed fifth part is here dispensed with, it is still a trespass offering, for his conscience tells him that he has trespassed against the Lord.

VI.

(1) **And the Lord spake.**—Like chap. v. 14, which begins with the same introductory formula, this is a further communication made to the lawgiver wherein other instances are specified which require a trespass offering. It is repeatedly stated, in some of our best commentaries, that verses 1—7 form part of chap. v. in the Hebrew Bible, and that our translators unfortunately adopted the division of the Septuagint, instead of following the Hebrew. Nothing can be more erroneous than this statement. The Hebrew Scriptures in manuscript have no division into chapters at all. The text is divided into sections, of which there are no less than 669 in the Pentateuch. The book of Leviticus has ninety-eight of these sections, while in our Authorised Version it has only twenty-seven chapters. The divisions into chapters, now to be found in the Hebrew Bibles, were adopted in the fourteenth century by the Jews from the Christians for polemical purposes, and the figures attached to each verse are of a still later period.

(2) **And commit a trespass against the Lord.**—It will be seen that the trespass against God is, strictly speaking, a violation of the rights of a neighbour's property. As fraud and plunder are most subversive of social life, a crime of this sort is described as an insult to God, who is the founder and sovereign ruler of his people.

In that which was delivered him to keep.—To deposit valuable property with a neighbour was, and still is, a common practice in the East where no responsible establishments exist for the reception of private treasure. Hence, when a man went on a journey, he concealed his precious things underground. This was connected with the danger of forgetting the spot where they were hidden, when search and digging had to be resorted to. This not only accounts for the fact that treasure is called in Hebrew by a name which denotes *hidden*, or things which men are in the habit of hiding underground, but explains such allusions as "hidden riches of secret places" (Isa. xlv. 3), "and searchest for her as for hid treasure" (Prov. ii. 4), "dig for it more than for hid treasure" (Job iii. 21). To avoid this danger, men entrusted their treasure to the custody of a neighbour. It is to this practice which the text before us refers, and it is from this practice that the apostle took the expression when he declares, "I am persuaded that he is able to keep that which I have committed unto him against that day" (2 Tim. i. 12; see also verse 14, and 1 Tim. vi. 20).

Or in fellowship.—Literally, *or in something that is placed in the hand*; that is, put in his hand, a deposit. It is similar in nature to the trust mentioned in the preceding clause, for which reason it is not repeated in the general recapitulation of the offences in verses 4 and 5.

Or in a thing taken away in violence.—Having specified two cases of embezzlement in connection with things voluntarily handed over to the defrauder, two

neighbour; (3) or have found that which
was lost, and lieth concerning it, and
[a] sweareth falsely; in any of all these
that a man doeth, sinning therein:
(4) then it shall be, because he hath sin-
ned, and is guilty, that he shall restore
that which he took violently away, or
the thing which he hath deceitfully
gotten, or that which was delivered him
to keep, or the lost thing which he
found, (5) or all that about which he
hath sworn falsely; he shall even [b] re-
store it in the principal, and shall add
the fifth part more thereto, *and* give it
unto him to whom it appertaineth, [1] [2] in
the day of his trespass offering. (6) And
he shall bring his trespass offering unto
the LORD, a ram without blemish out
of the [c] flock, with thy estimation, for a
trespass offering, unto the priest: (7) and
the priest shall make an atonement for
him before the LORD: and it shall be
forgiven him for any thing of all that
he hath done in trespassing therein.
(8) And the LORD spake unto Moses,
saying, (9) Command Aaron and his
sons, saying, This *is* the law of the
burnt offering: It *is* the burnt offering,
[3] because of the burning upon the altar
all night unto the morning, and the fire
of the altar shall be burning in it.
(10) And the priest shall put on his linen
garment, and his linen breeches shall he
put upon his flesh, and take up the ashes

a Num. 5. 6.

b ch. 5. 16.

1 Or, *in the day of his being found guilty.*

2 Heb., *in the day of his trespass.*

c ch. 5. 15.

3 Or, *for the burning.*

---

other frauds are adduced, in which the offender possessed himself of his neighbour's property by violence and extortion.

(3) **Or have found.**—The fifth instance adduced is of property which was neither entrusted nor exacted but accidentally found. For the law on lost property, see Exod. xxiii. 4; Deut. xxii. 1—3.

And sweareth falsely.—This refers to all the five instances specified—that is, if he denies with an oath that property had been entrusted to him, that he had robbed, or exacted, or found anything.

(4) **Then it shall be, because he hath sinned, and is guilty.**—Better, *And it shall come to pass, when he hath so sinned, and acknowledgeth his guilt.* (See chap. iv. 22.) That is, when he has committed any of the aforementioned offences, and denied the sin with an oath, but afterwards voluntarily acknowledges his guilt without having been found out.

That he shall restore that . . . which he hath deceitfully gotten.—Better, *then he shall restore,* &c.

(5) **And shall add the fifth part more thereto.**—The first thing the offender must do, when he realises and confesses his guilt, is to make restitution of the property which he had embezzled, if he still has it, or if that be impossible, he is to pay the value of it as estimated by the authorised tribunal. Besides this, the offender is to add a fifth part of the principal, to compensate for the loss which the owner sustained during the interval. It will be seen that in Exod. xxii. 1—9, when a person was guilty of any of the offences here specified, the offender was condemned to make a fourfold restitution, whilst in the passage before us the mulct is reduced to the restitution of the principal with the addition of a fifth part. The reason of this difference is that the law in Exodus deals with a culprit who is convicted of his crime in a court of justice by means of witnesses, whilst the law before us deals with an offender who, through compunction of mind, voluntarily confesses his offence, and to whom, without this voluntary confession, the offence could not be brought home. It is this difference which constitutes it a case for a trespass offering. (Comp. Num. v. 7.)

In the day of his trespass offering.—Better, *on the day of his guilt.* That is, as soon as he acknowledges his guilt, and brings the sacrifice for his offence, he is to make the requisite restitution.

(6) **With thy estimation.**—That is, according to the official valuation; the ram is to be so grown up as to be worth two shekels. (See chap. v. 15.)

(8) **And the Lord spake unto Moses, saying.**—This is the fourth instance in which this formula is used (see chaps. iv. 1, v. 14, vi. 1) in Leviticus, and, as in the former passages, introduces a further communication to the Lawgiver. Hitherto the law pointed out to the people under what circumstances and how they are to bring their sacred oblations, now directions are given to the priests how to conduct the sacrificial service of the people.

(9) **It is the burnt offering, because of the burning upon the altar.**—Better, *This, the burnt offering, shall be upon the fire on the altar.* That is, the continued burnt offering, with which the sacrifices here enumerated begin, is to remain burning upon the altar from the evening until the morning. (Comp. Exod. xxix. 38—42; Num. xxviii. 1—8).

Shall be burning in it.—Better, *shall burn by it.* That is, shall be fed and kept up by it. According to the practice which obtained during the second Temple, the fat pieces of the burnt offering began to be burned at midnight, thus feeding the fire till the break of day.

(10) **And the priest shall put on his linen garment.**—The officiating priest was to put on his sacerdotal garments, which consisted of four pieces—viz., (1) the tunic, which was a long close robe of fine linen, with sleeves but without folds, covering the whole body, and reaching down to the feet; (2) linen breeches—better, *linen drawers*—which, according to the authorities during the second Temple, reached to the knees and were fastened by ribbons above the flanks; (3) a linen girdle, which, according to the same authorities, was three fingers wide and thirty-two cubits long, and, like the veil of the court and of the sanctuary, was embroidered with figures; and (4) a mitre, or, better, *turban,* which was likewise of fine linen, and was fastened to the head by means of ribbons, to prevent its falling off (Exod. xxviii. 4, 40, xxix. 5—10; Lev. viii. 13). Though the second and third only are here mentioned, there can hardly be any doubt that all the four garments were meant, and that the third and fourth are either omitted for the sake of brevity, or because they are included in the first term, which is the reason why some of the ancient versions have it in the plural.

which the fire hath consumed with the
burnt offering on the altar, and he shall
put them beside the altar. (11) And he
shall put off his garments, and put on
other garments, and carry forth the
ashes without the camp unto a clean
place. (12) And the fire upon the altar
shall be burning in it; it shall not be
put out: and the priest shall burn wood
on it every morning, and lay the burnt
offering in order upon it; and he shall
burn thereon the fat of the peace offer-
ings. (13) The fire shall ever be burning
upon the altar; it shall never go out.
(14) [a] And this *is* the law of the meat
offering: the sons of Aaron shall offer
it before the LORD, before the altar.
(15) And he shall take of it his handful,
of the flour of the meat offering, and of
the oil thereof, and all the frankincense
which *is* upon the meat offering, and
shall burn *it* upon the altar *for* a sweet
savour, *even* the [b] memorial of it unto
the LORD. (16) And the remainder
thereof shall Aaron and his sons eat:
with unleavened bread shall it be eaten
in the holy place; in the court of the
tabernacle of the congregation they
shall eat it. (17) It shall not be baken
with leaven. I have given it *unto them*
for their portion of my offerings made
by fire; it *is* most holy, as *is* the sin
offering, and as the trespass offering.
(18) All the males among the children of

a ch. 2. 1; Num. 15. 4.

b ch. 2. 9.

Take up the ashes which the fire had consumed with the burnt offering.—Better, *take up the ashes into which the fire had consumed the burnt offering.* That is, the ashes into which the consuming fire had converted the victim.

He shall put them beside the altar.—During the second Temple, a priest was appointed by lot to take off from the altar every morning at least a shovelful of ashes and carry it without the camp, and when the ashes accumulated they were entirely removed to the same place.

(11) **And he shall put off his garments.**—That is, the priest shall change the sacred robes in which he ministered at the altar; for other garments, though less holy, were not common, since the removing of the ashes was still a sacerdotal function. The holy garments were deposited in the cells within the precincts of the sanctuary, till they were required again for the altar service (Ezek. xliv. 19; Ezra ii. 69; Neh. vii. 70). Great care was taken that the place to which the ashes were removed was well sheltered, so that the wind should not blow them about. The priest was not allowed to scatter them, but had to deposit them gently. No stranger was permitted to gather them, or to make profit by the ashes.

(12) **And the fire upon the altar shall be burning in it.**—Better, *and the fire upon the altar shall burn by it.* This is almost a literal repetition of the last clause in verse 9, and is here introduced to caution the priest whose function it is to remove the ashes. When engaged in this act, he is to take great care that in taking off the ashes from the altar, he does not knock away the fat pieces of the burnt offering, which constitute the fuel, from the fire, and thus cause it to go out, but let it burn by the fat all night.

And the priest shall burn wood on it every morning.—In the morning, however, the priest is to replenish the burning fuel on the altar with the wood provided at the expense of the congregation, and a store of which was kept in the precincts of the sanctuary. (See chap. i. 7.)

(13) **The fire shall ever be burning.**—This fire, which first came down from heaven (chap. ix. 24), was to be continually fed with the fuel especially provided by the congregation, and with the daily burnt offerings. During the second Temple, this perpetual fire consisted of three parts or separate piles of wood on the same altar: on the largest one the daily sacrifice was burnt; the second, which was called the pile of incense, supplied the fire for the censers to burn the morning and evening incense; and the third was the perpetual fire from which the other two portions were fed. It never was quenched till the destruction of the Temple by Nebuchadnezzar. Indeed, we are positively assured that the pious priests who were carried captives into Persia concealed it in a pit, where it remained till the time of Nehemiah, when it was restored to the altar (2 Macc. i. 19—22). The authorities in the time of Christ, however, assure us that the perpetual fire was one of the five things wanting in the second Temple.

(14) **And this is the law of the meat offering.**—In chap. ii. 1—3, where this meat offering is spoken of, the people are told of what the *mincha* is to consist, and what portion of it was the perquisite of the officiating priest. In the section before us (chap. vi. 14—18) additional directions are given to the priests about the eating of the portions which belong to them and about the treatment of the residue.

The sons of Aaron shall offer it.—Though in the chapter before us it literally means Aaron's own sons, the phrase is intended to comprise his lineal descendants who succeeded to the priestly office. They, and they only, shall offer the sacrifices, but not a layman.

Before the altar.—Or, *in* or *at the fore part of the altar.* That is, at the south-easterly corner of the altar. (See chap. ii. 8.)

(15) **And he shall take of it.**—That is, one of the sons of Aaron mentioned in the preceding verse, whose rotation it is to serve at the altar. For an explanation of these directions see chap. ii. 2.

(16) **With unleavened bread shall it be eaten.**—Better, *unleavened shall it be eaten.* That is, the remainder of the meal is to be made into unleavened cakes, and thus be eaten. (See chap. x. 12.) By adding the word *with*, which is not in the original, the Authorised Version says that the priests are to eat the meat offering with the addition of unleavened cakes.

(17) **I have given it unto them for their portion.**—It was ordained that those who ministered at the altar should live of the altar; hence the priests had no portion or inheritance in the land.

(18) **All the males among the children of Aaron.**—The sin offerings, the trespass offerings, and

Aaron shall eat of it. *It shall be* a
statute for ever in your generations concerning the offerings of the LORD made
by fire: [a]every one that toucheth them
shall be holy.

(19) And the LORD spake unto Moses,
saying, (20) This *is* the offering of Aaron
and of his sons, which they shall offer
unto the LORD in the day when he is
anointed; the tenth part of an [b]ephah of
fine flour for a meat offering perpetual,
half of it in the morning, and half thereof
at night. (21) In a pan it shall be made
with oil; *and when it is* baken, thou shalt
bring it in: *and* the baken pieces of the
meat offering shalt thou offer *for* a
sweet savour unto the LORD. (22) And
the priest of his sons that is anointed
in his stead shall offer it: *it is* a statute
for ever unto the LORD; it shall be
wholly burnt. (23) For every meat offering for the priest shall be wholly burnt:
it shall not be eaten.

(24) And the LORD spake unto Moses,

a Ex. 29. 37.

b Ex. 16. 36.

---

the remainder of the peace offerings being most holy, could only be eaten by the male members of the families of the priests within the court of the sanctuary; whilst the offerings of tithes, fruit, the shoulder and breast of the people's peace offerings, &c., being less holy, were not only eaten by the officiating priests in Jerusalem, but by their incapacitated sons, their daughters, &c., provided they were ritually clean. Any priest who ate the most holy things outside the wall of the courts, or the less holy things outside of the walls of Jerusalem, received forty stripes save one.

Every one that toucheth them shall be holy.—According to this rendering, which exhibits one of the views that obtained during the second Temple, the meaning is that any one who touches the sacrifices of the first order of holiness must not only be a descendant of Aaron and a male, but must have sanctified himself by undergoing the necessary ablutions. (See chap. xxii. 6, 7.) There is, however, another view of the passage which is of equal, if not of anterior, date. That is, *whoso* or *whatsoever toucheth them shall become holy.* Any layman or any ordinary utensil, &c., becomes sacred by touching one of the higher order of sanctity. (See Exod. xxix. 37, xxx. 29; Ezek. xliv. 19, xlvi. 20; Hag. ii. 12.)

(19) **And the Lord spake unto Moses.**—The new law, which is here introduced with this special formula (see verse 8), gives directions about the meat offering which the high priest is to bring on his consecration to the pontifical office (verses 19—23). It naturally follows the sacrificial instructions given for the priests in the preceding section.

(20) **This is the offering of Aaron and of his sons.**—This offering, which is called the oblation of initiation, was, according to the practice which obtained during the second Temple, the *mincha* "of Aaron and his sons," as the text before us declares; that is, of the high priest and of every common priest. The ordinary priest, however, only offered it once on the day of his consecration, whilst the high priest was bound to offer it every day after the regular holocaust, with its meat offering and before the drink offering (Eccles. xlv. 14, with Josephus, *Antiq.* III. x. § 7). It is to this practice that the apostle refers when he says, "For such a high priest became us . . . who needeth not daily, like those high priests, to offer up sacrifices first for his own sins, &c." (Heb. vii. 27).

In the day when he is anointed.—That is, when he is anointed (comp. Gen. ii. 4) or when his anointing ceremony is completed, and he entered upon the duties of his office, which was on the eighth day. (See chap. viii. 35, ix. 1.)

A meat offering perpetual.—That is, in the case of the high priest this oblation is to be offered every day as long as he lived or held the pontifical office. This perpetual meat offering is to consist of a tenth part of an ephah, which is an omer, half of which he is to offer in the morning and half in the evening.

In a pan it shall be made.—Better, *upon a flat plate.* (See chap. ii. 5.)

And when it is baken thou shalt bring it in.—Better, *thou shalt bring it well soaked.* That is, thoroughly saturated with oil.

And the baken pieces of the meat offering shalt thou offer.—That is, a meat offering consisted of small roasted cakes. After the flour was put into the pan, and was soaked in oil, it was divided into and baked in small pieces, apparently to represent the limbs into which the victim of the burnt offering was divided before it was burnt. (See chap. i. 8.) During the second Temple the following practice obtained. The high priest brought the whole tenth part of flour every morning. After sanctifying the whole, he divided it into halves with the measure kept in the sanctuary. He likewise brought three logs of oil, which he mingled with the flour, and kneaded six cakes of each half. After baking the cakes a little, he fried them upon the pan with some of the oil, taking care not to bake them too much, but that they should be between baked and raw, in accordance with the expression, *tuphinei*, which the authorities of those days explained in this manner, but which is rendered here in the Authorised Version by *baken*, and by us *roasted cakes.* Hereupon the high priest divided the six cakes into twelve cakes, being the same number as those of the shewbread, and offered six subdivided in two in the morning and six in the evening.

(22) **And the priest of his sons.**—That is, any one of his descendants who succeeds to the high priesthood is to do the same in all times to come, since it is a statute to last as long as the priesthood continues.

It shall be wholly burnt.—Unlike the ordinary meat offerings brought by the laity, which, with the exception of a handful, was the perquisite of the officiating priest (see chap. ii. 2, 3), the high priest could not eat of this *mincha* because he presented it himself, since it would be unseemly both to offer it to God and at the same time eat it himself. Nor was an ordinary priest allowed to eat it, because he was subordinate in rank to the officiating high priest.

(23) **For every meat offering for the priest.**—Better, *and every meat offering of a priest.* This rule applies to every meat offering brought by the priests themselves for the same reason.

(24) **And the Lord spake unto Moses.**—As is indicated by the special formula, this introduces a new law, or rather a more expanded law than the one contained in chap. iv. 1—5, giving more precise

saying, (25) Speak unto Aaron and to his
sons, saying, This *is* the law of the sin
offering: In the place where the burnt
offering is killed shall the sin offering
be killed before the LORD: it *is* most
holy. (26) The priest that offereth it for
sin shall eat it: in the holy place shall
it be eaten, in the court of the taber-
nacle of the congregation. (27) Whatso-
ever shall touch the flesh thereof shall
be holy: and when there is sprinkled
of the blood thereof upon any garment,
thou shalt wash that whereon it was
sprinkled in the holy place. (28) But
the earthen vessel wherein it is sodden
[a]shall be broken: and if it be sodden
in a brasen pot, it shall be both scoured,
and rinsed in water. (29) All the males
among the priests shall eat thereof: it *is*
most holy. (30) [b]And no sin offering,
whereof *any* of the blood is brought
into the tabernacle of the congregation
to reconcile *withal* in the holy *place*,
shall be eaten: it shall be burnt in the
fire.

a ch. 11. 33.

b Heb. 13. 11.

CHAPTER VII.—(1) Likewise this *is*
the law of the trespass offering: it *is*
most holy. (2) In the place where they
kill the burnt offering shall they kill the

---

directions to the priests about the sin offering of the laity (verses 24—30).

(25) **In the place where the burnt offering is killed.**—That is, the north side of the altar. (See chap. i. 11.)

It is most holy.—That is, the sin offering belongs to the class of sacrifices which is most holy. (See chap. ii. 3.)

(26) **The priest that offereth it for sin.**—Rather, *the priest that offereth it for expiation*, or, *the priest that expiateth sin by it.* That is, who makes atonement by the blood thereof. (See chap. ix. 15.)

Shall eat it.—God gave the sin offering as food for the priests to bear the iniquity of the congregation, and to make atonement for them (chap. x. 17). It constituted a part of their livelihood (Ezek. xliv. 28, 29). The officiating priest to whom fell this perquisite could invite not only his family but other priests and their sons to partake of it. Covetous priests abused this gift (Hos. iv. 8).

In the holy place shall it be eaten.—That is, within the forecourt of the sanctuary. Eight of the offerings had to be eaten in the precincts of the sanctuary: (1) the flesh of the sin offering (chap. iv. 26); (2); the flesh of the trespass offering (chap. vii. 6); (3) the peace offering of the congregation (chap. xxiii. 19, 20); (4), the remainder of the omer (chap. xxiii. 10, 11); (5), of the meat offering of the Israelites (chap. ii., 3—10); (6), the two loaves (chap. xxiii., 20); (7), the shew-bread (chap. xxiv. 9); and (8), the leper's log of oil (chap. xiv. 10—13).

(27) **Whatsoever shall touch the flesh thereof.**—Better, *every one that toucheth the flesh thereof*, as the Authorised Version rightly renders this phrase in verse 18 of this very chapter, where it is explained.

And when there is sprinkled . . . .—So peculiarly sacred was the sin offering, that when any of its blood chanced to spurt upon the garment of the officiating priest, or the one who brought the sacrifice, the spot which received the stain had to be washed in the room of the court provided for this purpose, wherein was a well which supplied the water for the sanctuary, thus preventing the blood from being profaned outside the holy place.

Thou shalt wash.—That is, Aaron, to whom the command was first given, and then his descendants, the priests, not the Israelite or layman.

(28) **But the earthen vessel.**—The earthen vessels used by the Hebrews were unglazed. The ordinary domestic vessels throughout the East are so to this day. From their porous character, therefore, they would absorb some of the fat juices of the flesh which was boiled in them for the priests to eat. And as the absorbed juices could not be washed out, the inexpensive earthenware was to be broken up. (See chap. xi. 33, 35). During the second Temple the fragments were carefully buried in the ground when there was a large accumulation of them.

And if it be sodden in a brasen pot.—Being a solid metal, no juices could sink into it, and any of the most holy flesh that might adhere to it could easily be removed by washing. During the second Temple the scouring was done with hot water, and the rinsing with cold.

(29) **All the males among the priests.**—Not only did the officiating priest, whose perquisite the flesh of the sin offering became, and his male children, partake of it, but he could invite any other priests and their sons to the meal. It is to this practice that the apostle refers when he says, "We have an altar whereof they have no right to eat which serve the tabernacle" (Heb. xiii. 10).

(30) **And no sin offering, whereof . . . .**—Better, *but no sin offering, &c.* The rule set forth in the preceding verse only applies to the sin offerings of the laity (chap. iv. 22, &c.); their flesh fell to the share of the priests, but the flesh of the sin offerings, the blood of which was brought into the tabernacle, "to make atonement in the sanctuary," was not to be eaten but to be burnt. Such were the sin offerings for the high priest (chap. iv. 3, 12), and the whole congregation (chaps. iv. 13—21), and the sin offering of the Day of Atonement (chap. xvi. 27).

To reconcile withal.—Better, *to make atonement for*, as the Authorised Version renders it in chap. i. 4, and generally wherever it occurs.

VII.

(1) **Likewise this is the law . . . .**—Better, *and this is the law, &c.* Just as chap. vi. 24—30 contains additional regulations addressed to the priest about the rites of the sin offering, so chap. vii. 1—10 gives more precise instructions about the trespass offering, supplementing chap. v. 1—13, also designed for the guidance of the priest.

(2) **In the place where they kill.**—That is, the north side of the altar (chap. i. 11).

Shall they kill the trespass offering.—That is, the people who bring these sacrifices shall kill them, since the offerers themselves slaughtered the victim. (See chap. i. 5.)

trespass offering: and the blood thereof
shall he sprinkle round about upon the
altar. (3) And he shall offer of it all the
fat thereof; the rump, and the fat that
covereth the inwards, (4) and the two
kidneys, and the fat that *is* on them,
which *is* by the flanks, and the caul *that*
is above the liver, with the kidneys, it
shall he take away: (5) and the priest
shall burn them upon the altar *for* an
offering made by fire unto the LORD: it
is a trespass offering. (6) Every male
among the priests shall eat thereof: it
shall be eaten in the holy place: it *is*
most holy. (7) As the sin offering *is*, so
is the trespass offering: *there is* one law
for them: the priest that maketh atone-
ment therewith shall have *it*. (8) And
the priest that offereth any man's burnt
offering, *even* the priest shall have to
himself the skin of the burnt offering
which he hath offered. (9) And all the
meat offering that is baken in the oven,
and all that is dressed in the fryingpan,
and [1]in the pan, shall be the priest's that
offereth it. (10) And every meat offering,
mingled with oil, and dry, shall all the
sons of Aaron have, one *as much* as
another.

(11) And this *is* the law of the sacri-
fice of peace offerings, which he shall
offer unto the LORD. (12) If he offer it
for a thanksgiving, then he shall offer
with the sacrifice of thanksgiving un-
leavened cakes mingled with oil, and
unleavened wafers anointed with oil,

1 Or, *on the flat plate*, or, *slice*.

The blood thereof shall he sprinkle.—Better, *throw the blood.* (See chap. i. 5.) Unlike the sin offering, the blood of which was thrown upon the horns of the altar (chap. iv. 25, 30, 34), that of the trespass offering was simply thrown upon the walls of the altar, or round about it. (See chap. v. 9.) During the second Temple there was a scarlet line or thread round the altar, exactly in the middle. The blood of the trespass offering and of the peace offering was thrown round about below the central line, whilst that of the whole burnt offering was thrown round about above the central line.

(3, 4) **And he shall offer.**—For the regulations here described, see chap. iii. 3, 4, 8, 9, &c.

(5) **And the priest shall burn.**—These fat pieces he shall burn, as in the case of the sin offering and peace offering (chap. iv. 26, 31).

(7) **There is one law for them.**—That is, the same rule, as stated in chap. vi. 27, 28, applies to both the sin offering and the trespass offering; hence what is omitted in the regulation of the one must be supplied from the directions given in the other.

(8) **The priest shall have to himself the skin.**—As the skin was the only part not consumed by the fire, in the case of the burnt offering, it fell to the share of the officiating priest. According to the rule which obtained during the second Temple, all the skins of the most holy things belonged to the officiating priests—*i.e.*, those of the trespass offering, the sin offerings of the laity, &c.—whereas those of the holy things—*i.e.*, those of the peace offerings—belonged to the owners of the victims. These skins, which accumulated during the week, the priests whose course it was to serve divided between them every Sabbath evening.

(9) **And all the meat offering.**—Better, *every meat offering.* That is, dressed in whichever of the three ways here mentioned. (See chap. ii. 4—7.)

Shall be the priest's.—With the exception of the memorial part, which was burnt upon the altar (see chap. ii. 4—10), the whole was to go to the particular priest who offered it.

(10) **And every meat offering . . . and dry.**—Better, *but every meat offering . . . or dry.* The only exception to the foregoing rule is the raw flour offering. That is, the voluntary offering of flour which was mingled with oil (chap. ii. 1), or the poor man's sin offering, which, though resembling a meat offering, had no oil put upon it (see chap. v. 11), and the offering of jealousy (Num. v. 15).

Shall all the sons of Aaron have.—That is, whether with or without oil, the remainder of this kind of raw offering is to be equally shared by all the priests.

One as much as another.—Literally, *a man as his brother;* that is, *every man alike.* From the expression *man,* which, as it will thus be seen, is used in the original but does not appear in the Authorised Version, the rule obtained in the time of Christ that neither a child nor woman, though of priestly descent, could partake of this offering; but a priest who was disqualified from officiating through a physical blemish had a share in it, as he comes under the designation of *man.*

(11) **And this is the law of the sacrifice of peace offerings.**—That is, the rites to be observed in connection with this sacrifice. As in the case of the sin offering (chap. iv. 24—31 with chap. vi. 24—30) and the trespass offering (chap. v. 1—13 with chap. vii. 1—10), so here (chap. vii. 11—21), we have more specific and fuller directions given to the priests with regard to the peace offerings, about which orders had previously been given to the people (chap. iii. 1—15).

Which he shall offer.—That is, he who feels it his duty to offer it to the Lord. This common Hebrew idiom of using a verb with *he* in it without an antecedent is better expressed in English by the impersonal, *which one shall offer,* or by the passive, *which shall be offered.* (See verses 20, 21, 29.) Three classes of peace offerings are specified—(1) an acknowledgment of mercies received, (2) as a vow offering, (3) as a free-will offering.

(12) **If he offer it for a thanksgiving.**—That is, acknowledgment of special mercies received from God, such as deliverance in travels, by land or sea, redemption from captivity, restoration to health, &c., enumerated in Ps. cvii. It is to this sacrifice that the apostle alludes when he says, "By him therefore let us offer the *sacrifice of praise* to God continually."

Then he shall offer with the sacrifice.—That is, with the bullock or cow if it be from the herd, or a lamb or goat if it be from the flock (chap. iii. 1).

Unleavened cakes mingled with oil.—From the fact that no mention is here made of the number

and cakes mingled with oil, of fine flour,
fried. (13) Besides the cakes, he shall
offer *for* his offering leavened bread with
the sacrifice of thanksgiving of his peace
offerings. (14) And of it he shall offer
one out of the whole oblation *for* an
heave offering unto the LORD, *and* it
shall be the priest's that sprinkleth the
blood of the peace offerings. (15) And
the flesh of the sacrifice of his peace
offerings for thanksgiving shall be eaten
the same day that it is offered; he shall
not leave any of it until the morning.
(16) But if the sacrifice of his offering *be*
a vow, or a voluntary offering, it shall
be eaten the same day that he offereth
his sacrifice: and on the morrow also
the remainder of it shall be eaten:
(17) but the remainder of the flesh of the
sacrifice on the third day shall be burnt
with fire. (18) And if *any* of the flesh of
the sacrifice of his peace offerings be
eaten at all on the third day, it shall
not be accepted, neither shall it be im-
puted unto him that offereth it: it shall
be an abomination, and the soul that
eateth of it shall bear his iniquity.
(19) And the flesh that toucheth any
unclean *thing* shall not be eaten; it shall
be burnt with fire: and as for the flesh,

---

of cakes or the quantity of oil, it is evident that this was left to the decision of the administrators of the laws and the spiritual guides of the people. The rule which obtained during the second Temple with regard to this offering was as follows:—The offerer brought twenty tenths or pottles of fine flour; ten of them he made leavened and ten he left unleavened. He made the leavened into ten cakes, and of the ten that were unleavened he made thirty cakes. These thirty leavened cakes, which were made with half a log of oil, were divided into three tens, and each ten was prepared in a different manner; that is, ten with an eighth of the oil were baked in the oven, ten with another eighth of the oil were made into wafers, and ten with a fourth of the oil were hastily fried. Of the forty cakes the priest received four, one of each sort, thus obtaining a tenth part.

(13) **Besides the cakes.**—That is, the thirty unleavened cakes which were made of half of the quantity of the flour brought by the offerer, as described in the previous verse, the ten leavened cakes made of the other half of the flour are to be brought. These had all to be baked before the victim was slaughtered. The only other occasion when leavened bread formed part of the offering was on Pentecost (Levit. xxiii. 17); but no portion of it was burnt on the altar as a memorial, for leaven was forbidden to be on the altar. (See chap. ii. 11, 12.)

(14) **And of it he shall offer one out of the whole.**—Better, *and he shall offer of it one out of each.* That is, the officiating priest waves one of each of the four kinds of cakes before the Lord as a heave offering (see Exod. xxix. 24, 28), and is to have these four loaves as his portion, while the rest or the remaining thirty-six cakes belonged to the owner of the sacrifice.

(15) **And the flesh of the sacrifice.**—That is, after the priest had the breast and the shoulder, the share of the victim which belongs to the offerer, together with the remaining loaves, he with his family and poor guests (see Deut. xii. 11—18) are to eat up before the morning, which at the time of the second Temple was limited to midnight. This limitation of time was designed both to encourage liberality to the poor, and to impress upon those who partook of it that it was a sacrificial and sacred feast, so as to prevent its being turned into unseemly conviviality.

(16) **Be a vow or a voluntary offering.**—The vow and the voluntary offering which constitute the second class of peace offerings are both entirely voluntary. The distinction between them, as defined by the canon law, which obtained in the time of Christ, is as follows:—A vow (*nĕdĕr*) is an obligation voluntarily imposed upon oneself with the formula, "Behold, I take it upon myself to bring a bullock, &c., for a peace offering." This undertaking is binding upon the person till he fulfils it. Hence, if the bullock in question dies, or is stolen, or becomes disqualified for a sacrifice, he must bring another. A free-will offering (*nedabah*) simply pledges voluntarily a certain animal for a peace offering, with the formula, "Behold, this animal I devote for a peace offering." Hence, if the animal in question dies, or is stolen, or has otherwise become disqualified for sacrifice, the obligation ceases, since it does not extend beyond the animal thus devoted.

It shall be eaten the same day.—As both these votive offerings were an indirect mode of supplication having respect to future favours, and hence were not a spontaneous expression of pious devotion, they were not so sacred as the former. They were, therefore, allowed to be eaten both on the day of presentation and on the following day.

(17) **But the remainder of the flesh.**—If, however, the sacrifices were very plentiful, or if through niggardliness of the owners a sufficient number of poor guests were not invited, so that the victim could not be eaten up within the time specified, all that remained on the third day was to be burnt.

(18) **And if any of the flesh . . . . be eaten.**—The owner of the sacrifice was responsible for the due observance of this injunction. If, through his neglect, any one ate of the sacrifice after the limited time here specified, the efficacy of the sacrifice was disannulled, and the offerer had to bring another votive offering.

It shall be an abomination.—That is, the flesh left so long in the Eastern climate begins to putrefy, and becomes loathsome and offensive on the third day; so that which is holy becomes desecrated.

And the soul that eateth of it.—Hence he who ate it after the prescribed time was regarded as eating carrion, he bore his guilt, *i.e.*, incurred the penalty of excision.

(19) **And the flesh that toucheth.**—Not only does the sacrificial flesh become desecrated when left by itself beyond the prescribed period, but when it comes in contact with what is unclean, man, woman, or animal, which might happen whilst it is carried from the altar to the place where it is eaten, it becomes defiled, and must be burnt, so that no profane use is made of it.

And as for the flesh, all that be clean shall eat thereof.—Better, *And as for the flesh,*

all that be clean shall eat thereof.
(20) But the soul that eateth *of* the flesh
of the sacrifice of peace offerings, that
pertain unto the LORD, [a]having his un-
cleanness upon him, even that soul shall
be cut off from his people. (21) More-
over the soul that shall touch any un-
clean *thing*, *as* the uncleanness of man,
or *any* unclean beast, or any abominable
unclean *thing*, and eat of the flesh of
the sacrifice of peace offerings, which
pertain unto the LORD, even that soul
shall be cut off from his people.
(22) And the LORD spake unto Moses,
saying, (23) Speak unto the children of
Israel, saying, [b] Ye shall eat no manner
of fat, of ox, or of sheep, or of goat.
(24) And the fat of the [1]beast that dieth
of itself, and the fat of that which is
torn with beasts, may be used in any
other use: but ye shall in no wise eat
of it. (25) For whosoever eateth the fat
of the beast, of which men offer an
offering made by fire unto the LORD,
even the soul that eateth *it* shall be cut
off from his people. (26) [c]Moreover ye
shall eat no manner of blood, *whether it*
be of fowl or of beast, in any of your
dwellings. (27) Whatsoever soul *it be*
that eateth any manner of blood, even
that soul shall be cut off from his
people.
(28) And the LORD spake unto Moses,
saying, (29) Speak unto the children of
Israel, saying, He that offereth the sac-
rifice of his peace offerings unto the
LORD shall bring his oblation unto the
LORD of the sacrifice of his peace
offerings. (30) His own hands shall bring
the offerings of the LORD made by fire,
the fat with the breast, it shall he bring,
that [d]the breast may be waved *for* a

a ch. 15. 3.

b ch. 3. 17.

1 Heb., *carcase.*

c Gen. 9. 4; ch. 3. 17. & 17. 14

d Ex. 29. 24.

---

every one that is clean may eat the flesh—that is, any one whom the offerer invites may partake of the sacrificial repast, provided he is legally clean.

(20, 21) **But the soul that eateth, &c.**—Any one who partakes of the Lord's holy peace offering in a state of legal defilement, arising either from contact with unclean men or objects (see chap. xi. 8—44; xv. 1—33), incurs the penalty of excision.

(22) **And the Lord spake unto Moses.**—This formula introduces a fresh communication made to the lawgiver (verses 22—27), containing explanations and restrictions of the precept laid down in chap. iii. 17, about the fat and blood of animals. The section before us, therefore, supplements and expands the previous law upon the same subject, just as the foregoing section supplemented and expanded the regulations about the different sacrifices.

(23) **Ye shall eat no manner of fat.**—That is, the fat of beeves, sheep, or goats. The fat of these three kinds of sacrificial quadrupeds is prohibited, even when they are not killed as sacrifices, but when slaughtered for private consumption; but the fat of other tame or wild clean quadrupeds, as stags, roes, &c. &c., was lawful. According to the practice which obtained during the second Temple, there are three kinds of fat for the eating of which a man incurred the penalty of excision: the fat (1) which is upon the inwards, (2) upon the two kidneys, and (3) upon the flanks (chap. ix. 10). The rump, the kidney, and the caul above the liver were not called fat, except in sacrifices. The fat which is covered with flesh is lawful, the fat upon the kidneys is forbidden; but that which is within the kidneys, as well as that of the heart, is lawful.

(24) **And the fat of the beast that dieth of itself.**—That is, of the aforesaid animals which died of any disease or accident, or were killed by wild beasts, and which, therefore, are entirely unclean (see chaps. xvii. 15; xxii. 8), might be used for common purposes in ordinary life, such as making candles, &c., &c.

(25) **The fat of the beast of which men offer an offering.**—That is, the fat of beeves, sheep, or goats. (See verse 23.) If he did it presumptuously he incurred the penalty of excision, and if he did it inadvertently he was beaten with forty stripes save one, and had to bring the sin offering appointed.

(26) **Moreover ye shall eat. . . .**—Better, *and ye shall eat no blood in all your dwellings.* That is, this law is binding upon the Israelites wherever they may dwell. (See chap. iii. 17.)

Whether it be of fowl or of beast.—It extends to all fowls and quadrupeds, whether they are legally prescribed as sacrifices or not; but not to fishes, locusts, creeping things, &c., which are not prescribed in the dietary laws as unclean.

(27) **That soul shall be cut off.**—According to the law which obtained during the second Temple, the punishment of excision was only inflicted for eating the life-blood (see chap. xvii. 11), that is, the blood in which the life of the animal resides, and the loss of which causes death. For eating the blood found in the limbs, or in any internal portion of the body, a sin offering had to be brought, and the offender was beaten with stripes.

(28) **And the Lord spake unto Moses.**—With this formula, which, as we have seen, indicates a fresh communication made by the Lord to the lawgiver, additional precepts are introduced, regulating God's portion of the peace offering.

(29) **He that offereth the sacrifice of his peace offerings.**—That is, if his peace offering is one of the three aforementioned classes. (See verse 11.)

Shall bring his oblation.—That is, those portions of the peace offering which the offerer devoted to the Lord and to the officiating priest.

(30) **His own hands shall bring.**—This act the owner himself was to perform, and it was not to be deputed to any one else. The manner in which this rite was performed in the time of Christ was as follows:—The offerer killed the sacrifice, and the priest sprinkled the blood. The victim was then flayed, and the officiating priest took out the inwards, cut the flesh into pieces, and separated the breast and the right shoulder. Whereupon he laid the fat first upon the owner's hands, then the breast, then the shoulder above it; the

wave offering before the LORD. (31) And the priest shall burn the fat upon the altar: but the breast shall be Aaron's and his sons'. (32) And the right shoulder shall ye give unto the priest *for* an heave offering of the sacrifices of your peace offerings. (33) He among the sons of Aaron, that offereth the blood of the peace offerings, and the fat, shall have the right shoulder for *his* part. (34) For the wave breast and the heave shoulder have I taken of the children of Israel from off the sacrifices of their peace offerings, and have given them unto Aaron the priest and unto his sons by a statute for ever from among the children of Israel. (35) This *is the portion* of the anointing of Aaron, and of the anointing of his sons, out of the offerings of the LORD made by fire, in the day *when* he presented them to minister unto the LORD in the priest's office; (36) which the LORD commanded to be given them of the children of Israel, in the day that he anointed them, *by* a statute for ever throughout their generations.

(37) This *is* the law of the burnt offering, of the meat offering, and of the sin offering, and of the trespass offering, and of the consecrations, and of the sacrifice of the peace offerings; (38) which the LORD commanded Moses in mount Sinai, in the day that he commanded the children of Israel to offer their oblations unto the LORD, in the wilderness of Sinai.

CHAPTER VIII.—(1) And the LORD spake unto Moses, saying, (2) Take Aaron and his sons with him, and [a]the garments, and [b]the anointing oil, and a bullock for the sin offering, and two rams, and a basket of unleavened bread; (3) and gather thou all the congregation

a Ex. 28. 2, 4.

b Ex. 30. 24.

---

two kidneys and the caul of the liver above them again, and the bread above the whole, put his own hand under that of the offerer, and waved it all before the Lord. Hereupon the priest salted the inwards, and burned them upon the altar. The breast and right shoulder, as well as the bread waved before the Lord, were eaten by him and his brother priests, whilst the remainder of the flesh and the rest of the bread were eaten by the owner and his friends. If two persons brought a peace offering in partnership, one of them waved for both; and if a woman brought it, the waving was performed by the officiating priest, since women were not allowed to wave except in the offering of jealousy and of a Nazarite (Numb. v. 25, vi. 20).

(34) **By a statute for ever.**—That is, the statute that these two parts of the peace offering are to be given to Aaron and his descendants who may officiate at this sacrifice, is binding upon the Israelites as long as the priesthood lasts.

(35) **This is the portion of the anointing of Aaron and of the anointing of his sons.**—Better, *this is the share of Aaron and the share of his sons.* That is, the wave breast and the heave shoulder.

(36) **Which the Lord commanded to be given them.**—That is, this command is binding upon every offerer to give the before-mentioned parts to the officiating priests, since this is their right by virtue of their office.

(37) **This is the law . . .**—This and the following verse sum up the whole sacrificial law contained in chap. i.—viii.

The burnt offering.—Described in chap. i. 3—17, with its supplement, chap. vi. 8—13.

The meat offering.—Described in chap. ii. 1—16, with its supplement, chap. vi. 14—18.

The sin offering.—Described in chap. iv. 1—35, with its supplement, chap. vi. 24—30.

The trespass offering.—Described in chap. v. 1—13, with its supplements, chaps. v. 14—26, vi. 1—7, vii. 1—10.

And of the consecrations.—Better, *and of the offering of consecration,* that is, the meat offering which the high priest is to bring on his consecration to the pontifical office, described in chap. vi. 19—23.

The peace offering.—Described in chap. iii. 1—17, with its supplements, chap. vii. 11—21 and 28—36.

VIII.

(1) **And the Lord spake unto Moses.**—As the consecration of Aaron and his sons to the priesthood which the Lord commanded Moses to effect (Exod. xxviii. 1—43) was to be accompanied by different kinds of sacrifices (Exod. xxix. 1—37), it was first of all necessary to define the ritual of each sacrifice. This was therefore done in chaps. i.—vii., and the lawgiver now proceeds to record the communication which he received from the Lord respecting the appointment to the sacerdotal office, thus resuming the narrative which was broken off at the end of Exodus.

(2) **Take Aaron and his sons.**—That is, order them to come and to bring with them the sacred vestments and the sacrifices to the entrance of the tent of meeting. (See verse 3.)

The garments.— Those which God had before commanded to be made. (See Exod. xxviii. 2, &c.; xxix. 1, &c.) For the anointing oil, see Exod. xxx. 23, &c.; xxxvii. 29.

And a bullock for the sin offering, and two rams, and a basket.—Better, *and the bullock, the two rams, and the basket.* That is the offering about which directions are given in Exod. xxix. 1—3, thus showing the intimate connection between this part of Leviticus and the latter part of Exodus.

(3) **And gather thou all the congregation together**—Better, *and gather all the assembly together.* The same word is rightly rendered assembly in the Authorised Version in verse 4. (See chap. iv. 13.) That is, call together the assembly of the elders, the heads of the tribes, and the principal men who represented the people. This is confirmed by chap. ix. 1, where it is distinctly said that "Moses called Aaron and

together unto the door of the tabernacle
of the congregation. (4) And Moses did
as the LORD commanded him; and the
assembly was gathered together unto
the door of the tabernacle of the con-
gregation.
(5) And Moses said unto the congre-
gation, [a]This *is* the thing which the
LORD commanded to be done. (6) And
Moses brought Aaron and his sons, and
washed them with water. (7) And he
put upon him the coat, and girded him
with the girdle, and clothed him with
the robe, and put the ephod upon him,
and he girded him with the curious
girdle of the ephod, and bound *it* unto
him therewith. (8) And he put the
breastplate upon him: also he [b]put in
the breastplate the Urim and the Thum-
mim. (9) And he put the mitre upon his
head; also upon the mitre, *even* upon
his forefront, did he put the golden
plate, the holy crown; as the LORD
[c]commanded Moses.
(10) And Moses took the anointing oil,
and anointed the tabernacle and all that
was therein, and sanctified them. (11) And
he sprinkled thereof upon the altar

a Ex. 29. 4.

b Ex. 28. 30.

c Ex. 28. 39, &c.

---

his sons, and *the elders* of Israel," and where these elders are called in the following verse "the children of Israel," by virtue of their representing the children of Israel.

Unto the door of the tabernacle of the congregation.—Better, *to the entrance of the tent of meeting*, that is, the courtyard of the same.

(4) **And Moses did as the Lord commanded him.**—That is, he not only summoned Aaron and his sons, but had their holy vestments, the oil, and the sacrifices brought, which were necessary for the consecration.

Unto the door of the tabernacle of the congregation.—Better, *to the entrance of the tent of meeting.* These representatives of the people, and as many more as the place would conveniently hold, occupied the court-yard, whilst the people at large who wished to witness the solemn consecration of the priesthood probably occupied the neighbouring places which overlooked the enclosure. According to a tradition which obtained in the time of Christ, this ceremony took place on the 23rd of the month Adar, or February.

(5) **This is the thing which the Lord commanded.**—That is, these are the instructions which are given in Exod. xxix. 1—37, and which Moses now published to the assembled representatives of the people.

(6) **And washed them with water.**—As the first initiatory rite of the consecration, Moses caused Aaron and his sons to bathe (see chap. xvi. 4), thus symbolising their purification from sin. Where the phrase "to wash with water" is used without specifying any particular part or parts of the body, as in Gen. xix. 2, xxiv. 32, Exod. xxx. 19, 21, Deut. xxi. 6, it denotes the washing or bathing of the entire body. This was not done in the presence of the people, but in a baptistry, behind a curtain. During the second Temple the sacerdotal immersion could not be effected in a vessel, but had to take place in a hollow made in the ground, containing at least twenty-four cubic feet of water. The installation of the priest, which is here conducted by Moses, as the giver and representative of the Divine law, was during the second Temple performed by the Sanhedrin, who "sat in Moses' seat."

(7) **And he put upon him the coat.**—Better, *and he put upon him the tunic.* For this garment see chap. vi. 10, and Exod. xxviii. 39. It will be seen that the first article of dress—viz., the drawers—distinctly mentioned in Exod. xxviii. 42, is here omitted. This arises from the fact that, being nearest to the skin, Aaron put them on himself behind the curtain, immediately after his ablution.

And girded him with the girdle.—Not the band of the ephod, which is mentioned further on by the name of "curious girdle," but the one made of needlework, with which the tunic was girded about the loins. (See chap. vi. 10, and Exod. xxviii. 39.)

The robe.—Called in Exod. xxviii. 31—35, "the robe of the ephod," which was woven without seam, and was wholly blue. (See chap. vi. 10.)

And put the ephod upon him.—The ephod, which was the distinctive vestment of the high priest, was a sleeveless garment, and was worn over the shoulders. It was made of blue, purple, scarlet, and fine-twined linen, interwoven with golden threads. (See Exod. xxviii. 6—7.)

And he girded him with the curious girdle.—Better, *and girded him with the band.* This band was not only made of the same costly materials as the ephod, but was woven out of the same piece on either side of the garment, so that the ephod had as it were two hands, which constituted the band. (See Exod. xxviii. 8.) It will be seen that this is entirely different from the girdle which was tied around the tunic, mentioned in the former part of this verse.

(8) **And he put the breast-plate upon him.**—Called more fully, "the breast-plate of judgment," which was also a distinctive pontifical garment, and which was made of the same costly materials and the same skilful work as the ephod. (See Exod. xxviii. 15, &c.)

Also he put in the breast-plate the Urim and the Thummim.—Better, *and he put into,* &c. (see Exod. xxviii. 30), that is, Moses put into the bag of the breast-plate (comp. Exod. xxv. 16) these material objects which were separate from the breast-plate, as well as from the gems set in the breast-plate. (See Exod. xxviii. 30.)

(9) **And he put the mitre.**—See Exod. xxviii. 36—38.

As the Lord commanded Moses.—That is, the making of these pontifical garments here enumerated, and the investiture of the high priest by Moses, were according to the Divine command given in Exod. xxviii. 1—43.

(10) **And Moses took the anointing oil.**—Having invested the high priest with the visible emblems of his office and holiness, Moses now, in accordance with the directions given in Exod. xxx. 26—30, xl. 9—11, first anointed the tabernacle and all that was therein—that is, the ark of the covenant, the altar of incense, the candlestick, the table of shewbread, with all the utensils belonging unto them. For the ingredients

seven times, and anointed the altar and
all his vessels, both the laver and his
foot, to sanctify them. (12) And he
[a] poured of the anointing oil upon Aaron's
head, and anointed him, to sanctify him.
(13) And Moses brought Aaron's sons,
and put coats upon them, and girded
them with girdles, and [1] put bonnets
upon them; as the LORD commanded
Moses.

(14) [b] And he brought the bullock for
the sin offering: and Aaron and his
sons laid their hands upon the head of
the bullock for the sin offering. (15) And
he slew *it;* and Moses took the blood,
and put *it* upon the horns of the altar
round about with his finger, and puri-
fied the altar, and poured the blood at
the bottom of the altar, and sanctified
it, to make reconciliation upon it.
(16) And he took all the fat that *was* upon
the inwards, and the caul *above* the
liver, and the two kidneys, and their fat,
and Moses burned *it* upon the altar.
(17) But the bullock, and his hide, his
flesh, and his dung, he burnt with fire
without the camp; as the LORD [c] com-
manded Moses.

(18) And he brought the ram for the
burnt offering: and Aaron and his sons
laid their hands upon the head of the
ram. (19) And he killed *it;* and Moses

a Ps. 133. 2; Ecclus. 45. 15.

1 Heb., *bound.*

b Ex. 29. 1.

c Ex. 29. 14.

---

of this oil, which is also called "oil of holy ointment" (Exod. xxx. 25), see Exod. xxx. 23—25.

And sanctified them.—That is, by this unction Moses separated them from the laity, and dedicated them to the service of God, so that they were not to come in contact with any defilement. (See Exod. xxix. 37, xxx. 29—30.)

(11) **And he sprinkled thereof upon the altar seven times.**—That is, the altar of burnt offering. This rite of sprinkling the altar seven times is not mentioned in the directions given in Exod. xxx. 28, xl. 10. For the import of the number seven, see Levit. iv. 6.

And anointed the altar and all his vessels.—That is, the same altar of burnt sacrifice. The altar, having thus been sanctified, was thenceforward considered as sanctifying the sacrifices and oblations offered upon it. Hence the remark of Christ, "Ye fools and blind, for whether is greater, the gift, or the altar that sanctifieth the gift?" (Matt. xxiii. 19).

(12) **And he poured of the anointing oil upon Aaron's head.**—In the anointing of Aaron, the oil was poured upon his head. (See also chap. xxi. 10—12; Exod. xxix. 7; Ps. cxxxiii. 2.) This profuse pouring of oil was repeated at the consecration of every successor to the high-priesthood, whilst the common priests were simply anointed, or were simply marked with the finger on the forehead on their first installation, and this anointing descended with them for all futurity. (See chap. vi. 3.) Tradition informs us that during the second Temple, the person who anointed the high priest first threw the oil upon his head, and then drew with his finger the sign of the letter *Caph,* being the initial of *Cohen, i.e.,* priest, between the eyebrows of the newly-consecrated pontiff.

(13) **And Moses brought Aaron's sons.**—Having consecrated the father as high priest, Moses now invests Aaron's four sons, Nadab, Abihu, Eleazar, and Ithamar, with the visible signs of the priestly office by robing them in the sacerdotal garments. For these articles of dress see Exod. xxviii. 40, 41, xxix. 30, xl. 14.

(14) **And he brought the bullock for the sin offering.**—Though duly consecrated, Aaron and his sons had first to be purged of their sins before they could commence their priestly functions in the sanctuary. Hence, Moses, as the mediator of the covenant delegated by God to perform the act of consecration, also performed the sacrificial rites, whilst the installed priests stood as penitent sinners by the side of the sin offering which was now offered for the first time. For the laying on of the hands by the offerer on the victim, see chap. i. 4.

(15) **And he slew it.**—Better, *and he killed it,* as it is rendered in the Authorised Version, in verse 19. In ordinary cases the offerer himself slaughtered the victim (see chap. i. 5), but in the case before us Moses performed this act in accordance with the command in Exod. xxix. 11.

And Moses took the blood.—That is, having caught the blood in the bowl, he threw it upon the four corners of the altar, as described in chap. i. 5—not, however, on the horns of the altar of incense, or in the tabernacle, as in the case of the sin offering for the high priest and for the nation. (See chap. iv. 7, 16—18.)

And purified the altar . . . and sanctified it.—Like the priest, the altar was consecrated to the service of God by the anointing oil (see verse 11), and hence, like the priest, the altar is also purified by the expiatory sacrifice from its defilements.

(16) **And he took all the fat.**—That is, in accordance with the directions given in Exod. xxix. 13. For the different portions of the sacrifice see chap. iii. 3—5.

(17) **But the bullock . . . he burnt . . .**—Though none of the blood of this sin offering was brought into the sanctuary, whereby it became excluded from the rule laid down in chap. vi. 30, yet the flesh was not allowed to be eaten, but like the sin offering of the high priest (chap. iv. 3—12), and for the whole congregation (chap. iv. 13—21), had to be burnt without the camp, since Moses could not eat it, because he was not a legally consecrated priest (see chap. vi. 25), and the priest could not eat it because it was against the law for the sinner to partake of the sin offering which he brought himself. (See chap. iv. 35.)

(18) **And he brought the ram.**—After their sins had been expiated by the sin offering, Moses offered for the consecrated priests one of the two rams which he was ordered to take (see verse 2) as a burnt offering. With the exception of performing the sacerdotal rites himself, the ritual here described is in accordance with rules laid down in chap. i. 3—9.

(19) **And he killed it.**—That is, Moses himself slaughtered the victim, and not the offerer, as was usually the case. (See verse 15.)

And Moses sprinkled the blood.—Better, *and Moses cast the blood.* The word here is not the same in the original as in verse 15.

sprinkled the blood upon the altar round
about. (20) And he cut the ram into
pieces; and Moses burnt the head, and
the pieces, and the fat. (21) And he
washed the inwards and the legs in
water; and Moses burnt the whole ram a Ex. 29. 31.
upon the altar: it *was* a burnt sacrifice
for a sweet savour, *and* an offering made
by fire unto the Lord; as the Lord
commanded Moses.
(22) And he [a] brought the other ram,
the ram of consecration: and Aaron and b Ex. 29. 24, &c.
his sons laid their hands upon the head
of the ram. (23) And he slew *it;* and
Moses took of the blood of it, and put *it*
upon the tip of Aaron's right ear, and
upon the thumb of his right hand, and
upon the great toe of his right foot. c Ex. 29. 26.
(24) And he brought Aaron's sons, and
Moses put of the blood upon the tip of
their right ear, and upon the thumbs of
their right hands, and upon the great
toes of their right feet: and Moses
sprinkled the blood upon the altar round d Ex. 29. 32.
about. (25) And he took the fat, and the
rump, and all the fat that *was* upon the
inwards, and the caul *above* the liver,
and the two kidneys, and their fat, and
the right shoulder: (26) and out of the
basket of unleavened bread, that *was*
before the Lord, he took one unleavened
cake, and a cake of oiled bread, and one
wafer, and put *them* on the fat, and
upon the right shoulder: (27) And he put
all [b] upon Aaron's hands, and upon his
sons' hands, and waved them *for* a wave
offering before the Lord. (28) And
Moses took them from off their hands,
and burnt *them* on the altar upon the
burnt offering: they *were* consecrations
for a sweet savour: it *is* an offering
made by fire unto the Lord. (29) And
Moses took the breast, and waved it *for*
a wave offering before the Lord: *for* of
the ram of consecration it was Moses'
[c] part; as the Lord commanded Moses.
(30) And Moses took of the anointing
oil, and of the blood which *was*
upon the altar, and sprinkled *it* upon
Aaron, *and* upon his garments, and
upon his sons, and upon his sons' gar-
ments with him; and sanctified Aaron,
and his garments, and his sons, and his
sons' garments with him.
(31) And Moses said unto Aaron and
to his sons, Boil the flesh *at* the door of
the tabernacle of the congregation: and
there [d] eat it with the bread that *is* in the

---

(22) **And he brought the other ram.**—That is, the second of the two rams mentioned in verse 2.

The ram of consecration.—That is, the sacrifice of consecration. This concluding sacrifice, which in form resembles the thank offering and the peace offering, was designed to express the gratitude which Aaron and his sons felt for having been chosen to the office of priests, and their peace and fellowship with God.

(23) **And he slew it.**—Better, *and he killed,* as the same word is rendered in the Authorised Version in verse 19, that is, Moses killed it.

And put it upon the tip of Aaron's right ear.—To teach him that, as the mediator between God and His people, it was his bounden duty to hearken to the commandments of the Lord.

And upon the thumb of his right hand.—To remind him that henceforth he is to execute God's will, and walk in the way of His commandments.

(24) **And he brought Aaron's sons.**—Having performed these symbolical acts upon the high priest, Moses now repeats the same in the case of the four ordinary priests. The right members were chosen for these symbolical acts because they are represented as the strongest, and are therefore most able to execute the will of God (see also Exod. xxix. 20). The cured leper had the same parts of the body touched with the blood of the trespass offering. (See chap. xiv. 14—17.)

(25) **And he took the fat, and the rump.**—Better, *and he took the fat and the fat-tail* (see chap. iii. 9). For the import of this verse see Exod. xxix. 22.

(26—28) **And out of the basket.**—The description in these three verses of the rites performed at the sacrifice of consecration is exactly in accordance with the orders given in Exod. xxix. 23—25. The right shoulder, and one cake of each of the three unleavened kinds, which formed the officiating priests' share of the sacrifices (see chap. vii. 12, 32), and which were ordinarily eaten by them and their families, Moses on this occasion burned upon the altar, after being placed in the hands of Aaron and his sons, and waved before the Lord.

(29) **And Moses took the breast.**—That is, the breast-piece, which was afterwards the perquisite of the officiating priest (see chap. vii. 34), fell in this instance to the share of Moses, in accordance with the directions given in Exod. xxix. 26, to be his sacrificial meal since he was divinely appointed to perform the priestly service.

(30) **And of the blood which was upon the altar.**—That is, some of the blood of the ram of consecration, which was probably kept in the bowl, and placed upon the altar for this purpose. Whether the anointing oil and the blood were sprinkled separately, or whether they were mixed together, cannot possibly be gathered either from this passage, or from Exod. xxix. 21, which gives the order. As the sacred garments were the badge of office, they received the same cleansing and sanctification as the priests themselves. Hence the remark of the apostle, "almost all things were by the law purged with blood" (Heb. ix. 22).

(31) **And Moses said . . . boil the flesh.**—That is, of the ram of consecration; with the exception of the fat parts and the right shoulder, which were burnt

basket of consecrations, as I commanded, saying, Aaron and his sons shall eat it. (32) And that which remaineth of the flesh and of the bread shall ye burn with fire. (33) And ye shall not go out of the door of the tabernacle of the congregation *in* seven days, until the days of your consecration be at an end: for [a] seven days shall he consecrate you. (34) As he hath done this day, *so* the LORD hath commanded to do, to make an atonement for you. (35) Therefore shall ye abide *at* the door of the tabernacle of the congregation day and night seven days, and keep the charge of the LORD, that ye die not: for so I am commanded. (36) So Aaron and his sons did all things which the LORD commanded by the hand of Moses.

CHAPTER IX.—(1) And it came to pass on the eighth day, *that* Moses called Aaron and his sons, and the elders of Israel; (2) and he said unto Aaron, [b] Take thee a young calf for a sin offering, and a ram for a burnt offering, without blemish, and offer *them* before the LORD. (3) And unto the children of Israel thou shalt speak, saying, Take ye a kid of the goats for a sin offering; and a calf and a lamb,

[a] Ex. 29. 35.

[b] Ex. 29. 1.

upon the altar, and the wave-breast, which was awarded to Moses as the officiating priest on the occasion (see verse 8, and Exod. xxix. 31, 32), the flesh of the victim is to be prepared by Aaron and his sons for the sacrificial meal (see chap. vii. 11, &c.). From the peculiar nature of this offering, however, it is ordained that the flesh is to be boiled *at the entrance of the tent of meeting*, not *at the door of the tabernacle of the congregation*, as the Authorised Version has it. According to Exod. xxix. 31, this is to take place " at the holy place," that is, in the court, and is to be eaten with unleavened bread, thus distinguishing it from the ordinary sacrificial meal of the peace offering.

Aaron and his sons shall eat it.—This is another distinguishing feature of the sacrifice in question. Whilst to the ordinary sacrificial feasts the offerer could invite his family and strangers (see chap. vii. 15), in this no layman or non-priest could partake of the meal, because the flesh and the bread were peculiarly holy (see Exod. xxix. 33), as this sacrifice had the same atoning virtue as the burnt offering. (See chap. i. 4.)

(32) **And that which remaineth.**—That is, if any of the flesh or cakes was not eaten upon the day on which the sacrifice was offered, it had to be burnt, which was the law in the case of the peace offering. (See chap. vii. 15, 17; Exod. xxix. 34.)

(33) **And ye shall not go out of the door of the tabernacle.**—Better, *and ye shall not go from the enclosure of the tent of meeting*, that is, Aaron and his sons are not to go out of the court, as the consecration was not performed within but at the entrance of the tent of meeting. This is most distinctly stated in verse 35.

In seven days.—Better, *for seven days.* As the ceremony of consecration lasted seven days, it was but natural that Aaron and his sons were enjoined not to quit the sacred enclosure for any secular transactions during the whole of this period.

For seven days shall he consecrate you.—That is, on each of these seven days the same sacrifices are to be repeated, the sin offering, the burnt offering, and the consecration offering are to be offered up, and Aaron and his sons, as well as their garments, are to be sprinkled with the sacrificial blood and the anointing oil. (See Exod. xxix. 36.)

(34) **As he hath done this day, so . . .**—Better, *As hath been done this day, so* . . . That is, the rites of consecration which have been performed upon you to-day, or the first day, the Lord hath commanded to be repeated every day for seven days.

IX.

(1) **And it came to pass on the eighth day.**—That is, the day following the seven days of consecration. (See chap. viii. 33, 53.) According to ancient tradition this was the first of the month Nisan, or March.

Moses called Aaron and his sons, and the elders.—That is, the same elders, the representatives of the people, who were called to attest the imposing ceremony of consecration (see chap. viii. 3), are now also summoned to witness how the newly-installed priests entered upon the active duties of their ministrations. Like newly-born children who remain seven days in a state of uncleanness and enter into the covenant privileges of the congregation on the eighth day (see chap. xii. 2, 3), so the newly-created priests after a purging of seven days commenced their sacred duties and partook of their privileges on this symbolical day.

(2) **A young calf for a sin offering.**—Literally, *a calf, the son of a bull*, which, according to the canonical law, was a calf of the second year, whilst a steer, the son of a bull, rendered in the Authorised Version by "young bullock," was defined to be three years old, or in its third year. (See chap. iv. 3.) Before they could mediate for the forgiveness of the people, Aaron and his sons had first to bring a sin offering for themselves, in expiation probably for the feeling of pride which they might have fostered at having been so highly distinguished and chosen to be the mediators of the people. This sin offering, however, showed him that, though a high priest, he was beset with the same infirmities, and stood in need of the same atonement, as the people whom he represented. As this is the only instance in which a calf is appointed for a sin offering, and as the offerer who is ordered to bring this exceptional sacrifice is Aaron, Jewish tradition will have it that it was designed to refer to the sin of the golden calf which he made for the people. (Exod. xxxii. 4—6.) So old and universal is this interpretation, that it is expressed in the ancient Chaldee Version of the Pentateuch. This sense seems to derive support from verse 7.

Before the Lord.—That is, before the door of the tent of meeting (see chap. i. 5, 11), on the altar of burnt offering.

(3) **And unto the children of Israel thou shalt speak.**—That is, Aaron, who was now constituted high priest, was to give the orders about the sacrifices.

both of the first year, without blemish,
for a burnt offering; (4) also a bullock
and a ram for peace offerings, to sac-
rifice before the LORD; and a meat
offering mingled with oil: for to day
the LORD will appear unto you.
(5) And they brought *that* which
Moses commanded before the taber-
nacle of the congregation: and all the
congregation drew near and stood be-
fore the LORD. (6) And Moses said,
This *is* the thing which the LORD
commanded that ye should do: and
the glory of the LORD shall appear
unto you.
(7) And Moses said unto Aaron, Go
unto the altar, and offer thy sin
offering, and thy burnt offering, and
make an atonement for thyself, and for
the people: and offer the offering of the
people, and make an atonement for
them; as the LORD commanded. (8) Aaron
therefore went unto the altar, and slew
the calf of the sin offering, which *was* for
himself. (9) And the sons of Aaron
brought the blood unto him: and he
dipped his finger in the blood, and put
it upon the horns of the altar, and poured
out the blood at the bottom of the altar:
(10) but the fat, and the kidneys, and
the caul above the liver of the
sin offering, he burnt upon the altar;
as the LORD commanded Moses. (11) And
the flesh and the hide he burnt with

It will be seen that the elders of the people whom Moses summoned in verse 1 to witness in behalf of the people the first ministrations of the priests, are here called "the children of Israel," thus showing that the representatives acted for the people. Hence the two terms are interchanged (see chap. viii. 2), which accounts for the fact that the Greek Version (LXX.) renders it here by "elders."

A kid of the goats . . . and a calf.—Better, *a shaggy-haired he-goat.* (See chap. iv. 23, &c.)

(4) **Also a bullock and a ram.**—The elders were thus to bring on behalf of the people, (1) a he-goat for a sin offering; (2) a yearling calf and a yearling sheep for a burnt offering; and (3) an ox and a ram for a peace offering.

A meat offering mingled with oil.—The oil was to be added, as, with the exception of the small portion offered to the Lord, the meat offering was the perquisite of the officiating priests who partook of it, together with their share of the victims, and the cakes had to be made palatable for the sacerdotal repast. (See chap. ii. 1.)

For to-day the Lord will appear unto you.—That is, prepare and sanctify yourselves with these sacrifices, for the Lord is to manifest himself in an especial manner to signify his approval of the inauguration of Aaron and his family to the priesthood.

(5) **And they brought.**—That is, Aaron and his sons, according to the command of Moses, and the elders on behalf of the people, and according to the order of Aaron, who was directed by Moses so to do, brought the aforenamed sacrifices.

And all the congregation . . .—That is, the elders who represented the people, whom Moses summoned (see verse 1), and as many of the people as could find room assembled before the sanctuary in the court-yard to witness the newly-installed priests officiating for the first time.

(6) **And Moses said.**—As the people now stood assembled in the court and around it, Moses explained to them the import of the ritual which they were about to witness in the presence of the Lord.

(7) **And Moses said unto Aaron.**—Though he was now the duly-installed high priest, yet he did not approach the altar till he was solemnly called upon by Moses to do it, thereby showing the authorised representatives of the people that Aaron did not take this honour to himself, but that it was the call of God by Moses. Hence, the remark of the Apostle, "And no man taketh this honour unto himself, but he that is called of God, as was Aaron; so also Christ glorified not himself to be made an high priest, but he that said unto him," &c. (Heb. v. 4, 5.)

Make atonement for thyself and the people.—The fact that these sacrifices which the high priest is to bring are here described as designed to make atonement for himself and the people, goes far to confirm the ancient interpretation that reference is here made to the particular sin which Aaron and the people committed in common, and that it is the sin of the golden calf (see verse 2), which is so emphatically described in the words "they made the calf which Aaron made" (Exod. xxxii. 35). Hence, whilst their share of the sin is to be atoned by a special sacrifice (see verse 15), they are yet to participate in the atoning virtue of Aaron's sacrifice because they prevailed on him to make the calf (Exod. xxxii. 1).

(8) **And slew the calf.**—As the sacrificer Aaron, like every ordinary offerer, slaughtered the victim himself (see chap. i. 5) on the north side of the altar. (See chap. i. 11.)

(9) **And the sons of Aaron brought the blood.**—His sons, for whom the sacrifice was offered as well as for himself, and who assisted at the ritual, after catching the blood in a bowl (see chap. i. 5), brought it to Aaron, who stood at the altar waiting to receive it. Unlike the ordinary law of the sin offering for the high priest and for the people, the blood of which was taken into the tabernacle (see chap. iv. 7, 16—18), Aaron on this occasion simply put some of it upon the four horns of the brazen altar as Moses had done in the sin offering of consecration (see chap. viii. 15), for, though high priest, he had not as yet access to the holy place of the sanctuary till he had qualified himself by this sacrifice in the court-yard.

(10) **But the fat . . . he burnt upon the altar.**—The fat portions of this sin offering Aaron was still to burn upon the altar as Moses had done before (see chap. viii. 14, 21, 28), since the miraculous fire from God did not issue forth till the burnt offering of the people was offered. (See verse 24.)

(11) **And the flesh and the hide he burnt.**—The flesh and the hide, which were ordinarily the perquisite of the officiating priest (see chap. vi. 26), were on this occasion to be burnt, because the priest

fire without the camp. (12) And he
slew the burnt offering; and Aaron's
sons presented unto him the blood,
which he sprinkled round about upon the
altar. (13) And they presented the burnt
offering unto him, with the pieces
thereof, and the head: and he burnt
them upon the altar. (14) And he did
wash the inwards and the legs, and
burnt *them* upon the burnt offering on
the altar.

(15) And he brought the people's
offering, and took the goat, which *was*
the sin offering for the people, and
slew it, and offered it for sin, as the
first. (16) And he brought the burnt
offering, and offered it according to the
[1] manner. (17) And he brought the meat
offering, and [2] took an handful thereof,
and burnt *it* upon the altar, [a] beside
the burnt sacrifice of the morning.
(18) He slew also the bullock and the
ram *for* a sacrifice of peace offerings,
which *was* for the people: and Aaron's
sons presented unto him the blood,
which he sprinkled upon the altar
round about, (19) and the fat of the
bullock and of the ram, the rump,
and that which covereth *the inwards*,
and the kidneys, and the caul *above*
the liver: (20) and they put the fat up-
on the breasts, and he burnt the fat
upon the altar: (21) and the breasts
and the right shoulder Aaron waved
for a wave offering before the LORD;
as Moses commanded.

(22) And Aaron lifted up his hand to-
ward the people, and blessed them,
and came down from offering of the
sin offering, and the burnt offering,
and peace offerings. (23) And Moses and
Aaron went into the tabernacle of

1 Or, *ordinance.*

2 Heb., *filled his hand out of it.*

a Ex. 29. 38.

---

was not permitted to partake of the sin offering which he offered for himself. (See chap. iv. 35.)

(12) **And he slew the burnt offering.**—As was the order of the sacrifices which Moses brought (see chap. viii. 18—21), so here the sin offering is followed by the burnt offering. The ram (see verse 2) which constituted this sacrifice Aaron slew at the north side of the altar (see chap. i. 11), and after the blood had been received into the bowl by his sons who assisted him, and had been handed to him, Aaron sprinkled it around the altar in the same manner as Moses had done before. (See chap. viii. 19.)

(13) **With the pieces thereof.**—Literally, *according to its pieces*, or *piece by piece*, that is, after it had been cut up into the pieces as ordered in chap. i. 6, and as the burnt-offering offered by Moses was cut up (see chap. viii. 20), his sons handed the dismembered victim to him piece by piece. The process of cutting up is not mentioned, because it is implied in the fact that the ritual on this occasion was exactly the same as in the offerings made by Moses.

(14) **And burnt them upon the burnt offering.**—That is, no special fire is to be kindled for it, but this burnt offering is to be put upon the top of the burning sin offering. (See chap. iv. 35.)

(15) **And he brought the people's offering.**—Being reconciled to God by the atoning sacrifice which he offered for his own share in the sin, Aaron was now qualified to offer the sin offering of the people.

As the first.—The ritual in this sacrifice Aaron conducted in the same manner as in the foregoing one offered for himself. (See verse 8.) He accordingly burnt the flesh without the camp, for which he was reproved by Moses.

(16) **And he brought the burnt offering.**—That is, the yearling calf and the lamb (see verse 3), which he offered according to the rites prescribed in chap. i. 3, &c. The same expression "manner," in the sense of prescribed ritual, also occurs in chap. v. 10, where, like here, it is rendered in the Margin by "ordinance."

(17) **And he brought the meat offering.**—This Aaron offered according to the rule in chap. ii. 1—3.

Beside the burnt sacrifice of the morning.—That is, in addition to the lamb which was daily offered as a burnt sacrifice, and was accompanied by a meat offering (Exod. xxix. 30, 40). Accordingly Aaron began his priestly functions by first offering the daily morning sacrifice which took precedence of all other sacrifices, and which was never superseded by the extra offerings; then followed the other sacrifices here described.

(18—21) **He slew also the bullock.**—Better, *and he slew*, &c. With this peace offering, which was carried out according to the rules prescribed in chap. iii. 1, &c., concluded the sacrificial ceremony of the installation of the priesthood and the sanctification of the people.

(22) **And Aaron lifted up his hand.**—Having now completed the rites of the various sacrifices, and whilst still standing on the elevation leading to the altar, Aaron with uplifted hands solemnly pronounces upon the assembled people the priestly benediction prescribed in Numb. vi. 24—26. As the Lord separated the tribe of Levi to bless the people in His name (Deut. x. 8, xxi. 5), the descendants of Aaron to this day pronounce this benediction upon the congregation in the synagogue at certain periods of the year. In accordance with the remark in the passage before us, they are obliged to turn their faces to the people. In lifting up their hands above their shoulders, stretching them forward towards the worshippers, each priest joins his hands together by the thumbs and the two forefingers, separating the other two fingers so as to produce a triple division. (See Num. vi. 24, &c.)

And came down from offering.—That is, from the elevated standing-place by the side of the altar, which was ascended by a gently sloping dam of earth, since no steps were allowed (see Exod. xx. 3), and which during the second Temple was three cubits high.

(23) **Went into the tabernacle of the congregation.**—Better, *went into the tent of meeting.* The sacrifices being ended, there still remained the burning of the incense on the golden altar which stood in the tabernacle. Hence Aaron, conducted by Moses, left the court where the altar of burnt offering stood, and where the sacrifices had been offered, and went into

the congregation, and came out, and
blessed the people: and the glory of
the LORD appeared unto all the people.
(24) And [a] there came a fire out from
before the LORD, and consumed upon
the altar the burnt offering and the
fat: *which* when all the people saw,
they shouted, and fell on their faces.

CHAPTER X.—(1) And [b] Nadab and
Abihu, the sons of Aaron, took either
of them his censer, and put fire there-

a Gen. 4. 4; 1 Kin. 18. 38; 2 Chron. 7. 1; 2 Mac. 2. 10, 11.

b Num. 3. 4 & 26. 61; 1 Chron. 24. 2.

the holy place where the altar of incense stood to perform this last act of the ritual. (See Exod. xxx. 7, &c.) Having already delivered to Aaron the charge of all the things connected with the sacrifices in the court, Moses now also committed to him the care of the things within the sanctuary, showing him, at the same time, how to offer the incense, how to arrange the shewbread on the table, how to light and trim the lamps of the candlestick, &c., all of which were in the sanctuary. There can, however, hardly be any doubt that whilst there they prayed, as tradition informs us, for the promised manifestation of the Divine presence.

And came out, and blessed the people.—According to an ancient tradition embodied in the Chaldee Version of the Pentateuch, the blessing which Moses and Aaron unitedly bestowed upon the people on coming out of the sanctuary, was as follows:—"May the word of the Lord accept your sacrifice with favour, and remit and pardon your sins."

And the glory of the Lord appeared.—To show his gracious acceptance of the institution of the priesthood, and of the whole service connected therewith, God manifested himself in the more luminous appearance of the cloudy pillar. This glorious appearance which, in a lesser degree, always filled the tabernacle, was now visible in greater effulgence to all the people who witnessed the installation. (Comp. Exod. xvi. 10, xl. 34; 1 Kings viii. 10—12.)

(24) **And there came a fire.**—As a further indication of His acceptance of all the forementioned rites, the Lord sent forth from the luminous cloud flashes of fire, which, on this occasion, suddenly consumed in the sight of the people the victims that ordinarily continued smouldering on the altar all the day and all the night. In this manner God afterwards testified His acceptance of the sacrifice of Gideon (Judges vi. 20, 21), of Elijah, (1 Kings xviii. 38), and of the sacrifices of Solomon at the dedication of the Temple (2 Chron. vii. 1, 2). Tradition assures us that the sacred fire which thus issued forth from the immediate presence of God continued to be nourished on the altar with the fuel especially provided by the congregation, and constituted the perpetual fire. (See chap. vi. 13.)

They shouted, and fell on their faces.—On seeing these visible tokens of the Divine acceptance of the services, the people expressed their thankfulness in the same manner as they showed it on a similar occasion. Thus we are told—"When all the sons of Israel saw how the fire came down, and the glory of the Lord shone upon the house, they bowed themselves with their faces to the ground upon the pavement, and worshipped and praised the Lord, saying, For he is good, for his mercy endureth for ever" (2 Chron. vii. 3).

X.

(1) **And Nadab and Abihu.**—Immediately after the Divine manifestation of God's acceptance of the services connected with the institution of the priesthood, and whilst the congregation are still giving utterance to their profound expressions of thankfulness and joy, the assembled people see a most daring act of sacrilege committed by two of the five newly-installed priests, and have to witness the most awful punishment which befals the offenders. The offenders are the two eldest sons of Aaron, who had received the high distinction to be invited to accompany their father and Moses to the summit of the hallowed mount (Exod. xxiv. 1); the lesson to the Israelites being that the priests, though mediators between God and the people, are beset with the same infirmities as the laity, and must not presume upon their office.

Took either of them his censer.—The sin of Nadab and Abihu was of a complicated nature, and involved and consisted of several transgressions:—(1) They each took *his* own censer, and not the sacred utensil of the sanctuary. (2) They both offered it together, whereas the incense was only to be offered by one. (3) They presumptuously encroached upon the functions of the high priest; for according to the Law the high priest alone burnt incense *in a censer*. (See chap. xvi. 12, 13; Num. xvii. 11.) The ordinary priests only burnt it on the golden altar in the holy place (Exod. xxx. 7, 8), or on the brazen altar as a part of the memorial. (See chap. ii. 2, 3, 16, &c.) The case of Korah and his company was an exception, since it was ordered by Moses for an especial purpose (Num. xvi. 6—25). (4) They offered the incense at an unauthorised time, since it was apart from the morning and evening sacrifice.

And offered strange fire.—They filled their vessels with common fire instead of taking it from the holy fire of the altar, which was always to be used in burning incense. (See chaps. ix. 24, xvi. 12.) It is with reference to this practice that we are told—"And the angel took the censer and filled it with fire off the altar" (Rev. viii. 5). Ancient tradition says that Nadab and Abihu had partaken too freely of the drink offering, and performed their service in a state of intoxication, when they were incapacitated to distinguish between what was legal and illegal. So general was this tradition that it is actually embodied in the Palestinian Chaldee Version of verse 9, which contains the solemn warning against wine to those engaged in the service of the sanctuary, and which is regarded as a sequel to this awful catastrophe. Others, however, suppose that the phrase "strange fire" denotes not offered according to the prescribed law, just as "strange incense" is used in the sense of incense not prepared in the manner ordered by the Law (Exod. xxx. 9).

Before the Lord.—This may mean before the door of the sanctuary (see chap. i. 5), or in front of the holy of holies. (See chap. iv. 6.) As the dead bodies are said in verse 4 to have lain in the court of the tabernacle, the former must be the meaning in the passage before us.

Which he commanded them not.—According to a figure of speech frequently used in Hebrew, where the negative form is used for the emphatic affirmative, this phrase is better rendered, "which he had strongly forbidden them." Though the command is only expressed in chap. xvi. 12, there can hardly be any doubt that it was previously given by Moses, since it is implied

in, and put incense thereon, and offered
strange fire before the LORD, which
he commanded them not.
(2) And there
went out fire from the LORD, and devoured them, and they died before the
LORD.
(3) Then Moses said unto Aaron,
This *is it* that the LORD spake, saying,
I will be sanctified in them that come
nigh me, and before all the people I
will be glorified. And Aaron held his
peace.
(4) And Moses called Mishael
and Elzaphan, the sons of Uzziel the
uncle of Aaron, and said unto them,
Come near, carry your brethren from
before the sanctuary out of the camp.
(5) So they went near, and carried
them in their coats out of the camp;
as Moses had said.
(6) And Moses
said unto Aaron, and unto Eleazar
and unto Ithamar, his sons, Uncover
not your heads, neither rend your
clothes; lest ye die, and lest wrath
come upon all the people: but let
your brethren, the whole house of

---

in chaps. i. 7, vi. 12. A similar reference to a well-known statement, though not here recorded, we have in the following verse.

(2) **And there went out fire from the Lord.**—By fire they sinned, and by fire they died. The Divine fire which issued forth to consume the sacrifices as a token of acceptance, now descended as the avenger of sin to consume the sacrificers, just as the same gospel is to one a savour of life unto life, and to another a savour of death unto death. (2 Cor. ii. 16.)

And devoured them.—That is, slay them, since we are told in verse 5 that not only were their bodies in a perfect state of preservation, but even their garments were not burnt. The word *consume*, however, is used here to keep up the connection between this verse and chap ix. 24.

They died before the Lord.—That is, in the court of the sanctuary (see verse 1), on the very spot where the sin was committed.

(3) **Then Moses said . . . This is it that the Lord spake.**—Here we have another instance of a reference to a well-known Divine communication made through Moses, which has not been previously recorded in the Pentateuch. Moses adduces this declaration to explain to the bereaved father the judgment of God.

I will be sanctified in them that come nigh me.—Better, *I will sanctify myself in them that come near to me.* God had sanctified to himself Aaron and his sons by the holy unction (see chap. viii. 10, 12), that they might sanctify Him in the strict performance of their sacred duties as the mediators between God and man. Having failed to do this, God sanctified himself in them by the awful punishment inflicted upon them for their transgression. (See Ezek. xxvii. 22, xxxviii. 16, 23.) The phrase, "that come near to God," is a frequent designation for the priest. (Exod. xix. 22; Numb. xvi. 5; Ezek. xlii. 13, xliii. 19.)

And before all the people I will be glorified.—Better, *and I will glorify myself before all the people.* By this judgment God vindicated His law, showing that it cannot be violated with impunity, and thus glorified Himself as the Holy One of Israel.

And Aaron held his peace.—He silently submitted to the righteous judgment which bereft him of his two sons. So the Psalmist, "I was dumb, I opened not my mouth; because thou didst it" (xxxix. 9).

(4) **And Moses called . . . the sons of Uzziel.**—Uzziel was the son of Kohath, the younger brother of Amram. As Amram was the father of Aaron, Uzziel was the uncle of Aaron. Uzziel had three sons, of whom Mishael and Elzaphan were two (Exod. vi. 18, 22). Eleazar and Ithamar, as ordinary priests, might have been employed in removing the remains of their slain brothers. (See chap. xxi. 1—4.) Naturally they were too much affected by this appalling scene; Moses therefore wanted to spare their feelings, and hence charged their cousins-german with the task of carrying away the dead bodies. The reason why Izar and Hebron, the two older uncles of Aaron, are here passed over is because the discontent of their children with the choice of Aaron and his sons to the priesthood, which afterward broke out in open rebellion on the part of Korah, Izar's son (Numb. xvi., xvii.), had evidently begun to show itself when they witnessed the imposing ceremonies of the consecration. It was necessary that those who suffered so signally for the transgression of the Divine institutions should be buried by men whose allegiance to God's law was unimpeachable.

Carry your brethren.—That is, your kinsmen. The expression brother is frequently used in the Bible in the sense of near relation. (See Gen. xiii. 8, xiv. 6, xxiv. 48, xxix. 12—15, &c.)

From before the sanctuary.—In the courtyard of the sanctuary, where the incense was offered in the midst of the rejoicing people, and where they were struck dead. (See chap. ix. 5.)

(5) **And carried them in their coats.**—Better, *and they carried them in their tunics*, the long white garments in which they ministered, and which were the most characteristic part of the sacerdotal vestments. In ordinary cases the cast-off dresses of the priests were converted into wick for the lamps of the sanctuary, but in this case they were buried with the persons, for, apart from their becoming unclean by their contact with the corpses, no one would have used them, having been worn at a time of so awful a visitation.

Out of the camp.—Burial places in ancient times were outside the towns in open fields. (See Gen. xxiii. 9, 17; Matt. xxvii. 71; Luke viii. 27.)

(6) **Uncover not your heads.**—Better, *let not your heads be dishevelled.* It was the custom for mourners to let their hair grow long, and let it fall in a disorderly and wild manner over the head and face. (See chaps. xiii. 45, xxi. 10; 2 Sam. xv. 30, xix. 4, &c.) For this reason the priests who are consecrated to the service of the Lord are even on ordinary occasions not to shave their heads nor suffer their locks to grow long. (Ezek. xliv. 20.) On this occasion more especially Aaron and his two surviving sons are forbidden to give way to these manifestations of grief, since it might be considered as a reflection upon the justice of the punishment.

Neither rend your clothes.—This was another ordinary manifestation of sorrow and mourning. (See Gen. xxxvii. 29, 34; Josh. vii. 6; 2 Sam. xiii. 21, &c.) To this day the Jews observe this custom of mourning for the death of their near relations; they tear their

Israel, bewail the burning which the
LORD hath kindled. (7) And ye shall
not go out from the door of the
tabernacle of the congregation, lest ye
die: for the anointing oil of the LORD *is*
upon you. And they did according to
the word of Moses.

(8) And the LORD spake unto Aaron,
saying, (9) Do not drink wine nor strong
drink, thou, nor thy sons with thee,
when ye go into the tabernacle of the
congregation, lest ye die: *it shall be*
a statute for ever throughout your
generations: (10) and that ye may put
difference between holy and unholy,
and between unclean and clean; (11) and
that ye may teach the children of
Israel all the statutes which the LORD
hath spoken unto them by the hand
of Moses.

(12) And Moses spake unto Aaron, and
unto Eleazar and unto Ithamar, his sons
that were left, Take the meat offering
that remaineth of the offerings of the
LORD made by fire, and eat it without leaven beside the altar: for it *is*

---

garments, let their hair and nails grow, and do not wash.

And lest wrath come upon all the people.—The transgression of this command would not only bring down upon Aaron and his sons the same awful judgment, but would expose the whole community to the Divine wrath. In virtue of the intimate connection which subsisted between the representative of the nation and the people, a sin committed by the high priest in his official position involved the whole community, and they had to share the consequences of the offence. (See chap. iv. 3.)

But let your brethren.—The afflicted relatives were, however, not to be deprived of all the customary expressions of mourning. The whole house of Israel, who are here designedly called "the brethren" of the bereaved, to show the depth of their sympathy, were allowed to mourn over the great calamity which had thus befallen them.

(7) **From the door of the tabernacle of the congregation.**—Better, *away from the entrance of the tent of meeting.* (See chap. i. 3.) But Aaron and his sons are not to quit the court of the sanctuary to take part in the burial.

For the anointing of the Lord is upon you.—The reason why they are not to join in the funeral rites is that they had been devoted by this holy unction to the service of God. Earthly relations were, therefore, not to interfere with the duties to God. Hence, it was sin for priests to mourn when they ministered before the Lord. (See chap. xxi. 10—12.) This law was strictly observed during the second Temple. When an officiating priest heard of the death of a relative, he did not quit the sanctuary, lest it should appear that he had greater love for the dead person than for the living God.

(8) **And the Lord spake unto Aaron.**—As half of the staff of the priesthood had thus been struck down, and the other half were not allowed to mourn over the departed, the chief of the survivors might have thought that God was altogether displeased with the newly-created pontificate. To comfort him, therefore, as well as to restore the prestige of this sacred office in the eyes of the people, who had witnessed the disobedience and punishment of the spiritual functionaries, the Lord, who hitherto made all such communications to Moses, now honours Aaron with speaking to him immediately.

(9) **Do not drink wine.**—As the command that the priests are to abstain from any intoxicating liquors when performing their sacred functions follows so closely upon the death of Nadab and Abihu, the opinion obtained as early at least as the time of Christ that there is a connection between the specific sin and the general law, that the two sons of Aaron drank wine to excess when they offered strange fire, and that the present prohibition is based upon that circumstance. Accordingly, the Apostle enjoins that a bishop "must not be given to wine," that "deacons must not be given to much wine" (1 Tim. iii. 2, 3). A similar law existed among the ancient Greeks and Persians, enjoining the priests to abstain from wine.

Nor strong drink.—The word (*shēchār*) here rendered strong drink, is the general name of intoxicating drinks, whether made of wheat, barley, millet, apples, dates, honey, or other fruits. One of the four intoxicating drinks which are prohibited among the Mahommedans in India is called "Sachar.

When ye go into the tabernacle of the congregation.—Better, *when ye go into the tent of meeting.* The Palestinian Chaldee adds here, "as thy sons did who died by the burning fire." The same precept is repeated in Ezek. xliv. 21, "Neither shall any priest drink wine when they enter into the inner court." The injunction that on these particular occasions the priests are to abstain from taking it clearly implies that, ordinarily, when not going into the tent of meeting—that is, when not performing their sacred functions in the sanctuary—they were not forbidden to use it if required.

(10) **And that ye may put difference.**—The motive here assigned for their abstinence from intoxicating liquor is, that by keeping sober they might be able to discriminate between the legal and illegal points in the prescribed observances, which required the greatest care. Thus, for instance, the rules as to which places and days and sundry portions of the offerings were holy or common, or as to holy fire and common fire, which Nadab and Abihu violated; or about ceremonially clean and unclean men, women, animals, and utensils. (See Ezek. xliv. 23.)

(11) **And that ye may teach.**—The priests were not only to keep sober to be able to decide the questions of ritual, but they were to teach the people, since the ceremonial law affected domestic life and social intercourse (Deut. xxxiii. 10; Mal. ii. 7). For neglecting these duties, the prophet charges them:—"Her priests have violated my law, and have profaned my holy things: they have put no difference between the holy and the profane, neither have they showed difference [*i.e.*, taught the people the difference] between the unclean and the clean" (Ezek. xxii. 26).

(12) **And Moses spake unto Aaron.**—This communication, which refers to the sacrifices offered on the eighth day, or the day after the consecration was finished, Moses made to Aaron and his two surviving

most holy: (13) and ye shall eat it in
the holy place, because it *is* thy due,
and thy sons' due, of the sacrifices
of the LORD made by fire: for so I
am commanded. (14) And [a] the wave
breast and heave shoulder shall ye eat
in a clean place; thou, and thy sons,
and thy daughters with thee: for *they*
be thy due, and thy sons' due, *which*
are given out of the sacrifices of peace
offerings of the children of Israel.
(15) The heave shoulder and the wave
breast shall they bring with the
offerings made by fire of the fat, to
wave *it for* a wave offering before the
LORD; and it shall be thine, and thy
sons' with thee, by a statute for ever;
as the LORD hath commanded.
(16) And Moses diligently sought the
goat of the sin offering, and, behold,
it was burnt: and he was angry with
Eleazar and Ithamar, the sons of
Aaron *which were* left *alive*, saying,
(17) Wherefore have ye not eaten the
sin offering in the holy place, seeing
it *is* most holy, and *God* hath given
it you to bear the iniquity of the
congregation, to make atonement for
them before the LORD? (18) Behold,
the blood of it was not brought in

a Ex. 29. 24.

---

sons immediately after the calamity that had befallen them. As Aaron lost his two eldest sons in consequence of their having violated the sacrificial regulations, Moses is most anxious to guard him and his two younger sons against transgressing any other part of the ritual connected with the same sacrifices, lest they also should incur a similar punishment.

Take the meat offering that remaineth of the offerings.—The meat offering which was offered by the nation the day after the consecration, when the calamity happened (see chap. ix. 17), and which was not as yet eaten. With the exception of the handful which was burnt on the altar, all belonged to the priests. (See chaps. ii. 1—3, vi. 14—18.)

And eat it without leaven beside the altar.—That is, in the court of the tent of meeting, where the altar of burnt offering stood. (See chap. vi. 16.)

For it is most holy.—Hence it could only be eaten by the male members of the families of the priests within the court of the sanctuary. (See chap. vi. 18.)

(13) **And ye shall eat it in the holy place.**—Better, *and ye shall eat it in a holy place*, that is, in any part of the holy court; it was not to be taken out of the precincts of the sanctuary.

(14) **And the wave breast and heave shoulder.**—That is, of the peace offering which was offered by the nation. (See chap. ix. 18—21.) As they were given to the priests for the maintenance of their families (see chap. vii. 34), these portions might be eaten anywhere within the camp, provided the place was not defiled by ceremonial uncleanness.

(15) **The heave shoulder and the wave breast shall they bring.**—That is, the offerers who devoted these portions of the peace offering to the Lord, are to bring them to the officiating priests. (See chap. vii. 29, 30.)

(16) **And Moses diligently sought the goat.**—That is, the flesh of the goat of the sin offering which was offered by the nation on the eighth day. (See chap. ix. 15.)

And, behold, it was burnt.—Being overwhelmed with grief at the loss of their brothers, Eleazar and Ithamar could not eat, and as none but priests were allowed to partake of the flesh of the sin offering, they burnt it on the altar, to prevent its corruption. They did this all the more readily since the flesh of Aaron's sin offering was just before burnt without the camp. (See chap. ix. 11.)

And he was angry with Eleazar and Ithamar.—As it was Aaron's duty quite as much as his two sons to eat of the flesh, Moses probably omitted to mention his name, because he wished to spare the honour of the pontiff in the sight of the people.

(17) **Wherefore have ye not eaten? . . .**—As enjoined in chap. vi. 26.

God hath given it.—That is, He has given to you the flesh of the sin offering to eat. (See chap. vi. 29.)

To bear the iniquity of the congregation.—Better, *to remove the iniquity of the congregation*, which the priests did by making atonement for them before the Lord, as is explained in the next clause. Accordingly the flesh of the sin offering is given to the priests, that by the act of eating it they may visibly show the offerer that God has graciously accepted the expiatory sacrifice, and that it is a most holy thing. The phrase "to bear iniquity" often signifies "to bear away, to remove, to forgive iniquity." (Comp. Gen. l. 17; Exod. xxxii. 32; Ps. xxxii. 1, 5, &c.) Hence the most ancient Versions translate it here, "that ye may take *away* or *remove*" (LXX., the Chaldee, the Syriac, &c.). The rendering of the Authorised Version, however, is that of the Vulgate, which has been followed by the Reformers both in England and on the continent, as well as by several modern expositors. This is supported by the meaning of the phrase "to bear the iniquity" in Exod. xxviii. 38; Num. xviii. 1; Ezek. iv. 4—6. Those who follow this rendering take the passage to mean that the priest, by eating or incorporating the victim on which the offerer had laid his guilt, actually took away the sin, or neutralised it in a mysterious way, by virtue of the sanctifying power belonging to the sacerdotal office. Others, again, who also take the phrase to mean that the priest literally takes the sin upon himself, do not explain it, but simply say, that by eating the sin-laden victim the sins of the offerer were, *in some sort*, laid upon the priest to be taken away by him, thus prefiguring Christ, who should be both priest and sacrifice.

(18) **Behold, the blood of it.**—According to the sacrificial law, the flesh of the sin offerings (the blood of which was not carried into the sanctuary) had to be eaten by the priests alone, in a holy place, as a part of the expiatory rites. (See chaps. vi. 25, 26, x. 17.) It was the flesh of those sin offerings, the blood of which was carried into the sanctuary, which had to be burnt. (See chaps. iv. 5, 16, vi. 23, 30.) Now the blood of the people's sin-offering which was offered on this occasion was not carried into the sanctuary. (See chap. ix. 9.)

Ye should indeed have eaten it.—Hence its flesh should have been eaten by Aaron and his two sons

within the holy *place:* ye should in-
deed have eaten it in the holy *place,*
[a]as I commanded. (19) And Aaron said
unto Moses, Behold, this day have
they offered their sin offering and
their burnt offering before the LORD;
and such things have befallen me:
and *if* I had eaten the sin offering to
day, should it have been accepted
in the sight of the LORD? (20) And
when Moses heard *that,* he was
content.

CHAPTER XI.

CHAPTER XI.—(1) And the LORD
spake unto Moses and to Aaron,
saying unto them, (2) Speak unto the
children of Israel, saying, [b]These *are*
the beasts which ye shall eat among
all the beasts that *are* on the earth.
(3) Whatsoever parteth the hoof, and is

a ch. 6. 26.

b Deut. 14. 4; Acts 10. 14.

---

in the court-yard of the sanctuary, as Moses commanded in chap. vi. 26.

(19) **And Aaron said.**—Though, according to verse 16, Moses only blamed Eleazar and Ithamar for this transgression of the law, yet there can hardly be any doubt that Aaron was included in this censure, and that the lawgiver abstained from expressing his anger against the pontiff because of the supreme dignity of his office, which he would not lower in the sight of the people. Aaron, however, was fully sensible of this, and hence replies to the charge brought against his sons.

They offered their sin offering.—Before proceeding to the transgression with which they are thus charged, Aaron adverts to the fact that all the other sacrificial duties in which he and his sons were engaged on the same day, prior to the great calamity, were performed in strict accordance with the prescribed ritual. His sons assisting him had offered "their"—*i.e.,* the people's—sin and burnt offerings (see chap. ix. 15, 16) thus far in due compliance with the requirements of the law, and hence could never have meant to transgress intentionally.

And such things have befallen me.—But whilst he, Eleazar, and Ithamar were thus duly performing the sacrificial rites, Nadab and Abihu, his other two sons, transgressed, and were suddenly struck down dead, thus overwhelming the survivors with sorrow, and rendering them unfit to partake of the sacrifices.

And if I had eaten.—Aaron submits that, unfitted as they thus were by mourning and the sense of their own sinfulness, if they had partaken of this solemn meal it would not have been acceptable to the Lord. In consequence of this declaration, the rule obtained during the second Temple, that when an ordinary priest heard of the death of a relative whilst on duty in the sanctuary, he had to cease from service, though he could not leave the precincts of the Temple otherwise he defiled the sacrifice; whilst the high priest, who could continue his sacred ministrations, was not allowed to partake of the sacrificial meal.

(20) **And . . . he was content.**—He acknowledged Aaron's plea to be just, and that he had himself spoken hastily. This is a remarkable instance of Moses' humility, and of the human side of his nature as a lawgiver. (See also Num. xxxii. 6, &c.) Hence Jewish tradition from time immemorial ascribes the mistake to Moses, and not to Aaron. The paraphrase of this verse in the Palestine Chaldee Version, which embodies the ancient opinions, is very instructive. It is as follows: "And when Moses heard it, he approved of this explanation. Whereupon he sent a herald through the whole camp of Israel, saying, It is I from whom the law had been hid, and my brother Aaron brought it to my remembrance."

XI.

(1) **And the Lord spake unto Moses and to Aaron.**—Lest the rebuke which Moses publicly administered to the priests (see chap. x. 16) should diminish their influence with the people, whom they had to teach the laws of clean and unclean things (see chap. x. 10, 11) laid down in the following chapters, the Lord here honours Aaron, as well as Moses, by making this communication to them conjointly. Besides, Aaron as minister was as much concerned in these laws as Moses the legislator. Hence, when a question of defilement had afterwards to be decided, it was brought for judgment before Moses and Aaron conjointly. (See Num. ix. 6.)

(2) **These are the beasts which ye shall eat among all . . .**—Better, *These are the animals which ye may eat of all* . . . . The dietary laws, which stand first in the general precepts about clean and unclean things, begin with the quadrupeds, or land animals, both domesticated and wild. This is in accordance with the Hebrew division of the animal kingdom into four principal classes:—(1) the land animals, (2) the water animals, (3) the birds of the air, and (4) the swarming animals. Though not specified here by name, yet the parallel regulations in Deut. xiv. 4, 5 enumerate the following ten animals:—the ox, the sheep, the goat, the hart, the roebuck, the fallow deer, the wild goat, the pygang, the wild ox, and the chamois, with their various kindred species, which are not mentioned. From the expression, "These are the animals," the opinion obtained during the second Temple that God actually caused specimens of every animal to pass before Moses and Aaron, in order to show them the veritable creatures which are clean and unclean, just as the Lord caused every species to come to Noah into the ark.

(3) **Whatsoever parteth the hoof, and is clovenfooted.**—Better, *Whatsoever is clovenfooted, and entirely separateth the hoofs.* The first rule laid down by which the clean quadruped is to be distinguished is that the hoofs must be completely cloven or divided above as well as below, or, as the parallel passage in Deut. xiv. 6 has it, "and cleaveth the cleft into two claws." Such is the case in the foot of the ox, the sheep, and the goat, where the hoof is wholly divided below as much as above. The foot of the dog, the cat, and the lion, though exhibiting a division into several distinct toes or claws, is contrary to the regulation here laid down, inasmuch as the division is simply on the upper side, the lower side being united by a membrane, and hence the hoof is not "entirely separated."

And cheweth the cud.—In addition to the foot being perfectly cloven, the quadruped to be clean is to be ruminating. The canon which obtained during the second Temple is thus formulated: "Every quadruped

clovenfooted, *and* cheweth the cud,
among the beasts, that shall ye eat.
(4) Nevertheless these shall ye not eat
of them that chew the cud, or of them
that divide the hoof: *as* the camel,
because he cheweth the cud, but di-
videth not the hoof; he *is* unclean
unto you. (5) And the coney, because
he cheweth the cud, but divideth not
the hoof; he *is* unclean unto you.
(6) And the hare, because he cheweth
the cud, but divideth not the hoof; he
is unclean unto you. (7) And [a] the
swine, though he divide the hoof, and
be clovenfooted, yet he cheweth not
the cud; he *is* unclean to you.

a 2 Mac. 6. 18.

which has no upper teeth is known to be ruminant, and when it is also clovenfooted is clean." According to the law of Manu the highest Hindoo castes were also forbidden to eat the flesh or drink the milk of quadrupeds with uncloven hoof. The same was the case with the Egyptian priests: they abstained from eating the flesh of any animal which had uncloven hoofs or many claws.

(4) **Nevertheless these shall ye not eat.**—As there are some quadrupeds which comply with only one of the two above-named conditions—*i.e.*, which ruminate but have not their hoofs perfectly parted in two, or, *vice versâ*, are bisulcous and not ruminant—it is here declared that such animals must not be eaten.

As the camel, because he cheweth the cud, but divideth not . . .—Better, *though he cheweth the cud, yet he divideth not*, as the same phrase is properly rendered in the Authorised Version in verse 7. The first animal adduced to illustrate this fact is the indispensable camel, or "the ship of the desert," as it is aptly called. Though cloven-footed above, the toes of the camel are united below in a large elastic pad on which the camel treads, and which is like the sole of a shoe. Hence it does not come within the category of those animals which are thoroughly bisulcate. The Egyptians, the Zebii, and the Hindus, too, did not eat camel's flesh, because they supposed it to be heating, and to engender cruelty and revenge; whilst the Persians, the ancient Arabians, and the Moslems feasted upon its milk and flesh.

(5) **And the coney, because he cheweth the cud, but divideth not . . .**—Better, *though he cheweth the cud, yet he divideth not.* (See verse 4.) The coney, which is the old English name for rabbit, is the meaning of the Hebrew expression *shaphan*, according to the definition of those who had to explain and administer this law at the time of Christ. As these interpreters lived in Palestine, where they saw the animals in question, the objection that the rabbit is not indigenous in Palestine falls to the ground. These shrewd administrators of the law must also have noticed that it was the habit of the feeble conies to seek refuge and build in the fissures of the rocks, which not unfrequently are on a level with the ground. The rabbit, moreover, well suits the hare, by which it is immediately followed. Modern expositors, however, identify it with the Syrian hyrax, or rock-badger, which is about the size of a well-grown rabbit. It resembles the guinea-pig or the Alpine marmot, has long hair of a brownish grey or brownish-yellow colour on the back, but white on the belly, a very short tail, and short round ears. The action of its jaws when it is at rest resembles that of the ruminants.

(6) **And the hare, because he cheweth the cud, but.**—Better, *though he cheweth the cud, yet.* Other nations, too, shunned the flesh of hares. The Parsees considered the hare as the most unclean of all animals, and the ancient Britons abstained from eating it because of the loathsome disorders to which the hare is subject. Like the rabbit, or the hyrax, the hare has not the peculiar stomach of the true ruminant; but, like the rabbit, the hare, when sitting at rest, so moves its jaws that it appears to masticate. As the object of the legislator was to furnish the people with marks by which they were to distinguish the clean from the unclean animals, he necessarily adopted those which were in common vogue, and which alone were intelligible in those days.

(7) **And the swine, though he divide the hoof, and be clovenfooted.**—Better, *And the swine, though he is clovenfooted, and entirely separateth the hoofs.* (See verse 3.) Having given these illustrations of animals which comply with the first condition only—*i.e.*, which are ruminant but not bisulcous—and hence must not be eaten, the lawgiver now concludes the list of prohibited quadrupeds with an illustration of a contrary nature—viz., the swine, which comply with the second condition only, but not with the first. Here, too, the description is according to appearance. The feet of the pig tribe generally have four toes enclosed in separate hoofs. The two middle hoofs, however, are much larger, and are divided by a deep cleft, and hence to all appearances the swine is bisulcous. Though the law before us simply describes the swine as wanting in one of the two criteria, like the camel, the coney, and the hare, yet the abhorrence which the Jews, as a nation, have always had of this animal, and the impurity which they have ascribed to it infinitely surpass their repulsion of any other unclean beast. For this reason it became the symbol of defilement and the badge of insult (Pss. lxv. 4, lxvi. 3, 17; Prov. xi. 22). The eating of pork was regarded as renouncing the Law, and as a sign of apostasy. Hence Antiochus Epiphanes adopted it as a test that those Jews who ate it had forsaken their religion and submitted to his rule. Hence we read that when swine's flesh was forced into the mouth of Eleazar, the aged scribe, he "spit it forth, choosing rather to die gloriously than to live stained with such an abomination" (2 Macc. vi. 18, 19). During the time of the commonwealth there were no swine in Judea. Hence it was in a "far country" that the prodigal son was sent into the field to feed the swine (Luke xv. 13—15). The swine in Galilee in our Lord's time (Matt. viii. 30) were undoubtedly kept by Gentiles for the Roman legion. The very name of swine (*chazir*) was discarded, and the animal was designated by the euphemistic expression, "the other thing." This "brutish of all animals" was, moreover, regarded as propagating cutaneous and many other disorders. The Talmud declares that "ten measures of pestilential diseases were spread over the earth, and nine of them fell to the share of pigs." On the other hand, many of the Pagan nations regarded the swine as an emblem of the productive power of nature. Hence they sacrificed them to those deities to whom they ascribed the fertility of the soil, and the fruitfulness of cattle. Thus, the Egyptians offered them in honour of Isis and Osiris once

(8) Of their flesh shall ye not eat, and
their carcase shall ye not touch;
they *are* unclean to you.
(9) These shall ye eat of all that *are*
in the waters: whatsoever hath fins
and scales in the waters, in the seas,
and in the rivers, them shall ye eat.
(10) And all that have not fins and
scales in the seas, and in the rivers,
of all that move in the waters, and of
any living thing which *is* in the
waters, they *shall be* an abomination
unto you: (11) they shall be even an
abomination unto you; ye shall not eat
of their flesh, but ye shall have their
carcases in abomination. (12) Whatso-
ever hath no fins nor scales in the
waters, that *shall be* an abomination
unto you.
(13) And these *are they which* ye shall
have in abomination among the fowls;
they shall not be eaten, they *are* an

---

a year at the festival of the full moon. The Athenians, too, offered the swine in their mysteries; so did the Boetians and the early Romans.

(8) **Of their flesh ye shall not eat.**—During the second Temple the prohibition was defined to extend to the smallest quantity. If any one ate a piece of flesh less even than the size of an olive he was chastised with stripes.

And their carcase shall ye not touch.—As contact with a human dead body, which was regarded as the most defiling of all, was only forbidden to the priests (see chap. xxi. 1—3), hence the prohibition here addressed to the whole nation was interpreted during the second Temple to apply simply to the occasions when the Israelites came to Jerusalem on the pilgrimage festivals. Contact with a carcase of an unclean animal on these visits precluded the worshipper from entering the sanctuary, from touching sacred things, and from partaking of the sacrificial meats.

(9) **These shall ye eat.**—The water animals, which, as we have seen, constitute the second division of the animal kingdom, now follow the land animals. They are discussed in verses 9—12. Like the clean quadrupeds, the salt-water and the fresh-water fish must comply with two conditions to bring them within the class of clean. They must have both scales and fins. It will be seen that in the case of the quadrupeds, not only are two criteria given by which the clean animals may be distinguished from the unclean, but that the law is illustrated by adducing ten land animals of the former kind (see verse 2), and four of the latter (see verses 4—7). In the case before us, however, not a single typical fish is given by name, and the law itself is expressed in the briefest and most generic manner possible. It was evidently left to those upon whom the administration of the law devolved to define it more minutely in order that it may be observed in practical life. Hence the following expanded definitions obtained during the second Temple:—(1) All fishes with scales have invariably also fins, but fishes which have fins have not always scales. Any fish, therefore, or even a piece of one exposed by itself for sale in the market, which exhibits scales may be eaten, for it is to be taken for granted that it had fins, or that the fins cannot be seen because of their extraordinary smallness. But, on the other hand, a fish with fins may exist without scales, and hence is unclean; (2) Clean fishes have a complete vertebral column, but the unclean have simply single joints, united by a gelatinous cord. To the former class belong, (*a*) "the soft fins," or the salmon and trout, the capellan and grayling, the herring, the anchovy and the sardine, the pike and carp families, the cod, the hake and the haddock, the sole, the turbot, and the plaice; (*b*) "the spiny fins," as the perch, the mackerel, and the tunny. To the latter class belong the shark tribe, the sturgeons with their caviare, the lamprey, and the nine-eyed eel; (3) The head of clean fishes is more or less broad, whilst that of the unclean kinds is more or less pointed at the end, as the eel, the mammalian species, &c.; (4) The swimming bladder of clean fishes is rounded at one end, and pointed at the other, whilst that of the unclean fishes is either rounded or pointed at both extremities alike. It is in allusion to this law that we are told in the parable of the fisherman, which is taken from Jewish life, that when they drew to shore the net with every kind of fishes, the fishermen sat down (*i.e.,* to examine the clean and the unclean), and gathered the good (*i.e.,* the clean), into the vessels, but cast the bad (*i.e.,* the unclean) away (Matt. xiii. 48). The orthodox Jews to this day strictly observe these regulations, and abhor eating those fishes which are enumerated under the four above-named criteria of not clean. It is moreover to be remarked that fishes without scales are also still regarded in Egypt as unwholesome, and that the Romans would not permit them to be offered in sacrifice.

(10) **Of all that move in the waters.**—That is, apart from the fishes exhibiting the above-named signs, all other inhabitants of the water are forbidden. Hence all shell-fish, whether molluscs or crustaceans, and cetaceous animals, are unclean.

(13) **Ye shall have in abomination among the fowls.**—The third of the four great divisions of the animal kingdom—viz., the birds of the air, in accordance with their proper sequence—is discussed in verses 13—19. It will be seen that, whilst in the case of the two preceding divisions of the animal kingdom certain signs are given by which to distinguish the clean from the unclean animals, in the division before us a list is simply given of the birds which are unclean and prohibited. This absence of all criteria is all the more remarkable, since after some of the birds mentioned it is added "after his kind," or "after her kind" (see verses 14—16, 19), thus showing that kindred species were included in the prohibition, and that it was left to those who had to administer this law, to lay down some general signs by which the proscribed species are to be known. Hence the following rules obtained during the second Temple. Those birds are unclean (1) which snatch their food in the air, and devour it without first dropping it on the ground; (2) which strike with their talons and press down with their foot the prey to the ground, and then tear off pieces with their beak for consumption; (3) which "divide their feet" when standing on an extended rope or branch, placing two toes on the one side and two on the other, and not three in front and one behind; and (4) whose eggs are equally narrow or equally round at both ends, and have the white in the middle and the yolk around it.

abomination: the eagle, and the ossifrage, and the ospray, (14) and the vulture, and the kite after his kind; (15) every raven after his kind; (16) and the owl, and the night hawk, and the cuckow, and the hawk after his kind,

The eagle.—As the king of the birds, the eagle stands first in the list. It denotes here all the species of the eagle proper. Arabian writers, scientific travellers, and the most distinguished naturalists, concur in their testimony that the eagle eats carrion when it is still fresh, thus harmonizing with the description in Job xxxix. 10; Prov. xxx. 17; Matt. xxiv. 28, &c. The assertion, therefore, that the bird here meant is the Egyptian vulture, because the eagle disdains dead bodies and feeds only on what it kills itself, is erroneous. Besides the kindred dialects, all the ancient versions and the best Hebrew scholars place it beyond a doubt that *Nesher* here denotes eagle. Afterwards, however, the carrion-kite and the golden vulture were also reckoned among the different species of eagles. Hence the allusion in Micah i. 16.

The ossifrage.—That is, the bone-breaker, or simply *the breaker*, is the literal translation of the expression here used in the original, which only occurs again in the parallel passage in Deut. xiv. 12. It is most probably the bearded griffin or *lammergeier*, which unites in itself the eagle and the vulture, and is therefore aptly called *gypaëtus* or vulture-eagle, and appropriately stands in the list here between the eagle and the vulture. The fitness of its name may be seen from its habits. It takes the bones of animals, which other birds of prey have denuded of the flesh, up into the air and then lets them fall upon a well-selected projecting rock, and thus literally breaks them in order to get at their marrow, or to render the fragments of the bones more digestible.

And the ospray, or sea-eagle. It is about the size of the golden-eagle, and preys principally upon fish, but also occasionally on birds and other animals, and when its extreme voracity is not satisfied, will devour the most putrid carrion. Hence its place in the catalogue of unclean birds. The word only occurs again in the parallel passage, Deut. xiv. 12.

(14) **And the vulture.**—Rather, *the kite.* Its name in the original (*dââh*), which literally denotes *the swift, majestic and gliding flier*, appropriately describes this bird, which sails with its expanded wings through the air, where it often pauses as if suspended, watching for its prey. Kites are very plentiful in Syria, and are frequently seen hovering over the plains, the villages, and the outskirts of towns, and looking out for garbage and offal, and hence are often seen in company with the vulture at their useful task of devouring the carrion. Their gregarious habits are referred to by Isaiah (xxxiv. 15), where they are mentioned in company with other raptatores as suitable inhabitants of devastated Edom. The kite is used by different Eastern tribes as food.

And the kite.—Rather, *the falcon.* "The greedy one" (*ayah*), as it is called in the original, fitly describes this most sagacious, sanguinary, and rapacious robber. Its piercing sight is referred to by Job (xxviii. 7), where it is translated *vulture* in the Authorised Version, though in the passage before us and in the parallel passage in Deut. xiv. 13, it is rendered *kite.* It exists in Syria in a great variety of species, for which reason the text adds "after his kind." The falcon is eaten in the Levant, and is considered rather delicate.

(15) **And every raven.**—The raven or the blackbird (Song of Songs v. 11), the bird of the night, as its name denotes in Heb., like the eagle, occurs frequently in the Bible. It preys upon putrid corpses (Prov. xxx. 17), and is especially eager to pick out the eyes of the dead, and sometimes even attacks the eyes of the living. So great is its gluttony that it fills the air with its wild shrieks when searching for food (Ps. cxlvii. 9; Job xxxviii. 41). Its rapacity makes the raven expel its own offspring from their nest and from the surrounding places as soon as they are able to fly, and before they are quite able to procure their own food. Indeed, the ancients believed that it forsook its young immediately after they were hatched. It was in consequence of their excessive greed and known aversion to part with anything, even for their own offspring, that the ravens were chosen to carry food to the prophet (1 Kings xvii. 4, 6), thus to make the miracle all the more striking. The phrase, "every raven after his kind," clearly shows that the whole genus of ravens is intended, with all the raven-like birds, such as the rook, the crow, the jackdaw, the jay, &c., which abound in Syria and Palestine.

(16) **And the owl.**—Better, *and the ostrich*, as the Authorised Version rightly renders it in the margin in three out of the eight passages in which it occurs, viz., Job xxx. 29, Isa. xxxiv. 13, xliii. 20; literally, *the daughter* or *inhabitant of the desert.* The ostrich, which is the largest bird and the swiftest of all cursorial animals, was associated by the Hebrews with the terrors of the wilderness, and was regarded by the ancients as an unnatural hybrid, as a kind of half bird and half quadruped. It dwells amongst desolated places (Isa. xiii. 21, xxxiv. 13; Jerem. l. 39), fills the air with its doleful and hideous wails (Micah i. 8) and cruelly neglects its eggs to be hatched by the sun or trodden down under foot (Lam. iv. 3; Job xxxix. 17, 18). Owing to its proverbial stupidity, this hybrid is selected with another monster to illustrate the abundant goodness of the Lord, by showing that even this creature will become sensible of gratitude and break forth into thanksgiving and praise (Isa. xliii. 20). The flesh of the ostrich was eaten by the ancient Ethiopians, Indians, and other nations. The Romans regarded ostrich brains as a great delicacy. The ostrich occasionally devours fowls and other small vertebrates like a bird of prey, and tradition assures us that ostriches consumed the body of Agag.

And the night hawk.—Of all the unclean birds constituting this list, the one here rendered night hawk is the most difficult to identify. The name in the original (*tachmâs*) simply describes the bird as "the violent" one, or the rapacious, or "the cruel," and this designation would apply to any bird of prey not already specified in this catalogue. Hence it has alternately been taken for the owl, the night hawk, the male ostrich, the falcon, the seabird gannet, the cuckoo, and the swallow. It will, however, be seen that all the large birds of prey which are here hazarded, have either already been mentioned or are mentioned in the sequel of this list, whilst the small birds, viz., the cuckoo and the swallow, are too insignificant and too harmless to be placed between the large raptorial companions. In this uncertainty of opinion it is best to leave the Authorised Version alone. The name only occurs again in the parallel passage in Deut. xiv. 15.

And the cuckow.—Rather, *and the sea-gull.* Like the foregoing bird of prey, the *shachaph* here

(17) and the little owl, and the cormorant, | and the great owl, (18) and the swan,

mentioned only occurs again in the duplicate list of unclean animals in Deut. xiv. 15. It literally means the *thin, slender,* or *cadaverous* bird, and is taken by the most ancient authorities to denote the sea-gull, which is "the raven of the sea." It darts down with great velocity upon its victim, like a bird of prey. It not only eats fishes, insects, and smaller aquatic animals, but feeds upon carrion. The eggs of the gulls and the flesh of the young birds are to this day eaten both in the East and in some northern countries of Europe.

And the hawk.—Besides the parallel passage in Deut. xiv. 15, the hawk (*netz*) also occurs in Job xxxix. 26, where it is described as a migratory bird, since it migrates to a more southern climate on the approach of winter. It feeds upon mammals, birds, and amphibia, and attacks even its own parent, mate, and offspring. It abounds in a variety of species in all parts of Asia. Hence the remark "after his kind." Some tribes regard the flesh of the hawk as very palatable.

(17) **And the little owl.**—With the exception of the parallel passage, Deut. xiv. 16, this bird only occurs once more, in Ps. cii. 6, where it is properly rendered in the Authorised Version by "owl," omitting the word "little," and is described as inhabiting deserted ruins. It not only feeds upon insects and molluscs, hares, rabbits, ducks, geese, and birds of prey, but devours mice and rats, which are especially detested by the Jews. Its flesh is, however, regarded by some tribes as very savoury. The name *kos* which is translated "owl" in the three above-named passages, is the common Hebrew word for "cup," and it is supposed that it has been given to this bird because the sitting owl especially widens towards the upper part, thus imparting to it a cup-like appearance.

And the cormorant.—Of all the web-footed birds which prey on fish, cormorants are the most voracious. They usually assemble in flocks on the rocks which overhang the sea, whence they drop down from the greatest height upon their victim, dive after it with the rapidity of a dart, and invariably gulp their prey head foremost. The cormorant is to be found in every climate, and is the destruction of all the finny tribe in any fresh-water river which he happens to occupy for a time. Hence he is called the feathered terror of the finny tribe. From the skill which he displays in casting himself down from a great height, and in plunging dart-like after his victim, he derives his Hebrew name, which denotes "darter." The flesh of the cormorant, though rank, is eaten in some regions; whilst the skin, which is tough, is made into garments. The Hebrew name only occurs again in the duplicate catalogue of unclean animals in Deut. xiv. 17. By comp. verses 17, 18 of the list before us with the parallel list in Deut. xiv. 16, 17, it will be seen that though the two catalogues respectively enumerate in these two verses the same six birds, yet the order is different. The cormorant, which is here second in verse 17, is in Deut. xiv. sixth in verse 17. There can, therefore, hardly be any doubt that the verse before us has been disturbed, and that by placing the cormorant here sixth, as it is in Deuteronomy, we obtain the two species of owls naturally following each other, as is the case in the parallel catalogue.

And the great owl.—Rather, *the night owl,* as the name in the original (*yanshûph*) denotes "night-bird." Besides the parallel passage in Deut. xiv. 16, this bird of prey only occurs again once more in Isa. xxxiv. 11, where the Authorised Version translates simply "owl," omitting the word "great," and where it is associated with the raven and other dismal birds as fit occupants of deserted ruins. According to the description of it which prevailed in the time of Christ, its eyes are directed forward, it utters frightful shrieks in the night, and has a face like a cat, and cheeks like a human being. In consequence of its repulsive visage and human appearance it was considered a bad omen if one saw an owl in a dream. That the two kinds of owls are here mentioned is probably owing to their disgusting habit of ejecting pellets, each one of which contains sometimes from four to seven skeletons of mice. Hence, instead of saying "after his kind," to include the other varieties, the lawgiver enumerates them separately.

(18) **And the swan.**—The word here translated "swan," which, besides the parallel list in Deut., also occurs in verse 30, among the names of the lizards, denotes, according to tradition, another variety of the owl. Whatever difficulty there may be about the true import of the word, it is certainly not the swan. It has, however, also been translated "ibis," "bat," "purple water-hen," "heron," "pelican," and "goose."

And the pelican.—The pelican is one of the largest and most voracious of the web-footed birds. It fills its capacious pouch with fish almost to suffocation, which it disgorges either for its own future consumption, or for the nourishment of its young, by pressing the under mandible against the neck and breast to assist the vomiting up of the contents. Hence its Hebrew name, which denotes "the vomiter." During this operation the red nail of the upper mandible comes in contact with the breast, thus imparting to it the appearance of blood, which is most probably the origin of the fable that it feeds its young with its own life-blood. The pelican often builds in deserted places as far as twenty miles from the shore. When it has filled its expansive pouch with prey, it retires to its lonely place of repose, where it remains with its head leaning against its breast almost motionless till impelled by hunger to fly to the water in search for a fresh store of victims. It is to this melancholy attitude of lonely desolation that the Psalmist refers when he says, "I am like a pelican of the wilderness" (Ps. cii. 6), and it is to its habit of building in deserted places that the prophets allude when they describe the desolation of Edom and Nineveh by saying that "the pelican shall possess" them (Isa. xxxiv. 11; Zeph. ii. 14). In the last two passages the Authorised Version, which wrongly translates it "cormorant" in the text, has rightly pelican in the margin.

And the gier eagle.—As the name of a bird, this word (*racham*), which is here in the masculine form, and denotes "the merciful," only occurs again in the parallel passage, Deut. xiv. 17, where, however, it is in the feminine (*rachamah*). The species here intended is most probably the Gyps, called alternately the sacred or Egyptian vulture and Pharaoh's hen, which is often figured on the ancient Egyptian monuments. It was regarded with religious veneration in Egypt, both because it prevented epidemics by acting as scavenger, and because of its extreme devotion and tenderness to its young, since it was believed to watch over its offspring

and the pelican, and the gier eagle,
(19) and the stork, the heron after her
kind, and the lapwing, and the bat.
(20) All fowls that creep, going

a hundred and twenty days every year, and to feed them, if necessary, with the blood of its thighs. Hence it was used to denote both "mother" and "merciful" in Egyptian, and hence, too, its name "merciful" in Hebrew. The ancients also believed that there were no male vultures, and that the females conceived through the wind. It was probably to counteract this superstitious belief that the lawgiver uses here the masculine form and the feminine form in the parallel passage in Deut. xiv. 17. The vulture is most loathsome in its habits, and feeds upon the foulest carrion, for which reason it is put in the list of unclean birds.

(19) **And the stork.**—Besides the parallel passage, Deut. xiv. 18, the word (*chasidah*) here rendered "stork" also occurs in Job xxxix. 13; Ps. civ. 17; Jer. viii. 7; Zech. v. 9, and is so translated, except Job xxxix. 13, where the Authorised Version has "wing" in the text and "stork" in the margin. Its name literally denotes in Hebrew "the pious," "the kind," and is so called because the ancients regarded it as a type of maternal and filial affection and tenderness. The mother has been known to prefer perishing with its offspring in the flames rather than desert them when its attempts to rescue them from a fire had failed. The white stork is one of the largest land birds. Its black and powerful wings strikingly contrast with the pure white of its plumage. Hence the remark "they had wings like the wings of the stork" (Zech. v. 9). The storks build on the loftiest towers and most conspicuous ruins, and also on the tops of high trees, where they may be seen to this day by the Sea of Galilee. It is to this that the Psalmist alludes: "as for the stork, the fir-trees are her home" (Ps. civ. 17). To these nests they regularly return at the proper season, which marks them as the most punctual of migratory birds; and it is tc this feature in their nature that the prophet refers: "the stork in heaven knoweth her appointed times" (Jer. viii. 7). The stork feeds on fish, reptiles, and all kinds of offal and garbage, for which reason it is here placed in the list of unclean birds.

The heron.—Whilst the two preceding birds are named after their good qualities, viz., "the merciful" and "the pious," this bird, which only occurs again in the parallel passage in Deut. xiv. 18, is termed (*anaphah*) "the angry," "the cruel," which aptly describes the heron. It is allied to the stork, and is of such a savage nature that it will defend itself with its beak against the dogs after it has had its legs shot and broken. It resides on the banks of rivers and in marshy places, and feeds on fish, frogs, lizards, snails, field-mice, and all sorts of insects, for which reason it is here included in the proscribed list of unclean birds. It exists in a variety of species. Hence the adjunct, "after her kind."

And the lapwing.—Better, *the hoopoe*. This dirty bird, which only occurs again in the parallel list in Deut. xiv. 18, and which according to the ancients builds its nest of human dung, feeds upon offal and garbage. Its loathsome smell during brooding-time, and for weeks after, is perfectly insufferable. Though its flesh, which in the autumn tastes like quail's, is eaten in some places, yet the Mohammedans regard it as proscribed. According to another ancient tradition the bird here meant is "the mountain cock."

And the bat.—The list which opens with the eagle, the king of the birds, fitly concludes with the hybrid bat, the vilest creature, which is between a bird and a mouse, and is appropriately associated in the Bible with the mole as the type of darkness (comp. Isa. ii. 20). From the fact that the air is its home; that like the swallow, which it resembles in mode of flight, it wheels through the air in every direction in search of the crepuscular and nocturnal insects on which it preys; and that it performs the most abrupt and skilful evolutions in its aerial course, the bat was classed among the birds. Bats abound in Syria in a great variety of species. They penetrate into the houses and make the rooms most offensive to live in. Those who have realised the sickening odour of these creatures in the East will readily understand why the loathsome bats are included in the list of unclean birds. Some of the ancient nations ate bats and regarded them as delicious food. Besides being the lowest, the bat is here placed last, because it forms the connecting link between the volatile bipeds and quadrupeds.

(20) **All the fowls that creep.**—Better, *all creeping things which have wings*. The swarming animals or insects, which, as we have seen, constitute the fourth class of the Hebrew division of the animal kingdom, are now discussed in verses 20—23. From the fact that in the following verse several kinds of locusts are exempted, it is evident that the phrase "creeping things which have wings" denotes insects.

Going upon all four.—That is, the insects in question not only fly but also creep. The phrase, however, "upon all four" does not refer to the exact number of feet, but, as in some modern languages, denotes walking with its body in a horizontal position, or near the ground, in contradistinction to the two-legged birds discussed in the foregoing verses. This is the sense which the administrators of the law in the time of Christ attached to the phrase. Hence the Chaldee paraphrase of Jonathan translates it, "And all creeping things which have wings going upon all four, the fly species and the wasp or hornet species and the bee species."

Shall be an abomination unto you.—As the bee species is included among "the creeping things which have wings," some have supposed that bee-honey comes within the unclean things which are here said "shall be an abomination unto you." Hence it is thought that the honey (*dabesh*) which is so frequently mentioned in the Bible as a special feature of the promised land (Exod. iii. 8, 17, xiii. 5, xvi. 14, xxxiii. 3; Lev. xx. 24, *etc.*), and which formed an important article of food among the Hebrews, was not the natural product of the bee, but is either the grape-honey, the *dibs*, which is still prepared in many parts of Syria and Palestine, and is exported in great quantities into Egypt; or the vegetable-honey, the exudation of certain trees and shrubs found in the peninsula of Sinai. Hence, too, it is supposed that the wild honey which Jonathan ate in the wood (1 Sam. xiv. 25), and which was the meat of John the Baptist (Matt. iii. 4), must refer to this vegetable-honey. But though it is true that the canon which obtained during the second Temple was "Whatsoever cometh from unclean creatures is unclean," and that in accordance with this law the milk of unclean quadrupeds and the eggs of unclean birds and fishes were fo bidden, yet the honey of bees was expressly permitted. The adminis-

upon *all* four, *shall be* an abomination
unto you. (21) Yet these may ye eat
of every flying creeping thing that
goeth upon *all* four, which have legs
above their feet, to leap withal upon
the earth; (22) *even* these of them ye
may eat; the locust after his kind, and
the bald locust after his kind, and

trators of the law in the time of Christ accounted for this exemption that it is not the direct produce of the insect itself, but is a preparation from gathered juices of clean herbs. The Chaldee paraphrase of Jonathan therefore adds, after "shall be an abomination unto you," the words, *nevertheless the honey of the bee ye may eat.* John the Baptist therefore acted in perfect obedience to the Law when he ate the honey which the bees deposited in the crevices of the rocks and in the hollow of trees. The prohibition to use honey in meat-offerings is not owing to its being unclean, but to its producing fermentation. (See chap. ii. 11.)

(21) **Of every flying creeping thing.**—Rather, *of all winged creeping things.* Having laid down the general rule that those creatures which creep along upon their feet in the manner of quadrupeds, and which have also wings, must not be eaten, the Lawgiver now mentions those which form an exception.

Which have legs above their feet.—Better, *which have knees above their hinder legs,* that is, those which have the third or hindmost pair of legs much longer and stronger than ordinary insects. Those insects, therefore, in whose hindermost legs the second joint is much larger and stronger, whereby they are enabled to leap *or raise* themselves up with great force and leap a great distance upon the earth, are excepted. These are the locusts. The canonical law which obtained during the second Temple defines more minutely the characteristics of clean locusts. A clean locust we are told has (1) four front feet, (2) four wings, (3) two springing feet, and (4) the wings so long and broad that they cover the greater portion of the back body of the insect. If it possesses these four characteristics it is clean, whether it is with a tail or without it, and whether it has an oblong or round head.

(22) **The locust after his kind.**—Of the four species of locusts here specified as permitted to be eaten, this one called *arbe* is the most frequently mentioned in the Bible. It occurs no less than twenty-four times, and is in four instances wrongly rendered in the Authorised Version by "grasshopper" (Judg. vi. 5, vii. 12; Job xxxix. 20; Jerem. xlvi. 23). It is the locust which constituted the eighth plague of Egypt (Exod. x. 4—19); which is described as committing the terrible ravages (Deut. xxviii. 38; Joel i. 4, ii. 25; Nah. iii. 7); and which swarmed in such innumerable quantities that it became a proverb in the Bible, "like the locusts in multitude" (Judg. vii. 12; Jerem. xlvi. 23). From these characteristics the *arbe* is supposed to be the flying migratory locust. The administrators of the law in the time of Christ described the *arbe* by the name *gubai,* which is the species most commonly eaten, and ordained the following benediction to be recited before eating it: "Blessed be He by whose word everything was created." The locusts which are still eaten by the Jews and other Eastern nations are prepared in different ways. Generally they are thrown alive into a pot of boiling water mixed with salt, and taken out after a few minutes, when the heads, feet, and wings are plucked off, and the trunks are dried in an oven or in the sun on the roofs of houses, and are kept in bags for winter use. They are also broiled or stewed, or fried in butter; or they are mixed with butter and spread on thin cakes of bread. In taste they resemble shrimps or prawns. There are shops in some Eastern towns where they only sell locusts, strung upon cords or by measure. The locusts thus form an antidote to the famine they create by the devastation which they commit. They formed, along with "wild honey," the food of John the Baptist (Matt. iii. 4).

And the bald locust.—This is the only place where *salam,* which is the name in the original, occurs as one of the edible kinds of leaping insects. Any attempt to identify the species is simply conjecture, since all which tradition tells us about it is that this kind of locust "has no tail but has a hump."

The beetle.—Rather, *the hopping locust.* Though it is difficult to identify the exact species, as the name (*chargol*) does not occur again in the Bible, yet it is perfectly certain that a sort of locust is here intended, since the context clearly shows that four different kinds of the same insect are enumerated. This is moreover confirmed by the administrators of the law in the time of Christ, who assure us the *chargol* is a species of locust having both a hump and a tail, the eggs of which Jewish women suspended in the ear as a remedy against ear-ache. This shows that it must have been a very large kind, and as the name denotes *the galloping* or *hopping one,* it is evidently designed to describe an unwinged species.

The grasshopper.—Rather, *the small locust.* This name (*chagab*) occurs four times more in the Bible (Num. xiii. 33; 2 Chron. vii. 13; Eccl. xii. 5; Isa. xl. 22), and is only in one place rightly rendered by *locust* (2 Chron. vii. 13) in the Authorised Version. From the fact that it is described as laying waste the fields (2 Chron. vii. 13), and that its insignificant appearance is contrasted with giant men (Num. xiii. 33) and with the great God of heaven (Isa. xl. 22), it is justly inferred that it denotes a small devastating locust which swarms in great quantities. According to the authorities in the time of Christ, it is a species which has a tail, but no hump. It was so common that the name (*chagab*) became a generic term for many of the locust tribe. Some kinds bearing this name were beautifully marked, and were eagerly caught by Jewish children as playthings, just as butterflies and cockchafers are sought after by children in the present day. Others again were caught in large numbers, sprinkled over with wine, and then sold. Hence the following two rules obtained during the second Temple: (1) No Israelite was allowed to buy them after the dealer had prepared them in this manner; and (2) he that vowed to abstain from flesh is not allowed to eat the flesh of fish and of (*chagabim*) locusts. Because the edible kinds of locusts are passed over in the parallel dietary laws in Deuteronomy, some have concluded that the eating of these insects was prohibited at the more advanced time when Deuteronomy was written. The fact, however, that John the Baptist ate locusts, and that a benediction was ordered during the second Temple to be recited at eating them, plainly shows the futility of the assertion. The Lawgiver never intended to repeat in Deuteronomy every particular point of legislation.

the beetle after his kind, and the
grasshopper after his kind. (23) But
all *other* flying creeping things, which
have four feet, *shall be* an abomination
unto you. (24) And for these ye shall
be unclean: whosoever toucheth the
carcase of them shall be unclean un-
til the even. (25) And whosoever beareth
ought of the carcase of them shall
wash his clothes, and be unclean un-
til the even.

(26) *The carcases* of every beast which
divideth the hoof, and *is* not cloven-
footed, nor cheweth the cud, *are* un-
clean unto you: every one that toucheth
them shall be unclean. (27) And what-
soever goeth upon his paws, among
all manner of beasts that go on *all*
four, those *are* unclean unto you:
whoso toucheth their carcase shall be
unclean until the even. (28) And he
that beareth the carcase of them shall
wash his clothes, and be unclean
until the even: they *are* unclean unto
you.

(29) These also *shall be* unclean unto
you among the creeping things that
creep upon the earth; the weasel, and

---

(23) **But all other flying creeping things.**—Better, *but all other winged creeping things.* Besides the above-named four species and their kindreds, all other locusts, as well as insects of any kind, are to be abhorred as food.

(24) **And for these ye shall be unclean.**—Rather, *and by these ye shall be defiled,* that is, the beasts and animals specified in verses 26 and 27.

Shall be unclean until the even.—For coming in contact with the dead body of the animals contracts defilement for the rest of the day, and till the beginning of a new day, which took place after sunset (comp. chap. xxiii. 32). During these hours of legal uncleanness he was not allowed to enter the sanctuary, touch any sacred thing, or have intercourse with those who were legally clean, since contact with one who has contracted legal defilement imparted defilement to both persons and things.

(25) **And whosoever beareth.**—But he who removed the carcase out of the camp or city, or from one place to another, not only contracted defilement for the rest of the day, but had to wash the clothes which he had on, since the pollution by carrying is greater than that by touching. During the time of the second Temple, the administrators of the law declared that wherever the Law enjoins that a man should "wash his clothes" because of the legal defilement which he contracted, it included the command of bathing the body, and that it was only omitted here and in verses 28 and 40 for the sake of brevity. The Samaritan text and some Hebrew manuscripts have actually the whole phrase "and wash his clothes and bathe himself in water," as in chap. xvii. 15 and Num. xix. 19. In allusion to this we are told that those who contracted pollution, and have come out of the great tribulation, "washed their robes and made them white in the blood of the Lamb" (Rev. vii. 14).

Ought of the carcase.—The uncleanness was contracted by not only carrying away the whole carcase, but by removing any portion of it. (See verse 32.) The expression *ought* is represented in the original, and is rightly printed in the ordinary type of the text in the Authorised Version of 1611. The printing it in italics is an unauthorised innovation, though it is followed in the *Speaker's Commentary,* which professes to give the text of 1611.

(26) **The carcases of every beast.**—The construction of this text constituted one of the differences between the Pharisees and the Sadducees during the second Temple. According to the Pharisees, or the National Church in the time of Christ, the phrase "that toucheth *them*" in the last part of this verse refers to "the carcases" of the unclean animals spoken of in the preceding verse. It was only when an unclean animal was dead, whether death was owing to natural causes, design, or accident, that contact with its body defiled (see verses 8, 31); but when alive, unclean animals were freely used. Hence camels, asses, horses, &c., were employed in daily life, though unclean (1 Chron. xii. 40; Zech. xiv. 15; Matt. xxi. 2; Luke xiii. 15, &c.). The Authorised Version rightly expresses this sense by inserting "the carcases" in italics at the beginning of the verse, thus showing that "them" in the latter part of the verse refers to the bodies of unclean animals when dead. Indeed some MSS. have actually "that toucheth their carcases," instead of "that toucheth them." The Sadducees, however, took the expression "them" to refer to the living unclean animals, and hence maintained that touching the body of any animal described in this dietary list as unclean defiled. The difference which this interpretation of the text produced in the domestic life and social intercourse of the Jews can hardly be described, since, according to the doctrine of the Sadducees, it was exceedingly difficult to remain undefiled as soon as one of them stepped outside their dwellings.

(27) **And whatsoever goeth upon his paws.**—Rather, *and whatsoever goeth upon his palms,* that is, those animals whose feet are not divided into two parts, but which have feet with fingers like a hand, such as the lion, the bear, the ape, the wolf, the cat, &c.

(28) **And he that beareth.**—This is simply a resumption of verse 25.

(29) **These also shall be unclean.**—Better, *And these shall be the most unclean.* As verses 24—28 have been occupied with the discussion of the defilement caused by the carcases of unclean quadrupeds, which, as we have seen, belong to the first class of the animal kingdom, the Lawgiver now enumerates those "creeping things" of the fourth class, which likewise cause defilement by touching them. The eight animals here adduced (verses 29, 30) are therefore a continuation of the things that go on their belly, mentioned in verses 20—23. They only differ in this respect, that in verses 20—23 the creeping things have also wings, whilst those described here are creeping things without wings. In a stricter sense, however, verse 29, &c., is a resumption of verse 20.

The weasel.—Though the Hebrew name (*choled*), which literally denotes "the gliding" or "slipping in" animal, does not occur again in the Bible, yet the ancient versions and the description given of it by the ad-

the mouse, and the tortoise after his | kind, (30) and the ferret, and the cha-

ministrators of the law in the time of Christ place it beyond a doubt that it is meant for weasel. According to these authorities the animal in question lodges in the holes of walls and in ditches, is inordinately voracious, kills other animals of prey much bigger than itself, and carries them off in its mouth. It is especially obnoxious to poultry, for which reason the ventilating holes in hen-roosts are made so small that it should not be able to get through them; it has pointed and crooked teeth, with which it pierces through the skull and brain of the hens; it attacks sleeping children and human corpses, and laps water from a vessel. It delights in pilfering bright objects, which it hides in holes. It will be seen that this description given by the administrators of the law during the second Temple, of the animal meant by *choled* can only apply to the weasel, and not to the mole. This is fully supported by the ancient versions, though the word denotes "mole" in Arabic, and is sometimes also used in this sense in the Talmud.

And the mouse.—Besides this passage, this word (*achbar*), which is taken to denote "the field," or "corn-destroyer," also occurs four times in Samuel (1 Sam. vi. 4, 5, 11, 18), and once in Isaiah (chap. lxvi. 17) and is uniformly translated "mouse." That this is the true rendering is fully confirmed by the ancient versions and the administrators of the law during the second Temple. Their insatiable voracity and great fecundity make mice destroy the entire produce of a harvest in an incredibly short time. For this reason they became the symbol of destruction in the Egyptian hieroglyphics, and obtained the appellation, "the scourge of the field" in the Bible (1 Sam. vi. 5). So great was the injury which they inflicted upon the fields in Palestine, that during the second Temple the administrators of the law permitted the Jews to destroy them by any means, even on the middle days of the two great pilgrimage festivals, the Feasts of Passover and of Tabernacles. The mischievous instinct which they have of gnawing at things which they cannot eat, and of penetrating into the sanctuary, and destroying the sacred food and scriptures, made mice peculiarly repulsive to the Jews, who gave them the appellation of "wicked mice," a name with which they brand any malicious and wicked person to this day.

And the tortoise.—This creature (*tzâb*), which literally denotes "the swollen," "the inflated" (see Num. v. 27), occurs nowhere else in the Bible. That it is not the tortoise is perfectly certain, since this animal, according to the highest legal authority, was not unclean. Thus Maimonides tells us "only those animals mentioned in the Law (Levit. xi. 29, 30) are defiling, but not the serpent, the frog, and the tortoise." It is certain that the authorities in the time of Christ took it to denote the toad. This is evident from the discussion as to the condition of the man who has touched an animal, and cannot decide whether it is a frog, which is not defiling, or a *tzâb*, which is defiling. As it is the toad, and not the tortoise or lizard, which has such a misleading resemblance to the frog, there can hardly be any doubt that the administrators of the law understood the reptile here to denote the toad. This agrees with the meaning of the name, which, as we have seen, denotes the "swollen one," and which is one of the peculiar characteristics distinguishing it from the frog, by its having a thick, squat, and more swollen body. The reason why the toad and not the frog is put into the defiling list of reptiles is probably owing to the fact that its shorter legs impart to it more the appearance of a creeping thing, and that it was believed that the limpid fluid which this reptile suddenly discharges when touched is poisonous. Some ancient versions, however, translate it "the land crocodile."

(30) **And the ferret.**—The ancient legal authorities explain this name (*anâkâh*), which only occurs here in the Hebrew Scriptures, by *kipôr* or *kipôd*, "an animal whose body is entirely covered with sharp prickles, and when touched the creature draws in its legs and rolls itself up in a ball." Its skin in ancient days was tied round the udder of cows to prevent other reptiles sucking out their milk. There can, therefore, be no doubt that the administrators of the law took it to be the hedgehog. Some ancient versions, however, render it by shrew mouse, whilst some modern expositors make it the gecko.

And the chameleon.—The ancient versions agree that by this animal (*khôach*), which denotes "strength," and which occurs nowhere else in the Bible as the name of a reptile, is meant the chameleon. Its power of enduring for a long time without food, which led the ancients to believe that it entirely subsisted upon air, may be the cause both of its Hebrew name (as specified above), and the name chameleon, *i.e.*, "a lion on the ground," a reptile with the strength of a lion, The belief that it lives upon the air had also given rise to its Aramaic name in the time of Christ (*zekitha*), which denotes the animal that fills itself with air. The perplexity which the administrators of the law experienced about its food, and the time of feeding this creature, may be gathered from the story in the Talmud attributed to one of the sons of Noah, of what happened in the Ark. Sem, the son of Noah, said, "We had much trouble with the chameleon, for whilst we fed the day animals by day and the night animals by night, we did not know what the chameleon fed on. One day, however, I broke open a pomegranate, and a worm fell out of it, which the creature immediately devoured. Afterwards I pounded together fruit, and when it bred maggots the chameleon ate them." The common chameleon is found in Syria and Palestine, and some eastern tribes believe that its flesh when eaten boiled is a remedy for leanness, and if eaten dry cures fever. In Spain chameleons are kept in rooms to destroy troublesome flies.

And the lizard.—Though the ancient authorities agree that the creature here named (*l'tââh*) is lizard, yet the description which the administrators of the law give of it, does not enable us to define the species to which it belongs. The characteristics which they give of the lizard are as follows: It has a thick though soft and smooth skin, and lays eggs in which the yolk and the white are not separated. Its tail when cut off will move for some time afterwards, and the creature itself when apparently dead will sometimes revive by pouring cold water over it.

And the snail.—This meaning of the Hebrew name (*chômet*) is attested by the highest Jewish authorities of ancient times. It denotes the testaceous kinds, whilst the word (*shabbel*) in Ps. lviii. 8 describes the naked species. Snails abound in a great variety of species in the East, and some kinds were eaten by the ancients as a great luxury. It was believed that the slime which it constantly emits as it crawls along brings about its death by a process of dissolution. Hence the

meleon, and the lizard, and the snail,
and the mole. (31) These *are* unclean
to you among all that creep: whoso-
ever doth touch them, when they be
dead, shall be unclean until the even.
(32) And upon whatsoever *any* of them,
when they are dead, doth fall, it shall
be unclean; whether *it be* any vessel
of wood, or raiment, or skin, or sack,
whatsoever vessel *it be*, wherein *any*
work is done, it must be put into
water, and it shall be unclean until
the even; so it shall be cleansed.
(33) And every earthen vessel, where-
into *any* of them falleth, whatsoever
is in it shall be unclean; and [a] ye
shall break it. (34) Of all meat which
may be eaten, *that* on which *such*
water cometh shall be unclean: and
all drink that may be drunk in every
such vessel shall be unclean. (35) And
every *thing* whereupon *any part* of
their carcase falleth shall be unclean;
whether it be oven, or ranges for pots,

a ch. 6. 28.

remark "as a snail which melteth, let every one of them pass away" (Ps. lviii. 8).

And the mole.—The word (*tinshemeth*) here translated "mole," is the same which is used in verse 18 for an unclean bird. That the Authorised Version, however, gives the correct rendering of the word is not only attested by the ancient versions, but by the following description, which the administrators of the law in the time of Christ give of the reptile here intended. It has no eyes, and burrows into the earth, and destroys the roots. For this reason, as well as for its carrying quantities of corn to its nest, it was ordained during the second Temple that the creature may be killed on the middle days of the two pilgrim festivals, *i.e.*, of the Feasts of Passover and of Tabernacles. In Isa. ii. 20, however, which is the only other passage where the mole occurs in the Hebrew Scriptures, the name for it is *châpar pêrah*. We have already seen in the case of the snail that two different names for the same creature are used designedly to describe the different characteristics of the same animal.

(31) **These are unclean.**—Better, *these are the most unclean,* as verse 29. That is, the eight animals thus enumerated are pre-eminently unclean of all the creeping things.

When they be dead.—The phrase, "whosoever doth touch them when they be dead," is simply another expression for "whosoever toucheth the carcase of them," which is used in verse 24. Defilement is only contracted when their dead bodies are touched, but not if touched when alive. According to the canon which obtained during the second Temple, "there is no kind of living creature that becomes defiled while it is alive, or defiles when it is alive, save man only."

(32) **And upon whatsoever any of them.**—Better, *and upon whatsoever aught of them,* that is, not only if the whole carcase fell upon any of the specified vessels were the vessels in question defiled, but if a portion of the carcase came in contact with the utensils it made them unclean. (See verse 25.) According to the law which obtained during the second Temple it was only when the portion of the carcase of an unclean animal had flesh on it that it defiled, but not otherwise. Hence the skins, hair, bones, horns, hoofs, sinews, &c. of all unclean creatures were exempted. These were made into different domestic utensils and implements. The use thus made of the parts in question also constituted one of the differences between the Pharisees and the Sadducees in the time of Christ. The Sadducees regarded every portion of every unclean animal in whatever state as defiling, and hence prohibited its being made up into any vessel.

Vessel of wood.—That is, vessels made of bulrushes (Isa. xviii. 2), reeds, wicker, shells of nuts, barks of trees, or of anything which grew out of the earth like wood.

Or raiment.—That is, any garment made of a woven material, such as wool, flax, hemp, or anything which grows on the dry land. Hence cloth made of a material which grows in the sea was not defiled, according to the canons which obtained during the second Temple.

Or skin.—This also, according to the same authorities, only applied to the skins of land animals; skins of aquatic creatures received no defilement.

Or sack.—From the parallel passage in Num. xxxi. 20, we see that by this expression here is meant garments made of stuffs of goats' hair, in contradistinction to the textures of which the garments were made, denoted by the expression *beged,* "raiment." (See also Isa. xx. 2.) Skins which were not made into garments or vessels, or which exhibited unfinished vessels, received no pollution.

(33) **And every earthen vessel.**—The case, however, is different with regard to vessels made of clay and burned in the kiln.

Whereinto any of them falleth.—Better, *whereinto aught of them falleth,* that is, into which any of the aforesaid portion of a defiling carcase falls (see verse 32). Whilst defiled vessels of other materials were made clean by water, earthen vessels, when they became defiled, had to be destroyed (see chap. vi. 28), and their contents were rendered polluted.

(34) **That on which such water cometh.**—Better, *upon which water cometh,* that is, all food which is prepared with water for eating becomes defiled when the carcase of such an unclean reptile falls on it. The same is the case with any beverage which is drank from any kind of vessel; if the said carcase falls into it, it is rendered unclean. According, however, to the canons which obtained during the second Temple, the import of the first part of this verse is that things which constitute man's meat, only then become defiled by the carcase in question when any water whatsoever has been poured upon them, though these articles of food have afterwards become dry; but when they have not been moistened they do not become defiled. By water these authorities understand any of the following seven liquids:—water, dew, oil, wine, milk, blood, and honey.

(35) **And every thing.**—That is, not only the above-named garments and utensils become defiled by the said carcases, or any portion of them, falling on them, but also everything else is subject to the same pollution.

Oven, as the context shows, is an earthen vessel or baking-pot for making thin unleavened cakes, which, according to the ancient description of it, was wide at the bottom and narrow at the top, so formed to keep the heat in longer. (See chap. ii. 4.)

they shall be broken down: *for* they
are unclean, and shall be unclean un-
to you. (36) Nevertheless a fountain or
pit, [1] *wherein there is* plenty of water,
shall be clean: but that which toucheth
their carcase shall be unclean. (37) And
if *any part* of their carcase fall upon
any sowing seed which is to be sown,
it *shall be* clean. (38) But if *any* water
be put upon the seed, and *any part*
of their carcase fall thereon, it *shall*
be unclean unto you.

[1] Heb., *a gathering together of waters.*

(39) And if any beast, of which ye
may eat, die; he that toucheth the
carcase thereof shall be unclean until
the even. (40) And he that eateth of
the carcase of it shall wash his clothes,
and be unclean until the even: he also
that beareth the carcase of it shall
wash his clothes, and be unclean until
the even.

(41) And every creeping thing that
creepeth upon the earth *shall be* an
abomination; it shall not be eaten.

Or ranges for pots.—According to the same ancient authorities this kind of oven was oblong, and was so made that two pots should be placed upon it, and that the fire should burn under both of them. Hence the rendering of the Authorised Version, "Ranges for pots." This name, however, does not occur again in the Hebrew Scriptures.

They shall be broken down.—Because earthen vessels could not be made clean by washing. (See chap. vi. 28.)

(36) **Nevertheless a fountain or pit, wherein there is plenty of water.**—Better, *But wells and cisterns being gatherings together of water.* But if the unclean carcase, or any portion of it, happens to fall or to be thrown into wells or cisterns, they are to be treated as large collections of water, such as pools, ponds, and lakes, and hence are exempt from contracting pollution. The constant change of water which takes place in these reservoirs counteracts the effects of the polluting carcase. When it is borne in mind how few are the wells and cisterns in the East, and how scarce water is, the merciful provision of this law will be apparent. According to the canon which obtained during the second Temple, this immunity was only applicable to receptacles of water actually in the ground, but not to collections of water in vessels.

But that which toucheth.—Better, *but he who toucheth.* But though the water into which the carcase has fallen is mercifully exempted, he who comes in contact with the carcase in the water and removes it from the water is unclean, because the carcase itself remains a source of defilement.

(37) **And if any part of their carcase.**—The principle which underlies the immunity from pollution of living water is also at the basis of the exception of living plants. Hence if the carcase or a portion of a dead reptile is found among grain destined for sowing, the quantity of wheat in which it is discovered does not become defiled, since the growing plant constantly derives new elements from below and fresh moisture from above, thus undergoing as many changes in its way as spring water. The law therefore which obtained during the second Temple was as follows:—"Whatever is fixed in the ground does not contract defilement. Plants are not defiled till they are gathered." Hence the ancient Chaldee version of Jonathan renders this verse: "If any part of their carcase falleth upon any seed that is sown in the manner in which it is commonly sown—that is, in its dry state—it is clean."

(38) **But if any water be put upon the seed.**—The case, however, is different when the grain is moistened, because the fluid softens the corn, and thus enables the defilement of the carcase to penetrate into its very fibres. The wet corn therefore is regarded in the same light as porous clay vessels which become saturated with defilement, and must be broken. (Comp. chap. vi. 28.) By water, according to the rule which obtained during the second Temple, the seven liquids mentioned in verse 34 are meant.

(39) **And if any beast.**—That is, a clean animal, which is both bisulcous and ruminant, but which has not been properly slaughtered, having died from any disease or accident. During the second Temple, the law here enacted was restricted to quadrupeds, domestic or wild, but was not applicable to birds and fishes.

He that toucheth the carcase.—The carcase, in this case, is to be regarded as the dead body of an unclean animal (see verses 24—28), and defiles by contact. (See also chap. xvii. 15.) This, however, only applies to the flesh of the quadruped. The skin, the bones, the sinews, the horns, and the claws are clean, the sacred Scriptures even being written on the prepared skins; and the horns used for the trumpets or horns of the sanctuary, according to the canons of the Pharisees, whilst the Samaritans and the Sadducees regarded them as polluting.

(40) **And he that eateth.**—That is, ignorantly, since for wilful transgression the transgressor incurred the penalty of excision. (See Num. xv. 30; Deut. xiv. 21.)

He also that beareth the carcase.—Removing the carcase of a clean quadruped which died, defiled the person who carried it quite as much as removing the carcase of an unclean beast. Hence the law of purification for the defilement arising in either case is the same. (See verse 25.)

(41) **And every creeping thing.**—Besides the eight reptiles which defile by touching their carcase, and which are enumerated in verses 29, 30, all other creeping things upon the earth, with the exception of those specified in verses 21, 22, are to be treated as an abomination, and must not be eaten, though their carcases do not defile by coming in contact with them. From the fact that the creeping things here proscribed are expressly described as "creeping upon the earth," the administrators of the law during the second Temple concluded that the small worms which do not creep upon the earth do not come within the operation of this prohibition. Hence worms bred in vegetables, fruit, and certain kinds of food are permitted. Thus the worms in figs, dates, and berries, the mites in peas, beans, and lentils, the maggots in cheese, the insects found in the flesh and under the skin of fishes, are not proscribed, and only when they quit the object wherein they have been generated, and creep about upon the ground, are they forbidden. Hence the Chaldee Version of Jonathan renders the passage "and every creeping thing that flieth is unclean unto you" (Deut. xiv. 19)

(42) Whatsoever goeth upon the belly,
and whatsoever goeth upon *all* four,
or whatsoever [1]hath more feet among
all creeping things that creep upon
the earth, them ye shall not eat; for
they *are* an abomination. (43) Ye shall
not make your [2]selves abominable
with any creeping thing that creepeth,
neither shall ye make yourselves un-
clean with them, that ye should be
defiled thereby. (44) For I *am* the
LORD your God: ye shall therefore
sanctify yourselves, and [a]ye shall be
holy; for I *am* holy: neither shall ye
defile yourselves with any manner of
creeping thing that creepeth upon the
earth. (45) For I *am* the LORD that
bringeth you up out of the land of
Egypt, to be your God: ye shall there-
fore be holy, for I *am* holy.
(46) This *is* the law of the beasts,
and of the fowl, and of every living
creature that moveth in the waters,
and of every creature that creepeth
upon the earth: (47) to make a differ-
ence between the unclean and the clean,
and between the beast that may be eaten
and the beast that may not be eaten.

1 Heb., *doth multiply feet.*

2 Heb., *souls.*

a ch. 19. 2 & 20. 7; 1 Pet. 1. 15.

CHAPTER XII.— (1) And the LORD

---

by "and all bees and wasps, and all worms of vegetables and of pulse which leave the objects of food and fly like birds, are unclean unto you."

(42) **Whatsoever goeth upon the belly.**—In explanation of the general statement made in the preceding verse, three classes of creeping things are here adduced. (1) Those which move by the aid of the under part of the stomach, here described as "going upon the belly," as serpents (see Gen. iii. 14) and serpentine worms.

And whatsoever goeth upon all four.—Those (2) which have four legs and yet move like reptiles, as scorpions, beetles, &c.

Or whatsoever hath more feet.—Better, *whatsoever hath many feet,* that is (3), those which have a number of such short feet that they cannot easily be discerned by the naked eye, and appear to crawl about upon their stomachs, as caterpillars, centipedes, millepedes, &c.

(43) **Ye shall not make your selves abominable.**—By eating the unclean creatures which are constantly characterised in this book as "abominable" (see chaps. vii. 21, xi. 10—13, 20, 23, 41, 42)—a term which only occurs twice more in the Hebrew Scriptures (Isa. lxvi. 17; Ezek. viii. 10)—those who do so render themselves abominable and repulsive; hence the admonition. The phrase only occurs once more, viz., chap. xx. 25, where it is translated in the Authorised Version, "Ye shall not make your souls abominable." This is the reason why "soul" is put here in the margin on the word "selves."

Neither shall ye make yourselves unclean.—But not only is it disgusting to eat these abominable creatures, but their carcases defile and debar him who comes in contact with them from entering into the sanctuary and from partaking of the sacrificial meal.

(44) **For I am the Lord your God.**—As the Lord who is their God is Himself holy, His people, in order to enjoy perfect communion with Him, must also be holy. Hence they must abstain from all these objects of defilement which mar that holy communion. Appealing to this declaration, the Apostle Paul uses the same admonition: "As he which hath called you is holy so be ye holy in all manner of conversation, because it is written, Be ye holy, for I am holy" (1 Peter i. 15, 16).

Ye shall therefore sanctify yourselves, and ye shall be holy.—Better, *Sanctify yourselves therefore, and be ye holy,* as the Authorised Version renders exactly the same phrase in chap. xx. 6.

(45) **That bringeth you up out of the land of Egypt.**—Having in a marvellous way delivered them from the land of bondage to be their God in a peculiar sense (comp. 2 Sam. vii. 23), the Holy One of Israel had a special claim upon His redeemed people that they should obey His laws and keep themselves holy as their Redeemer. This signal act of redemption is repeatedly appealed to in the Scriptures, both to show the obligations which the Israelites are under to obey God's commandments and to expose their ingratitude (Deut. viii. 14, xiii. 6, xx. 1; Josh. xxiv. 17; Judges ii. 12, &c.).

(46) **This is the law of the beasts.**—This is a recapitulation of the different classes of animals proscribed in the dietary laws. It will, however, be seen that in this summary they are not enumerated in the same order in which they are discussed in the chapter before us. In the dietary law the order of the four classes is as follows:—(1) the land animals, (2) the water animals, (3) the birds of the air, and (4) the swarming animals; whilst the order of the summary is:—(1) the land animals, (2) the birds of the air, (3) the water animals, and (4) the swarming animals. Exactly the same is the case in the summary of the sacrificial law. (See chap. vii. 37, 38.)

(47) **To make a difference.**—Better, *that ye may put difference,* as the Authorised Version renders the same word in chap. x. 10. That is, the design of the dietary law is to enable both the administrators of the law and the people to distinguish, by the characteristics and criteria specified above, between what is clean and unclean.

And between the beast that may be eaten.—From the fact that the same word, "beast," is used in both clauses with regard to the animal which may be eaten and the one which may not be eaten without the qualifying adjunct "clean" and "unclean," the administrators of the law during the second Temple concluded that the same clean animal is meant in both instances, under different conditions. The clean animal may be eaten when it is in a healthy state, but the same animal may not be eaten when it has organic defects, or is diseased. Hence they enacted the following canon: an animal is perfectly sound when it is capable of conceiving and bringing forth young. This is the reason why the LXX. renders the word beast here by *viviparous.*

XII.

(1) **And the Lord spake unto Moses.**—As the reason why God graciously addressed the regulation about the clean and unclean animals to Moses and Aaron conjointly (see chap. xi. 1), no longer operates here, the Lord now addresses the laws of purification to

spake unto Moses, saying, (2) Speak
unto the children of Israel, saying, If
a [a] woman have conceived seed, and
born a man child: then she shall be
unclean seven days; according to the
days of the separation for her infir-
mity shall she be unclean. (3) And in
the [b] eighth day the flesh of his fore-
skin shall be circumcised. (4) And she
shall then continue in the blood of
her purifying three and thirty days;
she shall touch no hallowed thing, nor
come into the sanctuary, until the
days of her purifying be fulfilled.
(5) But if she bear a maid child, then
she shall be unclean two weeks, as in

a ch. 15. 19.

b Luke 2. 21; John 7. 22.

---

the Lawgiver alone. The laws of defilement contracted from without by eating or coming in contact with unclean objects are naturally followed by precepts about defilement arising from within the human body itself. The spiritual guides in the time of Christ, however, account for the sequence of these laws by declaring that the arrangement follows the order of the Creation. Just as at the Creation God made the animals first, and then formed man, so in the laws of purity the animals take the precedence of man, and are treated of first.

(2) **If a woman have conceived seed.**—Rather, *if a woman bringeth forth seed*, that is, is delivered of a child. (See Gen. i. 11, 12, 29.) This general statement is afterwards specified by the phrases "and born a man child," and "bear a maid child," in the verse before us, and in verse 5. Thus the regulations about impurity naturally begin with the beginning of life. According to the administrators of the law during the second Temple, the regulations here set forth with regard to the deliverance are in force even when it is an untimely birth, or when the child is born dead, provided it has a perfect shape, which it assumes after forty days of its conception. Amongst the Hindoos, too, the mother in case of a miscarriage remains in a state of defilement as many nights as months have elapsed since her conception.

And born a man child.—Better, *and giveth birth to a male child.* The expression rendered here in the Authorised Version by "a man child" is translated in verse 7 simply "male." In so short a paragraph discussing the same enactment it is important that words identical in the original should be translated uniformly in English.

She shall be unclean seven days.—Though the issue of blood which succeeds child-birth generally only lasts three or four days, yet the period of uncleanness is extended to seven days to include exceptional cases.

According to the days . . . .—Better, *as in the days of the uncleanness of her monthly courses*, that is, her uncleanness is to be of the same duration, and she is to observe the same rules, and be subjected to the same restraints as during the period of her menstruation. (See chap. xv. 19.) The fact that reference is here made to the regulations about the periodical impurity of women which have not as yet been laid down shows that, like other laws, this law was already known to and generally practised by the Jews before it was finally fixed in the Levitical code.

(3) **And in the eighth day.**—When the seven days had passed by during which the mother remained unclean, the boy is to be circumcised, since on the eighth day the first period of her extreme state of impurity ceases, and she no more imparts defilement to whomsoever or to whatsoever she touches. For the rite of circumcision, see Gen. xvii. 10, 13.

(4) **Continue in the blood of her purifying.**—Better, *continue in the blood of purification*, that is, *pure blood.* Though the discharge consequent upon the birth ceases after two or three weeks, the period in this case, as in the former instance, is nearly doubled, to include exceptional cases. During these thirty-three days, which constituted the second stage, the mother was only debarred from touching holy things, such as first tithes, the flesh of thank- and peace-offerings, &c., and from entering the sanctuary. Having bathed at the end of the seven days which constituted the first and defiling period, she could now partake of the second tithes, and resume conjugal intercourse, since any blood that might now appear was regarded as *pure blood*, in contradistinction to the (*dam nidah*) blood of monthly courses. Her proximity, therefore, no longer defiled. The Sadducees and the Samaritans during the second Temple, and their followers, the Karaite Jews, interpreted this law more rigidly. Though admitting that there is a difference of degree in the two periods, they maintained that the woman was too unclean for conjugal intercourse even during the second period. They therefore pointed the text differently so as to yield the rendering "blood of *her* purifying." The Authorised Version, which, in this instance, follows the opinion of the Sadducees, departs from the received text.

(5) **But if she bear a maid child.**—Better, *but if she giveth birth to a female child.* (See verse 2.)

As in her separation.—Better, *as in the time of her monthly courses.* (See verse 2.) In the case of a daughter the days of purification in both stages is exactly double that prescribed at the birth of a son. The reason for this difference is probably owing to the fact that the ancients believed that the physical derangement of the system is far greater at the birth of a girl than at the birth of a boy, and that it requires a longer time for the effects to pass away. Similar laws obtained among other nations of antiquity, and exist to this day among many Eastern tribes. The Greeks held that the man who had been near a woman in childbirth defiled the altar if he approached it. One of the means adopted during the Peloponnesian war for purifying the island of Delos was to proscribe women keeping their confinement on the island. The Hindoos go so far as to regard all the relations of a new-born child as impure; the father has to undergo lustrations, and the mother remains unclean till the tenth day, when the child receives its name. Among the Arabs the mother continues unclean for forty days.

In the blood of her purifying.—Better, *in the blood of purification*, that is, *pure blood.* (See verse 4.) It will be seen that the law here only legislates for ordinary cases, and that it passes over in silence cases of twins. The administrators of the law during the second Temple had therefore, in this instance, as in many other points, to supplement the Mosaic legislation. They therefore enacted that when a mother had twins, and if they were a boy and a girl, the two stages of her uncleanness were those for a girl. If one of the twins was a boy and the other sexless, or bi-sexual, she continued unclean for both male and female. If, on the

her separation: and she shall continue
in the blood of her purifying three-
score and six days.
(6) And when the days of her puri-
fying are fulfilled, for a son, or for a
daughter, she shall bring a lamb [1]of
the first year for a burnt offering, and
a young pigeon, or a turtledove, for
a sin offering, unto the door of the
tabernacle of the congregation, unto
the priest: (7) who shall offer it before
the LORD, and make an atonement for
her; and she shall be cleansed from
the issue of her blood. This *is* the
law for her that hath born a male or
a female. (8) [a] And if [2]she be not able
to bring a lamb, then she shall bring
two turtles, or two young pigeons;
the one for the burnt offering, and the
other for a sin offering: and the
priest shall make an atonement for
her, and she shall be clean.

CHAPTER XIII.—(1) And the LORD
spake unto Moses and Aaron, saying,
(2) When a man shall have in the
skin of his flesh a [3]rising, a scab, or
bright spot, and it be in the skin of
his flesh *like* the plague of leprosy;
then he shall be brought unto Aaron

1 Heb., *a son of his year.*

a Luke 2. 24.

2 Heb., *her hand find not sufficiency of.*

3 Or, *swelling.*

---

contrary, one was a female and the other of neither sex, or bi-sexual, her separation was only for a female.

(6) **And when the days . . .**—Having described in the previous verses the conditions of defilement arising from childbirth, the legislator now prescribes the offerings to be brought for the purification of the woman. The offerings were brought at the expiration of the fortieth day in the case of a boy, and at the end of the eightieth day in the case of a girl, that is, on the forty-first and on the eighty-first respectively.

For a son, or for a daughter.—That is, with regard to a son or a daughter, to either of which she had given birth. The purification was for herself, and was owing to the defiling discharges connected with childbirth, and not for the child to which she gave birth, since the baby was not unclean.

She shall bring a lamb of the first year.—Or, as the Margin has it, *a son of his year,* that is, a lamb which was within the year of its birth. This burnt offering was an expression of gratitude for the Divine mercy vouchsafed to her in the hours of sorrow and danger, or, as some ancients suggest, it was designed as a confession of impatient and reproachful thoughts harboured by the mother during her pregnancy and the time of parturition (comp. Gen. xxv. 22); whilst the sin offering was to atone for sinful and violent expressions which she may have heedlessly uttered in the hours of labour and agony. Though when the two sacrifices are mentioned together, the sin offering generally precedes the burnt offering (see chaps. v. 7, xiv. 31, xv. 15, 30, xvi. 3, 5, &c.), here the burnt offering takes precedence, because it is the more costly of the two. Besides the mother after child-birth (chap. xii. 6, 8), there were three other unclean persons who had to bring a sin offering for their uncleanness: the leper (chap. xiv. 19, 31), the woman that had an issue (chap. xv. 15), and the man that had an issue (chap. xv. 30).

Unto the door of the tabernacle of the congregation.—Better, *to the entrance of the tent of meeting.* (See chap. i. 3.) During the time of the second Temple these sacrifices were brought to the eastern gate, called the Gate of Nicanor. Here the lying-in women were purified and the lepers cleansed. (See chap. xiv. 13.)

(7) **Who shall offer it.**—Better, *and he shall offer it,* that is, the priest shall offer the sin offering. Though two sacrifices were brought—a burnt offering and a sin offering—yet stress is laid on the sin offering, for on it depended the purification and atonement of the mother. Even if the mother gave birth to twins, the administrators of the law during the second Temple decided that the one sin offering here prescribed sufficed.

(8) **And if she be not able.**—As a merciful provision for those who were too poor to bring a lamb, the law permits them to bring a turtle-dove or a pigeon for a burnt offering, provided only it is the same kind of bird as the one brought for a sin offering; that is, they must either be both turtle-doves or both pigeons, and not one turtle-dove and one pigeon. Turtle-doves and pigeons were plentiful and cheap in Palestine (see chap. i. 14). It was therefore the poor woman's sacrifice which the mother of our Lord offered, when, in accordance with this commutation, she offered a pair of turtle-doves or two young pigeons, on presenting herself for purification at the Temple with the child Jesus, on the expiration of the prescribed term of uncleanness (Luke ii. 24), and the priest, after sprinkling her with the blood of the humble sacrifice, declared her cleansed.

XIII.

(1) **And the Lord spake unto Moses and Aaron.**—As laws of leprosy chiefly concerned the priests, who had to examine the symptoms and to decide whether they indicated the distemper or not, the Lord addressed the regulations to Aaron as well as to Moses. The leprosy discussed in this and the following chapters consists of three general classes: viz., (1) leprosy of man (chap. xiii. 2—46); (2) leprosy of garments (chap. xiii. 47—59); and (3) leprosy of houses (chap. xiv. 33—57).

When a man shall have in the skin of his flesh.—In discussing the leprosy of man, the lawgiver enumerates six different circumstances under which it may develop itself. The first circumstance adduced in verses 2—6 is of its developing itself without an apparent cause. Hence it was enjoined that if anyone should notice in the skin of his flesh a rising or swelling, he should be taken to the priest. As the description of these symptoms is very concise, and requires to be specified more minutely for practical purposes, the spiritual guides of Israel, who had to explain the law to the priests during the second Temple, and who came in personal contact with this distemper, defined them as follows:—

A rising.—That is, *a swelling,* or *swollen spot.*

Or bright spot.—That is, *a bright* or *glossy pimple.* But these symptoms, when indicative of leprosy, assume respectively one of two colours, a principal or a subordinate colour. The principal colour of the rising spot is like that of an egg-shell, and the

the priest, or unto one of his sons
the priests: (3) and the priest shall look
on the plague in the skin of the flesh:
and *when* the hair in the plague is
turned white, and the plague in sight
be deeper than the skin of his flesh,
it *is* a plague of leprosy: and the
priest shall look on him, and pronounce
him unclean. (4) If the bright spot *be*
white in the skin of his flesh, and in
sight *be* not deeper than the skin, and
the hair thereof be not turned white;
then the priest shall shut up *him that*
hath the plague seven days: (5) and
the priest shall look on him the seventh
day: and, behold, *if* the plague in his
sight be at a stay, *and* the plague
spread not in the skin; then the
priest shall shut him up seven days
more: (6) and the priest shall look on
him again the seventh day: and, be-
hold, *if* the plague *be* somewhat dark,
and the plague spread not in the skin,
the priest shall pronounce him clean:
it *is but* a scab: and he shall wash
his clothes, and be clean. (7) But if
the scab spread much abroad in the
skin, after that he hath been seen of
the priest for his cleansing, he shall
be seen of the priest again: (8) and *if*

secondary one resembles white wool; whilst the principal colour of the bright pimple is white as snow, and the subordinate resembles plaster on the wall.

Then he shall be brought unto Aaron.—The following rules obtained during the second Temple with regard to the examination of the patient. Though anyone may examine the disease except the patient himself or his relations, yet the priest alone can decide whether it is leprosy or not, because the law declares that the priests must decide cases of litigation and disease (Deut. xxi. 5); hence the patient must "be brought unto Aaron," &c. But though the priests only can pronounce the patient clean or unclean, even if he be a child or a fool, yet he must act upon the advice of a learned layman in those matters. If the priest is blind of one eye, or is weak-sighted, he is disqualified for examining the distemper. The inspection must not take place on the Sabbath, nor early in the morning, nor in the middle of the day, nor in the evening, nor on cloudy days, because the colour of the skin cannot properly be ascertained in those hours of the day; but it must take place in the third, fourth, fifth, seventh, eighth, and ninth hours.

(3) **When the hair in the plague is turned white.**—Better, *and the hair in the plagued spot, &c.* The first symptom indicating the existence of the disorder is that the hair, which is generally jet-black among the Hebrews, turns white on the affected spot. The authorities during the second Temple defined it that there must at least be two hairs white, at the root and in the body of the bright spot, before the patient can be declared unclean. The word *plague,* in accordance with a usage common in Hebrew—to put the abstract for the concrete—denotes here the plagued spot, or the spot affected by the plague, whilst in verse 4 it means the person affected by this disorder. Thus in chap. xix. 32, "the hoary head" stands for *hoary-headed person.*

And the plague in sight be deeper than the skin.—Better, *and the appearance of the plagued spot be deeper, &c.* The second symptom which shows the development of the disorder is that the spot affected by this plague appears to be deeper than the rest of the skin.

Pronounce him unclean.—Literally, *make him unclean.* According to the frequently occurring phraseology, a man is said to *do* that which in his official capacity *he* pronounces as done, or orders to be done. Thus Ezekiel is said "to destroy the city" when he simply foretold its destruction (Ezek. xliii. 3). The existence of these two symptoms made it incumbent upon the priest to declare the person unclean, and hence imparting defilement.

(4) **If the bright spot be white.**—But if upon inspection there merely appeared a white spot in the skin, and the above named two symptoms were absent, the case was not to be decided.

Then the priest shall shut up him that hath the plague.—The individual thus suspected was to be separated from the rest of the community for seven days, during which time it would be seen whether it actually developed itself into this disorder. According to the canons which obtained during the second Temple, if a bridegroom was seized with this distemper he could not be shut up during the nuptial week. It will be seen that the words "him that hath" are in italics, thus indicating that they are not in the text; but "plague" here, as we have seen in verse 3, denotes *plagued person.*

(5) **And the priest shall look on him.**—If at the end of a week there is no alteration in the symptoms, the case must be adjourned for another seven days. The same priest who inspected it at the first must examine it again, as another one could not tell whether it has spread or not. If the priest died in the interim, or was taken ill, another priest could examine the patient, but could not pronounce him unclean. If the seventh day happened to be a Sabbath or feast day, the case had to be put off to the following day.

If the plague in his sight be at a stay.—Better, *if the plagued spot remain the same in its colour,* that is, if the suspicious spot which caused the individual to be shut up had not altered its complexion. The expression here translated "sight" is the same which is rightly rendered by "colour" in the Authorised Version in verse 55 of this very chapter. (Comp. also Num. xi. 7.) It will thus be seen that though the affected spot had not spread, still it retained its unhealthy and suspicious complexion.

(6) **And the priest shall look on him again.**—If, on further examination at the end of another week, the priest finds that the bright spot looks darker, and that it has not spread, he is to pronounce the patient clean, and set him at liberty, since it was simply an ordinary scurf; but though not leprous, the eruption indicated some impurity in his blood, and he had therefore to wash his garments.

(7, 8) **But if the scab spread.**—As verse 5 prescribes that the priest who examines the patient after seven days' quarantine, and finds no spreading of the affected spot, is to give another seven days' quarantine,

the priest see that, behold, the scab
spreadeth in the skin, then the priest
shall pronounce him unclean: it *is* a
leprosy.
(9) When the plague of leprosy is in
a man, then he shall be brought unto
the priest; (10) and the priest shall see
him: and, behold, *if* the rising *be*
white in the skin, and it have turned
the hair white, and *there be* [1] quick
raw flesh in the rising; (11) it *is* an
old leprosy in the skin of his flesh,
and the priest shall pronounce him un-
clean, and shall not shut him up: for
he *is* unclean. (12) And if a leprosy
break out abroad in the skin, and the
leprosy cover all the skin of *him that*
hath the plague from his head even to
his foot, wheresoever the priest looketh;
(13) then the priest shall consider: and,
behold, *if* the leprosy have covered all
his flesh, he shall pronounce *him*
clean *that hath* the plague: it is all
turned white: he *is* clean. (14) But
when raw flesh appeareth in him, he
shall be unclean. (15) And the priest
shall see the raw flesh, and pronounce
him to be unclean: *for* the raw flesh
is unclean: it *is* a leprosy. (16) Or if
the raw flesh turn again, and be
changed unto white, he shall come
unto the priest; (17) and the priest shall
see him: and, behold, *if* the plague
be turned into white; then the priest
shall pronounce *him* clean *that hath*
the plague: he *is* clean.
(18) The flesh also, in which, *even* in
the skin thereof, was a boil, and is
healed, (19) and in the place of the
boil there be a white rising, or a

[1] Heb., *the quickening of living flesh.*

---

the verses before us declare what the examining priest is to do when he notices that the spot has spread.

For his cleansing.—That is, for the purpose of being declared clean. If, after he had appeared before the priest to be examined and declared not leprous, at the expiration of the first week of seclusion the priest finds that the spot has spread, he must pronounce him unclean, since the spreading indicates that it is leprosy.

(9) **When the plague of leprosy is in a man.**—The second case, discussed in verses 9—17, is of leprosy re-appearing after it has been cured, when a somewhat different treatment is enjoined. In its re-appearance, as in its first manifestation, the patient is forthwith to be brought to the priest.

(10) **If the rising be white.**—If the distemper actually returns, one of two symptoms indicates it. A white rising will be noticed in the skin, which changes the black hair into white. The white hair only then indicates the disorder when it co-exists with the white rising or swelling which produced it. If the original white swelling, which discoloured the hair, disappears, and a fresh white swelling forms itself around the existing white hair, it is no indication of uncleanness.

And there be quick raw flesh in the rising.—Rather, *or if there be,* or *and likewise if there be,* &c. This clause gives the second of the two symptoms, either of which indicates the return of the disorder. According to the administrators of the law during the second Temple, the phrase here translated "quick raw flesh" in the Authorised Version, which literally means "the quickening of live flesh," denotes "sound flesh," or a spot in the flesh assuming the appearance of life after it had been paled by the whiteness which overspread the whole surface. The size of this spot of live flesh, which indicated the disease and made the patient unclean, had to be at least that of a lentil. This rendering is given by the LXX., the Chaldee, &c. An insulated spot of sound flesh in the midst of a tubercle was considered a sign of the fretting and consuming progress which the disease made in the surrounding flesh.

(11) **It is an old leprosy.**—Either of these symptoms showed that it was the re-appearance of the old distemper, and rendered quarantine needless. The priest is, therefore, to pronounce him unclean at once.

(12, 13) **And if a leprosy break out abroad.**—There were, however, two phases of this returned distemper which exempted the patient from uncleanness. If the leprosy suddenly covered the whole body so that the patient became perfectly white, in which case there could be no appearance of live flesh, then he was clean. This indicated the crisis, as the whole evil matter thus brought to the surface formed itself into a scale, which dried and peeled off.

(14) **But when raw flesh appeareth.**—Rather, *but in the day when sound flesh appeareth again,* that is, whenever patches of natural flesh appear intermingled with the white scurf, he forthwith becomes unclean, since this showed that the disease had not exhausted itself. Because it is here said, "But in the day when sound flesh," &c., and not simply, "but when sound flesh," &c., the administrators of the law in the time of Christ concluded that there were days on which the examination of this distemper was not undertaken: viz., during the seven nuptial days, and the seven days of the great pilgrim festivals of Passover and Tabernacles.

(15) **And the priest shall see the raw flesh.**—Rather, *the sound flesh.* It will be seen that it is the sound flesh only, and not the white hair, which renders the patient unclean.

(16, 17) **Or if the raw flesh turn again.**—Rather, *yet if the sound flesh changeth again and becometh, &c.* As soon, however, as the patches of sound flesh resume the white colour, so that the whole body is again white, without exhibiting any spots, the patient is to betake himself to the priest, who, after assuring himself of the fact, will pronounce him clean.

(18) **The flesh also, in which.**—Rather, *and if there is in the skin of the flesh a boil.* The third case, discussed in verses 18—28, is of leprosy developing itself from a healed boil, or from an inflammation which has apparently been healed. According to those who administered the law in the time of Christ, the boil and inflammation here meant are such as arise from a stroke by a piece of wood or a stone, and from having come in contact with pitch or hot water, thus distinguishing it from the burn by fire mentioned in verse 24.

(19) **And in the place of the boil.**—If the cicatriced sore breaks out again, and exhibits the usual

bright spot, white, and somewhat red-
dish, and it be shewed to the priest;
(20) and if, when the priest seeth it,
behold, it *be* in sight lower than the
skin, and the hair thereof be turned
white; the priest shall pronounce him
unclean: it *is* a plague of leprosy
broken out of the boil. (21) But if the
priest look on it, and, behold, *there be*
no white hairs therein, and *if* it *be* not
lower than the skin, but *be* somewhat
dark; then the priest shall shut him
up seven days: (22) and if it spread
much abroad in the skin, then the
priest shall pronounce him unclean:
it *is* a plague. (23) But if the bright
spot stay in his place, *and* spread not,
it *is* a burning boil; and the priest
shall pronounce him clean.

(24) Or if there be *any* flesh, in the
skin whereof *there is* [1] a hot burning,
and the quick *flesh* that burneth have
a white bright spot, somewhat red-
dish, or white; (25) then the priest
shall look upon it: and, behold, *if* the
hair in the bright spot be turned
white, and it *be in* sight deeper than
the skin; it *is* a leprosy broken out
of the burning: wherefore the priest
shall pronounce him unclean: it *is* the
plague of leprosy. (26) But if the
priest look on it, and, behold, *there be*
no white hair in the bright spot, and
it *be* no lower than the *other* skin,
but *be* somewhat dark; then the
priest shall shut him up seven days:
(27) and the priest shall look upon him
the seventh day: *and* if it be spread
much abroad in the skin, then the
priest shall pronounce him unclean:
it *is* the plague of leprosy. (28) And if
the bright spot stay in his place, *and*
spread not in the skin, but it *be*
somewhat dark; it *is* a rising of the
burning, and the priest shall pronounce
him clean: for it *is* an inflammation
of the burning.

(29) If a man or woman have a plague

1 Heb., *a burning of fire.*

---

symptoms of leprosy, the patient is to show himself to the priest.

White, and somewhat reddish.—Better, *of a white-reddish colour.* This symptom is peculiar to re-opened cicatriced sores, and hence has not been mentioned before. The authorities in the time of Christ describe the mixture of red and white as follows:—"It has the appearance of red wine poured into water, and is either a palish white or somewhat darker."

(20) **Behold, it be in sight lower than the skin.**—Better, *Behold, its appearance is lower than the other skin.* If upon examination the priest finds that the spot has assumed a deeper appearance than the rest of the skin, and the hair turned white—which were the two critical symptoms—he forthwith declared it leprosy.

(21) **But if the priest.**—In the absence, however, of these two symptoms, the patient is to be put in quarantine for one week only.

(22) **And if it spread much abroad.**—If, on inspecting it again at the end of the seven days' seclusion, the priest finds that the spot has spread, it was evident that the blood was vitiated, and that the distemper began to develop in the body.

It is a plague.—That is, of leprosy. The word "leprosy," which has here dropped out of the text, is still preserved in some of the ancient versions.

(23) **But if the bright spot stay.**—As the spreading of the spot is a sure sign of the disease lurking in the system, its continuing in the same condition showed that it was simply the re-opening of the boil. The priest is therefore to pronounce the patient clean, or clear of leprosy.

(24) **Or if there be any flesh, in the skin whereof there is.**—Rather, *or if there is in the skin of the flesh.* As a burn or inflammation arising from contact with pitch or hot water was adduced in verse 18, the verse before us specifies a sore, pustule, or blister occasioned by "a burning of fire," as the Margin of the Authorised Version rightly has it, and not *a hot burning,* as it is in the text. The ancient canons distinctly define this by "that which is burnt with a coal or with embers, whatsoever is from the force of actual fire, is the burning here meant," in contradistinction to the burn or inflammation mentioned in verse 18.

And the quick flesh that burneth.—Rather, *and the sound flesh of the burning* (see verse 10), that is, the tender flesh which is renewed (after it has lost the purulent matter in it) and exhibits these symptoms.

(25) **Then the priest shall look.**—If upon examination the priest finds that the hair which was before black has now turned white.

And it be in sight deeper than the skin.—Better, *and its appearance is deeper than the other skin.* (See verses 3 and 20.)

(26) **But if the priest look on it.**—If these symptoms are absent, the same directions are to be followed as laid down in verse 21, in the case of a boil or an inflammation.

(27, 28) **And the priest shall look.**—The directions here given as to what the priest is to do at the end of the week's quarantine are the same as those given in verses 23 and 24. It will be seen that there is a difference in the treatment of the suspicious symptoms in case No. 1, and in the case before us, No. 3. In the former instance, where there is no apparent cause for the symptoms, the suspected invalid has to undergo two remands of seven days each before his case can be decided; whilst in the instance before us, where the boil, the inflammation, or the burn visibly supplies the reason for this suspicion, he is only remanded for one week, at the end of which his case is finally decided.

(29) **If a man or woman.**—The fourth case, discussed in verses 29—37, is leprosy on the head or chin. Cases where this distemper attacks first the hairy parts are not uncommon.

upon the head or the beard; (30) then
the priest shall see the plague: and, be-
hold, if it *be* in sight deeper than the
skin; *and there be* in it a yellow thin
hair; then the priest shall pronounce
him unclean: it *is* a dry scall, *even*
a leprosy upon the head or beard.
(31) And if the priest look on the plague
of the scall, and, behold, it *be* not in
sight deeper than the skin, and *that
there is* no black hair in it; then the
priest shall shut up *him that hath* the
plague of the scall seven days: (32) and
in the seventh day the priest shall look
on the plague: and, behold, *if* the scall
spread not, and there be in it no
yellow hair, and the scall *be* not in
sight deeper than the skin; (33) he shall
be shaven, but the scall shall he not
shave; and the priest shall shut up
him that hath the scall seven days
more: (34) and in the seventh day the
priest shall look on the scall: and,
behold, *if* the scall be not spread in
the skin, nor *be* in sight deeper than
the skin; then the priest shall pro-
nounce him clean: and he shall wash
his clothes, and be clean. (35) But if
the scall spread much in the skin
after his cleansing; (36) then the priest
shall look on him: and, behold, if the
scall be spread in the skin, the priest

(30) **Behold, if it be in sight deeper.**—Better, *Behold, if its appearance is deeper.* The first symptom of its existence is the same as usual—the depression of the affected spot.

And there be in it a yellow thin hair.—Whilst the symptom of leprosy in other parts of the body consisted of the hair turning white on the affected spot, in the case of this distemper breaking out on the head or chin it was indicated by the naturally black hair changing its colour into a golden appearance, and becoming short. According to the adminstrators of the law during the second Temple, the colour of the hair became like that of the new plumage of young pigeons after they have lost their first feathers, or, in other words, like the appearance of thin gold. By the "thin hair" those authorities who came in contact with the disorder understand *small* or *short* hair. Hence they laid down the following rule: The condition of the hair constituting one of the signs of leprosy is its becoming short; but if it be long, though it is as yellow as gold, it is no sign of uncleanness. Two yellow and short hairs, whether close to one another or far from each other, whether in the centre of the affected spot or on the edge thereof,—no matter whether the affection on the spot precedes the yellow hair, or the yellow hair precedes the affection on the spot,—are symptoms of uncleanness.

It is a dry scall, even a leprosy.—The ancient canons laid down by those authorities in the time of Christ who had the official treatment of this distemper define the word (*nethek*), which is translated "dry scall" by an affection on the head or chin, which causes the hair on those affected parts to fall off by the roots, so that the place of the hair is quite bare.

(31) **It be not in sight deeper than the skin.**—Better, *its appearance is not deeper than the other skin.* If the first symptom which manifests itself in the depression of the affected spot is absent.

And that there is no black hair in it.—Better, *but there is no black hair in it*; that is, the healthy black colour of the hair is absent, which is a suspicious sign. The phrase, "there is no black hair in it," is another way of saying "there is yellow hair in it." The presence of yellow hair, however, on the first inspection, though suspicious, did not necessarily indicate by itself leprosy, since the hair sometimes turned yellow temporarily in the case of an ordinary ulcer, and resumed its natural black colour when the patient returned to his usual health. Hence, the absence of the black hair was simply a suspicious symptom, which required the attention of the priest, for which reason the patient had to be put in quarantine for seven days. The alteration of the word "black" into "yellow," which has been adopted by those commentators who follow the LXX., is therefore unnecessary. Indeed, if this reading be adopted, both the unfavourable symptoms mentioned in verse 30, which indicate leprosy—viz., (1) the depression of the affected spot, and (2) the discolouring of the hair—would be absent. There would be no reason for quarantine, as the priest in the absence of these criteria would have to pronounce the man clean. (See verse 37.)

(32) **The scall be not in sight deeper than the skin.**—Better, *the appearance of the scall is not deeper than the other skin.* If at the expiration of the seven days' quarantine, the priest, on examining the spot which had a resemblance to leprosy, finds that it has not developed those signs which this distemper always discloses within this time.

(33) **He shall be shaven.**—The priest, for the sake of making sure, and to be able to examine the patient more thoroughly, is to have his head and beard shaved. This operation was performed by professional barbers, who were always on the spot.

But the scall shall he not shave.—The place, however, where the scall appeared was not to be shaved, so that the priest might be able to see the colour of the hair. The manner in which the shaving was performed during the second Temple was as follows: The hair round the scall was all shaved off, except two hairs on each side, which were close to the affected spot, to enable the priest to see whether the spot is spreading or not.

(34) **And in the seventh day.**—If at the expiration of the second week of quarantine the priest sees that none of the symptoms which generally indicate this distemper have appeared, he is to pronounce him clean, upon which, after performing the necessary ablutions, he is restored to the privileges of the sanctuary. (See verse 6.)

Be in sight deeper than the skin.—Better, *is in appearance deeper than the other skin.*

(35, 36) **But if the scall spread.**—If, after the scall had remained stationary for a fortnight, and the patient had been pronounced clean, he is brought again because the scall had spread after the lapse of the two quarantines, he is to be forthwith pronounced unclean, whether it was accompanied by yellow hair or not.

shall not seek for yellow hair; he *is*
unclean. (37) But if the scall be in his
sight at a stay, and *that* there is black
hair grown up therein; the scall is
healed, he *is* clean: and the priest shall
pronounce him clean.
(38) If a man also or a woman have
in the skin of their flesh bright spots,
even white bright spots; (39) then the
priest shall look: and, behold, *if* the
bright spots in the skin of their flesh
be darkish white; it *is* a freckled spot
that groweth in the skin; he *is* clean.
(40) And the man whose [1] hair is
fallen off his head, he *is* bald; *yet is*
he clean. (41) And he that hath his
hair fallen off from the part of his
head toward his face, he *is* forehead
bald: *yet is* he clean. (42) And if there
be in the bald head, or bald forehead,
a white reddish sore; it *is* a leprosy
sprung up in his bald head, or his
bald forehead. (43) Then the priest shall
look upon it: and, behold, *if* the rising
of the sore *be* white reddish in his bald
head, or in his bald forehead, as the
leprosy appeareth in the skin of the
flesh; (44) he is a leprous man, he *is*

[1] Heb., *head is pilled.*

---

(37) **But if the scall be in his sight at a stay.**—Better, *But if the appearance of the scall hath remained the same.*

And that there is black hair grown up therein.—Better, *And if black hair hath,* &c. If, in addition to its not spreading, the healthy colour of the hair has returned, it shows that the patient is cured of the leprosy, and the priest shall pronounce him clean. (See verse 31.) According to the adminstrators of the law, there had at least to be two black hairs, of such a length that the top could bow towards the root. If two hairs grew up on the healed scall, one black and the other white or yellow, or one long and the other short, the patient could not be declared clean.

(38) **If a man also or a woman.**—The fifth case, discussed in verses 38, 39, is the harmless leprosy, which does not render the patient unclean.

Bright spots, even white bright spots.—These white spots, which are of unequal size, and a little higher than the skin, generally appeared on the neck and face, and did not change the colour of the hair.

(39) **Then the priest shall look.**—If the priest, upon examination, finds that these elevated spots are of a dull or palish white colour, then he is to pronounce the patient clean, that is, free of leprosy, since it is simply a white eruption or tetter, which lasts for a few months, causes no inconvenience, and by degrees disappears of itself. Hence it is called *bahack,* or "white scurf," and not leprosy. This nameless disorder, which still prevails in the East, is to this day called by the Biblical name *bahack.*

(40) **And the man whose hair is fallen off.**—Better, *And if a man loseth the hair of his head.* The sixth and last case, discussed in verses 40—44, is leprosy either at the back or in the front of the head. Though baldness in itself was regarded as a disgrace, and often looked upon as a Divine punishment (2 Kings ii. 23; Isa. iii. 17; Jer. xlviii. 37), yet the simple fact of the mere falling of the hair is not to be taken as a sign of leprosy.

He is bald; yet is he clean.—Better, *if he is backhead bald, he is clean.* The baldness mentioned in the first part of the verse in general terms is now more minutely specified as consisting of two kinds of baldness.

Verses 41 and 42 distinctly show that the word (*kēreach*), here translated simply "bald" in the Authorised Version, denotes a person who has lost hair from the crown of his head downwards towards the channel of his neck, as the administrators of the law during the second Temple rightly define it, in contradistinction to the fore baldness which immediately follows.

(41) **And he that hath his hair fallen off.**—Rather, *And if he loseth the hair of his head.*

He is forehead bald.—This, which, according to the administrators of the law, was from the crown of the head descending to his face, and constituted the man a *gibbēach,* was also not a sign of leprosy.

(42) **And if there be in the bald head.**—Better, *But if there be in the bald backhead.* But if a reddish-white eruption appears either in the hinder or fore part of the bald head, resembling that which arises in the place of healed boils (see verses 19—24), then it indicates the existence of leprosy.

In his bald head.—Better, *in his bald backhead.*

(43) **Then the priest shall look.**—It is then the duty of the priest to ascertain whether the white-reddish rising in the bald backhead or bald forehead is in appearance like the leprosy in the skin of the flesh described in verse 2, excepting, of course, the white hair, which in this case could not exist.

As the leprosy appeareth in the skin of the flesh.—Better, *in appearance like the leprosy in the skin of the flesh.* Though the reddish-white eruption is the only symptom mentioned whereby head-leprosy is to be recognised, and nothing is said about remanding the patient if the distemper should appear doubtful, as in the other cases of leprosy, yet because it is here said "in appearance like the leprosy in the skin of the flesh," the administrators of the law during the second Temple inferred that *all* the criteria specified in one are implied in the other. They interpret this phrase, "they are, and therefore must be treated like, leprosy in the skin of the flesh." Hence they submit that there are two symptoms which render baldness in the front or at the back of the head unclean: viz., (1) live or sound flesh; and (2) spreading. "If live or sound flesh is found in the bright spot on the baldness at the back or in the front of the head, he is pronounced unclean; if there is no live flesh, he is shut up, and examined at the end of the week, and if live flesh has developed itself, and it has spread, he is declared unclean, and if not, he is shut up for another week. If it spreads during this time, or engenders live flesh, he is declared unclean, and if not, he is declared clean. He is also pronounced unclean if it spreads or engenders sound flesh after he has been declared clean." Of course, the fact that the distemper in this instance develops itself on baldness precludes white hair being among the criteria indicating uncleanness.

unclean: the priest shall pronounce him utterly unclean; his plague *is* in his head.

(45) And the leper in whom the plague *is*, his clothes shall be rent, and his head bare, and he shall put a covering upon his upper lip, and shall cry, Unclean, unclean. (46) All the days wherein the plague *shall be* in him he shall be defiled; he *is* unclean: he shall dwell alone; [a] without the camp *shall* his habitation *be*.

(47) The garment also that the plague of leprosy is in, *whether it be* a woollen garment, or a linen garment; (48) whether *it be* in the warp, or woof; of

[a] Num. 5. 2; 2 Kings 15. 5.

(45) **His clothes shall be rent.**—As leprosy was regarded as a visitation from God for sin committed by the person thus afflicted, the patient is to rend his garments like one mourning for the dead. (See chap. xxi. 10.) During the second Temple the administrators of the law exempted leprous women from rending their clothes, which was evidently owing to a feeling of decorum.

And his head bare.—Better, *and his hair be dishevelled.* This was another sign of mourning. (See chap. x. 6.) The legislators during the second Temple also exempted leprous women from letting their hair fall in the disorderly and wild manner over their heads and faces which was the custom for mourners to do.

And he shall put a covering upon his upper lip.—To veil the beard, which was the pride of the Oriental, was also a sign of mourning. (Comp. Ezek. xxiv. 17, 22; Micah iii. 7.) This was generally done by throwing the skirt of the garment over the lower part of the chin.

And shall cry, Unclean.—As leprosy was most defiling, and as the very entrance of a leper into a house rendered everything in it unclean, the person thus afflicted had to warn off the passers by, lest they should approach him, and by contact with him become defiled. In some instances this was done by a herald, who preceded the leper. Hence the rendering of the ancient Chaldee paraphrase of Jonathan by "a herald shall proclaim, and say, Depart, depart from the unclean!"

(46) **He shall dwell alone.**—In consequence of his extreme defilement, the leper had to live in seclusion outside the camp or city (Num. v. 1—4, xiii. 10—15; 2 Kings vii. 3, &c.). According to the legislation during the second Temple, if he stood under a tree and a clean person happened to pass by, he defiled the passer by. In the synagogue which he wished to attend they were obliged to make him a separate compartment, ten handbreadths high and four cubits long and broad. He had to be the first to go in and the last to leave the synagogue. Hence, leprosy was regarded as a living death, and as an awful punishment from the Lord (2 Kings v. 7; 2 Chron. xxvi. 20), which they invoked upon all their mortal enemies (2 Sam. iii. 29; 2 Kings v. 27). The leper was debarred from conjugal intercourse. These ancient Rabbinic laws were imported into the Christian Church during the Middle Ages. When any one was afflicted with this distemper, the priest, wearing his stole and holding the crucifix, conducted him into the church, where the leper had to exchange his clothes for a peculiar black garment, and the mass was read over him and the service for the dead. He was then taken to a sequestered house, where earth was thrown upon his feet as a sign of burial, and was admonished never to appear otherwise than in his black garment and barefooted. He was not allowed to enter a church, or any place where there was a mill or bread was baked, or come near a well or fountain. He forfeited both the right of inheritance and of disposing of his property, for he was considered a dead man.

(47) **The garment also that.**—Better, *And if a garment hath.* The fact that the same phrase, "plague of leprosy," is used both in the case of garments and of human beings, and that the symptoms and working of leprous garments and those of leprous men are identical, shows beyond doubt that the same distemper is meant. The theory, therefore, that "plague of leprosy" is here used figuratively of garments fretted by a species of animalculæ or vermin, which feed upon and corrode the finer parts of the texture in the manner of moths, is contrary to the uniform import of this phrase in the discussion of the disorder, and is against the testimony of the administrators of the law during the second Temple, who came in personal contact with the complaint. They assure us that leprosy of garments and houses was not to be found in the world generally, but was a sign and miracle in Israel to guard them against an evil tongue. Equally untenable is the theory that it denotes an infectious condition of clothes caused by contact with the leprous matter of wounds and boils, which is so strong that it corrodes and injures all kinds of texture. Neither the regulations here laid down, nor the further development of them exhibited in the canons which obtained during the second Temple, regard leprosy as contagious. This is evident from the fact that the priest was in constant and close contact with the leper; that the leper who was *entirely* covered was pronounced clean, and could mix with the community (see verses 12, 13); that the priest himself ordered all the things in a leprous house to be taken out before he entered it, in order that they might be used again (see chap. xiv. 36); that according to the ancient canons a leprous minor, a leprous heathen or proselyte, as well as leprous garments in houses of non-Israelites, do not render any one unclean, nor does a bridegroom who is seized with this malady during the nuptial week defile any one. All this most unquestionably implies that there was no fear of contagion on the part of the authorities who had personally to deal with this distemper.

Whether it be a woollen garment.—As among the ancient Egyptians and Greeks, woollen and linen garments were the only apparel worn by the Israelites. (Comp. Deut. xxii. 11; Hosea ii. 7, 11; Prov. xxxi. 13.) The administrators of the law during the second Temple, however, took this enactment literally as referring strictly to wool of sheep and flax, but not to hemp and other materials. Hence they declared that a material made of camels' hair and sheep's wool is not rendered unclean by leprosy if the camels' hair preponderates, but is unclean when the sheep's hair preponderates, or when both are equal. The same rule also applies to mixtures of flax and hemp. Dyed skins and garments are not rendered unclean by leprosy. We have here another proof that these authorities did not regard leprosy as contagious.

linen, or of woollen; whether in a skin, or in any [1] thing made of skin; (49) and if the plague be greenish or reddish in the garment, or in the skin, either in the warp, or in the woof, or in any [2] thing of skin; it *is* a plague of leprosy, and shall be shewed unto the priest: (50) and the priest shall look upon the plague, and shut up *it that hath* the plague seven days: (51) and he shall look on the plague on the seventh day: if the plague be spread in the garment, either in the warp, or in the woof, or in a skin, *or* in any work that is made of skin; the plague *is* a fretting leprosy; it *is* unclean. (52) He shall therefore burn that garment, whether warp or woof, in woollen or in linen, or any thing of skin, wherein the plague is: for it *is* a fretting leprosy; it shall be burnt in the fire.

(53) And if the priest shall look, and, behold, the plague be not spread in the garment, either in the warp, or in the woof, or in any thing of skin; (54) then the priest shall command that they wash *the thing* wherein the plague *is,* and he shall shut it up seven days more: (55) and the priest shall look on the plague, after that it is washed: and, behold, *if* the plague have not changed his colour, and the plague be not spread; it *is* unclean; thou shalt burn it in the fire; it *is* fret inward, [3] *whether* it *be* bare within or without. (56) And if the priest look, and, behold, the plague *be* somewhat dark after the washing of it; then he shall rend it out of the garment, or out of the skin, or out of the warp, or out of the woof: (57) and if it appear still in the garment, either in the warp, or in the woof, or in any thing of skin; it *is* a spreading *plague:* thou shalt burn that wherein the plague *is* with fire. (58) And the garment, either warp, or woof, or whatsoever thing of skin *it be,* which thou shalt wash, if the plague be departed from them, then it shall be washed the second time, and shall be clean.

(59) This *is* the law of the plague of leprosy in a garment of woollen or linen, either in the warp, or woof, or any thing of skins, to pronounce it clean, or to pronounce it unclean.

1 Heb., *work of.*

2 Heb., *vessel,* or, *instrument.*

3 Heb., whether it be *bald in the head thereof, or in the forehead thereof.*

---

(49) **And if the plague be greenish.**—If one of these symptoms manifests itself in a woollen or linen garment, or in a leathern vessel, it must forthwith be shown to the priest. The Jewish canons define the colour of the green symptom to be like that of herbs, and that of the red to be like fair crimson.

(50) **And the priest shall look.**—If upon examination the priest finds that the garment or vessel in question exhibits one of these symptoms, he must put it in quarantine for a week, as in the case of a human being. (See verse 4.)

(51) **And he shall look on the plague.**—If at the end of the week, when the priest examines it again, he finds that the distemper has spread, it undoubtedly indicates malignant leprosy. Here, again, the symptom of spreading is the same in the garment as in the human being. (See verses 5, 6, 8, &c.) The leprous garment, like a human leper, makes everything and everybody unclean by contact with it, or by coming into the house where it remains.

(52) **He shall therefore burn.**—As this distemper could never be eradicated from stuffs, the garments which have once become possessed of leprosy had to be burnt.

(53, 54) **And if the priest shall look.**—If, however, after a week's quarantine, the priest on examination finds that the disease has not spread, he must order the affected garments to be washed, and shut them up for another week, when it will be seen whether the colour has changed, and the distemper has disappeared or not.

(55) **And the plague be not spread.**—Better, *though the plague hath not spread.* If after the washing of the affected spot the priest finds that its appearance has not changed, it must nevertheless be burnt, since the retention of the suspicious colour indicates that it is leprosy.

It is fret inward, whether it be bare within or without.—Better, *it is a corroding in the fore baldness thereof, or in the back baldness thereof.* (See verses 42, 43.) That is, though it has not spread in breadth, the distemper has eaten into the fabric, either on the upper side, which is compared to the forehead, or into the under side, which is compared to the hinder part of the head in human head-leprosy.

(56) **Behold, the plague be somewhat dark.**—But if after the washing the priest finds that the suspicious colour has changed from green or red into a darkish colour, and the spot has contracted, he is to cut out the affected spot and burn it, and declare the garment itself clean. (See verse 6.)

(57) **And if it appear still.**—If, after the affected piece has been cut out and burnt, the distemper appears again in another part of the garment or skin, it indicates beyond doubt that it is spreading leprosy; the garment must therefore be entirely destroyed, as in stuffs this disorder is incurable.

(58) **And the garment . . .**—According to verses 54 and 56, the suspicious symptoms often disappeared after the stuffs had been washed and put in quarantine for a week, thus showing that it was not real leprosy. But though non-leprous, the garments had to be washed a second time before they could be pronounced fit for use.

(59) **This is the law of the plague of leprosy.**—That is, the above-mentioned regulations are to guide the priests in their decisions whether a garment or leathern utensil is leprous or not, and in their declaration of its being clean or defiling.

CHAPTER XIV.—(1) And the LORD
spake unto Moses, saying, (2) This shall
be the law of the leper in the day of
his cleansing: He [a] shall be brought
unto the priest: (3) and the priest shall
go forth out of the camp; and the
priest shall look, and, behold, *if* the
plague of leprosy be healed in the leper;
(4) then shall the priest command to
take for him that is to be cleansed two
[1] birds alive *and* clean, and cedar wood,
and scarlet, and hyssop: (5) and the
priest shall command that one of the
birds be killed in an earthen vessel
over running water: (6) as for the living
bird, he shall take it, and the cedar
wood, and the scarlet, and the hyssop,
and shall dip them and the living bird
in the blood of the bird *that was* killed
over the running water: (7) and he shall
sprinkle upon him that is to be cleansed
from the leprosy seven times, and shall

a Matt. 8. 2; Mark 1. 40; Luke 5. 12.

1 Or, *sparrows*.

XIV.

(1) **And the Lord spake unto Moses.**—The regulations for the purification of the leper are delivered to Moses alone, who is to communicate them to Aaron and his sons, whilst the rules by which the distemper is to be discerned were given both to Moses and Aaron. (See chap. xiii. 1.) The reason for this is probably that Moses was designed by God as the great law-giver and teacher of the priesthood as well as of the laity.

(2) **This shall be the law of the leper.**—That is, the manner in which an Israelite cured of his leprosy shall be purified and restored to the communion of the sanctuary on the day when he is pronounced clean.

He shall be brought unto the priest.—He is to be conducted from his place of seclusion (see chap. xiii. 46) to an appointed place on the borders of the camp. It was this coming to the priest to which Christ referred when He said to the leper whom He had healed, "Go, show thyself to the priest, and offer the gift that Moses commanded" (Matt. viii. 4).

(3) **And the priest shall go forth.**—To this appointed place the priest had to go to meet and examine the restored leper, and to satisfy himself that he was thoroughly cured.

(4) **Then shall the priest command to take.**—Literally, *And the priest shall command, and he shall take*, that is, the leper shall take. To avoid the ambiguity as to the person, the translators of the Authorised Version adopted the rendering in the text. As the relatives of the cured leper procured the things prescribed for the purification, some of the ancient versions render it, *And they shall take.*

Two birds alive and clean.—These were either sparrows, doves, turtledoves, or any other birds, provided they belonged to the clean species described in chap. xi. According to the canons which obtained during the second Temple, the birds had to be sparrows, and the reason assigned for it was that as leprosy was regarded as a Divine punishment for calumny, such birds were selected as were proverbial for their constant twitter. Hence the rendering of sparrow in the Latin Vulgate, and in the Margin of the Authorised Version.

And cedar wood.—This had to be a foot and a half long, and a quarter of the foot of the bed in thickness. Though this wood was primarily chosen for its antiseptic properties, which made it peculiarly suitable for the occasion, still, belonging to the loftiest of trees (Pss. ii. 13, xxvii. 24; Amos ii. 9), it also was designed to symbolise the haughtiness of mind which called down the affliction of leprosy.

And scarlet.—This was probably a band of scarlet wool with which the cedar and the hyssop were tied together. In later times the woollen band had to be the weight of a shekel, or weighing thirty-two grains of barley. It was taken to symbolise the purified and now healthy blood.

And hyssop.—This, according to the canons which obtained in the time of Christ, had at least to be a handbreadth in size. It could not be the so-called Greek, or the ornamental, or Roman, or wild hyssop, or any other hyssop which was distinguished by the name of the place where it grew, but had to be the common hyssop which grew in gardens. Though, like the cedar wood, it was primarily used on these occasions for its aromatic properties, yet this diminutive shrub was also most probably designed to symbolise the humility of the cured leper. Hence ancient tradition tells us, "Cedar wood and hyssop, the highest and the lowest, give the leper purity. Why these? Because pride was the cause of the distemper, which cannot be cured till man becomes humble, and keeps himself as low as hyssop." Cedar wood, hyssop, and scarlet were also burnt with the red heifer (Num. xix. 6), and were generally employed in purifications (Heb. ix. 19). Hence the Psalmist prays, "Purge me with hyssop, and I shall be clean" (Ps. li. 17).

(5) **And the priest shall command that one of the birds be killed.**—Rather, *And the priest shall command, and he shall kill the one bird*, that is, upon the priest ordering it, the cured leper is to kill the one which is the fairer and better bird of the two, as was the rule during the second Temple. Not being a sacrifice, the victim was killed outside the camp.

In an earthen vessel over running water.—Better, *over an earthen vessel upon* (or *into*) *living water*, that is, the bird was killed over the dish, so as to let the blood flow into the water. The vessel had to be a new one; into it was poured a fourth part of a log, or as much as an egg and a-half of "living water:" that is, water taken from a running stream or a perennial spring, where its continual motion resembles life, in contradistinction to stale or stagnant water. Water which had already been used for other purposes, salt water, rain water, or water which had been melted or warmed, was illegal. When the blood had thus been wrung into it, a hole was dug, and the bird was buried in the presence of the priest and the patient.

(6) **And shall dip them and the living bird.**—With the crimson thread the priest tied together lengthwise the bundle of hyssop and the cedar wood, extended about them the wings and the tail of the living bird, and then dipped all the four in the mixture of blood and water which was in the earthen vessel.

(7) **And he shall sprinkle.**—Having thus dipped the hyssop fastened to the cedar stick into the blood and water, the priest is to sprinkle with it the back of the hand and the forehead of the patient seven times. The seven times symbolised the complete cleansing.

pronounce him clean, and shall let the
living bird loose [1] into the open field.
(8) And he that is to be cleansed shall
wash his clothes, and shave off all his
hair, and wash himself in water, that
he may be clean: and after that he
shall come into the camp, and shall
tarry abroad out of his tent seven days.
(9) But it shall be on the seventh day,
that he shall shave all his hair off his
head and his beard and his eyebrows,
even all his hair he shall shave off: and
he shall wash his clothes, also he shall
wash his flesh in water, and he shall be
clean.
(10) And on the eighth day he shall
take two he lambs without blemish,
and one ewe lamb [2] of the first year
without blemish, and three tenth deals
of fine flour *for* a meat offering, mingled
with oil, and one log of oil. (11) And
the priest that maketh *him* clean shall
present the man that is to be made
clean, and those things, before the LORD,

1 Heb., *upon the face of the field.*

2 Heb., *the daughter of her year.*

(See chap. iv. 6.) Hence Naaman the leper washed himself seven times in the Jordan (2 Kings v. 10, 14).

And shall let the living bird loose.—Whereupon the priest not only pronounced the cured man clean and restored to his liberty, but at the same time liberated the bird also. The release of the bird symbolised the freedom restored to the patient, who, like the bird, was now at liberty to go where he liked without any restraint. Because it is here said that the bird is to be let loose "into the open field," or, more literally, *towards the face of the field*, the ancient canons decreed that he who lets it loose must not turn his face towards the sea, wilderness, or city, but towards the field. The cedar wood, the crimson thread, and the hyssop, as well as the bird, if caught again, could be used again in the cleansing of other lepers.

(8) **Shall wash his clothes.**—This was done not to disinfect them, for leprosy, as we have seen, was not contagious, but as an act of purification, which was performed after every kind of defilement. (See chaps. vi. 20, xi. 25, &c.)

And shave off all his hair.—The razor had to pass over the whole of his body, even his secret parts. A similar process was undertaken at the consecration of the Levites. (Comp. Num. viii. 7.)

And shall tarry abroad out of his tent.—But though permitted to return to the camp, yet he had to live the first week out of his own house. This the authorities during the second Temple rightly regarded as an euphemism for seclusion from connubial intercourse during the first seven days, in order that he might not contract impurity (see chap. xv. 10), and thus interrupt the period of holy preparation. Hence the ancient Chaldee Version of the so-called Jonathan translates it: "He shall sit without the tent of the house of his habitation, and shall not come near to the side of his wife seven days." With this ended the first stage of purification, which restored the convalescent to his social or civil privileges, but not to the sanctuary.

(9) **But it shall be . . .**—Better, *And it shall be.* The second stage of purification, which restored the convalescent to the communion of the sanctuary, began on the seventh day, when, as a first act, he had again to shave off the hair of the whole of his body.

Also he shall wash his flesh.—Better, *and he shall bathe himself*, or *his body.* The expression "flesh" simply means *self*, or *body*, as the Authorised Version rightly translates it in Eccles. ii. 3; Isa. x. 8; Ezek. x. 12. Besides Num. xix. 7, the full phrase, "to wash the flesh in water," occurs eight times, and always in Leviticus (chaps. xiv. 9, xv. 13, 16, xvi. 4, 24, 26, 28, xxii. 6), and is rendered in three different ways in the Authorised Version: by (1) "wash his flesh in water" (Lev. xiv. 9, xv. 16, xvi. 4); by (2) "wash his flesh with water" (chap. xvi. 24); by (3) "bathe his flesh in water" (chaps. xv. 13, xvi. 24, 26, 28; Num. xix. 7). When a peculiar ritual phrase designedly deviates in a single section in the original from another phrase which is used to express the same idea (comp. chaps. xiv. 8, xv. 5, 6, 7, 8, 10, 12, 16, 18, 21, 22, 27, xvii. 15), it is essential that it should be translated by the identical phrase in English. During the second Temple, restored lepers bathed in a chamber at the north-western corner of the Court of the Women, called the "chamber of the lepers."

(10) **And on the eighth day.**—Though restored to social intercourse with his fellow brethren, the recovered leper could not at once be admitted to the privileges of the sanctuary, but had to bring on the eighth day three kinds of sacrifices: viz., a trespass offering, a sin offering, and a burnt offering. The lamb for the sin offering had not only to be without blemish (see chap. i. 3), but of the first year (see chap. xii. 6).

And three tenth deals of fine flour.—Each of these three sacrifices is to be accompanied by a meat offering, consisting of a tenth part of an ephah (which is an omer) of flour. The omer, which is the same as "the tenth deal" (see Exod. xvi. 36), as it is here called, is equal to 43⅕ eggs, or about four pints. Ordinarily a meat offering did not accompany the trespass offering or the sin offering, and only one omer was brought with a lamb (see Num. xv. 4); but according to the administrators of the law during the second Temple, three omers are here prescribed as a substitute for the drink offering which should have accompanied the two expiatory sacrifices. For the manner in which the meat offering was prepared, see chap. xi. 1—4.

And one log of oil.—This oil, as we see afterwards (see verse 15, &c), was used to sprinkle seven times before the Lord, to sanctify the ear, the hand, the foot, and the head of the restored leper. The measure *log*, which occurs four times in this section (chap. xiv. 10, 12, 15, 21), is not to be found in any other part of the Hebrew Scriptures. According to the authorities at the time of Christ, a "log" is equal to six hen's eggs.

(11) **Shall present the man . . . before the Lord, at the door.**—As his purification was not yet effected, since expiation had not yet been made, the convalescent could not enter into the court of the Israelites. Hence, during the second Temple the priest who performed the function of purifying him went close to the gate of Nicanor, between the court of the Women and that of Israel. Here the patient stood with his face towards the sanctuary, which was taken to mean "before the Lord." The phrase "at the door of the tabernacle of the congregation," as usual, should be rendered *at the entrance of the tent of meeting.* (See chap. i. 3.)

at the door of the tabernacle of the congregation: (12) and the priest shall take one he lamb, and offer him for a trespass offering, and the log of oil, and [a] wave them *for* a wave offering before the LORD: (13) and he shall slay the lamb in the place where he shall kill the sin offering and the burnt offering, in the holy place: for [b] as the sin offering *is* the priest's, *so is* the trespass offering: it *is* most holy: (14) and the priest shall take *some* of the blood of the trespass offering, and the priest shall put *it* upon the tip of the right ear of him that is to be cleansed, and upon the thumb of his right hand, and upon the great toe of his right foot: (15) and the priest shall take *some* of the log of oil, and pour *it* into the palm of his own left hand: (16) and the priest shall dip his right finger in the oil that *is* in his left hand, and shall sprinkle of the oil with his finger seven times before the LORD: (17) and of the rest of the oil that *is* in his hand shall the priest put upon the tip of the right ear of him

a Ex. 29. 24.

b ch. 7. 7.

(12) **And offer him for a trespass offering.**—As leprosy was a Divine punishment for sin, the restored leper had to bring expiatory sacrifices. There is, however, a striking difference in the ritual of the leper's trespass offering and the ordinary trespass offering described in chap. v. 6, &c. In the case before us, not only did oil accompany it, but both the trespass offering and the oil were waved by the priest, which did not take place on any other occasion in connection with the trespass offering and sin offering. Indeed, in no other case was the entire victim waved before the Lord.

(13) **And he shall slay the lamb.**—Better, *And the lamb shall be killed.* On ordinary occasions the sacrificer himself slaughtered the victim on the north side of the altar (see chap. i. 5); but as the convalescent was not as yet allowed to enter the court, other persons appointed for these occasions killed the sacrifice. Hence the ancient Chaldee Version of the so-called Jonathan ben Uzziel rightly renders it, "And the slaughterer shall slay the lamb." The phrase is therefore better rendered in the passive, as is often the case in Hebrew. Before the sacrifice was slain the offerer had to lay his hands on the victim. (See chap. i. 4.) For the reason, however, already stated, the convalescent could not do it before the altar. The lamb was therefore brought to the door of the court where the leper stood, and the convalescent put his hands through the gate of Nicanor, and laid them on the victim. From this place the purification was performed of men who contracted defilement from a running issue, and of women when they brought their offerings after childbirth. (See chap. xii. 6.)

In the place where he shall kill the sin offering.—Better, *in the place where they kill,* &c., as exactly the same phrase is rendered by the Authorised Version in chap iv. 33: that is, in the court of the sanctuary, on the north side of the altar (see chaps. i. 11, vi. 25), which was more holy than the entrance where the convalescent stood.

For as the sin offering . . .—The flesh of both these sacrifices was the perquisite of the officiating priest, and could only be eaten by him and the male members of his family within the court of the sanctuary, being of the class of sacrifices which were most holy. (See chap. vi. 18.)

(14) **And the priest shall take some of the blood.**—During the second Temple two priests caught the blood of the trespass offering—one into a vessel, and the other into the hollow of his hand. The one who caught the blood in the vessel sprinkled it against the wall of the altar, whilst the other who had the blood in the hollow of his hand went to the convalescent, who was waiting in the porch of Nicanor opposite the eastern door, with his face turned to the west.

And the priest shall put it upon the tip of the right ear.—Still unable to enter the court of the sanctuary, because he had not as yet been cleansed, the restored leper put his head through the gate of Nicanor, when the priest who caught the blood in the hollow of his hand, and who stood within the court, close to the entrance, (because the blood of the expiatory sacrifices could not be brought beyond the limits of the court of Israel), put some of it on the cartilage of his right ear. He then put through his right hand, and the priest put some of the blood on his thumb; he then again put through his right foot, and the priest put some of the blood on the great toe. To expedite the process, the restored leper was also allowed to put through all the three members at once. If the cured leper had not a thumb on his right hand, or a toe on his right foot, or a right ear, he was never cleansed. The right members were chosen for these symbolical acts, as in the case of the consecration of the priest, because they are represented as the strongest, and are therefore the most able to execute the will of God, for which reason they were henceforth dedicated to His service. (See chap. vii. 24.)

(15) **Shall take some of the log of oil.**—This he had to do with his right hand, which is actually expressed in the ancient Chaldee paraphrase.

And pour it into the palm of his own left hand.—Better, *and he shall pour it into the palm of the priest's left hand,* that is, the priest who has hitherto performed the ceremony of cleansing the leper now takes some of the log of oil, and puts it into the left hand of his fellow priest. This is not only distinctly declared in the canons which obtained during the second Temple, but is expressed in the text, which is seen from the literal translation we have given of the clause in question. The same priest, however, was allowed to pour it into the palm of his own hands. To express this view, which the translators of the Authorised Version espoused, they omitted the word *priest,* which is to be found in the original, and substituted *his own,* which is not in the original.

(16) **And the priest shall dip.**—The priest did not take the oil into the sanctuary, but, holding it in the hollow of his hand, stood in the court, whilst the officiating priest, turning his face to the Holy of Holies, dipped his right finger in the oil, and sprinkled it seven times upon the floor of the court, which was understood to mean "before the Lord," dipping his finger every time he sprinkled the oil.

(17) **And of the rest of the oil.**—With the rest of the oil both priests returned to the leper, when the

that is to be cleansed, and upon the thumb of his right hand, and upon the great toe of his right foot, upon the blood of the trespass offering: (18) and the remnant of the oil that *is* in the priest's hand he shall pour upon the head of him that is to be cleansed: and the priest shall make an atonement for him before the LORD. (19) And the priest shall offer the sin offering, and make an atonement for him that is to be cleansed from his uncleanness; and afterward he shall kill the burnt offering: (20) and the priest shall offer the burnt offering and the meat offering upon the altar: and the priest shall make an atonement for him, and he shall be clean.

(21) And if he *be* poor, and [1] cannot get so much; then he shall take one lamb *for* a trespass offering [2] to be waved, to make an atonement for him, and one tenth deal of fine flour mingled with oil for a meat offering, and a log of oil; (22) and two turtledoves, or two young pigeons, such as he is able to get; and the one shall be a sin offering, and the other a burnt offering. (23) And he shall bring them on the eighth day for his cleansing unto the priest, unto the door of the tabernacle of the congregation, before the LORD. (24) And the priest shall take the lamb of the trespass offering, and the log of oil, and the priest shall wave them *for* a wave offering before the LORD: (25) and he shall kill the lamb of the trespass offering, and the priest shall take *some* of the blood of the trespass offering, and put *it* upon the tip of the right ear of him that is to be cleansed, and upon the thumb of his right hand, and upon the great toe of his right foot: (26) and the priest shall pour of the oil into the palm of his own left hand: (27) and the priest shall sprinkle with his right finger *some* of the oil that *is* in his left hand seven times before the LORD: (28) and the priest shall put of the oil that *is* in his hand upon the tip of the right ear of him that is to be cleansed, and upon the thumb of his right hand, and upon the great toe of his right foot, upon the place of the blood of the trespass offering: (29) and the rest of the oil that *is* in the priest's hand he shall put upon the head of him that is to be cleansed, to make an atonement for him before the LORD. (30) And he shall offer

1 Heb., *his hand reach not.*

2 Heb., *for a waving.*

---

officiating priest put it on those parts of the convalescent's body on which he had previously put blood, so that the oil now actually was "upon the blood of the trespass offering," on the tip of the ear, the thumb, and the toe of the cleansed leper. (See also verse 28.)

(18) **He shall pour upon the head.**—That which remains of the oil in the hollow of the priest's hand after some of it had been sprinkled seven times before the Lord, and after some had been put on the several organs of the leper's body, the priest is *to put,* not "pour," upon the convalescent's head—the quantity left in the hand not being sufficient to pour—whilst the bulk of the log from which the hollow handful has been taken was the perquisite of the officiating priests, and, like the flesh of the sacrifices, had to be consumed within the sacred precincts.

And the priest shall make an atonement.—According to the canons which obtained during the second Temple, it was the act of putting the oil on the several organs, but more especially on the head, which effected the atonement of the restored leper. Failing to do this, even if the prescribed sacrifices had been offered, no expiation was made. The atonement was made for the sins which brought leprosy upon the sinner.

(19) **And the priest shall offer the sin offering.**—The other ewe lamb mentioned in verse 10 the priest is now to offer as a sin offering, to expiate the sins which the restored leper had committed during his illness, having probably given vent to impatient and unbecoming expressions at his loathsome condition, not as due in consequence of having been in a state of uncleanness. The regulations in chap. v. 2, 3, refer to cases when through thoughtlessness the unclean person forgot his duty.

(20) **Shall offer the burnt offering.**—With the offering of the burnt offering, accompanied by the meat offering mentioned in verse 10, concluded the second and last stage of the purification of the leper, which completely restored him to the privileges of the sanctuary.

(21) **And if he be poor.**—The benign consideration for the poor which has been evinced on former occasions in connection with the sacrifices (see chaps. v. 7, 11, xii. 18) is also shown here. Three lambs and three tenth deals of flour were more than a poor leper could afford to bring. In such cases, therefore, all that was required was one lamb, which constituted the trespass offering, and one tenth deal of flour for a meat offering, and the log of oil which was needed for his consecration.

(22) **Two turtledoves, or two young pigeons**—which were plentiful and cheap in Palestine (see chap. i. 14), instead of the two lambs required of those who were able to bring them.

(23) **And he shall bring them on the eighth day.**—This premises that the poor man is to go through the first stage of purification which is prescribed in verses 3—8, and which admits him to social life, in exactly the same manner as the rich man, since the things prescribed for this stage are inexpensive.

(24–29) **And the priest shall take the lamb.**—The ritual for the poor man's sacrifices, however, is the same as that which is prescribed for the rich man. The solemnity and imposing nature of the service is not diminished, as both rich and poor are alike in the presence of the Lord. Hence the directions in verses 24

the one of the turtledoves, or of the
young pigeons, such as he can get;
(31) *even* such as he is able to get, the
one *for* a sin offering, and the other *for*
a burnt offering, with the meat offering:
and the priest shall make an atonement
for him that is to be cleansed before
the LORD.
(32) This *is* the law *of him* in whom *is*
the plague of leprosy, whose hand is
not able to get *that which pertaineth* to
his cleansing.
(33) And the LORD spake unto Moses and
unto Aaron, saying, (34) When ye be come
into the land of Canaan, which I give
to you for a possession, and I put the
plague of leprosy in a house of the land
of your possession; (35) and he that
owneth the house shall come and tell
the priest, saying, It seemeth to me
there is as it were a plague in the house:
(36) then the priest shall command that
they [1] empty the house, before the priest
go *into it* to see the plague, that all that
is in the house be not made unclean:
and afterward the priest shall go in to
see the house: (37) and he shall look
on the plague, and, behold, *if* the plague
be in the walls of the house with hollow
strakes, greenish or reddish, which in
sight *are* lower than the wall; (38) then
the priest shall go out of the house to the

[1] Or, *prepare.*

—29 in connection with the humbler sacrifices are simply a repetition of those ordained in verses 12—18, to be observed in the case of the more costly offerings.

(32) **This is the law of him . . . whose hand is not able to get.**—That is, that which is laid down in verses 21—31 constitutes the law for the restored leper who is too poor to offer the sacrifices prescribed in verses 10—20.

(33) **And the Lord spake unto Moses and unto Aaron.**—Whilst the law about the cleansing of restored lepers was addressed to Moses alone (see verse 1), the regulations about leprous houses, like those with regard to leprous garments and persons, are for the same reason delivered to Moses and Aaron conjointly. (See chap. xiii. 1.)

(34) **When ye be come into the land of Canaan.**—We have here the first of four instances in Leviticus of a law being given prospectively, having no immediate bearing on the condition of the people of Israel (see chaps. xix. 23; xxiii. 10; xxv. 2). This may be the reason why it is separated from the law of leprous men and garments, which we should naturally expect it would follow, instead of being preceded by the law of cleansing, and why it occupies the position of an appendix. Because it is here said "the land of Canaan," the authorities during the second Temple maintained that this supernatural plague of leprous houses was peculiar to Palestine, and was unknown in any other country. They moreover adduce the words "in a house of the land of your possession" to account for the fact that houses in Palestine not in the possession of the Israelites, —*i.e.,* houses of Gentiles—were exempt from this distemper, that the synagogues throughout the country which had no official dwelling-houses attached to them were never visited by this loathsome disease, and that none of the houses in Jerusalem were ever afflicted with it, because the holy city was never divided among the tribes. Whatever we may think of their interpretation, the testimony of these eye-witnesses who had to administer the laws of leprosy, that out of Palestine, that in certain houses in Palestine, and that in the whole of Jerusalem, this kind of distemper was unknown, remains unshaken.

And I put the plague of leprosy.—The plague is here described as a supernatural one, proceeding from the immediate hand of God. Ordinary leprosy, as we are told by the authorities in the time of Christ, comes upon man for the following sins: "for idolatry, for profaning the name of the Lord, unchastity, theft, slander, false witness, false judgment, perjury, infringing the borders of a neighbour, devising malicious plans, or creating discord between brothers." House leprosy is sent by God if the owner of a plot of land on the sacred soil builds his house with materials unlawfully acquired. Hence the ancient Chaldee Version of Jonathan renders the first part of this verse by, "And if there be a man who buildeth his house with stolen goods, then I will put the plague," &c.

(35) **He that owneth the house.**—As in the case of the suspicious symptoms in human beings, the suspected house is forthwith to be examined by the priest.

Saying, It seemeth to me . . .—According to the authorities in the time of Christ, this prescribes the formula which the owner of the house is to use when he communicates the fact to the priest. Hence they enacted that though he be himself an expert in these matters, and know certainly that it is leprosy, he is not to say positively to the priest, "The plague has appeared in my house," but "It seemeth to me . . . as it were," &c., because it was the office of the priest to pronounce a positive sentence on the subject.

(36) **That they empty the house.**—If the examination was made before the removal of the objects in it, and the priest pronounced the house leprous, all the furniture, &c., found therein would be defiled. Hence the benign law that everything should be removed previous to the priest's inspection, to save the household stuff. This assuredly shows that the law did not regard leprosy as infectious.

(37) **With hollow strakes, greenish or reddish.**—If the house is really leprous, the priest on inspecting it will find in the walls the same three symptoms which are visible in the skin of leprous human beings: (1) hollow strakes, or, rather, *deep cavities* or *depressions,* which the ancient canons define as a depression deeper than the rest of the wall, being the same symptom as in man (see chap. xiii. 3); (2) a *greenish* or (3) a *reddish* spot, which were the second and third symptoms of leprosy in men and garments. (Comp. chap. xiii. 49.) According to the canons which obtained during the second Temple, the size of this discoloured spot on the wall had to be that of two beans.

(38) **Shut up the house seven days.**—On finding these symptoms, the priest is to put the house in quarantine for seven days, in order to see what alteration will take place during this interval, adopting the same treatment as in the case of leprous garments. (See chap. xiii. 50.)

door of the house, and shut up the
house seven days: (39) and the priest
shall come again the seventh day, and
shall look: and, behold, *if* the plague
be spread in the walls of the house;
(40) then the priest shall command that
they take away the stones in which the
plague *is*, and they shall cast them into
an unclean place without the city:
(41) and he shall cause the house to be
scraped within round about, and they
shall pour out the dust that they scrape
off without the city into an unclean
place: (42) and they shall take other
stones, and put *them* in the place of
those stones; and he shall take other
morter, and shall plaister the house.
(43) And if the plague come again, and
break out in the house, after that he
hath taken away the stones, and after
he hath scraped the house, and after
it is plaistered; (44) then the priest shall
come and look, and, behold, *if* the
plague be spread in the house, it *is* a
fretting leprosy in the house: it *is* un-
clean. (45) And he shall break down the
house, the stones of it, and the timber
thereof, and all the morter of the house;
and he shall carry *them* forth out of the
city into an unclean place. (46) More-
over he that goeth into the house all
the while that it is shut up shall be
unclean until the even. (47) And he that
lieth in the house shall wash his clothes;
and he that eateth in the house shall
wash his clothes.

(48) And if the priest [1] shall come in,
and look *upon it*, and, behold, the plague
hath not spread in the house, after the
house was plaistered: then the priest
shall pronounce the house clean, because
the plague is healed. (49) And he shall
take to cleanse the house two birds,
and cedar wood, and scarlet, and hyssop:
(50) and he shall kill the one of the birds
in an earthen vessel over running
water: (51) and he shall take the cedar
wood, and the hyssop, and the scarlet,
and the living bird, and dip them in the
blood of the slain bird, and in the
running water, and sprinkle the house
seven times: (52) and he shall cleanse
the house with the blood of the bird,
and with the running water, and with
the living bird, and with the cedar
wood, and with the hyssop, and with
the scarlet: (53) but he shall let go the
living bird out of the city into the open
fields, and make an atonement for the
house: and it shall be clean.

[1] Heb., *in coming in shall come in, &c.*

(39, 40) **And the priest shall come again.**—If on inspecting it again at the end of the first week's quarantine, the priest finds that the depression or discolouring has spread in the walls, thus indicating the progress of the disease, just as in the case of leprous men and garments (see chap. xiii. 5, 50), he is to order the affected stones which exhibit these symptoms to be pulled out of the walls, and to be cast into the unclean receptacle which was prepared outside every city for carcases and filth of every kind, just as there was outside the city a clean place for the deposition of the ashes of the sanctuary. (See chap. iv. 11.) It will be seen that out of the eight verbs used in verses 40—42 in connection with the removing of the affected stones and the constitution of new ones, the scraping, and the plaistering, six are in the plural: viz., they shall take, they shall cast (verse 40); they shall pour out, they shall scrape off (verse 41); they shall take, they shall put them (verse 42); and two are in the singular: viz., he shall take other mortar, he shall plaister (verse 42). From this the authorities during the second Temple concluded, and hence enacted, that if the affected stones are in a partition wall which divides two houses occupied by two different owners, both alike must take part in the first six acts, whilst the new mortaring and the plaistering must be done by the owner of the affected house alone.

(43, 45) **And if the plague come again.**—If after these alterations and precautions the symptoms reappear, the house must be pulled down, just as the garment was destroyed under similar circumstances (see chap. xiii. 51), and the materials deposited in the unclean receptacle outside the city, since its re-appearance shows that it is an incurable leprosy. From the fact that the materials of the house here spoken of are stones, earth, and wood, the ancient canons enacted that no dwelling is exposed to the laws of leprosy unless it has four walls, and is built of stone, earth, and wood. Houses of brick and marble, therefore, do not come within these laws.

(46) **Moreover he that goeth into the house.**—If any one only momentarily entered the house whilst it was under quarantine, he contracted defilement, which lasted till sundown of the same day. After the priest declared it unclean, it defiled by simply touching it outside.

(47) **And he that lieth in the house.**—As abiding in it all night was graver than a momentary entrance, it involved the washing of the garments before the person so defiled could be clean. The same was the case if any one made a meal in it.

(48) **The plague hath not spread.**—If at the end of the second week's quarantine the distemper has not spread, having been checked by the means prescribed in verses 42, 43, the priest is to declare it clean, and fit for re-habitation. This is the same criterion adopted in the case of leprous men and garments. (See chap. xiii. 6, 58.)

(49—53) **And he shall take to cleanse the house.**—The same rites are prescribed for cleansing the house which were performed in cleansing the healed leper (see verses 3—7), with the exception of the sacrifices which the man brought afterwards, and which were necessarily absent in the case of the restored leprous house.

(54) This *is* the law for all manner of
plague of leprosy, and [a]scall, (55) and for
the leprosy of a garment, and of a
house, (56) and for a rising, and for a
scab, and for a bright spot: (57) to teach
[1] when *it is* unclean, and when *it is*
clean: this *is* the law of leprosy.

CHAPTER XV.—(1) And the LORD
spake unto Moses, and to Aaron, saying,
(2) Speak unto the children of Israel,
and say unto them, When any man
hath a [2] running issue out of his flesh,
because of his issue he *is* unclean.
(3) And this shall be his uncleanness in
his issue: whether his flesh run with
his issue, or his flesh be stopped from
his issue, it *is* his uncleanness. (4) Every
bed, whereon he lieth that hath the
issue, is unclean: and every [3] thing,
whereon he sitteth, shall be unclean.
(5) And whosoever toucheth his bed shall
wash his clothes, and bathe *himself* in
water, and be unclean until the even.
(6) And he that sitteth on *any* thing
whereon he sat that hath the issue shall
wash his clothes, and bathe *himself* in
water, and be unclean until the even.
(7) And he that toucheth the flesh of
him that hath the issue shall wash his
clothes, and bathe *himself* in water, and
be unclean until the even. (8) And if he
that hath the issue spit upon him that
is clean; then he shall wash his clothes,
and bathe *himself* in water, and be
unclean until the even. (9) And what

a ch. 13. 30.

1 Heb., *in the day of the unclean, and in the day of the clean.*

2 Or, *running of the reins.*

3 Heb., *vessel.*

(54–56) **This is the law for all manner of plague.**—These verses sum up the laws of leprosy given in chaps. xiii., xiv. The various names contained in verse 56 are repeated from chap. xiii. 2.

(57) **To teach when it is unclean.**—This verse is intimately connected with verse 54, viz.: "This is the law for all manner of plague of leprosy . . . to afford instruction in the day of uncleanness, and in the day of cleanness:" that is, to furnish them with instructions against the time when they would have to deal with these cases in taking possession of the promised land. The ancient authorities, however, insisted upon the literal rendering which is substantially exhibited in the Margin of the Authorised Version, viz., "To teach concerning the day of uncleanness and concerning the day of cleanness:" *i.e.*, to instruct the people on which days this distemper may be examined and decided. Hence the ancient Chaldee Version of Jonathan renders it, "That the priests may teach the people to discern between the dark days, when his leprosy is to be examined, and between the bright days." (See chap. xiii. 2.)

XV.

(1) **And the Lord spake unto Moses and to Aaron.**—This chapter, which lays down the laws of uncleanness arising from issues, discusses two diseased and three natural secretions.

(2) **A running issue out of his flesh.**—Flesh, as is frequently the case, euphemistically denotes private parts. (See Gen. vi. 10, vii. 13; chaps. vi. 3, xvi. 4; Ezek. xvi. 26, xxiii. 20, &c.)

Because of his issue he is unclean.—Better, *his issue is unclean.* Hence, any one coming in contact with it, or with the garment on which traces of the secretion are found, is thereby rendered unclean.

(3) **Whether his flesh run.**—This verse defines more minutely the statement in the preceding verse.

(4) **Every bed, whereon he lieth.**—So severely did the canonical law deal with these cases that they interpreted the defilement communicated to the bed, and hence also to his seat and saddle, by the patient in five different ways: by standing, sitting, lying, hanging, or leaning on it. The patient's polluting power is so great that even if the bed, seat, or saddle is under a stone, he defiles it through the stone by any of these actions. If he stood upon two beds, placing one foot upon each, he defiled both.

(5, 6) **And whosoever toucheth his bed.**—The defiling power of the patient was so great that the bed, seat, or saddle which he rendered unclean by any of the above-named five acts polluted again any one who came in contact with these articles in seven different ways: by standing, sitting, lying, hanging, leaning, touching, or bearing them. The person thus polluted had to remain in this condition, debarred from the privileges of the sanctuary, till sundown, when he had to wash his garments, and immerse his whole body in water.

(7) **And he that toucheth the flesh.**—With such intense loathing was the person regarded who had contracted this infirmity, that even the medical man who had professionally to examine him became defiled for the rest of the day. He had to wash his clothes and immerse the whole of his body in water before he could be admitted into the enjoyment of his own sacred privileges.

(8) **If he . . . spit upon him.**—Spitting in the face of a person was, and still is, commonly resorted to among Oriental nations as an expression of insult and contempt (Num. xii. 14; Deut. xxv. 9; Isa. l. 6; Job xxx. 10; Matt. xxvi. 67, &c.). Suffering from the disease here discussed, the patient would naturally be more irritable, and hence be liable to give vent more frequently to this mode of expressing his wrath. Now, any person upon whom he happened to heap this indignity became defiled by the spittle in the same manner, and had to go through the same purification, as he who chanced to touch his garments, or as the physician who had to examine him.

(9) **And what saddle soever.**—Better, *and any carriage.* The word here translated "saddle" only occurs twice more: viz., 1 Kings v. 6 in Hebrew, or chap. iv. 26 in English, where it is rendered "chariot" in the Authorised Version, and in Cant. iii. 10, where it is translated "covering," but where it manifestly denotes the seat inside the palanquin. With the feminine termination the word in question occurs no less than forty-four times, and is invariably translated in the Authorised Version "chariot." What kind of vehicle the masculine form of the expression in question denotes in the three passages in which it occurs must be decided

saddle soever he rideth upon that hath
the issue shall be unclean. (10) And
whosoever toucheth any thing that was
under him shall be unclean until the
even: and he that beareth *any of* those
things shall wash his clothes, and bathe
himself in water, and be unclean until
the even. (11) And whomsoever he touch-
eth that hath the issue, and hath not
rinsed his hands in water, he shall wash
his clothes, and bathe *himself* in water,
and be unclean until the even. (12) And
the [a] vessel of earth, that he toucheth
which hath the issue, shall be broken:
and every vessel of wood shall be rinsed
in water. (13) And when he that hath
an issue is cleansed of his issue; then
he shall number to himself seven days
for his cleansing, and wash his clothes,
and bathe his flesh in running water,

a ch. 6. 28.

from the context. In Kings, the horses which are used in connection with it show that it was a carriage drawn by animals. In Canticles it is a vehicle, or the essential part of it, carried by men, and this is the kind of vehicle meant in the passage before us. It is the well-known palanquin so largely used in the East.

Shall be unclean.—The conveyance used is to be unclean, and hence, is not to be used by any one else. It will be seen that the present text does not say how long the vehicle is to be defiled, though in every other instance the time is fixed. (See verses 5—11.) There can, therefore, hardly be any doubt that the reading in the LXX., which has here *until evening*, is the original one, and that the words have dropped out of the Hebrew text.

(10) **And whosoever toucheth any thing that was under him.**—That is, the seat in the palanquin on which the passenger sits. If touched by any one after the man with the issue has sat on it, he contracts defilement till sundown.

And he that beareth any of those things.—Better, *And he that beareth them.* That is, whoso carries the palanquin, with the patient in it, from one place to another, contracts defilement. (See chap. xi. 28, 40.)

(11) **And hath not rinsed his hands in water.**—If the patient happens to touch any one with his hands without having first washed his hands, the man who has thus been touched by the unwashen hands of the defiled invalid contracts pollution till sundown of the day on which he has been touched. He has to wash his clothes and immerse his whole body in water before he can partake of the privileges of the sanctuary. This is the only instance where the touch of the hand as imparting defilement is expressly mentioned, and where the washing of the hands alone is ordered in the Mosaic Law to prevent the communication of pollution. The washing of the hands over the heifer, ordered in Deut. xxi. 6, is of a different kind. It is meant to renounce any share in the guilt of the murder, or rather, to protest their innocence.

(12) **And the vessel of earth . . . shall be broken.**—For the reason why vessels of a porous clay must be destroyed when contaminated by defilement, see chaps. vi. 28, xi. 33. This, however, is the only instance where an earthen vessel touched on the outside was defiled, thus again showing the intense loathing with which the guilt of this kind of infirmity was regarded.

Every vessel of wood shall be rinsed in water.—As these kinds of vessels were both more expensive and more difficult to restore, the Law, which so frequently takes into consideration the circumstances of the people, mercifully spares the more costly utensils. These are to undergo the same baptism as human beings. The administrators of the law during the second Temple took the expression "wood" in a more generic sense, as denoting more enduring material than clay; hence they included vessels made of copper, brass, silver, &c. With regard to the manner in which the vessels thus polluted are to be immersed, they ordained that if the utensil is dipped with its mouth downward, or if the vessel, at the time of its immersion, contains any liquor except water, the baptism is illegal. They, moreover, ordained that all new vessels which are purchased, or otherwise acquired, must likewise be immersed, for fear lest the maker, or some of those who have handled them prior to the purchase, might have been in a state of defilement. Hence the orthodox Jews to this day literally baptize cups, plates, knives, forks, or any new utensil which they buy. It is to this law that Christ refers when He says, "And many other things there be, which they have received to hold, as the washing [literally, *the baptism*] of cups, and pots, brazen vessels, and of tables," or, as the Margin has it more correctly, "beds," or *couches* (Mark vii. 4).

(13) **And when he . . . is cleansed of his issue.**—That is, recovered or healed of his infirmity (see verse 28), as the real purification was not accomplished till he had performed the ritual prescribed in this and in the two following verses. He is, however, not to perform these rites as soon as he finds that the issue has ceased, but has to wait seven clear days, so as to afford sufficient time to ascertain whether the infirmity had actually disappeared. If any vestige of it was seen during these seven days, or even at the end of the seventh day, and after he was baptized, he had again to count seven other days.

Bathe his flesh in running water.—Or, more literally, *living water.* It will be seen that whilst all other defiled persons and things were to be immersed in a collection of water, the restored man who had suffered from the issue in question was ordered to bathe in a fountain or in spring water. For the phrase "living water," see chap. xiv. 5, 50. It is more than probable that the term "flesh" has here, too, the euphemistic sense in which it has hitherto been used in this section. (See verses 2, 3, 7.) This derives support from the fact that whenever bathing of the body is ordered, the phrase for it throughout this section is uniformly "bathe in water" simply, which occurs no less than ten times (chap. xv. 5—8, 10, 11, 18, 21, 22, 27), and where the Authorised Version has in all cases inserted *himself* in italics. This, moreover, seems to be confirmed by the fact that in the only passage in this section where the expression "flesh" is used in its literal sense for "body" (see verse 16), the sacred writer designedly added (*ĕth kol*) "all," so that it might be distinguished from the euphemistic sense in which it is used in all the other passages in this section. This, however, would not exclude the bathing of the body as well, but, on the contrary, premises it.

and shall be clean. (14) And on the
eighth day he shall take to him two
turtledoves, or two young pigeons, and
come before the LORD unto the door of
the tabernacle of the congregation, and
give them unto the priest: (15) and the
priest shall offer them, the one *for* a sin
offering, and the other *for* a burnt offer-
ing; and the priest shall make an atone-
ment for him before the LORD for his
issue.

(16) And if any man's seed of copula-
tion go out from him, then he shall
wash all his flesh in water, and be un-
clean until the even. (17) And every
garment, and every skin, whereon is the
seed of copulation, shall be washed with
water, and be unclean until the even.
(18) The woman also with whom man
shall lie *with* seed of copulation, they
shall *both* bathe *themselves* in water, and
be unclean until the even.

(19) And if a woman have an issue,
and her issue in her flesh be blood, she
shall be [1] put apart seven days: and
whosoever toucheth her shall be unclean

[1] Heb., *in her separation.*

(14) **And on the eighth day he shall take to him.**—If after the bathing on the eve of the seventh day no sign of the infirmity is seen, he is to bring on the eighth day the appointed sacrifices. It is very striking that whilst in other cases it was only the poor who, out of consideration, were allowed two turtledoves or two young pigeons (see chaps. v. 7, xii. 8, xiv. 22), in the case before us the meanest offering was prescribed for all alike who suffered from this infirmity, without giving them the choice of bringing a more costly sacrifice. The phrase "he shall take to him" is simply a Hebrew pleonastic way for saying "he shall take."

The door of the tabernacle of the congregation.—Better, *the entrance of the tent of meeting,* which here means the eastern gate, where the offerer would face the west, or Holy of Holies, the place of the Lord's Divine majesty, and hence, "before the Lord."

(15) **And the priest shall make an atonement.**—That is, for the sinful act which has brought about the infirmity. The severity with which people were treated who had contracted this disease may further be seen from the fact that they had to remain without the camp (Num. v. 1—4). During the second Temple they were debarred from partaking of the Paschal meal, and were banished from the precincts of the holy city. Hence, when David in his great indignation wanted to invoke an imprecation upon his adversaries, he exclaimed, "Let there not fail from the house of Joab one that hath an issue" (2 Sam. iii. 29).

(16) **And if any man's seed.**—The second case, discussed in this and the following verses, is that of an involuntary emission, as in Deut. xxiii. 10. The man who sustained it had simply to immerse his whole body in water the following morning, and remain unclean till sundown. Similar rites were performed by the ancients under the same circumstances. Thus the Egyptian priests when they were defiled by a dream purified themselves by bathing their bodies; and, according to the directions of the Koran, any faithful Mahommedan who meets with such an accident must not perform his prayers till he has gone through the prescribed oblation. (*Koran*, iv. 46.)

(17) **And every skin.**—That is, everything which a man wears or lies upon made of skin, in contradistinction to the ordinary garments made of stuffs (see chap. xiii. 48) with which it is associated. Any one of these thus defiled was cleansed by washing. It is from this circumstance that the apostle borrows the expression "hating even the garments spotted by the flesh" (Jude 23).

(18) **The woman also with whom man shall lie.**—Better, *And if a man lie with a woman,* that is, even when what is specified in verse 16 takes place in intercourse between man and woman lawfully married, it pollutes both the husband and the wife. They have accordingly both to immerse their whole bodies, and remain unclean till sundown, and were debarred from the privileges of the sanctuary during that day. Hence abstinence from conjugal intercourse was regarded as a necessary preparation for the performance of sacred duties. He who had approached his wife could not draw nigh to God (Exod. xix. 15), and was not allowed to partake of sacred meals. (Comp. 1 Sam. xxi. 5, 6.) The law of pollution was not designed to put a check upon marriage, since matrimony is a Divine institution (Gen. i. 27, 28, ii. 21—25), but it is intended to prevent husband and wife from making an immoderate use of their conjugal life, and thus to preserve them in health and vigour by prescribing such constant purifications after it. This is probably the reason why other nations of antiquity enacted similar laws. Thus the Hindoos and the Babylonians bathed after conjugal intercourse. The Egyptian priests abstained from it when they had to perform sacred duties, and the laity were not allowed to enter the precincts of the Temple unless they submitted to ablutions. Mahommed, for the same reason, enjoins lustrations upon all the faithful before reciting their prayers.

(19) **And if a woman have an issue.**—Having legislated for cases in connection with man—as well as for one case in which both the husband and the wife are concerned, the Law now lays down directions for two cases affecting the woman.

And her issue in her flesh be blood.—Better, *if her issue, &c.* This clause defines the preceding one, stating more minutely what the issue consists of and proceeds from.

She shall be put apart seven days.—Though as a rule the discharge ceases after three or four days, yet, as in the first stage after childbirth, the period of uncleanness is extended to seven days to include exceptional cases. (See chap. xii. 2.) To fully appreciate the merciful provisions of the laws here enacted, it is necessary to bear in mind not only the gross superstitions which obtained among the ancients about women in this condition, but the cruel treatment to which wives and daughters were subjected, and in some countries both in the Old and New Worlds still are subjected. It was believed that if a woman in this condition sat under a tree, all its fruit fell off; at her approach the edge of a tool became blunted, and copper utensils contracted a fetid smell, and meat got sour, and a thousand other things. Hence the Parsees

until the even. (20) And every thing that
she lieth upon in her separation shall
be unclean: every thing also that she
sitteth upon shall be unclean. (21) And
whosoever toucheth her bed shall wash
his clothes, and bathe *himself* in water,
and be unclean until the even. (22) And
whosoever toucheth any thing that she
sat upon shall wash his clothes, and
bathe *himself* in water, and be unclean
until the even. (23) And if it *be* on *her*
bed, or on any thing whereon she sitteth,
when he toucheth it, he shall be unclean
until the even. (24) And if any man lie
with her at all, and her flowers be
upon him, he shall be unclean seven
days; and all the bed whereon he lieth
shall be unclean.

(25) And if a woman have an issue of
her blood many days out of the time of
her separation, or if it run beyond the
time of her separation; all the days of
the issue of her uncleanness shall be as
the days of her separation: she *shall be*
unclean. (26) Every bed whereon she
lieth all the days of her issue shall be
unto her as the bed of her separation:
and whatsoever she sitteth upon shall
be unclean, as the uncleanness of her
separation. (27) And whosoever touch-
eth those things shall be unclean, and
shall wash his clothes, and bathe *him-
self* in water, and be unclean until the
even. (28) But if she be cleansed of her
issue, then she shall number to herself
seven days, and after that she shall be
clean. (29) And on the eighth day she
shall take unto her two turtles, or two
young pigeons, and bring them unto
the priest, to the door of the tabernacle
of the congregation. (30) And the priest
shall offer the one *for* a sin offering,
and the other *for* a burnt offering; and
the priest shall make an atonement for
her before the LORD for the issue of her
uncleanness.

(31) Thus shall ye separate the children
of Israel from their uncleanness; that

---

not only isolated her from the rest of the family, but forbade her speaking to any one, and those who took food to her in her seclusion had to put it at some distance from her. The Zabii purified with fire every place which she trod. Even if the wind which came from the quarter where she was blew upon any one, he became polluted. To this day the negroes in Issing, the Calmucks, and many others, have special houses for them outside each town and village; and at the River La Plata they are sewn into hammocks, with only a small aperture for the mouth, till they are well again. To restrain the Jews from sharing these superstitions, and from resorting to any of these inhuman acts, as well as for sanitary purposes, the Lawgiver ordained these benign and necessary rules.

Whosoever toucheth her shall be unclean.—Like other unclean persons, she defiled by being touched. Though not expressed here, it is implied that he who contracted this defilement had both to wash his garments and bathe his body as usual.

(21—22) **And whosoever toucheth her bed.**—The regulations in these three verses are the same as those laid down in verses 4—6.

(23) **And if it be on her bed.**—Better, *and if any object be on her bed*, that is, if anything happen to lie on her bed.

When he toucheth it.—Rather, *if he toucheth it.* Whilst the former two verses declare that if any one touches the bed itself, or the thing on which she sat, he contracts such a degree of defilement that he must wash his clothes, bathe his whole body, and remain in a state of pollution till sundown, the verse before us enacts that if he happens to touch any vessel, garment, or any other objects which are lying on the defiling bed or seat in question, he has only to remain unclean till sundown, without having to wash his garments. The defilement in this case is not primary, but secondary. It is no more the bed or seat which defiled by direct contact, but an object which the defiled bed or seat had defiled, the pollution in this case being indirect.

(24) **And if any man lie with her.**—For committing this gross act presumptuously, both parties to it were visited with death. (See chaps. xviii. 19, xx. 18.)

(25) **Have an issue . . . many days.**—The last case is that of a chronic issue, arising from a derangement in the constitution. This is the kind of complaint from which the woman suffered who came to Christ (Matt. ix. 20; Luke viii. 44). As long as she suffered from it, which lasted sometimes for many years, she defiled and was defiling in the same way as in her menses.

(26, 27) **Every bed whereon she lieth.**—The rules here laid down about her defilement and defiling are the same as those in verses 20—22.

(28) **But if she be cleansed.**—That is, cured or healed of her infirmity. The expression "cleansed" is used both here and in verse 13 for the disappearance of the complaint. From the time of its cessation she is to count seven days, during which no trace of the complaint must be observable, just as in the case of the less innocent disorder. (See verse 13.)

After that she shall be clean.—That is, after having performed the rites of lustration.

(29) **She shall take unto her . . .**—On the eighth day she is to bring the same sacrifices which are prescribed for the man who is cured of an issue (see verse 14), only that in the latter case the man had to be bathed in living water, because he brought the illness upon himself.

(30) **And the priest shall offer.**—Exactly in the same manner as described in verse 15.

(31) **Thus shall ye separate.**—That is, according to the regulations laid down in this chapter. "Ye"—*i.e.*, Moses and Aaron, to whom they were conjointly addressed (see verse 1)—are to restrain the children of Israel, lest they be punished with death when they approach the Lord in a defiled state.

they die not in their uncleanness, when
they defile my tabernacle that *is* among
them.
(32) This *is* the law of him that hath
an issue, and *of him* whose seed goeth
from him, and is defiled therewith;
(33) and of her that is sick of her flowers,
and of him that hath an issue, of the
man, and of the woman, and of him
that lieth with her that is unclean.

CHAPTER XVI. —(1) And the LORD
spake unto Moses after [a]the death of
the two sons of Aaron, when they
offered before the LORD, and died;
(2) and the LORD said unto Moses, Speak
unto Aaron thy brother, that he [b]come
not at all times into the holy *place*
within the vail before the mercy seat,
which *is* upon the ark; that he die not:
for I will appear in the cloud upon the
mercy seat. (3) Thus shall Aaron come
into the holy *place:* with a young
bullock for a sin offering, and a ram for

a ch. 10. 2.

b Ex. 30. 10; Heb. 9. 7.

Defile my tabernacle. — Better, *my dwelling-place*, which can here be used, though in chap. viii. 10, where it also occurs, the expression "dwelling-place" does not suit so well.

(32, 33) **This is the law.**—These two verses give a summary of the contents of the chapter. In the recapitulation, however, as we have already seen, the order of the enactments is not strictly adhered to.

XVI.

(1) **And the Lord spake unto Moses.**—As the observance of the minute regulations given in the preceding chapters about the daily sacrifices and purifications would necessarily be tainted with many imperfections and shortcomings, both on the part of the mediating priests and the offering laity, a general day of atonement is here instituted, when priest and people are alike to obtain atonement once a year for the sins which were mixed up even with their sacred worship. The day of atonement enacted in the chapter before us is therefore an appropriate conclusion of the laws of purification in the preceding chapters. It is an annual supplement and completion of all the ordinances which were daily practised, and the design of which was to obtain atonement and reconciliation.

After the death of the two sons of Aaron.—That is, after Nadab and Abihu, his two eldest sons, had died, in consequence of having presumptuously entered the sanctuary in a profane manner, and at an irregular time. (See chap. x. 1, 2.)

(2) **That he come not at all times.**—Moses is therefore to warn his brother Aaron, the high priest, that if he wishes to escape a similar fate, he is not to presume to enter the Holy of Holies except on one day of the year, the Day of Atonement. As Aaron here stands for all those who in future are to succeed him in the pontificate, so Moses, who teaches him his duty, stands for his successors who are hereafter to impart instruction to the high priests on these most solemn occasions. Hence during the second Temple the tuition and preparation of the high priest for his functions devolved upon the Sanhedrin, who prescribed most minute rules for his guidance. Seven days before the Day of Atonement he was separated from his wife, and lodged in a chamber in the Temple, lest he should contract defilement, which might unfit him for the performance of his pontifical duties. The elders or the representatives of the Sanhedrin read and expounded to him the ordinances contained in this chapter; which he had to practise in their presence, so as to make sure that he could rightly perform all the ceremonies. This continued during the whole night previous to the Day of Atonement, when he was kept awake, so as to prevent any pollution arising from a dream or accident by night. He read, in the silent hours of darkness, the Books of Job, Daniel, Ezra, and Chronicles; and if he was no scholar, and could not read, the elders read them to him. As it was deemed important that he should not fall asleep, the priests who surrounded him alternately snapped their fingers, and made him walk on the cold pavement of the court. When the chief of the thirteen priests who were appointed to perform the ordinary duties in connection with the service in the sanctuary had ascertained that the morning had dawned, that the ashes had been removed from the brazen altar, and that the time of the early sacrifice had arrived, the high priest was conducted to the baptistery, where he immersed his whole body in water.

Into the holy place.—This is here more minutely defined by "within the vail," thus showing that the Holy of Holies is meant. In the succeeding portions of this chapter, however, the expression "holy" is used for "Holy of Holies" without this adjunct. (See verses 3, 16, 17, 20, 27.)

Before the mercy seat, which is upon the ark.—Or, according to the accents of the received text, *nor come to the mercy seat, which,* &c. The present text exhibits the view of the Pharisees—that the high priest, though at some distance from the ark, is yet hid through the frankincense on the burning coals in the Holy of Holies itself (see verses 12, 13); whilst the Sadducees maintained that he must put it on the coals already in the court, because they deemed it improper to work in the presence of the Lord, and because the pontiff would otherwise see the ark. The Authorised Version, therefore, here, as elsewhere, follows the view of the Sadducees, and departs from the received accents, which are an essential part of the traditional text.

For I will appear in the cloud. — That is, because the Lord appeared over the mercy seat and between the cherubim in the bright luminous cloud which constituted the symbol of His Divine presence (see Exod. xxv. 22), therefore even the high priest must not approach it except on the occasion here prescribed. The Sadducees, however, render it, *only in the cloud of incense will I be seen on the cover,* that is, in the cloud arising from the burning incense which the high priest is to produce by fumigation before he enters the Holy of Holies, and which is to conceal the manifested Deity.

(3) **Thus shall Aaron come.**—Better, *With this shall,* &c., that is, with the following sacrifices, ritual, vestments, &c., shall he approach the most holy place, after having offered previously the daily morning sacrifice, and performed the ordinary daily service. During the performance of the morning service the high priest, at the time of Christ, wore the golden vestments. These he changed for the white garments

a burnt offering. (4) He shall put on
the holy linen coat, and he shall have
the linen breeches upon his flesh, and
shall be girded with a linen girdle, and
with the linen mitre shall he be attired:
these *are* holy garments; therefore shall
he wash his flesh in water, and *so* put
them on. (5) And he shall take of the
congregation of the children of Israel
two kids of the goats for a sin offering,
and one ram for a burnt offering. (6) And
Aaron shall offer his bullock of the sin
offering, which *is* for himself, and [a] make
an atonement for himself, and for his
house. (7) And he shall take the two
goats, and present them before the
LORD *at* the door of the tabernacle of
the congregation. (8) And Aaron shall
cast lots upon the two goats; one lot
for the LORD, and the other lot for the

a Heb. 9. 7.

before he commenced the special ritual prescribed for this day.

With a young bullock for a sin offering.—Which had to be of the second year (see Exod. xxix. 1), and which the high priest had to buy with his own money. It was to be his own property because the victim was to expiate his own sins, since he, like the meanest sinner, required Divine mercy and forgiveness, though, owing to his high office, he had to bring a more costly sacrifice.

(4) **He shall put on the holy linen coat.**—Better, *a holy linen tunic.* The four articles of clothing here mentioned, all of which were of white linen, constituted the sacerdotal "white vestments," in contradistinction to "the golden garments." Of the white garments he possessed two sets, one of Egyptian linen, and the other of Indian and less costly linen. The community allowed the high priest thirty minæ to purchase these garments, and he could add as much as he liked from his own money if he wished them to be more costly, provided the material was linen made of six double-twisted threads and of flax. It was the more costly vestments of Egyptian linen which the high priest wore on this occasion. The latter he put on in the after part of the day when he entered the Holy of Holies to bring out the censer. These garments were the same as those of the ordinary priests, except the turban, which was a little taller.

And he shall wash.—He had to bathe his body every time when he changed his vestments.

(5) **And he shall take of the congregation.**—On this occasion the high priest himself had to officiate, by virtue of his being the chief mediator between God and His people.

Two kids of the goats.—Better, *two shaggy he-goats.* (See chap. iv. 23.) These two goats, which were the sin offering for the people, and the ram, which was their burnt offering, were purchased with the money of the public some time before the Day of Atonement. During the second Temple the two goats had to be alike in value, equal in size, and of the same colour. If one of them happened to die after the decision of the lot, a new pair had to be purchased, and the surviving one of the original pair was kept and properly fed till it became ritually defective, whereupon it was sold, and the money paid into the sacred treasury.

(6) **And Aaron shall offer.**—Better, *And Aaron shall present,* or *bring near,* as the word literally denotes (comp. verses 9, 11, &c.), since the actual offering or killing took place afterwards, when the lots for the goats had been cast, as described in verse 11.

For himself, and for his house.—By this is meant that the atonement was for his own sins, for those of his family and for all the priests, the sons of Aaron. The ritual at this pontifical sacrifice during the second Temple was most solemn and impressive. By the side of the victim, which was placed between the porch and the altar towards the east, stood the high priest, arrayed in his white robes, with his face towards the west. In this attitude of a penitent sinner, the pontiff laid both his hands upon the sacrifice and confessed his sins in an audible voice in the sight of God and the assembled congregation as follows: "O Lord, I have sinned, I have committed iniquity, I have transgressed before thee, I and my house. O Lord, I beseech thee cover over my sins, iniquities, and transgressions which I have committed before thee, I and my house, even as it is written in the Law of Moses thy servant—For on that day He will cover over for you and cleanse you from all your sins," &c. To this the congregation replied: "Blessed be the name of His glorious kingdom for ever and ever." Whereupon the high priest repeated this confession a second time, including in it the children of Aaron, God's holy people. (See verse 11.)

(7) **And he shall take the two goats.**—Having presented his own sin-offering, the high priest, accompanied by the two chief priests, now came to the north of the altar. Here the one of his companions who was next in rank to the pontiff placed himself at his right side, whilst the other, who held the office of chief of the principal household (see 1 Chron. xxiv. 6), stood at his left. It was here that the two goats were presented with their faces to the west, where the Holy of Holies was, and where the Divine majesty was especially revealed.

(8) **And Aaron shall cast lots.**—The lots consisted of two small tablets which at an earlier time were of box or ebony wood, but which during the later part of the second Temple were made of gold, and were kept in a wooden chest. On the one was engraved the words "For Jehovah," and on the other "For Azazel," the expression in the original, which is translated *scapegoat* in the Authorised Version. The high priest, after shaking the chest, put both his hands into the urn and simultaneously took out the two tablets, one in each hand. Hereupon he put the tablet which he had in his right hand upon the goat that was standing on his right side, whilst the tablet in his left hand he put on the goat on his left side. If the tablet with the inscription "For Jehovah" was in his right hand the chief priest who stood at the right of the pontiff exclaimed "Hold up thy right hand on high!" and if it happened to be in the left hand, the chief of the principal household, who stood on his left, called out to him "Hold up thy left hand." Hereupon the high priest laid the two lots on the two goats, the one in the right hand on the goat at his right, and the one in the left hand on the animal at his left, exclaiming at the same time, "To the Lord a sin offering!"

And the other lot for the scapegoat.—Better, *and the other lot for Azazel.* The word, which only occurs in this chapter, probably denotes the utterly

[1] scapegoat. (9) And Aaron shall bring
the goat upon which the LORD's lot
[2] fell, and offer him *for* a sin offering.
(10) But the goat, on which the lot fell
to be the scapegoat, shall be presented
alive before the LORD, to make an
atonement with him, *and* to let him go
for a scapegoat into the wilderness.
(11) And Aaron shall bring the bullock
of the sin offering, which *is* for himself,
and shall make an atonement for him-
self, and for his house, and shall kill
the bullock of the sin offering which *is*
for himself: (12) and he shall take a
censer full of burning coals of fire from
off the altar before the LORD, and his
hands full of sweet incense beaten
small, and bring *it* within the vail:
(13) and he shall put the incense upon
the fire before the LORD, that the cloud
of the incense may cover the mercy
seat that *is* upon the testimony, that
he die not: (14) and [a] he shall take of
the blood of the bullock, and [b] sprinkle
it with his finger upon the mercy seat
eastward; and before the mercy seat

1 Heb., *Azazel*.

2 Heb., *went up*.

a Heb. 9. 13 & 10. 4.

b ch. 4. 6.

---

banished demon, the prince of the evil spirits, who with his legions occupies the desert regions and desolated places. (Comp. Isa. xiii. 21, xxxiv. 14; Matt. xii. 43; Luke xi. 24; Rev. xviii. 2.) As the removal or pardon of sin is often represented in the Bible by its being banished into the uttermost parts of the earth and seas (Micah vii. 19; Ps. ciii. 12), nothing could be more striking or convey to the people the idea of absolute forgiveness better than this symbolical act of sending the goat laden with the sins of the congregation to the wilderness, the abode of the prince of darkness, back to the author of all sin. The rendering, *scapegoat*, is contrary to the manifest antithesis of the verse. If the one member "For Jehovah" denotes a person, the second member "For Azazel," which forms the contrast, must, *primâ facie*, also denote a person. Besides, the translation *scapegoat* cannot be admitted in the next verse but one, where, if adopted, it would literally be "to send the goat to the scapegoat in the wilderness" (see verse 10), or in verse 26, where it is, "and he who taketh away the goat to the scapegoat."

(9) **The goat upon which the Lord's lot fell.**—Immediately after the lots decided the destiny of the two goats they were distinguished from each other by peculiar marks. The one which was "for Jehovah" had a red woollen thread tied around its neck, whilst the one "for Azazel" had the scarlet thread tied on the head or on the horns.

And offer him for a sin offering.—Better, *and shall present*, or *appoint it for a sin offering* (see verse 6), as the actual offering of it up took place afterwards. (See verse 15.)

(10) **On which the lot fell to be the scapegoat.**—Better, *on which the lot "for Azazel" fell.* This one with its distinctive scarlet badge was placed at the spot from whence he was sent away, and thus *stood alive*, not *presented*, before the Lord.

To make an atonement with him.—Better, *to make atonement for it*, that is, it was placed before the Lord in order that it might receive expiation and sanctification, and thus be fitted for the sacred purposes it was destined to fulfil. (See verses 16, 18.)

And to let him go for a scapegoat into the wilderness.—Better, *to send it to Azazel into the wilderness.*

(11) **And Aaron shall bring the bullock.**—Having formally dedicated the bullock for his own sin offering (see verse 6), and after the two goats which constituted the people's sin offering had been presented and their lots decided (verses 7—10), Aaron comes back to his own sin offering a second time. He again laid both his hands on the victim and repeated the confession for himself, for his house, and for the whole priesthood, as given in verse 6.

And shall make an atonement for himself.—His own sins had first to be expiated before he could offer the atoning sacrifices for the people. (Comp. Heb. v. 3, ix. 7.)

And shall kill the bullock.—Being a sacrifice offered up for himself the high priest, like any layman, had to slaughter the victim, and could not delegate this work to anyone else. (See chap. i. 5.) He received the blood in the sprinkling bowl, which he handed over to a priest to stir the blood lest it should coagulate while he performed the fumigation.

(12) **A censer full of burning coals.**—After the bullock was slain, and before its blood was sprinkled, the high priest took the censer, which on this occasion was a golden one, and filled it with brightly glowing coals. These he took off from that part of the ever-burning fire on the altar of burnt offering or brazen altar which was next to the west, towards the Holy of Holies, where the Lord had His dwelling. This is the sense which the canonical law attached to the phrase here "before the Lord."

And his hands full of sweet incense.—Having provided himself with two handfuls of the finest incense, and holding the censer with the fire in his right hand, and the cup with the incense in his left, he now entered for the first time through the second vail into the Holy of Holies, advanced to the ark of the covenant, and deposited the censer between its two staves. During the second Temple he stepped forward to the stone which was the substitute of the Ark, and placed the censer upon it.

(13) **And he shall put the incense.**—The high priest now threw the incense upon the coals in the censer, in the Holy of Holies, and stayed there till the whole place was filled with a cloud of smoke, taking special care that the mercy seat and the cherubim should be enveloped in the cloud. Whereupon he left the Holy of Holies, walking backward, with his face to the holy place and his back to the Temple. Upon his emerging from within the second vail, and arriving in the Holy place, he pronounced the following prayer:—"May it please Thee, O Lord my God, that if this year was intended to be one of drought, it be one of rain. May he who rules over the house of Judah not die. May Thy people not be in want, so that one should beg bread from another or from strangers; and let not the prayers of travellers come before Thee" [because they pray that no rain may fall].

(14) **And he shall take of the blood.**—Having left the Holy place and returned to the court, where the

shall he sprinkle of the blood with his
finger seven times.
(15) Then shall he kill the goat of the
sin offering, that *is* for the people, and
bring his blood within the vail, and do
with that blood as he did with the blood
of the bullock, and sprinkle it upon the
mercy seat, and before the mercy seat:
(16) and he shall make an atonement for
the holy *place*, because of the unclean-
ness of the children of Israel, and
because of their transgressions in all
their sins: and so shall he do for the
tabernacle of the congregation, that
[1]remaineth among them in the midst
of their uncleanness. (17) [a] And there
shall be no man in the tabernacle of
the congregation when he goeth in to
make an atonement in the holy *place*,
until he come out, and have made an
atonement for himself, and for his
household, and for all the congregation
of Israel. (18) And he shall go out unto
the altar that *is* before the LORD, and
make an atonement for it; and shall
take of the blood of the bullock, and
of the blood of the goat, and put *it*
upon the horns of the altar round about.
(19) And he shall sprinkle of the blood
upon it with his finger seven times, and
cleanse it, and hallow it from the un-
cleanness of the children of Israel.
(20) And when he hath made an end of
reconciling the holy *place*, and the
tabernacle of the congregation, and the
altar, he shall bring the live goat:
(21) and Aaron shall lay both his hands
upon the head of the live goat, and
confess over him all the iniquities of
the children of Israel, and all their

1 Heb., *dwelleth.*

a Luke 1. 10.

priest stood with the bowl of the blood of the bullock, stirring it, to prevent it coagulating (see verse 11), the high priest took it, and went back to the Holy of Holies, to the same place where he stood on his first entry.

Sprinkle it with his finger.—During the second Temple the high priest sprinkled the blood once upwards and seven times downwards, in such a manner that the eight sprinklings formed a continuous line on the ground. As he sprinkled he was obliged to count one, two, three, &c., lest he should make a mistake.

(15) **Then shall he kill the goat.**—As the act of expiation for himself and for the priesthood was thus completed by the sprinkling of the blood, the high priest again left the Holy of Holies in the same manner as before, put the vessel on a golden stand in the Temple, expressly prepared for this purpose, and returned to the court, to the altar of burnt offering. On the north side of the altar he slew the goat which the lot had destined for God, and which was the sin offering for the people. As in the case of the bullock, which was his own sin offering, he caught the blood in the bowl, and went within the Holy of Holies a third time. He placed himself in the same position as before, sprinkled and counted the sprinklings in the same manner, and, on his returning to the Holy place, put the vessel on another stand.

(16) **Make an atonement for the holy place.**—The transgressions of the Israelites during the year not only defiled them, but also drew defilement upon the very sanctuary with its utensils, which was pitched in the midst of them. For this purpose the high priest during the second Temple thoroughly mixed the blood of the bullock with that of the goat, and went out into the Holy place which he inspected first.

And so shall he do for the tabernacle of the congregation.—Better, *and so shall he do for the tent of meeting.* He next cleansed by the same process the tent of meeting, or the court of the sanctuary, where the Israelites were usually admitted; that is, the high priest sprinkled the court and the altar of burnt offering which was in it eight times with the mingled blood of the bullock and goat.

(17) **And there shall be no man.**—Whilst the high priest was performing this process of cleansing, no one, whether priest or Israelite, was permitted to be present, thus precluding the possibility of anyone being within the precincts who had unwittingly contracted defilement. The fact that the high priest was thus alone in the sanctuary, with no one to see how he conducted the ritual, gave rise to the practice of his being sworn, on the eve of the Day of Atonement, by the chief priests and the elders of the Sanhedrin that he would make no change whatever in the traditional ceremonies of the day, as follows:—"We adjure thee, by Him who hath caused His name to dwell in this house, that thou shalt not alter anything of all that we do say unto thee." This had especial reference to the points at issue between the Pharisees and Sadducees, as some of the high priests held the Sadducaic views. (See verse 2.)

(18) **And he shall go out unto the altar.**—The authorities during the second Temple took this to denote the golden altar, or the altar of incense which stood in the Holy place over against the Holy of Holies, as this was the altar for which expiation was made once a year on this day (see Exod. xxx. 10); hence it was cleansed next. Beginning at the north-eastern corner, the high priest then went to the north-western, then the south-western, and last round to the south-eastern corner.

(19) **And he shall sprinkle.**—He then sprinkled with his right finger, seven times, the middle or top of the altar, the coals and ashes having been previously removed so effectually, that the gold appeared. The remainder of the blood he poured out at the western and south-eastern side of the altar, where a drain communicated with the Kidron, whither it was conducted by a pipe.

(20) **And when he hath made an end.**—Having finished the expiation for himself, his fellow priests, and the sanctuary with its utensils, the goat destined by lot for Azazel, which was standing in the court before the Lord, was now brought to the high priest, that he might complete the sin-offering for the Israelites.

(21) **And Aaron shall lay both his hands.**—With the imposition of "both his hands," a phrase which only occurs in this ceremony, the high priest indicated in the most solemn manner possible that the animal was intended both for the priesthood and for the laity.

transgressions in all their sins, putting
them upon the head of the goat, and
shall send *him* away by the hand of [1]a
fit man into the wilderness: (22) and the
goat shall bear upon him all their ini-
quities unto a land [2]not inhabited: and
he shall let go the goat in the wilder-
ness.

(23) And Aaron shall come into the
tabernacle of the congregation, and
shall put off the linen garments, which
he put on when he went into the holy
place, and shall leave them there:
(24) and he shall wash his flesh with
water in the holy place, and put on his
garments, and come forth, and offer his
burnt offering, and the burnt offering
of the people, and make an atonement
for himself, and for the people. (25) And
the fat of the sin offering shall he burn
upon the altar.

(26) And he that let go the goat for
the scapegoat shall wash his clothes,
and bathe his flesh in water, and after-

1 Heb., *a man of opportunity.*

2 Heb., *of separation.*

And confess over him all the iniquities.—This confession, which was at first extempore, was formulated during the second Temple as follows: "O Lord, thy people, the house of Israel, have sinned, and done iniquity, and transgressed before thee. O Lord, I beseech thee, cover over the sins, the iniquities and the transgressions that thy people, the house of Israel, have sinned, have done iniquitously, and have transgressed before thee, as it is written in the Law of thy servant Moses" (Lev. xvi. 30). The priests and the people who stood in the court when they heard the high priest utter the Ineffable name, Jehovah—which in the time of Christ was only pronounced on this day, and that by the pontiff—prostrated themselves, and with their faces to the ground responded, "Blessed be the name of His glorious kingdom for ever and ever."

Putting them upon the head of the goat.—By this imposition of hands, and the confession, the high priest transferred the sins of the nation to the goat. He then turned to the people, and declared, "Ye shall be clean."

Send him away by the hand of a fit man.—The guilt-laden animal was then entrusted to a man previously appointed, to be conducted to the lonely region, the abode of Azazel, thus carrying back to him the sins which he enticed the people to commit during the year. The phrase which is here rendered by "a fit man," and which occurs nowhere else in the Bible, denotes more properly *a timely man, a man at hand,* one appointed for the occasion. The marginal rendering, "a man of opportunity," is still more objectionable.

(22) **Unto a land not inhabited.**—Literally, *unto a land cut off,* that is, a place the ground of which is separated from all around it, hence a summit, a peak standing out by itself, a precipice.

In the wilderness.—Where no human beings dwell, but which is the abode of evil spirits. It will be seen that the directions here are simply to conduct the goat into the wilderness, where it is apparently to be let loose to pursue its own course. During the second Temple, however, the authorities decreed that the animal must be destroyed. Accordingly one of the priests who was appointed to execute this mission led the goat to a rock called Zuck, in the wilderness, situate about twelve miles, or ninety furlongs, from Jerusalem. Between the holy city and this steep rock, ten booths were erected at intervals of one mile, and persons were located in every booth to accompany the messenger to the next tent, which was distant a Sabbath-day's journey. From the last booth to the rock, which was double this distance, the messenger had no companion, but he was carefully watched by the occupants of the last booth to see that he performed the ritual according to the prescribed order. On his arrival at the mountain he divided the crimson thread, which was the badge of the goat, into two; one half he fastened to the rock, and the other he tied between the two horns of the victim, and then pushed the animal down the projecting ledge of the rock, when it was dashed to pieces before it reached the bottom. Hereupon the persons stationed at the last booth to watch the proceedings waved linen cloths or white flags, thus signalling from station to station to the priests in the court of the Temple the arrival of the goat at its proper destination.

(23) **Shall come into the tabernacle of the congregation.**—Better, *shall come into the tent of meeting.* This was the fourth time that the high priest entered into the Holy of Holies on the Day of Atonement. The object of his going into the most Holy was to fetch the censer and the incense cup which he had left between the two staves (see verse 12). To do this he had again to bathe, which always accompanied the change of garments, and to put on his white robes. As it was no part of the actual service, but was simply a necessary act subsequent to the service, it is not fully described in the text. This was the last act on the Day of Atonement which the high priest performed in his white robes.

And shall leave them there.—The robes were now deposited in a chamber in the sanctuary especially set apart for this purpose, and the high priest was never allowed to minister in them again.

(24) **And he shall wash his flesh.**—That is, immerse his whole body. The baptistery, where the high priest performed these ablutions, was on the roof of a building in the sacred precincts. According to the authorities and practice during the second Temple the act described in this verse preceded the one ordered in the foregoing verse. The burnt offering, both for himself and for the people, the high priest offered in the golden garments. These he changed for the white robes when he afterwards went into the Holy of Holies to fetch the censer and the incense cup. The sacrifice consisted first of his own ram, then the ram of the people, and lastly the bullock of the people, and their seven lambs. (Comp. Num. xxix. 8).

(25) **And the fat of the sin offering.**—That is, the fat of the inwards of both the bullock (see verse 6) and the goat (see verse 15), which constituted the sin offering, as well as the fat of the other goat, which was the priest's sin offering, was to be burnt upon the brazen altar of burnt offering in the courtyard. (See chap. iv. 8—10.)

(26) **And he that let go the goat for the scapegoat.**—Better, *And he that leadeth away the goat to Azazel* (see verse 10). As the messenger who conducted the sin-laden animal to the author of sin

ward come into the camp. (27) And the
bullock *for* the sin offering, and the
goat *for* the sin offering, whose blood
was brought in to make atonement in
the holy *place*, shall *one* carry forth
[a]without the camp; and they shall burn
in the fire their skins, and their flesh,
and their dung. (28) And he that burneth
them shall wash his clothes, and bathe
his flesh in water, and afterward he
shall come into the camp.

(29) And *this* shall be a statute for ever
unto you: *that* in the seventh month,
on the tenth *day* of the month, ye shall
afflict your souls, and do no work at all,
whether it be one of your own country,
or a stranger that sojourneth among
you: (30) for on that day shall *the priest*

a ch. 6. 30; Heb. 13. 11.

contracted defilement by the impurity which the victim carried away, he had both to wash his clothes and immerse his whole body in water before he was admitted into the camp. During the second Temple he remained in the last booth, which was a mile from Jerusalem, till sundown, when he was re-admitted into the camp.

(27) **And the bullock.**—That is, the bodies of the sin offerings for the priests and the people (see verses 5, 6, 9, 11), whose blood the high priest carried into the Holy of Holies. (See verses 14, 15, with chap. iv. 11, 12.)

Shall one carry forth.—Better *shall be carried forth.* During the second Temple four men carried the carcases upon two poles to the place set aside outside Jerusalem for burning. (See chap. iv. 11.) Hence the ancient Palestinian Targum translates it, "they shall be carried out on poles by the hands of the younger priests." As has already been remarked, the priest performed this part of the service immediately after the goat was dispatched by the messenger to the wilderness. Whilst the victims were being burned outside the camp the high priest read in the women's court the appointed lessons for the Day of Atonement (viz., Lev. xxiii. 26; Num. xxix. 7—11) in the presence of the congregation, who were all standing, and at the conclusion of the reading pronounced the eight benedictions (1) on the Divine Law, (2) on the public service, (3) on confession, (4) forgiveness of sins, (5) on Jerusalem, (6) on the Temple, (7) on Israel, and (8) on the priesthood.

(28) **And he that burneth.**—That is, those who carried the carcases and burned them, like the messenger who conducted the sin-laden goat, contracted defilement from the atoning victims. They had, therefore, to undergo the same ablutions.

(29) **And this shall be a statute for ever.**—Literally, *a statute of eternity*, that is, an everlasting ordinance. That which is contained in verses 29, 30 is binding upon the Israelites as long as they exist, and is to be observed by them annually.

In the seventh month, on the tenth day.—This month, which is called *Tishri*, corresponds to September, and is the month of great festivals. On the first is the Feast of Trumpets (see chap. xxiii. 24), on the tenth the Day of Atonement, and on the fourteenth begins the Feast of Tabernacles which lasts eight days.

Ye shall afflict your souls.—From Isa. lviii. 3, 5, 10 it is evident that by the phrase "to afflict the soul" is meant fasting. This is expressed by the fuller form, "to afflict the soul with fasting," in Ps. xxxv. 13, where the Authorised Version inconsistently translates it, "humbled my soul." This is the only public fast ordained in the Mosaic Law; and the authorities during the second Temple defined more minutely in what this fasting consists. According to the canon law it consists not only in abstaining from eating and drinking, but from washing, anointing, wearing of shoes or sandals, and the marriage-bed, as they were the outward signs of joy. (Comp. Eccles. ix. 10.) If any one presumptuously ate as much as a date with a kernel, or drank as much as fills one cheek, he violated the Law, and incurred the penalty of excision. If he did it unintentionally he had to bring a sin offering. The fast lasted from evening to evening, and is rigorously kept by Jews to this day. Exception was and still is made in the case of pregnant women, invalids, and children. This is the fast which the Apostle refers to in Acts xxvii. 9. The marginal note on this passage, viz., "the fast was on the tenth day of the seventh month" (Lev. xxiii. 27, 29), is not to be found in the first edition of the Authorised Version. It was introduced by Bishop Lloyd in the Bible published in London, 1701, fol., who took it from the Geneva Version (Geneva, 1560), and it was adopted in the Oxford 4to edition, 1703. When Christ admonishes his followers, "When thou fastest, anoint thine head, and wash thy face" (Matt. vi. 17), He refers to the canonical law about fasting here given.

And do no work at all.—Better, *ye shall do no manner of work*, as the same phrase is rendered in the Authorised Version in chap. xxiii. 31. It is to be regretted that this legal phrase, which occurs five times in the Pentateuch, four of which are to be found in this very book (chaps. xvi. 29, xxiii. 3, 28, 31; Num. xxix. 7), should have been translated differently in the Authorised Version. This variation is all the more glaring in Num. xxix. 7, which is the parallel passage to this. The day was to be a rest from all manual and other secular work exactly as on the Sabbath, with this exception, that whilst work on the Sabbath was punished with stoning, labour on the Day of Atonement was punished with excision.

A stranger that sojourneth among you.—That is, one of non-Jewish descent who had renounced idolatry, and voluntarily joined the Jewish community. (See Exod. xii. 19, xx. 10.)

(30) **For on that day shall the priest make an atonement.**—Literally, *For on that day he shall make atonement for you*, which may either be the Lord, who is mentioned in the next clause, or, more probably, the high priest, who is mentioned five verses before. (See verse 25, and especially verse 32.)

That ye may be clean . . .—Better, *you shall be clean, &c.* Because it is here said "you shall be clean from all your sins before the Lord," the administrators of the law in the time of Christ declared that only the sins which a man commits before, *i.e.*, against the Lord, are atoned for on the Day of Atonement, but the sins which man commits against his fellow man are not forgiven on this day unless we have first satisfied our injured neighbour, and have obtained pardon from him. Again, he who sinneth in the hope that he will obtain absolution on the Day of Atonement, for him there is no forgiveness on this day.

make an atonement for you, to cleanse
you, *that* ye may be clean from all your
sins before the LORD. (31) It *shall be* a
sabbath of rest unto you, and ye shall
afflict your souls, by a statute for ever.
(32) And the priest, whom he shall anoint,
and whom he shall [1] consecrate to
minister in the priest's office in his
father's stead, shall make the atone-
ment, and shall put on the linen clothes,
even the holy garments: (33) and he shall
make an atonement for the holy sanc-
tuary, and he shall make an atonement
for the tabernacle of the congregation,
and for the altar, and he shall make an
atonement for the priests, and for all
the people of the congregation. (34) And
this shall be an everlasting statute unto
you, to make an atonement for the
children of Israel for all their sins
[a] once a year.

And he did as the LORD commanded
Moses.

CHAPTER XVII.—(1) And the LORD
spake unto Moses, saying, (2) Speak unto
Aaron, and unto his sons, and unto all the
children of Israel, and say unto them;

[1] Heb., *fill his hand.*

[a] Ex. 30. 10; Heb. 9. 7.

(31) **It shall be a Sabbath of rest unto you.**—Literally, *a resting day of solemn resting, a Sabbath of Sabbaths, i.e.*, a day of complete and perfect rest. This phrase, which occurs six times in the Bible, is only applied to weekly Sabbaths (Exod. xvi. 23, xxxi. 15, xxxv. 2; Lev. xxiii. 3), the Day of Atonement (chap. xvi. 31, xxiii. 32), and to the Sabbatical year, or the year of Jubilee (chap. xxv. 4), but not to the other festivals.

(32) **And the priest, whom he shall anoint.**—Better, *And the priest who shall be anointed.* Not only is Aaron to make atonement on this occasion, but, in future, the priest who shall be consecrated by the proper authorities as his successor to the pontificate shall perform this act of expiation on the Day of Atonement.

And whom he shall consecrate.—Better, *and who shall be consecrated.* According to the canonical interpretation which obtained during the second Temple, this clause makes the hereditary right to the high priesthood conditional. Unlike property, which descends to the heirs unconditionally, the son of the high priest can only succeed his father if he is morally and physically blameless. The decision upon these points was vested in the community, represented by their elders—the Sanhedrin—who pronounced whether the heir apparent was qualified or disqualified to step into the office of pontiff, and who appointed the delegates to anoint and invest the new high priest with the insignia of his functions.

And shall put on the linen clothes.—Better, *and shall put on the linen garments,* as it is rendered in the Authorised Version in verse 23. This phrase only occurs twice, and in this very section. To render it by two different expressions within so short a space is almost equivalent to depriving it of its identity. Now the priest who has thus been deemed worthy to succeed to this high office is to put on the holy white garments on the Day of Atonement.

(33) **And he shall make an atonement.**—Like Aaron, the successor to the pontificate is to perform the service of expiation as detailed in this chapter, a summary of which is here given.

(34) **And this shall be an everlasting statute.**—Better, *And this shall be a statute for ever,* as the Authorised Version has it in verse 29. Here, again, we have an instance of how the same phrase which occurs three times within four verses (see verses 29, 31, 34) is rendered in the Authorised Version by two different phrases, thus giving the idea to the English reader that there is a difference in the original. The thrice-repeated phrase emphasises the abiding nature of this law, and indicates the solemnity of the day.

And he did as the Lord commanded Moses—That is, Aaron performed the service for the first time, according to the ordinances which the Lord communicated to Moses. A similar remark occurs at the first observance of the Passover. (See Exod. xii. 50.) The solemn admonition, therefore, addressed to the priesthood at the beginning of this chapter (see verses 1, 2), not to presume on their office, but to submit to the Divine regulations, was duly observed by the first high priest. It may, however, also be designed to indicate that Aaron did not assume the dignity of the pontificate to exalt himself, but in obedience to the command God gave to Moses.

XVII.

(1) **And the Lord spake unto Moses.**—The Day of Atonement was instituted to purge, in an especial manner, the whole community from all their sins, and present them a holy nation before the Lord once a year. Hence it is now followed by regulations concerning every-day life, the observance of which is to foster the holiness secured on that particular day.

(2) **And unto all the children of Israel.**—To understand the import of this phrase, and its bearing upon the injunction in question, it is necessary to notice that the words "and unto all the children of Israel" are here used for the first time. Hitherto the Divine communications were made to (1) Moses alone, without his being ordered to speak to any one else (chaps. v. 14, 20, vi. 12, viii. 1, xiv. 1); (2) to Moses, with the command to speak to Aaron (chap. xvi. 1); (3) to Moses, with the command to speak to Aaron and his sons (chap. vi. 1, 17); (4) to Moses, with a command to speak to the children of Israel (chaps. i. 1, iv. 1, vii. 28, xii. 1); (5) to Moses and Aaron conjointly, without being ordered to speak to the children of Israel (chaps. xiii. 1, xiv. 33); (6) to Moses and Aaron conjointly, who are ordered to speak to the children of Israel (chaps. xi. 1, xv. 1); and (7) Aaron alone is addressed (chap. x. 8). In the chapter before us, however, the communication is made to Moses alone, and he is commanded not only to impart its contents to Aaron and his sons—*i.e.*, the priesthood—but "unto all the children of Israel," or their representatives, at the same time. The pontiff and the priests are thus put on a level with the ordinary Israelite or the laity, as far as this regulation is concerned. There are only two other occasions on which this phrase is used again, viz., chaps. xxi. 24, xxii. 18.

This is the thing which the Lord hath commanded.—To emphasise the importance of the following law Moses is ordered by God to use this additional

This *is* the thing which the LORD hath
commanded, saying, (3) What man soever
there be of the house of Israel, that
killeth an ox, or lamb, or goat, in the
camp, or that killeth *it* out of the camp,
(4) and bringeth it not unto the door of
the tabernacle of the congregation, to
offer an offering unto the LORD before
the tabernacle of the LORD; blood shall
be imputed unto that man; he hath
shed blood; and that man shall be cut
off from among his people: (5) to the
end that the children of Israel may
bring their sacrifices, which they offer
in the open field, even that they may
bring them unto the LORD, unto the
door of the tabernacle of the congre-
gation, unto the priest, and offer them
for peace offerings unto the LORD. (6) And
the priest shall sprinkle the blood upon
the altar of the LORD *at* the door of
the tabernacle of the congregation, and
burn the fat for a [a]sweet savour unto
the LORD. (7) And they shall no more
offer their sacrifices unto devils, after
whom they have gone a whoring. This
shall be a statute for ever unto them
throughout their generations.

a Ex. 29. 18: ch. 4. 31.

---

formula; whilst in other instances where it is used, when important statutes are enacted, Moses uses it of his own accord. (Comp. Exod. xvi. 16, xxxv. 4; Lev. viii. 5, ix. 6; Num. xxx. 2, xxxvi. 6.)

(3) **That killeth an ox, or lamb, or goat.**—The law which is thus solemnly laid down is that when one of the three kinds of the sacrificial quadrupeds (see chap. vii. 23) are intended for private use, they must not be slaughtered within or outside the camp. That the injunction here refers to the domestic animals in question, and not to the ordinary sacrifices, is not only evident from the expression "killeth," instead of "sacrificeth," but more especially from a comparison of verses 3, 4 with verses 8, 9.

(4) **And bringeth it not unto the door of the tabernacle of the congregation.**—Better, *and bringeth it not to the entrance of the tent of meeting;* that is, if he does not bring it to the place where the sacrifices are killed, and offer it first as a peace offering to Jehovah, he is to be regarded as wantonly shedding blood, and will be visited with the penalty of excision.

(5) **To the end that the children of Israel may bring.**—The reason why these three kinds of animals, when intended for private food, are to be brought to the precincts of the sanctuary, and are there to be offered first as a peace offering to the Lord, is to prevent the Israelites sacrificing them to the demons in the open fields.

Which they offer in the open field.—The first part of this verse is better rendered, *In order that the children of Israel may bring in* [*i.e.*, within the precincts of the sanctuary] *their sacrifices which they are sacrificing on the face of the field;* that is, which they have heretofore been in the habit of offering in the open fields to heathen deities, and which, in future, they might be inclined to do again. The phrase "open field" denotes the space outside the encampment, in contradistinction to the enclosed place where the Israelites sojourned. (See chap. xiv. 7, 53, &c.)

Even that they may bring them . . . unto the door of the tabernacle of the congregation.—Better, *and bring them . . . to the entrance of the tent of meeting.*

(6) **And the priest shall sprinkle.**—After the animals in question had been duly slaughtered by those who brought them, the officiating priest who caught the blood in a bowl is to throw it upon the walls of the altar of burnt offering. (See chap. i. 5.)

At the door of the tabernacle of the congregation.—Better, *at the entrance of the tent of meeting.*

And burn the fat.—See chap. iii. 3, 5.

(7) **And they shall no more offer their sacrifices unto devils.**—The word (*sĕirim*) here translated "devils," literally denotes *hairy* or *shaggy goats*, and then *goat-like deities*, or *demons*. The Egyptians, and other nations of antiquity, worshipped goats as gods. Not only was there a celebrated temple in Thmuis, the capital of the Mendesian Nomos in Lower Egypt, dedicated to the goat-image Pan, whom they called Mendes, and worshipped as the oracle, and as the fertilising principle in nature, but they erected statues of him everywhere. Hence the Pan, Silenus, satyrs, fauns, and the woodland gods among the Greeks and Romans; and hence, too, the goat-like form of the devil, with a tail, horns, and cloven feet, which obtain in medieval Christianity, and which may still be seen in some European cities. The terror which the devil, appearing in this Pan-like form, created among those who were thought to have seen him, has given rise to our expression *panic*. This is the form of idolatrous worship which the Jews brought with them from Egypt, and to which reference is continually made. (See Josh. xxiv. 14; Ezek. xx. 7, xxiii. 3, &c.; and especially 2 Chron. xi. 15.) The expression "and they shall *no more* offer" shows that the Israelites were hitherto in the habit of first dedicating their ordinary food to these deities; whilst the words "gone a whoring" indicate the orgies connected with this form of idol worship. It has been urged that the demand to offer up, in so confined a space as the entrance of the sanctuary, the domestic animals intended for the daily consumption of more than 600,000 people, imposed a task upon the people which it was impossible for them to carry out. Hence it has been urged that the injunction here (verses 2—7) must refer to sacrifices. But this difficulty arises from importing our modern notions into the ancient mode of living. The ancient Israelites, like the modern Orientals, especially the nomadic tribes, ate very little flesh meat apart from the seasons of sacrifice, which were the occasions of feasting. Besides, those who urge this difficulty ignore the fact that the injunction before us is restricted to the three kinds of animals; that none of the wild clean quadrupeds, as stags, roes, &c., nor any of the feathered tribes, as pigeons, turtledoves, &c., which formed an essential part of the daily diet, is here included; and that even the three kinds of sacrificial quadrupeds only come within this restriction when they are qualified by age, which was within two years, and by physical condition, which demanded that it should have no external defect, as blindness of one eye, lameness of one foot, &c., to be offered first to the

(8) And thou shalt say unto them,
Whatsoever man *there be* of the house
of Israel, or of the strangers which
sojourn among you, that offereth a
burnt offering or sacrifice, (9) and bring-
eth it not unto the door of the taber-
nacle of the congregation, to offer it
unto the LORD; even that man shall be
cut off from among his people.

(10) And whatsoever man *there be* of
the house of Israel, or of the strangers
that sojourn among you, that eateth
any manner of blood; I will even set
my face against that soul that eateth
blood, and will cut him off from among
his people. (11) For the life of the flesh
is in the blood: and I have given it to
you upon the altar to make an atone-
ment for your souls: for it *is* the blood
that maketh an atonement for the soul.
(12) Therefore I said unto the children of
Israel, No soul of you shall eat blood,
neither shall any stranger that sojourn-
eth among you eat blood.

(13) And whatsoever man *there be* of
the children of Israel, or of the strangers

Lord. Moreover, the injunction was only intended to operate temporarily, whilst the Jews sojourned and wandered about in the wilderness, where, besides the propensity to sacrifice these animals to idols, they would have been in danger of extirpating their most useful animals. The law was repealed when the Israelites entered the promised land. (Comp. Deut. xii. 13—15.)

(8, 9) **Whatsoever man there be.**—Better, *what man soever there be*, as it is in the Authorised Version in verse 3. Here again we have an instance of the same legislative phrase used four times in one short section (verses 3, 8, 10, 13), being translated differently in the Authorised Version. The law enacted in these two verses requires that all legitimate sacrifices should henceforth be presented in the appointed sanctuary, which was the centre of national unity, thus abolishing the liberty which, in accordance with patriarchal practice, had hitherto existed, that every head of a family could be his own priest, and offer up sacrifices wherever and whenever he liked. The commonwealth of Israel were now to acknowledge one altar, one high priest, and one sanctuary. This law was binding not only upon the Israelite by race, but upon strangers who took up their abode in and joined the Jewish community. For wilfully violating this law the offender incurred the penalty of excision.

(10) **And whatsoever man.**—Better, *and what man soever.* (See verse 8.)

Eateth any manner of blood.—This prohibition, which has already been mentioned twice in Leviticus, is in both instances joined to the prohibition of fat. (See chaps. iii. 17, vii. 26, 27.) Owing to its great importance, however, the law is enacted here *separately*, where it naturally follows the order that the blood of all animals sacrificed in the sanctuary is to be offered to the Lord upon the altar. According to the canons which obtained during the second Temple, the blood of clean fishes, of locusts, and of permissible creeping things is exempted.

I will even set my face against that soul.—That is, make him feel my anger. Though this phrase only occurs twice more in this book, and only once in connection with legal enactments (see chaps. xx. 3, 6, xxvi. 17), yet from its usages in other passages it is clear that the expression "face" denotes anger, which shows itself in the countenance. Thus the phrase, which is translated in the Authorised Version, "I will appease him" (Gen. xxx. 20), is in the original, "I will appease his face," where it manifestly stands for *anger*. Hence Lamen. iv. 16, which is in the original, "the face of the Lord hath divided them," is properly rendered in the Authorised Version in the text by "the anger of the Lord." (Comp. also 1 Pet. iii. 12.)

(11) **For the life of the flesh is in the blood.**—Better, *for the soul of the flesh is in the blood.* The word here rendered "life" in the Authorised Version occurs twice more in this very verse, and is in both instances properly translated *soul.* Though it is immaterial whether the word in question is translated *life* or *soul*, it is essential that it should be rendered uniformly throughout the passage. By translating it differently in the first clause, the Authorised Version has unnecessarily increased the difficulty of the verse. This clause assigns the reason why blood must not be eaten. It is the principle of vitality, it constitutes the soul of animal life. Hence blood and life are used interchangeably in the Scriptures. Thus, when the Psalmist exclaims, "what profit is there in my blood" (Ps. xxx. 9), he uses it for *life.*

I have given it to you upon the altar.—For the sake of emphasis, the words in the original denoting "upon the altar" are placed first in the Hebrew, and the Authorised Version follows this order. It is however better to translate this clause, *For I have ordained it upon the altar to make atonement for your souls.* Because it is the principle of life, therefore God has ordained it to be offered upon the altar as an expiation for the offerer's life.

For it is the blood that maketh an atonement for the soul.—Better, *for it is the blood that maketh atonement by means of the soul.* As the blood of the victim is identical with its life, and represents the soul of the animal, hence God has appointed it as a substitute for the sinner's life. Thus the life of the sacrifice atones for the life of the offerer. Hence the remark of the Apostle, "without shedding of blood there is no remission" (Heb. ix. 22).

(12) **Therefore I said . . .**—Because it is the vehicle of life, and has been ordained by God to atone for life, the children of Israel are here forbidden to eat it. The strangers are also prohibited eating blood, because they have submitted to the law of the land, and because their eating it would not only infringe the law which they have voluntarily adopted, but would lessen the horror with which such indulgence was regarded by the Jews. Hence the enforcement of this prohibition by the Apostle (Acts xv. 20, 29, xxi. 25).

(13) **And whatsoever man.**—Better, *what man soever* (see verse 3). Hitherto the law mainly discussed the blood of sacrificial animals, or those quadrupeds which were slaughtered at home. In this and the following verses the statute is extended to all other

that sojourn among you, [1] which hunteth and catcheth any beast or fowl that may be eaten; he shall even pour out the blood thereof, and cover it with dust. (14) [a] For *it is* the life of all flesh; the blood of it *is* for the life thereof: therefore I said unto the children of Israel, Ye shall eat the blood of no manner of flesh: for the life of all flesh *is* the blood thereof: whosoever eateth it shall be cut off.

(15) And every soul that eateth [2] that which died *of itself*, or that which was torn *with beasts*, *whether it be* one of your own country, or a stranger, he shall both wash his clothes, and bathe *himself* in water, and be unclean until the even: then shall he be clean. (16) But if he wash *them* not, nor bathe his flesh; then he shall bear his iniquity.

1 Heb., *that hunteth any hunting.*

a Gen. 9. 4.

2 Heb., *a carcase.*

CHAPTER XVIII.—(1) And the LORD spake unto Moses, saying, (2) Speak unto the children of Israel, and say unto

---

creatures which, though wild, are legally clean and used as food.

Which hunteth and catcheth.—Hunting, which was an amusement with other nations of antiquity, was with the serious Hebrew a matter of necessity. It was resorted to as a matter of necessity to exterminate dangerous beasts (Exod. xxiii. 29), but more especially to procure food (Gen. xxv. 27; Prov. xii. 27). Besides the numerous pitfalls, snares, traps, &c., which are so frequently mentioned in the Bible, the Hebrews also employed arms in catching game (Gen. xxvii. 3). When wounded, or when the game had to be killed to facilitate its being carried home, the hunters were liable to become careless about the blood, as is evident from the practice which obtained among some of the ancients. Thus we are told that the Zabians, when they slew a beast, put the blood into a vessel or into a hole which they dug in the ground, and then sat round and feasted on it. It is to prevent such outrages on the sacred blood, which the hunters were especially liable to commit when hungry, that the law is here enacted. An instance of the hungry army flying upon the spoil, killing the cattle in the field, and eating the flesh with the blood, is recorded in 1 Sam. xiv. 32—34. (Comp. also Ezek. xxxiii. 25.)

Any beast or fowl that may be eaten.—That is, those wild beasts or fowl which, according to the dietary law, were usually eaten. During the second Temple this was interpreted strictly to apply to the clean wild beasts, but not to those not permitted to be eaten.

He shall even pour out the blood.—The earth, from which all animals came forth at their creation (Gen. i. 24), is to receive back again the principle of their life. They proceeded from the womb of the earth, and their life-blood is to return to it. With such scrupulous care was this law observed during the second Temple, that the following Benediction was ordered to be recited when the blood was covered up: "Blessed art thou, O Lord our God, King of the universe, who hath sanctified us by His precepts, and hath commanded us to cover up the blood."

(14) **For it is the life of all flesh . . .**—Better, *for the soul of all flesh is its blood, in, or through, its soul,* that is, the sacredness of the blood arises from the fact that it contains the vital principle of all animal life. Or this clause may be rendered, *for the life of all flesh is its blood in, or during, its life,* that is, the life of all creatures consists in its blood; but only as long as the blood contains this life, for when it is dried up, or coagulated, the life has passed away from it.

For the life of all flesh.—Better, *for the soul of all flesh* (see verse 11), that is, even of those wild animals which, in contradistinction to the sacrificial quadrupeds, must not be offered upon the altar, the blood constitutes the vital principle.

(15) **That which died of itself.**—The law enacted here is a natural sequel to the one immediately preceding, since it is still based upon the sacredness of blood. As the body of the animal which either died a natural death, or has been torn by a wild beast, retains a great portion of its blood, it is forbidden to be eaten. The carcases, in which the blood has thus been coagulated in the veins and arteries, were given to the dogs (Exod. xxii. 31). The rigour with which this law was enforced may be seen from 1 Sam. xiv. 32—35; Ezek. iv. 14, xlvi. 36. According to the canonical law which obtained during the second Temple, the carcase was forbidden when the animal died a natural death, or met with an accident, or was strangled to death, or was torn by a wild beast. This explains the apostolic decision, in the council at Jerusalem, about "things strangled" (Acts xv. 20).

Whether it be one of your own country.—The law was not only binding upon the native Israelite, but upon the proselyte. The mere stranger, in the strict sense of the word, who had not joined the Jewish community, was allowed to eat such carcases. (See Deut. xiv. 21.)

He shall both wash his clothes.—If he ate any of it unwittingly, he had not only to wash his garments, but immerse his whole body in water, and be excluded from the sanctuary till sundown. The sin offering prescribed in chap. v. 2 was not for inadvertently touching the carcase, but for neglecting the prescribed purification. (See chap. v. 2.)

(16) **Then he shall bear his iniquity.**—If he neglects these acts of purification, and enters the sanctuary in a defiled state, or partakes of the sacrificial meal, he is to incur the penalty of excision for the former act, and to be beaten with stripes for the latter, according to the interpretation given to this law in the time of Christ.

XVIII.

(1) **And the Lord spake unto Moses.**—Unlike the preceding Divine communications, which treated of the ritual and ceremonial pollutions, the enactments which Moses is here commanded to communicate direct to the children of Israel, or their representatives, the elders, affect their moral life—precepts which form the basis of domestic purity, and which are the foundation of human happiness.

(2) **I am the Lord your God.**—The Lord is their recognised and sole sovereign, the children of Israel are therefore bound to obey His precepts, and not be led astray by the customs or statutes which prevailed among

them, I am the LORD your God. (3) After
the doings of the land of Egypt, wherein
ye dwelt, shall ye not do: and after the
doings of the land of Canaan, whither
I bring you, shall ye not do: neither
shall ye walk in their ordinances. (4) Ye
shall do my judgments, and keep mine
ordinances, to walk therein: I *am* the
LORD your God. (5) Ye shall therefore
keep my statutes, and my judgments:
[a]which if a man do, he shall live in
them: I *am* the LORD.
(6) None of you shall approach to any
that is [1]near of kin to him, to uncover
***their* nakedness: I *am* the LORD. (7) The**
nakedness of thy father, or the naked-

a Ezek. 20. 11; Rom. 10. 5; Gal. 3. 12.

1 Heb., *remainder of his flesh.*

---

the people whose country they are to possess. Moreover, as He is holy, the Israelites, by faithfully obeying His sacred laws, will attain to that holiness which will bring them in communion with Him in whose image they were created. This phrase, which is so emphatically repeated twice more in this chapter (verses 4, 30), has only been used once before in this book. (See chap. xi. 44.)

(3) **After the doings of the land of Egypt.**—During their sojourn in Egypt the Israelites became familiar with the practices which obtained in the land of their bondage, and as they adopted some of them (see chap. xvii. 7), they are here solemnly warned to eschew those which are especially proscribed in the sequel.

And after the doings of the land of Canaan.—The danger of imitating the customs which they had for centuries witnessed in the land they quitted, was greatly increased by the fact that these licentious practices obtained in worse forms in the land which they were to inherit. It is therefore against the past and the future that they are here warned.

Neither shall ye walk in their ordinances.—As some of "the doings" referred to may have been simple custom, not based upon the law of the country where they obtained, the Lawgiver here emphatically condemns the acts which were legalised, declaring them to have no authority whatever. (See verse 30.)

(4) **Ye shall do my judgments.**—The expression "my judgments and mine ordinances" is here used emphatically, in opposition to "their ordinances," and has here the force of *Mine only;* just as the phrase "Him shalt thou serve" (Deut. vi. 13) is explained by Christ "*Him only* shalt thou serve" (Matt. iv. 10).

(5) **Ye shall therefore keep my statutes.**—Better, *and ye shall keep my ordinances.* The word here rendered by "statutes" is the same which the Authorised Version translates *ordinances* in verses 3 and 4.

He shall live in them.—Better, *he shall live by* or *through them;* that is, by observing them the law-abiding will live a happy and prosperous life, since disobedience will expose the offender to the penalty of death. The spiritual authorities in the time of the second Temple interpreted this clause to mean that he who obeys these laws shall have eternal life. Hence the ancient Chaldee Versions translate it, "Shall have life eternal." This passage is quoted both in the Prophets (Ezek. xx. 11, 13, 21; Neh. ix. 29) and by St. Paul (Rom. x. 5; Gal. iii. 12), who contrasts this promise made to works with the promise of the Gospel made to faith.

(6) **None of you shall approach.**—Literally, *man, man, ye shall not approach.* It is part of the phrase used in chap. xvii. 3, 8, 13, and should accordingly be rendered by *no man whatsoever shall approach.* The absence of the words "of the house of Israel," which, in the other instances, form part of this phrase, as we are assured by the authorities in the time of Christ, shows that these prohibitions are also binding upon the stranger who took up his abode among the Israelites, lest the land be defiled by his transgressions. Though primarily addressed to man, who, in these cases, takes the initiative, the punishment for violating any of these laws was visited upon both man and woman.

Near of kin to him.—Literally, *the flesh of his flesh.* (See Pss. lxxiii. 26, lxxviii. 20, 27; Micah iii. 2, 3.) The combination of two synonymous expressions is often used to denote intensity. Thus the phrase rendered "my exceeding joy" in the Authorised Version (Ps. xliii. 4), literally means *the joy of my joy,* or, as the Margin has it, "the gladness of my joy." Accordingly, "the flesh of his flesh" signified "nearness of his flesh," his near kin. This technical sense is assigned to the first of these two words by itself in verses 12, 13, &c., where it is translated "near kinswoman." It expresses kinship of both consanguinity and mere affinity. (See verse 17.)

To uncover their nakedness.—Upon the import of this phrase depends the interpretation of the laws laid down in this chapter and chapter xx., inasmuch as it furnishes the clue to the definition whether the interdicts refer to illicit commerce or to incestuous marriages. In the only other passage in the Pentateuch where it occurs, it does not appear to imply any unseemly intention (Exod. xx. 23). This is also its sense in Isa. xlvii. 3. In the seven instances in Ezekiel, however (xvii. 36, 37; xxii. 10; xxiii. 10, 18, 29), which are the only other passages in the Bible where this phrase is used, it denotes unseemly exposure, sexual intercourse, etc. Hence some high authorities maintain that in the twenty-one instances in which it is used in this part of the legislation (chaps. xviii. 6—19; xx. 11, 17, 20, 21), it denotes extra-conjugal licentiousness, and is simply an explanatory addition to the phrase "approach to," with which it is combined in verses 6, 14, 18. From a comparison, however, of chap. xviii. 18 with verse 19 to chap. xx. 11, it will be seen that it is undoubtedly used to denote sexual intercourse both within and without the pale of matrimony. As cohabitation without any religious ceremony whatever constituted and consummated marriage amongst the early Hebrews, the euphemistic phrases "to take home," "to approach to," "to know," etc., as well as the less veiled expressions, "to lie with," "to uncover her nakedness," etc., denote marriage in Hebrew, not excluding, however, the primary sense of illicit commerce or incestuous marriages. The context in which the phrase occurs must determine the sense in which it is used. The administrators of the law during the second Temple, whilst rightly interpreting it here generally to denote incestuous marriages, also apply it in some instances to fornication and adultery.

(7) **The nakedness of thy father, or the nakedness of thy mother.**—The rendering of the Authorised Version is based upon the interpretation which obtained during the second Temple, according to

ness of thy mother, shalt thou not
uncover: she *is* thy mother; thou shalt
not uncover her nakedness. (8) [a]The
nakedness of thy father's wife shalt
thou not uncover: it *is* thy father's
nakedness. (9) The nakedness of thy
sister, the daughter of thy father, or
daughter of thy mother, *whether she be*
born at home, or born abroad, *even* their
nakedness thou shalt not uncover.
(10) The nakedness of thy son's daughter,
or of thy daughter's daughter, *even*
their nakedness thou shalt not uncover:
for their's *is* thine own nakedness. (11) The
nakedness of thy father's wife's daughter,
begotten of thy father, she *is* thy sister,

[a] ch. 20. 11.

---

which this injunction is addressed both to the daughter and the son. The daughter must not marry or have commerce with the father, nor the son with the mother. Hence the Chaldee Version of Jonathan translates it "the woman shall not lie with her father, and the man shall not lie with his mother." Accordingly the case here contemplated is that of Lot's daughters (Gen. xix. 31—38). This passage may, however, be translated literally, *the nakedness of thy father, and the nakedness of thy mother shalt thou not uncover.* That is, they being both one flesh, the nakedness of the one is the nakedness of the other. Amongst the Persians and other eastern nations, marriage between son and mother was allowed.

(8) **The nakedness of thy father's wife.**—Whilst the former prohibition refers to the son's own mother, this law is directed against illicit commerce with his stepmother. Here we have an instance where the phrase "to uncover the nakedness," denotes both illicit commerce and incestuous marriage. Accordingly the administrators of the law during the second Temple defined it as follows; a man's father's wife is for ever prohibited, whether she be simply betrothed or married to his father, whether she be divorced or not, whether she be a widow or not; all connection with her on the part of the father's son is forbidden. If he lie with her while her husband is alive, he is doubly guilty, first, because she is near of kin, and secondly, because she is another man's wife. This, therefore, includes the sin of Reuben with Bilhah, his father's concubine (Gen. xxxv. 22), and of Absalom with the wives of his father (2 Sam. xvi. 20—23; 1 Kings ii. 17), which was not incestuous marriage but adultery, since their husbands were alive and the wives were not divorced from them, as well as the sin practised among some of the Christians in Corinth, which consisted in sons actually marrying their divorced stepmothers in the lifetime of their fathers, and which the Apostle denounced with such severity (1 Cor. v. 1—4). Among the ancient Arabs, marriages with stepmothers were common, and to this day among some tribes in Africa, when a father is unable through advanced age to attend to his young wives, he voluntarily gives them over to his eldest son. The Koran, however, like the Mosaic law, proscribes these marriages (*Koran*, iv. 27).

(9) **The nakedness of thy sister.**—The fact that Adam married "bone of his bone and flesh of his flesh," and that his sons married their own sisters, encouraged the ancient Hebrew to imitate their example. Hence we find Abraham, the father of the faithful, married his half-sister (Gen. xx. 12). The same practice obtained amongst other nations of antiquity. Thus the Athenians married their half-sisters by their father's side, and the Spartans married half-sisters by the same mother, whilst the Assyrians and Egyptians married full sisters. Though nothing can be more explicit than the law here laid down, and though the transgression of it is denounced as an accursed and impious crime, to be visited with capital punishment (see chap. xx. 17; Deut. xxvii. 22), yet from the narrative of Amnon and his sister Tamar, and especially from the touching and melancholy remark of the outraged sister (2 Sam. xiii. 13, 16, 20), it is evident that the practice of the primitive parents of the human race and the example of the father of the Hebrew nation, continued to be followed in spite of this law. (Comp. Ezek. xxii. 11.)

Born at home or born abroad.—Literally, *the birth,* or *offspring of the house or the birth,* or *offspring from abroad.* According to the administrators of the law during the second Temple, the import of this precept is to forbid commerce between a brother and a sister, whether the sister is born in wedlock, which is meant by born at home, or whether she is illegitimate, which is meant by birth or offspring from abroad. Hence the ancient Chaldee Version of this clause, "whom thy father begot of another woman or of thy mother, or whom thy mother brought forth by thy father or by another man."

(10) **The nakedness of thy son's daughter.**—From this prohibition it is inferred that a man must not marry his own daughter. If a granddaughter, who is a degree further removed from him, is proscribed, how much more his own daughter. Hence the canonical law during the second Temple deduced from this passage that "whoso companieth with a woman, even by way of fornication, and begetteth a daughter, she is forbidden to him." Still, when the mother is expressly forbidden to the son (see verse 7), it is strange that the daughter should have been passed over in silence, and be left to inference. It is therefore more than probable that a word has dropped out of the text, and that originally it stood here, "the nakedness of thy daughter and of thy son's daughter," &c. That this is not a solitary instance where the text has suffered from disarrangement we shall presently have occasion to see in verse 11.

(11) **Thy father's wife's daughter.**—If this clause stood alone it would denote the daughter of a man's stepmother by another or previous husband, since "father's wife" in Hebrew always denotes *stepmother* (see verse 8, chap. xx. 11; Deut. xxiii. 1, xxvi. 20), in which case the man and the maiden, though no blood relations at all, would be forbidden to each other by virtue of the damsel's mother having married the man's father. It would thus differ from verse 9, where the maiden is a half-sister either by the same father or the same mother.

Begotten of thy father.—Literally, *the birth,* or *offspring of thy father* (see verse 9), that is, though the daughter of the stepmother, she is begotten by the same father, and hence is his half-sister on the father's side, which is exactly the same case already prohibited in the first clause of verse 9. Hence to avoid a senseless repetition of the same prohibition we must either regard this clause as having crept into the text from a marginal gloss, or we must correct the first letter of the disjunctive particle in verse 9, which would make it "the nakedness of thy sister, the daughter of thy father

thou shalt not uncover her nakedness.
(12)[a] Thou shalt not uncover the naked-
ness of thy father's sister: she *is* thy
father's near kinswoman. (13) Thou shalt
not uncover the nakedness of thy
mother's sister: for she *is* thy mother's
near kinswoman. (14) [b] Thou shalt not
uncover the nakedness of thy father's
brother, thou shalt not approach to his
wife: she *is* thine aunt. (15) [c] Thou shalt
not uncover the nakedness of thy
daughter in law: she *is* thy son's wife;
thou shalt not uncover her nakedness.
(16) [d] Thou shalt not uncover the naked-
ness of thy brother's wife: it *is* thy
brother's nakedness. (17) Thou shalt not
uncover the nakedness of a woman and
her daughter, neither shalt thou take
her son's daughter, or her daughter's
daughter, to uncover her nakedness;

a ch. 20. 19.
b ch. 20. 20.
c ch. 20. 12.
d ch. 20. 21.

---

and the daughter of thy mother." Accordingly, verse 9 prohibits marriage with a full sister, whilst the verse before us forbids it with a half-sister. The latter is the more probable, since intermarriage between entire step-brother and stepsister has always been, and still is, legitimate among the Jews.

(12) **Thy father's sister.**—According to the law which obtained in the time of Christ this prohibition not only extended to the father's half-sisters, but even when they were begotten by the grandfather illegitimately. It is remarkable that Moses himself was the offspring of such an alliance, since his father Amram married his own aunt Jochebed, who was the sister of his father. (See Exod. vi. 20.)

(13) **Thy mother's sister.**—Equally forbidden is the aunt by the mother's side. The law which obtained in the time of Christ also defines this prohibition to extend to a mother's sister or half-sister by the same father or mother, whether born in wedlock or out of it. It is remarkable that the administrators of the law during the second Temple understood this last prohibition strictly to apply to alliances between nephews and aunts, but not *vice versâ* to marriages between nieces and uncles. They regarded intermarriage between uncle and niece as an especially meritorious act, and interpreted the promises "then shalt thou call and the Lord shall answer" (Isa. lviii. 9) to refer more particularly to the man "who loves his neighbours, befriends his relations, *marries his brother's daughter*, and lends money to the poor in the hour of need." This is in accordance with the fact that not only do we find that Nahor married Milcah the daughter of his brother Haran (Gen. xi. 29), but that Othniel, the son of Kenaz, married his niece Achsah, being the daughter of Caleb, his father's brother (Josh. xv. 17; Judges i. 13). Hence among the Jews to this day intermarriages between uncles and nieces is of common occurrence.

(14) **Thy father's brother, thou shalt not approach to his wife.**—That is, according to the ancient legal interpretation, a nephew is to have no commerce with her during her husband's lifetime, nor marry her when his uncle is dead. Those who transgressed this law had not only to bear their sin, but were doomed to die without issue. (See chap. xx. 20.)

(15) **Thy daughter-in-law.** — The legislators in the time of Christ defined this prohibition as applicable not only to cases where marriage between them had actually been consummated, but to cases where the maiden had only been espoused, or when the daughter-in-law had been divorced by the son, or had become a widow. For an offence of this kind both parties were punished with death. (See chap. xx. 12.) Other nations regarded such alliances with the same abhorrence. (See *Koran*, iv. 27.)

(16) **The nakedness of thy brother's wife.**—Though alliance with a brother's wife is here forbidden—the prohibition, according to the administrators of the law during the second Temple, extending to illicit commerce or marriage in case she is divorced from her husband during the lifetime of her husband—and though the offenders are threatened with the curse of childlessness (see chap. xx. 21), yet the law on this point is by no means absolute. Under certain conditions the law enjoins it as a moral and civil duty for a man to marry his brother's widow. If a brother dies without issue, it is incumbent upon each surviving brother in succession to marry the widow, and if the brother-in-law refused to perform the sacred duty, the widow made him pass through a ceremony in which she heaped upon him the greatest indignity. This clearly shows that the prohibition here could not be based upon the ground of incest, since that which is inherently incestuous the Divine law itself would under no circumstances have set aside. This duty the surviving brother-in-law had to perform to the widows of as many of his brothers as happened to die without issue. A striking illustration of this fact occurred whilst Jehudah the Holy was president of the Sanhedrin. Twelve widows appealed to their brother-in-law to perform the duty of *Levir*. He refused to marry them because he saw no prospect how to maintain such an additional number of wives, and possibly a large increase of children. The case came before the President of the Sanhedrin, who not only decided that he must marry them all, but promised that if he would do the duty enjoined upon him by the Law of Moses, he himself would maintain the family, and their children in case there should be any, every Sabbatical year, when no produce was got from the land, which was at rest. The offer was accepted by the *Levir*, and he accordingly married his twelve sisters-in-law. After three years these twelve wives appeared with thirty-six children before Jehudah the Holy, to claim the promised alimony, as it was the Sabbatical year, and they actually obtained it. To this day this law is in force among the orthodox Jews. When a man dies without issue, the widow *ipso facto* belongs to the surviving brother, and she is not allowed to marry any one else unless her brother-in-law has gone through the ceremony of publicly renouncing her, which is tantamount to a divorce. This will explain the rendering of the clause before us in the ancient Chaldee Version, "thou shalt not uncover the nakedness of thy brother's wife in the lifetime of thy brother or after his death if he has children."

(17) **A woman and her daughter.**—That is, if a man marries a widow who has a daughter by a former husband, or if he forms an alliance with a woman who has a daughter out of wedlock, he is forbidden to marry also the daughter. But though this prohibition is directed against a peculiar form of polygamy.

for they *are* her near kinswomen: it *is*
wickedness. (18) Neither shalt thou take
[1]a wife to her sister, to vex *her*, to uncover her nakedness, beside the other in
her life *time*. (19) [a]Also thou shalt not
approach unto a woman to uncover her nakedness, as long as she is put apart for her uncleanness. (20) Moreover thou shalt not lie carnally with thy neighbour's wife, to defile thyself with her.

1 Or, *one wife to another.*

a ch. 20. 18.

there can hardly be any doubt that, as the administrators of the law during the second Temple interpreted it, if he married either of them and she died, he could not marry the other any more, and that this prohibition did not apply to cases of illicit commerce. Criminal intercourse with one did not preclude him from marrying the other. For contracting the kind of polygamy here forbidden, the offenders were punished with death by fire. (See chap. xx. 14.)

(18) **A wife to her sister.**—That is, a man is here forbidden to take a second sister for a wife to or in addition to the one who is already his wife, and who is still alive. This clause therefore forbids the Jews, who were permitted to have several wives, a particular kind of polygamy, *i.e.*, a plurality of sisters. According to the administrators of the law during the second Temple, the expression "sister" here not only denotes a full sister by the same father and the same mother, but a half-sister either by the same father or the same mother. The marginal rendering in the Authorised Version, "one wife to another," which makes this a prohibition of polygamy, and which was first proposed by Junius and Tremelius in 1575, is (1) contrary to the expressions "wife" and "sister," which, in every verse of these prohibitions (see verses 8, 9, 11—17), invariably mean wife and sister. (2) Whenever the phrase, "a man to his brother," or "a woman to her sister," is used metaphorically in the sense of "one to" or "one with another" (Exod. xxvi. 3, 5, 6, 17; Ezek. i. 9, 23; iii. 13, &c.), the words have always a distributive force, and are invariably preceded by a plural verb, and the things themselves to which they refer are mentioned by name. Thus, for instance, in Ezek. i. 23, it is, "their wings were straight one toward the other," which is not the case in the passage before us. (3) This rendering is at variance with the Mosaic code, which bases its legislation upon the existence of polygamy, and thus authorises it, as will be seen from the following facts. It permits a father, who had given his son a bondwoman for a wife, to give him a second wife of "freer birth," and prescribes how the first is to be treated under such circumstances (Exod. xxi. 9, 10). It ordains that a king "shall not multiply wives unto himself" (Deut. xvii. 17), which, as Bishop Patrick rightly remarks, "is not a prohibition to take more wives than one, but not to have an excessive number"; thus, in fact, legalising a moderate number. The law of primogeniture presupposes the case of a man having two wives (Deut. xxi. 15—17), and the Levitical law expressly enjoins that a man, though having a wife already, is to marry his deceased brother's widow (Deut. xxv. 17). Hence we find that the judges and kings of Israel had many wives (Judg. vii. 30, x. 4, xii. 9; 1 Sam. i. 2; 2 Sam. iii. 7). David, the royal singer of Israel, "their best king," as Bishop Patrick remarks, "who read God's word day and night and could not but understand it, took many wives without reproof; nay, God gave him more than he had before by delivering his master's wives to him" (2 Sam. xii. 8), and the case adduced in the previous verse plainly shows that polygamy continued among the Jews after the destruction of the second Temple (verse 10). (4) The Jews to whom this law was given to be observed in their every day life, and to whom the right understanding of its import was of the utmost importance, inasmuch as it involved the happiness of their families, the transgression of it being visited with capital punishment, have, as far as we can trace it, always interpreted this precept as referring to marriage with two sisters together. Hence the ancient canonical interpretation of it is embodied in the Chaldee Version, "a woman in the lifetime of her sister thou shalt not take," in the LXX., Vulg., the Syriac, and all the ancient versions.

To vex her.—That is, by marrying also the younger sister, the first, who is already the wife, would be roused to jealousy, and the natural love of sisters would thus be converted into enmity, thus precluding the occurrence of a case like that of Jacob with Leah and Rachel. (See Gen. xxix. 30.)

In her life-time.—This limits the prohibition to her lifetime, that is, as long as the sister who was first married is still living, he must not marry another of her sisters, but he may marry her when the first one is dead. According to the authorities during the second Temple, "in her lifetime" also includes a woman who had been divorced from her husband, and though she is no longer his wife, yet as long as she lives he is forbidden to marry her sister. When the wife died, he was not only free to marry her sister, but in case the deceased left issue, it was regarded as a specially meritorious thing for the widower to do so. Hence the Jews from time immemorial have afforded the bereaved husband special facilities to marry his deceased wife's sister, by allowing the alliance to take place within a shorter period after the demise of his first wife than is usually the case.

(19) **Also thou shalt not approach.**—Literally, *thou shalt not approach.* The marriage laws are now followed by sexual impurities, which to some extent are suggested by the subjects that had necessarily to be discussed or hinted at in regulating the alliance in question.

As long as she is put apart.—Put apart, *i.e.*, seven days. (See chap. xv. 19.) For consorting with her without being aware of her condition the man contracted defilement for seven days (see chap. xv. 24), and for committing this gross act presumptuously, both parties to it were visited with death. (See chap. xx. 18.) Ezekiel refers to the transgression of this law as one of the heinous sins perpetrated by the people of Israel (Ezek. xviii. 16; xxii. 10).

(20) **Thy neighbour's wife.**—For committing adultery, which is here branded as a defilement, whether with a betrothed or married woman, both guilty parties incurred the penalty of death by stoning. (See chap. xx. 10; Deut. xxii. 22; Ezek. xvi. 38, 40; John viii. 5.) In Egypt the adulterer received a thousand strokes with a stick, and the guilty woman had her nose cut off, and to this day the criminal wife among the Bedouins is executed by her husband, father, or brother, without any mercy. Both criminals were also punished with death among other Eastern nations.

(21) And thou shalt not let any of
thy seed [a] pass through *the fire* to
[b] Molech, neither shalt thou profane the
name of thy God: I *am* the LORD.
(22) Thou shalt not lie with mankind, as
with womankind: it *is* abomination.
(23) [c] Neither shalt thou lie with any beast
to defile thyself therewith: neither shall
any woman stand before a beast to lie
down thereto: it *is* confusion.
(24) Defile not ye yourselves in any of
these things: for in all these the nations
are defiled which I cast out before you:
(25) and the land is defiled: therefore I
do visit the iniquity thereof upon it,
and the land itself vomiteth out her
inhabitants. (26) Ye shall therefore keep
my statutes and my judgments, and
shall not commit *any* of these abomina-
tions; *neither* any of your own nation,
nor any stranger that sojourneth among
you: (27) (for all these abominations have
the men of the land done, which *were*
before you, and the land is defiled;)

a ch. 20. 2; 2 Kings 23. 10.

b Called, Acts 7. 43, *Moloch.*

c ch. 20. 15.

---

(21) **And thou shalt not let any of thy seed.**—Literally, *And thou shalt not give any of thy seed.* Those who violate the sanctity of the marriage ties will readily sacrifice their children. Hence the prohibition to offer up their children to idols follows the law about unchastity.

Pass through the fire to Molech.—Literally, *to let it pass to Molech,* that is, to put the child into the hands of the figure of Molech, when it fell into the fire which was kindled in the hollow statue of this idol. Molech, also called Milcom, which denotes king, is described as the hideous idol, or "the abomination of the Ammonites" (1 Kings xi. 5, 11). The following graphic description has been handed down traditionally of this idol and its worship:—"Our sages of blessed memory say that whilst all other idols had temples in Jerusalem, Molech had his temple outside Jerusalem, in a place by itself. It was a brass and hollow image, bull-headed, with arms stretched out like a human being who opens his hands to receive something from his neighbour. Its temple had seven compartments, into which the offerers went according to their respective gifts. If one offered a fowl, he went into the first compartment; if a sheep, into the second; if a lamb, into the third; if a ram, into the fourth; if a bullock, into the fifth; if an ox, into the sixth; and if he offered his son, he was conducted into the seventh compartment. He first kissed the image, as it is written, 'let the sacrificers of men kiss the calf' (Hosea xiii. 2), whereupon a fire was kindled in Molech till its arms became red hot; the child was then put into its hands, and drums were beaten to produce tremendous noises so as to prevent the shrieks of the child reaching the father's ears, lest he should be moved with pity towards his offspring." It was to this idol that Solomon erected a temple on the southern side of Mount Olivet (2 Kings xxiii. 13). This idolatrous worship was punished with death by stoning. (See chap. xx. 2.)

Neither shalt thou profane.—Better, *And thou shalt not profane,* that is, by causing other nations to say that the Israelites regard their God as an inferior deity, and hence offer unto him animals, whilst to Molech they sacrifice their own children. Hence any act which is done in violation of his commands, or misrepresents God, or by which He is put on a par with other gods, is called "profaning the name of God." (See chaps. xix. 12; xx. 3; xxi. 6; xxii. 2, 32, &c.)

(22) **As with womankind.**—This was the sin of Sodom (Gen. xix. 5), whence it derived its name, and in spite of the penalty of death enacted by the Law against those who were found guilty of it (see chap. xx. 13), the Israelites did not quite relinquish this abominable vice (Judges xix. 22; 1 Kings xiv. 24), to which the surrounding nations were addicted and which was so prevalent in the time of the Apostles (Rom. i. 27; 1 Cor. vi. 9; Gal. v. 19; 1 Tim. i. 10). By the law of Christ those who are guilty of this sin are excluded from the kingdom of God (1 Cor. vi. 9, 10), whilst the laws of civilised Europe rightly inflict the severest penalties upon offenders of this kind.

(23) **Any beast.**—The necessity for the prohibition of this shocking crime, for which the Mosaic law enacts the penalty of death (see chap. xx. 15, 16; Exod. xxii. 18), will appear all the more important when it is borne in mind that this degrading practice actually formed a part of the religious worship of the Egyptians in connection with the goat deities.

(24) **Defile not ye yourselves.**—The Lawgiver who solemnly introduced these precepts by five verses of preamble at the beginning of the chapter (verses 1—5), now concludes by an equally solemn appeal to God's people sacredly to observe them in all their integrity, since the violation of them (verses 6—23) has branded those nations with infamy, and brought about their national destruction, and expulsion from the very land which is now to be given to the Israelites.

(25) **The land itself vomiteth out her inhabitants.**—From the creation the earth shared in the punishment of man's guilt (Gen. iii. 17), and at the restitution of all things she is to participate in his restoration (Rom. viii. 19—22). The physical condition of the land, therefore, depends upon the moral conduct of man. When he disobeys God's commandments she is parched up and does not yield her fruit" (Deut. xi. 17). "The land is defiled" when he defiles himself. When he walks in the way of the Divine commands she is blessed (Levit. xxv. 19; xxvi. 4); "God is merciful unto his land and to his people" (Deut. xxxii. 43). Hence, "the earth mourneth" when her inhabitants sin (Isa. xxiv. 4, 5), and "the earth is glad" when God avenges the cause of His people (Ps. xcvi. 11—13). It is owing to this intimate connection between them that the land, which is here personified, is represented as loathing the wicked conduct of her children and being unable to restrain them. She nauseated them. The same figure is used in verse 28; chap. xx. 22; and in Rev. iii. 16.

(26) **Ye shall therefore keep my statutes.**—As the perpetration of the above named abominations entailed such disastrous consequences both to the land and to its inhabitants, the strict observance of the Divine statutes is enjoined upon all alike, whether they be Israelites by race or strangers who took up their abode amongst them and joined the Jewish community. (See chap. xvii. 9.)

(27) **For all these abominations.**—Though the contents of this verse are substantially the same as

(28) that the land spue not you out also,
when ye defile it, as it spued out the
nations that *were* before you. (29) For
whosoever shall commit any of these
abominations, even the souls that commit
them shall be cut off from among their
people. (30) Therefore shall ye keep mine
ordinance, that *ye* commit not *any one*
of these abominable customs, which
were committed before you, and that ye
defile not yourselves therein: I *am* the
LORD your God.

a ch. 11. 44 & 20. 7; 1 Pet. 1. 16.

CHAPTER XIX.—(1) And the LORD
spake unto Moses, saying, (2) Speak unto
all the congregation of the children of
Israel, and say unto them, *a*Ye shall be
holy: for I the LORD your God *am*
holy.
(3) Ye shall fear every man his mother,

those in verses 24, 25, yet the wording is different. In the former the Israelites are exhorted not *to pollute* themselves as the different tribes or nations have both polluted themselves and the land, whilst here *the inhabitants of Canaan* are more specifically described as having *practised* the abominations. The repetition of the same sentiments in different words, as is frequently the case in Hebrew, is designed to impart emphasis. The parentheses are unnecessary.

(28) **That the land spue not you out also.**—Better, *Lest the land vomit you out.* By unnecessarily translating the same word differently into "vomiteth" in verse 25, and "spue" here, as is done in the Authorised Version, the striking connection between the two verses is somewhat weakened.

(29) **For whosoever shall commit.**—This clause, according to the interpretation which obtained during the second Temple, particularises every individual, and is intended to indicate that any one, whether it be male or female, who is guilty, will incur the punishment prescribed for these sins.

Shall be cut off.—That is, in case the transgression escapes the ken of the tribunal, God himself will inflict the punishment upon the criminals, since some of the crimes specified in this chapter are, according to chap. xx., to be visited with death by the hand of man.

(30) **Therefore shall ye keep mine ordinance.** As God is no respecter of persons, and as He will assuredly visit His own people with the same punishment which He inflicted upon the former occupants of the land, the Israelites are to take special care to keep inviolate His ordinances.

Commit not any one of these abominable customs, which were committed before you.—Better, *Do not any one of these abominable statutes which were done*, as the Authorised Version translates the word in Deut. vi. 24, xvi. 12, xxvi. 16. These abominations were not practised simply as customs, but were legally enacted as statutes of the land, and formed part of their religious institutions (see verse 3). A similar state of degeneracy is described by Isaiah, who tells us that the Divine statutes, which is the same word used in the passage before us, were changed. By deviating here from the usual rendering of this phrase the Authorised Version mars the import of the passage.

I am the Lord your God.—This is the declaration with which this group of laws was introduced. Its repetition at the end imparts peculiar solemnity to these enactments. (See verse 1.)

XIX.

(1) **And the Lord spake unto Moses.**—The prohibitions in the preceding chapter, which are designed to regulate the moral conduct of relations and connections towards each other in their family circles, are now followed by precepts which affect the Israelite's life in all its bearings, both towards God and man. Hence the authorities during the second Temple regarded it as "embodying the Decalogue," for which reason, as well as for the fact that "it contains the sum and substance of the precepts of the Law, it is read in public." The precepts in this chapter are divided into sixteen groups, eight of which end with the emphatic reiteration, "I am the Lord your God" (verses 2—4, 10, 25, 31, 34, 36), and eight with the shorter formula, "I am the Lord" (verses 12, 14, 16, 18, 28, 30, 32, 37).

(2) **Speak unto all the congregation of the children of Israel.**—The importance which the Lawgiver Himself attaches to this epitome of the whole Law, as this section is called, may be seen from the fact that God commands Moses to address these precepts "to all *the congregation* of the children of Israel" —a phrase which occurs nowhere else in Leviticus in this formula, and which is only to be found once more in the whole Pentateuch (Exod. xii. 3), at the institution of the Passover, the great national festival which commemorates the redemption of the Israelites from Egypt.

I the Lord your God.—Around this solemn declaration, which is repeated no less than sixteen times, both in its full and shorter form (see verse 1), cluster the different precepts of this section. It is this solemn formula which links together the various injunctions in the chapter before us. As the Lord who is their God is Himself holy, they who are His people must also be holy, or as the saying which obtained during the second Temple expresses it, "the surroundings of the king must bear the moral impress of the sovereign;" or, in other words, your nearness to God not only demands that your conduct should not be in contradiction to His holy nature, but that your life should bear the impress and reflect the image of God. (See chap. xi. 44; Matt. v. 48; 1 Peter i. 15.)

(3) **Ye shall fear every man his mother, and his father.**—The first means to attain to the holiness which is to make the Israelite reflect the holiness of God, is uniformly to reverence his parents. Thus the group of precepts contained in this chapter opens with the fifth commandment in the Decalogue (Exod. xx. 12), or, as the Apostle calls it, the first commandment with promise (Eph. vi. 2). During the second Temple, already the spiritual authorities called attention to the singular fact that this is one of the three instances in the Scriptures where, contrary to the usual practice, the mother is mentioned before the father; the other two being Gen. xliv. 20 and Lev. xxi. 2. As children ordinarily fear the father and love the mother, hence they say precedence is here given to the mother in order to inculcate the duty of fearing them both alike. The expression "fear," however, they take to include the following:—(1) Not to stand or sit in the place set

and his father, and keep my sabbaths: I *am* the LORD your God.

(4) Turn ye not unto idols, nor make to yourselves molten gods: I *am* the LORD your God.

(5) And if ye offer a sacrifice of peace offerings unto the LORD, ye shall offer it at your own will. (6) It shall be eaten the same day ye offer it, and on the morrow: and if ought remain until the third day, it shall be burnt in the fire.

(7) And if it be eaten at all on the third day, it *is* abominable; it shall not be accepted. (8) Therefore *every one* that eateth it shall bear his iniquity, because he hath profaned the hallowed thing of the LORD: and that soul shall be cut off from among his people.

a ch. 23. 22.

(9) And [a] when ye reap the harvest of your land, thou shalt not wholly reap the corners of thy field, neither shalt thou gather the gleanings of thy

---

apart for the parents; (2) not to carp at or oppose their statements; and (3) not to call them by their proper names, but either to call them father or mother, or my master, my lady. Whilst the expression "honour," which is used in the parallel passage in Exodus xx. 12, they understand to include (1) to provide them with food and raiment, and (2) to escort them. The parents, they urge, are God's representatives upon earth; hence as God is both to be "honoured" with our substance (Prov. iii. 9), and as He is to be "feared" (Deut. vi. 13), so our parents are both to be "honoured" (Exod. xx. 12) and "feared" (chap. xix. 3); and as he who blasphemes the name of God is stoned (chap. xxiv. 16), so he who curses his father or mother is stoned (chap. xx. 9).

And keep my sabbaths.—Joined with this fifth commandment is the fourth of the Decalogue. The education of the children, which at the early stages of the Hebrew commonwealth devolved upon the parents, was more especially carried on by them on Sabbath days. In these leisure hours, when the Israelites were strictly forbidden to engage in any secular work, they found it a pleasant task and a welcome occupation to instruct their children in the many symbols, rites, and ceremonies which formed part of the service of the Sabbaths. Hence the observance of the day implied the instruction of the people in the fear and admonition of the Lord, and in acquiring the holiness which is the keynote of this chapter. Hence, too, the violation of the sanctity of the Sabbath is denounced as the greatest sin which the Israelites committed (Ezek. xx. 12, xxii. 8, xxiii. 38, &c.). It is probably for this reason that the administrators of the law during the second Temple say that the commandment about the Sabbath has here been selected to limit the duty of filial obedience. Its combination with the fifth commandment is to show that though children are admonished to obey their parents, yet if they should order the profanation of this holy day, the children must not obey. (See chap. xxiii. 3.)

(4) **Turn ye not unto idols.**—As the Lord is their God, and there is no other God besides Him, the Israelites must never turn their affections nor address prayers or enquiries to idols. This part of the verse therefore corresponds with the first commandment of the Decalogue (Exod. xx. 3). The expression here rendered "idols," which, apart from the Prophets and Hagiographa, only occurs once more (see chap. xxvi. 1), denotes *non-entities*—nothings, and it is in allusion to this import of the word that the Apostle remarks, "We know that an idol is *nothing* in the world" (1 Cor. viii. 4). According to the administrators of the law during the second Temple, the injunction here "turn not" means "face not," and forbids even the looking at or the examination of an idol.

Nor make yourselves molten gods.—This part of the verse corresponds with the second commandment in the Decalogue (Exod. xx. 4—6), though the phrase "molten gods" only occurs once more where the same prohibition is enforced (Exod. xxxiv. 17).

(5) **And if ye offer a sacrifice.**—From chap. xvii. 3—7, it will be seen that the Israelites were in the habit of sacrificing to idols the animals intended for private consumption, and that this practice gave rise to the enactment that when any of the three kinds of quadrupeds are to be slaughtered for daily meat, they should first be devoted to God as peace-offerings. Hence the transition here from the prohibition of idolatrous worship to the peace-offerings. The simple abstention from sacrifice to idols and offering them to God is not enough. If the Israelites bring a peace-offering to the Lord it must be offered in the prescribed manner.

Ye shall offer it at your own will.—Better, *ye shall offer it for your acceptance* (see chap. i. 3), that is, ye are to do it in such a manner as will secure for you the Divine acceptance.

(6) **It shall be eaten the same day . . . and on the morrow.**—The fact that the flesh of the animal might be eaten both on the day on which it was offered and on the following day, according to the authorities during the second Temple, shows that the second class of peace-offering is here meant, described in chap. viii. 16, since the flesh of the first class of peace-offerings had to be eaten on the same day. (See chap. vii. 15).

Until the third day.—See chap. vii. 17.

(7) **If it be eaten at all on the third day.**—See chap. vii. 18.

(8) **Therefore every one that eateth it.**—See chap. vii. 18—20.

That soul shall be cut off from among his people.—Better, *That soul shall be cut off from his people*, as the Authorised Version renders it in four out of the six instances (see chap. vii. 20, 21, 25, 27) in which this phrase occurs in the Book of Leviticus. When so important a legal formula, threatening death by excision, is used in a limited number of cases, it is most important that it should be rendered uniformly in a translation. (See Note on chap. xxii. 3.)

(9) **And when ye reap.**—Benevolent consideration for the poor is another means whereby the Israelite is to attain to that holiness which will enable him to reflect the holiness of God. As the Lord is merciful to all, and provides for the wants of every living creature (Ps. cxlv. 15, 16), the Israelite, too, is to regard the wants of the needy. By this injunction the Law moreover establishes the legal rights of the poor to a portion of the produce of the soil, and thus

harvest. (10) And thou shalt not glean
thy vineyard, neither shalt thou gather
every grape of thy vineyard; thou shalt
leave them for the poor and stranger: I
am the LORD your God.
(11) Ye shall not steal, neither deal
falsely, neither lie one to another.
(12) And ye shall not [a] swear by my name
falsely, neither shalt thou profane the
name of thy God: I *am* the LORD.
(13) [b] Thou shalt not defraud thy neighbour, neither rob *him*: [c] the wages of
him that is hired shall not abide with
thee all night until the morning.
(14) Thou shalt not curse the deaf,
[d] nor put a stumblingblock before the

a Ex. 20. 7; Deut. 5. 11; Matt. 5. 34; Jam. 5. 12.

b Ecclus. 10. 6.

c Deut. 24. 14; Tobit 4. 14.

d Deut. 27. 18.

---

releases him from private charity, which, in its exercise, might have been capricious and tyrannical.

The harvest of your land.—The expression "harvest," which is subject to this law, the administrators of the law during the second Temple defined to consist of the following produce of the soil (1) all edible and nutritious plants, but not those used for dyeing and colouring; (2) plants which are cultivated, but not those which grow wildly; (3) those which strictly belong to the soil, but not mushrooms, sponges, &c., since these are not so much dependent upon the soil for their growth, but upon humidity, and grow also upon wet wood, &c.; (4) those which ripen at the same time of the year and are all gathered in at the same time, thus excluding figs and similar fruits of trees which are gathered later and gradually, and (5) the produce which is not for immediate consumption, but is garnered up, thus excluding vegetables.

Thou shalt not wholly reap the corners of thy field.—The extent of the "corner" to be thus left for the poor, like that of filial duty and the study of the Divine law, has designedly been left undefined by the administrators of the law. It is among the things which have "no fixed measures." But though the maximum is not given, the minimum is stated to be no less than the sixtieth part of the field. The corner was generally left at the end of the field, so that the poor could easily get at it. The time when the poor came was morning, noon, and at the evening sacrifice, which was about three o'clock in the afternoon. The morning was intended for the accommodation of those mothers who had young children, who were then asleep; the middle of the day to accommodate the nurses, whilst the evening suited the elderly people.

The gleanings of thy harvest.—The expression "gleaning" is defined by the authorities during the second Temple to be the ears which fall from the hand or from the sickle in the time of reaping, provided that the quantity which has thus dropped from the hand of the plucker or cutter does not exceed one or two ears. When these ears have thus been dropped they belong to the proprietor and not to the gleaner. If a wind arose after the corn had all been cut, and scattered the harvest over the gleanings, the field was measured, and a certain quantity was allotted as gleanings; if the owner had gathered in all the harvest without leaving any gleanings, he was obliged to give a certain portion to the poor, though the corn had been ground into flour and baked; and if the harvest was lost or burnt after he had thus gathered it without leaving the gleanings, he was beaten with stripes.

(10) **And thou shalt not glean thy vineyard.**—In gathering in the vine care is to be taken only to cut off the large clusters, but not the *infantas*, as the expression literally denotes, which is here rendered by "glean." Those branches or twigs which had only one or two grapes on them were to be left to the poor.

Neither shalt thou gather every grape.—Better, *Nor shalt thou gather the scattered grapes*, that is, those single grapes which had either fallen to the ground during the process of cutting off the branches, or those which were scattered about the ground after the vintage was completed. Like the gleanings of the field these grapes were the portion of the poor both of Jewish origin and proselytes.

(11) **Ye shall not steal.**—This injunction, which forms the eighth commandment of the Decalogue (Exod. xx. 15), most probably has here a primary reference to the conduct of the owners of fields and vineyards. They are cautioned that by depriving the poor of his prescribed right to the corner of the fields, and to the gleanings of the harvest and vintage, they commit theft. Hence the Jewish canonists laid it down that he who puts a basket under a vine at the time of gathering grapes robs the poor.

(12) **And ye shall not swear.**—This corresponds with the third commandment of the Decalogue (Exod. xx. 7).

(13) **Thou shalt not defraud.**—Here oppression by fraud and oppression by violence are forbidden. It is probably in allusion to this passage that John the Baptist warned the soldiers who came to him: "And he said to them, Do violence to no man, neither accuse any falsely; and be content with your wages" (Luke iii. 14).

The wages of him that is hired.—From the declaration in the next clause, which forbids the retention of the wages over night, it is evident that the day labourer is here spoken of. As he is dependent upon his wages for the support of himself and his family, the Law protects him by enjoining that the earnings of the hireling should be promptly paid. This benign care for the labourer, and the denunciation against any attempt to defraud him, are again and again repeated in the Scriptures (Deut. xxiv. 14, 15; Jer. xxxii. 13; Mal. iii. 5; James v. 4). Hence the humane interpretation which obtained of this law during the second Temple: "He who treats a hireling with harshness sins as grievously as if he hath taken away life, and transgresses five precepts."

(14) **Thou shalt not curse the deaf.**—To revile one who cannot hear, and is therefore unable to vindicate himself, is both inexpressibly mean and wicked. The term deaf also includes the absent, and hence out of hearing (Ps. xxxviii. 14, 15). According to the administrators of the law during the second Temple, this prohibition was directed against all cursing whatsoever. For, said they, if to curse one who cannot hear, and whom, therefore, it cannot grieve, is prohibited, how much more is it forbidden to curse one who hears it, and who is both enraged and grieved by it.

Nor put a stumblingblock before the blind.—In Deut. xxvii. 18 a curse is pronounced upon those who lead the blind astray. To help those who were thus afflicted was always regarded as a meritorious act. Hence among the benevolent services which Job rendered to his neighbours, he says "I was eyes to the blind" (Job xxix. 15). According to the interpretation

blind, but shalt fear thy God: I *am* the
LORD.
(15) Ye shall do no unrighteousness in
judgment: thou shalt not [a] respect the
person of the poor, nor honour the per-
son of the mighty: *but* in righteousness
shalt thou judge thy neighbour.
(16) Thou shalt not go up and down
as a talebearer among thy people:
neither shalt thou stand against the
blood of thy neighbour: I *am* the
LORD.
(17) [b] Thou shalt not hate thy brother
in thine heart: thou shalt in any wise
rebuke thy neighbour, [1] and not suffer
sin upon him.

a Ex. 23. 3; Deut. 1. 17 & 16. 19; Prov. 24. 23; Jam. 2. 9.

b 1 John 2. 11; Matt. 18. 15; Ecclus. 19. 13.

1 Or, *that thou bear not sin for him.*

---

which obtained in the time of Christ, this is to be understood figuratively. It forbids imposition upon the ignorant, and misdirecting those who seek advice, thus causing them to fall. Similar tenderness to the weak is enjoined by the Apostle: "That no man put a stumblingblock or an occasion to fall in his brother's way" (Rom. xiv. 13).

But shalt fear thy God.—Deafness and blindness may prevent the sufferers from detecting the offender, and bringing him to justice before an earthly tribunal, but God on high hears it when the human ear is stopped up, and sees it when the human eye is extinct. Hence the prohibition against injustice to the infirm and the poor is enforced by an appeal to fear the Lord. (See verse 32.)

(15) **Do no unrighteousness in judgment.**—That is, the judges are not to abuse the authority vested in them by virtue of their office, by administering what ought to be justice in an arbitrary manner.

Thou shalt not respect the person of the poor.—The general statement in the preceding clause is here more minutely defined. The consideration for the infirm enjoined in verse 14 is not to influence the decision of the judge, who is to administer justice, even if the poor is thereby reduced to greater poverty, and though the rich party to the suit may benevolently desire a verdict against himself to save the needy (Exod. xxiii. 3). The authorities during the second Temple illustrate it as follows:—"If the rich man should say I am by law obliged to provide for the poor, I will therefore let him win the suit, and he will thus have his wants supplied without being subjected to the humiliation of receiving alms; for this reason it is said thou shalt not respect the person of the poor."

Nor honour the person of the mighty.—Jewish juries, in their extreme desire to be impartial, have gone so far as to urge, that whilst the case between a rich man and a poor is being tried, they should both be dressed alike, both alike should either stand or sit, both should have the same right of speech, and both should be addressed by the judge in the same courteous manner. "If ye have respect to persons," says the Apostle, in allusion to this passage, "ye commit sin, and are convinced of the law as transgressors" (James ii. 9, with verses 2—4).

(16) **Thou shalt not go up and down as a tale-bearer.**—Better, *Thou shalt not go about slandering,* as the Authorised Version has it in Jerem. vi. 28, ix. 4; Ezek. xxii. 9, Margin. Whilst giving just evidence in a court of justice is demanded by the law, it prohibits the circulation of slanderous reports about our neighbours. This dangerous habit, which has ruined the character and destroyed the life of many an innocent person (1 Sam. xxii. 9, 18; Ezek. xxii. 9, &c.), was denounced by the spiritual authorities in the time of Christ as the greatest sin. Three things they declared remove a man from this world, and deprive him of happiness in the world to come—idolatry, incest, and murder, but slander surpasses them all. It kills three persons with one act, the person who slanders, the person who is slandered, and the person who listens to the slander. Hence the ancient Chaldee Version of Jonathan translates this clause: "Thou shalt not follow the thrice accursed tongue, for it is more fatal than the double-edged devouring sword." (Comp. also Ecclus. xxviii. 14.)

Neither shalt thou stand against the blood.—This part of the verse is evidently designed to express another line of conduct whereby our neighbour's life might be endangered. In the former clause, "the going about" with slanderous reports imperilled the life of the slandered person, here "the standing still" is prohibited when it involves fatal consequences. The administrators of the law during the second Temple translating this clause literally, *thou shalt not stand still by the blood,* &c., interpreted it to mean that if we see any one in danger of his life, *i.e.,* drowning, attacked by robbers or wild beasts, &c., we are not to stand still by it whilst his blood is being shed, but are to render him assistance at the peril of our own life. Or if we know that a man has shed the blood of his fellow creature, we are not to stand silently by whilst the cause is before the tribunal. Hence the Chaldee Version of Jonathan renders it, "Thou shalt not keep silent the blood of thy neighbour when thou knowest the truth in judgment." Others, however, take it to denote to come forward, and try to obtain a false sentence of blood against our neighbours, so that this phrase is similar in import to Exod. xxiii. 1, 7.

(17) **Shalt not hate thy brother in thine heart.**—From the outward acts denounced in the preceding verse, the legislator now passes to inward feelings. Whatever wrong our neighbour has inflicted upon us, we are not to harbour hatred against him.

Thou shalt in any wise rebuke.—Better, *thou shalt by all means,* or *thou shalt freely rebuke him.* If he has done wrong he is to be reproved, and the wrong is to be brought home to him by expostulation. In illustration of this precept the Jewish canonists remark, "when any man sinneth against another he must not inwardly hate him and keep silence, as it is said of the wicked, 'And Absalom spake unto his brother Amnon neither good nor bad, for Absalom hated Amnon' (2 Sam. xiii. 22); but he is commanded to make it known unto him, and to say, 'Why hast thou done thus unto me?'" Similar is the admonition of Christ, "If thy brother sin against thee rebuke him, and if he repent forgive him" (Luke xvii. 3).

And not suffer sin upon him.—Better, *so that thou bear not sin on his account.* That is, by not reproving him, but harbouring inward hatred towards the offender, we not only become partakers of his offence, but incur the sin of bearing secret ill-will (Rom. i. 32; Eph. iv. 26; 1 Tim. v. 20, 22). According to the spiritual authorities during the second Temple, however, this clause denotes, "but thou shalt bear no sin by reason of it," as the Authorised Version

(18) Thou shalt not avenge, nor bear any grudge against the children of thy people, [a] but thou shalt love thy neighbour as thyself: I *am* the LORD. (19) Ye shall keep my statutes.

Thou shalt not let thy cattle gender with a diverse kind: thou shalt not sow thy field with mingled seed: neither shall a garment mingled of linen and woollen come upon thee.

a Matt. 5. 43. & 22. 39; Rom. 13. 9; Gal. 5. 14; Jam. 2. 8.

translates this phrase in Num. xviii. 32; that is, "execute the duty of reproof in such a manner that thou dost not incur sin by it," which they explain in the following manner: "Even if the reproof is ineffectual the first time, it must be repeated over and over again, but the rebuker must desist as soon as he sees blushes on the offender's face, for it shows that the reproofs have made an impression. Every step taken by the one who reproves, after the offender has thus indicated by his countenance that he realises the offence, is an unnecessary humiliation, and hence brings sin upon him who rebukes by reason of it."

(18) **Thou shalt not avenge.**—As the preceding verse enjoins upon us to reprove the offender, this verse forbids us to avenge the wrong even when the rebuke has proved ineffectual, thus demanding the greatest sacrifice on the part of the injured person. The administrators of the law during the second Temple illustrate what is meant by avenge by the following example. "When a disobliging person who is in need applies to you to lend him something, and you reply, 'I will not lend you even as you would not lend me,' this is to avenge." (Comp. also Rom. xii. 19.)

Nor bear any grudge.—The law goes further still. It enjoins that the injured man is to banish from memory the injury he has suffered, though the offender has made no reparation. The spiritual authorities during the time of Christ regarded the simple reference to the injury when a kindly act is performed to our adversary as a violation of this injunction. They illustrated it by the following example. When an adversary applies to you to lend him something, and you actually comply with his request, but in so doing you say, "I lend it you, I will not act as you have acted, for you have refused to lend me," this is a violation of the command not to bear any grudge. "He who at the reconciliation with his adversary readily forgives his transgressions, his own trespasses will also be readily forgiven in the day of judgment," is the oft-repeated precept of the sages during the second Temple. Again, "He who suffers injuries and does not return injury for injury, he who is reviled and does not revile again, fulfils acts of love and rejoices in suffering; of him it is said, 'Those that love him are like the sun, which comes forth in its might from all dark clouds beaming with light'" (Judges v. 31).

Thou shalt love thy neighbour as thyself.—This sublime precept formed the centre around which clustered the ethical systems propounded by some of the most distinguished Jewish teachers during the second Temple. When Hillel was asked by one who wished to learn the sum and substance of the Divine Law in the shortest possible time, this sage replied by giving a paraphrase of the precept before us in a negative form, "What thou dost not wish that others should do to thee, that do not thou to others; this is the whole Law, the rest is only its interpretation. Now go and learn." Christ gives it in the positive form (Matt. vii. 12; Luke vi. 31; Rom. xiii. 8—10).

(19) **Ye shall keep my statutes**—that is, the following ordinances, which though not of the same high moral nature as the precepts laid down in the preceding verses, are yet necessary to attain to holiness. The Holy God has made everything "after its kind" (Gen. i. 11, 12, 21, 24, 25, &c.), and has thus established a physical distinction in the order of His creation. For man to bring about a union of dissimilar things is to bring about a dissolution of the Divine laws and to act contrary to the ordinances of Him who is holy, and to whose holiness we are to attain.

Cattle gender with a diverse kind.—Such commixtures would not only contravene the Divine order of things, but would lessen the abhorrence of the crime prohibited in chap. xviii. 22, 23. The use, however, of animals produced from such mixtures was not forbidden. Hence we find that mules were largely employed by the Jews (2 Sam. xiii. 29, xviii. 9; 1 Kings i. 33, 38, x. 25, xviii. 5; Ezra ii. 66, &c.). These hybrids were either the issue of parents voluntarily coming together without the aid of the Israelites, or were imported from other countries. This law is binding upon the Jews to this day in every country where they happen to live, whether in Palestine or out of it.

Not sow thy field with mingled seed.—According to the administrators of the law during the second Temple, the prohibition is only applicable to diverse seeds for human food, mixed together for the purpose of sowing them in the same field, as, for instance, wheat and barley, beans and lentils. These an Israelite must neither sow himself nor allow a non-Israelite to do it for him. Seeds of grain and seeds of trees, as well as seeds of different kinds of trees, may be sown together. The opening words of the parable, "A certain man had a fig-tree planted in his vineyard" (Luke xiii. 6), do not contravene this law. Seeds which were not intended for human food, such as of bitter herbs, or of vegetables intended for drugs, were exempted from this law, and like the hybrids of mixed parents, the seeds of herbs sown with diverse kinds were allowed to be used. Unlike the law, however, about the commixture of animals, which, as we have seen, is of universal application, the law about mixed seeds was only applicable to the Holy Land, since the command here is, "thou shalt not sow *thy field*," which these authorities maintain means "the fields of their inheritance in the promised land. Though trees are not mentioned here, the law was applied to grafting. Hence it was forbidden to graft an apple-tree on a citron-tree, or herbs into trees. The fruit, however, which grew upon the trees of such graftings was allowed to be eaten. The law about the diverse graftings is binding upon the Jews in every country and to all ages.

A garment mingled of linen and woollen.—Not only is it forbidden to weave woollen and flaxen threads together into one material to make wearing apparel of it, but according to the administrators of the law during the second Temple, an Israelite must not mend a woollen garment with a flaxen thread, and *vice versâ*. One of the reasons which the ancient canonists assign for this prohibition is that "wool and linen were appointed for the priests alone." This law is observed by the orthodox Jews to this day. The law laid down

(20) And whosoever lieth carnally with
a woman, that *is* a bondmaid, [1] [2] be-
trothed to an husband, and not at all
redeemed, nor freedom given her; [3] [4] she
shall be scourged; they shall not be put
to death, because she was not free.
(21) And he shall bring his trespass offer-
ing unto the LORD, unto the door of
the tabernacle of the congregation,
even a ram for a trespass offering.
(22) And the priest shall make an atone-
ment for him with the ram of the tres-
pass offering before the LORD for his
sin which he hath done: and the sin
which he hath done shall be forgiven
him.
(23) And when ye shall come into the
land, and shall have planted all manner
of trees for food, then ye shall count
the fruit thereof as uncircumcised:
three years shall it be as uncircumcised
unto you: it shall not be eaten of.

1 Or, *abused by any.*

2 Heb., *reproached by*, or, *for man.*

3 Or, *they.*

4 Heb., *there shall be a scourging.*

---

in this verse is substantially repeated in Deut. xxii. 9–11.

(20) **And whosoever lieth.**—Better, *If a man lie*, as the same phrase is translated in the Authorised Version, chaps. xxii. 14, xxiv. 19, xxv. 29, xxvii. 14.

Betrothed to an husband.—Better, *betrothed to a man.* From the law about the mixed seeds the Lawgiver passes to heterogeneous alliances. The case here legislated for is that of seducing a bondwoman who is espoused to another man. This bondwoman might be either one of an intermediate kind, that is, one whose redemption money had been partially paid, or belong to that class who had no prospect of a free discharge. According to the administrators of the law during the second Temple, the case before us is that of a Canaanitish maid, partly free and partly servile, whom her master had espoused to a Hebrew slave. (See Exod. xxi. 4.)

And not at all redeemed.—Better, *not fully* or *entirely redeemed*, that is, only part of her redemption money had been paid, so that she was partly free and partly slave. According to the law which obtained during the second Temple, the espousal of such a woman was not legally complete, and hence she is not properly a married woman or the wife of another man.

Nor freedom given her.—That is, the legal document that she is a free woman and has ceased to be a slave. This was done upon payment of the full money, or of her master's free choice without redemption money at all. In either case, however, she was then only legally free when she received the bill of freedom. Hence the ancient Chaldee Version translates this clause, "Nor has freedom been given her by a bill of dismission."

She shall be scourged.—Literally, *there shall be visitation* or *inquisition;* then, as is frequently the case, the effect of this visitation or requisition, *i.e.*, punishment, which, according to the administrators of the law during the second Temple, consisted in giving the woman forty stripes with the thong of an ox-hide. This punishment, however, she only received when it was proved that she was a consenting party to the sin. Hence the rendering in the Authorised Version, "she shall be scourged." The Marginal rendering, "they shall be scourged," though supported by some ancient Versions, is contrary to the legislation during the second Temple. The punishment prescribed in this clause is for the woman alone, the man's punishment follows in the next verse.

They shall not be put to death.—As she was a slave, and her espousals were illegal, the punishment of death, which was ordinarily inflicted in cases of adultery or seduction of a free woman betrothed to a man (see chap. xx. 10; Deut. xxii. 23), was not inflicted on them.

(21) **And he shall bring his trespass offering.**—Unlike the woman, the man had to bring this sacrifice under any circumstances, whether he sinned ignorantly or presumptuously. She was exempted from offering a sacrifice because she was her master's property, and not being her own, she had no property.

Unto the door of the tabernacle of the congregation.—Better, *to the entrance of the tent of meeting*, whither all the sacrifices were brought. (See chap. xvii. 4, 5.) The ram here prescribed was the usual animal for such a sacrifice. (See chap. v. 17, 18.)

(22) **And the priest shall make an atonement.**—Having offered the trespass offering according to the prescribed ritual by the priest, the sinner expiated for his sin, and was declared free by the officiating son of Aaron. (See chap. iv. 20, 26.)

(23) **And when ye shall come.**—Rather, *And when ye be come*, as the Authorised Version renders the same phrase in chap. xiv. 34. This is one of the four instances in Leviticus of a law being given prospectively having no immediate bearing on the condition of the people of Israel (viz., chaps. xiv. 34, xix. 23, xxiii. 10, xxv. 2), and though all the four enactments are introduced by the same phrase, they are translated in three different ways in the Authorised Version:—"When ye be come into the land," in chaps. xiv. 34, xxiii. 10; "When ye shall come into the land," in chap. xix. 23; and "When ye come into the land," in chap. xxv. 2; thus giving the impression as if the phrases in the original were different in the different passages. In legislative formulæ it is of importance to exhibit uniformly the same phraseology in a translation.

Shall have planted all manner of trees for food.—From this declaration the administrators of the law during the second Temple inferred that the trees planted by the inhabitants of Canaan before the Israelites took possession of it, were exempt from this law, and that it only applies to fruit-trees intended for food, such as citron-trees, olive-trees, fig-trees, vines, &c. Trees which bore fruit unfit for human food, which grew up by themselves, or which were planted for hedges or timber, did not come under this law.

Then ye shall count the fruit thereof as uncircumcised.—Literally, *then shall ye circumcise its uncircumcision, its fruit*, that is, cut off or pinch off its uncircumcision, which the text itself explains as "its fruit." The metaphorical use of circumcision is thus explained by the text itself: it denotes the fruit as disqualified or unfit. In chap. xxvi. 41 the same metaphor is used for the heart which is stubborn or not ripe to listen to the Divine admonitions. And in other passages of Scripture it is used with reference to lips (Exod. vi. 12, 30) and ears (Jer. vi. 10) which do not perform their proper functions.

(24) But in the fourth year all the
fruit thereof shall be [1] holy to praise
the Lord *withal.* (25) And in the
fifth year shall ye eat of the fruit
thereof, that it may yield unto you the
increase thereof: I *am* the Lord your
God.
(26) Ye shall not eat *any thing* with
the blood: neither shall ye use enchant-
ment, nor observe times. (27) [a] Ye shall

[1] Heb., *holiness of praises to the LORD.*

[a] ch. 21. 5.

Three years shall it be.—The cutting off of the fruit is to be repeated every year during three successive years. As the produce of the earliest year when let to grow upon the trees is both stunted and tasteless, and, moreover, as by plucking off the fruit or pinching off the blossom the trees will thrive better and bear more abundantly afterwards, the Lawgiver enacts here as law that which was in vogue amongst careful husbandmen from time immemorial, thus debarring greedy owners from acting in a way which would ultimately be to their own material injury.

It shall not be eaten.—According to the authorities in the time of Christ, this interdict extended to any and every advantage to be derived from the first three years' produce. The fruits must not be sold, but must either be burnt, or buried in the ground; and if any one eat as much as an olive he received forty stripes save one.

(24) **But in the fourth year.**—Like the second tithes the fruits of the fourth year were taken up to Jerusalem, and there eaten by the owner, in company with the poor and needy whom he invited to the repast. The owner, however, was also allowed to redeem them. In this case he had to add the fifth part of their value, take up the money to the holy city, and there spend it in a repast to which he invited the poor. The grapes of the vineyards within a distance of a day's journey of Jerusalem had, however, to be taken up to decorate the streets of the holy city. Vineyards of the fourth year were exempt from the law laid down in verses 9 and 10, as well as from the law of first-fruits, tithes, and second tithes.

Shall be holy to praise the Lord withal.—Better, *shall be holy, a praise to the Lord,* that is, either the fruits themselves, or their equivalent in money, shall be spent in the holy city, thus offering them at this sacrificial repast in praise to the Lord. (Comp. Judges ix. 27.)

(25) **And in the fifth year.**—It was only in the fifth year that the owner was permitted to eat the fruits without redeeming them.

That it may yield unto you the increase thereof.—That is, refraining from using the fruits during the first three years, and consecrating to the Lord the fruit of the fourth year in the sacrificial repast, they will realise that hereafter the tree will yield them abundant fruit. So far, therefore, from being losers by waiting till the fifth year, they will actually be gainers.

(26) **Ye shall not eat any thing with the blood.**—According to the administrators of the law during the second Temple, there are no less than five different things forbidden here. It prohibits (1) eating the flesh of a legally slaughtered animal as long as its life is not quite gone, or whilst the flesh is still trembling; (2) eating the flesh of sacrificial animals whilst the blood is still in the sprinkling bowl, and before it has been sprinkled on the altar; (3) eating the meat of mourners by the relatives when a member of the family has been publicly executed, and his blood has been shed; (4) eating anything by the judicial court on the day when their sentence of death is being executed on the criminal; and (5) it warns the rebellious and gluttonous son "not to eat immoderately by the penalty of blood." The ancient Chaldee Version, therefore, which translates it "Ye shall not eat the flesh of any sacrifice whilst the blood is in the basin unsprinkled," exhibits the second of these prohibitions involved in this interpretation; and all the five premise the rendering of this phrase, "Ye shall not eat by the blood," which has the merit of being literal; whilst the Authorised Version follows the first of these five prohibitions. Others, again, who also translate it "Ye shall not eat by the blood," take it as a prohibition of the idolatrous practice which obtained among the Zabii, who, to obtain favour from the demons, gathered the blood of the sacrifices which they offered to them into a vessel or a hole dug in the earth, and then sat around it to consume the sacrificial meal by the blood, thinking that thereby they fraternised with these demons. This seems to be favoured by the next clause.

Neither shall ye use enchantment.—Better, *ye shall use no enchantment.* According to the authorities during the second Temple, this consisted in any one saying, "A morsel has dropped out of my mouth; the staff has fallen out of my hand; my child has called out behind me; a crow has cawed to me; a deer has crossed my path; a serpent crept on my right hand; a fox has gone by on my left;" and regarding these as bad omens for the day which has now began or for the work which he has just commenced. Or if he says to the man who raises the taxes, "Do not begin with me; it is still early in the day; it is the first of the month; it is the beginning of the week; I shall be unlucky the whole day, week, or month to be the first to be burdened;" this is enchantment.

Nor observe times.—This, according to the same authorities, consists in "taking notice of the seasons and days, and in saying this is a good day to begin a journey, to-morrow will be lucky to make a purchase."

(27) **Round the corners of your heads.**—That is, they are not to shave off the hair around the temples and behind the ears, so as to leave the head bald except a dish-like tuft upon the crown, thus imparting to their heads the form of a hemisphere. This was done by the Arabs, and other worshippers of the god Orotal. Hence the Arabs are ironically called "those with the corner of their hair polled," as it is rightly rendered in the Margin (Jer. ix. 26, xxv. 23, xlix. 32).

Mar the corners of thy beard.—The beard was regarded by the Hebrews and other eastern nations as the greatest ornament of a man, and was as dear to them as life itself. It was the object of salutation (2 Sam. xx. 9), and the mutilation of it was looked upon as the greatest disgrace and most degrading punishment (2 Sam. x. 4; Isa. vii. 20; Ezra v. 1—5, &c.). It was only in seasons of sorrow that the Hebrews neglected their beards; and sometimes, to show how deeply they were afflicted, they covered them up, or even cut them off, or tore them out (2 Sam. xix. 24; Isa. xv. 2; Jer. xli. 5, &c.). Because it was so precious a treasure, it was customary among some of the ancients to present to their gods the firstlings of their beards. The prohibition before us alludes to this practice.

not round the corners of your heads,
neither shalt thou mar the corners of
thy beard. (28) Ye shall not [a] make any
cuttings in your flesh for the dead, nor
print any marks upon you: I *am* the
LORD.
(29) Do not [1] prostitute thy daughter,
to cause her to be a whore; lest the
land fall to whoredom, and the land be-
come full of wickedness.
(30) Ye shall keep my sabbaths, and
reverence my sanctuary: I *am* the
LORD.
(31) Regard not them that have familiar
spirits, neither seek after wizards, to be
defiled by them: I *am* the LORD your
God.
(32) Thou shalt rise up before the
hoary head, and honour the face of the
old man, and fear thy God: I *am* the
LORD.
(33) And [b] if a stranger sojourn with

a Deut. 14. 1.

1 Heb., *profane.*

b Ex. 22. 21.

---

(28) **Cuttings in your flesh for the dead.**—It was not only the custom for mourners to let their hair grow long and wear it in a disorderly manner (see chap. x. 6), but the bereaved in the East to this day make cuts and incisions in their bodies in mourning for the dead. The Israelite, however, who is created in the image of God, and who is to be as holy as the Lord is holy, must not thus disfigure his body (see chap. xxi. 6; Deut. xiv. 1, &c.); he must not sorrow as others which have no hope. For transgressing this law the offender received forty stripes save one.

Nor print any marks upon you.—This, according to the ancient authorities, was effected by making punctures in the skin to impress certain figures or words, and then filling the cut places with stibium, ink, or some other colour. The practice of tattooing prevailed among all nations of antiquity, both among savages and civilised nations. The slave had impressed upon his body the initials of his master, the soldier those of his general, and the worshipper the image of his tutelar deity. To obviate this disfiguration of the body which bore the impress of God's image, and yet to exhibit the emblem of his creed, the Mosaic Law enacted that the Hebrew should have phylacteries which he is to bind as "a sign" upon his hand, and as "a memorial" between his eyes "that the Lord's law may be in his mouth" (Exod. xiii. 9, 16; Deut. vi. 8, xi. 18).

(29) **Do not prostitute thy daughter.**—This refers to the degrading worship of Astarte which prevailed in ancient times, and which at times also broke out among the Jews.

(30) **Ye shall keep my sabbaths.**—The greatest safeguard against the above-named abomination, and the surest way to fulfil the Divine commands, is by keeping the Sabbath day, and following the instruction imparted on this day of rest. (See verse 3.)

And reverence my sanctuary—which the Israelites frequented on the Sabbath. (See Exod. xlvi. 3.) The way to reverence the sanctuary, according to the definition of the Jewish canonists, was for an Israelite not to come into the sanctuary when legally defiled, not to ascend the mountain of the house of God with his staff in his hand, with his shoes on his feet, in his working clothes, with the dust on his feet, or carrying bags of money about his person, not to spit in the sacred precincts, or make them a thoroughfare. It is in reference to the last-mentioned rule that we are told Christ "would not suffer that any man should carry any vessel through the Temple" (Mark xi. 16)—He would not allow them to use the sacred precincts as a short cut.

(31) **Regard not.**—Better, *Turn ye not unto,* as the Authorised Version renders this very phrase in verse 4.

Them that have familiar spirits.—This phrase represents the single word *oboth* in the original, and the translators of our Authorised Version by adopting it implied that those who practised this craft were supposed to be attended by an invisible spirit who was subject to their call to supply them with supernatural information. According to the authorities during the second Temple it denotes one who has a spirit speaking from under his arm-holes, or chest, with a hollow voice, as if it came out of a bottle, which is the meaning of *ob* in Job xxxii. 19. They identified it with the spirit of Python, by which the ancient Chaldee Version renders it.

Neither seek after wizards.—The expression "wizard," which in old English denotes "wise man," "sage," is almost the exact equivalent of the word in the original. These cunning men pretended to tell people their fortunes, where their lost property was to be found, &c. According to ancient tradition, these wizards took in their mouth a bone of a certain bird called *yaduā,* burned incense, thus producing fumes which sent them off into an ecstacy, and then foretold future events. Hence their name, *yidonee,* as it is in the original. It occurs eleven times in the Bible, and always together with the word translated "familiar spirit."

(32) **Rise up before the hoary head.**—But though no regard is to be paid to these soothsayers and cunning men, the greatest reverence is to be shown to the aged, for "with the old is wisdom, and in length of days understanding" (Job xii. 12, xxxii. 7, &c.). If we, therefore, are to attain to the holiness which, as it is set forth in the beginning of this chapter, is to reflect the holiness of God, we must have reverence for the ancients, since God himself is called "the Ancient of days" (Daniel vii. 9, 13, 22). This precept, which is so often inculcated in Holy Writ, is beautifully enforced in the maxims of the authorities during the second Temple. "He who receives and takes care of an old man is rewarded as if he received and sought God," is one of their sayings. Again, "Prophets are only believed if they come armed with Divine miracles, but old men always." To this day, when, among the orthodox Jews, an aged person enters into a house where young people are, they all rise up, and will not sit down till he asks them to do it. An exception, however, is made with regard to workmen. When an aged person passes by artisans who are engaged in their work, they need not stand up, and thus be interrupted in their labour.

(33) **And if a stranger sojourn with thee.**—The stranger, for whose benefit the legislators enacted so many humane and benign laws, and with regard to whom the book of Leviticus has laid down so many precepts, is one of non-Jewish origin, but who had joined the Jewish faith. He had, therefore, to undergo the rite of circumcision; he had to fast on the great

thee in your land, ye shall not [1] vex
him. (34) [a] *But* the stranger that dwell-
eth with you shall be unto you as one
born among you, and thou shalt love
him as thyself; for ye were strangers in
the land of Egypt: I *am* the LORD
your God.
(35) Ye shall do no unrighteousness in
judgment, in meteyard, in weight, or in
measure. (36) [b] Just balances, just
[2] weights, a just ephah, and a just hin,
shall ye have: I *am* the LORD your God,
which brought you out of the land of
Egypt. (37) Therefore shall ye observe
all my statutes, and all my judgments,
and do them: I *am* the LORD.

CHAPTER XX.—(1) And the LORD
spake unto Moses, saying, (2) [c] Again,
thou shalt say to the children of Israel,
Whosoever *he be* of the children of
Israel, or of the strangers that sojourn

1 Or, *oppress.*

a Ex. 22. 21.

b Prov. 11. 1 & 16. 11 & 20. 10.

2 Heb., *stones.*

c ch. 18. 21.

Day of Atonement (chap. xvi. 29); he had to submit to the regulations about sacrifices (chaps. xvii. 8, 9, xxii. 18); he had to abstain from eating blood and the flesh of animals torn by wild beasts (*ibid.* verses 10, 15); he had to practise the laws of chastity (chap. xviii. 26); like the Israelite by birth, he had to refrain from blasphemy, and obey the moral precepts (chap. xxiv. 16—22). These were some of the conditions of his sojourning in the land.

Ye shall not vex him.—Having once been admitted into the community, the Israelites were forbidden to upbraid him with his nationality or throw at him the fact that he was originally an idolater. They are thus prohibited calling him foreigner or neophyte, a practice which every civilised nation and religious community are prone more or less to indulge in to this day, with regard to aliens and those who have embraced their faith.

(34) **But the stranger that dwelleth.**—Better, *The stranger that sojourneth.* The word "but" is not in the original, and its insertion mars the flow of the passage, whilst the expression rendered in the Authorised Version by "dwelleth" is the same which is translated "sojourn" in the preceding verse. This stranger is in every respect to be treated as any other member of the commonwealth, and as a native.

Shalt love him as thyself.—He is not simply to be treated with consideration and courtesy because he is a foreigner, and enjoy the rights and receive the justice due to every human being, but he is to be put on a perfect equality with the ordinary Israelite. Hence the precept laid down in verse 18, "thou shalt love thy neighbour as thyself," is here enacted with regard to the stranger. It was this humane law which attracted so many strangers to Palestine. Hence we find that in the days of Solomon there were 153,600 strangers in the Holy Land.

For ye were strangers in the land of Egypt.—To enforce these kindly sentiments towards strangers, which was so contrary to the practice of the surrounding nations, who had an inveterate hatred of all foreigners, the lawgiver appeals to their own bitter experience. They knew with what inhumanity they were treated in Egypt because they were strangers, how they had been humiliated and reduced to slavery. The very thought of this will not only soften their hearts, but will enable them to see that the safety of all classes consists in basing our legislation upon the principle of equal rights to all inhabitants. This pathetic appeal is to be found three times more in the Pentateuch to enforce this precept (Exod. xxii. 20, xxiii. 9; Deut. x. 19).

(35) **Ye shall do no unrighteousness in judgment.**—It will be seen that the Lawgiver uses here exactly the same phrase with regard to meting out right measure which he used in connection with the administration of justice in verse 15. He, therefore, who declares that a false measure is a legal measure is, according to this law, as much a corrupt judge, and defrauds the people by false judgment, as he who in the court of justice wilfully passes a wrong sentence. Owing to the fact that men who would otherwise disdain the idea of imposition often discard their scruples in the matter of weights and measures, the Bible frequently brands these dealings as wicked, and an abomination to the Lord, whilst it designates the right measure as coming from God himself (Deut. xxv. 13, 15; Ezek. xlv. 10, 12; Hosea xii. 8; Amos viii. 5; Micah vi. 10, 11; Prov. xi. 1, xvi. 11, xx. 10, 23). According to the authorities during the second Temple, he who gives false weight or measure, like the corrupt judge, is guilty of the following five things. He (1) defiles the land; (2) profanes the name of God; (3) causes the Shechinah to depart; (4) makes Israel perish by the sword, and (5) to go into captivity. Hence they declared that "the sin of illegal weights and measures is greater than that of incest, and is equivalent to the sin of denying that God redeemed Israel out of Egypt." They appointed public overseers to inspect the weights and measures all over the country; they prohibited weights to be made of iron, lead, or other metal liable to become lighter by wear or rust, and ordered them to be made of polished rock, of glass, &c., and enacted the severest punishment for fraud.

(36) **Just balances, just weights.**—That is, they were to be the same for buying as for selling.

Just ephah.—The ephah is the dry measure, and contained ten omers. (See chap. xiv. 10.) It is the same measure as the *bath* is for liquids.

A just hin.—The hin, which was a measure for liquids, contained as much as seventy-two hen's eggs. These two measures are here used as representative, including all other measures.

XX.

(1) **And the Lord spake unto Moses.**—It is difficult to account for the position of this chapter. Naturally we should expect it to follow chap. xviii. If chap. xx. contains the penalties attached to the sins enumerated in chap. xviii., we should expect it immediately to follow that chapter. It may, however, be that before enacting these severe punishments, the Lawgiver wanted to appeal to the high calling of the nation, to qualify them by the sublime precepts laid down in chap. xix. for obedience to the laws in chap. xviii., and that in the chapter before us the civil punishments are set forth as an alternative for those who will not be guided by the spiritual sentiments enunciated in chap. xix.

(2) **Again, thou shalt say.**—Better, *And thou shalt say.*

in Israel, that giveth *any* of his seed
unto Molech; he shall surely be put to
death: the people of the land shall
stone him with stones. (3) And I will
set my face against that man, and will
cut him off from among his people; be-
cause he hath given of his seed unto
Molech, to defile my sanctuary, and to
profane my holy name. (4) And if the
people of the land do any ways hide
their eyes from the man, when he giveth
of his seed unto Molech, and kill him
not: (5) then I will set my face against
that man, and against his family, and
will cut him off, and all that go a whor-
ing after him, to commit whoredom
with Molech, from among their people.
(6) And the soul that turneth after
such as have familiar spirits, and after
wizards, to go a whoring after them, I

Whosoever he be.—Better, *What man soever there be,* as the Authorised Version renders this phrase in chap. xvii. 3. (See Note on chap. xvii. 8.)

That giveth any of his seed unto Molech.—It will be seen that whilst in chap. xviii. 21 the law about Molech worship follows the laws of incest, the reverse is the case here, where it precedes those laws.

The people of the land.—That is, the whole community (see chap. iv. 27), who have selected the judges, and in whose name sentence is passed by the judges, are bound to execute the sentence.

Shall stone him with stones.—Lapidation was the first and the severest mode of capital punishment among the Hebrews, the three others being burning, beheading, and strangling. The Jewish canonists have tabulated the following eighteen cases in which death by stoning was inflicted: (1) of a man who has commerce with his own mother (chap xx. 11); (2) or with his father's wife (chap. xx. 12); (3) or with his daughter-in-law (chap. xx. 12); (4) or with a betrothed maiden (Deut. xxii. 23, 24); (5) or with a male (chap. xx. 13); (6) or with a beast (chap. xx. 15); (7) of a woman who was guilty of lying with a beast (chap. xx. 16); (8) the blasphemer (chap. xxiv. 10—16); (9) the worshipper of idols (Deut. xvii. 2—5); (10) the one who gives his seed to Molech (chap. xx. 2); (11) the necromancer; (12) the wizard (chap. xx. 27); (13) the false prophet (Deut. xiii. 6); (14) the enticer to idolatry (Deut. xiii. 11); (15) the witch (chap. xx. 17); (16) the profaner of the Sabbath (Num. xv. 32—36); (17) he that curses his parent (chap. xx. 9); and (18) the rebellious son (Deut. xxi. 18—21). As the Mosaic legislation only directs that the lapidation is to take place without the precincts of the city (chap. xxiv. 14; Num. xv. 36), and that the witnesses upon whose evidence the criminal has been sentenced to death are to throw the first stone (Deut. xvii. 7), the administrators of the law during the second Temple decreed the following mode of carrying out the sentence. On his way from the court of justice to the place of execution a herald preceded the criminal, exclaiming, "So-and-so is being led out to be stoned for this and this crime, and so-and-so are the witnesses; if any one has to say anything that might save him, let him come forward and say it." Within ten yards of the place of execution he was publicly admonished to confess his sins, within four yards he was stripped naked except a slight covering about his loins. After his hands had been bound, he was led upon a scaffolding about twice the height of a man. Here wine mingled with myrrh was mercifully given him to dull the pain of execution, and from here one of the witnesses pushed him down with great violence so that he fell upon his back. If the fall did not kill him, the other witness dashed a great stone on his breast, and if this did not kill him, all the people that stood by covered him with stones. The corpse was then nailed to the cross, and afterwards burnt. Hereupon the relatives visited both the judges and the witnesses to show that they bore no hatred towards them, and that the sentence was just. Not unfrequently, however, the excited multitude resorted to lapidation when they wished to inflict summary justice. This description will explain why the Jews said to Christ that the woman had to be stoned, and why He replied to her accusers that he who is without sin should cast the first stone (John viii. 5, 7); why the Jews wanted to stone Christ when they thought He was blaspheming (John x. 31), and why they offered Him wine mingled with myrrh before his crucifixion (Matt. xxvii. 34, 38; Mark xv. 23).

(3) **And I will set my face against that man.**—That is, make him feel my anger. (See chap. xvii. 10.)

And will cut him off.—As the preceding verse describes the offender as having been stoned to death by the people, the declaration on the part of God that He will cut off the sinner has occasioned some difficulty. Hence some take it simply to express the same thing—that the judicial execution is God's mode of cutting off the sinner from his people. According to the administrators of the law during the second Temple, however, the legislator supposes a case where the man has been actually guilty of the crime, and that there has not been a sufficient amount of evidence to convict him. In that case God himself would interpose and cut the offender off. This is more in accordance with what follows.

To defile my sanctuary.—By sinning, the Israelites contracted defilement, and they defiled the sanctuary which was in their midst. (See chaps. xv. 31, xvi. 16.) These very people, moreover, when they had sacrificed their children to Molech, afterwards came to the sanctuary to worship God (Jer. vii. 9, 10; Ezek. xxiii. 37—39).

Profane my holy name.—See chap. xviii. 21.

(4) **And if the people of the land . . .**—In the former verse the Legislator treated of cases where there was insufficient evidence. Here he declares what God would do if the community itself, whose duty it is to execute the sentence, either from culpable indifference or criminal sympathy with the sin, connive at it.

(5) **Then I will set my face.**—In that case God himself will show His anger. (See verse 3, and chap. xvii. 10.) He will interpose to execute just judgment.

And against his family.—Because they would naturally be privy to it, and aid and abet the father in this crime, they, as well as all those who joined in this idolatrous worship, will be cut off by God himself.

(6) **And the soul that turneth after such as have familiar spirits.**—The same punishment will be visited upon the man who consults necromancers. For the nature of this sin, see chap. xix. 31, and for the

will even set my face against that soul,
and will cut him off from among his
people.
(7) [a] Sanctify yourselves therefore, and
be ye holy: for I *am* the LORD your God.
(8) And ye shall keep my statutes, and
do them: I *am* the LORD which sanctify
you.
(9) [b] For every one that curseth his
father or his mother shall be surely put
to death: he hath cursed his father or
his mother; his blood *shall be* upon him.
(10) And [c] the man that committeth
adultery with *another* man's wife, *even*
he that committeth adultery with his
neighbour's wife, the adulterer and the
adulteress shall surely be put to death.
(11) [d] And the man that lieth with his
father's wife hath uncovered his father's

a ch. 11. 44 & 19. 2; 1 Pet. 1. 16.

b Ex. 21. 17; Prov. 20. 20; Matt. 15. 4.

c Deut. 22. 22; John 8. 4.

d ch. 18. 8.

e ch. 18. 22.

f ch. 18. 23.

nakedness: both of them shall surely be
put to death; their blood *shall be* upon
them.
(12) And if a man lie with his daughter
in law, both of them shall surely be put
to death: they have wrought confusion;
their blood *shall be* upon them.
(13) [e] If a man also lie with mankind,
as he lieth with a woman, both of them
have committed an abomination: they
shall surely be put to death; their blood
shall be upon them.
(14) And if a man take a wife and her
mother, it *is* wickedness: they shall be
burnt with fire, both he and they; that
there be no wickedness among you.
(15) [f] And if a man lie with a beast,
he shall surely be put to death: and ye
shall slay the beast. (16) And if a woman

---

execution of this sentence see 1 Chron. x. 13, 14. The soothsayers themselves were stoned to death by the community. (See verse 27.)

(7, 8) **Sanctify yourselves therefore, and be ye holy.**—Rather, *Ye shall therefore sanctify yourselves, and ye shall be holy,* as the same phrase is rendered in the Authorised Version in chap. xi. 44. Though it is immaterial which of the two renderings is adopted, it is important that it should be the same in both passages, since the phrase is exactly the same in the original. It is only by keeping the Divine ordinances that the Israelites will attain to that state of holiness which will not only arm them to resist the abominable rites and idolatrous practices denounced in the foregoing verses, but which will enable them to reflect the holiness of their Lord.

(9) **For every one that curseth his father.**—Though the administrators of the Law during the second Temple have laid down the most minute regulation with regard to filial obedience (see chap. xix. 3), and though nothing can exceed the tenderness with which they instilled into the hearts of children the Biblical precepts on this subject (Exod. xx. 12), yet they enacted that the child only incurred the penalty of death when he used the ineffable name God when cursing his parent, who was either alive or dead, and that if he used an attribute of the Deity, such as Almighty, the Merciful, &c., he was simply to be beaten with stripes. This will account for the rendering of this passage in the ancient Chaldee Version, "who curseth his father or his mother by the inexpressible name," *i.e.,* Jehovah.

Shall be surely put to death—That is, by stoning. (See verse 2.) This precept is also to be found in Exod. xxi. 17; Prov. xx. 20, and is referred to by our Lord (Matt. xv. 14; Mark vii. 10).

His blood shall be upon him—That is, he has brought it upon himself to be killed. (See Josh. ii. 19.) This phrase, which occurs seven times either in the singular or plural, is only to be found in this chapter (See verses 9, 11, 12, 13, 16, 27). According to the authorities during the second Temple, it carried with it death by lapidation.

(10) **Shall surely be put to death.**—This is, by penalty for the sin forbidden in chap. xviii. 20. According to Jewish tradition whenever the phrase "shall surely be put to death" occurs by itself, it denotes death by strangling. This death was inflicted for six crimes—(1) upon him who had commerce with another man's wife; (2) who smote his father or mother; (3) who stole an Israelite; (4) who being an elder rebelled against the decree of the senate (Deut. xvii. 12); (5) who played the false prophet; and (6) who prophesied in the name of another god.

(11) **His father's wife.**—Here the penalty is enacted for the sin prohibited in chap. xviii. 8.

(12) **With his daughter in law.**—See Notes on chap. xviii. 15.

(13) **Mankind.**—See chap. xviii. 22.

(14) **A wife and her mother.**—See chap. xviii. 17.

They shall be burnt with fire.—This, as we have seen, is the second of the four modes of capital punishment. (See verse 2.) In the following ten cases those guilty of the sins specified suffered this punishment: (1) the unchaste high priest's daughter (chap. xxi. 9); (2) he who had commerce with his daughter; (3) or with his daughter's daughter; (4) or with his son's daughter; (5) or with his wife's daughter; (6) or with her daughter's daughter; (7) or with her son's daughter; (8) or with his mother-in-law; (9) or with the mother of his mother-in-law; and (10), or with the mother of his father-in-law. It will thus be seen that with the exception of the high priest's daughter this death was only inflicted for incest. As the Bible nowhere states the precise mode in which this kind of death is to be carried out, the authorities during the second Temple maintained that it must be executed in such a manner as to leave the body externally unchanged by the flames, because, when God himself inflicted this punishment, the dead bodies of Nadab and Abihu were in a perfect state of preservation. (See chap. x. 2.) To effect this the criminal was put into dung up to his knees, a soft cloth containing a hard one was then tied around his throat, while the two witnesses who had secured his sentence drew tighter by the two cords till the criminal opened his mouth, when molten lead was poured down his throat, thus burning him to death. Hence the ancient Chaldee Version renders it here, "they shall be burnt with fire, with melted lead in their mouth."

(15, 16) **With a beast.**—See chap. xviii. 23.

approach unto any beast, and lie down
thereto, thou shalt kill the woman, and
the beast: they shall surely be put to
death: their blood *shall be* upon them.
(17) And if a man shall take his sister,
his father's daughter, or his mother's
daughter, and see her nakedness, and
she see his nakedness; it *is* a wicked
thing; and they shall be cut off in the
sight of their people: he hath uncovered
his sister's nakedness; he shall bear his
iniquity.
(18) [a] And if a man shall lie with a
woman having her sickness, and shall
uncover her nakedness; he hath [1] dis-
covered her fountain, and she hath un-
covered the fountain of her blood: and
both of them shall be cut off from
among their people.
(19) And thou shalt not uncover the
nakedness of thy mother's sister, nor of
thy father's sister: for he uncovereth
his near kin: they shall bear their
iniquity. (20) And if a man shall lie
with his uncle's wife, he hath uncovered
his uncle's nakedness: they shall bear
their sin; they shall die childless.
(21) And if a man shall take his brother's
wife, it *is* [2] an unclean thing: he hath
uncovered his brother's nakedness; they
shall be childless.
(22) Ye shall therefore keep all my
[b] statutes, and all my judgments, and do
them: that the land, whither I bring
you to dwell therein, [c] spue you not out.
(23) And ye shall not walk in the manners
of the nation, which I cast out before
you: for they committed all these
things, and [d] therefore I abhorred them.
(24) But I have said unto you, Ye shall
inherit their land, and I will give it
unto you to possess it, a land that
floweth with milk and honey: I *am* the
Lord your God, which have separated
you from *other* people.
(25) [e] Ye shall therefore put difference
between clean beasts and unclean, and
between unclean fowls and clean: and
ye shall not make your souls abominable
by beast, or by fowl, or by any manner
of living thing that [3] creepeth on the
ground, which I have separated from
you as unclean. (26) And ye shall be
holy unto me: [f] for I the Lord *am* holy,
and have severed you from *other* people,
that ye should be mine.

a ch. 18. 19.

1 Heb., *made naked.*

2 Heb., *a separation.*

b ch. 18. 26.

c ch. 18. 25.

d Deut. 29. 5.

e ch. 11. 2; Deut. 14. 4.

3 Or, *moveth.*

f ch. 19. 2 & 20. 7; 1 Pet. 1. 16.

---

(17) **Take his sister.**—See chap. xviii. 9.

(18) **Having her sickness.**—See chaps. xv. 24, xviii. 19.

(19) **Thy mother's sister.**—See chap. xviii. 12.

(20) **His uncle's wife.**—See chap. xviii. 14.

(21) **His brother's wife.**—See chap. xviii. 16.

(22) **Ye shall therefore keep all my statutes.**—Like the prohibitions (see chap. xviii. 26—30), the penalties here enacted for transgressing them conclude with an appeal to the Israelites to keep the Divine precepts, and not to be guilty of the crimes for which the former inhabitants of the land have been cast out.

That the land . . . spue you not out.—Better, *lest the land . . . vomit you out,* as in chap. xviii. 28. For this figure of speech see verse 25 of the same chapter.

(24) **But I have said unto you.**—That is, promised to your fathers Abraham, Isaac, and Jacob, and also to you, that he would expel the Canaanites, and give the land to the Israelites as an inheritance.

(25) **Ye shall therefore put difference.**—Better, *Ye shall therefore separate.* It is the same word which is used at the end of the preceding verse, and which is rendered "separate" in the Authorised Version. It is important that the word should be translated by the same expression, since it not only shows the intimate connection between the two verses, but brings out more forcibly the reason for the exhortation in the verse before us. Because the Lord has separated or distinguished the Israelites from all nations, and is about to give them the promised land, therefore the Israelites are to separate or to distinguish between the clean and unclean animals, as ordained in chap. xi. By strictly following out the dietary laws, the Israelites will always be able to keep separate from all other nations (Dan. i. 8).

(26) **And ye shall be holy unto me.**—Rather, *And ye shall be my holy ones,* in harmony with the remark in the last clause of this verse, where God says that He had separated them for the purpose that "ye should be mine." The phrase only occurs here, and is different from the one which has been used in chaps. xi. 44, 45, xx. 17.

And have severed you from other people.—Better, *and have separated you from other people,* as the Authorised Version renders this phrase in verse 24. That is, God has separated them from the rest of the nations to be His holy people, and to be an example to them. The spiritual guides during the second Temple have explained this separation of Israel as not implying the rejection of the other nations, but simply as the first instalment. They maintained that it implies that all other nations are gradually to follow, and that the Divine choice is to go on from people to people, till "many nations shall be joined to the Lord . . . and shall be my people" (Zech. ii. 11), where the same phrase, "shall be mine," is used as in the passage before us. The Divine plan of the redemption of mankind they set forth in the text before us as follows:—"If the Scripture had said, I have separated all the nations from you, there would be no future for the Gentiles; but since it is said, I have separated you from the nations, it is as one who first of all separates the best from the less good, and then goes on continually to separate the better ones. But he who separates the bad from the good, by this very process rejects the bad, and does not return to them." The Mosaic doctrine of

(27) [a] A man also or woman that hath a familiar spirit, or that is a wizard, shall surely be put to death: they shall stone them with stones: their blood *shall be* upon them.

CHAPTER XXI.—(1) And the LORD said unto Moses, Speak unto the priests the sons of Aaron, and say unto them, There shall none be defiled for the dead among his people: (2) but for his kin, that is near unto him, *that is*, for his mother, and for his father, and for his son, and for his daughter, and for his

[a] Deut. 18. 11; 1 Sam. 28. 7.

---

the separation of Israel, therefore, so far from tending to produce and harbour in the Jews contracted views of God's mercy, and a contempt for all other nations, has taught them to look upon themselves as simply having gone first to the mountain of the Lord, and that all other nations are to follow, and to become with them children of God.

(27) **A man also or woman.**—Better, *And a man or a woman.* The departure from the literal translation of the conjunction in the Authorised Version is both unnecessary and obscures the meaning of the sentence. It ought rather to be translated "but;" that is, but because the Israelites are God's holy ones, therefore every man or woman who pretends to disclose future events by means of necromancy, thus usurping the functions of God, is to be stoned to death. The case of these necromancers is here repeated, because in chap. xix. 31 the consulting them only is forbidden, and in the sixth verse of this chapter the penalty for consulting them is set forth, whilst in the passage before us the penalty is enacted which the persons themselves who are convicted of practising these secret arts are to suffer. The woman is here expressly added, both because this art seems to have been principally followed by women (Exod. xxii. 28; 1 Sam. xxviii. 7; Acts xvi. 16), and because men would naturally be inclined to treat women more mercifully.

Their blood shall be upon them.—That is, they have brought it upon themselves to be killed. (See verse 9.)

XXI.

(1) **And the Lord said unto Moses.**—The laws about the purity and holiness of the Jewish community, and of every individual lay member, enacted in chaps. xi. 1—xx. 27, are now followed by statutes respecting the purity and holiness of the priesthood who minister in holy things in behalf of the people, and who, by virtue of their high office, were to be models of both ceremonial and moral purity.

Speak unto the priests the sons of Aaron.—Moses is ordered to communicate these statutes to the priests as the sons of Aaron. The peculiar phrase "the priests the sons of Aaron," which only occurs here—since in all other six passages in the Pentateuch it is the reverse, "the sons of Aaron the priests" (see chaps. i. 5, 8, 11, ii. 2, iii. 2; Num. x. 8; Note on chap. i. 5), is designed to inculcate upon them the fact that they are priests by virtue of being the sons of Aaron, and not because of any merit of their own, and that they are to impress the same sentiments upon their issue. This fact, moreover, as the authorities during the second Temple remark, imposes upon the priests the duty of bringing up their children in such a manner as to make them morally and intellectually fit to occupy this hereditary office. They also deduce from the emphatic position of the term "priests," that it only applies to those of them who are fit to perform their sacerdotal duties, and not to the disqualified priests (see verse 15).

There shall none be defiled for the dead.—Better, *He shall not defile himself for a dead person;* that is, the priest is not to contract defilement by contact with the body of any dead person. What constitutes defilement is not specified, but, as is often the case, was left to the administrators of the Law to define more minutely. Accordingly, they enacted that not only touching a dead body, but coming within four cubits of it, entering the house where the corpse lay, entering a burial place, following to the grave, or the manifestation of mourning for the departed, pollutes the priest, and consequently renders him unfit for performing the services of the sanctuary, and for engaging in the services for the people. This they deduced from Num. xix. 11—16. The Egyptian priests were likewise bound to keep aloof from "burials and graves, from impure men and women." The Romans ordered a bough of a cypress-tree to be stuck at the door of the house in which a dead body was lying, lest a chief priest should unwittingly enter and defile himself.

Among his people—That is, among the tribes or people of Israel, the Jewish community (see Deut. xxxii. 8, xxxiii. 3, &c.). Hence the authorities during the second Temple concluded that when the corpse is among the people whose duty it is to see to its burial, the priest is forbidden to take part in it; but when a priest or even the high priest, finds a human body in the road where he cannot call on any one to bury it, he is obliged to perform this last sacred office to the dead himself. When it is borne in mind how much the ancient Hebrews thought of burial, and that nothing exceeded their horror than to think of an unburied corpse of any one belonging to them, this humane legislation will be duly appreciated.

(2) **But for his kin, that is near unto him.**—There are, however, seven exceptions to the general rule. According to the administrators of the Law during the second Temple, the phrase, "his kin that is near unto him," or rather, "his flesh that is near unto him" (comp. chap. xviii. 6 with Gen. ii. 24), denotes "wife." Hence the Chaldee version of Jonathan renders it, "but for a wife who is of kin to his flesh."

For his mother, and for his father.—This is the second of the three instances in the Bible where the mother is mentioned before the father (see chap. xix. 3). The Jewish canonists, who call attention to this unusual phrase, account for it by saying that she is placed first because the son's qualifications for the priesthood depend more upon his having a good mother (see verse 7). This will be readily understood when it is borne in mind that the regulations about the woman whom a priest was allowed to marry during the second Temple were of the most stringent nature, and that the slightest infringement of them disqualified the son for performing sacerdotal functions. Thus the daughter of a foreigner or of a released captive was forbidden to the priest, and when a city was besieged and taken by the enemy all the wives of the priests had to be divorced for fear lest they had suffered violence.

brother, (3) and for his sister a virgin,
that is nigh unto him, which hath had
no husband; for her may he be defiled.
(4) *But* he shall not defile himself, [1]*being*
a chief man among his people, to pro-
fane himself. (5) [a]They shall not make
baldness upon their head, neither shall
they shave off the corner of their beard,
nor make any cuttings in their flesh.
(6) They shall be holy unto their God,
and not profane the name of their God:
for the offerings of the LORD made by
fire, *and* the bread of their God, they
do offer: therefore they shall be
holy.
(7) They shall not take a wife *that is* a
whore, or profane; neither shall they
take a woman put away from her
husband: for he *is* holy unto his God.
(8) Thou shalt sanctify him therefore;
for he offereth the bread of thy God:
he shall be holy unto thee: for I the
LORD, which sanctify you, *am* holy.
(9) And the daughter of any priest, if

1 Or, being *an husband among his people, he shall not defile himself* for his wife, &c.

a ch 19. 27.

---

(3) **And for his sister a virgin, that is nigh unto him**—That is, his maiden sister who still remains in sole relationship with him. What this is the next clause explains more minutely.

Which hath had no husband.—When she is married she goes to her husband, and ceases to be near her brother. It then devolves upon her husband to attend to the funeral rites.

For her may he be defiled.—According to the administrators of the Law during the second Temple, the priest was not only allowed to contract defilement by attending to the funeral rites of these seven relations, but was obliged to do it.

(4) **But he shall not defile himself, being a chief man . . .** —Better, *A husband shall not defile himself among his people when he had profaned himself.* As the seven exceptions to the general rule began with his wife, whose funeral rites the priestly husband is allowed to attend, the verse before us restricts this permission to his legally prescribed wife. If he contracted a marriage which profaned him, he could not attend to her funeral ceremonies. The last clause, which is here translated, "when he had profaned him," literally denotes "to profane himself," "with respect to his profanation"—*i.e.,* with respect to a marriage by which he profaned himself. This is the interpretation which the administrators of the Law attached to the verse, and which is transmitted in the Chaldee version of Jonathan. It is not only in perfect harmony with the context, but does least violence to this manifestly disordered text. The translations exhibited in the Authorised version, both in the text and in the margin, as well as most of those suggested by modern commentators, leave the clause unexplained, since it manifestly means something else than defiling himself by contracting impurity through contact with the dead, as is evident from the fact that it is not added in the other instances where the priest is forbidden to defile himself by attending to the dead. (See verses 1—11.)

(5) **Make baldness upon their head.**—The natural expression of grief, however, which the priests were to manifest for the above-named departed relations, was not to show itself in the practices which disfigure their bodily appearance, and which obtained among other nations of antiquity in connection with funeral ceremonies. Thus, in the graphic description of the idolatrous priests mourning, we are told "the priests sit in their temples, having their clothes rent, and their heads and beards shaven, and nothing upon their heads." (*Baruch* vi. 31.) The three things here prohibited to the priests are also forbidden to the people at large under other circumstances. (See chap. xix. 27, 28; Deut. xiv. 1.) The ordinary Israelites, however, indulged in the same practices. (See Jer. xvi. 6; Ezek. vii. 18; Amos viii. 10.)

(6) **They shall be holy unto their God.**—This is the reason why the priests are not to disfigure themselves by maiming their outward appearance. Being sacred to the Lord, they are not to indulge in those outward manifestations of grief which would interfere with the discharge of their sacred duties, and thus cause the name of God to be profaned.

The offerings of the Lord made by fire, and the bread of their God.—Better, *the offerings of the Lord made by fire, being the food of God.* As the altar was the table, the sacrifice burnt on it was called His food. (See chap. iii. 11.)

(7) **Not take a wife.**—From the defilement arising through contact with the dead, the lawgiver passes to regulation about the priest's alliances with the living, which might be fraught with still more serious consequences to his sacred office. In selecting a wife he is to be careful both about her chastity and legitimate descent.

(8) **Thou shalt sanctify him therefore.**—This is addressed to the Jewish community. They are to take care that the priest does not contract such illegal marriages, and to sanctify him only who acts in obedience to these statutes. The Jewish priest is thus placed under the supervision of the people. His sacred office, and his duly performing the priestly functions, are their concern. If he refused to conform to the law of sanctity, the people, according to the administrators of the Law during the second Temple, were to compel him to do so by the penalty of administering to him the prescribed number of stripes.

He shall be holy unto thee.—On the other hand, when he acts in accordance with his sacred office, the people must reverence his holy person. Hence the administrators of the Law during the second Temple enacted that the priest is to take precedence on public occasions. Thus, when the people assemble, he opens the meeting by invoking God's blessing. At the reading of the Law of God in the synagogue, he is called up first to the rostrum to read the first portion, and at table he recites the benedictions over the repast. This honour the Jews assign to the priests to this day.

(9) **And the daughter of any priest.**—This statute, according to the administrators of the Law during the second Temple, applies only to betrothed and married daughters. Hence the ancient Chaldee version renders it, "and if the betrothed daughter."

She shall be burnt with fire.—Whilst the married daughter of a layman who had gone astray was punished with death by strangling (see chap. xx. 10; Deut. xxii. 23, 24), the daughter of a priest who had disgraced herself was to be punished with the severer

she profane herself by playing the whore, she profaneth her father: she shall be burnt with fire.

(10) And *he that is* the high priest among his brethren, upon whose head the anointing oil was poured, and that is consecrated to put on the garments, shall not uncover his head, nor rend his clothes; (11) neither shall he go in to any dead body, nor defile himself for his father, or for his mother; (12) neither shall he go out of the sanctuary, nor profane the sanctuary of his God; for the crown of the anointing oil of his God *is* upon him: I *am* the LORD. (13) And he shall take a wife in her virginity. (14) A widow, or a divorced woman, or profane, *or* an harlot, these shall he not take: but he shall take a virgin of his own people to wife. (15) Neither shall he profane his seed among his people: for I the LORD do sanctify him.

(16) And the LORD spake unto Moses,

---

death by burning. Though the doom of the guilty partner in the crime is not mentioned here, his sentence was death by strangulation.

(10) **And he that is the high priest among his brethren.**—That is, among his priestly brethren, the one who is distinguished among them by this office.

Upon whose head the anointing oil was poured.—This profuse pouring of oil was the distinctive feature in the consecration of the high priest. (See chap. viii. 12.)

Consecrated to put on the garments.—Better, *consecrated by putting on the garments.* The robing of the high priest by Moses, as well as the anointing him, constituted part of the consecration ceremony. (See chap. viii. 7—11.)

Shall not uncover his head.—Better, *shall not let his head be dishevelled,* which was a sign of mourning. (See chap. x. 6.)

Nor rend his clothes.—That is, "in the time of distress," as the ancient Chaldee version of Jonathan rightly adds after it. Sustaining this high position, and being the intercessor between God and man, such outward expressions of sorrow might lead those in whose behalf he ministers in the sanctuary to believe that he thereby impugns the justice of the Divine judgment.

(11) **Neither shall he go in to any dead body.**—Not only is he to abstain from the manifestation of sorrow for the troubles which befell the community, or those whom he loves, but in the case of death he is not to enter into a tent, house, or place where a human corpse was lying (Num. xix. 14), lest he should contract defilement. According to the administrators of the Law during the second Temple, the expression *any dead body* extends to any portion of it, so that when the pontiff entered a place where a certain quantity of the blood of the dead body was to be found, he became defiled. Accordingly, "any dead soul," which is literally the meaning of the phrase here translated by "dead body," denotes the blood which constitutes the soul or life. (See chap. xvii. 10—14.)

Nor defile himself for his father . . .—Better, *not for his father . . . shall he defile himself,* or, *not even for his father,* &c. As the rigorous enactment in the preceding clause constitutes already the difference between the high priest and the ordinary priest, this clause simply adduces an instance to illustrate it. Whilst the ordinary priest was not only permitted, but even obliged, to attend the funeral ceremonies of no less than seven of his relations (see verses 2, 3), the high priest was not even allowed to join in the obsequies of his parents. The only exception made in his case was when he found a human body in an isolated place. Under such circumstances he was not only permitted, but it was a meritorious act on his part, to bury it. (See verse 1.)

(12) **Neither shall he go out of the sanctuary.**—Better, *and he shall not go out of the sanctuary,* as in chap. x. 7. When the tidings of the death of a parent is brought to him during the service, he must not desist from the service and quit the sanctuary, lest it should appear that he has a greater regard for the dead than for the service of the living God. The difference between the ordinary priest and the high priest in this respect was, that when the former heard, during the service, of the death of any one of the seven relations for whom he had to mourn, he was obliged to discontinue the service, though he too could not leave the precincts of the sanctuary; whilst the former, under these circumstances, was bound to continue the service. The former, by becoming a mourner, profaned the service if he continued it; the latter never became a mourner, and hence profaned the service if he discontinued it.

(13) **A wife in her virginity.**—From this verse the administrators of the Law during the second Temple concluded that (1) the high priest must be the husband of one wife, though the ordinary priests might have several; (2) that she must be a virgin, under the age of thirteen; (3) that she must not even have been betrothed to another person; and that (4) she must be the daughter of Jewish parents by race, as it is stated in the next verse, though the ordinary priest was allowed to marry the daughter of proselytes. The first of these enactments is also enjoined by St. Paul on Christian bishops (1 Tim. iii. 2; Titus i. 16); whilst the fourth is actually expressed in the Greek version (LXX.), which has at the end of the verse, "of his own race."

(14) **A widow.**—By this the high priest was not only forbidden to marry the widow of an ordinary Israelite, or even the widow of a priest, but, according to the Jewish canons, a virgin who had been betrothed to another man, and whom she lost by death before they were married. If he, however, became engaged to a widow before he was elected to the pontificate, he could marry her after his consecration. He was, however, exempt from the obligation to marry the widow of his brother who died without issue. (See chap. xviii. 16.)

Or a divorced woman.—The classes of women which follow are also forbidden to the ordinary priests. (See verse 7.)

(15) **Neither shall he profane his seed.**—Better, *And he shall not profane;* that is, he is not to contract any of these forbidden marriages, lest he should thereby degrade his offspring, since the children of such an issue, as well as their mother, were debarred the privileges of the priesthood, and were not permitted to partake of those portions of the sacrifices which formed the perquisites of the officiating priests.

(16) **And the Lord spake unto Moses.**—In the preceding part of this chapter the priests were

saying, (17) Speak unto Aaron, saying,
Whosoever *he be* of thy seed in their
generations that hath *any* blemish, let
him not approach to offer the [1]bread of
his God. (18) For whatsoever man *he be*
that hath a blemish, he shall not
approach: a blind man, or a lame, or
he that hath a flat nose, or any thing
[a]superfluous, (19) or a man that is broken-
footed, or brokenhanded, (20) or crook-
backt, or [2]a dwarf, or that hath a
blemish in his eye, or be scurvy, or
scabbed, or hath his stones broken;
(21) no man that hath a blemish of the
seed of Aaron the priest shall come
nigh to offer the offerings of the LORD
made by fire: he hath a blemish; he
shall not come nigh to offer the bread
of his God. (22) He shall eat the bread
of his God, *both* of the most holy, and

1 Or, *food.*

a ch. 22. 23.

2 Or, *too slender.*

---

forbidden voluntarily to disfigure themselves, or to disqualify themselves and their descendants for their sacred office by illegal alliances. The legislator, therefore, now passes on to other blemishes, which, though not voluntarily contracted, likewise disqualify the priests for performing sacerdotal duties in the sanctuary.

(17) **Whosoever he be of thy seed.**—Better, *any man of thy seed throughout their generations;* that is, any of the descendants, to all future times, who have not been disqualified for service in the sanctuary by their parents contracting illegal alliances, are yet to be subject to the following regulations.

To offer the bread of his God.—That is, shall not officiate at the sacrifices. (See verse 6—chap. iii. 2.)

(18) **For whatsoever man . . .**—This part of the verse is simply an emphatic repetition of the same declaration at the end of the last verse to introduce the examples of the bodily blemishes which disqualified the priests for the service at the altar. A similar law obtained among the Greeks and Romans, that a priest should be perfect in all his parts; and according to the Hindoo law, Brahmins born with a bodily defect, or who received one before their sixteenth year, are excluded from the rites of consecration.

A blind man.—During the second Temple, this was not only interpreted to be partial blindness on both eyes, or on one eye, but was taken to include any blemish in the eye or in the eyelid, of which the administrators of the Law enumerate twenty-six cases, nineteen in the eye and seven in the eyelid.

Or a lame.—This was understood during the second Temple to refer to any imperfection in the gait of the priest, which might show itself in twenty different ways.

Or he that hath a flat nose.—Of the nasal deformity no less than nine different illustrations are given.

Or any thing superfluous.—That is, one member of the body more stretched out or longer than the others, or out of proportion, as an eye, shoulder, thigh, leg, &c.

(19) **Brokenfooted, or brokenhanded.**—That is, one with a badly cured fractured foot or hand, since in ancient days such accidents were scarcely ever properly cured. Owing to the imperfect knowledge of surgery, and to a want of skill in setting fractures, the evil effects of such accidents had to be endured by a considerable number of the members of the community.

(20) **Or crookbackt.**—Rather, *or whose eyebrows cover his eyes.* This is the sense given to this clause during the second Temple. Hence the ancient Chaldee version of Jonathan translates it, "whose eyebrows lying cover his eyes." That is, the hair, of the eyebrows are so thick, heavy, and long, that they join together and cover his eyes, thus interfering with his eyesight, and rendering him unsightly in appearance.

Or a dwarf, or that hath a blemish in his eye.—Better, *or hath a cataract or a fusion of the white and black in his eye,* as the administrators of the Law during the second Temple interpret the two defects here spoken of.

Or be scurvy, or scabbed.—According to the authorities in the time of Christ, both these are kinds of ulcers or scurvy; the former is a scab which is dry both within and without, whilst the second is a scab which is moist within and dry without, and which clings to a man till he dies.

Or hath his stones broken.—That is, one whose testicles are injured. This included several kinds of defectiveness, which are exhibited in the different renderings of the ancient versions, but all refer to the same seat of the blemish.

(21) **No man that hath a blemish.**—The addition of this general remark to the twelve instances adduced in the preceding verses, shows that the cases in question were simply typical, and that it was left to the administrators of the Law, not only to decide the minute details and various stages of these cases, but also to determine whether other bodily infirmities are included or not in this summary statement. Hence, during the second Temple, the authorities registered no less than one hundred and forty-two defects which disqualify the priest for serving at the altar. There was a chamber in the court of the Temple in which the Sanhedrim examined all the priests prior to their being received into the staff of those who officiated in the sanctuary. At the conclusion of this periodical examination, all the priests were divided into two classes. Those who were pronounced physically disqualified "put on black garments, wrapped themselves up in black cloaks, and went away in silence"; whilst those who were declared qualified put on white garments and white cloaks, and forthwith joined their brethren to assist in the sacred office. They celebrated the day by giving a feast to all their friends, which they opened with the following benediction: "Blessed be the Lord! Blessed be He because no blemish hath been found in the seed of Aaron, the priest; and blessed be He because He hath chosen Aaron and his sons to stand and to serve before the Lord in His most holy sanctuary." Those priests who were declared physically unfit, were employed in the chamber for wood at the north-east of the court of the women, to select the proper wood for the altar, since any piece which was worm-eaten could not be burnt on it. (See chap. i. 7.)

(22) **He shall eat the bread of his God.**—But though unfit for serving at the altar, and reduced to do the menial work connected with the sanctuary, he was not only allowed to partake of the less holy sacri-

of the holy. (23) Only he shall not go
in unto the vail, nor come nigh unto
the altar, because he hath a blemish;
that he profane not my sanctuaries:
for I the LORD do sanctify them.
(24) And Moses told *it* unto Aaron, and
to his sons, and unto all the children of
Israel.

CHAPTER XXII.—(1) And the LORD
spake unto Moses, saying, (2) Speak unto
Aaron, and to his sons, that they
separate themselves from the holy
things of the children of Israel, and
that they profane not my holy name *in*
those things which they hallow unto me:
I *am* the LORD. (3) Say unto them,
Whosoever *he be* of all your seed among
your generations, that goeth unto the
holy things, which the children of Israel
hallow unto the LORD, having his un-
cleanness upon him, that soul shall be
cut off from my presence: I *am* the
LORD. (4) What man soever of the seed
of Aaron *is* a leper, or hath a [1] running
issue; he shall not eat of the holy
things, until he be clean. And [a] whoso
toucheth any thing *that is* unclean *by*
the dead, or a man whose seed goeth
from him; (5) or whosoever toucheth
any creeping thing, whereby he may be
made unclean, or a man of whom he
may take uncleanness, whatsoever un-
cleanness he hath; (6) the soul which
hath touched any such shall be unclean
until even, and shall not eat of the holy
things, unless he wash his flesh with
water. (7) And when the sun is down,
he shall be clean, and shall afterward
eat of the holy things; because it *is*

1 Heb., *running of the reins.*

a ch. 15 2.

ficial gifts, such as the peace shoulder, the tithes, and the first-fruits, but also to eat what remained of the meat-offerings, the sin-offerings, and the trespass-offerings, which were most holy. (See chap. ii. 3.)

(23) **Only he shall not go in unto the vail.**—That is, into the holy place which was before the vail.

(24) **And unto all the children of Israel.**—These regulations about the conduct and qualifications of the priesthood, which God imparted to Moses, the latter not only communicated to the high priest and his sons the priests, but to the representatives of the people, who, as the community, had the supervision of the priests. The sacerdotal laws were administered and enforced by the elders or Sanhedrim, who were the representatives of the people. (See verse 21.)

XXII.

(1) **And the Lord spake unto Moses.**—In this chapter the laws regulating the conduct of the priests in their holy ministrations are continued. As the last chapter concluded with the permission to disqualified priests to eat of the sacrifices, this chapter opens with conditions under which even the legally qualified priests must not partake of the offerings.

(2) **Separate themselves from the holy things of the children of Israel.**—As parts of the sacrifices offered by the Israelites belonged to the priests, they are here warned that (see chap. vii. 20, 21) they are not to consider themselves absolutely entitled to them under all circumstances, and that there are times when they must abstain from them.

In those things which they hallow unto me.—That is, in their treatment of the sacrifices which the children of Israel have consecrated and offered to the Lord.

(3) **Whosoever he be of all your seed, among your generations.**—Better, *throughout your generations, every man.* So the Authorised version properly renders the expression here translated "among your generations" in chap. xxiii. 14, 21. (See chaps. iii. 17, xxi. 17.)

That goeth unto the holy things.—That is, who approaches the sacrifices to eat them, as is stated in verses 4, 6, 12.

Having his uncleanness upon him.—Not having first submitted to the prescribed lustrations (see chap. vii. 20), the defilement which he contracted rests upon him.

That soul shall be cut off from my presence.—This phrase, with the expression "from my presence," does not occur again in the Pentateuch when the Lord threatens with the penalty of excision. In Leviticus, where, besides the passage before us, the penalty is enacted six times, the formula is always, "that soul shall be cut off from his people" (chaps. vii. 20, 21, 25, 27, xix. 8, xxiii. 29). Its exceptional form here may therefore have reference to the peculiar circumstances. If the priest ventures to approach the altar presumptuously to partake in a defiled state of the holy sacrifices, God himself will banish him from His presence as He did Nadab and Abihu.

(4) **Is a leper.**—The different forms of uncleanness are now specified. (For the leper, see chap. xiii. 3.)

Or hath a running issue.—See chap. xv. 2.

Whoso toucheth any thing that is unclean by the dead.—That is, if he touches any person or anything that had been defiled through contact with a corpse. (See Num. xix. 11—14.)

Whose seed goeth from him.—This is the same case mentioned in chap. xv. 16. The two passages ought therefore to be uniform in the translation.

(5) **Or whosoever toucheth any creeping thing.**—See chap. xi. 24—44.

Or a man of whom he may take uncleanness.—Better, *or a man who is unclean to him,* that is, who is a leper (see chap. xiii. 45), or has an issue (see chap. xv. 5, &c.), and who imparts defilement by contact.

(6) **The soul which hath touched.**—Better, *the man who hath,* that is, the priest for whom these laws are here enacted. Hence the ancient Chaldee version renders it "the man a priest."

Shall be unclean until even.—When the day ends and another begins (see chap. xi. 24—32), and when he had to immerse his body in water.

(7) **And shall afterward eat . . . because it is his food.**—As the sacrifices which were the perquisites of the officiating priests were the only things

his food. (8) [a] That which dieth of itself,
or is torn *with beasts*, he shall not eat
to defile himself therewith: I *am* the
LORD. (9) They shall therefore keep
mine ordinance, lest they bear sin for
it, and die therefore, if they profane it:
I the LORD do sanctify them.
(10) There shall no stranger eat *of* the
holy thing: a sojourner of the priest,
or an hired servant, shall not eat *of* the
holy thing. (11) But if the priest buy
any soul [1] with his money, he shall eat
of it, and he that is born in his house:
they shall eat of his meat. (12) If the
priest's daughter also be *married* unto
[2] a stranger, she may not eat of an
offering of the holy things. (13) But if
the priest's daughter be a widow, or
divorced, and have no child, and is re-
turned unto her father's house, [b] as in
her youth, she shall eat of her father's
meat: but there shall no stranger eat
thereof. (14) And if a man eat *of* the
holy thing unwittingly, then he shall
put the fifth *part* thereof unto it, and
shall give *it* unto the priest with the

a Ex. 22. 31; Ezek. 44. 31.

1 Heb., *with the purchase of his money.*

2 Heb., *a man a stranger.*

b ch. 10. 14.

---

he had to live upon, the priest who had contracted defilement had virtually to go without food till sundown, when he purified himself by the prescribed lustrations.

(8) **That which dieth of itself.**—That is, clean animals or birds which have not been properly slaughtered, but have met with an accident. These have already been forbidden to every ordinary Israelite. (See chap. xvii. 15.) In the case of a priest eating the proscribed meat the consequences would be more serious, inasmuch as he would be debarred from his sacerdotal duties.

(9) **Keep my ordinance.**—That is, one laid down in the preceding verse with reference to animals which died a natural death, &c.

And die therefore, if they profane it.—The death here threatened for the transgression of the ordinance is one not to be inflicted by an earthly tribunal, but, as it was explained during the second Temple, "by the hand of heaven." Hence the Chaldee version of Jonathan renders it, "lest they be killed for it by a flaming fire" like Nadab and Abihu.

(10) **There shall no stranger eat of the holy thing.**—By "stranger" here is meant a non-Aaronite who was a stranger to the priestly family, though he was an Israelite, or even a Levite. The holy things are the peace offerings. (See chap. vii. 30.)

A sojourner of the priest.—This, during the second Temple, was a Hebrew servant whose ear had been pierced, and who thus became his master's property till the year of jubile. (See Exod. xxi. 6.)

Or an hired servant.—That is, a Hebrew servant who is hired for several years, and who goes out free after six years. (See Exod. xxi. 2.) Neither of them was the property of the priest, though his labour and services belonged to him. As these Hebrew servants could not be bought with money like a heathen slave, they were treated like strangers, or non-Aaronites, and hence were not permitted to partake of the holy food.

(11) **But if the priest buy any soul.**—The case, however, was different with heathen slaves whom the priest purchased. These were admitted into the Jewish community by the rite of circumcision, they were allowed to partake of the paschal lamb, and of every privilege of the Israelites. Hence they became incorporated in the priestly family, and were allowed to eat of the holy things. During the second Temple this privilege was extended to that kind of domestic whom the priest did not actually acquire by his own purchase-money, but whom the wife brought with her as part of her dowry, as well as to those whom the slaves of the priestly family purchased.

Born in his house.—That is, the house-born servant or the child of the slave. (See Gen. xvii. 12, 13.) Even when the priest himself could not eat of the holy things by reason of his having contracted some legal defilement, his wife, children, and slaves were permitted to partake of the sacrificial repast.

(12) **If the priest's daughter also be married.**—Better, *And if the priest's daughter be married.* By marrying a Hebrew of non-Aaronic descent, and thus leaving her paternal home, the daughter of the priest ceased to be part of the family circle, and lost her right to partake of the holy things. Her bread came from her husband, and she could therefore no longer partake of the priest's bread. During the second Temple the term "stranger" in this verse was also interpreted to include a man who ought to be a stranger to her, and hence it was enacted that if the priest's daughter had gone astray with a stranger (see chap. xxi. 7, 9), she is for ever forbidden to eat of the holy food.

(13) **Be a widow, or divorced, and have no child.**—An exception, however, to this rule is, when the priest's married daughter loses her husband either by death or by divorce, and has no children; under such circumstances she may resume her family ties under her paternal roof. Having lost her bread supplier, she may eat again her father's bread. She could, however, only eat of the heave-offerings, but not of the wave-breast and heave-shoulder.

Returned unto her father's house, as in her youth.—As an inference from these words, two canons were enacted during the second Temple. (1) If thus left a widow without children, her departed husband has a surviving brother, who, according to the law, must marry his sister-in-law (see chap. xviii. 16), and she is reserved for him, she cannot partake of the holy things, though she has temporarily "returned unto her father's house." Hence the Chaldee version renders this clause, "returned to her father's house, and is not reserved for her husband's brother." And (2) if she is with child at the death of her husband, and on her return home, she must not eat of the holy things. If the child dies she then is permitted to be incorporated again in her father's family.

(14) **Eat of the holy thing unwittingly.**—Or, *through ignorance*, as it is rendered in the Authorised version in all the other five passages where this expression occurs in this book. (See chap. iv. 2, 22, 27; v. 15, 18.) That is, when he ate of the things he was ignorant that they were holy.

He shall put the fifth part thereof unto it.—To make the people more careful, the offender,

holy thing. (15) And they shall not pro-
fane the holy things of the children of
Israel, which they offer unto the LORD;
(16) or [1] suffer them to bear the iniquity
of trespass, when they eat their holy
things: for I the LORD do sanctify them.
(17) And the LORD spake unto Moses,
saying, (18) Speak unto Aaron, and to
his sons, and unto all the children of
Israel, and say unto them, Whatsoever
he be of the house of Israel, or of the
strangers in Israel, that will offer
his oblation for all his vows, and for all
his freewill offerings, which they will
offer unto the LORD for a burnt offer-
ing; (19) *ye shall offer* at your own will
a male without blemish, of the beeves,
of the sheep, or of the goats. (20) *But*
whatsoever hath a blemish, *that* shall ye
not offer: for it shall not be acceptable
for you. (21) [a] And whosoever offereth a
sacrifice of peace offerings unto the
LORD to accomplish *his* vow, or a free-
will offering in beeves or [2] sheep, it shall
be perfect to be accepted; there shall
be no blemish therein. (22) Blind, or
broken, or maimed, or having a wen,
or scurvy, or scabbed, ye shall not offer
these unto the LORD, nor make an offer-
ing by fire of them upon the altar unto

1 Or, *lade themselves with the iniquity of trespass in their eating.*

a Deut. 15. 21 & 17. 1.

2 Or, *goats.*

---

though ignorant of the offence at the time when he committed it, had to pay the fifth part of the value of the holy property which he had eaten, in addition to the principal. For the way in which this was estimated see chap. v. 16.

And shall give it unto the priest with the holy thing.—Better, *And shall give back the holy thing to the priest.* "Holy thing" denotes here the equivalent of the holy thing which he has eaten. This he has to return to the priest with the fifth part. As eating holy things through ignorance was not so great an offence as withholding them altogether, or not delivering them up, restitution with a small fine was deemed a sufficient caution, whilst the case of ignorantly keeping them back was more serious, and hence the offender had also to bring a trespass-offering. (See chap. v. 14—17.)

(15) **And they shall not profane.**—That is, the priests are not to desecrate the holy gifts of the Israelites by carelessly exposing them, and by not treating them with that sacred regard which is due to their being the bread of God.

(16) **Or suffer them to bear the iniquity of trespass.**—Better, *Moreover, they shall not cause them to bear the iniquity.* That is, not only are the priests themselves prohibited to treat with profanity the sacred gifts, but they are to realise that it is incumbent upon them to guard these sacrifices so carefully as not to cause the Israelites to contract sin by transgressing the laws by eating holy things which are put in their way through culpable negligence.

(17) **And the Lord spake unto Moses.**—The laws about the physical features and ceremonial purity of the priests, who are to be devoted to the services of the altar, are now followed by kindred precepts about the animals which are to be offered upon the altar.

(18) **And unto all the children of Israel.**—As the following laws presented the condition of the animals which the Israelites are to offer, they are addressed to the laity as well as to the priests.

Whatsoever he be.—Better, *what man soever there be*, as it is translated in the Authorised version chap. xvii. 3 (and see Note on chap. xvii. 8).

Offer his oblation.—Better, *offer his offering*, as the Authorised version translates it in chaps. iii. 7, 14, vii. 12, xvii. 4, &c. It is difficult to divine why the translators gave here a different rendering of a fixed sacrificial formula which it is important to reproduce uniformly in a translation.

For all his vows, and for all his freewill offerings.—Better, *for any manner of vow, or for any manner of freewill offering.* That is, if an Israelite by race, or one who was originally a stranger but has joined the Jewish community, brings a sacrifice, be it in consequence of a vow which he has made, or be it a freewill offering. Both these kinds of sacrifices were entirely voluntary, and the difference between them is described in chap. vii. 16.

(19) **Ye shall offer at your own will a male.**—Better, *that it may be accepted for you it shall be a male;* or, *ye shall offer for your acceptance a male*, repeating the word offer; or, *for your acceptance it must be a male*, as the Authorised version renders the same phrase in verses 20, 21, 27 (see chap. i. 3).

(20) **But whatsoever hath a blemish.**—Better, *whatsoever hath*, &c., without the "but," which is not in the original, and is not wanted. The general rule is here repeated as an introduction to the cases which are immediately to be specified. It will be seen that only quadrupeds are given and that fowls are not alluded to, because when people brought birds the Law did not require any distinction to be made between male and female, and during the second Temple no blemish disqualified a bird except the entire absence of a limb.

(21) **A sacrifice of peace offerings.**—(See chap. iii. 1.)

To accomplish a vow.—In fulfilment of a vow made in time of impending danger (Gen. xxviii. 20—22; Jonah i. 16, &c.).

Freewill offering.—Generally brought in acknowledgment of mercies received.

(22) **Blind.**—Whether totally blind or only of one eye. This blemish also disqualified the priest for the service at the altar (see chap. xxi. 18).

Or broken.—Better, *broken-limbed* (see Exod. xxii. 9), extending to the head, ribs, &c.

Or maimed.—This was regarded in the time of the second Temple to describe a blemish in the eyebrow. Hence the Chaldee version translates it "one whose eye-brows are fallen off." It would thus correspond to the defect which unfitted the priest for ministering at the altar.

Or having a wen.—According to the Jewish canonists this denotes a disease of the eyes. Hence the Chaldee version translates it "one whose eyes are smitten with a mixture of white and black," thus corresponding to the blemish which unfits the priest mentioned in chap. xxi. 19.

the LORD. (23) Either a bullock or a
[1] lamb that hath any thing [a] superfluous
or lacking in his parts, that mayest
thou offer *for* a freewill offering; but for
a vow it shall not be accepted. (24) Ye
shall not offer unto the LORD that which
is bruised, or crushed, or broken, or
cut; neither shall ye make *any offering*
thereof in your land. (25) Neither from
a stranger's hand shall ye offer the
bread of your God of any of these; be-
cause their corruption *is* in them, *and*
blemishes *be* in them: they shall not be
accepted for you.
(26) And the LORD spake unto Moses,
saying, (27) When a bullock, or a sheep,
or a goat, is brought forth, then it shall
be seven days under the dam; and from
the eighth day and thenceforth it shall
be accepted for an offering made by

1 Or, *kid*.

a ch. 21. 18.

Or scurvy or scabbed.—These are exactly the same two defects specified with regard to the priests (see chap. xxi. 20).

Ye shall not offer these unto the Lord.—Though he must not offer animals with such blemishes, and though the man who vowed them for the sanctuary was beaten with stripes, yet the animals thus sanctified were no more his, he had to redeem them according to valuation, and with the money purchase another oblation.

(23) **Either a bullock or a lamb.**—Better, *And bullock and one of the flock.*

That hath any thing superfluous.—That is one member of the animal being more elongated or contracted than the other, being out of proportion. The same blemish also unfitted the priest for performing sacerdotal functions (see chap. xxi. 18).

Or lacking in his parts.—This, according to the authorities during the second Temple, denotes contracted hoofs, or undivided hoofs, making them resemble those of an ass or horse.

That mayest thou offer for a freewill offering.—Better, *that thou mayest make a freewill offering.* As verses 18—20 most emphatically declare that an animal with any blemish whatsoever must not be offered "for any manner of freewill offering," it is hardly conceivable that the lawgiver would contradict this enactment within the space of three verses, and say "that the animals with those serious organic defects enumerated in the verse before us, thou mayest offer for a freewill offering." Hence, during the second Temple, the passage before us was interpreted to mean that the animals in question were only allowed to be consecrated for the maintenance and repair of the sanctuary, but not to be offered as a sacrifice on the altar. They were sold, or the offerer paid the value himself, and the money was applied to these sacred purposes. The opinion that a freewill offering was of less importance than a vow, and that therefore the lawgiver allows animals with the two kinds of defects here described to be offered for a freewill offering but not for a vow, is contrary to the regulations laid down in verses 18—20, and is against the practice during the second Temple (see chap. vii. 16). It is far more probable that the text is disarranged, and that it originally was, "that thou mayest not offer for a freewill offering, and for a vow it shall not be accepted."

(24) **That which is bruised, or crushed, or broken, or cut.**—These four terms express the four ways which the ancients used to emasculate animals.

Neither shall ye make any offering thereof in your land.—Better, *and this shall ye not do in your land;* that is, not only are animals thus mutilated prohibited as offerings for the altar, but this practice of gelding is altogether forbidden to the Israelites with regard to any animal whatsoever throughout the country. This law is binding upon the orthodox Jews to this day, and the question has recently been discussed by some of their spiritual guides, since it seriously affects those of their community who are engaged in farming land.

(25) **Neither from a stranger's hand shall ye offer.**—That is, the prohibition to sacrifice these animals is not restricted to beasts castrated in the land, but extends to all such as have been so treated out of the land, and are imported and sold to the Israelites by the hands of foreigners.

Because their corruption is in them.—That is, their mutilation is in them, though not effected by an Israelite nor in the land. The circumstance that such an animal is purchased from the hand of a foreigner does not alter the case.

They shall not be accepted for you.—That is, if the Israelites bring such mutilated sacrifices, thinking that, because they have been procured from a stranger's hand, they do not transgress the law laid down in the preceding verse, they will not be accepted by God, who regards them as blemished and illegal. Jewish canonists, however, regard this verse as regulating the sacrifices offered by Gentiles, and maintain that the same law about defective animals is here laid down in their case. But the manifest contrast between the expression, when the deed is done "in your land," at the end of the preceding verse, and the words "from the hand of a foreigner," at the beginning of this verse; and more especially the declaration in the clause before us, "they shall not be acceptable for you," *i.e.*, the Israelites, show beyond doubt that the Israelites themselves are here spoken of as the offerers.

(26) **And the Lord spake unto Moses.**—Though beginning with a separate formula, and thus indicating that it is a distinct communication, the regulations here laid down about the age of the sacrificial animals are necessarily connected with the preceding statutes, and exhibit a logical sequence.

(27) **When a bullock, or a sheep, or a goat.**—The three sacrificial quadrupeds. (See verse 19 and chap. xvii. 3—6.)

Is brought forth.—From this expression it was enacted during the second Temple that the animal fit for a sacrifice had to be born naturally. One brought into the world by artificial aid was disqualified for the altar.

It shall be seven days under the dam.—Under seven days the animal is extremely weak, and unfit for human food, and hence must not be offered as the food of God, as sacrifices are called. (See verse 25.) For the same reason children could not be circumcised before the eighth day from their birth. (See Exod. xxii. 29.) Because the text here says that the newly born animal is to be with the dam seven days, it was enacted that if the mother died before the seven days (in which case it could not be with the dam seven days), it was for ever disqualified for a sacrifice.

fire unto the LORD. (28) And *whether it*
be cow or [1] ewe, ye shall not kill it [a] and
her young both in one day.
(29) And when ye will offer a sacrifice
of thanksgiving unto the LORD, offer *it*
at your own will. (30) On the same day
it shall be eaten up; ye shall leave [b] none
of it until the morrow: I *am* the LORD.
(31) Therefore shall ye keep my com-
mandments, and do them: I *am* the LORD.
(32) Neither shall ye profane my holy
name; but [c] I will be hallowed among
the children of Israel: I *am* the LORD
which hallow you, (33) that brought you
out of the land of Egypt, to be your
God: I *am* the LORD.

1 Or, *she goat.*
a Deut. 22. 6.
b ch. 7. 15.
c ch. 10. 3.
d Ex. 20. 9: Deut. 5. 13; Luke 13 14.
e Ex. 12. 18; Num. 28. 17.

CHAPTER XXIII.—(1) And the
LORD spake unto Moses, saying,
(2) Speak unto the children of Israel,
and say unto them, *Concerning* the feasts
of the LORD, which ye shall proclaim *to*
be holy convocations, *even* these *are* my
feasts.
(3) [d] Six days shall work be done: but
the seventh day *is* the sabbath of rest,
an holy convocation; ye shall do no
work *therein*: it *is* the sabbath of the
LORD in all your dwellings.
(4) These *are* the feasts of the LORD,
even holy convocations, which ye shall
proclaim in their seasons.
(5) [e] In the fourteenth *day* of the first

---

(28) **Not kill it and her young both in one day.**—According to the ancient canons, this prohibition to slaughter the dam and its youngling the same day was not only designed to remind the Israelites of the sacred relations which exist between parent and offspring, but was especially intended to keep up feelings of humanity. Hence the ancient Chaldee version begins this injunction with the words, "My people the children of Israel, as our Father is merciful in heaven, so be ye merciful on earth."

(29) **Offer it at your own will.**—Better, *offer it for your acceptance.* (See verse 19.) That is, offer it in such a manner that it should be accepted. (For this kind of offering, see chap. vii. 15, 16.)

(30) **On the same day it shall be eaten.**—This shows that the sacrifice here spoken of belonged to the first class of peace offerings, the flesh of which had to be eaten up on the same day. (See chap. vii. 15.)

(31) **Therefore shall ye keep my commandments.**—Better, *and ye shall keep my commandments.* The law about the priests and sacrifices now concludes with an appeal to both the priests and the people to faithfully observe these commandments.

(32) **Neither shall ye profane my holy name.**—Better, *and ye shall not profane.* The rendering of the conjunctives, both in the former verse and in this, by "therefore" and "neither," as is done in the Authorised version, is not only unnecessary, but mars the simple and dignified style of the original. For the manner in which God's name is profaned when His commandments are violated, see chap. xviii. 21.

(33) **That brought you out.**—By this signal act of redemption from bondage, and by choosing them as His peculiar people, God has a special claim upon His redeemed people that they should keep His commandments. (See chap. xi. 45.)

XXIII.

(1) **And the Lord spake unto Moses.**—The regulations about the holiness of the sanctuary and the sacrifices, the holiness of the priests and the people, are now followed by statutes about holy seasons.

(2) **Speak unto the children of Israel.**—As the festivals here discussed were to be solemnly kept by them, Moses is ordered to address these regulations to the people or their representatives.

Concerning the feasts of the Lord . . . Better, *the festivals of the Lord which ye shall proclaim as holy convocations, these are my festivals.* That is, the following festivals God claims as His, on which solemn assemblies are to be held in the sanctuary.

(3) **Six days shall work be done.**—Recurring every week, and being the most important as well as the oldest of all festivals, the sabbath introduces the holy seasons. Hence, during the second Temple it was declared that "the sabbath is in importance equal to the whole law; he who profanes the sabbath openly is like him who transgresses the whole law." The hour at which it began and ended was announced by three blasts of the trumpets.

Ye shall do no work therein.—Better, *ye shall do no manner of work,* as the Authorised version renders this phrase in verse 31 of this very chapter. (See chap. xvi. 29.) Whilst on all other festivals servile work only was forbidden (see verses 7, 8, 21, 25, 35, 36), and work connected with the preparation of the necessary food was permitted (see Exod. xii. 16), the sabbath and the day of atonement were the only days on which the Israelites were prohibited to engage in any work whatsoever. (See verses 28, 30; chap. xvi. 29.) Though manual labour on the sabbath was punished with death by lapidation (see Exod. xxxi. 14, 15, xxxv. 2; Num. xv. 35, 36), and though the authorities during the second Temple multiplied and registered most minutely the things which constitute labour, yet these administrators of the Law have enacted that in cases of illness and of any danger work is permitted. They laid down the principle that "the sabbath is delivered into your hand, but not you into the hand of the sabbath." Similar is the declaration of Christ (Matt. xii. 8, Mark ii. 27, 28).

(4) **These are the feasts of the Lord.**—Because the following are the festivals proper as distinguished from the sabbath (see verses 37, 38), and because they are now enumerated in their regular order, the introductory heading is here repeated.

Ye shall proclaim in their seasons.—By the blast of trumpets on the day of the month on which they are to be observed.

(5) **In the fourteenth day of the first month.**—This month is called *Abib* in the Pentateuch (Exod. xiii. 4, xxiii. 15; Deut. xvi. 1), and *Nisan* in the later books of Scripture (Neh. ii. 1; Esther iii. 7). The fourteenth day of this month is about the beginning of April. On this day, which was called both "the preparation for the Passover" (John xix. 14), and "the first day of Passover," all handicraftsmen, with the exception of tailors, barbers, and laundresses, were

month at even *is* the LORD's passover.
(6) And on the fifteenth day of the same
month *is* the feast of unleavened bread
unto the LORD: seven days ye must eat
unleavened bread. (7) In the first day
ye shall have an holy convocation: ye
shall do no servile work therein. (8) But
ye shall offer an offering made by fire
unto the LORD seven days: in the
seventh day *is* an holy convocation: ye
shall do no servile work *therein.*
(9) And the LORD spake unto Moses,
saying, (10) Speak unto the children of
Israel, and say unto them, When ye
be come into the land which I give unto you, and shall reap the harvest
thereof, then ye shall bring a [1][2] sheaf
of the firstfruits of your harvest unto

[1] Or, *handful.*

[2] Heb., *an omer.*

obliged to relinquish work either from morning or from noon, according to the custom of the different places in Palestine. Leaven was only eaten till midday, and it had to be burned in the afternoon. The time for desisting from and burning the leaven was thus indicated: "Two desecrated cakes of thanksgiving offerings were placed on a bench in the Temple; as long as they were thus exposed all the people ate leaven. When one of them was removed they abstained from eating, but did not burn it; but when the other was taken away all the people began burning the leaven." It was on this day that every Israelite who was not infirm, ceremonially defiled, uncircumcised, or beyond fifteen miles from the walls of Jerusalem, had to appear before the Lord in the holy city, with an offering in proportion to his means (Exod. xxiii. 5; Deut. xvi. 16, 17). Those who came from the country were gratuitously accommodated by the inhabitants with the necessary apartments (Luke xxii. 10—12; Matt. xxvi. 18), and the guests in acknowledgment of the hospitality they received left to their hosts the skins of the paschal lambs, and the vessels which they used in their religious ceremonies. Josephus, who was an eye-witness to the fact, tells us that at the Passover, in the reign of Nero, there were 2,700,000 people, when 256,500 lambs were sacrificed. Most of the Jews must therefore have encamped in tents without the walls of the city, as the Mohammedan pilgrims now do at Mecca. It was for this reason that the Romans took great precaution, using both force and conciliatory measures, during the festivals (Matt. xxvi. 5; Luke xiii. 1).

At even.—Or, *in the evening,* as the Authorised version renders this phrase in the parallel passage (Exod. xii. 6), literally, *denotes between the two evenings.* The interpretation of this expression constituted one of the differences between the Sadducees and the Pharisees during the second Temple, and seriously affected the time for offering up the paschal lamb and the evening sacrifices. According to the Sadducees it denotes the time between the setting of the sun and the moment when the stars become visible, or when darkness sets in, *i.e.*, between six and seven o'clock, a space of about one hour and twenty minutes. According to the Pharisees, however, "between the two evenings" means from the afternoon to the disappearing of the sun. The first evening is from the time when the sun begins to decline towards the west, whilst the second is when it goes down and vanishes out of sight. This is the reason why the paschal lamb in the evening sacrifice began to be killed and the blood sprinkled at 12.30 p.m. This is more in harmony with the fact that the large number of sacrifices on this day could only be offered up in the longer period of time.

The Lord's passover.—Also called "the feast of unleavened bread." (See verse 6.)

(6) **Seven days ye must eat unleavened bread.**—See Exod. xii. 15, 18—20.

(7) **In the first day.**—That is, the first of the seven days, or the fifteenth of the month Nisan. (See Exod. xii. 16.)

Ye shall do no servile work therein.—Servile work was defined during the second Temple to consist in building, pulling down edifices, weaving, reaping, threshing, winnowing, grinding, &c., whilst needful work which was allowed was killing beasts, kneading dough, baking bread, boiling, roasting, &c. For violating this law the offender was not to be stoned to death, as in the case of violating the sabbath, but to receive forty stripes save one.

(8) **But ye shall offer.**—Better, *and ye shall offer.* In addition to the daily ordinary sacrifices, there were offered on this day, and on the following six days, two young bullocks, a ram, and seven lambs of the first year, with meat offerings for a burnt offering, and a goat for a sin offering (Num. xxviii. 19—23). Besides these public sacrifices, there were the voluntary offerings which were made by every private individual who appeared before the Lord in Jerusalem (Exod. xxiii. 15; Deut. xvi. 16), and which, according to the practice during the second Temple, consisted of (1) a burnt offering of not less in value than sixteen grains of corn; (2) a festive offering called *chagigah,* the minimum value of which was thirty-two grains of corn; and (3) a peace or joyful offering (Deut. xxvii. 7), the value of which was left to be determined by the good will of the offerer in accordance with Deut. xxvii. 7. These victims were offered with the ritual prescribed in chaps. iii. 1—5, vii. 16—18, 29—34.

In the seventh day . . . . ye shall do no servile work.—This was, in all respects, celebrated like the first, with the exception that it did not commence with the paschal meal. During the intervening days the people indulged in public amusements, as dances, songs, games, &c., to fill up the time in harmony with the joyful and solemn character of the festival. They were also allowed to irrigate dry land, dig water-courses, repair conduits, reservoirs, roads, &c.

(9) **And the Lord spake unto Moses.**—As the celebration of the sheaf of first-fruits formed no part of the original institution of the Passover (Exod. xii. 1—20), and as the omer ritual could not be observed in the wilderness, where there was no sowing of corn, it is here enacted as a prospective part of the feast of unleavened bread, and hence is introduced by a separate formula.

(10) **When ye be come into the land.**—This is the third of the four instances in Leviticus where a law is given prospectively, having no immediate bearing on the condition of the people of Israel. (See chap. xix. 23.)

Then ye shall bring a sheaf of the first-fruits of your harvest.—Better, *ye shall bring the first-fruit omer of your harvest.* The omer had to be from the best and ripest standing corn of a field near

the priest: (11) and he shall wave the
sheaf before the LORD, to be accepted
for you: on the morrow after the sab-
bath the priest shall wave it. (12) And
ye shall offer that day when ye wave
the sheaf an he lamb without blemish
of the first year for a burnt offering un-
to the LORD. (13) And the meat offering
thereof *shall be* two tenth deals of fine
flour mingled with oil, an offering made
by fire unto the LORD *for* a sweet
savour: and the drink offering thereof
shall be of wine, the fourth *part* of an
hin. (14) And ye shall eat neither bread,
nor parched corn, nor green ears, until
the selfsame day that ye have brought
an offering unto your God: *it shall be*
a statute for ever throughout your gene-
rations in all your dwellings.
(15) And [a] ye shall count unto you from
the morrow after the sabbath, from the
day that ye brought the sheaf of the

a Deut. 16. 9.

Jerusalem. The measure of an omer was of the meal obtained from the barley offering. Hence three *seahs* = one *ephah*, or ten omers, were at first gathered in the following manner:—"Delegates from the Sanhedrim went into the field nearest to Jerusalem a day before the festival, and tied together the ears in bundles whilst still fastened to the ground."

(11) **And he shall wave the sheaf.**—Better, *and he shall wave the omer.* The priest mixed with the omer of meal a log of oil, put on a handful of frankincense (see chap. ii. 15), as on other meat-offerings, waved it, took a handful of it and caused it to ascend in smoke (see chap. ii. 16), and then consumed the residue in company with his fellow-priests. Immediately after this ceremony, bread, parched corn, green ears, &c., of the new crop were exposed for sale in the streets of Jerusalem, as, prior to the offering of the omer, no use whatever was allowed to be made of the new corn.

On the morrow after the sabbath.—The interpretation of this phrase also constituted one of the differences between the Pharisees and the Sadducees during the second Temple. According to the Pharisees, the term sabbath here, as elsewhere (see verses 24, 32, 39), is not the weekly sabbath, but the next day, or the first day of the holy convocation, the first day of Passover, on which the Israelites had to abstain from all unnecessary work. It is the 16th of Nisan. The Sadducees, however, maintained that it is to be understood in its literal sense as denoting the weekly sabbath in the Passover week, which might happen to fall within the seven days, and possibly the fifth or sixth day of the festival. But this is against the import of verse 15. Here the feast of Pentecost is to be reckoned from this sabbath, and if this sabbath might either be on the second or sixth day of the Passover, not only would the feast of Pentecost have no definite day, but the Passover itself would, in the course of time, be displaced from the fundamental position which it occupies in the order of the annual festivals. Hence the Pharisees, rightly regarding the word sabbath here as an alternative term for the day of holy convocation, took the morrow after the sabbath to denote Nisan 16. On the afternoon of this day, therefore, the inhabitants of the neighbouring towns of Jerusalem assembled together "so that the reaping might take place amidst great tumult." As soon as it became dark, each of the reapers asked, "Has the sun gone down?" To which the people replied, "Yes." They asked twice again, "Has the sun gone down?" to which the people each time replied, "Yes." Each reaper then asked three times, "Is this the scythe?" to which the people each time replied "Yes." "Is this the box?" they next asked three times. "Yes," was again thrice the reply of the people. "Is this the Sabbath?" the reaper asked three times; and three times the people replied, "Yes." "Shall I cut?" he asked three times; and three times the people replied, "Yes." When cut it was laid in boxes, brought into the court of the Temple, threshed with canes and sticks, that the grains might not be crushed, and laid in a roast with holes, so that the fire might touch each grain. Thereupon it was spread in the court of the sanctuary for the wind to pass over it, and ground in a barley mill which left the hulls unground. The flour thus obtained was sifted through thirteen different sieves, each one finer than its predecessor. In this manner was the prescribed omer or tenth part got from the seah.

(12) **And he shall offer.**—With the omer of the first-fruits a lamb was offered, besides the sacrifices for the feast enumerated in verse 8.

(13) **Two tenth deals of fine flour.**—Ordinarily only one-tenth deal of fine flour was required for a meat-offering (Exod. xxix. 40; Num. xv. 4, xxviii. 9, 13, &c.), to exhibit the plentiful harvest. With the exception of the handful of flour and oil, and of all the frankincense, this meat-offering was the perquisite of the priests. (See chap. ii. 2, 3.)

(14) **And ye shall eat neither bread.**—In acknowledgment of the bountiful Giver of the new harvest, it was ordained that the Israelites were not to taste any of it till they had dedicated the first-fruit to the Lord. By bread is meant the unleavened bread which they were now enjoined to eat. The unleavened bread for the first and the second days of Passover was prepared from the last year's harvest, but the bread for the following days could only be made from the new harvest after the formal dedication of it to the Lord.

Parched corn.—See chap. ii. 14.

Green ears.—The expression *carmel,* which the Authorised version renders "full ears" in chap. ii. 14, the authorities during the second Temple took to denote the five kinds of the new grain, viz., wheat, rye, oats, and two kinds of barley, which were forbidden to be used in any form whatsoever prior to this public dedication of the harvest to the Lord. The same custom of dedicating the first-fruits of the harvest to the divine beings also obtained amongst the Egyptians, Greeks, Romans, and other nations of antiquity.

A statute for ever . . .—See chaps. iii. 17, vii. 23—25.

(15) **Ye shall count . . . from the morrow after the sabbath.**—That is, from the day following the first day of holy convocation, which was a rest-day. As this was the fifteenth of Nisan, the counting began from the sixteenth (see verse 11), the day on which the omer of the first-fruits was presented to the Lord.

wave offering; seven sabbaths shall be
complete: (16) even unto the morrow
after the seventh sabbath shall ye number fifty days; and ye shall offer a new
meat offering unto the LORD. (17) Ye
shall bring out of your habitations two wave loaves of two tenth deals: they shall be of fine flour; they shall be baken with leaven; *they are* the firstfruits unto the LORD. (18) And ye shall
offer with the bread seven lambs without blemish of the first year, and one young bullock, and two rams: they shall be *for* a burnt offering unto the LORD, with their meat offering, and their drink offerings, *even* an offering made by fire, of sweet savour unto the
LORD. (19) Then ye shall sacrifice one
kid of the goats for a sin offering, and two lambs of the first year for a sacrifice of peace offerings. (20) And the
priest shall wave them with the bread of the firstfruits *for* a wave offering before the LORD, with the two lambs:

Seven sabbaths shall be complete.—Better, *seven weeks shall be complete.* That is, seven entire weeks, making forty-nine days. The expression sabbath denotes here a week, hence the parallel passage substitutes the word week, viz., "seven weeks shalt thou number unto thee" (Deut. xvi. 9). The same usage is to be found in the New Testament. Thus the passage rendered in the Authorised version, "the first day of the week," is "the first day of the sabbath" (Matt. xxviii. 1); and "I fast twice in the week" (Luke xviii. 12), is, "I fast twice in the sabbath." In accordance with the injunction here given, the Jews to the present day begin to count the forty-nine days at the conclusion of the evening service on the second day of Passover, and pronounce the following blessing every evening of the forty-nine days: "Blessed art thou, O Lord our God, King of the universe, who hast sanctified us with thy commandments, and hast enjoined us to count the omer. This is the first day of the omer. May it please thee, O Lord our God, and the God of our fathers, to rebuild the sanctuary speedily in our days, and give us our portion in thy Law."

(16) **Even unto the morrow after the seventh sabbath.**—That is, the day after the seven complete weeks, or the fiftieth day. Hence its name, "Pentecost, or fiftieth-day" feast in the New Testament (Acts ii. 1, xx. 16; 1 Cor. xvi. 8), and "feast of weeks" in the Old Testament (Exod. xxxiv. 12; Deut. xvi. 10, 16; 2 Chron. viii. 13). The fiftieth day, according to the Jewish canons, may fall on the 5th, 6th, or 7th of *Sivan*, the third month of the year, *i.e.*, from the new moon of May to the new moon of June.

Shall offer a new meat offering.—That is, of the first-fruits of the wheat-harvest in contradistinction to the omer first-fruits, which was of barley-harvest. Hence this festival is also called "the feast of harvest" (Exod. xxiii. 16), because it concluded the harvest of the later grain.

(17) **Ye shall bring out of your habitations.**—During the second Temple this clause was taken to be elliptical, and to denote ye shall *bring out of*, or *from, the land of your habitations*, that is, from Palestine (Num. xv. 2).

Two wave loaves of two tenth deals.—These two loaves were prepared in the following manner. Three seahs of new wheat were brought into the court of the Temple, were beaten and trodden and ground into flour. Two omers of the flour were respectively obtained from a seah and a half, and after having been sieved in the twelve different sieves, were kneaded separately with leaven into two loaves outside the Temple, but were baked inside the sanctuary on the day preceding the festival. Each loaf was seven hand-breadths long, four hand-breadths broad, and five fingers high. These were offered to the Lord as firstlings (Exod. xxxiv. 17), whence this festival is also called "the day of first-fruits" (Num. xxviii. 26).

(18) **And ye shall offer with the bread seven lambs.**—The additional sacrifices for the feast day consisted of two bullocks, one ram, and seven lambs, which were a burnt offering, and of a goat as a sin offering (Num. xxviii. 26, 27, 30). Besides these, however, the new meat offering of the two loaves mentioned in the text before us is to be brought, and with it are to be offered one bullock, two rams, and seven lambs, all for burnt offerings.

(19) **Then ye shall sacrifice.**—Better, *and ye shall sacrifice.* They were, moreover, to offer a goat for a sin offering, and two lambs for a peace offering. Hence Josephus, who was an eye-witness to the Temple service, in summing up the number of animal sacrifices on this festival, says that there were fourteen lambs, three young bullocks, and three goats, the number *two* instead of three goats being manifestly a transcriber's error (*Antiq.* III., x. 6). The two statements, therefore, viz., the one in the passage before us, and the other in Num. xxviii. 27, according to the authorities during the second Temple, refer to two distinct sacrifices. The one before us speaks of the sacrifices which are to accompany the wave loaves, whilst the order in Numbers refers to the properly appointed sacrifices for the festival. Those prescribed in Numbers were offered in the wilderness, whilst those prescribed here were only to be offered when the Israelites entered the Promised Land.

(20) **And the priest shall wave them . . . with the two lambs.**—During the second Temple this was done in the following manner:—The two lambs were brought into the Temple, and waved together or separately by the priest while yet alive. Whereupon they were slain, and the priest took the breast and shoulder of each one (see chap. vii. 30—32), laid them down by the side of the two loaves, put both his hands under them, and waved them all together or separately towards the east side forwards and backwards, up and down. He then burned the fat of the two lambs, after which the remainder of the flesh, which became the perquisite of the officiating priest, was eaten by him and his fellow-priests. Of the two loaves the high priest took one, and the other was divided between the officiating priests, who had to eat them up within the same day and half the following night, just as the flesh of the most holy things. After these prescribed sacrifices had been offered, each individual brought his free-will offering, which formed the cheerful and hospitable meal of the family, and to which the Levite, the widow, the orphan, the poor, and the stranger, were invited.

they shall be holy to the LORD for the
priest. (21) And ye shall proclaim on
the selfsame day, *that* it may be an holy
convocation unto you: ye shall do no
servile work *therein: it shall be* a statute
for ever in all your dwellings through-
out your generations.
(22) And [a] when ye reap the harvest of
your land, thou shalt not make clean
riddance of the corners of thy field when
thou reapest, [b] neither shalt thou gather
any gleaning of thy harvest: thou shalt
leave them unto the poor, and to the
stranger: I *am* the LORD your God.
(23) And the LORD spake unto Moses,
saying, (24) Speak unto the children of
Israel, saying, In the [c] seventh month,
in the first *day* of the month, shall ye
have a sabbath, a memorial of blowing
of trumpets, an holy convocation. (25) Ye
shall do no servile work *therein:* but ye
shall offer an offering made by fire un-
to the LORD.
(26) And the LORD spake unto Moses,

a ch. 19. 9.

b Deut. 24. 19.

c Num. 29. 1.

---

(21) **And ye shall proclaim on the selfsame day.**—This proclamation was made to the people by the priest with trumpet blasts.

Ye shall do no servile work.—For what constituted servile work, see verse 7.

A statute for ever . . . .—See verse 14, chaps. iii. 17, vii. 23—25. In accordance with this declaration, and with the fact that the Jews during the second Temple regarded it as the day on which the Decalogue was given, the Israelites to this day sacredly keep this festival on the 6th and 7th of *Sivan, i.e.*, between the second half of May and the first half of June. From their circumstances, however, the harvest character of the festival is now subordinate, and more prominence is given to its commemorating the giving of the Law on Sinai. Still the synagogues and the private houses are adorned with flowers and odoriferous herbs. The male members of the community purify themselves for its celebration by immersion and confession of sin, and many of them spend all night in their respective places of worship.

(22) **Thou shalt not make a clean riddance.**—Better, *thou shalt not wholly reap*, as the Authorised version translates the same phrase in chap. xix. 9. In the midst of rejoicing and thankfulness to God for a bountiful harvest, the Lawgiver again inculcates the duty of remembering the poor, and reminds the proprietors of the land that the needy have legally a share in the produce, as has been enacted in chap. xix. 9.

(23) **And the Lord spake unto Moses.**—The new festival about which regulations are given in verses 24—32, is introduced by a separate formula, which describes the subject matter as a separate and distinct Divine communication.

(24) **A memorial of blowing of trumpets.**—Literally, *remembrance blowing*, for which see Num. xxix. 1, the only place in the Old Testament where this festival is named as "the day of blessing," *i.e.*, the trumpets. As the first of *Ethanim*, as the month is called in the Bible (1 Kings viii. 2), or *Tishri*, as the Jews call it, in which this festival occurs, is the commencement of the civil new year, this festival was called "the Festival of New Year" ever since the time of the second Temple, and has been regarded as preparatory to the great day of Atonement, which is ten days later. The blowing of trumpets, therefore, which was the distinguishing feature of this festival, was designed to summon the Israelites to enter upon the work of sanctification, which will be accounted to them as a merit in the sight of God, and for which they are promised to be especially remembered before the Lord (Num. x. 9, 10). Hence its name, *Remembrance blowing*—the blowing of trumpets, which will make them to be remembered before the Lord. The synagogue, however, takes the name more in the sense of "reminding" God of the merits of the patriarchs and his covenant with them, and for this reason has appointed Gen. xxi. 1—34, xxii. 1—24, recording the birth and sacrifice of Isaac, as the lesson for this festival.

(25) **Ye shall do no servile work.**—With the exception of what was absolutely necessary, all handicraft and trade were stopped. (See verse 7.)

But ye shall offer.—As the festival is also the new moon, a threefold sacrifice was offered on it, viz. (1) the ordinary daily sacrifice which was offered first; (2) the appointed new moon sacrifice (Num. xxviii. 11—15); and (3) the sacrifice for this festival, which consisted of a young bullock, a ram, and seven lambs of the first year, with the usual meat offerings, and a kid for a sin offering (Num. xxix. 1—6). With the exception, therefore, of there being one bullock instead of two, this sacrifice was simply a repetition of the monthly offering by which it was preceded in the service. During the offering of the drink offering and the burnt offering the Levites engaged in vocal and instrumental music, singing the eighty-first and other psalms, whilst the priests at stated intervals broke forth with awful blasts of the trumpets. After the offering up of the sacrifices, the service was concluded by the priests, who pronounced the benediction (Num. vi. 23—27), which the people received in a prostrate position before the Lord. Having prostrated themselves a second time in the court, the congregation resorted to the adjoining synagogue, where the appointed lessons from the Law and the Prophets were read, consisting of Gen. xxi. 1—34; Num. xxix. 1—6; 1 Sam. i. 1—ii. 10; Gen. xxii. 1—24; Jer. xxxi. 2—20. Psalms were recited and the festival prayers were offered, beseeching the Lord to pardon the sins of the past year, and to grant the people a happy new year. This concluded the morning service, after which the families resorted to their respective homes, partook of the social and joyous repast, and in the evening went again into the Temple to witness the offering of the evening sacrifices, and to see the candlestick lighted with which the festival concluded, all wishing each other, "May you be written down for a happy new year; may the Creator decree for you a happy new year." To which was responded, "And you likewise." With the exception of the sacrifices, the Jews keep this festival to the present day. The trumpet which they use on this occasion consists of the curved horn of a ram, in remembrance of the ram which Abraham sacrificed instead of Isaac. This event, as we have seen, is also commemorated in the lesson of the day.

(26) **And the Lord spake unto Moses.**—The same formula which introduced the regulations about the feast of trumpets (see verse 23), now introduces the laws about the day of Atonement.

saying, (27) [a] Also on the tenth *day* of this
seventh month *there shall be* a day of
atonement: it shall be an holy convoca-
tion unto you; and ye shall afflict your
souls, and offer an offering made by fire
unto the LORD. (28) And ye shall do no
work in that same day: for it *is* a day
of atonement, to make an atonement
for you before the LORD your God.
(29) For whatsoever soul *it be* that shall
not be afflicted in that same day, he
shall be cut off from among his people.
(30) And whatsoever soul *it be* that doeth
any work in that same day, the same
soul will I destroy from among his
people. (31) Ye shall do no manner of
work: *it shall be* a statute for ever
throughout your generations in all your
dwellings. (32) It *shall be* unto you a
sabbath of rest, and ye shall afflict your
souls: in the ninth *day* of the month at
even, from even unto even, shall ye [1] cele-
brate your sabbath.

(33) And the LORD spake unto Moses,
saying, (34) Speak unto the children of
Israel, saying, [b] The fifteenth day of this
seventh month *shall be* the feast of
tabernacles *for* seven days unto the

[a] ch. 16. 30; Num. 29. 7.

[1] Heb., *rest*.

[b] Num. 29. 12; John 7. 37.

---

(27) **Also on the tenth.**—See chap. xvi. 29.

And ye shall afflict your souls.—That is, fast. (See chap. xvi. 29.)

And offer an offering.—See Num. xxix. 8—11.

(28) **And ye shall do no work.**—Better, *And ye shall do no manner of work*, as the Authorised version has it in verse 31 of this very chapter. (See chap. xvi. 29.) This is the only day which had to be kept like the sabbath, and on which no manner of work was allowed. (See verse 3.)

To make an atonement for you.—See chap. xvi. 30.

(29) **For whatsoever soul . . . he shall be cut off from among his people.**—Better, *For whatsoever soul . . . that shall be cut off from his people.* (See Note on chap. xix. 8.) Any member of the community who does not fast on this day God himself will punish with excision, except those who through old age or sickness are unable to endure it.

(30) **That doeth any work.**—That is, engages in any kind of work whatsoever, since this is the only festival which is to be kept like the sabbath.

Will I destroy. — Whilst in all other instances where God threatens the offender with the penalty of excision the expression "cut off" is used, in the passage before us the word is "destroy." This stronger term may be owing to the fact that the day of Atonement is the most solemn day in the whole year, and that violating its sanctity will be visited more severely. Hence the severer expression used on this occasion. It is, however, to be remarked that whilst working on the sabbath was punished with death by stoning, he who transgressed the law of labour on the day of Atonement was punished with excision.

(31) **Ye shall do no manner of work.**—Owing to the great sanctity of the day, the command to abstain from all work is repeated after the enactment of the penalty, in order to impress it more effectually upon the people.

A statute for ever . . .—See chap. iii. 17, vii. 23—25.

(32) **It shall be unto you a sabbath of rest.**—Rather, *It shall be a sabbath of rest unto you*, as the Authorised version renders it in chap. xvi. 31. It is most unaccountable why the translators varied this important formula, when it is exactly the same in the original in both passages. For the import of this phrase see chap. xvi. 31.

And ye shall afflict your souls.—Having set forth in verses 30 and 31, and in the first clause of this verse, the duty of abstaining from all work, and of celebrating this day as a day of solemn rest, the law-giver repeats the second feature of the day, which is of equal importance, viz., the fasting, lest some should think that doing the one and leaving the other undone would pass as having kept this law.

In the ninth day of the month at even.—In accordance with the ancient mode of counting the day, the tenth of the month began with the evening of the ninth. (See chap. xvi. 29.)

Celebrate your sabbath.—In chap. xxv. 2, where this phrase occurs again, the Authorised version inconsistently renders it *keep . . . sabbath.* In both instances, however, the margin has, "Heb., rest." This alternative rendering of part of the phrase has no meaning. To convey to the English reader an idea of the Hebrew idiom here used, which was the intention of the translators, the whole phrase should have been translated, which is, *rest the day of rest*, that is, to "keep rest," to "keep the day of rest." Just as to "fast a fast" (2 Sam. xii. 16; Zech. vii. 5) denotes "to keep a fast." In 2 Sam. xii. 16 the margin has consistently reproduced the Hebraism by remarking "Heb., fasted a fast."

(33) **And the Lord spake unto Moses.**—Like the festivals of new year and the day of Atonement (see verses 23, 26), the feast of Tabernacles, which is discussed in verses 34—43, is introduced by this special formula, thus indicating that it was a separate communication.

(34) **The fifteenth day of this seventh month.**—That is, the month Tishri, corresponding to the end of September and the beginning of October, and only four days after the day of Atonement.

Shall be the feast of tabernacles.—How and where these tabernacles are to be erected the law here gives no directions. The details, as in many other enactments, are left to the administrators of the Law. From the account of the first celebration of this festival after the return from Babylon, the Jews, according to the command of Ezra, made themselves booths upon the roofs of houses, in the courts of their dwellings, and of their sanctuary, in the streets of the Water-gate and the gate of Ephraim. These tabernacles they made of olive branches, pine branches, myrtle branches, palm branches, and branches of thick trees (Neh. viii. 15—18). The construction of these temporary abodes, however, was more minutely defined by Ezra's successors. It was ordained during the second Temple that the interior of each tabernacle must not be higher than twenty cubits, and not lower than ten palms, it must at least have three walls, with a thatched roof partially

LORD. (35) On the first day *shall be* an holy convocation: ye shall do no servile work *therein*. (36) Seven days ye shall offer an offering made by fire unto the LORD: on the eighth day shall be an holy convocation unto you; and ye shall offer an offering made by fire unto the LORD: it *is* a [1] solemn assembly; *and* ye shall do no servile work *therein*.

(37) These *are* the feasts of the LORD, which ye shall proclaim *to be* holy convocations, to offer an offering made by fire unto the LORD, a burnt offering, and a meat offering, a sacrifice, and drink offerings, every thing upon his day: (38) beside the sabbaths of the LORD, and beside your gifts, and beside all your vows, and beside all your free-

1 Heb., day of restraint.

---

open so as to admit a view of the sky and the stars. It must not be under a tree, nor must it be covered with a cloth, or with any material which contracts defilement. Only branches or shrubs which grow out of the ground are to be used for the covering. These booths the Israelites began to erect on the morrow after the Day of Atonement. On the fourteenth, which was the day of preparation, the pilgrims came up to Jerusalem, and on the eve of this day the priests proclaimed the approach of the holy convocation by the blasts of trumpets. As on the feasts of Passover and Pentecost, the altar of burnt-offering was cleansed in the first night watch, and the gates of the Temple, as well as those of the inner court, were opened immediately after midnight, for the convenience of the priests who resided in the city, and for the people, who filled the court before the cock crew, to have their sacrifices duly examined by the priests.

(35) **On the first day shall be an holy convocation.**—At daybreak of this day one of the priests, accompanied by a jubilant procession and a band of music, went with a golden pitcher to the pool of Siloam, and having filled it with water, returned with it to the Temple in time to join his brother-priests in the morning sacrifices. He entered from the south through the water-gate, when he was welcomed by three blasts of the trumpets. He then ascended the steps of the altar with another priest, who carried a pitcher of wine for the drink offering. The two priests turned to the left of the altar, where two silver basins were fixed with holes at the bottom, and simultaneously poured into their respective basins the water and the wine in such a manner that both were emptied at the same time upon the base of the altar. This ceremony of drawing the water was repeated every morning during the seven days of the festival. Another jubilant multitude, who went outside Jerusalem at the same time to gather willows, now returned. With great rejoicings and amidst blasts of trumpets they carried the willows into the Temple, and placed them at the altar in such a manner that their tops overhung and formed a kind of canopy.

Ye shall do no servile work therein.—For the difference between servile and necessary work see verse 7.

(36) **Seven days ye shall offer.**—The special sacrifices for this day consisted of a burnt offering of thirteen bullocks, two rams, and fourteen lambs, with an appropriate meat and drink offering, and a goat for a sin offering (Num. xxix. 12—38). Whereupon were offered the peace offerings, the vows and the free-will offerings which constituted the repasts of the people. Whilst these sacrifices were being offered up the Levites chanted the festive Hallel, as on the feasts of Passover and Pentecost. This was repeated every day during the seven days of the festival, only that the number of animals offered as sacrifices diminished daily during the middle days of the festival, according to the prescription in Num. xxix. 12—38. On the eve of the second day, or what is called the lesser festival, and on each of the five succeeding nights, was celebrated the "Rejoicing of the water-drawing" in the court of the Temple. Four huge golden candelabra were lighted in the centre of the court, and the light emanating from them was visible to the whole city. Around these lights pious men danced before the people with lighted flambeaux in their hands, singing hymns and songs of praise, whilst the Levites, who were stationed on the fifteen steps which led into the women's court, and which corresponded to the fifteen psalms of degrees, *i.e.*, steps (Ps. cxx.—cxxxiv.), accompanied the songs with instrumental music. It is supposed that on the last evening of the festival, when the splendid light of this grand illumination was to cease, Christ called attention to himself, "I am the light of the world" (John viii. 12), which is to shine for ever, and illuminate not only the Temple and the holy city, but all the world.

On the eighth day shall be an holy convocation.—That is, like the first day, since no servile work is to be done on it. As it is not only the finishing of the feast of Tabernacles, but the conclusion of the whole cycle of festivals, the dwelling in tabernacles is to cease on it.

Ye shall offer.—For this reason the sacrifices offered on this day are to be distinct, and unlike the sacrifices of the preceding days. The burnt sacrifice is to consist of one bullock, one ram, and seven lambs, with the appropriate meat and drink offerings, and one goat for a sin offering. (Num. xxix. 36—38.) Being, however, attached to the feast of Tabernacles, the two festivals are often joined together, and spoken of as one festival of eight days.

(37) **These are the feasts of the Lord.**—That is, the above-named six festivals, viz.—(1) the Passover (verses 4—14), (2) Pentecost (verses 15—22), (3) New Year (verses 23—25), (4) Day of Atonement (verses 26—32), (5) Tabernacles (33—36*a*), and (6) the concluding festival (verse 36*b*). Thus the list of these festivals concludes with the formula by which they were introduced in verse 4.

To offer an offering.—On these festivals sacrifices are to be offered as prescribed in Num. xxviii. and xxix.

(38) **Beside the sabbaths.**—By a figure of speech called metonymy, which is frequently used both in the Old and New Testaments, the expression sabbaths stands here for *the sacrifices of the sabbaths*, just as in chap. xxv. 6 "sabbath of the land" denotes the produce of the sabbath of the land, or of the sabbatic year, and as the phrase "it is written in the prophets" (Mark i. 2) is used for "it is written in *the writings* of the prophets." (Comp. also Matt. v. 17; vii. 12; xxii. 40, &c.) The meaning, therefore, of the passage before

will offerings, which ye give unto the
Lord. (39) Also in the fifteenth day of
the seventh month, when ye have ga-
thered in the fruit of the land, ye shall
keep a feast unto the Lord seven days:
on the first day *shall be* a sabbath, and
on the eighth day *shall be* a sabbath.
(40) And ye shall take you on the first
day the [1] boughs of goodly trees,
branches of palm trees, and the boughs
of thick trees, and willows of the brook;
and ye shall rejoice before the Lord
your God seven days. (41) And ye shall
keep it a feast unto the Lord seven days
in the year. *It shall be* a statute for
ever in your generations: ye shall cele-
brate it in the seventh month. (42) Ye
shall dwell in booths seven days; all
that are Israelites born shall dwell in
booths: (43) that your generations may
know that I made the children of Israel
to dwell in booths, when I brought
them out of the land of Egypt: I *am*
the Lord your God.
(44) And Moses declared unto the chil-
dren of Israel the feasts of the Lord.

[1] Heb., *fruit.*

---

us is that the sacrifices ordered for each of these festivals are to be in addition to the sacrifices appointed to each weekly sabbath in the year; so that when one of these festivals falls on a sabbath, the sacrifices due to the latter are not set aside by the former. Both must be offered in their proper order.

Beside your gifts.—Nor are they to interfere with the voluntary offerings which each individual brought privately (Deut. xvi. 10, 17; 2 Chron. xxv. 7, 8), or with the performance of vows (Deut. xii. 6—12).

(39) **Also in the fifteenth day.**—After the list of festivals discussed in this chapter has been summed up in verses 37 and 38, the next five verses recur to the feast of Tabernacles. The regulations are supplementary to those given before, and embody a separate enactment.

When ye have gathered in the fruit of the land.—That is, those productions which ripen in the autumnal season, as wheat, barley, oil, wine, &c.

Ye shall keep a feast unto the Lord.—The Israelites are then to keep a festival in which they are to acknowledge the bounties of the Lord and express their gratitude to the Giver of all good things. For this reason this festival is also called "the Feast of Ingathering" (Exod. xxiii. 16, xxxiv. 22).

On the first day shall be a sabbath.—Both on the first and last days of this festival there is to be abstention from all servile work. (See verses 35, 36.)

(40) **And ye shall take you on the first day.**—The four species of vegetable production here ordered are a distinctive feature of this festival. They have been most minutely defined during the second Temple.

Boughs of goodly trees.—Better, *the fruit of goodly trees*, as the margin rightly renders it. As this phrase is too indefinite, and may simply denote the fruit of any choice fruit-tree, there can hardly be any doubt that in this instance, as in many other cases, the lawgiver left it to the administrators of the Law to define its precise kind. Basing it therefore upon one of the significations of the term here translated "goodly," which is *to dwell, to rest*, the authorities during the second Temple decreed that it means the fruit which permanently rests upon the tree—*i.e.*, the citron, the paradise-apple. If it came from an uncircumcised tree (see chap. xix. 23), from an unclean heave-offering (comp. Num. xviii. 11, 12), or exhibited the slightest defect, it was ritually illegal.

Branches of palm trees.—During the second Temple this was defined as the shoot of the palm-tree when budding, before the leaves are spread abroad, and whilst it is yet like a rod. It is technically called *lulab*, which is the expression whereby it is rendered in the ancient Chaldee version. The *lulab* must at least be three hands tall, and must be tied together with its own kind.

The boughs of thick trees.—This, according to the same authorities, denotes *the myrtle branch*, whose leaves thickly cover the wood. To make it ritually legal it must have three or more shoots round the stem, and on the same level with it. If it is in any way damaged it is illegal. This accounts for the ancient Chaldee version rendering it by "myrtle branch."

Willows of the brook.—That species, the distinguishing marks of which are dark wood and long leaves with smooth margin. The palm, the myrtle, and the willow, when tied together into one bundle, constitute the Lulab. Whilst the psalms are chanted by the Levites during the sacrifices, the pilgrims, who held the Lulabs or palms, shook them thrice, viz., at the singing of Ps. cxviii. 1, then again at verse 25, and at verse 29. When the chant was finished, the priests in procession went round the altar once, exclaiming, "Hosanna, O Lord, give us help, O Lord! give prosperity!" (Ps. cxviii. 25). Whereupon the solemn benediction was pronounced by the priests, and the people dispersed amidst the repeated exclamations, "How beautiful art thou, O altar!" It is this part of the ritual which explains the welcome that the multitude gave Christ when they went to meet Him with palm-branches and shouts of hosanna (Matt. xxi. 8, 9, 15; John xii. 12, 13).

(41) **Seven days in the year.**—These seven days denote the feast of Tabernacles proper, whilst the eight days in verse 39 include the concluding festival of the last day. (See verse 36.)

In your generations.—Better, *throughout your generations*, as the Authorised version renders it in verses 14, 21, and 31 of this very chapter. (See chap. iii. 17.)

(42) **Dwell in booths seven days.**—Because the eighth day was a separate festival, when the booths were no more used. (See verse 36.)

(43) **That your generations may know.**—When their posterity are securely occupying the land of Canaan, the temporary dwelling in booths once a year may remind them of the goodness of God vouchsafed to their fathers in delivering them from the land of bondage, and sheltering them in booths in the wilderness.

(44) **And Moses declared.**—In accordance with the command which Moses received (see verse 2), he explained to the children of Israel the number and motive of these festivals. This verse therefore forms an appropriate conclusion to the whole chapter.

CHAPTER XXIV.—(1) And the LORD
spake unto Moses, saying, (2) Command
the children of Israel, that they bring
unto thee pure oil olive beaten for the
light, [1] to cause the lamps to burn con-
tinually. (3) Without the vail of the
testimony, in the tabernacle of the con-
gregation, shall Aaron order it from the
evening unto the morning before the
LORD continually: *it shall be* a statute
for ever in your generations. (4) He
shall order the lamps upon [a] the pure
candlestick before the LORD continually.
(5) And thou shalt take fine flour, and
bake twelve [b] cakes thereof: two tenth
deals shall be in one cake. (6) And thou
shalt set them in two rows, six on a
row, upon the pure table before the
LORD. (7) And thou shall put pure
frankincense upon *each* row, that it may
be on the bread for a memorial, *even*
an offering made by fire unto the LORD.

1 Heb., *to cause to ascend.*

a Ex. 31. 8.

b Ex. 25. 30.

XXIV.

(1) **And the Lord spake unto Moses.**—The regulations about the annual festivals and the ritual connected with them are now followed by directions with regard to the daily service and its ritual.

(2) **Command the children of Israel.**—This is the only other occasion in Leviticus on which God orders Moses to "command," instead of imparting or communicating His will. (See chaps. vi. 1 in Hebrew, and vi. 9 in English.) This command, however, occurs almost literally in Exod. xxvii. 20, 21.

(3) **Without the vail of the testimony.**—That is, the second vail, which divided the holy from the most holy. (See Exod. xxvii. 21.)

In the tabernacle of the congregation.—Better, *in the tent of meeting.*

A statute for ever in your generations.—Better, *a statute for ever throughout your generations,* as this phrase is rendered in the Authorised Version in chap. xxiii. 14, 31, &c. (See chap. iii. 17.)

(4) **The lamps upon the pure candlestick.**—Though it would appear from Exod. xxv. 31 that the candlestick was called pure because it was made entirely of pure gold, yet, according to the authorities during the second Temple, the order here is that "he shall arrange the lamps after having purified and made clean the candlestick, and removed all the cinders."

(5) **And bake twelve cakes.**—The next order is about the preparation of the shewbread, and the use to be made of it. It was made in the following manner. Twenty-four seahs of wheat, which were brought as a meat offering, were beaten and ground, and after passing through twelve different sieves each finer than the other, twenty-four tenth-deals of the finest flour were obtained. The dough was kneaded outside the court, and after it was put into a golden mould of a definite size and form to impart the prescribed size and shape to each cake, was brought into the court. Here it was taken out of the first golden mould, and put into a second of the same material and form, and baked in it. As soon as it was taken out of the oven the cake was put into a third mould of the like description, and when it was turned out of it the cake was ten handbreadths long, five broad, one finger thick, and square at each end. Each cake, therefore, was made of two omers of wheat, or, as it is here said, of two tenth-parts of an ephah, which is the same thing. (See chap. xiv. 10.) As an omer is the quantity which, according to the Divine ordinance (Exod. xvi. 16—19), supplies the daily wants of a human being, each of these cakes represents the food of a man and his neighbour, whilst the twelve cakes answered to the twelve tribes of Israel. Hence the ancient Chaldee version has, after the words "twelve cakes," "according to the twelve tribes." The baking of these cakes took place every Friday afternoon, or Thursday if a feast which required Sabbatical rest fell on Friday. According to the testimony of those who were eye-witnesses to the baking, these cakes were unleavened.

(6) **In two rows, six on a row.**—Better, *in two piles, six on a pile.* The table on which the cakes are here ordered to be put stood along the northern or most sacred side of the holy place. Like all the sacred furniture, except the Ark of the Covenant, it was ranged lengthways of the sanctuary. It was one cubit and a half, or nine handbreadths high; the surface-board or plate was two cubits, or twelve handbreadths long, and one cubit or six handbreadths broad. These twelve cakes were placed one upon another in two piles lengthwise on the breadth of the table. As the cakes were ten handbreadths long, and the table was only six handbreadths wide, the cakes projected two handbreadths at each side of the table.

Upon the pure table.—According to the interpretation which obtained during the second Temple, this denotes that the cakes are to be put upon the table itself, and not upon the hollow golden rods which were on the table to allow the air to pass through to prevent the shewbread becoming mouldy during the week. These hollow tubes are to be placed between the cakes, whilst the cakes themselves are to be put on the table itself and not on the tubes, so as to be raised above the table.

Before the Lord.—That is, the table which stood before the Lord, for it was placed in the sanctuary. The cakes, therefore, which were thus ranged upon it were constantly before God. Hence, not only is the table called "the table of His Presence" (Num. iv. 7), but the cakes are called "the bread of His Presence" (Exod. xxv. 30, xxxv. 13, xxxix. 36). The rendering of the Authorised Version, "table of shewbread," and "shewbread," is taken from Luther, and does not express the import of the names. The names, "the bread set in order," "the sets of bread," and the "table set in order," which were given to the cakes (1 Chron. ix. 32, xxiii. 29; 2 Chron. xiii. 11; Neh. x. 33) and to the table (2 Chron. xxix. 18) in later times, and which are unjustifiably obliterated in the Authorised Version, are derived from this verse where the cakes are ordered to be ranged in two "sets."

(7) **Shalt put pure frankincense upon each row.**—Better, *shalt place pure frankincense by each pile.* As the two piles of six cakes each measured together ten handbreadths in width, and as the length of the table was twelve handbreadths, there was a vacant space of two handbreadths left on the table for the two bowls with frankincense. The vacant place in question may, therefore, (1) have been divided between the two ends of the table, and a bowl with incense been put at each end on either side of the two piles; or (2) the dis-

(8) Every sabbath he shall set it in
order before the LORD continually, *being
taken* from the children of Israel by an
everlasting covenant. (9) And [a] it shall
be Aaron's and his sons'; and they
shall eat it in the holy place: for it *is*
most holy unto him of the offerings of
the LORD made by fire by a perpetual
statute.
(10) And the son of an Israelitish wo-
man, whose father *was* an Egyptian,
went out among the children of Israel:
and this son of the Israelitish *woman*
and a man of Israel strove together in

a Ex. 29. 33; ch. 8. 31; Matt. 12. 1, 5.

---

posable vacant space may have been left at one end of the table only, and the bowls put together on this end by one side of the two piles; or (3) each of the two piles of the cakes may have been put more or less closely to the other end of the table, thus leaving a vacant space between the two piles, into which the two bowls with the frankincense were placed. The last was the practice during the second Temple.

That it may be on the bread for a memorial.—Better, *that it may be for the bread as a memorial,* that is, that the frankincense may be offered up upon the altar, as God's portion, instead of the bread which was given to the priests. By this means the prayers of the children of Israel will be brought into grateful remembrance before the Lord. (See chap. ii. 2.)

(8) **Every sabbath he shall set it in order.**—That is, Aaron is to carry out these instructions in the first instance, as we are told in verse 3, and after him, or together with him, the priests are sacredly to attend to this duty every sabbath throughout the year. Of the manner in which the shewbread, or the "bread of His Presence," was renewed every Sabbath during the second Temple, we have a minute account. "Four priests entered the holy place, two of them carried in their hands the two piles of the cakes, and two carried in their hands the two incense cups, four priests having gone in before them, two to take off the two old piles, and two to take off the two incense cups. Those who brought in the new stood at the north side with their faces to the south, and those who took away the old stood at the south side with their faces to the north. As soon as the one party lifted up the old, the others put down the new, so that their hands were exactly over against each other, because it is written, "before my Presence continually" (Exod. xxv. 30). The authorities during the second Temple took the expression "continually" to denote that the cakes were not to be absent for one moment. Hence the simultaneous action of the two sets of priests, one lifting up the old, and the other at once putting down the new shewbread.

Being taken from the children of Israel.—Like the daily sacrifices, the offerings for the congregation, the salt for the sacrifices, the wood for the altar, the incense, the omer (see chap. xxiii. 10, 11), the two wave-loaves (chap. xxiii. 17), the scapegoat (chap. xvi. 5, &c.), the red heifer (Num. xix. 1—22), &c., the shewbread, or the "bread of His Presence," according to the canon that obtained during the second Temple, were purchased with the people's half-shekels, which every Israelite had to contribute annually toward the maintenance of the service in the sanctuary. (See Exod. xxx. 11—16.)

(9) **And it shall be Aaron's and his sons'.**—In accordance with this statute, the twelve cakes were divided during the second Temple between the high priest and the officiating priests, the former had six, and the latter had six, among them.

They shall eat it in the holy place.—Of the many things connected with the national service which became the perquisites of the priests, there were eight only which had to be consumed within the precincts of the sanctuary, and the shewbread is one of the eight, viz., (1) the remnant of the meat offering (chap. ii. 3, 10); (2) the flesh of the sin offering (chap. vi. 26); (3) of the trespass offering (chap. vii. 6); (4) the leper's log of oil (chap. xiv. 10); (5) the remainder of the omer (chap. xxiii. 10, 11); (6) the peace offering of the congregation; (7) the two loaves (chap. xiii. 19, 20); and (8) the shewbread.

Of the offerings of the Lord made by fire.—That is, the former part of the offering, as the frankincense, which was the other part, was burnt as an offering to God.

(10) **The son of an Israelitish woman, whose father was an Egyptian.**—The name of the Israelitish woman, whose son is the subject of the narrative before us, we are afterwards told was Shelomith. She had married an Egyptian whilst she and her people were still in Egypt. Though the father's nationality is here expressly given, yet from the fact that he does not personally come before us in this incident, it is evident that he remained in Egypt, whilst the son was of the "mixed multitude" who followed the Israelites in their exodus (Exod. xii. 38). This incident, therefore, which is so difficult satisfactorily to connect with the preceding legislation, brings before us a picture of the camp-life of the Israelites in the wilderness. According to tradition, the father of this blasphemer was the taskmaster under whom Shelomith's husband worked in Egypt, that he had injured Shelomith and then smote her husband, that this was the Egyptian whom Moses slew (Exod. ii. 11) for the injuries he had thus inflicted both upon the Hebrew and his wife, and that the culprit before us is the issue of the outraged Shelomith by the slain Egyptian. This will explain the rendering here of the ancient Chaldee version, "A wicked man, a rebel against the God of heaven, had come out of Egypt, the son of the Egyptian who slew an Israelite in Egypt, and outraged his wife, who conceived, and brought forth this son among the children of Israel."

Went out among the children of Israel.—Better, *he went out into the midst,* &c. This shows that he lived outside the camp and came where he had no right to be.

This son of the Israelitish woman and a man of Israel strove together.—The cause and the manner of their quarrel or contention are not given. But, according to tradition, the "man of Israel" was a Danite, and, as we are told in the next verse, his mother was of the tribe of Dan, this semi-Egyptian contended with this Danite that he had a right from the side of his mother to encamp among the children of Dan, whilst the Danite disputed this, maintaining that a son could only pitch his tent by the standard of his father's name (Num. ii. 2). This contention, moreover, took place before the rulers who tried the case (Exod. xix. 21, 22). Hence the ancient Chaldee version translates it, "And while the Israelites were dwelling in the wilderness, he sought to pitch his tent

the camp; (11) and the Israelitish
woman's son blasphemed the name *of*
the LORD, and cursed. And they brought
him unto Moses: (and his mother's
name *was* Shelomith, the daughter of
Dibri, of the tribe of Dan:) (12) and they
[a] put him in ward, [1] that the mind of the
LORD might be shewed them. (13) And
the LORD spake unto Moses, saying,
(14) Bring forth him that hath cursed
without the camp; and let all that
heard *him* [b] lay their hands upon his
head, and let all the congregation stone
him. (15) And thou shalt speak unto
the children of Israel, saying, Whoso-
ever curseth his God shall bear his sin.

a Num. 15. 34.

1 Heb., *to expound unto them according to the mouth of the LORD.*

b Deut. 13. 9 & 17. 7.

---

in the midst of the tribe of the children of Dan; but they would not let him, because, according to the order of Israel, every man, according to his order, dwelt with his family by the ensign of his father's house. And they strove together in the camp. Whereupon the son of the Israelitish woman and the man of Israel who was of the tribe of Dan went into the house of judgment."

(11) **Blasphemed the name of the Lord, and cursed.**—Better, *cursed the Name and reviled.* In accordance with the above interpretation, this happened after sentence was given against him, and when they had left the court. Being vexed with the Divine enactments which excluded him from encamping in the tribe of his mother, he both cursed God who gave such law, and reviled the judges who pronounced judgment against him. The expression, "the Name," which in after times was commonly used instead of the Ineffable Jehovah, has been substituted here for the Tetragrammaton by a transcriber who out of reverence would not combine cursing with it. The same shyness on the part of copyists has been the cause of inserting the word Lord (*Adonaï*) and God (*Elohîm*) for Jehovah in sundry passages of the Old Testament. During the second Temple, however, this passage was rendered, "*he pronounced the Name* and cursed." Hence it was enacted that the simple pronunciation of the Tetragrammaton was criminal. In accordance with the ancient interpretation, the Chaldee version translates this part of the verse, "And when they came out of the house of judgment, having been condemned, the son of the Israelitish woman pronounced and reviled the great and glorious name of manifestation which had been heard on Sinai, and he was defiant and annoying."

And they brought him unto Moses.—The contention about his right to pitch his tent among the tribe to which his mother belonged being a minor point, came within the jurisdiction of the rulers, according to the advice of Jethro (Exod. xviii. 22); whilst blaspheming God was considered too serious an offence, and hence the criminal was brought to Moses.

And his mother's name was Shelomith.—Whether we accept the traditional explanation, that Shelomith was no consenting party to her union with the Egyptian, or whether we regard her as having voluntarily married him, the fact that both her personal and tribal names are here so distinctly specified, indicates that the record of this incident is designed to point out the ungodly issue of so unholy an alliance, and to guard the Hebrew women against intermarriage with heathen.

(12) **And they put him in ward.**—That is, to keep him in safe custody till he had been tried. In the Mosaic legislation confinement in a prison for a certain period as a punishment for an offence is nowhere enacted.

That the mind of the Lord might be shewed them.—Better, *that he might direct them according to the command of the Lord,* as the Authorised Version renders this phrase in Exod. xvii. 1, Num. iv. 37, 41, 49, &c. Though this was a transgression of the third commandment, and though it was ordained that he who cursed his earthly parent should be put to death (see chap. xx. 9), yet no law existed as to the exact punishment which was to be inflicted upon him who cursed his heavenly Father (see Exod. xxii. 28); nor was it known whether such an offender should be left to God Himself to execute the sentence. For this reason the criminal was detained till Moses had appealed to the Lord for instruction, in order that he might direct the people accordingly. Similar instances of Moses appealing direct to the Lord for guidance in matters of law and judgment we have in Num. xv. 34, xxviii. 1—5.

(13) **And the Lord spake unto Moses.**—In none of these instances, however, is it stated how and where Moses made this appeal to God, whether he inquired by means of the Urim and Thummim, or otherwise. As God promised to reveal His will to Moses from the mercy-seat between the cherubim (Exod. xxv. 22), it is probable that the lawgiver received the Divine directions in the sanctuary.

(14) **Bring forth him that hath cursed.**—The sentence which God now passes upon the blasphemer is that he should be conducted from prison outside the camp, where all unclean persons had to abide (Num. v. 2, 3), and where malefactors were executed (Heb. xiii. 12, 13).

Let all that heard him lay their hands upon his head.—That is, the witnesses who heard him blaspheme, and upon whose evidence he was convicted, and the judges who found him guilty, are to lay their hands upon the criminal's head. Hence the Chaldee version translates it, "Let the witnesses who heard his blasphemy and the judges lay their hands upon his head." This imposition of hands upon a criminal was peculiar to the blasphemer who was sentenced to death, and according to the Jewish canonists, the witnesses and the judges thereby declared that the testimony and the sentence were faithful and righteous, and at the same time uttered the solemn words, "Let thy blood be upon thine own head; thou hast brought this upon thyself."

Let all the congregation stone him.—The witnesses, who are the representatives of the people, cast the first stone, and then all the people who stood by covered the convict with stones. (See chap. xx. 2.)

(15) **Whosoever curseth his God.**—As Moses had to appeal to God for direction, the Lord has not only declared what should be done with this particular offender, but lays down a general law for the punishment of blasphemers. As the criminal who is the immediate occasion of this enactment is an Egyptian, directions are given, in the first place, about the treatment of Gentiles who temporarily sojourn among the Hebrews, and who have not as yet renounced their faith in their own God. If such a Gentile curses his own God in whom he still professes to believe, he shall bear his sin; he must suffer the punishment for his sin from the

(16) And he that blasphemeth the name
of the LORD, he shall surely be put to
death, *and* all the congregation shall
certainly stone him: as well the stranger,
as he that is born in the land, when he
blasphemeth the name *of the LORD*, shall
be put to death.
(17) [a]And he that [1]killeth any man
shall surely be put to death. (18) And
he that killeth a beast shall make it
good; [2]beast for beast. (19) And if a
man cause a blemish in his neighbour;
as [b]he hath done, so shall it be done to
him; (20) breach for breach, eye for eye,
tooth for tooth: as he hath caused a
blemish in a man, so shall it be done
to him *again*. (21) And he that killeth
a beast, he shall restore it: and he that
killeth a man, he shall be put to death.
(22) Ye shall have [c]one manner of law,
as well for the stranger, as for one of
your own country: for I *am* the LORD
your God.
(23) And Moses spake to the children
of Israel, that they should bring forth
him that had cursed out of the camp,
and stone him with stones. And the
children of Israel did as the LORD com-
manded Moses.

CHAPTER XXV.—(1) And the LORD
spake unto Moses in mount Sinai, say-
ing, (2) Speak unto the children of Israel,
and say unto them, When ye come into
the land which I give you, then shall
the land [3]keep [d]a sabbath unto the

a Ex. 21. 12; Deut. 19. 21.

1 Heb., *smiteth the life of a man.*

2 Heb., *life for life.*

b Ex. 21. 24; Deut. 19. 21; Matt. 5. 38.

B.C. 1491.

c Ex. 12. 49.

3 Heb., *rest.*

d Ex. 23. 10.

---

hands of his co-religionists, whose feelings he has outraged. The Israelites are not to interfere to save him from the consequence of his guilt; for a heathen who reviles the god in whom he believes is not to be trusted in other respects, and sets a bad example to others, who might be led to imitate his conduct.

(16) **And he that blasphemeth the name of the Lord.**—Better, *And he that curseth the name of the Lord.* The case is, however, different when it is the God of Israel. It is henceforth to be the law that whosoever curses Jehovah is to suffer death by lapidation, which is to be inflicted upon the criminal by the Jewish community.

As well the stranger as he that is born in the land.—This law is applicable alike to the proselyte and to the Gentile, who does not even profess to believe in Jehovah.

When he blasphemeth the name of the Lord.—Better, *when he curseth the Name.* Here again the expression "Name" has, out of reverence, been substituted for Jehovah. (See verse 11.)

(17) **And he that killeth a man.**—The enactment that in case of blaspheming no difference is to be made between a non-Israelite and Israelite, is now followed by other laws respecting murder and personal injury which have been given before (Exod. xxi. 12, &c.), but which are here repeated in order to show that, like blasphemy, they apply alike to Gentile and Jew. It may also be that the repetition here of the law of murder is designed to draw a distinction between the judicial sentence of death carried out by the community, and the illegal taking away of life by individuals.

(18) **And he that killeth a beast.**—The law about killing a human being is now followed by the enactments with regard to killing a beast. He who kills an animal has to make it good by giving another animal for it. The case is not the same as that legislated for in Exod. xxi. 33, 34.

(19, 20) **And if a man cause a blemish.**—See Exod. xxi. 24, 25.

(21) **And he that killeth a beast.**—This verse contains a repetition of the laws enacted in verses 17, 18.

(22) **Ye shall have one manner of law.**—Not in the case of blasphemy (see verse 16), but in all the instances just adduced, the same penal statutes apply to the non-Israelite and stranger.

(23) **And Moses spake to the children of Israel.**—Having recited the laws which were promulgated in consequence of the appeal made to God, Moses now calls upon the people to execute the sentence which the Lord pronounced against the blasphemer.

XXV.

(1) **And the Lord spake unto Moses.**—This chapter should properly have followed chap. xxiii., since the institutions of the sabbatical year, and the jubile which it discusses, are closely connected with the regulations about the festivals laid down in that chapter. The isolation of these ordinances from the rest of the festivals cannot be satisfactorily explained on any other principle than that which the authorities during the second Temple laid down, viz., that many of the sections are transposed, and that "there is no strict sequence in the Law."

In Mount Sinai.—That is, in the mountainous regions of Sinai. The expression "mountain" is often used to denote a mountainous tract of country (Num. xii. 9; Deut. i. 2; Josh. xiv. 12, &c.). Accordingly, this divine communication was made to Moses when the Israelites were encamped in the neighbourhood of Sinai, where they remained in the wilderness for twelve months after their exodus from Egypt (Num. x. 11, 12).

(2) **When ye come into the land.**—Better, *When ye be come into the land*, as the Authorised Version renders the same phrase in chap. xiv. 34. (See Note on chap. xix. 23.) This is the fourth instance in Leviticus of a law being given prospectively which had no immediate bearing on the condition of Israel. (See chaps. xiv. 34, xix. 23, xxiii. 10.) According to the authorities during the second Temple this law came into operation in the twenty-first year after the Israelites entered Canaan. As the conquest of the promised land occupied them seven years (Josh. xiv. 10), and as the division of it between the different tribes took seven years more (Josh. xviii. 1, &c.), the real cultivation of the land only began at the end of the second seven years. Hence the first seventh year in which laws of the sabbatical year came into operation was the twenty-first year after their entrance into Canaan.

Then shall the land keep a sabbath.—For which the marginal rendering is "rest," *i.e.*, a sabbath. For the import of this phrase see Note on chap. xxiii.

LORD. (3) Six years thou shalt sow thy
field, and six years thou shalt prune thy
vineyard, and gather in the fruit there-
of; (4) but in the seventh year shall be
a sabbath of rest unto the land, a sab-
bath for the LORD: thou shalt neither
sow thy field, nor prune thy vineyard.
(5) That which groweth of its own
accord of thy harvest thou shalt not
reap, neither gather the grapes [1] of thy
vine undressed: *for* it is a year of rest
unto the land. (6) And the sabbath of
the land shall be meat for you; for thee,
and for thy servant, and for thy maid, and
for thy hired servant, and for thy stranger
that sojourneth with thee, (7) and for thy
cattle, and for the beast that *are* in thy
land, shall all the increase thereof be meat.

1 Heb., *of thy separations.*

---

32. The septennial sabbath is to be to the land what the weekly sabbath is to the whole earth. Just as the seventh day is dedicated to God in recognition of His being the Creator of the world, so the seventh year is to be consecrated to Him in acknowledgment that He is the owner of the land. Hence, like the weekly sabbath (Exod. xx. 10; chap. xxiii. 3; Deut. v. 14), the seventh year sabbath is belonging "unto the Lord." (See verse 4.)

(3) **Six years thou shalt sow.**—See Exod. xxiii. 10.

The fruit thereof.—That is, of the land which is mentioned in the preceding verse, and which includes fields, vineyards, olive-gardens, &c. (See Exod. xxiii. 11.)

(4) **The seventh year shall be a sabbath of rest.**—Literally, *the seventh year shall be a rest of solemn resting*, or *a sabbath of sabbaths*. For the import of this phrase see Note on chap. xvi. 31. Like the weekly sabbath, the seventh year is to be the Lord's sabbath. The soil is therefore to have a perfect rest.

Thou shalt neither sow thy field.—What constitutes cultivation, and how much of labour was regarded as transgressing this law, may be seen from the following canons which obtained during the second Temple. No one was allowed to plant trees in the sabbatical year, nor to cut off dried-up branches, to break off withered leaves, to smoke under the plants in order to kill the insects, nor to besmear the unripe fruit with any kind of soil in order to protect them, &c. Any one who committed one of these things received the prescribed number of stripes. As much land, however, might be cultivated as was required for the payment of taxes as well as for growing the barley required for the omer or wave sheaf at the Passover, and wheat for the two wave-loaves at Pentecost.

(5) **That which groweth of its own accord.**—Not only is every owner of land to desist from cultivating it, but the spontaneous growth of the fields from seeds which accidentally fell down at the harvest, as well as from old roots, are not to be gathered, or no harvest is to be made of it.

Neither gather the grapes of thy vine undressed.—Literally, *thy Nazarite vine*, the vine which bears the character of a Nazarite, or of being separated or consecrated to God. As the seventh year is the sabbath of the Lord, being consecrated to Him, the vine of this year is consecrated to Him. Hence the Greek version (LXX.) translates it "the grapes of thy consecration," and hence, too, the marginal rendering "of thy separations." The passage is also interpreted "thou shalt not gather the grapes from which thou hast separated and debarred other people, and which thou hast not declared common property."

(6) **And the sabbath of the land.**—That is, the growth or produce during this sabbath of the land. For the figure of speech see chap. xviii. 38.

Shall be meat for you.—That is, it shall serve as your food, but you must not trade with it, or store it up. Hence, during the second Temple the produce of the sabbatical year could only be used for direct consumption, and was not allowed to be converted first into other articles and then used. Thus, for instance, though wood of that year could be used as firewood, yet it was illegal to convert it first into coal and then use the coal thus obtained from the wood, nor was it legal to convert vegetables into medicines, or to give human food to animals.

For thee, and for thy servant . . .—The produce is to be left in the field for the free use of the poor, the servant, &c. (See also Exod. xxiii. 11.) Hence it was enacted during the second Temple that "whoso locks up his vineyard, or hedges in his field, or gathers all the fruit into his house in the sabbatical year breaks this law." Everything is to be left common, and every man has a right to every thing in every place. Every man could only bring into his house a little at a time, according to the manner of things that are in common."

(7) **And for thy cattle.**—In accordance with the benign legislation which obtained during the second Temple, the administrators of the law inferred from this verse, and hence enacted, that the fruit of the seventh year may only be eaten by man at home, as long as the kind is found in the field. "As long as the animals eat the same kind in the field thou mayest eat what there is of it in the house, but if the animal has consumed it all in the field thou art bound to remove this kind from the house into the field." (For the enactment which enjoins the remission of debts in the sabbatical year, see Deut. xv. 1—3.) During the second Temple the sabbatical year began on the first day of the month of Tishri, which was the beginning of the civil year. The tillage, however, and the cultivation of certain fields and gardens, were left off in the sixth year. The cultivation of corn-fields ceased from the Feast of Passover, and orchards from Pentecost of the sixth year. The reading of portions of the Law which is enjoined in Deut. xxxi. 10—13, was assigned during the second Temple to the king. At the termination of the seventh fallow year, which coincided with the first day of the Feast of Tabernacles of the eighth year, a wooden platform was erected in the outer court of the Temple, on which the king was seated. The chief of the synagogue took the Book of the Law, and gave it to the head of the synagogue, who gave it to the head of the priests. He gave it to the high priest, and the latter handed it to the king, who stood up to receive it. He then sat down again, and read the following seven sections:—(1) Deut. i. 1—vi. 3; (2) vi. 4—8; (3) xi. 13—22; (4) xiv. 22—xv. 23; (5) xvi. 12—19; (6) xvii. 14—20; (7) xxvii. 1—xxviii. 69. The king concluded with the same benedictions, which the high priest pronounced (see chap. xvi. 27), only that he substituted the blessing for the festival for the absolution of sins.

(8) And thou shalt number seven sabbaths of years unto thee, seven times seven years; and the space of the seven sabbaths of years shall be unto thee forty and nine years.
(9) Then shalt thou cause the trumpet [1] of the jubile to sound on the tenth *day* of the seventh month, in the day of atonement shall ye make the trumpet sound throughout all your land.
(10) And ye shall hallow the fiftieth year, and proclaim liberty throughout *all* the land unto all the inhabitants thereof: it shall be a jubile unto you; and ye shall return every man unto his possession, and ye shall return every man unto his family.
(11) A jubile shall that fiftieth year be unto you: ye shall not sow, neither reap that which groweth of itself in it, nor gather *the grapes* in it of thy vine undressed.
(12) For it *is* the jubile; it shall be holy unto you: ye shall eat the increase thereof out of the field.
(13) In the year of this jubile ye shall return every man unto his possession.

[1] Heb., *loud of sound.*

---

(8) **And thou shalt number.**—Better, *And thou shalt count unto thee,* as the Authorised Version renders the same phrase in chap. xxiii. 15.

Number seven sabbaths of years.—Better, *count seven weeks of years* (see chap. xxiii. 15). The seven days of each week stand for so many years, so that seven weeks of years make forty-nine years. Hence the explanation in the next clause: "Seven times seven years." As the observance of the jubile, like that of the sabbatical year, was only to become obligatory when the Israelites had taken possession of the promised land (see verse 2), and as the first sabbatical year, according to the authorities during the second Temple, came into operation in the twenty-first year after their entrance into Canaan (see verse 2), the first jubile was celebrated in the sixty-fourth year after they came into the land of promise.

(9) **Cause the trumpet of the jubile to sound.**—Better, *cause the blast of the cornet to sound;* literally, *cause to resound the cornet of loud sound.* According to the authorities during the second Temple, the cornets used on this occasion, like those of the Feast of Trumpets or New Year, were of rams' horns, they were straight, and had their mouth-piece covered with gold.

In the day of atonement shall ye make the trumpet sound.—Better, *In the day of atonement shall ye cause the cornet to sound.* On the close of the great Day of Atonement, when the Hebrews realised that they had peace of mind, that their heavenly Father had annulled their sins, and that they had become reunited to Him through His forgiving mercy, every Israelite was called upon to proclaim throughout the land, by nine blasts of the cornet, that he too had given the soil rest, that he had freed every encumbered family estate, and that he had given liberty to every slave, who was now to rejoin his kindred. Inasmuch as God has forgiven his debts, he also is to forgive his debtors.

(10) **And ye shall hallow the fiftieth year.**—Because it is here said "Ye shall hallow the fiftieth year," the authorities during the second Temple inferred that the good work of the jubile is to begin with the first day of Tishri, which is the beginning of the year, and which ought to be hallowed. Hence as new year was with the Hebrews the preparation for the Day of Atonement, so it also became the prelude to the acts of mercy which finally came into operation on the Day of Atonement. They therefore began counting the cycle of the jubile from the first of Tishri, or new year, though they proclaimed it on the tenth, or on the close of the Day of Atonement. In accordance with this the authorities during the second Temple record that "from the Feast of Trumpets [*i.e.,* Tishri 1] till the Day of Atonement [*i.e.,* Tishri 10], the slaves were neither manumitted to return to their homes, nor were made use of by their masters, but ate, drank, rejoiced, and wore garlands; and when the Day of Atonement came the judges blew the cornet, the slaves were manumitted to return to their homes, and the fields were set free."

And proclaim liberty . . . unto all the inhabitants.—That is, to all the Israelites, who are the true possessors of the land. Hence the ancient authorities conclude that the law of jubile was only in force as long as the whole Jewish nation dwelt in the land, but not after the tribes of Reuben and Gad, and half the tribe of Manasseh, were carried into captivity by Pul and Tilgath-Pilneser kings of Assyria (1 Chron. v. 26), because "all the inhabitants" of the land dwelt no longer in it. It is from this declaration to proclaim liberty that the year of jubile is also called "the year of freedom" (Ezek. xlvi. 17).

It shall be a jubile.—This is an abbreviation of the fuller form, "a year of jubile," used in the other passages of this chapter (see verses 13, 28, 40, 50, 52, 54), and denotes "a year proclaimed by the blast of the horn," since the word *yôbel* signifies both ram's horn and the sound emitted from it.

And ye shall return every man.—See verses 14—16, 23—28.

Every man unto his family.—See verses 39, 40.

(11) **A jubile shall that fiftieth year be unto you.**—According to the unanimous testimony of the authorities during the second Temple, including Philo (ii. 287—290) and Josephus (*Antt.* iii. 12, § 3), the jubile was observed every fiftieth year, as is plainly enjoined both in the verse before us and in verse 10. As the forty-ninth year is the sabbatical year and the fiftieth year the jubile, there were two successive fallow years.

Ye shall not sow.—As the fiftieth year is jubile, and partakes of the nature of the sabbatical year, sowing and reaping are forbidden.

Neither reap that which groweth of itself in it.—That is, the spontaneous growth of this year is not to be made into a regular harvest and stored up. (See verse 5.)

Vine undressed.—See verse 5.

(12) **Ye shall eat the increase thereof out of the field.**—Better, *Ye shall eat its produce from the field.* Because it is the jubile, which must be observed as a sacred institution, the spontaneous produce of this year is not to be stored, but as much of it must each time be taken direct from the field as is wanted for daily consumption.

(13) **Ye shall return every man unto his possession.**—In the year of jubile every man is to be restored to his landed property, whether he had disposed of it by sale or by gift.

(14) And if thou sell ought unto thy
neighbour, or buyest *ought* of thy neigh-
bour's hand, ye shall not oppress one
another: (15) according to the number of
years after the jubile thou shalt buy of
thy neighbour, *and* according unto the
number of years of the fruits he shall
sell unto thee: (16) according to the mul-
titude of years thou shalt increase the
price thereof, and according to the few-
ness of years thou shalt diminish the
price of it: for *according* to the number
of the years of the fruits doth he sell
unto thee.
(17) Ye shall not therefore oppress one
another; but thou shalt fear thy God:
for I *am* the LORD your God. (18) Where-
fore ye shall do my statutes, and keep
my judgments, and do them; and ye shall
dwell in the land in safety. (19) And
the land shall yield her fruit, and ye
shall eat your fill, and dwell therein in
safety.
(20) And if ye shall say, What shall we

---

(14) **Ye shall not oppress one another.**—Better, *ye shall not overreach any man his brother.* Not only does the Law provide against the poor man losing his land for ever, but enjoins that in the temporary sales the buyer and seller are not to take undue advantage of each other's circumstances. Hence it was enacted that if any one bought or sold anything for a sixth part more than its value the aggrieved party was entitled to have the excess returned to him, and if it amounted to more than a sixth part, the contract could be rescinded altogether. The fact that the phrase which is here translated "one another" in the Authorised Version is varied in the Hebrew in verse 17, where it is likewise rendered "one another," shows that it is not used in this idiomatic sense, but is designed to denote fellow-brethren, members of the same community, those who are related to each other by race and creed, as in Exod. xxxii. 27, Jer. xxxi. 34

(15) **According to the number of years . . . thou shalt buy.**—The promised land, according to the Law, was to be divided by lot in equal parts among the Israelites. The plot which should thus come into the possession of each family is to be absolutely inalienable, and for ever continue to be the property of the descendants of the original possessor. Hence it is here enacted that where a proprietor being pressed by poverty is compelled to sell a field, it could not be bought of him for a longer period than up to the time of the next jubile, when it reverted to the original possessor, or to his family. In purchasing a plot of land the purchaser is to reckon how many years had elapsed since the last jubile, since this would show him the exact period during which he would be entitled to hold it. It thus corresponds to what with us is buying the unexpired term of a lease.

Of thy neighbour.—From this it was deduced that the Israelite who was reduced to poverty could only sell his land to a fellow-Israelite, but not to a Gentile.

The number of years of the fruit he shall sell.—Whilst the purchaser is to take into consideration the number of years which the lease has still to run, the vendor has to consider how many sabbatical years there will be from the time of the sale till next jubile, since the sale was not so much of the land as of the produce of so many years. Hence the fallow sabbatical years are not to be included. As the plural "number of years" is here used, the authorities during the second Temple concluded that the vendor could not sell it for less than *two productive years*, exclusive of a sabbatical year, a year of barrenness, and of the first harvest if the purchase was effected shortly before the seventh month, with the ripe produce in the field.

(16) **According to the multitude of years . . . and according to.**—Better, *in proportion to the multitude of years . . . and in proportion to*, as the words in the original here are not the same which are used in verse 15 and at the end of this verse, which are translated "according" in the Authorised Version. Having laid down in the preceding verse the principles of equitable dealings both for the purchaser and vendor, the Lawgiver, in his anxiety lest the distressed seller should be taken advantage of, reverts again to the purchaser, who is enjoined strictly to regulate the purchase price in proportion to the number of years the lease of the field has still to run.

For according to the number of the years of the fruits doth he sell.—Better, *for a number of crops he selleth*, that is, the vendor does not sell the land but a certain number of harvests till the next jubile.

(17) **Ye shall not therefore oppress one another.**—Better, *And ye shall not overreach any man his neighbour.* (See verse 14.)

But thou shalt fear thy God—who pleads the cause of the oppressed, and avenges every injustice. (See chap. xix. 14.)

(18) **Wherefore ye shall do my statutes.**—Better, *And ye shall do . . .* that is, the above named statutes and ordinances respecting the sabbatical year and the jubile, which required great sacrifices.

Ye shall dwell in the land in safety.—As God is Israel's strong tower and wall of defence, it is by keeping His commandments that the Israelites will enjoy the security which other nations endeavour to obtain by great labour and mighty armies.

(19) **And the land . . . her fruit.**—He, moreover, who has given Israel these statutes, also controls the operations of nature. Hence, though the observance of His laws would necessitate the abstention from cultivating the soil, the Lord will cause the land to yield an abundant harvest which will richly supply all their wants, and they will safely and quietly dwell therein without being compelled to make raids upon their neighbours for food, or surrender themselves to their enemies for want of provision (1 Macc. vi. 49, 53; Josephus, *Antt.* xiv. 16, § 2; xv. 1, § 2).

(20) **What shall we eat the seventh year?**—The Lawgiver here anticipates an objection on the part of those who are called upon to abstain from cultivating the land in the sabbatical year, and who are over-anxious about the provisions of their families.

Behold, we shall not sow.—That is, are forbidden to sow. (See verse 4.)

Nor gather in our increase.—That is, we are even prohibited to gather the spontaneous growths and store them up, and are commanded to leave "the increase" in the field. (See verse 7.)

eat the seventh year? behold, we shall
not sow, nor gather in our increase:
(21) then I will command my blessing
upon you in the sixth year, and it shall
bring forth fruit for three years. (22) And
ye shall sow the eighth year, and eat
yet of old fruit until the ninth year;
until her fruits come in ye shall eat *of*
the old *store*.

(23) The land shall not be sold [1][2] for
ever: for the land *is* mine; for ye *are*
strangers and sojourners with me.
(24) And in all the land of your posses-
sion ye shall grant a redemption for
the land. (25) If thy brother be waxen
poor, and hath sold away *some* of his
possession, and if any of his kin come to
redeem it, then shall he redeem that

1 Or, *to be quite cut off.*

2 Heb., *for cutting off.*

(21) **Then I will command my blessing.**—That is, He will send out His Divine command to the soil in the sixth year that it should be a blessing to them, and it shall be done. (See Deut. xxviii. 8; Pss. xlii. 8, xliv. 4, lxviii. 29.)

It shall bring forth fruit for three years.—Better, *it shall bring forth produce.* This special blessing will be manifested in the abundant crop of the harvest preceding the sabbatical year. Just as at the institution of the weekly Sabbath, when God enjoined abstention from labour, He sent down a double portion of manna every sixth day to make up for the day of rest (Exod. xvi. 22—27), so He will exercise a special providence every sixth year by blessing the soil with a treble crop to compensate for giving the land a septennial sabbath. As the sabbatical year began the civil year, viz., 1 Tishri, which was in the autumn or in September, the three years here spoken of are to be distributed as follows: (1) the remainder of the sixth year after the harvest; (2) the whole of the seventh year; and (3) the period of the eighth year till the harvest is gathered in from the seeds sown in the eighth year. It will thus be seen that the question anticipated in verse 29, viz., "What shall we eat the seventh year?" properly applies to the eighth year, since the requirements for the seventh year are supplied by the regular harvest of the sixth year, and it is the eighth year for which the harvest of the seventh is wanted. To meet this difficulty, one of the most distinguished Jewish expositors of the Middle Ages translates verse 20: "And if ye shall say in the seventh year 'What shall we eat'" *i.e.*, in the eighth year. It may, however, be that the question expresses the anxiety which the people might feel in eating their ordinary share in the seventh year, lest there should be nothing left for the eighth year, since in all other years the harvest is ripening for the next year whilst the fruits of the past year are being consumed.

(22) **And ye shall sow the eighth year, and eat yet of old fruit.**—Better, *And when ye shall sow in the eighth year, ye shall yet eat of the old produce,* that is, when at the termination of the sabbatical year the Israelites resume the cultivation of the soil in the eighth year, the abundant crop of the sixth year—the year preceding the sabbatical year—will not only suffice for this year, but will reach till that part of the ninth year when the crops sown in the eighth are ripe and gathered in. Accordingly, the sixth year's harvest will suffice till the Feast of Tabernacles, or till Tishri 1 of the ninth year.

Until her fruits come in.—Better, *until its produce come in,* that is, the produce of the eighth year which was gathered in the ninth. Verse 20, therefore, which states the anticipated question, and verses 21 and 22, which contain the reply, ought properly to follow immediately after verse 7, since they meet the difficulty arising from the rest of the land during the sabbatical year. The redactor of Leviticus may, however, have inserted verses 20—22 here because the difficulty raised in them, and the reply given to the anticipated question, apply equally to the jubile year. The special Divine interposition which is here promised to meet the requirements of one year's cessation from cultivating the land will, as a matter of course, be all the more readily vouchsafed when the Israelites will have to exercise greater obedience and faith in the jubile, and abstain two successive years from tilling the ground.

(23) **The land shall not be sold for ever.**—That is, no plot of the land of Israel must be absolutely alienated from the original proprietor, who has been driven by poverty to sell his patrimony. We have here a resumption of the laws relating to the sale and purchase of land, which have already been briefly stated in verses 14—17. Having been interrupted by the insertion of the Divine promise with regard to the sabbatical year (verses 20—22), the legislation now proceeds with more directions about the limited sale of land.

For the land is mine.—The reason for this prohibition absolutely to cut off the patrimony from the family, is that God claims to be the supreme owner of the land (Exod. xv. 17; Isa. xiv. 2, 25; Jer. ii. 5; Ps. x. 16), and as the Lord of the soil He prescribes conditions on which he allotted it to the different tribes of Israel.

Ye are strangers and sojourners with me.—God has not only helped the Israelites to conquer the land of Canaan, but has selected it as His own dwelling-place, and erected His sanctuary in the midst of it (Exod. xv. 13; Num. xxxv. 34). He therefore is enthroned in it as Lord of the soil, and the Israelites are simply His tenants at will (chaps. xiv. 34, xx. 24, xxiii. 10; Num. xiii. 2, xv. 2), and as such will have to quit it if they disobey His commandments (chaps. xviii. 28, xx. 22, xxvi. 33; Deut. xxviii. 63). For this reason they are accounted as strangers and sojourners, and hence have no right absolutely to sell that which is not theirs.

(24) **Ye shall grant a redemption for the land.**—Being simply tenants at will, and having obtained possession of it on such terms, the land is not even to remain with the purchaser till the year of jubile, but the buyer is to grant every opportunity to the seller to redeem it before that time.

(25) **If thy brother be waxen poor, and hath sold . . .**—As poverty is the only reason which the Law here supposes might lead one to part with his field, the authorities during the second Temple concluded, and hence enacted, that it is not allowable for any one to sell his patrimony on speculation. This will account for the horror which Naboth expressed to Ahab of selling his patrimony: "The Lord forbid it me that I should give the inheritance of my fathers to thee" (1 Kings xxi. 3).

which his brother sold. (26) And if the
man have none to redeem it, and [1]him-
self be able to redeem it; (27) then let
him count the years of the sale thereof,
and restore the overplus unto the man
to whom he sold it; that he may return
unto his possession. (28) But if he be
not able to restore *it* to him, then that
which is sold shall remain in the hand
of him that hath bought it until the
year of jubile: and in the jubile it shall
go out, and he shall return unto his
possession.
(29) And if a man sell a dwelling house
in a walled city, then he may redeem it
within a whole year after it is sold;
within a full year may he redeem it.
(30) And if it be not redeemed within the
space of a full year, then the house that
is in the walled city shall be established

1 Heb., *his hand hath attained and found sufficiency.*

And if any of his kin come to redeem it, then shall he redeem.—Better, *then his nearest kinsman shall come and redeem.* If he has thus been compelled by pressure of poverty to sell part of his land, then it is the duty of the nearest relation, or, as the original literally denotes, "the redeemer that is nearest to him," to redeem the property which his impoverished relative has been obliged to sell. The expression "redeemer" is applied in Hebrew to one who, by virtue of being the nearest of kin, had not only to redeem the patrimony of the family, but to marry the childless widow of his brother (Ruth iii. 13), and avenge the blood of his relative (Num. xxxv. 19—28; Deut. xix. 6—12).

(26) **And if the man have none to redeem it.**—In case, however, he has either no nearest of kin, or if his nearest of kin is himself too poor to perform this duty, which is incumbent upon him, "and himself be able to redeem it," that is, after he was compelled, by stress of poverty, to sell the property he has become prosperous, so as to be able to redeem it himself; though not distinctly expressed, it is implied that under these altered circumstances he is obliged to redeem his patrimony himself. According to the canonical law, however, he must not borrow money to redeem it.

(27) **Count the years of the sale thereof.**—To regulate the price of the redemption money the crops were valued which the purchaser had enjoyed since he had acquired the property. This was deducted from what he originally paid for the plot of land, and the difference was returned to him by the vendor, to whom the patrimony reverted. Thus, for instance, if there were thirty years from the time the purchase was effected to the year of jubile, and the vendor or his next of kin redeemed the inheritance either ten or fifteen years after the transaction, he had to return to the purchaser either one-third or half of the purchase money, when the soil was restored to the seller or his next of kin. In the interest of the purchaser, however, it was enacted during the second Temple that the redemption should not take place before he had the benefit of the field for two productive years (see verse 15), and that he could claim compensation for outlay on improvements.

Restore the overplus unto the man to whom he sold it.—That is, an equitable estimate is to be made of what the land is likely to yield from the time of its redemption by the vendor to the jubile, which is to be allowed to the purchaser.

(28) **Not able to restore it to him.**—That is, if the vendor is unable to return to the purchaser the probable value of the crops between the contemplated redemption and the next jubile year.

Then that which is sold.—In that case the land thus sold is to continue with the purchaser till jubile, when it is to revert to the vendor without any repayment whatever. The design of this law was to secure to each family a permanent interest in the soil, and to prevent the accumulation of land on the part of the greedy few who are ever anxious to join field unto field, thus precluding the existence of landless beggars and too extensive landed proprietors. To the same effect were the laws of inheritance (Num. xxvii. 6—11, xxxvi. 5—13). Similar laws obtained among other nations of antiquity. Laws were enacted that the lots which were distributed among the inhabitants were neither to be sold nor bought. Solon made it a law that no one should acquire as much land as he wished; whilst Plato held that no individual person is to possess more than four times the quantity of land than the lowest owner, who had only a single lot.

(29) **A dwelling house in a walled city.**—It is, however, quite different in the case of houses in walled cities. These are not the creation of God (see verse 23), allotted by His command to the different tribes of Israel; they are the work of man, who build them up and raze them to the ground at their own will, and according to their fancy. Hence the law of jubile does not apply to these temporary human buildings. Though an Israelite could sell his house without being driven by stress of circumstances to do it, still, as he may feel attached to his home, the Divine law affords him some protection for a limited period, during which he or his family may redeem the building. During the second Temple "a dwelling house in a walled city" was defined to be a house standing within an area of land which was first walled round for the purpose of building upon it human habitations, and in which the houses were afterwards erected. But if the houses were built first, and the city wall afterwards, they do not come within the law here laid down.

Within a full year may he redeem it.—If within a year of the sale he wishes to redeem, the Law gives him the power, or in case he dies empowers his son, to repurchase the property at the same price which he received for it. Besides limiting the period to a year, the Law does not prescribe that the next of kin is to redeem, nor give him the power to do it. During the second Temple it was also enacted that the vendor could not redeem it with borrowed money.

(30) **If it be not redeemed within the space of a full year.**—That is, either by the vendor or his son. According to the interpretation which obtained during the second Temple, the phrase "full year" is here used for the benefit of the seller, inasmuch as it gives him the advantage of an intercalary year, when he has an additional month, up to the last day of which he could still effect the redemption. Moreover, as the purchaser sometimes concealed himself towards the end of the year, in order to prevent the seller from redeeming his house, it was enacted that the original

for ever to him that bought it through-
out his generations: it shall not go out
in the jubile. (31) But the houses of the
villages which have no wall round about
them shall be counted as the fields of
the country: [1] they may be redeemed,
and they shall go out in the jubile.
(32) Notwithstanding the cities of the
Levites, *and* the houses of the cities of
their possession, may the Levites re-
deem at any time. (33) And if [2] a man
purchase of the Levites, then the house
that was sold, and the city of his pos-
session, shall go out in *the year of* jubile:
for the houses of the cities of the Levites
are their possession among the children
of Israel. (34) But the field of the
suburbs of their cities may not be sold;
for it *is* their perpetual possession.
(35) And if thy brother be waxen poor,
and [3] fallen in decay with thee; then
thou shalt [4] relieve him: *yea, though he
be* a stranger, or a sojourner; that he
may live with thee. (36) [a] Take thou no

1 Heb., *redemption belongeth unto it.*

2 Or, one *of the Levites redeem* them.

3 Heb., *his hand faileth.*

4 Heb., *strengthen.*

a Ex. 22. 25; Deut. 23. 19; Prov. 28. 8; Ezek. 18. 8 & 22. 12.

---

proprietor should hand over the redemption money to the public authorities when the purchaser could not be found, break open the doors, and take possession of the house; and if the purchaser died during the year, the vendor could redeem it from his heir.

It shall not go out in the jubile.—If the vendor, however, failed to redeem the house within the prescribed period, it was not to be subject to the laws of jubile like the land, but is to remain for ever the property of the purchaser.

(31) **But the houses of the villages which have no wall.**—Houses in villages, however, form an exception. They are part of the landed property, and hence, like the cultivated land on which they are erected, are subject to the law of jubile.

(32) **Notwithstanding the cities of the Levites, and the houses.**—Better, *And as to the cities of the Levites, the houses,* that is, the houses which belong to the Levites, in the forty-eight cities given to them (see Num. xxxv. 1—8; Josh. xxi. 1—3), are to be exempt from this general law of house property.

May the Levites redeem at any time.—Having the same value to the Levites as landed property has to the other tribes, these houses are to be subject to the jubile laws for fields, and hence may be redeemed at any time.

(33) **And if a man purchase of the Levites.**—Better, *And if one of the Levites redeem it,* that is, even if a Levite redeemed the house which his brother Levite was obliged to sell through poverty, the general law of house property is not to obtain even among the Levites themselves. They are to treat each other according to the law of landed property.

Then the house that was sold, and the city of his possession, shall go out.—Better, *then the house that was sold in the city of his possession shall go out,* that is, in the year of jubile the house is to revert to the vendor just as if it were landed property. Thus, for instance, the house of the Levite A, which he, out of poverty, was obliged to sell to the non-Levite B, and which was redeemed from him by a Levite C, reverts in the jubile year from the Levite C to the original Levitical proprietor A. It is, however, more than probable that the negative particle has dropped out of the text, and that the passage as it originally stood was, "And if one of the Levites doth not redeem it." That is, if he does not act the part of the nearest of kin, then the house reverts in the year of jubile to the original Levitical owner, just as landed property. The Vulg. has still the negative particle.

For the houses of the cities of the Levites are their possession.—As these houses were all which the Levites possessed, they were as important to them as the land was to the other tribes, hence they were to be treated legally in the same way as the soil.

(34) **But the field of the suburbs of their cities may not be sold.**—The Levitical cities had both suburbs or commons for their cattle, &c., and fields which they cultivated (Num. xxxv. 4, 5). These outlying fields, which were beyond the suburbs, they are here forbidden to sell. According to the authorities during the second Temple the expression "to sell" here used is to be taken in a wider sense as including diverting any part of it from its original purpose. Hence they say it forbids the Levites not only to sell the field, but to convert it into a suburb, and *vice versâ.* What is field must always remain field, what is suburb must remain suburb, and what is city must continue to be city.

For it is their perpetual possession.—The estates belong to the whole tribe to all futurity, and the present occupiers have to transmit them intact to their successors. Hence no present owner, or all of them combined, have a right to dispose of any portion of the estates, or materially to alter it. They must hand these estates down to their successors as they receive them from their predecessors.

(35) **And if thy brother be waxen poor.**—This part of the jubile laws which relates to the manumission of the Israelites who through poverty are compelled to sell themselves as bondsmen (verses 39—55) is introduced by a pathetic appeal to the benevolence of the people to bestow brotherly help to the poor (verses 35—38).

And fallen in decay with thee.—Literally, *and his hand wavered with thee,* that is, when it is weak and can no longer render support, or gain a livelihood. As the laws of jubile guard the future interests of the Israelite who is driven by stress of poverty to sell his patrimony, the Lawgiver now points out the duties of each member of the community to the impoverished brother who has to wait till the year of jubile for the restoration of his property, but who in the meantime is unable to support himself.

Then thou shalt relieve him.—Literally, *thou shalt lay hold of him.* When his hand is thus trembling, it is the duty of every Israelite to support his weak hand, and enable it to gain a livelihood.

Though he be a stranger, or a sojourner.—Better, *as a stranger and a sojourner,* that is, he is not to be treated like an outcast because he has been compelled by poverty to sell his patrimony, but is to receive the same consideration which strangers and sojourners receive, who, like the unfortunate Israelite, have no landed property. (See chap. xix. 33, 34.)

(36) **Take thou no usury of him, or increase.**—The first thing to be done to the impoverished

usury of him, or increase: but fear thy
God; that thy brother may live with
thee. (37) Thou shalt not give him thy
money upon usury, nor lend him thy
victuals for increase. (38) I *am* the
Lord your God, which brought you
forth out of the land of Egypt, to give
you the land of Canaan, *and* to be your
God.

(39) And [a] if thy brother *that dwelleth*
by thee be waxen poor, and be sold unto
thee; thou shalt not [1] compel him to
serve as a bondservant: (40) *but* as an
hired servant, *and* as a sojourner, he
shall be with thee, *and* shall serve thee
unto the year of jubile: (41) and *then*
shall he depart from thee, *both* he and
his children with him, and shall return
unto his own family, and unto the pos-
session of his fathers shall he return.
(42) For they *are* my servants, which I
brought forth out of the land of Egypt:
they shall not be sold [2] as bondmen.
(43) [b] Thou shalt not rule over him with
rigour; but shalt fear thy God. (44) Both
thy bondmen, and thy bondmaids, which
thou shalt have, *shall be* of the heathen
that are round about you; of them
shall ye buy bondmen and bondmaids.
(45) Moreover of the children of the stran-
gers that do sojourn among you, of
them shall ye buy, and of their families

a Ex. 21. 2; Deut. 15. 12; Jer. 34. 14.

1 Heb., *serve thyself with him with the service, &c.*

2 Heb., *with the sale of a bondman.*

b Eph. 6. 9; Col. 4. 1.

Israelite is to supply him with the means to recover himself without any interest. The authorities during the second Temple defined the words which are translated "usury" (*neshech*) and "increase" (*tarbith*, or *marbith*) as follows: If a person lends to another a shekel worth four denarii, and gets in return five denarii, or if he lends him two sacks of wheat, and receives back three, this is usury. If one buys wheat for delivery at the market price of 25 denarii a measure, and when it rises to 30 denarii he says to the vendor, "Deliver me the wheat, for I want to sell it and buy wine," and the vendor replies, "I will take the wheat at 30 denarii and give thee wine for it," though he has no wine, this is increase. The "increase" lies in the fact that the vendor has no wine at the time, and that he may possibly lose again by the rise in wine. Accordingly the former is a charge upon money, whilst the latter is on products.

(37) **Thou shalt not give him.**—This is simply an emphatic repetition of the declaration in the foregoing verse, and favours the ancient distinction between the two terms.

(38) **Which brought you forth out of the land of Egypt.**—For this appeal to the signal act of redemption from Egypt, see chap. xii. 45.

(39) **And if thy brother that dwelleth by thee be waxen poor.**—Better, *And if thy brother be waxen poor by thee,* that is, after supporting his tottering hand, as prescribed in verses 35—38, and making all the charitable efforts to help him, they fail, and he still finds himself in extreme poverty, and unable to obtain a livelihood.

And be sold unto thee.—The voluntary disposal of his own liberty for a money consideration the Israelite could only effect by stress of poverty.

Thou shalt not compel him to serve as a bondservant.—Under these circumstances he is not to be treated like heathen slaves who are either purchased or captured, and made to do the menial service which these Gentile slaves have to perform. The authorities during the second Temple adduce the following as degrading work which the Israelite bondman is not to be put to: He must not attend his master at his bath, nor tie up or undo the latchets of his sandals, &c., &c.

(40) **But as an hired servant.**—The master is in all respects to treat him as one who disposes of his service for wages for a certain time, and will then be his own master again.

Shall serve thee unto the year of jubile.—Nor could he be kept beyond the year of jubile. This terminated the sale of his services just as it cancelled all the sales of landed property.

(41) **And then shall he depart from thee.**—At the same time that he regains his liberty, and takes with him his family, the patrimony which he sold also reverts to him.

(42) **For they are my servants.**—This is a clue to the whole system of Hebrew servitude. These poverty-stricken men, who are driven to sell themselves to their fellow-Israelites, God claims as His servants. God is their Lord as well as their master's Lord. He delivered them both alike from bondage to serve Him. There is, therefore, no difference between bond and free.

They shall not be sold as bondmen—That is, as personal property or chattels. The authorities during the second Temple, however, interpreted this clause to mean that an Israelite is not to be sold by proclamation or in public places, but privately, and in an honourable manner, with all possible consideration for his feelings.

(43) **Thou shalt not rule over him with rigour.**—The master is forbidden to tyrannise over him as if he were a slave without any rights.

(44) **Both thy bondmen, and thy bondmaids, which thou shalt have, shall be of the heathen.**—Rather, *As for thy bondmen and bondmaids which thou must have of the heathen,* &c. As the Law forbids the Israelites to have their brethren as bondmen, or employ them in menial work which belongs to the slaves, the Lawgiver anticipates a difficulty which the Hebrews might raise against these enactments. If they are not to be engaged in this work, who then is to do it? Hence the reply in the verse before us.

Of the heathen that are round about you.—These are to be purchased to do the necessary work. The Israelites, however, were restricted to the Ammonites, the Moabites, the Edomites, and the Syrians, who were their neighbours, but were not permitted to buy any slaves from the seven nations who were in the midst of them, and whom they were ordered to destroy (Deut. xx. 16—18).

(45) **Moreover of the children of the strangers.**—Besides the surrounding nations, the Hebrews are also permitted to obtain their slaves from those strangers who have taken up their abode in the Holy Land. By these strangers the ancient authorities understand

that *are* with you, which they begat in
your land: and they shall be your pos-
session. (46) And ye shall take them as
an inheritance for your children after
you, to inherit *them for* a possession;
[1] they shall be your bondmen for ever:
but over your brethren the children of
Israel, ye shall not rule one over another
with rigour.
(47) And if a sojourner or stranger [2] wax
rich by thee, and thy brother *that
dwelleth* by him wax poor, and sell him-
self unto the stranger *or* sojourner by
thee, or to the stock of the stranger's
family: (48) after that he is sold he may
be redeemed again; one of his brethren
may redeem him: (49) either his uncle,
or his uncle's son, may redeem him, or
any that is nigh of kin unto him of his
family may redeem him; or if he be
able, he may redeem himself. (50) And
he shall reckon with him that bought
him from the year that he was sold to
him unto the year of jubile: and the
price of his sale shall be according unto
the number of years, according to the
time of an hired servant shall it be with
him. (51) If *there be* yet many years *be-
hind*, according unto them he shall give
again the price of his redemption out
of the money that he was bought for.
(52) And if there remain but few years
unto the year of jubile, then he shall
count with him, *and* according unto his

1 Heb., *ye shall serve yourselves with them.*

2 Heb., *his hand obtain, &c.*

---

those who have been permitted to settle down among the Jews on condition that they submit to the seven commandments given to Noah, but have not embraced Judaism. Hence the Chaldee Version translates this phrase, "the children of uncircumcised strangers."

And they shall be your possession.—These, but not the Hebrews, the masters may hold as their absolute property.

(46) **And ye shall take them as an inheritance for your children.**—That is, they may appropriate them to themselves, as their personal property, which is transmissible as inheritance to posterity with the family land.

They shall be your bondmen for ever.—These are not subject to the laws of jubile. They remain in perpetual serfdom unless they or their friends redeem them, or their master has maimed any one of them. In case of injury the master is obliged to manumit him (Exod. xxi. 26, 27). The authorities during the second Temple enacted that the master's right, even with regard to this kind of bondmen, is restricted to their labour, but that he has no right to barter with them, to misuse them, or to put them to shame.

Over your brethren . . . . ye shall not rule . . . . with rigour.—In contrast to these heathen bondmen the Jewish bondmen are here designated "brethren." They are co-religionists, who have been reduced to temporary servitude, but who are, nevertheless, fellow-heirs with them in the land of their possession. Hence the greatest consideration was to be shown to them in these adverse circumstances. The authorities during the second Temple have therefore enacted that there must be no difference between the daily food, raiment, and dwelling of the master and his Hebrew slave, and that the master and the servant are alike in these respects.

(47) **And if a sojourner or stranger wax rich by thee.**—Better, *And if the hand of a stranger, and that a sojourner, attain riches by thee,* that is, a stranger who has become a sojourner, or who has taken up his abode among the Israelites, and become prosperous by trading. Such a one had only to submit to the seven commandments given to Noah, and hence had not joined the Jewish religion. For this reason the Chaldee Version translates it, "And if the hand of an uncircumcised sojourner with thee wax strong."

And thy brother that dwelleth by him wax poor.—Better, *and thy brother by him wax poor,* that is, the Israelite who traded with him is unfortunate in business, and is reduced to poverty.

And sell himself unto the stranger or sojourner by thee.—Better, *and sells himself unto the stranger-sojourner by thee.* The two terms as before describe the same person—the stranger who has become a sojourner. Hence the Chaldee Version translates it, "and sells himself to the uncircumcised stranger who is with thee."

Or to the stock of the stranger's family.—That is, the offshoot or descendant of a foreign family.

(48) **He may be redeemed again.**—The law which applies to a heathen who sold himself to a Hebrew is reversed in this case. Whilst the heathen cannot be redeemed, and is to remain a bondman for ever, the Israelite who sells himself to a heathen may be redeemed. Indeed, according to the interpretation which obtained during the second Temple, this passage enjoins it upon his relations and the congregation to redeem him as soon as possible. Hence the ancient Chaldee Version translates it, "his redemption must be effected forthwith."

(49) **Either his uncle, or his uncle's son, may redeem him.**—That is, any of his relatives are to redeem him, which is not the case when an Israelite sells himself to one of his own nation. Hence the Jewish canons enacted that "if a Hebrew is sold to a stranger, and is unable to redeem himself, his kinsmen must redeem, nay, the Sanhedrin are to compel his kinsmen to redeem him lest he should be lost among the heathen. If his kindred do not redeem him, and if he cannot redeem himself, every man of Israel is commanded to redeem him. But if he is sold to an Israelite his kindred may not redeem him, nor may he borrow money to redeem himself, nor redeem himself by instalments." In accordance with this injunction we find the Jews declare "we after our ability have redeemed our brethren the Jews which were sold unto the heathen, and will ye even sell your brethren, or shall they be sold unto us?" (Neh. v. 8).

(50—52) **And he shall reckon with him.**—That is, either the man himself when he is able to redeem himself, or his kindred. The authorities during the second Temple rightly point out that this passage enjoins the Hebrew to treat the heathen master fairly

years shall he give him again the price
of his redemption. (53) *And* as a yearly
hired servant shall he be with him: *and*
the other shall not rule with rigour over
him in thy sight. (54) And if he be not
redeemed [1] in these *years*, then he shall
go out in the year of jubile, *both* he,
and his children with him. (55) For unto
me the children of Israel *are* servants;
they *are* my servants whom I brought
forth out of the land of Egypt: I *am*
the LORD your God.

CHAPTER XXVI. — (1) Ye shall
make you [a] no idols nor graven image,
neither rear you up a [2] standing image,
neither shall ye set up *any* [3] [4] image
of stone in your land, to bow down
unto it: for I *am* the LORD your
God.

(2) [b] Ye shall keep my sabbaths,
and reverence my sanctuary: I *am* the
LORD.

(3) [c] If ye walk in my statutes, and
keep my commandments, and do them;

1 Or, *by these means.*

a Ex. 20. 4; Deut. 5. 8 & 16. 22; Ps. 97. 7.

2 Or, *pillar.*

3 Or, *figured stone.*

4 Heb., *a stone of picture.*

b ch. 19. 30.

c Deut. 28. 1.

---

by duly compensating and compounding for the number of years he has still to serve till jubile, and to take no advantage of the idolater.

(53) **And as a yearly hired servant shall he be.**—Better, *As a yearly servant*, &c., without the "and," which is not in the original, and is not wanted. That is, as long as he is in service his master must not treat him like a slave, but is to behave to him as if he were simply one who hires out his services from year to year, and who, after a short time, will be his own master again.

And the other shall not rule with rigour over him.—Better, *he shall not rule*, &c., that is, the heathen master. The words "and the other" are not in the original, and the sense of the passage is quite plain without them.

In thy sight.—The Israelite is here admonished not to be a tacit spectator of the cruel treatment of his brother Israelite by a heathen master, and though he is not to resent in the same way in which the Lawgiver himself resented it (Exod. ii. 11, 12), still he is to remonstrate with the cruel Gentile, and invoke the protection of the powers that be.

(54) **If he be not redeemed in these years.**—Better, *If he be not redeemed by these*, that is, by the relations or the means indicated in verses 48 and 49, he is to go out free in the year of jubile. (See verse 41.) The heathen is to submit to the laws of jubile as much as the Hebrew.

(55) **For unto me the children of Israel are servants.**—See verses 38, 42.

XXVI.

(1) **Ye shall make you no idols.**—The first two verses of this chapter are still a part of the previous section in the Hebrew original. By separating them from their proper position, and making them begin a new chapter, both the logical sequence and the import of these two verses are greatly obscured. As verses 47—55 legislated for cases where Israelites are driven by extreme poverty to sell themselves to a heathen, and when they may be compelled to continue in this service to the year of jubile, and thus be obliged to witness idolatrous practices, the Lawgiver solemnly repeats the two fundamental precepts of Judaism, which they might be in danger of neglecting, viz., to abstain from idol-worship and to keep the Sabbath, which are two essential commandments of the Decalogue. The same two commandments, but in reverse order, are also joined together in chap. xix. 3, 4.

Idols.—For this expression see chap. xix. 4.

Nor graven image, neither rear you up a standing image.—Better, *nor shall ye rear you up a graven image or pillar.* Graven image is not only a plastic image of a heathen deity, but a visible or sensuous representation of the God of Israel (Exod. xx. 19, 20; Deut. iv. 15, 16).

A standing image.—This expression, which only occurs once more in the text of the Authorised Version (Micah v. 13), and four times in the Margin (1 Kings xiv. 23; Jer. xliii. 13; Hosea iii. 4, x. 1), is the rendering of a Hebrew word (*matzebah*), which is usually and more correctly translated "pillar," or "statue" (Gen. xxviii. 18, 22, xxxi. 13, &c.). This was a plain and rude stone without any image engraved on it, and was not unfrequently erected to God himself, but in after-time more especially as a memorial to false deities. (Gen. xxviii. 18, 22, xxxi. 13, xxxv. 14, with Exod. xxiii. 24, xxxiv. 13, &c.)

Neither shall ye set up any image of stone.—The authorities during the second Temple interpreted the words here rendered "images of stone" to denote *beholding*, or *worshipping stones*—*i.e.*, stones set in the ground in places of worship upon which the worshippers prostrated themselves to perform their devotions. The stone was therefore a kind of signal, calling the attention of the worshipper to itself, so that he may fall down upon it. With such stones, these authorities assure us, the Temple was paved, since they were perfectly lawful in the sanctuary, but must not be used in worship out of the Temple, or rather, out of the land, as these authorities understood the words "in your land" here to denote. Hence the Chaldee Version paraphrases it, "and a painted stone ye shall not place in your land to prostrate yourselves upon it, but a pavement adorned with figures and pictures ye may put in the floor of your sanctuary, but not to bow down upon it," *i.e.*, in an idolatrous manner. Hence, too, the ancient canon, "in your own land" (*i.e.*, in all other lands) "ye must not prostrate yourselves upon stones, but ye may prostrate yourselves upon the stones in the sanctuary."

(2) **Ye shall keep my sabbaths . . .**—This is exactly the same precept laid down in chap xix. 30, and is here repeated because of the danger of desecrating the Sabbath to which the Israelite is exposed who sells himself to a heathen. The Israelite will effectually guard against idol-worship, by keeping the Sabbath holy, and reverencing God's sanctuary.

(3) **If ye walk in my statutes.**—We have already remarked that this verse begins the section in the Hebrew and ought to have begun the chapter in English. Having set forth the ceremonial and moral injunctions which are necessary for the development and maintenance of holiness and purity in the commonwealth, the legislator now concludes by showing the happiness which will accrue to the Israelites from a faithful observance of these laws, and the punishments

(4) then I will give you rain in due sea-
son, and the land shall yield her increase,
and the trees of the field shall yield
their fruit. (5) And your threshing
shall reach unto the vintage, and the
vintage shall reach unto the sowing
time: and ye shall eat your bread to
the full, and [a]dwell in your land safely.
(6) And I will give peace in the land,
and ye shall lie down, and none shall
make *you* afraid: and I will [1]rid evil
beasts out of the land, [b]neither shall
the sword go through your land.
(7) And ye shall chase your enemies, and
they shall fall before you by the sword.
(8) And [c]five of you shall chase an
hundred, and an hundred of you shall
put ten thousand to flight: and your
enemies shall fall before you by the
sword. (9) For I will have respect unto
you, and make you fruitful, and multi-
ply you, and establish my covenant with
you. (10) And ye shall eat old store, and
bring forth the old because of the new.
(11) [d]And I will set my tabernacle among
you: and my soul shall not abhor you.
(12) [e]And I will walk among you, and
will be your God, and ye shall be my
people. (13) I *am* the LORD your God,
which brought you forth out of the
land of Egypt, that ye should not be
their bondmen; and I have broken the
bands of your yoke, and made you go
upright.

a Job 11. 19.

1 Heb., *cause to cease.*

b Job 11. 19.

c Josh. 23. 10.

d Ezek. 37. 26.

e 2 Cor. 6. 16.

---

which await them if they transgress these Divine ordinances.

(4) **Then I will give you rain in due season.**—Better, *then I will give you your rains in due season,* that is, the former and latter rains (Deut. xi. 14). In Palestine the proper season for the early rain is from about the middle of October until December, thus preparing the ground for receiving the seed, whilst that of the latter or vernal rain is in the months of March and April, just before the harvest. Thus, also, in the covenant which God is to make with His people, a similar promise is made. "I will cause the showers to come down in his season; there shall be showers of blessing" (Ezek. xxxiv. 26).

(5) **And your threshing shall reach unto the vintage.**—That is, the corn crop shall be so plentiful that those who shall be employed in threshing about the month of March will not complete it before the vintage, which was about the month of July.

The vintage shall reach unto the sowing time.—The wine, again, is to be so abundant that those who shall be engaged in gathering and pressing the grapes will not be able to finish before the sowing time again arrives, which is about the month of October. A similar promise is made by Amos: "the plowman shall overtake the reaper, and the treader of grapes him who sowed seed" (Amos ix. 13).

(6) **And I will give peace.**—Not only are they to have rich harvests, but the Lord will grant them peace among themselves, so that they shall be able to retire at night without any anxiety, or fear of robbers (Pss. iii. 5, iv. 8).

I will rid evil beasts out of the land.—The promise to destroy the beasts of prey, which endanger life, and which abounded in Palestine, is also to be found in Ezekiel, where exactly the same words are rendered in the Authorised Version, "And will cause the evil beasts to cease out of the land" (Ezek. xxxiv. 25). The two passages should be uniform in the translation.

(7) **And ye shall chase your enemies.**—If, covetous of their prosperity, the enemies should dare to attack them, God will inspire His people with marvellous courage, so that they will not only pursue them, but put them to the sword.

(8) **And five of you shall chase an hundred.**—This is a proverbial saying, corresponding to our phrase "A very small number, or a mere handful, shall be more than a match for a whole regiment." The same phrase, with different proportions to the numbers, occurs in other parts of the Bible (Deut. xxxii. 30; Josh. xxiii. 10; Isa. xxx. 17).

(9) **For I will have respect unto you.**—Better, *And I will turn unto you,* as it is rendered in the Authorised Version in Ezek. xlvi. 9, the only other passage where this phrase occurs; that is, be merciful to them and bless them. (Comp. 2 Kings xiii. 23; Ps. xxv. 16, lxix. 17, &c.)

And multiply you, and establish my covenant with you.—That is, by multiplying them as the stars of heaven and the sand of the sea, God fulfil the covenant which He made with their fathers (Gen. xii. 2, xiii. 16, xv. 5, xxii. 17; Exod. xxiii. 26).

(10) **And ye shall eat old store.**—Better, *old store which hath become old.* Though they will thus multiply, there shall be abundant stores for them, which become old because it will take them so long to consume them.

And bring forth the old because of the new.—Better, *and remove the old on account of the new,* that is, they will always have such abundant harvests that they will be obliged to remove from the barns and garners the old stock of corn, in order to make room for the new.

(11) **And I will set my tabernacle among you.**—Better, *And I will set my dwelling-place among you.* (See chap. xv. 31.) Not only will God bless them with these material blessings, but will permanently abide with them in the sanctuary erected in their midst.

My soul shall not abhor you.—That is, God has no aversion to them; does not regard it below His dignity to sojourn amongst them, and to show them His favour.

(12) **And I will walk among you.**—This promise is quoted by St. Paul (2 Cor. vi. 16).

(13) **I have broken the bands of your yoke.**—The promises thus made to the Israelites of the extraordinary fertility of their land, of peace within and immunity from war without, and of the Divine presence constantly sojourning amongst them, if they will faithfully obey the commandments of the Lord, now conclude with the oft-repeated solemn appeal to the obligation they are under to the God who had so marvellously

(14) [a] But if ye will not hearken unto
me, and will not do all these commandments; (15) and if ye shall despise my
statutes, or if your soul abhor my judgments, so that ye will not do all my
commandments, *but* that ye break my
covenant: (16) I also will do this unto
you; I will even appoint [1] over you
terror, consumption, and the burning
ague, that shall consume the eyes, and
cause sorrow of heart: and ye shall sow
your seed in vain, for your enemies shall
eat it. (17) And I will set my face
against you, and ye shall be slain before
your enemies: they that hate you shall
reign over you; and [b] ye shall flee when
none pursueth you.
(18) And if ye will not yet for all this
hearken unto me, then I will punish you
seven times more for your sins. (19) And
I will break the pride of your power;
and I will make your heaven as iron,

[a] Deut. 28. 15; Lam. 2. 17; Mal. 2. 2.

[1] Heb., *upon you.*

[b] Prov. 28. 1.

---

delivered them from cruel bondage and made them His servants. To remind them of the abject state from which they were rescued, the illustration is taken from the way in which oxen are still harnessed in the East. The bands or the rods are straight pieces of wood, which are inserted in the yoke, or laid across the necks of the animals, to fasten together their heads and keep them level with each other. These bands, which are then attached to the pole of the waggon, are not only oppressive, but exhibit the beasts as perfectly helpless to resist the cruel treatment of the driver. This phrase is often used to denote oppression and tyranny (Deut. xxviii. 48; Isa. ix. 3, x. 27, xiv. 25, &c.), but nowhere are the words as like those in the passage before us as in Ezek. xxxiv. 27.

(14) **But if ye will not hearken unto me.**—The glowing promises of blessings for obedience are now followed by a catalogue of calamities of the most appalling nature, which will overtake the Israelites if they disobey the Divine commandments. The first degree of punishment with which this verse begins extends to verse 17.

(15) **And if ye shall despise my statutes.**—From passive indifference to the Divine statutes mentioned in the preceding verse, their falling away is sure to follow. Hence what was at first mere listlessness now develops itself into a contemptuous rejection of God's ordinances.

Or if your soul abhor my judgments.—Better, *and if your soul*, &c., as the picture of their apostasy goes on developing itself.

But that ye break my covenant.—Better, *that ye break*, &c., without the "but," which is not in the original, and obscures the sense of the passage, since it is the fact of their abhorrence of God's law which breaks the Divine covenant with them. (See Gen. xvii. 14.) The sense is more correctly given by rendering this clause "Thus breaking my covenant," or "Thereby breaking my covenant."

(16) **I also will do this unto you.**—That is, He will do the same unto them; He will requite them in the same way, and abhor them.

I will even appoint over you terror.—Better, *and I will appoint*, &c., that is, God will visit them with terrible things, consisting of consumption and burning ague. These two diseases also occur together in Deut. xxviii. 22, the only passage in the Bible where they occur again. The second of the two, however, which is here translated "burning ague" in the Authorised Version, is, in the Deuteronomy passage, rendered simply by "fever." The two passages ought to be uniformly rendered.

That shall consume the eyes, and cause sorrow of heart.—Better, *that shall extinguish the eyes, and cause life to waste away.* The rendering of the Authorised Version, "consume the eyes," though giving the sense, is misleading, inasmuch as it suggests that the verb "consume" is the same as the disease, "consumption" mentioned in the preceding clause. For the phrase "extinguish the eye"—the eye failing—see Job xi. 20, xvii. 5, xxxi. 16, &c., and for the whole phrase, comp. Deut. xxviii. 65; 1 Sam. ii. 23.

And ye shall sow your seed in vain, for your enemies shall eat it.—Besides these terrible diseases, the production of the soil, which is necessary for the sustenance of life, and which is to be so abundant and secure against enemies when the Israelites obey the Divine commandments (see verses 4—6), will be carried off by strangers. Similar threatenings in case of disobedience are to be found both in the Pentateuch (Deut. xxviii, 33, 51) and in the prophets (Jer. v. 17). The most striking parallel is the one in Micah, "Thou shalt sow, but thou shalt not reap; thou shalt tread the olives, but thou shalt not anoint thee with oil" (Micah vi. 15). For the reverse state of things, see Isa. lxii. 8, lxv. 22, 23.

(17) **And I will set my face against you.**—That is, make them feel his anger. (See Note on chap. xvii. 10.)

Be slain before your enemies.—Better, *be smitten before your enemies*, as this phrase is rendered in the Authorised Version (Num. xiv. 42; Deut. i. 42, xxviii. 25).

Shall reign over you.—Better, *shall rule over you*, as the Authorised Version renders it in Isa. xiv. 2; Ezek. xxix. 15, xxxiv. 4, &c.

(18) **And if ye will not yet for all this hearken unto me.**—Better, *and if up to these ye will not hearken unto me*, that is, if they should persist in their disobedience to the very end of those punishments mentioned in verses 16 and 17. This verse, therefore, introduces the second degree of punishments, which ends with verse 20.

I will punish you seven times more.—That is, indefinitely or unceasingly; many more times. Seven being a complete number is often used to denote thoroughness (see Note on chap. iv. 6), a large or indefinite number. Hence the declaration "He shall deliver thee in six troubles; yea, in seven there shall no evil touch thee" (Job v. 19), and "if he trespass against thee seven times in a day" (Luke xvii. 4), that is, an indefinite number of times. (Comp. also Ps. cxix. 164; Prov. xxiv. 16, &c.)

(19) **And I will break the pride of your power.**—That is, the strength which is the cause of your pride, the wealth which they derive from the abundant harvests mentioned in verses 4 and 5, as is evident from what follows immediately, where the punishment is threatened against the resources of this power or wealth. Comp. Ezek. xxx. 6, xxxiii. 28.) The authorities

and your earth as brass: (20) and your
strength shall be spent in vain: for your
land shall not yield her increase, neither
shall the trees of the land yield their
fruits.

(21) And if ye walk [1] contrary unto me,
and will not hearken unto me; I will
bring seven times more plagues upon
you according to your sins. (22) I will
also send wild beasts among you, which
shall rob you of your children, and destroy your cattle, and make you few in
number; and your *high* ways shall be
desolate.

(23) And if ye will not be reformed by
me by these things, but will walk contrary unto me; (24) [a] then will I also walk
contrary unto you, and will punish you
yet seven times for your sins. (25) And I
will bring a sword upon you, that shall
avenge the quarrel of *my* covenant: and
when ye are gathered together within
your cities, I will send the pestilence
among you; and ye shall be delivered
into the hand of the enemy. (26) *And*
when I have broken the staff of your
bread, ten women shall bake your bread
in one oven, and they shall deliver *you*
your bread again by weight: and ye
shall eat, and not be satisfied.

1 Or, *at all adventures with me*, and so ver. 24.

a 2 Sam 22. 27; Ps. 18. 26.

---

during the second Temple, however, took the phrase "the pride of your power" to denote the sanctuary, which is called "the pride of your power" in Ezek. xxiv. 21, the expression used here, but the identity of which is obliterated in the Authorised Version by rendering the phrase "the excellency of your strength." Hence the Chaldee Versions paraphrase it, "And I will break down the glory of the strength of your sanctuary."

I will make your heaven as iron.—That is, the heaven which is over them shall yield no more rain than if it were of metal. In Deut. xxviii. 23, where the same punishment is threatened, and the same figure is used, the metals are reversed, the heaven is brass, and the earth iron.

(20) **And your strength shall be spent in vain.**—That is, with the heaven over them as metal, their labour expended in ploughing, digging, and sowing will be perfectly useless.

Your land shall not yield her increase, as no amount of human labour will make up for the want of rain. In Deut. xi. 17, where the same punishment is threatened, and the same phrase is used, the Authorised Version unnecessarily obliterates the identity of the words in the original by rendering them "the land yield not *her fruit*."

(21) **And if ye walk contrary unto me.**—That is, continue the defiance of the Divine law, and rebel against God's authority. The third warning, contained in verses 21, 22, threatens them with destruction by wild beasts.

Seven times more plagues.—That is, a still greater number. (See verse 18.)

According to your sins.—This increased number of scourges will be in proportion to their sins, since their defiance, in spite of the two preceding classes of punishments, aggravates and enhances their guilt.

(22) **I will also send wild beasts.**—Better, *and I will send wild beasts.* Wild beasts, which abounded in Palestine (Exod. xxiii. 29), are used as a punishment for sin (Deut. xxxii. 24; 2 Kings xvii. 25; Isa. xiii. 21, 22; Ezek. xiv. 15, &c.).

(23) **And if ye will not be reformed.**—The fourth warning (verses 23—26) threatens the rebellious Israelites with a more intensified form of the punishment partially mentioned in the first warning. (See verse 17.)

(24) **Then will I also walk contrary unto you.**—By their increased hostility to God, they simply increase their calamities, since He whom they are defying now also assumes a hostile attitude towards those who are defiant.

And will punish you yet.—Better, *and I also will smite you.* (See verse 28.)

(25) **That shall avenge the quarrel of my covenant.**—Better, *that shall avenge my covenant*, that is, the sword, which shall avenge the breach of the Divine covenant; a war, which will devastate them because of their rebellion against the covenant God. Hence the Chaldee Versions render it, "that shall avenge on you the vengeance for that ye have transgressed against the words of the law."

And when ye are gathered together within your cities.—When, completely defeated in the battle-field, the Israelites escape from the avenging sword into their fortified cities, they will then become a prey to pestilence, so that the surviving remnant will prefer to deliver themselves over into the hands of the relentless enemy. (Comp. Jer. xxi. 6—9; Ezek. v. 12, vii. 15.)

(26) **And when I have broken the staff of your bread.**—Better, *when I break you the staff of bread*, that is, when God cuts off their supply of bread, which is the staff of life. "To break the staff of bread" denotes to take away or to destroy the staff or the support which bread is to man. This metaphor also occurs in other parts of Scripture (Isa. iii. 1; Ezek. iv. 16, v. 16, xiv. 13; Ps. cv. 16). This, in addition to the pestilence in the cities, which will drive them to deliver themselves up to the enemy, or rather the cause of this pestilence will be the famine which will rage in the town whither they fled for protection.

Ten women shall bake your bread in one oven.—Better, *then ten women*, &c., that is, so great will be the famine when God cuts off the supply, that one ordinary oven will suffice to bake the bread of ten families, who are represented by their ten women, whilst in ordinary times one oven was only sufficient for one family.

And they shall deliver you your bread again by weight.—When it is brought from the bake-house each one will not be allowed to eat as much as he requires, but will have his stinted allowance most carefully served out to him by weight. Parallel to this picture of misery is the appalling scene described by Ezekiel, "I will break the staff of bread in Jerusalem, and they shall eat bread by weight, and with care, and they shall drink water by measure, and with astonishment; that they may want bread and water, and be astonished one with another, and consume away for their iniquity" (Ezek. iv. 16, 17).

(27) And if ye will not for all this
hearken unto me, but walk contrary
unto me; (28) then I will walk contrary
unto you also in fury; and I, even I, will
chastise you seven times for your sins.
(29) [a] And ye shall eat the flesh of your
sons, and the flesh of your daughters
shall ye eat. (30) And I will destroy
your high places, and [b] cut down your
images, and cast your carcases upon the
carcases of your idols, and my soul shall
abhor you. (31) And I will make your
cities waste, and bring your sanctuaries
unto desolation, and I will not smell the
savour of your sweet odours. (32) And I
will bring the land into desolation: and
your enemies which dwell therein shall
be astonished at it. (33) And I will
scatter you among the heathen, and will
draw out a sword after you: and your
land shall be desolate, and your cities
waste.

a Deut. 28. 53.

b 2 Chron. 34. 7.

---

(27) **And if he will not for all this hearken unto me.**—Better, *And if, notwithstanding these, ye will not hearken unto me,* that is, if in spite of these awful punishments they persist in rebellion against God. With this reiterated formula the fifth warning is introduced (verses 27—33), which threatens the total destruction of the land and the people in the midst of the most appalling horrors.

(28) **Then I will walk contrary unto you also in fury.**—Whilst in verse 24 the persistent rebellion is responded to on the part of the defied God in the simple words, "then will I also work contrary unto you," we have here the addition "in fury" as the provocation is more intense.

And I, even I, will chastise you.—Better, *And I also will chastise you.* The verb here is different from the one in verse 24.

(29) **And ye shall eat the flesh of your sons.**—The harrowing scene here described is also depicted in Deut. xxviii. 53—57. This prediction actually came to pass at the siege of Samaria by the Syrians (2 Kings vi. 28, 29), and at the siege of Jerusalem by the Chaldæans, which Jeremiah thus bewails, "the hands of pitiful women have sodden their own children, they were their meat in the destruction of the daughter of my people" (Lam. iv. 10; comp. also Jer. xix. 9; Ezek. v. 10; Zech. xi. 9, &c.). This also happened at the siege of Jerusalem by Titus. A woman named Mary killed her infant child and boiled it during the height of the famine, and after she had eaten part of it, the soldiers found the rest in her house.

(30) **And I will destroy your high places.**—Though these eminences were also used for the worship of Jehovah (Judges vi. 25, 26, xiii. 16—23; 1 Sam. vii. 10; 1 Kings iii. 2; 2 Kings xii. 3; 1 Chron. xxi. 26, &c.), the context shows that the high places here are such as were dedicated to idolatrous worship (Num. xxii. 41, xxxiii. 52; Deut. xii. 2; Josh. xiii. 17, &c.). By the destruction of these places of idolatrous worship, the Israelites would see how utterly worthless those deities were whom they preferred to the God who had wrought such signal redemption for them.

And cut down your images.—Better, *and cut down your sun-images,* or *solar-statues,* that is, idolatrous pillars of the sun-god (Isa. xvii. 8; 2 Chron. xiv. 5, xxxiv. 7).

And cast your carcases upon the carcases of your idols.—Nothing could show a greater contempt both for the idol-worshippers and the idols than the picture here given. When the apostate Israelites have succumbed to the sword, famine, and pestilence, they will not even have a seemly burial, but their carcases will be mixed up with the shattered remains of their gods, and thus form one dunghill. Similar is the picture given by Ezekiel, "Your altars shall be desolate, and your images shall be broken, and I will cast down your slain men before your idols, and I will lay the dead carcases of the children of Israel before their idols, and I will scatter your bones round about your altars" (Ezek. vi. 4, 5).

(31) **I will make your cities waste.**—Not only will the elevated spots outside the cities with their idols be destroyed, and the carcases of the deluded worshippers be scattered among their remains, but the cities themselves will be converted into ruins and desolations (Jer. iv. 7, ix. 11; Ezek. vi. 6, xii. 20; Neh. ii. 17, &c.).

And bring your sanctuaries unto desolation.—Even the sanctuary with all its holy places (Jer. li. 51; Ezek. xxi. 7; Amos vii. 9; Pss. lxviii. 36, lxxiv. 7. &c.), sacred edifices, synagogues, &c. (chap. xxi. 23), will not be spared, God thus reversing the promise which He made to the Israelites, that He will set up His dwelling place in the midst of them (see verse 11) if they will walk according to His commandments.

I will not smell the savour of your sweet odours.—When this awful destruction of the sanctuary is to take place God will not regard the fact that the odour of sweet sacrifices is there being offered up. (See chap. i. 9.) The service which may then be performed to Him will not hinder Him from executing this judgment.

(32) **And I will bring the land into desolation.** Better, *And I myself will bring,* &c. From the ruin of the cities and the sanctuaries the desolation extends to the whole country. Whilst the devastations hitherto were the result of God permitting hostile invasions and conquests, the desolation of the whole country and the dispersion of the Israelites described in the following verses are to be the work of God Himself. He who has promised to bless the land in so marvellous a manner (verses 4—10) as a reward for their obedience, will Himself reduce it to the most astounding desolation as a punishment for their disobedience, so much so, that their very enemies will be amazed at it (Jer. ix. 11; Ezek. v. 15, xxxiii. 28, 29, xxxv. 10, xxxvi. 5).

(33) **And I will scatter you among the heathen.**—They will not even be permitted to tarry among the ruins of their favoured places, but God Himself, who brings about the desolation, will disperse the surviving inhabitants far and wide.

And will draw out a sword after you.—To show how complete this dispersion is to be, God is represented with a drawn sword in His hand pursuing them and scattering them, so that both their land and every city in it should be denuded of them, and that there should be no possibility of any of them turning back. Thus the sword which God promised should not go through their land (see verse 6) if they walk according to the Divine commandments, will now be wielded by Himself to bring about their utter dispersion from the

(34) Then shall the land enjoy her sab-
baths, as long as it lieth desolate, and
ye *be* in your enemies' land; *even* then
shall the land rest, and enjoy her sab-
baths. (35) As long as it lieth desolate
it shall rest; because it did not rest in
your sabbaths, when ye dwelt upon it.
(36) And upon them that are left *alive*
of you I will send a faintness into their
hearts in the lands of their enemies;
and the sound of a [1] shaken leaf shall
chase them; and they shall flee, as flee-
ing from a sword; and they shall fall
when none pursueth. (37) And they shall
fall one upon another, as it were before
a sword, when none pursueth: and ye
shall have no power to stand before your
enemies. (38) And ye shall perish among
the heathen, and the land of your
enemies shall eat you up. (39) And they
that are left of you shall pine away in
their iniquity in your enemies' lands;
and also in the iniquities of their
fathers shall they pine away with them.
(40) If they shall confess their iniquity,
and the iniquity of their fathers, with
their trespass which they trespassed
against me, and that also they have
walked contrary unto me; (41) and *that*
I also have walked contrary unto them,
and have brought them into the land of
their enemies; if then their uncircum-
cised hearts be humbled, and they then
accept of the punishment of their ini-

1 Heb., *driven.*

---

land. A similar appalling scene is described by Jeremiah: "I will scatter them also among the heathen, whom neither they nor their fathers have known: and I will send a sword after them, till I have consumed them" (Jer. ix. 16, with chap. xlii. 16—18; Ezek. xii. 14).

(34) **Then shall the land enjoy her sabbaths.**—The land, which participates both in the happiness and misery of the Israelites (see chap. xviii. 25), and which through their disobedience of the Divine laws would be deprived of her sabbatical rests as long as the rebellious people occupy it, would now at last be able to enjoy its prescribed legal rest, when it is ridden of these defiant transgressors, and as long as they remain in exile.

(35) **As long as it lieth desolate it shall rest; because it did not rest . . .**—Better, *All the days of its desolation shall it keep that rest which it did not rest,* &c., that is, the land during its desolation will not be cultivated but will lie fallow, and thus be enabled to make up by its long rest for the many sabbaths and sabbatical years of which it had been deprived by the lawless Israelites during their sojourn in it. (Comp. Jer. xxxiv. 17; 2 Chron. xxxvi. 21.)

(36, 37) **And upon them that are left alive of you.**—Better, *And as to those that remain of you,* as the Authorised Version generally renders this expression. This obviates the insertion of the expression "alive," which is not in the original, and is not put in the Authorised Version in verse 39, where the same phrase occurs. Where these will remain is explained in the next clause.

I will send a faintness into their hearts.—That is, He will implant in them such timidity and cowardice that they will be frightened at the faintest sound. He will make life a misery to them. (Comp. Deut. xxviii. 65—67.)

(38) **And ye shall perish among the heathen.**—Better, *And ye shall be lost among the heathen,* as the word here rendered "perish" is often translated. (See Deut. xxii. 3; 1 Sam. ix. 3, 20; Jer. l. 6; Ezek. xxxiv. 4, 16; Ps. cxix. 176, &c.) The context plainly shows that utter destruction is not meant here. The very next verse speaks of a remnant who are to pine away, whilst verse 40 speaks of their confessing their guilt.

The land of your enemies shall eat you up.—That is, they shall be so completely mixed up with the heathen nations amongst whom they are to be dispersed, and so utterly incorporated amongst them, that they will disappear, and have no separate existence. This is the sense of this peculiar phrase in Num. xiii. 32; Ezek. xxxvi. 13.

(39) **And they that are left of you shall pine away in their iniquity.**—Better, *But those that remain of you shall pine away because of their iniquity,* that is, those who will survive the terrible doom described under the five warnings, will pine away with grief, reflecting upon their sins which have brought upon them these tribulations.

And also in the iniquities of their fathers shall they pine away with them.—Better, *and also on account of the iniquity of their fathers with them shall they pine away,* that is, they shall pine away on account of their ancestral sins, which they repeat and reproduce. Hence the ancient Chaldee Versions render it, "And also on account of the evil sins of their fathers, which they hold fast in their hands, shall they pine away." It may, however, also be rendered, "And also on account of the iniquities of their fathers which are with them;" that is, which they must bear and expiate. (See Exod. xx. 5.)

(40) **If they shall confess their iniquity.**—Better, *And they shall confess,* that is, when their sufferings have reached this terrible point, the Israelites will realise and confess their iniquities and those of their fathers who have perished in these terrible punishments, on account of their sins, and who are no longer alive to confess their sins themselves. The whole description is present to the Lawgiver's mind; hence the different degrees of the sins, the various stages of the sufferings, and the ultimate penitence of the people are described as passing before our eyes, as if exhibited in a kaleidoscope.

With their trespass which they trespassed against me.—Better, *because of their trespass that they have,* &c., as this phrase is rendered in the Authorised Version in Dan. ix. 7.

(41) **And that I also have walked contrary unto them.**—That is, and they shall also confess that through their walking contrary unto God, He also walked contrary unto them, and brought them into the land of their enemies.

If then their uncircumcised hearts be humbled.—Better, or rather, *their uncircumcised*

quity: (42) then will I remember my
covenant with Jacob, and also my cove-
nant with Isaac, and also my covenant
with Abraham will I remember; and I
will remember the land.
(43) The land also shall be left of them,
and shall enjoy her sabbaths, while she
lieth desolate without them: and they
shall accept of the punishment of their
iniquity: because, even because they
despised my judgments, and because
their soul abhorred my statutes.
(44) And yet for all that, when they be in
the land of their enemies, [a] I will not
cast them away, neither will I abhor
them, to destroy them utterly, and to
break my covenant with them: for I *am*
the LORD their God. (45) But I will for
their sakes remember the covenant of
their ancestors, whom I brought forth
out of the land of Egypt in the sight of
the heathen, that I might be their God:
I *am* the LORD.
(46) These *are* the statutes and judg-
ments and laws, which the LORD made
between him and the children of Israel
in mount Sinai by the hand of Moses.

a Deut. 4. 31; Rom. 11. 26.

CHAPTER XXVII. — (1) And the
LORD spake unto Moses, saying, (2) Speak

hearts shall be humbled. This is a resumption of the statement made at the beginning of verse 40, viz., "And they shall confess their iniquity . . .;" or rather, *their uncircumcised hearts shall be humbled.* That is, perverse and stubborn hearts; too proud to make an humble confession. (See chap. xix. 23, with Jer. ix. 26.) The same metaphor is used by the Apostle: "Ye stiffnecked and uncircumcised in heart and ears, ye do always resist the Holy Ghost" (Acts vii. 51).

Accept of the punishment of their iniquity.—Rather, *accept willingly,* that is, they will acknowledge the justice of their punishment, and be in that frame of mind when they will freely own that the punishment is not commensurate with their guilt, and willingly accept the Divine retribution. The exact shade of meaning covered by this phrase in the original cannot adequately be given in a translation, since the verb here translated "accept," or "accept willingly," is the same which is translated "enjoy" in verse 34. The whole phrase denotes literally, *they shall rejoice in their iniquity,* or *in the punishment of their iniquity;* they will take it joyfully, as the best and most appropriate means to bring them to repentance. The nearest approach to it is the passage, "I will bear the indignation of the Lord, for I have sinned against him" (Micah vii. 9).

(42) **Then will I remember.**—That is, perform the covenant God made. The expression "remember" frequently denotes "to be mindful," "to perform," especially when used with regard to God; as, for instance, "I have remembered my covenant," &c. (Exod. vi. 5, 6); "He remembered for them his covenant" (Ps. cvi. 45).

My covenant with Jacob, and also my covenant with Isaac, and also my covenant with Abraham.—When thus brought to repentance, the Lord will perform towards them the covenant which He made with their ancestors, and in which He not only promised that the Israelites are to be a numerous people, but that they are to possess the land for ever (Exod. xxxii. 13). From the fact that the expression "covenant" is here exceptionally repeated before the name of each patriarch, the authorities during the second Temple rightly concluded that it refers to three distinct covenants made respectively with the patriarchs. Hence the Chaldee Versions render it, "And I will remember in mercy the covenant which I covenanted with Jacob at Bethel [Gen. xxxv. 9—15], and also the covenant which I covenanted with Isaac at Mount Moriah [Gen. xxii.], and the covenant which I covenanted with Abraham between the divided pieces [of the sacrifices (Gen. xv. 18—21)]." The ancients also call attention to the fact that whilst in all other passages where the three patriarchs are mentioned together, the order is according to their seniority, viz., Abraham, Isaac, and Jacob (Gen. l. 24; Exod. ii. 24, vi. 8, xxxii. 13; Deut. xxix. 13, xxxiv. 4; 2 Kings xiii. 23; Ps. cv. 8—10; 1 Chron. xvi. 16—17), this is the solitary instance where the regular order is inverted.

(43) **The land also shall be left of them.**—Better, *but the land shall be deserted by them.* The solemn warning is here reiterated, that before God will remember His covenant with the patriarchs, and also be mindful of the land, the land must be depopulated of its rebellious inhabitants, and enjoy the Sabbaths which have been denied to it. This verse, therefore, which is substantially a repetition of verses 33, 34, seems to have been inserted here to deprecate more solemnly the heinousness of their sins.

(44) **And yet for all that.**—Better, *And yet even so,* that is, even if it be so that they remain exiles in foreign lands for a long time, this is no proof that God has finally cast them off, has given them over to destruction, and abrogated His covenant with them. He is always their God, and will keep His covenant for ever.

(45) **But I will for their sakes remember the covenant.**—Better, *And will remember unto them the covenant,* that is, as their God He will execute to them the covenant which He made with their ancestors. This verse is therefore closely connected with the preceding verse.

(46) **These are the statutes and judgments.**—That is, the statutes and judgments contained in chaps. xxv. 1—xxvi. 45.

In Mount Sinai.—That is, in the mountainous district of Sinai. This group of statutes therefore concludes with the very phrase with which it began (see chap. xxv. 1), thus showing that it forms a section by itself.

XXVII.

(1) **And the Lord spake unto Moses.**—Like the group of enactments contained in chaps. xxv. 1—xxvi. 45, the regulations about the different kinds of vows are introduced with the formula which indicates that the section before us constitutes a separate Divine communication. As sundry allusions are made throughout this book to vows, thus legally acknowledging the

unto the children of Israel, and say unto
them, When a man shall make a singu-
lar vow, the persons *shall be* for the
LORD by thy estimation. (3) And thy
estimation shall be of the male from
twenty years old even unto sixty years
old, even thy estimation shall be fifty
shekels of silver, after the shekel of the
sanctuary. (4) And if it *be* a female,
then thy estimation shall be thirty she-
kels. (5) And if *it be* from five years old
even unto twenty years old, then thy
estimation shall be of the male twenty
shekels, and for the female ten shekels.
(6) And if *it be* from a month old even
unto five years old, then thy estimation
shall be of the male five shekels of sil-
ver, and for the female thy estimation
shall be three shekels of silver. (7) And
if *it be* from sixty years old and above;
if *it be* a male, then thy estimation shall
be fifteen shekels, and for the female

---

existence of the ancient practice of votive offerings (chaps. vii. 16, xxii. 18, 21, 23, xxiii. 38), the Levitical code, which is pre-eminently designed to uphold the holiness of the sanctuary and its sacrifices, as well as the holiness of the priests and the people, would be incomplete without defining the nature and obligation of these self-imposed sacrifices.

(2) **Shall make a singular vow.**—Better, *shall consecrate a vow.* (See chap. xxii. 21.) According to the interpretation of this phrase which obtained during the second Temple it denotes *shall pronounce a vow.* Hence the ancient Chaldee Versions render it, "shall distinctly pronounce a vow." Accordingly, no vow mentally made or conceived was deemed binding. It had to be distinctly pronounced in words. The form of the vow is nowhere given in the Bible. Like many other points of detail, the wording of it was left to the administrators of the law. They divided vows into two classes: (1) Positive vows, by which a man bound himself to consecrate for religious purposes his own person, those members of his family over whom he had control, or any portion of his property, and for this kind of vow the formula was "Behold I consecrate this to the Lord"; and (2) Negative vows, by which he promised to abstain from enjoying a certain thing, for which the formula was, "Such and such a thing be unlawful to me for so many days, weeks, or for ever."

The persons shall be for the Lord by thy estimation.—Better, *souls to the Lord according to thy estimation,* that is, the vow consists of consecrating persons to the Lord with the intention of redeeming by money the persons thus consecrated, according to the valuation put upon them by Moses. This part of the verse explains the nature of the vow, and takes it for granted that by consecrating a human being to God by a vow is meant to substitute the money value for him. By the suffix, "*thy* estimation," Moses is meant, to whom these regulations are here Divinely communicated, and upon whom it devolved in the first instance to carry out the law. (See chap. v. 15, 18.) During the second Temple any Israelite could estimate the money value of a person thus vowed to the Lord.

(3) **And thy estimation shall be of the male.**—Better, *Then thy estimation of the male shall be* (*as follows*).

From twenty years old even unto sixty years old.—The estimation not only begins with the male, who is the most important person, but takes special notice of his age. The years here specified represent the prime of his life, and he is to be rated not according to his rank or position, but according to the value of his services.

Fifty shekels of silver, after the shekel of the sanctuary.—Whether the person who makes this vow makes it with regard to himself, or whether he dedicates by it any other member of the community, he is to pay fifty silver shekels, which in our currency would be £6 9s. 2d., if the man thus consecrated is between twenty and sixty years of age. This sum he is to pay, whether rich or poor. For this sum he was liable, during the second Temple, if he said "My value be upon me," or "This man's value be upon me," or "Such a man's value be upon me."

(4) **And if it be a female . . . thirty shekels.**—As the woman is the weaker vessel, and her labour is of less value, if she vows herself or dedicates by a vow any other one of her own sex to the sanctuary, she is to pay thirty shekels, or £3 17s. 6d., provided she is within the above-named limits of age. This was the value of a slave (Exod. xxi. 32), and is the price at which Christ was sold (Matt. xxvii. 9). It is supposed that under this provision Jephtha might have redeemed his daughter whom he unwittingly vowed to the Lord (Judges xi. 30). (See, however, verse 29.)

(5) **If it be from five years old, even unto twenty years.**—From the fact that a child of five years is here mentioned it is evident that the vows here spoken of are not simply those which a man makes with regard to his own person, but which he also makes about others, since a vow involving the payment of a considerable sum of money on the part of a child was of no force. The case, therefore, here contemplated is of a father or mother vowing the male child unto the Lord or of any other person taking upon himself to pay the value of such and such a child to the sanctuary. This is still more manifest from the following verse.

The male twenty shekels.—As the services of a boy at the age here specified are of much less value, the parent, or anyone else, who vows him to the sanctuary is to pay £2 11s. 8d.

The female ten shekels.—For the girl, whose value is proportionately less, the vower is to pay £1 5s. 10d.; being the same value put on an old woman. (See verse 7.)

(6) **From a month old even unto five years old.**—That is, if a parent, or any other person, devotes his or anyone else's child to the sanctuary, he is obliged to be redeemed according to the prescribed valuation. The formula used in such a case during the second Temple was, "Behold the estimation of this my boy, or this my girl, or of that boy or that girl, be upon me."

The male five shekels of silver.—As at this tender age the service of a child is not of much value, the vower is to pay for a boy 12s. 11d.

The female . . . three shekels of silver.—The girl being proportionately less valuable, is to be redeemed at 7s. 9d.

(7) **From sixty years old and above.**—Being almost past labour, the old man is next in value to the child.

ten shekels. (8) But if he be poorer than
thy estimation, then he shall present
himself before the priest, and the priest
shall value him; according to his
ability that vowed shall the priest value
him.

(9) And if *it be* a beast, whereof men
bring an offering unto the LORD, all that
any man giveth of such unto the LORD
shall be holy. (10) He shall not alter it,
nor change it, a good for a bad, or a bad
for a good: and if he shall at all change
beast for beast, then it and the ex-
change thereof shall be holy. (11) And
if *it be* any unclean beast, of which they
do not offer a sacrifice unto the LORD,
then he shall present the beast before
the priest: (12) and the priest shall value
it, whether it be good or bad: [1]as thou
valuest it, *who art* the priest, so shall it
be. (13) But if he will at all redeem it,
then he shall add a fifth *part* thereof
unto thy estimation.

(14) And when a man shall sanctify his
house *to be* holy unto the LORD, then
the priest shall estimate it, whether it

[1] Heb., *according to thy estimation, O priest, &c.*

A male . . . fifteen shekels.—The old man is therefore to be redeemed at £1 18s. 9d.

The female ten shekels.—The old woman, from sixty and upwards, is estimated at exactly the same value as the girl from five to twenty years old (see verse 5), and hence is to be redeemed at £1 5s. 10d. It will be seen that the disproportion between a man and a woman is not the same in old age as in youth. The authorities during the second Temple account for it by adducing the adage, "An old man in the house is always in the way; an old woman in the house is a treasure, she manages all household affairs."

(8) **But if he be poorer than thy estimation.**—That is, if the person who makes the vow possesses less than the specified legal rates required to redeem it.

Then he shall present himself before the priest.—The man pleading poverty is to appear before the priest, who is to examine into his circumstances, and tax him accordingly. The minimum, however, which he was obliged to pay during the second Temple was one shekel. If anyone neglected paying his vows to the Temple treasury, his goods were seized by the officials. This, however, had to be done in such a manner as not to deprive the man of his means of subsistence. The bailiffs were obliged to leave a mechanic two sets of tools, a husbandman a yoke of oxen, and a donkey driver his donkey. They were bound to leave food sufficient for thirty days, and bedding for twelve months; and they could never seize the man's sandals or phylacteries, or his wife's property, or his children's clothes.

(9) **And if it be a beast, whereof men bring an offering.**—That is, if what a man vows consists of sacrificial quadrupeds, viz., bullocks, sheep, or goats.

Shall be holy.—That is, must not be redeemed at all. They were delivered to the sanctuary: they were sold by the priests to those Israelites who required them as sacrifices for the altar, and the money expended in the maintenance of the service.

(10) **He shall not alter it, nor change it.**—The identical animal vowed is to be delivered; no change whatever, even if it is in the substitution of a better for an inferior animal, is permitted. The stress laid upon this part of the enactment is indicated by the employment here of two verbs of the same import. If he who vows does change the one he dedicated to the Lord, both the animals, the one he originally vowed and the one he substituted for it, are alike holy, and must be delivered to the sanctuary.

(11) **And if it be any unclean beast.**—That is, if what he vows consists of an unclean beast, which does not belong to the three kinds of sacrificial quadrupeds, and which cannot therefore be sacrificed on the altar. According to the authorities during the second Temple, however, the expression "unclean beast" here denotes defective sacrificial animals, such as oxen, sheep, and goats with blemishes, which have become unlawful for the altar.

(12) **Whether it be good or bad.**—That is, the priest shall estimate its value according to the condition of the animal, whatever that may be, whether it is of good quality or bad.

(13) **But if he will at all redeem it.**—Better, *and if he wishes to redeem it*, that is, the man himself who vowed it for the sanctuary. The estimate put upon the animal in question was intended for anyone who wished to purchase it, not excluding, however, the person who vowed it.

He shall add a fifth part.—Whilst anyone else could purchase the animal at the valuation put upon it by the priest, its former owner is to pay a fifth more than the valuation price. This was probably intended as a fine for taking back a thing which he promised to the Lord. For the way in which the fifth part was computed during the second Temple see chap. v. 16.

(14) **And when a man shall sanctify his house.**—That is, devotes it to the service of God by a vow, when it has to be sold and the money used by the authorities for the maintenance and repair of the sanctuary, unless it is required as a dwelling for the priests, or for some other purpose connected with the duties of the Temple. The sale, however, can only take place after the priest has carefully examined it, ascertained and fixed its value, according to the condition of the house. It then can be bought by any one at the price so fixed. The expression "house" the authorities during the second Temple interpreted to mean not only the building itself but anything belonging to it, or any article of furniture in it which the owner could vow to the sanctuary separately, whilst from the expression "*his* house" they concluded that the house or the things therein must be absolutely his own, and that he has the exclusive right of disposal. Hence any house or property obtained by fraud neither the defrauder nor the defrauded could vow to the sanctuary, since the property was not properly in the possession of either, and could not be called *his*. Moreover, if anyone vowed a thing by mistake, it could not be claimed for the sanctuary, the vow under such circumstances was regarded as null and void. From these considerations, as well as from the fact that any article that was vowed could be redeemed, it is evident that the Mosaic vow of consecration to the sanctuary imparted no sacramental and

be good or bad: as the priest shall esti-
mate it, so shall it stand. (15) And if he
that sanctified it will redeem his house,
then he shall add the fifth *part* of the
money of thy estimation unto it, and it
shall be his.

(16) And if a man shall sanctify unto
the LORD *some part* of a field of his pos-
session, then thy estimation shall be
according to the seed thereof: [1]an
homer of barley seed *shall be valued* at
fifty shekels of silver. (17) If he sanctify
his field from the year of jubile, accord-
ing to thy estimation it shall stand.
(18) But if he sanctify his field after the
jubile, then the priest shall reckon unto
him the money according to the years
that remain, even unto the year of the
jubile, and it shall be abated from thy
estimation.

(19) And if he that sanctified the field
will in any wise redeem it, then he shall
add the fifth *part* of the money of thy
estimation unto it, and it shall be as-
sured to him. (20) And if he will not
redeem the field, or if he have sold the
field to another man, it shall not be re-
deemed any more. (21) But the field,
when it goeth out in the jubile, shall be
holy unto the LORD, as a field devoted;

[1] Or, *the land of an homer, &c.*

---

inalienable sanctity to the objects themselves in our ecclesiastical sense of consecration. It is not the gift, but its money value which had to be devoted to the holy cause.

(15) **And if he that sanctified it will redeem his house.**—Though the net price thus fixed by the priest is all that anyone else who wishes to buy it has to pay for the house, yet if the former owner of it, or, according to the practice which obtained during the second Temple, his son, wife, or nearest of kin, wishes to redeem it, he is to add one-fifth more than the valuation price, just as in the case of animals, and for the same reason, that is, for taking back a thing which he once promised to the Lord. (See verse 13.)

(16) **Some part of a field of his possession.**—That is, if he consecrates by a vow to the service of the sanctuary a portion of a field which he inherits from his forefathers, and which, therefore, constitutes a part of his inalienable patrimony, thus distinguishing it from a field which he has acquired by his own purchase. (See verse 22.) The words, *some part,* which are in italics, are implied in the Hebrew construction of these words. No man was allowed to vow the whole of his estates to the sanctuary, as he would thereby impoverish his own family.

Thy estimation shall be according to the seed thereof.—Better, *thy estimation shall be according to its seed,* that is, he is not to part with the field thus vowed for the sanctuary, but the priest is to value the area according to the quantity of seed required for sowing it.

An homer of barley seed shall be valued at fifty shekels of silver.—That is, if the piece of land which he vowed could properly be cropped with one homer, or five bushels and a half of barley seed, he is to value it at £6 9s. 2d. (See verse 3.) According to the authorities during the second Temple, these fifty shekels covered the value of the produce for the whole period of forty-nine years, that is, from one jubile year to another, so that a plot of land of the dimensions here described was estimated at a little more than one shekel per annum. The person who made the vow could, under these circumstances, always redeem it, as it would almost amount to a gift to let any stranger buy it at this price. The low value put upon it was evidently designed not to deprive the family of their means of subsistence, since the patrimonial estates were almost always the only source of their livelihood.

(17) **If he sanctify his field from the year of jubile.**—That is, the above-named valuation of fifty shekels only applies if he makes the vow immediately after the expiration of the year of jubile, when the period covered by this estimation is forty-nine years.

(18) **But if he sanctify his field after the jubile.**—If, however, the vow is made after the jubile, the priest is to value the field according to the number of years from the time of the vow to the next jubile year.

And it shall be abated from thy estimation.—That is, the years which have elapsed since the last jubile up to the time when he made the vow are to be deducted from the jubile cycle, and hence so many shekels are to be taken off from the original valuation of fifty shekels. Thus, for instance, if he vowed the field at the estimated value of fifty shekels twenty years after the jubile, the priest is only to reckon the thirty years which have to run to the next jubile, and is to deduct twenty shekels for the twenty years which have elapsed since the last jubile. Accordingly, the vower would only have to pay thirty shekels, exclusive of the fifth part above the estimated value.

(19) **And if he that sanctified the field will in any wise redeem it.**—Better, *and if he wishes to redeem the field that sanctified it.* (See verse 13.) This is sure to be the case, since the low value fixed per acre was designed that the field should be redeemed by him. According to the legislation during the second Temple, the rule here included his wife and his heirs, any one of whom had the right to redeem it. But the family in redeeming it had, as usual, to add one-fifth over and above the valuation price, for the reason already stated. (See verses 13, 15.)

(20) **And if he will not redeem the field.**—That is, if after all the advantages which the law affords to the vower to redeem his patrimonial inheritance before the jubile year, he is base enough to forego the privilege of redemption, thus showing no desire to perpetuate his family name,—

Or if he have sold the field to another man.—Better, *and if he yet sells the field to another man,* that is, if in addition to this absence of family honour he surreptitiously sells the field which he has vowed to the sanctuary to another man, thus adding sacrilege to baseness,—

It shall not be redeemed any more,—then he loses all right ever to redeem it at all.

(21) **But the field, when it goeth out in the jubile.**—That is, when it quits the hand of the purchaser, since in jubile every buyer was to part with the land which he bought, (see chap. xxv. 25—28)—

the possession thereof shall be the
priest's.
(22) And if *a man* sanctify unto the
LORD a field which he hath bought,
which *is* not of the fields of his posses-
sion; (23) then the priest shall reckon
unto him the worth of thy estimation,
even unto the year of the jubile: and he
shall give thine estimation in that day,
as a holy thing unto the LORD. (24) In
the year of the jubile the field shall re-
turn unto him of whom it was bought,
even to him to whom the possession of
the land *did belong*.
(25) And all thy estimations shall be
according to the shekel of the sanctuary:
[a] twenty gerahs shall be the shekel.
(26) Only the [1]firstling of the beasts,
which should be the LORD's firstling,
no man shall sanctify it; whether *it be*
ox, or sheep: it *is* the LORD's. (27) And
if *it be* of an unclean beast, then he shall
redeem *it* according to thine estimation,
and shall add a fifth *part* of it thereto:
or if it be not redeemed, then it shall
be sold according to thy estimation.
(28) [b]Notwithstanding no devoted thing,
that a man shall devote unto the LORD
of all that he hath, *both* of man and
beast, and of the field of his possession,

[a] Ex. 30. 13; Num. 3. 47; Ezek. 45. 12.

[1] Heb., *first born, &c.*

[b] Josh. 6. 19.

Shall be holy unto the Lord, as a field devoted.—It shall not revert to the original owner who first vowed it and, after refusing to redeem it, fraudulently sold it, but becomes God's property, like all devoted or banned things. (See verse 28.) According to the authorities during the second Temple, however, the import of the law laid down in verses 20 and 21 is as follows:—If the vower of the field does not redeem it before the jubile year, and the field is then still in the possession of the Temple treasurer, who has the control of all the things thus consecrated by vow; or if the Temple treasurer has sold the field to another person who has it in his possession, the original owner or vower can no longer redeem it, but in the year of jubile it reverts either from the Temple treasurer or the purchaser to the priests who are on duty in that year, who add it to their pasture fields. These priests, however, have to pay for it the valuation money.

(22) **And if a man sanctify unto the Lord a field which he hath bought.**—But if a man vows a field which he has acquired by purchase, and which is only his till the next jubile, when it reverts to its original owner (see chap. xxv. 25—28), the case is necessarily different. Such a leased field, when vowed to the Lord, is to be dealt with as follows:—

(23) **Then the priest shall reckon unto him.**—In this case the vower is not to pay the low rate fixed for a field which is the family inheritance (see verse 16), but the priest is to value it in proportion to the number of crops which it will produce up to the year of jubile, in the same way as fields are valued in ordinary purchases. (See chap. xxv. 14—16.)

And he shall give thine estimation in that day.—This valuation the vower or his relatives had to pay all at once, without, however, the additional fifth part of its value; whilst in the case of vowing an hereditary field, the vower had the advantage of paying the small sum by yearly instalments.

(24) **The field shall return unto him of whom it was bought.**—In accordance with the law laid down in chap. xxv. 23—28, the field thus vowed did not return to the purchaser in the year of jubile, but to the hereditary owner, of whom the person who had vowed it to the Lord had bought it.

(25) **According to the shekel of the sanctuary.**—As the proceeds of these vows were devoted to the maintenance and repair of the sanctuary, all the valuations are to be made and paid according to the standard weight of the sanctuary shekel. (See Exod. xxx. 13.)

(26) **Only the firstling of the beasts.**—Better, *nevertheless the firstlings, &c.*, as this rendering also suits verse 28, which begins with the same particle, and which is translated in the Authorised Version, "notwithstanding." Having laid down the regulations about the four classes of objects which may be vowed to the Lord—viz.: 1, persons (verses 2—8); 2, animals (verses 9—13); 3, houses (verses 14, 15); and 4, lands (verses 16—25)—the legislator concludes by pointing out two exceptions to the rules about votive offerings hitherto discussed. The two classes of objects which are forbidden to be vowed are (1) the firstlings of beasts and (2) devoted things. The firstlings belonged already to the Lord by an express statute (Exod. xiii. 2). To vow, therefore, to the Lord that which was His own is a mockery.

Which should be the Lord's firstling.—Rather, *which is born as a firstling to the Lord*, that is, one which, by virtue of its being a firstling, and by its very birth, is the property of the Lord.

(27) **And if it be of an unclean beast.**—That is, if he vows the firstling of an unclean beast he could redeem it according to the valuation of the priest with the addition of one-fifth over and above the fixed value. If he did not redeem it the treasurer of the sanctuary sold it to anyone who liked to buy it at this valuation, and the proceeds were devoted to the maintenance and repairs of the sanctuary. As this is at variance with the law laid down in Exod. xiii. 13; xxxiv. 20, where it is enacted that the firstborn of an ass is either to be redeemed with a sheep, or is to be put to death, the authorities during the second Temple interpreted the precept in the passage before us as not applying to the firstborn of the unclean animals, but to unclean animals generally which are dedicated for the repairs of the sanctuary.

(28) **Notwithstanding no devoted thing.**—Better, *Nevertheless, no banned thing* (see verse 26), that is, unlike those things consecrated to God by the vow hitherto spoken of, anything which the vower devoted to God under a solemn ban cannot be redeemed.

Both of man and beast, and of the field of his possession.—This shows the extent to which a man may go in exercising his power to devote things to God in this manner. He was perfectly at liberty to ban not only his cattle and his otherwise inalienable inherited land, but also those human beings over whom he had control—his children and slaves.

Every devoted thing is most holy unto the Lord.—Being most holy, any thing or person thus

shall be sold or redeemed: every devoted
thing *is* most holy unto the LORD.
(29) None devoted, which shall be de-
voted of men, shall be redeemed; *but*
shall surely be put to death.

(30) And all the tithe of the land,
whether of the seed of the land, *or* of
the fruit of the tree, *is* the LORD'S: *it is*
holy unto the LORD. (31) And if a man
will at all redeem *ought* of his tithes, he
shall add thereto the fifth *part* thereof.
(32) And concerning the tithe of the herd,
or of the flock, *even* of whatsoever passeth
under the rod, the tenth shall be holy
unto the LORD. (33) He shall not search
whether it be good or bad, neither shall
he change it: and if he change it at all,
then both it and the change thereof
shall be holy; it shall not be redeemed.

(34) These *are* the commandments,
which the LORD commanded Moses for
the children of Israel in mount Sinai.

---

devoted to the Lord could neither be sold by the officials of the sanctuary nor be redeemed by the vower who had in this manner banned the objects of his vow. All gifts devoted under the ban became the property of the priests. (See verse 17; Num. xviii. 14; Ezek. xliv. 29.)

(29) **None devoted, which shall be devoted of men.**—Better, *Every one banned, which shall be banned of men,* that is, every one banned from amongst men, or every human being banned, is not to be redeemed. Like the cattle and the patrimonial estates, when once devoted to God by a vow of banning, the man thus banned by a vow comes irretrievably under the class of "most holy unto the Lord," or one irrevocably withdrawn from the power of man.

But shall surely be put to death.—Not as a sacrifice to God, but, on the contrary, to be removed out of His sight. This is the apparent import of the passage, and seems to be confirmed by the melancholy narrative of Jephtha and his daughter (Judges xi. 30). This seems to have been the interpretation put on the law in question during the second Temple, since it is embodied in the Chaldee Versions, which render the verse as follows: "Every vow that shall be vowed of man, shall not be redeemed with money, but with burnt offerings and with hallowed victims, and with supplications for mercy before the Lord, because such are to be put to death." It is, however, supposed that this awful vow of banning could only be exercised on notorious malefactors and idolaters as dangerous to the faith of the Israelites, that it could not be made by any private individual on his own responsibility, and that when such cases occurred the community or the Sanhedrin carried out the ban as an act of judicial necessity, thus showing it to be "most holy unto the Lord." Accordingly, verses 28 and 29 treat of two different cases. The former regulates objects "banned unto the Lord," which differs from the vow of dedication discussed in verses 2—8 only in so far that it is unredeemable, whilst verse 29 regulates the banning enacted by the law itself (Exod. xxii. 19), or pronounced by the court of justice on a man who is irretrievably to be put to death.

(30) **And all the tithe of the land.**—That is, of the soil, or what grows on it, in contradistinction to the tithes of the land mentioned in verse 32. The last things mentioned which cannot be dedicated to the Lord by a vow are tithes. Like the firstborn of animals (see verse 26), they already belong to God by another statute. A man, therefore, cannot vow to God what is not his own.

Whether of the seed of the land.—That is, what the seed when sown produced in the soil (Num. xviii. 21—24; Deut. xiv. 22—29).

(31) **And if a man will at all redeem.**—Better, *And if a man wishes to redeem.* (See verses 13, 19. Though a man may not vow tithes, being already the Lord's, yet if he wishes he may redeem them by adding one-fifth to the actual value of them. According to the authorities during the second Temple, anyone was allowed to redeem the tithes due from another person by paying the exact value for them, without the addition of the fifth part. The tithes could then be eaten in any place, but the redemption money had to be taken to Jerusalem, where it was spent in sociable feasts, to which the Levite, the stranger, and the poor were invited.

(32) **Whatsoever passeth under the rod.**—That is, for the purpose of counting and tithing them. The manner in which this was done is described by the Jewish canonists as follows: "The owner is to gather all his lambs or all his calves into the fold and make a little door to it, so that two should not be able to go out at once. He is to place their dams without. As they bleat the lambs hear their voice and go out of the fold to meet them, as it is said, 'whatsoever passeth under the rod' (Lev. xxvii. 32), since it must pass of itself, and not be brought out by his hand. And as they come out of the fold one after another he counts them with the rod, one, two, three, etc., and the tenth which comes out, whether it be male or female, whether it be perfect or blemished, he marks it with a red mark, and says, 'This is the tithe.'" It is to this custom that the prophet alludes when he says, "I will cause you to pass under the rod, and I will bring you into the bond of the covenant" (Ezek. xx. 37), that is, shall once more claim you, being marked as belonging to the Lord.

(33) **He shall not search whether it be good or bad.**—That is, the owner is not to pick out the good ones from the bad, but, as described above, is to mark every tenth one as it comes out of the fold as belonging to the Lord.

And if he change it at all.—See verse 10.

(34) **These are the commandments.**—That is, the laws laid down in chap. xxvii. 1—34.

In Mount Sinai.—In the mountainous district of Sinai. (See chap. xxvi. 46.)

THE FOURTH BOOK OF MOSES, CALLED

NUMBERS

INTRODUCTION

TO

THE FOURTH BOOK OF MOSES, CALLED

NUMBERS

THE appellation commonly given by the Jews to the fourth Book of the Pentateuch, as in the case of the titles of the other Books, is derived from one of the words which occur in the first verse of the first chapter —viz., *bemidbar:* "in the desert." The names given to it in the Greek, Latin, and English versions—viz., Ἀριθμοὶ, Numeri, Numbers—are derived from the account which it contains of the results of the census which was taken shortly after the Exodus, and of that which was taken at the expiration of the wanderings in the wilderness.

The contents of this book may be described as follows:—

CHAPTERS I. 1—X. 10.

The preparations for the departure from Mount Sinai, and for the march into the land of Canaan: including (1) the numbering of the males of eleven tribes, from twenty years old and upwards, who were capable of bearing arms; (2) the numbering of the Levites, from one month old and upwards; (3) the numbering of the firstborn, and the substitution of the Levites for the firstborn; (4) the order of encampment and of the march; (5) the regulations for the preservation of order in the camp; (6) some additional legislation, either supplementary to, or explanatory of, that which is contained in the Books of Exodus and Leviticus; (7) the law of the Nazarites; (8) the form of priestly blessing; (9) the offerings of the princes for the service of the Tabernacle; (10) instructions concerning lighting the lamps of the golden candlestick, the consecration of the Levites, and the respective ages at which they were to enter on the various parts of their service; (11) the celebration of the first Passover after the Exodus; (12) the appointment of the Passover of the second month; (13) the description of the miraculous guidance of the people; and (14) the directions respecting the use of the silver trumpets.

CHAPTERS X. 11—XIV. 45.

These chapters contain the account of (1) the departure of the Israelites from Sinai; (2) the order of the march; (3) the invitation of Moses to Hobab; (4) the watchwords of the march; (5) the murmurings of the people against God and against Moses; (6) the fire at Taberah; (7) the prophesying of Eldad and Medad; (8) the miraculous supply of quails; (9) the plague at Kibroth-hattaavah; (10) the insurrection of Miriam and Aaron against Moses, and the leprosy of Miriam; (11) the expedition of the spies into the land of Canaan, and their report; (12) the judgment denounced against the generation which was numbered at Sinai; and (13) the presumptuous attempt to enter Canaan by way of the Negeb, and the discomfiture at Hormah.

CHAPTERS XV. 1—XIX. 22.

These chapters contain (1) some legislative enactments which were to be held in abeyance during the sojourn in the wilderness, and which were to come into operation after the entrance into Canaan; (2) the account of the insurrection of Korah, Dathan, and Abiram, and the plague which followed upon it; (3) the miraculous confirmation of the Aaronic priesthood by the blossoming of Aaron's rod; (4) a more accurate definition of the respective duties of the priests and Levites; and (5) the law for the purification of those who were defiled by contact with the dead, by means of the ashes of the red heifer.

CHAPTERS XX. 1—XXV. 18.

These chapters contain the account of (1) the abode in Kadesh-Barnea; (2) the second recorded miraculous supply of water; (3) the sentence pronounced against Moses and Aaron; (4) the refusal of the King of Edom to grant the Israelites a passage through his land; (5) the death of Aaron; (6) the expedition against the King of Arad; (7) the plague of the fiery serpents, and the construction and erection of the brazen serpent; (8) the march to Mount Pisgah; (9) the victory over Sihon, the King of the Amorites, and Og, the King of Bashan; (10) the history of Balak and Balaam; and (11) the plague at Shittim.

CHAPTERS XXVI. 1—XXXVI. 13.

These chapters contain the account of (1) the second census of the people; (2) the inheritance of the daughters of Zelophehad; (3) the consecration of Joshua; (4) the enlargement of the law respecting the two daily lambs and the Sabbath-day offerings; (5) the law respecting the vows of women; (6) the war against Midian; (7) the assignment of the land on the eastern side of the Jordan to the tribes of Reuben and Gad and the half tribe of Manasseh; (8) a list of the encampments; (9) the renewed command concerning the expulsion of the Canaanites and the destruction of their idolatrous images; (10) the determination of the boundaries of the land, and the list of men appointed to distribute it; (11) the regulations respecting the Levitical cities and the cities of refuge; and (12) laws respecting the tribal inheritance, and the limitation of the right of marriage in regard to heiresses.

THE CHRONOLOGY OF THE BOOK OF NUMBERS.

The period of time embraced in the Book of Numbers is clearly defined. The narrative begins with the command which was given to Moses to take a census of the people "on the first day of the second month, in the second year after they were come out of the land of Egypt" (chap. i. 1). The death of Aaron, as recorded in chap. xxxiii. 38, took place "in the fortieth year after the children of Israel were come out of the land of Egypt, in the first day of the fifth month." The interval between these two events is exactly thirty-eight years and three months; and inasmuch as the last recorded events in the Book of Numbers took place on the eastern side of the Jordan, and the rehearsal of the law, as contained in the Book of Deuteronomy, took place in the beginning of the eleventh month of the fortieth year (Deut. i. 3), and the passage of the Jordan was effected under Joshua on the tenth day of the first month of the following year (Josh. iv. 19), it will appear that the entire period embraced in the Book of Numbers is somewhat short of thirty-nine years.

Antiquity of the Book of Numbers.

The antiquity of this Book is proved by the numerous references which are found in the later books to the events which are recorded in it. The following will suffice by way of illustration:—

(1) In Joshua i. 7 reference is made to the charge which Moses gave to Joshua by the commandment of the Lord (Num. xxvii. 23). It may be observed that the same Hebrew word which is here rendered "gave a charge," is used also in Josh. i. 7, where it is rendered "commanded."

(2) In Joshua ii. 10 we find a reference to the utter destruction of Sihon and Og, which is recorded in Numbers xxi. 24—35.

(3) In Joshua v. 6 we find a reference to the oath which the Lord sware that He would not show the land of promise to the men of war who came out of Egypt, and to the fact that all the men of war who came out of Egypt were consumed in the wilderness, "because they obeyed not the voice of the Lord." In Numbers xiv. 28—32 we find the oath to which reference is made; and in Numbers xxvi. 63—65 we find a statement that at the later census there was not left a man of those who were numbered at the former census, save Joshua and Caleb. Nor is this all: for we find an agreement in the two accounts which is corroborative of the historical accuracy of both. It has been alleged as a discrepancy between the threat and its recorded accomplishment, that Eleazar, who acted as a priest shortly after the Exodus, and who was therefore, in all probability, upwards of twenty years of age at the first census, was not only engaged in making the second census, but is found amongst those who entered into the land of Canaan. On a closer examination, however, of the threat of exclusion, as recorded in the Book of Numbers, and its fulfilment, as recorded both in the Book of Numbers and in the Book of Joshua, it will be found to refer only to those who were enrolled at the first census taken at Sinai as men of war over twenty years of age, and consequently that the tribe of Levi, which was not included in that census, was not included in the sentence of extermination. In like manner, in Joshua v. 6, it is stated, not as it has been commonly supposed, that all the Israelites who were over twenty years of age perished in the wilderness, but "all the people that were men of war" —*i.e.*, the "six hundred thousand and three thousand and five hundred and fifty," who are expressly described in Numbers i. 45 as "all that were able to go forth to war in Israel."

(4) The reference in Joshua xvii. 4 to the inheritance of the daughters of Zelophehad accords verbally with that contained in Numbers xxvii. 7. In the latter place Moses is said to have received a command to "give them a possession of an inheritance among their father's brethren." In the former place it is said that Joshua, "according to the commandment of the Lord, gave them an inheritance among the brethren of their father."

(5) The reference to the Kenites in 1 Sam. xv. 6 not only derives elucidation from Numbers x. 29—32, but reflects light upon that passage. The result of the invitation which Moses gave to Hobab to accompany the Israelites on their march through the wilderness is not recorded in the Book of Numbers. We learn, however, from Judges i. 16 that "the children of the Kenite" accompanied the children of Judah into the wilderness of Judah; and in 1 Sam. xv. 6 Saul refers to the kindness which the Kenites showed to the children of Israel as a well-established fact.

(6) One of the most conclusive indications of the reception of the Book of Numbers by the later writers of Holy Scripture, as containing a true history of the events which are recorded in it, will be found in the incidental allusion to the order of the marches through the wilderness, which we find in Ps. lxxx. 2, "Before Ephraim and Benjamin and Manasseh stir up Thy strength, and come and save us." This Psalm was manifestly composed, as it is implied in the first verse, whilst the Temple of Solomon was still standing, but subsequently to the separation of the kingdom in the time of Rehoboam. The combination of the tribes of Ephraim, Benjamin, and Manasseh, though partially explained by their common origin as descendants of Jacob by Rachel, presents upon the surface the obvious difficulty that Benjamin was attached to the southern, and Ephraim and Manasseh to the northern kingdom. A closer examination, however, of the Psalm, when elucidated by the order of the march, as prescribed in the second chapter of Numbers, will suffice to make the allusion of the Psalmist obvious. The reference in verse 1 is to the supernatural guidance of the hosts of Israel, and the mind of the writer would naturally revert to that period of the history of his people when Divine guidance was most needed and most manifestly displayed. Now we find from Numbers ii. 18—22, that during their encampments in the wilderness the three tribes here mentioned pitched together on the west side of the Tabernacle; and we find in verse 17 of the same chapter a direction which we are told (see Numbers x. 21, 22), was observed when the camp broke up and the Israelites commenced their journeys out of the wilderness of Sinai—viz., that the Tabernacle of the congregation was to set forward in such order that the eastern and southern camps were to precede it, and that the western camp, which, as we have seen, was composed of the three tribes here named, was to follow it. When, moreover, we bear in mind that the sacred Ark was commonly regarded and designated as the ark of God's strength (Ps. cxxxii. 8), there can remain little doubt of the reference of the writer of Psalm lxxx. to the prescribed order of the encampment and to the marches through the wilderness, as recorded in the Book of Numbers, when he gave utterance to the prayer, "Before Ephraim and Benjamin and Manasseh stir up Thy strength and come and save us."

(7) A few other references in the later Books to the Book of Numbers may be more briefly noticed.

(1) In 1 Sam. xv. 29 we find a quotation from Num. xxii. 19.

(2) In 1 Sam. xxx. 7, 8, and elsewhere, we find allusions to the mode of inquiry of the Lord, of which the first mention is found in Num. xxvii. 21.

(3) In Ps. lxxviii. 16, there appears to be an allusion to the miraculous supply of water at Kadesh, as related in Num. xx. 7—11, the word rendered *rock* being *sela*, as in Numbers, not *zur*,* as in Exod. xvii. 6.

(4) In Jer. xlviii. 45, we find a reference to, or rather a quotation from, Num. xxi. 28, and an obvious allusion to Num. xxiv. 17.

(5) In Josh. xxii. 17, Ps. cvi. 28, and Hosea ix. 10, we find an allusion to the idolatrous abominations of Baal-peor, as recorded in Num. xxv.

(6) In Amos ii. 9, we find an allusion to the gigantic size of the Anakim, as related in Num. xiii. 33.

(7) In Obad. verses 4, 19, we find allusions to Num. xxiv. 18, 21.

The above will suffice as illustrations of references, which might be almost indefinitely multiplied, to the history of the Israelites, and to events connected with that history, as they are recorded in the Book of Numbers. It is scarcely too much to affirm that no inconsiderable portion of the contents of this Book might be recovered from the various references and allusions to it which are dispersed over the later Books of the Old Testament.

The Authorship of the Book of Numbers.

Much which has been said upon the Mosaic authorship of the Pentateuch generally applies with special force to the authorship of the Book of Numbers. One portion of this Book, viz. the catalogue of the stations or encampments of the Israelites, as recorded in chap. xxxiii, is expressly ascribed to Moses in the following words: "And Moses wrote their goings out according to their journeys, by the commandment of the Lord" (verse 2). Some of the legislative enactments which are found only in the Book of Numbers, or which are recapitulated in the Book of Deuteronomy, are expressly assigned to Moses in the Book of Joshua. Such, *e.g.*, are the following: (1) the law that the Levites were to have no separate inheritance of land amongst the children of Israel (Josh. xiii. 14, 33; xiv. 3, 4, compared with Num. xviii. 20—24; Deut. x. 9; xiv. 27; xviii. 1, 2), but only cities to dwell in, with their suburbs taken out of the inheritance of the other tribes (Josh. xxi. 2, compared with Num. xxxv. 1—4); and (2) the assignment by lot † of the inheritance of the nine tribes and a half on the west of the Jordan, and of the two tribes and a half on the east of the Jordan (Josh. xiv. 2, 3; xviii. 7, compared with Num. xxvi. 55; xxxii. 33, xxxiii. 54; xxxiv. 13).

The presumption thus afforded that the Book of Numbers was written by Moses, is confirmed by the numerous indications which it contains that it is the work of a contemporary writer, who lived in the desert, and who was familiar with the history, customs, and institutions of Egypt. The minuteness of the details which the Book of Numbers contains respecting the order of the march through the wilderness, and the various incidents which occurred in the course of it, the remarkable manner in which the history and the legislation are interwoven,‡ and more particularly the insertion of additional legislation arising out of the protracted wanderings in the desert (as *e.g.*, that contained in xix. 14), point to the conclusion that the writer of the Book was either an eye-witness of the scenes which he records, or a forger whose skill has been unequalled in after ages. The topographical notices, again, testify to an aquaintance with the history of Egypt (as *e.g.*, xiii. 22), and also with that of the surrounding nations, previously to the entrance into the land of Canaan (as *e.g.*, xxi. 13); whilst the allusions to Egyptian customs, products and institutions, and also to particular incidents of Egyptian history, are such as cannot, with any great amount of probability, be ascribed to any writer between the days of Moses and those of Solomon (*e.g.*, xi. 5, 6, 7;* xxi. 5—9; † xxxiii. 4; ‡ xxxiii. 6—8).

Again, the contrast between the general allusions to the topography of Canaan, such as might well have been obtained from traditional sources, or from the reports of the spies, as compared with the more minute descriptions given in the Book of Joshua, precisely corresponds with the recorded history of Moses. Thus, while in the Book of Joshua the boundaries of Canaan are expressed with great minuteness, in the Book of Numbers they are laid down in general terms § (comp. Josh. xv. with Num. xxxiv.). It may be observed further, that the fact that the boundaries assigned to the promised land were never actually realised, even in the days of David and of Solomon, affords a strong argument in support of the belief that the Books in which they are described were not written at the late period to which they are assigned by some modern critics, in which case the original assignment would naturally have been made to accord with the actual extent of the kingdom. It must be observed further, that the statistics of the Book of Numbers stop short of the death of Moses, and that the records of families are restricted to the Mosaic era. Thus, *e.g.*, we read of the promise given to Phinehas and to his seed after him of an everlasting priesthood (xxv. 13), and we find mention of the part which Phinehas took in one of the latest expeditions in which Moses was engaged (xxxi. 6), but we must have recourse to the Books of Chronicles and of Ezra if we desire to obtain information concerning his descendants.

Objections to the Mosaic Authorship of the Book of Numbers.

It will be desirable in this place to notice some of the principal objections which have been urged against the historical accuracy, and the Mosaic authorship, of the Book of Numbers, premising only that those objections which rest upon passages in which Moses speaks as a prophet, not as an historian, do not fall within the scope of a work such as the present.

* The word *zur* occurs in Ps. lxxviii. 15, and in Is. xlviii. 21, in which places, however, there may be a reference to the later miracle at Kadesh, as well as to the earlier miracle at Rephidim.

† The assignment of the inheritances by lot, in regard to their relative position, and by the instrumentality of particular individuals appointed for the purpose, in regard to the amount of territory to be possessed by each tribe, as commanded by Moses, and as carried into execution by Joshua, is deserving of particular attention.

‡ Dr. Smith has some interesting and important remarks on the identity of the historian and the legislator throughout the Pentateuch, showing that those who acknowledge Moses to have been the legislator, must also acknowledge Moses as the historian (*The Pentateuch and its Authorship*, pp. 365—375).

* The best coriander seed is said by Pliny to come from Egypt. See Smith's *Pentateuch and its Authorship*, &c., p. 319.

† Ib., p. 340.

‡ We find the prediction in Exod. xii. 12, "Against all the gods of Egypt I will execute judgment," but we find no express account of its fulfilment. The allusion in Num. xxxiii. 4, to the fulfilment of the prediction, shows that the writer understood how the plagues of Egypt had a direct bearing upon the superstitious objects of Egyptian worship. (See Smith's *Pentateuch and its Authorship*, pp. 322—329, and Canon Cook's notes on the plagues in *The Speaker's Commentary*.)

§ The difference in the minuteness with which the northern and the southern boundaries of Canaan are described in the Book of Numbers, is deserving of notice; but the difference in the minuteness with which the latter, which must have been the boundary best known to those who were for so many years in its vicinity, is described in the Book of Numbers and in that of Joshua, is yet more remarkable.

NUMBERS.

I.—The Account of the First Census.

The difficulties in the account of the census which was taken on the plain of Sinai, as it is related in Numbers 1, may be enumerated as follows:—

(1) The precise agreement in the number of Israelites above twenty years of age as recorded in this census, with the number which is recorded in Ex. xxxviii. 26, where the reference is to a transaction which probably took place about six or seven months previously.

(2) The fact that the numbers of the respective tribes are round numbers, and, with the exception of the tribe of Gad, which has a complete fifty, that all the numbers are in round hundreds.

It has been suggested, in regard to the first difficulty, that there is nothing impossible in the fact that the number of the Israelites should not have been diminished by deaths in the course of six or seven months. This supposition, however, independently of its improbability, does not meet the real difficulty, inasmuch as there must in all probability have been many at the later date who had completed their twentieth year who could not have been included in the census of those who were twenty years old and upwards, which was taken six or seven months previously. The supposition that the number of those who died in the course of the following six or seven months was exactly equal to the number of those who attained their twentieth year in the interval, is equally improbable with the supposition that no deaths occurred in the interval; and, in any case, the difficulty attending the round numbers, on the supposition that they represent accurately the results of two distinct censuses, taken at two distinct periods, is one which, in the absence of any indication of miraculous agency, seems to be insuperable.

Both of the difficulties, however, which have been stated above, vanish, or may in any case be regarded as capable of a satisfactory solution, if it be admitted that it was one and the same census to which reference is made in the Book of Exodus and in that of Numbers.

The following reasons may be assigned for the belief that there was only one general census taken in the plain of Sinai:—

(1) The time occupied in taking the census, which is recorded in 2 Sam. xxiv.—viz., nine months and twenty days—suggests the inference that a complete census of the population, even in the time of Moses, must have occupied some considerable time.

(2) No adequate reason can be assigned for the necessity of a second census within six or seven months of a previous census.

(3) It is obvious, from the agreement of the numbers, that the tribe of Levi, which, we are expressly told, was not included in the census recorded in Numbers (see Num. i. 48, 49, ii. 33), was not included in the census to which reference is made in Exod. xxxviii., where no such exemption is mentioned, and no allusion is made to the subsequent command to number the males of the tribe of Levi from one month and upwards And, further, whereas the atonement number is expressly mentioned in Exod. xxxviii., no allusion is made to it in Num. i.

(4) We find reference made in Num. xxvi. 64, 65, to two numberings only, viz., that which was taken on the plain of Sinai, and that which was taken in the steppes of Moab, from which fact it seems reasonable to infer that two numberings only of the people were made.

Now, since the atonement money which was paid at the numbering recorded in Exod. xxxviii. was used in the construction of the Tabernacle, it is obvious that that money must have been paid previously to the first day of the first month of the year after the Exodus, at which time the Tabernacle was erected. Inasmuch, however, as the census was thus directly connected with the Tabernacle; and the census of the Levites, and also that of the firstborn, both of which were made previously to the twentieth day of the second month, in the year after the Exodus (Num. x. 11), and included all who were one month old and upwards, may be reasonably supposed to have included all who were born during the first month after the erection of the Tabernacle, and who were consequently a month old and upwards on the first day of the second month of the year after the Exodus (Num. iii. 15, 40); a reasonable probability arises that the day of the erection of the Tabernacle was that which was regarded in every case as the day by reference to which the age of the Israelites was to be ascertained and recorded. The census of the males of the several tribes, from twenty years old and upwards, being taken with reference to military service, would naturally be made in companies, which companies probably consisted of fifty or a hundred; and inasmuch as the number was taken of necessity some time previously to the erection of the Tabernacle (the atonement money being required, as already stated, for the service of the Tabernacle), it was impossible to ascertain with minute accuracy the number of those who would be alive on the day at which the Tabernacle was to be set up; and hence the odd numbers in excess of the last fifty or a hundred of those who would have completed their twentieth year at the erection of the Tabernacle, or of whose birthdays no record had been kept during the bondage in Egypt, may have been set over against the probable diminutions by death during the interval, and omitted from the sum total of each tribe. It is impossible to determine accurately the precise details which were obtained at the earlier and at the later enumeration. The amount of silver received at the earlier period sufficed to determine the number of those who paid, every man his half shekel. It is reasonable to suppose that the names of those who paid the half shekel were duly registered, and probably under their respective tribes, although there is no record of the number of each tribe in Exodus. Such a registration would naturally form the basis of the more complete census described in Numbers i., in which every man was enrolled, not only under his own tribe, but according to the two subdivisions of the tribes into "families" and "fathers' houses," according to the "number of names" included in the earlier registration. Other particulars may or may not have been included in the later registration, but if the supposition be correct that the object of the census was to associate the people with the Tabernacle, as the dwelling-place of Jehovah, it is reasonable to suppose that the same day—viz., the day of the erection of the Tabernacle—was that to which reference was made alike in the earlier and in the later registration.

In regard to the round numbers of the tribes at the later registration in the plains of Moab—in which all are recorded in tens, and all, except the tribe of Reuben, in hundreds—it is reasonable to suppose that, as on the former occasion, the registration took place in military companies of tens, fifties, or hundreds. And inasmuch as during the disbandment of the people, after their first arrival at Kadesh-Barnea, it is probable that no exact registration of births was kept, it is not unreasonable to suppose that the odd numbers were disregarded, or rather set off against the number of those whose ages could not be precisely ascertained.

It remains only that some reasonable account be given of the round number of the Levites—viz., 22,000, and of the discrepancy between the sum total and the amount of the numbers of the three families of the Kohathites, Gershonites, and Merarites, when taken separately—viz., 22,300. One solution which has been proposed of the discrepancy of the numbers is mentioned in the notes—viz., the probability that it has its origin in an error of transcription. Another proposed solution is, that some of the Levites must themselves have been firstborn, and as such could not be exchanged for the firstborn of the other tribes. The number of 300, may, it has been thought, have represented the number of Levites who were themselves firstborn; whilst in the absence of a more probable suggestion, the round numbers, both of the three families, taken separately, and of the sum total of 22,000, may be accounted for in a similar manner to that in which the round numbers of the other tribes have been explained—viz., that as the other tribes were probably registered in military companies of fifties and hundreds, so the Levites were registered in similar companies, with a view to their service in the Sanctuary—a service which is described by the Hebrew word *zaba*, which means *warfare* (Num. iv. 35).

The difficulty of accounting for the round numbers in the case of the Levites is increased by the fact that the time at which they were numbered is not specified. The injunction that the Levites were not to be numbered amongst the children of Israel (Num. i. 49), implies that their census followed that of the other tribes, but it does not clearly appear whether it preceded or followed the erection of the Tabernacle. The place in which the enumeration is recorded—viz., the Third chapter of Numbers, might seem to favour the latter supposition; but inasmuch as the command respecting Aaron and his sons, which is recorded in the same chapter (v. 10), was given previously to the erection of the Tabernacle (See Exodus, xxviii. 1), it is obvious that no certain inference respecting the time at which the injunction was given can be drawn from the place in which it is recorded. The case appears to stand thus. A command was given to Moses at the time of the Exodus to sanctify to the Lord the firstborn males of man and beast (Exod. xii. 1, 2). This command appears, from Exod. xii. 11—13, to have been given with a prospective reference to the land of Canaan, and consequently not to have come at once into operation. But when, at the expiration of the year of the Exodus, the people were still found in the wilderness, God was pleased to give some additional commands, in virtue of which the law assumed a retrospective character. The cattle of the Levites, as has been already stated, appear to have been taken as an equivalent for the firstborn cattle of the other tribes, which had been born during the preceding year. It remained that a similar arrangement should be made in regard to the firstborn of men. Some of these firstborn, both of the Levites and of the other tribes, must in all probability have died during the year, of whom no exact account may have been kept. An exact census appears to have been taken of the actual number of the firstborn then living, which was found to be 22,273. The Levites, whose sum, taken in round numbers, amounted to 22,000, were accepted as an equivalent for the same number of firstborn, the odd numbers being probably set over against those of the firstborn who had died during the year, and who, consequently, had been unredeemed. A sum of five shekels apiece was exacted as the redemption price of the surplus of the firstborn, and may, as it has been conjectured, have been levied on the parents of the youngest children; or the total amount may have been raised by a tax uniformly imposed upon the parents of all the firstborn; and from that time the sum of five shekels appears to have been exacted as the redemption price of each firstborn son.

II.—The Number of the Firstborn.

A second objection to the historical accuracy of the narrative contained in the Book of Numbers is based upon the alleged disproportion between the number of the firstborn males, viz. 22,273, and that of the entire number of the males, which is estimated at about nine hundred thousand or one million, a proportion which may be represented roughly as that of one to forty or forty-four. The fact that this disproportion exists in a narrative which affords abundant evidence of accurate computation, suggests the inference that the objection is apparent rather than real. Two solutions of the difficulty appear to be specially entitled to consideration. The first is, that the command contained in Exodus xiii. 2, respecting the sanctification of the firstborn was prospective, and that the census of the firstborn comprised only those who were born between the date of the Exodus and the beginning of the first month of the year which followed it. The second is, that the census included only the firstborn amongst those who were under twenty years of age at the time at which the general census was taken. In support of the former, and, as it should seem, the more probable of these solutions, much stress may be fairly laid upon the similar mode of reckoning the firstborn of the cattle. It is reasonable to suppose that the command to sanctify, or set apart for the Divine service, the firstborn of the cattle must have been designed to be of prospective, not retrospective, operation. This reasonable supposition is strongly corroborated by the fact that the cattle of the Levites was taken in exchange for the firstborn of the cattle of all the Israelites belonging to the other tribes. Now the male Levites of all ages bore nearly the same proportion as the firstborn of the sons of the Israelites to the entire number of the males of the other tribes. If then we assume that the cattle possessed by the Levites, previously to the time of their selection for the service of the Tabernacle, was not disproportionate to their numbers,* it will follow that about one in forty-five was given as an equivalent for the firstborn of the cattle belonging to the whole of the other tribes. This was probably an approximate equivalent for the firstborn cattle which had been born during the preceding twelve or thirteen months, but was obviously a number wholly disproportionate to the entire number of firstborn of the cattle possessed by the Israelites.

The obvious difficulty which arises in regard to this view is, that the number, 22,273, instead of being too small, appears to be much larger than that of the firstborn sons who were likely to have been born during the eleven and a half months after the Exodus. It may be fairly urged, however, in answer to this objec-

* It is not improbable that the cattle of the Levites was below rather than above the average of the cattle possessed by the other tribes. At a later period, two of the other tribes, the Reubenites and the Gadites, are said to have possessed much cattle (See Num. xxxii. 1, 4; Deut. iii. 19). It is quite possible, however, that this may have been the result, exclusively, of the recent wars in which they had been engaged.

tion, that the circumstances of the Israelites at the close of their period of bondage in Egypt, would be such as naturally to diminish to a great extent the number of marriages; whilst, on the other hand, the natural result of their deliverance from bondage would be to increase the rate of marriages much beyond the ordinary average. Under exceptionally favourable circumstances, there is no insuperable difficulty in the supposition that the number of firstborn sons in the course of nearly twelve months, out of a population of about two millions, should amount to a number even greater than that which is recorded in Num. iii. 43; and if, as some maintain, the eldest son, whether a daughter had or had not been born previously, was in every case included amongst the firstborn, the objection which has been stated loses much, if not all, of its weight. In regard to the second solution of the difficulty—viz., that the number of the firstborn sons includes only those who were under twenty years of age at the Exodus, and who had not been included in the earlier census—it may be urged—

(1) That the phraseology employed—"Number the firstborn of the males of (or belonging to) the children of Israel" (Num. iii. 40)—appears to refer to those who, like the Levites, had not been numbered already, and not to the "children of Israel" themselves, who had been already numbered, and who had already paid the half shekel, "every man a ransom for his soul" (Exod. xxx. 12).

(2) That the judgment inflicted upon the Egyptians appears to have been limited to the lowest generation, and not to have included father, grandfather, and great-grandfather, when such happened to be themselves firstborn sons. The same rule must, in all probability, have applied to the cattle. Otherwise, the distinctive character of the judgment could not have been equally apparent; as it is unreasonable to suppose that any record was kept of first births in the case of cattle which had arrived at maturity. The case is well stated by Professor Birks, in the following words:—

"The Levites 22,000, and the firstborn 22,273, are nearly equal to one-fortieth of the probable total of males in the twelve tribes, for one-fortieth of 900,000 is 22,300. This, at first sight, requires in every family, or for each mother, the enormous and incredible amount of forty sons and forty daughters. But the true comparison is with non-adult males under twenty years; and this reduces the number to thirteen and one-third of each sex. Again, it is firstborn males, and not eldest sons who had an elder sister, which alone are numbered; and this reduces the number to one-half, or six and two-thirds of either sex. But the mean number of children who survive at all the ages from 0 to 20, compared with the births, are two-thirds. Hence the probably surviving firstborn would be two-thirds for the whole period, and the number of sons and daughters in each family is reduced to four and four-ninths, only with the condition that those who died in infancy are not reckoned." (*The Exodus of Israel*, p. 75, 2nd edition, 1863.)

III.—The Results of the Earlier and Later Census.

Another objection which has been urged against the historical accuracy of the Book of Numbers is based upon a comparison of the results of the census which was taken at Sinai (Num. ii.), and that which was taken after the lapse of more than thirty-eight years, on the plains of Moab (Num. xxvi.).

The following table will show the increase or decrease in each tribe:—

	First Census.	Second Census.
Reuben,	46,500	43,730
Simeon,	59,300	22,200
Gad,	45,650	40,500
Judah,	74,600	76,500
Issachar,	54,400	64,300
Zebulon,	57,400	60,500
Ephraim,	40,500	32,500
Manasseh,	32,200	52,700
Benjamin,	35,400	45,600
Dan,	62,700	64,400
Asher,	41,500	53,400
Naphtali,	53,400	45,400
	603,550	601,730
Levi	22,000	23,000

(Num. iii. 39, compared with Num. xxvi. 62.)

It might, indeed, at first sight appear as though the remarkable increase of the Israelites in the land of Egypt would warrant the expectation of an increase of a somewhat corresponding character during the sojourn in the wilderness. It will appear, however, on a closer examination of the history, not only that the general results of the census, but also that in some cases the specific results in regard to some of the tribes, afford a strong confirmation of the general truth of the facts recorded in the Books of Exodus and Numbers.

In the first place, it must be remembered that the judgment of total extinction, with only two exceptions, was denounced against the males of all the tribes (except that of Levi), who were upwards of twenty years of age at the Exodus—*i.e.*, of all those who were included in the first census. And inasmuch as this sentence was pronounced, and began to be executed, at an early period of the wanderings in the wilderness—*i.e.*, at the time of the return of the spies (Num. xiv. 29), the result must necessarily have been a great diminution in the number of the next generation. But it is not so much in comparison of the total numbers, included respectively in the earlier and the later census, as in that of the respective numbers of the individual tribes, that we trace a correspondence between the allusions to these tribes, whether prophetical or historical, which we find in the Books of Genesis and of Numbers, and the results of the census which was taken on the plains of Moab. Thus, *e.g.*, by far the most striking decrease in numbers is observed in the case of the tribe of Simeon, which numbered at the later census little more than one-third of its amount at the first census. The case of the tribe of Levi, in which the total increase of males *from one month old and upward* was only 1,000, is almost if not quite as remarkable, more especially if it is borne in mind that that tribe does not appear to have been included in the general sentence of extermination of the males who were above twenty years of age at the Exodus. Looking back, however, to Gen. xlix. 5—7, we find Simeon and Levi associated in the prediction "I will divide them in Jacob, and scatter them in Israel." Again, in Num. xxv. we find that Zimri, the son of Salu, who took a prominent part in the idolatrous and lascivious rites of Baal-peor, was "a prince of a chief house among the Simeonites"; and hence it is not unreasonable to assume that a large number of the same tribe were concerned in that apostacy. Some indication of the tendency of this tribe to intermixture with foreign elements, and hence to the dispersion which was predicted in the prophecy of Jacob, is not wanting; for we find in Gen. xlvi. 10, notice of "the son of a Canaanitish woman" among the descendants of Simeon. Now, the laws which regulated the tribal relations were not given until the expiration of the wanderings in the wilderness, and consequently changes in those relations may have tended to a greater diminution of the tribe of Simeon than of any other tribe. Nor is it unworthy of notice that we find in 1 Chron. iv. 27 a passing allusion to the fact that the brethren of one of the heads of the tribe of Simeon—viz., Shimei—"had not many children," "neither," it is added, "did all their family multiply, like to the children of Judah." A strong confirmation of the actual fact of the paucity of numbers of the tribe of Simeon is found in Joshua xix. 9, where we find that the inheritance of the children of Simeon was taken "out of the portion of the children of Judah," because the part of the land which had been assigned to Judah was found to be "too much for them."

As regards the tribe of Levi, we find (1) that the two elder sons of Aaron, Nadab and Abihu, died childless (Num. iii. 4); and (2) we gather from the fact that the sons of Korah are expressly said not to have died with their father (Num. xxvi. 11), that a large number of the Levites who joined in the insurrection against Moses and Aaron (Num. xvi.) perished at that time. The diminution of the Reubenites may also be accounted for by the participation of the three Reubenites—Dathan, Abiram, and On—and probably of a large number of the adherents belonging to the same tribe, in the conspiracy of Korah, and in the signal punishment by which that conspiracy was avenged.

IV.—The Support of Life in the Wilderness.

Another objection which has been raised against the historical truth of the Book of Numbers, is based upon the alleged impossibility of supporting the life of nearly two millions of people and their cattle for forty years in the Sinaitic peninsula. This objection may be met in different ways; but it is probable that a full solution of the difficulty is to be found only in a more accurate aquaintance than it is now possible to obtain of the physical conditions of the country at the time of the Exodus. It may be observed, however, that if by the wilderness of Sinai we understand only the district in the immediate neighbourhood of Mount Sinai, the residence of the Israelites within that district must be reduced from forty years to about fourteen or fifteen months. In respect to the resources of the district in which the thirty-eight years of the wanderings were spent, the mode of life which was adopted by the Israelites, and the number of cattle which they possessed, we know extremely little. And again, although it may be fairly alleged that the miraculous supplies of food and water were neither required nor bestowed to the extent which some have alleged, it must not be forgotten that the miraculous elements of the history are closely interwoven into its entire fabric; and hence, whilst it is open to unbelievers to deny the historical truth of the whole of the history, the impossibility of the sustenance of life, both in regard to the people and the cattle, without miraculous intervention, so far from furnishing any argument against the account which is given in the Book of Numbers, must rather be regarded as an indication of the historical truth of a narrative in which miraculous intervention is alleged both to have been required, and also to have been vouchsafed.

It may be observed, moreover, generally, that nothing can be more uncertain than deductions as to the resources of any country, based upon evidence obtained more than three thousand years after the occurrence of the events to which the inquiry has reference. In regard to the particular region in question, we possess information which warrants the inference that its physical condition has undergone great and important changes. The conclusive evidence which exists that the population of the Sinaitic peninsula was at one time considerable, warrants the inference that its capabilities for the support of life must have been proportionate to the number of its inhabitants. It admits of no doubt that the mines, of which traces still remain, could not have been worked without the consumption of a large amount of fuel; neither could the Israelites have encamped for many months in the district without the destruction of a considerable quantity of the trees and brushwood, on which the amount of rain and its absorption so greatly depend. We have further evidence that water and pasturage still exist at many of those places at which we have reasons to believe that the Israelites encamped. Thus, *e.g.*, the plain at the foot of Mount Sinai, which is represented by Dr. Colenso as "one of the most desolate parts of the whole peninsula,"* is described by Dean Stanley as one of the "chief centres of vegetation in the whole peninsula."† It may be observed further, in regard to the region which was occupied by the Israelites during the protracted period of the wanderings, that we possess no definite information as to the precise spots which their encampments occupied, or the extent of space over which they were dispersed.

When all these circumstances are taken into account, in conjunction with the distinct statements which the Books of Exodus, Numbers and Deuteronomy contain respecting the miraculous supplies which the Israelites received, it will follow that there is no difficulty involved in the alleged sustentation of life during forty years in the wilderness which does not admit of a reasonable solution, provided only that the miraculous elements, which are essentially interwoven into the history, be not rejected on the ground of their inherent incredibility.

V.—Alleged Inconsistencies in the Laws respecting Tithes.

A more plausible ground of objection to the historical truth of the Book of Numbers arises out of the difficulty of reconciling the various and apparently conflicting laws which are found in it and in the Books of Leviticus and Deuteronomy, respecting the tithes and offerings of the Israelites, and their apportionment amongst the Priests, the Levites, the owners, and the poor. Some light has been thought to be thrown upon this subject by the usage of the Jews in later times. Independently, however, of the amount of uncertainty which attaches to the late interpretation of the Mosaic legislation generally, sufficient consideration does not appear to have been given to the two following points—viz., (1) What portion of these laws was applicable only to the wilderness? and (2) Did the laws which, as originally delivered, have reference to the land of Canaan undergo some later modification or amplification? It is obvious that if some of the laws had reference only to the wilderness, and, still further, if those laws may have undergone some further amplification, and possibly some modification, no adverse inference respecting the historical truth of the Books in which those laws are contained can fairly be deduced from the diversities which have been observed, unless it can be shown that they exist in laws which were

* *The Pentateuch and Book of Joshua Critically Examined:* Part 1, p. 71.

† *Sinai and Palestine*, p. 19.

designed to be carried simultaneously into operation. It is obvious that a complete examination of all the passages which bear upon this subject, would be as impracticable as it would be out of place in an introduction to the Book of Numbers. It must suffice if it can be shown here that the laws prescribed in Num. xviii. are not inconsistent with the earlier legislation of Exodus and Leviticus, or with the later legislation of Deuteronomy.

The general law respecting tithes, as given to Moses on Mount Sinai, is laid down in Lev. xxvii. 30—33, where it is stated that the tenth of the produce of the land and of the herds and flocks was "holy unto the Lord." In Num. xviii. 24, it is said that all the tenth in Israel was given (apparently from that time, as there is no earlier intimation of the mode of application) to the Levites, but it is not stated whether this tenth comprised the tithe of the cattle as well as that of the produce of the field. In Neh. x. 37, the tithe paid to the Levites is described as the tithes of the *ground* (comp. Neh. xii. 44). It is enjoined upon the Levites in the same chapter (verse 26) that they were to give a tenth of this tenth to the priests (comp. Neh. x. 38), and that after this tenth had been duly paid, the remaining nine-tenths might be eaten by themselves and by their households *in every place*. Now, as regards the predial produce, it is reasonable to suppose that this law must have had primary, if not exclusive, reference to the land of Canaan, not to the wilderness;* whilst it seems to follow from the words, *in every place*, that if the cattle were included in the tithe due to the Levites, the reference of the law must, in this case also, be to the land of Canaan, inasmuch as the slaughter of animals, so long as the Tabernacle remained in the wilderness, could lawfully take place only in one spot. In the legislation of Deuteronomy (chap. xii. 11—18) it is enacted that the Israelites were to bring their tithes—*i.e.*, of the land, consisting of corn, wine, and oil (verse 17), together with the firstlings of their flocks and herds, to the place which the Lord should choose, and should feast upon them there, together with their families and the Levites. A further provision is made in chap. xiv. 24—27, that if the distance to the Sanctuary should be too great, the tithe might be converted into its equivalent in money, and the money expended in food, which was to be consumed in the same manner at the place which should be selected for the Sanctuary. It is further enacted, in verses 28, 29 of the same chapter, that at the end of three years the whole of the tithe of that year's increase—*i.e.*, of the vegetable produce—was to be laid up within the gates of the cities in which the Israelites lived, and to be consumed there by "the Levites and the stranger and the fatherless and the widow." It is also enjoined in Deut. xxvi. 12—14, that at the end of the tithing of the third year, which is there described as "the year of tithing," the produce—*i.e.*, of the land—was to be given to the Levite, the stranger, the fatherless, and the widow, to be consumed within the gates of the cities, and that a solemn affirmation should be made by the owner that he had duly discharged all that devolved upon him in this respect.

When these ordinances are carefully examined and compared, it will appear that they present no inconsistency, except upon the wholly arbitrary assumption that there was but one tithe to which reference is made. The preposterous character of such a supposition is obvious, from the simple consideration that, inasmuch as that tithe was to be consumed, at least in the first and second year, at the Sanctuary, it will follow that no stated provision whatever was made for the Levites, and that they were dependent upon the feasts to which they were to be invited at certain seasons of the first and second year, and upon the portion which might fall to their lot in the third year.

It may, indeed, be fairly regarded as an open question whether the tithes of the third year were in lieu of, or were supplementary to, the second tithes of the first and second years; which (or their equivalent in money) were consumed at the Sanctuary. In the absence, as it should seem, of any direct information on this point, all that can be alleged with confidence is, that on the first and second of each of the triennial periods the tenth of the predial produce (and perhaps of the herds and flocks), was to be set apart for the maintenance of the Priests and Levites; and that a second tenth of the produce of the field, and also the firstlings of the flock, were appointed to be consumed by the owner and his family, together with the Levites, at the Sanctuary; and that on the third year, either (as some think) in addition to these two tenths, or (as others maintain) in lieu of the second tenth, a tenth of the predial produce was to be laid up in the cities in which the people lived, and to be consumed by the poor and friendless, together with the Levites. On the seventh year the land was to rest, and the law of tithes would necessarily be in abeyance.

We now proceed to take notice of some few additional passages or expressions which have been adduced as inconsistent with the Mosaic authorship of the Book of Numbers.

(1) It has been inferred from the words which occur in chap. xv. 32—"While the children of Israel were in the wilderness," that they were no longer in the wilderness when the incident which is there recorded was committed to writing, and, consequently, that Moses was not the author of this portion of the narrative. It might suffice to reply to this objection, that inasmuch as Moses lived to conduct the Israelites into the steppes of Moab, there is nothing inconsistent with the Mosaic authorship of the narrative in the statement that a certain incident happened while the people were still in the wilderness. There may, however, have been another and a special reason for the insertion of these words. The punishment of death, though not the mode of its infliction, had already been denounced against those who should violate the Sabbath (Exod. xxxi. 14, 15). It is obvious, however, that much of the legislation which is contained in the Book of Exodus (See, *e.g.*, chaps. xxii., xxiii.), was not designed to come into operation until after the entrance into the land of Canaan; and so, likewise, in regard to some of the legislation contained in the fifteenth chapter of the Book of Numbers, in which the incident of the man who gathered sticks on the Sabbath is recorded, it is expressly stated that it has reference to the land whither God was about to bring his people (verse 18). It is not unreasonable, therefore, to infer that the uncertainty which existed in the minds of Moses and of the congregation as to the punishment which should be inflicted on the Sabbath-breaker, may have arisen from the fact that the violation of the law took place in the *wilderness*, and that the same reason may be assigned why a prominent place is given in the narra-

* It would be rash to assert that corn may not have been sown and reaped during some portion of the thirty-eight years of the wanderings in the wilderness. There is, however, no evidence in support of an affirmative proposition on this subject.

tive to the fact that the people were still "in the wilderness" when this incident occurred.

(2) Some remarks will be found in the note on chap. xxii. 1 in respect to the use of the same Hebrew expression to denote the territory on the eastern and on the western side of the Jordan. It has been urged, as an objection to the Mosaic authorship of the Pentateuch, that the Hebrew phrase, which is commonly rendered "*beyond*," or "*on the other side* Jordan" (as, *e.g.*, in Num. xxii. 1, where, in the A.V., it is incorrectly rendered "on this side Jordan"), could not have been used by Moses, but must have been used by one who wrote in the land of Canaan. It has been fairly alleged, in reply to this objection, that during the long residence of the Hebrews in Canaan, previously to the descent into Egypt, this phrase may have become a generally recognised description of the country on the east of the Jordan, just as the expressions *Cisalpine Gaul* and *Transalpine Gaul* might have been used without reference to the abode of the writer on the north or south of the Alps, and as the name of *Peræa* was given to a particular province on the east of the Jordan. The fact, however, is that the phrase in question is used by the same writers or speakers with reference to the country *on both sides* of the Jordan, and in one instance—viz., Num. xxxii. 19—in the very same sentence (see Note *in loc.*). It follows, then, whatever may have been the origin of the expression, that no argument against the Mosaic authorship of the Pentateuch generally, or of the Book of Numbers in particular, can be fairly urged from the use of this expression by the writer in regard to the country either on the eastern or on the western side of the Jordan.

(3) Objection has been taken to the Mosaic authorship of the Book of Numbers on the ground of the use of the word *nabi*, *prophet*, instead of *roeh*, *seer*, in chapters xi. 29 and xii. 6, such use being, as it is alleged, inconsistent with the statement which is contained in 1 Sam. ix. 6, that he who was at that time called a *prophet* (*nabi*), was aforetime called a *seer* (*roeh*). It might suffice to observe, in reply to this objection, that if the reference be—as seems probable, and as the LXX. (who appear to have followed a different reading) understood the passage—to the popular use of the terms, there is no inconsistency in the fact that a writer such as Moses should have used the word *nabi* (*prophet*), whilst the people, in their ordinary conversation, used the word *roeh* (*seer*). The whole objection, however, is based upon an arbitrary interpretation of the word, which is rendered *beforetime* in 1 Sam. ix. 9. A long period had elapsed between the time of Moses and that of Samuel; and it is both possible and probable that during that interval there may have been a great fluctuation in the use of words. It follows, then, that there is no difficulty involved in the supposition that during a portion of that period the word *roeh* (*seer*) may have been in ordinary use, although in the time of Moses, as in subsequent periods of Jewish history, the word *nabi* (*prophet*) may have been more commonly employed to denote the same class of persons who had, *during an intermediate period*, been known as *seers*. It is not unreasonable, moreover, to suppose that the suspension of prophetical utterances, which appears to have prevailed from the days of Deborah to those of Samuel, may afford an adequate explanation of the reason why the people had ceased to employ the word *nabi* (*prophet*), and had become familiar with a word which does not denote the communication of any supernatural revelation through the agency of those to whom it was applied.

(4) There are other passages which have been alleged as inconsistent with the Mosaic authorship of the Book of Numbers, which may have been inserted at a later period, or which are capable of an explanation which is consistent with the supposition that they proceeded from the pen of Moses. Such, *e.g.*, is Num. xii. 3: "Now the man Moses was very meek, above all the men which were upon the face of the earth." It is quite possible that these words may have been inserted by Ezra or some other reviser of the Book of Numbers; or, as it is stated in the Note upon this passage, the word rendered *meek* may mean *afflicted* or *oppressed*. There is, however, no necessity for the adoption of either of these suppositions on the part of those who believe that Moses wrote by the inspiration of the Holy Ghost. If St. Paul, writing under the influence of the same Divine guidance, could speak of himself both as "the chief of sinners" (1 Tim. i. 15), and also as "not a whit behind the very chiefest Apostles" (2 Cor. xi. 5), it may well be that the same Moses who recorded the sentence of exclusion from the land of Canaan which was pronounced upon his own unbelief (Num. xx. 12), may have been inwardly moved by the Spirit to record also his possession, in an eminent degree, of that virtue, the reward of which has been declared by our Lord to be the future inheritance of the earth (St. Matt. v. 5).

A similar explanation may be given of some verses in chapter xiv. in which Joshua is associated with Caleb as protesting against the rebellious spirit of the people, whilst, in portions of chapters xiii. and xiv., it would seem as if Caleb alone had stilled the people, and as if to him alone of that generation had been promised an entrance into the land of Canaan.

In regard to these and some other passages—such, *e.g.*, as those which relate to geographical and historical circumstances—it is not always possible, nor is it of any real importance, that we should attempt to determine whether the whole formed part of the original narrative, or whether—as in the case of Deut. xxxiv.—some later interpolations and additions may have been admitted into it. It is enough if it be shown (as it may and has been) that there is no contrariety which does not admit of reasonable explanation.

(5) Another objection to the historical truth of the narrative contained in the Book of Numbers is based upon the alleged insufficiency of the time which is allotted to the transactions of the fortieth year. It is urged that the events which are said to have transpired between the death of Aaron, which took place on the first day of the fifth month in that year, and the defeat of Og, the king of Bashan, must have occupied a space of at least six months, and that we are thus brought to the beginning of the eleventh month, the time at which Moses is said to have addressed the assembled hosts of Israel on the plains of Moab (Deut. i. 3). No room, it is alleged, is left for a number of other events which are said to have taken place between these limits—as, *e.g.*, the march to the plains of Moab, the messages sent to Balaam and his arrival and prophesyings, the abode of the people in Shittim, and the plague which destroyed 24,000, the second census, and the Midianitish war. It appears, however, upon examination, that the time allotted to the several events which happened during these six months is, with one exception, purely arbitrary. The single exception is the period of mourning which ensued upon the death of Aaron—viz., one month. There is no evidence, however, that the whole of the Israelitish army abstained from action during this period; and it is probable that both the

attack of the king of Arad and his discomfiture may have taken place within a very few days after the death of Aaron. The events which followed may have taken place in rapid succession, and in some cases simultaneously.

Professors Birks and McCaul, by opposing conjecture to conjecture have shown that the whole may have been accomplished within the specified period; and the latter, by reference to the extraordinary results of the battle of Jena, has shown that such conjectures "concerning the possible and probable rapidity of Israelitish conquest, are confirmed by historic facts within the personal knowledge of many still living."

No Introduction to the Book of Numbers would be complete which failed to notice the peculiar proofs of its Divine inspiration which arise out of the typical occurrences which are related in it. These occurrences are, in some respects, even more remarkable, and more beyond the range of invention, than the symbolism of the ceremonial ordinances of the Levitical law. It is impossible to read, with candour and with attention, the account of the march of the Israelites through the wilderness, the miraculous guidance vouchsafed to them by the pillar of cloud and of fire, the invitation of Moses to Hobab, the miraculous supply of manna and of water, the expedition of the spies, the rash and abortive attempt to enter the land of Canaan, the repeated provocations in the wilderness, and the consequent exclusion from the land of promise of those who were included in the Sinaitic census, the intercession of Aaron as he stood between the living and the dead, the history of the fiery serpents and of the brazen serpent, the death of Moses and the appointment of Joshua as his successor, and lastly, the appointment of the cities of refuge—it is impossible, it may be affirmed, to read all these in a candid spirit and not to be struck with the remarkable types and foreshadowing which these events contain of the spiritual realities of the Christian life, and the impossibility either of the accidental occurrence of events which present so many points of spiritual correspondence, or of the arbitrary invention of such a chain of historical circumstances, even at the latest period to which certain modern critics have assigned the composition of the Book of Numbers.

Literature.

The following list contains some of the most valuable contributions to the critical and exegetical exposition of the Book of Numbers, which are either written in the English language or which have been translated into English. Of them many have been consulted, and valuable aid has been derived from them, in the composition of the present Commentary:—Keil on *The Pentateuch*, 3 vols., T. and T. Clark, Edinburgh, 1864; Bishop Wordsworth's *Commentary on the Bible*, part ii., Rivingtons, 1865; *The Speaker's Commentary*, vol. ii., J. Murray, 1871; Lange's *Commentary on the Old Testament*, vol. iii., T. and T. Clark, Edinburgh (no date); Patrick Lowth and Whitby on *The Old and New Testament*, 4 vols., imp. 8vo, Tegg, 1844; *A Practical and Explanatory Commentary on the Old Testament*, by the Rev. Robert Jamieson, D.D., imp. 4to, London, Virtue and Co.

Much valuable information may be obtained from the following works, which bear more or less fully upon the elucidation of the Book of Numbers. Some of them, however, and more particularly that of Bleek, must be consulted with much caution:—*The Historic Character of the Pentateuch Vindicated*, Skeffington, 1863; *The Mosaic Origin of the Pentateuch Considered*, Skeffington, 1864; *The Book of Moses, or the Pentateuch, in its Authorship, Credibility, and Civilisation*, by the Rev. W. Smith, Ph.D., vol. i., Longmans, 1868; *The Exodus of Israel*, by the Rev. T. R. Birks, M.A., Rector of Kelshall, Herts, Second Ed., 1863; Hengstenberg on *The Genuineness of the Pentateuch*, translated by Ryland, J. D. Lowe, Edinburgh, 2 vols., 8vo, 1847; Hävernick's *Historico-Critical Introduction to the Pentateuch*, translated by Thompson, T. and T. Clark, Edinburgh, 1850; Bleek's *Introduction to the Old Testament*, translated by Venables, 2 vols., 8vo, Bell and Daldy, 1869.

THE FOURTH BOOK OF MOSES, CALLED

NUMBERS

B. C. 1490.

CHAPTER I. — (1) And the LORD
spake unto Moses in the wilderness of
Sinai, in the tabernacle of the congre-
gation, on the first *day* of the second
month, in the second year after they
were come out of the land of Egypt,
saying, (2) [a] Take ye the sum of all the
congregation of the children of Israel,
after their families, by the house of
their fathers, with the number of *their*
names, every male by their polls;
(3) from twenty years old and upward,
all that are able to go forth to war in
Israel: thou and Aaron shall number
them by their armies. (4) And with you
there shall be a man of every tribe;
every one head of the house of his
fathers.
(5) And these *are* the names of the men
that shall stand with you: of *the tribe
of* Reuben; Elizur the son of Shedeur.
(6) Of Simeon; Shelumiel the son of
Zurishaddai. (7) Of Judah; Nahshon the
son of Amminadab. (8) Of Issachar;
Nethaneel the son of Zuar. (9) Of Zeb-
ulun; Eliab the son of Helon. (10) Of
the children of Joseph: of Ephraim;
Elishama the son of Ammihud: of
Manasseh; Gamaliel the son of Ped-
ahzur. (11) Of Benjamin; Abidan the
son of Gideoni. (12) Of Dan; Ahiezer
the son of Ammishaddai. (13) Of Asher;
Pagiel the son of Ocran. (14) Of Gad;
Eliasaph the son of Deuel. (15) Of
Naphtali; Ahira the son of Enan.
(16) These *were* the renowned of the con-
gregation, princes of the tribes of their
fathers, heads of thousands in Israel.

a Ex. 30. 12.

---

(1) **In the tabernacle of the congregation.**—The tabernacle of the congregation, or *tent of meeting*, so called because it was there that God met with Moses (chap. xvii. 4; Ex. xxv. 22), had been set up one month previously (Ex. xl. 17), nearly a year after the exodus.

(2) **After their families.**—The family or clan, *mishpahah*, included several fathers' houses (see Kurtz's *Hist. of the Old Covenant*, ii., pp. 8—10).

With the number of their names.—Better, *according to the number of names.* The reference is probably to the previous numbering recorded in Ex. xxx. 12. There is no corresponding clause in the account of the later numbering in chap. xxvi. 2.

By their polls—*i.e.*, man by man. The word *gulgoleth* denotes *a man's head*, or *skull.* Cf. Matt. xxvii. 33.

(3) **From twenty years old and upward.**—The result of the previous numbering (Ex. xxx. 12, xxxviii. 26), which was made about six months earlier, and which was probably obtained by counting the number of half-shekels which were paid, as Ithamar appears to have done (Ex. xxxviii. 2), exactly corresponds with the result of the present census (verse 46). But the complete census, or numbering and enrolment of the persons according to tribes, families, and fathers' houses, appears to have been deferred until after the erection of the tabernacle, towards the construction of which the atonement money had been paid. If the whole was done in obedience to the command contained in Ex. xxx. 12, and was regarded as one transaction, those only would be numbered on the second occasion who had already paid their atonement money. There is nothing impossible in the supposition that the whole of those who had been numbered six months previously were still alive, but no allowance is made, on this supposition, for the number of those who were below twenty years of age at the earlier period, and who had exceeded that age at the later period. Inasmuch, however, as the sum-total in both cases is divisible by ten, and inasmuch as the separate items in this chapter are given in tens (the smallest subdivision of the people which was adopted by Moses, on the recommendation of Jethro, Ex. xviii. 21), no objection to the historical accuracy of both records can be sustained if it be allowed that the number of those who had attained the age of twenty years since the earlier census corresponded nearly with the number of deaths during the same period. The whole of the objection, however, is removed in a far more satisfactory manner by the supposition that there was only one census. (See the Introduction.)

By their armies.—Better, *their hosts or companies.*

(4) **Of every tribe.**—Or, *for every tribe.*

Every one head . . .—The words may be rendered *every one a head . . .* There were many heads of fathers' houses in each tribe; but it appears from verse 16 (chap. vii. 10, 11) that in each case the tribal *prince* was selected to preside over the census.

(5) **Of the tribe of Reuben.**—Hebrew, *for Reuben.*

(16) **The renowned of the congregation.**—Lit., *the called men of the congregation*, i.e., the men chosen as representatives of their respective tribes, and appointed

(17) And Moses and Aaron took these
men which are expressed by *their*
names: (18) and they assembled all the
congregation together on the first *day*
of the second month, and they declared
their pedigrees after their families, by
the house of their fathers, according to
the number of the names, from twenty
years old and upward, by their polls.
(19) As the LORD commanded Moses, so
he numbered them in the wilderness of
Sinai.

(20) And the children of Reuben,
Israel's eldest son, by their generations,
after their families, by the house of
their fathers, according to the number
of the names, by their polls, every male
from twenty years old and upward, all
that were able to go forth to war;
(21) those that were numbered of them,
even of the tribe of Reuben, *were* forty
and six thousand and five hundred.

(22) Of the children of Simeon, by their
generations, after their families, by the
house of their fathers, those that were
numbered of them, according to the
number of the names, by their polls,
every male from twenty years old and
upward, all that were able to go forth
to war; (23) those that were numbered
of them, *even* of the tribe of Simeon,
were fifty and nine thousand and three
hundred.

(24) Of the children of Gad, by their
generations, after their families, by
the house of their fathers, according
to the number of the names, from
twenty years old and upward, all that
were able to go forth to war; (25) those
that were numbered of them, *even* of
the tribe of Gad, *were* forty and five
thousand six hundred and fifty.

(26) Of the children of Judah, by their
generations, after their families, by the
house of their fathers, according to the
number of the names, from twenty years
old and upward, all that were able to
go forth to war; (27) those that were
numbered of them, *even* of the tribe
of Judah, *were* threescore and fourteen
thousand and six hundred.

(28) Of the children of Issachar, by their
generations, after their families, by the
house of their fathers, according to the
number of the names, from twenty years
old and upward, all that were able to
go forth to war; (29) those that were
numbered of them, *even* of the tribe of
Issachar, *were* fifty and four thousand
and four hundred.

(30) Of the children of Zebulun, by
their generations, after their families,
by the house of their fathers, accord-
ing to the number of the names, from
twenty years old and upward, all that
were able to go forth to war; (31) those
that were numbered of them, *even* of the
tribe of Zebulun, *were* fifty and seven
thousand and four hundred.

(32) Of the children of Joseph, *namely*,
of the children of Ephraim, by their
generations, after their families, by the
house of their fathers, according to
the number of the names, from twenty
years old and upward, all that were
able to go forth to war; (33) those that
were numbered of them, *even* of the
tribe of Ephraim, *were* forty thousand
and five hundred.

(34) Of the children of Manasseh,
by their generations, after their fami-
lies, by the house of their fathers, ac-
cording to the number of the names,
from twenty years old and upward,
all that were able to go forth to
war; (35) those that were numbered

---

to act in that capacity in regulating the affairs of the nation.

Heads of thousands in Israel.—Better, *they were the heads of the thousands of Israel.* Comp. Exod. xviii. 21, 25, where rulers, or princes of thousands, are the highest class of officers recommended by Jethro, and appointed by Moses. See also chap. x. 4.

(18) **Declared their pedigrees.**—More literally, *announced themselves as having been born—i.e.*, caused themselves to be enrolled. The people appear to have been enrolled by their polls, *i.e.*, individually, under three heads—(1) according to the tribe to which they belonged; (2) according to the *mishpahah*, or family, which, as it appears from chap. iii. 22, included in some cases two or three thousand persons; and (3) according to their father's house. The importance of this enrolment, as affording the means of tracing the genealogy of Christ, must not be overlooked.

According to the number of the names.—The words are the same as in verse 2, and should be rendered in the same manner.

(20) **By their generations.**—The *toledoth*, or generations, included the whole of the descendants of the head of the tribe (Gen. v. 1, vi. 9).

(27) **Threescore and fourteen thousand and six hundred.**—The superiority of Judah in point of numbers over all the other tribes deserves notice in connection with the blessing pronounced on that tribe by Jacob in Gen. xlix. 8: "Thou art he whom thy brethren shall praise." In like manner it should be

of them, *even* of the tribe of Manasseh, *were* thirty and two thousand and two hundred.

(36) Of the children of Benjamin, by their generations, after their families, by the house of their fathers, according to the number of the names, from twenty years old and upward, all that were able to go forth to war; (37) those that were numbered of them, *even* of the tribe of Benjamin, *were* thirty and five thousand and four hundred.

(38) Of the children of Dan, by their generations, after their families, by the house of their fathers, according to the number of the names, from twenty years old and upward, all that were able to go forth to war; (39) those that were numbered of them, *even* of the tribe of Dan, *were* threescore and two thousand and seven hundred.

(40) Of the children of Asher, by their generations, after their families, by the house of their fathers, according to the number of the names, from twenty years old and upward, all that were able to go forth to war; (41) those that were numbered of them, *even* of the tribe of Asher, *were* forty and one thousand and five hundred.

(42) Of the children of Naphtali, throughout their generations, after their families, by the house of their fathers, according to the number of the names, from twenty years old and upward, all that were able to go forth to war; (43) those that were numbered of them, *even* of the tribe of Naphtali, *were* fifty and three thousand and four hundred.

(44) These *are* those that were numbered, which Moses and Aaron numbered, and the princes of Israel, *being* twelve men: each one was for the house of his fathers. (45) So were all those that were numbered of the children of Israel, by the house of their fathers, from twenty years old and upward, all that were able to go forth to war in Israel; (46) even all they that were numbered were six hundred thousand and three thousand and five hundred and fifty.

(47) But the Levites after the tribe of their fathers were not numbered among them. (48) For the LORD had spoken unto Moses, saying, (49) Only thou shalt not number the tribe of Levi, neither take the sum of them among the children of Israel: (50) but thou shalt appoint the Levites over the tabernacle of testimony, and over all the vessels thereof, and over all things that *belong* to it: they shall bear the tabernacle, and all the vessels thereof; and they shall minister unto it, and shall encamp round about the tabernacle. (51) And when the tabernacle setteth forward, the Levites shall take it down: and when the tabernacle is to be pitched, the Levites shall set it up: and the stranger that cometh nigh shall be put to death. (52) And the children of Israel shall pitch their tents, every man by his own camp, and every man by his own standard, through-

---

observed that the number of the tribe of Ephraim (verse 33) exceeded that of the tribe of Manasseh (verse 35). (See Gen. xlviii. 19, 20.)

(46) **Six hundred thousand and three thousand and five hundred and fifty.**—It is obvious that the odd numbers were not reckoned. In chap. xi. 21, as in Ex. xii. 37, the whole number is reckoned roughly at six hundred thousand.

(48) **For the Lord had spoken . . .**—Better, *And the Lord spake . . .* (chap. iii. 1, 5, 6, 14, 15). It is true that the Levites were not included in the earlier numbering, and consequently that they must have been exempted by divine direction. It does not appear, however, that there is a reference to any previous command respecting the Levites, or that the specific destination of the Levites had been previously declared.

(50) **The tabernacle of testimony.**—The testimony (sometimes described as the two tables of the testimony (Ex. xxxi. 18, xxxiv. 29) denotes in the first instance the tables of the law which were directed to be placed in the ark (Ex. xxv. 16, 21). Hence the ark is described as the ark of the testimony (Ex. xxv. 22, xxvi. 33), and the tabernacle as the tabernacle of the testimony (Ex. xxxviii. 21), and the tent, including the outer covering of the *mishkan*, or wooden building, is called the tent of the testimony (chap. ix. 15). Also the veil which separated the holy place from the most holy is called the veil of the testimony (Lev. xxiv. 3).

And shall encamp round about the tabernacle.—The tent of meeting was like a royal palace, and the Levites served as a guard of honour round about it, to protect it from every sort of desecration.

(51) **And the stranger that cometh nigh shall be put to death.**—The word *zar* (stranger) here denotes one who was not of the tribe of Levi (Lev. xxii. 10, 12).

(52) **By his own standard.**—It appears from chap. ii. 3, 10, 18, 25, that there were four standards—viz., those of Judah, Reuben, Ephraim, and Dan—corresponding to the four camps, each consisting of three tribes, which pitched round the tent of meeting.

out their hosts. (53) But the Levites shall pitch round about the tabernacle of testimony, that there be no wrath upon the congregation of the children of Israel: and the Levites shall keep the charge of the tabernacle of testimony.

(54) And the children of Israel did according to all that the LORD commanded Moses, so did they.

CHAPTER II. — (1) And the LORD spake unto Moses and unto Aaron, saying, (2) Every man of the children of Israel shall pitch by his own standard, with the ensign of their father's house: [1] far off about the tabernacle of the congregation shall they pitch.

(3) And on the east side toward the rising of the sun shall they of the standard of the camp of Judah pitch throughout their armies: and Nahshon the son of Amminadab *shall be* captain of the children of Judah. (4) And his host, and those that were numbered of them, *were* threescore and fourteen thousand and six hundred. (5) And those that do pitch next unto him *shall be* the tribe of Issachar: and Nethaneel the son of Zuar *shall be* captain of the children of Issachar. (6) And his host, and those that were numbered thereof, *were* fifty and four thousand and four hundred. (7) *Then* the tribe of Zebulun: and Eliab the son of Helon *shall be* captain of the children of Zebulun. (8) And his host, and those that were numbered thereof, *were* fifty and seven thousand and four hundred. (9) All that were numbered in the camp of Judah *were* an hundred thousand and fourscore thousand and six thousand and four hundred, throughout their armies. These shall first set forth.

(10) On the south side *shall be* the standard of the camp of Reuben according to their armies: and the captain of the children of Reuben *shall be* Elizur the son of Shedeur. (11) And his host, and those that were numbered thereof, *were* forty and six thousand and five hundred. (12) And those which pitch by him *shall be* the tribe of Simeon: and the captain of the children of Simeon *shall be* Shelumiel the son of Zurishaddai. (13) And his host, and those that were numbered of them, *were* fifty and nine thousand and three hundred. (14) Then the tribe of Gad: and the captain of the sons of Gad *shall be* Eliasaph the son of Reuel. (15) And his host, and those that were numbered of them, *were* forty and five thousand and six hundred and fifty. (16) All that were numbered in the camp of Reuben *were* an hundred thousand and fifty and one thousand and four hundred and fifty, throughout their armies. And they shall set forth in the second rank.

(17) Then the tabernacle of the congregation shall set forward with the camp of the Levites in the midst of the

[1] Heb., *over against.*

---

(53) **That there be no wrath upon the congregation of the children of Israel.**—The word *kezeph* (wrath) is used to denote some immediate visitation of the hand of God, as, *e.g.*, the plague. Thus, after the plague which broke out in consequence of the sin of Korah, Dathan, and Abiram, we read in chap. xviii. 5 "that there be no wrath (*kezeph*) any more upon the children of Israel." In chap. viii. 19 the word *negeph* (plague) is used in the same sense as *kezeph* is used here. (Cf. Josh. ix. 20; 2 Kings iii. 27; 1 Chron. xxvii. 24.)

II.

(2) **With the ensign.**—Better, *the signs* or *ensigns.* Probably each father's house had its own smaller ensign or flag.

Far off about the tabernacle of the congregation . . .—Better, *over against the tent of meeting shall they pitch round about it.* The word *minneged* (over against) generally implies the idea of distance as well as that of opposition. At the same time it is more correctly rendered *over against* than *far off.* The meaning seems to be that the four camps which encircled the tent of meeting were pitched opposite to, but at some distance from it; and this is implied in the directions given in the following chapter for the encamping of the Levites immediately round the tent of meeting. It has been supposed that the nearest tents were above 2,000 cubits, which was probably a Sabbath day's journey, from the tabernacle (cf. Josh. iii. 4); and on this supposition the area of the camp has been computed at about three square miles. The form of encampment was probably circular.

(9) **These shall first set forth.**—It is quite possible that there may be a *primary* reference in Gen. xlix. 10 to the position which the camp of Judah should occupy in the marches of the Israelites.

(14) **Reuel.**—There is good authority for reading *Deuel* here, as in chaps. i. 14, vii. 42, x. 20.

(16) **Throughout their armies.**—Better, *according to their hosts.* So in verses 3 and 24. In verse 31 the words "with their standards" seem to be used in the same manner. Each tribe had probably the common standard (*degel*) of its leading tribe as well as its own smaller ensigns.

(17) **In the midst of the camp.**—Or, *host.* The word *mahaneh* (camp) here denotes evidently the whole of the four united camps or hosts. As the tent of

camp: as they encamp, so shall they
set forward, every man in his place by
their standards.

(18) On the west side *shall be* the
standard of the camp of Ephraim
according to their armies: and the
captain of the sons of Ephraim *shall
be* Elishama the son of Ammihud.
(19) And his host, and those that were
numbered of them, *were* forty thousand
and five hundred. (20) And by him
shall be the tribe of Manasseh: and the
captain of the children of Manasseh
shall be Gamaliel the son of Pedahzur.
(21) And his host, and those that were
numbered of them, *were* thirty and two
thousand and two hundred. (22) Then
the tribe of Benjamin: and the captain
of the sons of Benjamin *shall be* Abidan
the son of Gideoni. (23) And his host,
and those that were numbered of them,
were thirty and five thousand and four
hundred. (24) All that were numbered
of the camp of Ephraim *were* an hun-
dred thousand and eight thousand and
an hundred, throughout their armies.
And they shall go forward in the third
rank.

(25) The standard of the camp of Dan
shall be on the north side by their
armies: and the captain of the children
of Dan *shall be* Ahiezer the son of
Ammishaddai. (26) And his host, and
those that were numbered of them,
were threescore and two thousand and
seven hundred. (27) And those that
encamp by him *shall be* the tribe of
Asher: and the captain of the chil-
dren of Asher *shall be* Pagiel the son
of Ocran. (28) And his host, and those
that were numbered of them, *were* forty
and one thousand and five hundred.
(29) Then the tribe of Naphtali: and
the captain of the children of Naph-
tali *shall be* Ahira the son of Enan.
(30) And his host, and those that were
numbered of them, *were* fifty and three
thousand and four hundred. (31) All
they that were numbered in the camp
of Dan *were* an hundred thousand and
fifty and seven thousand and six hun-
dred. They shall go hindmost with
their standards.

(32) These *are* those which were num-
bered of the children of Israel by the
house of their fathers: all those that
were numbered of the camps through-
out their hosts *were* six hundred
thousand and three thousand and five
hundred and fifty. (33) But the Levites
were not numbered among the children
of Israel; as the LORD commanded
Moses. (34) And the children of Israel
did according to all that the LORD com-
manded Moses: so they pitched by their
standards, and so they set forward, every
one after their families, according to the
house of their fathers.

---

meeting was compassed about by the four camps when stationary, so it was placed in the centre when they were in motion, having the camps of Judah and Reuben before it, and those of Ephraim and Dan behind it. As the sanctuary of God was in the midst of the camp of the Israelites, and set forward in the midst of their hosts as they marched, so God is represented by the Psalmist as being in the midst of His Church (Ps. xlvi. 5). The collocation of the tribes was evidently determined in accordance with their mutual relationship. Thus, the eastern camp was composed exclusively of the descendants of the sons of Leah; the southern of those of the two remaining sons of Leah (the tribe of Levi being encamped around the Tabernacle) and a son of Zilpah, Leah's handmaid; the western of those of one of the sons and of the two grandsons of Rachel; and the northern of those of the two sons of Bilhah and of the remaining son of Zilpah. If this arrangement is examined, it will be found that, if allowance be made for the separation of the tribe of Levi, none could have been made in which the relationship by birth would be more closely adhered to. We may learn from this arrangement that the ties of nature should strengthen those of Christian communion. The grouping of the tribes in Ezek. xlviii. 30—34 is different, but the family relationship is still more closely preserved. In Rev. vii. 5—8, where the reference is to a state in which they neither marry nor are given in marriage, the twelve tribes are enumerated without any regard to family relationship. It is deserving of notice that when the lots of the several tribes were finally determined, we find that the temporary association established during their encampments in the wilderness was to a great extent preserved. Thus we see, in regard to the three tribes which formed the eastern camp, that Issachar and Zebulun had adjoining territories; that of those which formed the southern camp, Reuben and Gad had adjoining territories on the east of the Jordan; that this was also the case with the three tribes which formed the western camp, viz., Benjamin, Manasseh, and Ephraim; and that of those which formed the northern camp, Asher and Naphtali had adjoining territories.

(32) **These are those which were numbered.**—The number of the Israelites was very large, considering in how short a time, and under what adverse circumstances, the small company which went down into Egypt had multiplied into 600,000 men capable of bearing arms, independently of the tribe of Levi. But the spiritual Israel of Rev. vii. 9 is represented as "a great multitude which no man could number."

The subjoined plan will suffice to convey a general

CHAPTER III. — (1) These also *are*
the generations of Aaron and Moses in
the day *that* the LORD spake with Moses
in mount Sinai. (2) And these *are* the
names of the sons of Aaron; Nadab
the [a] firstborn, and Abihu, Eleazar, and
Ithamar. (3) These *are* the names of
the sons of Aaron, the priests which
were anointed, [1] whom he consecrated to
minister in the priest's office. (4) [b] And
Nadab and Abihu died before the LORD,
when they offered strange fire before
the LORD, in the wilderness of Sinai,
and they had no children: and Eleazar
and Ithamar ministered in the priest's
office in the sight of Aaron their father.

B. C. 1491.

a Ex. 6. 23.

1 Heb., *whose hand he filled.*

B. C. 1490.

b Lev. 10. 1; ch. 26. 61; 1 Chr. 24. 2.

(5) And the LORD spake unto Moses,
saying, (6) Bring the tribe of Levi near,
and present them before Aaron the
priest, that they may minister unto
him. (7) And they shall keep his charge,
and the charge of the whole congre-
gation before the tabernacle of the
congregation, to do the service of the
tabernacle. (8) And they shall keep all
the instruments of the tabernacle of
the congregation, and the charge of
the children of Israel, to do the ser-
vice of the tabernacle. (9) And thou
shalt give the Levites unto Aaron and
to his sons: they *are* wholly given
unto him out of the children of Israel.

---

idea of the position of the twelve tribes with respect to the tent of meeting during their encampments in the wilderness. It does not clearly appear what was the position of the leading or standard tribe in regard to the two other tribes which constituted together with it one camp.

		ASHER, DAN, NAPHTALI.		
		MERARITES.		
MANASSEH, EPHRAIM, BENJAMIN.	GERSHONITES.	[TENT OF MEETING.]	MOSES, AARON AND HIS SONS.	ISSACHAR, JUDAH, ZEBULUN.
		KOHATHITES.		
		SIMEON, REUBEN, GAD.		

III.

(1) **These also are the generations of Aaron and Moses . . .**—The name of Aaron is placed first, not only because he was the elder brother, but also because the ministry of Moses was restricted to his own person, and his sons are merely classed amongst the rest of the Levitical families in 1 Chron. xxiii. 14; whereas the office of Aaron was perpetuated in the persons of his descendants. Hence we find no mention made in this place of the sons of Moses, but only of those of Aaron. The word *generations* here, as in the book of Genesis (*e.g.*, chaps. vi. 9, xxv. 19) and elsewhere, is used to denote the *history;* and in this sense the present and the following chapters pertain as much to Moses as to Aaron. Or the reference may be to the fact that Moses and Aaron were made the heads of the whole tribe of Levi, and therefore that the Levitical families generally are traced up equally to both.

(3) **Whom he consecrated . . .**—Literally, *filled their hand.* The rites of consecration are described at length in Exod. xxix. 1—37, where the command given to Moses is related, and in Lev. viii. 1—13, where the account is given of the actual consecration, on which occasion the appointed sacrificial offerings were placed by Moses in the hands of Aaron and in the hands of his sons. The act of consecration was performed by Moses in the case of Aaron's sons, as well as in that of Aaron himself.

(4) **Died before the Lord.**—The account is given in Lev. x. 1, 2, where the same expression "before the Lord" is used both in regard to the offering of strange fire by Nadab and Abihu, and also in regard to their death.

And they had no children.—To die childless was regarded not only as a reproach, but also as a judgment. This was especially the case in regard to Nadab and Abihu, inasmuch as the sons of one, or of *both* (as was the case in regard to the sons of Eleazar and of Ithamar), would have succeeded to the high priesthood.

(7) **And they shall keep his charge.**—The word rendered *charge* may mean the directions which the Levites should receive from Aaron (comp. Gen. xxvi. 5); or—as seems more probable from the use of the same word in this and the following verse with reference to the congregation—it may refer to the charge which was laid upon Aaron and upon the whole congregation in matters pertaining to the public worship of God.

(9) **They are wholly given unto him.**—Hebrew, *Given, given are they to him.* This repetition of

(10) And thou shalt appoint Aaron and
his sons, and they shall wait on their
priest's office: and the stranger that
cometh nigh shall be put to death.
(11) And the LORD spake unto Moses,
saying, (12) And I, behold, I have taken
the Levites from among the children of
Israel instead of all the firstborn that
openeth the matrix among the children
of Israel: therefore the Levites shall be
mine; (13) because all the firstborn *are*
mine; [a]*for* on the day that I smote all
the firstborn in the land of Egypt I
hallowed unto me all the firstborn in
Israel, both man and beast: mine shall
they be: I *am* the LORD.
(14) And the LORD spake unto Moses
in the wilderness of Sinai, saying,
(15) Number the children of Levi after
the house of their fathers, by their
families: every male from a month old
and upward shalt thou number them.
(16) And Moses numbered them accord-
ing to the [1] word of the LORD, as he was
commanded. (17) [b] And these were the
sons of Levi by their names; Gershon,
and Kohath, and Merari. (18) And these
are the names of the sons of Gershon
by their families; Libni, and Shimei.
(19) And the sons of Kohath by their
families; Amram, and Izehar, Hebron,
and Uzziel. (20) And the sons of Merari
by their families; Mahli, and Mushi.
These *are* the families of the Levites
according to the house of their fathers.
(21) Of Gershon *was* the family of the
Libnites, and the family of the Shimites:
these *are* the families of the Gershonites.
(22) Those that were numbered of them,
according to the number of all the males,
from a month old and upward, *even*
those that were numbered of them *were*
seven thousand and five hundred.
(23) The families of the Gershonites shall
pitch behind the tabernacle westward.
(24) And the chief of the house of the
father of the Gershonites *shall be* Elia-
saph the son of Lael. (25) And the charge
of the sons of Gershon in the tabernacle
of the congregation *shall be* the taber-
nacle, and the tent, the covering thereof,
and the hanging for the door of the

a Ex. 13. 1; Lev. 27. 26; ch. 8. 16; Luke 2. 23.

1 Heb., *mouth.*

b Gen. 46. 11; Ex. 6. 16; ch. 26. 57; 1 Chr. 6. 1.

---

the word *nethunim* (given) is emphatic. The same repetition occurs in chap. viii. 16, where the Levites are represented as "wholly given" to the Lord instead of the firstborn; and in verse 19 of that chapter, as in verse 12 of this chapter, they are represented as being given by Him to Aaron and his sons. The word *nethunim* must not be confounded with *Nethinim,* the name given at a later date (1 Chron. ix. 2; Ezra ii. 43; Neh. iii. 26, 31) to the Gibeonites, who were made "hewers of wood and drawers of water for the congregation and for the altar of the Lord" (Josh. ix. 27). The tribe of Levi had proved themselves the most zealous for the honour of the Lord at the time of the worship of the golden calf (Exod. xxxii. 26—29), and it was then that Moses gave them the charge to consecrate themselves (literally, *to fill their hands,* comp. verse 3 of this chapter) to the Lord. There was, therefore, a special reason for the selection of this tribe, independently of the fact that Moses and Aaron (and consequently the priests, as the descendants of Aaron) belonged to it.

(10) **Thou shalt appoint.**—Or, *number.* The word is the same as that which is used for the numbering of the Israelites generally (chap. i. 19) and for the numbering of the Levites (verse 15).

(13) **On the day that I smote all the firstborn.**—The command given to Moses respecting the sanctification or separation of the firstborn, both of man and of beast, is recorded immediately after the account of the exodus and of the institution of the Passover (Exod. xiii. 1, 2). It does not clearly appear, however, from the terms employed whether the sanctification or separation applied to the firstborn then in existence — which appears to be by far the more probable supposition—or whether, as some suppose, the command was simply prospective. The whole nation of Israel is described in Exod. iv. 22 as the Lord's firstborn son, and the firstborn sons appear to have been regarded in the light of representatives of the entire nation.

Mine shall they be: I am the Lord.—Or, *They shall be* (*i.e.,* belong) *to me,* (even) *to me, Jehovah.* (Comp. Gen. iv. 26: "And to Seth, to him also." Literally, *And to Seth, even him.*)

(15) **From a month old and upward . . .**—The males of the other tribes had been numbered "from twenty years old and upward" (chap. i. 3). The firstborn males, however, among all the children of Israel, in whose place the Levites were taken, were directed to be numbered "from a month old and upward" (verses 40, 43); and this was the age afterwards fixed for their redemption (chap. xviii. 16).

(23) **Behind the tabernacle westward.**—As the position of the twelve tribes in respect of the tent of meeting had been already determined, so in this and the following verses the position of the priests and Levites is fixed. On the east side of the tent Moses and Aaron and Aaron's sons were to encamp, on the south the Kohathites, on the west the Gershonites, on the north the Merarites.

(25) **In the tabernacle of the congregation.**—Better, *in the tent of meeting.* It is important to distinguish between the *ohel*—*i.e.,* the tent—and the *mishkan*—*i.e.,* the tabernacle—which was the building of shittim wood with its curtains which was within the tent. The word *ohel,* where it occurs in the second place in this verse, evidently means the outer covering, as in Exod. xxvi. 7, where the passage may be literally rendered thus:—"And thou shalt make curtains (or hangings) of goats' (hair) for an *ohel* upon (or over) the *mishkan.*"

The covering thereof.—The *mikseh* (covering) appears to include the two coverings described in Exod.

tabernacle of the congregation, (26) and
the hangings of the court, and the cur-
tain for the door of the court, which *is*
by the tabernacle, and by the altar round
about, and the cords of it for all the
service thereof.
(27) And of Kohath *was* the family of
the Amramites, and the family of the
Izeharites, and the family of the Hebron-
ites, and the family of the Uzzielites:
these *are* the families of the Kohathites.
(28) In the number of all the males, from
a month old and upward, *were* eight
thousand and six hundred, keeping the
charge of the sanctuary. (29) The fami-
lies of the sons of Kohath shall pitch on
the side of the tabernacle southward.
(30) And the chief of the house of the
father of the families of the Kohathites
shall be Elizaphan the son of Uzziel.
(31) And their charge *shall be* the ark,
and the table, and the candlestick, and
the altars, and the vessels of the sanc-
tuary wherewith they minister, and the
hanging, and all the service thereof.
(32) And Eleazar the son of Aaron the
priest *shall be* chief over the chief of the
Levites, *and have* the oversight of them
that keep the charge of the sanctuary.
(33) Of Merari *was* the family of the
Mahlites, and the family of the Mush-
ites: these *are* the families of Merari.
(34) And those that were numbered of
them, according to the number of all the
males, from a month old and upward,
were six thousand and two hundred.
(35) And the chief of the house of the
father of the families of Merari *was*
Zuriel the son of Abihail: *these* shall
pitch on the side of the tabernacle
northward. (36) And [1]*under* the custody
and charge of the sons of Merari *shall be*
the boards of the tabernacle, and the
bars thereof, and the pillars thereof, and
the sockets thereof, and all the vessels
thereof, and all that serveth thereto,
(37) and the pillars of the court round
about, and their sockets, and their pins,
and their cords.
(38) But those that encamp before the
tabernacle toward the east, *even* before
the tabernacle of the congregation east-
ward, *shall be* Moses, and Aaron and his
sons, keeping the charge of the sanc-
tuary for the charge of the children of
Israel; and the stranger that cometh
nigh shall be put to death. (39) All that
were numbered of the Levites, which

1 Heb., *the office of the charge.*

---

xxvi. 14—viz., the covering of rams' skins and that of badgers' skins or seals' skins.

The hanging for the door of the tabernacle of the congregation—*i.e., for the entrance or opening of the tent of meeting.* This hanging was of blue, and purple, and scarlet, and fine-twined linen, and was hung at the entrance—*i.e.,* the eastern or open end of the tent (Exod. xxvi. 36). The word rendered door (*pethach,* not *deleth*) means an opening. At a later period, when the Tabernacle was at Shiloh, it had *doors* (1 Sam. iii. 15). Both words occur in 1 Kings vi. 31: "And for the entering (or at the *opening*) of the oracle he made *doors,*" &c.

(26) **And the hangings of the court . . .**—See Exod. xxvii. 9 and Note.

And the cords of it for all the service thereof.—The pronominal suffixes do not seem to refer to the court, the cords belonging to which appear to have been under the custody of the Merarites (verse 37), but to the *mishkan* or Tabernacle itself. Or, the latter suffix (*its* service, or the service *thereof*) may be designed to refer to each of the various things mentioned, as in verse 31, inasmuch as the words *for all the service thereof* may mean for everything which had to be done in connection with the things mentioned.

(29) **On the side of the tabernacle southward.**—The south has its name in Hebrew (*Teman*) from *Yamin, the right hand,* because when a man stands with his face towards the east the south is on his right hand.

(32) **And Eleazar the son of Aaron the priest . . .**—In virtue, as it should seem, of the descent of Moses and Aaron from Kohath, the Kohathites had the most honourable portion of the service of the Tabernacle assigned to them; and hence, as the priests belonged to the Amramites, one of the four families of the Kohathites, Eleazar, the eldest surviving son of Aaron, was chosen to have the oversight over the whole body of the Levites.

(37) **And the pillars of the court round about . . .**—See Notes on Exod. xxvii. 9—19.

(38) **Keeping the charge of the sanctuary . . .**—The word *mikdash* (sanctuary) appears to be of a more comprehensive import than *mishkan,* the shittim-wood building, or *ohel,* the tent which covered it, and it seems to include the court which surrounded the Tabernacle, as in Lev. xii. 4, xxi. 12.

For the charge of the children of Israel—*i.e.,* to attend to everything which was commanded the children of Israel.

(39) **And Aaron . . .**—In the Hebrew text the word Aaron has certain marks over it, known as *puncta extraordinaria,* denoting that it is to be regarded as spurious or doubtful. It is omitted in the Samaritan and Syriac versions and in a few MSS. There appears, however, to be no sufficient reason for its rejection from the text.

Twenty and two thousand.—The total of the three several items—viz., 7,500, 8,600, and 6,200—amounts to 22,300. It appears, however, from verse 46 that the total is correctly given as 22,000, inasmuch as the number of the firstborn, 22,273, exceeded that of the Levites by 273. It has been suggested that in verse 28 we should read שלש (*shalosh*), three, for שש (*shesh*), six—*i.e.,* 8,300 instead of 8,600; or, if the numbers were denoted, as it has been commonly sup-

Moses and Aaron numbered at the commandment of the LORD, throughout their families, all the males from a month old and upward, *were* twenty and two thousand.

(40) And the LORD said unto Moses, Number all the firstborn of the males of the children of Israel from a month old and upward, and take the number of their names. (41) And thou shalt take the Levites for me (I *am* the LORD) instead of all the firstborn among the children of Israel; and the cattle of the Levites instead of all the firstlings among the cattle of the children of Israel.
(42) And Moses numbered, as the LORD commanded him, all the firstborn among the children of Israel. (43) And all the firstborn males by the number of names, from a month old and upward, of those that were numbered of them, were twenty and two thousand two hundred and threescore and thirteen.

(44) And the LORD spake unto Moses, saying, (45) Take the Levites instead of all the firstborn among the children of Israel, and the cattle of the Levites instead of their cattle; and the Levites shall be mine: I *am* the LORD. (46) And for those that are to be redeemed of the two hundred and threescore and thirteen of the firstborn of the children of Israel, which are more than the Levites;
(47) Thou shalt even take five shekels

---

posed, by the letters of the alphabet, it is quite possible that one letter may have been substituted by the scribe for another. Some suppose that the three hundred were themselves firstborn sons, who had been born since the command to sanctify the firstborn, and that it is on this account that they were not included in the census. (See Bishop Wordsworth's Notes *in loc.*, where the reasons which may be assigned for the extreme paucity of this tribe, as compared with the other tribes, are discussed.) The later census, which also included the children from a month old and upwards, shows but a very small increase in the number of this tribe, the number on that occasion amounting only to 23,000 (chap. xxvi. 62).

(41) **And thou shalt take the Levites for me (I am the Lord) . . .**—Or, *And thou shalt take the Levites for Me—for Me, Jehovah.* The assertions which have been frequently made respecting the transference of the priesthood of the firstborn to the Levites appear to be altogether without foundation. For (1) the priesthood which was exercised in patriarchal times was not restricted to the firstborn, but appears to have been common to the head of every family. (2) This priesthood was exercised previously to the exodus, and consequently previously to the command given to Moses to sanctify the firstborn. And (3) the priesthood, which belonged not to the firstborn exclusively, but to the Israelites at large, was thenceforth strictly confined to the family of Aaron, who inherited it not as the substitutes of the firstborn, but in the place of the whole nation.

(43) **Twenty and two thousand two hundred and threescore and thirteen.**—The extremely small number of the firstborn in proportion to a male population of 600,000 of twenty years of age and upwards—*i.e.*, to a population of about 1,000,000 males—has been a fruitful source of difficulty, and, in some cases, a ground for the rejection of the historical truth of the narrative, which involves, it has been alleged, the incredible conclusion that there was only *one* firstborn to *forty-four* males. It might suffice, in answer to those who urge this difficulty as a ground for rejecting the truth of the narrative, to reply that it is difficult, if not impossible, to conceive that a writer who has recorded, or, according to the theory in question, *invented* so many complicated calculations, should have inserted amongst them one which is fraught with so much apparent improbability. Many solutions of the problem have been proposed which relieve the apparent disproportion of the number of the firstborn not only of its alleged impossibility, but even of improbability. Some have urged that we are constrained by every principle of analogy to restrict the firstborn sons to those who were under twenty years of age, and who had not been included in the census which had been already taken. The destruction of the firstborn of the Egyptians was clearly subject to a somewhat similar limitation. Pharaoh himself was, in all probability, a firstborn son; and in regard to the Egyptians generally there does not appear to have been above one death in each house (Exod. xii. 30), although there must have been very many houses in which the father (and it may be the grandfather) as well as the son was a firstborn child. Another opinion is that by the firstborn in every *family* we are to understand the firstborn in every *household*, including the children of concubines and slaves. When due allowance has been made, on either of these hypotheses, for the average proportion of the sexes, the average number of early deaths, and also for the limitation of the term *firstborn* to those who were the firstborn on the side of the father as well as of the mother, it has been contended that the number of the firstborn is consistent with the supposition that each family of the Israelites consisted of about eight or nine children—a supposition which, considering how prolific the Hebrew women are said to have been, cannot be regarded as deserving of rejection on the ground of its incredibility. The most probable solution of the difficulty, however, appears to be that which is given in the Introduction.

(45) **And the cattle of the Levites instead of their cattle.**—There appears to have been no numbering of the cattle. Had it been otherwise, an argument might have been used in support of the prospective reference of the command to number the firstborn, derived from the fact that it would have been impossible to ascertain the number of firstborn among the cattle. It appears, however, that the whole of the cattle of the Levites was given in redemption of the firstborn of all the cattle of the other tribes.

(47) **Thou shalt even take five shekels apiece by the poll.**—It is not stated in what manner the 273 families of whom the redemption money was exacted were determined. Inasmuch, however, as the law of

apiece by the poll, after the shekel of the
sanctuary shalt thou take *them*: ([a] the
shekel *is* twenty gerahs:) (48) and thou
shalt give the money, wherewith the odd
number of them is to be redeemed, unto
Aaron and to his sons. (49) And Moses
took the redemption money of them that
were over and above them that were
redeemed by the Levites: (50) of the first-
born of the children of Israel took he
the money; a thousand three hundred
and threescore and five *shekels*, after the
shekel of the sanctuary: (51) And Moses
gave the money of them that were re-
deemed unto Aaron and to his sons,
according to the word of the LORD, as
the LORD commanded Moses.

CHAPTER IV. — (1) And the LORD
spake unto Moses and unto Aaron, say-
ing, (2) Take the sum of the sons of Ko-
hath from among the sons of Levi, after
their families, by the house of their
fathers, (3) from thirty years old and
upward even until fifty years old, all
that enter into the host, to do the
work in the tabernacle of the congrega-
tion.

(4) This *shall be* the service of the sons
of Kohath in the tabernacle of the con-
gregation, *about* the most holy things:
(5) and when the camp setteth forward,
Aaron shall come, and his sons, and they
shall take down the covering vail, and
cover the ark of testimony with it:
(6) and shall put thereon the covering of
badgers' skins, and shall spread over *it*
a cloth wholly of blue, and shall put in
the staves thereof. (7) And upon the
[b] table of shewbread they shall spread a
cloth of blue, and put thereon the dishes,
and the spoons, and the bowls, and
covers to [1] cover withal: and the con-
tinual bread shall be thereon: (8) And
they shall spread upon them a cloth of
scarlet, and cover the same with a
covering of badgers' skins, and shall put
in the staves thereof. (9) And they shall
take a cloth of blue, and cover the
[c] candlestick of the light, and his lamps,
and his tongs, [d] and his snuffdishes, and
all the oil vessels thereof, wherewith

a Ex. 30. 13; Lev. 27. 25; ch. 18. 16; Ezek. 45. 12.

b Ex. 25. 30.

1 Or, *pour out withal.*

c Ex. 25. 31.

d Ex. 25. 38.

---

the redemption of the firstborn by the payment of five shekels came into operation from this time (chap. xviii. 16), it seems probable that the money was exacted in the case of those who had been most recently born; or it may be that the matter was decided by lot.

After the shekel of the sanctuary. — See Exod. xxx. 13, where the expression occurs for the first time, and the value of the shekel is stated, as in this verse.

(48) **And thou shalt give the money . . .**— The verse may be rendered thus: *And thou shalt give the money to Aaron and to his sons: even the redemption money of those who are over and above amongst them.*

(49) **Redeemed by the Levites.**—*i.e.*, who were redeemed by the substitution of the Levites in their place.

(51) **The money of them that were redeemed.** —Better, *the ransom* (or, *redemption*) *money.*

IV.

(2) **Of the sons of Kohath . . .**—Kohath appears to have been the second son of Levi (chap. iii. 17), but the Kohathites here stand first because Moses and Aaron belonged to them, and it was their office to bear the Ark.

(3) **From thirty years old and upward even until fifty years old.**—The previous census of the Levites was from a month old. The present census was with a view to the discharge of duties requiring a considerable amount of physical strength, and hence the prescribed age for entering upon these duties was fixed at this time at thirty, and limited to fifty. It has been supposed by some that five years were spent in preparation for the service, and that it is in this way that the apparent discrepancy between this verse and chap. viii. 24, where the age for entering upon the service is fixed at twenty-five, is to be reconciled. (See Note on chap. viii. 24.) In Eastern countries the strength fails at an earlier period than in colder and more temperate climates. Thirty was the age at which John the Baptist and our Lord entered upon their public ministry.

All that enter into the host.—Or, *every one who enters upon the service.* The word *zaba*, commonly rendered *host*, and used elsewhere to denote military service, is here used to denote the service of the sanctuary.

(5) **Aaron shall come, and his sons . . .**— Under ordinary circumstances the high priest himself might only enter the most holy place on one day in the year. At the time of the moving of the camp, however, the Divine Presence seems to have departed from the Holy of Holies, and to have ascended in the cloud which gave the signal for the removal.

The covering vail.—Better, *the vail of the hanging or curtain*—viz., that which separated the Holy of Holies from the Holy Place. (Comp. chap. iii. 31.)

(6) **And shall put in the staves thereof.**—The staves had been removed whilst the Ark was being covered; otherwise they remained in their places (Exod. xxv. 15). (Comp. 2 Chron. v. 9.)

(7) **And covers to cover withal.**—Better, *and the cups for the drink-offering* (or *libation*).

And the continual bread.—The shew-bread is so called because it was renewed every Sabbath day, and was continually before the face of the Lord even (as it appears from this verse) during the marches of the Israelites through the desert (Exod. xxv. 30; Lev. xxiv. 5).

(8) **And cover the same.**—Better, *and cover it* (the table).

they minister unto it: (10) and they shall put it and all the vessels thereof within a covering of badgers' skins, and shall put *it* upon a bar. (11) And upon the golden altar they shall spread a cloth of blue, and cover it with a covering of badgers' skins, and shall put to the staves thereof: (12) and they shall take all the instruments of ministry, wherewith they minister in the sanctuary, and put *them* in a cloth of blue, and cover them with a covering of badgers' skins, and shall put *them* on a bar: (13) and they shall take away the ashes from the altar, and spread a purple cloth thereon: (14) and they shall put upon it all the vessels thereof, wherewith they minister about it, *even* the censers, the fleshhooks, and the shovels, and the [1] basons, all the vessels of the altar; and they shall spread upon it a covering of badgers' skins, and put to the staves of it. (15) And when Aaron and his sons have made an end of covering the sanctuary, and all the vessels of the sanctuary, as the camp is to set forward; after that, the sons of Kohath shall come to bear *it*: but they shall not touch *any* holy thing, lest they die. These *things are* the burden of the sons of Kohath in the tabernacle of the congregation.

(16) And to the office of Eleazar the son of Aaron the priest *pertaineth* the oil for the light, and the [a] sweet incense, and the daily meat offering, and the [b] anointing oil, *and* the oversight of all the tabernacle, and of all that therein *is*, in the sanctuary, and in the vessels thereof.

(17) And the LORD spake unto Moses and unto Aaron, saying, (18) Cut ye not off the tribe of the families of the Kohathites from among the Levites: (19) but thus do unto them, that they may live, and not die, when they approach unto the most holy things: Aaron and his sons shall go in, and appoint them every one to his service and to his burden: (20) but they shall not go in to see when the holy things are covered, lest they die.

1 Or, *bowls.*

a Ex. 30. 34.

b Ex. 30. 23.

---

(10) **Upon a bar.**—Better, *upon a pole, or frame made for bearing.* (Comp. chap. xiii. 23, where the same word *mot* is rendered "a staff.")

(11) **And shall put to the staves thereof.**—Better, *And shall put in the staves thereof,* as in verses 6, 8; so also in verse 14.

(13) **And they shall take away the ashes from the altar.**—In Exod. xxvii. 3 we find a direction to make pans for removing the ashes from the brazen altar, and also to make all the brazen vessels mentioned in the next verse.

(14) **The censers.**—Better, *the fire-pans,* as in Exod. xxvii. 3.

(15) **And all the vessels of the sanctuary.**—No mention is here made of the laver (Exod. xxx. 18). The LXX. and the Samaritan text supply a statement respecting the covering and conveyance of the brazen laver. The clause in the LXX. is as follows:—"And they shall take a purple cloth, and cover the laver and its foot (or base), and they shall put it into a blue cover of skin, and put it on bars." There is no sufficient ground, however, for supposing that the present Hebrew text is deficient in this place; and it seems more probable to suppose that the laver was not to be covered during its transport.

After that, the sons of Kohath shall come to bear it.—Better, *to bear, or carry*—viz., the whole of the vessels of ministry which had been previously enumerated. The distinction between the service of the priests and that of the Levites in regard to the removal of the Tabernacle and its furniture is here clearly marked.

But they shall not touch any holy thing, lest they die.—The word which is rendered "any holy thing" may here, as elsewhere, denote *the sanctuary.* This injunction is repeated in chap. xviii. 3. We find in 2 Sam. vi. 6, 7 an instance of the fatal result of the violation of this command by Uzzah, who being, as is most probable, a Levite, and of the family of Kohath, ought to have been acquainted with the law respecting the removal of the Ark. It is obvious that the Kohathites, as the immediate assistants of the priests, in regard to the vessels of the Sanctuary, were specially exposed to the risk of violating the law by touching the most holy things.

(16) **The oil for the light.**—Or, *for the candlestick* (Exod. xxv. 6).

The sweet incense.—Or, *the incense of spices* (Exod. xxv. 6).

The daily meat offering.—Better, *the continual meat offering—i.e.,* the morning and evening *minchah* (Exod. xxix. 38—42).

The anointing oil.—*i.e.,* "the oil of holy ointment" with which the tent of meeting, the vessels of the Sanctuary, and the priests were to be anointed (Exod. xxx. 23—31).

(18) **Cut ye not off the tribe . . .**—The word *shebet* (tribe) is here used in a very peculiar sense, and denotes one division only of the tribe of Levi. In this and the following verses the injunction already given (chap. v. 15) is renewed, and Moses and Aaron are charged not to be guilty of such negligence in respect of it as might expose the Kohathites to death in consequence of their unlawful treatment of the holy things. Moses and Aaron might be said to do that which would be the result of their negligence. In like manner St. Paul enjoins the Roman Christians in these words: "Destroy not him with thy meat for whom Christ died" (Rom. xiv. 15).

(20) **But they shall not go in to see when the holy things are covered.**—Better, *But they shall not go in to see the holy things* (or, the sanctuary) *for a moment.* The Levites were not permitted to enter the holy place in which the priests ministered, much less the Holy of Holies. Whether this rule was or was not relaxed at the time of the removal

(21) And the Lord spake unto Moses,
saying, (22) Take also the sum of the
sons of Gershon, throughout the
houses of their fathers, by their families;
(23) from thirty years old and upward
until fifty years old shalt thou number
them; all that enter in [1] to perform the
service, to do the work in the tabernacle
of the congregation.

(24) This *is* the service of the families
of the Gershonites, to serve, and for
[2] burdens: (25) and they shall bear the
curtains of the tabernacle, and the taber-
nacle of the congregation, his covering,
and the covering of the badgers' skins
that *is* above upon it, and the hanging
for the door of the tabernacle of the
congregation, (26) and the hangings of
the court, and the hanging for the door
of the gate of the court, which *is* by the
tabernacle and by the altar round about,
and their cords, and all the instruments
of their service, and all that is made for
them: so shall they serve. (27) At the
[3] appointment of Aaron and his sons shall
be all the service of the sons of the
Gershonites, in all their burdens, and in
all their service: and ye shall appoint
unto them in charge all their burdens.
(28) This *is* the service of the families of
the sons of Gershon in the tabernacle
of the congregation: and their charge
shall be under the hand of Ithamar the
son of Aaron the priest.

(29) As for the sons of Merari, thou
shalt number them after their families,
by the house of their fathers; (30) from
thirty years old and upward even unto
fifty years old shalt thou number them,
every one that entereth into the [4] service,
to do the work of the tabernacle of the
congregation.

(31) And this *is* the charge of their
burden, according to all their service in
the tabernacle of the congregation; [a] the
boards of the tabernacle, and the bars
thereof, and the pillars thereof, and
sockets thereof, (32) and the pillars of the
court round about, and their sockets,
and their pins, and their cords, with all
their instruments, and with all their
service: and by name ye shall reckon
the instruments of the charge of their
burden. (33) This *is* the service of the
families of the sons of Merari, according
to all their service, in the tabernacle of
the congregation, under the hand of
Ithamar the son of Aaron the priest.

(34) And Moses and Aaron and the
chief of the congregation numbered the
sons of the Kohathites after their fami-
lies, and after the house of their fathers,
(35) from thirty years old and upward
even unto fifty years old, every one that
entereth into the service, for the work
in the tabernacle of the congregation:
(36) and those that were numbered of
them by their families were two thou-
sand seven hundred and fifty. (37) These
were they that were numbered of the
families of the Kohathites, all that might
do service in the tabernacle of the con-
gregation, which Moses and Aaron did
number according to the commandment
of the Lord by the hand of Moses.

(38) And those that were numbered

1 Heb., *to war the warfare.*

2 Or, *carriage.*

3 Heb., *mouth.*

4 Heb., *warfare.*

a Ex. 35 15.

---

of the Tabernacle, as the prohibition against entrance into the Holy of Holies must have been in regard to the priests, the Levites were not permitted in any case to look upon the Ark and the other holy things until they were covered.

(25) **And the tabernacle of the congregation.**—Better, *And the tent of meeting.* The *mishkan* or dwelling-place is distinguished in chap. iii. 25 from the *ohel* or tent which covered it. The curtains of the *mishkan* are represented in Exod. xxvi. 6 as constituting the *mishkan* itself, the woodwork being apparently regarded as subsidiary to the curtains. These curtains were of fine-twined linen, while the curtains of the *ohel* or tent were of goats' hair (Exod. xxvi. 1, 7).

His covering.—*i.e.*, the covering of rams' skins, which is here distinguished from the outer covering of badgers' skins (Exod. xxvi. 14).

And the hanging for the door of the tabernacle of the congregation.—Better, *the hanging* (or covering) *for the entrance of the tent of meeting* (Exod. xxvi. 36).

(26) **Which is by the tabernacle and by the altar round about.**—Or, *which are . . .* The curtains or hangings enclosed the whole of the court.

(28) **Under the hand of Ithamar.**—It appears from Exod. xxxviii. 21 that Ithamar had been actively concerned in the construction of the Tabernacle. As the special duties of Eleazar, the eldest son of Aaron, had been already assigned (verse 16), so also are those of Ithamar, the younger son. These duties consisted in the superintendence of the Gershonites, as stated in this verse, and in the superintendence of the Merarites, as stated in verse 33.

(31) **The boards of the tabernacle, and the bars thereof . . .**—The duty of the Merarites was to carry the heavier and more cumbersome parts of the Tabernacle and the court; and it is probably on this account that, in their case, the specific duties of each were assigned to them by name (verse 32). The description of the several portions of the Tabernacle and Court here enumerated is found in Exod. xxvi. and xxxvi.

(32) **Ye shall reckon.**—Better, *ye shall assign, or appoint.* (See Note on the preceding verse.)

of the sons of Gershon, throughout their
families, and by the house of their fathers,
(39) from thirty years old and upward
even unto fifty years old, every one that
entereth into the service, for the work
in the tabernacle of the congregation,
(40) even those that were numbered of a Lev. 13. 3.
them, throughout their families, by the
house of their fathers, were two thousand
and six hundred and thirty. (41) These
are they that were numbered of the
families of the sons of Gershon, of all
that might do service in the tabernacle b Lev. 15. 2.
of the congregation, whom Moses and
Aaron did number according to the commandment of the Lord.

(42) And those that were numbered of
the families of the sons of Merari,
throughout their families, by the house of
their fathers, (43) from thirty years old and c Lev. 21. 1.
upward even unto fifty years old, every
one that entereth into the service, for
the work in the tabernacle of the congregation, (44) even those that were numbered of them after their families, were
three thousand and two hundred. d Lev. 6. 3.
(45) These *be* those that were numbered
of the families of the sons of Merari,
whom Moses and Aaron numbered according to the word of the Lord by the
hand of Moses.

(46) All those that were numbered of
the Levites, whom Moses and Aaron and e Lev. 6. 5
the chief of Israel numbered, after their
families, and after the house of their
fathers, (47) from thirty years old and
upward even unto fifty years old, every
one that came to do the service of the
ministry, and the service of the burden
in the tabernacle of the congregation,
(48) even those that were numbered of
them, were eight thousand and five
hundred and fourscore. (49) According
to the commandment of the Lord they
were numbered by the hand of Moses,
every one according to his service, and
according to his burden: thus were
they numbered of him, as the Lord commanded Moses.

CHAPTER V. — (1) And the Lord
spake unto Moses, saying, (2) Command
the children of Israel, that they put out
of the camp every [a] leper, and every one
that hath an [b] issue, and whosoever is
defiled by the [c] dead: (3) both male and
female shall ye put out, without the
camp shall ye put them; that they
defile not their camps, in the midst
whereof I dwell. (4) And the children of
Israel did so, and put them out without
the camp: as the Lord spake unto
Moses, so did the children of Israel.

(5) And the Lord spake unto Moses,
saying, (6) Speak unto the children of
Israel, [d] When a man or woman shall
commit any sin that men commit, to do
a trespass against the Lord, and that
person be guilty; (7) then they shall
confess their sin which they have done:
and he shall recompense his trespass
[e] with the principal thereof, and add unto
it the fifth *part* thereof, and give *it* unto
him against whom he hath trespassed.
(8) But if the man have no kinsman to
recompense the trespass unto, let the

---

(48) **Eight thousand and five hundred and fourscore.**—This number of men between the ages of twenty and fifty bears a just proportion to that of all the males from a month old and upwards—viz., 22,000.

V.

This chapter contains laws for the preservation of sanctity amongst the people in the midst of whom Jehovah was pleased to dwell.

(2) **Every leper.**—On the nature of this disease and the laws prescribed with regard to it, see Lev. xiii., xiv., and Notes.

Whosoever is defiled by the dead.—The law respecting defilement contracted by contact with the dead bodies of unclean animals and insects is contained in Lev. xi. 24, 25; and the law respecting defilement contracted by the priests, by contact with the dead, is contained in Lev. xxi. The law concerning defilement, in regard to the Israelites generally, is found at greater length in chap. xix. of this book.

(6) **To do a trespass.**—The noun *maal,* which is here employed in conjunction with its cognate verb, implies stealth, or secrecy in the action.

And that person be guilty.—Better, *then that person shall be guilty,* as in Lev. v. 3.

(7) **And add unto it the fifth part thereof.**—The law contained in this and the following verses appears to be supplementary to that which is found in Lev. v. 16. It is prescribed in Leviticus that both in the case of trespass committed in the holy things of the Lord, and also in the case of private wrongs, restitution should be made to the full amount of the injury done, with the addition of one-fifth to that amount. It is here not only provided by implication that in the case of the death of the person who suffered the injury, restitution should be made to his *goel,* or near kinsman, but also, that in the event of there being no near kinsman, restitution should be made to the Lord in the person of the priest.

(8) **Let the trespass be recompensed unto the Lord, even to the priest.**—Better, *the guilt offering with which restitution is made shall be the Lord's, even the priest's.*

trespass be recompensed unto the LORD, *even* to the priest; beside the ram of the atonement, whereby an atonement shall be made for him. (9) And every [1] offering of all the holy things of the children of Israel, which they bring unto the priest, shall be his. (10) And every man's hallowed things shall be his: whatsoever any man giveth the priest, it shall be [a] his.

(11) And the LORD spake unto Moses, saying, (12) Speak unto the children of Israel, and say unto them, If any man's wife go aside, and commit a trespass against him, (13) and a man lie with her carnally, and it be hid from the eyes of her husband, and be kept close, and she be defiled, and *there be* no witness against her, neither she be taken *with the manner;* (14) and the spirit of jealousy come upon him, and he be jealous of his wife, and she be defiled: or if the spirit of jealousy come upon him, and he be jealous of his wife, and she be not defiled: (15) then shall the man bring his wife unto the priest, and he shall bring her offering for her, the tenth *part* of an ephah of barley meal; he shall pour no oil upon it, nor put frankincense thereon; for it *is* an offering of jealousy, an offering of memorial, bringing iniquity to remembrance.

(16) And the priest shall bring her near, and set her before the LORD: (17) and the priest shall take holy water in an earthen vessel; and of the dust that is in the floor of the tabernacle the priest shall take, and put *it* into the water: (18) and the priest shall set the woman before the LORD, and uncover the woman's head, and put the offering of memorial in her hands, which *is* the jealousy offering: and the priest shall have in his hand the bitter water that causeth the curse: (19) and the priest shall charge her by an oath, and say unto the woman, If no man have lain with thee, and if thou hast not gone aside to uncleanness [2] *with another* instead of thy husband, be thou free from this bitter water that causeth the curse: (20) but if thou hast gone aside *to another* instead of thy husband, and if thou be defiled, and some man have lain with thee beside thine husband: (21) then the priest shall charge the woman with an oath of cursing, and the priest shall say unto the woman, The LORD make thee a curse

1 Or, *heave offering.*

a Lev. 10. 12.

2 Or, being *in the power of thy husband.* Heb., *under thy husband.*

---

(9) **And every offering.**—The word rendered *offering, terumah* (properly, *heave-offering*) may denote specifically the *heave-offering, i.e.,* the *shoulder,* or rather *leg,* of the sacrificial victim (as in Exod. xxix. 27; Lev. vii. 14, 32), or it may be used here (as in Exod. xxv. 2; xxx. 13) in the general sense of an *offering dedicated to the Lord by elevation.* A comparison of this passage with Exod. xxix. 28, and with chap. xviii. 8, 9, seems to warrant the conclusion that the reference here is, at least primarily, to the heave-offerings of the sacrifices, which were the portion, not of the priests generally, but of the particular priest who offered the sacrifice.

(12) **And commit a trespass against him.**—The word rendered *commit a trespass* is the same as in verse 6 (see Note). As the law of marriage lies at the very foundation of the civil commonwealth, it was of the greatest importance that stringent measures should be adopted for the detection and punishment of the sin of adultery.

(13) **Taken with the manner.**—Better, *caught,* or, *taken in the act.*

(15) **The tenth part of an ephah of barley meal.**—The fine wheaten flour appointed to be used in the morning and evening sacrifice was not allowed on this occasion, but barley flour, which was used by the poorer classes, or by the people generally, in time of great distress, and which appears to have been worth about one-half the price of wheaten flour (2 Kings vii. 1). "A cake of barley bread" is used to denote something base and contemptible (Judges vii. 13). Oil and incense, the symbols of the Holy Spirit's influences and of prayer, were not allowed to be used.

(16) **And the priest shall bring her near, and set her before the Lord**—*i.e.,* shall bring her before the Tabernacle, wherein was the ark of the Lord, over which He was pleased to manifest His presence (comp. Lev. i. 3).

(17) **Shall take holy water.**—This appears to be the only place in which this expression occurs. The water was probably taken from the laver of brass which stood between the Tabernacle and the brazen altar (Exod. xxx. 18). It is possible, however, that the reference may be to water in which the ashes of the red heifer had been cast (chap. xix. 9). The Jews have a tradition that it was on the day after the erection of the Tabernacle that Eleazar the priest burnt the red heifer, and sprinkled all Israel.

In an earthen vessel.—The vessel was to be of the most common material, not one of the brazen vessels of the Sanctuary.

And of the dust . . .—It was appointed that the serpent should eat dust, as the curse of sin (Gen. iii. 14). This dust, however, was sacred, as being the dust of the Tabernacle.

(18) **And uncover the woman's head.**—The word, which is rendered *uncover,* is the same which is used of the leper (Lev. viii. 45), "And his head *bare.*" It is thought to denote not only the removal of the head-covering, but also letting the hair become loose and dishevelled. (Comp. 1 Cor. xi. 5—10.)

The offering of memorial. (See verses 15, 26.)

(19) **With another instead of thy husband.**—Or, *whilst under thy husband, i.e.,* whilst in the marriage state, as in the margin. (See Ezek. xxiii. 5 for the use of the same Hebrew preposition.)

and an oath among thy people, when the
LORD doth make thy thigh to [1] rot, and
thy belly to swell; (22) and this water
that causeth the curse shall go into thy
bowels, to make *thy* belly to swell, and
thy thigh to rot: And the woman shall
say, Amen, amen. (23) And the priest
shall write these curses in a book, and
he shall blot *them* out with the bitter
water: (24) and he shall cause the woman
to drink the bitter water that causeth
the curse: and the water that causeth
the curse shall enter into her, *and become*
bitter.

(25) Then the priest shall take the
jealousy offering out of the woman's
hand, and shall wave the offering before
the LORD, and offer it upon the altar:
(26) and the priest shall take an handful
of the offering, *even* the memorial there-
of, and burn *it* upon the altar, and after-
ward shall cause the woman to drink the
water. (27) And when he hath made her
to drink the water, then it shall come to
pass, *that*, if she be defiled, and have
done trespass against her husband, that
the water that causeth the curse shall
enter into her, *and become* bitter, and
her belly shall swell, and her thigh shall
rot: and the woman shall be a curse
among her people. (28) And if the
woman be not defiled, but be clean;
then she shall be free, and shall conceive
seed.

(29) This *is* the law of jealousies, when
a wife goeth aside *to another* instead of
her husband, and is defiled; (30) or when
the spirit of jealousy cometh upon him,
and he be jealous over his wife, and
shall set the woman before the LORD,
and the priest shall execute upon her all
this law. (31) Then shall the man be
guiltless from iniquity, and this woman
shall bear her iniquity.

CHAPTER VI. — (1) And the LORD
spake unto Moses, saying, (2) Speak unto
the children of Israel, and say unto them,
When either man or woman shall [2] sepa-
rate *themselves* to vow a vow of a Naza-
rite, to separate *themselves* unto the
LORD: (3) he shall separate *himself* from
wine and strong drink, and shall drink
no vinegar of wine, or vinegar of strong
drink, neither shall he drink any liquor
of grapes, nor eat moist grapes, or dried.
(4) All the days of his [3] separation shall
he eat nothing that is made of the [4] vine

1 Heb., *fall.*

2 Or, *make themselves Nazarites.*

3 Or, *Nazariteship.*

4 Heb., *vine of the wine.*

---

(23) **And he shall blot them out with the bitter water.**—Better, *and he shall blot them out into the bitter water.* The curses were to be written upon a roll, and the roll washed in the bitter water, so that the water should be impregnated with the curse before it was drunk.

(24) **And he shall cause the woman to drink the bitter water . . .**—These words appear to be inserted here by way of anticipation, inasmuch as it appears from verse 26 that it was not until after the presentation of the offering upon the altar that the woman was required to drink the water. The offering was not presented until after the woman's oath of purification, but her guilt or innocence was not finally established until the effects of drinking the bitter water were ascertained.

(31) **And this woman shall bear her iniquity.**—Better, *and that woman.* Unlike the ordeals of other nations, the guilty were infallibly detected by the test thus imposed, and were constrained to endure the righteous judgment of God.

VI.

(2) **When either man or woman shall separate themselves to vow a vow . . .**—Better, *When a man or woman shall make a special* (or singular) *vow* (as in Lev. xxvii. 2)—*the vow of a Nazirite.* The verb which is here used denotes the doing something wonderful or extraordinary, and the spiritual lesson seems to be that Christ's servants are expected and required to do something more than others (Matt. v. 46, 47). The vows here referred to were made for a specific period. At a later time, however, some were consecrated or set apart as Nazirites during the entire period of their lives, as in the case of Samson, Samuel, and John the Baptist. This consecration, however, appears to have been made rather as the result of Divine revelation than of arbitrary appointment on the part of their parents. The meaning of the word *Nazirite* (Hebrew *nazir*) is contained in the concluding words of the verse—*to separate* (*i.e.*, himself) *unto Jehovah*—where the cognate verb is used.

(3) **He shall separate himself from wine and strong drink . . .**—The law of the Nazirite in this respect, as in regard to defilement from the dead, was more strict than that which was enjoined upon the priests, thus typifying the entire surrender of the heart and life to God, and freedom from the distraction of earthly ties. The ideal of this separation, however, was not that of a life of monastic seclusion, but of action, and of uninterrupted devotion to the Divine service. The priests were forbidden to drink wine, or strong drink, when they entered the tabernacle to perform service there, but were not prohibited the use of wine at other times. Strong drink (*shecar*) is supposed to have been made of barley and dates or honey. The prohibition to eat any of the produce of the vine, even of that which was not intoxicating, seems designed to denote the entire consecration of the Nazirite to the Divine service, and the obligation which rested upon him to abstain from all the desires and delights of the flesh. The love of cakes made of raisins is coupled in Hos. iii. 1 with idolatry.

(4) **From the kernels even to the husk.**—The word which is rendered *kernels* is supposed by some to denote sour grapes, and by others the kernels of berries. The word *zag* denotes the shell or husk.

tree, from the kernels even to the husk.
(5) All the days of the vow of his separa-
tion there shall no [a] razor come upon his
head: until the days be fulfilled, in the
which he separateth *himself* unto the
LORD, he shall be holy, *and* shall let the
locks of the hair of his head grow.
(6) All the days that he separateth *him-
self* unto the LORD he shall come at no
dead body. (7) He shall not make him-
self unclean for his father, or for his
mother, for his brother, or for his sister,
when they die: because the [1] consecra-
tion of his God *is* upon his head. (8) All
the days of his separation he *is* holy
unto the LORD. (9) And if any man die
very suddenly by him, and he hath de-
filed the head of his consecration; then
he shall shave his head in the day of his
cleansing, on the seventh day shall he
shave it. (10) And on the eighth day he
shall bring two turtles, or two young
pigeons, to the priest, to the door of the
tabernacle of the congregation: (11) And
the priest shall offer the one for a sin
offering and the other for a burnt offer-
ing, and make an atonement for him, for
that he sinned by the dead, and shall
hallow his head that same day. (12) And
he shall consecrate unto the LORD the
days of his separation, and shall bring a
lamb of the first year for a trespass offer-
ing: but the days that were before shall
[2] be lost, because his separation was de-
filed.

(13) And this *is* the law of the Nazarite,
when the days of his separation are ful-

a Judg. 13. 5; 1 Sam. 1. 11.

1 Heb., *separation*

2 Heb., *fall.*

b Acts 21. 24.

c Ex. 29. 27.

filled: he shall be brought unto the door
of the tabernacle of the congregation:
(14) and he shall offer his offering unto
the LORD, one he lamb of the first year
without blemish for a burnt offering,
and one ewe lamb of the first year with-
out blemish for a sin offering, and one
ram without blemish for peace offerings,
(15) and a basket of unleavened bread,
cakes of fine flour mingled with oil, and
wafers of unleavened bread anointed
with oil, and their meat offering, and
their drink offerings. (16) And the priest
shall bring *them* before the LORD, and
shall offer his sin offering, and his burnt
offering: (17) and he shall offer the ram
for a sacrifice of peace offerings unto the
LORD, with the basket of unleavened
bread: the priest shall offer also his
meat offering, and his drink offering.
(18) [b] And the Nazarite shall shave the
head of his separation *at* the door of the
tabernacle of the congregation, and shall
take the hair of the head of his separ-
ation, and put *it* in the fire which *is*
under the sacrifice of the peace offer-
ings. (19) And the priest shall take the
sodden shoulder of the ram, and one un-
leavened cake out of the basket, and one
unleavened wafer, and shall put *them* upon
the hands of the Nazarite, after *the hair
of* his separation is shaven: (20) and the
priest shall wave them [c] *for* a wave offer-
ing before the LORD: this *is* holy for the
priest, with the wave breast and heave
shoulder: and after that the Nazarite
may drink wine. (21) This *is* the law of

(5) **There shall no razor come upon his head.**—The hair was to be suffered to grow in all its luxuriance during the days of the Nazirite vow. The meaning may be illustrated by reference to Lev. xxv. 4, 5, 11, where it is prescribed that in the seventh year the vine was not to be pruned, and that the grapes of "the undressed vine" (literally, *the grapes of the Nazirite*) should not be gathered.

(7) **He shall not make himself unclean . . .**—The law of the Nazirite in this respect was equally stringent with that of the high priest (Lev. xxi. 11), and more stringent than that which was imposed upon the priests generally (Lev. xxi. 2, 3).

The consecration.—Better, *the separation* (Hebrew, *nezer*). So also in verse 9.

(11) **And the priest shall offer . . .**—The word which is here rendered "offer" (*asah*), like the Greek *poiein*, means literally "do." Its sacrificial signification, however, in this place, is entirely dependent upon the context.

By the dead.—*i.e.*, by reason of, or on account of the dead body with which he had been brought in contact.

(14) **And he shall offer.**—The word which is here rendered *offer* is different from that which is used in verse 11, and means literally *to bring near.* The cognate noun is *Corban*—a word which St. Mark translates into Greek *dovon,* and which means a gift offered to God. (Comp. St. Matt. xv. 5, 6; St. Mark vii. 11). The sin-offering was an offering of atonement for sins committed during the period of the consecration of the Nazirite, and the burnt-offering typified the entire consecration of the body, soul, and spirit of the offerer to the Lord.

(15) **And their meat offering, and their drink offerings.**—*i.e.*, the offerings of fine flour and oil and wine which belonged to the burnt-offerings and the peace-offerings (chap. xv. 3, &c.).

(18) **And the Nazarite shall shave . . .**—The consignment of his hair to the sacrificial fire formed a solemn and suitable termination of the days of his separation to the Lord during the continuance of his Nazirite vow.

(21) **Beside that that his hand shall get.**—*i.e.*, besides any voluntary offerings which it may be in his power to make.

the Nazarite who hath vowed, *and of* his
offering unto the LORD for his separation,
beside *that* that his hand shall get: ac-
cording to the vow which he vowed, so he
must do after the law of his separation.
(22) And the LORD spake unto Moses,
saying, (23) Speak unto Aaron and unto
his sons, saying, On this wise ye shall
bless the children of Israel, saying unto
them,
(24) The LORD bless thee, and keep thee:
(25) the LORD make his face shine upon
thee, and be gracious unto thee: (26) the
LORD lift up his countenance upon thee,
and give thee peace.
(27) And they shall put my name upon
the children of Israel; and I will bless
them.

CHAPTER VII. — (1) And it came to
pass on the day that Moses had fully
[a] set up the tabernacle, and had anointed
it, and sanctified it, and all the instru-
ments thereof, both the altar and all the
vessels thereof, and had anointed them,
and sanctified them; (2) that the princes
of Israel, heads of the house of their
fathers, who *were* the princes of the
tribes, [1] and were over them that were
numbered, offered: (3) and they brought
their offering before the LORD, six covered
wagons, and twelve oxen; a wagon for
two of the princes, and for each one
an ox: and they brought them before
the tabernacle. (4) And the LORD spake
unto Moses, saying, (5) Take *it* of them,
that they may be to do the service of the
tabernacle of the congregation; and
thou shalt give them unto the Levites,
to every man according to his service.
(6) And Moses took the wagons and the
oxen, and gave them unto the Levites.
(7) Two wagons and four oxen he gave
unto the sons of Gershon, according to
their service: (8) and four wagons and
eight oxen he gave unto the sons of
Merari, according unto their service,
under the hand of Ithamar the son of
Aaron the priest. (9) But unto the sons
of Kohath he gave none: because the
service of the sanctuary belonging unto
them *was that* they should bear upon
their shoulders.
(10) And the princes offered for dedi-
cating of the altar in the day that it was
anointed, even the princes offered their
offering before the altar. (11) And the
LORD said unto Moses, They shall offer
their offering, each prince on his day,
for the dedicating of the altar.

a Ex. 40. 18.

1 Heb. *who stood.*

---

(23) **On this wise ye shall bless the children of Israel.**—The occasions on which this blessing was used are not recorded. The blessing itself, which marks in a special manner the spiritual character of the chosen people, consists of three double clauses. In each of these three clauses the sacred name Jehovah is repeated, and there is a rising gradation in the blessing invoked, until it culminates in that peace which is the highest of those gifts that God can bestow and that man can possess. There has been commonly recognised in this blessing an allusion to the doctrine of the Trinity. Mention is made in Lev. ix. 22 of a blessing pronounced by Aaron upon the people, but no form of words is found there.

VII.

(1) **On the day that Moses had fully set up the tabernacle.**—Better, *had finished the setting up of the tabernacle.* The offerings of the princes occupied twelve days, the sacrifices being too numerous to be offered at the same time. It follows, therefore, that the expression "on the day" here and in verse 10 must be understood, as in Gen. ii. 4, as meaning "at the time." The verse, however, may be read thus: "And it came to pass on the day . . . that he anointed it . . . ;" in which case the following verse would begin thus: "And the princes of Israel . . ." It should be observed, however, on the other hand, that verse 10 connects the time of the offerings with that of the anointing of the altar. In any case, the expression "on the day" needs to be interpreted in the wider sense, which it not unfrequently requires, inasmuch as the Tabernacle was set up on the first day of the *first* month of the second year (Exod. xl. 17), and the events recorded in this and the preceding chapters appear to have taken place on and after the first day of the *second* month of that year (chap. i. 1). The account of the setting up of the Tabernacle and the altar, &c., is contained in Exod. xl. 17—33, and the account of the anointing and consecration is contained in Lev. viii. 10, 11. It appears from a comparison of Exod. xl. 17 with Num. x. 11 that fifty days intervened between the erection of the Tabernacle and the beginning of the march from Sinai.

(2) **And were over them that were numbered.**—The first mention of these princes is found in connection with the numbering of the tribes (chap. i. 4).

(3) **Six covered wagons.**—In Isa. lxvi. 20 the word which is here rendered *covered,* and which is a noun, occurs in the plural, and is rendered in the Authorised Version *litters.* It occurs nowhere else in the same sense. It seems probable, however, that the Vulgate, which the Authorised Version follows, has the right signification: *plaustra tecta.*

(7) **Two wagons and four oxen.**—The Gershonites had charge of the hangings of the Tabernacle and court (chap. iv. 25, 26), whilst the Merarites had charge of the boards, pillars, &c., which were of much greater weight (chap. iv. 31, 32). The Kohathites were required to bear their burdens on poles upon their shoulders (verse 9), and therefore did not require any wagons.

(10) **For dedicating of the altar.**—Literally, *the dedication of the altar—i.e.,* the gifts made at the dedication of the altar.

(12) And he that offered his offering the first day was Nahshon the son of Amminadab, of the tribe of Judah: (13) and his offering *was* one silver charger, the weight thereof *was* an hundred and thirty *shekels*, one silver bowl of seventy shekels, after the shekel of the sanctuary; both of them *were* full of fine flour mingled with oil for a [a] meat offering: (14) one spoon of ten *shekels* of gold, full of incense: (15) one young bullock, one ram, one lamb of the first year, for a burnt offering: (16) one kid of the goats for a [b] sin offering: (17) and for a sacrifice of peace offerings, two oxen, five rams, five he goats, five lambs of the first year: this *was* the offering of Nahshon the son of Amminadab.

(18) On the second day Nethaneel the son of Zuar, prince of Issachar, did offer: (19) he offered *for* his offering one silver charger, the weight whereof *was* an hundred and thirty *shekels*, one silver bowl of seventy shekels, after the shekel of the sanctuary; both of them full of fine flour mingled with oil for a meat offering: (20) one spoon of gold of ten *shekels*, full of incense: (21) one young bullock, one ram, one lamb of the first year, for a burnt offering: (22) one kid of the goats for a sin offering: (23) and for a sacrifice of peace offerings, two oxen, five rams, five he goats, five lambs of the first year: this *was* the offering of Nethaneel the son of Zuar.

(24) On the third day Eliab the son of Helon, prince of the children of Zebulun, *did offer*: (25) his offering *was* one silver charger, the weight whereof *was* an hundred and thirty *shekels*, one silver bowl of seventy shekels, after the shekel of the sanctuary; both of them full of fine flour mingled with oil for a meat offering: (26) one golden spoon of ten *shekels*, full of incense: (27) one young bullock, one ram, one lamb of the first year, for a burnt offering: (28) one kid of the goats for a sin offering: (29) and for a sacrifice of peace offerings, two oxen, five rams, five he goats, five lambs of the first year: this *was* the offering of Eliab the son of Helon.

(30) On the fourth day Elizur the son of Shedeur, prince of the children of Reuben, *did offer*: (31) his offering *was* one silver charger of the weight of an hundred and thirty *shekels*, one silver bowl of seventy shekels, after the shekel of the sanctuary; both of them full of fine flour mingled with oil for a meat offering: (32) one golden spoon of ten *shekels*, full of incense: (33) one young bullock, one ram, one lamb of the first year, for a burnt offering: (34) one kid of the goats for a sin offering: (35) and for a sacrifice of peace offerings, two oxen, five rams, five he goats, five lambs of the first year: this *was* the offering of Elizur the son of Shedeur.

(36) On the fifth day Shelumiel the son of Zurishaddai, prince of the children of Simeon, *did offer*: (37) his offering *was* one silver charger, the weight whereof *was* an hundred and thirty *shekels*, one silver bowl of seventy shekels, after the shekel of the sanctuary; both of them full of fine flour mingled with oil for a meat offering: (38) one golden spoon of ten *shekels*, full of incense: (39) one young bullock, one ram, one lamb of the first year, for a burnt offering: (40) one kid of the goats for a sin offering: (41) and for a sacrifice of peace offerings, two oxen, five rams, five he goats, five lambs of the first year: this *was* the offering of Shelumiel the son of Zurishaddai.

(42) On the sixth day Eliasaph the son of Deuel, prince of the children of Gad, *offered*: (43) his offering *was* one silver charger of the weight of an hundred and thirty *shekels*, a silver bowl of seventy shekels, after the shekel of the sanctuary; both of them full of fine flour mingled with oil for a meat offering: (44) one golden spoon of ten *shekels*, full of incense: (45) one young bullock, one ram, one lamb of the first year, for a burnt offering: (46) one kid of the goats for a sin

a Lev. 2. 1.

b Lev. 4. 23.

---

(12) **And he that offered his offering the first day . . .**—It should be observed that the order in which the offerings were made is not that of chap. i., but that observed in the encampments, as prescribed in chap. ii.

(13) **And his offering was one silver charger . . .**—The offerings of the twelve princes, or rather of the tribes which the princes represented, was the same in each case. The repetition of the description of the offerings, which occupies the remaining portion of this chapter, may serve to denote the special regard which God has to the offerings of His people, as may be learned from the notice which our Lord took of the offerings which were made for the Temple service, and His commendation of that of the poor widow who cast her two mites into the treasury (Mark xii. 41—44).

offering: (47) and for a sacrifice of peace offerings, two oxen, five rams, five he goats, five lambs of the first year: this *was* the offering of Eliasaph the son of Deuel.

(48) On the seventh day Elishama the son of Ammihud, prince of the children of Ephraim, *offered:* (49) his offering *was* one silver charger, the weight whereof *was* an hundred and thirty *shekels,* one silver bowl of seventy shekels, after the shekel of the sanctuary; both of them full of fine flour mingled with oil for a meat offering: (50) one golden spoon of ten *shekels,* full of incense: (51) one young bullock, one ram, one lamb of the first year, for a burnt offering: (52) one kid of the goats for a sin offering: (53) and for a sacrifice of peace offerings, two oxen, five rams, five he goats, five lambs of the first year: this *was* the offering of Elishama the son of Ammihud.

(54) On the eighth day *offered* Gamaliel the son of Pedahzur, prince of the children of Manasseh: (55) his offering *was* one silver charger of the weight of an hundred and thirty *shekels,* one silver bowl of seventy shekels, after the shekel of the sanctuary; both of them full of fine flour mingled with oil for a meat offering: (56) one golden spoon of ten *shekels,* full of incense: (57) one young bullock, one ram, one lamb of the first year, for a burnt offering: (58) one kid of the goats for a sin offering: (59) and for a sacrifice of peace offerings, two oxen, five rams, five he goats, five lambs of the first year: this *was* the offering of Gamaliel the son of Pedahzur.

(60) On the ninth day Abidan the son of Gideoni, prince of the children of Benjamin, *offered:* (61) his offering *was* one silver charger, the weight whereof *was* an hundred and thirty *shekels,* one silver bowl of seventy shekels, after the shekel of the sanctuary; both of them full of fine flour mingled with oil for a meat offering: (62) one golden spoon of ten *shekels,* full of incense: (63) one young bullock, one ram, one lamb of the first year, for a burnt offering: (64) one kid of the goats for a sin offering: (65) and for a sacrifice of peace offerings, two oxen, five rams, five he goats, five lambs of the first year: this *was* the offering of Abidan the son of Gideoni.

(66) On the tenth day Ahiezer the son of Ammishaddai, prince of the children of Dan, *offered:* (67) his offering *was* one silver charger, the weight whereof *was* an hundred and thirty *shekels,* one silver bowl of seventy shekels, after the shekel of the sanctuary; both of them full of fine flour mingled with oil for a meat offering: (68) one golden spoon of ten *shekels,* full of incense: (69) one young bullock, one ram, one lamb of the first year, for a burnt offering: (70) one kid of the goats for a sin offering: (71) and for a sacrifice of peace offerings, two oxen, five rams, five he goats, five lambs of the first year: this *was* the offering of Ahiezer the son of Ammishaddai.

(72) On the eleventh day Pagiel the son of Ocran, prince of the children of Asher, *offered:* (73) his offering *was* one silver charger, the weight whereof *was* an hundred and thirty *shekels,* one silver bowl of seventy shekels, after the shekel of the sanctuary; both of them full of fine flour mingled with oil for a meat offering: (74) one golden spoon of ten *shekels,* full of incense: (75) one young bullock, one ram, one lamb of the first year, for a burnt offering: (76) one kid of the goats for a sin offering: (77) and for a sacrifice of peace offerings, two oxen, five rams, five he goats, five lambs of the first year: this *was* the offering of Pagiel the son of Ocran.

(78) On the twelfth day Ahira the son of Enan, prince of the children of Naphtali, *offered:* (79) his offering *was* one silver charger, the weight whereof *was* an hundred and thirty *shekels,* one silver bowl of seventy shekels, after the shekel of the sanctuary; both of them full of fine flour mingled with oil for a meat offering: (80) one golden spoon of ten *shekels,* full of incense: (81) one young bullock, one ram, one lamb of the first year, for a burnt offering: (82) one kid of the goats for a sin offering: (83) and for a sacrifice of peace offerings, two oxen, five rams, five he goats, five lambs of the first year: this *was* the offering of Ahira the son of Enan.

(84) This *was* the dedication of the altar, in the day when it was anointed, by the princes of Israel: twelve chargers of silver, twelve silver bowls, twelve spoons of gold: (85) each charger of silver *weighing* an hundred and thirty *shekels,* each bowl seventy: all the silver vessels

weighed two thousand and four hundred
shekels, after the shekel of the sanctuary:
(86) the golden spoons *were* twelve, full of
incense, *weighing* ten *shekels* apiece, after
the shekel of the sanctuary: all the
gold of the spoons *was* an hundred and
twenty *shekels.* (87) All the oxen for the
burnt offering *were* twelve bullocks, the
rams twelve, the lambs of the first year
twelve, with their meat offering: and
the kids of the goats for sin offering
twelve. (88) And all the oxen for the
sacrifice of the peace offerings *were*
twenty and four bullocks, the rams sixty,
the he goats sixty, the lambs of the first
year sixty. This *was* the dedication of
the altar, after that it was anointed.
(89) And when Moses was gone into
the tabernacle of the congregation to
speak with [1] him, then he heard the
voice of one speaking unto him from
off the mercy seat that *was* upon
the ark of testimony, from between
the two cherubims: and he spake unto
him.

CHAPTER VIII. — (1) And the LORD
spake unto Moses, saying, (2) Speak unto
Aaron, and say unto him, When thou
[a] lightest the lamps, the seven lamps shall
give light over against the candlestick.
(3) And Aaron did so; he lighted the
lamps thereof over against the candle-
stick, as the LORD commanded Moses.
(4) [b] And this work of the candlestick *was*
of beaten gold, unto the shaft thereof,
unto the flowers thereof, *was* [c] beaten
work: according unto the pattern which
the LORD had shewed Moses, so he made
the candlestick.
(5) And the LORD spake unto Moses,
saying, (6) Take the Levites from among
the children of Israel, and cleanse them.
(7) And thus shalt thou do unto them, to
cleanse them: Sprinkle water of purify-
ing upon them, and [2] let them shave all

1 That is, *God.*

a Ex. 25. 37; & 40. 25.

b Ex. 25. 31.

c Ex. 25. 18.

2 Heb., *let them cause a rasor to pass over, &c.*

---

(89) **And when Moses was gone . . .**—Better, *And when Moses went—i.e.,* as often as he went.

To speak with him—*i.e.,* with God. Inasmuch as the tent of meeting took its name from the promise made to Moses (Exod. xxv. 22) that God would meet with him there, it was not necessary to supply the Divine name. The terms in which the promise is expressed seem to denote that it was in the Holy of Holies that God met with Moses.

The voice of one speaking unto him.—Better, *the voice speaking unto him.* (Comp. Rev. i. 12; vi. 6.)

From off the mercy seat.—Or, *from over the mercy seat.*

The ark of testimony.—Better, *the ark of the testimony*—so called from the fact that the Testimony (*i.e.,* the two tables of the Law) was put in it (Exod. xxv. 16).

VIII.

(2) **When thou lightest the lamps.**—Better, *When thou settest up the lamps.* (Comp. Exod. xxv. 37.) The golden candlestick was placed against the south wall of the Tabernacle, opposite to the table of shewbread, so that its seven branches were parallel to that wall, with its branches east and west, and consequently the seven lamps, one of which rested upon each of the seven branches, threw their light in front of the candlestick, *i.e.,* towards the north wall, by which arrangement the furniture of the holy place was more effectually lighted than it would have been had the candlestick been placed facing the entrance, with its branches north and south.

Over against.—Or, *in front of.*

(3) **He lighted.**—Better, *he set up.*

(4) **And this work of the candlestick . . .**—Better, *And this was the work of the candlestick, i.e.,* the material of which it was made.

Beaten gold.—Better, *turned* (or *twisted*) *gold.*

Unto the shaft thereof, unto the flowers thereof.—Literally, *unto its base, unto its flower or blossom, i.e.,* the whole of the candlestick, from its base to its flowers. The several parts of the candlestick, beginning with the base and ending with the flowers, are enumerated in Exod. xxv. 31.

(5) **And the Lord spake unto Moses.**—As Moses had already officiated in the consecration of the priests (Lev. viii.), so now, notwithstanding the fact that Aaron and his sons were already consecrated, he is commanded to officiate at the cleansing of the Levites.

(7) **Water of purifying.**—Literally, *water of sin,* or, *of sin-offering* (Hebrew, *hattath*). As in the case of the holy water, to which reference is made in chap. vi. 17, so here also there is no explanation given of the particular water which was to be used in cleansing the Levites. The bullock which was appointed to be offered as a sin-offering at the consecration of Aaron and his sons (Exod. xxix. 14; Lev. viii. 14) is described by the same word which is here employed (in the Authorised Version, *sin-offering*); and in Lev. iv. 14, the sacrifice which was appointed to be offered for the expiation of sin (in the Authorised Version, *the sin*) is also spoken of under the same name; so also is the sin-offering of the Levites in verse 8 of this chapter. The sin-water evidently denotes the water appointed to be used in the purification of sin; and the reference is probably (as in chap. vi. 17) to the water which was kept in the brazen laver in front of the Tabernacle. It is possible, however, that some direction which is not here recorded may have been given respecting putting the ashes of the sin-offering into water. (Comp. chap. xix. 9, where the water of purification is described under the same name: "it is a purification for sin." Literally, it is *hattath.*) In this case, however, the sin-offering, which is not mentioned until verse 8, must have been sacrificed previously to the sprinkling.

Let them shave all their flesh.—Literally, *cause the razor to pass over all their flesh.* A different word is used in Lev. xiv. 8, 9 to denote the more complete

their flesh, and let them wash their clothes, and *so* make themselves clean. (8) Then let them take a young bullock with his meat offering, *even* fine flour mingled with oil, and another young bullock shalt thou take for a sin offering. (9) And thou shalt bring the Levites before the tabernacle of the congregation: and thou shalt gather the whole assembly of the children of Israel together: (10) and thou shalt bring the Levites before the LORD: and the children of Israel shall put their hands upon the Levites: (11) and Aaron shall [1] offer the Levites before the LORD *for* an [2] offering of the children of Israel, that [3] they may execute the service of the LORD. (12) And the Levites shall lay their hands upon the heads of the bullocks: and thou shalt offer the one *for* a sin offering, and the other *for* a burnt offering, unto the LORD, to make an atonement for the Levites. (13) And thou shalt set the Levites before Aaron, and before his sons, and offer them *for* an offering unto the LORD. (14) Thus shalt thou separate the Levites from among the children of Israel: and the Levites shall be [a] mine. (15) And after that shall the Levites go in to do the service of the tabernacle of the congregation: and thou shalt cleanse them, and offer them *for* an offering. (16) For they *are* wholly given unto me from among the children of Israel; instead of such as open every womb, *even instead of* the firstborn of all the children of Israel, have I taken them unto me. (17) [b] For all the firstborn of the children of Israel *are* mine, *both* man and beast: on the day that I smote every firstborn in the land of Egypt I sanctified them for myself. (18) And I have taken the Levites for all the firstborn of the children of Israel. (19) And I have given the Levites *as* [4] a gift to Aaron and to his sons from among the children of Israel, to do the service of the children of Israel in the tabernacle of the congregation, and to make an atonement for the children of Israel: that there be no plague among the children of Israel, when the children of Israel come nigh unto the sanctuary.

(20) And Moses, and Aaron, and all the congregation of the children of Israel, did to the Levites according unto all that the LORD commanded Moses concerning the Levites, so did the children of Israel unto them. (21) And the Levites were purified, and they washed their clothes; and Aaron offered them *as* an offering before the LORD; and

1 Heb., *wave.*

2 Heb., *wave offering.*

3 Heb., *they may be to execute, &c.*

a ch. 3. 45.

b Ex. 13. 2; ch. 3. 13; Luke 2. 23.

4 Heb., *given.*

---

removal of the hair which was enjoined at the cleansing of the leper.

And let them wash their clothes.—The bodies of the priests were washed at their consecration (Lev. xiv. 8, 9), and those of the lepers at their cleansing (Lev. viii. 6); but the Levites, who were not brought into such immediate contact with the holy things as the priests, were only required to wash their clothes, which was an ordinary preparation for Divine worship (Exod. xix. 10; comp. Gen. xxxv. 2).

(9) **The whole assembly of the children of Israel**—*i.e.,* as elsewhere, the representatives of the people.

(10) **Shall put their hands upon the Levites.**—The same phrase is here used as in verse 12, and elsewhere, of the offerer who was required to lay his hand upon the victim which he offered in sacrifice. By this symbolical act the obligation which rested upon the whole nation in regard to the dedication of the firstborn was transferred to the Levites, who were thenceforth to be dedicated to the service of the Lord, and given over to the priests as the representatives of the Lord.

(11) **And Aaron shall offer the Levites before the Lord for an offering.**—Literally, *and Aaron shall wave the Levites as a wave-offering before the Lord.* The manner in which the Levites were thus set apart to the Lord is not expressed. It may have been done by leading them backwards and forwards in front of the Tabernacle and in the presence of the people, or by the waving of Aaron's hands. The same word is used elsewhere in reference to offerings of different kinds—as, *e.g.,* of gold in Exod. xxxv. 22. (Comp. verses 13, 15, 21 of this chapter.) The symbolical meaning of the ceremony is obvious from the concluding words of the verse, and is further explained in verses 13, 14. (Comp. Lev. vii. 30 and Note.)

(13) **And offer them for an offering.**—Literally, *and wave them as a wave-offering,* as in verse 11. So also in verse 15.

(15) **And after that shall the Levites go in . . .**—*i.e.,* into the court of the Tabernacle to keep watch there, and to assist the priests at the altar of burnt-offering, and to take down and set up the Tabernacle as occasion might require.

(16) **Instead of such as open every womb, even instead of the firstborn of all the children of Israel.**—It is difficult to determine whether the second clause is to be regarded as an exact equivalent, or as a limitation of the first. If an exact equivalent, a different meaning must be assigned to the *firstborn* from that which it commonly bears in the Pentateuch, where it appears to be restricted to the firstborn son on the father's side. (Cf. Exod. xiii. 2.)

(19) **As a gift.**—Hebrew, *given,* as in verse 16.

That there be no plague among the children of Israel.—The appointment of the Levites in the place of the firstborn was calculated to insure the reverent and orderly discharge of the duties of the Sanctuary, and to operate as a safeguard against those sins of omission and commission into which the

Aaron made an atonement for them to cleanse them. (22) And after that went the Levites in to do their service in the tabernacle of the congregation before Aaron, and before his sons: as the LORD had commanded Moses concerning the Levites, so did they unto them.

(23) And the LORD spake unto Moses, saying, (24) This *is it* that *belongeth* unto the Levites: from twenty and five years old and upward they shall go in [1] to wait upon the service of the tabernacle of the congregation: (25) and from the age of fifty years they shall [2] cease waiting upon the service *thereof*, and shall serve no more: (26) but shall minister with their brethren in the tabernacle of the congregation, to keep the charge, and shall do no service. Thus shalt thou do unto the Levites touching their charge.

CHAPTER IX. — (1) And the LORD spake unto Moses in the wilderness of Sinai, in the first month of the second year after they were come out of the land of Egypt, saying, (2) Let the children of Israel also keep [a] the passover at his appointed season. (3) In the fourteenth day of this month, [3] at even, ye shall keep it in his appointed season: according to all the rites of it, and according to all the ceremonies thereof, shall ye keep it. (4) And Moses spake unto the children of Israel, that they should keep the passover. (5) And they kept the passover on the fourteenth day of the first month at even in the wilderness of Sinai: according to all that the LORD commanded Moses, so did the children of Israel.

(6) And there were certain men, who

1 Heb., *to war the warfare of, &c.*

2 Heb., *return from the warfare of the service.*

a Ex. 12. 1, &c.; Lev. 23. 5; ch. 28. 16; Deut. 16. 2.

3 Heb., *between two evenings.*

---

firstborn would have been more likely to be betrayed, and which would have provoked the Divine wrath against the Israelites generally.

(24) **From twenty and five years old and upward.**—This regulation may be understood as referring to the age at which the Levites were to enter upon their duties after the people had taken possession of the land of Canaan, and it appears to have remained in force until the time of David, who substituted the age of twenty for that of twenty-five, because the necessity of carrying the Tabernacle and its furniture from place to place, which arose but seldom after the entrance into Canaan, finally ceased after the removal of the ark to Mount Zion. The time of service during the wanderings in the wilderness was from thirty to fifty (chap. iv. 3, 23, 30), during which time the constant removal of the Tabernacle required the services of men in the full vigour of life. The chronological order of events is not always observed in this book, and the directions contained in verses 23—26 may have been given at a later period, but inserted here in connection with the account of the appointment of the Levites to their office. On the other hand, it is quite possible that from the first the Levites entered upon the lighter parts of their office at the age of twenty-five years, but were not employed before they were thirty years of age in the more onerous duties of removing the Tabernacle, or in bearing on their shoulders the sacred vessels, as in the case of the Kohathites.

To wait upon the service.—Literally, *to war the warfare, or to serve the (military) service.* Similarly, in the following verse, *he shall return from the warfare of the service.*

(26) **To keep the charge.**—A clear distinction is here made between the *service* which involved heavy manual labour in carrying the furniture of the Tabernacle and in slaughtering the victims, and the *charge* or oversight of the furniture and the vessels of the Sanctuary.

IX.

(1) **In the first month of the second year.**—The celebration of the Passover, as recorded in this chapter, preceded in order of time the numbering of the people recorded in chap. i., and the other events which were connected with it. No provision had hitherto been made for the celebration of the Passover in the wilderness. A special injunction was, therefore, required for this purpose. Had it not been for the rebellion of the people, the next Passover after the original Egyptian Passover would have been celebrated in the land of Canaan, and it was for that one only that provision had been made (Exod. xii. 25).

(3) **At even.**—Hebrew, *between the two evenings.* (See Note on Exod. xii. 6.)

According to all the rites of it, and according to all the ceremonies thereof.—Better, *according to all the statutes and ordinances thereof.* It is obvious that some of the directions concerning the Egyptian Passover could not be observed in the wilderness. The reference must, therefore, be to those statutes and ordinances respecting the Passover which were of permanent obligation. (Comp. verse 12, where the ordinance respecting the time of observance is necessarily excluded.) Some of these are found in Exod. xii., whilst others of a later date are recorded in Lev. xvii. and Deut. xvi. It has been objected that three priests (for Nadab and Abihu were dead) could not sprinkle the blood of the large number of lambs which must have been slain. It must be remembered, however, (1) that there is no express injunction respecting the sprinkling of the blood on this occasion; and (2) that the priests were probably assisted at this time in the performance of some of their duties—as we are expressly informed that they were at the Passovers celebrated by Hezekiah and by Josiah (2 Chron. xxx. 16, xxxv. 11)—by the Levites.

(5) **And they kept the passover on the fourteenth day . . .**—There is no mention here of the observance of the feast of unleavened bread for seven days, as it was enjoined in Exod. xii. 18. It might not have been practicable to obtain a sufficient quantity of flour to last so large a number of people for seven days, though it may have been easy to procure from Midian or elsewhere a sufficient quantity for one meal.

(6) **And there were certain men . . .**—It has been supposed that the reference is to Mishael and Elzaphan, who appear to have buried their cousins,

were defiled by the dead body of a man,
that they could not keep the passover
on that day: and they came before
Moses and before Aaron on that day:
(7) and those men said unto him, We *are*
defiled by the dead body of a man:
wherefore are we kept back, that we
may not offer an offering of the LORD in
his appointed season among the children
of Israel? (8) And Moses said unto
them, Stand still, and I will hear what
the LORD will command concerning you.
(9) And the LORD spake unto Moses,
saying, (10) Speak unto the children of
Israel, saying, If any man of you or of
your posterity shall be unclean by rea-
son of a dead body, or *be* in a journey
afar off, yet he shall keep the passover
unto the LORD. (11) The fourteenth day
of the second month at even they shall
keep it, *and* eat it with unleavened bread
and bitter *herbs*. (12) They shall leave
none of it unto the morning, [a] nor break
any bone of it: according to all the
ordinances of the passover they shall
keep it. (13) But the man that *is* clean,
and is not in a journey, and forbeareth
to keep the passover, even the same soul
shall be cut off from among his people:
because he brought not the offering of
the LORD in his appointed season, that
man shall bear his sin. (14) And if a
stranger shall sojourn among you, and
will keep the passover unto the LORD;
according to the ordinance of the pass-
over, and according to the manner
thereof, so shall he do: [b] ye shall have
one ordinance, both for the stranger,
and for him that was born in the land.
(15) And [c] on the day that the taber-
nacle was reared up the cloud covered
the tabernacle, *namely*, the tent of the
testimony: and at even there was upon
the tabernacle as it were the appearance

a Ex. 12. 46; John 19. 36.

b Ex. 12. 49.

c Ex. 40. 34.

Nadab and Abihu, about this time (Blunt's "Script. Coincidences," pp. 66, 67, 1850). If the consecration of Aaron and his sons began on the first day of the first month (Exod. xl. 2, 12), and the death of Nadab and Abihu could not have taken place until the eighth day (Lev. ix. 1, 12; x. 19), inasmuch as the defilement caused by contact with the dead lasted for seven days (Num. xix. 11), it will follow, if this law was already in force, that those who buried Nadab and Abihu must have been unclean on the fourteenth day of the first month. Independently, then, of the doubtful inference which Professor Blunt draws from the identity of the numbers of the other tribes at the two numberings taken, the one before and the other after this time, from which he concludes that the deaths must have occurred amongst those who belonged to the tribe of Levi, which was not included in the census, this circumstance may fairly be adduced as one of the numerous undesigned coincidences with which Holy Scripture abounds. It may be observed further that, whilst reference would naturally be made to Moses on all doubtful occasions, none would be so likely to have recourse to him with the inquiry contained in verse 7 as those who had been employed by his direction (Lev. x. 4) in the burial of Nadab and Abihu. The law contained in Lev. vii. 21 appears to have been understood to refer to all sacrificial meals. The legal uncleanness which disqualified the Israelites for participation in the Passover may be regarded as typical of the moral and spiritual disqualifications which render men unfit for participation in the Lord's Supper.

(7) **An offering.**—Better, *the offering*, or *oblation*.

(10) **In a journey afar off.**—Or, *on a distant journey*. This is one of the ten passages in the Pentateuch in which one or more words are marked with certain dots, known as *puncta extraordinaria*. In this case these dots stand over the word *rehokah, distant*. The Rabbinical explanation is that the word is either spurious, as not being found in verse 13, or is not to be interpreted in its literal signification, but in a qualified sense.

(12) **According to all the ordinances.**—The word rendered *ordinances* is in the singular number: *according to all the ordinance* (or *statute*). The primary reference is probably to the law respecting the Paschal Lamb. According to Jewish tradition the feast was only observed for one day instead of seven, and it was not necessary to put away leaven.

(13) **Shall bear his sin**—*i.e.*, shall be put to death. (Comp. Lev. xxiv. 15; Num. xviii. 22.)

(14) **And if a stranger . . .**—The law respecting the stranger is contained in Exod. xii. 48, 49.

(15) **The cloud covered the tabernacle, namely, the tent of the testimony.**—Better, *the tabernacle of* (or, belonging to) *the tent of the testimony*. It is stated in Exod. xl. 34, after the account of the erection of the Tabernacle, that the cloud covered the Tent of Meeting, and that the glory of the Lord filled the Tabernacle. There is, therefore, no sufficient ground for the supposition that the cloud rested on that part of the Tabernacle exclusively in which the two tables of the testimony were kept, *i.e.*, the Holy of Holies. On the contrary, it is stated in Exod. xl. 35 that Moses could not enter the Tent of Meeting, because the cloud abode upon it, where there is no reference to any particular part of the erection. It is true, however, that it was from above the mercy-seat that the presence of Jehovah was specially manifested, and that it was in the most holy place, in which the ark of the testimony was kept, that He met with Moses and communed with him (Exod. xxv. 21—23). The account of the cloud covering the Tabernacle is repeated in this place, inasmuch as the history which follows relates the removal of the Tabernacle under the guidance of the same cloud which covered it at its erection.

And at even.—The dark side of the cloud afforded a grateful shade by day, and the bright side of the cloud served to supply light by night. Comp. Ps. lxxviii. 14: "In the day-time also He led them with a cloud, and all the night with a light of fire;" and Neh. ix. 12: "Thou leddest them in the day by a cloudy pillar, and in the night by a pillar of fire, to give them light in the way

of fire, until the morning. (16) So it was
alway: the cloud covered it *by day*,
and the appearance of fire by night.
(17) And when the cloud was taken up
from the tabernacle, then after that the
children of Israel journeyed: and in the
place where the cloud abode, there the
children of Israel pitched their tents.
(18) At the commandment of the LORD
the children of Israel journeyed, and at
the commandment of the LORD they
pitched: [a]as long as the cloud abode
upon the tabernacle they rested in
their tents. (19) And when the cloud
[1]tarried long upon the tabernacle many
days, then the children of Israel kept
the charge of the LORD, and journeyed
not. (20) And *so* it was, when the cloud
was a few days upon the tabernacle;
according to the commandment of the
LORD they abode in their tents, and
according to the commandment of the
LORD they journeyed. (21) And *so* it
was, when the cloud [2]abode from even
unto the morning, and *that* the cloud
was taken up in the morning, then
they journeyed: whether *it was* by day
or by night that the cloud was taken
up, they journeyed. (22) Or *whether it*
were two days, or a month, or a year,
that the cloud tarried upon the taber-
nacle, remaining thereon, the children
of Israel [b]abode in their tents, and jour-
neyed not: but when it was taken up,
they journeyed. (23) At the command-
ment of the LORD they rested in the
tents, and at the commandment of the
LORD they journeyed: they kept the
charge of the LORD, at the command-
ment of the LORD by the hand of Moses.

a 1 Cor. 10. 1.

1 Heb., *prolonged.*

2 Heb., *was.*

b Ex. 40. 36, 37.

CHAPTER X.—(1) And the LORD
spake unto Moses, saying, (2) Make thee
two trumpets of silver; of a whole piece
shalt thou make them: that thou
mayest use them for the calling of the
assembly, and for the journeying of the
camps. (3) And when they shall blow
with them, all the assembly shall as-
semble themselves to thee at the door
of the tabernacle of the congregation.
(4) And if they blow *but* with one

---

wherein they should go;" also Isa. iv. 5: "And the Lord will create upon every dwelling-place of Mount Zion, and upon her assemblies, a cloud and smoke by day, and the shining of a flaming fire by night."

(16) **The cloud covered it by day.**—There is no need for the insertion of the words in italics. It was the same cloud which was "alway" over the Tabernacle during the continuance of the journeyings through the wilderness.

And the appearance of fire by night.—Better, *and there was the appearance of fire by night.* (Comp. Exod. xiii. 21—22.)

(17) **And when the cloud was taken up. . .**—Only one instance is recorded of disregard of the Divine direction thus miraculously vouchsafed, viz., in chap. xiv. 40—42. It was necessary that the hosts of Israel should be always in a watchful state, and ready to obey at once the intimations given to them of the Divine will, thus affording a striking type and pattern to the Christian Church, and teaching it both collectively and individually to seek and to follow the guidance of its Divine Head, whose promise is "Lo, I am with you alway, even unto the end of the world."

(19) **Kept the charge of the Lord.**—The same expression is used of Aaron and his sons in Lev. viii. 35, and also in respect to the office of the Levites in chap. iii. 7, as keeping the charge of Aaron and of the congregation. It is also used of the people generally in 2 Chron. xxiii. 6, in regard to the charge or "watch" of the Lord. It may imply that the people were to engage in acts of religious worship, or it may denote adherence to the Divine commands and ordinances generally, as in Ezek. xlviii. 11.

(20) **And so it was . . .**—Better, *And sometimes*, &c., *i.e.*, there were times or occasions in which, &c. So in verse 21.

(21) **By day or by night.**—It is obvious from this verse that there must have been sentinels constantly watching by night as well as by day, whose office it was to give notice when the cloud was removed. (Comp. Ps. cxxxiv. 1.)

(22) **Or a year.**—Literally, *days* (comp. Gen. iv. 3, xl. 4, and Notes). If the rendering of the Authorised Version, "a year," is correct, as it probably is, it will follow that these words could not have been written until after the first arrival at Kadesh (chap. xiii. 26), and probably not until after the end of the wanderings in the wilderness. The elaborate manner in which the statement is made and repeated in almost identical terms shows the great importance which the writer ascribed to the Divine guardianship which was exercised over the Israelites, and to their submission to the miraculous guidance which was given to them.

X.

(2) **Of a whole piece.**—Better, *of beaten* (or, *turned*) *work.* (See Notes on Exod. xxv. 18, 31.) The trumpets here spoken of are supposed to have been straight, like that on the triumphal arch of Titus at Rome and on the old Egyptian monuments. In this respect the *hazozerah* is supposed to have differed from the cornet or horn, *keren* or *shophar* (which is interchanged with *keren*), which was crooked. (See Josh. vi. 5, compared with vi. 4, 6, 8, 13.) We find reference to the jubilee trumpet in Lev. xxv. 9, from which it has been inferred that the trumpets here mentioned were not first made at this time. It is true, indeed, that the first verse might be rendered: "Now the Lord had spoken unto Moses, saying"; but the word used in Lev. xxv. 9 is *shophar*, not *hazozerah*, and the latter word occurs in this place for the first time.

(4) **With one trumpet.**—Or, *but once* (or, *at the same time*). (Comp. Job. xxxiii. 14; Prov. xxviii. 18;

trumpet, then the princes, *which are*
heads of the thousands of Israel, shall
gather themselves unto thee. (5) When
ye blow an alarm, then the camps that
lie on the east parts shall go forward.
(6) When ye blow an alarm the second
time, then the camps that lie on the
south side shall take their journey:
they shall blow an alarm for their
journeys. (7) But when the congrega-
tion is to be gathered together, ye shall
blow, but ye shall not sound an alarm.
(8) And the sons of Aaron, the priests,
shall blow with the trumpets; and they
shall be to you for an ordinance
for ever throughout your generations.
(9) And if ye go to war in your land
against the enemy that oppresseth you,
then ye shall blow an alarm with the
trumpets; and ye shall be remembered
before the LORD your God, and ye shall
be saved from your enemies. (10) Also in
the day of your gladness, and in your
solemn days, and in the beginnings of
your months, ye shall blow with the
trumpets over your burnt offerings, and
over the sacrifices of your peace offer-
ings; that they may be to you for a
memorial before your God: I *am* the
LORD your God.

(11) And it came to pass on the twen-
tieth *day* of the second month, in the
second year, that the cloud was taken
up from off the tabernacle of the tes-
timony. (12) And the children of Israel
took their journeys out of the wilderness

Jer. x. 8.) Some suppose that the meaning is that the trumpets were to be blown at the same time with one even or uniform sound, and that not a continuous one.

(5) **When ye blow an alarm.**—The word *teruah, alarm,* is supposed to denote a loud and continuous blast, by which the signal for the moving of the camps was distinguished from those which were used for the summoning of the congregation, or of the princes (verse 7). In the former of these cases some suppose that both trumpets were blown, and in the latter only one (verse 4 and Note. Comp. Lightfoot's *Temple Service,* chap. vii. 5, 2.) The fuller directions respecting the order in which the camps were to break up are given in chap. ii. Here the order of the eastern and southern camps only is prescribed. In the LXX., however, we read thus: "And ye shall sound a third alarm, and the camps pitched by the sea (*i.e.,* westward), shall move forward; and ye shall sound a fourth alarm, and they that encamp toward the north shall move forward; they shall sound an alarm at their departure."

(7) **But ye shall not sound an alarm.**—A clear and intelligible distinction was to be made between the summons to the princes, or to the congregation, to assemble at the entrance of the Tent of Meeting and the signal for the moving of the camps. So the gospel trumpet must at no time give an uncertain sound (1 Cor. xiv. 8), but must be used faithfully and diligently by the spiritual watchmen, whether it be to warn the ungodly, to arouse the careless, or to speak to the hearts of God's people.

(8) **And the sons of Aaron, the priests, shall blow with the trumpets.**—As Aaron had only two sons at this time, there was need only of two trumpets. In most of the places in which the word *hazozerah* (trumpet) occurs (as, *e.g.,* Num. xxxi. 6; 1 Chron. xv. 24), this instrument appears to have been used by the priests. There are cases, however, in the later history (as 2 Kings xi. 14; 1 Chron. xvi. 42), in which the trumpets appear to have been used by the Levites, and perhaps by those who were neither priests nor Levites. The number of these trumpets was increased in the time of David and Solomon. We read in 1 Chron. xv. 24 of seven priests blowing with them before the ark of God, and in 2 Chron. v. 12 of one hundred and twenty priests blowing with them. Josephus says that Solomon made 200,000 trumpets, according to the command of Moses (Antiq., Book viii., chap. 3).

(9) **And if ye go to war.**—Better, *And when ye shall go to war.* In chap. xxxi. 6 we read that in the war against the Midianites, Phinehas, the son of Eleazar, had these trumpets of alarm (*hazozeroth*) in his hand. So also Abijah, in his address to Jeroboam, previously to the battle, lays great stress upon the fact that Judah had on their side the priests with the trumpets of alarm (2 Chron. xiii. 12, 14). On the other hand, the seven priests who compassed the city of Jericho carried the *shophar,* or *keren—i.e.,* rams' horn—not the *hazozerah,* or silver trumpet.

(10) **In the day of your gladness.**—As, *e.g.,* at the dedication of Solomon's temple (2 Chron. v. 13), and at the cleansing of the Temple by Hezekiah (2 Chron. xxix. 27, 28). Compare Ps. xcviii. 6.

For a memorial.—Compare Lev. xxiii. 24.

Before your God: I am the Lord your God.—Or, *Before your God,* (even) *before me, Jehovah, your God.* (Comp. chap. iii. 13 and Note.)

(11) **On the twentieth day of the second month.**—It appears from Exod. xix. 1 that the Israelites encamped before Mount Sinai in the third month of the preceding year, and, as is generally supposed, on the first day of the month. In this case the encampment at the foot of Mount Sinai had lasted eleven months and nineteen days. No day of the month, however, is specified in Exod. xix 1, and no *certain* reliance can be placed upon the Jewish tradition that the Law was delivered fifty days after the Exodus. There is the same omission of the day of the month in Num. ix. 1 and xx. 1.

(12) **And the cloud rested in the wilderness of Paran.**—The fact is here mentioned by way of anticipation (see verse 33). The spot referred to is probably Kibroth-hattaavah, which may have been at the southernmost extremity of the wilderness of Paran. In Deut. i. 19 it is called "that great and terrible wilderness." This wilderness is supposed to have been bounded by the land of Canaan on the north, by the valley of Arabah on the east, and by the desert of Sinai on the south. Its western boundary appears to have been the wilderness of Shur, or rather the river,

of Sinai; and the cloud rested in the
wilderness of Paran. (13) And they first
took their journey according to the
commandment of the LORD by the hand
of Moses.
(14) [a] In the first *place* went the stan-
dard of the camp of the children of
Judah according to their armies: and
over his host *was* [b] Nahshon the son of
Amminadab. (15) And over the host of
the tribe of the children of Issachar *was*
Nethaneel the son of Zuar. (16) And over
the host of the tribe of the children of
Zebulun *was* Eliab the son of Helon. (17)
And the tabernacle was taken down; and
the sons of Gershon and the sons of Merari
set forward, bearing the tabernacle.
(18) And the standard of the camp of
Reuben set forward according to their
armies: and over his host *was* Elizur
the son of Shedeur. (19) And over the
host of the tribe of the children of
Simeon *was* Shelumiel the son of
Zurishaddai. (20) And over the host of
the tribe of the children of Gad *was*
Eliasaph the son of Deuel. (21) And the
Kohathites set forward, bearing the
[c] sanctuary: and [1] *the other* did set up
the tabernacle against they came.
(22) And the standard of the camp of
the children of Ephraim set forward ac-
cording to their armies: and over his
host *was* Elishama the son of Ammihud.
(23) And over the host of the tribe of the
children of Manasseh *was* Gamaliel the
son of Pedahzur. (24) And over the host
of the tribe of the children of Benjamin
was Abidan the son of Gideoni.
(25) And the standard of the camp of
the children of Dan set forward, *which*
was the rereward of all the camps
throughout their hosts: and over his
host *was* Ahiezer the son of Ammishaddai.
(26) And over the host of the tribe of the
children of Asher *was* [a] Pagiel the son of
Ocran. (27) And over the host of the
tribe of the children of Naphtali *was*
Ahira the son of Enan. (28) [2] Thus *were*
the journeyings of the children of Israel
according to their armies, when they set
forward.
(29) And Moses said unto Hobab, the
son of Raguel the Midianite, Moses'
father in law, We are journeying unto

[a] ch. 2. 3.

[b] ch. 1. 7.

[c] ch. 4. 4.

1 That is, *the Gershonites and the Merarites:* See ver. 17.

2 Heb. *These.*

---

or brook, of Egypt (*Wady-el-Arish*), which divides the wilderness into two parts, of which the western part is sometimes known as the wilderness of Shur. The sojourn of the Israelites was confined to the eastern part. (See Kurtz's *History of the Old Covenant*, iii. p. 221.)

(17) **And the tabernacle was taken down . . .** —The order of precedence as regards the twelve tribes which were encamped on the four sides of the Tabernacle is clearly laid down in chap. ii., where it is ordered that the camp of the Levites should set forward "in the midst of the camps" (verse 17). The precise position which the three bodies of Levites were to occupy in the marches is defined in this chapter. The Gershonites, who had the charge of the curtains and hangings of the Tabernacle and the court (chap. iv. 25, 26), with their two wagons, and the Merarites, who had the charge of the heavier and more bulky materials (chap. iv. 31, 32), with their four wagons, were to set forward after the first or eastern camp, which was composed of the tribes of Judah, Issachar, and Zebulon, in order that they might have time to erect the Tabernacle before the arrival of the Kohathites, "bearing the sanctuary" (or sacred things). Next in order after the Gershonites and Merarites followed the southern camp, consisting of the three tribes of Reuben, Simeon, and Gad. Then followed the Kohathites in the centre of the procession, "bearing the sanctuary." After them marched the three tribes of Ephraim, Manasseh, and Benjamin, who formed the western camp, and as the rereward, the three tribes of Dan, Asher, and Naphtali, which formed the northern camp. This arrangement serves to throw light upon Ps. lxxx. 2: "Before Ephraim and Benjamin and Manasseh stir up thy strength, and come and save us.

(28) **When they set forward.**—Better, *and they set forward.*

(29) **Hobab, the son of Raguel the Midianite, Moses' father in law.**—Raguel is the same as Reuel (Exod. ii. 18), and the orthography should be the same in all places. Reuel is commonly supposed to be identical with Jether (Exod. iv. 18), or Jethro (Exod. iii. 1), who is frequently described as the *hothen* (in the Authorised Version, "father-in-law") of Moses (chap. xviii. 2, 5, 6, &c.). But, according to the ordinary rules of Hebrew syntax, Hobab, not Jethro, is here spoken of as the *hothen* of Moses; and in Judg. iv. 11 he is expressly so called. Inasmuch, however, as the cognate noun *hathan* is used to designate any near relation by marriage—as, *e.g.*, the sons-in-law of Lot (Gen. xix. 14)—the word *hothen* may here and in Judg. iv. 11 be rendered *brother-in-law.* Some, however, think that Hobab, whether identical with Jethro or not, was the son of Reuel, and that Zipporah was the daughter of Hobab. But when it is remembered that more than forty years had elapsed since Moses left the land of Egypt and came into that of Midian, and that he was now upwards of eighty years of age, it is much more probable that he should seek the aid of a guide through the wilderness amongst those of the same generation with Zipporah than amongst those of a generation above her. Whether Hobab accompanied Jethro on the occasion of the visit to Moses which is recorded in Exod. xviii., whilst the Israelites were encamped at Sinai, and remained with them after Jethro's departure (verse 27), or whether the Israelites had already commenced their journey (compare the words of Moses, "We are journeying," or, *setting forward,* with the concluding words of verse 28, *and they set forward,* and were at this time passing through the territory in which

the place of which the LORD said, I will give it you: come thou with us, and we will do thee good: for the LORD hath spoken good concerning Israel.
(30) And he said unto him, I will not go; but I will depart to mine own land, and to my kindred.
(31) And he said, Leave us not, I pray thee; forasmuch as thou knowest how we are to encamp in the wilderness, and thou mayest be to us instead of eyes.
(32) And it shall be, if thou go with us, yea, it shall be, that what goodness the LORD shall do unto us, the same will we do unto thee.
(33) And they departed from the mount of the LORD three days' journey: and the ark of the covenant of the LORD went before them in the three days' journey, to search out a resting place for them.
(34) And the cloud of the LORD *was* upon them by day, when they went out of the camp.
(35) And it came to pass, when the ark set forward, that Moses said, [a] Rise up, LORD, and let thine enemies be scattered; and let them that hate thee flee before thee.
(36) And when it rested, he said, Return, O LORD, unto the [1] many thousands of Israel.

a Ps. 68. 1, 2.

1 Heb., *ten thousand thousands.*

Hobab, as the chief of a nomad tribe, was living, cannot positively be determined.

We are journeying unto the place . . .—These words imply a strong faith in God's promise on the part of Moses, and a desire, not indeed altogether devoid of reference to mutual advantages, that those with whom he was connected by ties of earthly relationship should be partakers with himself and his people in the peculiar blessings which were promised to the chosen people of God. In any case, the invitation of Moses, when viewed as the mouthpiece of the Jewish Church, may be regarded in the light of an instructive lesson to the Church of Christ in all ages. It is alike the duty and the privilege of all who have heard and obeyed the Gospel invitation themselves to become the instruments of its communication to others. "The Spirit and the bride say, Come. And let him that heareth say, Come" (Rev. xxii. 17).

(30) **And he said unto him, I will not go . . .**—It is not expressly stated in the narrative whether Hobab did or did not ultimately accompany the Israelites on their march. It appears most probable, however, that the renewed solicitation of Moses proved effectual. In any case, it is certain from Judg. i. 16 that the Kenites, as a body, "went up out of the city of palm trees with the children of Judah into the wilderness of Judah," and that "they went and dwelt among the people." (See Judg. i. 16, iv. 11; 1 Sam. xv. 6; 2 Kings x. 15; compared with 1 Chron. ii. 55.)

(31) **How we are to encamp . . .**—It is clear from these words, as well as from many indications of the same nature, that notwithstanding the direct guidance which was vouchsafed from heaven, and the miraculous interpositions of Providence which the Israelites experienced throughout their journeys, Moses did not neglect to take advantage of all the ordinary precautions of which it was incumbent upon him as the leader of his people to avail himself. The line of march and the places of encampment were clearly marked out by the cloud, but many difficulties would arise in the course of the journeys, and at the places of encampment, which Hobab's familiarity with the desert would enable him to meet.

(33) **Three days' journey.**—The place at which the first protracted halt was made appears to have been either at Taberah, which means *burning*, or at Kibroth-hattaavah, *the graves of lust.* (Comp. chaps. xi. 3, xxxiii. 16; see also Note on chap. xi. 34.)

And the ark of the covenant of the Lord went before them.—It has been inferred from the fact that the Kohathites had the charge of the ark (chap. iii. 31), and that they were to set forward, "bearing the sanctuary," after the second or southern camp, *i.e.*, in the midst of the host, that the position of the ark during the journeys was in that place, and not in front. The obvious objection to this supposition arising out of the fact that the cloud which directed the march rested upon, or over, the ark may be overcome by the consideration that the cloud appears to have extended over the whole of the host during the journeys, and to have served as a protection from the scorching heat (see verse 34; also Exod. xiii. 21; Neh. ix. 12; Ps. cv. 39). On the other hand, the natural interpretation of this verse is that the ark was borne in front of the host, and did not merely serve to direct its line of march as a general, whose station might be in any part of an army. This interpretation is confirmed by Exod. xiii. 21, Deut. i. 33, and also by the position which the ark occupied at the passage of the Jordan. In the latter case the people were expressly directed to go after the ark (Josh. iii. 3); and in verse 11 the same word is used which occurs in this verse, "the ark of the covenant of the Lord of all the earth passeth over *before* you into Jordan." It will not follow, however, as a necessary inference, that the ark uniformly occupied the same position in all the journeys, and it cannot be denied that verse 21 presents a difficulty, partly arising from the ambiguity of meaning which is to be attached to the word *mikdash*, *sanctuary*, and partly from the omission of any word in the Hebrew corresponding to the words in italics, *the other.* Ibn Ezra thinks that this three days' journey was different from all the other journeys in respect of the position of the ark.

(35–36) **And it came to pass . . .**—It appears from these words that the marches of the Israelites began and ended with prayer, a significant lesson to the Church of all after ages. It is deserving of observation that the prayers were offered by Moses, not by Aaron. The inverted *nuns*, or parenthetical marks, which are found in a large number of Hebrew manuscripts at the beginning and end of these verses, are thought by some to denote their insertion as a break in the narrative whilst others have ascribed to them a mystical meaning. The words, "Return, O Lord," Bishop Wordsworth observes, "pre-announced the blessed time of rest and peace, when God *would abide with His Church on earth*, by the gift of the Holy Ghost, and will *tabernacle* for ever with His people in heavenly rest and joy." (Rev. vii. 15; xxi. 3.)

CHAPTER XI. — (1) And *when* the
people [1] complained, [2] it displeased the
LORD: and the LORD heard *it;* and his
anger was kindled; and the fire of the
LORD burnt [a] among them, and consumed
them that were in the uttermost parts of
the camp. (2) And the people cried unto
Moses; and when Moses prayed unto the
LORD, the fire [3] was quenched. (3) And
he called the name of the place [4] Ta-
berah: because the fire of the LORD
burnt among them.
(4) And the [b] mixt multitude that *was*
among them [5] fell a lusting: and the
children of Israel also [6] wept again, and
said, [c] Who shall give us flesh to eat?
(5) We remember the fish, which we did
eat in Egypt freely; the cucumbers, and
the melons, and the leeks, and the
onions, and the garlick: (6) but now our
soul *is* dried away: *there is* nothing at
all, beside this manna, *before* our eyes.
(7) And [d] the manna *was* as coriander
seed, and the [7] colour thereof as the
colour of bdellium. (8) *And* the people
went about, and gathered *it,* and ground
it in mills, or beat *it* in a mortar, and
baked *it* in pans, and made cakes of it:

1 Or, *were as it were complainers.*
2 Heb., *it was evil in the ears of, &c.*
a Ps. 78. 21.
3 Heb. *sunk.*
4 That is, *A burning.*
b As Ex. 12. 38.
5 Heb., *lusted a lust.*
6 Heb., *returned and wept.*
c 1 Cor. 10. 6.
d Ex. 16. 14, 31.
7 Heb., *eye of it as the eye of.*

XI.

(1) **And when the people complained . . .**—Better, *And the people were as those who complained* (or *murmured*), (which was) *evil in the ears of the Lord.* The LXX. has, "And the people murmured sinfully before the Lord." Comp. 1 Cor. x. 10: "Neither murmur ye as some of them also murmured."

And consumed them that were in the uttermost parts of the camp.—Better, *and devoured at the extremity of the camp.* Most commentators have remarked, and justly, upon the great severity of the Divine judgments which were inflicted after the giving of the Law, as compared with those which were inflicted before it. Reference may be made in illustration of this point to Exod. xiv. 11—14, xv. 24, 25, xvi. 2—8, xvii. 3—7. The writer of the Epistle to the Hebrews argues from the just recompense of reward which every transgression and disobedience received under the Law, the impossibility of the escape of those who neglect the great salvation of the Gospel. See Heb. ii. 2, 3. Comp. also Heb. x. 28, 29, xii. 25.

(2) **The fire was quenched.**—Better, *subsided* or *sunk down.* No precise information is given as to the extent of the fire, or as to the objects which it destroyed. It broke out in the extremity of the encampment, and it was arrested in its progress at the supplication of Moses. It seems, however, more probable that it consumed some of the Israelites themselves, than that it consumed only some of their tents. Some suppose that the reference is to the *simoom,* or fiery south wind, which sometimes blows in the Eastern desert, and which stifles those over whom it sweeps.

(3) **Taberah**—*i.e., burning,* a word cognate to the verb which is rendered *burnt* in verse 1 and in this verse.

(4) **And the mixt multitude.**—The Authorised Version follows the LXX. and the Vulgate in rendering the word *asaph-suph,* which occurs only in this place, and which is derived from a verb which means to collect, in the same way as the *ereb* of Exod. xii. 38, *a mixed multitude, vulgus promiscuum*—in many cases, probably, the children of Hebrew women by Egyptian fathers. This mixed multitude appears to have been very considerable, and they may have become, as the Gibeonites at a later period, servants to the Israelites, as hewers of wood and drawers of water (Deut. xxix. 11). It is probable that this mixed multitude may have partaken even more largely than the Israelites of the fish and vegetables of Egypt, and they appear to have instigated the Israelites to repine at the deprivations to which they were exposed in the wilderness. There is no mention in Exod. xvi. 3 of weeping, but the same craving after the flesh-pots of Egypt was probably manifested in the same manner in both cases.

Who shall give us flesh to eat?—The word *basar,* which is rendered *flesh,* seems here to include—it may be to have primary reference to—*fish.* It is used of fish in Lev. xi. 11, and it is obvious from verse 22 that it was understood by Moses in this general signification. Cp. the use of *flesh* (1 Cor. xv. 39).

(5) **We remember the fish . . .**—Classical writers and modern travellers agree in bearing testimony to the abundance of the fish in the Nile and in the neighbouring canals and reservoirs. The cucumbers in Egypt are of great size and finely flavoured. The water-melons serve to moderate the internal heat which the climate produces. (See *The Land and the Book,* p. 508.) The word rendered *leeks* (in Ps. civ. 14, *grass* for cattle) is supposed by some to denote a species of clover which is peculiar to Egypt, and of which the young and fresh shoots are said to be used as food and to be an excellent stomachic. The onions of Egypt are said to be the sweetest in the world, and they constitute the common food of the lowest class of the people. Garlic is still much used by the modern Arabs. It is only the fish, which was probably equally within the reach of all, of which the Israelites are said to have eaten *freely, i.e.,* not *abundantly,* but *gratuitously.* It is probable, however, that many of them cultivated the land to a greater or lesser degree, and so procured vegetables for themselves.

(6) **There is nothing at all . . .**—Better, *there is nothing, except that our eyes* (*look*) *upon, the manna.*

(7) **And the manna was . . .**—The design of the description of the manna in this place (comp. Exod. xvi. 14, 31, and Notes *in loc.;* also Article *Manna,* in "Smith's Dictionary of the Bible") was probably to exhibit in its just light the sinfulness of the Israelites in repining at the merciful provision which God had made for the supply of their wants. The dissatisfaction of the Israelites with the sweet bread of heaven, and their craving after the more savoury and more stimulating food of Egypt may be regarded as typical of man's natural repugnance to the spiritual food which is provided in the Gospel, and his restless cravings after the pleasures of the world.

(8) **As the taste of fresh oil.**—Or, *of a fat cake of oil.* In Exod. xvi. 31 the taste of the manna is said to have been "like wafers made with honey." The ancients used flour cakes mixed with oil and honey.

and the taste of it was as the taste of
fresh oil. (9) And when the dew fell
upon the camp in the night, the manna
fell upon it.
(10) Then Moses heard the people weep
throughout their families, every man in
the door of his tent: and the anger of
the LORD was kindled greatly; Moses
also was displeased. (11) And Moses said
unto the LORD, Wherefore hast thou
afflicted thy servant? and wherefore
have I not found favour in thy sight,
that thou layest the burden of all this
people upon me? (12) Have I conceived
all this people? have I begotten them,
that thou shouldest say unto me, Carry
them in thy bosom, as a nursing father
beareth the sucking child, unto the land
which thou swarest unto their fathers?
(13) Whence should I have flesh to give
unto all this people? for they weep unto
me, saying, Give us flesh, that we may
eat. (14) I am not able to bear all this
people alone, because *it is* too heavy for
me. (15) And if thou deal thus with me,
kill me, I pray thee, out of hand, if I
have found favour in thy sight; and let
me not see my wretchedness.
(16) And the LORD said unto Moses,
Gather unto me seventy men of the
elders of Israel, whom thou knowest to
be the elders of the people, and officers
over them; and bring them unto the
tabernacle of the congregation, that
they may stand there with thee. (17) And
I will come down and talk with thee
there: and I will take of the spirit
which *is* upon thee, and will put *it* upon
them; and they shall bear the burden
of the people with thee, that thou bear
it not thyself alone. (18) And say thou
unto the people, Sanctify yourselves
against to morrow, and ye shall eat
flesh: for ye have wept in the ears of
the LORD, saying, Who shall give us
flesh to eat? for *it was* well with us in
Egypt: therefore the LORD will give you
flesh, and ye shall eat. (19) Ye shall not
eat one day, nor two days, nor five days,
neither ten days, nor twenty days;
(20) *But* even a [1] whole month, until it
come out at your nostrils, and it be loath-
some unto you: because that ye have
despised the LORD which *is* among you,
and have wept before him, saying, Why
came we forth out of Egypt?

1 Heb., *month of days.*

---

(10) **Moses also was displeased.**—Or, *And it was evil* (or, *displeasing*) *in the eyes of Moses.* Moses was displeased with the people on account of their murmuring, and he was oppressed with the heavy burden of responsibility to which he felt himself unequal.

(11) **Wherefore hast thou afflicted.**—Literally, *done evil to:* the same verb, in a different conjugation, which is rendered "displeased" in verse 10.

(12) **Have I conceived . . ?**—The personal pronoun is emphatic in this and the following clause: *Is it I who have conceived all this people? Is it I who have brought them forth?* (or, *begotten them*), as in Gen. iv. 18, x. 8.

(13) **Whence should I have flesh . . ?**—Moses does not justify the murmuring of the people, and was doubtless conscious of their sinfulness. At the same time, he displays a spirit of discontent, and almost of despair, at God's dealings with himself; and he appears to treat the demand of the Israelites for flesh as one which was not altogether unreasonable.

(14) **To bear all this people alone.**—In accordance with the advice of Jethro, able men had been chosen out of all Israel who heard and determined the small matters which arose among them (Exod. xviii. 25, 26), but they were of no avail on occasions such as the present.

My wretchedness.—Or, *my evil.* This is one of the eighteen places in which the scribes are said to have altered the text, and to have substituted *my* for *Thy.*

(15) **Kill me, I pray thee, out of hand.**—Or, *Make an utter end of me.*

(16) **Seventy men of the elders of Israel . . .**—We find mention made of *elders* of the people in Exod. iii. 16, and of officers (*shoterim*) in Exod. v. 16; also of seventy elders in Exod. xxiv. 1. Frequent mention is made in Scripture of the number *seventy*—a number which is composed of the two sacred numbers *seven* and *ten*—the former being the seal of the covenant, and the latter probably denoting perfection. The seventy who were chosen on the present occasion may have consisted of some of those who were appointed as judges at the suggestion of Jethro, but there is no evidence of their identity with any persons previously selected.

(17) **And I will come down . . .**—The cloud which hovered over the Tabernacle appears to have descended to the entrance of it (verse 25). (Comp. Exod. xxxiii. 9; Num. xii. 5; Deut. xxxi. 15).

I will take of the spirit which is upon thee . . .—These words do not imply that there was any diminution of the gifts bestowed upon Moses, but that a portion of those spiritual gifts was bestowed upon the seventy. Rashi compares the mode of bestowal with the manner in which the other lamps of the Sanctuary were lighted at the golden candlestick without diminishing the light from which theirs was taken.

(18) **Sanctify yourselves against to-morrow.**—(Comp. Exod. xix. 10.) The Israelites were required to sanctify themselves by purification for the more immediate manifestation of the Divine presence, although their request was a sinful one, and was granted in judgment as well as—or even more than—in mercy. Comp. Ps. cvi. 15: "And he gave them their request; but sent leanness into their soul."

(19) **Ye shall not eat one day . . .**—The quails which had been sent the preceding year appear to have covered the camp only during one day (Exod. xvi. 13).

(21) And Moses said, The people,
among whom I *am*, *are* six hundred
thousand footmen; and thou hast said,
I will give them flesh, that they may eat
a whole month. (22) Shall the flocks and
the herds be slain for them, to suffice
them? or shall all the fish of the sea be
gathered together for them, to suffice
them? (23) and the LORD said unto Moses,
[a] Is the LORD's hand waxed short? thou
shalt see now whether my word shall
come to pass unto thee or not.

(24) And Moses went out, and told the
people the words of the LORD, and
gathered the seventy men of the elders
of the people, and set them round about
the tabernacle. (25) And the LORD came
down in a cloud, and spake unto him,
and took of the spirit that *was* upon him,
and gave *it* unto the seventy elders: and
it came to pass, *that*, when the spirit
rested upon them, they prophesied, and
did not cease. (26) But there remained
two *of the* men in the camp, the name
of the one *was* Eldad, and the name of
the other Medad: and the spirit rested
upon them; and they *were* of them that
were written, but went not out unto the
tabernacle: and they prophesied in the
camp. (27) And there ran a young man,
and told Moses, and said, Eldad and
Medad do prophesy in the camp. (28) And
Joshua the son of Nun, the servant of
Moses, *one* of his young men, answered
and said, My lord Moses, forbid them.
(29) And Moses said unto him, Enviest
thou for my sake? would God that all
the LORD's people were prophets, *and*
that the LORD would put his spirit upon
them! (30) And Moses gat him into the
camp, he and the elders of Israel.

(31) And there went forth a [b] wind from
the LORD, and brought quails from the
sea, and let *them* fall by the camp [1] as
it were a day's journey on this side, and
as it were a day's journey on the other
side, round about the camp, and as it
were two cubits *high* upon the face of

a Is. 50. 2; & 59. 1.

b Ex. 16. 13; Ps. 78. 26.

1 Heb., *as it were the way of a day.*

---

(21) **Six hundred thousand footmen.**—In chap. i. 46 the number is stated to be 603,550; but here, as elsewhere, a round number is mentioned.

(22) **Shall the flocks and the herds . . ?**—Rather, *Shall flocks and herds . . ?* The definite article is not used here, nor the possessive pronoun, as elsewhere, where the flocks and herds of the Israelites are denoted. (Comp. Exod. x. 9, xxxiv. 3; Deut. xii. 6.) There is no evidence, therefore, that Moses alluded exclusively, or even primarily, to the flocks and herds which the Israelites had brought out of Egypt. Moreover, a large number of the sheep and goats must have been recently slain at the Passover. Whether the encampment was, or was not within an easy distance of the Ælanitic Gulf, the gathering together of the fish of the sea in sufficient quantities to satisfy such a multitude for so long a time would require a miraculous agency; and the same agency could also bring together from unknown sources flocks and herds. The expression may be regarded as a form of natural hyperbole.

(24) **And Moses went out . . .**—*i.e.*, as it should seem, from the tabernacle of the congregation, where he had been conversing with God.

Round about the tabernacle.—This does not necessarily imply that the seventy men were placed so that they surrounded the whole of the tent of meeting. Comp. Exod. vii. 24, where the word means *on both sides of the river;* also Job xxix. 5, where the same word is rendered *about.*

(25) **In a cloud.**—Hebrew, *In the cloud.*

And gave it unto . . .—Better, *and put it upon,* as in Lev. ii. 15.

They prophesied, and did not cease.—Better, *they prophesied, but did so no more.* Comp. Gen. viii. 12; Exod. xi. 6; 2 Sam. ii. 28; so the LXX. The word *prophesy* does not necessarily denote the prediction of future events. It is elsewhere employed to denote the celebration of the praises of God, either with the voice or with instruments of music. (Comp. 1 Sam. x. 6; 1 Kings xviii. 29; 1 Chron. xxv. 1, 2, 3; Jer. xxix. 26.)

(28) **My lord Moses, forbid them.**—The motive which prompted Joshua in making this request appears to have been similar to that which led St. John to forbid the man to cast out devils who did not follow with the Apostles (Mark ix. 38, 39; Luke ix. 49, 50). But as the man did not cast out devils in his own name, but in that of Christ, so in this case Eldad and Medad prophesied in virtue of the spirit which rested upon them from above, of which the Holy Ghost, not Moses, was the giver. The motives which deterred Eldad and Medad from going to the tent of meeting are unknown. The history teaches the freeness and the sovereignty of the Holy Spirit's influences, as afterwards did that of Cornelius, when the Holy Ghost fell upon him and upon those who were with him, previously to the reception of baptism, and they spoke with tongues and magnified God (Acts x. 44—48).

(29) **Enviest thou for my sake?**—Better, *Art thou zealous for me? or, Art thou displeased on my account?* (Comp. chap. xxv. 13; 1 Kings xix. 10, 14.)

(31) **And there went forth a wind.**—In Ps. lxxviii. 26 we read thus: "He caused an east wind to blow in the heaven: and by his power he brought in the south wind." A south-east wind would bring the quails from the neighbourhood of the Red Sea, where they abound.

And let them fall.—Better, *and scattered them* (or, *spread them out*). Comp. 1 Sam. xxx. 16: "They were spread abroad upon all the earth," or, over all the ground.

Round about.—See Note on verse 24.

As it were two cubits high upon the face of the earth.—Or, *about two cubits over* (or, *above*) *the ground.* Had the quails lain upon the earth in a heap for any considerable time, life could only have been preserved by miraculous interference with the ordinary laws of nature, and the Israelites were not

the earth. (32) And the people stood up
all that day, and all *that* night, and all
the next day, and they gathered the
quails: he that gathered least gathered
ten homers: and they spread *them* all
abroad for themselves round about the
camp. (33) And while the [a] flesh *was* yet
between their teeth, ere it was chewed,
the wrath of the LORD was kindled a-
gainst the people, and the LORD smote
the people with a very great plague.
(34) And he called the name of that place
[1] Kibroth-hattaavah: because there they
buried the people that lusted.

(35) *And* the people journeyed from
Kibroth-hattaavah unto Hazeroth; and
[2] abode at Hazeroth.

CHAPTER XII. — (1) And Miriam
and Aaron spake against Moses because
of the [3] Ethiopian woman whom he had
married: for he had [4] married an Ethio-
pian woman. (2) And they said, Hath
the LORD indeed spoken only by Moses?
hath he not spoken also by us? And the
LORD heard *it*. (3) (Now the man Moses
was [b] very meek, above all the men
which *were* upon the face of the earth.)

a Ps. 78. 31.

1 That is, *The graves of lust.*

2 Heb., *they were in*, &c.

3 Or, *Cushite.*

4 Heb., *taken.*

b Ecclus. 45. 4.

---

allowed to eat of that which had died of itself. Quails commonly fly low, and when wearied with a long flight might fly only about breast-high. On the other hand, the more obvious interpretation of the words is that the quails were spread over the ground, and covered it in some places to the height of two cubits. They were probably taken and killed immediately on their descent, as the following verse seems to indicate, and then spread out and dried and hardened in the sun. Some think that the word which is here rendered *quails* denotes *cranes*.

(32) **Ten homers.**—The *homer*, which was equal to ten ephahs, or a hundred omers, appears to have contained between five and six bushels, according to the Rabbinists, but according to Josephus about double that quantity.

(33) **With a very great plague.** — The noun, *maccah*, plague, is cognate to the verb which is rendered *smote*. It is frequently used of a stroke inflicted by God, as, *e.g.*, pestilence or any epidemic sickness. A surfeit, such as that in which the Israelites had indulged, especially under the circumstances in which they were placed, would naturally produce a considerable amount of sickness. Here, then, as in the account of the plagues of Egypt and in other parts of the sacred history, the natural and the supernatural are closely combined.

(34) **Kibroth-hattaavah**—*i.e., the graves of lust* (or, *desire*). In Numbers xxxiii. 16, Kibroth-hattaavah is mentioned as the first station after the departure from Sinai, whereas it is obvious that there must have been an encampment at Taberah. Taberah may have been the name given to a part of Kibroth-hattaavah, or the two names may have belonged to the same place.

XII.

(1) **And Miriam and Aaron spake against Moses.**—Miriam appears to have been the leader in this insurrection against the authority of Moses. Her name occurs before that of Aaron, either as the nearer or as the more prominent subject; and the verb which is rendered "spake" is in the feminine gender. Moreover, the judgment which was inflicted (verse 10) fell upon Miriam, not upon Aaron, who seems to have yielded to the suggestions of Miriam, as he had previously done to the request of the Israelites in regard to the golden calf.

Because of the Ethiopian woman whom he had married.—Some suppose that the reference is to Zipporah, who may have been included amongst the Asiatic division of the Ethiopians, or Cushites (comp. Hab. iii. 7, where the tents of Cushan, or Cush, are coupled with the curtains of Midian), and that the occasion of the opposition to Moses was the undue influence which he is supposed to have allowed Hobab and other members of Zipporah's family to exercise over him. This supposition, however, seems improbable on many accounts. The words, "for he had married an Ethiopian (or Cushite) woman," naturally point to some recent occurrence, not to one which had taken place more than forty years previously, and which is, therefore, very unlikely to have given occasion to the murmuring of Miriam and Aaron at this time. Moreover, the murmuring is expressly connected with the Cushite herself, not with any of the subsequent or incidental results of the marriage. It seems, therefore, much more probable that Zipporah was dead, and that Moses had married one of the African Cushites who had accompanied the Israelites in their march out of Egypt, or one of the Cushites who dwelt in Arabia, and who were found at this time in the neighbourhood of Sinai. A similar marriage had been contracted by Joseph, and such marriages were not forbidden by the Law, which prohibited marriage with the Canaanites (Exod. xxxiv. 16).

(2) **Hath the Lord indeed spoken only by Moses?**—There is probably a reference in these words to the facts related in Exod. iv. 10—16, where Moses speaks of his own slowness of speech (verse 10), and where it is said of Aaron, "And he shall be thy spokesman unto the people" (verse 16). Miriam also is spoken of in Exod. xv. 20 as "the prophetess." "Such is the depravity of human nature," writes Calvin, "that they not only abuse the gifts of God towards the brother whom they despise, but by an ungodly and sacrilegious glorification extol the gifts themselves in such a manner as to hide the Author of the gifts."

(3) **Now the man Moses was very meek . . .**—These words have been urged by some as an argument against the Mosaic authorship of the Pentateuch generally, or of the Book of Numbers in particular, but whether they may or may not have been inserted by a later writer, this inference is altogether unfounded. It is possible that the writer of Deut. xxxiv. 10 may have inserted these words in this place. On the other hand, there is no necessity for such a supposition. An objective statement, such as that contained in these words, is perfectly consistent with true humility and with a deep sense of sinfulness and frailty. When such expressions are required in order to a full understanding of all the circumstances of the history, they afford no just ground of objection either against the writer, or against the genuineness of the writing; and least of all can they be justly objected to in the case of those who, like Moses and St. Paul, were ever ready to sacrifice their

(4) And the LORD spake suddenly unto
Moses, and unto Aaron, and unto Miriam,
Come out ye three unto the tabernacle
of the congregation. And they three
came out. (5) And the LORD came down in
the pillar of the cloud, and stood *in* the
door of the tabernacle, and called Aaron
and Miriam: and they both came forth.
(6) And he said, Hear now my words:
If there be a prophet among you, *I* the
LORD will make myself known unto him
in a vision, *and* will speak unto him in a
dream. (7) My servant Moses *is* not so,
[a] who *is* faithful in all mine house.
(8) With him will I speak [b] mouth to
mouth, even apparently, and not in dark
speeches; and the similitude of the
LORD shall he behold: wherefore then
were ye not afraid to speak against my
servant Moses? (9) And the anger of the
LORD was kindled against them; and he
departed. (10) And the cloud departed
from off the tabernacle; and, behold,
Miriam *became* leprous, *white* as snow:
and Aaron looked upon Miriam, and, be-
hold, *she was* leprous. (11) And Aaron
said unto Moses, Alas, my lord, I beseech
thee, lay not the sin upon us, wherein we
have done foolishly, and wherein we
have sinned. (12) Let her not be as one

a Heb., 3. 2.

b Ex. 33. 11.

---

own personality in the cause to which they had devoted their lives (comp. 2 Cor. xi. 5). It may be observed, further, that the word *anav*, meek, is frequently interchanged with the cognate word *ani*, and that the meaning may be *bowed down*, or *oppressed*.

(4) **Come out ye three . . .**—There is nothing in these words which implies that Miriam entered into the Tabernacle itself. Moses, Aaron, and Miriam were summoned to go out of the camp (comp. chap. xi. 30), and to come to the entrance of the Tabernacle, or rather of the court, inasmuch as the command to come as far as the entrance into the Sanctuary appears to have been given afterwards (verse 5). It must be remembered that there was but one court at this time.

(6) **If there be a prophet . . .**—Better, *If there be to* (or, *among*) *you a prophet of Jehovah, I will make myself known unto him in a vision, and speak unto him.* The LXX. and Vulgate connect the word "Jehovah" with the former, not with the latter part of the clause. The mode of communication between God and Moses differed in the respects which are enumerated in verse 8 from the mode of communication by visions or dreams, in which God communicated His will to others.

(7) **My servant Moses . . .**—Better, *Not so (in regard to) my servant Moses: he is faithful.* Reference is made to these words in Heb. iii. 5: "And Moses verily was faithful in all his house," *i.e.*, in the whole of the Mosaic economy or dispensation, or the house of Israel, which is spoken of as God's house. A contrast is drawn in verse 6 between the vocation of Moses as a servant *in* the house of God and that of Christ as a Son *over* His own house.

(8) **With him will I speak.**—Better, *do I speak, mouth to mouth.* Comp. Exod. xxxiii. 11.

Even apparently.—The noun *mareh*, which is here used, is cognate with that which occurs with the preposition in verse 6, and which is rendered "a vision." It differs from it only in punctuation, and is sometimes identical in meaning. It appears, however, here to denote an objective reality, as in Exod. iii. 3, where it is rendered *sight*. The clause might be rendered, *and* (*as*) *an appearance, and not in riddles* (or, *enigmas*).

And the similitude of the Lord . . .—Or, *and the form of Jehovah doth he behold.* The word which is here rendered *similitude* (*temunah*) is the same which occurs in Exod. xx. 4; Deut. iv. 15, 16, 23, 25, v. 8; Ps. xvii. 15. It is sometimes rendered *likeness*, and sometimes *similitude*. The noun *mareh*, which is here rendered "*apparently*," and that which is rendered *similitude*, are found in conjunction in Job iv. 16: "I could not discern the form (or appearance), *mareh*, thereof: an image (or form), *temunah*, was before mine eyes." (Comp. Exod. xxxiii. 20—23.)

(10) **And the cloud departed . . .**—The withdrawal of the cloud was the visible token of the Divine displeasure. The word *sar, departed*, which is here used, is an entirely different word from that which occurs in chap. ix. 17: "When the cloud was *taken up* from the tabernacle." The *lifting up* of the cloud was the signal for the breaking up of the camp and the resumption of the march; the *withdrawal* of the cloud was the token of the withdrawal of the Divine presence and direction.

Leprous, white as snow.—Better, *was leprous as snow*, as in Exod. iv. 6, where the same words occur; or, *a leper* (as white), *as snow*, as in 2 Kings v. 27. In an ordinary case of leprosy, when the disease covered the whole body, and the whole of the flesh had turned white, the man was to be pronounced clean. It was otherwise in cases in which persons were smitten with leprosy by the immediate hand of God, as in the case of Moses and in that of Gehazi.

And Aaron looked upon Miriam . . .—Or, *and Aaron turned towards Miriam—i.e.*, directed his attention to her, &c. This may have been the first case in which Aaron was required to carry into execution the laws laid down in Lev. xiii., xiv., respecting the inspection of the leper; and the duties which devolved upon him must have been doubly painful from the fact that the leper stood in a near relationship to himself, and that he had been a participator in the sin which had called for so severe a punishment.

(11) **Alas, my lord.**—The word rendered *alas!* is an exclamation of entreaty rather than of lamentation. It is used towards superiors in conjunction with *adoni* (my lord) in Gen. xl. 20; 1 Kings iii. 17.

Lay not the sin upon us . . .—Better, *lay not sin* (*i.e.*, the punishment which is due to it) *upon us, for that* (or, *inasmuch as*) *we have done foolishly*, &c. Aaron does not seek to shift the guilt which had been incurred from himself and Miriam to any others, but prays that they may not be constrained to bear the punishment which their sin had justly deserved. In Zech. xiv. 19 the same word *hattath* is rendered *punishment*.

(12) **Let her not be as one dead.**—This is another of the places in which the Scribes are said to have altered the text. The original is said to have been as follows:—*Let her not be as one dead, who proceeded from the womb of our mother, and half of our flesh be consumed.* The leper was "as one dead" in two respects—(1) as being shut out from inter-

dead, of whom the flesh is half consumed
when he cometh out of his mother's
womb. (13) And Moses cried unto the
LORD, saying, Heal her now, O God, I
beseech thee. (14) And the LORD said
unto Moses, If her father had but spit in
her face, should she not be ashamed
seven days? let her be [a] shut out from
the camp seven days, and after that let
her be received in *again*. (15) And Miriam
was shut out from the camp seven days:
and the people journeyed not till Miriam
was brought in *again*.

(16) And afterward the people removed
from Hazeroth, and pitched in the wil-
derness of Paran.

CHAPTER XIII. — (1) And the LORD
spake unto Moses, saying, (2) Send thou
men, that they may search the land
of Canaan, which I give unto the chil-
dren of Israel: of every tribe of their
fathers shall ye send a man, every one a
ruler among them. (3) And Moses by
the commandment of the LORD sent them
from the wilderness of Paran: all those
men *were* heads of the children of Israel.
(4) And these *were* their names: of the
tribe of Reuben, Shammua the son of
Zaccur. (5) Of the tribe of Simeon, Shap-
hat the son of Hori. (6) Of the tribe of
Judah, Caleb the son of Jephunneh.
(7) Of the tribe of Issachar, Igal the son
of Joseph. (8) Of the tribe of Ephraim,
Oshea the son of Nun. (9) Of the tribe
of Benjamin, Palti the son of Raphu.
(10) Of the tribe of Zebulun, Gaddiel, the
son of Sodi. (11) Of the tribe of Joseph,

[a] Lev. 13. 46.

---

course with his brethren; and (2) as causing ceremonial defilement in the case of those who were brought into contact with him, similar to that which was caused by touching a dead body. "He was," as Archbishop Trench has remarked, "a dreadful parable of death" (*On the Miracles*, p. 214). In the most severe types of leprosy there was, as the same writer has observed, "a dissolution, little by little, of the whole body, so that one limb after another actually decayed and fell away" (*Ibid*, p. 213).

(13) **Heal her now, O God, I beseech thee.**—Better, *O God, I beseech thee, heal her, I beseech thee.*

(14) **If her father had but spit in her face.**—Or, *in her presence.* Spitting in the presence of any one, much more spitting in the face of any one, is regarded in the East as an indication of the utmost degree of abhorrence and indignation. Comp. Deut. xxv. 9; Job xxx. 10; Is. l. 6; Matt. xxvi. 67.

Seven days.—This was the time during which the person suspected of being leprous was to be shut up in the first instance (Lev. xiii. 4, 21, &c.); and this was also the time during which the leper, when cleansed, was to "tarry abroad out of his tent," after he had come into the camp, before the appointed sacrifices were offered on his behalf (Lev. xiv. 8, 10). It was thus that she who had placed herself on a level with the divinely-appointed head and ruler of her nation was to be excluded for seven days from any part or lot in the privileges which were enjoyed by the humblest member of the congregation.

(15) **And the people journeyed not . . .**—The law for the purification of the leper, as prescribed in Lev. xiv., had already been delivered.

(16) **In the wilderness of Paran.**—See Note on chap. x. 12. It appears from the 26th verse of the following chapter that the encampment was at Kadesh, which has been supposed by some to be identical with Rithmah (chap. xxxiii. 18).

XIII.

(1) **And the Lord spake unto Moses . . .**—There is no inconsistency between this statement and that which is contained in Deut. i. 22, where the sending of the spies is represented as having originated with the people. It is there said that the saying pleased Moses well; but it would be wholly inconsistent with the character and conduct of Moses to suppose that in a matter of such importance he should have acted in accordance with the suggestion of the people, or upon his own judgment, without seeking direction from God. The command which was given to Moses must not be regarded as implying of necessity that the expedition of the spies was, in the first instance, ordained by God, any more than the command which was afterwards given to Balaam to accompany the messengers of Balak was any indication that God originally commanded, or approved of his journey.

(2) **Every one a ruler among them.**—Or, *a prince among them*, as in chap. i. 16. A comparison of the names which follow with those which are given in chap. i. 5—15 will show that the persons selected were not the tribal princes who are mentioned in connection with the census. The tribe of Levi, as in the former case, is not represented, as the Levites were to have no inheritance in the land, and the number of twelve, as in chap. i., is made up by the division of the tribe of Joseph into the two tribes of Ephraim and Manasseh.

(3) **And Moses, by the commandment of the Lord, sent them, &c.**—Better, *And Moses sent them from the wilderness of Paran, according to the command* (literally, the mouth) *of the Lord, i.e.*, as appears from Deut. i. 19. from Kadesh-barnea.

(6) **Caleb the son of Jephunneh.**—In three places—viz., in chap. xxxii. 12; and in Josh. xiv. verses 6 and 14—Caleb is described as the Kenezite (or rather, the Kenizzite). Now in Gen. xv. 19 the Kenizzites are mentioned as one of the Canaanite tribes, and in Gen. xxxvi. 11, 15, Kenaz occurs as an Edomite name. It has been conjectured from these facts, but, as it should seem, on insufficient grounds, that Caleb was of foreign origin, and that he had been incorporated into the tribe of Judah.

(8) **Of the tribe of Ephraim.**—It has been supposed that there is some displacement of the text in this verse. Thus far the order of the tribes is the same as in chap. i. 5—8. After Issachar, Zebulun (the sixth son of Leah) would naturally follow, as in chap. i. 9, and Ephraim and Manasseh would naturally be connected, as in chap. i. 10. This supposition is supported

namely, of the tribe of Manasseh, Gaddi
the son of Susi. (12) Of the tribe of Dan,
Ammiel the son of Gemalli. (13) Of the
tribe of Asher, Sethur the son of Michael.
(14) Of the tribe of Naphtali, Nahbi the
son of Vophsi. (15) Of the tribe of Gad,
Geuel the son of Machi. (16) These *are*
the names of the men which Moses sent
to spy out the land. And Moses called
Oshea the son of Nun Jehoshua.

(17) And Moses sent them to spy out
the land of Canaan, and said unto them,
Get you up this *way* southward, and go
up into the mountain: (18) and see the
land, what it *is;* and the people that
dwelleth therein, whether they *be* strong
or weak, few or many; (19) and what the
land *is* that they dwell in, whether it *be*
good or bad; and what cities *they be*
that they dwell in, whether in tents, or
in strong holds; (20) and what the land *is,*
whether it *be* fat or lean, whether there
be wood therein, or not. And be ye of
good courage, and bring of the fruit of
the land.

(21) Now the time *was* the time of the
firstripe grapes. So they went up, and
searched the land from the wilderness of
Zin unto Rehob, as men come to Hamath.
(22) And they ascended by the south, and
came unto Hebron; where Ahiman, She-
shai, and Talmai, the children of Anak,
were. (Now Hebron was built seven
years before Zoan in Egypt.) (23) [a] And
they came unto the [1] brook of Eshcol,
and cut down from thence a branch
with one cluster of grapes, and they bare
it between two upon a staff; and *they*

a Deut. 1. 24.

1 Or, *valley.*

---

by the occurrence of the name of Joseph in verses 7, 11. The order of the remaining four tribes is the same as in chap. i., except that the tribe of Naphtali is placed before, instead of after, that of Gad.

(16) **And Moses called Oshea . . .**—It is not distinctly stated that the change of name took place at this time. It may have taken place at an earlier period, and have been confirmed on the present occasion, as in the case of *Israel* (Gen. xxxii. 28, xxxv. 10), and of *Bethel* (Gen. xxviii. 19, xxxv. 15). On the other hand, it is quite possible that the name may have been proleptically adopted in Exod. xvii. 9, 13, xxiv. 13, xxxii. 17, xxxiii. 11, and Num. xi. 28. The original name *Hoshea* means *help,* or *salvation.* The name *Joshua,* or *Jehoshua,* means *Jehovah is help,* or *salvation.*

(17) **Get you up this way southward.**—Rather, *by the Negeb,* or *south country* (comp. verse 22). The southern part of Palestine was known by the name of *the Negeb.* It formed the transition from the desert to the more highly cultivated land, and was more fitted for grazing than for agricultural purposes. (See Wilton's *The Negeb.*)

Into the mountain.—The word which is here used commonly denotes the hill country, *i.e.,* the mountainous part of Palestine, which was inhabited by the Hittites, Jebusites, and Amorites. It is called "the mount of the Amorites" in Deut. i. 7, inasmuch as the Amorites were the strongest of the Canaanite tribes. The same word is rendered "the mountains" in verse 29. The reference here, however, may be to the particular mountain which was nearest to the encampment of the Israelites (see chap. xiv. 40).

(18) **And see the land.**—Or, *inspect the land.* The same word is used of the inspection of the leper by the priest in Lev. xiii. 3, 5, 6, 10, 13, &c.

(19) **Whether in tents.**—Better, *in camps, i.e.,* in open villages and hamlets, as contrasted with strongholds or fortified places.

(20) **Now the time . . .**—The first grapes ripen in Palestine as early as August, or even July, although the vintage does not take place until September or October.

(21) **From the wilderness of Zin.**—The name of the wilderness of Zin, in which Kadesh was situated, appears to have been given to the northern or north-eastern part of the wilderness of Paran. Comp. chap. xx. 1, xxvii. 14, xxxiii. 36, xxxiv. 3, 4; Deut. xxxii. 51; Josh. xv. 1, 3.

Unto Rehob, as men come to Hamath.—Or, *unto Rehob, at the entrance of Hamath.* Rehob is supposed to be identical with the Beth-rehob of Judges xviii. 28, in the tribe of Naphtali, which was near Dan-Laish. "The entrance of Hamath" formed the northern boundary of the land assigned to the Israelites (Num. xxxiv. 8).

(22) **And they ascended by the south, and came.**—The latter verb is in the singular number in the Hebrew text: *he came.* It is quite possible that the twelve spies may not always have been together, and that one only may have gone to Hebron.

Ahiman, Sheshai, and Talmai.—Some suppose these to be the names of tribes, not of individuals. It is quite possible, however, that the same individuals may have been still alive when the city of Hebron was assigned to Caleb, about fifty years later, and when he drove out these three sons of Anak (Josh. xv. 14).

The children of Anak.—Better, *the children of the Anakim.* (Comp. Deut. i. 28, ix. 2.) When Anak, as an individual, is mentioned, as in verse 33, the article is omitted.

Before Zoan in Egypt.—Zoan, or Tanis, on the eastern bank of the Tanitic arm of the Nile, appears to have been the residence of Pharaoh in the days of Moses (Ps. lxxviii. 12). Hebron was in existence in the days of Abraham (Gen. xiii. 18, xxiii. 2, &c.).

(23) **The brook of Eshcol.**—This is commonly identified with the valley of Hebron. Ritter says that the reputation of the grapes of Hebron is so great throughout all Palestine that there is no difficulty in believing that the valley of Eshcol was that which is directly north of the city of Hebron. The valley may have derived its name originally from Eshcol, the brother of Mamre the Amorite (Gen. xiv. 13). In like manner the name of Mamre appears to have been transferred to the tree, or grove, of Mamre, which was opposite to the cave of Machpelah (Gen. xxiii. 17); and in this manner Eshcol is closely connected with Hebron in Gen. xxiii. 19 as it is in the present chapter.

Upon a staff.—The majority of travellers concur in estimating the weight of the largest clusters commonly produced in Palestine at about ten or twelve pounds.

brought of the pomegranates, and of the
figs. (24) The place was called the [1] brook
[2] Eshcol, because of the cluster of grapes
which the children of Israel cut down
from thence. (25) And they returned from
searching of the land after forty days.
(26) And they went and came to Moses,
and to Aaron, and to all the congre-
gation of the children of Israel, unto the
wilderness of Paran, to Kadesh; and
brought back word unto them, and unto
all the congregation, and shewed them
the fruit of the land. (27) And they told
him, and said, We came unto the land
whither thou sentest us, and surely it
floweth with [a] milk and honey; and this
is the fruit of it. (28) Nevertheless the
people *be* strong that dwell in the land,
and the cities *are* walled, *and* very great:
and moreover we saw the children of
Anak there. (29) The Amalekites dwell
in the land of the south: and the Hit-
tites, and the Jebusites, and the Amo-
rites, dwell in the mountains: and the
Canaanites dwell by the sea, and by the
coast of Jordan.
(30) And Caleb stilled the people before
Moses, and said, Let us go up at once,
and possess it; for we are well able to
overcome it. (31) But the men that went
up with him said, We be not able to go
up against the people; for they *are*
stronger than we. (32) And they brought
up an evil report of the land which they
had searched unto the children of Israel,
saying, The land, through which we have
gone to search it, *is* a land that eateth
up the inhabitants thereof; and all the
people that we saw in it *are* [3] men of a
great stature. (33) And there we saw the
giants, the sons of Anak, *which come* of
the giants: and we were in our own
sight as grasshoppers, and so we were in
their sight.

1 Or, *valley.*

2 That is, *a cluster of grapes.*

a Ex. 33. 3.

Kitto, however, mentions an instance of a bunch of Syrian grapes produced in our own country weighing nineteen pounds, which was sent by the Duke of Portland to the Marquis of Rockingham, and which was carried more than twenty miles by four labourers, two of whom bore it by rotation upon a staff. The greatest diameter of this cluster was nineteen inches and a half (*Pictorial Bible*, in loc., 1855). The arrangement referred to in the text was probably made, not because the weight was too great for one person to carry, but in order to prevent the grapes from being crushed. The pomegranates and figs, which are still some of the most important fruits of Hebron (see *The Land and the Book*, p. 583), were probably carried on the same pole. The words may be rendered thus: "*And they bare it between two upon a staff; also some of the pomegranates and of the figs.*" This incident has obvious reference to the homeward journey of the spies. As the grapes of Eshcol were to the Israelites both a pledge and a specimen of the fruits of Canaan, so the communion which believers have with God on earth is a pledge as well as a foretaste of the blessedness of heaven.

(24) **The place was called . . .**—This verse states the reason why the valley was so called by the Israelites, but does not determine the question whether it originally derived its name from Eshcol or not.

(25) **After forty days.**—This time allowed a full and careful exploration of the land.

(26) **To Kadesh.**—Robinson and others identify Kadesh with *Ain-el-Weibeh*, which is in the Arabah, about ten miles north of the place in which Mount Hor abuts on that valley. On the other hand, Mr. Wilton, in *The Negeb* (pp. 79, 80), and Mr. Palmer in the *Desert of the Exodus* (chap. xxv.), maintain the identity of Kadesh with el-Ain, which is about sixty miles west of Mount Hor, and about fifty miles west of Ain-el-Weibeh. The former of these views is maintained in a very elaborate note on this verse in *The Bible Commentary*.

(28) **Nevertheless the people be strong . . .**—The spies adopted the words of Exod. iii. 8, "flowing with milk and honey," as descriptive of the fertility of the land of Canaan, but at the same time they discouraged the hearts of their brethren by their description of the strength of the fortified cities and the gigantic stature of the inhabitants.

The children of Anak.—Better, *of the Anakim.* (See verse 22, and Note.)

(29) **The land of the south.**—Better, *of the south country*, or *the Negeb.* See Gen. xxxvi. 12, and also verse 17 of this chap. and Note.

The mountains.—See Gen. x. 15, 16, and verse 17 of this chap. and Note.

The Canaanites.—See Gen. x. 15—18, xiii. 7, and Notes.

(30) **And Caleb stilled the people.**—The fact that Caleb alone is mentioned in this place is by no means inconsistent with the statement which is contained in chap. xiv. 6—9, from which it appears that Joshua and Caleb concurred in exhorting the people to go up and take possession of the land of promise. It appears, moreover, from Deut. i. 29, &c., that Moses also remonstrated earnestly with the people, and yet neither here nor in the following chapter is mention made of that remonstrance.

(32) **A land that eateth up the inhabitants thereof.**—Some understand by this phrase a land of scarcity, unable to support its inhabitants; others understand it as denoting an unhealthy land, in which sense it appears to be still used in the East. (See Roberts' *Oriental Illustrations*, p. 101, 8vo, 1844.) It seems more probable, however, that the allusion is to the strife and discord which prevailed amongst the various tribes who contended for its possession. (Comp. Lev. xxvi. 38.)

Men of great stature.—Literally, *men of measures* (comp. Isa. xlv. 14), where the word *middah*, *measure*, occurs in the singular number, "men of stature." Such persons did undoubtedly exist in the land of Canaan, but there is no evidence that the inhabitants generally were of extraordinary size.

(33) **And there we saw the giants.**—The same word, *nephilim*, is here used which is found in Gen. vi. 4. See Note *in loc.*

CHAPTER XIV. — (1) And all the
congregation lifted up their voice, and
cried; and the people wept that night.
(2) And all the children of Israel mur-
mured against Moses and against Aaron:
and the whole congregation said unto
them, Would God that we had died in
the land of Egypt! or would God we had
died in this wilderness! (3) And where-
fore hath the LORD brought us unto this
land, to fall by the sword, that our
wives and our children should be a prey?
were it not better for us to return into
Egypt? (4) And they said one to another,
Let us make a captain, and let us return
into Egypt.

(5) Then Moses and Aaron fell on their
faces before all the assembly of the
congregation of the children of Israel.
(6) And Joshua the son of Nun, and Caleb
the son of Jephunneh, *which were* of
them that searched the land, rent their
clothes: (7) and they spake unto all the
company of the children of Israel, saying,
The land, which we passed through to
search it, *is* an exceeding good land.
(8) If the LORD delight in us, then he will
bring us into this land, and give it us;
a land which floweth with milk and
honey. (9) Only rebel not ye against the
LORD, neither fear ye the people of the
land; for they *are* bread for us: their
[1] defence is departed from them, and the
LORD *is* with us: fear them not. (10) But
all the congregation bade stone them
with stones.

And the glory of the LORD appeared
in the tabernacle of the congregation
before all the children of Israel.
(11) And the LORD said unto Moses, How
long will this people provoke me? and
how long will it be ere they believe me,
for all the signs which I have shewed
among them? (12) I will smite them
with the pestilence, and disinherit them,
and will make of thee a greater nation
and mightier than they.

(13) And [a] Moses said unto the LORD,
Then the Egyptians shall hear *it*, (for
thou broughtest up this people in thy
might from among them;) (14) and they
will tell it to the inhabitants of this land:

1 Heb. *shadow*.

a Ex. 32. 12.

XIV.

(2) **And all the children of Israel murmured.**—When the people murmured in like manner in the wilderness of Sin (Exod. xvi. 2, 3) against Moses and Aaron because they had brought them forth into the wilderness, Moses assured them that at even they should know that it was Jehovah Himself who had brought them out from the land of Egypt (*Ibid*, ver. 6). On the present occasion their murmuring was not against Moses and Aaron only, but they openly rebelled against Jehovah Himself, to whom they ascribed, in the way of reproach, their exodus from the land of Egypt.

(3) **And wherefore hath the Lord brought us unto this land . . .?**—Better, *And wherefore doth the Lord bring us into this land?—i.e.*, the land of Canaan, as clearly appears from the words which follow (comp. chap. xv. 18, where the same Hiphil participle is used). The destruction which the Israelites apprehended at this time was not a destruction by famine or drought, but by the sword of the Amorites and of the children of the Anakim. (Comp. Deut. i. 27, 28.)

That our wives and our children should be a prey—*i.e.*, should fall into the hands of the enemy after their entrance into the land of Canaan. (Comp. Exod. xv. 14—17.) It is possible, however, that the land through which the Israelites were passing may be included here and in verse 14.

(6) **Rent their clothes.**—Comp. Lev. x. 6 and Note.

(9) **Their defence is departed from them.**—Literally, *their shadow*. This is a natural and frequently recurring figure of speech in the East, where protection from the scorching rays of the sun is a boon of incalculable worth. (Comp. Gen. xix. 8; Ps. xvii. 8, xci. 1; Is. xxv. 4, xxx. 2.) The measure of the iniquity of the Canaanites was now full, and they were ripe for destruction. (Comp. Gen. xv. 16; Lev. xviii. 25, xx. 23.)

(10) **But all the congregation bade stone them with stones.**—All the congregation here, as elsewhere, seems to denote the princes or chief men of the congregation; otherwise it is difficult to understand to whom the order was addressed to stone Joshua and Caleb. Stoning appears to have been a mode of death commonly adopted in Egypt (Exod. viii. 26). Under the Jewish law stoning was the ordinary, and, as some think, the only prescribed mode of death, and was inflicted as the punishment for crimes such as adultery (Deut. xxii. 22, 24), idolatry (Deut. xiii. 10), witchcraft (Lev. xx. 27), sabbath-breaking (Num. xv. 35), and blasphemy (Lev. xxiv. 16). Moses had apprehended the same outbreak of popular violence on a former occasion (Exod. xvii. 4), and, at a later period, David was threatened in a similar manner (1 Sam. xxx. 6).

And the glory of the Lord appeared in the tabernacle of the congregation.—The meaning probably is in the court of the Tabernacle, or, as some think, above the Tabernacle. (See the Targum of Jonathan and the Vulgate and Septuagint Versions.) The children of Israel could not have seen the glory of the Lord had it been manifested within the Tabernacle.

(12) **And will make of thee a greater nation and mightier than they.**—A similar promise had been given to Moses on occasion of the rebellion at Sinai, and Moses on that occasion interceded with God on behalf of His people in like manner as at this time (Exod. xxxii. 10—12).

(13, 14) **And Moses said unto the Lord . . .**—There is considerable difficulty as to the correct rendering of these verses. They may be rendered in accordance with the Authorised Version, or they may be rendered as follows:—*And Moses said unto the*

for they have heard that thou LORD *art*
among this people, that thou LORD art
seen face to face, and *that* [a] thy cloud
standeth over them, and *that* that thou
goest before them, by day time in a
pillar of a cloud, and in a pillar of fire
by night. (15) Now *if* thou shalt kill *all*
this people as one man, then the nations
which have heard the fame of thee will
speak, saying, (16) because the LORD was
not [b] able to bring this people into the
land which he sware unto them, there-
fore he hath slain them in the wilder-
ness. (17) And now, I beseech thee, let
the power of my Lord be great, ac-
cording as thou hast spoken, saying,
(18) The LORD *is* [c] longsuffering, and of
great mercy, forgiving iniquity and
transgression, and by no means clearing
the guilty, [d] visiting the iniquity of
the fathers upon the children unto
the third and fourth *generation.*
(19) Pardon, I beseech thee, the iniquity
of this people according unto the great-
ness of thy mercy, and as thou hast
forgiven this people, from Egypt even
[1] until now.
(20) And the LORD said, I have par-
doned according to thy word: (21) But *as*
truly *as* I live, all the earth shall be
filled with the glory of the LORD.
(22) Because all those men which have
seen my glory, and my miracles, which
I did in Egypt and in the wilderness,
and have tempted me now these ten
times, and have not hearkened to my
voice; (23) [2] Surely they shall not see the
land which I sware unto their fathers,
neither shall any of them that provoked
me see it: (24) But my servant [e] Caleb,
because he had another spirit with him,
and hath followed me fully, him will I
bring into the land whereinto he went;
and his seed shall possess it. (25) (Now
the Amalekites and Canaanites dwelt in
the valley.) To-morrow turn you, and

a Ex. 13. 21.
b Deut. 9. 28.
c Ex. 34. 6; Ps. 103. 8.
d Ex. 20. 5; & 34. 7.
1 Or, *hitherto.*
2 Heb., *If they see the land.*
e Josh. 14. 6.

LORD, *The Egyptians have both heard that thou hast brought up this people from among them by thy might, and they have also told* (*it*) *to the inhabitants of this land* (*i.e.,* the land of Canaan, as in verse 3); *they* (*i.e.,* the Egyptians and the Canaanites) *have heard that thou* LORD *art in the midst of this people, for thou* LORD *art seen face to face, and thy cloud standeth over them, and thou goest before them,* &c. &c. Reference may be made to the following passages in illustration of the argument by which Moses enforced his intercessory prayer on behalf of Israel:—Deut. xxxii. 26, 27; Josh. vii. 9; Isaiah xlviii. 9, 11; Ezek. xxxvi. 22, 23.

(17, 18) **And now, I beseech thee, let the power of my Lord be great.**—The word *Lord* in verse 17 should not be printed in large capitals in this place, as in the Authorised Version of 1611, inasmuch as it is the rendering of *Adonai,* not of *Jehovah,* as in verse 18. Moses here employs a second argument, founded on the revelation of God's name (*i.e.,* His nature), as made to him on Mount Sinai (Exod. xxxiv. 6, 7), the substance of which he here recites in the same terms.

(20) **I have pardoned according to thy word.**—The holiness and justice of the Lord required that punishment should overtake the transgressors, as it had been foretold in Exod. xxxii. 34. Nevertheless the prayer of Moses was heard and answered, and the people were not wholly exterminated.

(21, 22, 23) **But as truly as I live . . .**—The three verses may be rendered as follows:—*Nevertheless, as truly as I live, and all the earth shall be filled with the glory of the Lord, none of those men who have seen my glory and my signs which I did in Egypt and in the wilderness, and* (*who*) *tempted me these ten times, and hearkened not unto my voice, shall see the land which I sware unto their fathers,* &c. Some have explained the words *these ten times* by adding to the eight murmurings which are recorded—(1) at the Red Sea (Exod. xiv. 11, 12); (2) at Marah (Exod. xv. 23); (3) in the wilderness of Sin (Exod. xvi. 2); (4) at Rephidim (Exod. xvii. 1); (5) at Horeb (Exod. xxxii.); (6) at Taberah (Num. xi. 1); (7) at the graves of lust (Num. xi. 4); and (8) at Kadesh (Num. xiv.)—the transgressions of certain individuals—(1) in keeping the manna until the morning of the day after that on which it was gathered (Exod. xvi. 20); and (2) in going out to gather the manna on the seventh day, when none fell (Exod. xvi. 27). It is more probable, however, that the number *ten* is used here, as elsewhere (comp. Gen. xxxi. 7), as denoting a full measure. The persons to whom the penalty applied are specified in verse 29: viz., those who were included in the first census. The principal exceptions to the threat of exclusion from the land of promise are specified in verses 30 and 31: viz., Joshua and Caleb, and the generation which had not reached twenty years of age at the exodus. The other exception, or exceptions, if such there were, belonged to the tribe of Levi, which was not included in the census which was first taken, nor represented by the spies. It has been inferred from the fact that Nadab and Abihu only went up into the mountain with Moses and Aaron, that Eleazar, who entered Canaan with Joshua (chap. xiv. 1), was under twenty years of age at the exodus. It may be observed that it does not follow that the regulation respecting the age of the Levites at the time of entering upon their service applied also to the priests, and consequently Eleazar *may* have been under twenty years of age at the time of his consecration. (Comp. 2 Chron. xxxi. 17.) There seems, however, to be no sufficient authority for such a supposition.

(24) **And his seed shall possess it.**—It appears from Joshua xiv. 6—14 that Moses had specially promised Hebron to Caleb, and that the mountainous country which the Anakim inhabited, and which only he and Joshua of the twelve spies believed that the Israelites were able to take possession of, was afterwards allotted to him by Joshua "for an inheritance."

(25) **Now the Amalekites and the Canaanites dwelt in the valley.**—There is considerable difficulty in regard to the meaning and connection of these

get you into the wilderness by the way
of the Red Sea.
(26) And the LORD spake unto Moses
and unto Aaron, saying, (27) How long
shall I bear with this evil congregation,
which murmur against me? I have heard
the murmurings of the children of
Israel, which they murmur against me.
(28) Say unto them, [a] *As truly as* I live,
saith the LORD, as ye have spoken in
mine ears, so will I do to you: (29) Your
carcases shall fall in this wilderness;
and all that were [b] numbered of you, ac-
cording to your whole number, from
twenty years old and upward, which have
murmured against me, (30) doubtless ye
shall not come into the land, *concerning*
which I [1] sware to make you dwell there-
in, save Caleb the son of Jephunneh, and
Joshua the son of Nun. (31) But your

a ch. 26. 65; & 32. 10.

b Deut. 1. 35.

1 Heb., *lifted up my hand.*

2 Or, *feed.*

c Ps. 95. 10; Ezek. 4. 6.

3 Or, *altering of my purpose.*

little ones, which ye said should be a
prey, them will I bring in, and they shall
know the land which ye have despised.
(32) But *as for* you, your carcases, they
shall fall in this wilderness. (33) And
your children shall [2] wander in the wil-
derness forty years, and bear your
whoredoms, until your carcases be wasted
in the wilderness. (34) After the number
of the days in which ye searched the
land, *even* [c] forty days, each day for a
year, shall ye bear your iniquities, *even*
forty years, and ye shall know my [3] breach
of promise. (35) I the LORD have said, I
will surely do it unto all this evil con-
gregation, that are gathered together
against me: in this wilderness they shall
be consumed, and there they shall die.
(36) And the men, which Moses sent to
search the land, who returned, and made

---

words. They may be attached to the words which precede: "And his seed shall possess it, and the Amalekites and the Canaanites dwelling in the valley"—*i.e.*, shall possess the land occupied by them. There are strong objections, however, to this rendering, as well as to the rendering adopted by the Authorised Version, if the latter be understood as an historical statement respecting the geographical position of the Amalekites and Canaanites, of which Moses can scarcely be supposed to have been ignorant, and which may be assigned with greater probability to the "hill" than to the "valley." (Comp. verse 45 and Note; also Deut. i. 44, where one or both of these races are spoken of under the name of *Amorites* or *mountaineers.*) The word which is rendered "dwelt" is often used in reference to a temporary sojourn, as, *e.g.*, in Josh. viii. 9 of the ambuscade sent by Joshua, which "abode" between Bethel and Ai, and in 1 Sam. xxv. 13 of a portion of David's men who "abode by the stuff." It is used also in verse 45 of this chapter in respect to the position of the Amalekites and Canaanites, whether temporary or permanent, in the "hill," which appears to be used in contrast with the "valley." The passage may be rendered thus: "Now the Amalekites and the Canaanites are abiding in the valley," *i.e.*, are lying in ambuscade in the valley, and waiting for an opportunity to attack the Israelites (comp. verse 43). If this interpretation of the words, which is that of Ibn Ezra, be adopted, they afford a strong reason for the command which follows:—"To morrow turn you, and get you into the wilderness by the way of the Red Sea"—*i.e.*, do not fall into the snare which is laid for you, but turn and go in a contrary direction.

(27) **How long shall I bear with this evil congregation . . .?**—Or, *How long shall I pardon* (or *forgive*), &c. The verb is not expressed in the Hebrew. It is probable that one of the verbs in verse 19, *pardon* or *forgive*, should be supplied.

(28) **As ye have spoken in mine ears, so will I do unto you.**—The Israelites had exclaimed in their sinful murmuring against God, "Would God we had died in the wilderness" (verse 2) and God declares in His wrathful displeasure that the judgment which they had thus invoked should be inflicted upon them, and that their carcases should fall in the wilderness.

(29) **From twenty years old and upward.**—Rashi thinks that these words were employed to show that the Levites who were numbered from a month old and upwards were not included in the general sentence of destruction, and hence that it is no just cause of astonishment that some of them, as, *e.g.*, Eleazar, should have entered the land of Canaan.

(30) **Concerning which I sware.**—Literally, *I lifted up my hand.* Lifting up the hand is the attitude of swearing. (See Gen. xiv. 22 and Note; Deut. xxxii. 40.) The reference appears to be to the original covenant made with Abraham, and renewed to Isaac and Jacob, respecting the possession of the land of Canaan. (Comp. Gen. xv. 7, 18, xvii. 8, xxii. 16—18, xxvi. 3, 4, xxviii. 13; Exod. vi. 8.)

(32) **But as for you, your carcases, they shall fall.**—Better, *but your carcases, even yours, shall fall.*

In this wilderness.—The very words which the Israelites themselves had used. (See verse 2.)

(33) **And your children shall wander.**—Better, *shall be shepherds*, or, *shall feed their flocks.*

Forty years.—The forty years were reckoned from the exodus, not from the return of the spies to Kadesh. (See verse 34 and Note.)

And bear your whoredoms.—The children were doomed to bear the penalty of their fathers' apostasy. (Comp. Exod. xxxiv. 16.)

(34) **Even forty days, each day for a year.**—The numbering which is recorded in chapter xxvi. took place after the death of Aaron, which happened on the first day of the fifth month of the fortieth year after the exodus (chap. xxxiii. 38). Hence it follows that the year and a half which had elapsed since the exodus must be included in the forty years of shepherd life in the wilderness.

My breach of promise.—The noun which is thus rendered occurs only in one other place, viz., Job xxxiii. 10. The cognate verb, however, occurs several times in this book in the sense of *refuse, disallow*, or *hinder.* (See chaps. xxx. 5, 8, 11, xxxii. 7.) The meaning here appears to be *rejection* or *alienation.*

all the congregation to murmur against
him, by bringing up a slander upon the
land, (37) even those men that did bring
up the evil report upon the land, [a] died by
the plague before the LORD. (38) But
Joshua the son of Nun, and Caleb the
son of Jephunneh, *which were* of the men
that went to search the land, lived *still.*
(39) And Moses told these sayings unto
all the children of Israel: and the people
mourned greatly. (40) And they rose up
early in the morning, and gat them up
into the top of the mountain, saying, Lo,
we [b] *be here*, and will go up unto the
place which the LORD hath promised:
for we have sinned. (41) And Moses said,
Wherefore now do ye transgress the
commandment of the LORD? but it shall
not prosper. (42) Go not up, for the LORD
is not among you; that ye be not
smitten before your enemies. (43) For
the Amalekites and the Canaanites *are*
there before you, and ye shall fall by the
sword: because ye are turned away
from the LORD, therefore the LORD will
not be with you.
(44) But they presumed to go up unto
the hill top: nevertheless the ark of
the covenant of the LORD, and Moses,
departed not out of the camp. (45)
Then the Amalekites came down, and
the Canaanites which dwelt in that hill,
and smote them, and [c] discomfited them,
even unto Hormah.

CHAPTER XV. — (1) And the LORD
spake unto Moses, saying, (2) [d] Speak
unto the children of Israel, and say
unto them, When ye be come into the
land of your habitations, which I give

[a] 1 Cor. 10. 10; Heb. 3. 17; Jude 5.
[b] Deut. 1. 41.
[c] Deut. 1. 44.
[d] Lev. 23. 10.

(37) **By the plague.**—The word *maggephah,* which is here rendered *plague,* denotes *a stroke.* In Exod. ix. 14 it is used of the ten plagues of Egypt. In Num. xvi. 48, 49, it is used of the plague which broke out after the insurrection of Korah, Dathan, and Abiram, and in chap. xxv. 9—18 of that which broke out after the Israelites had joined in the idolatrous and lascivious rites of the Moabites and Midianites. In 1 Sam. iv. 17, 2 Sam. xvii. 9, xviii. 7, it is used of destruction by the sword. It appears to denote in this place sudden death, inflicted by the immediate visitation of the Lord.

(39) **And the people mourned greatly.** — It appears from what follows that the sorrow which the Israelites felt was sorrow for the punishment which their sin had entailed, not godly sorrow for the sin itself.

(40) **Into the top of the mountain.**—Or, *towards the top of the mountain.* This appears to have been the same route as that by which the spies had gone into the south country of Judæa. (See chap. xiii. 17.) It seems to be implied in vv. 44, 45 that the people did not actually ascend the top of the adjoining mountain.

(42) **Go not up, for the Lord is not among you.**—Moses had already received the command which is contained in verse 25. He knew, therefore, that the Israelites would not have the guidance of the cloud, the visible token of the Divine presence.

(43) **Are there before you.**—Or, *will be there before you.* If the same persons are here spoken of as in verse 25, it will follow that they had left their temporary abode, and gone up into the hill country. It is possible, however, that the reference is to different portions of the same nations.

(44) **They presumed to go up.**—*i.e., they made a bold attempt to ascend the mountain.* Their enemies appear to have encountered and discomfited them before they had actually gained the summit.

(45) **Then the Amalekites came down . . .**—The words "which dwelt in that hill" may refer to the Canaanites only, or to the Amalekites and the Canaanites, and may denote either permanent residence or temporary occupation. If the reference is, as seems most natural, to a permanent abode, it will follow verse 25, for the latter verse cannot be intended to describe the geographical position of the Canaanites.

Even unto Hormah.—Or, *the place of the ban.* The definite article is used in this place, *the Hormah.* If the Hormah which is here mentioned is identical with the Hormah of chap. xxi. 3, where the definite article is not used, and with the Hormah of Judges i. 17, we must conclude that the name is used proleptically, as is not unfrequently the case in Scripture. It is probable, however, that in each case a different place is denoted by a common name. The cognate verb is employed in Deut. xx. 17, where the command is given to devote the Canaanitish nations to utter destruction, *i.e.,* to a state of *hormah.*

XV.

(1, 2) **And the Lord spake unto Moses, saying . . .**—We learn from Deut. i. 46 that the Israelites "abode in Kadesh many days," and from Deut. ii. 1 that afterwards they "turned," in obedience to the command given in the preceding chapter of this book, and "took their journey into the wilderness by the way of the Red Sea." It appears, further, from Num. xx. 1 that in the first month of the fortieth year they came again into the desert of Zin, and "abode in Kadesh." In regard to the transactions recorded in this and in the four following chapters we have no certain chronological data. The fact that additional laws were given during the long period of the wanderings in the wilderness furnished a practical proof of the continuance of the covenant which had been made with Israel at Sinai. Bishop Wordsworth supplies the following answer to the inquiry how the Israelites were able to find a sufficient quantity of cattle and of birds in the wilderness to fulfil the requirements of the Levitical law:—"God," he writes, "promulgated that law on Mount Sinai in order that it might be observed in Canaan; and when he gave it, the Israelites had not as yet incurred the sentence of exclusion, and they *might*—and if they had not been disobedient, they would—have been in Canaan within a fortnight of its delivery. The Levitical law was given under the presumption that they would obey Him who gave it, and that they would be soon afterwards in Canaan, when they would be able to comply with that law. (Comp. Deut. iv. 14.) But they

unto you, (3) and will make an offering
by fire unto the LORD, a burnt offering,
or a sacrifice [a] in [1] performing a vow, or
in a freewill offering, or in your solemn
feasts, to make a [b] sweet savour unto the
LORD, of the herd, or of the flock: a Lev. 22. 21.
(4) Then [c] shall he that offereth his offer-
ing unto the LORD bring a meat offering
of a tenth deal of flour mingled with the
fourth *part* of an hin of oil. (5) And the
fourth *part* of an hin of wine for a drink
offering shalt thou prepare with the 1 Heb., *separating.*
burnt offering or sacrifice, for one lamb.
(6) Or for a ram, thou shalt prepare *for* a
meat offering two tenth deals of flour
mingled with the third *part* of an hin of
oil. (7) And for a drink offering thou
shalt offer the third *part* of an hin of b Ex. 29. 18.
wine, *for* a sweet savour unto the LORD.
(8) And when thou preparest a bullock
for a burnt offering, or *for* a sacrifice in
performing a vow, or peace offerings
unto the LORD: (9) Then shall he bring
with a bullock a meat offering of three c Lev. 2. 1.
tenth deals of flour mingled with half
an hin of oil. (10) And thou shalt bring
for a drink offering half an hin of wine,
for an offering made by fire, of a sweet
savour unto the LORD. (11) Thus shall it
be done for one bullock, or for one ram, d Ex. 12. 49; ch. 9. 14.
or for a lamb, or a kid. (12) According
to the number that ye shall prepare, so
shall ye do to every one according to
their number. (13) All that are born of
the country shall do these things after
this manner, in offering an offering made
by fire, of a sweet savour unto the LORD.
(14) And if a stranger sojourn with you,
or whosoever *be* among you in your
generations, and will offer an offering
made by fire, of a sweet savour unto the
LORD; as ye do, so he shall do. (15) [d] One
ordinance *shall be both* for you of the
congregation, and also for the stranger
that sojourneth *with you,* an ordinance
for ever in your generations: as *ye are,*
so shall the stranger be before the
LORD. (16) One law and one manner
shall be for you, and for the stranger
that sojourneth with you.

(17) And the LORD spake unto Moses,
saying, (18) Speak unto the children of
Israel, and say unto them, When ye
come into the land whither I bring you,
(19) Then it shall be, that when ye eat of
the bread of the land, ye shall offer up
an heave offering unto the LORD. (20) Ye
shall offer up a cake of the first of your
dough *for* an heave offering: as *ye do*
the heave offering of the threshingfloor,
so shall ye heave it. (21) Of the first of
your dough ye shall give unto the LORD
an heave offering in your generations.

(22) And if ye have erred, and not ob-
served all these commandments, which
the LORD hath spoken unto Moses,
(23) *even* all that the LORD hath com-
manded you by the hand of Moses, from

---

murmured against God at Kadesh-barnea, and thus they forfeited His favour—they, as it were, excommunicated themselves. They forfeited the *privileges of obedience.* They had kept one Passover at Mount Sinai, but there is no evidence that they were ever *permitted* to keep another Passover during the whole term of their wanderings. They themselves felt and acted as men under a ban; they did not even administer circumcision in the wilderness, nor until they were admitted into Canaan under Joshua; then—but not till then—they were again allowed to eat the Passover." The words which follow were evidently addressed to those of the Israelites who were under twenty years of age at the time of the exodus.

(4) **A meat offering of a tenth deal of flour . . .**—The meal offering and the drink offering which are here ordered to be brought when a lamb was offered in performance of a vow, or as a free will offering, or at the solemn feasts, are the same as those which were appointed to be offered with the morning and evening lamb. (Exod. xxix. 38—40.) Meal offerings and drink offerings had already been prescribed in connection with the three great feasts. (Lev. xxiii. 13, 18, 37.)

(8) **In performing a vow.**—Rather, *in making a special vow.* (See chap. vi. 2.)

(13) **All that are born of the country.**—The Targum of Jonathan is, "all that are born in Israel, and not among the people." It seems clear, however, from verse 14 that the reference in this verse is to the indigenous Israelites.

(15) **One ordinance shall be both for you of the congregation . . .**—Literally, *As for the congregation, there shall be one ordinance for you and for the stranger that sojourneth.* Some render the words thus:—*O congregation, one ordinance shall be for you and for the stranger,* &c.

(20) **Of the first of your dough.**—Or, *mixed meal.* The word *arisoth* is used only in the plural number, and is found only in Neh. x. 37 and Ezek. xliv. 30, besides this and the following verse.

(22) **And if ye have erred, and not observed.**—Rather, *And if ye shall err and not observe.*

(23) **And henceforward.**—Rather, *and onward,* or *thenceforward.* There is nothing in the word which is here used to denote whether the reference is or is not to legislation of a later date than that at which the words were spoken. The *terminus a quo* is expressed in the preceding words. Comp. Is. xviii. 2, where the meaning seems to be *up to the present time,* and Ezek. xxxix. 22, where the reference is to the *indefinite future.*

the day that the LORD commanded *Moses*,
and henceforward among your genera-
tions; (24) then it shall be, if *ought* be
committed by ignorance [1] without the
knowledge of the congregation, that all
the congregation shall offer one young
bullock for a burnt offering, for a sweet
savour unto the LORD, with his meat
offering, and his drink offering, according
to the [2] manner, and one kid of the goats
for a sin offering. (25) And the priest
shall make an atonement for all the
congregation of the children of Israel,
and it shall be forgiven them; for it *is*
ignorance: and they shall bring their
offering, a sacrifice made by fire unto
the LORD, and their sin offering before
the LORD, for their ignorance: (26) And
it shall be forgiven all the congregation
of the children of Israel, and the
stranger that sojourneth among them;
seeing all the people *were* in ignorance.
(27) And if [a]any soul sin through ig-
norance, then he shall bring a she goat
of the first year for a sin offering.
(28) And the priest shall make an atone-
ment for the soul that sinneth ignorantly,
when he sinneth by ignorance before the
LORD, to make an atonement for him;
and it shall be forgiven him. (29) Ye
shall have one law for him that [3] sinneth
through ignorance, *both for* him that is
born among the children of Israel, and
for the stranger that sojourneth among
them.
(30) But the soul that doeth *ought*[4]
presumptuously, *whether he be* born in
the land, or a stranger, the same re-
proacheth the LORD; and that soul
shall be cut off from among his people.
(31) Because he hath despised the word
of the LORD, and hath broken his com-
mandment, that soul shall utterly be
cut off; his iniquity *shall be* upon him.
(32) And while the children of Israel
were in the wilderness, they found a
man that gathered sticks upon the
sabbath day. (33) And they that found
him gathering sticks brought him unto
Moses and Aaron, and unto all the con-
gregation. (34) And they put him [b]in
ward, because it was not declared what
should be done to him. (35) And the
LORD said unto Moses, The man shall
be surely put to death: all the con-
gregation shall stone him with stones
without the camp. (36) And all the
congregation brought him without the
camp, and stoned him with stones, and
he died; as the LORD commanded Moses.

1 Heb., *from the eyes.*
2 Or, *ordinance.*
a Lev. 4. 27.
3 Heb., *doeth.*
4 Heb., *with an high hand.*
b Lev. 24. 12.

---

(24) **By ignorance.**—The word *shegagah* is used to denote transgressions committed unwittingly in contrast to sins committed presumptuously (verse 30). (See Lev. iv. 2 and Note.) Provision had already been made in Lev. iv. for sins of commission committed unwittingly by the whole congregation, but no provision appears to have been made for the guilt contracted in the case of sins of omission. It is possible, also, that in this place transgressions committed by an individual, but affecting the whole of the congregation, may be included. In Lev. iv. 14 a young bullock is appointed as a sin offering; in the present case a young bullock is appointed for a burnt offering and a kid of the goats for a sin offering. It must be remembered, moreover, that the commandments delivered in this chapter have express reference to the land of Canaan, whereas many of the commandments previously delivered had already become obligatory.

(25) **For it is ignorance.**—Rather, *for it is a sin of ignorance*, or *an error*. So also at the end of the verse.

(26) **Seeing all the people were in ignorance.**—Rather, *for in regard to all the people, it was done in ignorance*, or *unwittingly*.

(27) **And if any soul sin through ignorance.**—There is no restriction here, as in Lev. iv. 27, to sins of commission.

(30) **That doeth ought presumptuously.**—Literally, *with a high hand.*

Reproacheth the Lord.—Rather, *blasphemeth*, as in 2 Kings xix. 6, 22.

(32) **And while the children of Israel were in the wilderness . . .**—Better, *Now the children of Israel were in the wilderness, and they found*, &c. It is probable that the incident which is here recorded is designed to illustrate the presumptuous sins which were to be punished by death. The offence may have been committed shortly after the promulgation of the commandments contained in this chapter, but all that is certain is that it was committed "in the wilderness," *i.e.*, according to Ibn Ezra, in the wilderness of Sinai, but more probably during the period of the wanderings in the wilderness after the arrival at Kadesh. No inference can be drawn from this verse as to the time at which the account was committed to writing. The observance of the Sabbath was obligatory in the wilderness as well as in the land of Canaan (comp. Exod. xvi. 27—30), and the punishment of death had already been denounced against those who profaned it by doing any work thereon (see Exod. xxxi. 15, xxxv. 2), but the manner in which death was to be inflicted does not appear to have been hitherto declared. The same verb which is here rendered "declared" occurs in the parallel case of the blasphemer in Lev. xxiv. 12, where it is rendered "shewed":—"And they put him in ward, that the mind of the Lord might be shewed them." The punishment of death had already been denounced against those who cursed father or mother (Lev. xx. 9). It could hardly be thought that a lighter punishment was to be inflicted on one who blasphemed the name of Jehovah, but in that case, as in this, the mode of death does not appear to have been previously enjoined.

(37) And the LORD spake unto Moses,
saying, (38) Speak unto the children of
Israel, and bid [a]them that they make
them fringes in the borders of their
garments throughout their generations,
and that they put upon the fringe of
the borders a ribband of blue: (39) and
it shall be unto you for a fringe, that ye
may look upon it, and remember all
the commandments of the LORD, and do
them; and that ye seek not after your
own heart and your own eyes, after
which ye use to go a whoring: (40) that
ye may remember, and do all my com-
mandments, and be holy unto your
God. (41) I *am* the LORD your God,
which brought you out of the land of
Egypt, to be your God: I *am* the LORD
your God.

CHAPTER XVI.—(1) Now [b]Korah,
the son of Izhar, the son of Kohath, the
son of Levi, and Dathan and Abiram,
the sons of Eliab, and On, the son of
Peleth, sons of Reuben, took *men:* (2)
and they rose up before Moses, with
certain of the children of Israel, two
hundred and fifty princes of the as-
sembly, [c]famous in the congregation,
men of renown: (3) and they gathered
themselves together against Moses and
against Aaron, and said unto them,
[1] *Ye take* too much upon you, seeing all
the congregation *are* holy, every one of

[a] Deut. 22. 12; Matt. 23. 5.

[b] ch. 27. 3; Ecclus. 45. 21; Jude 11.

[c] ch. 26. 9.

[1] Heb., It is *much for you.*

---

(38) **That they make them fringes . . .**—Better, *That they make them tassels on the corners of their garments throughout their generations, and that they put upon the tassel of the corner* (*i.e., on each tassel*) *a thread* (*or cord*) *of blue.* The *tassels* (*zirith*) appear to be the same as the *gedilim* (*fringes*) of Deut. xxii. 12. The outer garment of the Jews was a four-cornered cloth, which was also used by the poor as a counterpane (Exod. xxii. 26, 27). It appears to have been commonly used with a hole in the centre, through which the head was put, so that one-half covered the front and the other the back of the body. These tassels, or fringes (LXX. κράσπεδα—*craspeda*), were enlarged by the Pharisees to exhibit their punctilious fulfilment of the Law (Matt. xxii. 5). Great sanctity was attached to these fringes or tassels, and for this cause the woman with the issue of blood desired to touch a *kraspedon* of our Saviour's garment (Matt. ix. 20).

(39) **That ye seek not after your own heart.**—Or, *That ye go not about,* or *search not out,* &c.

XVI.

(1) **Now Korah, the son of Izhar . . .**—Some suppose that the copula before "Dathan and Abiram" should be omitted, and that the verse should be rendered thus: *Now Korah, the son of Izhar, the son of Kohath, the son of Levi, took Dathan and Abiram,* &c. The rebellion of Korah, Dathan, and Abiram is the only important event which is recorded in connection with the protracted wandering in the desert. The time and place of its occurrence cannot be positively determined. The circumstances out of which it appears to have arisen render it probable that it took place during one of the early years of the wanderings in the wilderness, either during the abode at Kadesh or subsequently to the departure from it. In favour of the supposition that the occurrence took place during the sojourn at Kadesh, it may be urged—(1) that the history of the Israelites between the first and the second encampments at Kadesh appears to be designedly regarded and treated as a blank; and (2) that during that interval they appear to have been dispersed over the face of the wilderness, whilst the narrative of the rebellion of Korah seems to assume the concentration of the people in one place. The whole of the narrative bears the clear impress of historical truth. The leaders of the rebellion, amongst whom Korah holds the most conspicuous place (comp. chaps. xvi. 1, xxvi. 9; Jude, ver. 11), belonged to the tribes of Levi and Reuben. Korah, as the descendant of Izhar, the brother of Amram, who was the father (or, as some maintain, the more distant ancestor) of Moses and Aaron, may well be supposed to have been jealous of the peculiar prerogatives of the priestly family, and also of the leadership of Elizaphan, the son of Uzziel (chap. iii. 30), who appears to have been the youngest son of Kohath, whilst the name of Izhar stands next to that of Amram (chap. iii. 19). Dathan and Abiram, moreover, as the sons of Eliab, the son of Pallu, the son of Reuben (chap. xxvi. 5—9), who was the eldest son of Jacob, may, on like grounds, be supposed to have been discontented on account of the transference of the birthright, and the consequent loss of the leadership which had been possessed by their tribe, and which was now held by the tribe of Judah. It is possible that they may have regarded the priesthood also as amongst the prerogatives of the firstborn which should have descended to them. The proximity of the Kohathites to the Reubenites—for both were encamped on the south side of the Tabernacle—afforded opportunity for their common deliberations; and it has been inferred by some, from verses 24—27, that they had erected a tabernacle in rivalry with the Tabernacle of the Congregation. No further mention is made of the name of On, nor is he expressly included in the account of the final punishment.

(2) **And they rose up . . .**—*i.e.,* in rebellion.

Two hundred and fifty princes . . .—It has been inferred from chap. xxvii. 3, where it is stated that Zelophehad, the Manassite, did not take part in the rebellion, that these princes, or chief men of the congregation, belonged to the other tribes of Israel as well as that of Levi. They are called Korah's company because he was their leader, and it is probable from verse 8 that a large number of them belonged to the tribe of Levi.

(3) **Ye take too much upon you . .**—Or, *enough for you* (comp. Gen. xlv. 28), *i.e.,* you have held the priesthood and the government long enough; or, *Let it be enough for you to be numbered amongst the holy people without usurping dominion over them.* It is evident from the whole tenour of the address that Korah laid claim to a universal priesthood on behalf of

them, and the LORD *is* among them:
wherefore then lift ye up yourselves
above the congregation of the LORD?
(4) And when Moses heard *it*, he fell
upon his face: (5) and he spake unto
Korah and unto all his company, say-
ing, Even to morrow the LORD will
shew who *are* his, and *who is* holy;
and will cause *him* to come near unto
him: even *him* whom he hath chosen
will he cause to come near unto him.
(6) This do; Take you censers, Korah,
and all his company; (7) and put fire
therein, and put incense in them before
the LORD to morrow: and it shall be
that the man whom the LORD doth
choose, he *shall be* holy: *ye take* too
much upon you, ye sons of Levi.
(8) And Moses said unto Korah, Hear,
I pray you, ye sons of Levi: (9) *seemeth
it but* a small thing unto you, that the
God of Israel hath separated you from
the congregation of Israel, to bring you
near to himself to do the service of the
tabernacle of the LORD, and to stand
before the congregation to minister
unto them? (10) And he hath brought
thee near *to him*, and all thy brethren
the sons of Levi with thee: and seek ye
the priesthood also? (11) For which
cause *both* thou and all thy company
are gathered together against the
LORD: and what *is* Aaron, that ye
murmur against him?
(12) And Moses sent to call Dathan
and Abiram, the sons of Eliab: which
said, We will not come up: (13) *is it* a
small thing that thou hast brought us
up out of a land that floweth with milk
and honey, to kill us in the wilderness,
except thou make thyself altogether a
prince over us? (14) Moreover thou hast
not brought us into a land that floweth
with milk and honey, or given us in-
heritance of fields and vineyards: wilt
thou [1] put out the eyes of these men?
we will not come up.
(15) And Moses was very wroth, and
said unto the LORD, [a] Respect not thou
their offering: I have not taken one ass
from them, neither have I hurt one of
them. (16) And Moses said unto Korah,
Be thou and all thy company before the
LORD, thou, and they, and Aaron, to
morrow: (17) and take every man his
censer, and put incense in them, and

1 Heb., *bore out.*

a Gen. 4. 4.

---

the people, designing probably to secure the chief place in that priesthood for himself.

(5) **And he spake unto Korah and unto all his company.**—The words seem to have been addressed only to Korah and his company, not to Dathan and Abiram, who do not appear to have been present on this occasion. (See verse 12, where Moses is represented as sending for Dathan and Abiram.)

Even to-morrow.—Literally, *In the morning.* It may be that On and also the sons of Korah profited by this suspension of the judgment which was about to overtake those who persisted in their rebellion.

(6) **Take you censers.**—The offering of incense was the peculiar prerogative and the holiest function of the priesthood. The destruction of Nadab and Abihu ought to have served as a warning to Korah and his company not to provoke a similar exhibition of the Divine displeasure.

(7) **Ye take too much upon you . . .**—Moses here adopts the language of Korah in verse 3. The meaning appears to be, as more fully explained in verses 9, 10, that it ought to have sufficed Korah and the other Levites that they had been chosen from amongst their brethren to discharge the inferior offices of the sanctuary.

(10) **And seek ye the priesthood also?**—The Targums of Onkelos and Jonathan understand the reference to be to the high priesthood. As the other Levites who belonged to Korah's company sought the priesthood, so Korah may have aimed at the high priesthood.

(12) **And Moses sent to call Dathan and Abiram . . .**—If, as seems probable from verse 3, Dathan and Abiram had joined Korah and his company in the address to Moses which is contained in verse 3, they must have subsequently withdrawn themselves and retired to their own tents, from which they refused to go up at the bidding of Moses.

(13) **A land that floweth with milk and honey.**—The description of the land of promise is here applied perversely and ironically to the land of Egypt.

(14) **Moreover thou hast not brought us . . .**—The words which the Lord had spoken to Moses (Exod. iii. 8) concerning the deliverance from Egypt, and the bringing of the people into a land flowing with milk and honey, had been communicated by Aaron to the people (Exod. iv. 30). Dathan and Abiram reproach Moses, as though he was responsible for their protracted sojourn in the wilderness.

Wilt thou put out the eyes of these men?—Hebrew, *those men.* The same expression is employed in its literal signification in regard to Samson (Judges xvi. 21). It is probably used here in the same manner; or, it may be, to denote an alleged attempt on the part of Moses to blind the eyes of the people to the violation of promises solemnly made to them, and to impose upon them a law of blind obedience to his own arbitrary injunctions.

(15) **I have not taken one ass from them . . .**—In answer to the accusation preferred against him in verse 13, Moses vindicates himself from the charge of oppression or extortion.

(17) **Take every man his censer.**—These censers may have been household vessels resembling censers, and available for the same purpose; or they may have been vessels which were used by the heads of houses, as priests, before the order of priesthood was restricted to

bring ye before the LORD every man his
censer, two hundred and fifty censers;
thou also, and Aaron, each *of you* his
censer.
(18) And they took every man his
censer, and put fire in them, and laid
incense thereon, and stood in the door
of the tabernacle of the congregation
with Moses and Aaron. (19) And Korah
gathered all the congregation against
them unto the door of the tabernacle
of the congregation: and the glory of
the LORD appeared unto all the con-
gregation.
(20) And the LORD spake unto Moses
and unto Aaron, saying, (21) Separate
yourselves from among this congrega-
tion, that I may consume them in a
moment. (22) And they fell upon their
faces, and said, O God, the God of the
spirits of all flesh, shall one man sin,
and wilt thou be wroth with all the
congregation? (23) And the LORD spake
unto Moses, saying, (24) Speak unto the
congregation, saying, Get you up from
about the tabernacle of Korah, Dathan,
and Abiram.
(25) And Moses rose up and went unto
Dathan and Abiram; and the elders of
Israel followed him. (26) And he spake
unto the congregation, saying, Depart,
I pray you, from the tents of these
wicked men, and touch nothing of
their's, lest ye be consumed in all their
sins. (27) So they gat up from the
tabernacle of Korah, Dathan, and
Abiram, on every side: and Dathan
and Abiram came out, and stood in
the door of their tents, and their
wives, and their sons, and their little
children. (28) And Moses said, Hereby
ye shall know that the LORD hath sent
me to do all these works; for *I have*
not *done them* of mine own mind. (29) If
these men die [1]the common death of
all men, or if they be visited after the
visitation of all men; *then* the LORD
hath not sent me. (30) But if the LORD
[2]make a new thing, and the earth open
her mouth, and swallow them up, with
all that *appertain* unto them, and they
go down quick into the pit; then ye
shall understand that these men have
provoked the LORD.
(31) [a]And it came to pass, as he had
made an end of speaking all these
words, that the ground clave asunder
that *was* under them: (32) and the earth
opened her mouth, and swallowed them
up, and their houses, and all the men

B. C. cir. 1471.

1 Heb., *as every man dieth.*

2 Heb., *create a creature.*

a ch. 27. 3; Deut. 11. 6; Ps. 106. 17.

---

the family of Aaron; or they may have been made by Korah and his company for their own use.

(19) **All the congregation.**—It is evident from these words that there was a general disposition on the part of the people to favour the insurrection of Korah against Moses and Aaron.

(21) **Separate yourselves from among this congregation . . .**—By their obedience to the summons of Korah the congregation generally, or at least a large portion of it, had made themselves partakers in his sin, and had become obnoxious to the Divine wrath.

(24) **Get you up from about the tabernacle of Korah, Dathan, and Abiram.**—It is not easy to determine what is the meaning of the word *mishkan* (tabernacle) in this and in the 27th verse. The word, in the singular number, commonly denotes the tabernacle of the congregation—*i.e.*, the boarded erection which was covered by the *ohel*, or tent. The word means simply a "dwelling-place," and it may denote in this and in the 27th verse a rival tabernacle which had been erected by Korah and the other conspirators; or it may denote, in a collective sense, the tent of Korah, which may have been contumaciously pitched near that of the Reubenites, and also the tents of Dathan and Abiram, which were in proximity to those of the Kohathites, but further removed from the Tabernacle. The substitution of the word "tents" in verse 26, in which Moses delivers to the people the command contained in verse 24, seems to favour the latter of these explanations.

(27) **And Dathan and Abiram came out . . .**—No mention is made of the position of Korah at this time, neither is any mention made of his sons, who, as we learn from chap. xxvi. 11, "died not" when the company of Korah died. His descendants are mentioned in 1 Chron. vi. 22—38, and mention is made of "the sons of Korah" in the titles of eleven of the Psalms. Samuel the prophet and Heman the singer were of this family (1 Chron. vi. 22, 33).

(28) **To do all these works.**—*i.e.*, to bring the people out of the land of Egypt, to exchange the firstborn for the Levites, to consecrate Aaron and his sons to the priesthood, and generally to declare the will of the Lord to the people.

(30) **Make a new thing.**—Literally, *create a creation—i.e.*, do something hitherto unknown.

Into the pit.—Literally, *into Sheol.*

(32) **And the earth opened her mouth . . .**—Had this verse stood alone it might have been inferred that Korah and his family shared the fate of Dathan and Abiram and their families and households. In regard to the sons of Korah, however, there is direct evidence that they did not share in the punishment of Dathan and Abiram (see Note on verse 27); and in regard to Korah there is ground for the belief that he perished by fire with the 250 men who offered incense with him. It is true, indeed, that in chap. xxvi. 10 Korah is mentioned in conjunction with Dathan and Abiram (see Note *in loc.*); but in the other places in which reference is made to the conspiracy, the fate of the chief conspirators is separated. Thus, in Deut. xi. 6 we read only of what God did unto Dathan and Abiram and their households and tents; and in Ps. cvi. 17 we read that "The earth opened and swallowed

that *appertained* unto Korah, and all
their goods. (33) They, and all that
appertained to them, went down alive
into the pit, and the earth closed upon
them: and they perished from among
the congregation. (34) And all Israel
that *were* round about them fled at the
cry of them: for they said, Lest the
earth swallow us up *also*. (35) And there
came out a fire from the LORD, and
consumed the two hundred and fifty
men that offered incense.

(36) And the LORD spake unto Moses,
saying, (37) Speak unto Eleazar the son
of Aaron the priest, that he take up the
censers out of the burning, and scatter
thou the fire yonder; for they are
hallowed. (38) The censers of these
sinners against their own souls, let
them make them broad plates *for* a
covering of the altar: for they offered
them before the LORD, therefore they
are hallowed: and they shall be a sign
unto the children of Israel. (39) And
Eleazar the priest took the brasen
censers, wherewith they that were
burnt had offered; and they were
made broad *plates for* a covering of
the altar: (40) *to be* a memorial unto
the children of Israel, that no stranger,
which *is* not of the seed of Aaron, come
near to offer incense before the LORD;
that he be not as Korah, and as his
company: as the LORD said to him by
the hand of Moses.

(41) But on the morrow all the con-
gregation of the children of Israel
murmured against Moses and against
Aaron, saying, Ye have killed the
people of the LORD. (42) And it came
to pass, when the congregation was
gathered against Moses and against
Aaron, that they looked toward the
tabernacle of the congregation: and,
behold, the cloud covered it, and the
glory of the LORD appeared. (43) And
Moses and Aaron came before the
tabernacle of the congregation. (44)
And the Lord spake unto Moses, say-
ing, (45) Get you up from among this
congregation, that I may consume
them as in a moment. And they fell
upon their faces. (46) And Moses said
unto Aaron, Take a censer, and put

---

up Dathan, and covered the company of Abiram," whilst in the following verse it is added that "The flame burned up the wicked." If Korah's tent remained in its appointed place amongst the Kohathites, it may reasonably be supposed that the chasm did not extend beyond the tents of Dathan and Abiram; or if Korah had pitched a tent for himself adjoining the tents of Dathan and Abiram, it may be inferred that those only of his household remained in it who shared in the conspiracy, and that his sons remained amongst the other Kohathites, or withdrew with the rest of the congregation at the command of Moses. It is most natural to suppose that Korah was at this time before the door of the Tabernacle, with the 250 men of his company who had presumed to offer incense, and that he shared their doom. Ibn Ezra observes that in the song of the Red Sea there is no mention made of the drowning of Pharaoh, but only of his chariots and hosts; whilst in Ps. cxxxvi. 15 we read that Pharaoh and his host were overthrown in the Red Sea.

(35) **And there came out a fire from the Lord . . .**—It was thus, as Bishop Wordsworth has observed, that "Korah and his company were punished by the same element as that by which they had sinned."

(37) **Speak unto Eleazar the son of Aaron . . .**—Aaron was shortly to be employed in an act of sacerdotal ministration and intercession, for which he would have become disqualified had he been ceremonially defiled by contact with things pertaining to the dead.

(38) **These sinners against their own souls.**—*i.e.*, men who have forfeited their lives by their sin.

Let them make them broad plates . . .—It was thus that the sacrilegious act of Korah and his company was made the occasion of a permanent warning against all similar profanation of holy things. The altar of burnt-offering had already a covering of brass; but, as the altar was made of wood, an additional covering afforded further security against the fire which was continually burning on it. The censers of Korah and his company were made of brass (verse 39). Those of Aaron and his sons are thought by some to have been made of silver, but there seems to be no sufficient authority for this supposition; and in Exod. xxxviii. 3, where the same Hebrew word is used, but which in the English version is rendered "firepans," it is said that all the vessels of the altar were made of brass. In the time of Solomon the censers were made of gold (1 Kings vii. 50). That used by Aaron on the great day of atonement was of gold. (Comp. Heb. ix. 4; Rev. viii. 3.)

(39) **Wherewith they that were burnt had offered.**—Or, *which they who were burnt had brought nigh* (*i.e.*, unto the Lord).

(40) **To be a memorial unto the children of Israel.**—The Apostle Jude warns Christians by the same example against the profanation of Divine ordinances (verse 11).

(41) **But on the morrow . . .**—It is difficult to conceive of a more striking illustration of the depravity of the human heart than is afforded by this outbreak of the same spirit of rebellion which had been so signally punished on the preceding day.

(42) **And, behold, the cloud covered it.**—The cloud had probably been removed on the preceding day when the rebels were consumed, and was now again restored in order to encourage Moses and Aaron.

(46) **Take a censer.**—Better, *the censer*. The reference appears to be to the golden censer of the high priest. Incense was an emblem of prayer, and a figure of the intercession and mediation of Christ. (See Ps. cxli. 2; Rev. viii. 3, 4.)

fire therein from off the altar, and put on incense, and go quickly unto the congregation, and make an atonement for them: for there is wrath gone out from the LORD; the plague is begun. (47) And Aaron took as Moses commanded, and ran into the midst of the congregation; and, behold, the plague was begun among the people: and he put on incense, and made an atonement for the people. (48) And he stood between the dead and the living; and the plague was stayed. (49) Now they that died in the plague were fourteen thousand and seven hundred, beside them that died about the matter of Korah. (50) And Aaron returned unto Moses unto the door of the tabernacle of the congregation: and the plague was stayed.

CHAPTER XVII.—(1) And the LORD spake unto Moses, saying, (2) Speak unto the children of Israel, and take of every one of them a rod according to the house of *their* fathers, of all their princes according to the house of their fathers twelve rods: write thou every man's name upon his rod. (3) And thou shalt write Aaron's name upon the rod of Levi: for one rod *shall be* for the head of the house of their fathers. (4) And thou shalt lay them up in the tabernacle of the congregation before the testimony, [a]where I will meet with you. (5) And it shall come to pass, *that* the man's rod, whom I shall choose, shall blossom: and I will make to cease from me the murmurings of the children of Israel, whereby they murmur against you.

(6) And Moses spake unto the children of Israel, and every one of their princes gave him [1]a rod apiece, for each prince one, according to their fathers' houses, *even* twelve rods: and the rod of Aaron *was* among their rods. (7) And Moses laid up the rods before the LORD in the tabernacle of witness.

(8) And it came to pass, that on the morrow Moses went into the tabernacle of witness; and, behold, the rod of Aaron for the house of Levi was budded, and brought forth buds, and bloomed blossoms, and yielded almonds. (9) And Moses brought out all the rods from

a Ex. 25. 22.

1 Heb., *a rod for one prince, a rod for one prince.*

And go quickly.—Or, *and carry it quickly.*

(47) **And ran into the midst of the congregation.**—The whole occasion was an extraordinary one. On ordinary occasions incense might only be offered on the golden altar within the holy place in which the priests ministered.

(48) **And he stood between the dead and the living . . .**—Aaron was, in this respect, a striking type of Christ, who "hath given himself for us an offering and a sacrifice to God for a sweet-smelling savour" (Eph. v. 2).

XVII.

(2) **And take of every one of them . . .**—Better, *And take of them a rod for each father's house.*

Twelve rods.—Some suppose that Aaron's rod was not included amongst the twelve. Others suppose that one rod only was taken for the tribes of Ephraim and Manasseh. The latter supposition is more accordant with the terms here employed than the former, and is supported by Deut. xxvii. 12, 13, where Joseph stands for the two tribes of Ephraim and Manasseh, and Levi is included amongst the twelve tribes.

Write thou every man's name upon his rod.—This was in accordance with an Egyptian custom. (See Wilkinson's *Ancient Egyptians*, III. 388.) The prophet Ezekiel received a similar injunction (Ezek. xxxvii. 16).

(3) **And thou shalt write Aaron's name upon the rod of Levi.**—Aaron was descended from the *second* son of Levi. He was not, therefore, the natural, but the divinely-appointed head of his father's house, and hence it would not have sufficed for the purpose contemplated to have inscribed the name of Levi upon the rod. Aaron was constituted the head alike of the priests and of the Levites, into which two classes the tribe of Levi was divided.

(4) **Where I will meet with you.**—Rather, *where I meet with you.*

(5) **The man's rod, whom I shall choose, shall blossom.**—Or, *shall sprout forth* or *put forth—i.e.*, leaves or blossoms. Achilles, when enraged against Agamemnon, is made to swear a solemn oath by his sceptre which, having once left its stock on the mountains, shall never again grow. King Latinus is represented by Virgil as confirming his covenant with Æneas by a similar oath.

(8) **Behold, the rod of Aaron for the house of Levi was budded . . .**—As the budding of Aaron's rod was the divinely appointed proof of the establishment of the priesthood in his person and in his posterity, so our Lord proved Himself to be the true High Priest over the House of God by coming forth as "a rod [or shoot] out of the stem of Jesse" (Isa. xi. 1), and as "a root out of a dry ground" (Isa. liii. 2). The miraculous shooting forth of Aaron's dry rod may be regarded as a type of the mode of the Spirit's operation in the Church, and more especially in the work of the ministry; "Not by might, nor by power, but by my spirit, saith the Lord of hosts" (Zech. iv. 6).

And yielded almonds.—Better, *and brought almonds to maturity*, or *yielded ripe almonds.* The word *shaked* (almond-tree) is a cognate form of the verb *shakad—to keep watch.* The name is supposed to have been given to the almond-tree because it blossoms at a time when vegetation is lying in the sleep of winter. (See Jer. i. 11, 12; also, *The Land and the Book*, p. 319.)

before the LORD unto all the children
of Israel: and they looked, and took
every man his rod.
(10) And the LORD said unto Moses,
Bring [a]Aaron's rod again before the
testimony, to be kept for a token
against the [1]rebels; and thou shalt
quite take away their murmurings
from me, that they die not. (11) And
Moses did *so*: as the LORD commanded
him, so did he.
(12) And the children of Israel spake
unto Moses, saying, Behold, we die, we
perish, we all perish. (13) Whosoever
cometh anything near unto the taber-
nacle of the LORD shall die: shall we
be consumed with dying?

CHAPTER XVIII.—(1) And the LORD
said unto Aaron, Thou and thy sons
and thy father's house with thee shall
bear the iniquity of the sanctuary:
and thou and thy sons with thee shall
bear the iniquity of your priesthood.
(2) And thy brethren also of the tribe
of Levi, the tribe of thy father, bring
thou with thee, that they may be joined
unto thee, and minister unto thee: but
thou and thy sons with thee *shall
minister* before the tabernacle of wit-
ness. (3) And they shall keep thy
charge, and the charge of all the
tabernacle: only they shall not come
nigh the vessels of the sanctuary and
the altar, that neither they, nor ye
also, die. (4) And they shall be joined
unto thee, and keep the charge of the
tabernacle of the congregation, for all
the service of the tabernacle: and a
stranger shall not come nigh unto you.
(5) And ye shall keep the charge of the
sanctuary, and the charge of the altar:
that there be no wrath any more upon
the children of Israel. (6) And I, behold,
I have [b]taken your brethren the Levites
from among the children of Israel: to
you *they are* given *as* a gift for the
LORD, to do the service of the taber-
nacle of the congregation. (7) Therefore
thou and thy sons with thee shall keep
your priest's office for every thing of
the altar, and within the vail; and ye
shall serve: I have given your priest's
office *unto you as* a service of gift: and
the stranger that cometh nigh shall be
put to death.

a Heb. 9. 4.

1 Heb., *children of rebellion.*

b ch. 3 45.

---

(10) **Bring Aaron's rod again before the testimony.**—Better, *Put back* (literally, *make to return*) *Aaron's rod* . . . It is not stated here that the rod was put within the ark. Nor is it so stated in Exod. xvi. 33 with regard to the pot of manna. Neither of these was within the ark when it was brought into Solomon's temple (1 Kings viii. 9); but this statement is by no means inconsistent with that contained in Heb. ix. 4, inasmuch as the assertion that there was nothing but the tables of the law in the ark at that time does not prove that there were not other things in it at an earlier period, and may be thought to suggest the inference that such was actually the case. The Jews have a tradition that when King Josiah ordered the ark to be put in the house which King Solomon built, the rod of Aaron and the pot of manna and the anointing oil were hidden with the ark, and that at that time the rod of Aaron had buds and almonds.

(12, 13) **And the children of Israel spake unto Moses . . .**—The special manifestations of Divine power which the Israelites had witnessed excited within them salutary emotions of awe and of anxious apprehension, but do not seem to have awakened within them any corresponding sense of gratitude either for their deliverance from the plague, or for the privileges which they enjoyed by reason of the Divine presence amongst them. The true answer to their inquiry whether they were doomed utterly to perish is contained in the following chapter, in which the priesthood of Christ is typically set forth as bearing the iniquity of the sanctuary, and thus making reconciliation for the sins and securing the acceptance of the imperfect service of His people.

XVIII.

(1) **Shall bear the iniquity of the sanctuary . . .**—It must be remembered that the iniquity of the sanctuary, and the iniquity of the priesthood, extended not only to the defilement of the sanctuary by the transgressions of priests and people (Lev. xvi. 11, 15, 16), but also to its defilement by the imperfections connected with the services of the priests and the offerings of the people (Exod. xxviii. 38).

(2) **That they may be joined unto thee.**—There is an allusion here to the meaning of the name Levi, which was given to Leah's third son. (See Gen. xxix. 34.) The Hebrew verb is the same as that which occurs in the speech of Leah.

And minister unto thee: but thou and thy sons . . .—Or, *and they shall minister unto thee, both unto thee and to thy sons with thee, before the tent of witness.* The service of the Levites was executed before the tent—*i.e.*, in the court; that of the priests was in the holy place, as well as in the court (verse 7).

(4) **And keep the charge . . .**—See chaps. i. 53, iii. 7.

(5, 6) **And ye shall keep the charge of the sanctuary . . .**—See chap. viii. 19.

(7) **And within the vail.**—*i.e.*, the vail which separated the holy place from the most holy. The word which is employed in this place (*parocheth*) is used only of the second vail. (See Lev. xvi. 12.) When the outer vail or *hanging* is designed to be understood, the word used is *masak.* The reference appears to be to the whole of the priestly duties which were discharged by Aaron and his sons, from those con-

(8) And the LORD spake unto Aaron,
Behold, I also have given thee the
charge of mine heave offerings of all
the hallowed things of the children of
Israel; unto thee have I given them by
reason of the anointing, and to thy
sons, by an ordinance for ever. (9) This
shall be thine of the most holy things,
reserved from the fire: every oblation
of their's, every meat offering of their's,
and every sin offering of their's, and
every trespass offering of their's, which
they shall render unto me, *shall be* most
holy for thee and for thy sons. (10) In
the most holy *place* shalt thou eat it;
every male shall eat it: it shall be holy
unto thee. (11) And this *is* thine; the
heave offering of their gift, with all the
wave offerings of the children of Israel:
I have given them unto [a]thee, and to
thy sons and to thy daughters with
thee, by a statute for ever: every one
that is clean in thy house shall eat of
it. (12) All the [1]best of the oil, and all
the best of the wine, and of the wheat,
the firstfruits of them which they shall
offer unto the LORD, them have I given
thee. (13) *And* whatsoever is first ripe
in the land, which they shall bring unto
the LORD, shall be thine; every one
that is clean in thine house shall eat
of it. (14) [b]Every thing devoted in Israel
shall be thine. (15) Every thing that
openeth [c]the matrix in all flesh, which
they bring unto the LORD, *whether it be*
of men or beasts, shall be thine: never-
theless the firstborn of man shalt thou
surely redeem, and the firstling of un-
clean beasts shalt thou redeem. (16) And
those that are to be redeemed from a
month old shalt thou redeem, according
to thine estimation, for the money of
five shekels, after the shekel of the
sanctuary, [d]which *is* twenty gerahs.
(17) But the firstling of a cow, or the
firstling of a sheep, or the firstling of
a goat, thou shalt not redeem; they
are holy: thou shalt sprinkle their
blood upon the altar, and shalt burn
their fat *for* an offering made by fire,
for a sweet savour unto the LORD. (18)
And the flesh of them shall be thine, as
the [e]wave breast and as the right
shoulder are thine. (19) All the heave
offerings of the holy things, which the
children of Israel offer unto the LORD,
have I given thee, and thy sons and thy
daughters with thee, by a statute for
ever: it *is* a covenant of salt for ever
before the LORD unto thee and to thy
seed with thee.

(20) And the LORD spake unto Aaron,
Thou shalt have no inheritance in their
land, neither shalt thou have any part

a Lev. 10. 14.

1 Heb., *fat*

b Lev. 27. 28.

c Ex. 13. 2, & 22. 29; Lev. 27. 26; ch. 3. 13.

d Ex. 30. 13; Lev. 27. 25; ch. 3. 47; Ezek. 45. 12.

e Ex. 29. 26.

---

nected with the altar of burnt offering to those which were performed in the most holy place.

(8) **The charge of mine heave offerings.**—See Lev. vii. 34, and verse 11 of this chapter.

Unto thee have I given them by reason of the anointing.—Better, *unto thee have I given them for an anointing portion.* (See Lev. vii. 35, and Note.)

By an ordinance for ever.—Better, *as an eternal statute.*

(9) **From the fire.**—*i.e.,* from the fire which was kindled upon the altar of burnt offering.

Every oblation of their's, every meat offering of their's . . .—Or, *every oblation of their's for all their meat offerings, and for all their sin offerings, and for all their trespass offerings* (or, *guilt offerings*).

(10) **In the most holy place . . .**—These gifts were to be eaten, as most holy, in the court of the Tabernacle (see Lev. vi. 16, 26, vii. 6), and only by the priests and the male members of their families.

(11) **The heave offering of their gift, with all the wave offerings . . .**—See Lev. vii. 34.

Every one that is clean in thy house shall eat of it.—See Lev. xxii. 10—13.

(12) **All the best . . .**—Hebrew, *all the fat,* as in Gen. xlv. 18.

The firstfruits of them . . .—The quantity is not defined. St. Jerome, in his Commentary on Ezek. xlv., mentions the fortieth part as a liberal contribution, and the sixtieth as a scanty one, according to Jewish tradition.

(14) **Every thing devoted . . .**—See Lev. xxvii. 21—28.

(15) **Every thing that openeth the matrix . . .**—(See Lev. xxvii. 6, 26, 27.) Five shekels was the redemption-price paid for each of the firstborn who were not redeemed by the Levites (chap. iii. 47).

(16) **According to thine estimation.**—See Lev. xviii. 3—7, and Notes.

(18) **And the flesh of them shall be thine . . .**—In Deut. xii. 17, 18, the firstlings of the herd and of the flock are directed to be eaten by the owners in the place which the Lord should choose. Either the law as prescribed in Numbers was subsequently modified, or the second clause of this verse explains and qualifies the preceding clause, and assigns only the wave breast and the right shoulder (or, rather, *leg*) to the priests. (Comp. Lev. x. 14, 15.)

(19) **It is a covenant of salt.**—*i.e.,* an indissoluble covenant. (See Lev. ii. 13, and Note; also 2 Chron. xiii. 5.) Hence the phrases used by the Greeks to denote the breach of a covenant, "Where is the salt?" and "They overstepped the salt." (Comp. Pliny, *H. N.,* xxxi. 41; Cic., *De Div.,* ii. 16; Virgil, *Ecl.,* viii. 82.)

(20) **Thou shalt have no inheritance . . .**—Aaron is addressed in this verse as the representative of the priesthood. He himself did not enter into the land of Canaan.

among them: [a]I *am* thy part and thine
inheritance among the children of
Israel. (21) And, behold, I have given
the children of Levi all the tenth in
Israel for an inheritance, for their
service which they serve, *even* the
service of the tabernacle of the con-
gregation. (22) Neither must the children
of Israel henceforth come nigh the
tabernacle of the congregation, lest
they bear sin, [1]and die. (23) But the
Levites shall do the service of the
tabernacle of the congregation, and
they shall bear their iniquity: *it shall
be* a statute for ever throughout your
generations, that among the children
of Israel they have no inheritance. (24)
But the tithes of the children of Israel,
which they offer *as* an heave offering
unto the LORD, I have given to the
Levites to inherit: therefore I have said
unto them, Among the children of
Israel they shall have no inheritance.
(25) And the LORD spake unto Moses,
saying, (26) Thus speak unto the Levites,
and say unto them, When ye take of
the children of Israel the tithes which
I have given you from them for your
inheritance, then ye shall offer up an
heave offering of it for the LORD, *even*
a tenth *part* of the tithe. (27) And *this*
your heave offering shall be reckoned
unto you, as though *it were* the corn
of the threshingfloor, and as the ful-
ness of the winepress. (28) Thus ye also
shall offer an heave offering unto the
LORD of all your tithes, which ye
receive of the children of Israel; and
ye shall give thereof the LORD's heave
offering to Aaron the priest. (29) Out
of all your gifts ye shall offer every
heave offering of the LORD, of all the
[2]best thereof, *even* the hallowed part
thereof out of it. (30) Thereof thou shalt
say unto them, When ye have heaved
the best thereof from it, then it shall
be counted unto the Levites as the
increase of the threshingfloor, and as
the increase of the winepress. (31) And
ye shall eat it in every place, ye and
your households: for it *is* your reward
for your service in the tabernacle of the
congregation. (32) And ye shall bear no
sin by reason of it, when ye have heaved
from it the best of it: neither shall ye
pollute the holy things of the children
of Israel, lest ye die.

CHAPTER XIX.—(1) And the LORD
spake unto Moses and unto Aaron,
saying, (2) This *is* the ordinance of the
law which the LORD hath commanded,

a Deut. 10. 9. & 18. 2; Josh. 13. 14, 33; Ezek. 44. 28.

1 Heb., *to die.*

2 Heb. *fat.*

I am thy part and thine inheritance . . .—All that are admitted into the number of Christ's royal priesthood have God for their portion and inheritance—in life, in death, and throughout eternity. (Comp. Pss. lxxiii. 26, cxlii. 5.)

(21) **All the tenth in Israel.**—The reference here is to the first tithe, or tenth of the whole of the produce of the land.

(22) **Lest they bear sin and die.**—*i.e.,* lest they bring sin upon themselves, the penalty of which they would have to bear. This appears to be the primary meaning of the phrase, from which the secondary meaning, viz., that of bearing sin in the sense of atoning for it, is derived. (Comp. Lev. xix. 17, xxii. 9.)

(24) **But the tithes . . .**—Better, *for the tithes . . .* This verse assigns the reason why the Levites were to have no inheritance among the children of Israel.

(25) **And the Lord spake unto Moses . . .**—The law respecting the Levitical dues was given to Aaron, and communicated through him to the people. The law respecting the tithe which the Levites were to give to the priests, in which Aaron's family were directly concerned, was communicated to Moses, and by him to the Levites.

(26) **Even a tenth part of the tithe.**—Better, *a tithe of the tithe.*

(27) **And as the fulness of the wine-press.**—The word which is here rendered *fulness* is the same which occurs in Exod. ii. 29, and is there rendered "the first of thy ripe fruits." It is used to denote either the fully ripe grain, or the produce of the vine. The tithe which the Levites paid to the priests was regarded in the same light as if it had been the produce of their own labour.

(30) **As the increase of the threshing-floor.**—As the tithe rendered to the priests was to be regarded in the same light as if it had been the produce of their own labour (verse 27), so what remained after the heave-offerings had been duly set apart was to be reckoned as much the property of the Levites, and to be treated in the same manner, as the corn of the threshing-floor and the wine of the wine-press of the rest of the Israelites.

(31) **And ye shall eat it in every place.**—When the tenth which was due to the priests had been duly paid, the remainder of the tithe received from the people became the rightful portion of the Levites, as their ordinary means of subsistence, and might be eaten by them in every place, not being subject to the restrictions laid upon the priests in regard to the place in which the holy things were to be eaten. (See v. 10.)

(32) **And ye shall bear no sin . . .**—*i.e.,* shall not incur any guilt, or become liable to any punishment. (See Note on verse 22.)

XIX.

(2) **This is the ordinance of the law . . .**—This combination of the two words denoting "law" and "statute or ordinance" is peculiar. It occurs once more in chap. xxxi. 21, and seems to imply the importance of

saying, Speak unto the children of
Israel, that they bring thee a red
heifer without spot, wherein *is* no
blemish, *and* upon which never came
yoke: (3) And ye shall give her unto
Eleazar the priest, that he may bring
her [a]forth without the camp, and *one*
shall slay her before his face: (4) and
Eleazar the priest shall take of her
blood with his finger, and [b]sprinkle
of her blood directly before the taber-
nacle of the congregation seven times:
(5) and *one* shall burn the heifer in his
sight; [c]her skin, and her flesh, and
her blood, with her dung, shall he
burn: (6) and the priest shall take
cedar wood, and hyssop, and scarlet,
and cast *it* into the midst of the burn-
ing of the heifer. (7) Then the priest
shall wash his clothes, and he shall
bathe his flesh in water, and afterward
he shall come into the camp, and the
priest shall be unclean until the even.
(8) And he that burneth her shall wash
his clothes in water, and bathe his
flesh in water, and shall be unclean
until the even. (9) And a man *that is*
clean shall gather up the ashes of the
heifer, and lay *them* up without the
camp in a clean place, and it shall be
kept for the congregation of the
children of Israel for a water of
separation: it *is* a purification for
sin. (10) And he that gathereth the
ashes of the heifer shall wash his
clothes, and be unclean until the even:
and it shall be unto the children of
Israel, and unto the stranger that
sojourneth among them, for a statute
for ever.

(11) He that toucheth the dead body
of any [1]man shall be unclean seven
days. (12) He shall purify himself with
it on the third day, and on the seventh
day he shall be clean: but if he purify
not himself the third day, then the
seventh day he shall not be clean. (13)
Whosoever toucheth the dead body of
any man that is dead, and purifieth not
himself, defileth the tabernacle of the
LORD; and that soul shall be cut off
from Israel: because the water of
separation was not sprinkled upon
him, he shall be unclean; his unclean-
ness *is* yet upon him. (14) This *is* the
law, when a man dieth in a tent: all

a Heb. 13. 11.

b Heb. 9. 13.

c Ex. 29. 14; Lev. 4. 11, 12.

1 Heb., *soul.*

---

the law which was about to be given. The extraordinary mortality which the Israelites had sustained (chap. xvi. 49) may have called for some special rites of purification from the defilement caused by contact with the dead. There is no distinct intimation, however, of the time at which this law was first promulgated, which Ibn Ezra and others suppose to have been previously to the departure from Sinai. The words "which the Lord hath (or had) commanded" are consistent with the fact of the previous existence of the ordinance, though not necessarily suggestive of it. This institution was one which admitted of observance in the wilderness under circumstances in which other requirements of the Levitical law could not be observed.

Without spot.—The word so translated may be taken in connection with that which precedes it, and may denote that the heifer was to be entirely red: or it may, more probably, be taken in connection with the words which follow, and may be understood as defining more precisely the freedom of the animal from every defect. (Comp. Lev. xxii. 19, 20.)

(4) **And Eleazar the priest shall take of her blood . . .**—The appointed rites were to be discharged by Eleazar, not by Aaron, who would otherwise have been temporarily disqualified by legal impurity from the discharge of his high-priestly functions.

Before the tabernacle of the congregation . . .—*i.e.*, opposite to the entrance of the Tabernacle, but, as stated in the preceding verse, outside the camp, because the act had reference to the uncleanness of death.

(6) **And the priest shall take cedar wood, and hyssop, and scarlet.**—According to the Targum of Jonathan, another priest was to do this, but the reference seems to be to Eleazar. Cedar-wood may be regarded as the emblem of fragrance and incorruption; hyssop as the emblem of purification; and scarlet (or crimson) wool or cloth may be regarded as emblematical both of sin, which is compared to it in Isa. i. 18, and also of the blood, which is the life, the shedding of which was needful in order to the remission of sin. All of these were used in the purification of the leper (Lev. xiv. 4). In both cases there appears to be a typical reference to the sprinkling of the blood of Christ. (See. Heb. ix. 13, 14).

(7) **Then the priest . . .**—The Targum of Jonathan refers these words to the priest who killed the heifer, and Ibn Ezra to the priest who burnt it; but the reference is more probably, as in the preceding verse, to Eleazar.

(10) **And it shall be unto the children of Israel, and unto the stranger . . .**—So the promise of the remission of sins through Christ Jesus was not only to the Jews and to their children, but also to all that were afar off. (See Acts ii. 39.)

(11) **He that toucheth the dead body . . .**—The defilement caused by touching the dead body of a beast lasted only until the evening (Lev. xi. 24). The death of man was the wages of sin; and hence contact with the dead body of a man was attended by ceremonial defilement of longer duration.

(12) **He shall purify himself . . .**—The verse may be rendered thus: *He shall purify himself with it on the third day and on the seventh day; so shall he be clean; but if he purify not himself on the third day and on the seventh day,* then *he shall not be clean:* so the LXX. and Vulg. (See verse 19.)

that come into the tent, and all that
is in the tent, shall be unclean seven
days. (15) And every open vessel, which
hath no covering bound upon it, *is*
unclean. (16) And whosoever toucheth
one that is slain with a sword in the
open fields, or a dead body, or a bone
of a man, or a grave, shall be unclean
seven days.

(17) And for an unclean *person* they
shall take of the [1]ashes of the burnt
heifer of purification for sin, and [2]run-
ning water shall be put thereto in a
vessel: (18) and a clean person shall take
hyssop, and dip *it* in the water, and
sprinkle *it* upon the tent, and upon all
the vessels, and upon the persons that
were there, and upon him that touched
a bone, or one slain, or one dead, or a
grave: (19) and the clean *person* shall
sprinkle upon the unclean on the third
day, and on the seventh day: and on
the seventh day he shall purify himself,
and wash his clothes, and bathe himself
in water, and shall be clean at even.
(20) But the man that shall be unclean,
and shall not purify himself, that soul
shall be cut off from among the con-
gregation, because he hath defiled the
sanctuary of the LORD: the water of
separation hath not been sprinkled
upon him; he *is* unclean. (21) And it
shall be a perpetual statute unto them,
that he that sprinkleth the water of
separation shall wash his clothes; and
he that toucheth the water of separa-
tion shall be unclean until even. (22)
And whatsoever the unclean *person*
toucheth shall be unclean; and the
soul that toucheth *it* shall be unclean
until even.

CHAPTER XX.—(1) Then came the
children of Israel, *even* the whole con-
gregation, into the desert of Zin in the
first month: and the people abode in
Kadesh; and Miriam died there, and
was buried there.

(2) And there was no water for the
congregation: and they gathered
themselves together against Moses
and against Aaron. (3) And the people
chode with Moses, and spake, saying,
Would God that we had died [a]when

1 Heb., *dust.*

2 Heb., *living waters shall be given.*

a ch. 11. 33.

---

(17) **Of the ashes of the burnt heifer of purification for sin.**—Better, *of the ashes of the burnt sin-offering;* literally, *of the burning of the sin-offering.*

(19) **He shall purify himself, and wash . . .** —The rendering should be, *he* (*i.e.*, the clean person) *shall purify him* (*i.e.*, the unclean person), and *he* (the unclean person) *shall wash . . .*

XX.

(1) **Then came . . .**—It would be better to translate thus: *And* (or, *Now*) *the children of Israel came* (or, *had come*) . . . , inasmuch as the interval of time between the events related in the preceding chapters and in this chapter is unknown.

In the first month.—It has been commonly supposed that the reference is to the first month of the fortieth year, when the Israelites are thought to have arrived for the second time at Kadesh. Some, however, are of opinion that the journey is the same as that which is mentioned in chap. xii. 16, and in Deut. i. 19; and that the arrival at Kadesh was on the first month of the third year, *i.e.*, the year which followed the departure from Sinai, which departure took place on the twentieth day of the second month, in the second year after the exodus.

And the people abode in Kadesh.—It is evident that the sojourn in Kadesh was a protracted one, whether Kadesh did, or did not serve as the head-quarters of the people from the second or third year of the exodus until that in which they entered into the land of Canaan. See Deut. i. 46, where Moses describes the length of the sojourn in Kadesh by the words "many days," the same words which he employs in Num. xx. 15 to denote the length of the sojourn in the land of Egypt. It cannot, however, be inferred from the simple use of the word which is here rendered *abode* that the sojourn at Kadesh at the beginning of the fortieth year was of long duration (see Judg. xi. 17, where the same word is used). Hence no legitimate conclusion can be drawn from the use of this word respecting the reference of the verse to an arrival at Kadesh at the beginning of the third or of the fortieth year after the exodus. (See xx. 14, and Note).

(2) **And there was no water . . .**—Kadesh may have comprised a considerable portion of the wilderness of Zin, and there may have been a supply of water in some parts of the district and a scarcity in others; or the supply may have proved insufficient for the wants of so great a multitude; or the miraculous supply which was given at Rephidim may have continued, with more or less frequent intermissions, up to the time to which this statement refers, and may have been suddenly withdrawn at this time in order to try the faith of the Israelites.

(3) **Would God that we had died . . .**—The reference seems to be to the plague which broke out after the insurrection of Korah. The language of the murmurers is very similar to that which is recorded in chap. xvi. 14, and the word *gava* (die, or expire), which is twice used in this verse, and which occurs in chap. xvii. 26, 28, in connection with the history of Korah, Dathan, and Abiram, is found only in one other place throughout the last four books of the Pentateuch—viz., Num. xx. 29. The probability that that plague was of comparatively recent occurrence, and not separated from the present murmuring by a period of nearly forty years, has been inferred from the use of the word *brethren* in this verse. The generation which was contemporary with those who perished in the plague which followed the rebellion of Korah is supposed by some to

B. C. 1453.

our brethren died before the LORD!
(4) And [a]why have ye brought up the
congregation of the LORD into this
wilderness, that we and our cattle
should die there? (5) And wherefore
have ye made us to come up out of
Egypt, to bring us in unto this evil
place? it *is* no place of seed, or of
figs, or of vines, or of pomegranates;
neither *is* there any water to drink.
(6) And Moses and Aaron went from
the presence of the assembly unto the
door of the tabernacle of the congre-
gation, and they fell upon their faces:
and the glory of the LORD appeared
unto them. (7) And the LORD spake
unto Moses, saying, (8) Take the rod,
and gather thou the assembly together,
thou, and Aaron thy brother, and speak
ye unto the rock before their eyes; and
it shall give forth his water, and thou
shalt bring forth to them water out of
the rock: so thou shalt give the con-
gregation and their beasts drink.
(9) And Moses took the rod from before
the LORD, as he commanded him. (10)
And Moses and Aaron gathered the
congregation together before the rock,
and he said unto them, Hear now, ye
rebels; must we fetch you water out
of this rock? (11) And Moses lifted up
his hand, and with his rod he smote the
rock twice: and the water came out
abundantly, and the congregation
drank, and their beasts *also*.
(12) And the LORD spake unto Moses
and Aaron, Because ye believed me not,
to sanctify me in the eyes of the
children of Israel, therefore ye shall
not bring this congregation into the
land which I have given them.
(13) [b]This *is* the water of [1]Meribah;

[a] Ex. 17.

[b] Ps. 106. 32, &c.

[1] That is, *Strife*.

---

have been almost extinct at the time to which the events recorded in this chapter are commonly referred, and the word *fathers*, it is alleged, would, in that case, have been more applicable to those who perished than *brethren*. It may be observed, further, that the inquiry, "Wherefore have ye made us to come up out of Egypt?" is more natural when regarded as the language of the generation which had come up out of Egypt as adults, and who looked back to the exodus as to a recent event, than when regarded as that of a generation of which a large number had been born in the wilderness, and the rest had left Egypt nearly forty years previously. These considerations, however, do not appear to be entitled to much weight. The older portion of the congregation, who would naturally be the spokesmen, would speak of those who perished in the insurrection of Korah as their *brethren*, whether the event itself was of recent occurrence or not; and the words which are rendered "Why have ye brought up, &c.?" may, with equal propriety, be rendered "Why did ye bring up, &c.?" (Comp. verse 16 and Note).

(8) **Take the rod.**—It has been supposed by some, from the fact that the rod is represented as being taken "from before the Lord" (verse 9), that the reference is to the rod of Aaron which was kept "before the testimony" (chap. xvii. 10). On the other hand, the natural presumption that the rod was the same as that with which some of the previous miracles in Egypt and those at the Red Sea and at Rephidim had been wrought is confirmed by the facts that the name of Aaron is not mentioned in this verse until after the mention of the rod, and that Moses is said, in verse 11, to have smitten the rock "with his rod."

(10) **Must we fetch you water out of this rock?**—In the case of the former miracle at Rephidim the rock is spoken of only under the Hebrew word *zur* (Exod. xvii. 6). Throughout the present narration the rock is invariably spoken of under the word *sela*. In Ps. lxxviii. 15, 16, where reference appears to be made to both miracles, both words are used.

(12) **And the Lord spake unto Moses and Aaron.**—We read in Ps. cvi. 33 that the Israelites "provoked (literally, *made to rebel*) his spirit, so that he spake unadvisedly with his lips." Whatever was the nature of the sin thus committed, it is clear that Aaron was a participator in it with Moses. Some have thought that the sin of Moses consisted in addressing the people as rebels (or as rebellious ones); but this is the charge repeatedly brought against them in the book of Deuteronomy (see chaps. i. 26, 43, ix. 23, xxxi. 27), under circumstances in which it is impossible to suppose that Moses committed the same sin. It has also been thought that the sin of Moses and Aaron consisted in arrogating to themselves the honour which was due only to God, "Must *we* fetch you water?" but the personal pronoun does not occur in the Hebrew, as it might, and probably would, have occurred, if intended to be emphatic. The more probable explanation appears to be that, notwithstanding the miraculous supply of water which had begun at Rephidim, and which had been subsequently continued, Moses and Aaron distrusted the word and power (verse 12) of God, and that they yielded to the impulse of impatience and anger, as betrayed both by the language which they used and by the double smiting of the rock, to which Moses had been commanded only to speak. To what degree Aaron was concerned in these sins can be inferred only from the facts that he, as well as Moses, was charged with the sin of unbelief, and that the punishment of exclusion from the land of Canaan was inflicted upon both.

(12) **Therefore ye shall not bring this congregation . . .**—In chap. xiv. 30 Caleb and Joshua are mentioned as the only exceptions to the general sentence of exclusion pronounced against the generation which had come out of Egypt, and which consisted of those who were above twenty years of age. It does not appear, however, from that passage whether the sentence pronounced against Moses and Aaron had, or had not, been delivered at that time, inasmuch as they were the speakers on that occasion, and they belonged to the tribe of Levi, which was not included in the numbering to which reference is made in verse 29.

(13) **This is the water of Meribah.**—*i.e.*, of strife. (See Exod. xvii. 7, and Note; also Num. xxvii. 14, where the words "in Kadesh, in the wilderness of

because the children of Israel strove with
the LORD, and he was sanctified in them.
(14) And Moses sent messengers from
Kadesh unto the king of Edom,
Thus saith thy brother Israel, Thou
knowest all the travel that hath [1]be-
fallen us: (15) how our fathers went
down into Egypt, and we have dwelt in
Egypt a long time; and the Egyptians
vexed us, and our fathers: (16) and when
we cried unto the LORD, he heard our
voice, and sent an angel, and hath
brought us forth out of Egypt: and,
behold, we *are* in Kadesh, a city in the
uttermost of thy border: (17) let us pass,
I pray thee, through thy country: we
will not pass through the fields, or
through the vineyards, neither will we
drink *of* the water of the wells: we
will go by the king's *high* way, we will
not turn to the right hand nor to the
left, until we have passed thy borders.
(18) And Edom said unto him, Thou
shalt not pass by me, lest I come out
against thee with the sword. (19) And
the children of Israel said unto him,
We will go by the high way: and if I
and my cattle drink of thy water, then
I will pay for it: I will only, without
doing any thing *else*, go through on my
feet. (20) And he said, Thou shalt not
go through. And Edom came out
against him with much people, and
with a strong hand. (21) Thus Edom
refused to give Israel passage through
his border: wherefore Israel turned
away from him.
(22) And the children of Israel, *even*
the whole congregation, journeyed from
[a]Kadesh, and came unto mount Hor.
(23) And the LORD spake unto Moses
and Aaron in mount Hor, by the coast
of the land of Edom, saying, (24) Aaron
shall be gathered unto his people: for
he shall not enter into the land which
I have given unto the children of Israel,

1 Heb., *found us.*

a ch. 33. 37.

Zin," are added to distinguish the latter from the earlier miracle.) In Deut. xxxii. 51 the waters are spoken of as those of "Meribah of Kadesh."

And he was sanctified in them.—The reference in the words *in them* seems to be either to the word *waters*, which is plural in Hebrew, or, more probably, to the children of Israel, amongst whom Moses and Aaron were included. It has been supposed that the place derived its name of *Kadesh* (or, more fully, Kadesh-Barnea, chap. xxxii. 8) from the cognate verb, which is rendered *sanctify* in this and the preceding verse. It was in Kadesh that the sentence of exclusion had been pronounced upon the people generally (chap. xiv. 22, 23), and upon Moses and Aaron in particular, and it was thus that the Lord sanctified Himself in dealing with the transgressors. If the place derived its name, Kadesh, from these circumstances, it must have been called by that name proleptically in Gen. xiv. 7—a supposition which is entirely consistent with the manner in which the place is mentioned in that verse ("*En-mishpat*, which is Kadesh.")

(14) **And Moses sent messengers from Kadesh . . .**—The date of the occurrence related in this and the following verses is not stated. It might be inferred from Judges xi. 16, 17 that the message to the Kings of Edom and Moab was sent soon after the exodus, and that it was in consequence of their refusal that the sojourn in Kadesh was prolonged: "And (or, So) Israel abode in Kadesh" (Judges xi. 17). The account, however, is too summary to admit of any certain inference in regard to time. No difficulty is involved in the fact that Edom is represented in Gen. xxxvi. as being governed by dukes, or chiefs (*alluphim*), whilst in this place we read of a king. It is possible that the form of government may have been changed, or, as in the case of the rulers of Midian, the same persons who in one place are described as kings may, in another place, be described as dukes, *duces*, or leaders. Comp. Num. xxxi. 8, where the five rulers of Midian are described as *kings*, with Joshua xiii. 21, where the same persons are described as *princes* or *chiefs*.

Thus saith thy brother Israel.—The Edomites, as the descendants of Esau, who received the name of Edom (Gen. xxv. 30), were closely connected with the descendants of Jacob.

(15) **Vexed us.**—Better, *dealt ill with.*

(16) **And sent an angel.**—See Exod. iii. 2, xiv. 19.

And hath brought us forth. — Better, *And brought us forth.*

(17) **We will go by the king's highway.**—It is supposed that this military road led through the broad Wady *el Ghuweir*, which is celebrated for its excellent pasture and its numerous springs. (See Keil *in loc.*)

(19) **I will only, without doing anything else . . .**—Literally, *Only—it is nothing—let me pass through on my feet.*

(22) **And the children of Israel . . .**—Better, *And they journeyed from Kadesh; and the children of Israel, even the whole congregation, came unto Mount Hor.* The insertion of the words "the whole congregation," as in verse 1, probably denotes that the people were broken up and dispersed during a considerable portion of their wilderness life, and that it was only on particular occasions that they were gathered together.

And came unto Mount Hor.—It cannot be inferred from this statement that Mount Hor, near Petra, the modern Hârûn (see Stanley's "Sinai and Palestine," p. 86), was only one day's journey from Kadesh. It is evident from chap. x. 33 that the places of encampment may have been distant from each other several days' journey. The name *Hor* is thought by some to be another form of the Hebrew *har*, a mountain. The same name is given in chap. xxxiv. 7 to a mountain which is supposed by some to be a branch of Lebanon. (See Note *in loc.*)

(24) **Shall be gathered unto his people.**—This expression does not refer to the place of sepulture. (See Gen. xxv. 8, and Note.)

because ye rebelled against my [1]word
at the water of Meribah. (25) [a]Take
Aaron and Eleazar his son, and bring
them up unto mount Hor: (26) And strip
Aaron of his garments, and put them
upon Eleazar his son: and Aaron shall
be gathered *unto his people*, and shall
die there. (27) And Moses did as the
LORD commanded: and they went up
into mount Hor in the sight of all the
congregation. (28) And Moses stripped
Aaron of his garments, and put them
upon Eleazar his son; and [b]Aaron died
there in the top of the mount: and
Moses and Eleazar came down from
the mount. (29) And when all the con-
gregation saw that Aaron was dead,
they mourned for Aaron thirty days,
even all the house of Israel.

CHAPTER XXI.—(1) And *when* [c]king
Arad the Canaanite, which dwelt in the
south, heard tell that Israel came by
the way of the spies; then he fought
against Israel, and took *some* of them
prisoners. (2) And Israel vowed a vow
unto the LORD, and said, If thou wilt
indeed deliver this people into my hand,
then I will utterly destroy their cities.
(3) And the LORD hearkened to the
voice of Israel, and delivered up the
Canaanites; and they utterly destroyed
them and their cities: and he called
the name of the place [2]Hormah.
(4) And they journeyed from mount
Hor by the way of the Red sea,
to compass the land of Edom: and
the soul of the people was much
[3][4]discouraged because of the way.

1 Heb., *mouth*.
a ch. 33. 38; Deut. 32. 50.
b Deut. 10. 6; & 32. 50.
c ch. 33. 40.
2 That is, *Utter destruction*.
3 Or, *grieved*.
4 Heb., *shortened*.

---

(26) **And strip Aaron of his garments.**—Thus the same hands which had invested Aaron with the sacred garments were employed in divesting him of them, and, in both cases, in obedience to the express command of God. The removal of the priestly robes from Aaron may be regarded as typical of the future disannulling of his priesthood when a priest after the order of Melchizedek should arise. "The succession of the priesthood," says Dean Stanley (who refers to Ewald's *Geschichte*, v. 13), "was made through that singular usage, preserved even to the latest days of the Jewish hierarchy, by the transference of the vestments and drapery of the dead High Priest to the living successor." (*Lectures on Jewish History*, i. 182.)

(27) **And they went up into Mount Hor . . .**—Some would render *to the summit of the mountain*, and regard these words as equivalent to those which occur in the following verse, "the top of the mount;" but the same words occur in the fourth verse of the following chapter, where they cannot be thus understood.

In the sight of all the congregation.—The place where the people encamped is called *Moseroth* in chap. xxxiii. 30, and *Mosera* in Deut. x. 6.

(28) **And Aaron died there in the top of the mount.**—The date of Aaron's death, as we learn from chap. xxxiii. 38, was the first day of the fifth month, in the fortieth year after the exodus, and his age a hundred and twenty-three years (verse 39), which accords with the statement contained in Exod. vii. 7, that "Moses was fourscore years old, and Aaron fourscore and three years old, when they spake unto Pharaoh." The difference in the circumstances of the death of the two brothers is remarkable. Both Moses and Aaron were excluded from the land of promise by reason of transgression. Both died upon the top of a mountain. But whilst Moses died in solitary grandeur, and the place of his burial was unknown, Aaron ascended the mount "in the sight of all the people," and died in the presence of Moses and Eleazar. The death of Aaron was an indication of the imperfection of the Levitical priesthood. "They truly were many priests, because they were not suffered to continue by reason of death; but this man because he continueth ever, hath an unchangeable priesthood" (Heb. viii. 23, 24).

XXI.

(1) **And when king Arad . . .**—The verse may be rendered thus: *Now the Canaanite, the King of Arad, which dwelt in the south country* (or, *Negeb*) *heard* (or, *had heard*) *that Israel had come by the way of Atharim* (or, *of the spies*), *and he fought* . . . The date of this occurrence is uncertain. The district of Arad appears to have extended to the southern frontier of Canaan. (Comp. chap. xxxiii. 40; Josh. xii. 14; Judg. i. 16, 17.) The attack probably took place either in the interval between the departure of the messengers to Edom and their return, or at the time at which the Israelites broke up from Kadesh, and before the direction of their march had been ascertained. The word *Atharim*, which is rendered in the Authorised Version *spies*, may be another form of the word which occurs in chap. xiv. 6, and which is there rendered *them that searched*; or, as appears more probable, it may be the name of a place which does not occur elsewhere.

(3) **And they utterly destroyed them and their cities.**—The meaning of the verb which is here employed is to *devote to destruction*, and hence to *destroy utterly*. It does not clearly appear whether this destruction was effected at once, or whether the fulfilment of the vow took place at a later period. (See Josh. xii. 14; Judg. i. 17.) If the attack of the Canaanites was made at the time of the final departure from Kadesh, the latter view must be maintained, as it can scarcely be supposed that the cities could have been rebuilt and again destroyed in so short an interval.

And he called the name of the place Hormah.—Better, *And the name of the place was called Hormah.* The word *Hormah—i.e., a devoted thing*—is cognate with the verb which occurs in this and the preceding verse, and which is rendered *utterly destroy*. The place is so called by anticipation in chap. xiv. 45, and, as in regard to other names (*e.g., Bethel* and *Jacob*), the name was probably given anew to the place on a later occasion (Judg. i. 17).

(4) **Because of the way.**—Better, *in* (or, *on*) *the way*. In addition to all the hardships and dangers of the journey, they were conscious that they were turning their backs upon the land of Canaan, instead of marching by a direct course into it.

(5) And the people spake against God,
and against Moses, Wherefore have ye
brought us up out of Egypt to die in
the wilderness? for *there is* no bread,
neither *is there any* water; and [a]our
soul loatheth this light bread.
(6) And [b]the LORD sent fiery serpents
among the people, and they bit the
people; and much people of Israel died.
(7) Therefore the people came to Moses,
and said, We have sinned, for we have
spoken against the LORD, and against
thee; pray unto the LORD, that he take
away the serpents from us. And Moses
prayed for the people. (8) And the LORD
said unto Moses, Make thee a fiery
serpent, and set it upon a pole: and it
shall come to pass, that every one that
is bitten, when he looketh upon it, shall
live. (9) And [c]Moses made a serpent of
brass, and put it upon a pole, and it
came to pass, that if a serpent had
bitten any man, when he beheld the
serpent of brass, he lived.

(10) And the children of Israel set
forward, and [d]pitched in Oboth.
(11) And they journeyed from Oboth,
and pitched at [1]Ije-abarim, in the
wilderness which *is* before Moab,
toward the sun-rising.
(12) From thence they removed, and
pitched in the valley of Zared.
(13) From thence they removed, and
pitched on the other side of Arnon,
which *is* in the wilderness that cometh
out of the coasts of the Amorites: for
Arnon *is* the border of Moab, between
Moab and the Amorites. (14) Wherefore
it is said in the book of the wars of the
LORD, [2]What he did in the Red sea, and
in the brooks of Arnon, (15) and at the
stream of the brooks that goeth down
to the dwelling of Ar, and [3]lieth upon
the border of Moab.
(16) And from thence *they went* to
Beer: that *is* the well whereof the LORD
spake unto Moses, Gather the people
together, and I will give them water.

a ch. 11. 6.

b Wisd. 16. 1, 5; 1 Cor. 10. 9.

c 2 Kings 18. 4; John 3. 14.

d ch. 33. 43.

1 Or, *Heaps of Abarim.*

2 Or, *Vaheb in Suphah.*

3 Heb., *leaneth.*

---

(5) **This light bread.**—The word rendered *light* denotes something vile or worthless. It was thus that the Israelites regarded the manna which was given to them from heaven; even as the "spiritual meat" which is given to Christ's Church in His word and ordinances is too commonly regarded amongst ourselves.

(6) **And the Lord sent fiery serpents . . .**—Hebrew, *the serpents, the seraphim* (*i.e.,* the burning ones). (See Deut. viii. 15; Isa. xiv. 29, xxx. 6.) The word appears to denote a particular kind of serpent, as in the following verse. Some think that they were so called because of the bright fiery red upon their heads; others because of the blazing sunbeams on their scales; and others because of their inflammatory and poisonous bite. Venomous snakes are said to abound still in the Arabah.

(8) **Make thee a fiery serpent.**—The single Hebrew word which is here employed is *saraph* (a seraph), or *burning one,* as in verse 6, where the word *nehashim*—*serpents*—occurs also. The meaning is explained in the following verse, in which it is said that Moses made "a serpent of brass."

Set it upon a pole.—Better, *a standard.* The LXX. have σημεῖον, the Vulgate *signum.* The Hebrew word (*nes*) is the same which occurs in Exod. xvii. 15, "Jehovah-nissi"—*i.e.,* Jehovah is my standard or banner.

(9) **And Moses made a serpent of brass.**—The old serpent was the cause of death, temporal and spiritual. Christ Jesus, "in the likeness of sinful flesh" (Rom. viii. 3), was made sin for us (2 Cor. v. 21), and thus fulfilled, as He Himself explained to Nicodemus, the type of the brazen serpent (John iii. 14, 15). The meaning of this type, or "sign of salvation," is explained in the Book of Wisdom in these words, "He that turned himself toward it was not saved by the thing that he saw, but by Thee, that art the Saviour of all" (chap. xvi. 7). This serpent was preserved by the Israelites, and taken into Canaan, and was ultimately destroyed by King Hezekiah, after it had become an object of idolatrous worship (2 Kings xviii. 4).

(10) **And pitched in Oboth.**—The intermediate stations between Mount Hor and Oboth were Zalmonah and Punon (chap. xxxiii. 41—43). The former of these places is thought by some to have derived its name from the Hebrew word *zelem* (image, or likeness), and to have been the place at which the likeness of the serpents which bit the Israelites was set up.

(11) **At Ije-abarim.**—This word seems to denote *the heaps* (or, *ruins*) *of passages or of coast or river lands*—*i.e.,* of districts bordering upon the sea or a river. It is called *Iim* or *Iyim* simply in chap. xxxiii. 45.

(13) **On the other side of Arnon.**—Better, *by the side of the Arnon.* (Comp. Deut. ii. 24, 26.) The Hebrew word which is here used does not determine on which side of the Arnon the encampment was. (Comp. chap. xxii. 1, and Note.)

(14, 15) **The book of the wars of the Lord.**—Nothing is known about this book. The last days of Moses, as Baumgarten has observed may have been a suitable time for the commencement of such a work. The history of the journey from Kadesh to the *Arboth Moab* was not written by Moses until after the defeat of the two kings of the Amorites, and the subjugation of the land on the east of the Jordan.

What he did in the Red Sea . . .—The original is very obscure. It is probable that some such verb as *They conquered* (or, *subdued*) is understood, and that the words may be rendered *Vaheb in Suphah and the valleys* (by) *Arnon, and the bed* (or, *ravine*) *of the valleys which inclines towards the dwelling of Ar, and leans upon the border of Moab.* Vaheb was probably the name of a town, and Suphah the district in which that town was situated, so called from its reeds and rushes. Some, however, think that Suphah here denotes a storm or hurricane, as in other places. Ar is supposed to be the same as Areopolis.

(17) Then Israel sang this song, [1]Spring
up, O well; [2]sing ye unto it: (18) the
princes digged the well, the nobles of
the people digged it, by *the direction of*
the lawgiver, with their staves. And
from the wilderness *they went* to
Mattanah:
(19) And from Mattanah to Nahaliel:
and from Nahaliel to Bamoth: (20) And
from Bamoth *in* the valley, that *is* in
the [3]country of Moab, to the top
of [4]Pisgah, which looketh toward
[5]Jeshimon.
(21) And Israel sent messengers unto
Sihon king of the Amorites, saying, (22)
[a]Let me pass through thy land: we will
not turn into the fields, or into the
vineyards; we will not drink *of* the
waters of the well: *but* we will go along
by the king's *high* way, until we be past
thy borders. (23) [b]And Sihon would not
suffer Israel to pass through his border:
but Sihon gathered all his people together,
and went out against Israel
into the wilderness: and he came to
Jahaz, and fought against Israel. (24)
And [c]Israel smote him with the edge
of the sword, and possessed his land
from Arnon unto Jabbok, even unto the
children of Ammon: for the border of
the children of Ammon *was* strong. (25)
And Israel took all these cities: and
Israel dwelt in all the cities of the
Amorites, in Heshbon, and in all the
[6]villages thereof. (26) For Heshbon *was*
the city of Sihon the king of the
Amorites, who had fought against the
former king of Moab, and taken all his
land out of his hand, even unto Arnon.
(27) Wherefore they that speak in proverbs
say, Come into Heshbon, let the
city of Sihon be built and prepared: (28)
for there is a fire gone out of Heshbon,
a flame from the city of Sihon: it hath
consumed Ar of Moab, *and* the lords of
the high places of Arnon. (29) Woe to
thee, Moab! thou art undone, O people
of [d]Chemosh: he hath given his sons
that escaped, and his daughters, into
captivity unto Sihon king of the
Amorites. (30) We have shot at them;
Heshbon is perished even unto Dibon,
and we have laid them waste even unto
Nophah, which *reacheth* unto Medeba.

1 Heb., *Ascend*

2 Or, *answer*

3 Heb., *field.*

4 Or *The hill.*

5 Or, *The wilderness.*

a Deut. 2. 27; Judg. 11. 19.

B. C. 1452.

b Deut. 29. 7.

c Josh. 12. 2; Ps. 135. 11; Amos 2. 9.

6 Heb., *daughters.*

d 1 Kings 11. 7, 33.

---

(18) **By the direction of the lawgiver.**—Better, *with the ruler's staff.* The same word occurs in Gen. xlix. 10, where it stands in parallelism to "the sceptre." (See Note *in loc.*)

And from the wilderness they went to Mattanah.—The Targums interpret this and verses 19 and 20 of the well, *And from the wilderness it was given to them for a gift, and from thence it was given to them in Mattanah, &c.* The Targum of Onkelos is as follows: "And from the time that it was given to them, it descended with them to the rivers, &c." The Targum of Palestine is—"And from the wilderness, &c." (as above).

(20) **And from Bamoth in the valley.**—Better, *and from Bamoth to the valley that is . . .* The *country* (or, rather, *field*) of Moab was a portion of the table-land which stretches from Rabbath Ammân to the Arnon. The valley in this table-land was upon the height of Pisgah—*i.e.*, the northern part of the mountains of Abarim.

Toward Jeshimon.—Or, *across the waste* (or, *desert*).

(24) **For the border of the children of Ammon was strong.**—These words assign the reason why the conquests of the Amorites were arrested, not why the children of Israel did not take possession of the land of the Ammonites, with whom they were forbidden to meddle, and whose land they were not to occupy. (See Deut. ii. 19.)

(25) **And Israel dwelt in all the cities of the Amorites.**—If, as appears most probable, this and the thirty-first verse form a part of the original narrative, the word which is rendered *dwelt* should be rendered *sojourned*, or *abode*, and understood, in accordance with the frequent use of the word (as, *e.g.*, in chap. xxii. 5, 8), of a temporary occupation or encampment. The permanent occupation of the eastern side of the Jordan by the Israelites was subsequent to the death of Moses.

(26) **And taken all his land . . .**—*i.e.*, the land between the Arnon and the Jabbok, as it is explained in the last clause of the verse.

(27—30) **Come into Heshbon.**—These verses appear to commemorate first the victory of the Amorites over the Moabites, and then that of the Israelites over the Amorites. They may be rendered thus:—

> "*Come ye to Heshbon!*
> *Let the city of Sihon be built up and restored!*
> *For a fire went out from Heshbon—*
> *A flame from the city of Sihon:*
> *It devoured Ar (or, the city) of Moab—*
> *The lords of the high places of Arnon.*
>
> *Woe to thee, Moab!*
> *Thou art perished, O people of Chemosh:*
> *He (i.e., Chemosh) gave up his sons as fugitives,*
> *And his daughters into captivity,*
> *Unto Sihon, the King of the Amorites.*
>
> *We cast them down:*
> *Heshbon is perished even unto Dibon:*
> *Yea, we laid them waste even unto Nophah,*
> *Which (reacheth) even unto Medeba.*"

Or, if we read *esh* (fire) instead of *asher* (which), a reading which derives some support from the Masoretic point over the last letter and from the context (verse 28), as well as from the LXX., the last words may be rendered, "With fire, even unto Medeba."

The Targum understands by "the lords of the high places of Arnon" the priests and worshippers in the temples and at the altars of the idols in Moab. Medeba, now Medaba, was situated at the south of Heshbon. The position of Nophah is unknown. It has been

(31) Thus Israel dwelt in the land of
the Amorites. (32) And Moses sent to
spy out Jaazer, and they took the
villages thereof, and drove out the
Amorites that *were* there.
(33) [a] And they turned and went up by
the way of Bashan: and Og the king
of Bashan went out against them, he,
and all his people, to the battle at
Edrei. (34) And the LORD said unto
Moses, Fear him not: for I have
delivered him into thy hand, and all
his people, and his land; and [b] thou
shalt do to him as thou didst unto
Sihon king of the Amorites, which
dwelt at Heshbon. (35) So they smote
him, and his sons, and all his people,
until there was none left him alive:
and they possessed his land.

CHAPTER XXII.—(1) And the
children of Israel set forward, and
pitched in the plains of Moab on this
side Jordan *by* Jericho.

a Deut. 3. 1. & 29. 7.

b Ps. 135. 11.

c Josh. 24. 9.

1 Heb., *eye.*

(2) And Balak the son of Zippor saw
all that Israel had done to the Amorites.
(3) And Moab was sore afraid of the
people, because they *were* many: and
Moab was distressed because of the
children of Israel. (4) And Moab said
unto the elders of Midian, Now shall
this company lick up all *that are* round
about us, as the ox licketh up the grass
of the field. And Balak the son of
Zippor *was* king of the Moabites at
that time. (5) [c] He sent messengers
therefore unto Balaam the son of Beor
to Pethor, which *is* by the river of the
land of the children of his people, to
call him, saying, Behold, there is a
people come out from Egypt: behold,
they cover the [1] face of the earth, and
they abide over against me: (6) come
now therefore, I pray thee, curse me
this people; for they *are* too mighty
for me: peradventure I shall prevail,
that we may smite them, and *that* I may
drive them out of the land: for I wot

---

supposed that it may be the same as Nebo, which is mentioned in connection with Dibon and Medeba in Isa. xv. 2, or with Arneibah, which lies to the east of Medeba.

(31) **Thus Israel dwelt . . .**—Better, *And Israel sojourned,* &c. (See Note on verse 25.)

XXII.

(1) **In the plains of Moab.**—The *Arboth Moab* extended from *Beth Jeshimoth* (the house of wastes) to *Abel Shittim* (the meadow of acacias) (chap. xxxiii. 49), in the upper Arabah, the present *Ghor.* These plains had belonged to Moab, and, since the victory over the Amorites, were possessed by the Israelites.

On this side Jordan.—Better, *alongside of the Jordan.* It cannot be determined, from the use of the word *eber*, or *me-eber*, to which side of the Jordan reference is made. (See chap. xxxii. 19, where *me-eber* occurs twice, and is rendered in the Authorised Version *on yonder side* in the first case, and *on this side* in the second case. See Deut. i. 1, and Note, and Isa. ix. 1, where Galilee is described by Isaiah as "beyond Jordan.")

(3) **And Moab was sore afraid of the people.**—There was no ground for this apprehension, inasmuch as the Divine command given to Moses was "Distress not the Moabites, neither contend with them in battle" (Deut. ii. 9). It does not appear, however, that Balak was aware of the prohibition; and the recent conquests of the Israelites naturally filled the Moabites with alarm, especially inasmuch as when the Israelites sent to the King of Moab to ask permission to pass through his land he did not consent (Judg. xi. 17).

(4) **And Moab said unto the elders of Midian.**—It has been thought that Balak was a Midianite, who had been imposed upon the Moabites as their king by their Amoritish conquerors. (Comp. chap. xxi. 26.) The concluding words of the verse may be understood as denoting a recent change in the dynasty.

As the ox licketh up the grass of the field.—The comparison is one which well accords with the occupation of the Moabites as a pastoral people.

(5) **Balaam the son of Beor.**—The name of Balaam is probably derived from *bala* (to devour), with the terminal syllable *am*, or from the two words *bala* (he devoured), and *am* (people). His father's name (*Beor*), from *baär* (to consume), has been thought to denote that Balaam belonged to a family in which the magical art was hereditary. He is described in Josh. xiii. 22 as "the soothsayer" (Hebrew, *kosem*)—*i.e.*, one of that class of persons who were not to be tolerated amongst the Israelites, and who are spoken of as "an abomination unto the Lord" (Deut. xviii. 10—12). The form *Bosor* (2 Pet. ii. 15) probably arose from a peculiar mode of pronouncing the guttural letter *Ain* in *baar*. (See Keil, *On the Pentateuch*, iii. p. 159, and Note.) On the character and history of Balaam, reference may be made to Bishop Butler (Serm. vii.); Waterland (Works, ix. 397); Keil, *On the Pentateuch, in loc.;* Hengstenberg (*Dissertation on the Histories and Prophecies of Balaam*, p. 747, Clark, 1848); and to the Article in Smith's *Dictionary of the Bible*, by Professor Stanley Leathes.

To Pethor, which is by the river of the land . . .—Better, *To Pethor, which is by the river,* (even to) *the land of the children of his people.* Pethor was in Mesopotamia (chap. xxiii. 7), where Lot, from whom the Moabites were descended, had dwelt (Gen. xii. 5). "The river" is the Euphrates here, as elsewhere. (See, *e.g.*, Gen. xv. 18, xxxi. 21; Exod. xxiii. 31; 2 Chron. ix. 26.)

They cover the face of the earth.—Literally, *the eye of the earth* (or, *the land*). (Comp. Exod. x. 5.)

(6) **Curse me this people.**—Balak undoubtedly believed in the efficacy of Balaam's magical incantations. It is deserving of observation, moreover, that, as has been remarked by Keil (*in loc.*), "it is frequently celebrated as a great favour displayed towards Israel

that he whom thou blessest *is* blessed,
and he whom thou cursest is cursed.
(7) And the elders of Moab and the
elders of Midian departed with the
rewards of divination in their hand;
and they came unto Balaam, and
spake unto him the words of Balak.
(8) And he said unto them, Lodge here
this night, and I will bring you word
again, as the LORD shall speak unto
me: and the princes of Moab abode
with Balaam.

(9) And God came unto Balaam, and
said, What men *are* these with thee?
(10) And Balaam said unto God, Balak
the son of Zippor, king of Moab, hath
sent unto me, *saying*, (11) Behold, *there*
is a people come out of Egypt, which
covereth the face of the earth: come
now, curse me them; peradventure [1]I
shall be able to overcome them, and
drive them out. (12) And God said unto
Balaam, Thou shalt not go with them;
thou shalt not curse the people: for
they *are* blessed.

(13) And Balaam rose up in the morn-
ing, and said unto the princes of Balak,
Get you into your land: for the LORD
refuseth to give me leave to go with
you. (14) And the princes of Moab rose
up, and they went unto Balak, and said,
Balaam refuseth to come with us.

(15) And Balak sent yet again princes,
more, and more honourable than they.
(16) And they came to Balaam, and said
to him, Thus saith Balak the son of
Zippor, [2]Let nothing, I pray thee,
hinder thee from coming unto me:
(17) For I will promote thee unto very
great honour, and I will do whatsoever
thou sayest unto me: come therefore,
I pray thee, curse me this people.
(18) And Balaam answered and said unto
the servants of Balak, [a]If Balak would
give me his house full of silver and gold,
I cannot go beyond the word of the
LORD my God, to do less or more.
(19) Now therefore, I pray you, tarry ye
also here this night, that I may know
what the LORD will say unto me more.

(20) And God came unto Balaam at
night, and said unto him, If the men
come to call thee, rise up, *and* go with
them; but yet the word which I shall
say unto thee, that shalt thou do.

(21) And Balaam rose up in the morn-

1 Heb., *I shall prevail in fighting against him.*

2 Heb., *Be not thou letted from, &c.*

a ch. 24. 13.

---

that the Lord did not hearken to Balaam, but turned the curse into a blessing" (Deut. xxiii. 5; Josh. xxiv. 10; Neh. xiii. 2).

(7) **And the elders of Moab and the elders of Midian.**—The close alliance which existed between the two nations appears throughout the whole of the narrative.

The rewards of divination.—Literally, *the divinations.* Some think the meaning to be *instruments of divination;* but as *besorah* means not only *tidings,* but also the *reward for tidings* (2 Sam. iv. 10), so *kesamim* may mean not only *divinations,* but also the *rewards of divination.*

(8) **Lodge here this night.**—These words indicate the true character of Balaam. As a prophet of the Lord, he must have known that in seeking to curse the Israelites he was sinning against the Lord, who had chosen them for His own people.

As the Lord shall speak unto me.—It appears from this verse, as from verses 18, 19, that the name of Jehovah was known to Balaam.

(9) **What men are these with thee?**—This inquiry, like that addressed to Elijah, "What doest thou here?" (1 Kings xix. 9), or that to Hezekiah, "What said these men? and from whence came they unto thee?" and "What have they seen in thine house?" (Isa. xxxix. 3, 4) was calculated to arouse the slumbering conscience of Balaam, and to open his eyes to a perception of his sin and of his danger.

(11) **A people come out of Egypt . . .**—Better, *the people which came out from Egypt, it covereth . . .*

(14) **Balaam refuseth to come with us.**—It does not appear that Balaam had told the messengers of Balak the ground of the Divine prohibition; viz., "for they are blessed." Balak accordingly entertained the hope that stronger inducements would prevail with Balaam.

(18) **I cannot go beyond the word of the Lord . . .**—These words may have been nothing more than an ostentatious semblance of disinterestedness and superiority to worldly considerations; or it is possible that Balaam may have been conscious that "he spake not of himself," and that, as regards his prophetic utterances, he was but the mouthpiece of the Lord.

(19) **Tarry ye also here this night.**—Balaam knew that God was "not a man, that he should lie; neither the son of man, that he should repent" (chap. xxiii. 19); and yet he indulged the vain expectation that he might be allowed to curse those whom God had declared to be blessed.

(20) **If the men come to call thee.**—The words may be rendered *Since* (or, *forasmuch as*) *the men have come to call thee.* The messengers had already come for that purpose, as it is stated in verse 16, where the same verb is used. The phrase which is here rendered to "call" occurs also in verse 5.

Rise up, and go with them.—There is no real inconsistency with verse 12. The absolute and immutable prohibition had reference to the cursing. The going with the messengers, which was forbidden in mercy at first, was enjoined in judgment at last. God often punishes disobedience to His declared will by permitting the transgressors to "eat the fruit of their own way, and to be filled with their own devices" (Prov. i. 31). "He gave them their request, but sent leanness into their soul" (Ps. cvi. 15). Comp. Ps. lxxxi. 12; Isa. lxvi. 4; Jer. ii. 19.

ing, and saddled his ass, and went with
the princes of Moab. (22) And God's
anger was kindled because he went:
and the angel of the Lord stood in the
way for an adversary against him. Now
he was riding upon his ass, and his two
servants *were* with him. (23) And [a]the
ass saw the angel of the Lord standing
in the way, and his sword drawn in his
hand: and the ass turned aside out of
the way, and went into the field: and
Balaam smote the ass, to turn her into
the way. (24) But the angel of the Lord
stood in a path of the vineyards, a wall
being on this side, and a wall on that
side. (25) And when the ass saw the
angel of the Lord, she thrust herself
unto the wall, and crushed Balaam's
foot against the wall: and he smote her
again. (26) And the angel of the Lord
went further, and stood in a narrow
place, where *was* no way to turn either
to the right hand or to the left. (27) And
when the ass saw the angel of the Lord,
she fell down under Balaam: and
Balaam's anger was kindled, and he
smote the ass with a staff. (28) And the
Lord opened the mouth of the ass, and
she said unto Balaam, What have I
done unto thee, that thou hast smitten
me these three times? (29) And Balaam
said unto the ass, Because thou hast
mocked me: I would there were a sword
in mine hand, for now would I kill thee.
(30) And the ass said unto Balaam, *Am*
not I thine ass, [1]upon which thou hast
ridden [2]ever since *I was* thine unto this
day? was I ever wont to do so unto
thee? And he said, Nay.

(31) Then the Lord opened the eyes of
Balaam, and he saw the angel of the
Lord standing in the way, and his
sword drawn in his hand: and he bowed
down his head, and [3]fell flat on his face.

[a] 2 Pet. 2. 16; Jude 11.

1 Heb., *who hast ridden upon me.*

2 Or, *ever since thou wast, &c.*

3 Or, *bowed him self.*

---

(22) **Because he went.**—Literally, *because he was going.* The participle denotes the continuous act. He deliberately and resolutely proceeded on his journey with the messengers of Balak, in defiance of the warnings which he had received.

Stood in the way.—Better, *placed* (or, *stationed*) *himself in the way.*

(24) **In a path of the vineyards.**—Better, *in the hollow pass of the vineyards.*

A wall.—Or, *a fence.*

(28) **And the Lord opened the mouth of the ass.**—Many critics, who admit the miraculous character of the events recorded in this and the following verses, maintain the subjective character of some of the incidents, and they adduce arguments to show that, whilst the same results might have been brought about in either manner, it is more in accordance with the general analogy of Scripture to assign a subjective than an objective interpretation to the language which is here employed. The following remarks may be made in regard to this interpretation:—(1) Consistency requires that the whole of the narrative should be interpreted either objectively or subjectively; and hence, that if the voice of the ass be interpreted as a subjective impression made upon the mind of Balaam, the appearance of the angel must be understood in the same manner. In this case, however, a difficulty arises which is as great, or greater, than that which the subjective theory is thought to remove. If the appearance of the angel to Balaam was subjective, the appearance must have been subjective also to the ass. In this case, moreover, it may be fairly alleged that if the line which divides the intelligent from the brute creation is transgressed by ascribing articulate speech to the ass, much more is that line transgressed by the supposition that an impression was produced in a subjective manner upon the mind of the ass. But (2) the real question at issue is not whether the recorded results might have been accomplished on the supposition that the incidents are to be explained subjectively, but what is the interpretation which the narrative itself suggests, and which the words of St. Peter (2 Pet. ii. 16) require? In regard to the narrative itself, there is no intimation given that its respective portions are to be differently interpreted; nor is it possible, without doing violence to its obvious meaning, to interpret some parts of it objectively and other parts subjectively; whilst in regard to the testimony of St. Peter, it would be impossible to conceive of a statement couched in terms more directly suggestive of a literal fact than the following—"The dumb ass, speaking with man's voice, forbad the madness of the prophet." In regard to the objections which have been raised to the literal interpretation, grounded on the absence of any expression of surprise on the part of Balaam, and of any allusion to the effect produced upon the Moabitish princes and Balaam's servants, it will suffice to observe (1) that here, as elsewhere, no just inference can be drawn from the silence of Scripture; and (2) that, as in the case of those who were with St. Paul as he went to Damascus, we have no means of determining, on the assumption of the presence of witnesses throughout the miraculous occurrences described, what amount of those occurrences they may have seen and heard. The angel was visible, in the first instance, only to the ass. In like manner the angel may have been visible only to Balaam, not to those who were with him. So also in regard to the voice: it may have been audible only to him to whom it was addressed.

(30) **Ever since I was thine.**—Literally, *ever since thou livedst,—i.e., all thy life long.* The Targums of Jonathan and of Jerusalem paraphrase thus—"upon which thou hast ridden from thy youth unto this day." "An Arabic writer," says Dr. Gill, in his *Commentary*, in loc., "makes mention of an ass that the owner rode on forty years."

Unto this day.—The use of these words in this place serves to throw light upon such passages as Deut. iii. 14, "called them after his own name . . . unto this day," and shows that they do not necessarily denote that the events to which reference is made were separated by any very long interval.

(32) And the angel of the LORD said unto
him, Wherefore hast thou smitten thine
ass these three times? behold, I went
out [1]to withstand thee, because *thy*
way is perverse before me: (33) and the
ass saw me, and turned from me these
three times: unless she had turned from
me, surely now also I had slain thee,
and saved her alive. (34) And Balaam
said unto the angel of the LORD, I have
sinned; for I knew not that thou
stoodest in the way against me: now
therefore, if it [2]displease thee, I will
get me back again. (35) And the angel
of the LORD said unto Balaam, Go with
the men: but only the word that I
shall speak unto thee, that thou shalt
speak. So Balaam went with the
princes of Balak.

(36) And when Balak heard that
Balaam was come, he went out to
meet him unto a city of Moab, which
is in the border of Arnon, which *is* in
the utmost coast. (37) And Balak said
unto Balaam, Did I not earnestly send
unto thee to call thee? wherefore
camest thou not unto me? am I not
able indeed to promote thee to honour?
(38) And Balaam said unto Balak, Lo, I
am come unto thee: have I now any
power at all to say any thing? the word
that God putteth in my mouth, that
shall I speak. (39) And Balaam went with
Balak, and they came unto [3]Kirjath-
huzoth. (40) And Balak offered oxen and
sheep, and sent to Balaam, and to the
princes that *were* with him.

(41) And it came to pass on the
morrow, that Balak took Balaam,
and brought him up into the high
places of Baal, that thence he might
see the utmost *part* of the people.

CHAPTER XXIII.—(1) And Balaam
said unto Balak, Build me here seven
altars, and prepare me here seven oxen
and seven rams. (2) And Balak did as
Balaam had spoken; and Balak and
Balaam offered on *every* altar a bullock
and a ram. (3) And Balaam said unto

1 Heb., *to be an adversary unto thee.*

2 Heb., *be evil in thine eyes.*

3 Or, *A city of streets.*

---

(32) **Because thy way is perverse before me.**—Or, *because the way leads to destruction in my sight.*

(33) **Unless she had turned from me.**—There may be an aposiopesis in this verse. *Perhaps she turned aside from* (or, *before*) *me . . . for* (otherwise) *now I had killed thee, &c.* According to this view the angel does not assign a reason why the ass turned aside, but leaves this to be inferred by Balaam. (Comp. Keil, *in loc.*)

(35) **Go with the men: but only the word that I shall speak unto thee . . .**—The command contained in verse 20 is here repeated, and the unrighteous prophet is punished by being constrained to reap the fruit of his own perversity. It should be observed that here, as elsewhere, the angel who speaks to Balaam identifies himself with Him who sent him: "The word that *I* shall speak unto thee, that thou shalt speak." (Comp. verse 20, where God Himself is represented as delivering to Balaam the same injunction.)

(36) **A city of Moab.**—Better, *the city of Moab.* (Comp. chap. xxi. 15.)

Which is in the utmost coast.—Or, *which flows at the extremity of the border.* Sihon, the Amorite, had taken possession of the Moabitish territory as far as the Arnon.

(40) **And Balak offered . . .**—Better, *and Balak slew* (or, *slaughtered in sacrifice*), *&c.* The word rendered *offered* does not necessarily denote anything more than to *slay.* It is very commonly used, however, to denote slaying in sacrifice; and it is most probable that Balak made a sacrificial feast, and sent portions of the flesh to Balaam and the princes who were with him. Kings not unfrequently acted as priests of old, as, *e.g.*, Melchizedek. (Comp. *Rex Anius, rex idem hominum Phoebique sacerdos,* Aen. iii. 80.)

(41) **Into the high places of Baal.**—Or, *to Bamoth-Baal.* Bamoth-Baal was probably the first height on the way to the steppes of Moab from which the Israelitish camp could be seen. Hengstenberg observes that "Balak started with the supposition that Balaam must necessarily have the Israelites in view if his curse was to take effect."

That thence he might see the utmost part of the people.—Better, *And he saw from thence, &c.* If the Authorised Version of chap. xxiii. 13 is correct, it seems necessary to understand these words as denoting that Balaam had a view from Bamoth-Baal of the whole army of Israel, even to the very extremity, or utmost part of the camp. This verse, however, is more commonly interpreted as denoting that Balaam saw only the extremity of the camp. So the Targum of Palestine: "He saw from thence the camp of Dan, which went at the rear of the people." (See Note on chap. xxiii. 13.)

XXIII.

(1) **Build me here seven altars.**—The patriarchs of old, as their pious descendants after the giving of the Law, never erected more than one altar in one place. A plurality of altars was the badge of idolatry. Hengstenberg adduces several instances in proof that the ancients were accustomed to have recourse to sacrifice and conjuration in order to avert calamity and produce prosperity. (*History of Balaam and his Prophecies,* p. 392.) The number *seven* was regarded as significant among the Greeks and Romans, as well as among the Israelites.

(2) **And Balak and Balaam offered.**—It is more probable that Balak, as a king, performed priestly functions than that Balaam performed them alone. (See Note on chap. xxii. 40.)

(3) **To an high place.**—Rather, *to a bare or barren height.* The heathen augurs were accustomed to choose elevated places for their auspices with an extensive prospect, especially the barren summits of mountains.

Balak, Stand by thy burnt offering,
and I will go: peradventure the LORD
will come to meet me: and whatsoever
he sheweth me I will tell thee. And
[1]he went to an high place. (4) And God
met Balaam: and he said unto him,
I have prepared seven altars, and I
have offered upon *every* altar a bullock
and a ram. (5) And the LORD put a
word in Balaam's mouth, and said,
Return unto Balak, and thus thou
shalt speak. (6) And he returned unto
him, and, lo, he stood by his burnt
sacrifice, he, and all the princes of Moab.
(7) And he took up his parable, and said,

Balak the king of Moab hath brought
me from Aram, out of the mountains
of the east, *saying*, Come, curse me
Jacob, and come, defy Israel. (8) How
shall I curse, whom God hath not
cursed? or how shall I defy, *whom* the
LORD hath not defied? (9) For from the
top of the rocks I see him, and from
the hills I behold him: lo, the people
shall dwell alone, and shall not be
reckoned among the nations. (10) Who
can count the dust of Jacob, and the
number of the fourth *part* of Israel?
Let [2]me die the death of the righteous,
and let my last end be like his!

(11) And Balak said unto Balaam,
What hast thou done unto me? I
took thee to curse mine enemies, and,
behold, thou hast blessed *them* alto-
gether. (12) And he answered and said,
Must I not take heed to speak that
which the LORD hath put in my mouth?
(13) And Balak said unto him, Come,
I pray thee, with me unto another place,
from whence thou mayest see them:
thou shalt see but the utmost part of
them, and shalt not see them all: and
curse me them from thence. (14) And
he brought him into the field of Zophim,

1 Or, *he went solitary.*

2 Heb., *my soul,* or, *my life.*

---

(5) **The Lord put a word in Balaam's mouth.**—"God, who had opened the mouth of the ass," says Bishop Wordsworth, *in loc.*, "in a manner contrary to her nature, now opens Balaam's mouth in a manner contrary to his own will."

(9) **For from the top of the rocks I see him . . .**—From the summit of the rocky mountain on which Balak had erected his seven altars, Balaam, according to one interpretation (see chap. xxii. 41, and Note), had a full view of the outstretched camps of Israel.

Lo, the people shall dwell alone . . .—Better, *Lo, it is a people that dwelleth alone, and that is not numbered, &c.* In the fact that the host of Israel dwelt by itself in a separate encampment, Balaam discerned a type of the essential separation of Israel from the surrounding nations. When Israel adopted the ways of the heathen nations it speedily lost its external independence. Hengstenberg observes upon the last clause of this verse as follows:—"How truly Balaam said that Israel 'did not reckon itself with the heathen' appears from the fact that while all the powerful empires of the ancient world—the Egyptian, Assyrian, Babylonian, and others—have utterly perished, Israel (which even under the Old Covenant was rescued from so many dangers that threatened its entire destruction, particularly in being brought back from exile) flourishes anew in the Church of the New Covenant, and continues also to exist in that part of it which, though at present rejected, is destined to restoration at a future period." (*History of Balaam,* &c., p. 409.)

(10) **Who can count the dust of Jacob?**—These words point back to the promise made to Abraham: "And I will make thy seed as the dust of the earth," &c. (Gen. xiii. 16).

And the number of the fourth part of Israel.—The Israelites were divided into four great encampments (chap. ii). It is probable that Balaam could only see one of these encampments from Bamoth-Baal (chap. xxii. 41); but see below on verse 13.

The death of the righteous.—The Hebrew word *yesharim* (upright, or righteous) is applied to Israel because God, who is just and right (Deut. xxxii. 4), had chosen His people to be a *Jeshurun* (Deut. xxxii. 15, xxxiii. 5, 26)—a holy and peculiar people, following after righteousness and judgment. The end of Balaam (chap. xxxi. 8) presented a strange contrast to his prayer, and showed that even the prayer of the wicked is abomination in the sight of the Lord. (See Prov. xxviii. 9.)

(11) **Thou hast blessed them altogether.**—Hebrew, *Thou hast blessed, to bless:* an emphatic mode of stating that Balaam had continued to give utterance to nothing but blessings.

(13) **Thou shalt see but the utmost part of them . . .**—If this rendering be correct, it strongly confirms that interpretation of chap. xxii. 41 according to which Balaam saw the whole host of Israel from Bamoth-Baal. The words may, however, be rendered thus: *Thou seest* (*i.e.*, here) *but the utmost part of them, and thou dost not see them all.* If the interpretation of chap. xxii. 41 is adopted, which restricts the view from Bamoth-Baal to the extremity of the host of Israel, the meaning of this verse would seem to be that if Balaam could obtain a full view of the entire army he would not only perceive the ground which existed for Balak's alarm, but would be induced to put forth more strenuous efforts to deliver him from so formidable an invasion. On the other hand, if that interpretation of chap. xxii. 41 be adopted, which implies that from Bamoth-Baal Balaam had a view of the whole of the host of Israel from one extremity of their camps to the other, the meaning of this verse would be that although the sight of so vast and orderly a mass produced so powerful an effect upon Balaam that he was unable to utter the curses which he had desired to pronounce upon Israel, such an effect would not be equally likely to be produced if only a portion of the camps was visible at the same time.

(14) **The field of Zophim.**—*i.e.*, of watchers. The spot seems to be identified with that from which Moses afterwards surveyed the promised land (Deut. iii. 27),

to the top of [1]Pisgah, and built seven
altars, and offered a bullock and a ram
on *every* altar. (15) And he said unto
Balak, Stand here by thy burnt offer-
ing, while I meet *the* LORD yonder.
(16) And the LORD met Balaam, and
[a]put a word in his mouth, and said,
Go again unto Balak, and say thus.
(17) And when he came to him, behold,
he stood by his burnt offering, and the
princes of Moab with him. And Balak
said unto him, What hath the LORD
spoken? (18) And he took up his
parable, and said,
Rise up, Balak, and hear; hearken
unto me, thou son of Zippor: (19) God
is not a man, that he should lie; neither
the son of man, that he should repent:
hath he said, and shall he not do *it?* or
hath he spoken, and shall he not make
it good? (20) Behold, I have received
commandment to bless: and he hath
blessed; and I cannot reverse it.
(21) He hath not beheld iniquity in
Jacob, neither hath he seen perverse-
ness in Israel: the LORD his God *is*
with him, and the shout of a king *is*
among them. (22) [b]God brought them
out of Egypt; he hath as it were the
strength of an unicorn. (23) Surely *there*
is no enchantment [2]against Jacob,
neither *is there* any divination against
Israel: according to this time it shall
be said of Jacob and of Israel, What
hath God wrought! (24) Behold, the
people shall rise up as a great lion,
and lift up himself as a young lion:
he shall not lie down until he eat
of the prey, and drink the blood of the
slain.
(25) And Balak said unto Balaam,
Neither curse them at all, nor bless
them at all. (26) But Balaam answered
and said unto Balak, Told not I thee,
saying, All that the LORD speaketh,
that I must do?
(27) And Balak said unto Balaam,
Come, I pray thee, I will bring thee
unto another place; peradventure it
will please God that thou mayest curse
me them from thence. (28) And Balak
brought Balaam unto the top of Peor,
that looketh toward Jeshimon. (29) And
Balaam said unto Balak, Build me here
seven altars, and prepare me here seven
bullocks and seven rams. (30) And Balak

1 Or, *The hill.*
a ch. 22. 35.
b ch. 24. 8.
2 Or, *in.*

---

and which is described in Deut. xxxiv. 1 as "the mountain of Nebo," or Mount Nebo. It is possible, however, that Pisgah may have had more than one of such summits.

(17) **What hath the Lord spoken?**—Balak here speaks of God under the name *Jehovah.*

(19) **Neither the son of man, that he should repent.**—The adoption of these words, with slight variation, by Samuel (1 Sam. xv. 29) affords evidence of his familiarity with this portion of the Pentateuch.

(21) **He hath not beheld iniquity . . .**—The same combination of the words *aven* (iniquity, or injustice) and *amal* (perverseness, or, rather, suffering or grievance) occurs in Hab. i. 3.

The shout of a king.—The word which is rendered shout (*teruah*) is the same which occurs in Lev. xxiii. 24, and which is there rendered *blowing of trumpets.* (Comp. Josh. vi. 5, 20, where the same word is rendered *shout* as here.)

(22) **God brought them out of Egypt.**—Literally, *is bringing them.* The use of the participle denotes the continuance of the action. He who brought them forth out of Egypt was still conducting them on their march. There is an obvious allusion in these words to those of Balak in chap. xxii. 5: "Behold, there is a people come out from Egypt." Seeing that the people did not come out of Egypt in obedience to their own caprice, but under Divine guidance, it was vain for Balak to resist them on their course, seeing that to contend with them was to contend against God.

The strength of an unicorn.—Better, *of a buffalo.* (Comp. Deut. xxxiii. 17—a passage closely resembling the present—from which it appears that the *reem* had more than one horn.)

(23) **Surely there is no enchantment against Jacob . . .**—The verse may be rendered as follows: *For there is no augury in Jacob, and there is no divination in Israel. At the* (*set*) *time it is told to Jacob and to Israel what God hath done* (or, *doth*). The ordinary meaning of the words *nahash* (omen, or augury) and *kesem* (soothsaying, or divination), the use of the same preposition in verse 21 which is there rendered *in,* and more especially the second clause of the verse, seem to decide the meaning of the former clause to be as it is here given. The Israelites had no need of augury and divination, seeing that God revealed to them His acts, His counsel, and His will. "What is here affirmed of Israel," says Hengstenberg, "applies to the Church of all ages, and also to every individual believer. The Church of God knows from His own Word what God does, and what it has to do in consequence. The wisdom of this world resembles augury and divination. The Church of God, which is in possession of His word, has no need of it." (*History of Balaam and his Prophecies,* p. 441).

(24) **As a great lion.**—Better, *as a lioness.* (Comp. Gen. xlix. 9.) Balaam transfers to the whole nation that which Jacob had prophesied of Judah.

(27) **Peradventure it will please God . . .**—Here Balak makes mention of God as *Elohim.* He appears to be satisfied that Balaam was hindered by God from uttering the curses which he desired him to pronounce upon Israel (comp. chap. xxiv. 11). Or the words may have been spoken ironically (comp. chap. xxiv. 11, and Note).

(28) **Unto the top of Peor.**—Mount Peor was one peak of the northern part of the mountains of Abarim. It was nearer than the other heights to the camp of the

did as Balaam had said, and offered a
bullock and a ram on *every* altar.

CHAPTER XXIV.—(1) And when
Balaam saw that it pleased the LORD
to bless Israel, he went not, as at [a]other
times, [1]to seek for enchantments, but
he set his face toward the wilderness.
(2) And Balaam lifted up his eyes, and
he saw Israel abiding *in his tents* accord-
ing to their tribes; and the spirit of
God came upon him. (3) [b]And he took
up his parable, and said,

Balaam the son of Beor hath said,
and the man [2]whose eyes are open hath
said: (4) He hath said, which heard the
words of God, which saw the vision of
the Almighty, falling *into a trance*, but
having his eyes open: (5) How goodly
are thy tents, O Jacob, *and* thy taber-
nacles, O Israel! (6) As the valleys are
they spread forth, as gardens by the
river's side, as the trees of lign aloes
which the LORD hath planted, *and* as
cedar trees beside the waters. (7) He
shall pour the water out of his buckets,
and his seed *shall be* in many waters,
and his king shall be higher than Agag,
and his kingdom shall be exalted.
(8) [c]God brought him forth out of
Egypt; he hath as it were the strength
of an unicorn: he shall eat up the
nations his enemies, and shall break
their bones, and pierce *them* through
with his arrows. (9) [d]He couched, he
lay down as a lion, and as a great lion:

a ch. 23. 3, 15.

1 Heb., *to the meeting of enchantments.*

b ch. 23. 7, 18.

2 Heb., *who had his eyes shut, but now open.*

c ch. 23. 22.

d Gen. 49. 9.

Israelites. It looked toward, or over the face of *Jeshimon, i.e.*, the waste (or, desert). See chap. xxi. 20.

XXIV.

(1) **He set his face toward the wilderness.** —*i.e.*, towards the place where the Israelites were encamped on the steppes of Moab.

(2) **Abiding in his tents . . .**—*i.e.*, encamped according to the order prescribed for the respective tribes. The cognate noun is rendered *tabernacles* in verse 5.

And the spirit of God came upon him.—In regard to the two former utterances, it is said that Jehovah put a word in the mouth of Balaam (chap. xxiii. 5, 15). In the present case the Spirit of God came upon (or, over) him. The same expression is used of the messengers of Saul (1 Sam. xix. 20), and of Saul himself (*Ibid*, ver. 23). The prophecy of Caiaphas (John xi. 15) affords another instance of the sovereign power of the Spirit as displayed through the medium of wicked men.

(3) **Balaam the son of Beor hath said.**—The Hebrew word (*neum*) is imperfectly rendered by *hath said.* It is the word which is commonly used in the prophetical books of Scripture to denote a Divine saying, and is rarely used when a human author is named. It occurs in the Pentateuch only in Gen. xxii. 16, Num. xiv. 28, and in this chapter, where it is found in verses 3, 4, 15, and 16.

The man whose eyes are open.—There is great diversity of opinion respecting the meaning of the word which is here rendered *open*, and which, as it is here written, occurs in no other place. If *shatham* is identified with *satham*, it means to close, not to open. The meaning, however, of this verse is sufficiently explained by that which follows, whichever rendering of the word *shethum* is adopted. Balaam appears to have been thrown into an ecstatic state, as was Saul, and as were many of the ancient prophets; and whilst the eye of the outer senses was closed, the eye of the inner senses was preternaturally opened.

(4) **Falling into a trance, but having his eyes open.**—Better, *falling* (*upon his face*), *and having his eyes opened.* The physical effect produced upon Balaam appears to have been the same as that which was produced upon Saul (1 Sam. xix. 24), upon Ezekiel (chap. i. 28), upon Daniel (chap. viii. 17, 18), and upon St. John (Rev. i. 17). The word which is here rendered "open" (*gelui*) is a different word from that which is so rendered in verse 2, and is frequently used in reference to Divine communications and spiritual intuition. There may be a reference to the events which befel Balaam on his journey (chap. xxii. 31).

(6) **As gardens by the river's side.**—It is probable that the allusion may be to the Euphrates, although the definite article is not prefixed to the word *nahar* (river) in the Hebrew. (Comp. Isa. vii. 20.)

As cedar trees beside the waters.—The difference between cedars which grow beside running water which their roots can reach, and the ordinary type of cedars which throw out their strength in lateral branches is illustrated in Ezek. xxxi. 3, 4, where the proud Assyrian is compared to a cedar having "his top among the thick boughs" (or, the clouds), which "the waters made great." (Comp. Pss. i. 3, xcii. 12.)

(7) **He shall pour the water out of his buckets.**—Better, *Water shall flow from his buckets;* or, *he shall flow with water from his buckets.* The nation is personified as a man carrying two buckets full of water, which was the type and leading source of blessing and prosperity in the East. This is a beautiful image, as Bishop Wordsworth has observed, of the true Israel "pouring out the living waters of salvation, the pure streams of the Spirit, and making the wilderness of the world to rejoice and be glad."

His seed shall be in many waters.—This may mean that Israel should inhabit Canaan—"a land of brooks of water" (Deut. viii. 7, xi. 11); or it may mean that, like seed sown and trees planted by the waters (Isa. xxxii. 20, xliv. 4, lxv. 22, 23), they should inherit the richest blessings.

His king shall be higher than Agag . . .—Agag appears to have been the title (*nomen dignitatis*) of the Amalekite kings, as *Pharaoh* of the Egyptian and *Abimelech* of the Philistine kings. The reference does not seem to be to any particular king, but to the kingdom which should hereafter be established in Israel—to the kings, generally, which should come out of the loins of Abraham (Gen. xvii. 6, xxxv. 11).

(8) **God brought him forth out of Egypt.**—(Comp. chap. xxiii. 22, and Note.)

(9) **He couched, he lay down as a lion, and as a great lion.**—The Hebrew *labi* (great lion) should

who shall stir him up? Blessed *is* he
that blesseth thee, and cursed *is* he that
curseth thee.
(10) And Balak's anger was kindled
against Balaam, and he smote his
hands together: and Balak said unto
Balaam, I called thee to curse mine
enemies, and, behold, thou hast alto-
gether blessed *them* these three times.
(11) Therefore now flee thou to thy place:
I thought to promote thee unto great
honour; but, lo, the LORD hath kept
thee back from honour.
(12) And Balaam said unto Balak,
Spake I not also to thy messengers
which thou sentest unto me, saying,
(13) If Balak would give me his house
full of silver and gold, I cannot go
beyond the commandment of the LORD,
to do *either* good or bad of mine own
mind; *but* what the LORD saith, that
will I speak? (14) And now, behold, I
go unto my people: come *therefore, and*
I will advertise thee what this people
shall do to thy people in the latter days.
(15) And he took up his parable, and said,
Balaam the son of Beor hath said,
and the man whose eyes are open hath
said: (16) He hath said, which heard the
words of God, and knew the knowledge
of the most High, *which* saw the vision
of the Almighty, falling *into a trance*,
but having his eyes open: (17) I shall see
him, but not now: I shall behold him,
but not nigh: there shall come a Star
out of Jacob, and a Sceptre shall rise

---

be rendered "a lioness," as in chap. xxiii. 24. The image of a lion connects this verse with the preceding verse: "he shall eat up the nations." (See Note on chap. xxiii. 24.)

Blessed is he that blesseth thee . . .—Compare the original blessing which was pronounced upon Abraham by the Lord (Gen. xii. 3), and which was afterwards adopted by Isaac in the blessing which he pronounced upon Jacob (Gen. xxvii. 29).

(10) **And he smote his hands together.**—The smiting the hands was a token of strong feeling, whether of scorn, of indignation, or of despair. (Comp. Job xxvii. 23; Lam. ii. 15.)

(11) **The Lord hath kept thee back from honour.**—These words may have been spoken ironically, or Balak may have been convinced of the supernatural influence under which the words of Balaam were uttered. (See chap. xxiii. 27, and Note.)

(13) **I cannot go beyond the commandment of the Lord.**—Hebrew, *the mouth of the Lord:* the same expression which is used in chap. xxii. 18, where the Authorised Version has "*the word* of the Lord."

(14) **I go unto my people.**—Such was, probably, the intention of Balaam when he spoke these words. The account of the death of Balaam, however, shows that he still lingered amongst the Moabites.

I will advertise thee . . .—The word which is here employed generally means to *advise.* The announcement which Balaam made to Balak virtually included advice, inasmuch as it foretold the supremacy of Israel over all their foes, and, consequently, implied the folly of opposition to their progress. It does not appear whether it was or was not at this time that Balaam "taught Balac to cast a stumbling block before the children of Israel, to eat things sacrificed unto idols, and to commit fornication" (Rev. ii. 14). In any case, there does not appear to be any reference to such advice in this verse, although it is inserted in the Targum of Palestine in this place.

In the latter days.—Literally, *in the end of the days.* (See Gen. xlix. 1, where the same expression occurs, and Note.) The prophecy which follows refers exclusively to the future; and it is divided into four parts by the recurrence of the words "He took up his parable" at verses 15, 20, 21, 23.

(16) **Which heard . . . and knew.**—Better, *which heareth . . . and knoweth.*

Which saw.—Better, *he seeth.*

(17) **I shall see him . . .**—Better, *I see him* (or, *it*), *but not now; I behold him* (or, *it*), *but not nigh.* The reference cannot be to Israel, whose armies were encamped before the eyes of Balaam. His words must be understood as having reference to One whom he beheld with the eyes of his mind, not with his bodily sight. This is obvious from the words which follow. Balaam beholds in vision a Star and a Sceptre, not as having already appeared, but as about to appear in the future.

There shall come a Star out of Jacob . . .—Literally, *There hath come forth a Star out of Jacob,* &c. The verb is in the prophetic past or historic tense of prophecy, denoting the certainty of the event predicted. (Comp. Jude, verse 14: "Behold the Lord cometh"—literally, *came.*) If there is any ambiguity in the first symbol it is removed in the second. A star is a fitting image of an illustrious king or ruler, and the mention of the *sceptre* in the words which follow (comp. Gen. xlix. 10) shows that it is so employed in the present instance. The Targum of Onkelos is as follows:—"When the King shall arise out of Jacob, and the Messiah shall be anointed from Israel." The Targum of Palestine reads thus:—"A King is to arise from the house of Jacob, and a Redeemer and Ruler from the house of Israel." Ibn Ezra interprets these words of David, but he says that many interpret them of the Messiah. It seems to have been with reference to this prophecy that the pretender to the title of the Messiah in the days of the Emperor Adrian took the name of *Bar-cochab,* or *Bar-cochba* (the son of a star). The words of the Magi, "We have seen his star in the East" (Matt. ii. 2), appear to have reference to this prophecy.

And shall smite the corners of Moab.—Or, *the two sides of Moab.* The prophecy was partially, or typically, fulfilled in the time of David (2 Sam. viii. 2). Moab and Edom represented symbolically the enemies of Christ and of His Church, and as such will eventually be subdued by the King of kings. (Comp. Ps. lx. 8.)

And destroy all the children of Sheth.—Better, *and destroy* (or, *break down;* comp. Isa. xxii. 5)

out of Israel, and shall [1]smite the corners of Moab, and destroy all the children of Sheth. (18) And Edom shall be a possession, Seir also shall be a possession for his enemies; and Israel shall do valiantly. (19) Out of Jacob shall come he that shall have dominion, and shall destroy him that remaineth of the city.

(20) And when he looked on Amalek, he took up his parable, and said,

Amalek *was* [2]the first of the nations; but his latter end [3]*shall be* that he perish for ever.

(21) And he looked on the Kenites, and took up his parable, and said,

Strong is thy dwellingplace, and thou puttest thy nest in a rock.

1 Or, *smite through the princes of Moab.*

2 Or, *the first of the nations that warred against Israel*, Ex. 17. 8.

3 Or, shall be *even to destruction.*

---

all the sons of tumult. Such appears to be the most probable rendering of these words according to the present Hebrew text. It has been conjectured, however, that the word which is rendered "destroy" (*karkar*) should be read *kodkod* (crown of the head), as in the parallel passage of Jer. xlviii. 45, in which case the clause may be rendered, *And the crown of the head of all the sons of tumult.*

(18) **And Edom shall be a possession, Seir also . . .**—Better, *And Edom shall be a possession, and Seir shall be a possession, for his enemies* (*i.e.*, the enemies of Israel, or, rather, of the Ruler who was to rise out of Israel). The Hebrew word (*oyebaiv*) which is rendered "his enemies" appears to stand in apposition to Edom and Seir, as the word *zaraiv* (his enemies, or adversaries) in verse 8 to "the nations." Edom was the name of the people, Seir of the country. (See Gen. xxxii. 3.) The prophecy received its primary accomplishment in the time of David (2 Sam. viii. 14), but the ultimate accomplishment is to be found in the person and work of Christ (Isa. lxiii. 1—4).

And Israel shall do valiantly.—Or, *shall acquire power or wealth.* (Comp. Deut. viii. 17, 18; Ruth iv. 11.)

(19) **He that shall have dominion.**—The reference is explained in Ps. lxxii. 8, "He shall have dominion also from sea to sea, and from the river unto the ends of the earth," where the same verb occurs which is in both places rendered in the Authorised Version "shall have dominion."

And shall destroy him that remaineth of the city.—Or, *and He shall destroy the remnant from the cities.* The *city*, which is in the singular number here as in Ps. lxxii. 16, may be used collectively to denote cities generally, though some have understood the reference to be to the city of Jerusalem. But the reference seems to be rather to the chief city, or the cities generally, of Edom. (Comp. Obad., verse 18, where the same word occurs which is here rendered "him that remaineth," and which is there rendered "any remaining.")

(20) **And when he looked on Amalek . . .**—From the mountain of Peor, on which Balaam then stood, he had a view of the country of the Amalekites, which lay to the south of the land of Canaan (chap. xiii. 29; Gen. xxxvi. 12).

Amalek was the first of the nations.—The ancestor of the Amalekites was Eliphaz, the son of Esau (Gen. xxxvi. 12). It has been supposed that the Amalekites separated themselves at a very early period from the rest of the Edomites. The word *reshith*, which is here rendered "first," may denote priority in rank, but more frequently denotes priority in time. The corresponding word in the second clause of the verse, *aharith* (latter end), may be thought to denote that the reference is to time, not to rank. On the other hand, the reference in verse 7 to the kings of the Amalekites may be urged in favour of the reference to rank. Some understand the allusion to be to the fact that the Amalekites were the first nation which attacked Israel when they had come out of Egypt (Exod. xvii. 8). It is possible, however, that there may be a reference both to time and to rank. (Comp. Amos vi. 1.)

But his latter end shall be that he perish for ever.—Or, *come to destruction.* More literally, *But his latter end shall be even to one perishing—i.e.*, he shall come to the position of one who is perishing. The destruction of the Amalekites began in the reign of Saul (1 Sam. xiv. 48, xv. 7), was continued by David (1 Sam. xxvii. 8, xxx. 17; 2 Sam. viii. 12), and was completed by Hezekiah (1 Chron. iv. 42, 43).

(21–22) **And he looked on the Kenites . . .**—According to the ordinary interpretation of these verses the continuous destruction of the Kenites is foretold until the Israelites should be taken captive by the Assyrians. The Kenites are included amongst the tribes whose country Abraham's descendants were to possess (Gen. xv. 19). A portion of this tribe, however (for there is no evidence that the Canaanitish and the Midianitish Kenites had a different origin), joined the Israelites, and settled on the southern border of Judah (Judg. i. 16). If the Authorised Version of these verses be adopted, it is reasonable to conclude that the Kenites to whom Balaam's prophecy referred must have been included amongst the enemies of Israel, whose destruction, in common with their other foes, is here predicted. It is obvious that this interpretation is open to two serious objections:—(1) that the natural reference of the words "carry thee away captive" is to the Kenites, not to the Israelites; and (2) that as the later history, as well as the Book of Numbers, makes mention only of those Kenites who allied themselves with the Israelites, we should naturally expect that in accordance with the promise which was given to Hobab by Moses (chap. x. 29), the Kenites should be distinguished from the enemies of Israel, and be exempted from the destruction with which they were threatened. Another rendering of verse 22, and one which appears to be more agreeable to the context in which it stands, is the following:—"For surely the Kenites shall not be destroyed until Asshur shall carry thee into captivity." This version has the support of the Targum of Palestine and other authorities. It is true that there is no express record of the fulfilment of this prophecy, but it is not probable that the Assyrians spared the Kenites who were settled amongst the Israelites; and we know from Jer. xxxv. 11 that after the invasion of Nebuchadnezzar, the Rechabites, who were of the Kenite race (1 Chron. ii. 55), came to Jerusalem for fear of the armies of the Chaldeans and Syrians. If *Asshur* denotes in this place *the Assyrians* in the later acceptation of the term, it must be remembered that one branch of the Kenites settled in Naphtali, near Kadesh (Judg. iv. 11). *Asshur*, however, appears to be used in a wider sense,

(22) Nevertheless [1]the Kenite shall be
wasted, [2]until Asshur shall carry thee
away captive.
(23) And he took up his parable, and
said,
Alas, who shall live when God doeth
this! (24) And ships *shall come* from the
coast of Chittim, and shall afflict
Asshur, and shall afflict Eber, and he
also shall perish for ever.
(25) And Balaam rose up, and went
and returned to his place: and Balak
also went his way.

CHAPTER XXV.—(1) And Israel
abode in [a]Shittim, and the people began
to commit whoredom with the daughters
of Moab. (2) And they called the people
unto the sacrifices of their gods: and
the people did eat, and bowed down to
their gods. (3) And Israel joined him-
self unto Baal-peor: and the anger of
the LORD was kindled against Israel.
(4) And the LORD said unto Moses, [b]Take
all the heads of the people, and hang
them up before the LORD against the
sun, that the fierce anger of the LORD
may be turned away from Israel. (5) And
Moses said unto the judges of Israel,
Slay ye every one his men that were
joined unto Baal-peor.
(6) And, behold, one of the children of
Israel came and brought unto his
brethren a Midianitish woman in the
sight of Moses, and in the sight of all
the congregation of the children of
Israel, who *were* weeping *before* the door
of the tabernacle of the congregation.
(7) And [c]when Phinehas, the son of
Eleazar, the son of Aaron the priest,
saw *it*, he rose up from among the con-
gregation, and took a javelin in his

1 Heb., *Kain.*

2 Or, *how long shall it be ere Asshur carry thee away captive?*

a ch. 33. 49.

b Deut. 4. 3; Josh. 22. 17.

c Ps. 106. 30; 1 Mac. 2. 54.

---

so as to include all the nations which proceeded from it (see verse 24). Even the Persian king is called, as Keil has observed, King of Asshur (Ezra vi. 22). If this interpretation of the text be received, the antithesis between the doom of the Amalekites and the deliverance of the Kenites exactly corresponds to the attitude assumed by those tribes respectively in regard to Israel.

(23) **When God doeth this.**—These words may be rendered, *since* (or, *from the time that*) *God sets* (or, *determines*) *it* (or, *this*)—*quando faciet ista Deus* (Vulgate); or, *because God determines it* (or, *this*).

(24) **And ships shall come from the coast of Chittim.**—The *Chittim* (or, *Kittim*) are said to have migrated from Phœnicia to Cyprus, and there founded the city of Citium, the modern *Chitti.* (See Josephus, "Antiq." i. 6, 1.) The name probably applies to the islands and coasts of the Mediterranean generally. The rendering of the Vulgate is *Venient in trieribus de Italiâ;* and in Dan. xi. 30, which is obviously founded upon this verse, the Vulgate identifies the *Kittim* with the *Romans.*

And shall afflict Asshur, and shall afflict Eber.—Some understand by *Eber* the *Hebrews* only. The word, however, appears to be used in a wider signification, as comprising "all the children of Eber" (Gen. x. 21). Perhaps the word *Asshur* may here be used to denote the *Eastern Shemites*, and *Eber* the *Western Shemites.*

And he also shall perish for ever—*i.e.*, the victorious power which was to afflict Asshur and Eber. "The overthrow of this last power of the world," says Keil, *in loc.*, "concerning which the prophet Daniel was the first to receive and proclaim new revelations, belongs to 'the end of the days,' in which the star out of Jacob is to rise upon Israel as 'a bright morning-star'" (Rev. xxii. 16). There is no evidence as to the manner in which Balaam's prophecies came into the hands of the Israelites. It is possible that he may have communicated them to Moses, in the expectation of receiving from him the reward which he had failed to obtain from Balak, or, if captured, in the hope of thereby saving his life.

(25) **And returned to his place.**—Balaam probably set out with the intention of returning home. He turned *towards* his place. The sequel shows that he remained amongst the Midianites, and perished with them.

XXV.

(1) **Abode in Shittim**—*i.e., Abel-Shittim* (chap. xxxiii. 49). (See Note on chap. xxii. 1.)

(2) **And they called the people . . .**—The Moabitish women invited the Israelites to their sacrificial feasts, which were celebrated in honour of Baal-peor, who was worshipped in the city of Beth-peor (Deut. iii. 29). He is supposed to be identical with *Chemosh*, the Moabitish god of war.

(4) **Take all the heads of the people.**—The "heads" or "chiefs" of the people seem to be identical with the "judges" of the following verse. Some understand by "all the heads" those only who had been the chief offenders, whilst others understand the word "take" as equivalent to "assemble," or "bring before thee," and refer the word "them" to the offenders.

Hang them up . . .—It is obvious from verse 5 that the punishment of impaling or crucifying was not to be inflicted until after death. The LXX. renders the Hebrew verb which is here used (and which is found also in 2 Sam. xxi. 6, 9) by the same word which occurs in Heb. vi. 6, and is there translated "to put to an open shame."

(7) **And when Phinehas, the son of Eleazar, the son of Aaron the priest . . .**—In accordance with this punctuation, the designation *the priest* (which generally denotes the high priest) refers to Aaron, not to Phinehas. Eleazar was the high priest at this time (chap. xx. 26); and consequently—although as a general rule any designation which follows the words "the son of such an one" refers to the former, not to the latter noun—it appears most probable that the designation *the priest* has reference here to Aaron, not to Phinehas, who, although a priest, was not the high priest at this time. He was invested, however, with civil as well as ecclesiastical authority.

hand; (8) and he went after the man of
Israel into the tent, and thrust both of
them through, the man of Israel, and
the woman through her belly.

So the plague was stayed from the
children of Israel. (9) And [a] those that
died in the plague were twenty and
four thousand.

(10) And the LORD spake unto Moses,
saying, (11) [b] Phinehas, the son of Eleazar,
the son of Aaron the priest, hath turned
my wrath away from the children of
Israel, while he was zealous for my sake
among them, that I consumed not the
children of Israel in my jealousy.
(12) Wherefore say, [c] Behold, I give unto
him my covenant of peace: (13) and he
shall have it, and his seed after him,
even the covenant of an everlasting
priesthood; because he was zealous for
his God, and made an atonement for
the children of Israel.

(14) Now the name of the Israelite that
was slain, *even* that was slain with the
Midianitish woman, *was* Zimri, the son
of Salu, a prince of a [1] chief house among
the Simeonites. (15) And the name of
the Midianitish woman that was slain
was Cozbi, the daughter of Zur; he *was*
head over a people, *and* of a chief house
in Midian.

(16) And the LORD spake unto Moses,
saying, (17) [d] vex the Midianites, and
smite them: (18) for they vex you with
their wiles, wherewith they have be-
guiled you in the matter of Peor, and
in the matter of Cozbi, the daughter of
a prince of Midian, their sister, which
was slain in the day of the plague for
Peor's sake.

a 1 Cor. 10. 8.

b Ps. 106. 30.

c Ecclus. 45. 24; 1 Mac. 2. 54.

1 Heb., *house of a father.*

d ch. 31. 2.

(See 1 Chron. ix. 20, where he is described as *a ruler*—Hebrew, *nagid.*)

(8) **Into the tent.**—The word *kubbah* (tent, or alcove) occurs only in this place. The reference may be to the inner part of the ordinary tent which was occupied by the women; or it may denote an arched or vaulted tent (probably of skins), which the Israelites had erected whilst joining with the Moabites and Midianites in the lascivious worship of Baal-peor. The LXX. has *kaminos,* the Vulgate *lupanar.*

Through her belly.—Or, *within her tent.* It is thought by some that the word which is here used was originally the same word which occurs in the earlier part of the verse, and which is there rendered *tent.*

So the plague was stayed . . .—It is probable that the judges were not duly obedient to the command of Moses, and, consequently, that a plague broke out from the Lord upon the people.

(9) **Twenty and four thousand.**—In 1 Cor. x. 8 the number of those who "fell in one day" is said to have been "three and twenty thousand." It has been supposed that a thousand were put to death by the judges, and that these were not included in St. Paul's enumeration. Presuming, however, that there has been no error in either place on the part of the scribes in recording the numbers, the words "in one day" may account for the apparent discrepancy.

(11) **Phinehas, the son of Eleazar, the son of Aaron the priest . . .**—The description of Phinehas, as in verse 7, is repeated in full, as if to denote that he was not a private individual, but one invested with public authority.

While he was zealous for my sake among them.—Better, *in that he was jealous with my jealousy* (or, *in that he displayed my jealousy*).

(12) **My covenant of peace.**—Phinehas, as one who was zealous for the honour of God and of the house of the Lord, was a fitting type of Christ, in whom the prediction of the Psalmist received its accomplishment, "The zeal of thine house hath eaten me up" (Ps. lxix. 9; John ii. 17). The covenant of grace is described in Isa. liv. 10 and in Mal. ii. 5 as the covenant of peace.

(13) **And he shall have it, and his seed after him.**—The covenant of peace, which was made by the blood of the Cross, and all the blessings which belong to that covenant, stand fast with Christ, and are secured to His spiritual seed. (Comp. Ps. lxxxix. 28, 29.)

Even the covenant of an everlasting priesthood.—Phinehas succeeded his father Eleazar as high priest (Judg. xx. 28). After a temporary interruption in the succession, which existed in the time of Eli, and continued until the time of David, when there appears to have been a joint high-priesthood, the office was restored by Solomon to Zadok, the descendant of Phinehas, and so continued until the gradual dissolution of the Jewish state. Christ's priesthood is "an unchangeable priesthood" (Heb. vii. 24): "Thou art a priest for ever after the order of Melchisedec" (Heb. vii. 17).

(14) **A prince of a chief house among the Simeonites.**—Better, *of a father's house,* &c. It is probable that the tribe of Simeon was deeply implicated in the transgression, and that those who belonged to that tribe were the chief sufferers in the plague. (See chap. xxvi. 14, and Note.)

(15) **Head over a people, and of a chief house in Midian.**—Better, *head of the tribes* (or, *communities*) *of a father's house in Midian.* Several of the Midianitish tribes, or smaller divisions of a father's house, may have descended from one tribe-father. In chap. xxxi. 8, Zur is described as one of the five kings of Midian who were slain by the Israelites.

(17) **Vex the Midianites, and smite them.**—The Midianites appear to have been joint actors with the Moabites throughout the whole of the opposition which was offered to Israel, and the chief actors in the wiles by which the Israelites were seduced. As the descendants of Abraham, the father of the faithful, the Midianites ought to have feared and obeyed Abraham's God, and to have shown brotherly kindness to His people, who were their own kindred. The special judgments of God are directed against the sins of apostacy and of seduction. (Comp. Rev. ii. 14, xviii. 6.) Although the Moabites were not to be smitten with the Midianites (see Deut. ii. 9), nevertheless they did not escape punishment, but were shut out, even to

CHAPTER XXVI.—(1) And it came
to pass after the plague, that the Lord
spake unto Moses and unto Eleazar the
son of Aaron the priest, saying, (2) Take
the sum of all the congregation of the
children of Israel, [a] from twenty years [a] ch. 1. 3.
old and upward, throughout their
fathers' house, all that are able to go
to war in Israel. (3) And Moses and
Eleazar the priest spake with them in
the plains of Moab by Jordan *near* [b] ch. 1. 1.
Jericho, saying, (4) *Take the sum of the*
people, from twenty years old and up-
ward; as the Lord [b] commanded Moses
and the children of Israel, which went
forth out of the land of Egypt.
(5) [c] Reuben, the eldest son of Israel: [c] Gen. 46. 8; Ex. 6. 14; 1 Chr. 5. 1.
the children of Reuben; Hanoch, *of*
whom cometh the family of the Hano-
chites: of Pallu, the family of the
Palluites: (6) of Hezron, the family of
the Hezronites: of Carmi, the family of
the Carmites. (7) These *are* the families [d] ch. 16. 2.
of the Reubenites: and they that were
numbered of them were forty and three
thousand and seven hundred and thirty.
(8) And the sons of Pallu; Eliab. (9) And
the sons of Eliab; Nemuel, and Dathan,
and Abiram. This *is that* Dathan and
Abiram, *which were* famous in the con-
gregation, who [d] strove against Moses
and against Aaron in the company of
Korah, when they strove against the
Lord: (10) and the earth opened her
mouth, and swallowed them up together
with Korah, when that company died,
what time the fire devoured two hundred
and fifty men: and they became a sign.
(11) Notwithstanding the children of
Korah died not.
(12) The sons of Simeon after their
families: of Nemuel, the family of the
Nemuelites: of Jamin, the family of the
Jaminites: of Jachin, the family of the
Jachinites: (13) of Zerah, the family of
the Zarhites: of Shaul, the family of
the Shaulites. (14) These *are* the families
of the Simeonites, twenty and two
thousand and two hundred.
(15) The children of Gad after their
families: of Zephon, the family of the
Zephonites: of Haggi, the family of the
Haggites: of Shuni, the family of the
Shunites: (16) of Ozni, the family of the

---

the tenth generation, from the congregation of the Lord. (See Deut. xxiii. 3, 4.) Their exemption at this time from the judgment executed upon the Midianites was probably due, not to their descent from Lot (for the Midianites were descended from Abraham), but to the fact that the measure of their sin was not yet full. (Comp. Gen. xv. 16.)

XXVI.

(1) **And it came to pass after the plague . . .**—The plague probably destroyed the remnant of the generation which had come out of Egypt, and which had been numbered in the wilderness of Sinai.

(2) **Take the sum . . .**—The same command had been given to Moses and Aaron (chap. i. 2, 3). In that case a man taken out of every tribe, the head of his father's house, was appointed to assist Moses and Aaron in taking the census. It is probable that the same arrangement was made in the present instance, though it is not recorded.

(4, 5) **Take the sum of the people . . .**—The verses may be rendered thus: *From twenty years old and upward, as the Lord commanded Moses. And the children of Israel which went forth out of the land of Egypt* were these: *Reuben, the eldest son of Israel*, &c. The expression "as the Lord commanded Moses" is one of very frequent occurrence in this book. The command was given to Moses, not to the children of Israel generally. The form of enumeration is concise. The omissions may be supplied thus:—Reuben—he was the eldest son of Israel. The sons of Reuben were—Hanoch—of him, the family of the Hanochites, &c. (Comp. Gen. xlvi. 9; Exod. vi. 14; 1 Chron. v. 3.)

(7) **Forty and three thousand and seven hundred and thirty.**—As compared with the former census, the tribe of Reuben had decreased by 2,770. (See chap. i. 21.) Dathan and Abiram had probably enlisted many of the tribe to which they belonged in their rebellion against Moses and Aaron. (See verses 9, 10 of this chapter, and chap. xvi. 1, and Note.)

(10) **And the earth opened her mouth, and swallowed them up together with Korah . . .**—Hebrew, *and Korah.* It would appear from this verse that Korah perished in the earthquake with Dathan and Abiram. The Samaritan Pentateuch, however, has a different reading here. It transposes the words "and Korah," and combines them with the words "and the two hundred and fifty men": thus—"when the fire devoured Korah and the two hundred and fifty men." (See Notes on chap. xvi. 32, 35.) It is possible that there may have been an omission here of the words which are found in chap. xvi. 32, "all the men that appertained unto," or of words denoting "all the goods belonging to."

(11) **Notwithstanding the children of Korah died not.**—See Notes on chap. xvi. 27, 32.

(14) **Twenty and two thousand and two hundred.**—This shows a decrease of 37,100 in the tribe of Simeon. Zimri, the chief offender in the matter of Baal-peor, belonged to this tribe, and, as in the case of the Reubenites, it is probable that he had led astray many of his tribe with him. It is remarkable that this is the only tribe on which, according to the present Hebrew text,* no blessing was pronounced by Moses (Deut. xxxiii.), and that in the allotment of the land of Canaan the inheritance of Simeon was only

* The "Codex Alexandrinus" inserts a clause: "Let Simeon be many in number."

Oznites: of Eri, the family of the Erites:
(17) of Arod, the family of the Arodites:
of Areli, the family of the Arelites.
(18) These *are* the families of the children
of Gad according to those that were
numbered of them, forty thousand and
five hundred.

(19) [a]The sons of Judah *were* Er and
Onan: and Er and Onan died in the
land of Canaan. (20) And the sons of
Judah after their families were; of
Shelah, the family of the Shelanites:
of Pharez, the family of the Pharzites:
of Zerah, the family of the Zarhites.
(21) And the sons of Pharez were; of
Hezron, the family of the Hezronites:
of Hamul, the family of the Hamulites.
(22) These *are* the families of Judah ac-
cording to those that were numbered of
them, threescore and sixteen thousand
and five hundred.

(23) *Of* the sons of Issachar after their
families: *of* Tola, the family of the
Tolaites: of Pua, the family of the Pun-
ites: (24) of Jashub, the family of the
Jashubites: of Shimron, the family of
the Shimronites. (25) These *are* the
families of Issachar according to those
that were numbered of them, threescore
and four thousand and three hundred.

(26) *Of* the sons of Zebulun after their
families: of Sered, the family of the
Sardites: of Elon, the family of the
Elonites: of Jahleel, the family of the
Jahleelites. (27) These *are* the families
of the Zebulunites according to those
that were numbered of them, threescore
thousand and five hundred.

(28) The sons of Joseph after their
families *were* Manasseh and Ephraim.
(29) Of the sons of Manasseh: of [b]Machir,
the family of the Machirites: and
Machir begat Gilead: of Gilead *come*
the family of the Gileadites. (30) These
are the sons of Gilead: *of* Jeezer, the
family of the Jeezerites: of Helek, the
family of the Helekites: (31) and *of* Asriel,
the family of the Asrielites: and *of*
Shechem, the family of the Shechemites:
(32) and *of* Shemida, the family of the
Shemidaites: and *of* Hepher, the family
of the Hepherites. (33) And [c]Zelophehad
the son of Hepher had no sons, but
daughters: and the names of the
daughters of Zelophehad *were* Mahlah,
and Noah, Hoglah, Milcah, and Tirzah.
(34) These *are* the families of Manasseh,
and those that were numbered of them,
fifty and two thousand and seven hun-
dred.

(35) These *are* the sons of Ephraim
after their families: of Shuthelah, the
family of the Shuthalhites: of Becher,
the family of the Bachrites: of Tahan,
the family of the Tahanites. (36) And
these *are* the sons of Shuthelah: of Eran,
the family of the Eranites. (37) These
are the families of the sons of Ephraim
according to those that were numbered
of them, thirty and two thousand and
five hundred. These *are* the sons of
Joseph after their families.

(38) The sons of Benjamin after their
families: of Bela, the family of the
Belaites: of Ashbel, the family of the
Ashbelites: of Ahiram, the family of the
Ahiramites: (39) of Shupham, the family
of the Shuphamites: of Hupham, the
family of the Huphamites. (40) And the
sons of Bela were Ard and Naaman: *of*
Ard, the family of the Ardites: *and* of
Naaman, the family of the Naamites.
(41) These *are* the sons of Benjamin after
their families: and they that were

a Gen. 38. 2, &c.; & 46. 12.
b Josh. 17. 1.
c ch. 27. 1.

---

the remnant of that which was assigned to Judah (Josh. xix. 9).

(18) **Forty thousand and five hundred.**—This shows a decrease of 5,150. Reuben, Simeon, and Gad encamped together on the south of the Tabernacle (chap. ii. 10), and had probably been mutually contaminated by each other's evil example.

(19) **Er and Onan died in the land of Canaan.**—See Gen. xxxviii. 6—10, and Note.

(21) **Of Hezron . . .**—Judah had five sons, but inasmuch as Er and Onan died childless, Hezron and Hamul were substituted in their place. (Comp. Gen. xlvi. 12.)

(29) **Machir begat Gilead.**—It is stated in 1 Chron. vii. 14, and in the LXX. of Gen. xlvi. 20, that Machir's mother was an Aramitess. This may account for the name which was given to his son, *Gilead*, the border land between Syria and Canaan, and that in which Laban overtook Jacob (Gen. xxxi. 25).

(37) **Thirty and two thousand and five hundred.**—This shows a decrease of 8,000. Jacob foretold that Ephraim should be greater than Manasseh (Gen. xlviii. 19); and at the former census the number of the Ephraimites was considerably greater than that of the Manassites (chap. i. 33, 35), and Ephraim was made a standard-bearer (chap. ii. 18). At the present census, however, the number of the Manassites exceeded that of the Ephraimites by 20,200; and yet, in the face of the great increase of Manasseh and the diminution of Ephraim, Moses renewed and confirmed the prediction of Jacob as to the ultimate superiority of Ephraim, and whilst ascribing only "thousands" to Manasseh, he speaks of the "ten thousands of Ephraim" (Deut. xxxiii. 17).

numbered of them *were* forty and five
thousand and six hundred.
(42) These *are* the sons of Dan after
their families: of Shuham, the family
of the Shuhamites. These *are* the fami-
lies of Dan after their families. (43) All
the families of the Shuhamites, accord-
ing to those that were numbered of
them, *were* threescore and four thousand
and four hundred.
(44) *Of* the children of Asher after their
families: of Jimna, the family of the
Jimnites: of Jesui, the family of the
Jesuites: of Beriah, the family of the
Beriites. (45) Of the sons of Beriah: of
Heber, the family of the Heberites: of
Malchiel, the family of the Malchielites.
(46) And the name of the daughter of
Asher *was* Sarah. (47) These *are* the
families of the sons of Asher according
to those that were numbered of them;
who were fifty and three thousand and
four hundred.
(48) *Of* the sons of Naphtali after their
families: of Jahzeel, the family of the
Jahzeelites: of Guni, the family of the
Gunites: (49) of Jezer, the family of the
Jezerites: of Shillem, the family of the
Shillemites. (50) These *are* the families
of Naphtali according to their families:
and they that were numbered of them
were forty and five thousand and four
hundred.
(51) These *were* the numbered of the
children of Israel, six hundred thousand
and a thousand seven hundred and
thirty.
(52) And the LORD spake unto Moses,
saying, (53) Unto these the land shall
be divided for an inheritance accord-
ing to the number of names. (54) [a]To
many thou shalt [1]give the more inheri-
tance, and to few thou shalt [2]give the
less inheritance: to every one shall his
inheritance be given according to those
that were numbered of him. (55) Not-
withstanding the land shall be [b] divided
by lot: according to the names of the
tribes of their fathers they shall inherit.
(56) According to the lot shall the posses-
sion thereof be divided between many
and few.
(57) [c]And these *are* they that were num-
bered of the Levites after their families:
of Gershon, the family of the Gershon-
ites: of Kohath, the family of the
Kohathites: of Merari, the family of the
Merarites. (58) These *are* the families of
the Levites: the family of the Libnites,
the family of the Hebronites, the family
of the Mahlites, the family of the Mush-
ites, the family of the Korathites. And
Kohath begat Amram. (59) And the
name of Amram's wife *was* [d] Jochebed,
the daughter of Levi, whom *her mother*
bare to Levi in Egypt: and she bare
unto Amram Aaron and Moses, and
Miriam their sister. (60) And unto Aaron
was born Nadab, and Abihu, Eleazar, and
Ithamar. (61) And [e] Nadab and Abihu
died, when they offered strange fire
before the LORD. (62) And those that
were numbered of them were twenty and
three thousand, all males from a month
old and upward: for they were not
numbered among the children of Israel,
because there was no inheritance given
them among the children of Israel.

a ch. 33. 54.

1 Heb., *multiply his inheritance.*

2 Heb., *diminish his inheritance.*

b ch. 33. 54; Josh. 11. 23. & 14. 2.

c Ex. 6. 16, 17, 18, 19.

d Ex. 2. 2. & 6. 20.

e Lev. 10. 2; ch. 3. 4; 1 Chron. 24. 2.

---

(51) **Six hundred thousand and a thousand seven hundred and thirty.**—The sum total exhibits a decrease of 1,820, as compared with the census taken at Sinai thirty-eight years previously. On this decrease Bishop Wordsworth observes as follows:—"When the Israelites were suffering persecution in Egypt they 'multiplied exceedingly' (Exod. i. 7, 20); but after their deliverance from Egypt they rebelled against God, and 'He consumed their days in vanity, and their years in trouble' (Ps. lxxviii. 33). . . . Here there is comfort and warning to the Church and every soul in it—comfort in time of affliction, and warning in days of prosperity."

(53–56) **Unto these the land shall be divided . . .**—The general apportionment of the land, as regarded the relative position of each tribe, was to be decided by lot, which was commonly looked upon as the determination of God Himself, and in this instance was undoubtedly so. The extent of territory was to be determined by the number of names—*i.e.*, of persons—in each tribe, and each inheritance was to bear the name of the ancestor of the tribe. Rashi says that the names of the twelve tribes were written on twelve scrolls of parchment, and twelve borders, or limits of land, on twelve others, and that they were mixed together in an urn.

(59) **Jochebed, the daughter of Levi, whom her mother bare to Levi . . .**—Or, *who was born to Levi*, &c. There is a similar omission of the subject of the verb in 1 Kings i. 6. Some writers have supposed that Jochebed was the granddaughter, or possibly even some more remote descendant of Levi, and that Amram, the father of Moses, was not the same as Amram, the son of Kohath. (See Keil, "On the Pentateuch," i. 469—471; but for a defence of the view which has been more commonly adopted, see Birks' "Exodus of Israel," pp. 153—199.)

(62) **Twenty and three thousand.**—At the former census the number was 22,000 or 22,300. (See chap. iii. 39, and Note.)

(63) These *are* they that were numbered by Moses and Eleazar the priest, who numbered the children of Israel in the plains of Moab by Jordan *near* Jericho. (64) But among these there was not a man of them whom Moses and Aaron the priest numbered, when they numbered the children of Israel in the wilderness of Sinai. (65) For the LORD had said of them, They [a]shall surely die in the wilderness. And there was not left a man of them, save Caleb the son of Jephunneh, and Joshua the son of Nun.

CHAPTER XXVII.—(1) Then came the daughters of [b]Zelophehad, the son of Hepher, the son of Gilead, the son of Machir, the son of Manasseh, of the families of Manasseh the son of Joseph: and these *are* the names of his daughters; Mahlah, Noah, and Hoglah, and Milcah, and Tirzah. (2) And they stood before Moses, and before Eleazar the priest, and before the princes and all the congregation, *by* the door of the tabernacle of the congregation, saying, (3) Our father [c]died in the wilderness, and he was not in the company of them that gathered themselves together against the LORD in the company of Korah; but died in his own sin, and had no sons. (4) Why should the name of our father be [1]done away from among his family, because he hath no son? Give unto us *therefore* a possession among the brethren of our father.

(5) And Moses brought their cause before the LORD. (6) And the LORD spake unto Moses, saying, (7) The daughters of Zelophehad speak right: thou shalt surely give them a possession of an inheritance among their father's brethren; and thou shalt cause the inheritance of their father to pass unto them. (8) And thou shalt speak unto the children of Israel, saying, If a man die, and have no son, then ye shall cause his inheritance to pass unto his daughter. (9) And if he have no daughter, then ye shall give his inheritance unto his brethren. (10) And if he have no brethren, then ye shall give his inheritance unto his father's brethren. (11) And if his father have no brethren, then ye shall give his inheritance unto his kinsman that is next to him of his family,

[a] ch. 14. 28; 1 Cor. 10. 5, 6.

[b] ch. 26. 33; Josh. 17. 3.

[c] ch. 14. 35 & 26. 64, 65.

[1] Heb., *diminished.*

---

(64) **But among these . . .**—Thus the prediction contained in chap. xiv. 29—32 was fulfilled. The fact that the fulfilment of this prediction is stated after verse 62, which contains the result of the census as regards the Levites, viewed in connection with the statement contained in verse 65, might seem to favour the inference that the sentence of exclusion was applicable to the tribe of Levi as well as to the other tribes. On the other hand, the second clause of verse 62 may be alleged in support of the opposite view. (See chap. xiv. 29, and Note.)

When they numbered . . .—Or, *who numbered,* as in verse 63.

XXVII.

(3) **Our father died in the wilderness.**—The preceding chapter records the fulfilment of the sentence of exclusion pronounced on the generation which came out of Egypt after the completion of the twentieth year of their age. The argument used by the daughters of Zelophehad appears to be that their father was not one of those who signally provoked the Divine displeasure, so that he might justly have forfeited for himself and his descendants a share in the possession of the promised land. "He died," they say, "in his own sin." There is a Jewish tradition that Zelophehad was the man who gathered sticks on the Sabbath day, and was stoned (chap. xiv. 32). The more common interpretation of the expression is that he committed only the ordinary sins of human frailty (see chap. v. 6), and that he died "the common death of all men," and was "visited after the visitation of all men" (see chap. xvi. 29), and consequently did not entail upon his posterity any special punishment for the sins which he had committed. In obedience to the directions contained in the preceding chapter (verses 52—56), the land of Canaan was to be portioned out, in accordance with the results of the census which had recently been taken, amongst the males who were upwards of twenty years of age; and consequently the daughters of Zelophehad would not have shared in the inheritance. Keil (*in loc.*) quotes several instances in which the sons of mothers who possessed landed property were received through that inheritance into the family of their mothers, and included in the tribe to which the mothers belonged. In this case the desire of the daughters of Zelophehad was that their father's name should be perpetuated—*i.e.*, that their sons should be enrolled as descendants of Zelophehad, and should succeed to that portion of the land which, under ordinary circumstances, would have fallen to his sons, had he left any behind him. Bishop Wordsworth observes that, inasmuch as we are to regard the inheritance of Canaan as being a figure of the heavenly possession, the answer which was returned to the inquiry of Moses respecting the daughters of Zelophehad may be regarded as an indication that "in Christ Jesus there is neither male nor female," and that women, no less than men, are "heirs according to the promise" (Gal. iii. 28, 29).

(7) **Thou shalt surely give them . . .**—The pronoun *them* is in the masculine gender in the Hebrew. Either the reference must be to the sons of Zelophehad's daughters, or the daughters must be regarded in the light of sons.

(8) **If a man die, and have no son . . .**—On the general law of inheritance which is here laid down, see Selden's *De Successionibus,* London, 1636, and Keil's *Archæol.,* ii., s. 142.

and he shall possess it: and it shall be
unto the children of Israel a statute of
judgment, as the LORD commanded
Moses.
(12) And the LORD said unto Moses,
[a]Get thee up into this mount Abarim,
and see the land which I have given
unto the children of Israel. (13) And
when thou hast seen it, thou also shalt
be gathered unto thy people, as [b]Aaron
thy brother was gathered. (14) For ye
[c]rebelled against my commandment in
the desert of Zin, in the strife of the
congregation, to sanctify me at the water
before their eyes: that *is* the [d]water of
Meribah in Kadesh in the wilderness
of Zin.
(15) And Moses spake unto the LORD,
saying, (16) Let the LORD, the God of the
spirits of all flesh, set a man over the
congregation, (17) which may go out
before them, and which may go in
before them, and which may lead them
out, and which may bring them in; that
the congregation of the LORD be not as
sheep which have no shepherd.
(18) And the LORD said unto Moses,
Take thee Joshua the son of Nun, a man
in whom *is* the spirit, and lay thine hand
upon him; (19) and set him before Eleazar
the priest, and before all the congrega-
tion; and give him a charge in their
sight. (20) And thou shalt put *some* of
thine honour upon him, that all the
congregation of the children of Israel
may be obedient. (21) And he shall stand
before Eleazar the priest, who shall ask
counsel for him [e]after the judgment of
Urim before the LORD: at his word shall
they go out, and at his word they shall
come in, *both* he, and all the children of
Israel with him, even all the congrega-
tion.
(22) And Moses did as the LORD com-
manded him: and he took Joshua, and
set him before Eleazar the priest, and
before all the congregation: (23) and he
laid his hands upon him, and gave him a

a Deut. 32. 49.
b ch. 20. 24.
c ch. 20. 24.
d Ex. 17. 7.
e Ex. 28. 30.

---

(12) **Get thee up into this mount Abarim.**—The position of this command, in immediate connection with the answer returned to the request of the daughters of Zelophehad, is very remarkable. They were to enter into the land of promise, and their descendants were to inherit it. The great lawgiver himself was to be excluded on account of his transgression. He does not, however, shrink from recording the sentence of exclusion in immediate connection with an incident which brings out that exclusion into greater prominence. The fulfilment of the announcement made to Moses is related in Deut. xxxii. 48—52. The mountains of Abarim form the Moabitish table-land, the northern portion of which bore the name of Pisgah. It is here that we must look for Mount Nebo, which is sometimes described as one of the mountains of Abarim (Deut. xxxii. 49), and at other times as the top of Pisgah (Deut. iii. 27, xxxiv. 1).

And see the land which I have given unto the children of Israel.—"The law," says Bishop Wordsworth, "led men to 'see the promises afar off, and to embrace them' [rather, *to see and greet the promises from afar*, Heb. xi. 13], and it brought them to the borders of Canaan, but could not bring them into it: that was reserved for Joshua, the type of Jesus." It must not be overlooked, however, that, although he was shut out during his lifetime from entering into the land of Canaan, Moses was permitted to stand with Elijah upon the Mount of Transfiguration (Matt. xvii. 3).

(13) **Gathered unto thy people.**—See Gen. xxv. 8, and Note. In the case of Moses, as in that of Abraham, the expression cannot be understood in reference to the place of his burial.

(14) **To sanctify me . . .**—See chap. xx. 12, 13, where the same expression is used.

(16) **Let the Lord . . .**—We have a remarkable instance here of the true greatness of Moses, as a type of Him whose words were, "Weep not for me, but weep for yourselves and for your children" (Luke xxiii. 28). Instead of indulging in excessive grief, or in unavailing remorse, the mind of Moses was intently fixed upon the welfare of those for whose sake he had been willing that his own name should be blotted out of the Book (Exod. xxxii. 32): and instead of appointing one of his own family, or the man of his own choice, as his successor, he commits the matter to God, and prays that He will appoint one who would be a true shepherd to the flock.

(17) **Which may go out before them . . .**—The expression going out and coming in is used here, as in many other places, to denote the ordinary life of man (Deut. xxviii. 6, xxxi. 2). Leading out and bringing in (literally, *causing to go out and to come in*), as a shepherd in respect of his flock (John x. 3—9), denotes the direction of the conduct of others.

(18) **In whom is the spirit . . .**—The definite article is not used in the original. The word translated "spirit" appears to denote spiritual endowment and qualifications.

And lay thine hand upon him.—It is to be observed that the spiritual qualifications of Joshua did not supersede the necessity of an outward consecration to his office. Nay, more; it seems that special qualifications for the office were bestowed in connection with the imposition of the hands of Moses, for it is written in Deut. xxxiv. 9 that "Joshua the son of Nun was full of the spirit of wisdom; for Moses had laid his hands upon him."

(19) **And give him a charge . . .**—Comp. Deut. xxxi. 23, "And he gave Joshua the son of Nun a charge, and said, Be strong and of a good courage."

(21) **After the judgment of Urim . . .**—See Exod. xxviii. 30, and Note.

At his word . . .—*i.e.*, Joshua and the children of Israel were to abide by the decision of the high priest, which was obtained by means of Urim and Thummim.

charge, as the LORD commanded by the
hand of Moses.

CHAPTER XXVIII. — (1) And the
LORD spake unto Moses, saying, (2) Com-
mand the children of Israel, and say
unto them, My offering, *and* my bread
for my sacrifices made by fire, *for* [1] a
sweet savour unto me, shall ye observe
to offer unto me in their due season.
(3) And thou shalt say unto them, [a] This
is the offering made by fire which ye
shall offer unto the LORD; two lambs of
the first year without spot [2] day by day,
for a continual burnt offering. (4) The
one lamb shalt thou offer in the morn-
ing, and the other lamb shalt thou offer
[3] at even; (5) and a tenth *part* of an
ephah of flour for a [b] meat offering,
mingled with the fourth *part* of an [c] hin
of beaten oil. (6) *It is* a continual burnt
offering, which was ordained in mount
Sinai for a sweet savour, a sacrifice
made by fire unto the LORD. (7) And
the drink offering thereof *shall be* the
fourth *part* of an hin for the one lamb:
in the holy *place* shalt thou cause the
strong wine to be poured unto the LORD
for a drink offering. (8) And the other
lamb shalt thou offer at even: as the
meat offering of the morning, and as
the drink offering thereof, thou shalt
offer *it*, a sacrifice made by fire, of a
sweet savour unto the LORD.

(9) And on the sabbath day two lambs
of the first year without spot, and two
tenth deals of flour *for* a meat offering,
mingled with oil, and the drink offer-
ing thereof: (10) *this is* the burnt offering
of every sabbath, beside the continual
burnt offering, and his drink offering.

(11) And in the beginnings of your
months ye shall offer a burnt offering
unto the LORD; two young bullocks, and
one ram, seven lambs of the first year
without spot; (12) and three tenth deals
of flour *for* a meat offering, mingled
with oil, for one bullock; and two tenth
deals of flour *for* a meat offering, min-
gled with oil, for one ram; (13) and a
several tenth deal of flour mingled with
oil *for* a meat offering unto one lamb;
for a burnt offering of a sweet savour, a
sacrifice made by fire unto the LORD.

1 Heb., *a savour of my rest.*

a Ex. 29. 38.

2 Heb., *in a day.*

3 Heb., *between the two evenings.*

b Lev. 2. 1.

c Ex. 29. 40.

XXVIII.

(1) **And the Lord spake unto Moses . . .**—The sacrificial laws had been to a great extent in abeyance during the wanderings of the Israelites in the wilderness. It was needful, therefore, that before the entrance into the land of Canaan those laws should be promulgated afresh.

(2) **My offering, and my bread . . .**—Better, *My oblation* (even) *my bread,* &c. The offering, though presented by the hands of men, was God's, not theirs. "The silver is mine, and the gold is mine, saith the Lord of hosts" (Haggai ii. 8). "Every beast of the forest is mine, and the cattle upon a thousand hills" (Ps. l. 10). The word *korban* is a general term for an oblation. It may denote in this place the *minchah,* or meal offering, or the shew-bread, offerings which were directly connected with a settled life in Canaan rather than with a nomadic life in the wilderness. Or the word *lehem* (bread) may be used to denote food generally, the sacrificial offerings being symbolically regarded as the Lord's food. (Comp. Lev. iii. 11, 16, where the same word is rendered *food,* and where the reference is to a portion of the flesh of the lamb and of the goat of the peace offering. See also Mal. iii. 7.)

(3) **Two lambs of the first year . . .**—See Exod. xxix. 38—42.

A continual burnt offering.—The morning and evening lamb offered as "a continual burnt offering" afforded a striking type of the Lamb of God offered "once for all" (Heb. vii. 3, x. 12, 14).

(4) **At even.**—Hebrew, *between the two evenings.* (See Exod. xii. 6, and Note.)

(5) **Beaten oil.**—See Exod. xxvii. 20, and Note.

(6) **Which was ordained in mount Sinai . . .** Or, *which was offered* (Hebrew, *made*) *in Mount Sinai.* Ibn Ezra adduces this passage as a proof that the Israelites ceased to offer burnt sacrifices after they left the encampment at Sinai throughout the time of their wanderings in the wilderness.

(7) **Shalt thou cause the strong wine to be poured . . .**—Better, *pour out the drink offering of strong drink.* The word *shecar,* which is here rendered "strong wine," denotes any kind of intoxicating drink, whether made from grapes, honey, or grain; but it is more frequently used to denote a drink which is not made from grapes, as, *e.g.,* in Lev. x. 9, where the command is given to Aaron and his sons not to drink "wine nor strong drink" (*shecar*) when they went into the tent of meeting. In the parallel passage in Exodus, the drink offering was to consist of "the fourth part of an hin of wine" (chap. xxix. 40). (Comp. chap. xv. 5.) In Exod. xxx. 9 it is forbidden to pour any drink offering upon the altar of incense, from which passage it has been inferred that the drink offerings were poured upon the altar of burnt sacrifice.

(9) **And on the sabbath day two lambs . . .**—The Sabbath offering which was to be added to the daily sacrifice is here enjoined for the first time. The rule respecting the drink offering which was to accompany the burnt offering is laid down in chap. xv. 5. The law of the Sabbath is laid down in Exod. xx. 8—11, and Lev. xxiii. 3.

(11) **In the beginnings of your months . . .**—The beginning of the month was announced by the blowing of the silver trumpets (chap. x. 10). Increased respect was paid to the beginning of the month in later times. Trade was suspended (Amos viii. 5), and religious instruction appears to have been given at this time (2 Kings iv. 23).

(14) And their drink offerings shall be
half an hin of wine unto a bullock, and
the third *part* of an hin unto a ram, and
a fourth *part* of an hin unto a lamb:
this *is* the burnt offering of every month
throughout the months of the year.
(15) And one kid of the goats for a sin
offering unto the LORD shall be offered,
beside the continual burnt offering, and
his drink offering. a Ex. 12. 18; Lev. 23. 5.
(16) [a]And in the fourteenth day of the
first month *is* the passover of the LORD.
(17) And in the fifteenth day of this
month *is* the feast: seven days shall
unleavened bread be eaten. (18) In the
[b]first day *shall be* an holy convocation;
ye shall do no manner of servile work
therein: (19) but ye shall offer a sacrifice b Lev. 23. 7.
made by fire *for* a burnt offering unto
the LORD; two young bullocks, and one
ram, and seven lambs of the first year:
they shall be unto you without blemish:
(20) and their meat offering *shall be of*
flour mingled with oil: three tenth deals
shall ye offer for a bullock, and two
tenth deals for a ram; (21) a several
tenth deal shalt thou offer for every c Lev. 23. 24.
lamb, throughout the seven lambs:
(22) and one goat *for* a sin offering, to
make an atonement for you. (23) Ye
shall offer these beside the burnt offer-
ing in the morning, which *is* for a con-
tinual burnt offering. (24) After this
manner ye shall offer daily, throughout
the seven days, the meat of the sacrifice
made by fire, of a sweet savour unto
the LORD: it shall be offered beside the
continual burnt offering, and his drink
offering. (25) And on the seventh day
ye shall have an holy convocation; ye
shall do no servile work.

(26) Also in the day of the firstfruits,
when ye bring a new meat offering unto
the LORD, after your weeks *be out*, ye
shall have an holy convocation; ye shall
do no servile work: (27) but ye shall offer
the burnt offering for a sweet savour
unto the LORD; two young bullocks,
one ram, seven lambs of the first year;
(28) and their meat offering of flour
mingled with oil, three tenth deals unto
one bullock, two tenth deals unto one
ram, (29) a several tenth deal unto one
lamb, throughout the seven lambs;
(30) *and* one kid of the goats, to make an
atonement for you. (31) Ye shall offer
them beside the continual burnt offering,
and his meat offering, (they shall be
unto you without blemish) and their
drink offerings.

CHAPTER XXIX.

— (1) And in the
seventh month, on the first *day* of the
month, ye shall have an holy convoca-
tion; ye shall do no servile work: [c]it
is a day of blowing the trumpets unto
you. (2) And ye shall offer a burnt
offering for a sweet savour unto the
LORD; one young bullock, one ram, *and*
seven lambs of the first year without

(16, 17) **And in the fourteenth day of the first month . . .**—The observance of the Passover had been in abeyance for thirty-eight years. The law is now promulgated afresh. The observance of the first and seventh days of the feast are enjoined in Exod. xii. 16 and Lev. xxiii. 7, 8; and in the latter place it is enjoined that an offering made by fire should be offered for seven days. The nature of that offering is stated in the 19th verse of this chapter, and the fact that the details are not found in Lev. xxiii. may be adduced in proof of the prospective character of much of the Levitical legislation.

(26) **In the day of the firstfruits.**—See Exod. xxiii. 16, xxxiv. 22; Lev. xxiii. 15—21, and Notes.

A new meat offering . . .—See Lev. xxiii. 16.

After your weeks be out.—Hebrew, *in your weeks—i.e.,* at the expiration of a week of weeks from the morrow after the chief day of the feast of the Passover.

(27) **Two young bullocks, one ram, seven lambs of the first year.**—In Lev. xxxii. 18 the animal sacrifices enjoined are one young bullock, two rams, and seven lambs without blemish. The Mishnah (Menach. iv. 2) considers that these animals were to be presented together with the loaves, whereas those named in Numbers were additional sacrifices of the day. Josephus also thinks that three bullocks, two [three] rams, and fourteen sheep were offered at this time (*Antt.* iii. 10, § 6).

XXIX.

(1) **And in the seventh month . . .**—This chapter contains an account of the days which were to be observed as religious ordinances in the seventh or Sabbatical month—a month which contained more of those days than any other month in the year.

It is a day of blowing the trumpets unto you.—Literally, *of loud or joyful clang.* The silver trumpets were blown at every new moon (chap. x. 10), but the first day of the seventh month was emphatically the day for blowing of trumpets—"a memorial of blowing of trumpets," which, according to Jewish writers, was continued from sun-rising to sun-setting. (See Lev. xxiii. 24, and Note.) The word "trumpets" is not expressed either in Lev. xxiii. 24, or in this place; and in Ps. lxxxi. 3, which is used at the Feast of Trumpets in the modern Jewish services, the word used is *shophan*—a word which is interchanged with *keren* (the cornet, or ram's horn)—not *hazozerah*, the straight silver trumpet mentioned in chap. x. 2. The

blemish: (3) and their meat offering *shall be of* flour mingled with oil, three tenth deals for a bullock, *and* two tenth deals for a ram, (4) and one tenth deal for one lamb, throughout the seven lambs: (5) and one kid of the goats *for* a sin offering, to make an atonement for you: (6) beside the burnt offering of the month, and his meat offering, and the daily burnt offering, and his meat offering, and their drink offerings, according unto their manner, for a sweet savour, a sacrifice made by fire unto the LORD.

(7) And [a]ye shall have on the tenth *day* of this seventh month an holy convocation; and ye shall afflict your souls: ye shall not do any work *therein*: (8) but ye shall offer a burnt offering unto the LORD *for* a sweet savour; one young bullock, one ram, *and* seven lambs of the first year; they shall be unto you without blemish: (9) and their meat offering *shall be of* flour mingled with oil, three tenth deals to a bullock, *and* two tenth deals to one ram, (10) a several tenth deal for one lamb, throughout the seven lambs: (11) one kid of the goats *for* a sin offering; beside the sin offering of atonement, and the continual burnt offering, and the meat offering of it, and their drink offerings.

(12) And on the fifteenth day of the seventh month ye shall have an holy convocation; ye shall do no servile work, and ye shall keep a feast unto the LORD seven days: (13) and ye shall offer a burnt offering, a sacrifice made by fire, of a sweet savour unto the LORD; thirteen young bullocks, two rams, *and* fourteen lambs of the first year; they shall be without blemish: (14) and their meat offering *shall be of* flour mingled with oil, three tenth deals unto every bullock of the thirteen bullocks, two tenth deals to each ram of the two rams, (15) and a several tenth deal to each lamb of the fourteen lambs: (16) and one kid of the goats *for* a sin offering; beside the continual burnt offering, his meat offering, and his drink offering.

(17) And on the second day *ye shall offer* twelve young bullocks, two rams, fourteen lambs of the first year without spot: (18) and their meat offering and their drink offerings for the bullocks, for the rams, and for the lambs, *shall be* according to their number, after the manner: (19) and one kid of the goats *for* a sin offering; beside the continual burnt offering, and the meat offering thereof, and their drink offerings.

(20) And on the third day eleven bullocks, two rams, fourteen lambs of the first year without blemish; (21) and their meat offering and their drink offerings for the bullocks, for the rams, and for the lambs, *shall be* according to their number, after the manner: (22) and one goat *for* a sin offering; beside the continual burnt offering, and his meat offering, and his drink offering.

(23) And on the fourth day ten bullocks, two rams, *and* fourteen lambs of the first year without blemish: (24) their meat offering and their drink offerings

a Lev. 16. 29; & 23. 27.

---

word *teruah*, which is here rendered "blowing the trumpets," is coupled with *shophar* in Lev. xxv. 9—"the trumpet of loud clang or joyful sound." The details of the fire offering prescribed in Lev. xxiii. 25 are here given.

(6) **Beside the burnt offering of the month.**—Better, *of the new moon.* (See chap. xxviii. 11, where the burnt offering of the beginning of the month is described.)

(7) **The tenth day of this seventh month . . .**—The law respecting the observance of the great Day of Atonement is contained in Lev. xvi. and xxiii. 26—32. The sacrifices prescribed in verses 8—11, which are the same as those prescribed for the first day of the seventh month, were to be offered in addition to the sin offerings of atonement prescribed in Lev. xvi. and to the daily burnt offerings. (See Notes on Lev. xvi., xxiii. 26—32.)

And ye shall afflict your souls.—See Lev. xvi. 29. This affliction or humiliation appears to have included in it fasting (comp. Acts xxvii. 9), although the word which denotes fasting is not employed, nor is there any express injunction respecting fasting in the Pentateuch.

(12) **And on the fifteenth day of the seventh month . . .**—See Lev. xxiii. 33—36, 39—43. A larger number of burnt offerings was appointed for this feast than for any other festival. Seventy oxen in all were to be offered on the seven days of the feast, the number being diminished by one daily—viz., thirteen on the first day, twelve on the second, eleven on the third, and in like manner until the seventh day, on which seven oxen, the perfect number, were to be offered. In addition to the oxen, two rams and fourteen lambs were to be offered daily as burnt offerings, and a he-goat as a sin offering, in addition to the daily burnt offering. The appointed meal offerings and drink offerings were to be offered with all the burnt offerings. The large number of the sacrifices offered at this time may be accounted for from the consideration that at this feast the people not only expressed their gratitude for the Divine presence and protection, but also for the rich fruits of the harvest which had been recently ingathered.

for the bullocks, for the rams, and for the lambs, *shall be* according to their number, after the manner: (25) and one kid of the goats *for* a sin offering; beside the continual burnt offering, his meat offering, and his drink offering.

(26) And on the fifth day nine bullocks, two rams, *and* fourteen lambs of the first year without spot: (27) and their meat offering and their drink offerings for the bullocks, for the rams, and for the lambs, *shall be* according to their number, after the manner: (28) and one goat *for* a sin offering; beside the continual burnt offering, and his meat offering, and his drink offering.

(29) And on the sixth day eight bullocks, two rams, *and* fourteen lambs of the first year without blemish: (30) and their meat offering and their drink offerings for the bullocks, for the rams, and for the lambs, *shall be* according to their number, after the manner: (31) and one goat *for* a sin offering; beside the continual burnt offering, his meat offering, and his drink offering.

(32) And on the seventh day seven bullocks, two rams, *and* fourteen lambs of the first year without blemish: (33) and their meat offering and their drink offerings for the bullocks, for the rams, and for the lambs, *shall be* according to their number, after the manner: (34) and one goat *for* a sin offering; beside the continual burnt offering, his meat offering, and his drink offering.

(35) On the eighth day ye shall have a [a] solemn assembly: ye shall do no servile work *therein:* (36) but ye shall offer a burnt offering, a sacrifice made by fire, of a sweet savour unto the LORD: one bullock, one ram, seven lambs of the first year without blemish: (37) their meat offering and their drink offerings for the bullock, for the ram, and for the lambs, *shall be* according to their number, after the manner: (38) and one goat *for* a sin offering; beside the continual burnt offering, and his meat offering, and his drink offering.

(39) These *things* ye shall [1] do unto the LORD in your set feasts, beside your vows, and your freewill offerings, for your burnt offerings, and for your meat offerings, and for your drink offerings, and for your peace offerings.

(40) And Moses told the children of Israel according to all that the LORD commanded Moses.

CHAPTER XXX. — (1) And Moses spake unto the heads of the tribes concerning the children of Israel, saying, This *is* the thing which the LORD hath commanded. (2) If a man vow a vow unto the LORD, or swear an oath to bind his soul with a bond; he shall not [2] break his word, he shall do accord-

a Lev. 23. 36.

1 Or, *offer.*

2 Heb., *profane.*

---

(35) **On the eighth day ye shall have a solemn assembly.**—Or, *closing feast day.* The word *azereth,* which is here and in the parallel passage in Lev. xxiii. 36 (comp. Neh. viii. 18; 2 Chron. vii. 9) rendered "solemn assembly," is used in Deut. xvi. 8 of the seventh or closing day of the Feast of the Passover. It is used in Jer. ix. 2 and Amos v. 2 in a more general manner. In the former of these passages it is used of an assembly or confederacy of false dealers, and in the latter it appears to include solemn festivals generally, without limitation to the last day of their duration. The primary notion appears to be that of restraint—*i.e.,* from the performance of servile work. The sacrifices of the eighth day were the same as those which were appointed for the first day of the seventh month, *i.e.,* the Feast of Trumpets, and also for the tenth day, or Day of Atonement. (See Lev. xxiii. 36, and Note.)

(39) **These things ye shall do unto the Lord in your set feasts.**—Better, *These sacrifices shall ye offer unto the Lord at your set seasons.*

For your burnt offerings . . .—The sacrifices prescribed in this chapter were appointed to be offered independently of all the burnt offerings, meal offerings, drink offerings, and peace offerings, which were made in performance of special vows, or as freewill offerings. (See Lev. xxii. 18—21; Num. xv. 1—13.)

(40) **And Moses told the children of Israel . . .**—In the Hebrew Bible this verse forms the beginning of the 30th chapter.

XXX.

(2) **If a man vow a vow unto the Lord . . .**—Two kinds of vows are spoken of in this verse—viz., the *neder,* which is here rendered *vow,* and which denotes primarily a positive vow, or vow of performance, and the *issar,* which is here rendered *bond,* and which denotes a negative vow, or a vow of abstinence. It is natural to suppose that at the expiration of the protracted wanderings in the wilderness the pious Israelites would be desirous of testifying their gratitude by dedicating themselves, or some portion of their substance beyond that which the law demanded, to the service of the Lord. And hence, although some regulations respecting vows had already been made (see Lev. xxvii.), it was needful that before their entrance into the land of Canaan some additions should be made to the law which pertained to the nature and obligation of vows.

He shall not break his word . . .—The sacred character of a vow is enforced in these words; and a timely caution was thus given to the Israelites that it was better for them not to vow than to vow and not to pay. (Comp. Eccles. v. 2—5.)

ing to all that proceedeth out of his
mouth.
(3) If a woman also vow a vow unto
the LORD, and bind *herself* by a bond,
being in her father's house in her youth;
(4) and her father hear her vow, and her
bond wherewith she hath bound her
soul, and her father shall hold his peace
at her: then all her vows shall stand,
and every bond wherewith she hath
bound her soul shall stand. (5) But if
her father disallow her in the day that
he heareth; not any of her vows, or of
her bonds wherewith she hath bound
her soul, shall stand: and the LORD
shall forgive her, because her father
disallowed her.
(6) And if she had at all an husband,
when [1]she vowed, or uttered ought out
of her lips, wherewith she bound her
soul; (7) and her husband heard *it*, and
held his peace at her in the day that he
heard *it*: then her vows shall stand, and
her bonds wherewith she bound her
soul shall stand. (8) But if her husband
disallowed her on the day that he heard
it; then he shall make her vow which she
vowed, and that which she uttered with
her lips, wherewith she bound her soul,
of none effect: and the LORD shall for-
give her.
(9) But every vow of a widow, and of
her that is divorced, wherewith they
have bound their souls, shall stand
against her.
(10) And if she vowed in her husband's
house, or bound her soul by a bond
with an oath; (11) and her husband
heard *it*, and held his peace at her,
and disallowed her not: then all her
vows shall stand, and every bond
wherewith she bound her soul shall
stand. (12) But if her husband hath
utterly made them void on the day he
heard *them; then* whatsoever proceeded
out of her lips concerning her vows, or
concerning the bond of her soul, shall
not stand: her husband hath made
them void; and the LORD shall for-
give her. (13) Every vow, and every
binding oath to afflict the soul, her
husband may establish it, or her hus-
band may make it void. (14) But if her
husband altogether hold his peace at
her from day to day; then he estab-
lisheth all her vows, or all her bonds,
which *are* upon her: he confirmeth
them, because he held his peace at her
in the day that he heard *them*. (15) But
if he shall any ways make them void
after that he hath heard *them;* then he
shall bear her iniquity.
(16) These *are* the statutes, which the
LORD commanded Moses, between a man
and his wife, between the father and his
daughter, *being yet* in her youth in her
father's house.

CHAPTER XXXI.—(1) And the LORD
spake unto Moses, saying, (2) [a]Avenge

1 Heb., *her vows were upon her.*

a ch. 25. 17.

(3) **If a woman also . . .**—Four distinct cases are contemplated in the following verses in regard to vows taken by women:—(1) that of an unmarried woman, living, in her youth, in the house of her father; (2) that of a woman who is unmarried at the time of making a vow, but enters into the state of marriage before the vow is fulfilled; (3) that of a widow, or of a divorced woman; and (4) that of a married woman. The sanctity and obligations of the fifth commandment are distinctly recognised and enforced in these verses. (See Matt. xv. 4, 5.) Whenever the vow which the young daughter had made should come to the ears of her father, he had the power either to ratify or to disannul it. If he remained silent the vow was ratified; if he disallowed the vow, the obligation to fulfil it no longer remained in force.

(5) **The Lord shall forgive her**—*i.e.*, she would not incur the guilt or punishment which would otherwise have been incurred by neglecting to fulfil the vow which she had made.

(6) **And if she had at all an husband . . . .**—Better, *And if she should be married to a husband whilst her vows are upon her, or the rash utterance of her lips wherewith she hath bound her soul.* The case here contemplated appears to be that of a woman who married whilst under a vow. On the other hand the case of a woman who takes a vow after marriage is treated of further on in verses 10—13. The cognate verb of the word *mibta, rash utterance,* occurs in Lev. v. 4, and seems to denote something which is uttered without reflection.

(10) **And if she vowed in her husband's house, or bound her soul . . .**—*i.e.*, if she took a vow of performance or of abstinence whilst in the house of her husband.

(13) **Every vow, and every binding oath to afflict the soul.**—Reference is again made to the two kinds of vows which are treated of in this chapter —viz., a vow to do anything, and a vow to abstain from anything.

XXXI.

(1) **Avenge the children of Israel of the Midianites.**—The time had now come for the fulfilment of the command which had already been given (see chap. xxv. 16—18), after which Moses was to be gathered unto his people, as it had been revealed to him (chap. xxvii. 13). After Balaam had been dismissed by Balak, he appears to have gone, not to the Moabites, but to the Midianites; and it was in consequence of the

the children of Israel of the Midianites:
afterward shalt thou [a]be gathered unto
thy people.
(3) And Moses spake unto the people,
saying, Arm some of yourselves unto
the war, and let them go against the
Midianites, and avenge the LORD of
Midian. (4) [1] Of every tribe a thousand,
throughout all the tribes of Israel, shall
ye send to the war. (5) So there were
delivered out of the thousands of Israel,
a thousand of *every* tribe, twelve thou-
sand armed for war. (6) And Moses
sent them to the war, a thousand of
every tribe, them and Phinehas the son
of Eleazar the priest, to the war, with
the holy instruments, and the trumpets
to blow in his hand. (7) And they
warred against the Midianites, as the
LORD commanded Moses; and they slew
all the males. (8) And they slew the
kings of Midian, beside the rest of them
that were slain; *namely*, [b]Evi, and
Rekem, and Zur, and Hur, and Reba,
five kings of Midian: Balaam also the
son of Beor they slew with the sword.
(9) And the children of Israel took *all*
the women of Midian captives, and
their little ones, and took the spoil of
all their cattle, and all their flocks, and
all their goods. (10) And they burnt all
their cities wherein they dwelt, and all

a ch. 27. 13.

1 Heb., *A thousand of a tribe, a thousand of a tribe.*

b Josh. 13. 21.

---

counsel which he gave to the Midianites (chap. v. 16) that the Israelites were reduced into the idolatrous and lascivious worship of Baal Peor. It is possible, also, that the Midianites, as the descendants of Abraham, may have possessed clearer light and greater privileges than the Moabites. They may have had many men as enlightened as Jethro amongst them, and consequently they may have incurred the greater guilt, and rendered themselves obnoxious to the severer punishment of those who, "after they have known the way of righteousness, turn from the holy commandment delivered unto them" (2 Pet. ii. 21). But whether satisfactory reasons can or cannot be assigned why a more exemplary judgment should have been inflicted upon the Midianites than upon the Moabites, who were not left unpunished (see Deut. xxiii. 3, 4), those only can maintain that the destruction of the Midianites is inconsistent with the justice or the goodness of God who deny that He has absolute control over the destinies of all the creatures of His hands, and that when it is His pleasure to recall the life which He has bestowed, it is for Him to determine what agents or what instruments it is best to employ.

(3) **Arm some of yourselves . . .**—Better, *Arm from among you* (or, *from those with you*) *men for the war.* The details of the selection are contained in the next verse.

(6) **With the holy instruments, and . . .**—Or, *with the holy instruments, even, &c.* It does not appear whether the ark did or did not accompany the expedition. It has been inferred from chap. xiv. 44 that the reference may be to the ark, but it does not appear probable that the ark would be so described. Moreover, Phinehas was not the high priest, and therefore would not have the ephod with the breastplate, which was worn at this time by Eleazar. The reference may be only to the silver trumpets (see chap. x. 9), or it may include other sacred instruments. This was emphatically a holy war; and we may learn, from the command given to the Israelites to take with them "the holy instruments," that they who would engage in the war against sin and Satan must "take to them the whole armour of God" (Ephes. vi. 13).

(7) **They slew all the males.**—The reference appears to be to those who were engaged in the war. The words do not refer to the whole of the male population, as appears from verse 17; and it is probable that many of the Midianites who were not engaged in the war withdrew from the scene of conflict. The reference in this verse, unless the words are inserted proleptically, seems to be to the whole of the adult males who fell into the hands of the Israelites during the war.

(8) **And they slew the kings of Midian . . .**—Those persons who are here described as kings appear to have been chiefs of the more powerful Midianitish tribes, just in the same way as Zur is represented in chap. xxv. 15. They are described in Josh. xiii. 21 as "princes" or "chiefs," and as "dukes" or "princes" of Sihon, by which expression it appears that they were his vassals.

Balaam also the son of Beor they slew with the sword.—The death of Balaam by the sword of the Israelites presents a strange and instructive contrast to the prayer which he uttered that he might die the death of the righteous (chap. xxiii. 10). Few of the ancient prophecies are more remarkable, as Bishop Wordsworth has observed, than those of Balaam for "spirituality of conception and sublimity of expression." And if, as some think, we are to understand Micah vi. 8 as containing the actual words which were addressed by Balaam to Balak, few men possessed a clearer perception of moral truth than that which is expressed in the words, "He hath shewed thee, O man, what is good; and what doth the Lord require of thee, but to do justly, and to love mercy, and to walk humbly with thy God?" And yet, notwithstanding the light which Balaam possessed, the sublimity of the prophecies which he uttered, and the purity of the motives by which he professed to be actuated, he "loved the wages of unrighteousness," and gave himself up to do Satan's bidding in "casting a stumbling-block before the children of Israel," and miserably perished amongst the enemies of God and of His people. Bishop Wordsworth draws a striking and instructive contrast between Balaam and Moses, both of whom had visions of Christ and prophesied of Him, whilst one loved the wages of unrighteousness, and the other did all for God's glory.

(10) **All their cities wherein they dwelt.**—Better, *all their cities in their dwelling-places.* This expression is explained by a reference to Josh. xiii. 21, from which it appears that the five kings or chiefs of the Midianites who are mentioned in chap. v. 8 dwelt in the territory which Sihon, king of the Amorites, had wrested from the Moabites. The Midianites were a nomad people, and were not likely to have built cities for themselves.

their goodly castles, with fire. (11) And
they took all the spoil, and all the prey,
both of men and of beasts. (12) And they
brought the captives, and the prey, and
the spoil, unto Moses, and Eleazar the
priest, and unto the congregation of the
children of Israel, unto the camp at the
plains of Moab, which *are* by Jordan
near Jericho.

(13) And Moses, and Eleazar the priest,
and all the princes of the congregation,
went forth to meet them without the
camp. (14) And Moses was wroth with
the officers of the host, *with* the cap-
tains over thousands, and captains over
hundreds, which came from the [1] battle.
(15) And Moses said unto them, Have ye
saved all the women alive? (16) Behold,
[a] these caused the children of Israel,
through the [b] counsel of Balaam, to
commit trespass against the LORD in
the matter of Peor, and there was a
plague among the congregation of the
LORD. (17) Now therefore [c] kill every
male among the little ones, and kill
every woman that hath known man by
lying with [2] him. (18) But all the wo-
men children, that have not known a
man by lying with him, keep alive for
yourselves. (19) And do ye abide with-
out the camp seven days: whosoever
hath killed any person, and [d] whosoever
hath touched any slain, purify *both*
yourselves and your captives on the
third day, and on the seventh day.
(20) And purify all *your* raiment, and all
[3] that is made of skins, and all work
of goats' *hair*, and all things made of
wood.

(21) And Eleazar the priest said unto
the men of war which went to the bat-
tle, This *is* the ordinance of the law
which the LORD commanded Moses;
(22) only the gold, and the silver, the
brass, the iron, the tin, and the lead,
(23) every thing that may abide the fire,
ye shall make *it* go through the fire,
and it shall be clean: nevertheless it
shall be purified with the water of
separation: and all that abideth not the
fire ye shall make go through the water.
(24) And ye shall wash your clothes on the
seventh day, and ye shall be clean, and
afterward ye shall come into the camp.

(25) And the LORD spake unto Moses,
saying, (26) Take the sum of the prey
[4] that was taken, *both* of man and of
beast, thou, and Eleazar the priest, and
the chief fathers of the congregation:
(27) and divide the prey into two parts;
between them that took the war upon
them, who went out to battle, and be-
tween all the congregation: (28) and levy
a tribute unto the LORD of the men of
war which went out to battle: one soul
of five hundred, *both* of the persons, and
of the beeves, and of the asses, and of
the sheep: (29) take *it* of their half, and
give *it* unto Eleazar the priest, *for* an
heave offering of the LORD. (30) And of

1 Heb., *host of war.*
a ch. 25. 2.
b Pet. 2. 15.
c Judg. 21. 11.
2 Heb. *a male.*
d ch. 19. 11, &c.
3 Heb., *instrument,* or, *vessel of skins.*
4 Heb., *of the captivity.*

---

(12) **The captives, and the prey, and the spoil.**—The first word denotes the women and children; the second, which in chap. v. 11 includes both the captives and the cattle, appears in this place to refer to the animals only; whilst the third refers to the rest of the spoil.

(15) **Have ye saved all the women alive?**—It was the women, as is expressed in the following verse, who had been the cause, at the instigation of Balaam, of the apostacy of the Israelites; and consequently the command to "avenge the Lord of Midian," implied the punishment of those who had been the instruments employed in the seduction of the Israelites.

(18) **Keep alive for yourselves.**—The Israelites were allowed to make slaves of their captives. Shortly after the capture of these Midianitish women, and, it may be, as arising out of it, the law concerning marriage with captives was enacted. (See Deut. xxi. 10—14.)

(27) **And divide the prey into two parts . . .**—It was reasonable that those who had encountered the perils and hardships of the war should receive a larger share of the spoil than those who had remained in the camp. It was equally reasonable that the latter should not be left without some substantial benefit from the victory miraculously achieved over the enemies of the Lord and of His people. A similar direction is found in Josh. xxii. 8 in regard to the division of spoil taken from enemies, but no general ordinance appears to have been made in regard to the division of the spoils of war until the time of David. (See 1 Sam. xxx. 24, 25.)

(28) **And levy a tribute unto the Lord.**—Literally, *and thou shalt lift up* (or, *heave*), &c. The portion assigned to the priests, which was taken from the prey that fell to the lot of the warriors, and which is described in verse 29 as "the heave offering of the Lord," was one-five-hundredth part of the maidens and of the cattle which had fallen to their share. The maidens were probably employed as slaves, and the cattle used for the maintenance of the priests. Inasmuch, then, as the entire booty consisted of 32,000 maidens, 675,000 small cattle, 72,000 oxen, and 61,000 asses, the portion which fell to the lot of the 12,000 warriors was 16,000 maidens, 337,500 sheep and goats, 36,000 oxen, and 30,500 asses, of which the portion of the priests was 32 maidens, 675 sheep and goats, 72 oxen, and 61 asses.

(30) **One portion of fifty.**—The Levites were much more numerous than the priests, and consequently it was ordered that they should have two per cent. of the

the children of Israel's half, thou shalt
take one portion of fifty, of the per-
sons, of the beeves, of the asses, and of
the [1] flocks, of all manner of beasts, and
give them unto the Levites, which keep
the charge of the tabernacle of the
LORD. (31) And Moses and Eleazar the
priest did as the LORD commanded
Moses.

(32) And the booty, *being* the rest of
the prey which the men of war had
caught, was six hundred thousand and
seventy thousand and five thousand
sheep, (33) and threescore and twelve
thousand beeves, (34) and threescore and
one thousand asses, (35) and thirty and
two thousand persons in all, of women
that had not known man by lying with
him.

(36) And the half, *which was* the por-
tion of them that went out to war,
was in number three hundred thousand
and seven and thirty thousand and five
hundred sheep: (37) and the LORD's tri-
bute of the sheep was six hundred and
threescore and fifteen. (38) And the
beeves *were* thirty and six thousand; of
which the LORD's tribute *was* threescore
and twelve. (39) And the asses *were*
thirty thousand and five hundred; of
which the LORD's tribute *was* threescore
and one. (40) And the persons *were* six-
teen thousand; of which the LORD's
tribute *was* thirty and two persons.
(41) And Moses gave the tribute, *which
was* the LORD's heave offering, unto
Eleazar the priest, as the LORD com-
manded Moses.

(42) And of the children of Israel's
half, which Moses divided from the men
that warred, (43) (now the half *that
pertained unto* the congregation was
three hundred thousand and thirty
thousand *and* seven thousand and five
hundred sheep, (44) and thirty and six
thousand beeves, (45) and thirty thou-
sand asses and five hundred, (46) and
sixteen thousand persons;) (47) even of
the children of Israel's half, Moses took
one portion of fifty, *both* of man and of
beast, and gave them unto the Levites,
which kept the charge of the tabernacle
of the LORD; as the LORD commanded
Moses.

(48) And the officers which *were* over
thousands of the host, the captains of
thousands, and captains of hundreds,
came near unto Moses: (49) and they
said unto Moses, Thy servants have
taken the sum of the men of war which
are under our [2] charge, and there lacketh
not one man of us. (50) We have there-
fore brought an oblation for the LORD,
what every man hath [3] gotten, of jewels
of gold, chains, and bracelets, rings, ear-
rings, and tablets, to make an atone-
ment for our souls before the LORD.
(51) And Moses and Eleazar the priest
took the gold of them, *even* all wrought
jewels. (52) And all the gold of the
[4] offering that they offered up to the
LORD, of the captains of thousands, and
of the captains of hundreds, was sixteen
thousand seven hundred and fifty she-
kels. (53) (*For* the men of war had taken
spoil, every man for himself.) (54) And
Moses and Eleazar the priest took the
gold of the captains of thousands and of
hundreds, and brought it into the taber-
nacle of the congregation, *for* a memorial
for the children of Israel before the
LORD.

1 Or, *goats.*

2 Heb., *hand.*

3 Heb., *found.*

4 Heb., *heave offering.*

---

spoil which fell to the congregation, whereas the priests had only one-fifth per cent. of a like amount. The portion of the Levites, therefore, was 320 maidens, 6,750 sheep and goats, 720 oxen, and 610 asses.

(32) **And the booty, being the rest of the prey . . .**—The reference may be to the residue of the captives after the slaughter of all the males and of a large number of the women, and to the cattle which were brought to the camp, some, it may be, having been lost or slaughtered for food; or it may be to the booty which had been taken in captives and animals, as distinguished from the gold and silver, &c.

(49) **There lacketh not one man of us.**—It is obvious from the smallness of the number of the Israelitish warriors, as well as from the reference to those chiefs only of the Midianites who were the vassals of Sihon, and from the strength of the Midianitish nation in the time of Gideon (Judges vi.—viii.), that the attack was made only upon that particular portion of the nation which had been concerned in the seduction of the Israelites to the worship of Baal Peor. The Midianites were probably attacked in an unprepared and defenceless state. After due allowance, however, has been made for all these circumstances, the fact that not a single Israelitish warrior perished can be satisfactorily explained only on the supposition that God vouchsafed to grant to His people miraculous aid and protection.

(52) **Sixteen thousand seven hundred and fifty shekels.**—This quantity of golden ornaments is quite in harmony with the well-known habits of nomad and even barbarous tribes. The peculiar affection of the Midianites for such ornaments is shown further in the account which is contained in Judges viii. 26 of the weight of the golden earrings which were given to Gideon after his victory over that nation

CHAPTER XXXII. — (1) Now the
children of Reuben and the children of
Gad had a very great multitude of cat-
tle: and when they saw the land of
Jazer, and the land of Gilead, that,
behold, the place *was* a place for cattle;
(2) the children of Gad and the children
of Reuben came and spake unto Moses,
and to Eleazar the priest, and unto the
princes of the congregation, saying,
(3) Ataroth, and Dibon, and Jazer, and
Nimrah, and Heshbon, and Elealeh, and
Shebam, and Nebo, and Beon, (4) *even*
the country which the LORD smote be-
fore the congregation of Israel, *is* a land
for cattle, and thy servants have cattle:
(5) wherefore, said they, if we have found
grace in thy sight, let this land be
given unto thy servants for a possession,
and bring us not over Jordan.

(6) And Moses said unto the children
of Gad and to the children of Reuben,
Shall your brethren go to war, and shall
ye sit here? (7) And wherefore [1]discour-
age ye the heart of the children of
Israel from going over into the land
which the LORD hath given them?
(8) Thus did your fathers, when I sent
them from Kadesh-barnea to see the
land. (9) For [a]when they went up unto
the valley of Eshcol, and saw the land,
they discouraged the heart of the chil-
dren of Israel, that they should not go
into the land which the LORD had given
them. (10) And the LORD's anger was
kindled the same time, and he sware,
saying, (11) Surely none of the men that
came up out of Egypt, [b]from twenty
years old and upward, shall see the land
which I sware unto Abraham, unto
Isaac, and unto Jacob; because they
have not [2]wholly followed me: (12) save
Caleb the son of Jephunneh the Kenez-
ite, and Joshua the son of Nun: for
they have wholly followed the LORD.
(13) And the LORD's anger was kindled
against Israel, and he made them wan-
der in the wilderness forty years, until
all the generation, that had done evil
in the sight of the LORD, was consumed.
(14) And, behold, ye are risen up in your
fathers' stead, an increase of sinful men,
to augment yet the fierce anger of the
LORD toward Israel. (15) For if ye turn
away from after him, he will yet again
leave them in the wilderness; and ye
shall destroy all this people.

(16) And they came near unto him, and
said, We will build sheepfolds here for
our cattle, and cities for our little ones:
(17) but we ourselves will go ready armed
before the children of Israel, until we

1 Heb., *break*.

a ch. 13. 24.

b ch. 14. 28, 29

2 Heb., *fulfilled after me.*

XXXII.

(1) **Now the children of Reuben and the children of Gad . . .**—These tribes had occupied a contiguous position in their encampments for the space of thirty-eight years (chap. ii. 10, 14), and it was natural that they should desire to be permanently located near each other.

The land of Jazer.—See chap. xxi. 32. This district was remarkable for its rich pasture-land.

The land of Gilead.—This land lay north and south of the Jabbok, and even in its present desolation shows traces of its great fertility.

(5) **Bring us not over Jordan.**—These words may be understood either simply as a request that the inheritance of the speakers might be assigned to them on the eastern side of the Jordan, or, as they appear to have been understood by Moses, and as they were in all probability designed to be understood, as a request that the conquest of the western side of the Jordan might be left to the other tribes, and that the Reubenites and Gadites might be permitted at once to establish themselves in the land which had been already subjugated. It is possible that the speakers, judging from the ease and rapidity with which the eastern side of the Jordan had been conquered, might have thought that their brethren were well able to subdue the western side without their aid. Be this as it may, their language indicated a selfish consideration of their own interests, and it was calculated to discourage and dishearten their brethren, and consequently it was strongly reproved by Moses. It is deserving of notice that the tribes of Reuben and Gad and the half tribe of Manasseh were amongst the first who were taken into captivity by the King of Assyria (1 Chron. v. 26).

(7) **And wherefore discourage ye the heart . . .**—The verb which is rendered *discourage*, and which occurs again in verse 9, means rather to "alienate," or "avert." The cognate noun occurs in chap. xiv. 34, in the same connection in which it is used in verse 9. (See Note *in loc.*)

(12) **For they have wholly followed the Lord.**—See chap. xiv. 24.

(13) **And he made them wander in the wilderness forty years.**—Moses here declares the fulfilment of the prediction which he had announced in obedience to the Divine commandment at the time when the spies brought up an evil report of the land. (See chap. xiv. 33, 34.)

(16) **We will build sheepfolds . . .**—The sheepfolds were commonly constructed of loose stones piled up on one another.

And cities for our little ones.—The word which is rendered "build" often means to "build up" or "repair," and it probably has that meaning in this place, as applied to the cities. (See verse 26.)

(17) **Will go ready armed . . .**—Or, *will equip ourselves in haste.*

And our little ones shall dwell . . .—The word *taph*, which is here rendered "little ones," ap-

have brought them unto their place:
and our little ones shall dwell in the
fenced cities because of the inhabitants
of the land. (18) We will not return
unto our houses, until the children of
Israel have inherited every man his in-
heritance. (19) For we will not inherit
with them on yonder side Jordan, or
forward; because our inheritance is
fallen to us on this side Jordan east-
ward.
(20) And [a] Moses said unto them, If ye
will do this thing, if ye will go armed
before the LORD to war, (21) and will go
all of you armed over Jordan before the
LORD, until he hath driven out his ene-
mies from before him, (22) and the land
be subdued before the LORD: then after-
ward ye shall return, and be guiltless
before the LORD, and before Israel; and
this land shall be your possession before
the LORD. (23) But if ye will not do so,
behold, ye have sinned against the
LORD: and be sure your sin will find
you out. (24) Build you cities for your
little ones, and folds for your sheep;
and do that which hath proceeded out
of your mouth.
(25) And the children of Gad and the
children of Reuben spake unto Moses,
saying, Thy servants will do as my lord
commandeth. (26) Our little ones, our
wives, our flocks, and all our cattle,
shall be there in the cities of Gilead:
(27) [b] but thy servants will pass over,
every man armed for war, before the
LORD to battle, as my lord saith.
(28) So concerning them Moses com-
manded Eleazar the priest, and Joshua
the son of Nun, and the chief fathers of
the tribes of the children of Israel: (29) and
Moses said unto them, If the children of
Gad and the children of Reuben will pass
with you over Jordan, every man armed
to battle, before the LORD, and the land
shall be subdued before you; then ye
shall give them the land of Gilead for
a possession: (30) but if they will not
pass over with you armed, they shall
have possessions among you in the land
of Canaan. (31) And the children of Gad
and the children of Reuben answered,
saying, As the LORD hath said unto thy
servants, so will we do. (32) We will
pass over armed before the LORD into
the land of Canaan, that the possession
of our inheritance on this side Jordan
may be our's.
(33) And [c] Moses gave unto them, *even*
to the children of Gad, and to the chil-
dren of Reuben, and unto half the tribe
of Manasseh the son of Joseph, the

a Josh. 1. 13.
b Josh. 4. 12.
c Deut. 3. 12; Josh. 13. 8, & 22. 4.

pears to include all the defenceless portion of the nation. (See Exod. xii. 37.)

(19) **For we will not inherit with them on yonder side Jordan, or forward . . . on this side Jordan eastward.**—This is one of the critical passages which determine the meaning of the word which is rendered "on yonder side" in the first clause of the verse, and "on this side" in the second clause. It is true that the meaning of the word in the first clause is defined by the addition of the word which is rendered "or forward," and which is more correctly rendered *and forward—i.e.,* "further off," or "to a greater distance;" and that its meaning in the second clause is defined by the addition of the word "eastward," or "towards the sun-rising;" but the application of the same word to the country on both sides of the Jordan shows that it cannot be inferred, with any degree of certainty, from the use of this word, whether the position of the writer was on the eastern or western side of the river. (See verse 32, where the same word occurs without any addition.) The language of the Gadites and the Reubenites must not be interpreted as if it were spoken in a defiant spirit, but as disclaiming their right to any portion of the inheritance on the west of the Jordan if they obtained their request to settle on the eastern side.

(20) **If ye will go armed before the Lord . . .**—The same verb and the same preposition are here used which are used in verse 17. It may be inferred from this expression that the army of the Israelites was regarded as the army of the Lord; and it seems probable that there is a reference to the ark of the Lord as being carried on certain occasions into the war. If the order of march prescribed in the second chapter of this Book was still observed, there may be a reference to the fact that the tribes of Reuben and Gad, which encamped on the south side of the Tabernacle, immediately preceded the ark (see chap. x. 18—22), just as those of Ephraim, Benjamin, and Manasseh immediately followed it (Ps. lxxx. 2). At the time of the passage of the Jordan, the priests who bare the ark stood still in the river until the whole of the people had passed over "before the ark of the Lord" (Josh. iv. 5, 11); but at the siege of Jericho it appears that the ark was carried in the midst of the host, some of the armed men going before it, and some following after it (Josh. vi. 9). If this is the true meaning of the word "before the Lord," it was natural that the Reubenites, or their spokesman, should first use the words "before the children of Israel" in verse 17, and should not adopt the expression "before the Lord," as in verse 32, until it had been previously employed by Moses.

(22) **And this land shall be your possession before the Lord.**—See Deut. iii. 12—20; Josh. xiii. 15—33.

(33) **And unto half the tribe of Manasseh . . .**—This is the first mention of the tribe of Manasseh. The application for a grant of the land on the eastern side of the Jordan appears to have been made only by the tribes of Reuben and Gad. The explanation, how-

kingdom of Sihon king of the Amorites,
and the kingdom of Og king of Bashan,
the land, with the cities thereof in the
coasts, *even* the cities of the country
round about.
(34) And the children of Gad built
Dibon, and Ataroth, and Aroer, (35) and
Atroth, Shophan, and Jaazer, and Jog-
behah, (36) and Beth-nimrah, and Beth-
haran, fenced cities: and folds for sheep.
(37) And the children of Reuben built
Heshbon, and Elealeh, and Kirjathaim,
(38) and Nebo, and Baal-meon, (their
names being changed,) and Shibmah:
and [1] gave other names unto the cities
which they builded.
(39) And the children of [a] Machir the
son of Manasseh went to Gilead, and
took it, and dispossessed the Amorite
which *was* in it. (40) And Moses gave
Gilead unto Machir the son of Manas-
seh; and he dwelt therein. (41) And [b] Jair
the son of Manasseh went and took the
small towns thereof, and called them
Havoth-jair. (42) And Nobah went and
took Kenath, and the villages thereof,
and called it Nobah, after his own
name.

1 Heb., *they called by names the names of the cities.*

a Gen. 50. 23.

B. C. 1491.

b Deut. 3. 14.

c Ex. 12. 37.

d Ex. 13. 20.

CHAPTER XXXIII. — (1) These *are*
the journeys of the children of Israel,
which went forth out of the land of
Egypt with their armies under the hand
of Moses and Aaron. (2) And Moses
wrote their goings out according to
their journeys by the commandment of
the LORD: and these *are* their journeys
according to their goings out.
(3) And they [c] departed from Rameses
in the first month, on the fifteenth day
of the first month; on the morrow after
the passover the children of Israel went
out with an high hand in the sight of
all the Egyptians. (4) For the Egyp-
tians buried all *their* first-born, which
the LORD had smitten among them:
upon their gods also the LORD executed
judgments. (5) And the children of
Israel removed from Rameses, and
pitched in Succoth. (6) And they de-
parted from [d] Succoth, and pitched in
Etham, which *is* in the edge of the

---

ever, of this mention of the half tribe of Manasseh is found in verse 39, from which it appears that a portion of that tribe had been chiefly, if not exclusively, engaged in the conquest of certain portions of Gilead and Bashan, and had, therefore, justly acquired a claim to the possession of the districts which they had subjugated. (See Deut. iii. 13—15.)

(34) **And the children of Gad built Dibon . . .** Better, *repaired* or *fortified.* Some of the cities mentioned in this and the following verses—as, *e.g.*, Dibon and Heshbon—are mentioned also in chap. xxi. in connection with the conquest of the Amoritish territory. It is not probable that new cities would have been built at this time, nor did the circumstances of the Israelites admit of the delay which would have been involved in such an undertaking. It was at Dibon that the Moabite stone was discovered by Mr. Klein in 1868. For the geographical position and modern names of the towns mentioned in these verses, see Keil (*in loc.*). In the distribution of the towns by Joshua, some of the southernmost towns repaired or fortified by the Gadites appear to have fallen to the tribe of Reuben. (See Josh. xiii. 16, 17.) Heshbon, on the other hand, appears to have fallen to the lot of the tribe of Gad, and to have been assigned to the Levites (1 Chron. vi. 80, 81).

(39) **And the children of Machir the son of Manasseh went . . .**—Better, *Now the children of Machir the son of Manasseh had gone to Gilead, and taken it, &c.* (See Note on verse 33.)

(41) **And Jair the son of Manasseh . . .**—Jair was the son of Segub, the son of Hezron, who married the daughter of Machir, the son of Manasseh (1 Chron. ii. 21, 22). Jair was, therefore, the great-grandson of Manasseh, and was one of those Israelites who were reckoned as belonging to their maternal tribe.

XXXIII.

(1) **These are the journeys of the children of Israel . . .**—The word which is rendered *journey* appears to denote primarily *the breaking up* of the encampments, which lasted for very different periods, and which, during the protracted wanderings in the wilderness, may have been of the average duration of a twelvemonth. The list of the encampments is expressly said to have been written by Moses, and it served as a permanent memorial, on the one hand, of the sin and rebellion of the nation, and, on the other hand, of the faithfulness and long-suffering of God in leading and sustaining His people throughout their sojourn in the wilderness.

(2) **By the commandment of the Lord.**—It does not clearly appear whether these words should be understood of the record of the journeys of the Israelites as being made by Moses in obedience to a Divine command, or whether they should be understood of the journeys themselves as being taken in obedience to the Divine command.

(3—5) **And they departed . . .**—In these verses the departure from Rameses, at which place the Israelites seem to have been gathered together previously to the exodus, is related as in Exod. xii. 37. The places of encampment from Succoth to the wilderness of Sinai (verses 6—15) agree with those which are recorded in Exod. xiii. 20 (Succoth and Etham), xiv. 2 (Pi-hahiroth and Migdol), xv. 22 (the wilderness, *i.e.*, of Shur), xv. 23—27 (Marah and Elim), xvi. 1 (wilderness of Sin), xvii. 1 (Rephidim), except that there is no mention in Exodus of the station at the Red Sea (verse 10), and of the stations at Dophkah and Alush (verses 12, 13). The first two stations named after the departure from Sinai, viz., Kibroth-hattaavah, or the *graves of lust,* and

wilderness. (7) And they removed from
Etham, and turned again unto Pi-
hahiroth, which *is* before Baal-zephon:
and they pitched before Migdol. (8) And
they departed from before Pi-hahiroth,
and [a] passed through the midst of
the sea into the wilderness, and went
three days' journey in the wilderness
of Etham, and pitched in Marah.
(9) And they removed from Marah, and
[b] came unto Elim: and in Elim *were*
twelve fountains of water, and three-
score and ten palm trees; and they
pitched there. (10) And they removed
from Elim, and encamped by the Red
sea. (11) And they removed from the
Red sea, and encamped in the [c] wilder-
ness of Sin. (12) And they took their
journey out of the wilderness of Sin,
and encamped in Dophkah. (13) And
they departed from Dophkah, and en-
camped in Alush. (14) And they re-
moved from Alush, and encamped at
[d] Rephidim, where was no water for the
people to drink. (15) And they departed
from Rephidim, and pitched in the [e] wil-
derness of Sinai. (16) And they removed
from the desert of Sinai, and pitched [f] at

a Ex. 15. 22.
b Ex. 15. 27.
c Ex. 16. 1.
d Ex. 17. 1
e Ex. 19. 1.
f ch. 11. 34.
1 That is, *The graves of lust.*
g ch. 11. 35.
B. C. 1490.
h Deut. 10. 6.

[1] Kibroth-hattaavah. (17) And they de-
parted from Kibroth-hattaavah, and
[g] encamped at Hazeroth. (18) And they
departed from Hazeroth, and pitched in
Rithmah. (19) And they departed from
Rithmah, and pitched at Rimmon-parez.
(20) And they departed from Rimmon-
parez, and pitched in Libnah. (21) And
they removed from Libnah, and pitched
at Rissah. (22) And they journeyed
from Rissah, and pitched in Kehelathah.
(23) And they went from Kehelathah,
and pitched in mount Shapher. (24) And
they removed from mount Shapher, and
encamped in Haradah. (25) And they
removed from Haradah, and pitched in
Makheloth. (26) And they removed from
Makheloth, and encamped at Tahath.
(27) And they departed from Tahath, and
pitched at Tarah. (28) And they re-
moved from Tarah, and pitched in
Mithcah. (29) And they went from
Mithcah, and pitched in Hashmonah.
(30) And they departed from Hashmonah,
and [h] encamped at Moseroth. (31) And
they departed from Moseroth, and
pitched in Bene-jaakan. (32) And they
removed from Bene-jaakan, and en-

Hazeroth, *enclosures*, agree with those which are found in chap. xi. 34, 35. The next station named in this list is Rithmah. Now, according to chap. xii. 16, the next encampment after Hazeroth was in the wilderness of Paran, from whence Moses, in obedience to the Divine command, sent the spies to search out the land of Canaan (chap. xiii. 3). If, then, we compare these two accounts, and take into further consideration the fact that the Wady *Abu Retemat* is not far distant from Kadesh, and that, according to Robinson (I., p. 279), it abounds with the *retem*, or broom, and that near it there is a copious spring of water called *Ain el Kudeirât*, it seems reasonable to infer that the encampment at Rithmah which is recorded in this chapter is the same as that at Kadesh, "in the wilderness of Paran," as recorded in chap. xii. 16. If this inference be admitted, it is reasonable to conclude further that the seventeen places of encampment which are mentioned in verses 19—36 between Rithmah and Kadesh are those at which the Israelites pitched their camps during the thirty-eight years of wandering in the wilderness. An apparent difficulty, however, arises on this supposition out of a comparison of verses 30—33 of this chapter with Deut. x. 6, 7, where we find mention made of four places which appear to be identical with those named in this chapter, viz., Beeroth of the children of Jaakan, Mosera, Gudgodah, and Jotbath, which correspond to Bene-jaakan, *i.e., the children of Jaakan* (an abbreviation, probably, of *Beeroth-bene-Jaakan, i.e.,* the wells of the sons of Jaakan), Moseroth, the plural form of Mosera, Hor-hagidgad, *i.e., the cave of Gidgad or Gudgodah*, and Jotbathah, an alternative form of Jotbath. The apparent difficulty, however, of the identification arises out of the fact that whereas in this chapter the Israelites are said to have journeyed from Moseroth to Bene-jaakan, they are represented in Deut. x. 6 to have journeyed "from Beeroth of the children of Jaakan to Mosera." It is evident, however, that in Deut. x., where the account is manifestly parenthetical, the reference is to the journeys of the Israelites after the final breaking up of the encampment at Kadesh, at the expiration of the thirty-eight years of wandering in the wilderness; whereas, if the supposition stated above is correct, the reference in this chapter is to the period of the wanderings in the wilderness after the first departure from Kadesh. In this case a change in the order of encampments presents no difficulty, inasmuch as whilst the Israelites, at the later period, must, in all probability, have taken the most direct course open to them from Kadesh to Ezion-geber, there is no improbability involved in the supposition that at the earlier period, whilst wandering about in the wilderness, their places of encampment should have been determined not so much by geographical considerations as by the particular advantages which each spot presented in regard to pasturage and water. It may be observed, further that if the supposition above stated is correct, it will account for the fact that, whereas seventeen places of encampment between Rithmah and Ezion-geber are named in verses 19—35, no intermediate stations between Ezion-geber and Kadesh are mentioned in verse 36, the same places of encampment, as may reasonably be inferred, being selected (if, indeed, any formal encampments were made during so hasty a journey) on the return to Kadesh as had been previously occupied on the journey from Kadesh to Ezion-geber, which is at the northern extremity of the Elanitic Gulf.

camped at Hor-hagidgad. (33) And they
went from Hor-hagidgad, and pitched
in Jotbathah. (34) And they removed
from Jotbathah, and encamped at Eb-
ronah. (35) And they departed from
Ebronah, and encamped at Ezion-gaber.
(36) And they removed from Ezion-gaber,
and pitched in the [a] wilderness of Zin,
which *is* Kadesh. (37) And they removed
from [b] Kadesh, and pitched in mount
Hor, in the edge of the land of Edom.

(38) And [c] Aaron the priest went up
into mount Hor at the commandment
of the LORD, and died there, in the
fortieth year after the children of Israel
were come out of the land of Egypt, in
the first *day* of the fifth month. (39) And
Aaron *was* an hundred and twenty and
three years old when he died in mount
Hor.

(40) And [d] king Arad the Canaanite,
which dwelt in the south in the land of
Canaan, heard of the coming of the
children of Israel.

a ch. 20. 1.

b ch. 20. 22.

c ch. 20. 25; Deut. 32. 50.

B. C. 1453.

d ch. 21. 1, &c.

e ch. 21. 4.

1 Or, *Heaps of Abarim.*

2 Or, *The plains of Shittim.*

f ch. 25. 1.

(41) And they departed from mount
[e] Hor, and pitched in Zalmonah. (42) And
they departed from Zalmonah, and
pitched in Punon. (43) And they de-
parted from Punon, and pitched in
Oboth. (44) And they departed from
Oboth, and pitched in [1] Ije-abarim, in
the border of Moab. (45) And they de-
parted from Iim, and pitched in Dibon-
gad. (46) And they removed from Dibon-
gad, and encamped in Almon-diblathaim.
(47) And they removed from Almon-dibla-
thaim, and pitched in the mountains of
Abarim, before Nebo. (48) And they de-
parted from the mountains of Abarim,
and pitched in the plains of Moab by
Jordan *near* Jericho. (49) And they
pitched by Jordan, from Beth-jesimoth
even unto [2] [f] Abel-shittim in the plains
of Moab.

(50) And the LORD spake unto Moses
in the plains of Moab by Jordan *near*
Jericho, saying, (51) Speak unto the chil-
dren of Israel, and say unto them,

(37, 38) **And they removed from Kadesh . . .**—See chap. xx. 22—29, and Notes.

(40) **And King Arad . . .**—See chap. xxi. 1, and Note.

(43, 44) **And pitched in Oboth . . .**—See chap. xxi. 10, 11.

(45) **From Iim.**—Instead of the seven intermediate stations between Ijim, or Ije-abarim, and the plains of Moab, which are mentioned in chap. xxi. 11—20, we find only three mentioned in this chapter: viz., Dibon of Gad, Almon-diblathaim, and Mount Abarim before Nebo, none of which agree in name with the stations mentioned in chap. xxi. In regard to the number of stations, the diversity may probably be explained on the supposition that chap. xxi. mentions those stations only which were of historical importance—as, *e.g.*, those from which any military expedition was made—whilst chap. xxxiii. appears to mention every place in which an organised camp was erected, and in which the Tent of Meeting was formally set up. If this supposition be correct, no difficulty is involved in the fact that fewer stations are named between Mount Hor and Ije-abarim in chap. xxi. than in chap. xxxiii., whilst more stations are named between Ije-abarim and Arboth-Moab in chap. xxxiii. than in chap. xxi. There is a further diversity, however, in the two accounts as regards the names of the intermediate stations between Ije-abarim and the plains of Moab. In respect of the stations between Mount Hor and Ije-abarim, if we suppose Zalmonah to have been the station at which the brazen serpent was set up (see chap. xxi. 10, and Note), the difference between the two accounts consists only in the insertion in chap. xxxiii. of the station at Punon, between Zalmonah and Oboth. In respect of the stations, however, between Ije-abarim and Arboth-Moab there is not only a difference in the number, but also in the names of the stations. But this difference is easily accounted for when it is remembered that a host consisting of 600,000 men, with their wives, children, and cattle, must have extended over a large area, and, in the case of an inhabited country in which towns and villages abounded, may have occupied more than one of these at the same time. (Comp. verse 49, where the Israelites are represented as encamping "from Beth-jesimoth even unto Abel-shittim.") Hence there is no difficulty in connecting the formal encampment at Dibon of Gad (chap. xxxiii. 45) with some one or more of the stations on the north of the Arnon mentioned in chap. xxiii. 13—19, or in connecting Almon-diblathaim, which appears to have been situated on the north or north-west of Dibon (Comp. Jer. xlviii. 22, where Beth-diblathaim is mentioned in conjunction with Dibon and Nebo) with Bamoth—*i.e., heights*—which, if identical with Bamoth-Baal (chap. xxii. 4), is mentioned by Joshua (chap. xiii. 17) in immediate connection with Dibon. In regard to the last station named in this chapter before the encampment in the plains of Moab—viz., "the mountains of Abarim, before Nebo"—there can be no doubt as to the identity of the station with that in "the valley in the country (or, field) of Moab, at the top of Pisgah," in chap. xxi. 20. According to Deut. xxxiv. 1, Mount Nebo was a peak of Pisgah, which, as we learn from Deut. xxxii. 49, was one of the mountains of Abarim; and the place of the burial of Moses, who died upon the top of Pisgah, is described as "the valley"—*i.e.*, the well-known valley—"in the land of Moab" (Deut. xxxiv. 6).

In Dibon-gad.—Or, *Dibon of Gad.* The reference is probably to the fact which has already been mentioned in chap. xxxii. 34, that the children of Gad rebuilt or fortified Dibon, which stood on the northern side of the river Arnon, and which is one of the towns named in chap. xxxii. 3 as situated in that portion of the country which the Reubenites and the Gadites desired to possess.

(49) **Beth-jesimoth even unto Abel-shittim . . .**—See chap. xxii. 1, and Note, and chap. xxv. 1, where Abel-shittim is mentioned as Shittim.

[a] When ye are passed over Jordan into
the land of Canaan; (52) then ye shall
drive out all the inhabitants of the land
from before you, and destroy all their
pictures, and destroy all their molten
images, and quite pluck down all their
high places: (53) and ye shall dispossess
the inhabitants of the land, and dwell
therein: for I have given you the land
to possess it. (54) And [b] ye shall divide
the land by lot for an inheritance among
your families: *and* to the more ye shall
[1] give the more inheritance, and to the
fewer ye shall [2] give the less inheri-
tance: every man's *inheritance* shall be
in the place where his lot falleth; ac-
cording to the tribes of your fathers ye
shall inherit. (55) But if ye will not
drive out the inhabitants of the land
from before you; then it shall come to
pass, that those which ye let remain of
them *shall be* [c] pricks in your eyes, and
thorns in your sides, and shall vex you
in the land wherein ye dwell. (56) More-
over it shall come to pass, *that* I shall
do unto you, as I thought to do unto
them.

CHAPTER XXXIV. — (1) And the
LORD spake unto Moses, saying, (2) Com-
mand the children of Israel, and say unto
them, When ye come into the land of
Canaan; (this *is* the land that shall fall
unto you for an inheritance, *even* the land
of Canaan with the coasts thereof:)
(3) Then [d] your south quarter shall be
from the wilderness of Zin along by the
coast of Edom, and your south border
shall be the outmost coast of the salt
sea eastward: (4) and your border shall
turn from the south to the ascent of
Akrabbim, and pass on to Zin: and the
going forth thereof shall be from the
south to Kadesh-barnea, and shall go on
to Hazar-addar, and pass on to Azmon:
(5) and the border shall fetch a compass
from Azmon unto the river of Egypt, and
the goings out of it shall be at the sea.
(6) And *as for* the western border,
ye shall even have the great sea for

a Deut. 7. 2; Josh. 11. 12.

b ch. 26. 53.

1 Heb., *multiply his inheritance.*

2 Heb., *diminish his inheritance.*

c Josh. 23. 13; Judg. 2. 3.

d Josh. 15 1.

---

(52) **And destroy all their pictures.**—The word which is here rendered "pictures" denotes "imagery," or "engraved figures." In Lev. xxvi. 1 the material named is stone—"a stone of imagery," *i.e.*, a stone which has been formed into an idol. (Comp. Exod. xxxiv. 13, where, however, a different word is used for "images.")

All their high places.—Hebrew, *bamoth.* The reference here is probably to the altars which were frequently erected on the high places. (Comp. chap. xxii. 41, where Balaam is brought by Balak "up into the high places of Baal.")

(54) **And ye shall divide the land by lot . . .**—See chap. xxvi. 53—56, and Note.

(56) **Moreover it shall come to pass . . .**—Better, *And it shall come to pass that, as I have thought* (or, *determined*) *to do unto them, so will I do unto you.* It must be borne in mind that the idolatrous inhabitants of Canaan were never wholly exterminated, and the pernicious influence which they exercised was felt throughout the whole of the history of the Israelites until the judgments threatened against them were finally executed in the Assyrian and Babylonian captivities.

XXXIV.

(2, 3) **When ye come . . .**—Better, *Ye are entering into the land of Canaan; this is the land which shall fall unto you for an inheritance,* (even) *the land of Canaan, according to the borders thereof. And your south quarter* (or, *district*) *shall be from the wilderness of Zin by the side of Edom; and your south border shall be from the extremity of the salt sea eastward* (or, *on the east*). It was important for the Israelites to be taught that, whilst divinely commissioned to exterminate the idolatrous inhabitants of the land of Canaan, they had no commission to make aggressive wars upon the surrounding nations which were beyond the confines of the land which was allotted to them. The southern boundary which is here described is the same as that of the tribe of Judah, as described in Josh. xv. 1, 2. The land of the Israelites was to extend towards the south as far as the wilderness of Zin, which was to divide their territory from that of the Edomites.

(4) **And your border shall turn from the south . . .**—Better, *And your border shall turn on* (or, *to*) *the south side of the ascent of Akrabbim, and shall pass over to Zin; and the goings forth thereof shall be on the south of Kadesh-barnea.* The meaning appears to be that the boundary line was to go in a south-westerly direction from the southern point (or, tongue) of the Dead Sea, as far as the height (or, ascent) of Akrabbim; and was to be continued from this point in a westerly direction as far as Kadesh-barnea, which was at the western extremity of the desert of Zin, and was to be included within the Israelitish territory. What is here called the height of Akrabbim is supposed to be a row of white cliffs, which run obliquely across the Arabah, at a distance of about eight miles from the Dead Sea. (Comp. Josh. xv. 3, 4.)

(5) **And the border shall fetch a compass . . .**—Although the exact spots of some of the places which determined the southern border have not been positively ascertained, there seems, on the whole, very little doubt that the boundary line ran along the valleys which form a natural division between the cultivated land and the desert, from the Arabah on the east to the Mediterranean on the west, the Brook of Egypt—*i.e.*, the Wady-el-Arish—forming the western boundary until it reached the sea.

(6) **And as for the western border . . .**—Better, *And as for the western border, ye shall have the great sea and* (its) *border* (*i.e.*, its coast). (See Josh. xv. 47 "the great sea and the border thereof.")

a border: this shall be your west border.

(7) And this shall be your north border: from the great sea ye shall point out for you mount Hor: (8) from mount Hor ye shall point out *your border* unto the entrance of Hamath; and the goings forth of the border shall be to Zedad: (9) and the border shall go on to Ziphron, and the goings out of it shall be at Hazar-enan: this shall be your north border.

(10) And ye shall point out your east border from Hazar-enan to Shepham: (11) and the coast shall go down from Shepham to Riblah, on the east side of Ain; and the border shall descend, and shall reach unto the [1] side of the sea of Chinnereth eastward: (12) and the border shall go down to Jordan, and the goings out of it shall be at the salt sea: this shall be your land with the coasts thereof round about.

(13) And Moses commanded the children of Israel, saying, This *is* the land which ye shall inherit by lot, which the LORD commanded to give unto the nine tribes, and to the half tribe: (14) [a] for the tribe of the children of Reuben according to the house of their fathers, and the tribe of the children of Gad according to the house of their fathers, have received *their inheritance;* and half the tribe of Manasseh have received their inheritance: (15) the two tribes and the half tribe have received their inheritance on this side Jordan *near* Jericho eastward, toward the sunrising.

(16) And the LORD spake unto Moses, saying, (17) These *are* the names of the men which shall divide the land unto you: [b] Eleazar the priest, and Joshua the son of Nun. (18) And ye shall take one prince of every tribe, to divide the land by inheritance. (19) And the names of the men *are* these: Of the tribe of Judah, Caleb the son of Jephunneh. (20) And of the tribe of the children of Simeon, Shemuel the son of Ammihud. (21) Of the tribe of Benjamin, Elidad the son of Chislon. (22) And the prince of the tribe of the children of Dan, Bukki the son of Jogli. (23) The prince of the children of Joseph, for the tribe of the children of Manasseh, Hanniel the son of Ephod. (24) And the prince of the tribe of the children of Ephraim, Kemuel the son of Shiphtan. (25) And the prince of the tribe of the children of Zebulun, Elizaphan the son of Parnach. (26) And the prince of the tribe of the children of Issachar, Paltiel the son of Azzan. (27) And the prince of the tribe of the children of Asher, Ahihud the son of Shelomi. (28) And the prince of the tribe of the children of Naphtali, Pedahel the son of Ammihud.

(29) These *are they* whom the LORD commanded to divide the inheritance unto the children of Israel in the land of Canaan.

1 Heb., *shoulder.*

a ch. 32. 33; Josh. 14. 2, 3.

b Josh. 19. 51.

---

(7) **Mount Hor.**—It has been thought by some that Hermon is the mountain to which reference is made. But, as Ritter has observed ("Comparative Geography of Palestine," iii., p. 176), "Hermon stands too far eastward to answer the conditions of the problem," and he thinks that some peak very near the Mediterranean must be meant. Von Raumer considers that it was probably one of the peaks belonging to the Lebanon range, and discernible from Sidon. (*Ib.*)

(8) **From Mount Hor . . .**—From Mount Hor the boundary line was to pass the unknown Ziphron to the village of Enan, or Hazar-enan, which is likewise unknown. (Comp. Ezek. xlvii. 16, 17, 18.) This line probably crossed the northern portion of the Lebanon.

(11) **Riblah, on the east side of Ain.**—Ain (Heb., *a fountain*) is supposed to be the great fountain of Neba Anjar at the foot of Antilibanus, in which case Riblah must be distinguished from the Riblah in the land of Hamath, which is mentioned in 2 Kings xxiii. 33 and in Jer. xxxix. 9. From this point the boundary went further southward by the side (Heb., *shoulder*) of the lake of Chinnereth, or Sea of Galilee, from whence the eastern boundary was the Jordan down to the Dead Sea. This was to be the land of the Israelites, according to its borders on every side.

The sea of Chinnereth.—Chinnereth, or *Cinnereth,* appears to have been the name of a district, and also of a town. The name is supposed to be derived from *kinnor,* a "harp." In later times the city was called *Genusar,* whence the name *Gennesareth,* as we find it in the Gospels.

(15) **On this side Jordan.**—Better, *Along the side or bank of Jordan.* (See Note on chapter xxxii. 19.)

(17) **Which shall divide the land unto you.**—Better, *Which shall give* (or, *allot*) *the land as an inheritance unto you.*

(18) **And ye shall take one prince of every tribe . . .**—In addition to Eleazar the high priest, and Joshua the commander of the army, one chief man, or prince, was to be selected out of each of the ten tribes which were interested in the division, as at the first census one out of each tribe was associated with Moses and Aaron (chap. i. 4), and as was *probably* the case at the second census under Moses and Eleazar. (Comp. chap. xxvii. 2.) Security was thus afforded for the equity and impartiality of the allotment; the position of the territory only, and not its dimensions, being determined by lot. With the exception of Caleb, the names of the princes selected for this purpose are not mentioned elsewhere.

CHAPTER XXXV. — (1) And the
LORD spake unto Moses in the plains of
Moab by Jordan *near* Jericho, saying,
(2) [a]Command the children of Israel, that
they give unto the Levites of the in-
heritance of their possession cities to
dwell in; and ye shall give *also* unto
the Levites suburbs for the cities round
about them. (3) And the cities shall
they have to dwell in; and the suburbs
of them shall be for their cattle, and
for their goods, and for all their beasts.
(4) And the suburbs of the cities, which
ye shall give unto the Levites, *shall*
reach from the wall of the city and out-
ward a thousand cubits round about.
(5) And ye shall measure from without
the city on the east side two thousand
cubits, and on the south side two thou-
sand cubits, and on the west side two
thousand cubits, and on the north side
two thousand cubits; and the city *shall*
be in the midst: this shall be to them
the suburbs of the cities. (6) And among
the cities which ye shall give unto the
Levites *there shall be* [b]six cities for
refuge, which ye shall appoint for the
manslayer, that he may flee thither:

B. C. 1451.

a Josh. 21. 2.

b Deut. 4. 41; Josh. 20. 2, & 21. 3.

XXXV.

(2) **Cities to dwell in.**—The object of the dispersion of the Levites throughout the other tribes seems to have been primarily with a view to the instruction of their brethren in the law of the Lord (Deut. xxxiii. 10). It is probable that the Levites also discharged all those other functions which are now discharged by the learned professions.

And ye shall give also unto the Levites suburbs . . .—The word *migrash*, "suburb," denotes, probably, pasture ground into which flocks are driven.

(3) **For their cattle . . .**—The word which is rendered "cattle" generally denotes oxen and beasts of burden. The word which is rendered "goods" probably refers here to the sheep and goats. (Cf. 2 Chron. xxi. 14; xxxv. 7.) The passage may be rendered, *for their cattle and for their substance, even for all their beasts.*

(5) **And ye shall measure from without the city on the east side two thousand cubits . . .**—The explanation of this passage commonly given by Jewish writers is that the area included by four lines drawn at a distance of 1,000 cubits from the walls of the city was to be allotted to the Levites for their cattle, and a larger area included by four lines drawn at a distance of 2,000 cubits from the inner suburbs was to be allotted to them for vineyards, &c. The explanation of J. D. Michaelis is, that only an area included by four lines drawn at a distance of 1,000 cubits from the walls of the city was to be assigned to the Levites, and that the length of the city walls, supposing the city to be square, was to be added to the 2,000 cubits of the four boundary lines. The Greek text has 2,000 in verse 4 as in verse 5. According to the former of these explanations it is supposed that the space included in the first thousand cubits from the city walls was designed for the cattle, and that the space included in the 2,000 cubits beyond the walls was designed for vineyards, &c., or *vice versâ*. According to the explanation of this passage which has been suggested by J. D. Michaelis, it is supposed that the length of the city wall was added to the 2,000 cubits in every case, so that, *e.g.*, in the case of a city the walls of which were 1,000 cubits in length and breadth, the suburbs would be 3,000 cubits in length and breadth; and in the case of a city the walls of which were 500 cubits in length and breadth, the suburbs would measure 2,500 cubits in length and breadth. It is obvious that, if this supposition be correct, the size of the suburbs would vary in each case with that of the city, so that the suburbs of the larger city, in which there would, in all probability, be a greater number of resident Levites, would be greater than those of a smaller

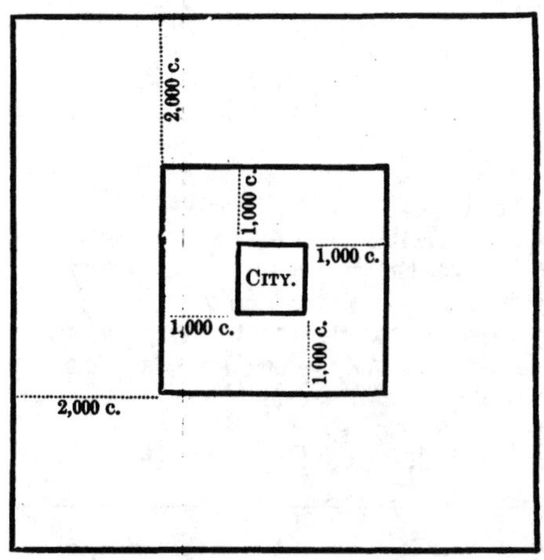

city, in which the number of Levites would probably be less. At the same time, the explanation does not accord so nearly as the preceding with the direction that in every case the measure was to be 2,000 cubits.

(6, 7, 8) **And among the cities which ye shall give . . .**—The construction of this verse is involved; or, rather, there is a suspension of the subject in verse 6, and a resumption of it in verses 7 and 8. The verses may be rendered thus: *And as to the cities which ye shall give to the Levites, viz., the six cities of refuge which ye shall give that the manslayer may flee thither (and in addition to these ye shall give forty and two cities); as to all the cities which ye shall give to the Levites, viz., forty and eight cities, them and their suburbs; now as to the cities which ye shall give from the possession of the children of Israel; from the many ye shall take many, and from the few ye shall take few . . .* It had already been announced in general terms that a place should be appointed whither any one should flee who had unintentionally smitten a man so that he died, and had not lain in wait with a view to commit murder (Exod. xxi. 12, 13). In the verses which follow, the law is delivered at length, and

and [1]to them ye shall add forty and
two cities. (7) *So* all the cities which ye
shall give to the Levites *shall be* forty
and eight cities: them *shall ye give*
with their suburbs. (8) And the cities
which ye shall give *shall be* of the pos-
session of the children of Israel: from
them that have many ye shall give many;
but from *them that have* few ye shall
give few: every one shall give of his
cities unto the Levites according to his
inheritance which [2]he inheriteth.

(9) And the LORD spake unto Moses,
saying, (10) Speak unto the children of
Israel, and say unto them, [a]When ye
be come over Jordan into the land of
Canaan; (11) then ye shall appoint you
cities to be cities of refuge for you;
that the slayer may flee thither, which
killeth any person [3]at unawares. (12) And
they shall be unto you cities for refuge
from the avenger; that the manslayer
die not, until he stand before the con-
gregation in judgment. (13) And of
these cities which ye shall give six cities
shall ye have for refuge. (14) Ye shall
give three cities on this side Jordan,
and three cities shall ye give in the land
of Canaan, *which* shall be cities of re-
fuge. (15) These six cities shall be a
refuge, *both* for the children of Israel,
and for the stranger, and for the so-
journer among them: that every one
that killeth any person unawares may
flee thither.

(16) [b]And if he smite him with an in-
strument of iron, so that he die, he *is*
a murderer: the murderer shall surely
be put to death. (17) And if he smite
him [4]with throwing a stone, wherewith
he may die, and he die, he *is* a mur-
derer: the murderer shall surely be put

1 Heb., *above them ye shall give.*

2 Heb., *they inherit.*

a Deut. 19. 2; Josh. 20. 2.

3 Heb., *by error.*

b Ex. 21. 14.

4 Heb., *with a stone of the hand.*

---

is repeated and further expanded in Deut. xix. 1—13. There were many reasons why all the cities of refuge were Levitical cities. Of these reasons the chief probably were:—(1) That these cities were specially consecrated to the Lord (see Josh. xx. 7, "And they appointed," &c.—Heb., *consecrated*); and (2) that it was to the priests and Levites that the people looked as administrators of justice.

(10, 11) **When ye be come over Jordan . . .**—Or, *Ye are going over the Jordan into the land of Canaan; and ye shall appoint . . .*

(12) **And they shall be unto you cities for refuge . . .**—Better, *And the cities shall be unto you for refuge* (or, *as a place of refuge*) *from the avenger, that the manslayer may not die until he stand before the congregation for judgment.* The avenger (Heb., *goel*) was the near kinsman whose office it was to redeem the person or inheritance of his kinsman, if that kinsman was reduced by poverty to sell himself into slavery, or to sell his inheritance; and also to avenge his blood in the event of his being slain. (See Lev. xxv. 25—55, and Notes.) The law of the *goel*, as contained in this chapter, served to keep in check the excited passions of the near relations of the man who had been slain, and to secure for him a fair and impartial trial. The duties which devolved upon the congregation are stated in verses 24, 25. Christ, as our "Redeemer" (Heb., *goel*), ever lives (Job xix. 25). He has redeemed the persons and the inheritance of His people by His death; and He will in the last great day, ransom them from the power of the grave, and redeem them from death (Hos. xiii. 4, where the cognate verb to *goel* occurs), and will avenge their blood on them that dwell on the earth (Rev. vi. 10).

(14) **Ye shall give three cities on this side Jordan.**—The meaning of the Hebrew word which is here rendered "on this side" is determined by the words "in the land of Canaan," which describe the position of the three cities on the west of the Jordan. Otherwise the Hebrew word is applicable equally to the cities on the east and to those on the west of the Jordan. Moses himself appointed the three cities on the east of the Jordan—viz., Bezer, in the country of the Reubenites; Ramoth in Gilead, in the country of the Gadites; and Golan in Bashan, in the country of the Manassites (Deut. iv. 43). The three cities on the west of the Jordan were not appointed until the land had been allotted amongst the nine tribes and a half (Josh. xx. 7), when the original appointment of Moses in regard to the three cities on the east of the Jordan was confirmed (Josh. xx. 8). It is supposed that the six cities were so selected that no one should be above thirty miles from the nearest city of refuge.

(15) **For the stranger, and for the sojourner . . .**—The word *ger*, "stranger," properly denotes a foreigner who took up a temporary abode amongst the Israelites; whereas *toshab*, "sojourner," denotes one who was settled in Israel. Sometimes, however, the words *ger* and *toshab* appear to be used as a compound term, as in Lev. xxv. 47, where they occur with the conjunctive (or disjunctive) particle in the former part of the verse, and without it in the latter. "The cities of refuge," says Dr. Gill, "were of God's appointing: so Christ, as a Saviour and rock of refuge to His people, is appointed and foreordained of God; they were well known for refuges, as the Lord is in the palaces of Zion; they were open for all at all times, as Christ is for all sinners, even the chief of sinners —Jews or Gentiles; they are all one in Christ—the Israelites, and the stranger and sojourner; all impediments were removed out of the way of them, and plain directions given, as are in the Gospel, and by the ministers of it; and there is always room in Christ for such that flee to Him, as there was in those cities; and being in Him, they are safe from the curse and condemnation of the law, from wrath to come, and from the second death; and their redemption and atonement, peace and reconciliation, liberty, life and salvation, are owing to the death of Christ, their High Priest." (Comp. chap. xxv. 29.)

(17) **And if he smite . . .**—Better, *And if he smote . . .*

With throwing a stone.—Literally, *with a stone of the hand—i.e.,* a stone held in the hand, whether thrown or used as the "weapon of wood" of verse 18.

And he die.—Better, *and he died.*

to death. (18) Or *if* he smite him with an hand weapon of wood, wherewith he may die, and he die, he *is* a murderer: the murderer shall surely be put to death. (19) The revenger of blood himself shall slay the murderer: when he meeteth him, he shall slay him. (20) But if [a] he thrust him of hatred, or hurl at him by laying of wait, that he die; (21) or in enmity smite him with his hand, that he die: he that smote *him* shall surely be put to death; *for* he *is* a murderer: the revenger of blood shall slay the murderer, when he meeteth him.

(22) But if he thrust him suddenly [b] without enmity, or have cast upon him any thing without laying of wait, (23) or with any stone, wherewith a man may die, seeing *him* not, and cast *it* upon him, that he die, and *was* not his enemy, neither sought his harm: (24) then the congregation shall judge between the slayer and the revenger of blood according to these judgments: (25) and the congregation shall deliver the slayer out of the hand of the revenger of blood, and the congregation shall restore him to the city of his refuge, whither he was fled: and he shall abide in it unto the death of the high priest, which was anointed with the holy oil.

(26) But if the slayer shall at any time come without the border of the city of his refuge, whither he was fled; (27) and the revenger of blood find him without the borders of the city of his refuge, and the revenger of blood kill the slayer; [1] he shall not be guilty of blood: (28) because he should have remained in the city of his refuge until the death of the high priest: but after the death of the high priest the slayer shall return into the land of his possession.

(29) So these *things* shall be for a statute of judgment unto you throughout your generations in all your dwellings.

(30) Whoso killeth any person, the murderer shall be put to death by the [c] mouth of witnesses: but one witness shall not testify against any person *to cause him* to die. (31) Moreover ye shall take no satisfaction for the life of a murderer, which *is* [2] guilty of death: but he shall be surely put to death. (32) And ye shall take no satisfaction for him that is fled to the city of his refuge, that he should come again to dwell in the land, until the death of the priest.

(33) So ye shall not pollute the land wherein ye *are*: for blood it defileth the

a Deut. 19. 21.

b Ex. 21. 13.

1 Heb., *no blood shall be to him.*

c Deut. 17. 6, & 19. 15; Matt. 18. 16; 2 Cor. 13. 1; Heb. 10. 28.

2 Heb., *faulty to die.*

---

(20) **But if he thrust him . . .**—Better, *And if . . .*

That he die.—Better, *that he died.* So in verses 21, 23.

(22, 23) **But if he thrust him suddenly . . .**—See Deut. xix. 4, 5, where the meaning of the law is illustrated.

(25) **And he shall abide in it unto the death of the high priest.**—Although the death which had been occasioned was accidental, not intentional, nevertheless the shedding of blood demanded expiation. The manslayer was, therefore, required to remain an exile from his own home until the death of the high priest who had been anointed with the holy oil. As the high priest, by reason of the anointing with the holy oil, became qualified to act as the representative of the nation, and in that capacity acted as their mediator on the great day of atonement, so the death of the high priest assumed a symbolical or representative character, and became a type of that of the great High Priest who, through the eternal Spirit, offered Himself without spot to God, and who by His death made a propitiation for the sins of the world. Thus, as by the death of the Jewish high priest a typical atonement was made for the sin of the Israelitish manslayer, and he was restored thereupon to "the land of his possession" amongst his brethren, so by the death of our High Priest they who have fled for refuge to lay hold on the hope set before them, are restored to the inheritance which had been forfeited by sin, and made joint heirs with Christ of those mansions which He has gone before to prepare for those who love Him.

(26) **But if the slayer shall at any time come without the border of the city . . .**—As the bodily safety of the Israelite who had slain a man depended upon his strict observance of the law which required him to remain within the city of refuge until the death of the high priest, so in the same way the spiritual safety of the believer depends upon his exclusive reliance upon the merits and efficacy of the atoning death and righteousness of Christ, seeing that "there is none other name under heaven given among men whereby we may be saved; neither is there salvation in any other" (Acts iv. 12).

(30) **By the mouth of witnesses.**—The number of witnesses is not here specified. In Deut. xvii. 6 it is ordained that the crime of idolatry should be punished with death "at the mouth of two witnesses, or of three witnesses;" and in Deut. xix. 15 it is ordained in general terms that "one witness shall not rise up against a man for any iniquity, or for any sin that he sinneth: at the mouth of two witnesses, or at the mouth of three witnesses, shall the matter be established."

(31, 32) **Moreover ye shall take no satisfaction for the life of a murderer . . .**—The Israelites were not allowed to make terms with the relatives of the man who had been slain, as is not unfrequently the case at the present time; nor were they permitted to

land: and [1] the land cannot be cleansed
of the blood that is shed therein, but
by the blood of him that shed it. (34) De-
file not therefore the land which ye
shall inhabit, wherein I dwell: for I
the LORD dwell among the children of
Israel.

CHAPTER XXXVI. — (1) And the
chief fathers of the families of the
children of Gilead, the son of Ma-
chir, the son of Manasseh, of the
families of the sons of Joseph, came
near, and spake before Moses, and
before the princes, the chief fathers of
the children of Israel: (2) and they said,
[a] The LORD commanded my lord to give
the land for an inheritance by lot to the
children of Israel: and my lord was
commanded by the LORD to give the in-
heritance of Zelophehad our brother
unto his daughters. (3) And if they be
married to any of the sons of the *other*
tribes of the children of Israel, then
shall their inheritance be taken from
the inheritance of our fathers, and shall
be put to the inheritance of the tribe
[2] whereunto they are received: so shall
it be taken from the lot of our inherit-
ance. (4) And when the jubile of the
children of Israel shall be, then shall
their inheritance be put unto the inherit-
ance of the tribe whereunto they are
received: so shall their inheritance be
taken away from the inheritance of the
tribe of our fathers.

(5) And Moses commanded the children
of Israel according to the word of the
LORD, saying, The tribe of the sons of
Joseph hath said well. (6) This *is* the
thing which the LORD doth command
concerning the daughters of Zelophehad,
saying, Let them [3] marry to whom they
think best; [b] only to the family of the
tribe of their father shall they marry.
(7) So shall not the inheritance of the
children of Israel remove from tribe to
tribe: for every one of the children of
Israel shall [4] keep himself to the inheri-
tance of the tribe of his fathers. (8) And
every daughter, that possesseth an in-
heritance in any tribe of the children of
Israel, shall be wife unto one of the
family of the tribe of her father, that
the children of Israel may enjoy every
man the inheritance of his fathers.
(9) Neither shall the inheritance remove
from *one* tribe to another tribe; but
every one of the tribes of the children
of Israel shall keep himself to his own
inheritance.

(10) Even as the LORD commanded

1 Heb., *there can be no expiation for the land.*

a ch. 27 1; Josh. 17. 3.

2 Heb., *unto whom they shall be*

3 Heb., *be wives.*

b Tob. 1. 9.

4 Heb., *cleave to the, &c.*

---

allow the man who had slain any one unintentionally to return home from the city of refuge before the death of the high priest, on the payment of a sum of money by way of compensation.

XXXVI.

(1, 2, 3) **And the chief fathers of the families . . .**—Better, *And the heads of the fathers of the family . . .* It was at the instance of the daughters of Zelophehad that an ordinance had been enacted, in accordance with which the inheritance of a man who left no sons should pass to his daughters, if he had any, and in default of any issue, to his brethren (chap. xxvii. 1—11). The result of this ordinance would naturally have been that the inheritance of the tribes would have undergone constant change, inasmuch as the inheritance of the daughters would have passed into the possession of the children of their husbands, to whatever tribe those husbands might happen to belong. The Machirites were anxious to avoid such a transference of a portion of the possessions of the tribe of Manasseh, which, after the next jubile, would have become inalienable. They, therefore, came before Moses and the princes, and represented to them what would be the result of the ordinance which had been made at the instigation of the daughters of Zelophehad, if they should marry into another tribe.

(4) **And when the jubile of the children of Israel shall be.**—Up to the year of jubile it was possible that the inheritance might revert to the tribe of Manasseh, either by purchase, or as the result of the marriages of the daughters proving childless. At the jubile the transfer of the inheritance to the tribe or tribes into which the daughters of Zelophehad might have married would become permanent.

(5) **And Moses commanded the children of Israel according to the word of the Lord.**—In regard to the application made by the daughters of Zelophehad to Moses and Eleazar and the princes, it is said that "Moses brought their cause before the Lord" (chap. xxvii. 5). In the present case there is no express declaration made to the same effect; but there can be no doubt that the statement contained in this verse, that Moses commanded the children of Israel "according to the word of the Lord," and that contained in ver. 6, "This is the thing which the Lord doth command," imply that Moses had committed this cause also to the Lord, and that he had received direction from Him.

(8, 9) **And every daughter, that possesseth an inheritance . . .**—The particular direction which was given in the case of the daughters of Zelophehad is extended in these verses into a general and permanent law that no heiress in Israel should marry out of her father's tribe, in order that the inheritance might not be transferred from one tribe to another, and thus, in process of time, the division of the land amongst the tribes, which was made under Divine direction, be materially changed.

Moses, so did the daughters of Zelophe-
had: (11) [a] for Mahlah, Tirzah, and Hog-
lah, and Milcah, and Noah, the daughters
of Zelophehad, were married unto their
father's brothers' sons: (12) *and* they
were married [1] into the families of the
sons of Manasseh the son of Joseph,
and their inheritance remained in the
tribe of the family of their father.

(13) These *are* the commandments and
the judgments, which the LORD com-
manded by the hand of Moses unto the
children of Israel in the plains of Moab
by Jordan *near* Jericho.

a ch. 27. 1.

1 Heb., to some that were *of the families.*

(11) **Were married unto their father's brothers' sons.**—Better, *unto the sons of their near kinsmen.* The word *dod* generally denotes *an uncle* on the father's side, and probably does so in the present case; but in Jer. xxxii. 12 it seems to denote *a cousin.*